The Complete
Learning
Disabilities
Directory

2013
Eighteenth Edition

The Complete Learning Disabilities Directory

Associations • Products • Resources • Magazines
Books • Services • Conferences • Web Sites

A SEDGWICK PRESS Book

Grey House
Publishing

PUBLISHER:	Leslie Mackenzie
EDITOR:	Richard Gottlieb
EDITORIAL DIRECTOR:	Laura Mars
PRODUCTION MANAGER:	Kristen Thatcher
PRODUCTION ASSISTANTS:	Dawn Jenkins, David Wittmer
MARKETING DIRECTOR:	Jessica Moody

A Sedgwick Press Book
Grey House Publishing, Inc.
4919 Route 22
Amenia, NY 12501
518.789.8700
FAX 845.373.6390
www.greyhouse.com
e-mail: books@greyhouse.com

First edition published 1993
Eighteenth edition published 2012
Printed in Canada
The complete learning disabilities directory. -- 2012-

    v. ; 27.5 cm.
    Annual
    Continues: Complete directory for people with learning disabilities
    Includes index.

1. Learning disabled--Education--United States--Directories. 2. Learning disabilities--United States--Bibliography. 3. Education, Special--United States--Bibliography. 4. Education, Special--United States--Directory. 5. Learning Disorders--rehabilitation--United States--Bibliography. 6. Learning Disorders--rehabilitation--United States--Directory. 7. Rehabilitation Centers--United States--Bibliography. 8. Rehabilitation Centers--United States—Directory.

LC4704.6 .C66
371.9025
ISBN 10: 1-59237-873-9   ISBN 13: 978-1-59237-873-9   softcover

Table of Contents

Introduction

The Complete Learning Disabilities Directory has been a comprehensive and sought-after resource for professionals, families and individuals with learning disabilities since 1992.

It is estimated that one in five people in the United States today suffer from a learning disability – nearly 54.5 million individuals. Of that number, 11 million are 6 years old or younger.

According to the *National Institute of Child Health & Human Development*, "learning disabilities…affect the way the brain processes information and can impact how someone learns to read, write, hear, speak and calculate. They are, but are not limited to, language-based (dyslexia), mathematics-based (dyscalculia), writing-based (dysraphia), related to processing information received through the five senses, or related to age-appropriate communication such as speaking, listening, reading, spelling and writing."

Following this Introduction are two elements designed to help those individuals and families dealing with a learning disability, whether for the first time, or for a number of years. The first is a short article from the *National Institute of Child Health & Human Development* that defines a number of specific learning disabilities, and discusses not only what to look for when diagnosing a leaning disability, but also what treatment options are available. The second is an in-depth Glossary from *ldonline,* a leading web site about learning disabilities and ADHD. This Glossary provides more than 200 clear, detailed definitions of acronyms and specialized terms frequently used in books, articles, medical offices and educational environments that are devoted to individuals with learning disabilities and their network of family, friends, and professionals.

This edition of *The Complete Learning Disabilities Directory*, with 4,608 listings, provides a comprehensive look at the variety of resources available for the many different types of learning disabilities, from those that occur in spoken language, to those that affect organizational skills. It includes a wide array of testing resources, crucial for early diagnosis, and is arranged in subject-specific chapters for quick, effective research.

Five-Star Review:
*"This is a must-have resource for individuals who work with people with different types of learning disabilities . . . any professional, parent, or student wanting to learn more. This is **by far the best** of all the resources available for learning disabled individuals. No need to search the Internet to find this information; this book provides it all at your fingertips!"*
Doody's Review Service

Award Winner:
. . . named a Silver National Health Information Winner for providing "... the Nation's Best Consumer Health Information Programs and Materials in the category of Health Promotion/Disease and Injury Prevention Information."
Health Information Resource Center

The Table of Contents is your guide to this database in print form. *The Complete Learning Disabilities Directory's* listings are arranged into 21 major chapters and 100 subchapters, making it easy to pinpoint the exact type of desired reference, including Associations, National/State Programs, Publications, Audio/Video, Web Sites, Products, Conferences, Schools, Learning/Testing Centers, and Summer Programs. Listings provide thousands of valuable contact points, including more than 7,000 key executives, web sites, fax numbers, descriptions, founding year, designed-for age for products, and size of LD population for schools.

The Complete Learning Disabilities Directory provides comprehensive and far-reaching coverage not only for individuals with LD, but for parents, teachers and professionals. Users will find answers to legal and advocacy questions, as well as specially designed computer software and a full range of assistive devices.

As information overload distracts to immobility, *The Complete Learning Disabilities Directory* gives you the confidence that this one resource with important LD information is all you need. It assures those in the LD community that this crucial information is readily available at every school and library across the country, not just at state or district level special education resource centers. Now, every special education teacher, student, and parent can have, right at their fingertips, a wealth of information on the critical resources that are available to help individuals achieve in school and in their community.

This valuable resource includes three indexes: Entry Name; Geographic; and Subject.

This data in *The Complete Learning Disabilities Directory* is also available for subscription on G.O.L.D. – Grey House OnLine Databases. Subscribers to G.O.L.D. can access their subscription via the Internet and do customized searches that make finding information quicker and easier. Visit http://gold.greyhouse.com for more information.

Learning Disabilities
What are learning disabilities?

Learning disabilities are caused by a difference in brain structure that is present at birth and is often hereditary. They affect the way the brain processes information. This processing is the main function involved in learning.

Learning disabilities can impact how someone learns to read, write, hear, speak, and calculate. There are many kinds of learning disabilities and they can affect people differently.

Learning disabilities do not reflect IQ (intelligence quotient) or how smart a person is. Instead, a person with a learning disability has trouble performing specific types of skills or completing a task.

Learning disabilities are not the same as mental or physical disabilities, such as intellectual and developmental disabilities, deafness, or blindness. But, learning disabilities may occur together with mental or physical disabilities.

Children with learning disabilities cannot be identified on the basis of acuity (such as vision or hearing) or other physical signs, nor can they be diagnosed solely based on neurological findings. Learning disabilities are widely regarded as variations on normal development and are only considered disabilities when they interfere significantly with school performance and adaptive functions.

What are the signs and symptoms of learning disabilities?

A delay in achieving certain developmental milestones, when most other aspects of development are normal, could be a sign of a learning disability. Such delays may include problems with language, motor delays, or problems with socialization.

If you think your child may have a learning disability, talk to your child's health care provider or educator to discuss options for evaluation and treatment. These professionals can screen for potential difficulties, but it is essential that someone specializing in the diagnosis of learning disabilities do a full evaluation to confirm the presence of a learning disability.

What are some types of learning disabilities?

The term "learning disabilities" includes a variety of disorders that affect the ability to learn. Some examples include (but are not limited to):

- **Reading Disability** is a reading and language-based learning disability, also commonly called **dyslexia**. For most children with learning disabilities receiving special education services, the primary area of difficulty is reading. People with reading disabilities often have problems recognizing words that they already know. They may also be poor spellers and may have problems with decoding skills. Other symptoms may include trouble with handwriting and problems understanding what they read. About 15 percent to 20 percent of people in the United States have a language-based disability, and of those, most have dyslexia.

- **Dyscalculia** (dis-kal-**kyoo**-lee-*uh*) is a learning disability related to math. Those with dyscalculia may have difficulty understanding math concepts and solving even simple math problems.
- **Dysgraphia** (dis-**graf**-ee-*uh*) is a learning disability related to handwriting. People with this condition may have problems forming letters as they write or may have trouble writing within a defined space.
- **Information-processing disorders** are learning disorders related to a person's ability to use the information that they take in through their senses – seeing, hearing, tasting, smelling, and touching. These problems are not related to an inability to see or hear. Instead, the conditions affect the way the brain recognizes, responds to, retrieves, and stores sensory information.
- **Language-related learning disabilities** are problems that interfere with age-appropriate communication, including speaking, listening, reading, spelling, and writing.

What is the treatment for learning disabilities?

While there is no direct cure for a learning disability, early screening and intervention from specialists can often provide great benefits. Early intervention can prevent learning difficulties, thus reducing the number of children requiring special education services.

Under the 2004 reauthorization of the Individuals with Disabilities Education Improvement Act, legislators made significant changes in how people with learning disabilities could be identified as eligible for special education services. This reauthorization allows for the optional use of the Response to Intervention (RTI) approach to determine whether a child has a specific learning disability and may receive special education services. There is evidence that the IQ-discrepancy model normally used is ineffective in identifying all students with learning disabilities; therefore many schools are implementing an RTI approach.

RTI is a tiered approach to educational intervention; the most common is a 3-tier model. The first tier provides high quality reading instruction to all students, with careful progress monitoring by teachers in the classrooms. Tier 2 is the same high quality instruction but with increased intensity for those not progressing well enough. If students do not progress with this more intensive instruction, they are identified for Tier 3, which is targeted special education intervention. Tier 3 students would have full evaluations and the establishment of an Individualized Education Program (IEP).

Most children with learning disabilities are eligible for special assistance at school. An IEP should be developed for students who need special education and related services. An IEP includes specific academic, communication, motor, learning, functional, and socialization goals for a child based on his or her educational needs.

A number of parents' organizations, both national and local, provide information on therapeutic and educational services and how to get these services for a child. Visit http://www.nlm.nih.gov/medlineplus/learningdisorders.html for a listing of these organizations.

Eunice Kennedy Shriver National Institute of Child Health and Human Development (NICHD), NIH, DHHS; http://www.nichd.nih.gov.

LD Online Glossary of Learning Disabilities and Terms

A

Academic Achievement Standards

Academic achievement standards refer to the expected performance of students on measures of academic achievement; for instance, "all students will score at least 76% correct on the district-developed performance-based assessment." Also known as performance standards. See also academic content standards.

Academic Content Standards

Academic content standards are developed by state departments of education to demonstrate what they expect all students to know and be able to do in the core content areas. According to NCLB, ELL students "will meet the same challenging State academic content and student academic achievement standards as all children are expected to meet." See also academic achievement standards.

Academic English

The English language ability required for academic achievement in context-reduced situations, such as classroom lectures and textbook reading assignments. This is sometimes referred to as Cognitive/Academic Language Proficiency (CALP).

Accommodation (For English Language Learners)

Adapting language (spoken or written) to make it more understandable to second language learners. In assessment, accommodations may be made to the presentation, response method, setting, or timing/scheduling of the assessment (Baker, 2000; Rivera & Stansfield, 2000).

Accommodation (For Students With Disabilities)

Techniques and materials that allow individuals with LD to complete school or work tasks with greater ease and effectiveness. Examples include spellcheckers, tape recorders, and expanded time for completing assignments.

Accuracy

The ability to recognize words correctly.

Adequate Yearly Progress (AYP)

An individual state's measure of yearly progress toward achieving state academic standards. "Adequate Yearly Progress" is the minimum level of improvement that states, school districts and schools must achieve each year.

Affective Filter

The affective filter is a metaphor that describes a learner's attitudes that affect the relative success of second language acquisition. Negative feelings such as lack of motivation, lack of self-confidence and learning anxiety act as filters that hinder and obstruct language learning. This term is associated with linguist Stephen Krashen's Monitor Model of second language learning.

Affix

Part of word that is "fixed to" either the beginnings of words (prefixes) or the endings of words (suffixes). The word *disrespectful* has two affixes, a prefix (*dis-*) and a suffix (*-ful*).

Age Equivalent Score

In a norm-referenced assessment, individual student's scores are reported relative to those of the norming population. This can be done in a variety of ways, but one way is to report the average age of people who received the same score as the individual child. Thus, an individual child's score is described as being the same as students that are younger, the same age, or older than that student (e.g. a 9 year old student my receive the same score that an average 13 year old student does, suggesting that this student is quite advanced).

Alphabetic Principle

The basic idea that written language is a code in which letters represent the sounds in spoken words.

Americans With Disabilities Act (ADA)

A federal law that gives civil rights protections to individuals with disabilities similar to those provided to individuals on the basis of race, color, sex, national origin, age, and religion. It guarantees equal opportunity for individuals with disabilities in public accommodations, employment, transportation, state and local government services, and telecommunications.

For more information, go to The Americans with Disabilities Act.

Analogy-Based Phonics

In this approach, students are taught to use parts of words they have already learned to read and decode words they don't know. They apply this strategy when the words share similar parts in their spellings, for example, reading screen by analogy to green. Students may be taught a large set of key words for use in reading new words.

Analytic Phonics

In this approach, students learn to analyze letter-sound relationships in previously learned words. They do not pronounce sounds in isolation.

Annual Measurable Achievement Objectives (AMAO)

Within Title III of NCLB, each state is required to determine Annual Measurable Achievement Objectives (AMAOs). AMAOs indicate how much English language proficiency (reading, writing, speaking, listening, and comprehension) children served with Title III funds are expected to gain each year. See also AYP, for similar content area requirements

The AMAO requirements include reporting on these three things:

1. Annual increases in the number or percentage of children making progress in learning English.
2. Annual increases in number or percentage of children attaining English proficiency.
3. ELL children making AYP.

Aphasia

see Developmental Aphasia

Assessment

Assessment is a broad term used to describe the gathering of information about student performance in a particular area. See also formative assessment and summative assessment.

Assistive Technology

Equipment that enhances the ability of students and employees to be more efficient and successful. For more information, go to "LD Topics: Technology.

Attention Deficit / Hyperactivity Disorder (ADHD)

Any of a range of behavioral disorders in children characterized by symptoms that include poor concentration, an inability to focus on tasks, difficulty in paying attention, and impulsivity. A person can be predominantly inattentive (often referred to as ADD), predominantly hyperactive-impulsive, or a combination of these two.

Attention Deficit Disorder (ADD)

see ADHD

Auditory Discrimination

Ability to detect differences in sounds; may be gross ability, such as detecting the differences between the noises made by a cat and dog, or fine ability, such as detecting the differences made by the sounds of letters "m" and "n."

Auditory Figure-Ground

Ability to attend to one sound against a background of sound (e.g., hearing the teacher's voice against classroom noise).

Auditory Memory

Ability to retain information which has been presented orally; may be short term memory, such as recalling information presented several seconds before; long term memory, such as recalling information presented more than a minute before; or sequential memory, such as recalling a series of information in proper order.

Auditory Processing Disorder (APD)

An inability to accurately process and interpret sound information. Students with APD often do not recognize subtle differences between sounds in words.

Authentic Assessment

Authentic assessment uses multiple forms of evaluation that reflect student learning, achievement, motivation, and attitudes on classroom activities. Examples of authentic assessment include performance assessment, portfolios, and student self-assessment.

Automaticity

Automaticity is a general term that refers to any skilled and complex behavior that can be performed rather easily with little attention, effort, or conscious awareness. These skills become automatic after extended periods of training. With practice and good instruction, students become automatic at word recognition, that is, retrieving words from memory, and are able to focus attention on constructing meaning from the text, rather than decoding.

B

Base Words

Words from which many other words are formed. For example, many words can be formed from the base word *migrate*: *migration, migrant, immigration, immigrant, migrating, migratory*.

Basic Interpersonal Communication Skills (BICS)

Basic Interpersonal Communication Skills (BICS) is often referred to as "playground English" or "survival English." It is the basic language ability required for face-to-face communication where linguistic interactions are embedded in a situational context called context-embedded language. BICS is part of a theory of language proficiency developed byJim Cummins, which distinguishes this conversational form of language from CALP (Cognitive Academic Language Proficiency).

BICS, which is highly contextualized and often accompanied by gestures, is cognitively undemanding and relies on context to aid understanding. BICS is much more easily and quickly acquired than CALP, but is not sufficient to meet the cognitive and linguistic demands of an academic classroom .

Behavior Intervention Plan (BIP)

A plan that includes positive strategies, program modifications, and supplementary aids and supports that address a student's disruptive behaviors and allows the child to be educated in the least restrictive environment (LRE).

Bicultural

Identifying with the cultures of two different ethnic, national, or language groups. To be bicultural is not necessarily the same as being bilingual. In fact, you can even identify with two different language groups without being bilingual, as is the case with many Latinos in the U.S.

Bilingual Education

An educational program in which two languages are used to provide content matter instruction. Bilingual education programs vary in their length of time, and in the amount each language is used.

Bilingual Education, Transitional

An educational program in which two languages are used to provide content matter instruction. Over time, the use of the native language is decreased and the use of English is increased until only English is used.

Bilingualism

Bilingualism is the ability to use two languages. However, defining bilingualism can be problematic since there may be variation in proficiency across the four language dimensions (listening, speaking, reading and writing) and differences in proficiency between the two languages. People may become bilingual either by acquiring two languages at the same time in childhood or by learning a second language sometime after acquiring their first language.

Biliteracy

Biliteracy is the ability to effectively communicate or understand written thoughts and ideas through the grammatical systems, vocabularies, and written symbols of two different languages.

Blend

A consonant sequence before or after a vowel within a syllable, such as *cl*, *br*, or *st*; it is the written language equivalent of consonant cluster.

C

California English Language Development Test (CELDT)

CELDT is a language proficiency test developed for the California Department of Education. Progress on language proficiency assessments like the CELDT is a requirement for ELLs under the No Child Left Behind Act .

Center For Applied Linguistics (CAL)

CAL is a private, non-profit organization consisting of a group of scholars and educators who use the findings of linguistics to identify and address language-related problems. CAL carries out a wide range of activities including research, teacher education, analysis and dissemination of information, design and development of instructional materials, technical assistance, conference planning, program evaluation, and policy analysis. Visit the CAL website.

Central Auditory Processing Disorder (CAPD)

A disorder that occurs when the ear and the brain do not coordinate fully. A CAPD is a physical hearing impairment, but one which does not show up as a hearing loss on routine screenings or an audiogram. Instead, it affects the hearing system beyond the ear, whose job it is to separate a meaningful message from non-essential background sound and deliver that information with good clarity to the intellectual centers of the brain (the central nervous system).

Cloze Passage

A cloze passage is a reading comprehension exercise in which words have been omitted in a systematic fashion. Students fill in the blanks, and their responses are counted correct if they are exact matches for the missing words. Cloze exercises assess comprehension and background knowledge, and they are also excellent indicators of whether the reading level and language level of the text are appropriate for a given student.

Cognates

Words in different languages related to the same root, e.g. *education* (English) and *educación* (Spanish).

Cognitive/Academic Language Proficiency (CALP)

Cognitive/Academic Language Proficiency (CALP) is the language ability required for academic achievement in a context-reduced environment. Examples

of context-reduced environments include classroom lectures and textbook reading assignments, where there are few environmental cues (facial expressions, gestures) that help students understand the content. CALP is part of a theory of language developed by Jim Cummins, and is distinguished from Basic Interpersonal Communication Skills (BICS).

Collaborative Writing

Collaborative writing is an instructional approach in which students work together to plan, draft, revise, and edit compositions.

Comprehension Strategies

Techniques to teach reading comprehension, including summarization, prediction, and inferring word meanings from context.

Comprehension Strategy Instruction

The explicit teaching of techniques that are particularly effective for comprehending text. The steps of explicit instruction include direct explanation, teacher modeling ("think aloud"), guided practice, and application. Some strategies include *direct explanation* (the teacher explains to students why the strategy helps comprehension and when to apply the strategy), *modeling* (the teacher models, or demonstrates, how to apply the strategy, usually by "thinking aloud" while reading the text that the students are using), *guided practice* (the teacher guides and assists students as they learn how and when to apply the strategy) and *application* (the teacher helps students practice the strategy until they can apply it independently).

Connected Instruction

A way of teaching systematically in which the teacher continually shows and discusses with the students the relationship between what has been learned, what is being learned, and what will be learned.

Content Area

Content areas are academic subjects like math, science, English/language arts, reading, and social sciences. Language proficiency may affect these areas, but is not included as a content area. Assessments of language proficiency differ from those of language arts.

Context Clues

Sources of information outside of words that readers may use to predict the identities and meanings of unknown words. Context clues may be drawn from the immediate sentence containing the word, from text already read, from pictures accompanying the text, or from definitions, restatements, examples, or descriptions in the text.

Context-Embedded Language

Context-embedded language refers to communication that occurs in a context of shared understanding, where there are cues or signals that help to reveal the meaning (e.g. visual clues, gestures, expressions, specific location).

Context-Reduced Language

Context-reduced language refers to communication where there are few clues about the meaning of the communication apart from the words themselves. The language is likely to be abstract and academic. Examples: textbook reading, classroom lecture.

Continuous Assessment

An element of responsive instruction in which the teacher regularly monitors student performance to determine how closely it matches the instructional goal.

Cooperative Learning

A teaching model involving students working together as partners or in small groups on clearly defined tasks. It has been used successfully to teach comprehension strategies in content-area subjects.

Criterion-Referenced Test

Criterion-referenced tests are designed to determine whether students have mastered specific content, and allow comparisons with other students taking the same assessment. They are nationally and locally available.

Curriculum-Based Assessment

A type of informal assessment in which the procedures directly assess student performance in learning-targeted content in order to make decisions about how to better address a student's instructional needs.

D

Decoding

The ability to translate a word from print to speech, usually by employing knowledge of sound-symbol correspondences. It is also the act of deciphering a new word by sounding it out.

Developmental Aphasia

A severe language disorder that is presumed to be due to brain injury rather than because of a developmental delay in the normal acquisition of language.

Developmental Spelling

The use of letter-sound relationship information to attempt to write words (also called *invented spelling*)

Dialogue Journal

A type of writing in which students make entries in a notebook on topics of their choice, to which the teacher responds, modeling effective language but not overtly correcting the student's language (O'Malley & Valdez-Pierce, 1996, p.238).

Differentiated Instruction

An approach to teaching that includes planning out and executing various approaches to content, process, and product. Differentiated instruction is used to meet the needs of student differences in readiness, interests, and learning needs.

Direct Instruction

An instructional approach to academic subjects that emphasizes the use of carefully sequenced steps that include demonstration, modeling, guided practice, and independent application.

Direct Vocabulary Learning

Explicit instruction in both the meanings of individual words and word-learning strategies. Direct vocabulary instruction aids reading comprehension.

Domain-Specific Words And Phrases*

Vocabulary specific to a particular field of study (domain), such as the human body, in the Standards, domain-specific words and phrases are analogous to Tier Three words.

Dominant Language

The dominant language is the language with which a bilingual or multilingual speaker has greatest proficiency and/or uses more often. See primary language.

Dual Language Program/Dual Immersion

Also known as two-way immersion or two-way bilingual education, these programs are designed to serve both language minority and language majority students concurrently. Two language groups are put together and instruction is delivered through both languages. For example, in the U.S., native English-speakers might learn Spanish as a foreign language while continuing to develop their English literacy skills and Spanish-speaking ELLs learn English while developing literacy in Spanish. The goals of the program are for both groups to become biliterate, succeed academically, and develop cross-cultural understanding. See the ERIC Two-way Online Resource Guide or the NCELA publication, Biliteracy for a Global Society.

Dyscalculia

A severe difficulty in understanding and using symbols or functions needed for success in mathematics.

Dysgraphia

A severe difficulty in producing handwriting that is legible and written at an age-appropriate speed.

Dyslexia

A language-based disability that affects both oral and written language. It may also be referred to as reading disability, reading difference, or reading disorder.

Dysnomia

A marked difficulty in remembering names or recalling words needed for oral or written language.

Dyspraxia

A severe difficulty in performing drawing, writing, buttoning, and other tasks requiring fine motor skill, or in sequencing the necessary movements.

E

Early Childhood English Language Learner (ECELL)

An ECELL is a child who is between the ages of zero and five (early stages of development) and who is in the process of learning English as a second language.

Editing*

A part of writing and preparing presentations concerned chiefly with improving the clarity, organization, concision, and correctness of expression relative to task, purpose, and audience; compared to revising, a smaller-scale activity often associated with surface aspects of a text; see also revising, rewriting.

ELD

English language development (ELD) means instruction designed specifically for English language learners to develop their listening, speaking, reading, and writing skills in English. This type of instruction is also known as "English as a second language" (ESL), "teaching English to speakers of other languages" (TESOL), or "English for speakers of other languages" (ESOL). ELD, ESL, TESOL or ESOL are versions of English language arts standards that have been crafted to address the specific developmental stages of students learning English.

ELL

See English language learner.

Embedded Phonics

In this approach, students learn vocabulary through explicit instruction on the letter-sound relationships during the reading of connected text, usually when the teacher notices that a student is struggling to read a particular word. Letter-sound relationships are taught as part of sight word reading. If the sequence of letter-sounds is not prescribed and sequenced, but is determined by whatever words are encountered in text, then the program is not systematic or explicit.

Emergent Literacy

The view that literacy learning begins at birth and is encouraged through participation with adults in meaningful reading and writing activities.

Emergent Reader Texts*

Texts consisting of short sentences comprised of learned sight words and CVC words; may also include rebuses to represent words that cannot yet be decoded or recognized; see also rebus.

English As A Second Language

English as a Second Language (ESL) is an educational approach in which English language learners are instructed in the use of the English language. Their instruction is based on a special curriculum that typically involves little or no use of the native language, focuses on language (as opposed to content) and is usually taught during specific school periods. For the rest of the school day, students may be placed in mainstream classrooms, an immersion program, or a bilingual education program. Every bilingual education program has an ESL component (U.S. General Accounting Office, 1994). See also ELD, pull-out ESL, ESOL.

English Language Learner (ELL)

Students whose first language is not English and who are in the process of learning English.

Entry Criteria

Entry criteria are a set of guidelines that designate students as English language learners and help place them appropriately in bilingual education, ESL, or other language support services. Criteria usually include a home language survey and performance on an English language proficiency test.

ESL

See English As A Second Language

ESOL

ESOL stands for 'English for speakers of other languages' (see ESL).

Evidence*

Facts, figures, details, quotations, or other sources of data and information that provide support for claims or an analysis and that can be evaluated by others; should appear in a form and be derived from a source widely accepted as appropriate to a particular discipline, as in details or quotations from a text in the study of literature and experimental results in the study of science.

Exceptional Students Education (ESE)

Refers to special education services to students who qualify.

Executive Function

The ability to organize cognitive processes. This includes the ability to plan ahead, prioritize, stop and start activities, shift from one activity to another activity, and to monitor one's own behavior.

Exit Criteria

Exit criteria are a set of guidelines for ending special services for English language learners and placing them in mainstream, English-only classes as fluent English speakers. This is usually based on a combination of performance on an English language proficiency test, grades, standardized test scores, and teacher recommendations. In some cases, this redesignation of students may be based on the amount of time they have been in special programs.

Experimental Writing

Efforts by young children to experiment with writing by creating pretend and real letters and by organizing scribbles and marks on paper.

Expressive Language

The aspect of spoken language that includes speaking and the aspect of written language that includes composing or writing.

F

Family Educational Right To Privacy Act (FERPA)

A federal law that protects the privacy of student education records.

Fluency

The ability to read a text accurately, quickly, and with proper expression and comprehension. Because fluent readers do not have to concentrate on decoding words, they can focus their attention on what the text means.

Focused Question*

A query narrowly tailored to task, purpose, and audience, as in a research query that is sufficiently precise to allow a student to achieve adequate specificity and depth within the time and format constraints.

Formal Assessment

The process of gathering information using standardized, published tests or instruments in conjunction with specific administration and interpretation procedures, and used to make general instructional decisions.

Formal English

See Standard English.

Formative Assessment

Formative assessments are designed to evaluate students on a frequent basis so that adjustments can be made in instruction to help them reach target achievement goals.

Free Appropriate Public Education (FAPE)

A requirement of IDEA; all disabled children must receive special education services and related services at no cost.

Functional Behavioral Assessment (FBA)

A problem-solving process for addressing student problem behavior that uses techniques to identify what triggers a given behavior(s) and to select interventions that directly address them.

G

General Academic Words And Phrases*

Vocabulary common to written texts but not commonly a part of speech; in the Standards, general academic words and phrases are analogous to Tier Two words and phrases.

Grade Equivalent Scores

In a norm-referenced assessment, individual student's scores are reported relative to those of the norming population. This can be done in a variety of ways, but one way is to report the average grade of students who received the same score as the individual child. Thus, an individual child's score is described as being the same as students that are in higher, the same, or lower grades than that student (e.g. a student in 2nd grade my earn the same score that an average forth grade student does, suggesting that this student is quite advanced).

Grapheme

A letter or letter combination that spells a single phoneme. In English, a grapheme may be one, two, three, or four letters, such as *e*, *ei*, *igh*, or*eigh*.

Graphic Organizers

Text, diagram or other pictorial device that summarizes and illustrates interrelationships among concepts in a text. Graphic organizers are often known as maps, webs, graphs, charts, frames, or clusters.

I

Independent Educational Evaluation (IEE)

An evaluation conducted by a qualified examiner, who is not employed by the school district at the public's expense.

Independent School District (ISD)

ISD is a commonly-used acronym in education plans to refer to the school system the child attends.

Independent(Ly)*

A student performance done without scaffolding from a teacher, other adult, or peer; in the Standards, often paired with proficient(ly) to suggest a successful student performance done without scaffolding; in the Reading standards, the act of reading a text without scaffolding, as in an assessment; see also proficient(ly), scaffolding.

Indirect Vocabulary Learning

Vocabulary learning that occurs when students hear or see words used in many different contexts — for example, through conversations with adults, being read to, and reading extensively on their own.

Individualized Education Program (IEP)

A plan outlining special education and related services specifically designed to meet the unique educational needs of a student with a disability.

Individualized Transition Plan (ITP)

A plan developed by the IEP team to help accomplish the student's goals for the transition from high school into adulthood.

Individuals With Disabilities Education Act (IDEA)

The Individuals with Disabilities Education Act is the law that guarantees all children with disabilities access to a free and appropriate public education.

Informal Assessment

The process of collecting information to make specific instructional decisions, using procedures largely designed by teachers and based on the current instructional situation.

Information Gap

'Information gap' is an oral language activity in which a student is rated on his or her success in verbally describing visual information that is hidden from a partner, such as a picture, map, or object (O'Malley & Valdez-Pierce, 1996).

Instructional Conversations

[D]iscussion-based lessons geared toward creating opportunities for students' conceptual and linguistic development. They focus on an idea or a student. The teacher encourages expression of students' own ideas, builds upon information students provide and experiences they have had, and guides students to increasingly sophisticated levels of understanding (Goldenberg, 1991).

Intelligence Quotient (IQ)

A measure of someone's intelligence as indicated by an intelligence test, where an average score is 100. An IQ score is the ratio of a person's mental age to his chronological age multiplied by 100.

L

Language Learning Disability (LLD)

A language learning disability is a disorder that may affect the comprehension and use of spoken or written language as well as nonverbal language, such as eye contact and tone of speech, in both adults and children.

Language Majority

Language majority refers to a person or language community that is associated with the dominant language of the country.

Language Minority (LM)

Language minority refers to a person from a home where a language other than the dominant, or societal, language is spoken. So, that person may (1) be fully bilingual, (2) speak only the home language, (3) speak only English, or (4) speak mostly the home language but have limited English proficiency.

Language Proficiency

To be proficient in a second language means to effectively communicate or understand thoughts or ideas through the language's grammatical system and its vocabulary, using its sounds or written symbols. Language proficiency is composed of oral (listening and speaking) and written (reading and writing) components as well as academic and non-academic language (Hargett, 1998).

Lau Remedies

Lau Remedies are policy guidelines for the education of English language learners, based on the ruling in the Lau vs. Nichols suit, mandating school districts' compliance with the civil rights requirements of Title VI (Lyons, 1992).

Lau V. Nichols

'Lau vs. Nichols' is a lawsuit filed by Chinese parents in San Francisco in 1974, which led to a landmark Supreme Court ruling that identical education does not constitute equal education under the Civil Rights Act. School districts must take "affirmative steps" to overcome educational barriers faced by non-English speakers (Lyons, 1992).

Learning Disability (LD)
A disorder that affects people's ability to either interpret what they see and hear or to link information from different parts of the brain. It may also be referred to as a learning disorder or a learning difference.

Least Restrictive Environment (LRE)
A learning plan that provides the most possible time in the regular classroom setting.

LEP
See Limited English Proficient.

Limited English Proficient (LEP)
Limited English proficient is the term used by the federal government, most states, and local school districts to identify those students who have insufficient English to succeed in English-only classrooms. Increasingly, English language learner (ELL) or English learner (EL) are used in place of LEP.

Linguistically And Culturally Diverse (LCD)
The term 'linguistically and culturally diverse' is commonly used to identify communities where English is not the primary language of communication, although some individuals within the community may be bilingual or monolingual English speakers.

Listening Comprehension
Understanding speech. Listening comprehension, as with reading comprehension, can be described in "levels" – lower levels of listening comprehension would include understanding only the facts explicitly stated in a spoken passage that has very simple syntax and uncomplicated vocabulary. Advanced levels of listening comprehension would include implicit understanding and drawing inferences from spoken passages that feature more complicated syntax and more advanced vocabulary.

Literacy
Reading, writing, and the creative and analytical acts involved in producing and comprehending texts.

Literacy Coach
A reading coach or a literacy coach is a reading specialist who focuses on providing professional development for teachers by providing them with the additional support needed to implement various instructional programs and practices. They provide essential leadership for the school's entire literacy program by helping create and supervise a long-term staff development process that supports both the development and implementation of the literacy program over months and years.
For more information visit the International Reading Association website.

Local Education Agency (LEA)
A public board of education or other public authority within a state that maintains administrative control of public elementary or secondary schools in a city, county, township, school district or other political subdivision of a state.

M
Mainstream
"Mainstream" is a term that refers to the ordinary classroom that almost all children attend. Accommodations may be made for children with disabilities or who are English language learners, as part of the general educational program.

Metacognition

Metacognition is the process of "thinking about thinking." For example, good readers use metacognition before reading when they clarify their purpose for reading and preview the text.

Monitor Model

In the monitor model, linguist Stephen Krashen proposes that language learning is accomplished either through learning (formal, conscious learning about language) or through acquisition (informal, subconscious learning through experience with language). He suggests that there is an internal "monitor," which is developed through formal learning which is a part of the conscious process of error correction in when speaking a new language. The monitor plays only a minor role in developing fluency, compared to the role of acquisition. This model later became part of Krashen and Terrell's Natural Approach to language teaching (Krashen & Terrell, 1983).

Monitoring Comprehension

Readers who monitor their comprehension know when they understand what they read and when they do not. Students are able to use appropriate "fix-up" strategies to resolve problems in comprehension.

More Sustained Research Project*

An investigation intended to address a relatively expansive query using several sources over an extended period of time, as in a few weeks of instructional time.

Morpheme

The smallest meaningful unit of language. A morpheme can be one syllable (*book*) or more than one syllable (*seventeen*). It can be a whole word or a part of a word such as a prefix or suffix. For example, the word*ungrateful* contains three morphemes: *un*, *grate*, and *ful*.

Morphemic Relationship

The morphemic relationship is the relationship between one morpheme and another. In the word books, book is a free morpheme (it has meaning by itself) and -s is a bound morpheme (it has meaning only when attached to a free morpheme).

Morphology

The study of how the aspects of language structure are related to the ways words are formed from prefixes, roots, and suffixes (e.g., *mis-spell-ing*), and how words are related to each other.

Morphophonology

Using a word's letter patterns to help determine, in part, the meaning and pronunciation of a word. For example, the morpheme *vis* in words such as *vision* and *visible* is from the Latin root word that means *to see*; and the *ay* in *stay* is pronounced the same in the words *gray* and *play*.

Mother Tongue

This term variably means (a) the language learned from the mother, (b) the first language learned, (c) the native language of an area or country, (d) the stronger (or dominant) language at any time of life, (e) the language used most by a person, (f) the language toward which the person has the more positive attitude and affection (Baker, 2000). See also native language.

Multiple Intelligences

A theory that suggests that the traditional notion of intelligence, based on IQ testing, is far too limited. Instead, it proposes eight different intelligences to account for a broader range of human potential in children and adults. These intelligences are: linguistic, logical-mathematical, spatial, bodily-kinesthetic, musical, interpersonal, intrapersonal, naturalist.

Multiple Literacies

Multiple literacies reach beyond a traditional 'reading and writing' definition of literacy to include the ability to process and interpret information presented through various media.

Multisensory Structured Language Education

An educational approach that uses visual, auditory, and kinesthetic-tactile cues simultaneously to enhance memory and learning. Links are consistently made between the visual (what we see), auditory (what we hear), and kinesthetic-tactile (what we feel) pathways in learning to read and spell.

N

Naming Speed

The rate at which a child can recite "overlearned" stimuli such as letters and single-digit numbers.

Native Language

The first language a person acquires in life, or identifies with as a member of an ethnic group (Baker, 2000). See also mother tongue.

Natural Approach

The Natural Approach is a methodology for second language learning which focuses on communicative skills, both oral and written. It is based on linguist Stephen Krashen's theory of language acquisition, which assumes that speech emerges in four stages: (1) preproduction (listening and gestures), (2) early production (short phrases), (3) speech emergence (long phrases and sentences), and (4) intermediate fluency (conversation). This approach was developed by Krashen and teacher Tracy Terrell (1983) (Lessow-Hurley, 1991).

Newcomer Program

A newcomer program addresses the needs of recent immigrant students, most often at the middle and high school level, especially those with limited or interrupted schooling in their home countries. Major goals of newcomer programs are to acquire beginning English language skills along with core academic skills and to acculturate to the U.S. school system. Some newcomer programs also include primary language development and an orientation to the student's new community (Genesee, et al, 1999).

No Child Left Behind (NCLB)

The No Child Left Behind Act of 2001 is the most recent reauthorization of the Elementary and Secondary Education act of 1965. The act contains President George W. Bush's four basic education reform principles: stronger accountability for results, increased flexibility and local control, expanded options for parents, and an emphasis on teaching methods based on scientifically-based research.

Nonverbal Learning Disability

A neurological disorder which originates in the right hemisphere of the brain. Reception of nonverbal or performance-based information governed by this hemisphere is impaired in varying degrees, causing problems with visual-spatial, intuitive, organizational, evaluative, and holistic processing functions. For more information, go to Nonverbal LD.

Norm-Referenced Assessment

A type of assessment that compares an individual child's score against the scores of other children who have previously taken the same assessment. With a norm-referenced assessment, the child's raw score can be converted into a comparative score such as a percentile rank or a stanine.

Norm-Referenced Test

Norm-referenced tests (NRTs) are designed to discriminate among groups of students, and allow comparisons across years, grade levels, schools, and other variables. They are nationally, commercially available.

O

Occupational Therapy (OT)

A rehabilitative service to people with mental, physical, emotional, or developmental impairments. Services can include helping a student with pencil grip, physical exercises that may be used to increase strength and dexterity, or exercises to improve hand-eye coordination.

Office For Civil Rights (OCR)

A branch of the U.S. Department of Education that investigates allegations of civil rights violations in schools. It also initiates investigations of compliance with federal civil rights laws in schools that serve special student populations, including language-minority students. The office has developed several policies with regard to measuring compliance with the Lau v. Nichols decision. OCR is also responsible for enforcing Title VI of the Civil Rights Act of 1964. For more information, see the OCR resources about ELLs and OCR Disability Discrimination: Overview of the Laws.

Office Of Special Education Programs (OSEP)

An office of the U.S. Department of Education whose goal is to improve results for children with disabilities (ages birth through 21) by providing leadership and financial support to assist states and local districts.

Onset

The initial consonant sound(s) in a monosyllabic word. This unit is smaller than a syllable but may be larger than a phoneme (the onset of *bag* is *b-*; of *swim* is *sw-*).

Onset And Rime

Onsets and rimes are parts of monosyllabic words in spoken language. These units are smaller than syllables but may be larger than phonemes. An onset is the initial consonant sound of a syllable (the onset of bag is b-; of swim is sw-). The rime is the part of a syllable that contains the vowel and all that follows it (the rime of bag is -ag; of swim is -im).

Onset-Rime Phonics Instruction

In this approach, students learn to break monosyllabic words into their onsets (consonants preceding the vowel) and rimes (vowel and following consonants). They read each part separately and then blend the parts to say the whole word.

Onset-Rime Segmentation

Onset-rime segmentation is separating a word into the onset, the consonant(s) at the start of a syllable, and the rime, the remainder of the syllable. For example, in swift, sw is the onset and ift is the rime.

Oral Language Difficulties

A person with oral language difficulties may exhibit poor vocabulary, listening comprehension, or grammatical abilities for his or her age.

Orthographic Knowledge

The understanding that the sounds in a language are represented by written or printed symbols.

Orton-Gillingham

A multisensory approach to remediating dyslexia created by Dr. Samuel Orton, a neuropsychiatrist and pathologist, and Anna Gillingham, an educator and psychologist.

Other Health Impairments (OHI)

A category of special education services for students with limited strength, vitality or alertness, due to chronic or acute health problems (such as asthma, ADHD, diabetes, or a heart condition).

P

Paraprofessional Educator

Also known as instructional aides and teachers' aides, these individuals provide assistance to teachers in the classroom. They do not provide primary direct instruction, but may help clarify material to students through home language or other supports. In classrooms funded through Title I, instructional paraprofessionals must have at least an Associates' degree or its equivalent, or have passed a test.

Pervasive Developmental Disorder (PDD)

The category of special education services for students with delays or deviance in their social/language/motor and/or cognitive development.

Phoneme

The smallest unit of speech that serves to distinguish one utterance from another in a language.

Phonemic Awareness

The ability to notice, think about, and work with the individual sounds in spoken words. An example of how beginning readers show us they have phonemic awareness is combining or blending the separate sounds of a word to say the word (/c/ /a/ /t/ – cat.)

Phonics

Phonics is a form of instruction to cultivate the understanding and use of the alphabetic principle. It emphasizes the predictable relationship between phonemes (the sounds in spoken language) and graphemes (the letters that represent those sounds in written language) and shows how this information can be used to read or decode words.

See also: Analogy-based phonics, Analytic phonics, Embedded phonics, Onset-rime phonics instruction, Phonics through spelling, Synthetic phonics, Systematic and explicit phonics instruction.

Phonological Awareness

A range of understandings related to the sounds of words and word parts, including identifying and manipulating larger parts of spoken language such as words, syllables, and onset and rime. It also includes phonemic awareness as well as other aspects of spoken language such as rhyming and syllabication.

Physical Therapy (PT)

Instructional support and treatment of physical disabilities, under a doctor's prescription, that helps a person improve the use of bones, muscles, joints and nerves.

Point Of View*

Chiefly in literary texts, the narrative point of view (as in first- or third-person narration); more broadly, the position or perspective conveyed or represented by an author, narrator, speaker, or character.

Portfolio Assessment

A portfolio assessment is a systematic collection of student work that is analyzed to show progress over time with regard to instructional objectives (Valencia 1991, cited in O' Malley & Valdez-Pierce, 1996). Student portfolios may include responses to readings, samples of writing, drawings, or other work.

Pre-Reading

Prereading activities are activities used with students before they interact with reading material. They're designed to provide students with needed background knowledge about a topic, or to help students identify their purpose for reading.

Prefix

A prefix is a word part added to the beginning of a root or base word to create a new meaning. The most common prefixes include dis- (as in disagree), in- (as invaluable), re- (as in repeat), and -un (as in unfriendly).

Prewriting

Prewriting is any activity designed to help students generate or organize their ideas before writing.

Primary Language

The primary language is the language in which bilingual/multilingual speakers are most fluent, or which they prefer to use. This is not necessarily the language first learned in life. See also dominant language.

Print Awareness

Basic knowledge about print and how it is typically organized on a page. For example, print conveys meaning, print is read left to right, and words are separated by spaces.

Print Or Digital (Texts, Sources)*

Sometimes added for emphasis to stress that a given standard is particularly likely to be applied to electronic as well as traditional texts; the Standards are generally assumed to apply to both.

Proficient(Ly)*

A student performance that meets the criterion established in the Standards as measured by a teacher or assessment; in the Standards, often paired with independent(ly) to suggest a successful student performance done without scaffolding;

in the Reading standards, the act of reading a text with comprehension; see also independent(ly), scaffolding.

Pull-Out ESL

Pull-out ESL is a program in which LEP students are "pulled out" of regular, mainstream classrooms for special instruction in English as a second language.

Push-In ESL

In contrast with pull-out ESL instruction, a certified ESL teacher provides ELLs with instruction in a mainstream or content-area classroom.

R

Readability

Readability refers to the level of difficulty in a written passage. This depends on factors such as length of words, length of sentences, grammatical complexity and word frequency.

Reading Coach

See Literacy Coach.

For more information visit the International Reading Association website.

Reading Comprehension

See text comprehension.

Reading Disability

Another term for dyslexia, sometimes referred to as reading disorder or reading difference.

Reading First

Reading First is a federal program that focuses on putting proven methods of early reading instruction in classrooms. Through Reading First, states and districts receive support to apply scientifically based reading research and the proven instructional and assessment tools consistent with this research to ensure that all children learn to read well by the end of third grade.

For more information visit the USDOE website.

Rebus*

A mode of expressing words and phrases by using pictures of objects whose names resemble those words.

Receptive Language

The aspect of spoken language that includes listening, and the aspect of written language that includes reading.

Reciprocal Teaching

Reciprocal teaching is a multiple-strategy instructional approach for teaching comprehension skills to students. Teachers teach students four strategies: asking questions about the text they are reading; summarizing parts of the text; clarifying words and sentences they don't understand; and predicting what might occur next in the text.

Repeated And Monitored Oral Reading

In this instructional activity, students read and reread a text a certain number of times or until a certain level of fluency is reached. This technique has been shown to improve reading fluency and overall reading achievement. Four re-readings are usually sufficient for most students. Students may also practice reading orally through the use of audiotapes, tutors, peer guidance, or other means.

Response To Intervention (RTI)

Response to Intervention is a process whereby local education agencies (LEAs) document a child's response to scientific, research-based intervention using a tiered approach. In contrast to the discrepancy criterion model, RTI provides early intervention for students experiencing difficulty learning to read. RTI was authorized for use in December 2004 as part of the Individuals with Disabilities Education Act (IDEA).

Responsive Instruction

A way of making teaching decisions in which a student's reaction to instruction directly shapes how future instruction is provided.

Revising*

A part of writing and preparing presentations concerned chiefly with a reconsideration and reworking of the content of a text relative to task, purpose, and audience; compared to editing, a larger-scale activity often associated with the overall content and structure of a text; see also editing, rewriting.

Rewriting*

A part of writing and preparing presentations that involves largely or wholly replacing a previous, unsatisfactory effort with a new effort, better aligned to task, purpose, and audience, on the same or a similar topic or theme; compared to revising, a larger-scale activity more akin to replacement than refinement; see also editing, revising.

Rime

The vowel and all that follows it in a monosyllabic word (the rime of *bag* is -*ag*; of *swim* is -*im*).

Root Word

Words from other languages that are the origin of many English words. About 60 percent of all English words have Latin or Greek origins.

S

Scaffolding

A way of teaching in which the teacher provides support in the form of modeling, prompts, direct explanations, and targeted questions — offering a teacher-guided approach at first. As students begin to acquire mastery of targeted objectives, direct supports are reduced and the learning becomes more student-guided. The teacher provides contextual supports for meaning during instruction or assessment, such as visual displays, classified lists, or tables or graphs (O' Malley & Valdez-Pierce, 1996, p.240).

Scaffolding*

Temporary guidance or assistance provided to a student by a teacher, another adult, or a more capable peer, enabling the student to perform a task he or she otherwise would not be able to do alone, with the goal of fostering the student's capacity to perform the task on his or her own later on.

Self-Advocacy

The development of specific skills and understandings that enable children and adults to explain their specific learning disabilities to others and cope positively with the attitudes of peers, parents, teachers, and employers.

Self-Monitoring

The ability to observe yourself and know when you are doing an activity act according to a standard. For example, knowing if you do or do not understand what you are reading. Or whether your voice tone is appropriate for the circumstances or too loud or too soft.

Semantic Maps

A semantic map is a strategy for graphically representing concepts. As a strategy, semantic maps involve expanding a student's vocabulary by encouraging new links to familiar concepts. Instructionally, semantic maps can be used as a pre-reading activity for charting what is known about a concept, theme, or individual word. They can also be used during reading as a way to assimilate new information learned from the text.

Semantic Organizers

Graphic organizers that look somewhat like a spider web where lines connect a central concept to a variety of related ideas and events.

Sentence Combining

Sentence combining is an instructional approach that involves teaching students to combine two or more simple sentences to form a more complex or sophisticated sentence.

Short Research Project*

An investigation intended to address a narrowly tailored query in a brief period of time, as in a few class periods or a week of instructional time.

Sight Words

Words that a reader recognizes without having to sound them out. Some sight words are "irregular," or have letter-sound relationships that are uncommon. Some examples of sight words are *you*, *are*, *have* and *said*.

Small Learning Communities

Small learning communities are an increasingly popular approach for teaching adolescents. This approach uses personalized classroom environments where teachers know each individual student and can tailor instruction to meet their academic and social/emotional needs. The goal is to increase students' sense of belonging, participation, and commitment to school.

Social English

Often referred to as "playground English" or "survival English", this is the basic language ability required for face-to-face communication, often accompanied by gestures and relying on context to aid understanding. Social English is much more easily and quickly acquired than academic English, but is not sufficient to meet the cognitive and linguistic demands of an academic classroom. Also referred to as Basic Interpersonal Communication Skills (BICS).

Source*

A text used largely for informational purposes, as in research.

Special Education (SPED)

Services offered to children who possess one or more of the following disabilities: specific learning disabilities, speech or language impairments, mental retardation, emotional disturbance, multiple disabilities, hearing impairments, orthopedic impairments, visual impairments, autism, combined deafness and blindness, traumatic brain injury, and other health impairments.

Specific Learning Disability (SLD)

The official term used in federal legislation to refer to difficulty in certain areas of learning, rather than in all areas of learning. Synonymous with learning disabilities.

Speech Impaired (SI)

A category of special education services for students who have difficulty with speech sounds in their native language.

Speech Language Pathologist (SLP)

An expert who can help children and adolescents who have language disorders to understand and give directions, ask and answer questions, convey ideas, and improve the language skills that lead to better academic performance. An SLP can also counsel individuals and families to understand and deal with speech and language disorders.

Standard English*

In the Standards, the most widely accepted and understood form of expression in English in the United States; used in the Standards to refer to formal English writing and speaking; the particular focus of Language standards 1 and 2.

State Education Agency (SEA)

A state education agency is the agency primarily responsible for the state supervision of public elementary and secondary schools.

Story Structure

In story structure, a reader sees the way the content and events of a story are organized into a plot. Students learn to identify the categories of content (setting, characters, initiating events, internal reactions, goals, attempts, and outcomes). Often students recognize the way the story is organized by developing a story map. This strategy improves students' comprehension and memory of story content and meaning.

Strategic Instructional Model (SIM)

SIM promotes effective teaching and learning of critical content in schools. SIM strives to help teachers make decisions about what is of greatest importance, what we can teach students to help them to learn, and how to teach them well.

For more information visit the University of Kansas Center for Research on Learning website.

Striving Readers Act

Striving Readers is aimed at improving the reading skills of middle school- and high school-aged students who are reading below grade level. Striving Readers supports the implementation and evaluation of research-based reading interventions for struggling middle and high school readers in Title I eligible schools that are at risk of not meeting or are not meeting adequate yearly progress (AYP) requirements under the No Child Left Behind Act, or that have significant percentages or number of students reading below grade level, or both.

For more information visit the USDOE website.

Striving Readers Legislation

Striving Readers is a government program designed to improve the reading skills of middle and high school students who read below grade level. Authorized in 2005 as part of the No Child Left Behind Act, this program supports initiatives to improve literacy instruction across the curriculum and works to build a scientific research base for strategies that improve literacy skills for adolescents.

Suffix

"A suffix is a word part that is added to the end of a root word. The four most frequent suffixes account for 97 percent of suffixed words in printed school English. These include -ing, -ed, -ly, and -es."

Summarizing

Summarizing is a process in which a reader synthesizes the important ideas in a text. Teaching students to summarize helps them generate main ideas, connect central ideas, eliminate redundant and unnecessary information, and remember what they read.

Summative Assessment

Summative assessment is generally carried out at the end of a course or project. In an educational setting, summative assessments are typically used to assign students a course grade.

Supplemental Services

Services offered to students from low-income families who are attending schools that have been identified as in need of improvement for two consecutive years. Parents can choose the appropriate services (tutoring, academic assistance, etc.) from a list of approved providers, which are paid for by the school district.

Syllabication

The act of breaking words into syllables.

Syllable

A part of a word that contains a vowel or, in spoken language, a vowel sound (*e-vent*, *news-pa-per*).

Synthetic Phonics

In this instructional approach, students learn how to convert letters or letter combinations into a sequence of sounds, and then how to blend the sounds together to form recognizable words.

Systematic And Explicit Phonics Instruction

The most effective way to teach phonics. A program is systematic if the plan of instruction includes a carefully selected set of letter-sound relationships that are organized into a logical sequence. Explicit means the programs provide teachers with precise directions for the teaching of these relationships.

T

Teachers Of English To Speakers Of Other Languages (TESOL)

TESOL is a professional association of teachers, administrators, researchers and others concerned with promoting and strengthening instruction and research in the teaching of English to speakers of other languages.

Technical Subjects*

A course devoted to a practical study, such as engineering, technology, design, business, or other workforce-related subject; a technical aspect of a wider field of study, such as art or music.

Text Complexity Band*

A range of text difficulty corresponding to grade spans within the Standards; specifically, the spans from grades 2–3, grades 4–5, grades 6–8, grades 9–10, and grades 11–CCR (college and career readiness).

Text Complexity*

The inherent difficulty of reading and comprehending a text combined with consideration of reader and task variables; in the Standards, a three-part assessment of text difficulty that pairs qualitative and quantitative measures with reader-task considerations.

Text Comprehension

The reason for reading: understanding what is read by reading actively (making sense from text) and with purpose (for learning, understanding, or enjoyment).

Textual Evidence

See evidence.

Total Physical Response (TPR)

Total Physical Response is a language-learning approach based on the relationship between language and its physical representation or execution. TPR emphasizes the use of physical activity for increasing meaningful learning opportunities and language retention. A TPR lesson involves a detailed series of consecutive actions accompanied by a series of commands or instructions given by the teacher. Students respond by listening and performing the appropriate actions.

Transition

Commonly used to refer to the change from secondary school to postsecondary programs, work, and independent living typical of young adults. Also used to describe other periods of major change such as from early childhood to school or from more specialized to mainstreamed settings.

Transitional Bilingual Education

An educational program in which two languages are used to provide content matter instruction. Over time, the use of the native language is decreased and the use of English is increased until only English is used.

U

Unified School District (USD)

USD is a common acronym used in education plans to refer to the elementary, middle, and high schools within the school district.

Universal Design For Learning (UDL)

UDL provides a framework for creating flexible goals, methods, materials, and assessments that accommodate learner differences.

For more information visit the Center for Applied Special Technology website.

V

Vocabulary

Vocabulary refers to the words a reader knows. Listening vocabulary refers to the words a person knows when hearing them in oral speech. Speaking vocabulary refers to the words we use when we speak. Reading vocabulary refers to the words a person knows when seeing them in print. Writing vocabulary refers to the words we use in writing.

W

With Prompting And Support/With (Some) Guidance And Support

See scaffolding.

Word Attack

Word attack is an aspect of reading instruction that includes intentional strategies for learning to decode, sight read, and recognize written words.

Word Parts

Word parts include affixes (prefixes and suffixes), base words, and word roots.

Word Roots

Word roots are words from other languages that are the origin of many English words. About 60 percent of all English words have Latin or Greek origins.

Working Memory

The ability to store and manage information in one's mind for a short period of time. In one test of working memory a person listens to random numbers and then repeats them. The average adult can hold 7 numbers in their working memory. Working memory is sometimes called Short-term memory

These terms and definitions were collected from the following sources: Dr. Jean Lokerson, ERIC Digest; Southwest Educational Laboratory (SEDL); Dr. Linda Wilmshurst and Dr. Alan Brue, A Parent's Guide to Special Education, *American Management Association, 2005; The Partnership for Reading; Learning Disabilities Council; Dr. Don Deshler, University of Kansas.*

*Source: Common Core State Standards. National Governors Association Center for Best Practices, Council of Chief State School Officers, 2010.

User Key

1 → **Record Number**: Entries are listed alphabetically within each category and numbered sequentially. The entry numbers, rather than page numbers, are used in the indexes to refer to listings.

2 → **Organization Name**: Formal name of organization. Where organization names are completely capitalized, the listing will appear at the beginning of the alphabetized section. In the case of publications, the title of the publication will appear first, followed by the publisher.

3 → **Address**: Location or permanent address of the organization.

4 → **Phone Number**: The listed phone number is usually for the main office of the organization, but may also be for sales, marketing, or public relations as provided by the organization.

5 → **Fax Number**: This is listed when provided by the organization.

6 → **Toll-Free Number**: This is listed when provided by the organization.

7 → **TDY**: This is listed when provided by the organization. It refers to Telephone Device for the Deaf.

8 → **E-Mail**: This is listed when provided by the organization and is generally the main office e-mail.

9 → **Web Site**: This is listed when provided by the organization and is also referred to as an URL address. These web sites are accessed through the Internet by typing http:// before the URL address.

10 → **Key Personnel**: Name and title of key executives within the organization.

11 → **Organization Description**: This paragraph contains a brief description of the organization and their services.

The following apply if the listing is a publication:

12 → **Price:** The cost of each issue or subscription, often with frequency information. If the listing is a school or program, you will see information on age group served and enrollment size.

13 → **Number of Pages**: Total number of pages for publication.

14 → **Paperback:** The available format of the publication: paperback; hardcover; spiral bound.

User Guide

Descriptive listings in *The Complete Learning Disabilities Directory (LDD)* are organized into 21 chapters and 84 subchapters. You will find the following types of listings throughout the book:

- National Agencies & Associations
- State Agencies & Associations
- Camps & Summer Programs
- Exchange Programs
- Classroom & Computer Resources
- Print & Electronic Media
- Schools & Learning Centers
- Testing & Training Resources
- Conferences & Workshops

Below is a sample listing illustrating the kind of information that is or might be included in an entry. Each numbered item of information is described in the paragraphs on the following page.

▪▶ 1234

2 ▶ **Association for Children and Youth with Disabilities**

3 ▶ **1704 L Street NW**

Washington, DC 20036

4 ▶ **075-785-0000**

5 ▶ **FAX: 075-785-0001**

6 ▶ **800-075-0002**

7 ▶ **TDY: 075-785-0002**

8 ▶ **info@AGC.com**

9 ▶ **www.AGC.com**

10 ▶ Peter Rancho, Director
Nancy Williams, Information Specialist
Tanya Fitzgerald, Marketing Director
William Alexander, Editor

11 ▶ Advocacy organization that ensures children and youth with learning disabilities receive the best possible education. Services include speaking with an informed specialist, free publications, database searches, and referrals to other organizations.

12 ▶ *$6.99*

13 ▶ *204 pages*

14 ▶ *Paperback*

National

1 AVKO Educational Research Foundation
3084 Willard Rd
Birch Run, MI 48415-9404   810-686-9283
                                   866-285-6612
                              FAX 810-686-1101
                              http://www.avko.org
                              e-mail: webmaster@avko.org

Don Mc Cabe, President

AVKO is a non-profit membership organization that focuses
on the development and production of materials and especially techniques to teach reading and spelling, handwriting
(manuscript and cursive) and key boarding.

2 America's Health Insurance Plans
601 Pennsylvania Ave NW
S Bldg, Ste 500
Washington, DC 20004-2601   202-778-3200
                               FAX 202-331-7487
                               http://www.ahip.org
                               e-mail: ahip@ahip.org

Karen Ignagni, President/CEO
Scott Styles, Senior VP Legislative Affairs
Carmella Bocchino, Senior VP Medical Affairs
Purpose is to represent the interests of members on legislative and regulatory issues at the federal and state levels, and
with the media, consumers, and employers. Provides information and services such as newsletters, publications, a
magazine and on-line services. Conducts education, research, and quality assurance programs and engages in a host
of other activities to assist members.
1,300 members

**3 American Association of Collegiate Registrars and Ad-
missions Officers**
1 Dupont Circle NW
Ste 520
Washington, DC 20036-1148   202-293-9161
                               FAX 202-872-8857
                               http://www.aacrao.org
                               e-mail: corporateinfo@aacrao.org

Betty Huff, President

Provides professional development, guidelines and voluntary standards to be used by higher education officials regarding the best practices in records management,
admissions, enrollment management, administrative information technology and student services. It also provideess a
forum for discussion regarding policy initiation and development, interpretation and implementation at the institutional level and in the global educational community.
9,500 members

**4 American Bar Association Center on Children and the
Law: Information Line**
740 15th St NW
Fl 8
Washington, DC 20005-1019   202-662-1720
                               FAX 202-662-1755
                               http://www.abanet.org/child
                               e-mail: ctrchildlaw@abanet.org

Stephen N Zack, President
Henry F White Jr, Executive Director
Robert Horowitz, Associate Director
Aims to improve children's lives through advances in law,
justice, knowledge, practice and public policy.
400,000 members

5 American Camp Association
5000 State Road 67 N
Martinsville, IN 46151-7902   765-342-8456
                               FAX 765-342-2065
                               http://www.acacamps.org
                               e-mail: acacamps@acacamps.org

Peter Surgenor, President
Scott Brody, VP
Peg Smith, Executive Director/CEO
A community of camp professionals who, for more than 100
years, have joined together to share knowledge and experience and to ensure the quality of camp programs. Just as our
membership is diverse and programs distinct, so are the children who participate in the camp experience. Through what
we teach, the opportunities we offer, and the example we set,
children become part of a sharing community.
6,700+ members

6 American College Testing
500 Act Dr
Iowa City, IA 52243-0168   319-337-1000
                              FAX 319-339-3021
                              http://www.act.org

Richard L Ferguson, CEO/Chairman
Cynthia Board Schmeiser, President/COO
Janet Godwin, VP Operations
An independent, not-for-profit organization that provides
more than a hundred assessment, research, information, and
program management services in the broad areas of education and workforce development.
1959

7 American Counseling Association
5999 Stevenson Ave
Alexandria, VA 22304-3304   703-823-9800
                                    800-347-6647
                               FAX 703-823-0252
                               http://www.counseling.org
                               e-mail: aca@counseling.org

Marcheta Evans, President
Debra Bass, Marketing Director
Richard Yep, Executive Director
A not-for-profit, professional and educational organization
that is dedicated to the growth and enhancement of the counseling profession. The largest association exclusively representing professional counselors in various practice settings.
45,000 members 1952

8 American Dance Therapy Association (ADTA)
10632 Little Patuxent Pkwy
Ste 108
Columbia, MD 21044-3263   410-997-4040
                             FAX 410-997-4048
                             http://www.adta.org
                             e-mail: info@adta.org

Robyn Flaum Cruz, President

Works to establish and maintain high standards of professional education and competence in the field of dance/move-
ment therapy. ADTA stimulates communication among
dance/movement therapists and members of allied professions through publication of the ADTA Newsletter, the
American Journal of Dance Therapy, monographs, bibliog-
raphies, and conference proceedings.
1966

9 American Occupational Therapy Association
PO Box 31220
Bethesda, MD 20824-1220   301-652-2682
                             FAX 301-652-7711
                             http://www.aota.org
                             e-mail: praota@aota.org

Florence Clark, President
Frederick P Somers, Executive Director

Founded to represent the interests and concerns of occupational therapy practitioners and students of occupational
therapy and to improve the quality of occupational therapy
services. Advances the quality, availability, use, and support of occupational therapy through standard-setting, advocacy, education and research on behalf of its members and
the public.
36,000 members 1917

10   American Psychological Association
750 1st St NE
Washington, DC 20002-4242
202-336-5500
800-374-2721
FAX 202-336-5518
TDD:202-336-6123
http://www.apa.org
e-mail: psycinfo@apa.org
Carol D Goodheart, President
Nancy Gordon Moore, Staff Liaison

Its objectives are to advance psychology as a science and profession and as a means of promoting health, education and human welfare.
148,000 members

11   American Public Human Services Association (APHSA)
1133 19th St NW
Ste 400
Washington, DC 20036-3623
202-682-0100
FAX 202-289-6555
http://www.aphsa.org
e-mail: carolyn.marshall@aphsa.org
Carl Desantis, Interim Executive Director

A nonprofit, bipartisan organization of state and local human service agencies and individuals who work in or are interested in public human service programs. Mission is to develop and promote policies and practices that improve the health and well-being of families, children, and adults
1930

12   American Red Cross American Red Cross National Headquarters
2025 E Street NW
Washington, DC 20006
202-303-4498
FAX 518-459-8268
http://www.redcross.org
e-mail: info@usa.redcross.org
Gail J McGovern, President/CEO
Bonnie McElveen Hunter, Chair, Board of Governors

Founded in 1881. A humanitarian organization led by volunteers, guided by its Congressional Charter and the fundamental principles of the International Red Cross Movement to provide relief to victims of disasters and help people prevent, prepare for, and respond to emergencies.

13   American Rehabilitation Counseling Association (ARCA)
5999 Stevenson Ave
Alexandria, VA 22304-3304
703-823-9800
800-347-6647
FAX 703-461-9260
TDD:937-775-3153
http://www.arcaweb.org
Frank Lane, President

An organization of rehabilitation counseling practitioners, educators, and students who are concerned with improving the lives of people with disabilities. The mission is to enhance the lives of people with disabilities and to promote excellence in the rehabilitation counseling profession.

14   American Speech-Language-Hearing Association
2200 Research Blvd
Rockville, MD 20850-3289
301-296-5700
800-498-2071
FAX 301-296-8580
TTY: 301-296-5650
http://www.asha.org
e-mail: actioncenter@asha.org
Tommie L Robinson Jr, President
Arlene Pietranton PhD, Executive Director

Promotes the interests of and provide the highest quality services for professionals in audiology, speech-language pathology, and speech and hearing science, and to advocate for people with communication disabilities.
127,000 members 1958

15   Association On Higher Education and Disability (AHEAD)
107 Commerce Center Dr
Ste 204
Huntersville, NC 28078
704-947-7779
FAX 704-948-7779
http://www.ahead.org
Tri Do, Operations Manager
Richard Allegra, Professional Development Dir
Oonh Huvnh, Assoc Executive Director
A professional membership organization for individuals invloved in the development of policy and the provision of quality services to meet the needs of persons with disabiities in all aspects of higher education.

16   Association of Educational Therapists
11300 W Olympic Blvd
Ste 600
Los Angeles, CA 90064-1663
310-909-1490
800-286-4267
FAX 310-437-0585
http://www.aetonline.org
e-mail: aet@aetonline.org
Risa Graf, President

A national professional organization dedicated to establishing ethical professional standards, defining the roles and responsibilities of the educational therapist, providing opportunities for professional growth, and to studying techniques and technologies, philosophies and research related to the practice of educational therapy.

17   Attention Deficit Disorder Association
15000 Commerce Pkwy
Suite C
Mount Laurel, NJ 08054-2212
856-439-9099
FAX 856-439-0525
http://www.add.org
e-mail: mail@add.org
Evelyn Polk Green, MS.Ed, President
Linda Roggli, PCC, Vice President
Janet Kramer, M.D., Treasurer
The National Attention Deficit Disorder Association is an organization focused on the needs of adults and young adults with ADD/ADHD, and their children and families. We seek to serve individuals with ADD, as well as those who love, live with, teach, counsel and treat them.
1989

18   Autism Research Institute
4182 Adams Ave
San Diego, CA 92116-2599
619-281-7165
866-366-3361
FAX 619-563-6840
http://www.autismresearchinstitute.com
e-mail: matt@autism.com
Steve Edelson, Director

Founded to conduct and foster scientific research designed to improve methods of diagnosing, treating and preventing autism. ARI also disseminates research findings to parents and others worldwide seeking help.
1967

19   Autism Society
4340 East West Highway
Ste 350
Bethesda, MD 20814-3067
301-657-0881
800-328-8476
FAX 301-657-0869
http://www.autism-society.org
e-mail: info@autism-society.org

Lee Grossman, President/CEO
Jennifer Repella, Director of Programs

Works to increase public awareness about the day-to-day issues faced by those on the autism spectrum. Offers a national contact center, local chapters throughout the country, a quarterly magazine and an annual conference.
120,000 members 1965

20   Autism Treatment Center of America

2080 S Undermountain Rd
Sheffield, MA 01257-9643   413-229-2100
                                         877-766-7473
                                  FAX 413-229-3202
                     http://www.autismtreatmentcenter.org
Barry Kausman, Founder
Samahria Lyte Kaufman, Co-Founder
Bryn Hogan, Executive Director
Provides innovative training programs for parents and professionals caring for children challenged by Autism, Autism Spectrum Disorders, Pervasive Developmental Disorder (PDD) and other developmental difficulties. The Son-Rise Program teaches a specific yet comprehensive system of treatment and education designed to help families and caregivers enable their children to dramatically improve in all areas of learning.

21   Best Buddies International

100 SE 2nd St
Ste 2200
Miami, FL 33131-2151   305-374-2233
                                         800-892-8339
                                  FAX 305-374-5305
                          http://www.bestbuddies.org
                          e-mail: info@bestbuddies.org
Anthony Shriver, Founder/Chairman

A nonprofit organization dedicated to enhancing the lives of people with intellectual disabilities by providing opportunities for one-to-one friendships and integrated employment. Best Buddies is a vibrant, international organization that has grown from one original chapter to more that 1,300 middle school, high school and college campuses across the country and abroad.
1989

22   Birth Defect Research for Children (BDRC)

800 Celebration Ave
Ste 225
Celebration, FL 34747-5155   407-566-8304
                                  FAX 407-566-8341
                          http://www.birthdefects.org
                          e-mail: staff@birthdefects.org
Betty Mekdeci, Founder
Mike Mekdeci, Co-Founder

A non-profit organization that provides parents and expectant parents with information about birth defects and support services for children. BDRC also has a parent-matching program that links families who have children with similar birth defects.
1982

23   Boy Scouts of America
Scouting for the Handicapped Services
PO Box 152079
Irving, TX 75015-2079   972-580-2000
                                  FAX 972-580-2502
                             http://www.scouting.org
Robert Mazzuca, CEO

Provides an educational program for boys and young adults to build character, to train in the responsibilities of participating citizenship, and to develop personal fitness.
1910

24   Brain Injury Association of America

1608 Spring Hill Rd
Ste 110
Vienna, VA 22182-2241   703-761-0750
                                         800-444-6443
                                  FAX 703-761-0755
                               http://www.biausa.org
                          e-mail: info@biausa.org
Susan H Connors, President/CEO

A national organization serving and representing individuals, families and professionals who are touched by a life-altering traumatic brain injury.
1980

25   Career College Association (CCA)

1101 Connecticut Ave NW
Ste 900
Washington, DC 20036-4346   202-336-6700
                                         866-711-8574
                                  FAX 202-336-6828
                               http://www.career.org
                          e-mail: cca@career.org
Harris Miller, President/CEO
Bruce Leftwich, VP Legislation
Milt Girdner, CFO
CCA has over 1,400 members that educate and prepare two million students each year for employment in over 200 occupational fields.
1,400 members

26   Center for Adult English Language Acquisition (CAELA)

4646 40th St NW
Washington, DC 20016-1859   202-362-0700
                                  FAX 202-362-3740
                               http://www.cal.org/caela
                          e-mail: caelanetwork@cal.org
Joy Peyton, Director
Donna Christian, President

A national center focusing on literacy education for adults and out-of-school youth learning English as a second language. CAELA publishes many documents on its website.

27   Center for Applied Linguistics

4646 40th St NW
Washington, DC 20016-1867   202-362-0700
                                  FAX 202-362-3740
                               http://www.cal.org
                          e-mail: info@cal.org
Donna Christian, President

A private, nonprofit organization working to improve communication through better understanding of language and culture. Dedicated to providing a comprehensive range of research-based language tools and resources related to language and culture.
1959

28   Center for Applied Special Technology (CAST)

40 Harvard Mills Sq
Ste 3
Wakefield, MA 01880-3233   781-245-2212
                                  FAX 978-531-0192
                               http://www.cast.org
                          e-mail: cast@cast.org
Ada Sullivan, President

CAST has earned international recognition for innovative, technology-based educational resources and strategies based on the principals of Universal Design for Learning (UDL). The mission is to expand opportunities for all individuals, especially those with disabilities, through the research and development of innovative, technology-based educational resources and strategies.
1984

29 **Closing the Gap**
Computer Technology in Special Education & Rehab.
PO Box 68
Henderson, MN 56044-0068   507-248-3294
                                  FAX 507-248-3810
                    http://www.closingthegap.com
                    e-mail: info@closingthegap.com
Dolores Hagen, Founder
Budd Hagan, Co-Founder
Connie Kneip, VP/General Manager
An organization that focuses on computer technology for
people with special needs through its bi-monthly newsletter,
annual international conference and extensive web site.
                    1983

30 **College Board Services for Students with Disabilities**
PO Box 6226
Princeton, NJ 08541-6226   609-771-7137
                                  FAX 609-771-7944
                                  TTY: 609-882-4118
                    http://www.collegeboard.org
                    e-mail: ssd@info.collegeboard.org
Gaston Caperton, President

Founded in 1900. Offers testing accommodations that mini-
mize the effect of disabilities on test performance. The SAT
Program tests eligible students with documented visual,
physical, hearing, or learning disabilities who require testing accommodations for SAT.

31 **Commission on Accreditation of Rehabilitation Facilities (CARF)**
6951 E Southpoint Rd
Tucson, AZ 85756   520-325-1044
                                  888-281-6531
                                  FAX 520-318-1129
                                  TDD:888-281-6531
                    http://www.carf.org
                    e-mail: feedback@carf.org
Brian J Boon PhD, President/CEO

An independent, nonprofit accreditor of human service providers in the areas of aging services, behavioral health, child
and youth services, DMEPOS, employment and medical rehabilitation.
                    1966

32 **Council for Exceptional Children (CEC)**
1110 N Glebe Rd
Ste 300
Arlington, VA 22201-5704   703-243-0446
                                  888-232-7733
                                  FAX 703-264-9494
                                  TTY: 866-915-5000
                    http://www.cec.sped.org
                    e-mail: service@cec.sped.org
Bruce Ramirez, Executive Director
Dan Ratner, Asst Executive Director

An international professional organization dedicated to improving educational outcomes for individuals with
exceptionalities, students with disabilities, and/or the
gifted. Advocates for appropriate governmental policies,
sets professional standards, provides continual professional
development, advocates for underserved individuals with
exceptionalities, and helps professionals obtain resources
necessary for effective professional practice.

33 **Council for Learning Disabilities**
11184 Antioch
PO Box 405
Overland Park, KS 66210   913-491-1011
                                  FAX 913-491-1012
                    http://www.cldinternational.org
                    e-mail: CLDinfo@ie-events.com
Caroline Dunn, President
Linda Nease, Executive Director

An international organization concerned about issues related to students with learning disabilities. Working to build
a better future for students with LD has been the primary
goal of CLD for more than 20 years. Involvement in CLD
helps members stay abreast of current issues that are shaping
the field, affecting the lives of students, and influencing
professional careers.

34 **Council on Rehabilitation Education**
1699 Woodfield Rd
Ste 300
Schaumburg, IL 60173-2088   847-944-1345
                                  FAX 847-944-1346
                    http://www.core-rehab.org
                    e-mail: sdenys@cpcredentialing.com
Dr Marvin D Kuehn, Executive Director
Dr Tom Evenson, President

Seeks to provide effective delivery of rehabilitation services
to individuals with disabilities by stimulating and fostering
continuing review and improvement of master's degree
level rehabilitation counselor education programs.

35 **Culturally & Linguistically Diverse Exceptional Learn-
ers Division of CEC**
Council for Exceptional Children
1110 N Glebe Rd
Ste 300
Arlington, VA 22201-5704
                                  888-232-7733
                                  FAX 703-264-9494
                                  TTY: 866-915-5000
                    http://www.ddelcec.org
                    e-mail: admin@ddelcec.org
Sandra Nichols, President
Drew Allbritten MD, Executive Director

The official division of the Council for Exceptional Children, that promotes tha advancement and improvement of
educational opportunities for culturally and linguistically
diverse learners with disabilities and/or gifts and talents,
their families, and the professionals who serve them.

36 **Disability Rights Education & Defense Fund (DREDF)**
2212 6th St
Berkeley, CA 94710-2219   510-644-2555
                                  800-348-4232
                                  FAX 510-841-8645
                                  TTY: 510-644-2555
                    http://www.dredf.org
                    e-mail: info@dredf.org
Susan Henderson, Executive Director

A national civil rights law and policy center directed by individuals with disabilities and parents who have children with
disabilities. Advances the civil and human rights of people
with disabilities through legal advocacy, training, education, and public policy and legislative development.
                    1979

37 **Distance Education and Training Council (DETC)**
1601 18th St NW
Suite 2
Washington, DC 20009-2529   202-234-5100
                                  FAX 202-332-1386
                    http://www.detc.org
                    e-mail: brianna@detc.org
Michael P Lambert, Executive Director
Brianna Bates, Information Specialist

A nonprofit educational association founded to promote
sound educational standards and ethical business practices
within the correspondence field.
                    1926

38   Division for Communicative Disabilities and Deafness (DCDD)
1110 N Glebe Rd
Ste 300
Arlington, VA 22201-5704

703-243-0446
888-232-7733
FAX 703-264-9494
TTY: 866-915-5000
http://www.dcdd.us
e-mail: info@dcdd.us

Marguerite Vasconcellos, Director
David Conway, Secretary

The DCDD is concerned with the well-being, development, and education of infants, toddlers, children, and youth with communication and learning disorders, ranging from mild to profound and/or who are deaf or hard of hearing. ims to provide information to families regarding the development of communicationa and learning disabilities.

39   Division for Early Childhood of CEC
27 Fort Missoula
Ste 2
Missoula, MT 59804-7200

406-543-0872
FAX 406-543-0887
http://www.dec-sped.org
e-mail: dec@dec-sped.org

Sarah Mulligan, Executive Director

An international membership association for those who work with or on behalf of children with disabilities, birth through age eight and their families.
1973

40   Division on Career Development & Transition (DCDT)
1110 N Glebe Rd
Ste 300
Arlington, VA 22201-5704

703-620-3660
888-232-7733
FAX 703-264-9494
TDD:866-915-5000
TTY: 703-264-9446
http://www.dcdt.org
e-mail: dalun@tamu.edu

Dalun Zhang, President

Promotes national and international efforts to improve the quality of and access to career, vocational and transition services. Works to influence policies affecting career development and transition services for persons with disabilities.

41   Dyscalculia International Consortium (DIC)
7420 Calhoun Street
Dearborn, MI 48126

FAX 888-710-0951
http://www.dyscalculia.org
e-mail: help@dyscalculia.org

Renee M Newman, President
Mahesh Sharma, Dyscaculia Expert
Shad Moraif, Psychologist
A non-profit educational organization dedicated to advancing understanding and treatment of specific learning disabilities in mathematics AKA dyscaculia. Aims to provide free to the public, information about math learning disability and the best practices for diagnosis and treatment.

42   Easter Seals
233 S Wacker Dr
Ste 2400
Chicago, IL 60606-6410

312-726-6200
800-221-6827
FAX 312-726-1494
TDD:312-726-4258
http://www.easterseals.com
e-mail: info@easterseals.com

F. Timothy Muri, President/CEO
Sara Brewster, VP Communications
Rosemary Garza, Information/Referral Specialist

Easter Seals' mission is to create solutions that change lives for children and adults with disabilities, their families, and their communities. We work to identify the needs of people with disabilities and to provide appropriate developmental and rehabilitation services. Easter Seals operates 550 web sites that provide services to children and adults with disabilities and their families.

43   Eden Autism Services
1 Eden Way
Princeton, NJ 08540-5711

609-987-0099
FAX 609-987-0243
http://www.edenautismservices.org
e-mail: info@edenservices.org

Tom Mc Cool EdD, President/CEO

Provides year round educational services, early intervention, parent training, respite care, outreach services, community based residential services and employment opportunities for individuals with autism.

44   Educational Equity Center at Academy for Educational Development
100 5th Ave
Fl 8
New York, NY 10011-6903

212-243-1110
FAX 212-627-0407
TTY: 212-243-1110
http://www.edequity.org
e-mail: lcolon@aed.org

Merle Froschl, Co-Founder/Director
Barbara Sprung, Co-Founder/Co-Director
Linda Colon, Program Manager
A national not-for-profit organization that promotes bias-free learning through innovative programs and materials. The mission is to decrease discrimination based on gender, race/ethnicity, disability, and level of family income

45   Edvantia
PO Box 1348
Charleston, WV 25325-1348

304-347-0400
800-624-9120
FAX 304-347-0487
http://www.edvantia.org
e-mail: info@edvantia.org

Doris Redfield, President/CEO

Edvantia is an education research and development not-for-profit corporation.
1966

46   Families and Advocates Partnership for Education
PACER Center
8161 Normandale Blvd
Minneapolis, MN 55437-1044

952-838-9000
888-248-0822
FAX 952-838-0199
TTY: 952-838-0190
http://www.fape.org
e-mail: fape@fape.org

Paula Goldberg, Executive Director

The FAPE project is a strong partnership that aims to improve the educational outcomes for children with disabilities. FAPE links families, advocates, and self-advocates to information about the Individuals with Disabilities Education Act (IDEA). The project represents the needs of seven million children with disabilities.

47   Federation for Children with Special Needs
1135 Tremont St
Ste 420
Boston, MA 02120-2199

617-236-7210
800-331-0688
FAX 617-572-2094
TDD:617-236-7210
http://www.fcsn.org
e-mail: fcsninfo@fcsn.org

Richard Robison, Executive Director
Sara Miranda, Associate Executive Director

The mission of the Federation is to provide information, support and assistance to parents of children with disabilities, their professional partners and their communities. Major services are information and referral and parent and professional training.
1974

48   Friends-In-Art
4317 Vermont Ct
Columbia, MO 65203
573-445-5564
http://www.acb.org
e-mail: info@acb.org

Peter Altschut, President

Aims to enlarge the art experience of blind people, encourages blind people to visit museums, galleries, concerts, the theater and other enjoyable public places, offers consultation to program planners establishing accessible art and museum exhibits and presents Performing Arts Showcases at the American Council of the Blinds' national convention.
1961

49   Independent Living Research Utilization Program
Institute of Rehabilitation and Research
2323 S Shepher Dr
Ste 1000
Houston, TX 77019-7031
713-520-9058
FAX 713-520-5785
TTY: 713-520-0232
http://www.ilru.org
e-mail: ilru@ilru.org

Lex Frieden, Director

A national center for information, training, research, and technical assistance in independent living. Its goal is to expand the body of knowledge in independent living and to improve utilization of results of research programs and demonstration projects in this field.
1977

50   Institute for Educational Leadership
4455 Connecticut Ave NW
Ste 310
Washington, DC 20008-2328
202-822-8405
FAX 202-872-4050
http://www.iel.org
e-mail: iel@iel.org

Martin J Blank, President/CEO
Louise A Clarke, Chief Administrative Officer

Mission is to improve education and the lives of children and their families through positive and visionary change.

51   Institute for Human Centered Design
Adaptive Environments
200 Portland St
Ste 1
Boston, MA 02114
617-695-0085
800-949-4232
FAX 617-482-8099
TTY: 617-695-1225
http://adaptiveenvironments.org
e-mail: info@humancentereddesign.org

Marie Trottier, President
Oce Harrison, Project Director
Valerie Fletcher, Executive Director
Provides information and guidance on the Americans with Disabilities Act, Section 508, and accessible information technology to individuals in New England.
1978

52   Institutes for the Achievement of Human Potential
8801 Stenton Ave
Wyndmoor, PA 19038-8397
215-233-2050
800-736-4663
FAX 215-233-9312
http://www.iahp.org
e-mail: institutes@iahp.org

Janet Doman, Founder/Director
Dr. Leland Green, Medical Director
Dr Mihai Dimencescu, Chairman
Nonprofit educational organization that serves children by introducing parents to the field of child brain development. Parents learn how to enhance significantly the development of their children physically, intellectually and socially in a joyous and sensible way.
1955

53   International Dyslexia Association
40 York Rd
4th Floor
Baltimore, MD 21204
410-296-0232
FAX 410-321-5069
http://www.interdyslexia.org
e-mail: info@interdys.org

Guinevere Eden Ph.D., President
Stephen Peregoy, Executive Director

The International Dyslexia Association is an international organization that concerns itself with the complex issues of dyslexia. The IDA membership consist of a variety of professionals in partnership with people with dyslexia and their families and all others interested in The Association's mission.
13,000 members

54   International Reading Association
800 Barksdale Rd.
PO Box 8139
Newark, DE 19714-8139
302-731-1600
800-336-7323
FAX 302-731-1057
http://www.reading.org
e-mail: customerservice@reading.org
Patricia A Edwards, President
Victoria J Risko, President-Elect
Mark Mullen, Acting Executive Director
The mission of the International Reading Association is to promote reading by continuously advancing the quality of literacy instruction and research worldwide.
1956

55   LD Online Math & Dyscalculia
2775 South Quincy Street
Arlington, VA 22206
FAX 703-998-2060
Noel Gunther, Executive Director
Christian Lindstrom, Director, Learning Media
Rachel Walker, Outreach Counselor
Provides information and referrals to both parents and educators dealing with children that are diagnosed with disabilities in mathematics also known as dyscalculia.

56   Landmark School Outreach Program
Landmark School
429 Hale Street
P.O. Box 227
Prides Crossing, MA 01965-0227
978-236-3216
FAX 978-927-7268
http://www.landmarkoutreach.org
e-mail: outreach@landmarkschool.org
Dan Ahearn, Director of Outreach
Patricia Newhall, Associate Director of Outreach
Kathryn Frye, Outreach Registrar
Our professional development programs and publications offer research-based practical strategies for educators so that they may empower stydents with language-based learning disabilities and differences to become more effective and efficient learners.

57 Learning Ally
205 Badger Road
Oak Ridge, TN 37830   865-482-3496
                                        800-221-4792
                                    FAX 865-483-9934
                          http://www.LearningAlly.org
                       e-mail: cmorris@LearningAlly.org
Cecelia Morris, Production Director

Part of the national, nonprofit organization is dedicated to
serving individuals with visual and learning disabilities by
providing educational content, products and services to individuals for whom access and reading are barriers to learning.

58 Learning Disabilities Association of America
4156 Library Rd
Pittsburgh, PA 15234-1349   412-341-1515
                                    FAX 412-344-0224
                          http://www.LDAAmerica.org
                       e-mail: info@ldaamerica.org
Mary-Clare Reynolds, Executive Director

LDA is a grassroots, membership organization for learning
disabilities.
                    15,000+ members 1964

59 Learning Resource Network
PO Box 9
River Falls, WI 54022-0009   715-426-9777
                                        800-678-5376
                                    FAX 888-234-8633
                              http://www.lern.org
                           e-mail: info@lern.org
William A Draves, President
Julie Coates, VP Information Services

We are an international association of lifelong learning and
offer programming, information and resources to providers
of lifelong leraning programs.

60 MATRIX: A Parent Network and Resource Ctr
94 Galli Dr
Ste C
Novato, CA 94949-5739   415-884-3535
                                        800-578-2592
                                    FAX 415-884-3555
                                    TDD:415-884-3554
                        http://www.matrixparents.org
                     e-mail: info@matrixparents.org
Nora Thompson, Executive Director

Providing families who have children with disabilities and
other special needs with the tools they need to effectively advocate for themselves.
                    1983

**61 Marshall University HELP (Higher Education for
Learning Problems)**
520 18th St
Huntington, WV 25703-1530   304-696-6252
                                    FAX 304-696-3231
                                    TDD:202-272-2074
                          http://www.marshall.edu/help
                       e-mail: moorek@marshall.edu
Lynne Weston, HELP Program Director

Provides educational support, remediation, and mentoring
to individuals diagnosed with a learning disability and/or
ADD/ADHD. Comprise of Community H.E.L.P., College
H.E.L.P., Medical/Law H.E.L.P., and Diagnostic H.E.L.P.

62 Menninger Clinic: Center for Learning Disabilities
2801 Gessner Dr
PO Box 809045
Houston, TX 77280-9045   713-275-5000
                                        800-351-9058
                                    FAX 713-275-5107
                         http://www.menningerclinic.com
                        e-mail: info@menninger.edu
Ian Aitken, President/CEO
John Oldham, VP/Chief of Staff
Pam Greene, VP/CNO
The mission of Menninger is to be a national resource providing psychiatric care and treatment of the highest standard, searching for better understanding of mental illness
and human behavior, teaching what we know and what we
learn, and applying this knowledge in useful ways to promote individual growth and better mental health.
             1925Grade Range: All Ages

63 National ARD/IEP Advocates
PO Box 16111
Sugar Land, TX 77496-6111   281-265-1506
                                    FAX 253-295-9954
                              http://www.narda.org
                           e-mail: louis@narda.org
Louis Geigerman, Founder/President

National ARD Advocates is dedicated to obtaining the appropriate educational services for children with special
needs.

**64 National Adult Education Professional Development
Consortium**
444 N Capitol St NW
Ste 422
Washington, DC 20001-1557   202-624-5250
                                    FAX 202-624-1497
                              http://www.naepdc.org
                       e-mail: lmclendon@naepdc.org
Lennox Mc Lendon, Executive Director

Incorporated in 1990 by state and adult education directors,
provides professional development, policy analysis, and
dissemination of information important to state staff in adult
education.

**65 National Association for Adults with Special Learning
Needs**
1143 Tidewater Ct
Westerville, OH 43082-5402
                                        888-562-2756
                                    FAX 614-392-1559
                              http://www.naasln.org
Richard Cooper, President
Joan Hudson-Miller, President

An association for those who serve adults with special learning needs. Members include educators, trainers, employers
and human service providers

66 National Association for Child Development
549 27th St
Ogden, UT 84504-2422   801-621-8606
                                    FAX 801-621-8389
                              http://www.nacd.org
                           e-mail: mail@nacd.org
Robert J Doman Jr, Director

Provides neurodevelopmental evaluations and individualized programs for children and adults, updated on a quarterly
basis. Stresses parent training and parent implementation of
the program.

67   National Association for Community Mediation
1959 2 Power Rd
Ste 103-279
Mesa, CA 85206   602-633-4213
http://www.nafcm.org
e-mail: info@nafcm.org
Justin R Corbett, Executive Director

Supports the maintenance and growth of community-based
mediation programs and processes; acts as a resource for mediation information; locates a center to help individuals and
groups resolve disputes.

68   National Association for Gifted Children
1707 L St NW
Ste 550
Washington, DC 20036-4212   202-785-4268
FAX 202-785-4248
http://www.nagc.org
e-mail: nagc@nagc.org
Ann Robinson, President
Nancy Green, Executive Director

An organization of parents, teachers, educators, other professionals, and community leaders who unite to address the
unique needs of children and youth with demonstrated gifts
and talents as well as those children who may be able to develop their talent potential with appropriate educational
experiences.
8,000+ members

**69   National Association for the Education of Young Chil-
dren (NAEYC)**
1313 L St NW
Ste 500
Washington, DC 20005-4110   202-232-8777
800-424-2460
FAX 202-328-1846
http://www.naeyc.org
e-mail: naeyc@naeyc.org
Stephanie Fanjul, President
Roberta R Schumburg, VP
Jerlean Daniel, Executive Director
Dedicated to improving the well-being of all children, with
particular focus on the quality of educational and developmental services for children from birth through age 8. Also
the largest organization working on behalf of young adults
with nearly 100,000 members, a national network of over
300 local, state and regional affiliates, and a growing global
alliance of like-minded organizations.
1926

**70   National Association of Councils on Disabilities
(NACDD)**
1660 L St NW
Ste 700
Washington, DC 20036   202-506-5813
FAX 202-506-5846
http://www.nacdd.org
e-mail: info@nacdd.org
Deborah Swingley, President
Shari Lynn Cooper, VP
Michael Brogioli, Executive Director/CEO
A national member-driven organization consisting of 55
State and Territorial Councils. Places high value on mean-
ingful participation and contribution by Council members
and staff of all Member Councils, and continually work to-
wards positive system change on behalf of individuals with
developmental disabilities and their families. Founded in
2002.

**71   National Association of Parents with Children in Special
Education**
1431 W South Fork Dr
Phoenix, AZ 85045   800-754-4421
FAX 800-424-0371
http://www.napcse.org
e-mail: contact@napcse.org
Dr George Giuliani, President

A national membership organization dedicated to rendering
all possible support and assistance to parents whose children
receive special education services, both in and outside of
school. NAPCSE was founded to promote a sense of community and provide a national forum for ideas.

**72   National Association of Private Special Education Cen-
ters (NAPSEC)**
601 Pennsylvania Ave NW
Ste 900
Washington, DC 20004   202-434-8225
FAX 202-434-8224
http://www.napsec.org
e-mail: napsec@aol.com
Sherry Kolbe, Executive Director

A nonprofit association whose mission is to ensure access
for individuals to private special education as a vital component of the continuum of appropriate placement and services
in American education. The association consists solely of
private special education programs that serve both both pri-
vately and publicly placed individuals of all ages with
disabilities.

**73   National Association of Special Education Teachers
(NASET)**
1250 Connecticut Ave NW
Ste 200
Washington, DC 20036-2643   202-296-7739
800-754-4221
FAX 800-754-4221
http://www.naset.org
e-mail: contactus@naset.org
Dr Roger Pierangelo, Executive Director
Dr George Giuliani, Executive Director

A national membership organization dedicated to rendering
all possible support and assistance to those preparing for or
teaching in the field of special education.

**74   National Association of the Education of African Ameri-
can Children with Learning Disabilities**
PO Box 09521
Columbus, OH 43209-0521   614-237-6021
FAX 614-238-0929
http://www.aacld.org
e-mail: info@aacld.org
Nancy R Tidwell, President/Founder

The NAEAACLD links information and resources provided
by an established network of individuals and organizations
experienced in minority research and special education with
parents, educators and others responsible for providing an
appropriate education for African American students.

75   National Business and Disability Council
201 I U Willets Rd
Albertson, NY 11507-1516   516-465-1516
FAX 516-465-1591
http://www.nbdc.com
e-mail: jtowles@abilitiesonline.org
Edmund L Cortez, President/CEO

A leading resource for employers seeking to integrate people with disabilities into the workplace and companies seeking to reach them in the consumer marketplace. The NBDC has played a major role in helping businesses create accessible work conditions for employees and accessible products and services for consumers.

76   National Center for Family Literacy (NCFL)
325 W Main St
Ste 300
Louisville, KY 40202-4237   502-584-1133
                                    877-326-5481
                                    FAX 502-584-0172
                                    http://www.famlit.org
                                    e-mail: ncfl@famlit.org
Sharon Darling, President/Founder

Mission is to create a literate nation by leveraging the power of family. Family literacy is an intergenerational approach based on the indisputable evidence that low literacy is an unfortunate and debilitating family tradition.
1989

77   National Center for Learning Disabilities (NCLD)
381 Park Ave S
Ste 1401
New York, NY 10016-8829   212-545-7510
                                  888-575-7373
                                  FAX 212-545-9665
                                  http://www.ld.org
                                  e-mail: help@ncld.org
James Wendorf, Executive Director

Works to ensure that that nation's 15 million children, adolescents and adults with learning disabilities have every opportunity for succees in school, work and life. NCLD also provides essential information to parents, professionals and individuals with learning disabilities, promotes research and programs to foster effective learning and advocates for policies to protect and strengthen educational rights and opportunities.
1977

78   National Center for Youth Law
405 14th St
15th Fl
Oakland, CA 94612-2715   510-835-8098
                                 FAX 510-835-8099
                                 http://www.youthlaw.org
                                 e-mail: info@youthlaw.org
Peter B Edelman, President
John O'Toole, Director

Uses the law to improve the lives of low-income children. Also works to ensure that low-income children have the resources, support, and opportunities they need for a healthy and productive future. Much of NCYL's work is focused on poor children who are additionally challenged by abuse and neglect, disability, or other disadvantage.

79   National Council for Support of Disability Issues
3870 Mountain Rd
Haymarket, VA 20169   703-753-9148
                              FAX 703-753-9148
Jason Perry, President
Trisha Fink, Executive Director

The council's goal is to provide a means for sharing information, resources, ideas and support between people with all types of disabilities.

80   National Council of Juvenile and Family Court Judges (NCJFCJ)
PO Box 8970
Reno, NV 89507-8970   775-784-6012
                               FAX 775-784-6628
                               http://www.ncjfcj.org
                               e-mail: staff@ncjfcj.org

Judge R Michael Key, President
Cheryl Davidek, Director
Mary Mentaberry, Executive Director
The vision of the NCJFCJ is that every child and young person be reared in a safe, permanent, and nuturing family, where love, self-control, concern for others, and responsibility for the consequences of one's actions are experienced and taught as fundamental values for a successful life. Also advocates that every family in need of judicial oversight has access to fair, effective and timely justice.
1973 Grade Range: Professional Ed

81   National Council on Rehabilitation Education
California State University
5005 N Maple Ave
Fresno, CA 93740   559-906-0787
                            FAX 559-412-2550
                            http://www.rehabeducators.org
                            e-mail: info@rehabeducators.org
David R Strauser, President
Charles Arokiasamy, COO

A professional organization of educators dedicated to quality services for persons with disabilities through education and research. NCRE advocates-up-to-date education and training and the maintenance of professional standards in the field of rehabilitation
1955

82   National Disabilities Rights Network
900 2nd St NE
Ste 211
Washington, DC 20002-3560   202-408-9514
                                     FAX 202-408-9520
                                     TDD:202-408-9521
                                     http://www.ndrn.org
                                     e-mail: info@ndrn.org
Curtis Decker, Executive Director

Nonprofit membership organization for the federally mandated Protection and Advocacy (P&A) Systems and Client Assistance Programs (CAP) for individuals with disabilities. Serves a wide range of individuals with disabilities including, but not limited to, those with cognitive, mental, sensory, and physical disabilities. Services include guarding against abuse; advocating for basic rights; and ensuring accountability in health care, education, employment, housing, and transportation.

83   National Dissemination Center for Children with Disabilities
1825 Connecticut Ave NW
Suite 700
Washington, DC 20009   202-884-8200
                                800-695-0285
                                FAX 202-884-8441
                                TDD:800-695-0285
                                http://www.nichcy.org
                                e-mail: nichcy@aed.org
Stephen D Luke EdD, Project Director

NICHCY provides a website full of information on special education, early intervention, disabilities in children.

84   National Education Association (NEA)
1201 16th St NW
Washington, DC 20036-3290   202-833-4000
                                     FAX 202-822-7974
                                     http://www.nea.org
Dennis Van Roekel, President
John Wilson, Executive Director

The nation's largest professional employee organization, it is committed to advancing the cause of public education. NEA's members work at every level of education, from pre-school to university graduate programs. Also has affiliate organization in every state and in more than 14,000 communities across the United States.
3.2 million mem

85 **National Federation of the Blind**
200 E. Wells St. at Jernigan Place
Baltimore, MD 21230-4998   410-659-9314
FAX 410-685-5653
http://www.nfb.org
e-mail: nfb@nfb.org
Marc Maurer, President

The largest and most influential membership organization of
blind people in the United States. The NFB improves blind
people's lives through advocacy, education, research, technology, and programs encouraging independence and
self-confidence. It is also the leading force in the blindness
field today and the voice of the nation's blind.
50,000 members 1940

86 **National Institute of Art and Disabilities**
551 23rd St
Richmond, CA 94804-1626   510-620-0290
FAX 510-620-0326
http://www.niadart.org
e-mail: admin@niadart.org
Patricia Coleman, Executive Director

An innovative visual arts center assisting adults with developmental and other physical disabilities. Provides an art program that promotes creativity, independence, dignity, and
community integration for people with developmental and
other disabilities.
1982

87 **National Jewish Council for Disabilities Summer Program**
YACHAD East Coast Adventure
11 Broadway
13th Fl
New York, NY 10004-1303   212-613-8229
FAX 212-613-0796
http://www.njcd.org
e-mail: njcd@ou.org
Jeffrey Lichtman, National Director

Yachad/NJCD is dedicated to addressing the needs of all individuals with disabilities and including them in the Jewish
community. Summer Programs include a variety of summer
experiences for youth and adults with developmental
disabilities.

88 **National Joint Committee on Learning Disabilities**
2775 South Quincy Street
Arlington, VA 22206   301-296-5707
http://www.ldonline.org/njcld
e-mail: sdublinske@asha.org
Mary Beth Klotz, Chairman
Stan Dublinski, Secretary/Treasurer

The mission of the National Joint Committee on Learning
Disabilities (NJCLD) is to provide multi-organizational
leadership and resources to optimize outcomes for individuals with learning disabilities.

89 **National Organization for Rare Disorders (NORD)**
PO Box 1968
Danbury, CT 06813-1968   203-744-0100
800-999-6673
FAX 203-798-2291
TDD:203-797-9590
http://www.rarediseases.org
e-mail: orphan@rarediseases.org
Peter Saltonstall, President/CEO

A unique federation of voluntary health organizations dedicated to helping people with rare diseases and assisting the
organizations that serve them. Committed to the identification, treatment, and cure of rare disorders through programs
of education, advocacy, research, and service.
1983

90 **National Organization on Disability (NOD)**
1625 K St NW
Ste 802
Washington, DC 20006   202-293-5960
FAX 202-293-7999
TTY: 202-293-5968
http://www.nod.org
e-mail: ability@nod.org
Carol Glazer, President

The mission of the National Organization on Disability is to
expand the participataion and contribution of America's 54
million men, women and children with disabilities in all aspects of life.

91 **National Rehabilitation Association**
633 S Washington St
Alexandria, VA 22314-4109   703-836-0850
888-258-4295
FAX 703-836-0848
TDD:703-836-0849
http://www.nationalrehab.org
e-mail: info@nationalrehab.org
Bonnie Hawley, President
Tom Wilson, President-Elect
Beverlee Stafford, Executive Director
A membership organization that promotes ethical and state
of the art practice in rehabilitation with the goal of the personal and economic independence of persons with disabilities. Members include rehabilitation counselors, physical,
speech and occupational therapists, job trainers, consultants, independent living instructors, students in rehabilitation programs, and other professionals involved in the
advocacy of programs and services for people with
disabilities.

92 **National Rehabilitation Information Center**
8400 Corporate Dr
Ste 500
Landover, MD 20785-2245   301-459-5900
800-346-2742
FAX 301-459-4263
TTY: 301-459-5984
http://www.naric.com
e-mail: naricinfo@heitechservices.com
Mark X Odum, Director

The gateway to an abundance of disability-and rehabilita-
tion-oriented information organized in a variety of formats
designed to make it easy to find and use. The mission of the
Center is to collect and disseminate the results of research
funded by the National Institute in Disability and Rehabilitation Research (NIDRR).

93 **Nonverbal Learning Disorders Association**
507 Hopmeadow St
Simsbury, CT 06070-2456   860-658-5522
FAX 860-658-6688
http://www.nlda.org
e-mail: info@nlda.org
Patricia Carrin, Founder/ President
Marcia Rubinstein, Founder/Executive Liaison

A non-profit corporation dedicated to research, education,
and advocacy for nonverbal learning disorders.

94 **Office for Civil Rights U.S. Department of Education**
5 Post Office Square
8th Floor
Boston, MA 02109-3921   617-289-0111
800-421-3481
FAX 617-289-0130
TTY: 877-521-2172
http://www.ed.gov
e-mail: ccr.boston@ed.gov

95   **Parent Advocacy Coalition for Educational Rights (PACER)**
8161 Normandale Blvd
Bloomington, MN 55437-1044   952-838-9000
                                    800-537-2237
                                    FAX 952-838-0199
                                    TTY: 952-838-0190
                                    http://www.pacer.org
                                    e-mail: pacer@pacer.org
Paula Goldberg, Executive Director

The mission of PACER is to expand opportunities and enhance the quality of life of children and young adults with disabilities and their families, based on the concept of parents helping parents.
1977

96   **Parent Educational Advocacy Training Center (PEATC)**
100 N Washington Street
Suite 234
Falls Church, VA 22046-4523   703-923-0010
                                     800-869-6782
                                     FAX 800-693-3514
                                     TTY: 703-923-0010
                                     http://www.peatc.org
                                     e-mail: partners@peatc.org
Michael Heaney, President
Cherie Takemoto, Executive Director

A non-profit that believes children with disabilities reach their full potential when families and professionals enjoy an equal, respectful partnership. PEATC also provides support education, and training to families, schools and other professionals committed to helping children with disabilities.
1978

97   **Parents Helping Parents**
Sabrato Center for Nonprofits-San Jose
1400 Parkmoor Ave
Ste 100
San Jose, CA 95126-3797   408-727-5775
                                 866-747-4040
                                 FAX 408-286-1116
                                 http://www.php.com
                                 e-mail: info@php.com
Mary Ellen Peterson, Executive Director/CEO

Helping children with special needs receive the resources, love, hope, respect, health care, education and other services they need to achieve their full potential by helping to create strong families and dedicated professionals.

98   **Rehabilitation Engineering and Assistive Technology Society of North America (RESNA)**
1700 N Moore St
Ste 1540
Arlington, VA 22209-1917   703-524-6686
                                  FAX 703-524-6630
                                  TTY: 703-524-6639
                                  http://www.resna.org
                                  e-mail: info@resna.org
Nell Bailey, Executive Director
Jerry Weisman, President

An interdisciplinary association of people with a common interest in technology and disability. The purpose is to improve the potential of people with disabilities to achieve their goals through the use of technology.
1979

99   **Rehabilitation International**
25 2 21st St
4th Fl
New York, NY 10010-6207   212-420-1500
                                 FAX 212-505-0871
                                 http://www.riglobal.org
                                 e-mail: ri@riglobal.org
Anne Hawker, President
Venus Ilagan, Secretary General

A global network of people with disabilities, service providers, researchers, government agencies and advocates promoting and implementing the rights and inclusion of people with disabilities.
700 members 1922

100   **Research Division of CEC**
Council for Exceptional Children
Ste 300
1110 N Glebe Rd
Arlington, VA 22201-5704   703-620-3660
                                  888-232-7733
                                  FAX 703-264-9494
                                  TTY: 866-915-5000
                                  http://www.cecdr.org
                                  e-mail: service@cec.sped.org
Timothy Landrum, President

Devoted to the advancement of research related to the education of individuals with disabilities and/or who are gifted. The goals of CEC-DR include the promotion of equal partnership with practitioners in designing, conducting and interpreting research in special education.

101   **Resource Room**
608 S Race St
Urbana, IL 61801-4131   217-367-6218
                               http://www.resourceroom.net
                               e-mail: info@resourceroom.net
Susan Jones, President

Tools, strategies, and structured explorations for interesting learners. Resources for people who learn differently, or have learning difficulties or learning disabilities such as dyslexia, dysgraphia, or dyscalculia.

102   **Seratoma Inc**
1912 E Meyer Blvd
Kansas City, MO 64132-1141   816-333-8300
                                    FAX 816-333-4320
                                    http://www.sertoma.org
                                    e-mail: infosertoma@sertoma.org
Steven Murphy, Executive Director
Holly Walls, Director of Development

Activities focus on helping people with speech and hearing problems, but also have programs in the areas of youth, national heritage, drug awareness and community services.

103   **Son-Rise Program®**
Autism Treatment Center of America
2080 S Undermountain Rd
Sheffield, MA 01257-9643   413-229-2100
                                  800-714-2779
                                  FAX 413-229-3202
                                  http://www.autismtreatment.com
                                  e-mail: correspondence@option.org
Barry Neil Kaufman, CEO
Bryn Hogan, Director
Samahria Lyte Kaufman, Co-Founder/Co-Creator
Autism Treatment Center of America provides innovative training programs for parents and professionals caring for children challenged by Autism, Autism Spectrum Disorders, Pervasive Developmental Disorder (PDD) and other developmental difficulties. The Son-Rise Program teaches a specific yet comprehensive system of treatment and education designed to help families and caregivers enable their children to dramatically improve in all areas of learning.
1983

104 **Stuttering Foundation of America**
PO Box 11749
Memphis, TN 38111-0749   901-452-7343
                                       800-992-9392
                                   FAX 901-761-0484
                       http://www.stutteringhelp.org
                       e-mail: info@stutteringhelp.org
Jane Fraser, President

Founded with the goal to provide the best and most
up-to-date information and help available for the prevention
of stuttering in young children and the most effective treatment available for teenagers and adults.
1947

105 **Team of Advocates for Special Kids**
100 W Cerritos Ave
Anaheim, CA 92805-6546   714-533-8275
                                       866-828-8275
                                   FAX 714-533-2533
                             http://www.taskca.org
                             e-mail: task@.taskca.org
Marta Anchondo, Executive Director

TASK's mission is to enable children with disabilities to
reach their maximum potential by providing them, their families and the professionals who serve them, with training,
support information resources and referrals, and by providing community awareness programs. TASK's TECH Center
is a place for children, parents, adult consumers, and professionals to learn about assistive technology by providing
hands-on access to computer hardware, software and
adaptive equipment.

106 **Technology and Media Division**
Council for Exceptional Children
1110 N Glebe Rd
Ste 300
Arlington, VA 22201-5704   703-245-3660
                                       888-232-7733
                                   FAX 703-264-9494
                                   TTY: 866-915-5000
                             http://www.tamcec.org
                       e-mail: contactus@tamcec.org
Joel Mittler, President
Brenda Heiman, Past President
Maragret Bausch, President Elect
TAM works to promote the availability and effective use of
technology and media for children, birth to 21, with disabili-
ties and/or who are gifted.

107 **The American Printing House for the Blind, Inc.**
1839 Frankfort Avenue
P.O. Box 6085
Louisville, KY 40206-0085   502-895-2405
                                       800-223-1839
                                   FAX 502-899-2274
                                   http://www.aph.org
                             e-mail: info@aph.org
Tuck Tinsley, President
Bob Brasher, VP Advisory Services/Research
John Spiegelhalter, Business Development Manager
The world's largest nonprofit organization creating educa-
tional, work place, and independent living products and ser-
vices for people who are visually impaired.

108 **Thinking and Learning Connection**
239 Whitclem Ct
Palo Alto, CA 94306-4111   650-493-3497
                                   FAX 650-494-3499
Lynne Stietzel, Director
Eric Stietzel, Co-Director

It is our goal to assist students in understanding their style of
learning in order to promote success. We also actively advocate for our students in their schools, helping teachers and
administrators develop supportive, individulaized
programs.

109 **Very Special Arts**
818 Connecticut Ave NW
Ste 600
Washington, DC 20006-2719   202-628-2800
                                       800-933-8721
                                   FAX 202-429-0868
                                   TDD:202-737-0645
                                   http://www.vsarts.org
                             e-mail: info@vsarts.org
Soula Antoniou, President

An international, nonprofit organization founded to create a
society where all people with disabilities learn through, participate in and enjoy the arts. VSA arts is committed to driving change - changing perceptions and practice, classroom
by classroom, community by community.
1974

110 **Visual Impairments Division of CEC**
Council for Exceptional Children
1110 N Glebe Rd
Ste 300
Arlington, VA 22201-5704   703-245-3660
                                       888-232-7733
                                   FAX 703-264-9494
                                   TTY: 866-915-5000
                                   http://www.cecdvi.org
Loana Mason, President

An organization whose membership represents a diverse
group of individuals committed to the education of students
who are blind or visually impaired. DVI attracts members
committed to promoting effective educational practices and
outcomes through collaborative efforts in partnership with
families and colleagues.
1,000 members 1948

111 **Washington PAVE: Specialized Training of Military
Parents (STOMP)**
6316 S 12th St
Ste B
Tacoma, WA 98465-1900   253-565-2266
                                       800-572-7368
                                   FAX 253-566-8052
                                   TDD:800-572-7368
                                   TTY: 800-573-7368
                                   http://www.wapave.org
                             e-mail: pave@wapave.org
Tracy Kahlo, Founder/Program Director
Joanne Butts, Executive Director

STOMP, a parent directed project exists to empower military parents, individuals with disabilities, and service providers with knowledge, skills and resources so that they
might access services to create a collaborative environment
for a family and professional partnerships without regard to
geographic location.
100,000 members 1979

112 **World Institute on Disability (WID)**
510 16th St
Ste 100
Oakland, CA 94612-1520   510-763-4100
                                   FAX 510-763-4109
                                   TTY: 510-208-9493
                                   http://www.wid.org
                             e-mail: wid@wid.org
Anita Shafer Aaron, Executive Director

A nonprofit public policy center dedicated to promoting independence and full societal inclusion of people with disabilities. Since its founding in 1983 by Ed Roberts, WID has
earned a reputation for high quality research and public education on a wide range of issues. Newsletter is published on a
regular basis.
1983

113 YAI Network
460 West 34th Street
New York, NY 10001-2382   212-273-6100
                                      http://www.yai.org
                                   e-mail: staff@yai.org
Philip Levy, President

A national leader in the provision of services, education and training in the field of developmental and learning disabilities.
1957

Alabama

114 Easter Seals Alabama
5960 E Shirley Ln
Montgomery, AL 36117-1963   334-395-4489
                                      800-388-7325
                                  FAX 334-395-4492
                         http://alabama.easterseals.com
                         e-mail: info@al.easterseals.com
Lynne Stokley, CEO

Easter Seals provides services to children and adults with disabilities and other special needs, and support to their families.

115 Easter Seals Central Alabama
2125 E South Blvd
Montgomery, AL 36116-2409   334-288-0240
                                  FAX 334-288-7171
                          http://www.eastersealsca.org
                          e-mail: info@eastersealsca.org
Debbie Lynn, Administrator/Executive Director

Provides quality life enhancing programs and services to meet the individual needs of our consumers.

116 Easter Seals West Alabama
1110 Dr Edward Hillard Dr
Tuscaloosa, AL 35401-7446   205-759-1211
                                  FAX 205-349-1162
                         http://www.eastersealswestal.org
Loie S Robinson, Administrator

Serves children and adults with disabilities while maintaining a reputation for quality, and comprehensive services.

117 Easter Seals of the Birmingham Area
200 Beacon Parkway West
Birmingham, AL 35209-3102   205-942-6277
                                  FAX 205-945-4906
                         http://www.eastersealsbham.org
Lori Senn, Executive Director

Easter Seals has been helping individuals with disabilities and special needs, and their families, live better lices for more than 80 years. From child development centers to physical rehabilitation and job training for people with disabilities, Easter Seals offers a variety of services to help people with disabilities address life's challenges and achieve personal goals.

118 International Dyslexia Association of Alabama
2510 Monteview Drive
Huntsville, AL 35803   256-551-1442
                                  FAX 205-942-2688
                          http://www.idaalabama.org
                          e-mail: info@idaalabama.org
Marcia Ramsey, President

ALIDA will provide dyslexic individuals in Alabama with a unified voice to represent their interests to the public, to the educational community, to the legislature, and to others. ALIDA will also serve as a vehicle to increase awareness and understanding of dyslexia in Alabama.

119 Learning Disabilities Association of Alabama
PO Box 11588
Montgomery, AL 36111-0588   334-277-9151
                                  FAX 334-284-9357
                                   http://www.ldaal.org
Mattie Ray, President

A non-profit grassroots organization whose members are individuals with learning disabilities, their families, and the professionals who work with them. LDAA is dedicated to identifying causes and promoting prevention of learning disabilities and to enhance the quality of life for all individuals with learning disabilities and their families by encouraging effective identification and intervention, fostering research, and protecting their rights inder the law.

Alaska

120 Center for Human Development (CHD)
University of Alaska Anchorage
2702 Gambell St
Ste 103
Anchorage, AK 99503-2836   907-272-8270
                                     800-243-2199
                                 FAX 907-274-4802
                             TTY: 907-264-6206
                          http://www.alaskachd.org
                      e-mail: webmaster@alaskachd.org
Karen Ward, Director

One of 61 University Centers located in every state and territoyr, which attempts to bring together the resources of the university and the community in support of individuals with developmental disabilities.

121 Easter Seals Alaska
670 W Fireweed Ln
Ste 105
Anchorage, AK 99503-2562   907-277-7325
                                 FAX 907-272-7325
                         http://www.alaska.easterseals.com
V Gutierrez Osborne, Executive Director

Easter Seals assists more than one million children and adults with disabilities and their families annually through a nationwide network of more than 450 service sites.

Arizona

122 Arizona Center for Disability Law
5025 E Washington St
Ste 202
Phoenix, AZ 85034   602-274-6287
                                      800-927-2260
                                  FAX 602-274-6779
                              TTY: 520-327-9547
                               http://www.acdl.com
                      e-mail: center@azdisabilitylaw.org
Peri Jude Radecic, Executive Director
Randall Howe, President

Advocates for the legal rights of persons with disabilities to be free from abuse, neglect and discrimination; and to have access to education, healthcare, housing and jobs, and other services in order to maximize independence and achieve equality.

123 Institute for Human Development: Northern Arizona University
PO Box 5630
Flagstaff, AZ 86011-5630   928-523-4791
                                  FAX 928-523-9127
                              TTY: 928-523-1695
                               http://www.nau.edu
                      e-mail: elizabeth.reeg@nau.edu

Elizabeth Reeg, Executive Director

The Institute values and supports the independence, productivity and inclusion of Arizona's citizens with disabilities. Based on the values and beliefs, the Institute conducts training, research and services that further these goal.

124   International Dyslexia Association of Arizona
PO Box 6248
Scottsdale, AZ 85261-6284   480-941-0308
http://www.dyslexia-az.org
e-mail: arizona.ida@gmail.com
Mary Wennersten, President

The Arizona Branch of The International Dyslexia Association (AIDA) is a 501 (c)(3) non-profit, scientific organization dedicated to educating the public about the learning disability, dyslexia. The Arizona Branch has four objectives: to increase awareness in the dyslexic and general community; to network with other learning disability groups and legislators in education; to increase membership; to raise funds for future projects that will make a difference in our community.

125   Parent Information Network
Arizona Department of Education
2384 N Steves Blvd
Flagstaff, AZ 86004-6105   928-679-8106
800-352-4558
FAX 928-679-8124
http://www.ade.az.gov
e-mail: pins@azed.gov
Becky Raabe, Director

Provides free training and information to parents on federal and state laws and regulations for special education, parental rights and responsibilities, parent involvement, advocacy, behavior, standards and disability related resources. Provides a clearinghouse of information targeted to parents of children with disabilities. Also assists schools in promoting positive parent/professional/ regional partnerships.

126   Recording for the Blind & Dyslexic: Phoenix Studio
3627 E Indian School Rd
Ste 108
Phoenix, AZ 85018   602-468-9144
800-221-4792
FAX 609-987-8116
http://www.rfbd.org
e-mail: custserv@rfbd.org
Pam Bork, Production Director

To create opportunities for individuals, from Kindergarten through Graduate Level, who cannot read standard print because of a visual impairment, learning disability or other physical disability, to succeed in school by providing accessible educational materials.

127   Recording for the Blind & Dyslexic: Sun Cities Studio
9449 N 99th Ave
Peoria, AZ 85345-6913   623-977-6020
http://www.rfbd.org
Michael Kaminer, Production Director
Wendy White, Production Assistant

To create opportunities for individuals, from Kindergarten through Graduate Level, who cannot read standard print because of a visual impairment, learning disability or other physical disability, to succeed in school by providing accessible educational materials.

Arkansas

128   Center for Applied Studies in Education Learning (CASE)
ASU/SSFD
951 S Cady Mall
Social Sciences 144
Tempe, AZ 85287   480-965-6349
FAX 480-965-6779
e-mail: rhbradley@ualr.edu
Bob Bradley, Professor

Improves the quality of education and human services in Arkansas and globally through a number of inter-related activities: conducting research on the effectiveness of programs and practices in education and human services; providing technical assistance in statistics, research design, measurement methodologies, data management, and program evaluation to students, faculty, and external groups and agencies; providing formal and informal consultation, technical assistance and instruction.

129   Easter Seals Arkansas
3920 Woodland Heights Rd
Little Rock, AR 72212-2495   501-227-3600
FAX 501-227-4021
http://ar.easterseals.com
Stephanie Smith, Executive Director

Easter Seals' mission is to provide exceptional services to ensure that all people with disabilities or special needs have equal opportunities to live, learn, work and play in their communities.

130   Learning Disabilities Association of Arkansas (LDAA)
PO Box 95255
North Little Rock, AR 72190-5255   501-666-8777
FAX 501-666-4070
http://www.ldaarkansas.org
e-mail: ldaarkansas@yahoo.com
Tricia Smith, President

A nonprofit, volunteer organization of parents and professionals. LDAA is devoted to defining and finding solutions to the broad spectrum of learning disabilities.

California

131   Berkeley Policy Associates
440 Grand Ave
Ste 500
Oakland, CA 94610-5085   510-465-7884
FAX 510-465-7885
TDD:510-465-4493
http://www.berkeleypolicyassociates.com
e-mail: info@bpacal.com
Dwayne A Banks, President/CEO

Conducts social policy research and program evaluations in various topic areas, including disability policy. Although the research typically does not focus on specific disabilities, the reports or other deliverables deriving from the projects may include specific information relating to particular disabilities, and are available for purchase.

132   California Association of Private Special
520 Capitol Mall
Suite 280
Sacramento, CA 95814   916-447-7061
FAX 916-447-1320
http://www.capses.com
e-mail: director@capses.com

Suzy Fitch, President
Janeth Rodriguez, M.A., Executive Director
Rebecca Foo, Secretary

Dedicated to preserving and enhancing the leadership role of the private sector in offering quality alternative services to students with disabilities.
191 members 1973

133   Community Alliance for Special Education (CASE)

1550 Bryant St
Ste 738
San Francisco, CA 95814   415-431-2285
                                         FAX 415-431-2289
                            http://www.caseadvocacy.org
                            e-mail: info@caseadvocacy.org
Joseph Feldman, Director

Provides special education advocacy, representation at individual education program (IEP) meetings and due process proceedings, free technical assistance consultations and training throughout the San Francisco Bay area.
1979

134   Dyslexia Awareness and Resource Center

928 Carpinteria St
Ste 2
Santa Barbara, CA 93103-3477   805-963-7339
                                         FAX 805-963-6581
                            http://www.dyslexiacenter.org
                            e-mail: info@dyslexiacenter.org
Joan Esposito, Program Director
Leslie V Esposito, Executive Director

Provides it services, free of charge, to help educate, advocate, support and raise the awareness of the public about dyslexia, attention deficit disorder and other learning differences and the means to learn about and rise above these differences.
1990

135   Easter Seals Central California

9010 Soquel Dr
Aptos, CA 95003-4002   831-684-2166
                                            800-400-0671
                                         FAX 831-684-1018
                            http://www.centralcal.easterseals.com
Bruce Hinman, President

Create solutions that change lives of children and adults with disabilities or other special needs and their families.

136   Easter Seals Southern California

1801 E Edinger Ave
Ste 190
Santa Ana, CA 92705-4770   714-834-1111
                                         FAX 714-834-1128
                            http://southerncal.easterseals.com
Mark Whitley, President

Provides excpetional services to ensure that all peopel with disabilities or other special needs and their families have equal opportunities to live, learn, work and play in their communities.

137   Easter Seals: Lakeport

501 B N. Main Street
Lakeport, CA 95453-4811   707-263-3949
                                            877-263-3994
                                         FAX 707-263-3985
                            http://noca.easterseals.com
                            e-mail: bbonnett@noca.easterseals.com
Bonnie Bonnett, Site Manager
Susan Armiger, Interim CEO
Pat Straub, Administrative Assistant
Easter Seals provides services to children and adults with disabilities and other special needs and support to their families.

138   Easter Seals: Novato

20 Pimentel Court
Suite A1
Novato, CA 94949-5656   415-382-7450
                                         FAX 415-382-6052
                            http://noca.easterseals.com
                            e-mail: pstraub@noca.easterseals.com
Pat Straub, Exec. Asst.
Susan Armiger, Interim CEO

Easter Seals provides services to children and adults with disabilities and other special needs and support to their families.

139   International Dyslexia Association of Los Angeles

PO Box 8943
Calabasas, CA 91372-0808   818-506-8866
                                         FAX 818-222-9260
                            http://dyslexiala.org
                            e-mail: info@dyslexiala.org
Lainie Donnell, President

The Los Angeles County Branch of The International Dyslexia Association believes that all individuals have the right to realize their potential, that individual learning abilities can be strengthened, and that language and reading skills can be achieved.

140   International Dyslexia Association of Northern California

PO Box 5010
San Mateo, CA 94402-0010   650-328-7667
                                         FAX 650-375-8504
                            http://www.dyslexia-ncbida.org
                            e-mail: office@dyslexia-ncbida.org
Nancy Redding, President

Formed to increase public awareness of dyslexia in Northern California and Northern Nevada. Have been serving individuals with dyslexia, their families and professionals in the field in this community for 30 years.

141   International Dyslexia Association of San Diego

808 W Balboa Blvd
Newport Beach, CA 92661   949-673-3612
                            http://www.dyslexiasd.org
                            e-mail: sdidainfo@gmail.com
Tracy Block, President

A nonprofit scientific and educational organization dedicated to the study and treatment of the learning disability. This branch was informed to increase public awareness of dyslexia.

142   Learning Disabilities Association of California

808 W Balboa Blvd
Newport Beach, CA 92661   949-673-3612
                                            866-532-6322
                            http://www.ldaca.org
                            e-mail: ca-ida@sbcglobal.net
Louise Fundenberg, President

A non-profit volunteer organization of parents, professionals and adults with learning disabilities. Its purpose is to promote and support the education and general welfare of children and adults of potentially normal intelligence who manifest learning, perceptual, and/or behavioral handicaps.

143   Legal Services for Children

1254 Market St
Fl 3
San Francisco, CA 94102-4816   415-863-3762
                                         FAX 415-863-7708
                            http://www.lsc-sf.org
Shannan Wilber, Executive Director

15

Nonprofit law firm for children and youth. Legal Services for Children provides free legal and social services to children and youth under 18 years old in the San Francisco Bay area.
1975

144   Lutheran Braille Workers
PO Box 5000
Yucaipa, CA 92399-1450   909-795-8977
                                                 800-925-6092
                                                 FAX 909-795-8970
                                                 http://www.lbwinc.org
                                                 e-mail: lbw@lbwinc.org
Phillip Pledger, Executive Director

The mission of Lutheran Braille Workers is to provide the message of salvation, through faith in Jesus Christ, to individuals who are blind or visually impaired throughout the world.
1943

145   Orange County Learning Disabilities Association
PO Box 25772
Santa Ana, CA 92799-5772   714-547-4206
                                                 http://www.oclda.org
                                                 e-mail: info@oclda.org
Joyce Riley, President

A private, self-help, volunteer, non-profit, charitable organization of parents and professionals who are concerned with the welfare of children and adults who have learning disabilities.
1960

146   Recording for the Blind & Dyslexic: Los Angeles
5022 Hollywood Blvd
Los Angeles, CA 90027-6104   323-664-5525
                                                 800-732-text
                                                 http://www.rfbd.org
                                                 e-mail: volunteers@rfbdla.org
Maragaret Harty, Regional Programs/Services Dir

A nonprofit organization that serves individuals who cannot read standard print because of a vision, physical or learning disability, by providing them with educational materials in accessible formats.

147   Recording for the Blind & Dyslexic: Northern California
2455 Faber Place
Ste 103
Palo Alto, CA 94303-4103   650-493-3717
                                                 866-732-8398
                                                 FAX 650-493-5513
                                                 http://www.rfbd.org
Trish Bobenik, Area Director

Our territory covers nine counteis including San Francisco, San Mateo, Santa Clara, Santa Cruz, Monterey, Alameda, Contra Costa, Marin, and Sonoma. We have 3 field educational outreach offices in San Francisio, the South Bay, and the East Bay serving individual students and 160 schools in those local areas.
4,500 members 1967

148   Recording for the Blind & Dyslexic: Santa Barbara
5638 Hollister Ave
Ste 210
Goleta, CA 93117-3484   805-681-0531
                                                 FAX 805-681-0532
                                                 http://www.rfbd.org
Tim Schwartz, Executive Director

Our mission is to create opportunities for individual success by providing, and promoting the effective use of, accessible educational materials.

149   Recording for the Blind and Dyslexic: Inland Empire-Orange County Unit
Inland Empire Studio
1844 W 11th St
Ste C
Upland, CA 91786-3586   909-949-4316
                                                 800-732-8398
                                                 FAX 909-981-8457
                                                 http://www.rfbd.org
                                                 e-mail: mdavis@rfbd.org
Michael Davis, Executive Director
Maureen Ahrens, Production Director

Volunteers record textbooks on computer disks for the visually, physically and perceptually disabled.

Colorado

150   Easter Seals Colorado
2644 Alvarado Road
Empire, CO 80436   303-569-2333
                                                 FAX 303-569-3857
                                                 http://www.co.easterseals.com
                                                 e-mail: campinfo@eastersealscolorado.org
Lynn Robinson, President
Kelly Housman, Director Camp & Recreation

Provides services to children and adults with disabilities and other special needs, and support to their families.

151   Learning Ally: Colorado-Rocky Mountain Unit
1355 S. Colorado Blvd.
Suite C-406
Denver, CO 80222-3305   303-757-0787
                                                 http://www.learningally.org
                                                 e-mail: bjanowski@learningally.org
Bob Janowski, Production Director

Produces the textbooks that students and professionals with print impairments need for the academic and career success that lead to lifelong self-sufficiency and self-fulfillment. Also provide and educational outreach program to schools to help them use and understand the program and our services.

152   Learning Disabilities Association of Colorado
55 Madison St
Ste 750
Denver, CO 80206   303-894-0992
                                                 FAX 303-830-1645
                                                 http://ldaco.org
                                                 e-mail: info@ldaco.com
Bobbi Neiss, Executive Director
Jill Marrs, President

The Learning Disabilities Association of Colorado is committed to supporting the potential of individuals with learning and attention disabilities through accurate identification, advocacy, and education.

153   PEAK Parent Center
611 N Weber St
Ste 200
Colorado Springs, CO 80903-1072   719-531-9400
                                                 800-284-0251
                                                 FAX 719-531-9452
                                                 http://www.peakparent.org
                                                 e-mail: info@peakparent.org
Barbara Buswell, Executive Director

A federally-designated Parent Traning and Information Center (PTI). As a PTI, PEAK supports and empowers parents, providing them with information and strategies to use when advocating for their children with disabilities by expanding knowledge of special education and offering new strategies for success.

154 Rocky Mountain Disability and Business Technical Assistance Center
3630 Sinton Road
Suite 103
Colorado Springs, CO 80907-5072   719-444-0268
                                          800-949-4232
                                     FAX 719-444-0269
                                     TTY: 719-444-0268
                          http://www.adainformation.org
                          e-mail: rmdbtac@mtc-inc.com
Jana Copeland, Executive Director

Provides information on the Americans with Disabilities Act to Colorado, Utah, Montana, Wyoming, North Dakota and South Dakota.

155 Rocky Mountain International Dyslexia Association
PO Box 461010
Glendale, CO 80246-5010   303-721-9425
                                  FAX 303-557-9750
                          http://www.dyslexia-rmbida.org
                          e-mail: ida_rmb@yahoo.com
Elenn Steinberg, President

The mission of the International Dyslexia Association of Colorado is to pursue and provide the most comprehensive range of evidence-based information, education, and services that address the full scope of dyslexia and other associated learning disabilities and to have a meaningful impact on the lives of individuals and families affected by dyslexia so they may advocate for themselves and achieve their highest potential.
300+ members 1949

Connecticut

156 Capitol Region Education Council
111 Charter Oak Ave
Hartford, CT 06106-1912   860-247-2732
                                       877-850-2832
                                  FAX 860-246-3304
                          http://www.crec.org
                          e-mail: bdouglas@crec.org
Bruce Douglas, Executive Director

Will promote cooperation and collaboration with local school districts and other organizations committed to the improved quality of public education; provide cost-effective services to member districts and other clients; listen and respond to client needs for the improved quality of public education; and provide leadership in the region through the quality of its services and its ability to identify and share quality services of its member districts and other organizations to public education.
1966

157 Connecticut Association for Children and Adults with Learning Disabilities
25 Van Zant Street
Suite 15-5
Norwalk, CT 06855-1713   203-838-5010
                                  FAX 203-866-6108
                          http://www.cacld.org
                          e-mail: cacld@optonline.net
Beryl Kaufman, Executive Director

A regional, non-profit organization that supports individuals, families and professionals by providing information, education, and consultation while promoting public awareness and understanding. CACLD's goal is to ensure access to the resources needed to help children and adults with learning disabilities and attention deficit disorders achieve their full potential.
1963

158 Connecticut Association of Private Special Education Facilities (CAPSEF)
330 Main Street
3rd Floor
Hartford, CT 06106-1851   860-525-1318
                                  FAX 860-541-6484
                          http://www.capsef.org
                          e-mail: info@capsef.org
Jill Bourbeau, President

A voluntary association of provate schools which provides quality, cost effective, special education and related services to the special needs of children and adolescents (birth to 21 years) of Connecticut. The focus of these education services is social and vocation programs designed to enable students to succeed in the least restrictive environment
2,500 members 1974

159 Easter Seals Connecticut
85 Jones Street
P.O. Box 198
Hebron, CT 06248-0100   860-228-9496
                                       800-874-7687
                          http://ct.easterseals.com
Dot Shugrue, Executive Director

Easter Seals Connecticut creates solutions that change the lives of children adn adults with disabilities or special needs, their families and communities.
1966

160 Learning Disabilities Association of Conneecticut
999 Asylum Avenue
5th Floor
Hartford, CT 06105-2416   860-560-1711
                                  FAX 860-560-1750
                          http://www.ldact.org
                          e-mail: ldact@idact.org
Carrie Berman, President
Fran Ficocelli, Program Coordinator

LDA of Connecticut is a non-profit organization of parents, professionals, and persons with learning disabilities. We are dedicated to promoting a better understanding of learning disabilities, securing appropriate educational and employment opportunities for children and adults with learning disabilities and improving the quality of life for this population.

161 Nonverbal Learning Disorders Association
507 Hopmeadow St
Simsbury, CT 06070-2456   860-658-5522
                                  FAX 860-658-6688
                          http://www.nlda.org
                          e-mail: info@nlda.org
Patricia Carrin, President

A non-profit corporation dedicated to research, education and advocacy for nonverbal learning disorders.

162 Recording for the Blind & Dyslexic: Connecticut
2067 Massachusetts Avenue
3rd Floor chusetts Ave
Cambridge, MA 02140-1337   617-577-1111
                                  FAX 617-500-2712
                          http://www.rfbd.org
                          e-mail: jdougherty@rfbd.org
Jennifer Dougherty, Director

Provides textbooks on tape and computer disks to individuals who cannot read standard print because of a visual, perceptual or physical disability. Books span the entire educational spectrum from kindergarten through post graduate work and professional support. Master Tape Library contains almost 80,000 books on tape including a wide variety of science and technology books.
1959

163 State Education Resources Center of Connecticut
25 Industrial Park Rd
Middletown, CT 06457-1516   860-632-1485
                                          FAX 860-632-8870
                                          http://www.ctserc.org
                                          e-mail: info@ctserc.org
Marianne Kirner PhD, Executive Director

Non-profit educational organization. Provides high-quality
Profession Development to teachers, educators, parents and
families throughout the state of CT.
1969

Delaware

164 Easter Seals Delaware & Maryland's Eastern Shore
61 Corporate Cir
New Castle, DE 19720-2439   302-324-4444
                                              800-677-3800
                                          FAX 302-324-4441
                                          TDD:302-324-4442
                                          http://de.easterseals.com
William Adami, President

Provides exceptional services to ensure that all people with
disabilities or special needs and their families have equal opportunities to live, learn, work and play in their
communities.

165 Easter Seals Georgetown
22317 Dupont Blvd
Georgetown, DE 19947-2153   302-253-1100
                                          FAX 302-856-7296
                                          http://www.de.easterseals.com
Ford C Waggoner, Marketing Director

Provides exceptional services to ensure that all people with
disabilities or special needs and their families have equal opportunities to live, learn, work and play in their
communities.

166 Parent Information Center of Delaware
5570 Kirkwood Hwy
Orchard Commons Business Center
Wilmington, DE 19808-5002   302-999-7394
                                              888-547-4412
                                          FAX 302-999-7637
                                          http://www.picofdel.org
Marie-Anne Aghazadian, Executive Director

A statewide non-profit organization dedicated to providing
information, education and support, to families and caregivers of children with disabilites or special needs from birth
to age 26. We strive to promote partnerships among families,
educators, policy makers and the greater Delaware
Community.

District of Columbia

167 Center for Child and Human Development
Georgetown University
P.O.Box 571485
Washington, DC 20057-1485   202-687-5000
                                          FAX 202-687-8899
                                          http://www.gucchd.georgetown.edu
                                          e-mail: gucdc@georgetown.edu
Phyllis Magrab PhD, Executive Director

Established over four decades ago to improve the quality of
life for all children and youth, especially those with, or at
risk for, special needs and their families. Brings together
policy, research and clincal practice for the betterment of individuals and families, especially childre, youth and those
with special needs including: developmental disabilities and
special health care needs, mental health needs, young children and those in the child welfare system.

**168 Recording for the Blind & Dyslexic of Metropolitan
Washington**
5225 Wisconsin Avenue NW
Suite 312
Washington, DC 20015-2055   202-244-8990
                                          FAX 202-244-1346
                                          http://www.rfbd.org
                                          e-mail: csanzi@rfbd.org
Chris Smith, Production
Cheri Sanzi, Area Director

Provides unlimited numbers of recorded textbooks to students with documented learning disability. Serves students
in the District of Columbia, Montgomery and Prince Georges counties Maryland, and Northern Virginia.

Florida

169 Florida Advocacy Center for Persons with Disabilities
2728 Centerview Drive
Suite 102
Tallahassee, FL 32301-6298   850-488-9071
                                               800-342-0823
                                          FAX 850-488-8640
                                          TDD:800-346-4127
                                          http://www.advocacycenter.org
                                          e-mail: webmaster@advocacycenter.org
Gary Weston, Executive Director

The Advocacy Center for Persons with Disabilities is a non-
profit organization providing protection and advocacy services in the State of Florida. Our mission is to advance the
dignity, equality, self-determination and expressed choices
of individuals with disabilities.

170 International Dyslexia Association of Florida
3750 San Jose Place
Suite 35
Jacksonville, FL 32257-8861   904-803-9591
                                          http://www.idafla.org
                                          e-mail: kilpatricksnell@idafla.org
Dr Gayle Cane, President

A non-profit, scientific and educational organization, which
was formed to increase public awareness of dyslexia in
Florida.
1949

171 Learning Disabilities Association of Florida
894 Gary Hillery Drive
Winter Springs, FL 32708   941-637-8957
                                          FAX 941-637-0617
                                          http://www.lda-fl.org
                                          e-mail: graceparrish@lda-fl.org
Mark Halpert, President

A nonprofit volunteer organization of parents, professionals, and LD adults. It is devoted to defining and finding solutions to the broad spectrum of learning issues.

172 Miami Lighthouse for the Blind and Visually Impaired
601 SW 8th Ave
Miami, FL 33130-3209   305-856-2288
                                          FAX 305-285-6967
                                          http://www.miamilighthouse.com
                                          e-mail: info@miamilighthouse.com
Virginia Jacko, President

The oldest and largest private agency in Florida to serve people of all ages who are blind or the visually impaired.

173 **Recording for the Blind & Dyslexic: Florida**
777 Glades Road
Boca Raton, FL 33431   561-297-4444
http://www.rfbd.org
e-mail: shedrick@rfbd.org
Sonia Hedrick, Production

Georgia

174 **Easter Seals North Georgia**
Ste 250
1200 Lake Hearn Dr NE
Atlanta, GA 30319-1454   404-943-1070
FAX 404-943-0890
http://northgeorgia.easterseals.com
Donna Davidson, President

Provides information and referral, physical, occupational, and speech therapy, child care, Head Start and teacher training.

175 **Easter Seals Southern Georgia**
1906 Palmyra Rd
Albany, GA 31701-1575   229-439-7061
800-365-4583
FAX 229-435-6278
http://southerngeorgia.easterseals.com
Beth English, Executive Director

Creates solutions that change the lives of children, adults and families with disabilities or special needs by offering a variety of programs and services that enable individuals to lead lives of equality, dignity and independence.

176 **International Dyslexia Association - Georgia**
1951 Greystone Rd NW
Atlanta, GA 30318-2622   404-256-1232
http://www.idaga.org
e-mail: info@idaga.org
Jennifer Topple, President
Ann Marie Lewis, Outreach Coordinator

Formed to increase public awareness about dyslexia in the State of Georgia. The Branch encourages teachers to train in multisensory language instruction. Provides a network for individuals with dyslexia, their families and professionals in the educational and medical fields.
300 members

177 **Learning Disabilities Association of Georgia**
2566 Shallowford Rd NE, Suite 105
P.O. Box 353
Atlanta, GA 30345-1200   404-303-7774
FAX 404-467-0190
http://www.ldag.org
e-mail: ldaga@bellsouth.net
Tia Powell, President

One of 50 volunteer state organizations which comprise the Learning Disabilities Association of America. For over 30 years, LDAG has been enhancing the quality of life for individuals of all ages with Learning Disabilities and/or Attention Deficit and Hyperactivity Disorders.

178 **Recording for the Blind & Dyslexic: Georgia**
120 Florida Ave
Athens, GA 30605-1128   706-549-1313
FAX 706-227-6161
http://www.rfbd.org
e-mail: ecotton@rfbd.org
Eleanor Cotton, Production Director

A nonprofit volunteer organization, is the nation's educational library serving people who cannot effectively read standard print because of visual impairment, dyslexia and other physical disability. Our mission is to create opportunities for individual success by providing and, in the state of Georgia, promoting the effective use of, accessible educational materials.

Hawaii

179 **Aloha Special Technology Access Center**
710 Green St
Honolulu, HI 96813-2119   808-523-5547
FAX 808-536-3765
http://www.alohastac.org
e-mail: astachi@yahoo.com
Eric Anderson, Executive Director

Provide individuals with disabilities and their families access to computers, peripheral tools, and appropriate software. Aloha Stac aims to increase awareness, understanding, and implementation of microcomputer technology by establishing a program of activities and events to educate the community about what computers make possible for persons with disabilities.
1988

180 **Assistive Technology Resource Centers of Hawaii (ATRC)**
414 Kuwili Street
Suite 104
Honolulu, HI 96817-5362   808-532-7110
800-645-3007
FAX 808-532-7120
TTY: 808-532-7110
http://www.atrc.org
e-mail: atrc-info@atrc.org
Barbara Fischlowitz-Leong, Executive Director

A statewide, non-profit organization committed to ensuring access to assistive technology for persons with disabilities. ATRC links individuals with technology so all people can participate in every aspect of community life. Also empowers individuals to maintain dignity and control their lives by promoting technology thorough, advocacy, training, information, and education.

181 **Easter Seals Hawaii**
710 Green St
Honolulu, HI 96813-2119   808-536-1015
888-241-7450
FAX 808-536-3765
http://hawaii.easterseals.com
John Howell, President & CEO

Provide exceptional services to ensure that all people with disabilities of special needs and their families have equal opportunities to live, learn, work and play in their communities.

182 **International Dyslexia Association Of Hawaii**
705 S. King Street
Suite 206
Honolulu, HI 96822-3001   808-538-7007
866-773-4432
FAX 808-538-7009
http://www.dyslexia-hawaii.org
e-mail: hida@dyslexia-hawaii.org
Margaret Higa, Program Manager
Betty Ishii, President

HIDA's mission is to increase awareness of dyslexia in the community, provide support for parents and teachers, and promote teacher training. We also provide tutoring and testing referrals and information about other resources in Hawaii.
1986

183 Learning Disabilities Association of Hawaii (LDAH)

245 N. Kukui Street
Suite 205
Honolulu, HI 96817-3921   808-536-9684
                                  FAX 808-537-6780
                            http://www.ldahawaii.org
                         e-mail: MMoore@LDAHawaii.org
Neil Aoki, President
Michael Moore, Executive Director

A non-profit organization founded in 1968 by parents of children with learning disabilities.
1968

Idaho

184 Disability Rights - Idaho

4477 W. Emerald Street
Suite B100
Boise, ID 83706-2066   208-336-5353
                                 800-632-5125
                             FAX 208-336-5396
                             TDD:208-336-5353
                    http://www.disabilityrightsidaho.org
                  e-mail: info@disabilityrightsidaho.org
James R Baugh, Executive Director

The designated Protection and Advocacy System for Idaho provides advocacy for people with disabilities who have been abused/neglected; denied services or benefits; have experienced rights violations or discrimination because of their disability; or have voting accessibility problems. Also provides information & referral; negotiation & mediation; short term & technical assistance; legal advice/representation.
1977

Illinois

185 Child Care Association of Illinois

413 West Monroe Street
1st Floor
Springfield, IL 62704-1885   217-528-4409
                             FAX 217-528-6498
                          http://www.cca-il.org
                       e-mail: ilccamb@aol.com
Margaret Bergland, President & CEO

A voluntary, not-for-profit organization dedicated to improving the delivery of social services to the abused, neglected, and troubled children, youth and families of Illinois.
1964

186 Easter Seals Metropolitan Chicago

Ste 300
1939 W 13th St
Chicago, IL 60608-1226   312-491-4110
                                 866-GIV-2ESC
                             FAX 312-733-0247
                     http://chicago.easterseals.com
                 e-mail: mmorgan@eastersealschicago.org
F. Timothy Muri, President & CEO
Pat Straub, Exec. Asst.

Provides comprehensive services for individuals with disabilities or other special needs and their families to improve quality of life and maximize independence.

187 Guild for the Blind

180 N. Michigan Avenue
Suite 1700
Chicago, IL 60601-7463   312-236-8569
                             FAX 312-236-8128
                      http://www.guildfortheblind.org
                  e-mail: kathya@guildfortheblind.org
David Tabak, Executive Director

Support and information for families and individuals with visual disabilities.

188 Illinois Protection & Advocacy Agency: Equip for Equality

20 N Michigan Ave
Ste 300
Chicago, IL 60602-4861   312-341-0022
                                 800-537-2632
                             FAX 312-341-0295
                             TTY: 800-610-2779
                      http://www.equipforequality.org
                e-mail: contactus@equipforequality.org
Zena Naiditch, President

Advances the human and civil rights of children and adults with physical and mental disabilities in Illinois. The only statewide, cross-disability, comprehensive advocacy organization providing self-advocacy assistance, legal services, and disability rights education while also engaging in public policy and legislative advocacy and conducting abuse investigations and other oversight activities.
1985

189 International Dyslexia Association - Illinois/Missouri

751 Roosevelt Rd
Ste 116
Glen Ellyn, IL 60137-5905   630-469-6900
                             FAX 630-469-6810
                       http://www.readibida.org
                     e-mail: info@readibida.org
Maureen O'Connor, President
Maria Logan, Business Manager

Dedicated to the study and remediation of dyslexia and to the support and encouragement of individuals with dyslexia and their families.

190 Jewish Child & Family Services

Ste 800
216 W Jackson Blvd
Chicago, IL 60606-6920   312-444-2090
                             FAX 312-855-3754
                          http://www.jcfs.org
                 e-mail: robertbloom@jcbchicago.org
John Trossman, President
Robert Bloom, Executive Director

Provides a range of comprehensive programs designed to enable individuals and families to grow and develop positively throughout their lives.

191 Learning Disabilities Association of Illinois

10101 S Roberts Rd
Ste 205
Palos Hills, IL 60465-1556   708-430-7532
                             FAX 708-430-7592
                          http://www.ldail.org
                   e-mail: ldaofil@ameritech.net
Sharon Schussler, Administrative Assistant

A resource office with information for parents, professionals and adults with learning disabilities.

192   National Council of Teachers of English
1111 W Kenyon Rd
Urbana, IL 61801-1096   217-328-3870
                                          877-369-6283
                                     FAX 217-328-0977
                              http://www.ncte.org
                     e-mail: public_info@ncte.org
Kent Williamson, Executive Director
Lori Bianchini, Communications Specialist
Keith Gilyard, President 2011-2012
The National Council of Teachers of English, with over
30,000 members and subscribers worldwide, is dedicated to
improving the teaching and learning of English and the lan-
guage arts at all levels of education.

**193   Recording for the Blind & Dyslexic: Chicago Loop Stu-
dio**
180 N. Michigan Avenue
Suite 620
Chicago, IL 60601-7425   312-236-8715
                                     FAX 312-236-8719
                              http://www.rfbd.org
                     e-mail: jmilkovich@rfbd.org
Janet Milkovich, State Director

Provides equal access to the printed word for their members.

194   Recording for the Blind & Dyslexic: Lois C Klein Studio

9612c W 143rd St
Orland Park, IL 60462-2091   708-349-9356
                              http://www.rfbd.org
                     e-mail: selhenicky@rfbd.org
Sandy Elhenicky, Studio Director

Provides equal access to the printed word for their members.

Indiana

195   Easter Seal Arc of Northeast Indiana
4919 Coldwater Rd
Fort Wayne, IN 46825-5532   260-456-4534
                                          800-234-7811
                                     FAX 260-745-5200
                       http://neindiana.easterseals.com
Steven Hinkle, President

Provides services to children and adults with disabilities and
other special needs, and support to their families.

196   International Dyslexia Association of Indiana
2511 E. 46th Street
Suite 02
Indianapolis, IN 46205-2460   317-926-1450
                                     FAX 317-705-2067
                              http://www.inbofida.org
                     e-mail: inbofida@hotmail.com
Tracey Horth-Kreuger, President

A non-profit organization dedicatedt to helping individuals
with dyslexia, their families and the communities that support them. Promotes and disseminates researched-based
knowledge for early identification, effective teaching approaches and intervention strategies for dyslexics.
1971

197   Learning Disabilities Association of Indiana
1427 W. 86th Street
Suite 110
Indianapolis, IN 46260   317-872-4331
                                          800-284-2519
                                     FAX 574-272-3058
                              http://www.ldaofindiana.org

Sharon Harris, President

A non-profit, volunteer organization of parents, educators,
and other individuals who are committed to promoting
awareness, knowledge and acceptance of individuals with
learning disabilities and associated disorders such as attention deficit/hyperactivity disorders.
1972

198   Southwestern Indiana Easter Seal
Rehabilitation Center
3701 Bellemeade Ave
Evansville, IN 47714-0137   812-479-1411
                                     FAX 812-437-2634
                         http://www.in-sw.easterseals.com
Ray Raisor, President

The Easter Seals Rehabilitation Center in Evansville, IN
provides services to children and adults with disabilities and
other special needs and support to their families.

Iowa

199   Center for Disabilities and Development
University of Iowa Children's Hospital
100 Hawkins Dr
Iowa City, IA 52242-1016   319-353-6900
                                          877-686-0031
                                     FAX 319-356-8284
                                     TTY: 877-686-0032
               http://www.healthcare.uiowa.edu/cdd/index.asp
               e-mail: disabililtyresources@uiowa.edu
Judy Stephenson, Director

Improve the health and independence of people with disabilities and advance the community systems on which they
rely.
1947

200   International Dyslexia Association of Iowa
P.O.Box 11188
Cedar Rapids, IA 52410-1188   319-377-8371
                                          866-782-2930
                              http://www.ida-ia.org

Richard Bradford, President

Provides workshops, hands-on simulations, and resources to
incease public awareness of dyslexia.

201   Iowa Program for Assistive Technology
Center for Disabilities and Development
100 Hawkins Drive
Suite 295
Iowa City, IA 52242-1016   319-353-8777
                                          800-779-2001
                                     FAX 319-356-8284
                                     TDD:877-686-0032
                                     TTY: 877-686-0032
                         http://www.uiowa.edu/infotech
                         e-mail: jane-gay@uiowa.edu
Jane Gay, Director

IPAT's goals are to promote and create systems change in
the state with regards to assistive technology (AT) and it's
use. IPAT works with consumers and family members, service providers, and state and local agencies/organizations to
promote assistive technology through awareness, training,
and policy work. IPAT accomplishes this through five
specifi goal areas: education, employment, health, community living and recreation, telecommunication and
information technology.

202 **Learning Disabilities Association of Iowa**
5665 Greendale Rd
Ste D
Johnston, IA 50131-1903
515-280-8558
888-690-5324
FAX 515-243-1902
http://www.lda-ia.org
e-mail: kathylda@askresource.org
Kathy Specketer, State Coordinator

Dedicated to identifying causes and promoting prevention of learning disabilities and to enhancing the quality of life for all individuals with learning disabilities and their families by: encouraging effective identification and intervention, fostering research, and protecting the rights of individuals with learning disabilities under the law.

Kansas

203 **Disability Rights Center of Kansas (DRC)**
635 SW Harrison Street
Suite 100
Topeka, KS 66603-3726
785-273-9661
877-776-1541
FAX 785-273-9414
TTY: 877-335-3725
http://www.drckansas.org
e-mail: info@ksadv.org
Rocky Nichols, Executive Director

Formerly Kansas Advocacy & Protection Services, a public interest legal advocacy agency empowered by federal law to advocate for the civil and legal rights of Kansans with disabilities.

204 **Easter Seals Capper Foundation**
3500 SW 10th Ave
Topeka, KS 66604-1995
785-272-4060
FAX 785-272-7912
http://capper.easterseals.com
Jim Leiker, President & CEO

A community resource providing services to enhance the independence of people with disabilities, primarily children.

205 **Goodwill Industries of Kansas**
3636 N Oliver St
Wichita, KS 67220-3403
316-744-9291
FAX 316-744-1428
http://goodwillkansas.easterseals.com
Emily Compton, President

Education, training and employment for people with disabilities and other barriers to employment.

206 **Learning Disabilities Association of Kansas**
P.O.Box 4603
Olathe, KS 66063-4603
785-273-4505
FAX 785-228-9527
http://www.lda.of.ks.com
e-mail: marciasu@aol.com
Cindy Swarner, President

LDAK is a nonprofit, volunteer organization whose purpose is to advance the education and general well-being of children and adults with learning disabilities.

Kentucky

207 **Learning Disabilities Association of Kentucky**
2210 Goldsmith Lane
Suite 118
Louisville, KY 40218-1038
502-473-1256
877-587-1256
FAX 502-473-4695
http://www.ldaofky.org
e-mail: info@LDAofky.org
Tim Woods, Executive Director

A non-profit organization of individuals with learning differences and attention difficulties, their parents, educators, and other service providers.

208 **Recording for the Blind & Dyslexic: Kentucky**
180 N. Michigan Avenue
Suite 620
Chicago, IL 60601-7425
312-236-8715
FAX 312-236-8719
http://www.rfbd.org
e-mail: strester@rfbd.org
Janet Milkovich, Executive Director

Utilizes volunteers in multiple areas of operation including board and committee, membership, ausio production, educational outreach, public information and fundraising.

Louisiana

209 **Advocacy Center**
1010 Common Street
Suite 2600
New Orleans, LA 70112-2429
504-237-2337
800-960-7705
FAX 504-522-5507
TTY: 866-935-7348
http://www.advocacycenter@advocacyla.org
Lois Simpson, Executive Director

Protects and advocates for the human and legal rights of persons living in Louisiana who are elderly or disabled.

210 **Lafayette Advocacy Center**
Ste 812
600 Jefferson St
Lafayette, LA 70501-6982
337-237-7380
800-822-0210
FAX 337-237-0486
http://www.advocacyla.org
Nell Hahn, CAP Client Advocate

Protects and advocates for the human and legal rights of persons living in Louisiana who are elderly or disabled.

211 **New Orleans Advocacy Center**
1010 Common Streeet
Suite 2600
New Orleans, LA 70112-2401
504-237-2337
800-960-7705
FAX 504-522-5507
TTY: 866-935-7348
http://www.advocacycenteradvocacyla.org
e-mail: advocacycenter@advocacyla.org
Lois Simpson, Executive Director
Susan Bushnell, Advocacy Services Director

Protects and advocates for the human and legal rights of persons living in Louisiana who are elderly or disabled.

212 Shreveport Advocacy Center
2620 Centenary Blvd.
Suite 248
Shreveport, LA 71104-3356   318-227-6186
800-839-7688
FAX 318-227-1841
http://www.advocacyla.org
Jackolyn Sanchez, Intake Specialist Coordinator
Diane Mirvis, Client Asst Program Director

Protects and advocates for the human and legal rights of persons living in Louisiana who are elderly or disabled.

Maine

213 Easter Seals Maine
125 Presumpscot St
Portland, ME 04103-5225   207-828-0754
FAX 207-828-5355
http://maine.easterseals.com
Michael Fagone, Chairman

Creates solutions that change lives of children and adults with disabilities or other special needs and their families.

214 Learning Disabilities Association of Maine (LDA)
P.O.Box 67
Oakland, ME 04963-0067   207-861-7823
877-208-4029
FAX 207-861-7823
http://www.ldame.org
e-mail: info@ldame.org
Gene Kucinkas Jr, President
Brenda Bennett, Executive Director

Dedicated to assisting individuals with learning and attention disabilities through support, education and advocacy.

215 Maine Parent Federation
Ste 7
12 Shuman Ave
Augusta, ME 04330-6020   207-623-2144
800-870-7746
FAX 207-623-2148
http://www.mpf.org
e-mail: parentconnnect@mpf.org
Janice La Chance, Executive Director

The Maine Parent Federation is a statewide organiztion that provides information, advocacy, education, and training to benefit all children. We promote individual aspirations and community inclusion for people with disabilities.
1984

Maryland

216 Association for Childhood Education International (ACEI)
17904 Georgia Avenue
Suite 215
Olney, MD 20832-2277   301-570-2111
800-423-3563
FAX 301-570-2212
http://www.acei.org
e-mail: headquarters@acei.org
James Hoot, President
Diane Whitehead, Executive Director

Mission is to promote and support in global community the optimal education and development of children, from birth through early adolescence, and to influence the professional growth of educators and the efforts of others who are committed to the needs of children in a changing society.

217 Disability Support Services
University of Maryland
Susquehanna Hall
4th Floor
College Park, MD 20742-0001   301-314-7651
FAX 301-405-0813
http://www.counseling.umd.edu/dss
Jo Ann Hutchinson RhD, Director

Coordinates services that ensure individuals with disabilities equal access to University of Maryland College Park programs.
800 members

218 Division of Rehabilitation Services
Maryland State Department of Education
2301 Argonne Dr
Baltimore, MD 21218-1628   410-554-9442
888-554-0334
FAX 410-554-9412
TTY: 410-554-9411
http://www.dors.state.md.us
e-mail: dors@dors.state.md.us
Robert Burns, Director

Enables persons with disabilities to achieve employment, economic self-sufficiency and independence.

219 Easter Seals Greater Washington Baltimore Region
1420 Spring St
Silver Spring, MD 20910-2701   301-588-8700
800-886-3771
FAX 301-920-9770
http://gwbr.easterseals.com
Lisa Reeves, President

Provides exceptional services to ensure that all people with disabilities or special needs and their families have equal opportunities to live, learn, work and play in their communities. Proudly servinf Washington-Baltimore Region and the surrounding communities in Maryland, Northern Virginia and West Virginia.

220 International Dyslexia Association of Maryland
P.O. Box 233
Brooklandville, MD 21022   443-632-4149
FAX 410-321-5069
http://www.interdys.org
e-mail: info@idamd.org
Rob Hott, President
Bob Mauro, Interim Executive Director

Believes that all individuals have the right to achieve their full potential and that individual learning abilities can be strengthen. MBIDA will promote and organize classes and workshops to provide informtion and training for dyslexic individuals, educators, parents and others.

221 Learning Disabilities Association of Maryland
P.O.Box 744
Dunkirk, MD 20754
888-265-6459
http://www.ldamd.org
e-mail: ldamd@ldamd.org
Simone Martinez, President
Peggy Dansford, Vice President

Dedicated to enhancing the quality of life for all individuals with learning disabilities and their families through awareness, advocacy, education, service and collaborative efforts.

222 Maryland Association of University Centers on Disabilities
Ste 920
1010 Wayne Ave
Silver Spring, MD 20910-5646   301-588-8252
FAX 301-588-2842
http://www.aucd.org
e-mail: aucdinfo@aucd.org
Tamar Heller, President

The mission of AUCD is to advance policy and practice for and with people living with developmental and other disabilities, their families, and communities by supporting our members to engage in research, education, and service activities that achieve our vision

223 National Data Bank for Disabled Service
University of Maryland
Susquehanna Hall
4th Floor
College Park, MD 20742-0001   301-314-7651
FAX 301-314-9478
http://www.counseling.umd.edu/dss
e-mail: jahutch@umd.edu
Jo Ann Hutchinson RhD, Director
Evalyn Hamilton, Customer Service Coordinator

Coordinates services that ensure individuals with disabilities equal access to University of Maryland College Park programs.
800 members 1976

224 National Federation of Families for Children's Mental Health
9605 Medical Center Drive
Suite 280
Rockville, MD 20850-6390   240-403-1901
FAX 240-403-1909
http://www.ffcmh.org
e-mail: ffcmh@ffcmh.org
Sandra Spencer, Executive Director
Marilyn Mealing, Administrative Assistant

Dedicated exclusively to helping children with mental health needs and their families achieve a better quality of life.

Massachusetts

225 Adaptive Environments
Institute for Human Centered Design
200 Portland Street
Suite 1
Boston, MA 02114   617-695-1225
FAX 617-482-8099
TTY: 617-695-1225
http://www.adaptiveenvironments.org
e-mail: info@humancentereddesign.org
Valerie Fletcher, Executive Director

Committed to advancing the role of design in expanding opportunity and enhancing experience for people of all ages and abilites.
1978

226 Easter Seals Massachusetts
484 Main St
Worcester, MA 01608-1893   800-244-2756
FAX 508-831-9768
http://www.ma.easterseals.com
e-mail: info@eastersealsma.com
Kirk N Joslin, President

Statewide, community based organization that has been helping people with disabilities to live full and independent lives for over 60 years.

227 International Dyslexia Association of Massachusetts
P.O.Box 662
Lincoln, MA 01773   617-650-0011
http://www.dyslexia-ma.org
e-mail: mabida@comcast.net
Pamela Hook, President

The Massachusetts Branch of The International Dyslexia Association (MABIDA) is a 501(c)(3) non-profit, scientific and educational organization dedicated to the study and treatment of dyslexia. This Branch was formed to increase public awareness of dyslexia in Massachusetts.

228 Learning Disabilities Worldwide (LDW)
P.O.Box 142
Weston, MA 02493-0005   978-897-5399
FAX 978-897-5355
http://www.ldam.org
Teresa Citro, Executive Director

Formerly the Learning Disabilities Association of Massachusetts, works to enhance the lives of individuals with learning disabilities, with a specail emphasis on the underserved. The purpose is to identify and support the unrecognized strengths and capabilities of a person with learning disabilities. We strive to increase awareness and understanding of learning disabilities through our multilingual media productions and publications that serve populations across cultures and nations.
15,000 members 1965

229 Massachusetts Association of Approved Private Schools (MAAPS)
607 North Avenue
Wakefield, MA 01880-1647   781-245-1220
FAX 781-245-5294
TTY: 781-245-5145
http://www.maaps.org
e-mail: info@maaps.org
James Major, Executive Director

Nonprofit association of Chapter 766 approved private schools dedicated to providing educational programs and services to students with special needs throughout Massachusetts. Concerned that children with special needs have appropriate, quality education and that they and their families know the rights, policies, procedures and options that make the education process a productive reality for special needs children.

230 Recording for the Blind & Dyslexic: Berkshire/Williamstown
55 Pittsfield-Lenox Road
Lenox, MA 01240   413-637-0889
800-221-4792
http://www.rfbd.org
e-mail: jgolin@rfbd.org
Jennifer Golin, Production Director

The Berkshire United Way operates recording studios in both Lenox and Williamstown. The studios offer information on recordings of books on audio cassette and computer disk, and provides outreach to: four western counties of Massachusetts; Albany, Columbia, Rensselaer, Saratoga, Schenectady and Washington counties in New York; Bennington County in Vermont; Litchfield County in Connecticut.

231 Recording for the Blind & Dyslexic: Boston
2067 Massachusetts Ave
Cambridge, MA 02140-2128   617-577-1111
FAX 617-577-1113
http://www.rfbd.org
Christina Raimo, Executive Director

A nonprofit volunteer organization and educational library serving people who cannot effectively read standard print because of visual impairment, dyslexia or other physical disability. We strive to create opportunities for individual success by providing accessible educational material. Comprehensive source of recorded textbooks and other educational printed matter. One-time registration fee of $50.00 plus a $25.00 annual fee. School memberships are available.

Michigan

232   Easter Seals- Michigan, Inc.
2399 E. Walton Blvd.
Auburn Hills, MI 48326-2759   248-475-6400
                                          800-649-3777
                             http://www.mi.easterseals.com
John Cocciolone, CEO

Offers programs and services for children and adults with disabilities and special needs.

233   International Dyslexia Association of Michigan
1443 Kings Point Road
Grand Blanc, MI 48439-8614
                                          888-432-6424
                             e-mail: info@idamichigan.org
Pat Frazier, President

The purpose of the Michigan Branch of the International Dyslexia Association is to develop awareness and provide information about Dyslexia.

234   Learning Disabilities Association of Michigan (LDA)
200 Museum Drive
Suite 101
Lansing, MI 48933-1914   517-485-8160
                                          888-597-7809
                                    FAX 517-485-8462
                             http://www.ldaofmichigan.org
                        e-mail: ldamichigan@sbcglobal.net
Lori Parks, President

A nonprofit, volunteer association that is dedicated to enhancing the quality of life for all individuals with learning disabilities and their families through advocacy, education, training, services and support of research. Our goal is to see LD understood and addressed and the individuals with learning disabilities will thrive and participate fully in society.
1,200 Members

235   Michigan Citizens Alliance to Uphold Special Education (CAUSE)
Ste 130e
6412 Centurion Dr
Lansing, MI 48917-8258   517-886-9167
                                          800-221-9105
                                    FAX 517-886-9366
                                    TDD:888-814-4013
                             http://www.causeonline.org
                        e-mail: info@causeonline.org
Sue Pratt, Acting Executive Director

CAUSE shall provide a collaborative forum where consumers and providers can actively support an individualized Free Appropriate Public Education (FAPE) that enables all students to maximize their options in the world community. Our priority is to protect and advocate for all the educational rights of students with disabilities.
1970

236   Recording for the Blind & Dyslexic Learning
180 N. Michigan Avenue
Suite 620
Chicago, IL 60601-7425   312-236-8715
                                    FAX 312-236-8719
                                    http://www.rfbd.org
                             e-mail: creeb@rfbd.org
Janet Milkovich, Executive Director

Recording for the Blind & Dyslexic is the nation's educational library serving people who cannot effectively read standard print because of visual impairment, dyslexia or other physical disability. We provide textbooks, educational and professional materials in an audio format. The Michigan Unit's outreach volunteers offer students and their parents training sessions at the studio by appointment.
    1958

Minnesota

237   Learning Disabilities Association of Minnesota
6100 Golden Valley Rd
Golden Valley, MN 55422   952-582-6000
                                    FAX 952-922-8102
                             http://www.ldaminnesota.org
                        e-mail: info@ldaminnesota.org
Kitty Christiansen, Executive Director

Nonprofit educational agency helping children, youth, and adults at risk for learning disabilities and other learning difficulties.

238   Technical Assistance Alliance for Parent Centers: PACER Center
8161 Normandale Blvd
Minneapolis, MN 55437-1044   952-838-9000
                                          888-248-0822
                                    FAX 952-838-0199
                                    TTY: 952-838-0190
                             http://www.taalliance.org
                        e-mail: alliance@taalliance.org
Paula Goldberg, Executive Director

An innovative project that supports a unified technical assistance system for the purpose of developing, assisting and coordinating Parent Training Information Projects and Community Parent Resource Centers.

239   Upper Midwest Branch of the International Dyslexia Association
5021 Vernon Ave #159
Minneapolis, MN 55436-2102   612-486-4242
                                    http://www.ida.umb.org
                             e-mail: info@umbida.org
Cindee McCarthy, President

Informs and educates people about dyslexia and related difficulties in learning to read and write, in a way that supports and encourages, promotes effective change, and gives individuals the opportunity to lead productive and fulfilling lives, which benefits society with the resource that is liberated.

Mississippi

240   Learning Disabilities Association of Mississippi
P.O.Box 4477
Jackson, MS 39216   601-362-1667
                                    FAX 301-362-9180
                                    http://www.ldams.org
                             e-mail: ldams@bellsouth.net
Martha Kabbes Burns, Contact

A non-profit, volunteer organization that is an informational Support Center for parents of children with learning disabilities, adults with learning disabilities, and professionals providing services related to learning disabilities.

Missouri

241   Easter Seals - Heartland

13975 Manchester Rd
Manchester, MO 63011-4500   636-227-6030
                                          800-664-5025
                                      FAX 636-779-2270
                              http://mo.easterseals.com
                          e-mail: mail@mo.easterseals.com
Craig Byrd, President

Provides exceptional services to ensure all people with disabilities have equal opportunities to live, learn, work and play in their communities.

242   Learning Disabilities Association of Missouri

P.O.Box 3303
Springfield, MO 65808-3303   417-864-5110
                                      FAX 417-864-7290
                                   http://www.ldamo.org
Cathy Einhorn, President

Provides information and support to parents, individuals with learning disabilities and professionals.

243   Missouri Protection & Advocacy Services

925 S Country Club Dr
Jefferson City, MO 65109-4510   573-893-3333
                                          866-777-7199
                                      FAX 573-893-4231
                                      TDD:800-735-2966
                               http://www.moadvocacy.org
                         e-mail: mopasjc@embargmail.com
Cathy Enfield, Chair

A federally mandated system in the state which provides protection of the rights of persons with disabilities through leagally-based advocacy. The mission is to protect the rights of individuals with disabilities by providing advocacy and legal services.
1977

244   St. Louis Learning Disabilities Association

13537 Barrett Parkway Drive
Ste 110
Ballwin, MO 63021-5896   314-966-3088
                                      FAX 314-966-1806
                                   http://www.ldastl.org
                                  e-mail: info@ldastl.org
Pam Kortum, Executive Director

A non-profit organization dedicated to enhancing the understanding and acceptance of learning disabilities. Education, support, and consultation are provided to children, parents, and professionals to help reach their full potential.
1993

Montana

245   Learning Disabilities Association of Montana

3544 Toboggan Rd
Billings, MT 59101-9121   406-259-3110
                                   http://www.ldaofmt.org
                                  e-mail: info@ldaofmt.org
Mark Taylor, President

The Learning Disabilities Association of Montana assists individuals with learning disabilities through information, advocacy and support.

246   Montana Parents, Let's Unite for Kids (PLUK)

516 N 32nd St
Billings, MT 59101-6003   406-255-0540
                                          800-222-7585
                                      FAX 406-255-0523
                                     http://www.pluk.org
                            e-mail: info@pluk@pluk.org
Roger Holt, Executive Director

PLUK is a private, nonprofit organization formed by parents of children with disabilities and chronic illnesses. Its purpose is to provide information, support, training and assistance to aid parents with their children at home, in school and as adults. We keep current on best practices in education, medicine, law, human services, rehabilitation, and technology to insure families with disabilites have access to high quality services.
1984

Nebraska

247   Easter Seals Nebraska

638 N 109th Plz
Omaha, NE 68154-1722   402-345-2200
                                          800-650-9880
                                      FAX 402-345-2500
                             http://www.ne.easterseals.com
Karen Carlson, President

Provides exceptional services to help ensure all people with disabilities have an equal opportunity to live, learn, work and play.

248   International Dyslexia Association of Nebraska

5921 Sunrise Rd
P.O. Box 6302
Lincoln, NE 68506-0302   402-434-6434
                                      FAX 410-321-5069
                                   http://www.ne-ida.com
                                  e-mail: info@ne-ida.com
Joan Stoner, President

Nebraska Branch works to enhance the public's perception and understanding of dyslexia and related language/learning disabilities.
1984

249   Learning Disabilities Association of Nebraska

3135 N 93rd St
Omaha, NE 68134-4717   402-348-1567
                                      FAX 402-934-1479
                               http://www.ldanebraska.org
                             e-mail: ldaofneb@yahoo.com
Deb Carlson, President

Support groups for parents and teachers, information for school and the community about ADHD and LD children/adults. Offers book and video library, educational seminars and conferences, parent panels. Quarterly newsletter.
1984

Nevada

250   Children's Cabinet

1090 S Rock Blvd
Reno, NV 89502-7116   775-856-6200
                                      FAX 775-856-6208
                              http://www.childrenscabinet.org
                         e-mail: mail@childrenscabinet.org
Michael J. Pomi, Executive Director

The Children's Cabinet strives to ensure every child and family in our community has the services and resources to meet fundamental development, care, and learning needs.

251 Easter Seals Southern Nevada
6200 W Oakey Blvd
Las Vegas, NV 89146-1103
702-870-7050
FAX 702-870-7649
http://sn.easterseals.com
Brian Patchett, President

Provides services to children and adults with disabilities and other special needs, and support to their families.

252 Learning Disabilities Association of Nevada
2970 Idlewild Drive
Reno, NV 89509
http://www.ldaamerica.org
e-mail: nevspedlaw@aol.com
Candy Von Ruden, Contact

To create opportunities for success for all individuals affected by learning disabilities and to reduce the incidence of learning disabilities in future generations.

New Hampshire

253 Crotched Mountain
1 Verney Dr
Greenfield, NH 03047-5000
603-547-3311
FAX 603-547-6212
http://www.nhassistivetechnology.org
e-mail: development@crotchedmountain.org
Donald Shumway, President

Serves individuals with disabilities and their families, embracing personal choice and development, and building communities of mutual support.

254 Easter Seals New Hampshire
555 Auburn St
Manchester, NH 03103-4803
603-623-8863
800-870-8728
FAX 603-625-1148
http://www.nheasterseals.com
Larry Gammon, President

Easter Seals New Hampshire is one of the most comprehensive affiliates in the nation, assisting more than 18,000 children and adults with disabilities through a network of more than a dozen service sites around the state and in Vermont. Each center provides top-quality, family-focused and innovative services tailored to meet the specific needs of the particular community it serves.
1936

255 International Dyslexia Association of New Hampshire
PO Box 3724
Concord, NH 03302-3724
603-229-7355
http://www.nhida.org
e-mail: info@nhida.org
Kathy McGhee, President

The New Hampshire Branch of The International Dyslexia Association (NH/IDA) is a 501(c)(3) non-profit, scientific and educational organization dedicated to the study and treatment of the learning disability, dyslexia. The New Hampshire Branch was formed in 2002 to increase public awareness of dyslexia. The New Hampshire Branch serves New Hampshire, Maine and Vermont

256 New Hampshire Disabilities Rights Center (DRC)
18 Low Ave
Concord, NH 03301-4971
603-228-0432
800-834-1721
FAX 603-225-2077
TDD:603-228-0432
http://www.drcnh.org
e-mail: advocacy@drcnh.org
Richard Cohen, Executive Director

A statewide organization that is independent from state government or service providers and is dedicated to the full and equal enjoyment of civil and other legal rights by people with disabilities. The DRC is New Hampshire's designated Protection and Advocacy agency and authorized by federal statute to pursue legal, administrative and other appropriate remedies on behalf of individuals with disabilities.
1978

257 Parent to Parent of New Hampshire
12 Flynn St
Lebanon, NH 03766-1311
603-448-6393
800-698-5465
http://www.p2pnh.org
e-mail: p2p@nhsupport.net
Phillip Eller, Executive Director

If you are a parent of a child with special challenges and you would like to speak to a parent whose child has similar needs - someone who will understand, Parent to Parent is a network of families willing to share experiences. Should you call a Supporting Parent will contact you by phone or visit within 24 hours. All information will be kept confidential and there is no cost for the service.

New Jersey

258 ASPEN Asperger Syndrome Education Network
9 Aspen Cir
Edison, NJ 08820-2832
732-321-0880
http://www.aspennj.org
e-mail: info@aspennj.org
Lori Shery, President
Claudia Loomis, Executive VP
Amanda Vogler, VP
Provides families and individuals whose lives are affected by Autism Spectrum Disorders (Asperger Syndrome, Pervasive Developmental Disorder-NOS, High Functioning Autism), and Nonverbal Learning Disabilities with education, support and advocacy.

259 Disability Rights New Jersey
210 S Broad St
Ste 3
Trenton, NJ 08608
609-292-9742
800-922-7233
FAX 609-777-0187
TTY: 609-633-7106
http://www.drnj.org
e-mail: advocate@drnj.org
Joseph B Young, Executive Director

A consumer-directed, non-profit organization that serves as New Jersey's designated protection and advocacy system for people with disabilities in the state.

260 Easter Seals New Jersey
25 Kennedy Blvd
Ste 600
East Brunswick, NJ 08816
732-257-6662
FAX 732-257-7373
TDD:732-535-3217
http://eastersealsnj.org
Brian J Fitzgerald, President/CEO

To enable individuals with disabilities or special needs and their families to live, learn, work and play in their communities with equality, dignity and independence.

261 Family Resource Associates, Inc.
35 Haddon Ave
Shrewsbury, NJ 07702-4007
732-747-5310
FAX 732-747-1896
http://www.frainc.org
e-mail: info@frainc.org
Bill Sheeser, President

A non-profit agency with the mission of helping children, adolescents and people of all ages with disabilities to reach their fullest potenttial. Provides home-based early intervention for infants, therapeutic recreation programs and assistive technology services, along with family and sibling support groups.

262 Family Support Center of New Jersey
2516 Highway 35
Manasquan, NJ 08736-1925
732-528-8080
800-372-6510
FAX 732-528-4744
http://www.fscnj.org
e-mail: jacqui.moskowitz@fscnj.org
Jacqueline Moskowitz, Executive Director

The Family Support Center of New Jersey (FSCNJ) is a clearing house of up-to-date information on national, state and local family support programs, services and disabilities. FSCNJ offers a one stop shopping approach to individuals seeking information on disabilities and services by providing them with easy acces to a comprehensive array of services.

263 International Dyslexia Association of New Jersey
PO Box 32
Long Valley, NJ 07853-0032
908-876-1179
FAX 908-876-3621
http://www.interdys.org
e-mail: njida@msn.com
Susan Tramaglini, President

An international nonprofit, scientific and educational organization dedicated to the study of dyslexia. We offer tutoring and testing referrals, as well as support teacher education and hold outreach programs. Teacher Scholarships are offered to our Annual Fall Conferences, Wilson Reading Overviews and Project Read programs. Newsletter published bi-annually.
700 members

264 Learning Disabilities Association of New Jersey
P.O.Box 492
Towaco, NJ 07082-0492
973-265-4303
FAX 973-265-4303
http://www.ldaamerica.org
e-mail: ldanj@optonline.net
Terry Cavanaugh, State President

To create opportunities for success in all individuals affected by learning disabilities and to reduce the incidence of learning disabilities in future generations.

265 New Jersey Self-Help Group Clearinghouse
375 E McFarlan St
Dover, NJ 07801-3628
973-989-1122
800-367-6274
FAX 973-989-1159
http://www.njgroups.org
e-mail: abroderick@saintclares.org
Ed Madara, Executive Director

Puts callers in touch with any of several hundred national and international self-help groups covering a wide range of illnesses, disabilities, addictions, bereavement and stressful life situations.

New Mexico

266 Easter Seals Santa Maria El Mirador
P.O.Box 39
Alcalde, NM 87511-0039
505-852-4243
FAX 505-852-4138
http://smem.easterseals.com
Mark Johnson, CEO

Provides an array of quality supports for individuals with developmental disabilities in community integrated environments centered on personl choice, self value, and dignity.

267 International Dyslexia Association Southwest Branch
3915 Carlisle Blvd NE
Albuquerque, NM 87107-4503
505-255-8234
http://www.southwestida.com
e-mail: info@southwestida.com
Linda Curry, President

Deeply committed to the training of teachers, speech pathologists, parents, literacy volunteers, and other professionals in appropriate instructional methods for individuals with dyslexia. IDA's Southwest Branch encourages the use of Orton-Gilligham multisensory structured language based (MSL-based) methodology, which has proven to be the most effective way to teach individuals with dyslexia and related learning disabilities.
1985

268 Learning Disabilities Association of New Mexico: Albuquerque
Ste 556
6301 Menaul Blvd NE
Albuquerque, NM 87110-3323
505-821-2545
http://www.vivanewmexico.com/nm/nmlda
e-mail: bp@peavler.org
Penny White, President

A nonprofit volunteer organization affiliated with the Learning Disabilities Association of America (LDAA). LDAA gives support and information to persons with learning disabilities, parents, teachers, and other professionals through 50 state affiliates and 800 local units.

269 Learning Disabilities Association of New Mexico: Las Cruces
P.O.Box 30001/3spe
Las Cruces, NM 88003
505-867-3396
FAX 505-867-3398
http://www.education.nmsu.edu/projects/nmlda
e-mail: epoel@nmsu.edu
Selma Nevarez, President

LDA is a non-profit organization of volunteers including individuals with learning disabilities, their families and professionals. LDA is dedicated to identifying causes and promoting prevention of learning disabilities and to enhancing the quality of life for all individuals with learning disabilities and their families by encouraging effective identification and intervention, fostering research, and protecting their rights under the law.

New York

270 Advocates for Children of New York
151 West 30th Street
5th Floor
New York, NY 10001-4197
212-947-9779
FAX 212-947-9790
http://www.advocatesforchildren.org
e-mail: info@advocatesforchildren.org
Kim Sweet, Executive Director

Works on behalf of children from infancy to age 21 who are at greatest risk for school-based discrimination and/or academic failure. AFC provides a full range of services: free individual case advocacy, technical assistance, and training for parents, students, and professionals about children's educational entitlements and due process rights in New York City.

271   Dyslexia Association Long Island Island
728 Fort Salonga Rd
Northport, NY 11768-3176   631-261-7441
                                           FAX 631-261-7834
                                    http://www.lidyslexia.org
                              e-mail: information@lidyslexia.org
Lynne Burke, President

Our objectives are to increase awareness of dyslexia in the
community; provide support for parents and teachers; promote teacher training. We offer a telephone message system
for information requests; sponsor an annual conference and
four topic workshops as well as a summer Orton-Gillingham
course. We have a network of local school officials, parents,
attorneys and other professionals to help parents navigate
the channels of the school system.

272   International Dyslexia Association New York
Ste 1527
71 W 23rd St
New York, NY 10010-4197   212-691-1930
                                           FAX 212-633-1620
                                     http://www.nybida.org
                                    e-mail: info@nybida.org
Joanne Simon, President
Jo Haines, Executive Director

This is a nonprofit organization whose mission is to provide
continuing education in appropriate diagnostic remedial approaches and to support the rights of people with dyslexia in
order that they may lead fulfilling lives. To this end, the
NYB-IDA disseminates information, publishes a quarterly
newsletter, and provides information and referral services,
teacher training, conferences, adult support groups, and
workshops for parents. Annual teen conference.

**273   International Dyslexia Association of Western New
York**
2491 Emery Rd
South Wales, NY 14139-9408   716-687-2030
                                     http://www.wnyida.org
                                    e-mail: bufida@gow.org
Joseph W. Gullo, President

Strives to be a resource for information and services that address the full scope of dyslexia in a way that builds cooperation, partnership and understanding among professional
communities and dyslexic individuals so that everyone is
valued and has the opportunity to be productive and fulfilled
in life. Newsletter and teacher training scholarships.

274   LDA Life and Learning Services
1650 South Avenue
Suite 200
Rochester, NY 14620   585-263-3323
                                           FAX 585-224-7100
                                    http://www.LDARochester.org
                              e-mail: info@ldarochester.org
Robert S. Moore, President
Colin Garwood, Executive Director
Amanda Hartman, Deputy Executive Director
A non-profit agency that partners with individuals who seek
hlep in learning, so that they can succeed in school, work,
and community life. The primaty constituents include people who are working to overcome cognitive or developmental barriers to learning. Also serve as a resource to people
who are involved in the lives of these individuals, such as
family members, employers, teachers and health care
professionals.

275   Learning Disabilities Association of Central New York
722 W Manlius St
East Syracuse, NY 13057-2178   315-432-0665
                                           FAX 315-431-0606
                                     http://www.ldacny.org
                                    e-mail: ldacny@ldacny.org
Paulette Purdy, Executive Director

Enhances the quality of life for children and adults with
learning disabilities by providing advocacy, programs and
educational resources. Serving the counties of Cayuga,
Cortland, Madison, Onondaga and Owsego.

276   Learning Disabilities Association of New York City
27 West 20th Street
Suite 303
New York, NY 10011-3731   212-645-6730
                                           FAX 212-924-8896
                                     http://www.ldanyc.org
                                    e-mail: info@ldanyc.org
Susan Ingram, President
Donald Fann, Executive Director

Serves the counties of Brooklyn, Bronx, Manhattan, Queens
and Staten Island. Facilitates access to needed services for
all New Yorkers with Learning Disabilities, especially those
in the more disadvantaged communities, and provides support to those individuals and their families.
    1989

277   Learning Disabilities Association of Western New York
2555 Elmwood Ave
Kenmore, NY 14217-1939   716-874-7200
                                           FAX 716-874-7205
                                     http://www.ldaofwny.org
                              e-mail: information@ldaofwny.org
Mike Helman, Executive Director

To create conditions under which persons with learning disabilities, neurological impairments, and developmental disabilities are given opportunities to make choices and
develop and achieve independence. The association also addresses each individual's health, future, participation in the
community, and personal relationships. LDA Southern
Fredonia Tier branch can be reached at 716-679-1601.

278   New York Easter Seals Society
40 West 37th Street
Suite 503
New York, NY 10018   212-943-4364
                                           FAX 212-695-4807
                                    http://www.ny.easterseals.com
John W McGrath, SVP Organizational Development

Provides programs and services to children and adults with
disabilities and other special needs, and their families. The
goal is to help individuals with special needs gain dignity,
equality and independence. Also provide the highest quality
services in the most caring and cost-effective manner.
    1922

279   Recording for the Blind & Dyslexic
545 5th Ave
New York, NY 10017-3609   212-557-5720
                                     http://www.rfbd.org
                                    e-mail: jfernandes@rfbd.org
John Fernandes, Production Director

Serves New Yorkers who are blind, visually impaired, physically disabled or have a learning disability.

280   Resources for Children with Special Needs
116 E. 16th Street
5th Floor
New York, NY 10003-2164   212-677-4650
                                           FAX 212-254-4070
                                    http://www.resourcesnyc.org
                              e-mail: info@resourcesnyc.org
Rachel Howard, Executive Director

An information, referral, advocacy, tranining and support
center for NYC parents/professionals looking for services
for children-birth to 26 with learning, developmental, emotional of physical disabilities. Publications available on
website.

281 Strong Center for Developmental Disabilities
Golisano Children's Hospital at Strong
601 Elmwood Ave
Rochester, NY 14642-0001   585-341-9000
                                    FAX 585-275-0355
                        http://www.urmc.rochester.edu
                   e-mail: scdd@cc.urmc.rochester.edu
Steven Sulkes, MD, Director
Susan C. Hyman, MD, Division Chief

A University Center of Excellence for Developmental Disabilities, Education, Research and Service. Provides services, advocacy, education, technical assistance, and research to ensure full inclusion of persons with developmental disabilities in their communities and to maximize their potential for leading independent and productive lives.

282 Westchester Institute for Human Development
Westchester Medical Center
Cedarwood Hall
Valhalla, NY 10595   914-493-8150
                                    FAX 914-493-1973
                                http://www.wihd.org
                             e-mail: wihd@wihd.org
Ansley Bacon, PhD, President/CEO

WIHD advances policies and practices that foster the healthy development and ensure the safety of all children, strenghten families and communities, and promote health and well-being among people of all ages with disabilities and special health care needs.
           1950

283 Yellin Center for Mind, Brain, and Education
104 W 29th St
12th Fl
New York, NY 10001   646-775-6646
                                    FAX 646-775-6602
                          http://www.yellincenter.com
                       e-mail: info@yellincenter.com
Dr. Paul B. Yellin, MD, FAAP, Director

Comprehensive Neurodevelopmental and Psychoeducational Evaluation for students in Pre-K, K-12, College, Graduate and Professional Schools, and for adults. Ongoing support including Academic Coaching, Medication Management, Progress Monitoring and College Transition Support. Outreach to School, Teachers, and other providers where indicated. Professional development presentations for schools and parent organizations. Sliding scale available.

North Carolina

284 Mind Matters
Southeast Psych
6060 Piedmont Row Drive South
Ste 120
Charlotte, NC 28287   704-552-0116
                                    FAX 704-552-7550
                          http://www.southeastpsych.com
                   e-mail: cpohlman@southeastpsych.com
Craig Pohlman PhD, Director

Mind Matters at Southeast Psych believes in describing learners (not just labeling them), identifying strengths (not just weaknesses), explaining findings clearly (not just reporting scores), collaborating to support struggling learners, and improving the self-insight of all learners.

285 Success in Mind
324 Blackwell St
Ste 1240
Durham, NC 27701   919-680-8921
                                         877-680-8921
                                    FAX 919-680-8949
                         http://www.success-in-mind.org
                     e-mail: info@success-in-mind.org
Beth Briere MD, Executive Director and Neurodeve
Elizabeth Hodgson M.Ed., Learning Specialist

Provides students, families, teachers and others involved in a student's educatoin with a deep understanding and a common language that demystifies learning, values individual learning differences, and promotes success for each learner.

Ohio

286 Easter Seals: Youngstown
299 Edwards St
Youngstown, OH 44502-1599   330-743-1168
                                    FAX 330-743-1616
                                    TTY: 320-743-1616
                         http://www.mtc.easterseals.com
Ken Sklenar, Executive Director

Easter Seals of Mahoning, Trumbull and Columbiana Counties pledges to help persons with disabilities or special needs live with equality, dignity and independence.

287 International Dyslexia Association of Central Ohio
P.O. Box 340426
Columbus, OH 43234   614-899-5711
                                http://www.interdys.org
                             e-mail: info@cobida.org
Cyndi Schultz, President

Increases awareness of dyslexia and related learning disabilities; assist professionals, dyslexics and their families; promote use of effective teaching methods; and disseminate research-based knowledge. Serves Central Ohio and parts of West Virginia.

288 International Dyslexia Association of Northern Ohio
P.O.Box 2141
Hudson, OH 44236-0141   216-556-0883
                          http://www.dyslexia-nohio.org
                      e-mail: info@dyslexia-nohio.org
Monica Gordon Pershey, President

A non-profit, scientific and educational organization dedicated to the study and treatment of the language-based reading disability, dyselxia.

289 International Dyslexia Association: Ohio Valley Branch
P.O. Box 9084
Cincinnati, OH 45209   513-651-4747
                        http://www.cincinnatidyslexia.org
                       e-mail: andersonjl@fuse.net
Martha Chiodi, President

A non-profit, scientific and educational organization dedicated to the study and treatment of the learning disability, dyslexia. This Branch was formed to increase public awareness of dyslexia on the Southern Ohio, Southeast Indiana, Kentucky and Huntington, West Virginia areas.

290 Learning Disabilities Association of Cuyahoga County
30100 Chagrin Blvd.
Suite 302
Celveland, OH 44124   216-292-4549
                                    FAX 216-292-7076
                                http://www.ldaneo.org
                             e-mail: info@ldaneo.org
Ellen Fishman, Executive Director

Empowers those with Specific Learning Disabilities to realize their potential and achieve their goals.

Oklahoma

291 Easter Seals Oklahoma
701 NE 13th St
Oklahoma City, OK 73104-5003
405-239-2525
FAX 405-239-2278
http://ok.easterseals.com
Paula Porter, President

Provides services to children and adults with disabilities and other special needs, and support to their families.

292 Learning Disabilities Association of Oklahoma
P.O.Box 1134
Jenks, OK 74037-1134
918-298-1600
http://www.ldao.org
e-mail: ldao2002@sbcglobal.net
Linda Modenbach, President

A nonprofit organization committed to enhancing the lives of individuals with learning disabilities and their families through education, advocacy, research, and service

Oregon

293 Easter Seals Oregon
5757 SW Macadam Ave
Portland, OR 97239-3797
503-228-5108
800-556-6020
FAX 503-228-1352
http://or.easterseals.com
David Cheveallier, CEO

Provides services to children and adults with disabilities and other special needs, helping them to live with equality, dignity and independence.

294 International Dyslexia Association of Oregon
2525 NW Lovejoy Street
Suite 406
Portland, OR 97210-2865
503-228-4455
800-530-2234
FAX 503-228-3152
http://www.orbida.org
e-mail: info@orbida.org
Judith L Wright, President

The Oregon Branch of the International Dyslexia Association (ORBIDA) focuses on increasing public awareness of how dyslexia affects both children and adults.

295 Learning Disabilities Association of Oregon
P.O.Box 1221
Beaverton, OR 97008
503-968-0140
http://www.ldaor.org
e-mail: wisechoice@comcast.net
Myrna Soule, President

Works to promote the welfare of children and adults with learning disabilities. A non-profit organization that serves as a resource, referral, and information center for adults with learning disabilities, parents of children with learning disabilities, and profesionals working in the field of learning disabilities.

296 Oregon's Deaf and Hard of Hearing Services
500 Summer Street NE, E-16
Salem, OR 97301
503-947-5183
800-521-9615
FAX 503-947-5184
http://www.odc.state.or.us
e-mail: odhhs.info@state.or.us

Patricia O'Sullivan, Manager

Provides information and referral source on deafness and hearing loss issues; training on deaf awareness and sensitivity, and how to communicate with those with hearing loss.

297 University of Oregon Center for Excellence in Developmental Disabilities
Center on Human Development College of Education
5252 University of Oregon
Eugene, OR 97403-5252
541-346-3591
FAX 541-346-2594
http://ucedd.uoregon.edu
e-mail: uocedd@uoregon.edu
Jane Squires, Director

The mission of our UCEDD in Developmental Disabilities is to be of assistance in improving the quality of life for Oregonians and all persons with developmental disabilities and their families. To accomplish this mission, we provide training, technical assistance, interdisciplinary training, dissemination, networking and model development that responds effectively, and in a culturally competent fashion, to the multiple needs of individuals and their families.

Pennsylvania

298 AAC Institute
1401 Forbes Avenue
Suite 206
Pittsburgh, PA 15219-2627
412-523-6424
http://www.aacinstitute.org
e-mail: khill@aacinstitute.org
Katya Hill PhD, Executive Director

Established in 2000, a resource for all who are interested in enhancing the communication of people who rely on AAC. A not-for-profit charitable organization, offers information and provides services worldwide.

299 Easter Seals Society of Western Pennsylvania: Fayette
2525 Railroad St
Pittsburgh, PA 15222-4608
412-281-7244
800-587-3257
FAX 412-281-9333
http://www.westernpa.easterseals.com
Larry Rager, President

Speech, language, learning disabilities and hearing evaluations and therapy for all ages. PA licensed preschool on the premises. Open five days per week; 12 months. Call for an appointment or information on the programs provided.
1934

300 Huntingdon County PRIDE
1301 Mount Vernon Ave
Huntingdon, PA 16652-1149
814-643-5724
FAX 814-643-6085
http://www.huntingdonpride.org
e-mail: sbair@huntingdonpride.org
Sandy Bair, Executive Director

Provide programs which enable people who are developmentally and/or physically disabled to function at their optimal level of performance.

301 International Dyslexia Association of Pennsylvania
1062 E Lancaster Ave
Rosemontr, PA 19010-0251
610-527-1548
FAX 610-527-5011
http://www.pbida.org
e-mail: dyslexia@pbida.org

The Pennsylvania Branch of the International Dyslexia Association (PBIDA), serving Pennsylvania and Delaware provides support and information for individuals, families and educational professionals concerned with the issues of dyslexia and learning differences.

302   Learning Disabilities Association of Pennsylvania
4751 Lind Road
Suite 114
Harrisburg, PA 17111   717-939-3731
                                     888-775-3272
                         http://www.ldapa.org
Debbie Rodes, President

A nonprofit organization dedicated to serving Pennsylvania residents by providing accurate, up-to-date information regarding learning disabilities as well as support.

303   Pennsylvania Center for Disability Law and Policy
1515 Market Street
Suite 1300
Philadelphia, PA 19102-1819   215-557-7112
                                     888-745-2357
                               FAX 215-557-7602
                               TDD:215-557-7112
                   http://www.equalemployment.org
                   e-mail: info@equalemployment.org
Stephen Pennington, Executive Director

An advocacy program for people with disabilities administered by the Center for Disability Law & Policy. CAP helps people who are seeking services from the Office of Vocational Rehabilitation, Blindness and Visual Services, Centers for Independent Living and other progrmas funded under federal law. Hep is provided to you at no charge, regardless of income. Dedicated to ensuring that the rehabilitation system in Pennsylvania is open and responsive to your needs.

304   Recording for the Blind & Dyslexic
215 W Church Road
Suite 111
King of Prussia, PA 19406-3200   610-265-8090
                          http://www.rfbd.org
                   e-mail: dgoldenberg@rfbd.org
Dave Goldenberg, Executive Director

Serves Bucks, Chester, Delaware, Montgomery and Philadelphia counties with teacher training and technical assistance, information sessions about the RFB&D library of recorded textbooks, reference library services and our expanding line of tape and CD players and software designed to play RFB&D books.

Rhode Island

305   International Dyslexia Association of Rhode Island
8080 Ferry Road
Saunderstown, RI 02874   401-521-0020
                               FAX 401-847-6720
                          http://www.interdys.org
                   e-mail: ribida@yahoo.com
Melissa Chafee, President

A non-profit, scientific and educational organization dedicated to the study and treatment of dyslexia.

South Carolina

306   Easter Seals South Carolina
P.O.Box 5715
Columbia, SC 29250-5715   803-256-0735
                                     800-951-4090
                               FAX 803-356-6902
                         http://sc.easterseals.com
Provides services to children and adults with disabilities and other special needs, and support to their families.

307   International Dyslexia Association of South Carolina
30 South Hampton Drive
Charleston, SC 29407   864-483-0707
                          http://www.interdys.org
                   e-mail: scbida@gmail.com
Susan McLeod, President

The South Carolina Branch provides general information about dyslexia and makes referrals to various professionals and schools serving individuals with learning disabilities.
130 members

South Dakota

308   Learning Disabilities Association of South Dakota
1021 S. Courtland Street
Chamberlin, SD 57325   605-234-0115
                                     888-388-5553
                               FAX 305-787-7848
                          http://www.ldanatl.org
                   e-mail: maryalicelarson@yahoo.com
Mary Alice Larson, President

The Association conducts workshops and conferences, assists local communities, collaborates with other organizations with similar missions and concerns, and provides 1-on-1 assistance to individuals and families. Most visible among its efforts is the Association's statewide annual conference.
1996

309   South Dakota Center for Disabilities
Sanford School of Medicine USD
1400 W 22nd St
Sioux Falls, SD 57105-1505   605-357-1439
                                     800-658-3080
                               FAX 605-357-1438
                               TDD:800-658-3080
                               TTY: 800-658-3080
                          http://www.usd.edu
                   e-mail: cd@usd.edu
Judy Struck, Executive Director

A division of the Department of Pediatrics at the Sanford School pf Medicine at the University of South Dakota. The Center for Disabilities is South Dakota's University Center for Excellence in Developmental Disabilities Education, Research and Service sometimes referred to as University Centers for Excellence in Developmental Disabilities.

Tennessee

310   Easter Seals Tennessee
3011 Armory Drive
Suite 100
Nashville, TN 37204-3721   615-292-6640
                               FAX 615-251-0994
                               TDD:615-385-3485
                   http://www.tn.easterseals.com
Rita Baumgartner, President

Creates solutions that change the lives of children and adults with disabilities or other special needs and their families.

311   International Dyslexia Association: Tennessee Branch
Box 5074
Cookeville, TN 38505
                                     877-836-6432
                               FAX 931-528-3916
                          http://www.tnida.org
                   e-mail: htdainty@gmail.com
Helen Dainty, President

The Tennessee Branch of the International Dyslexia Association (TN-IDA) was formed to increase awareness about Dyslexia in the state of Tennessee. TN-IDA supports efforts to provide information regarding appropriate language arts instruction to those involved with language-based learning differences and to encourage the identity of these individuals at-risk for such disorders as soon as possible. This branch also serves individuals in the state of Kentucky.

312   **Learning Disabilities Association of Tennessee**
P.O.Box 40237
Memphis, TN 38174-0237   901-788-5328
http://www.learningdisabilities-tn.org
e-mail: info@learningdisabilities-tn.org
Sue Marsh, President

The Learning Disabilities Association of Tennessee has a mission to provide information concerning awareness, advocacy, parent information, and community education to maximize the quality of life for individuals and families affected by Learning Disabilities and related disorders in the state of Tennessee.

313   **Recording for the Blind & Dyslexic: Tennessee**
205 Badger Rd
Oak Ridge, TN 37830-6216   865-482-3496
FAX 865-483-9934
http://www.rfbd.org
e-mail: cmorris@rfbd.org
Cecelia Morrise, Production Director

Part of the national, nonprofit organization which records educational and career-related materials for print impaired students and professionals. The special focus is educational books. Blind and other print impaired students at every level, from elementary through graduate school, depend on RFBD tapes for the texts they need.
1952

Texas

314   **Easter Seals of Central Texas**
1611 Headway Circle
Building 2
Austin, TX 78754-5165   512-478-2581
FAX 512-476-1638
http://www.centraltx.easterseals.com
Jean Langendorf, Interim CEO/President

Easter Seals Central Texas provides exceptional services so people with disabilities and their families can fully participate in their communities.

315   **Easter Seals of North Texas**
1424 Hemphill St
Fort Worth, TX 76104-4703   817-332-7171
888-617-7171
FAX 817-332-7601
http://www.ntx.easterseals.com
e-mail: info@easterseals.com
Monica Prather, President

Created by the merger of Easter Seals of Greater Dallas and Easter Seals Greater Northwest Texas. Creates opportunities that advance the independence of individuals with disabilities and other special needs.

316   **International Dyslexia Association of Austin**
P.O.Box 92604
Austin, TX 78709-2604   512-452-7658
http://www.austinida.org
Monica Clark, President

The Austin Area Branch of the International Dyslexia Association is a 501(c)(3) non profit organization dedicated to promoting reading excellence for all children through early identification of dyslexia, effective literacy education for adults and children with dyslexia, and teacher training.

317   **International Dyslexia Association of Dallas**
14070 Proton Road
Suite 100
Dallas, TX 75244-3601   972-233-9107
FAX 972-490-4219
http://www.dbida.org
e-mail: hotline@dbida.org
H.B. Stern, President

The Dallas Branch of The International Dyslexia Association is committed to leadership and advocacy for people with dyslexia by providing: support for individuals and group interactions; programs to inform and educate; information for professionals and the general public.

318   **International Dyslexia Association of Houston**
P.O.Box 540504
Houston, TX 77254-0504   832-282-7154
FAX 972-490-4219
http://www.houstonida.org
e-mail: info@houstonida.org
Jim Carter MA CCC SLP, President

A non-profit organization dedicated to helping individuals with dyslexia and related learning disorders, their families and the communities that support them.

319   **Learning Disabilities Association of Texas**
PO Box 831392
Richardson, TX 75083-1392   512-458-8234
800-604-7500
http://www.ldat.org
e-mail: contact@ldat.org
Jean Kueker, President

Promotes the educational and general welfare of individuals with learning disabilities.
1963

320   **North Texas Rehabilitation Center**
1005 Midwestern Pkwy
Wichita Falls, TX 76302-2211   940-322-0771
800-861-1322
FAX 940-766-4943
http://www.ntrehab.org
Mike Castles, President

A not-for-profit organization providing nationally accredited outpatient medical, academic, and developmental rehabilitation to North Texas and Southern Oklahoma. From the Early Childhood Intervention program to the Aquatics programs, these services are designed to help our patients acheive their highest level of independence.
1948

Utah

321   **International Dyslexia Association of Utah**
4649 W. 10600N
Highland, VT 84003   801-756-1933
FAX 801-718-2222
http://www.ubida.org
e-mail: dyslexiacenterofutah.org
Shelley Hatch, Director

Dedicated to ensuring that every student with the learning difference of Dyslexia will receive scientifically based instruction and services consistent with his/her needs.

322   Learning Disabilities Association of Utah
PO Box 900726
Sandy, UT 84090-0726   801-553-9156
                                                  http://www.ldau.org
                                          e-mail: lda.utah@gmail.com
A non-profit volunteer organization supporting people with
learning disabilities and their families. Our mission is to create opportunities for individuals with learning abilities to
succeed and for their families to participate in their success.

Vermont

323   Vermont Protection & Advocacy
141 Main Street
Suite 7
Montpelier, VT 05602-2916   802-229-1355
                                                  800-834-7890
                                             FAX 802-229-1359
                                             TTY: 802-229-2603
                                                  http://www.vtpa.org
                                               e-mail: info@vtpa.org

Ed Paquin, Executive Director

Dedicated to addressing problems, questions and complaints
brought to it by Vermonters with disabilities. VP&A's mission is to promote the equality, dignity, and self-determination of people with disabilities. VP&A provides
infomration, referral and advocacy services, including leagl
representation when appropriate, to individuals with
disabilities throughout Vermont.

Virginia

324   Easter Seals UCP North Carolina & Virginia
8003 Franklin Farms Dr
Richmond, VA 23229-5107   804-287-1007
                                                  866-874-4153
                                             FAX 804-287-1008
                                        http://eastersealsucp.com
Connie Cochran, President/CEO

A lifelong partner fo people managing disabilities and mental health challenges. Services are centered around each person's individual needs to live, learn and participate fully in
his or her community.

325   International Dyslexia Association of Virginia
P.O.Box 17605
Richmond, VA 23226-7605   804-272-2881
                                             FAX 804-272-0277
                                                  http://vbida.org
                                              e-mail: info@vbida.org

Leslie Daise, President

Formed to increase public awareness of dyslexia in the State
of Virginia. We serve the entire state, with the exception of
Northern Virginia, which is part of the DC-Capital Branch in
Washington, DC. We serve individuals with dyslexia, their
families, and professionals in the field.

Washington

326   Disability Rights Washington
Ste 850
315 5th Ave S
Seattle, WA 98104-2691   206-324-1521
                                                  800-562-2702
                                             FAX 206-957-0729
                                             TTY: 206-957-0728
                                http://www.disabilityrightswa.org
                                            e-mail: info@dr-wa.org
Mark Stroh, Executive Director

Is a private, non-profit organization that has been protecting
the rights of people with disabilities.
1974

327   Easter Seals Washington
220 W. Mercer Street
Suite 120W
Seattle, WA 98119-4347   206-281-5700
                                                  800-678-5708
                                             FAX 206-284-0938
                                          http://wa.easterseals.com

Cathy Bisaillon, President

Provides exceptional services to ensure that people living
with autism and other disabilities have equal opportunities
to live, learn, work and play.

328   International Dyslexia Association of Washington
P.O.Box 27435
Seattle, WA 98165-2435   206-382-1020
                                                  http://www.wabida.org
                                            e-mail: info@wabida.org

Bonnie Meyer, President

The Washington State Branch of the International Dyslexia
Association is a 501 (c)(3) non-profit, scientific and educational organization dedicated to the study and treatment of
dyslexia. Our all volunteer board of directors seeks to increase public awareness of dyslexia in our branch's area
which includes Washington, Alaska, Idaho, and western
Montana.

329   Learning Disabilities Association of Washington
Family Resource Center Campus
16315 NE 87th Street
Suite B11
Redmond, WA 98052-3537   425-882-0820
                                                  800-536-2343
                                             FAX 425-558-4773
                                                  http://www.ldawa.org
                                         e-mail: cimel@ldawa.org
Robert Blumenfeld, Executive Director
Elizabeth Smith, President

Promotes and provides services and support to improve the
quality of life for individuals and families affected by learning and attentional disabilities
1965

330   Washington Parent Training Project: PAVE
6316 South 12th Street
Suite B
Tacoma, WA 98465-1900   253-565-2266
                                                  800-572-7368
                                             FAX 253-566-8052
                                             TDD:800-572-7368
                                             TTY: 800-572-7368
                                                  http://www.wapave.org
Joanne Butts, Executive Director

PAVE, a parent directed organization, exists to increase independence, empowerment, future opportunities and
choices for consumers with special needs, their families and
communities, through training, information, referral and
support.
1979

331   Washington State Branch of IDA
P.O.Box 27435
Seattle, WA 98165   206-382-1020
                                                  http://www.wabida.org
                                            e-mail: info@wabida.org

Bonnie Meyer, President

The Washington State Branch of the International Dyslexia Association is a 501 (c)(3) non-profit, scientific and educational organization dedicated to the study and treatment of dyslexia. Our all volunteer board of directors seeks to increase public awareness of dyslexia in our branch's area which includes Washington, Alaska, Idaho, and western Montana.

West Virginia

332   Easter Seals West Virginia
Rehabilitation Center
1305 National Rd
Wheeling, WV 26003-5705   304-242-1390
                                            800-677-1390
                                       FAX 304-243-5880
                                  http://wv.easterseals.com
Dr. Ellen Kitts, Medical Director

The Rehabilitaiton Center primary service area includes Ohio, Marshal, Wetzel, Tyler, Brooke and Hancock counties in West Virginia and Belmont, Monroe, Jefferson and Harrison Counties in Ohio.

Wisconsin

333   Easter Seals Southeast Wisconsin
3090 N 53rd St
Milwaukee, WI 53210   414-571-5566
                                            800-470-5463
                                       FAX 414-571-5568
                                       TTY: 414-571-9212
                              http://www.eastersealswise.com
Bob Glowacki, President
Michelle Schaefer, Executive VP
Carrie Cianciola, Early Intervention Services Dir
Provides services across the lifespan to individuals with autism and other disabilities. Services include: autism therapies, early intervention, day services and work service training.

334   International Dyslexia Association of Wisconsin
P.O.Box 284
Bayside, WI 53217   608-355-0911
                                    http://www.wibida.org
                                 e-mail: wibida@gmail.com

Cheryl Ward, President

We believe all individuals have the right to achieve their potential, that individual learning abilities can be strengthened and that social, educaitonal, and cultural barriers to language acquisition and use must be removed.

National Programs

335 Attention Deficit Disorder Association
15000 Commerce Pkwy
Suite C
Mount Laurel, NJ 08054-2212   856-439-9099
                                      FAX 856-439-0525
                                      http://www.add.org
                                      e-mail: mail@add.org
Evelyn Polk Green, MS.Ed, President
Linda Roggli, PCC, Vice President
Janet Kramer, M.D., Treasurer
The National Attention Deficit Disorder Association is an organization focused on the needs of adults and young adults with ADD/ADHD, and their children and families. We seek to serve individuals with ADD, as well as those who love, live with, teach, counsel and treat them.

336 Children and Adults with Attention Deficit Hyperactivity Disorder (CHADD)
8181 Professional Place
Suite 150
Landover, MD 20785-2264   301-306-7070
                                  800-233-4050
                                  FAX 301-306-7090
                                  http://www.chadd.org
                                  e-mail: national@chadd.org
Steven Peer, President

Children and Adults with Attention-Deficit/Hyperactivity Disorder (CHADD), is a national non-profit, tax-exempt (Section 501) organization providing education, advocacy and support for individuals with AD/HD. In addition to an informative Web site, CHADD also publishes a variety of printed materials to keep members and professionals current on research advances, medications and treatments affecting individuals with AD/HD.
16,000 members

337 Council for Exceptional Children (CEC)
1110 North Glebe Road
Suite 300
Arlington, VA 22201-5704   888-232-7733
                                   FAX 703-264-9494
                                   TTY: 866-915-5000
                                   http://www.cec.sped.org
                                   e-mail: service@cec.sped.org
Bruce Ramirez, Executive Director

The Council for Exceptional Children (CEC) is an international organization dedicated to improving educational outcomes for individuals with exceptionalities, students with disabilities, and/or the gifted. CEC advocates for appropriate governmental policies, sets professional standards, provides continual professional development, advocates for newly and historically underserved individuals with exceptionalities, and helps professionals obtain resources necessary for professional practice.

338 Council for Learning Disabilities CLD
11184 Antioch Rd
Overland Park, KS 66210-2420   913-491-1011
                                       FAX 913-491-1012
                                       http://www.cldinternational.org
                                       e-mail: cldinfo@ie-events.com
Christina Curran, President
Linda Nease, Executive Director

The mission of the Council for Learning Disabilities/CLD is to enhance the education and life span development of individuals with learning disabilities. CLD establishes standards of excellence and promotes innovative strategies on research and practice through interdisciplinary education, collaboration, and advocacy. CLD's publication, Learning Disability Quarterly, focuses on the latest research in the field of learning disabilities with an applied focus.

339 Dyslexia Research Institute
5746 Centerville Rd
Tallahassee, FL 32309-2893   850-893-2216
                                     FAX 850-893-2440
                                     http://www.dyslexia-add.org
                                     e-mail: dri@dyslexia-add.org
Patricia Hardman, Director
Robyn A Rennick MS, Director

Addresses academic, social and self-concept issues for dyslexic and ADD children and adults. College prep courses, study skills, advocacy, diagnostic testing, seminars, teacher training, day school, tutoring and an adult literacy and life skills program is available using an accredited MSLE approach.

340 *Learning Disabilities Association of America*
Learning Disabilities Association of America
4156 Library Rd
Pittsburgh, PA 15234-1349   412-341-1515
                                    888-300-6710
                                    FAX 412-344-0224
                                    http://www.ldanatl.org
                                    e-mail: info@ldaamerica.org
Patricia Lilly, President

An information and referral center for parents and professionals dealing with Attention Deficit Disorders, and other learning disabilities. Free materials and referral service to nearest chapter.

341 National Alliance on Mental Illness (NAMI)
3803 N. Fairfax Drive
Suite 100
Arlington, VA 22203   703-524-7600
                              888-999-6264
                              FAX 703-524-9094
                              http://www.nami.org
                              e-mail: info@nami.org
Michael J Fitzpatrick, Executive Director

NAMI/National Alliance on Mental Illness is a mental health organization dedicated to improving the lives of persons living with serious mental illness and their families. NAMI members, leaders, and friends work across all levels to meet a shared NAMI mission of support, education, advocacy, and research for people living with mental illness.

342 National Center for Learning Disabilities(NCLD)
381 Park Avenue South
Suite 1401
New York, NY 10016-8829   212-545-7510
                                  888-575-7373
                                  FAX 212-545-9665
                                  http://www.ncld.com
                                  e-mail: mg@ncld.org
James Wendorf, Executive Director
Sara Anderson, Development Program Assistant

NCLD develops and delivers programs and promotes research to improve instruction, assessment and support services for individuals with learning disabilities. They create and disseminate essential information for parents and educators, providing help and hope.

343 National Clearinghouse of Rehabilitation Training Materials (NCRTM)
Utah State University
6524 Old Main Hill
Logan, UT 84322-6524
                                  866-821-5355
                                  FAX 435-797-7537
                                  http://www.nchrtm.okstate.edu
                                  e-mail: ncrtm@cc.us.edu
Michael Millington PhD, Director
Jared Schultz, Principal Investigator

The mission of the NCRTM is to advocate for the advancement of best practice in rehabilitation counseling through the development, collection, dissemination, and utilization of professional information, knowledge and skill.

344   National Dissemination Center for Children with Disabilities

1825 Connecticut Ave NW
Suite 700
Washington, DC 20009   202-884-8200
                                     800-695-0285
                                     FAX 202-884-8441
                                     http://www.nichcy.org
                                     e-mail: nichcy@aed.org
Suzanne Ripley, Director

National Dissemination Center for Children with Disabilities is a central source of information on: disabilities in infants, toddlers, children, and youth; IDEA, which is the law authorizing special education; No Child Left Behind (as it relates to children with disabilities); and research-based information on effective educational practices.

345   National Institute of Mental Health (NIMH) Nat'l Institute of Neurological Disorders and Stroke

NIMH Neurological Institute
P.O. Box 5801
Bethesda, MD 20824-0001
                                     800-352-9424
                                     FAX 301-496-5751
                                     TTY: 301-408-5981
                                     e-mail: nimhinfo@nih.gov
Story C Landis Ph.D, Director NINDS
Thomas Inseo, Director NIMH

NINDS is part of the National Institutes of Health which support research on developmental disorders such as ADHD. Research programs of the NINDS, the National Institute of Mental Health (NIMH), and the National Institute of Child Health and Human Development (NICHD) seek to address unanswered questions about the causes of ADHD, as well as to improve diagnosis and treatment.

346   National Resource Center on AD/HD

8181 Professional Place
Suite 150
Landover, MD 20785-2264   301-306-7070
                                     800-233-4050
                                     FAX 301-306-7090
                                     http://www.help4adhd.org/
Timothy J MacGeorge MSW, Director

The National Resource Center on AD/HD (NRC): A Program of CHADD (Children and Adults with Attention-Deficit/Hyperactivity Disorder), was established in 2002 to be the national clearinghouse for the latest evidence-based information on AD/HD. The NRC provides comprehensive information and support to individuals with AD/HD, their families and friends, and the professionals involved in their lives.

347   U.S. Department of Health & Human Services Administration on Developmental Disabilities

370 L'Enfant Promenade SW
Mailstop HHH 405-D
Washington, DC 20447-0001   202-690-6590
                                     FAX 202-690-6904
                                     http://www.acf.hhs.gov/programs/add
                                     e-mail: fmccormick@acf.hhs.gov
Faith McCormick, Director

The Administration on Developmental Disabilities ensures that individuals with developmental disabilities and their families participate in the design of and have access to culturally competent services, supports, and other assistance and opportunities that promotes independence, productivity, and integration and inclusion into the community.

Publications/Videos

348   A New Look at ADHD: Inhibition, Time, and Self-Control

Guilford Publications
72 Spring St
New York, NY 10012-4019   212-431-9800
                                     800-365-7006
                                     FAX 212-966-6708
                                     http://www.guilford.com
                                     e-mail: info@guilford.com
Russell A Barkley PhD, Author

This video provides an accessible introduction to Russell A. Barkley's influential theory of the nature and origins of ADHD. The companion manual reviews and amplifies key ideas and contains helpful suggestions for further reading. The package also includes a leader's guide, providing tips on the optimal use of the video with a variety of audiences. *$99.00*
   Video & Manual
   ISBN 1-593854-21-8

349   AD/HD For Dummies

American Psychiatric Publishing, Inc (APPI)
Ste 1825
1000 Wilson Blvd
Arlington, VA 22209-3924   703-907-7322
                                     800-368-5777
                                     FAX 703-907-1091
                                     http://www.appi.org
                                     e-mail: appi@psych.org
John McDuffie, Editorial Director, Books
Jeff Strong, Author
Michael O Flanagan, Author
This book provides answers for parents of children who may have either condition, as well as for adult sufferers. Written in a friendly, easy-to-understand style, it helps people recognize and understand ADD and ADHD symptoms and offers an authoritative, balanced overview of both drug and non-drug therapies. *$29.95*
   Paperback
   ISBN 0-764537-12-7

350   ADD and Creativity: Tapping Your Inner Muse

Taylor Publishing
7211 Circle S Road
Austin, TX 78745   512-444-0571
                                     800-225-3687
                                     FAX 512-440-2160
                                     http://www.taylorpublishing.com
                                     e-mail: Yearbooks@balfour.com
Lynn Weiss PhD, Author

Raises and answers questions about the dynamic between the two components and shows how they can be a wonderful gift but also a painful liability if not properly handled. Real-life stories and inspirational affirmations throughout.
   216 pages Paperback
   ISBN 0-878339-60-4

351   ADD and Romance: Finding Fulfillment in Love, Sex and Relationships

Taylor Publishing
7212 Circle S Road
Austin, TX 78745   512-444-0571
                                     800-225-3687
                                     FAX 512-440-2160
                                     http://www.taylorpublishing.com
                                     e-mail: Yearbooks@balfour.com
Jonathan Halverstadt, Author

A look at how attention deficit disorder can damage romantic relationships when partners do not take time, or do not know how to address this problem. This book provides the tools needed to build and sustain a more satisfying relationship.
240 pages Paperback
ISBN 0-878332-09-X

352 **ADD and Success**
Taylor Publishing
7213 Circle S Road
Austin, TX 78745
512-444-0571
800-225-3687
FAX 512-440-2160
http://www.taylorpublishing.com
e-mail: Yearbooks@balfour.com
Lynn Weiss PhD, Author

Presents the stories of 13 individuals and their experiences and challenges of living with adult attention disorder and achieving success.
224 pages Paperback
ISBN 0-878339-94-9

353 **ADD in Adults**
Taylor Publishing
7214 Circle S Road
Austin, TX 78745
512-444-0571
800-225-3687
FAX 512-440-2160
http://www.taylorpublishing.com
e-mail: Yearbooks@balfour.com
Lynn Weiss PhD, Author

Updated version of this best-selling book on the topic of ADD helps others to understand and live with the issues related to ADD. *$17.95*
192 pages Paperback
ISBN 0-878338-50-0

354 **ADD/ADHD Behavior-Change Resource Kit:**
Ready-to-Use Strategies & Activities for Helping Children
With Attention Deficit Disorder
Ste 1825
1000 Wilson Blvd
Arlington, VA 22209-3924
703-907-7322
800-368-5777
FAX 703-907-1091
http://www.appi.org
e-mail: appi@psych.org
John McDuffie, Editorial Director, Books
Grad L Flick Ph.D, Author
Rebecca D. Rinehart, Publisher
For teachers, counselors and parents, this comprehensive new resource is filled with up-to-date information and practical strategies to help kids with attention deficits learn to control and change their own behaviors and build the academic, social, and personal skills necessary for success in school and in life. The Kit first explains ADD/ADHD behavior, its biological bases and basic characteristics and describes procedures used for diagnosis and various treatment options. *$29.95*
Paperback
ISBN 0-876281-44-4

355 **ADHD - What Can We Do?**
Guilford Publications
72 Spring St
New York, NY 10012-4019
212-431-9800
800-365-7006
FAX 212-966-6708
http://www.guilford.com
e-mail: info@guilford.com
Seymour Weingarten, Editor-in-Chief
Russell A Barkley PhD, Author
Bob Matloff, President

This program introduces viewers to a variety of the most effective techniques for managing ADHD in the classroom, at home, and on family outings. Illustrated are ways that parents, teachers, and other professionals can work together to implement specific strategies that help children with the disorder improve their school performance and behavior. Informative interviews, demonstrations of techniques, and commentary from Dr. Barkley illuminate the significant difference that treatment can make. *$99.00*
Manual-DVD/VHS
ISBN 1-593854-25-0

356 **ADHD - What Do We Know?**
Guilford Publications
72 Spring St
New York, NY 10012-4019
212-431-9800
800-365-7006
FAX 212-966-6708
http://www.guilford.com
e-mail: info@guilford.com
Seymour Weingarten, Editor-in-Chief
Bob Matloff, President
Russell A Barkley PhD, Author
Covering all the basic issues surrounding ADHD, this program is highly instructive. Through commentary from Dr. Barkley and interviews with parents, teachers, and children, viewers gain an understanding of: the causes and prevalence of ADHD; effects on children's learning and behavior; other conditions that may accompany ADHD; and, long-term prospects for children with the disorder. *$99.00*
Manual-DVD/VHS
ISBN 1-593854-17-X

357 **ADHD Challenge Newsletter**
PO Box 2277
Peabody, MA 01960-7277
800-233-2322
FAX 978-535-3276
http://www.dyslexiacenter.org/ar/000039.shtml
e-mail: info@dyslexiacenter.org
Joan T Esposito, Founder and Program Director
Leslie V. Esposito, C.F.R.E, Development Director
Valerie Allen, Center Coordinator
National newsletter on ADD/ADHD that presents interviews with nationally-known scientists, as well as physicians, psychologists, social workers, educators, and other practitioners in the field of ADHD. *$35.00*
Bimonthly

358 **ADHD Report**
Guilford Publications
72 Spring St
New York, NY 10012-4019
212-431-9800
800-365-7006
FAX 212-966-6708
http://www.guilford.com
e-mail: info@guilford.com
Seymour Weingarten, Editor-in-Chief
Russell A Barkley PhD, Author
Bob Matloff, President
Presents the most up-to-date information on the evaluation, diagnosis and management of ADHD in children, adolescents and adults. This important newsletter is an invaluable resource for all professionals interested in ADHD. *$79.00*
16 pages Bimonthly
ISSN 1065-8025

359 **ADHD and the Nature of Self-Control**
Guilford Publications
72 Spring St
New York, NY 10012-4019
212-431-9800
800-365-7006
FAX 212-966-6708
http://www.guilford.com
e-mail: info@guilford.com
Seymour Weingarten, Editor-in-Chief
Russell A Barkley PhD, Author
Bob Matloff, President

This instructive program integrates information about ADHD with the experiences of adults from different walks of life who suffer from the disorder. Including interviews with these individuals, their family members, and the clinicians who treat them, the program addresses such important topics as the symptoms and behaviors that are characteristic of the disorder, how adult ADHD differs from the childhood form, the effects of ADHD on the family, and successful coping strategies. *$55.00*

Hardcover
ISBN 1-593853-89-0

360 ADHD in Adolescents: Diagnosis and Treatment
Guilford Publications
72 Spring St
New York, NY 10012-4019   212-431-9800
                                 800-365-7006
                         FAX 212-966-6708
                    http://www.guilford.com
                    e-mail: info@guilford.com
Seymour Weingarten, Editor-in-Chief
Arthur L Robin, Author
Russell A Barkley PhD, Co-Author
This highly practical guide presents an empirically based approach to understanding, diagnosing, and treating ADHD in adolescents. Practitioners learn to conduct effective assessments and formulate goals that teenagers can comprehend, accept, and achieve. Educational, medical, and family components of treatment are described in depth, illustrated with detailed case material. Included are numerous reproducible handouts and forms. *$32.00*

Paperback
ISBN 1-572305-45-2

361 ADHD in Adults: What the Science Says
Guilford Publications
72 Spring St
New York, NY 10012-4019   212-431-9800
                                 800-365-7006
                         FAX 212-966-6708
                    http://www.guilford.com
                    e-mail: info@guilford.com
Seymour Weigarten, Editor-in-Chief
Russell Barkley PhD, Author
Kevin R. Murphy, Author
Providing a new perspective on ADHD in adults, this book analyzes findings from two major studies directed by leading authority Russell A. Barkley. Information is presented on the significant impairments produced by the disorder across major functional domains and life activities, including educational outcomes, work, relationships, health behaviors, and mental health. Accessible tables, figures, and sidebars encapsulate the study results and offer detailed descriptions of the methods. *$50.00*

Hardcover
ISBN 1-593855-86-9

362 ADHD in the Schools: Assessment and Intervention Strategies
Guilford Publications
72 Spring St
New York, NY 10012-4019   212-431-9800
                                 800-365-7006
                         FAX 212-966-6708
                    http://www.guilford.com
                    e-mail: info@guilford.com
Seymour Weigarten, Editor-in-Chief
George J DupPaul, Author
Gary Stoner, Author
This popular reference and text provides essential guidance for school-based professionals meeting the challenges of ADHD at any grade level. Comprehensive and practical, the book includes several reproducible assessment tools and handouts. A team-based approach to intervention is emphasized in chapters offering research-based guidelines for identifying and assessing children with ADHD and those at risk. *$29.00*

Paperback
ISBN 1-593850-89-1

363 ADHD/Hyperactivity: A Consumer's Guide For Parents and Teachers
P.O.Box 746
Syracuse, NY 13214-0746   315-446-4849
                                 800-550-2343
                         FAX 315-446-2012
                    http://www.gsi-add.com
                    e-mail: info@gsi-add.com
The publication is designed to assist parents and teachers in understanding ADHD/Hyperactivity, providing guidance in the selection of educational programs, effective evaluations, and offers suggestions for choosing medications. Dr. Gordon discusses 30 easy-to-understand principles that will help parents, teachers, and clinicians avoid the many pitfalls along the path to effective diagnosis and treatment. *$14.95*

364 ADHD: Attention Deficit Hyperactivity Disorder in Children, Adolescents, and Adults
Oxford University Press
198 Madison Ave
New York, NY 10016-4308   212-726-6000
                                 800-445-9714
                         FAX 919-677-1303
                    http://www.oup.com/us
                    e-mail: custserv.us@oup.com
Paul H. Wender, Author

ADHD provides parents and adults whose lives have been touched by this disorder an indispensable source of help, hope, and understanding. Explains the vital importance of drug therapy in treating ADHD; provides practical and extensive instructions for parents of ADHD sufferers; includes personal accounts of ADHD children, adolescents, and adults; and, offers valuable advice on where to find help. *$13.95*

ISBN 0-195113-49-7

365 Assessing ADHD in the Schools
Guilford Publications
72 Spring St
New York, NY 10012-4019   212-431-9800
                                 800-365-7006
                         FAX 212-966-6708
                    http://www.guilford.com
                    e-mail: info@guilford.com
Seymour Weingarten, Editor-in-Chief
George J DuPaul, Author
Gary Stoner, Author
This dynamic program demonstrates an innovative model for assessing ADHD in the schools. In a departure from other approaches, DuPaul and Stoner depict assessment as a collaborative, problem-solving process that is inextricably linked to the planning of individualized interventions. A range of crucial assessment techniques are considered, including parent interviews, behavior and academic performance rating scales, and direct observation. *$99.00*

Manual-DVD/VHS
ISBN 1-572304-14-6

366 Attention Deficit Disorder Warehouse
Ste 102
300 NW 70th Ave
Plantation, FL 33317-2360   954-792-8100
                                   800-233-9273
                           FAX 954-792-8545
                      http://www.addwarehouse.com
                      e-mail: websales@addwarehouse.com
Roberta Parker, Co-Founder/Owner/Manager
Harvey Parker PhD, Co-Founder/Owner/Manager

A comprehensive resource for the understanding and treatment of all developmental disorders, including ADHD and related problems, the ADD Warehouse provides a vast collection of ADHD-related books, videos, training programs, games, professional texts and assessment products.

367 **Attention Deficit Disorder in Adults Workbook**
Taylor Publishing
7214 Circle S Road
Austin, TX 78745   512-444-0571
                                    800-225-3687
                                    FAX 512-440-2160
                     http://www.taylorpublishing.com
                     e-mail: Yearbooks@balfour.com

Lynn Weiss, Author

Dr. Lynn Weiss's best-selling Attention Deficit Disorder In Adults has sold over 125,000 copies since its publication in 1991. This updated volume still contains all the original information — how to tell if you have ADD, ways to master distraction, ADD's impact on the family, and more—plus the newest treatments available. *$17.99*
    192 pages Paperback
    ISBN 0-878338-50-0

368 **Attention Deficit Disorder: A Concise Source of Information for Parents**
Temeron Books
PO Box 896
Bellingham, WA 98227   360-738-4016
                                  FAX 360-738-4016
                     http://www.temerondetselig.com
                     e-mail: temeron@telusplanet.net

Hossein Moghadam MD, Author
Lauri Seidlitz, Managing Editor
Fraser Seely, Partner
The authors travel from a brief historical review of ADD, through a description of symptoms and consequences, to a discussion of treatment. *$12.95*
    128 pages Paperback
    ISBN 1-550590-82-0

369 **Attention Deficit Hyperactivity Disorder: Handbook for Diagnosis & Treatment**
Guilford Publications
72 Spring St
New York, NY 10012-4019   212-431-9800
                                  800-365-7006
                                  FAX 212-966-6708
                     http://www.guilford.com
                     e-mail: info@guilford.com

Bob Matloff, President
Russell Barkley PhD, Author
Seymour Weingarten, Editor-in-Chief
This second edition helps clinicians diagnose and treat Attention Deficit Hyperactivity Disorder. Written by an internationally recognized authority in the field, it covers the history of ADHD, its primary symptoms, associated conditions, developmental course and outcome, and family context. A workbook companion manual is also available.
    700 pages Hardcover

370 **Attention Deficit/Hyperactivity Disorder Fact Sheet**
National Dissemination Center for Children
1825 Connecticut Ave NW
Suite 700
Washington, DC 20009   202-884-8200
                                  800-695-0285
                                  FAX 202-884-8441
                http://www.nichcy.org/pubs/factshe/fs19txt.htm
                     e-mail: nichcy@fhi360.org

Stephen F Moseley, President

An 8 page informational fact sheet, a publication of the National Dissemination Center for Children with Disabilities, that provides information on attention deficit/hyperactivity disorder in infants, toddlers, children, and youth. The brochure provides suggestions and tips for parents and teachers in addition to providing links to organizations where individuals can obtain further details on ADHD.

371 **Attention-Deficit Disorders and Comorbidities in Children, Adolescents, and Adults**
American Psychiatric Publishing, Inc (APPI)
1000 Wilson Blvd
Ste 1825
Arlington, VA 22209-3924   703-907-7322
                                  800-368-5777
                                  FAX 703-907-1091
                     http://www.appi.org
                     e-mail: appi@psych.org

John McDuffie, Editorial Director, Books
Thomas E. Brown, Editor
Rebecca D. Rinehart, Publisher
Book provides in-depth discussion of both ADD/Attention Deficit Disorders and that of ADHD/Attention Deficit-Hyperactivity Disorders, providing readers with information that focuses on several perspectives including learning disorders in children and adolescents; cognitive therapy for adults with ADHD; educational interventions for students with ADDs; tailoring treatments for individuals with ADHD; clinical and research perspectives, etc. *$82.00*
    Hardcover
    ISBN 0-880487-11-9

372 **Attention-Deficit Hyperactivity Disorder: A Clinical Workbook**
Guilford Publications
72 Spring St
New York, NY 10012-4019   212-431-9800
                                  800-365-7006
                                  FAX 212-966-6708
                     http://www.guilford.com
                     e-mail: info@guilford.com

Seymour Weingarten, Editor-in-Chief
Russell A Barkley PhD, Author
Kevin R. Murphy, Co-Author
The revised and expanded third edition of this user-friendly workbook provides a master set of the assessment and treatment forms, questionnaires, and handouts recommended by Barkley in the third edition of the Handbook. Formatted for easy photocopying, many of these materials are available from no other source. Includes interview forms and rating scales for use with parents, teachers, and adult clients; checklists and fact sheets; daily school report cards for monitoring academic progress. *$34.00*
    Paperback
    ISBN 1-593852-27-4

373 **Attention-Deficit/Hyperactivity Disorder: A Clinical Guide To Diagnosis and Treatment**
American Psychiatric Publishing, Inc (APPI)
1000 Wilson Blvd.
Suite 1825
Arlington, VA 22209   703-907-7322
                                  800-368-5777
                                  FAX 703-907-1091
                     http://www.appi.org
                     e-mail: appi@psych.org

Robert S Pursell, Marketing Director
Larry B Silver, Author

This new edition of Dr. Larry Silver's groundbreaking clinical book incorporates recent research findings on attention-deficit/hyperactivity disorder (ADHD), covering the latest information on diagnosis, associated disorders, and treatment, as well as ADHD in adults. The publication thoroughly reviews disorders often found to be comorbid with ADHD, including specific learning disorders, anxiety disorders, depression, anger regulation problems, obsessive-compulsive disorder, and tic disorders. *$52.00*
    Paperback
    ISBN 1-585621-31-6

374   CHADD Educators Manual
CHADD
Ste 150
8181 Professional Pl
Landover, MD 20785-2264   301-306-7070
                                            800-233-4050
                                    FAX 301-306-7090
                                    http://www.chadd.org
                                    e-mail: national@chadd.org
Barbara S. Hawkins, BA, President
Ruth Hughes, PhD, CEO
Susan Buningh, MRE, Executive Editor
An in-depth look at Attention Deficit Disorders from an educational perspective. *$10.00*

375   Children with ADD: A Shared Responsibility
Council for Exceptional Children
2900 Crystal Drive
Suite 1000
Arlington, VA 22202-3557   703-620-3660
                                            888-232-7733
                                    FAX 703-264-9494
                                    TDD:866-915-5000
                                    TTY: 703-264-9446
                                    http://www.cec.sped.org
                                    e-mail: service@cec.sped.org
George J DuPaul, Author
Gary Stoner, Co-Author
Margaret J. McLaughlin, President
This book represents a consensus of what professionals and parents believe ADD is all about and how children with ADD may best be served. Reviews the evaluation process under IDEA and 504 and presents effective classroom strategies.
      35 pages
      ISBN 0-865862-33-8

376   Classroom Interventions for ADHD
Guilford Publications
72 Spring St
New York, NY 10012-4019   212-431-9800
                                            800-365-7006
                                    FAX 212-966-6708
                                    http://www.guilford.com
                                    e-mail: info@guilford.com
Seymour Weingarten, Editor-in-Chief
George J DupPaul, Author
Gary Stoner, Co-Author
This informative video provides an overview of intervention approaches that can be used to help students with ADHD enhance their school performance while keeping the classroom functioning smoothly. The video features an illuminating discussion among DuPaul, Stoner, and Russell A. Barkley, addressing provocative questions on the benefits of proactive, preventive measures, on the one hand, and reactive techniques, on the other. *$99.00*
      Manual-DVD/VHS
      ISBN 1-572304-15-4

377   Coping: Attention Deficit Disorder: A Guide for Parents and Teachers
Temeron Books
PO Box 896
Bellingham, WA 98227   360-738-4016
                                    FAX 360-738-4016
                                    http://www.temerondetselig.com
                                    e-mail: temeron@telusplanet.net
Mary Ellen Beugin, Author
Lauri Seidlitz, Managing Editor
Fraser Seely, Partner
The author investigates medical and behavioral interventions that can be tried with ADD children and gives suggestions on coping with these children at home and at school. *$15.95*
      173 pages Paperback
      ISBN 1-550590-13-8

378   Driven to Distraction: Attention Deficit Disorder from Childhood Through Adulthood
Hallowell Center
144 North Rd
Suite 2450
Sudbury, MA 01776-1142   978-287-0810
                                    FAX 978-287-5566
                                    http://www.drhallowell.com/hallowell_center/
                                    e-mail: drhallowell@gmail.com
Edward M Hallowell, Author
John J. Ratey MD, Co-Author

Through vivid stories of the experience of their patients, Drs. Hallowell and Ratey show the varied forms ADD takes — from the hyperactive search for high stimulation to the floating inattention of daydreaming — and the transforming impact of precise diagnosis and treatment. *$10.40*
      336 pages
      ISBN 0-684801-28-0

379   E-ssential Guide: A Parent's Guide to AD/HD Basics
Schwab Learning
160 Spear Street
Suite 1020
San Francisco, CA 94105   650-655-2410
                                    FAX 650-655-2411
                                    http://www.schwablearning.org
Bill Jackson, Founder, President, and CEO
Matthew Nelson, Chief Operating Officer
Gretchen Anderson, Vice President, Product
This guide covers the fundamental facts about Attention-Deficit/Hyperactivity Disorder (AD/HD) that will provide a better understanding of AD/HD. Included is: A general overview of AD/HD and helpful strategies for managing your child's AD/HD at home and at school.

380   Fact Sheet-Attention Deficit Hyperactivity Disorder
Attention Deficit Disorder Association
Ste C
15000 Commerce Pkwy
Mount Laurel, NJ 08054-2212   856-439-9099
                                    FAX 856-439-0525
                                    http://www.add.org/articles/factsheet.html
                                    e-mail: mail@add.org
Evelyn Polk Green, MS.Ed, President
Linda Roggli, PCC, Vice President
Janet Kramer, M.D., Treasurer
A pamphlet offering factual information on ADHD. *$10.00*

381   Family Therapy for ADHD - Treating Children, Adolescents, and Adults
Guilford Publications
72 Spring St
New York, NY 10012-4019   212-431-9800
                                            800-365-7006
                                    FAX 212-966-6708
                                    http://www.guilford.com
                                    e-mail: info@guilford.com
Seymour Weingarten, Editor-in-Chief
Craig A. Everett, Author
Sandra Volgy Everett, Co-Author
Presents an innovative approach to assessing and treating ADHD in the family context. Readers learn strategies for diagnosing the disorder and evaluating its impact not only on affected young persons but also on their parents and siblings. From expert family therapists, the volume outlines how professionals can help families mobilize their resources to manage ADHD symptoms; improve functioning in school and work settings; and develop more effective coping strategies. *$ 29.00*
      Paperback
      ISBN 1-572307-08-0

382 Focus Magazine
Attention Deficit Disorder Association
Ste C
15000 Commerce Pkwy
Mount Laurel, NJ 08054-2212   856-439-9099
                                     FAX 856-439-0525
                                     http://www.add.org
                                     e-mail: mail@add.org
Evelyn Polk Green, MS.Ed, President
Linda Roggli, PCC, Vice President
Janet Kramer, M.D., Treasurer
Comprehensive magazine of the National Attention Deficit
Disorder Association. It focuses on the needs of adults and
young adults with ADD/ADHD, their children and families,
teachers and friends. Free with membership.
Quarterly

383 Getting a Grip on ADD: A Kid's Guide to Understanding & Coping with ADD
Educational Media Corporation
4256 Central Ave NE
Box 21311
Minneapolis, MN 55421-2920   763-781-0088
                                     800-966-3382
                                     FAX 763-781-7753
                                     http://www.educationalmedia.com
                                     e-mail: emedia@educationalmedia.com
Kim T. Frank, Author
Susan Smith, Co-Author

Help your elementary and middle school students cope more
effectively with Attention Deficit Disorders. *$9.95*
64 pages Paperback
ISBN 0-932796-60-5

384 How to Reach & Teach Teenagers With ADHD
John Wiley & Sons Inc
Ste 5
111 River St
Hoboken, NJ 07030-5774   201-748-6000
                                     800-225-5945
                                     FAX 201-748-6088
                                     http://http://as.wiley.com
                                     e-mail: info@wiley.com
Grad L Flick PhD, Author
Stephen M. Smith, President
Ellis E. Cousens, Executive Vice President
This comprehensive resource is pack with tested, up-to-date
information and techniques to help teachers, counselors and
parents understand and manage adolescents with attention
deficit disorder, including step-by-step procedures for behavioral intervention at school and home and reproducible
handouts, checklists and record-keeping forms. *$29.00*

ISBN 0-130320-21-6

385 Hyperactive Child Book
St. Martin's Press
175 5th Ave
New York, NY 10010-7703   646-307-5151
                                     888-330-8477
                                     FAX 212-674-6132
                                     http://www.stmartins.com
                                     e-mail: customerservice@mpsvirginia.com
Patricia Kennedy, Author
Lief G Terdal, Co-Author

The Hyperactive Child Book contains a comprehensive review of information about raising, treating, and educating a
child with Attention Deficit-Hyperactivity Disorder. The
book will be useful to parents, teachers, and health care professionals in their efforts to provide for the ADHD child.
$12.95
288 pages
ISBN 0-312112-86-6

386 Hyperactive Child, Adolescent and Adult
Oxford University Press
198 Madison Ave
New York, NY 10016-4308   212-726-6000
                                     800-445-9714
                                     FAX 919-677-1303
                                     http://www.oup.com/us
                                     e-mail: custserv.us@oup.com
Paul H Wender, Author

How does one know if a youngster is hyperactive? How do
you know if you are hyperactive yourself? The answers may
lie in this easy-to-read and comprehensive volume written
by one of the leading researchers in the field. *$27.00*
172 pages Hardcover
ISBN 0-195042-91-3

387 Hyperactive Children Grown Up: ADHD in Children, Adolescents, and Adults
Guilford Publications
72 Spring St
New York, NY 10012-4019   212-431-9800
                                     800-365-7006
                                     FAX 212-966-6708
                                     http://www.guilford.com
                                     e-mail: info@guilford.com
Seymour Weingarten, Editor-in-Chief
Gabrielle Weiss, Author
Lily Trokenberg Hechtman, Co-Author
Based on the McGill prospective studies, research that now
spans more than 30 years, the volume reports findings on the
etiology, treatment, and outcome of attention deficits and
hyperactivity at all stages of development. This second edi-
tion includes entirely new chapters that describes new devel-
opments in Attention Deficit Hyperactivity Disorder
(ADHD) in addition to the assessment, diagnosis, and treatment of ADHD adults. *$35.00*
Paperback
ISBN 0-898625-96-3

388 I Would if I Could: A Teenager's Guide To ADHD/Hyperactivity
PO Box 746
DeWitt, NY 13214   315-446-4849
                                     800-550-2343
                                     FAX 315-446-2012
                                     http://www.gsi-add.com
                                     e-mail: info@gsi-add.com
Michael Gordon Ph.D, Author
Janet H. Junco, Illustration
Arthur L. Robin, PhD., Co-Author
Provides youngsters with straightforward information about
the disorder in addition to exploring its impact on family relationships, self-esteem, and friendships. Dr. Gordon uses
humor and candor to educate and encourage teenagers who
too often find themselves confused and frustrated, providing
youngsters with straightforward information about the disorder and exploring its impact on family relationships,
self-esteem, and friendships. *$12.50*

389 I'd Rather Be With a Real Mom Who Loves Me: A Story for Foster Children
PO Box 746
DeWitt, NY 13214   315-446-4849
                                     800-550-2343
                                     FAX 315-446-2012
                                     http://www.gsi-add.com
                                     e-mail: info@gsi-add.com
Michael Gordon Ph.D, Author
Janet H. Junco, Illustration

This book tells the story of a young boy who's lived most of
his life away from his birth parents. It's an honest, realistic
account of the frustrations and heartache he endures. This
fully illustrated book sensitively but forthrightly deals with
the entire range of concerns that confront foster children
with ADHD/Hyperactivity disorder. *$12.00*

390 **Identifying and Treating Attention Deficit Hyperactivity Disorder: A Resource for School and Home**
U S Department of Education/Special Ed-Rehab Srvcs
PO Box 1398
Jessup, MD 20794-1398

877-433-7827
FAX 301-470-1244
TDD:877-576-7734
http://www.ed.gov/rschstat/research/pubs/adhd
e-mail: edpubs@inet.ed.gov

Alexa Posny, Editor
Danny Harris, Chief Information Officer
Arne Duncan, Secretary of Education
Publication from the U S Department of Education that provides comprehensive information on attention deficit hyperactivity disorders, including causes, medical evaluation and treatment options in addition to helpful hints and tips for both the home and school environments. *$6.00*

391 **International Reading Association Newspaper: Reading Today**
International Reading Association
PO Box 8139
800 Barksdale Rd.
Newark, DE 19714-8139

302-731-1600
800-336-7323
FAX 302-731-1057
http://www.reading.org
e-mail: customerservice@reading.org

Alan Farstrup, Editor
Carrice C. Cummins, President
Jill Lewis-Spector, Vice-President
Reading Today, the Association's bimonthly newspaper, is the first choice of IRA members for news and information on all these topics and more. It is available in print exclusively as an IRA membership benefit.
Bimonthly

392 **Jumpin' Johnny**
Gordon Systems, Inc.
PO Box 746
DeWitt, NY 13214

315-446-4849
800-550-2343
FAX 315-446-2012
http://www.gsi-add.com
e-mail: info@gsi-add.com

Michael Gordon Ph.D, Author
Janet H. Junco, Illustration and Design
Harvey C. Parker, PhD., Co-Author
This entertaining and informative book will help children understand the basic ideas about the evaluation of ADHD/Hyperactivity. Jumpin' Johnny tells what it is like to be inattentive and impulsive, and how his family and school work with him to make life easier. Children find this book amusing, educational, and accurate in its depiction of the challenges that confront them daily. *$11.00*

393 **LD Child and the ADHD Child**
1406 Plaza Dr
Winston Salem, NC 27103-1470

336-768-1374
800-222-9796
FAX 336-768-9194
http://www.blairpub.com
e-mail: sakowski@blairpub.com

Steve Kirk, Editor
Suzanne H Stevens, Author
Carolyn Sakowski, President
It is a brief, upbeat, always realistic look at what learning disabilities are and what problems LD children and parents face at home and at school. It contains a wealth of valuable suggestions, and its tempered optimism may dimish one's sense of futility and helplessness. *$12.95*
261 pages Paperback
ISBN 0-895871-42-4

394 **Learning Times**
Learning Disabilities Association of Georgia
Suite 104 PMB 353
2566 Shallowford Rd NE
Atlanta, GA 30345-1200

404-303-7774
FAX 404-467-0190
http://www.ldag.org
e-mail: ldaga@bellsouth.net

Tia Powell, Editor

Information and helpful articles on learning disabilities.
$40.00
Bimonthly

395 **Making the System Work for Your Child with ADHD**
Guilford Publications
72 Spring St
New York, NY 10012-4019

212-431-9800
800-365-7006
FAX 212-966-6708
http://www.guilford.com
e-mail: info@guilford.com

Seymour Weingarten, Editor-in-Chief
Perter S Jensen, Co-Author
Bob Matloff, President
Child psychiatrist Dr. Peter Jensen guides parents over the rough patches and around the hairpin curves in this empowering, highly informative book. Readers learn the whats, whys, and how-tos of making the system work and in getting their money's worth from the healthcare system, cutting through red tape at school, and making the most of fleeting time with doctors and therapists. *$17.95*
Paperback
ISBN 1-572308-70-2

396 **Managing Attention Deficit Hyperactivity Disorder: A Guide for Practitioners**
John Wiley & Sons Inc
Ste 5
111 River St
Hoboken, NJ 07030-5774

201-748-6000
800-225-5945
FAX 201-748-6088
http://http://as.wiley.com
e-mail: info@wiley.com

Sam Goldstein, Author
Michael Goldstein, Co-Author
Ellis E. Cousens, Executive Vice President
A valuable working resource for practitioners who manage children with ADHD, Managing Attention Deficit Hyperactivity in Children, Second Edition features: in-depth reviews of the latest research into the etiology and development of ADHD; Step-by-step guidelines on evaluating ADHD-medically, at home, and in school; a multidisciplinary approach to treating ADHD that combines medical, family, cognitive, behavioral, and school interventions; and critical discussions of controversial new treatments. *$130.00*
Hardcover
ISBN 0-471121-58-9

397 **Mastering Your Adult ADHD A Cognitive-Behavioral Treatment Program**
Oxford University Press
198 Madison Ave
New York, NY 10016-4308

212-726-6000
FAX 212-726-6453
http://www.oup.com/us
e-mail: custserv.us@oup.com

Steven A Safren, Author

Used in conjunction with the corresponding client workbook, this therapist guide offers effective treatment strategies that follow an empirically-supported treatment approach. It provides clinicians with effective means of teaching clients skills that have been scientifically tested and shown to help adults cope with ADHD. *$35.00*

ISBN 0-195188-18-7

398 **Maybe You Know My Kid: A Parent's Guide to Identifying ADHD**
119 West 40th Street
New York, NY 10018
212-407-1500
800-221-2647
FAX 212-935-0699
http://www.kensingtonbooks.com/
e-mail: ecommerce@us.penguingroup.com
Mary Cahill Fowler, Author
Steven Zacharius, President

A guide for parents of children diagnosed with ADD discusses the recent changes in the education of these children and offers practical guidelines for improving educational performance.

399 **Meeting the ADD Challenge: A Practical Guide for Teachers**
Research Press
PO Box 9177
Champaign, IL 61826-9177
217-352-3273
800-519-2707
FAX 217-352-1221
http://www.researchpress.com
e-mail: orders@researchpress.com
Steve B Gordon, Author
Michael J Asher, Co-Author

Provides educators with practical information about the needs and treatment of children and adolescents with ADD. The book addresses the defining characteristics of ADD, common treatment approaches, myths about ADD, matching intervention to student, use of behavior-rating scales and checklists evaluating interventions, regular verses, special class placement, helps students regulate their own behavior and more. Case examples are used throughout. *$17.95*
196 pages
ISBN 0-878223-45-2

400 **My Brother is a World Class Pain A Sibling's Guide To ADHD/Hyperactivity**
Gordon Systems, Inc.
P.O.Box 746
DeWitt, NY 13214-0746
315-446-4849
800-550-ADHD
FAX 315-446-2012
http://www.gsi-add.com
e-mail: info@gsi-add.com
Michael Gordon Ph.D, President

A book for the often forgotten group of those affected by ADHD, the brothers and sisters of ADHD children, this story about an older sister's efforts to deal with her active and impulsive brother sends the clear message to siblings of the ADHD child that they can play an important role in a family's quest for change. *$11.00*

401 **NIMH-Attention Deficit-Hyperactivity Disorder Information Fact Sheet**
National Institute of Mental Health
6001 Executive Blvd.
Room 8184, MSC 9663
Bethesda, MD 20892-9663
301-443-4513
FAX 301-443-4279
TTY: 301-443-8431
http://www.nimh.nih.gov
e-mail: nimhinfo@nih.gov
Story C Landis Ph.D, Director NINDS

NINDS (National Institute of Neurological Disorders and Stroke) is part of the National Institutes of Health several components of which support research on developmental disorders such as ADHD. Informational fact sheet provides data relative to research, symptons and diagnosis, in addition to links for organizational resources relative to the disorder.

402 **National Alliance on Mental Illness (NAMI) Attention-Deficit/Hyperactivity Disorder Fact Sheet**
3803 N. Fairfax Drive
Suite 100
Arlington, VA 22203
703-524-7600
888-999-6264
FAX 703-524-9094
TDD:703-516-7227
http://www.nami.org
e-mail: info@nami.org
Michael J Fitzpatrick, Executive Director

NAMI/National Alliance on Mental Illness is a mental health organization dedicated to improving the lives of persons living with serious mental illness and their families. ADHD fact sheet provides information on attention-deficit/hyperactivity disorder through NAMI's mission of support, education, advocacy, and research for people living with mental illness.

403 **Natural Therapies for Attention Deficit Hyperactivity Disorder**
Comprehensive Psychiatric Resources, Inc.
20 Hope Avenue
Suite 107
Waltham, MA 02453-2741
781-647-0066
FAX 781-899-4905
http://www.comprehensivepsychiatricresources.co
James M Greenblatt MD, Director

A full day workshop professionally recorded on six audiotapes featuring Dr. James M. Greenblatt, M.D., neuropsychiatrist. Dr. Greenblatt explores updated research on nutrition and ADD, food additives, food allergies, fatty acids and more, provides practical treatment strategies and helps you make informed choices between effective and worthless therapies. *$59.95*

404 **Nutritional Treatment for Attention Deficit Hyperactivity Disorder**
Comprehensive Psychiatric Resources, Inc.
20 Hope Avenue
Suite 107
Waltham, MA 02453
781-647-0066
FAX 781-899-4905
http://www.comprehensivepsychiatricresources.co
James M Greenblatt MD, Director

A full day workshop professionally recorded on six audiotapes featuring Dr. James M. Greenblatt, M.D., neuropsychiatrist. Dr. Greenblatt explores updated research on nutrition and ADD, food additives, food allergies, fatty acids and more, provides practical treatment strategies and helps you make informed choices between effective and worthless therapies.

405 **Power Parenting for Children with ADD/ADHD A Practical Parent's Guide for Managing Difficult Beha**viors
111 River St
Hoboken, NJ 07030-5774
201-748-6000
FAX 201-748-6088
http://www.wiley.com
e-mail: info@wiley.com

Grad L Flick, Author

A Practical Parent's Guide for Managing Difficult Behaviors. Written in clear, non-technical language, this much-needed guide provides practical, real-life techniques and activities to help parents. *$19.95*

ISBN 0-876288-77-1

406 Putting on the Brakes Young People's Guide to Understanding Attention Defici
American Psychological Association
750 First Street Northeast
Washington, DC 20002-4242   202-336-5500
                                         800-374-2721
                                    TDD:202-336-6123
                                    TTY: 202-336-6123
            http://www.maginationpress.com/4414576.html
                          e-mail: magination@apa.org
Patricia O Quinn, Author
Judith Stern, Co-Author

This book allows children to put their understanding of ADHD into action. Using pictures, puzzles, and other techniques to assist in the learning of a range of skills, this book helps teach problem solving, organizing, setting priorities, planning, maintaining control — all of those hard-to-learn skills that make everyday life just a little more manageable. *$14.95*

         ISBN 0-945354-57-6

407 Rethinking Attention Deficit Disorders
Brookline Books
34 University Road
Brookline, MA 02445   617-734-6772
                                    FAX 617-734-3952
                      http://www.brooklinebooks.com
Susan Sharp, Author
Jonathan Stolzenberg, Author

This ground-breaking work argues that the two behavioral manifestations of attention deficit disorder—hyperactivity and impulsivity—represent a person's attempts at self-regulation. The authors view Attention Deficit Disorder as a problem with control and fluency of attention; people with ADD have sustaining focus when faced with novel and/or intense stimulae. *$27.95*
         272 pages
         ISBN 1-571290-37-0

408 Ritalin Is Not The Answer: A Drug-Free Practical Program for Children Diagnosed With ADD or ADHD
John Wiley & Sons Inc
Ste 5
111 River St
Hoboken, NJ 07030-5774   201-748-6000
                                    FAX 201-748-6088
                           http://www.wiley.com
                           e-mail: info@wiley.com
David P Stein, Author

Ritalin Is Not the Answer confronts and challenges what has become common practice and teaches parents and educators a healthy, comprehensive behavioral program that really works as an alternative to the epidemic use of medication-without teaching children to use drugs in order to handle their behavioral and emotional problems. *$15.00*
         Paperback
         ISBN 0-787945-14-5

409 Shelley, the Hyperactive Turtle
Woodbine House
6510 Bells Mill Rd
Bethesda, MD 20817-1636   301-897-3570
                                         800-843-7323
                                    FAX 301-897-5838
                      http://www.woodbinehouse.com
                      e-mail: info@woodbinehouse.com
Deborah M Moss, Author

Shelley the turtle has a very hard time sitting still, even for short periods of time. During a visit to the doctor, Shelley learns that he is hyperactive, and that he can take medicine every day to control his wiggly feeling. *$ 14.95*
         20 pages Hardcover
         ISBN 1-890627-75-5

410 Stimulant Drugs and ADHD Basic and Clinical Neuroscience
Oxford University Press
198 Madison Ave
New York, NY 10016-4308   212-726-6000
                                    FAX 212-726-6453
                             http://www.oup.com/us
                        e-mail: custserv.us@oup.com
Mary Solanto, Editor

This volume is the first to integrate advances in the basic and clinical neurosciences in order to shed new light on this important question. The chapter topics span basic research into the neuroanatomy, neurophysiology and neuropsychology of catecholamines, animal models of ADHD, and clinical studies of neuroimaging, genetics, pharmacokinetics and pharmacodynamics, and the cognitive pharmacology of stimulants. *$81.50*

         ISBN 0-195133-71-4

411 The ADD/ADHD Checklist
American Psychiatric Publishing, Inc (APPI)
1000 Wilson Blvd.
Suite 1825
Arlington, VA 22209   703-907-7322
                                         800-368-5777
                                    FAX 703-907-1091
                             http://www.appi.org
                           e-mail: appi@psych.org
Robert E Hales MD, Editor
Sandra F Rief MA, Author

Written by a nationally known educator with two decades of experience in working with ADD/ADHD students. This unique resource is packed with up-to-date facts, findings, and proven strategies and techniques for understanding and helping children and adolescents with attention deficit problems and hyperactivity- all in a handy list format. *$12.95*
         Paperback
         ISBN 0-137623-95-2

412 The ADHD Book of Lists: A Practical Guidefor Helping Children and Teens With ADD
American Psychiatric Publishing, Inc (APPI)
1000 Wilson Blvd.
Suite 1825
Arlington, VA 22209   703-907-7322
                                         800-368-5777
                                    FAX 703-907-1091
                             http://www.appi.org
                           e-mail: appi@psych.org
Robert E Hales MD, Editor
Sandra F Rief MA, Author

The ADHD Book of Lists is a comprehensive, reliable source of answers, practical strategies, and tools written in a convenient list format. Created for teachers (K-12), parents, school psychologists, medical and mental health professionals, counselors, and other school personnel, this important resource contains the most current information about Attention Deficit/Hyperactivity Disorder (ADHD). *$29.95*
         Paperback
         ISBN 0-787965-91-4

413 The Down & Dirty Guide to Adult ADD
Gordon Systems, Inc.
P.O.Box 746
DeWitt, NY 13214-0746   315-446-4849
                                         800-550-ADHD
                                    FAX 315-446-2012
                             http://www.gsi-add.com
                           e-mail: info@gsi-add.com
Michael Gordon Ph.D, Editor

A book about Adult ADD that is informative, and uncomplicated. Drs. Gordon and McClure spare no effort or humor in clearly describing concepts essential to understanding how this disorder is best identified and treated. You'll find a refreshing absence of jargon and an abundance of common sense, practical advice, and healthy skepticism. This fine brew of scientific evidence and clinical wisdom is so cleverly presented that even the most inattentive reader will breeze through its pages. *$16.95*

414 The Hidden Disorder: A Clinician's Guide to Attention Deficit Hyperactivity Disorder in Adults
American Psychological Association
750 First Street Northeast
Washington, DC 20002-4242   202-336-5500
                                       800-374-2721
                                   FAX 202-336-5500
                        http://www.apa.org/publications
                                e-mail: order@apa.org
Robert J Resnick PhD, Author

Through accessible writing and engaging case studies, Robert J. Resnick, PhD, provides expert clinical guidance on etiology, differential diagnosis, assessment, and treatment. Adults with ADHD often require intermittent treatment at different points in their lives. This book provides various treatment interventions over the livespan. Also covered are the various co-morbid and look alike disorders that can confound diagnosis and lead to unsuccessful treatment. *$34.95*
Hardcover
ISBN 1-557987-24-2

415 Treating Huckleberry Finn: A New Narrative Approach to Working With Kids Diagnosed ADD/ADHD
John Wiley & Sons Inc
Ste 5
111 River St
Hoboken, NJ 07030-5774   201-748-6000
                                 FAX 201-748-6088
                                http://www.wiley.com
                              e-mail: info@wiley.com
David Nylund, Author

Ritalin Is Not the Answer confronts and challenges what has become common practice and teaches parents and educators a healthy, comprehensive behavioral program that really works as an alternative to the epidemic use of medication-without teaching children to use drugs in order to handle their behavioral and emotional problems. *$32.00*
Paperback
ISBN 0-787961-20-6

416 Understanding and Teaching Children With Autism
John Wiley & Sons Inc
111 River St
Hoboken, NJ 07030-5774   201-748-6000
                                 FAX 201-748-6088
                                http://www.wiley.com
                              e-mail: info@wiley.com
Rita Jordan, Author
Stuart Powell, Co-Author

The triad of impairment: social, language and communication and thought behavior aspects of development discussed. Difficulties in interacting, transfer of learning and bizarre behaviors are part of syndrome. Many LD are associated with autism. *$65.00*
188 pages Paperback
ISBN 0-471957-14-3

417 Understanding and Treating Adults With Attention Deficit Hyperactivity Disorder
American Psychiatric Publishing, Inc (APPI)
1000 Wilson Blvd.
Suite 1825
Arlington, VA 22209   703-907-7322
                                        800-368-5777
                                   FAX 703-907-1091
                                   http://www.appi.org
                               e-mail: appi@psych.org
Robert E Hales MD, Editor
Brian B Doyle MD, Author

Understanding the evolution of the concept and treatment of ADHD in children illuminates current thinking about the disorder in adults. Dr. Doyle presents guidelines for establishing a valid diagnosis, including clinical interviews and standardized rating scales. He covers genetic and biochemical bases of the disorder. He also addresses the special challenges of forming a therapeutic alliance-working with coach caregivers; cultural, ethnic, and racial issues; and legal considerations. *$52.00*
Paperback
ISBN 1-585622-21-4

418 What Causes ADHD?: Understanding What Goes Wrong and Why
Guilford Press
72 Spring St
New York, NY 10012-4019
                                        800-365-7006
                                   FAX 212-966-6708
                                http://www.guilford.com
                            e-mail: info@guilford.com
Seymour Weingarten, Editor
Joel T Nigg, Author

This book focuses on the multiple pathways by which attention-deficit/ hyperactivity disorder (ADHD) develops. Joel T. Nigg discusses the processes taking place within the symptomatic child's brain and the reasoning for such activity, tracing intersecting causal influences of genetic, neural, and environmental factors. Specific suggestions are provided for studies that might further refine the conceptualization of the disorder, with significant potential benefits for treatment and prevention. *$44.00*
Hardcover
ISBN 1-593852-67-3

419 Why Can't My Child Behave?
Feingold Association of the United States
Ste 301
554 E Main St
Riverhead, NY 11901-2671   631-369-9340
                                        800-321-3287
                                   FAX 631-369-2988
                          http://www.feingold.org/book.html
         e-mail: help@feingold.org OR janefaus@aol.com
Jane Hersey, Author

This book shows how foods and food additives can trigger learning and behavior problems in sensitive people. It provides practical guidance on using a simple diet to uncover the causes of ADD and ADHD. *$22.00*
473 pages Paperback
ISBN 0-965110-50-8

420 You Mean I'm Not Lazy, Stupid or Crazy?
Simon & Schuster, Inc.
1230 Avenue of the Americas
New York, NY 10020-1513   212-698-7000
                                        800-622-6611
                                   FAX 212-698-7007
                                http://www.simonsays.com
Peggy Ramundo, Author
Kate Kelly, Co-Author

This book is written by ADD adults for other ADD adults. A comprehensive guide, it provides accurate information, practical how-to's, and moral support. Among other issues, readers will get information on: unique differences in ADD adults; the impact on their lives; up-to-date research findings; treatment options available for adults; and much more. *$16.00*
    464 pages
    ISBN 0-743264-48-7

Web Sites

421 **LD Online**
WETA Public Television
2775 S Quincy St
Arlington, VA 22206   703-998-2060
                                      http://www.ldonline.org
Noel Gunther, Executive Director

LD OnLine seeks to help children and adults reach their full potential by providing accurate and up-to-date information and advice about learning disabilities and ADHD. The site features hundreds of helpful articles, monthly columns by noted experts, first person essays, children's writing and artwork, a comprehensive resource guide, very active forums, and a Yellow Pages referral directory of professionals, schools, and products.

422 **www.add.org**
Attention Deficit Disorder Association

The National Attention Deficit Disorder Association is an organization focused on the needs of adults and young adults with ADD/ADHD, and their children and families. We seek to serve individuals with ADD, as well as those who love, live with, teach, counsel and treat them.

423 **www.addhelpline.org**
ADD Helpline for Help with ADD

A site dedicated to providing information and support to all parents, regardless of their choice of treatment, belief or approach toward ADD/ADHD.

424 **www.additudemag.com**
Attitude Magazine

Information and inspiration for adults and children with attention deficit disorder.

425 **www.addvance.com**
ADDvance Online Newsletter

A resource for individuals with ADD and ADHD.

426 **www.addwarehouse.com**
ADD Warehouse

The world's largest collection of ADHD-related books, videos, training programs, games, professional texts and assessment products.

427 **www.adhdnews.com/ssi.htm**

Guidance in applying for Social Security disability benefits on behalf of a child who has ADHD.

428 **www.cec.sped.org**
Council for Exceptional Children

Dedicated to improving educational outcomes for individuals with exceptionalities, students with disabilities, and/or the gifted.

429 **www.chadd.org**
National Resource Center on AD/HD

CHADD works to improve the lives of people affected by AD/HD.

430 **www.childdevelopmentinfo.com**
Child Development Institute

Online information on child development, child psychology, parenting, learning, health and safety as well as childhood disorders such as attention deficit disorder, dyslexia and autism. Provides comprehensive resources and practical suggestions for parents.

431 **www.dyslexia.com**
Davis Dyslexia Association International

Links to internet resources for learning. Includes dyslexia, Autism and Asperger's Syndrome, ADD/ADHD and other learning disabilities.

432 **www.ncgiadd.org**
National Center for Gender Issues and AD/HD

Offers knowledge and understanding of girls and women with ADHD to improve their lives.

433 **www.nichcy.org**
Nat'l Dissemination Center for Children Disabiliti

Provides information on disabilties in children and youth and programs and services.

434 **www.oneaddplace.com**
One A D D Place

A virtual neighborhood of information and resources relating to ADD, ADHD and learning disorders.

435 **www.therapistfinder.net**

Locate psychologists, psychiatrists, social workers, family counselors, and more specializing in all disorders.

436 **www.webmd.com**
Web MD Health

Medical website with information which includes learning disabilities, ADD/ADHD, etc.

Publications

437 Guide to ACA Accredited Camps
American Camping Association
5000 State Road 67 N
Martinsville, IN 46151-7902 765-342-8456
800-428-2267
FAX 765-342-2065
TDD:765-342-8456
http://www.acacamps.org
e-mail: bookstore@acacamps.org
Peg Smith, Chief Executive Officer
Brigitta Adkins, Executive Director
Rhonda Begley, Chief Financial Officer
A national listing of accredited camping programs. Listed by activity, special clientele, camp name, and specific disabilities. *$14.95*
285 pages Annually
ISBN 0-876031-66-1

438 Guide to Summer Programs
Porter Sargent Handbooks
2 LAN Drive
Suite 100
Westford, MA 01886 978-692-9708
800-342-7470
FAX 978-692-2304
http://www.portersargent.com
e-mail: info@portersargent.com
Daniel P. McKeever, Senior Editor
Leslie A. Weston, Production Manager

Covers a broad spectrum of recreational and educational summer opportunities in the US and abroad. Current facts from 1650 camps and schools, as well as programs for those with special needs and disabilities. *$27.00*
960 pages Biannual/Paper
ISBN 9-780875-58-7

439 Resources for Children with Special Needs: Camp Guide
116 E 16th St
Fl 5
New York, NY 10003-2164 212-677-4650
FAX 212-254-4070
http://www.resourcesnyc.org/rcsn.htm
e-mail: info@resourcesnyc.org
Rachel Howard, Executive Director
Hilda Melendez, Family & Community Educator
Vicky Garwood Burton, Executive/Development Assistant
Resources for Children with Special Needs' Camp Guide, includes new camps, expanding both the range of special needs camps beyond the New York area and the northeast, and the types of disabilities served. It provides up-to-date information on more than 300 camps and programs that provide a wide range of summer activities for children with emotional, developmental, learning and physical disabilities and special needs.

440 Summer Camps for Children with Disabilities
National Dissemination Center for Children
1825 Connecticut Ave NW
Suite 700
Washington, DC 20009 202-884-8200
800-695-0285
FAX 202-884-8441
TTY: 800-695-0285
http://www.nichcy.org/pubs/genresc/camps.htm
e-mail: nichcy@fhi360.org
Suzanne Ripley, Executive Director

Extensive listing of resources available providing information on a variety of summer camps for children with disabilities. Address and contact info in addition to Website links are included.

Alabama

441 Camp ASCCA
Easter Seals of Alabama
P.O.Box 21
Jacksons Gap, AL 36861-0021 256-825-9226
800-843-2267
FAX 256-825-8332
http://www.campascca.org
e-mail: info@campascca.org
Matt Rickman, Camp Director
John Stevenson, Administrator

Helps children and adults with disabilities achieve equality, dignity and maximum independence. This is to be accomplished through a safe and quality program of camping, recreation and education in a year-round barrier-free environment. Founded 1976.

442 Good Will Easter Seals
2448 Gordon Smith Dr
Mobile, AL 36617-2319 251-471-1581
800-411-0068
FAX 251-476-4303
TTY: 800-411-0068
http://www.alabama.easterseals.com
e-mail: esmob@zebra.net
Frank Harkins, CEO

Easter Seals camping and recreation programs serve children, adults and families of all abilities. Various programs are available with the united purpose of giving disabled individuals a fun and safe camping or recreational experience. Camperships are available.

Arizona

443 Camp Civitan
Civitan Foundation
3509 E. Shea Blvd. #117
Phoenix, AZ 85028 602-953-2944
FAX 602-953-2946
http://www.campcivitan.org
e-mail: info@campcivitan.org
Shannon Valenzuela, Director of Shelter Operations
Mike Horne, Partner & COO
Gary Holliday, Pharmacy Director
Week-long camp sessions for developmentally disabled children and adults. The camp offers a variety of recreational programs that promote self-esteem, teamwork and socialization.

Arkansas

444 Easter Seals Adult Services Center
Easter Seals Arkansas
11801 Fairview Rd
Little Rock, AR 72212-2406 501-221-1063
877-533-3600
FAX 501-227-7180
TTY: 501-227-3686
http://www.ar.easterseals.com
e-mail: mail@easter-seals.org
Lauren Zilk, President

Easter Seals camping and recreation programs serve children, adults and families of all abilities. Various programs are available with the united purpose of giving disabled individuals a fun and safe camping or recreational experience.

California

445

Camp Harmon
Easter Seals Of Central California
9010 Soquel Dr
Aptos, CA 95003-4002 831-684-2166
FAX 831-684-1018
http://www.centralcal.easterseals.com
e-mail: jennifer@es-cc.org OR info@easterseals.com.
Bruce Hinman, Director

The following are camping and recreational services offered: Easter Seals own and operated camps and residential camping programs.

446

Camp Krem: Camping Unlimited
4610 Whitesands Ct
El Sobrante, CA 94803-1820 510-222-6662
FAX 510-223-3046
http://www.campingunlimited.com
e-mail: campkrem@yahoo.com
Mary Farfaglia, Executive Director

Provides year-round, recreation programs for children and adults with disabilities, Down Syndrome, Cerebral Palsy, Autism, wide range of physical/emotional disabilities.

447

Camp ReCreation
2110 Broadway
Sacramento, CA 95818-2518 916-733-0136
FAX 916-733-0195
http://www.camprec.org
e-mail: mail@camprec.org
Vicky Flaig MEd RD, Camp Director

Camp ReCreation is a residential summer camp program for persons with developmental disabilities, offering participants opportunities for fun, social interaction, and spiritual growth while providing valuable respite for parents and care givers. Camp ReCreation is held at Camp Ronald McDonald at Eagle Lake, owned and operated by Ronald McDonald House Charities Northern California and is sponsored by the Catholic Diocese of Sacramento.

448

Camp Ronald McDonald at Eagle Lake
2555 49th St
Sacramento, CA 95817-2306 916-734-4230
FAX 916-734-4238
http://www.campronald.org
e-mail: vicky@campronald.org
Catherine Ithurburn, Camp Director

Camp Ronald McDonald at Eagle Lake is a fully accessible residential summer camp for children who are at-risk with a variety of special medical needs, economic hardship and/or emotional, developmental or physical disabilities. Traditional camping activities include arts & crafts, hikes, fishing, canoeing, sports, swimming, talent show and campfires.

449

Easter Seals Bay Area: San Jose
Easter Seals Bay Area
180 Grand Avenue
Suite 300
Oakland, CA 94612-3705 510-835-2131
http://bayarea.easterseals.com
e-mail: info@easterseals.com.
Peter Olson, Manager

Easter Seals camping and recreation programs serve children, adults and families of all abilities. Various programs are available with the united purpose of giving disabled individuals a fun and safe camping or recreational experience.

450

Easter Seals Northern California
20 Pimentel Court
Suite A-1
Novato, CA 94949-5656 415-382-7450
800-234-7325
FAX 415-382-6052
TTY: 415-382-7454
http://www.noca.easter-seals.com
e-mail: cking@noca.easterseals.com
Craig King, CEO

Easter Seals camping and recreation programs serve children, adults and families of all abilities. arious programs are available with the united purpose of giving disabled individuals a fun and safe camping or recreational experience. The following are camping and recreational services offered: camp respite for adults, camperships, recreational services for adults and recreational services for children. Speech and language therapy and occupational therapy for children ages 0-3.

451

Easter Seals Northern California: Rohnert Park
5440 State Farm Drive
Rohnert Park, CA 94928 707-584-1443
800-234-7325
FAX 707-584-3438
TDD:707-584-1889
TTY: 707-584-1889
http://www.noca.easterseals.com
e-mail: skreuzer@ca-no.easter-seals.org
Susanne Kreuzer, Director

Easter Seals camping and recreation programs serve children, adults and families of all abilities. Various programs are available with the united purpose of giving disabled individuals a fun and safe camping or recreational experience. The folllowing are camping and recreational services offered: Camp respite for adults, camperships, day camping for children, recreational services for children and residential camping programs.

452

Easter Seals Superior California: Stockton
3205 Hurley Way
Sacramento, CA 95864-7132 916-485-6711
888-887-3257
FAX 916-485-2653
http://www.superiorca.easterseals.com
e-mail: info@easterseals.com
Joanna Budd, Manager

Easter Seals camping and recreation programs serve children, adults and families of all abilities. Various programs are available with the united purpose of giving disabled individuals a fun and safe camping or recreational experience. Camping and recreational services offered are: Swim programs.

453

Easter Seals Tri-Counties California
National Organization of Easter Seals
10730 Henderson Rd
Ventura, CA 93004-1898 805-647-1141
FAX 805-647-1148
http://centralcal.easterseals.com
e-mail: ca-tr.easterseals.com
Mary London, Director

Easter Seals camping and recreation programs serve children, adults and families of all abilities. Various programs are available with the united purpose of giving disabled individuals a fun and safe camping or recreational experience. Camping and recreational services offered are: Camperships and swim programs.

454 Grizzly Creek Camp
Easter Seals Northern California
20 Pimentel Court
Suite A-1
Novato, CA 94949   415-382-7450
                                      800-234-7325
                    http://www.noca.easterseals.com
              e-mail: kjohnson@noca.easterseals.com
Helen Gale, Manager

Easter Seals camping and recreation programs serve children, adults and families of all abilities. Various programs are available with the united purpose of giving disabled individuals a fun and safe camping or recreational experience. Camperships are available.

455 Kaleidoscope After School Program
Easter Seals - Bay Area
7425 Larkdale Ave
Dublin, CA 94568-1500   925-828-8857
                                  FAX 925-828-5245
                http://http//bayarea.easterseals.com
                      e-mail: info@easterseals.com
Toby Lupton, Manager

Easter Seals camping and recreation programs serve children, adults and families of all abilities. Various programs are available with the united purpose of giving disabled individuals a fun and safe camping or recreational experience.

456 Via West
2851 Park Ave
Santa Clara, CA 95050-6006   408-243-7861
                                  FAX 408-243-0452
                       http://www.viaservices.org
                     e-mail: camp@viaservices.org
Richard Frazier, Camp Director
Kay Walker, President/CEO

Camp Costanoan is a residential, respite and recreational camp for children and adults, ages 5 and older, with physical and/or developmental disabilities. Camp Costanoan enhances camper self-esteem, improves socialization skills and provide hands-on learning and therapeutic recreation opportunities. Additionally, Camp provides respite for families of individuals with disabilities.

Colorado

457 Rocky Mountain Village Camp
Easter Seals of Colorado
P.O.Box 115
Empire, CO 80438-0115   303-569-2333
                                  FAX 303-569-3857
                     http://http://co.easterseals.com
            e-mail: campinfo@eastersealscolorado.org
Krasimir Koev, Camp Director

Camping and recreational services are: Adventure, camp respite for adults, camp respite for children, camperships, conference rental, family retreats, recreational services for adults, recreational services for children, residential camping programs, swim programs and therapeutic horseback riding.

458 The Learning Camp
P.O.Box 1146
Vail, CO 81658-1146   970-524-2706
                                  FAX 970-524-4178
                       http://www.learningcamp.com
              e-mail: information@learningcamp.com
Ann Cathcart, Director

Summer camp that focuses on helping children with learning disabilities, such as dyslexia, ADD, ADHD and other learning challenges. The Learning Camp provides adventurous summer camp fun for boys and girls ages 7 - 14 combined with carefully designed academic programs. Camp activities include swimming, horseback riding, backpacking, archery, arts and crafts, fishing, canoeing, board games, and Colorado River rafting.

Connecticut

459 Camp Shriver
The ARC Of Greater Enfield
75 Hazard Avenue
Enfield, CT 06082-4001   860-763-5411
                            http://www.arcct.com
           e-mail: enfieldarc@sbcglobalnet.com
John Gallacher, Superintendent

Year round recreational programs for children and young adults with cognitive, intellectual and developmental delays.

460 Cyber Launch Pad Camp
Learning Incentive/American School for the Deaf
139 N Main St
West Hartford, CT 06107-1264   860-236-5807
                                  FAX 860-233-9945
                   http://www.learningincentive.com
            e-mail: Inquire@learningincentive.com
Aileen Stan-Spence, Director

Half days camp where children and their parents learn to use CyberSlate which is learning keyboarding, word processing, programming and remedial sessions in reading, writing and arithmetic for learning disabled children.

461 Eagle Hill Summer Program
Eagle Hill School
45 Glenville Rd
Greenwich, CT 06831-5331   203-622-9240
                                  FAX 203-861-9745
                      http://www.eaglehillschool.org
               e-mail: 0nfo@eaglehillschool.org
Nelson Dorta, Director
Brian Dayton, Summer Activities Director

Designed for children experiencing academic difficulty. Open to boys and girls ages 5-11. Some of the programs offered are mathematics, spelling, reading tutorials, writing workshops, oral language, handwriting, and study skills. Students attending the morning classes may also sign up for the Summer Activities Extended Program which is held in the afternoon.

462 Easter Seals Camp Hemlocks
Easter Seals Of Connecticut
85 Jones Street
P.O. Box 198
Hebron, CT 06248-0198   860-228-9496
                                      800-832-4409
                                  FAX 860-228-2091
                                  TTY: 860-228-2091
                    http://www.ct.easterseals.com
             e-mail: campinfo@eastersealsct.org
Sunny Ku, Director

Offers an environment that allows campers with disabilities optimal independence. Camping and recreational services are: Aquatics, Family Camp, Recreational Services for Adults and Children, Residential Camping Programs, Adventure/Traveling Program.

463   Horizons, Inc.
127 Babcock Hill Road
P.O. Box 323
South Windham, CT 06266-0323   860-456-1032
                                    FAX 860-456-4721
                        http://www.horizonsct.org
                    e-mail: staffpage@camphorizons.org
Scott Lambeck, Director of Camp & Facilities
Michelle Heimall, Director of Health & Operations

The mission of Horizons is to provide high quality residential, recreational support and work programs for people who have developmental disablties or who have other challenging social and emotional needs.

464   Our Victory Day Camp
46 Vineyard Ln
Stamford, CT 06902-1112   203-329-3394
                                        800-329-3394
                                    FAX 203-329-3394
                        http://www.ourvictory.com/
                        e-mail: ourvictory@aol.com
Fred Tunick, Executive Director

Our Victory Day Camp is a 7-week day camping program for children from 5 to 12 years of age. It is oriented toward children with learning disabilities and/or attention deficit disorder. The program is designed to expose each camper to a wide variety of activities. The goal is to create an opportunity for each camper to achieve success, whatever the camper's ability. Activities include arts and crafts, drama, music, nature, dancing, hiking, jewelry making, swimming, and sports.

465   Summer Day Programs
Middletown Parks and Recreation Department
100 Riverview Ctr
Suite 140
Middletown, CT 06457-3401   860-343-6620
                                    FAX 860-344-3319
                        http://www.cityofmiddletown.com
                    e-mail: john.milardo@cityofmiddletown.com
Raymond Santostefano, Director

These camps offer a variety of recreational and social activities. Each camp will be integrated with at least 12% population of children with disabilities. Campers must be Middletown residents.

466   Timber Trails Camps
Connecticut Valley Girl Scout Council
340 Washington St
Hartford, CT 06106-3317   860-522-0163
                                        800-922-2770
                                    FAX 860-548-0325
                        http://www.gsofct.org
                        e-mail: general@gsofct.org
Theresa Miller, Camp Director

All girls age 6 to 17 who can function in a group in a mainstream environment are welcome, including those with chronic illnesses, learning disabilities, and physical or emotional needs.

467   Valley-Shore YMCA
201 Spencer Plains Road
P.O. Box 694
Westbrook, CT 06498-0694   860-399-9622
                                    FAX 860-399-8349
                        http://www.vsymca.org
                        e-mail: vsymca@vsymca.org
Michael Sherman, Director

Family Play Dates, an adaptive recreation program designed for special language need children ages 3-7 years. (Pervasive Developmental Disorder and high functioning Autism, Asperger's, Down Syndrome). Daycamp with swimming, hiking, sports, games, nature study, archery and low ropes course.

468   Wheeler Regional Family YMCA
149 Farmington Avenue
Plainville, CT 06062   860-793-9631
                        http://www.ghymca.org
                    e-mail: kevin.washington@ghymca.org
Michelle Hill, Director

The Wheeler Regional Family YMCA is a non-profit charitable community organization. The YMCA provides a wide variety of programs for all ages. The YMCA's main programs include Child Care, Aquatic Programs, Day Camp, Teen programs, Wellness and Fitness Programs. The Wheeler Regional Family YMCA serves Plainville, Bristol, Farmington, Burlington and Plymouth.

469   Winston Prep School Summer Program
57 West Rocks Road
Norwalk, CT 06851-2213   203-229-0465
                        http://www.winstonprep.edu
                    e-mail: bsugerman@winstonprep.edu.
Jordan Yannotti, Director
Stephanie Mori, Director

For 6th through 12th grade students with learning differences such as dyslexia, nonverbal learning disabilities, expressive or receptive language disorders and attention deficit problems. The Summer Enrichment Program at their New York City branch school is designed to enhance academic skills. Students from area parochial, public and private schools attend the program every year. They receive daily one-on-one instruction in addition to attending class in the courses they have selected.

Florida

470   3D Learner Program
3D Learner, Inc.
7100 W. Camino Real
Suite 215
Boca Raton, FL 33433-7049   561-361-7495
                                        561-361-7497
                                    FAX 954-796-3883
                        http://www.3dlearner.com
Mark Halpert, Director
Mira Halpert, Director

3D Learner Program, a one-week program for struggling students who learn best when they see and experience information. We have had students from all over the US. We address attention, self-esteem and reading with a natural and effective method. Our students make immediate gains and often see significant gains with 3 months. Free learning survey and 10 minute consult. Also speak toparents and professionals.

471   Camp Challenge
Easter Seals Florida
31600 Camp Challenge Rd
Sorrento, FL 32776-9729   352-383-4711
                                        800-377-3257
                                    FAX 321-383-0744
                        http://www.fl.easeterseals.com
                    e-mail: camp@fl.easter-seals.com
John K Hazelton, Director

At Easter Seals Camp Challenge, campers participate in arts & crafts, nature activities, a universal high and low ropes course, music and dancing, outside entertainers, farm animals and other camp activities.

472 **Camp Kavod**
Adolph & Rose Levis Jewish Community Center
9801 Donna Klein Blvd
Boca Raton, FL 33428-1755   561-852-3200
http://www.levisjcc.org
e-mail: mariannej@levisjcc.org
Marty Schneer, Executive Director
Marianne Jacobs, Special Needs Director

Programs at the Center preserve and strengthen Jewish continuity by enriching personal, cultural, social and physical development. The Center shall foster leadership, enhance education, create a neighborhood of commonality for Jews of all beliefs, promote the welfare of the Jewish community and the community as a whole, and affirm the significance of the State of Israel.

473 **Camp Thunderbird**
909 E Welch Road
Apopka, FL 32712   407-889-8088
888-807-8378
FAX 407-218-4301
http://www.questinc.org
e-mail: rcage@questinc.org
Robert Cage, Director
Rosa Figueroa, LPN, Site Coordinator
Dustin Schwab, Program Coordinator
Since 1969, Quest's Camp Thunderbird has been dedicated to providing a real summer camp experience for people with special needs. Because of the physical and behavioral challenges associated with Down syndrome, autism, Cerebral Palsy and other developmental disabilities, these children and adults aren't typically eligible to attend traditional camps. Quest's Camp Thunderbird is their chance to learn new skills and focus on the remarkable things they can do, while making new friends and unforgett

474 **Easter Seals Florida**
2010 Mizell Avenue
Winter Park, FL 32792-2405   407-629-7881
http://www.fl.easterseals.com
Lynn Sinnot, President

Easter Seals camping and recreation programs serve children, adults and families of all abilities. Various programs are available with the united purpose of giving disabled individuals a fun and safe camping or recreational experience. Camping and recreational services are: Day camping for children.

Georgia

475 **Camp Hollywood**
FOCUS
3825 Presidential Parkway
Suite 103
Atlanta, GA 30340   770-234-9111
FAX 770-234-7131
http://www.focus-ga.org
e-mail: inquiry@focus-ga.org
Saxon Dasher, President
Lucy Cusick, Executive Director
Joy Trotti, Associate Director
Unique camp for children with developmental delays, neurological involvement, cerebral palsy, heart problems and immune deficiencies. Campers enjoy art projects and games. FOCUS also hosts Camp TEAM and Camp Infinity.

476 **Camp Merrimack**
Merrimack Hall Performing Arts Center
3320 Triana Blvd.
Huntsville, AL 35805   256-534-6455
http://www.merrimackhall.com
e-mail: adinges@merrimackhall.com
Debra Jenkins, Founder
Ashley Dinges, Executive Director
Kim Simari, Managing Director

Performing arts education camp for children ages 3-12 with Autism, Down Syndrome, Cerebral Palsy and cancer.

477 **Easter Seals Southern Georgia**
1906 Palmyra Rd
Albany, GA 31701-1575   229-439-7061
800-365-4583
FAX 229-435-6278
http://www.southerngeorgia.easterseals.com
e-mail: benglish@swga-easterseals.org
Beth English, President

Easter Seals camping and recreation programs serve children, adults and families of all abilities. Various programs are available with the united purpose of giving disabled individuals a fun and safe camping or recreational experience. Camping and recreational services offered are: Camp respite for adults, camp respite for children, day camping for children and therapeutic horseback riding.

478 **United Cerebral Palsy Of Georgia**
3300 Northeast Expressway
Building 9
Atlanta, GA 30341   770-676-2000
888-827-9455
FAX 770-455-8040
http://www.ucp.org
e-mail: info@ucpga.org
Stephen Bennett, President and CEO
Connie Garner, Executive Vice President
Michael E. Hill, Senior Vice President
UCP offers afterschool programs that help to develop cognitive, motors, language and communication skills, while fostering self-image and independence.

Hawaii

479 **Easter Seals Hawaii: Oahu Service Center**
710 Green St
Honolulu, HI 96813-2119   808-536-3764
888-241-7450
FAX 808-536-3765
http://www.eastersealshawaii.org
e-mail: info@eastersealshawaii.org
John F. Howell, Capital Projects
Mikio Sato, Chief Operating Officer
Esther Underwood, Vice President
Easter Seals camping and recreation programs serve children, adults and families of all abilities. Various programs are available with the united purpose of giving disabled individuals a fun and safe camping or recreational experience. Camping and recreational services offered are: Residential camping programs.

Idaho

480 **SUWS Wilderness Program**
Aspen Education Group
911 Preacher Creek Rd
Shoshone, ID 83352-5061   208-886-2565
888-879-7897
FAX 208-886-2153
http://www.suws.com
Kathy Rex, CTRS, Executive Director

Programs specialize in helping troubled teens and defiant teens with behavioral and emotional problems. Operating in southern Idaho since 1981, SUWS wilderness programs have assisted young people to identify and work through internal conflicts and emotional obstacles that have kept them from responding to parental efforts, schools, and treatment.

Illinois

481   Camp Free To Be
UCP Easter Seals In Southwestern Illinois
2720 N. Center Street
P.O. Box 367
Maryville, IL 62062   618-288-2218
                                              FAX 618-288-2249
http://http://www.ucpheartland.org
e-mail: plunkf@ucpheartland.org
Stephen Bennett, President and CEO
Connie Garner, Executive Vice President
Michael E. Hill, Senior Vice President
Day camp for ages 5-12 with disabilities and their siblings.
Activities include picnicking, swimming, fishing, outdoor
games, and arts & crafts.

**482   Camp Little Giant: Touch of Nature Environmental
Center**
Southern Illinois University
1208 Touch of Nature Rd
Carbondale, IL 62901   618-453-5348
                                              FAX 618-453-1188
http://www.tonec.siu.edu
e-mail: camplittlegiant99@yahoo.com
Randy Osborn, Program Coordinator

A residential camp program designed to meet the recreational needs of adults and children with disabilities. The
programs are designed for individuals with physical/devel-
opmental disabilities, visual & hearing impairments, mus-
cular dystrophy, cerebral palsy, autism, ADD/ADHD,
traumatic brain injury and special needs.

483   Camp Timber Pointe
Easter Seals Central Illinois
20 Timber Pointe Lane
Hudson, IL 61748   309-365-8021
                                              FAX 309-365-8934
http://http://ci.easterseals.com
Steve Thompson, President & CEO
David Bateman, Community President
Kory Kaeb, EVP
Camping and respite program for children and adults ages 7
& up with disabilities or special needs and their families.
Campers can participate in recreational activities susch as
fishing, boating, swimming, music, sports, horseback riding
and arts and crafts.

484   Easter Seals Camping and Recreation List
National Easter Seals Society
233 S. Wacker Drive
Suite 400
Chicago, IL 60606-4851
                                                 800-221-6827
                                              TTY: 312-726-4258
e-mail: info@easter-seals.com
James E Williams Jr, CEO

Various programs with the united purpose of giving disabled
children a fun and safe camping or recreational experience.
Call for information on activities in your state.

485   Easter Seals Central Illinois
Easter Seals Peoria & Bloomington-Normal & Decatur
2715 N 27th St
Decatur, IL 62526-2171   217-429-1052
                                              FAX 217-423-7605
http://www.easterseals-ci.org
Debbie England, President

Easter Seals camping and recreation programs serve children, adults and families of all abilities. Various programs
are available with the united purpose of giving disabled individuals a fun and safe camping or recreational experience.
The following are Camping and Recreational services offered: Recreational services for adults and recreational
services for children.

486   Easter Seals Joliet
Easter Seals Joliet Region, Inc.
212 Barney Dr
Joliet, IL 60435-5272   815-725-2194
                                              FAX 815-725-5150
http://www.joliet.easterseals.com
e-mail: dcondotti@il-wg.easter-seals.org
Debbie Condotti, President

Easter Seals camping and recreation programs serve children, adults and families of all abilities. Various programs
are available with the united purpose of giving disabled individuals a fun and safe camping or recreational experience.
The following are camping and recreational services
offered: Camperships.

487   Easter Seals UCP: Peoria
Easter Seals of Peoria Bloomington
507 East Armstrong Avenue
Peoria, IL 61603   309-686-1177
                                              FAX 306-686-7722
http://www.ci.easterseals.com
Mark Holstein, President/CEO

Easter Seals camping and recreation programs serve children, adults and families of all abilities. Various programs
are available with the united purpose of giving disabled individuals a fun and safe camping or recreational experience.
The following are Camping and Recreational services offered: Recreational services for adults and recreational
services for children.

488   Jayne Shover Center
Easter Seals DuPage and the Fox Valley Region
799 S McLean Blvd
Elgin, IL 60123-6704   847-742-3264
                                              FAX 847-742-9436
http://www.dfvr.easterseals.com
e-mail: admin@il-js.easterseals.com
Kim Garcia, CEO

Easter Seals camping and recreation programs serve children, adults and families of all abilities. Various programs
are available with the united purpose of giving disabled individuals a fun and safe camping or recreational experience.
The following are Camping and Recreational services offered: Recreational services for adult and recreational
services for children.

Indiana

489   Easter Seals ARC of Northeast Indiana
4919 Coldwater Rd
Fort Wayne, IN 46825-5532   260-456-4534
                                                 800-234-7811
                                              FAX 260-745-5200
http://neindiana.easterseals.com
e-mail: damstutz@esarc.org
Steven Hinkle, CEO

Easter Seals camping and recreation programs serve children, adults and families of all abilities. Various programs
are available with the united purpose of giving disabled individuals a fun and safe camping or recreational experience.
The following are camping and recreational services offered: Recreational services for adults and camp respite for
adults and children.

490   Easter Seals Crossroads
4740 Kingsway Dr
Indianapolis, IN 46205-1521   317-466-1000
                                              FAX 317-466-2000
                                              TTY: 317-479-3232
http://www.crossroads.easterseals.com
James Vento, President/CEO

Easter Seals camping and recreation programs serve children, adults and families of all abilities. Various programs are available with the united purpose of giving disabled individuals a fun and safe camping or recreational experience. The following are camping and recreational services offered: Camperships and recreational services for children.

Iowa

491 Camp Albrecht Acres
14837 Sherrill Road
P.O. Box 50
Sherrill, IA 52073   563-552-1771
                                             FAX 563-552-2732
                          http://www.albrechtacres.org
                          e-mail: info@albrechtacres.org
Deb Rahe, Executive Director
Dick McGrane, President
Randy Judge, Vice President
For children with special needs. Activities include cookouts, swimming, fishing, hay wagon rides, volleyball, dances and arts and crafts.

492 Camp Courageous
12701 Waterville-Swanton Road
Whitehouse, OH 43571   419-875-6828
                  http://www.campcourageous.com
                  e-mail: stevek@campcourageous.com
Charlie Becker, Executive Director
Jeanne Muellerleile, Camp Director

Camp Courageous is a year-round recreational and respite facility for individuals with disabilities. The camp provides the opportunity to campers for social and personal growth within a supportive environment while helping them to develop enhanced self-esteem. Some of the recreational activities include bocce ball, canoeing, games, hikes, scavenger hunts and arts & crafts.

493 Camp Sunnyside
Easter Seals Of Iowa
401 NE 66th Ave
Des Moines, IA 50313-1243   515-289-1933
                                     FAX 515-289-1281
                                     TTY: 515-289-4069
                          http://www.ia.easterseals.com
                          e-mail: clecroy@eastersealsia.org
Sherri Nielsen, President
Claire Lecroy, Director Camping & Respite Svcs.

Easter Seals camping and recreation programs serve children, adults and families of all abilities. Various programs are available with the united purpose of giving disabled individuals a fun and safe camping or recreational experience. The following are Camping and Recreational services offered: Adventure, camp respite for children, day camping for children, easter seals own and operated camps and residential camping programs.

Kansas

494 Camp Encourage
PO Box 10433
Kansas City, MO 64171   816-830-7171
                          http://www.campencourage.org
                          e-mail: camp.encourage@sbcglobal.net
Eric Lanham, J.D., President
Kelly Lee, M.S.Ed., Executive Director
Marita Burrow, Ph.D., Secretary
For children and young adults with Autism Spectrum disorders. The camp offers activities such as horseback riding, archery, fishing, swimming, hayrides, horseback riding, and art activities.

Louisiana

495 Camp Without Barriers
Easter Seals Of Louisiana
1010 Common Street
Suite 2000
New Orleans, LA 70112-2411   504-523-3465
                                         800-695-7325
                                     FAX 504-523-3465
                          http://www.louisiana.easterseals.com
Daniel Underwood, President

A non-profit, community-based health agency whose mission is to help children and adults with disabilities achieve independence through a variety of programs and services. Campers enjoy boating, nature walks, swimming, arts & crafts and campfire sing-a-longs.
                              1951

496 Easter Seals Louisiana
New Orleans Corporate Office
1010 Common Street
Suite 2000
New Orleans, LA 70112-2411   504-523-7325
                                         800-695-7325
                                     FAX 504-523-3465
                          http://www.louisiana.easterseals.com
                          e-mail: info@easterseals.org
Daniel Underwood, Corporate Program Director

Easter Seals camping and recreation programs serve children, adults and families of all abilities. Various programs are available with the united purpose of giving disabled individuals a fun and safe camping or recreational experience. The following are camping and recreational services offered: Camperships.

Maryland

497 Camp Fairlee Manor
Easter Seals of Delaware-Maryland
Fairlee Manor Recreation/Education
22242 Bay Shore Road
Chestertown, MD 21620   410-778-0566
                                 FAX 410-778-0567
                          http://www.easterseals.com
                          e-mail: contact@esdel.org
Pam Reuther, Director

For children with physical disabilities and/or cognitive impairments. Activities include arts & crafts, sports, games, nature walks, fishing, swimming and much more.

498 Kamp A-Kom-plish
9035 Ironsides Rd
Nanjemoy, MD 20662-3432   301-870-3226
                                 FAX 301-870-2620
                          http://www.kampakomplish.org
                          e-mail: kampakomplish@melwood.com
Bekah Carmichael, Exec. Assistant/Project Director

A sleep-away camp for for children and teens aged 8 to 16 years old. Located on 108 acres there are air-conditioned cabins, fishing, boating and trails for hiking. We welcome children with a variety of disabilities, such as developmental, physical and emotional however we are not able to support children with extreme behavioral issues or intense medical needs.

Massachusetts

499 Bridges To Independence Programs
The Bridge Center
470 Pine St
Bridgewater, MA 02324-2112   508-697-7557
FAX 508-697-1529
http://www.thebridgectr.org
e-mail: info@TheBridgeCtr.og

Mary Gallant, Director

Program offers teens and young adults the skills necessary for independent living and vocational success, as well as structured social and recreational opportunities

500 Camp Barefoot
The Fowler Center For Outdoor Learning
2315 Harmon Lake Road
Mayville, MI 48744   989-673-2050
FAX 989-673-6355
http://www.thefowlercenter.org
e-mail: director@thefowlercenter.org

Jack Fowler, Chairman/Founder
Kyle L. Middleton, CTRS, Executive Director
Lynn M. Seeloff, CTRS, Assistant Director
Specifically designed for teens and young adults age 18 and older with traumatic brain injuries or closed head injuries. Campers can request their daily activities.

501 Camp Connect
The Bridge Center
470 Pine St
Bridgewater, MA 02324-2112   508-697-7557
FAX 508-697-1529
http://www.thebridgectr.org
e-mail: info@TheBridgeCtr.org

Mary Gallant, Director

Camp for children and teens with high functioning Autism and Asperger's Syndrome. The programs offers to help support social skills and thinking development and practice.

502 Camp Discovery
The Bridge Center
470 Pine Street
Bridgewater, MA 02324   508-697-7557
FAX 508-697-1529
http://www.thebridgectr.org
e-mail: info@TheBridgeCtr.org

Anita Howards, Director of Administration
Karen Ellis, Office Manager
Spencer Nichols, Program Director
For campers with intellectual and developmental disabilities who benefit from extensive or pervasive support. Campers have access to all activities and also have staff support with daily living activities.

503 Camp Endeavor
The Bridge Center
470 Pine Street
Bridgewater, MA 02324   508-697-7557
FAX 508-697-1529
http://www.thebridgectr.org
e-mail: info@TheBridgeCtr.org

Anita Howards, Director of Administration
Karen Ellis, Office Manager
Spencer Nichols, Program Director
For children and adolescents with learning, intellectual and developmental disabilities. The program offers campers the chance to meet new people, try new activities and feel successfull.

504 Camp Joy
Boston Centers for Youth & Families
1483 Tremont St
Boston, MA 02120-2908   617-635-4920
FAX 617-635-4524
TTY: 617-635-5041
http://www.cityofboston.gov/bcyf
e-mail: BCYF@cityofboston.gov

Daphne Griffin, Executive Director

A therapeutic recreational program for special needs children and adults. Currently serving over 700 participants with a professionally qualified staff of 290 at 15 sites throughout the city. Serves the physically and cognitively challenged, multi-handicapped, behaviorally involved, legally blind/visually impaired, deaf/hearing impaired, learning disabled, and pre-school special needs children.

505 Camp Lapham
119 Myrtle Street
Duxbury, MA 02332   781-834-2700
FAX 781-834-2701
http://www.crossroads4kids.org
e-mail: office@crossroads4kids.org

Deb Samuels, Executive Director

Designed to meet the needs of children who thrive in a small, structured environment. The program emphasis includes anger and behavior management, along with strong self-image building all in a fun, noncompetitive camp atmosphere. With a maximum of 50 children enrolled per session and a low camper to counselor ratio of 1 to 4, the campers experience success in a more family-like atmosphere which enables each child to focus on personal goals and nonviolent methods of interaction.

506 Camp Ramah
2 Commerce Way
Norwood, MA 02062-3056   781-702-5290
FAX 781-702-5239
http://www.campramahne.org
e-mail: sallyr@campramahne.org

Rabbi Ed Gelb, Director
Davey Rosen, Assistant Director

Young people have fun while developing skills, strong friendships and a Jewish conciousness that lasts a lifetime through a variety of experiences such as sports, nature, music, arts and crafts, boating, study, Shabbat and Judaica. Campers have developmental disabilities. Some campers with LD are included in typical divisions.

507 Camp Summit
The Bridge Center
470 Pine Street
Bridgewater, MA 02324   508-697-7557
FAX 508-697-1529
http://www.thebridgectr.org
e-mail: info@TheBridgeCtr.org

Anita Howards, Director of Administration
Karen Ellis, Office Manager
Spencer Nichols, Program Director
For children and adolescents ages 4-22 who struggle with behavior control.

508 Creative Expressions Program
The Bridge Center
470 Pine St
Bridgewater, MA 02324-2112   508-697-7557
FAX 508-697-1529
http://www.bridgectr.org
e-mail: info@TheBridgeCtr.org

Mary Gallant, Director

Visual and performing arts, music, drama and dance. Children learn how to express themselves with art specific skills.

509 Crossroads for Kids
119 Myrtle St
Duxbury, MA 02332-2903
781-834-2700
888-543-7284
FAX 781-834-2701
http://www.crossroads4kids.org
e-mail: office@crossroads4kids.org
Victoria Nicastro, Overnight Camp Registrar
Bonnie Bowler, Day Camp Registrar

The daily programs provide a good balance between active and quiet, sport, cultural, group and individual activities. We place campers into smaller, age appropriate groups so they receive the extra support, care and encouragement they need to feel at home here at camp.

510 Explorer Camp
Easter Seals Massachusetts
484 Main St
Worcester, MA 01608-1893
800-244-2756
FAX 508-831-9768
TTY: 800-564-9700
http://www.eastersealsma.org
e-mail: camp@eastersealsma.org
Colleen Flanagan, Camp & Youth Leadership Manager

The following are camping and recreational services offered: Camp respite for adults, camp respite for children, canoeing, computer camp, computer program, day camping for children, residential camping programs, sailing, swim programs, therapeutic horseback riding and water skiing.

511 Handi Kids Camp
The Bridge Center
470 Pine St
Bridgewater, MA 02324-2112
508-697-7557
FAX 508-697-1529
http://www.thebridgectr.org
e-mail: info@TheBridgeCtr.org
Mary Gallant, Director

Handi Kids is a non-profit, recreational facility for children and young adults with physical and cognitive disabilities. Handi Kids provides therapeutic recreation to hundreds of individuals on a year-round basis, the goal of which is to benefit each child emotionally, physically and socially while helping those who require individualized attention and guidance enjoy and participate in recreational activities.

512 Hillside School Summer Program
404 Robin Hill Road
Marlborough, MA 01752-1099
508-485-2824
FAX 508-485-4420
http://www.hillsideschool.net
e-mail: admissions@hillsideschool.net
David Beecher, Director

Hillside School is an independent boarding and day school for boys, grades 5-9. Hillside provides educational and residential services to boys needing to develop their academic and social skills while building self-confidence and maturity. The 200-acre school is located in a rural section of Marlborough and includes a working farm. Hillside accommodates both traditional learners who want a more personalized education, and those boys with learning difficulties and/or attention problems.

513 Hippotherapy Camp Program
The Bridge Center
470 Pine St
Bridgewater, MA 02324-2112
508-697-7557
FAX 508-697-1529
http://www.thebridgectr.org
e-mail: info@TheBridgeCtr.org
Mary Gallant, Director

Occupational & Physical Therapists use horseback activities to help clients meet individual clinical goals such as mobility, strength, improved gait & balance, endurance and independence. The center also offers Therapeutic Riding which helps to improve posture, balance, communication & sensory processing. The Therapeutic Carriage Driving program allows those who do not ride horses the opportunity to sit with their instructor and learn how to control a horse when it is pulling a carriage.

514 Horse Camp
The Bridge Center
470 Pine Street
Bridgewater, MA 02324
508-697-7557
FAX 508-687-1529
http://www.thebridgectr.org
e-mail: info@TheBridgeCtr.org
Anita Howards, Director of Administration
Karen Ellis, Office Manager
Spencer Nichols, Program Director
For ages 8 and up who love to ride horses. The camp offers riding center activities and mounted riding lessons.

515 Landmark School Summer Boarding Program
Landmark School
429 Hale Street
P.O. Box 227
Prides Crossing, MA 01965
978-236-3216
FAX 978-921-7268
http://www.landmarkoutreach.org
e-mail: outreach@landmarkschool.org
Robert Broudo, Headmaster

Our Summer Program accepts boys and girls age 7-20, in grades 1-12, who possess average to superior intelligence, a history of healthy emotional development, and have been diagnosed with a language-based learning disability. Landmark's Summer Boarding Program excels at providing a safe, fun, and exciting summer experience.

516 Landmark Summer Program: Exploration and Recreation
PO Box 227
412 Hale Street
Prides Crossing, MA 01965
978-236-3010
FAX 978-921-0361
http://www.landmarkschool.org
e-mail: admission@landmarkschool.org
Robert Broudo, President and Headmaster
Mark R. Brislin, Vice President
Maureen Flores, Chief Development Officer
For students in grades 3-6, Landmark's Exploration Program provides the opportunity to combine a half-day of academic classes with a half-day Marine Science/Adventure Ropes experience. Students entering grades 1-5 may choose the Recreation Program which combines a half-day of academics with an afternoon of recreational activities. Both programs provide intensive academic study for students with language-based learning disabilities, and daily one-to-one tutorials.

517 Landmark Summer Program: Marine Science
PO Box 227
412 Hale Street
Prides Crossing, MA 01965
978-236-3010
FAX 978-921-0361
http://www.landmarkschool.org
e-mail: admission@landmakrschool.org
Robert Broudo, President and Headmaster
Mark R. Brislin, Vice President
Maureen Flores, Chief Development Officer

Landmark's Marine Science Summer Program enrolls students in grades 7-12, who have been diagnosed with a language-based learning disability, and are interested in marine studies. Students spend half the day exploring local coastal ecosystems, working on research teams and collecting data. The other half of the day is spent developing their language skills in an academic classroom setting and in one-to-one tutorial sessions.

518 Landmark Summer Program: Musical Theater

PO Box 227
412 Hale Street
Prides Crossing, MA 01965   978-236-3010
                                   FAX 978-921-0361
              http://www.landmarkschool.org
              e-mail: admission@landmarkschool.org
Robert Broudo, President and Headmaster
Mark R. Brislin, Vice President
Maureen Flores, Chief Development Officer
Landmark's new Musical Theater program gives students the opportunity to perform on stage or develop technical theater skills behind-the-scenes. The class culminates in a full-scale theatrical production at the end of six weeks. On-stage performers learn to act, dance, and sing as part of a musical company. Technical theater students try their hand at set-design and building, sound and lighting, and produce the summer's musical production.

519 Linden Hill School & Summer Program

154 S Mountain Rd
Northfield, MA 01360-9701   413-498-2906
                                   FAX 413-498-2908
              http://www.lindenhs.org/
              e-mail: office@lindenhs.org
James Mc Daniel, Headmaster

The Linden Hill Summer Program provides a balance of academic work and traditional camp experiences. Support and remdiation is offered through a multi-sensory approach to language training based in the renowned and clinically-proven Orton-Gillingham method. Honesty, integrity and pride in their success are goals for each of our participants. Linden Hill has hundreds of acres of fields, woods, ponds and streams, as well as a comfortable dormitory lodging and healthy, delicious home-cooked meals.

520 Moose Hill Nature Day Camp

293 Moose Hill Street
Sharon, MA 02067   781-784-5691
              http://www.massaudubon.org
              e-mail: moosehillcamp@massaudubon.org
Kay Andberg, Camp Director

Nature Day Camp is a welcoming environment with fewer than one hundred campers in each weekly session. The goal is to educate children and enrich their lives through outdoor exploration, focused activities, games, hikes, and crafts. Most weeks include special visitors and camp-wide theme days. The camp day runs from 9 a.m. to 3 p.m. with before and after camp programs available. The camp uses the Nature Center of Moose Hill Wildlife Sanctuary as its base.

521 Patriots' Trail Girl Scout Council Summer Camp

95 Berkeley St
Boston, MA 02116-6239
                                   800-882-1662
                                   FAX 617-482-9045
                                   TDD:800-882-1662
              http://www.ptgirlscouts.org/properties_camps/
              e-mail: info@ptgirlscouts.org
Ruth Bramson, CEO

Canoeing, swimming, windsurfing, life-saving, sailing, biking and trips.

522 Summer@Carroll

The Carroll School
25 Baker Bridge Rd
Lincoln, MA 01773-3199   781-259-8342
                                   FAX 781-259-8842
              http://www.carrollschool.org
              e-mail: summer@carrollschool.org
Stephen Wilkins, Headmaster

Summer at Carroll is designed to offer academic intervention and remediation to children diagnosed with primary language learning difficulties, such as dyslexia. Small group teaching, individualized instruction and attention to the needs of goals of the students are what Carroll prides themselves on.

523 The Drama Play Connection, Inc.

298 Crescent St
Waltham, MA 02453-3803   781-899-1160
                                   FAX 781-899-1180
              http://www.dramaplayconnection.com
              e-mail: info@dramaplayconnection.com
Liana P Morgens, Ph.D., Director

The Summer Pragmatic Language Drama Program serves primarily children and adolescents with Asperger's Disorder, Nonverbal Learning Disabilities, and those with related social pragmatic difficulties. The pragmatic program is designed to help children acquire the skills necessary to function more competently with their peers. The program includes drama curriculum that focuses on teaching nonverbal language skills through the use of improvisation and other drama techniques.

524 The Kolburne School Summer Program

Kolburne School
343 NM Southfield Rd
New Marlborough, MA 01230-2035   413-229-8787
                                   FAX 413-229-4165
              http://www.kolburne.net
              e-mail: info@kolburne.net
Jeane K Weinstein, Executive Director

A family operated residential treatment center located in the Berkshire Hills of Massachusetts. Through integrated treatment services, effective behavioral management, recreational programming, and positive staff relationships, our students develop the emotional stability, interpersonal skills and academic/vocational background necessary to return home with success.

Michigan

525 Adventure Learning Center at Eagle Village

4507 170th Ave
Hersey, MI 49639-8785   231-832-2234
                                  800-748-0061
                                  FAX 231-832-1729
              http://www.eaglevillage.org
              e-mail: info@eaglevillage.org
Craig Weidner, Director

Adventure Learning Center at Eagle Village offers a variety of fun camp experiences for any child, including those with emotional and/or behavioral impairments. Challenging activities make the camps rewarding experiences.

526 Children's Therapy Programs

Easter Seals - Michgan, Inc.
2399 E. Walton Avenue
Auburn Hills, MI 48326-4761   248-475-6400
                                  800-757-3257
              http://www.mi.easterseals.com
Julie Dorcey, Manager

Various programs designed for children with autism, speech and language delays, amotional, motor and social skill issues.

527 Easter Seals Genesee County Greater Flint Therapy Center
1420 University Ave
Flint, MI 48504-6208
810-238-0475
FAX 810-238-9270
http://mi.easterseals.com
Diane Austin, Program Manager

Children and adults with mental and physical disabilities and other special needs have access to services designed to meet their individual needs. Health professionals from a variety of disciplines work with each person to overcome obstacles to independence, and to reach his/her personal goals through person centered planning. The following are camping and recreational services offered: Recreational services for adults and children, residential camping programs, therapeutic horseback riding.

528 Easter Seals Of Michigan
2399 E. Walton Blvd.
Auburn Hills, MI 48326-6249
248-475-6400
http://mi.easterseals.com

John Kersten, President

Offers a variety of programs to individuals with disabilities and special needs.

529 The Fowler Center For Outdoor Learning
2315 Harmon Lake Rd
Mayville, MI 48744-9737
989-673-2050
FAX 989-673-6355
http://www.thefowlercenter.org
e-mail: info@thefowlercenter.org
Lynn Sealoff, Director

The Fowler Center is an outdoor recreation and education facility that provides programs for children, teens and adults with disabilities. Along with day camp programs, the camp also offers autism weekend camps and respite camps.

530 The JCC Center
Jewish Community Center of Metropolitan Detroit
D. Dan & Betty Kahn Building
6600 West Maple
West Bloomfield, MI 48322-3022
248-661-1000
FAX 248-661-3680
http://www.jccdet.org
e-mail: dstone@jccdet.org
Mark A. Lit, Executive Director
Dave Stone, Associate Executive Director

Programs that support Jewish unity, ensure Jewish continuity and enrich Jewish life while conveying the importance of well-being within the Jewish and general community and the people of Israel.

Minnesota

531 Camp Buckskin
4124 Quebec Avenue North
Suite 300
Minneapolis, MN 55427
763-208-4805
FAX 763-208-8668
http://www.campbuckskin.com
e-mail: info@campbuckskin.com
Tom Bauer, Director

Overnight summer camp program that specializes in serving boys and girls ages 6 - 18 who are experiencing social skill and academic difficulties. While not an entrance requirement, the majority of our campers have a primary diagnosis of AD/HD, Learning Disabilities, or Aspergers while others may have a secondary or related diagnosis.

532 Camp Confidence
1620 Mary Fawcett Memorial Dr
East Gull Lake, MN 56401-7538
218-828-2344
FAX 218-828-2618
http://www.campconfidence.com
e-mail: info@campconfidence.com
Jeff Olson, Executive Director
Bob Slaybaugh, Camp Director

A year-round center for persons with developmental disabilities specializing in recreation and outdoor education. Aimed at promoting self confidence and self esteem and the necessary skills to become full, contributing members of society.

533 Camp Friendship
Friendship Ventures
10509 108th St NW
Annandale, MN 55302-2912
952-852-0101
800-450-8376
FAX 952-852-0123
http://www.friendshipventures.org
e-mail: fv@friendshipventures.org
Georgann Rumsey, President

A summer resident camp that is open to anyone five or older who has developmental and/or physical disabilities.

534 Camp New Hope
Friendship Ventures
10509 108th Street NW
Annandale, MN 55302-4598
952-852-0101
800-450-8376
FAX 952-852-0123
http://www.friendshipventures.org
e-mail: fv@friendshipventures.org
Laurie Tschetter, President

A summer resident camp that is open to anyone five or older who has developmental and/or physical disabilities.

535 Camp Winnebago
19708 Camp Winnebago Rd
Caledonia, MN 55921-5738
507-724-2351
FAX 507-724-3786
http://www.campwinnebago.org
e-mail: director@campwinnebago.org
Rande Gustafson, Director

Individuals with developmental disabilities, six years of age and older, are eligible to attend Camp Winnebago. A variety of traditional summer camp activities abound: swimming, cooking over a fire, games, arts and crafts, hay-wagon rides, dancing and more. Activities are adapted to the age and ability of each camper to ensure maximum participation.

Missouri

536 H.O.R.S.E.
C/O BJ Wright
19021 Long Grove Road
Higginsville, MO 64037
660-909-5381
http://www.horsehelpspeople.org
e-mail: Brenda@HORSEhelpspeople.org
Brenda Wright, Executive Director
Athena Sharp, Director
Colleen White, Director

Combines the healing power of horses to deliver alternative therapeutic services to children with autism spectrum disorders and emotionally troubled individuals. The programs help to develop emotional awareness & expression, social skills and relationship building, as well as to help them build more self-esteem and self confidence.

Nebraska

537 **Camp Kitaki**
YMCA Of Lincoln Nebraska
570 Fallbrook Blvd.
Suite 210
Lincoln, NE 68521-3110   402-434-9222
                                   FAX 402-434-9226
                         http://www.ymcalincoln.org
                   e-mail: CampKitaki@ymcalincoln.org
Chris Klingberg, Executive Director

A Christian camp for children with ADD and other disabilities. Archery, climbing, horseback riding, fishing and aquatic activities are some of the activities.

538 **Easter Seals Nebraska**
638 N 109th Plz
Omaha, NE 68154-1722   402-345-2200
                                         800-650-9880
                                   FAX 402-345-2500
                           http://ne.easterseals.com
                  e-mail: mtufte@ne.easterseals.com
Karen C. Carlson, President & CEO
Michael Tufte, Vice President of Development
Angela Howell, Vice President of Employment
The following are camping and recreational services offered: Camp respite for adults, camp respite for children, camperships, recreational services for children and residential camping programs.

New Hampshire

539 **Calumet Camp**
Calumet Lutheran Ministries
1090 Ossipee Lake Road
P.O. Box 236
West Ossipee, NH 03890-0236   603-539-4773
                                   FAX 603-539-5343
                              http://www.calumet.org
                            e-mail: karl@Calumet.org
Karl Ogren, Camp Director

Camp Calumet is for kids, adults, seniors, singles, church groups, families and the developmentally disabled.

540 **Camp Starfish**
1121 Main Street
Lancaster, MA 01523   978-368-6580
                                   FAX 978-368-6578
                          http://www.campstarfish.org
                       e-mail: info@campstarfish.org
Emily Golinsky, Executive Director
Michelle Cyr, MSW, Associate Director
Jill Connell, Development/Admin. Assistant
Year round camp for children and young adults with ADHD, Aspergers, behavioral issues and learning disabilities. The focus is on teaching the children how to interact appropriately in a soocial group, and work on individual goals, while developing self-esteem and self-confidence.

541 **Easter Seals New Hempshire**
555 Auburn St
Manchester, NH 03103-4803   603-623-8863
                                         800-870-8728
                                   FAX 603-625-1148
                             http://www.eastersealsnh.org
                   e-mail: vbottino@eastersealsnh.org

Larry J. Gammon, President & CEO
Elin A. Treanor, Senior Vice President and CFO
Karen Van Der Beken, Senior Vice President
Easter Seals camping and recreation programs serve children, adults and families of all abilities. Various programs are available with the united purpose of giving disabled individuals a fun and safe camping or recreational experience. The following are camping and recreational services offered: Camp respite for adults, camperships, day camping for children, recreational services for children and residential camping programs.

New Jersey

542 **Camp Merry Heart**
Easter Seals Of New Jersey
21 O Brien Rd
Hackettstown, NJ 07840-4839   908-852-3896
                                   FAX 908-852-9263
                            http://www.easterseals.com
                  e-mail: msimpson@nj.easterseals.org
Richard Schuman, AVP, Camping/Recreational Svcs.

Camp Merry Heart provides a safe, supervised and beautiful setting for iindividuals with disabilities and special needs. Activities include swimming, boating, fishing, arts and crafts, singing, dance and nature studies.

543 **Camp Moore**
New Jersey State Elks Association
P.O. Box 1596
Woodbridge, NJ 07095   732-326-1300
                                   FAX 732-326-1319
                                   TDD:609-271-0138
                                 http://www.njelks.org
                    e-mail: njhcchq@gmail.com
Todd Garmer, Camp Director

Elks Camp Moore offers a fun filled vacation away from home for children with special needs. A week at Elks Camp Moore is a remarkable experience not soon to be fogotten. The primary goal of the camp is to further develop the recreational and social skills of each child. In a relaxed and accepting atmosphere, each camper experiences new adventures, lasting friendships, and opportunities that promote independence and greater self-confidence.

544 **Round Lake Camp**
21 Plymouth St
Fairfield, NJ 07004-1615   973-575-3333
                                   FAX 973-575-4188
                           http://www.roundlakecamp.org
                        e-mail: rlc@njycamps.org
David Friedman, Camp Director

A camp for children with learning differences and social communication disorders. The camp is designed so that all the educational, recreational and social activities are planned to meet the capabilities of each child.

New Mexico

545 **Camp Without Barriers**
Easter Seals Of New Mexico - Santa Fe
2041 S. Pacheco Street
Suite 100
Santa Fe, NM 87505   505-424-7700
                                   FAX 505-424-7707
                          http://www.smem.easterseals.com
Jane Carr, Camp Director

Camp Easter Seals New Mexico provides fun for children and adults with disabilities. Its unique combination of comfortable accessible facilities and energetic, outgoing staff offers a fun, exciting, summer experience with memories to last a lifetime. Camp Easter Seals is held at Kamp Kiwanis' site, located in Vanderwagen, New Mexico.

New York

546 Adirondack Leadership Expeditions
82 Church St
Saranac Lake, NY 12983-1858   518-897-5011
                                        FAX 518-897-5017
                http://www.adirondackleadership.com
                        e-mail: rtheisen@adkle.com
Robert Theisen, Ph.D, Executive Director

Specializes in helping young adults age 13 to 17 who are experiencing / exhibiting any of the following: entitlement, manipulation, family conflict, isolation, low self-esteem, substance use, defiant behavior, attention deficit, learning differences, school failure, and negative peer relationships.

547 Camp Bari Tov
92ny Street Y
1395 Lexington Ave
New York, NY 10128-1612   212-415-5573
                                http://www.92y.org
Melanie Mandel, Dir of Svcs for Children/Adults

Summer recreational program for children and young adults ages 5-13 with severe developmental disabilities. Campers participate in a variety of camp activities which include adaptive sports, music, art, nature and more.

548 Camp Colonie
Easter Seals New York
P.O. Box 5
Troy, NY 12181-2408   518-222-3932
                        http://www.ny.easterseals.com
Larry Gammon, President

Week long sessions for children and young adults age 5-21 years of age with developmental, emotional or physical disabilities.

549 Camp Dunnabeck at Kildonan School
425 Morse Hill Rd
Amenia, NY 12501-5240   845-373-8111
                                        FAX 845-373-9793
                        http://www.kildonan.org
                e-mail: admissions@kildonan.org
Benjamin Powers, Head Master

Specializes in helping intelligent children with specific reading, writing and spelling disabilities. Provides Orton-Gillingham tutoring with camp activities, including swimming, sailing, waterskiing, horseback riding, ceramics, tennis and woodworking.

550 Camp Huntington
Registration & Billing Office
P.O. Box 37
High Falls, NY 12440-0037   866-514-5281
                                        FAX 845-853-1172
                http://www.camphuntington.com
                e-mail: dfalk@camphuntington.com
Daniel Falk, Executive Director

Coed camp for children and young adults ages 6-21 who have learning and developmental disabililties, Autism Spectrum Disorders, Aspserger's, and ADD/ADHD. Programs emphasize development of social skills and independent living, vocational orientation, speech and language.

551 Camp Kehilla
Sid Jacobson JCC
300 Forest Dr
East Hills, NY 11548-1231   516-484-1545
                                        FAX 516-484-7354
                        e-mail: MPlotkin@sfy.org
Michelle Laser, L.C.S.W., Program Director/Special Needs
Sharon Hanover M.S.W., Camp Director

A summer day camp for children and teens with special needs.

552 Camp Northwood
132 State Route 365
Remsen, NY 13438-5700   315-831-3621
                                        FAX 315-831-5867
                        http://www.nwood.com
        e-mail: northwoodprograms@hotmail.com
Gordon Felt, Camp Director

Coed camp providing structured programs and activities to children and young adults ages 8-18 with Asperger's Syndrome, HFA, and Attention Deficit Disorders.

553 Camp Sunshine-Camp Elan
Mosholu Montefiore Community Center
3450 Dekalb Ave
Bronx, NY 10467-2302   718-882-4000
                                        FAX 718-882-6369
                        http://www.mmcc.org
                e-mail: daycamp@mmcc.org
Donald Bluestone, Executive Director

Provides programs, services and seasonal camping for children and adults. The camp serves children who are intellectually limited, emotionally impaired, and/or those who demonstrate special learniing disabilities.

554 Camp Tova
1395 Lexington Avenue
New York, NY 10128   212-415-5500
                                        FAX 212-415-5788
                                http://www.92y.org
Melanie Mandel, Director
Stuart J. Ellman, President
Sol Adler, Executive Director
Camp Tova is for children and young adults ages 6-13 with learning and other developmental disabilities. Campers develop a wide variety of social and creative skills while enjoying a variety of camp activites.

555 Clover Patch Camp
55 Helping Hand Ln
Glenville, NY 12302-5801   518-384-3081
                                        FAX 518-384-3001
                http://www.cloverpatchcamp.org
                e-mail: cloverpatchcamp@cfdsny.org
Laura Taylor, Camp Director

Clover Patch is a summer camp for individuals with disabilities where each camper is encouraged to reach his or her fullest potential. Campers enjoy a wide variety of programs and are able to make new friends and create everlasting memories.

556 EBL Coaching Summer Programs
17 E 89th St
Ste 1D
New York, NY 10128-0615   212-249-0147
                                        FAX 212-937-2305
                        http://www.eblcoaching.com
                e-mail: info@eblcoaching.com
Emily Levy, Director
Lauren Hosking, Education Coordinator

Provides one-on-one tutoring and small group summer programs for students with learning disabilities and ADHD. They use all research-based, multi-sensory strategies, including the Orton Gillingham technique.

557   Easter Seals Albany
292 Washington Avenue Ext
Ste 112
Albany, NY 12203-6385
518-456-0828
800-727-8785
FAX 518-456-5094
http://ny.easterseals.com
e-mail: info@ny.easter-seals.org
Chuck Paravella, Camp Director
Rita Stella, Director of Vocational Services
Chris Blake-Jeremias, Team Manager
Easter Seals camping and recreation programs serve children, adults and families of all abilities. Various programs are available with the united purpose of giving disabled individuals a fun and safe camping or recreational experience. The following are camping and recreational services offered: Camp respite for children, camperships, day camping for children and recreational services for children.

558   Gow School Summer Programs
PO Box 85
South Wales, NY 14139-0085
716-652-3450
FAX 716-652-3457
http://www.gow.org
e-mail: summer@gow.org
David Mendlewski, Director
Doug Cotter, Admissions Director

For boys and girls who have experienced past academic difficulties and have learning differences but possess the potential for success. The five week co-educational Gow School Summer Program (GSSP) serves students ages 8-16. Academic classes are combined with traditional camp activities and weekend trips.

559   Kamp Kiwanis
NY District Kiwanis Foundation
9020 Kiwanis Rd
Taberg, NY 13471-2727
315-336-4568
FAX 315-336-3845
http://www.kiwanis.org
e-mail: kamp@kiwanis-ny.org
Rebecca Lopez, Executive Director

Coed camp for children aged 8-14 who have special needs, are austistic, or physically/mentally challenged.

560   Mainstreaming at Camp
Frost Valley YMCA
2000 Frost Valley Rd
Claryville, NY 12725-5221
845-985-2291
FAX 845-985-0056
http://www.frostvalley.org
e-mail: campdirector@frostvalley.org jmedler@yai.org
Joe Medler, Camp Director

Serves children with developmental disabilities. The YMCA's 'Mainstreaming at Camp' allows campers to integrate with other campers throughout the day and reside in their own village with specially trained staff in the evenings.

561   Rockland County Association for the Learning Disabled (YAI/RCALD)
2 Crosfield Avenue
Suite 411
West Nyack, NY 10994-2212
845-358-2032
FAX 845-358-6119
http://www.yai.org
e-mail: link@yai.org
Melissa Yu, MD, CEO

YAI/RCALD conducts a wide variety of programs, supervised by experienced and professional staff, designed to build life skills, promote self-esteem, provide information exchange and offer other support services for individuals with learning and other developmental disabilities. The programs include, vocational evaluation and placements, recreational, residential, camping, service coordination and support groups.

562   Samuel Field Y
58-20 Little Neck Pkwy
Little Neck, NY 11362-2595
718-225-6750
FAX 718-423-8276
http://sfysummercamps.org
e-mail: sfy@sfy.org
Steven Goodman, Camp Director

Day camps specialize in serving children who have developmental disabilities 5-21 years old. Younger campers enjoy the center-based Childhood Program where they swim, play in the gym, cook, dance, as well as share arts and crafts activities and music. Activities for older campers include swimming, nature fun, an overnight at the Little Neck Site, community field trips, as well as a wide variety of specialty activities, such as drama, music, sports and arts and crafts.

563   School Vacation Camps: Youth with Developmental Disabilities
YWCA of White Plains-Central Westchester
515 North St
White Plains, NY 10605-3002
914-949-6227
FAX 914-949-8903
http://www.ywca.whiteplains.org
e-mail: jkrentsa@ywcawhiteplains.com
Amy Kohn, CEO

Camp for people with developmental disabilities.

564   Shield Summer Play Program
144-61 Roosevelt Avenue
Flushing, NY 11354-6252
718-939-8700
FAX 718-961-7669
http://www.shield.org
e-mail: ecohen@shield.org
Dr. Susan Provenzano, Ed.D, Executive Director
Beth Anisman, B&Co., LLC, President
Michael E. Katz, Treasurer
The School Program provides a school for children, adolescents, and young adults, ages 6 to 21, who have been diagnosed with either mental retardation or other developmental disabilities. The program provides special education and related services based on each student's skills and potential for independence. Instruction focuses on developing and enhancing skills in community, recreational, and vocational settings. Year-round services are available.

565   Summit Camp
Summit Camp & Travel Programs
322 Route 46 West
Suite 210
Parsippany, NJ 07054-6266
973-732-3230
FAX 973-732-3226
http://www.summitcamp.com
e-mail: info@summitcamp.com
Mayer Stiskin, Executive Director

Summit offers co-ed 4 week and 8 week programs, along with a 10 day Mini-Camp, providing many camp activities that feature a heated swimming pool, complete lake activities, climbing wall, go-karts, computer labs, adventure programs, field trips, etc. The programs and staffing are tailored to the needs of the children dealing with social/emotional challenges, Aspergers, Tourette's, Non-verbal LD, Bipolar Disorder. The camp serves 300 children and provides a staff of 270.

North Carolina

566   Camp Sky Ranch
634 Sky Ranch Rd
Blowing Rock, NC 28605-8231
                                828-264-8600
                            FAX 828-265-2339
                    http://www.campskyranch.com
                    e-mail: jsharp1@triad.rr.com

Jack Sharp, Director

Serves developmentally and mentally disabled individuals of all ages, from all over the world. Children and adults with Down Syndrome, Prader-Willie Syndrome, ADD/HD, Fragile X Syndrome, and Autism attend our camp each year.

567   Discovery Camp
Talisman Camps & Programs
64 Gap Creek Rd
Zirconia, NC 28790-8791
                                888-458-8226
                            FAX 828-697-6249
                    http://www.talismancamps.com
                    e-mail: info@talismancamps.com

Linda Tatsapaugh, Camp Director

Discovery Camp is a 2-week program designed for children ages 8-11, who may have ADD, learning disabilities, or experiencing some social anxiety. The activity packed schedule and 1:2.5 staff-camper ratio allows campers to have a positive experience at camp. In a nurturing yet structured environment, campers are challenged to become more independent and outgoing within the emotionally and physically safe setting that small group living provides. A good introduction to camp for younger kids.

568   SOAR Adventure Programs
SOAR
NC Base Camp
P.O. Box 388
Balsam, NC 28707-0388
                                828-456-3435
                            FAX 828-456-3449
                    http://www.soarnc.org
                    e-mail: admissions@soarnc.org

Laura Pate, Director

Emphasis is placed on developing self-confidence, social skills, problem-solving techniques, a willingness to attempt new challenges and the motivation which comes through successful goal orientation. Full semester and summer programs are available.

569   Talisman Camps & Programs
64 Gap Creek Rd
Zirconia, NC 28790-8791
                                828-697-6313
                                888-458-8226
                            FAX 828-697-6249
                    http://www.talismancamps.com
                    e-mail: info@talismancamps.com

Linda Tatsapaugh, Camp Director

Programs are co-educational, for children ages 9-13 who have been diagnosed with LD, ADD, ADHD, and mild behavior issues. Participants live on campus in rustic cabins participating in a variety of activities designed to promote better communication and cooperation skills. Limited enrollment helps to facilitate an extended-family environment. The 2.5 to 1 camper-to-staff ratio ensures that no child is lost in the crowd.

570   Talisman Summer Camp
64 Gap Creek Rd
Zirconia, NC 28790-8791
                                855-588-8254
                            FAX 828-697-6249
                    http://www.talismancamps.com
                    e-mail: info@talismancamps.com

Linda Tatsapaugh, Camp Director
Doug Smathers, Program Director

Includes three programs for children with learning disabilities, high functioning Autism and Asperger's Snydrome.

571   Victory Junction Gang Camp
4500 Adams Way
Randleman, NC 27317-8242
                                336-498-9055
                            FAX 336-498-9090
                    http://www.victoryjunction.org

Pattie Petty, CEO

Enriches the lives of children with chronic medical conditions or serious illnesses by providing life-changing camping experiences that are exciting, fun, and empowering, in a safe and medically sound environment.

572   Wilderness Experience
Ashe County 4-H
512 Brickhaven Rd.
Raleigh, NC 27606
                                336-219-2650
                            FAX 919-515-7812
                    http://www.nc4h.org
                    e-mail: larry_hancock@ncsu.edu

Ken Burgess, Extension Associate
Larry Hancock, Extension Associate
Keith Russell, Director

The type of 4-H Camp program operating in North Carolina offers campers a greater chance to learn, develop life skills and form attitudes that will help them to become self-directing and productive members of society. At camp, youth focus on subjects that might be difficult to handle at home due to need for special equipment. Camp then becomes a learning laboratory that allows youth to apply their new knowledge to real-life situations.

Ohio

573   Academic Fun & Fitness Camp
Creative Education Institute
120 North Main Street
Chagrin Falls, OH 44022
                                440-914-0200
                            FAX 440-542-1504
                    http://www.cei4learning.org
                    e-mail: caroler@cei4learning.org

Carole Richards, Director/President

For children ages 6-18 with special needs and learning differences such as ADD/ADHD, Asperger's Syndrome, and Dyslexia. 6 weeks in June & July; 5 to 1 camper/counselor ratio.

574   Akron Rotary Camp
4460 Rex Lake Dr
Akron, OH 44319-3430
                                330-644-4512
                            FAX 330-644-1013
                    http://www.akronymca.org
                    e-mail: rotarycamp@akronymca.org

Dan Reynolds, Camp Director

Rotary Camp was founded in 1924 with the purpose of providing children with special needs a place to spend their summers - a place where disabilities and limits do not hold kids back. Children ages 6-17 and who have physical or developmental disabilities are eligible to participate in this fun-filled camping experience.

575   Camp Echoing Hills
36272 County Road 79
Warsaw, OH 43844-9770
                                740-327-2311
                                800-419-6513
                            FAX 740-327-6371
                    http://www.echoinghillsvillage.org
                    e-mail: ckuhns@echoinghillsvillage.org

Buddy Busch, Camp Director

Camp Echoing Hills is a ministry of Echoing Hills Village, which specializes in providing various programs for individuals with developmental disabilities in six locations across Ohio and Ghana West Africa. Camp Echoing Hills provides a safe and encouraging residential camping experience where campers develop friendships, skills and life-long memories.

576   Camp Happiness
Catholic Charities Disability Services
7911 Detroit Ave
Cleveland, OH 44102-2815   216-334-2963
                                          FAX 216-334-2905
            http://www.clevelandcatholiccharities.org
        e-mail: mjscott@clevelandcatholiccharities.org
Dennis McNulty, Director
John Klee, Executive Director

A summer camp program for persons with developmental disabilities, Camp Happiness is a six-week day camp offered at several sites throughout the Diocese of Cleveland that provides educational, social and recreational services to children and adults with developmental disabilities during the summer months.

577   Camp Nuhop
404 Hillcrest Dr
Ashland, OH 44805-4152   419-289-2227
                                          FAX 419-289-2227
                http://www.campnuhop.org
            e-mail: campnuhop@zoominternet.net
Trevor Dunlap, Executive Director

A residential camp for all children with learning disabilities, attention deficit disorders and behavior disorders.

578   Easter Seals Broadview Heights
Easter Seals North East Ohio
1929 A East Royalton Road
Broadview Heights, OH 44147-2809   440-838-0990
                                            888-325-8532
                                          FAX 440-838-8440
                                          TTY: 440-838-0990
                http://neohio.easterseals.com
            e-mail: spowers@noh.easterseals.com
Sheila Dunn, CEO
Alex Barge, Camp Director
Colleen Flanagan, Camp Manager
The following are camping and recreational services offered: Camperships and day camping for children. Through our summer campership program, funding is available to children and adults with disabilities so they can select a summer day or residential camp of their choice. The program provides individuals with the opportunity to attend a camp specifically designed for their special needs and optimal enjoyments.

579   Easter Seals Central and Southeast Ohio
3830 Trueman Court
Hilliard, OH 43026   614-228-5523
                                            800-860-5523
                                          FAX 614-228-8249
                http://centralohio.easterseals.com
            e-mail: info@easterseals-cseohio.org
Karin A Zuckerman, CEO
Katherine Jones, Re-entry Specialist

The following are camping and recreational services offered: Aquatics. Summer Day Camp is open to toddlers, ages 18 months to 2 years, and preschoolers and young school-aged children from 3-8 years of age with and without disabilities.

580   Easter Seals Cincinnati
2901 Gilbert Ave
Cincinnati, OH 45206-1211   513-281-2316
                                            800-288-1123
                                          FAX 513-475-6787
                http://swohio.easterseals.com
        e-mail: buildingability@eastersealswrc.org
Pam Green, President and CEO
Peter Bloch, Executive Vice President
David Dreith, Executive Vice President
Easter Seals camping and recreation programs serve children, adults and families of all abilities. Various programs are available with the united purpose of giving disabled individuals a fun and safe camping or recreational experience. The following are camping and recreational services offered: Adventure.

581   Easter Seals Marietta
Easter Seals
PO Box 31
Marietta, OH 45750   740-374-8876
                                            800-860-5523
                                          FAX 740-374-4501
                http://www.eastersealscentralohio.org
            e-mail: matt@campascca.org
Karin A Zuckerman, CEO
Colleen Flanagan, Camp Manager
Alex Barge, Camp Director
Easter Seals camping and recreation programs serve children, adults and families of all abilities. Various programs are available with the united purpose of giving disabled individuals a fun and safe camping or recreational experience. The following are camping and recreational services offered: Camp respite for children and therapeutic horseback riding.

582   Easter Seals Northeast Ohio
Ste 124
3085 W Market St
Akron, OH 44333-3651   330-836-9741
                                            800-589-6834
                                          FAX 330-836-4967
                http://neohio.easterseals.com
            e-mail: spowers@noh.easterseals.com
Jenny Mason, Director
Susan Powers
Bryan Waugh
Easter Seals camping and recreation programs serve children, adults and families of all abilities. Various programs are available with the united purpose of giving disabled individuals a fun and safe camping or recreational experience. The following are camping and recreational services offered: Swim programs.

583   Easter Seals Youngstown
299 Edwards St
Youngstown, OH 44502-1599   330-743-1168
                                          FAX 330-743-1616
                                          TTY: 330-743-1616
                http://mtc.easterseals.com
            e-mail: matt@campascca.org
Vickie Villano, Director
Colleen Flanagan, Camp Manager
Alex Barge, Camp Director
Easter Seals camping and recreation programs serve children, adults and families of all abilities. Various programs are available with the united purpose of giving disabled individuals a fun and safe camping or recreational experience. The following are camping and recreational services offered: Recreationsl/Day care for Ages 6-12.

584   Marburn Academy Summer Programs
1860 Walden Dr
Columbus, OH 43229-3627   614-433-0822
                                          FAX 614-433-0812
                http://www.marburnacademy.org
        e-mail: marburnadmission@marburnacademy.org
Earl B Oremus, Headmaster

A four program academic day camp for children with LD and dyslexia, offering remediation in reading, math, phonemic awareness, or writing.

585   Pilgrim Hills Camp
Ohio Conference United Church of Christ
33833 Township Road 20
Brinkhaven, OH 43006   740-599-6314
                                     800-282-0740
                                   FAX 740-599-9790
                             http://www.ocucc.org
                   e-mail: campregistrar@ocucc.org
Jeff Thompson, Camp Director

Many camp programs for all children including learning disabled. Pilgrim Hills Camp is located on 375 acres of woodlands, meadows, ponds and trails. The facilities includes a large dining hall and full kitchen to feed up to 300 with full food service and menu options available.

586   Recreation Unlimited Farm and Fun
Recreation Unlimited Foundation
7700 Piper Rd
Ashley, OH 43003-9741   740-548-7006
                                   FAX 740-747-2640
                      http://www.recreationunlimited.org
                   e-mail: info@recreationunlimited.org
Jeremy James, Director

Provides year round programs in recreation, sports and education for individuals with developmental or physical disabilities. Campers build self-confidence and self-esteem while gaining positive relationships, attitudes and behaviors.

Oklahoma

587   Easter Seals Oklahoma
701 NE 13th St
Oklahoma City, OK 73104-5003   405-239-2525
                                   FAX 405-239-2278
                             http://ok.easterseals.com
                      e-mail: esok1@coxinet.net
Paula K. Porter, President
Vida Wasinger, Director of Operations
Aundria Goree, Programs Director
Easter Seals camping and recreation programs serve children, adults and families of all abilities. Various programs are available with the united purpose of giving disabled individuals a fun and safe camping or recreational experience. The following are camping and recreational services offered: Camperships.

Oregon

588   Easter Seals Medford
406 S Riverside Ave
Suite 101
Medford, OR 97501   541-842-2199
                                     800-244-5289
                                   FAX 541-842-4048
                             http://www.or.easterseals.com
                      e-mail: matt@campascca.org
J. David Cheveallier, President
Colleen Flanagan, Camp Manager
Alex Barge, Camp Director
Programs offered in Medford include summer day camp, Recreation & Respite, and the popular First Saturday dance and social event. Programs are held at various community centers in Medford.

589   Easter Seals Oregon
Easter Seals National
5757 SW Macadam Ave
Portland, OR 97239-3797   503-228-5108
                                     800-556-6020
                                   FAX 503-228-1352
                             http://www.or.easterseals.com
                      e-mail: matt@campascca.org
J. David Cheveallier, President
Colleen Flanagan, Camp Manager
Alex Barge, Camp Director
Easter Seals camping and recreation programs serve children, adults and families of all abilities. Various programs are available with the united purpose of giving disabled individuals a fun and safe camping or recreational experience. The following are camping and recreational services offered: Residential camping programs. In addition, the Portland program center hosts a warm water aquatic facility.

Pennsylvania

590   Camp Lee Mar
805 Redgate Road
Dresher, PA 19025-9612   215-658-1708
                                   FAX 215-658-1710
                             http://www.leemar.com
                      e-mail: gtour400@aol.com
Ariel Segal, Director

Private residential special needs camp for children and young adults with mild to moderate learning and developmental challenges, including but not limited to the following: mental retardation, developmental disabilities, down syndrome, autism, learning disabilities, Williams Syndrome, Asperger Syndrome, ADD, Prader Willi, and ADHD. A structured environment, individual attention and guidance are emphasized at all times.

Texas

591   Charis Hills
498 Faulkner Rd
Sunset, TX 76270-6683   940-964-2145
                                     888-681-2173
                                   FAX 940-964-2147
                             http://www.charishills.org
                      e-mail: info@charishills.org
Rand Southard, Director

Those with special learning needs have an opportunity to come to a place of acceptance. Here they meet others, both children and their counselors, who share similar experiences who are on the road to success. They have the opportunity to learn new activities in an environment that is safe, physically and socially.

Utah

592   Summer Reading Camp at Reid Ranch
2965 East 3435 South
Salt Lake City, UT 84109   801-466-4214
                                   FAX 801-466-4214
                             http://www.reidschool.com
                      e-mail: ereid@xmission.com
Dr. Mervin R Reid, President
Dr. Ethna R. Reid, Director

The camp offers daily reading and language arts programs for children and young adults. Recreational activities include horseback riding, swimming, paddle boats and canoes, mountain climbing, volleyball and other other sports.

Vermont

593   **Camp Akeela**
3 New King Street
White Plains, NY 10604   866-680-4744
                                       FAX 866-462-2828
                              http://www.campakeela.com
                              e-mail: info@campakeela.com
Eric Sasson, Director

Akeela campers thrive in a world in which they are sur-
rounded by peers with similar experiences and a staff who
understands and embraces them. Not only do they have the
time of their lives at camp, but they return home with skills
and a newfound self-confidence that they carry with them
throughout the year.

Virginia

594   **Summer PLUS Program**
Blue Ridge Autism and Achievement Center
312 Whitwell Drive
Roanoke, VA 24019   540-366-7399
                                       FAX 540-366-5523
                           http://www.achievementcenter.org
                          e-mail: braac.roanoke@gmail.com
Angela Leonard, BA Education, Executive Director
Lisa Hensley, BS Accounting, Business Manager
Patti Cook, BS Business, Administrative Director
Summer camp program for children with learning disabili-
ties and Autism. Programs put emphasis on social play and
social skill development, communication and social skills
all while targeting learning goals.

Wisconsin

595   **YMCA Camp Glacier Hollow**
Stevens Point Area YMCA
1000 Division St
Stevens Point, WI 54481-2700   715-342-2999
                                       FAX 715-342-2987
                              http://www.glacierhollow.com
                              e-mail: pmatthai@spymca.org
Pete Matthai, Camp Director

Offers a one week camp for children with learning disabilities.

Language Arts

596 Analogies 1, 2 & 3
Educators Publishing Service
PO Box 9031
Cambridge, MA 02139-9031   617-547-6706
                                   800-225-5750
                              FAX 617-547-3805
                        http://www.epsbooks.com
e-mail: CustomerService.EPS@schoolspecialty.com
Arthur Liebman, Author
Kathryn Hansen, Key Accounts Coordinator
Jeff Belanger, Regional Sales Manager
Studying analogies helps students to sharpen reasoning ability, develop critical thinking, understand relationships between words and ideas, learn new vocabulary, and prepare for the SAT's and for standardized tests.

597 AtoZap!
Sunburst Technology
1550 Executive Dr
Elgin, IL 60123-9311
                                   800-321-7511
                              FAX 888-608-0344
                        http://store.sunburst.com
                   e-mail: service@sunburst.com
Michael Guillory, Channel Sales/Marketing Manager

A whimsical world of magical talking alphabet blocks and energetic playful characters this program provides young children with exciting opportunities to explore new concepts through open-ended activities and games. Mac/Win CD-ROM

598 Basic Signing Vocabulary Cards
Harris Communications
15155 Technology Dr
Eden Prairie, MN 55344-2273   952-906-1180
                                   800-825-6758
                              FAX 952-906-1099
                        TTY: 800-825-9187
                   http://www.harriscomm.com
                   e-mail: info@harriscomm.com
Dr. Robert Harris, President
Darla Hudson, Customer Service
Lori Foss, Marketing Director
Harris Communications is the sign language superstore and sells a full line of sign language materials for children, students, teachers and interpreters. Please visit us on-line to view all of our sign language products. Catalog is also available to view on-line or sent via USPS. *$7.95*
          100 cards/set

599 Bubbleland Word Discovery
Sunburst Technology
1550 Executive Dr
Elgin, IL 60123-9311
                                   800-321-7511
                              FAX 888-608-0344
                        http://store.sunburst.com
                   e-mail: service@sunburst.com
Michael Guillory, Channel Sales/Marketing Manager

Build and sharpen language arts skills with this multimedia dictionary. Students explore ten familiar locations that include a pet shop, zoo, toy store, hospital, playground, beach and airport where they engage in 40 activities that build word recognition, pronunciation and spelling skills.

600 Carolina Picture Vocabulary Test (CPVT): For Deaf and Hearing Impaired Children
Pro-Ed
8700 Shoal Creek Blvd
Austin, TX 78757-6897   512-451-3246
                                   800-897-3202
                              FAX 800-397-7633
                        http://www.proedinc.com
                   e-mail: info@proedinc.com
Cheri Richardson, Permissions Editor
Thomas Layton, Author
David Holmes, Co-Author
A norm-referenced, validated, receptive sign vocabulary test for deaf and hearing-impaired children. *$147.00*

601 Curious George Pre-K ABCs
Sunburst Technology
1550 Executive Dr
Elgin, IL 60123-9311
                                   800-321-7511
                              FAX 888-608-0344
                        http://store.sunburst.com
                   e-mail: service@sunburst.com
Michael Guillory, Channel Sales/Marketing Manager

Children go on a lively adventure with Curious George visiting six multi level activities that provide an animated introduction to letters and their sounds. Students discover letter names and shapes, initial letter sounds, letter pronunciations, the order of the alphabet and new vocabulary words during the fun exursions with Curious George. Mac/Win CD-ROM

602 Early Communication Skills for Childrenwith Down Syndrome
Therapro
225 Arlington St
Framingham, MA 01702-8773   508-872-9494
                                   800-257-5376
                              FAX 508-875-2062
                        http://www.theraproducts.com
                   e-mail: info@theraproducts.com
Libby Kumin PhD, Author
Karen Conrad, President

Provides professional expertise in understandable terms. Parents and professionals learn how their skills are evaulated by professionals, and what activities they can practice with a child immediately to encouarge a childs's communication skill development. *$19.95*
          368 pages

603 Early Listening Skills
Therapro
225 Arlington St
Framingham, MA 01702-8773   508-872-9494
                                   800-257-5376
                              FAX 508-875-2062
                        http://www.theraproducts.com
                   e-mail: info@theraproducts.com
Diana Williams, Author
Karen Conrad, President

Two hundred activities designed to be photocopied for classroom or home. Includes materials on auditory detection, discrimination, recognition, sequencing and memory. Describes listening projects and topics for the curriculum. Activity sheets for parents are included. A practical, comprehensive and effective manual for professionals working with preschool children or the older child with special needs. *$63.50*

604 Earobics Step 2: Home Version
Abilitations Speech Bin
PO Box 1579
Appleton, WI 54912-1579

888-388-3224
FAX 888-388-6344
http://www.speechbin.com
e-mail: customercare@schoolspecialty.com
Michael P. Lavelle, President, CEO
Rick Holden, Executive Vice President
Gerald T. Hughes, Executive Vice Presiden, CFO
Step 2 teaches critical language comprehension skills and trains the critical auditory skills children need for success in learning. It offers hundreds of levels of play, appealing graphics, and entertaining music to train the critical auditory skills young children need for success in learning. Item number C483. *$58.99*

605 Earobics Step 2: Specialist/Clinician Version
Abilitations Speech Bin
PO Box 1579
Appleton, WI 54912-1579

888-388-3224
FAX 888-388-6344
http://www.speechbin.com
e-mail: customercare@schoolspecialty.com
Michael P. Lavelle, President, CEO
Rick Holden, Executive Vice President
Gerald T. Hughes, Executive Vice President
Earobics features: tasks and level counter with real time display; adaptive training technology for individualized programs; and reporting to track and evaluate each individual's progress. Step 2 teaches critical language comprehension skills and trains the critical auditory skills children need for success in learning. Item number C484. *$298.99*

606 Every Child a Reader
Sunburst Technology
1550 Executive Dr
Elgin, IL 60123-9311

800-321-7511
FAX 888-608-0344
http://store.sunburst.com
e-mail: service@sunburst.com
Michael Guillory, Channel Sales/Marketing Manager

Traditional reading strategies in a rich literary context. Designed to promote independent reading and develop oral and written language expression.

607 Explode the Code: Wall Chart
Educators Publishing Service
PO Box 9031
Cambridge, MA 02139-9031

617-547-6706
800-225-5750
FAX 617-547-3805
http://www.epsbooks.com
e-mail: CustomerService.EPS@schoolspecialty.com
Nancy M Hall, Author
Kathryn Hansen, Key Accounts Coordinator
Jeff Belanger, Regional Sales Manager
Learning sounds is exciting with the new Explode The Code alphabet chart! Each letter is represented by a colorful character from the series and is stored inside a felt pocket embroidered with the letter's name.

608 First Phonics
Sunburst Technology
1550 Executive Dr
Elgin, IL 60123-9311

800-321-7511
FAX 888-608-0344
http://store.sunburst.com
e-mail: service@sunburst.com
Michael Guillory, Channel Sales/Marketing Manager

Targets the phonics skills that all children need to develop, sounding out the first letter of a word. This program offers four different engaging activities that you can customize to match each child's specific need.

609 Fun with Language: Book 1
Therapro
225 Arlington St
Framingham, MA 01702-8773

508-872-9494
800-257-5376
FAX 508-875-2062
http://www.theraproducts.com
e-mail: info@theraproducts.com
Kathleen Yardley, Author
Karen Conrad, President

A wonderful reproducible workbook of thinking and language skill exercises for children ages 4-8. Perfect when you need something on a moment's notice. Over 100 beautifully illustrated exercises in the following categories: Spatial Relationships; Opposites; Categorizing; Following Directions; Temporal Concepts; Syntax & Morphology; Same and Different; Plurals; Memory; Reasoning; Storytelling; and Describing. Targets both receptive and expressive language as well as problem- solving skills. *$59.50*

610 Goldman-Fristoe Test of Articulation: 2nd Edition
Abilitations Speech Bin
PO Box 1579
Appleton, WI 54912-1579

888-388-3224
FAX 888-388-6344
http://www.speechbin.com
e-mail: customercare@schoolspecialty.com
Michael P. Lavelle, President, CEO
Ronald Goldman, Author
Macalyne Fristoe, Co-Author
It systematically measures a child's production of 39 consonant sounds and blends. Its age range is 2-21 years, and age based standard scores have separate gender norms. In this revised edition, inappropriate stimulus words have been replaced based on multicultural review, and all new artwork is featured. Item number 190915116. *$229.99*

611 HearFones
Abilitations Speech Bin
PO Box 1579
Appleton, WI 54912-1579

888-388-3224
FAX 888-388-6344
http://www.speechbin.com
e-mail: customercare@schoolspecialty.com
Michael P. Lavelle, President, CEO
Rick Holden, Executive Vice President

This unique nonelectronic self-contained headset is made of composite and plastic materials, and it's easy to clean. It lets users hear themselves more directly and clearly so they can analyze their own speech sound production and voice quality. Item number N261. *$28.99*

612 I Can Say R
Abilitations Speech Bin
PO Box 1579
Appleton, WI 54912-1579

888-388-3224
FAX 888-388-6344
http://www.speechbin.com
e-mail: customercare@schoolspecialty.com
Michael P. Lavelle, President, CEO
Rick Holden, Executive Vice President

Helping children overcome problems saying R sounds is one of the most perplexing dilemmas speech and language pathologists face in their caseloads. Here's a terrific book packed with innovative practice materials to make that task easier. Item number 190728116. *$26.99*

613 Idiom's Delight
Academic Therapy Publications
20 Commercial Blvd
Novato, CA 94949-6120

415-883-3314
800-422-7249
FAX 888-287-9975
http://www.academictherapy.com
e-mail: sales@academictherapy.com

Jim Arena, President
Joanne Urban, Manager
Cynthia Coverston
Offers 75 idioms and accompanying reproducible activities. Delightful illustrations portraying humorous literal interpretations of idioms are sprinkled throughout the book to enhance enjoyment. *$14.00*
64 pages
ISBN 0-878798-89-7

614 Island Reading Journey
Sunburst Technology
1550 Executive Dr
Elgin, IL 60123-9311

800-321-7511
FAX 888-608-0344
http://store.sunburst.com
e-mail: service@sunburst.com

Michael Guillory, Channel Sales/Marketing Manager

Enhance your reading program with meaningful summary and extension activities for 100 intermediate level books. Students read for meaning while they engage in activities that test for comprehension, build writing skills with reader response and essay questions, develop usage skills with cloze activities and improve vocabulary/word attack skills.

615 Kaufman Speech Praxis Test
Abilitations Speech Bin
PO Box 1579
Appleton, WI 54912-1579

888-388-3224
FAX 888-388-6344
http://www.speechbin.com
e-mail: customercare@schoolspecialty.com

Nancy R. Kaufman, Author
Michael P. Lavelle, President, CEO
Rick Holden, Executive Vice President
This standardized test utllizes a hierarchy of simple to complex motor-speech movements, from oral movement and simple phonemic/syllable to complex phonemic/syllable level. The complete kit contains manual, guide, and 25 test booklets. Item number 192126116. *$185.00*

616 LILAC
Abilitations Speech Bin
PO Box 1579
Appleton, WI 54912-1579

888-388-3224
FAX 888-388-6344
http://www.speechbin.com
e-mail: customercare@schoolspecialty.com

Michael P. Lavelle, President, CEO
Rick Holden, Executive Vice President
Gerald T. Hughes, Executive Vice President
LILAC uses direct and naturalistic teaching in a creative approach that links spoken language learning to reading and writing. Activities to develop semantic, syntactic, expressive, and receptive language skills are presented sequentially from three-to five-year-old developmental levels. Item number 190825116. *$27.99*

617 Language Activity Resource Kit: LARK
Abilitations Speech Bin
PO Box 1579
Appleton, WI 54912-1579

888-388-3224
FAX 888-388-6344
http://www.speechbin.com
e-mail: customercare@schoolspecialty.com

Michael P. Lavelle, President, CEO
Richard A Dressler, Author
Gerald T. Hughes, Executive Vice President
The LARK: Language Activity Resource Kit has been revised! This perennially popular language kit is now more portable and versatile for use with persons who have moderate to severe language disorders. Item number 190613116. *$217.99*

618 Max's Attic: Long & Short Vowels
Sunburst Technology
1550 Executive Dr
Elgin, IL 60123-9311

800-321-7511
FAX 888-608-0344
http://store.sunburst.com
e-mail: service@sunburst.com

Michael Guillory, Channel Sales/Marketing Manager

Filled to the rafters with phonics fun, this animated program builds your students' vowel recognition skills.

619 Pair-It Books: Early Emergent Stage 2
Houghton Mifflin Harcourt
6277 Sea Harbor Dr
5th Floor
Orlando, FL 32887

800-531-5015
FAX 800-699-9459
http://www.harcourtachieve.com
e-mail: greatservice@hmhpub.com

Michael Opitz, Author
Linda K. Zecher, President and CEO
Eric Shuman, Chief Financial Officer
John K. Dragoon, EVP
A series of 20 books, each containing 16 pages, that gradually become more difficult and reflect more complex text structures such as dialogue, content vocabulary and question and answer formats. All stories are available on audio cassette, and four are available in big book format.

620 PhonicsMart CD-ROM
HMH Supplemental Publishers
5th Floor
6277 Sea Harbor Dr
Orlando, FL 32887

800-531-5015
FAX 800-699-9459
http://www.harcourtachieve.com
e-mail: greatservice@hmhpub.com

Linda K. Zecher, President and CEO
Eric Shuman, Chief Financial Officer
John K. Dragoon, EVP
Five interactive games offer practice and reinforcement in 19 phonics skills at a variety of learning levels! Over 700 key words are vocalized, and each is accompanied by sound effects, colorful illustrations, animation, or video clips!

621 Polar Express
Sunburst Technology
1550 Executive Dr
Elgin, IL 60123-9311

800-321-7511
FAX 888-608-0344
http://store.sunburst.com
e-mail: service@sunburst.com

Michael Guillory, Channel Sales/Marketing Manager

Share the magic and enchantment of the holiday season with this CD-ROM version of Chris Van Allsburg's Caldecott-winning picture book.

622 Python Path Phonics Word Families
Sunburst Technology
1550 Executive Dr
Elgin, IL 60123-9311

800-321-7511
FAX 888-608-0344
http://store.sunburst.com
e-mail: service@sunburst.com
Michael Guillory, Channel Sales/Marketing Manager

Your students improve their word-building skills by playing three fun strategy games that involve linking one-or two-letter consonant beginnings to basic word endings.

623 Ridgewood Grammar
Educators Publishing Service
PO Box 9031
Cambridge, MA 02139-9031

617-547-6706
800-225-5750
FAX 617-547-3805
http://www.epsbooks.com
e-mail: CustomerService.EPS@schoolspecialty.com
Terri Wiss, Author
Nancy Bison, Co-Author
Kathryn Hansen, Key Accounts Coordinator
Grammar is an important part of any student's education. This new series, from the school district that developed the popular Ridgewood Analogies books, teaches 3rd, 4th, and 5th graders about the parts of speech and their use in sentences.

624 Sequential Spelling 1-7 with Student Respose Book
AVKO Educational Research Foundation
3084 Willard Rd
Birch Run, MI 48415-9404

810-686-9283
866-285-6612
FAX 810-686-1101
http://www.avko.org
e-mail: webmaster@avko.org
Don McCabe, Research Director/Author
Barry Chute, President
Julie Guyette, Vice President
Sequential Spelling uses immediate student self-correction. It builds from easier words of a word family such as all and then builds on them to teach; all, tall, stall, install, call, fall, ball, and their inflected forms such as: stalls, stalled, stalling, installing, installment. *$89.95*
  72 pages
  ISBN 1-664003-00-0

625 Soaring Scores CTB: TerraNova Reading and Language Arts
HMH Supplemental Publishers
5th Floor
6277 Sea Harbor Dr
Orlando, FL 32887

800-531-5015
FAX 800-699-9459
http://www.harcourtachieve.com
e-mail: greatservice@hmhpub.com
Linda K. Zecher, President and CEO
Eric Shuman, Chief Financial Officer
John K. Dragoon, EVP
Through a combination of targeted instructional practice and test-taking tips, these workbooks help students build better skills and improve CTB-TerraNova test scores. Initial lessons address reading comprehension and language arts. The authentic practice test mirrors the CTB's format and content.

626 Soaring Scores in Integrated Language Arts
HMH Supplemental Publishers
5th Floor
6277 Sea Harbor Dr
Orlando, FL 32877

800-531-5015
FAX 800-699-9459
http://www.harcourtachieve.com
e-mail: greatservice@hmhpub.com
Linda K. Zecher, President and CEO
Eric Shuman, Chief Financial Officer
John K. Dragoon, EVP
Help your students develop the right skills and strategies for success on integrated arts assessments. Soaring Scores presents three sets of two lengthy, thematically linked literature selections. Students develop higher-order thinking skills as they respond to open-ended questions about the selections.

627 Soaring Scores on the CMT in Language Arts& on the CAPT in Reading and Writing Across Disciplines
HMH Supplemental Publishers
5th Floor
6277 Sea Harbor Dr
Orlando, FL 32887

800-531-5015
FAX 800-699-9459
http://www.harcourtachieve.com
e-mail: greatservice@hmhpub.com
Linda K. Zecher, President and CEO
Eric Shuman, Chief Financial Officer
John K. Dragoon, EVP
Make every minute count when you are preparing for the CMT or CAPT. Fine tune your language arts test preparation with the program developed specifically for the Connecticut's assessments. Questions are correlated to Connecticut's content standards for reading and responding, producing text, applying English language conventions, and exploring and responding to texts.

628 Soaring Scores on the NYS English Language Arts Assessment
HMH Supplemental Publishers
5th Floor
6277 Sea Harbor Dr
Orlando, FL 32887

800-531-5015
FAX 800-699-9459
http://www.harcourtachieve.com
e-mail: greatservice@hmhpub.com
Linda K. Zecher, President and CEO
Eric Shuman, Chief Financial Officer
John K. Dragoon, EVP
With these workbooks, students receive instructional practice for approaching the assessment's reading, listening and writing questions.

629 Soaring on the MCAS in English Language Arts
HMH Supplemental Publishers
5th Floor
6277 Sea Harbor Dr
Orlando, FL 32887

800-531-5015
FAX 800-699-9459
http://www.harcourtachieve.com
e-mail: greatservice@hmhpub.com
Linda K. Zecher, President and CEO
Eric Shuman, Chief Financial Officer
John K. Dragoon, EVP
Instructional practice in the first section builds skills for the MCAS language, literacy, and composition questions. A practice test models the MCAS precisely in design and length.

630 Spelling: A Thematic Content-Area Approach
HMH Supplemental Publishers
5th Floor
6277 Sea Harbor Dr
Orlando, FL 32887

800-531-5015
FAX 800-699-9459
http://www.harcourtachieve.com
e-mail: greatservice@hmhpub.com
Linda K. Zecher, President and CEO
Eric Shuman, Chief Financial Officer
John K. Dragoon, EVP
Help students master the words they will use most frequently
in the classroom. Organized lessons incorporate word analysis of letter patterns, correlations to appropriate literature,
writing exercises, and application and extension activities.

631 Stories and More: Time and Place
Riverdeep, Inc.
100 Pine Street
Suite 1900
San Francisco, CA 94111-5205

415-659-2000
FAX 415-659-2020
http://http://web.riverdeep.net
e-mail: info@riverdeep.net
Barry O'Callaghan, Executive Chairman/CEO

Combines three well-loved stories - The House on Maple
Street, Roxaboxen, and Galimoto with engaging activities
that strengthen students' reading comprehension.

632 Sunken Treasure Adventure: Beginning Blends
Sunburst Technology
1550 Executive Dr
Elgin, IL 60123-9311

800-321-7511
FAX 888-608-0344
http://store.sunburst.com
e-mail: service@sunburst.com
Michael Guillory, Channel Sales/Marketing Manager

Focus on beginning blends sounds and concepts with three
high-spirited games that invite students to use two letter consonant blends as they build words.

633 Teaching Phonics: Staff Development Book
HMH Supplemental Publishers
5th Floor
6277 Sea Harbor Dr
Orlando, FL 32887

800-531-5015
FAX 800-699-9459
http://www.harcourtachieve.com
e-mail: greatservice@hmhpub.com
Linda K. Zecher, President and CEO
Eric Shuman, Chief Financial Officer
John K. Dragoon, EVP
Fine-tune your instructional approach with fresh insights
from phonics experts. This resource offers informative articles and timely tips for teaching phonics in the integrated
language arts classroom.

634 Test of Early Language Development
Pro-Ed, Inc.
8700 Shoal Creek Blvd
Austin, TX 78757-6897

512-451-3246
800-897-3202
FAX 800-397-7633
http://www.proedinc.com
e-mail: info@proedinc.com
Wayne Hresko, Author
D Kim Reid, Co-Author
Don Hammill, Co-Author

A normed test appropriate for children 0-2 through 7-11. It
quickly and easily measures Receptive and Expressive language and yields an overall Spoken Language Score.
$295.00

635 Vocabulary Connections
HMH Supplemental Publishers
5th Floor
6277 Sea Harbor Dr
Orlando, FL 32887

800-531-5015
FAX 800-699-9459
http://www.harcourtachieve.com
e-mail: greatservice@hmhpub.com
Linda K. Zecher, President and CEO
Eric Shuman, Chief Financial Officer
John K. Dragoon, EVP
Keep students engaged in building vocabulary through
crossword puzzles and cloze passages, and by using words in
context and making analogies. Lessons build around thematically organized literature and nonfiction selections provide
meaningful context for essential vocabulary words.

636 Workbook for Aphasia
Wayne State University Press
4809 Woodward Ave
Detroit, MI 48201-1309

313-577-6120
800-978-7323
FAX 313-577-6131
http://www.wsupress.wayne.edu
e-mail: bookorders@wayne.edu
Susan Howell Brubaker, Author

This book gives you materials for adults who have recovered
a significant degree of speaking, reading, writing, and comprehension skills. It includes 106 excercises divided into
eight target areas. *$65.00*
500 pages

637 Workbook for Language Skills
Wayne State University Press
4809 Woodward Ave
Detroit, MI 48201-1309

313-577-6120
800-978-7323
FAX 313-577-6131
http://wsupress.wayne.edu
e-mail: bookorders@wayne.edu
Susan Howell Brubaker, Author

This workbook features 68 real-world exercises designed for
use with mildly to severely cognitive and language-impaired
individuals. The workbook is divided in seven target areas:
Sentence Completion; General Knowledge; Word Recall;
Figurative Language; Sentence Comprehension; Sentence
Construction and Spelling. *$50.00*
288 pages

Life Skills

638 Activities for the Elementary Classroom
Curriculum Associates
153 Rangeway Rd
North Billerica, MA 01862-2013

978-667-8000
800-225-0248
FAX 800-366-1158
http://www.curriculumassociates.com
e-mail: cainfo@curriculumassociates.com
Ernest L Kern, Editor
Robert Waldron, President and CEO
Dave Caron, Chief Financial Officer
Challenge your students to make a hole in a 3x5 index card
large enough to poke their heads through. Or offer to pour
them a glass of air. You'll have their attenion — the first step
toward learning — when you use the high-interest, hands-on
activities in these exciting teacher resource books.

639   **Activities of Daily Living: A Manual of Group Activities and Written Exercises**
Therapro
225 Arlington St
Framingham, MA 01702-8773   508-872-9494
                                    800-257-5376
                              FAX 508-875-2062
                        http://www.theraproducts.com
                        e-mail: info@theraproducts.com
Karen McCarthy COTA, Author
Karen Conrad, President

Designed to provide group leaders easy access to structured plans for Activities of Daily Living (ADL) Groups. Organized into five modules: Personal Hygiene; Laundry Skills; Money Management; Leisure Skills and Nutrition. Each includes introduction, assessment guidelines, worksheets to copy, suggested board work, and wrap-up discussions. Appropriate for adult or adolescent programs, school systems and programs for the learning disabled. *$25.00*
136 pages

640   **Aids and Appliances for Independent Living**
Maxi-Aids
42 Executive Blvd
Farmingdale, NY 11735-4710   631-752-0521
                                     800-522-6294
                              FAX 631-752-0689
                              TTY: 631-752-0738
                        http://www.maxiaids.com
Elliot Zaretsky, President

Thousands of products to make life easier. Eating, dressing, communications, bed, bath, kitchen, writing aids and more.

641   **Changes Around Us CD-ROM**
5th Floor
6277 Sea Harbor Dr
Orlando, FL 32887
                                     800-531-5015
                              FAX 800-699-9459
                        http://www.harcourtachieve.com
                        e-mail: greatservice@hmhpub.com
Linda K. Zecher, President and CEO
Eric Shuman, Chief Financial Officer
John K. Dragoon, EVP
Nature is the natural choice for observing change. By observing and researching dramatic visual sequences such as the stages of development of a butterfly, children develop a broad understanding of the concept of change. As they search this multimedia database for images and information about plant and animal life cycles and seasonal change, students strengthen their abilities in research, analysis, problem-solving, critical thinking and communication.

642   **Classroom Visual Activities**
Therapro
225 Arlington St
Framingham, MA 01702-8773   508-872-9494
                                    800-257-5376
                              FAX 508-875-2062
                        http://www.theraproducts.com
                        e-mail: info@theraproducts.com
Regina G Richards MA, Author
Karen Conrad, President

This work presents a wealth of activities for the development of visual skills in the areas of pursuit, scanning, aligning, and locating movements; eye hand coordination, and fixation activity. Each activity lists objectives and criteria for success and gives detailed instuctions. *$15.00*
80 pages

643   **Cognitive Strategy Instruction for Middleand High Schools**
Brookline Books
PO Box 1209
Brookline, MA 02446   617-734-6772
                              800-666-2665
                        FAX 617-734-3952
                  http://www.brooklinebooks.com
                  e-mail: brbooks@yahoo.com
Eileen Wood, Editor
Vera E Woloshyn, Editor
Teena Willoughby, Editor
Presents cognitive strategies empirically validated for middle and high school students, with an emphasis for teachers on how to teach and support the strategies. *$26.95*
286 pages
ISBN 1-571290-07-9

644   **Fine Motor Activities Guide and Easel Activities Guide**
Therapro
225 Arlington St
Framingham, MA 01702-8773   508-872-9494
                                    800-257-5376
                              FAX 508-875-2062
                        http://www.theraproducts.com
                        e-mail: info@theraproducts.com
Jayne Berry OTR, Author
Carol Ann Meyers OTR, Co-Author
Karen Conrad, President
Useful for activity plans or teacher-educator-parent consultations. Perfect hand-outs as part of your inservice packet (no need to write out ideas, photocopy materials, etc). Package of 10 booklets. *$19.00*

645   **Finger Frolics: Fingerplays**
Therapro
225 Arlington St
Framingham, MA 01702-8773   508-872-9494
                                    800-257-5376
                              FAX 508-875-2062
                        http://www.theraproducts.com
                        e-mail: info@theraproducts.com
Liz Cromwell, Author
Dixie Hibner, Co-Author
John Faitel, Editor
Invaluable for occupational therapists, speech/language pathologists and teachers. Over 350 light and humorous fingerplays help children with rhyming and performing actions which develop fine motor and language skills. *$13.25*

646   **Hands-On Activities for Exceptional Students**
Sage/Corwin Press
2455 Teller Rd
Thousand Oaks, CA 91320-2218   805-499-9734
                                       800-233-9936
                                 FAX 805-499-5323
                           http://www.corwinpress.com
                           e-mail: order@corwin.com
Mike Soules, President
Beverly Thorne, Author
Lisa Shaw, Executive Director Editorial
This execptional new release is developed for educators of students who have cognitive delays who will eventually work in a sheltered employment environment. If you need new ideas at your fingertips, this practical book is for you. *$25.95*
112 pages Special Ed
ISBN 1-890455-31-8

647   **Health**
HMH Supplemental Publishers
5th Floor
6277 Sea Harbor Dr
Orlando, FL 32887
                                     800-531-5015
                              FAX 800-699-9459
                        http://steckvaughn.harcourtachieve.com
                        e-mail: greatservice@hmhpub.com

Linda K. Zecher, President and CEO
Eric Shuman, Chief Financial Officer
John K. Dragoon, EVP
Lessons and projects focus on nutrition, outdoor safety, smart choices, and exercise. Designed to make children more health conscious. Activity formats include fill in the blank, word puzzles, multiple choice, crosswords, and more.

648   Life-Centered Career Education Training
Council for Exceptional Children
2900 Crystal Drive
Ste 1000
Arlington, VA 22202-3557   703-620-3660
                                      888-232-7733
                                 FAX 703-264-9494
                                 TDD:866-915-5000
                                 TTY: 866-915-5000
                           http://www.cec.sped.org
                           e-mail: service@cec.sped.org
Bruce A. Ramirez, Executive Director
Margaret J. McLaughlin, President
Christy A. Chambers, President Elect
LCCE teaches you to prepare students to function independently and productively as family members, citizens, and workers, and to enjoy fulfilling personal lives. LCCE is a motivating and effective classroom, home, and community-based curriculum.

649   MORE: Integrating the Mouth with Sensory & Postural Functions
Therapro
225 Arlington St
Framingham, MA 01702-8773   508-872-9494
                                      800-257-5376
                                 FAX 508-875-2062
                           http://www.theraproducts.com
                           e-mail: info@theraproducts.com
Patricia Oetter OTR, Author
Eileen Richter OTR, Co-Author
Karen Conrad, President
MORE is an acronym for Motor components, Oral organization, Respiratory demands and Eye contact and control; elements of toys and items that can be used to facilitate integration of the mouth with sensory and postural development, as well as self-regulation and attention. A theoretical framework for the treatment of both sensorimotor and speech/language problems is presented, methods for evaluating therapeutic potential of motor toys, and activities designed to improve functions. *$49.95*

650   Memory Workbook
Therapro
225 Arlington St
Framingham, MA 01702-8773   508-872-9494
                                      800-257-5376
                                 FAX 508-875-2062
                           http://www.theraproducts.com
                           e-mail: info@theraproducts.com
Karen Conrad, President
Kathleen Anderson, Author
Pamela Crow Miller, Co-Author
Recalling daily activities, seasons, months of the year, shapes, words and pictures. *$12.50*

651   One-Handed in a Two-Handed World
Therapro
225 Arlington St
Framingham, MA 01702-8773   508-872-9494
                                      800-257-5376
                                 FAX 508-875-2062
                           http://www.theraproducts.com
                           e-mail: info@theraproducts.com
Tommye K Mayer, Author
Karen Conrad, President

A personal guide to managing single handed. Written by a woman who has lived one-handed for many years, this book shares a methodology and mindset necessary for managing. It details a wide array of topics including personal care, daily chores, office work, traveling, sports, relationships and many more. A must for patients and therapists. *$19.95*
    250 pages

652   People at Work
Pearson AGS Globe
PO Box 2500
Lebanon, IN 46052-3009
                                      800-992-0244
                                 FAX 877-260-2530
                           http://www.pearsonschool.com
Marjorie Scardino, CEO
Victor Coira, Sales Representative
Victoria Ramos, Digital Sales Rep
With an interest level of High School through Adult, ABE and ESL and a reading level of Grades 3-4, this program is a simple, thorough teaching plan for every day of the school year. The program's 180 sessions are divided into eighteen study units that each survey an entire occupational cluster of eight jobs while focusing on one or two writing skills. *$26.95*

653   Responding to Oral Directions
Pro-Ed
8700 Shoal Creek Blvd
Austin, TX 78757-6897   512-451-3246
                                      800-897-3202
                                 FAX 800-397-7633
                           http://www.proedinc.com
                           e-mail: info@proedinc.com
Robert A Mancuso, Author

Help children of all ages who function at first through sixth-grade levels learn to identify unclear directions and ask for clarification. Nine units teach them how to handle: recognizing directions, carryover and generalization; unreasonable, distorted, vague, unfamiliar, lenngthy, unknown, and mixed directions. Item number 190575116. *$59.00*

654   So What Can I Do?
Therapro
225 Arlington St
Framingham, MA 01702-8773   508-872-9494
                                      800-257-5376
                                 FAX 508-875-2062
                           http://www.theraproducts.com
                           e-mail: info@theraproducts.com
Gail Kushnir, Author
Karen Conrad, President

A book to help children develop their own solutions to everyday problems. Cartoon illustrations feature common situations for children to analyze. The adult asks the child, so what can you do? The child is then encouraged to think of creative solutions, developing their emotional intelligence and improving coping skills. 58 problems to solve. *$10.95*

655   Special Needs Program
Dallas Metro Care
1380 River Bend Drive
Dallas, TX 75247   214-743-1200
                                      877-283-2121
                                 FAX 214-630-3469
                           http://www.metrocareservices.org
                           e-mail: metrocare@metrocareservices.org
Cecilia Castillo, Director
John Gorman, Supervisor
Cary Thomas, Manager
The special needs curriculum teaches students with disabilities the life skills they need to achieve self-sufficiency. The program focuses on and enhances coping skills.

656 Stepwise Cookbooks

Therapro
225 Arlington St
Framingham, MA 01702-8773

508-872-9494
800-257-5376
FAX 508-875-2062
http://www.theraproducts.com
e-mail: info@theraproducts.com

Beth Jackson, Author
Karen Conrad, President

A chance for children and adults at all developmental levels to participate in fun-filled hands-on cooking activities while developing independence. These cookbooks were developed by an OT working with children and teenagers with cognitive and physical challenges. Only one direction is presented on a page to reduce confusion. Recipes are represented by large Boardmaker symbols from Mayer Johnson. Large, easy-to-read text with dividing lines for visual clarity. *$52.50*

657 Strategies for Problem-Solving

Houghton Mifflin Harcourt
6277 Sea Harbor Dr
5th Floor
Orlando, FL 32887

800-531-5015
FAX 800-699-9459
http://steckvaughn.harcourtachieve.com
e-mail: greatservice@hmhpub.com

Arnold Yellin, Author
Linda K. Zecher, President and CEO
Eric Shuman, Chief Financial Officer
Show students more than one way to approach a problem, and you hand them the key to effective problem solving. These reproducible activities build math reasoning and critical thinking skills, reinforce core concepts, and reduce math anxiety too. *$11.99*

658 Survey of Teenage Readiness and Neurodevelopmental Status

Educators Publishing Service
PO Box 9031
Cambridge, MA 02139-9031

617-547-6706
800-225-5750
FAX 617-547-3805
http://www.epsbooks.com
e-mail: CustomerService.EPS@schoolspecialty.com

Melvin D Levine MD FAAP, Author
Stephen R. Hooper, Ph.D., Co-Author
Kathryn Hansen, Key Accounts Coordinator
Developed by Dr. Mel Livine and Dr.Stephen Hooper, The Survey of Teenage Readiness and Neurodevelopmental Status capitalizes on adolescents' evolving metacognitive abilities by directly asking them for their perceptions of how they are functioning in school and how they process information across a variety of neurocognitive and psychosocial domains.

659 Swallow Right 2nd Edition

Therapro
225 Arlington St
Framingham, MA 01702-8773

508-872-9494
800-257-5376
FAX 508-875-2062
http://www.theraproducts.com
e-mail: info@theraproducts.com

Roberta B Pierce, Author
Karen Conrad, President

This 12-session program evaluates and treats oral myofunctional disorders. 40 reproducible sequential exercises train individuals from five years to adult how to swallow correctly. Easy-to-use evaluation and tracking forms, checklist, and carryover strategies make this book a real time-saver! Item number Q858. *$55.00*

660 Target Spelling

Houghton Mifflin Harcourt
6277 Sea Harbor Dr
5th Floor
Orlando, FL 32887

800-531-5015
FAX 800-699-9459
http://steckvaughn.harcourtachieve.com
e-mail: greatservice@hmhpub.com

Linda K. Zecher, President and CEO
Eric Shuman, Chief Financial Officer
John K. Dragoon, EVP
You can differentiate instructions to address a variety of learning styles and profiles and meet the needs of special education students.

661 Teaching Dressing Skills: Buttons, Bowsand More

Therapro
225 Arlington St
Framingham, MA 01702-8773

508-872-9494
800-257-5376
FAX 508-875-2062
http://www.theraproducts.com
e-mail: info@theraproducts.com

Marcy Coppelman Goldsmith, Author
Karen Conrad, President

Consists of 5 fold-out pamphlets for teaching children and adults of varying abilities the basic dressing skills: shoe tying, buttoning, zippering, dressing and undressing. Each task is broken down with every step clearly illustrated and specific verbal directions given to avoid confusion and to eliminate excess verbiage that can distract the learner. The author, an experienced OT, has included the needed prerequisites for each task, many great teaching tips and more. *$10.50*

5 Pamphlets

662 ThemeWeavers: Animals Activity Kit

Riverdeep
222 Berkeley Street
Boston, MA 02116

617-351-5000
888-242-6747
FAX 877-892-9820
http://www.riverdeep.net
e-mail: IIEcustomerservice@hmhpub.com

Linda K. Zecher, President and CEO
Eric Shuman, Chief Financial Officer
John K. Dragoon, EVP
ThemeWeavers: Animals is the essential companion for theme-based teaching. Dozens of animal-themed, interactive activities immediately engage your students to practice fundamental skills in math, language arts, science, social studies and more. Easy-to-use tools allow you to modify these activities or create your own to meet specific classroom needs.

663 ThemeWeavers: Nature Activity Kit

Riverdeep
222 Berkeley Street
Boston, MA 02116

617-351-5000
888-242-6747
FAX 877-892-9820
http://www.riverdeep.net
e-mail: IIEcustomerservice@hmhpub.com

Linda K. Zecher, President and CEO
Eric Shuman, Chief Financial Officer
John K. Dragoon, EVP
ThemeWeavers: Nature Activity Kit is an all-in-one solution for theme-based teaching. In just a few minutes, you can select from dozens of ready-to-use activities centering on the seasons and weather and be ready for the next day's lesson! Interactive and engaging activities cover multiple subject areas such as language arts, math, science, social studies and art.

664 Thinkin' Science ZAP
Riverdeep
222 Berkeley Street
Boston, MA 02116

617-351-5000
888-242-6747
FAX 877-892-9820
http://www.riverdeep.net
e-mail: IIEcustomerservice@hmhpub.com
Linda K. Zecher, President and CEO
Eric Shuman, Chief Financial Officer
John K. Dragoon, EVP
It is a dark and stormy night as you step backstage to be guest director at the Wonder Dome, the world-famous auditorium of light, sound, and electricity. But great zotz! The Theater has been zapped by lightning, and the Laser Control System is on the fritz! Can you learn all about light, sound and electricity to rescue the show? *$69.95*

665 Time: Concepts & Problem-Solving
Houghton Mifflin Harcourt
6277 Sea Harbor Dr
5th Floor
Orlando, FL 32887

800-531-5015
FAX 800-699-9459
http://steckvaughn.harcourtachieve.com
e-mail: greatservice@hmhpub.com
Linda K. Zecher, President and CEO
Eric Shuman, Chief Financial Officer
John K. Dragoon, EVP
Develop concepts of telling time, identifying intervals, calculating elapsed time, and solving problems that deal with time changes, lapses, and changes over the AM/PM cusp.

666 Travel the World with Timmy Deluxe
Riverdeep
222 Berkeley Street
Boston, MA 02116

617-351-5000
888-242-6747
FAX 877-892-9820
http://www.riverdeep.net
e-mail: IIEcustomerservice@hmhpub.com
Linda K. Zecher, President and CEO
Eric Shuman, Chief Financial Officer
John K. Dragoon, EVP
France and Russia are the newest destinations for Edmark's favorite world traveler, Timmy! In this delightful and improved program, students will enjoy expanding their understanding of the world around them. With wonderful stories, songs, games, and printable crafts, early learners discover how their international neighbors live, dress, sing, eat and play.

667 Workbook for Reasoning Skills
Wayne State University Press
4809 Woodward Ave
Detroit, MI 48201-1309

313-577-6120
800-978-7323
FAX 313-577-6131
http://wsupress.wayne.edu
e-mail: bookorders@wayne.edu
Susan Howell Brubaker, Author

This workbook is designed for adults and children who need practice in reasoning, thinking, and organizing. Includes 67 exercises created for individuals with closed head injuries and mild to moderate cognitive deficits. Item number W332. *$60.00*
328 pages

Math

668 Algebra Stars
Sunburst Technology
1550 Executive Dr
Elgin, IL 60123-9311

800-321-7511
FAX 888-608-0344
http://store.sunburst.com
e-mail: service@sunburst.com
Michael Guillory, Channel Sales/Marketing Manager

Students build their understanding of algebra by constructing, categorizing, and solving equations and classifying polynomial expressions using algebra tiles.

669 Attack Math
Educators Publishing Service
PO Box 9031
Cambridge, MA 02139-9031

617-547-6706
800-225-5750
FAX 617-547-3805
http://www.epsbooks.com
e-mail: CustomerService.EPS@schoolspecialty.com
Carole Greenes, Author
George Immerzeel, Co-Author
Linda Schulman, Co-Author
This series, for grades 1-6, teaches the four arithmetic operations: addition, subtraction, multiplication and division. Each operation is covered in three books, with book one teaching the basic facts and books two and three teaching multi-digit computation with whole numbers. A checkpoint and testpoint monitor progress at the middle and end of each book.

670 Awesome Animated Monster Maker Math
Sunburst Technology
1550 Executive Dr
Elgin, IL 60123-9311

800-321-7511
FAX 888-608-0344
http://store.sunburst.com
e-mail: service@sunburst.com
Michael Guillory, Channel Sales/Marketing Manager

With an emphasis on building core math skills, this humorous program incorporates the monstrous and the ridiculous into a structured learning environment. Students choose from six skill levels tailored to the 3rd to 8th grade.

671 Basic Essentials of Math: Whole Numbers, Fractions, & Decimals Workbook
Houghton Mifflin Harcourt
6277 Sea Harbor Dr
5th Floor
Orlando, FL 32887

800-531-5015
FAX 800-699-9459
http://steckvaughn.harcourtachieve.com
e-mail: greatservice@hmhpub.com
James T Shea, Author
Linda K. Zecher, President and CEO
Eric Shuman, Chief Financial Officer
Ideal for basic math skill instruction, test practice, or any situation requiring a thorough, confidence-building review. It provides a complete lesson - instruction, examples, and computation exercises. *$19.00*

672 Building Mathematical Thinking
Educators Publishing Service
PO Box 9031
Cambridge, MA 02139-9031

617-547-6706
800-225-5750
FAX 617-547-3805
http://www.epsbooks.com
e-mail: CustomerService.EPS@schoolspecialty.com

Marsha Stanton, Author
Kathryn Hansen, Key Accounts Coordinator
Jeff Belanger, Regional Sales Manager
In this new math program, the units covered are presented as a series of Skinny Concepts that serve as manageable building blocks that eventually become entire topics. The Students Journal provides exercises for each Skinny Concept, encourages students to seek their own conclusions for problem solving, and provides space for the students ideas.

673   Building Perspective
Sunburst Technology
1550 Executive Dr
Elgin, IL 60123-9311

800-321-7511
FAX 888-608-0344
http://store.sunburst.com
e-mail: service@sunburst.com
Michael Guillory, Channel Sales/Marketing Manager

Develop spatial perception and reasoning skills with this award-winning program that will sharpen your students' problem-solving abilities.

674   Building Perspective Deluxe
Sunburst Technology
1550 Executive Dr
Elgin, IL 60123-9311

800-321-7511
FAX 888-608-0344
http://store.sunburst.com
e-mail: service@sunburst.com
Michael Guillory, Channel Sales/Marketing Manager

New visual thinking challenges await your students as they engage in three spacial reasoning activities that develop their 3D thinking, deductive reasoning and problem solving skills

675   Combining Shapes
Sunburst Technology
1550 Executive Dr
Elgin, IL 60123-9311

800-321-7511
FAX 888-608-0344
http://store.sunburst.com
e-mail: service@sunburst.com
Michael Guillory, Channel Sales/Marketing Manager

Students discover the properties of simple geometric figures through concrete experience combining shapes. Measurements, estimating and operation skills are part of this fun program.

676   Concert Tour Entrepreneur
Sunburst Technology
1550 Executive Dr
Elgin, IL 60123-9311

800-321-7511
FAX 888-608-0344
http://store.sunburst.com
e-mail: service@sunburst.com
Michael Guillory, Channel Sales/Marketing Manager

Your students improve math, planning and problem solving skills as they manage a band in this music management business simulation.

677   Creating Patterns from Shapes
Sunburst Technology
1550 Executive Dr
Elgin, IL 60123-9311

800-321-7511
FAX 888-608-0344
http://store.sunburst.com
e-mail: service@sunburst.com
Michael Guillory, Channel Sales/Marketing Manager

Students discover patterns by exploring the properties of radiating and tiling patterns through Native American basket weaving and Japanese fish print themes.

678   Data Explorer
Sunburst Technology
1550 Executive Dr
Elgin, IL 60123-9311

800-321-7511
FAX 888-608-0344
http://store.sunburst.com
e-mail: service@sunburst.com
Michael Guillory, Channel Sales/Marketing Manager

This easy-to-use CD-ROM provides the flexibility needed for eleven different graph types including tools for long-term data analysis projects.

679   Decimals: Concepts & Problem-Solving
Houghton Mifflin Harcourt
6277 Sea Harbor Dr
5th Floor
Orlando, FL 32887

800-531-5015
FAX 800-699-9459
http://steckvaughn.harcourtachieve.com
e-mail: greatservice@hmhpub.com
Linda K. Zecher, President and CEO
Eric Shuman, Chief Financial Officer
John K. Dragoon, EVP
This easy to implement, flexible companion to the classroom mathematics curriculum emcompasses decimal concepts such as values and names, equivalent decimals, mixed decimals, patterns, comparing, ordering, estimating and more.

680   Equation Tile Teaser
Sunburst Technology
1550 Executive Dr
Elgin, IL 60123-9311

800-321-7511
FAX 888-608-0344
http://store.sunburst.com
e-mail: service@sunburst.com
Michael Guillory, Channel Sales/Marketing Manager

Students develop logic thinking and pre-algebra skills solving sets of numbers equations in three challenging problem-solving activities.

681   Factory Deluxe
Sunburst Technology
1550 Executive Dr
Elgin, IL 60123-9311

800-321-7511
FAX 888-608-0344
http://store.sunburst.com
e-mail: service@sunburst.com
Michael Guillory, Channel Sales/Marketing Manager

Five activities explore shapes, rotation, angles, geometric attributes, area formulas, and computation. Includes journal, record keeping, and on-screen help. This program helps sharpen geometry, visual thinking and problem solving skills.

682 **Focus on Math**
Houghton Mifflin Harcourt
6277 Sea Harbor Dr
5th Floor
Orlando, FL 32887

800-531-5015
FAX 800-699-9459
http://steckvaughn.harcourtachieve.com
e-mail: greatservice@hmhpub.com
Linda K. Zecher, President and CEO
Eric Shuman, Chief Financial Officer
John K. Dragoon, EVP
omnsists of four sections and in each you will learn more about addition and subtraction, multiplication and division, fractions, decimals, measurements, geometry and problem solving.

683 **Fraction Attraction**
Sunburst Technology
1550 Executive Dr
Elgin, IL 60123-9311

800-321-7511
FAX 888-608-0344
http://store.sunburst.com
e-mail: service@sunburst.com
Michael Guillory, Channel Sales/Marketing Manager

Build the fraction skills of ordering, equivalence, relative sizes and multiple representations with four, multi-level, carnival style games.

684 **Fractions: Concepts & Problem-Solving**
Houghton Mifflin Harcourt
6277 Sea Harbor Dr
5th Floor
Orlando, FL 32887

800-531-5015
FAX 800-699-9459
http://steckvaughn.harcourtachieve.com
e-mail: greatservice@hmhpub.com
Linda K. Zecher, President, CEO
Eric Shuman, Chief Financial Officer
John K. Dragoon, Executive Vice President
This companion to the classroom mathematics curriculum emcompasses many of the standards established at each grade level. Each activity page targets a specific skill to help bolster students who need additional work in a particular area of fractions.

685 **GEPA Success in Language Arts Literacy and Mathematics**
Houghton Mifflin Harcourt
6277 Sea Harbor Dr
5th Floor
Orlando, FL 32887

800-531-5015
FAX 800-699-9459
http://steckvaughn.harcourtachieve.com
e-mail: greatservice@hmhpub.com
Estell Kleinman, Author
Linda K. Zecher, President and CEO
Eric Shuman, Chief Financial Officer
Build skills as you improve scores on the GEPA. Better test scores don't always mean better skills. With these workbooks, you can ensure that your students are becoming more proficient users of language and math as well as more skilled test-takers. Your students will gain valuable practice answering the types of questions found on the GEPA, such as open-ended and enhanced multiple-choice items. *$17.60*

686 **Geometry for Primary Grades**
Houghton Mifflin Harcourt
6277 Sea Harbor Dr
5th Floor
Orlando, FL 32887

800-531-5015
FAX 800-699-9459
http://steckvaughn.harcourtachieve.com
e-mail: greatservice@hmhpub.com
Linda K. Zecher, President and CEO
Eric Shuman, Chief Financial Officer
John K. Dragoon, EVP
Self-explanatory lessons ideal for independent work or as homework. Transitions from concrete to pictorial to abstract.

687 **Get Up and Go!**
Sunburst Technology
1550 Executive Dr
Elgin, IL 60123-9311

800-321-7511
FAX 888-608-0344
http://store.sunburst.com
e-mail: service@sunburst.com
Michael Guillory, Channel Sales/Marketing Manager

Students interpret and construct timelines through three descriptive activities in the animated program. Students are introduced to timelines as they participate in an interactive story.

688 **Grade Level Math**
Houghton Mifflin Harcourt
6277 Sea Harbor Dr
5th Floor
Orlando, FL 32887

800-531-5015
FAX 800-699-9459
http://steckvaughn.harcourtachieve.com
e-mail: greatservice@hmhpub.com
Linda K. Zecher, President
Eric Shuman, Chief Financial Officer
John K. Dragoon, Executive Vice President
Easy to understand practice exercises help students build conceptual knowledge and computation skills together. Each book addresses essential grade appropriate math areas.

689 **Graphers**
Sunburst Technology
1550 Executive Dr
Elgin, IL 60123-9311

800-321-7511
FAX 888-608-0344
http://store.sunburst.com
e-mail: service@sunburst.com
Michael Guillory, Channel Sales/Marketing Manager

Students develop data analysis skills with this easy to use graphing tool. With over 30 pictorial data sets and 16 lessons, students learn to construct and interpret six different graph types.

690 **Green Globs & Graphing Equations**
Sunburst Technology
1550 Executive Dr
Elgin, IL 60123-9311

800-321-7511
FAX 888-608-0344
http://store.sunburst.com
e-mail: service@sunburst.com
Michael Guillory, Channel Sales/Marketing Manager

As students explore parabolas, hyperbolas, and other graphs, they discover how altering an equation changes a graph's shape or position.

691   Hidden Treasures of Al-Jabr
Sunburst Technology
1550 Executive Dr
Elgin, IL 60123-9311

800-321-7511
FAX 888-608-0344
http://store.sunburst.com
e-mail: service@sunburst.com
Michael Guillory, Channel Sales/Marketing Manager

Beginning algebra students undertake three challenges that develop skills in the areas of solving linear equations, substituting variables, grouping like variables, using systems of equations and translating algebra word problems into equations.

692   High School Math Bundle
Sunburst Technology
1550 Executive Dr
Elgin, IL 60123-9311

800-321-7511
FAX 888-608-0344
http://store.sunburst.com
e-mail: service@sunburst.com
Michael Guillory, Channel Sales/Marketing Manager

Each program in this bundle focuses on a specific area to ensure that your students master the math skills they need. This bundle allows students to master basics of Algebra, explore equations and graphs, practice learning with algebra graphs, use trigonometric functions, apply math concepts to practical situations and improve problem solving and data analysis skills.

693   Higher Scores on Math Standardized Tests
Harcourt Achieve
6277 Sea Harbor Dr
5th Floor
Orlando, FL 32887

800-531-5015
FAX 800-699-9459
http://www.harcourtachieve.com
e-mail: greatservice@hmhpub.com
Linda K. Zecher, President and CEO
Eric Shuman, Chief Financial Officer
John K. Dragoon, EVP
These grade level math test preparation series provide focused practice in areas where students have shown a weakness in previous standardized tests. Improves test scores by zeroing in on the skills requiring remediation.

694   Hot Dog Stand: The Works
Sunburst Technology
1550 Executive Dr
Elgin, IL 60123-9311

800-321-7511
FAX 888-608-0344
http://store.sunburst.com
e-mail: service@sunburst.com
Michael Guillory, Channel Sales/Marketing Manager

Students practice math, problem-solving, and communication skills in a multimedia business simulation that challenges students with unexpected events.

695   How the West Was 1+3x4
Sunburst Technology
1550 Executive Dr
Elgin, IL 60123-9311

800-321-7511
FAX 888-608-0344
http://store.sunburst.com
e-mail: service@sunburst.com
Michael Guillory, Channel Sales/Marketing Manager

Students use order of operations to construct equations and race along number line trails.

696   Ice Cream Truck
Sunburst Technology
1550 Executive Dr
Elgin, IL 60123-9311

800-321-7511
FAX 888-608-0344
http://store.sunburst.com
e-mail: service@sunburst.com
Michael Guillory, Channel Sales/Marketing Manager

Elementary students learn important problem solving, strategic planning and math operation skills, as they become owners of a busy ice cream truck.

697   Intermediate Geometry
Houghton Mifflin Harcourt
6277 Sea Harbor Dr
5th Floor
Orlando, FL 32887

800-531-5015
FAX 800-699-9459
http://steckvaughn.harcourtachieve.com
e-mail: greatservice@hmhpub.com
Linda K. Zecher, President and CEO
Eric Shuman, Chief Financial Officer
John K. Dragoon, EVP
Prepares intermediate and middle school students for a successful experience in high school geometry. Intermediate geometry provides a study of the concepts, computation, problem-solving, and enrichment of topics identified by NCTM standards. This three-book series links the informal explorations of geometry in primary grades to more formalized processes taught in high school.

698   Introduction to Patterns
Sunburst Technology
1550 Executive Dr
Elgin, IL 60123-9311

800-321-7511
FAX 888-608-0344
http://store.sunburst.com
e-mail: service@sunburst.com
Michael Guillory, Channel Sales/Marketing Manager

Students discover patterns found in art and nature, exploring linear and geometric designs, predicting outcomes and creating patterns of their own.

699   Mastering Math
Houghton Mifflin Harcourt
6277 Sea Harbor Dr
5th Floor
Orlando, FL 32887

800-531-5015
FAX 800-699-9459
http://steckvaughn.harcourtachieve.com
e-mail: greatservice@hmhpub.com
Linda K. Zecher, President and CEO
Eric Shuman, Chief Financial Officer
John K. Dragoon, EVP

Now low level readers can succeed at math with this easy to read presentation. Makes basic math concepts accessible to all students.

700 Measurement: Practical Applications
Houghton Mifflin Harcourt
6277 Sea Harbor Dr
5th Floor
Orlando, FL 32887

800-531-5015
FAX 800-699-9459
http://steckvaughn.harcourtachieve.com
e-mail: greatservice@hmhpub.com
Linda K. Zecher, President and CEO
Eric Shuman, Chief Financial Officer
John K. Dragoon, EVP
Concentrated practice on the measurement skills we use on a daily basis. This practical presentation of both customary and metric units helps the student to understand the importance of measurement skills in everyday life. Hands on activities and real life situations create logical applications so measurements make sense.

701 Memory Fun!
Sunburst Technology
1550 Executive Dr
Elgin, IL 60123-9311

800-321-7511
FAX 888-608-0344
http://store.sunburst.com
e-mail: service@sunburst.com
Michael Guillory, Channel Sales/Marketing Manager

Welcome to Tiny's attic where students build memory, matching, counting and money sense through a variety of fun matching activities.

702 Middle School Math Bundle
Sunburst Technology
1550 Executive Dr
Elgin, IL 60123-9311

800-321-7511
FAX 888-608-0344
http://store.sunburst.com
e-mail: service@sunburst.com
Michael Guillory, Channel Sales/Marketing Manager

This bundle helps improve student's logical thinking, number sense and operation skills. This product comes with Math Arena, Building Perspective Deluxe, Equation Tile Teasers and Easy Sheet.

703 Middle School Math Collection Geometry Basic Concepts
Houghton Mifflin Harcourt
6277 Sea Harbor Dr
5th Floor
Orlando, FL 32887

800-531-5015
FAX 800-699-9459
http://steckvaughn.harcourtachieve.com
e-mail: greatservice@hmhpub.com
Linda K. Zecher, President
Eric Shuman, Chief Financial Officer
John K. Dragoon, Executive Vice President
Provides students with enough comprehensive, skill specific practice in the key areas of geometry to ensure mastery. Ideal for junior high or high school students in need of remediation.

704 MindTwister Math
Riverdeep
222 Berkeley Street
Boston, MA 02116

617-351-5000
888-242-6747
FAX 877-892-9820
http://www.riverdeep.net
e-mail: IIEcustomerservice@hmhpub.com
Linda K. Zecher, President and CEO
Eric Shuman, Chief Financial Officer
John K. Dragoon, EVP
MindTwister Math provides a challenging review of third grade math and problem-solving skills in a fast-paced, multi-player game show format. Thousands of action-packed challenges encourage students to practice essential math facts including addition, subtraction, mutiplication and division and develop more advanced mathematical problem-solving skills such as visualization, deduction, sequencing, estimating and pattern recognition.

705 Mirror Symmetry
Sunburst Technology
1550 Executive Dr
Elgin, IL 60123-9311

800-321-7511
FAX 888-608-0344
http://store.sunburst.com
e-mail: service@sunburst.com
Michael Guillory, Channel Sales/Marketing Manager

Students advance their understanding of geometric properties and spatial relationships by exploring lines of symmetry within a single geometric shape.

706 Multiplication & Division
Houghton Mifflin Harcourt
6277 Sea Harbor Dr
5th Floor
Orlando, FL 32887

800-531-5015
FAX 800-699-9459
http://steckvaughn.harcourtachieve.com
e-mail: greatservice@hmhpub.com
Linda K. Zecher, President and CEO
Eric Shuman, Chief Financial Officer
John K. Dragoon, EVP
Skill specific activities focus on the concepts and inverse relationships of multiplication and division. Explains in simplified terms how the process of multiplication undoes the process of division, and vice versa.

707 My Mathematical Life
Sunburst Technology
1550 Executive Dr
Elgin, IL 60123-9311

800-321-7511
FAX 888-608-0344
http://store.sunburst.com
e-mail: service@sunburst.com
Michael Guillory, Channel Sales/Marketing Manager

Students discover the math involved in everyday living as they take a character from high school graduation to retirement, advising on important health, education, career, and financial decisions.

708 Nimble Numeracy: Fluency in Counting and Basic Arithmetic
Oxton House Publishers
PO Box 209
Farmington, ME 04938

207-779-1923
800-539-7323
FAX 207-779-0623
http://www.oxtonhouse.com
e-mail: info@oxtonhouse.com

Dr. Phyllis E. Fischer, Author
William Berlinghoff PhD, Managing Editor
Bobby Brown, Marketing Director
Dr. Phyllis Fischer, Author
This is a richly detailed handbook for teachers, tutors, and parents who want to help children develop fluent arithmetric skills. It provides explicit techniques for teaching counting and basic arithmetic, with special emphasis on the language of our base-ten, place-value system for speaking about and writing numbers. *$19.95*
> *136 pages*
> *ISBN 1-881929-19-1*

709 **Number Meanings and Counting**
Sunburst Technology
1550 Executive Dr
Elgin, IL 60123-9311
> 800-321-7511
> FAX 888-608-0344
> http://store.sunburst.com
> e-mail: service@sunburst.com
Michael Guillory, Channel Sales/Marketing Manager

Students develop their understanding of number meaning and uses with experiences practicing estimating, using number meanings, and making more-and-less comparisons.

710 **Number Sense & Problem Solving CD-ROM**
Sunburst Technology
1550 Executive Dr
Elgin, IL 60123-9311
> 800-321-7511
> FAX 888-608-0344
> http://store.sunburst.com
> e-mail: service@sunburst.com
Michael Guillory, Channel Sales/Marketing Manager

Build number and operation skills with these three programs: How the West Was One + Three x Four, Divide and Conquer and Puzzle Tanks.

711 **Numbers Undercover**
Sunburst Technology
1550 Executive Dr
Elgin, IL 60123-9311
> 800-321-7511
> FAX 888-608-0344
> http://store.sunburst.com
> e-mail: service@sunburst.com
Michael Guillory, Channel Sales/Marketing Manager

As children try to solve the case of missing numbers, they practice telling time, measuring and estimating, counting, and working with money.

712 **Penny Pot**
Sunburst Technology
1550 Executive Dr
Elgin, IL 60123-9311
> 800-321-7511
> FAX 888-608-0344
> http://store.sunburst.com
> e-mail: service@sunburst.com
Michael Guillory, Channel Sales/Marketing Manager

Students learn about money as they count combinations of coins in this engaging program.

713 **Problemas y mas**
Houghton Mifflin Harcourt
6277 Sea Harbor Dr
5th Floor
Orlando, FL 32887
> 800-531-5015
> FAX 800-699-9459
> http://steckvaughn.harcourt.com
> e-mail: greatservice@hmhpub.com
Alan Handel, Author
Linda K. Zecher, President and CEO
Eric Shuman, Chief Financial Officer
This ESL math practice and strategy tool is in three levels the same as Problems Plus, but expressly for your Spanish fluent ESL learners. *$13.40*

> *ISBN 0-811495-93-0*

714 **Problems Plus Level H**
Houghton Mifflin Achieve
6277 Sea Harbor Dr
5th Floor
Orlando, FL 32887
> 800-531-5015
> FAX 800-699-9459
> http://steckvaughn.harcourtachieve.com
> e-mail: greatservice@hmhpub.com
Francis J Gardella, Author
Linda K. Zecher, President
Eric Shuman, Chief Financial Officer
A one-of-a-kind guide to solving open-ended math problems. Doesn't just give answers to test questions. With its innovative problem-solving plan, this series teaches math thinking and problem attack strategies, plus offers practice in higher order thinking skills students need to solve open-ended math problems successfully. *$15.10*

715 **Puzzle Tanks**
Sunburst Technology
1550 Executive Dr
Elgin, IL 60123-9311
> 800-321-7511
> FAX 888-608-0344
> http://store.sunburst.com
> e-mail: service@sunburst.com
Michael Guillory, Channel Sales/Marketing Manager

A problem-solving program that uses logic puzzles involving liquid measurements.

716 **Representing Fractions**
Sunburst Technology
1550 Executive Dr
Elgin, IL 60123-9311
> 800-321-7511
> FAX 888-608-0344
> http://store.sunburst.com
> e-mail: service@sunburst.com
Michael Guillory, Channel Sales/Marketing Manager

In this investigation students work with one interpretation of a fraction and the relationship between parts and wholes by working with symbolic and visual representations.

717 **Sequencing Fun!**
Sunburst Technology
1550 Executive Dr
Elgin, IL 60123-9311
> 800-321-7511
> FAX 888-608-0344
> http://store.sunburst.com
> e-mail: service@sunburst.com
Michael Guillory, Channel Sales/Marketing Manager

Text, pictures, animation, and video clips provide a fun-filled program that encourages critical thinking skills.

718 Shape Up!
Sunburst Technology
1550 Executive Dr
Elgin, IL 60123-9311

800-321-7511
FAX 888-608-0344
http://store.sunburst.com
e-mail: service@sunburst.com
Michael Guillory, Channel Sales/Marketing Manager

Students actively create and manipulate shapes to discover important ideas about mathematics in an electronic playground of two and three dimensional shapes.

719 Shapes Within Shapes
Sunburst Technology
1550 Executive Dr
Elgin, IL 60123-9311

800-321-7511
FAX 888-608-0344
http://store.sunburst.com
e-mail: service@sunburst.com
Michael Guillory, Channel Sales/Marketing Manager

Students identify shapes within shapes, then rearrange them to develop spatial sense and deepen their understanding of the properties of shapes.

720 Spatial Relationships
Sunburst Technology
1550 Executive Dr
Elgin, IL 60123-9311

888-492-8817
FAX 888-608-0344
http://store.sunburst.com
e-mail: service@sunburst.com
Michael Guillory, Channel Sales/Marketing Manager

Students explore location by identifying the positions of objects and creating paths between places. Children develop spatial abilities and language needed to communicate about our world.

721 Speed Drills for Arithmetic Facts
Oxton House Publishers
PO Box 209
Farmington, ME 04938

207-779-1923
800-539-7323
FAX 207-779-0623
http://www.oxtonhouse.com
e-mail: info@oxtonhouse.com
William Berlinghoff PhD, Managing Editor
Bobby Brown, Marketing Director
Dr. Phyllis Fischer, Author
This looseleaf packet is a set of 48 pages of carefully constructed exercises to promote automaticity with basic arithmetic facts. The worksheets reinforce the interrelationship of three numbers in addition/subtraction and multiplication/division statements. Also included are six pages of detailed teaching advice and a chart template for tracking student progress. *$24.95*
54 pages
ISBN 1-881929-16-7

722 Splish Splash Math
Sunburst Technology
1550 Executive Dr
Elgin, IL 60123-9311

800-321-7511
FAX 888-608-0344
http://store.sunburst.com
e-mail: service@sunburst.com
Michael Guillory, Channel Sales/Marketing Manager

Students learn and practice basic operation skills as they engage in this high interest program that keeps them motivated. Great visual rewards and three levels of difficulty keep students challanged.

723 Strategies for Problem-Solving
Houghton Mifflin Harcourt
6277 Sea Harbor Dr
5th Floor
Orlando, FL 32887

800-531-5015
FAX 800-699-9459
http://steckvaughn.harcourtachieve.com
e-mail: greatservice@hmhpub.com
Arnold Yellin, Author
Linda K. Zecher, President and CEO
Eric Shuman, Chief Financial Officer
Show students more than one way to approach a problem, and you hand them the key to effective problem solving. These reproducible activities build math reasoning and critical thinking skills, reinforce core concepts, and reduce math anxiety, too. *$11.99*

ISBN 0-817267-61-1

724 Strategies for Success in Mathematics
Houghton Mifflin Harcourt
6277 Sea Harbor Dr
5th Floor
Orlando, FL 32887

800-531-5015
FAX 800-699-9459
http://steckvaughn.harcourtachieve.com
e-mail: greatservice@hmhpub.com
June Coultas, Author
Linda K. Zecher, President and CEO
Eric Shuman, Chief Financial Officer
Teach your students specific problem-solving skills and test taking strategies for success with math and math assessments. Practice thoroughly covers five math clusters: numerical operations, patterns and functions, algebraic concepts, measurement and geometry, and data analysis. *$16.60*

725 Sunbuddy Math Playhouse
Sunburst Technology
1550 Executive Dr
Elgin, IL 60123-9311

800-321-7511
FAX 888-608-0344
http://store.sunburst.com
e-mail: service@sunburst.com
Michael Guillory, Channel Sales/Marketing Manager

An entertaining play, hidden math-related animations, and four multi-level interactive activities encourage children to explore math and reading.

726 Ten Tricky Tiles
Sunburst Technology
1550 Executive Dr
Elgin, IL 60123-9311

800-321-7511
FAX 888-608-0344
http://store.sunburst.com
e-mail: service@sunburst.com
Michael Guillory, Channel Sales/Marketing Manager

Students develop their arithmetic and logic skills with three levels of activities that involve solving sets of numbers sentences.

727   **Tenth Planet: Combining and Breaking Apart Numbers**

Sunburst Technology
1550 Executive Dr
Elgin, IL 60123-9311

800-321-7511
FAX 888-608-0344
http://store.sunburst.com
e-mail: service@sunburst.com
Michael Guillory, Channel Sales/Marketing Manager

Students develop their number sense as they engage in real life dilemmas, which demonstrates the basic concepts of operations.

728   **Tenth Planet: Comparing with Ratios**

Sunburst Technology
1550 Executive Dr
Elgin, IL 60123-9311

800-321-7511
FAX 888-608-0344
http://store.sunburst.com
e-mail: service@sunburst.com
Michael Guillory, Channel Sales/Marketing Manager

Students learn that ratio is a way to compare amounts by using multiplication and division. Through five engaging activities, students recognize and describe ratios, develop proportional thinking skills, estimate ratios, determine equivalent ratios, and use ratios to analyze data.

729   **Tenth Planet: Equivalent Fractions**

Sunburst Technology
1550 Executive Dr
Elgin, IL 60123-9311

800-321-7511
FAX 888-608-0344
http://store.sunburst.com
e-mail: service@sunburst.com
Michael Guillory, Channel Sales/Marketing Manager

This exciting investigation develops students' conceptual understanding that every fraction can be named in many different but equivalent ways.

730   **Tenth Planet: Fraction Operations**

Sunburst Technology
1550 Executive Dr
Elgin, IL 60123-9311

800-321-7511
FAX 888-608-0344
http://store.sunburst.com
e-mail: service@sunburst.com
Michael Guillory, Channel Sales/Marketing Manager

Students build on their concepts of fraction meaning and equivalence as they learn how to perform operations with fractions.

731   **Tenth Planet: Grouping and Place Value**

Sunburst Technology
1550 Executive Dr
Elgin, IL 60123-9311

800-321-7511
FAX 888-608-0344
http://store.sunburst.com
e-mail: service@sunburst.com
Michael Guillory, Channel Sales/Marketing Manager

Students develop their understanding of our number system, learning to think about numbers in groups of ones, tens, and hundreds, and discovering the meaning of place value.

732   **Zap! Around Town**

Sunburst Technology
1550 Executive Dr
Elgin, IL 60123-9311

800-321-7511
FAX 888-608-0344
http://store.sunburst.com
e-mail: service@sunburst.com
Michael Guillory, Channel Sales/Marketing Manager

Students develop mapping and direction skills in this easy-to-use, animated program featuring Shelby, your friendly Sunbuddy guide.

Preschool

733   **2's Experience Fingerplays**

Building Blocks
38w567 Brindlewood Ln
Elgin, IL 60124-7976

800-233-2448
FAX 847-742-1054
http://www.bblocksonline.com
e-mail: sales@bblocksonline.com
Liz Wilmes, Author
Dick Wilmes, Co-Author

A wonderful collection of fingerplays, songs and rhymes for the very young child. Fingerplays are short, easy to learn, and full of simple movement. Chant or sing the fingerplays and then enjoy the accompanying games and activities. *$12.95*

     144 pages

734   **Curious George Preschool Learning Games**

Sunburst Technology
1550 Executive Dr
Elgin, IL 60123-9311

800-321-7511
FAX 888-608-0344
http://store.sunburst.com
e-mail: service@sunburst.com
Michael Guillory, Channel Sales/Marketing Manager

Join Curious George in Fun Town and play five arcade-style games that promote the visual and auditory discrimination skills all students need before they begin to read. Mac/Win CD-ROM

735   **Devereux Early Childhood Assessment(DECA)**

Kaplan Early Learning Company
1310 Lewisville Clemmons Rd
Lewisville, NC 27023-9635

336-766-7374
800-334-2014
FAX 800-452-7526
http://www.kaplanco.com
e-mail: info@kaplanco.com
Paul A. LeBuffe, Author
Jack A Naglieri, Co-Author
Hal Kaplan, President & CEO
Strength-based standardized, norm-referenced behavior rating scale designed to promote resilience and measure protective factors in children ages 2-5. Through the program, early childhood professionals and families learn specific strategies to support young children's social and emotional development and to enhance the ovall quality of early childhood programs. *$125.95*

736 Devereux Early Childhood Assessment: Clinical Version (DECA-C)
Kaplan Early Learning Company
1310 Lewisville Clemmons Rd
Lewisville, NC 27023-9635
336-766-7374
800-334-2014
FAX 800-452-7526
http://www.kaplanco.com
e-mail: info@kaplanco.com
Paul A. LeBuffe, Author
Jack A Naglieri, Co-Author
Hal Kaplan, President & CEO
DECA-C is designed to support early intervention efforts to reduce or eliminate significant emotional and behavioral concerns in preschool children. This can be used for guide interventions, identify children needing special services, assess outcomes and help programs meet Head Start, IDEA, and similar requirements. Kit includes: 1 Manual, 30 Record Forms, and 1 Norms Reference Card. *$125.95*

737 Early Movement Skills
Therapro
225 Arlington St
Framingham, MA 01702-8773
508-872-9494
800-257-5376
FAX 508-875-2062
http://www.theraproducts.com
e-mail: info@theraproducts.com
Naomi Benari, Author
Karen Conrad, President

Easy to follow, reproducible gross motor activities are graded from very simple (even for the passive child) to more demanding (folk dancing). Each of the 150 pages offers an activity with its objective, a clear instruction of the activity, rationale, and alternative movements and games. Many activities involve music and rythm. A great source for early intervention and early childhood programs. *$58.00*

738 Early Screening Inventory: Revised
Pearson Assessments
5601 Green Valley Dr
Bloomington, MN 55437-1099
800-627-7271
FAX 800-232-1223
http://www.pearsonassessments.com
e-mail: clinicalcustomersupport@pearson.com
Samuel J Meisels, Author
Martha S Wiske, Co-Author
Laura W Henderson, Co-Author
A developmental screening instrument for 3-to-6-year olds. Provides a norm-referenced overview of visual-motor/adaptive, language and cognition, and gross motor development. Meets IDEA and Head Start requirements for early identification and parental involvement. Test in English or Spanish in 15-20 minutes. Training video and materials available.

739 Early Sensory Skills
Therapro
225 Arlington St
Framingham, MA 01702-8773
508-872-9494
800-257-5376
FAX 508-875-2062
http://www.theraproducts.com
e-mail: info@theraproducts.com
Jackie Cooke, Author
Karen Conrad, President

A wonderful book filled with practical and fun activities for stimulating vision, touch, taste and smell. Invaluable for anyone working with children 6 months to 5 years, this manual outlines basic principals followed by six sections containing activities, games and topics to excite the senses. Introductions are easy to follow, and materials for the sensory work are readily accessible in the everyday environment. *$57.75*

740 Early Visual Skills
Therapro
225 Arlington St
Framingham, MA 01702-8773
508-872-9494
800-257-5376
FAX 508-875-2062
http://www.theraproducts.com
e-mail: info@theraproducts.com
Diana Williams, Author
Karen Conrad, President

A beautifully designed, easy to follow reproducible book for working with young children on visual perceptual skills. Most of the activities are nonverbal and can be used with children who have limited language. Each section has both easy and challenging activities for school and for parents working with children at home. Activities include sorting, color and shape matching, a looking walk, games to develop visual memory and concentration and many more. *$62.50*
208 pages

741 HELP for Preschoolers at Home
Therapro
225 Arlington St
Framingham, MA 01702-8773
508-872-9494
800-257-5376
FAX 508-875-2062
http://www.theraproducts.com
e-mail: info@theraproducts.com
Karen Conrad, President

Three hundred pages of practical, home-based activities that can be easily administered by the parents or the child's home-care provider. Upon completion of their assessments, teachers and therapists provide parents with these handouts to help them work on skills at home in conjunction with the program. *$72.50*

742 LAP-D Kindergarten Screen Kit
Kaplan Early Learning Company
1310 Lewisville Clemmons Rd
Lewisville, NC 27023-9635
336-766-7374
800-334-2014
FAX 800-452-7526
http://www.kaplanco.com
e-mail: info@kaplanco.com
Hal Kaplan, President & CEO

Concise, standardized screening deice normed on 5 year old children. Tasks are in four domains: fine, motor, gross motor, cognititve, and language. The Kindergarten Kit includes the technical manual, examiners, manual, and materials to assist in determining pure outcomes. *$124.95*

743 Learning Accomplishment Profile Diagnostic Normed Screens for Age 3-5
Kaplan Early Learning Company
1310 Lewisville Clemmons Rd
Lewisville, NC 27023-9635
336-766-7374
800-334-2014
FAX 800-452-7526
http://www.kaplanco.com
e-mail: info@kaplanco.com
Hal Kaplan, President & CEO

For 3-5 years. Create reliable developmental snapshots in fine motor, gross motor, cognitive, language, personal/social, and self-help skill domains. *$349.95*

744 Learning Accomplishment Profile (LAP-R) KIT
Kaplan Early Learning Company
1310 Lewisville Clemmons Rd
Lewisville, NC 27023-9635
336-766-7374
800-334-2014
FAX 800-452-7526
http://www.kaplanco.com
e-mail: info@kaplanco.com

Hal Kaplan, President & CEO
Mike Mathers, Author

A criterion-referenced assessment instrument measuring development in six domains: gross motor, fine motor, cognitive, language, self-help and social/emotional. Kit includes all materials necessary for assessing 20 children. *$299.95*

745   Learning Accomplishment Profile Diagnostic Normed Assessment (LAP-D)
Kaplan Early Learning Company
1310 Lewisville Clemmons Rd
Lewisville, NC 27023-9635   336-766-7374
                                     800-334-2014
                                FAX 800-452-7526
                            http://www.kaplanco.com
                            e-mail: info@kaplanco.com
Belinda J. Hardin, Ph.D., Author
Ellen S. Peisner-Feinberg, Ph.D, Co-Author
Stephanie W. Weeks, Ph.D., Co-Author
A comprehensive developemtal assessment tool for children between the ages of 30 and 72 months. LAP-D consists of a hierarchy of developmental skills arranged in four developmental domains: fine motor, gross motor, cognitive and language. *$624.95*

746   Partners for Learning (PFL)
Kaplan Early Learning Company
1310 Lewisville Clemmons Rd
Lewisville, NC 27023-9635   336-766-7374
                                     800-334-2014
                                FAX 800-452-7526
                            http://www.kaplanco.com
                            e-mail: info@kaplanco.com
Hal Kaplan, President & CEO

This resource uses cards, books, posters, and support materials to supply teaching ideas and to support child development. PARTNERS for Learning encourages cognitive, social, motor, and language development. The kit provides materials for curriculum planning and self-assessment. *$199.95*

747   Right from the Start: Behavioral Intervention for Young Children with Autism
Therapro
225 Arlington St
Framingham, MA 01702-8773   508-872-9494
                                     800-257-5376
                                FAX 508-875-2062
                         http://www.theraproducts.com
                         e-mail: info@theraproducts.com
Sandra Harris PhD, Author
Mary Jane Weiss PhD, Co-Author
Karen Conrad, President
This informative and user-friendly guide helps parents and service providers explore programs that use early intensive behavioral intervention for young children with autism and related disorders. Within these programs, many children improve in intellectual, social and adaptive functioning, enabling them to move on to regular elementary and preschools. Benefits all children, but primarily useful for children age five and younger. *$16.95*
138 pages

748   Sensory Motor Activities for Early Development
Therapro
225 Arlington St
Framingham, MA 01702-8773   508-872-9494
                                     800-257-5376
                                FAX 508-875-2062
                         http://www.theraproducts.com
                         e-mail: info@theraproducts.com
Chia Swee Hong, Author
Helen Gabriel, Co-Author
Cathy St John, Co-Author

A complete package of tried and tested gross and fine motor activities. Many activities to stimulate sensory and body awareness, encourage basic movement, promote hand skills, and enhance spatial/early perceptual skills. Master handouts throughout to give to parents for home practice activities for working in small groups. *$51.50*
93 pages

Reading

749   Animals of the Rainforest Classroom Library
HMH Supplemental Publishers
6277 Sea Harbor Dr
5th Floor
Orlando, FL 32887
                                     800-531-5015
                                FAX 800-699-9459
                        http://www.harcourtachieve.com
                        e-mail: greatservice@hmhpub.com
Linda K. Zecher, President and CEO
Eric Shuman, Chief Financial Officer
John K. Dragoon, EVP
When reading is a struggle, academic success is even harder to achieve. Now you can put social studies and science curriculum content within reach of every student with this series. Designed specifically for limited readers. *$46.50*

ISBN 0-739849-32-8

750   Ants in His Pants: Absurdities and Realities of Special Education
Sage Publications
2455 Teller Rd
Thousand Oaks, CA 91320-2218   805-499-9774
                                     800-818-7243
                                FAX 800-583-2665
                            http://www.sagepub.com
                            e-mail: orders@sagepub.com
Michael Giangreco, Author
Kevin Ruelle, Co-Author
Blaise R. Simqu, President
With wit, humor and profound one liners, Michael Giangreco will transform your thinking as you take a lighter look at the sometimes comical and occasionally harsh truths in the ever changing field of special education. *$20.95*
128 pages
ISBN 1-890455-42-3

751   AppleSeeds
Cobblestone Publishing
Ste C
30 Grove St
Peterborough, NH 03458-1453   603-924-7209
                                     800-821-0115
                                FAX 603-924-7380
                         http://www.cobblestonepub.com
                         e-mail: customerservice@caruspub.com
Susan Buckley, Editor

An award winning magazine of adventure and exploration for children ages 7 to 9. Provides kids with themed issues that explore a different topic with insightful articles, cool photographs, and a unique you-are-there perspective on culture and history. *$29.95*
36 pages 9 times a year

752   Basic Level Workbook for Aphasia
Wayne State University Press
4809 Woodward Ave
Detroit, MI 48201-1309   313-577-6120
                                     800-978-7323
                                FAX 313-577-6131
                          http://wsupress.wayne.edu
                          e-mail: bookorders@wayne.edu
Susan Howell Brubaker MS, Author

If you work with adolescents and adults with mild to moderate language deficits or limited, impaired, or emerging reading skills, this workbook is what you've been waiting for! The mMaterial is relevant to their lives, interests, experiences, and vocabulary. Item number W324. *$50.00*
> *360 pages*
> *ISBN 0-814326-20-X*

753 Beyond the Code
Educators Publishing Service
PO Box 9031
Cambridge, MA 02139-9031   617-547-6706
                                   800-225-5750
                              FAX 617-547-3805
                         http://www.epsbooks.com
        e-mail: CustomerService.EPS@schoolspecialty.com
Nancy M Hall, Author
Kathryn Hansen, Key Accounts Coordinator
Jeff Belanger, Regional Sales Manager
Beyond the Code gives beginning readers experience reading original stories as well as thinking about what they have read. This companion series follows the same phonetic progression as the frist 4 books of the popular Explode the Code program.

754 Chess with Butterflies
Oxton House Publishers
PO Box 209
Farmington, ME 04938   207-779-1923
                               800-539-7323
                          FAX 207-779-0623
                     http://www.oxtonhouse.com
                  e-mail: info@oxtonhouse.com
William Berlinghoff PhD, Managing Editor
Bobby Brown, Marketing Director
Sandi Hawkins, Representative
This is a phoneticaly controlled sequel to 'Fishing with Balloons.' It continues the adventures of the main character as it develops more sophisticated word families. Lists for those word families and notes on using them for reading instruction are included in the back of the book. *$5.95*
> *66 pages*
> *ISBN 1-881929-43-4*

755 Claims to Fame
Educators Publishing Service
PO Box 9031
Cambridge, MA 02139-9031   617-547-6706
                                   800-225-5750
                              FAX 617-547-3805
                         http://www.epsbooks.com
        e-mail: CustomerService.EPS@schoolspecialty.com
Carol Einstein, Author
Kathryn Hansen, Key Accounts Coordinator
Jeff Belanger, Regional Sales Manager
The three exercises after each reading are tailored to the content of each story. In Thinking About What You Have Read, students check and extend their understanding of the story. Working with Words asks students to think about and experiment with vaious word meanings.

756 Clues to Meaning
Educators Publishing Service
PO Box 9031
Cambridge, MA 02139-9031   617-547-6706
                                   800-225-5750
                              FAX 617-547-3805
                         http://www.epsbooks.com
        e-mail: CustomerService.EPS@schoolspecialty.com
Ann L Staman, Author
Kathryn Hansen, Key Accounts Coordinator
Jeff Belanger, Regional Sales Manager
A versatile series which teaches beginning readers to use the sounds of letters as one strategy among many in learning to read.

757 Concept Phonics
Oxton House Publishers
PO Box 209
Farmington, ME 04938   207-779-1923
                               800-539-7323
                          FAX 207-779-0623
                     http://www.oxtonhouse.com
                  e-mail: info@oxtonhouse.com
William Berlinghoff PhD, Managing Editor
Bobby Brown, Marketing Director
Dr. Phyllis Fischer, Author
This is a remarkably effective, research-based, multisensory program for teaching reading-decoding and speech to students with learning disabilities at any age or grade level. Its 13 component pieces include a book on understanding phonics, detailed teacher's guides, and sets of contrast cards, speed drills, worksheets, visual teaching aids, and comprehensive word lists. *$315.00*

> *ISBN 1-881929-36-1*

758 Cosmic Reading Journey
Sunburst Technology
1550 Executive Dr
Elgin, IL 60123-9311
                                   800-321-7511
                              FAX 888-608-0344
                         http://store.sunburst.com
                  e-mail: service@sunburst.com
Michael Guillory, Channel Sales/Marketing Manager

This reading comprehension program provides meaningful summary and writing activities for the 100 books that early readers and their teachers love most.

759 Creepy Cave Initial Consonants
Sunburst Technology
1550 Executive Dr
Elgin, IL 60123-9311
                                   800-321-7511
                              FAX 888-608-0344
                         http://store.sunburst.com
                  e-mail: service@sunburst.com
Michael Guillory, Channel Sales/Marketing Manager

Help your students develop letter recognition and phonemic awareness skills matching words with the same initial consonant letter in a Creepy Cave.

760 Decoding Automaticity Materials for Reading Fluency
Oxton House Publishers
PO Box 209
Farmington, ME 04938   207-779-1923
                               800-539-7323
                          FAX 207-779-0623
                     http://www.oxtonhouse.com
                  e-mail: info@oxtonhouse.com
William Berlinghoff PhD, Managing Editor
Bobby Brown, Marketing Director
Dr. Phyllis Fischer, Author
This six-part set is designed to bring students from decoding to automaticity in reading words. The two sets of worksheets train the brain's visual processor to recognize letter units in words; the contrast cards train the brain's speech processor to say the sounds for the letter units; and the speed drills put these two tasks together for reading whole words automatically. Also included are comprehensive sets of lists of one-and two syllable words for designing customized materials. *$150.00*

> *ISBN 1-881929-37-X*

761 Dyslexia Training Program
Educators Publishing Service
PO Box 9031
Cambridge, MA 02139-9031   617-547-6706
                                 800-225-5750
                              FAX 617-547-3805
                        http://www.epsbooks.com
        e-mail: CustomerService.EPS@schoolspecialty.com
Kathryn Hansen, Key Accounts Coordinator
Ryan Todd, Sales Consultant
Jeff Belanger, Regional Sales Manager
Introduces reading and writing skills to dyslexic children
through a two-year, cumulative series of daily one-hour vid-
eotaped lessons and accompanying student's books and
teacher's guides.

762 Earobics® Clinic Version Step 1
Abilitations Speech Bin
PO Box 1579
Appleton, WI 54912-1579
                                 888-388-3224
                              FAX 888-388-6344
                        http://www.speechbin.com
        e-mail: customercare@schoolspecialty.com
Michael P. Lavelle, President, CEO
Rick Holden, Executive Vice President

Earobics is a dazzling software that teaches phonological
awareness and auditory processing. It systematically — anf
enjoyably — trains these critical skills for development ages
four to seven years. Item number C482. *$298.99*

763 EarobicsM® Step 1 Home Version
Abilitations Speech Bin
PO Box 1579
Appleton, WI 54912-1579
                                 888-388-3224
                              FAX 888-388-6344
                        http://www.speechbin.com
        e-mail: customercare@schoolspecialty.com
Michael P. Lavelle, President, CEO
Rick Holden, Executive Vice President

Step 1 offers hundreds of levels of play, appealing graphics,
and entertaining music to train the critical auditory skills
young children need for success in learning. Item number
C481. *$58.99*

764 Emergent Reader
Sunburst Technology
1550 Executive Dr
Elgin, IL 60123-9311
                                 800-321-7511
                              FAX 888-608-0344
                        http://store.sunburst.com
                     e-mail: service@sunburst.com
Michael Guillory, Channel Sales/Marketing Manager

This story-reading program supports the efforts of beginning readers by developing their sight word vocabularies.

765 Every Child a Reader
Sunburst Technology
1550 Executive Dr
Elgin, IL 60123-9311
                                 800-321-7511
                              FAX 888-608-0344
                        http://store.sunburst.com
                     e-mail: service@sunburst.com
Michael Guillory, Channel Sales/Marketing Manager

Traditional reading strategies in a rich literary context. Designed to promote independent reading and develop oral and
written language expression.

766 Explode the Code
Educators Publishing Service
PO Box 9031
Cambridge, MA 02139-9031   617-547-6706
                                 800-225-5750
                              FAX 617-547-3805
                        http://www.epsbooks.com
        e-mail: CustomerService.EPS@schoolspecialty.com
Nancy M Hall, Author
Kathryn Hansen, Key Accounts Coordinator
Jeff Belanger, Regional Sales Manager
Explode the Code provides a sequential, systematic ap-
proach to phonics in which students blend sounds to build
vocabulary and read words, phrases, sentences, and stories.

767 Fishing with Balloons
Oxton House Publishers
PO Box 209
Farmington, ME 04938   207-779-1923
                                 800-539-7323
                              FAX 207-779-0623
                        http://www.oxtonhouse.com
                     e-mail: info@oxtonhouse.com
William Burlinghoff PhD, Owner
Bobby Brown, Marketing Director
Dion , Author
This is a phonetically controlled chapter book about a 10
year old who learns how his physical disability need not be a
barrier to his aspirations. As the story holds the reader's interest, it also emphasizes certain families of words. Lists for
those word families and notes on using them for reading instruction are included in the back of the book. *$5.95*
    68 pages
    ISBN 1-881929-34-5

768 Great Series Great Rescues
HMH Supplemental Publishers
5th Floor
6277 Sea Harbor Dr
Orlando, FL 32887
                                 800-531-5015
                              FAX 800-699-9459
                        http://www.harcourtachieve.com
                     e-mail: greatservice@hmhpub.com
Henry Billings, Author
Linda K. Zecher, President, CEO
Eric Shuman, Chief Financial Officer
Human drama makes beginning reading worth the effort.
Eight exciting titles build confidence as they build skills.
Short, easy-to-read selections enable limited readers to suc-
ceed with material that matters. *$15.00*

    ISBN 0-811441-76-8

769 Handprints
Educators Publishing Service
PO Box 9031
Cambridge, MA 02139-9031   617-547-6706
                                 800-225-5750
                              FAX 617-547-3805
                        http://www.epsbooks.com
        e-mail: CustomerService.EPS@schoolspecialty.com
Ann L Staman, Author
Kathryn Hansen, Key Accounts Coordinator
Jeff Belanger, Regional Sales Manager
Handprints is a set of 50 storybooks and 4 workbooks for be-
ginning readers in kindergarten and first grade. The
storybooks increase in difficulty very gradually and encourage the new readers to use meaning, language, and print cues
as they read.

770   High Noon Books
Academic Therapy Publications
20 Commercial Blvd
Novato, CA 94949-6120   415-883-3314
                                          800-422-7249
                                       FAX 888-287-9975
                      http://www.academictherapy.com
                      e-mail: sales@academictherapy.com
Jim Arena, President
Joanne Urban, Manager
Cynthia Coverston
Serving the field of learning disabilities for the past 25
years. High-interest books for reluctant readers. Reading so-
lution programs, phonics, spelling, writing, visual tracking
materials.

771   I Can Read
Teddy Bear Press
3703 S Edmunds St
Ste 67
Seattle, WA 98118   206-402-6947
                                       FAX 866-870-7323
                      http://www.teddybearpress.com
                      e-mail: fparker@teddybearpress.net
Fran Parker, Author

A series of 7 reading books and 7 workbooks, a set of 52
flashcards and teacher manual which uses a sight word approach to teach beginning readers. These teacher created
books and workbooks present an easy to use beginning reading program which provides repetition, visual motor, visual
discrimination and word comprehension activities. It was
created to teach young, learning disabled children and has
been successfully employed to teach beginning readers of
varying ages and abilities. *$90.00*

772   I Can See the ABC's
Teddy Bear Press
3703 S Edmunds St
Ste 67
Seattle, WA 98118   206-402-6947
                                       FAX 866-870-7323
                      http://www.teddybearpress.com
                      e-mail: fparker@teddybearpress.net
Fran Parker, Author

A big 11x17 which contains the pre-primer words found in
the I Can Read program while introducing the alphabet.
$25.00

773   Inclusion: Strategies for Working with Young Children
Corwin Press
2590 Conejo Spectrum Drive
Thousand Oaks, CA 91320-2218   805-499-9734
                                          800-233-9936
                                       FAX 805-499-5323
                      http://www.corwinpress.com
Lorraine O Moore PhD, Author

This exceptional resource is a gold mine of developmentally
based ideas to help children between the ages of 3-7 or older
students who may be developmentally delayed. This is a
very practical and easy-to-use publication which is appropriate for early childhood teachers, K-2 general and special
education teachers. *$28.95*
            144 pages Educators
            ISBN 1-890455-33-4

774   Island Reading Journey
Sunburst Technology
1550 Executive Dr
Elgin, IL 60123-9311
                                          800-321-7511
                                       FAX 888-608-0344
                      http://store.sunburst.com
                      e-mail: service@sunburst.com
Michael Guillory, Channel Sales/Marketing Manager

Enhance your reading program with meaningful summary
and extension activities for 100 intermediate level books.
Students read for meaning while they engage in activities
that test for comprehension, build writing skills with reader
response and essay questions, develop usage skills with
cloze activities and improve vocabulary/word attack skills.

775   Kids Media Magic 2.0
Sunburst Technology
1550 Executive Dr
Elgin, IL 60123-9311
                                          800-321-7511
                                       FAX 888-608-0344
                      http://store.sunburst.com
                      e-mail: service@sunburst.com
Michael Guillory, Channel Sales/Marketing Manager

The first multimedia word processor designed for young
children. Help your child become a fluent reader and writer.
The Rebus Bar automatically scrolls over 45 vocabulary
words as students type.

776   Let's Go Read 1: An Island Adventure
Riverdeep
222 Berkeley Street
Boston, MA 02116   617-351-5000
                                          888-242-6747
                                       FAX 877-892-9820
                      http://www.riverdeep.net
                      e-mail: IIEcustomerservice@hmhpub.com
Linda K. Zecher, President, CEO
Eric Shuman, Chief Financial Officer
John K. Dragoon, Executive Vice President
Take off with Robby the Raccoon, Emily the Squirrel and the
Reading Rover on an exciting adventure to an island inhab-
ited by the alphabet. Motivated by the delight of mastering
new challenges, your child will play through more than 35
fun activties that install and reinforce the essential skills for
successful reading.

777   Let's Go Read 2: An Ocean Adventure
Riverdeep
222 Berkeley Street
Boston, MA 02116   617-351-5000
                                          888-242-6747
                                       FAX 877-892-9820
                      http://www.riverdeep.net
                      e-mail: IIEcustomerservice@hmhpub.com
Linda K. Zecher, President and CEO
Eric Shuman, Chief Financial Officer
John K. Dragoon, EVP
Building upon your child's mastery of letters, Let's Go
Read: 2 explores how letters combine to form words, and
how words combine to express meaning. Dozens of captivating, skill-building activities teach your child the skills to
sound out, recognize, build and comprehend hundreds of
new words. It's an endlessly fun voyage toward reading
fluency!

778   Let's Read
Educators Publishing Service
PO Box 9031
Cambridge, MA 02139-9031   617-547-6706
                                          800-225-5750
                                       FAX 617-547-3805
                      http://www.epsbooks.com
                      e-mail: CustomerService.EPS@schoolspecialty.com
Leonard Bloomfield, Author
Clarence L Barnhart, Co-Author
Robert K Barnhart, Co-Author
Using a linguistic approach to teaching reading skills, this
series emphasizes relationship of spelling to sound, presenting the concepts together, and providing nine reading books
and accompanying workbooks for practice. Provides classroom directions and suggestions for supplementary
exercises.

779 Lighthouse Low Vision Products
Lighthouse International
111 E 59th St
New York, NY 10022-1202 212-821-9200
800-829-0500
FAX 212-821-9707
TTY: 212-821-9713
http://www.lighthouse.org
e-mail: info@lighthouse.com
Mark G. Ackermann, President, CEO
Maura J. Sweeney, Senior Vice President

Empowers people of all ages who are visually impaired to lead safe, active and independent lives

780 Megawords
Educators Publishing Service
PO Box 9031
Cambridge, MA 02139-9031 617-547-6706
800-225-5750
FAX 617-547-3805
http://www.epsbooks.com
e-mail: CustomerService.EPS@schoolspecialty.com
Kristin Johnson, Author
Polly Baird, Co-Author
Kathryn Hansen, Key Accounts Coordinator
A series with a systematic, multisensory approach to learning the longer words encountered from fourth grade on. Students first work with syllables, then combine the syllables into words, use them in context, and work to increase their reading and spelling proficiency. Teacher's Guide and Answer Key available.

781 Mike Mulligan & His Steam Shovel
Houghton Mifflin
215 Park Ave S
New York, NY 10003-1603 212-420-5846
FAX 212-420-5850
http://www.houghtonmifflinbooks.com
e-mail: trade_publicity@hmco.com
Virginia Lee Burton, Author

This CD-ROM version of the Caldecott classic lets students experience interactive book reading and participate in four skills-based extension activities that promote memory, matching, sequencing, listening, pattern recognition and map reading skills.

ISBN 0-395664-99-3

782 More Primary Phonics
Educators Publishing Service
PO Box 9031
Cambridge, MA 02139-9031 617-547-6706
800-225-5750
FAX 617-547-3805
http://www.epsbooks.com
e-mail: CustomerService.EPS@schoolspecialty.com
Barbara W Makar, Author
Kathryn Hansen, Key Accounts Coordinator
Jeff Belanger, Regional Sales Manager
Reinforces and expands skills developed in Primary Phonics. Workbooks and storybooks contain the same phonetic elements, sight words and phonetic sequences as workbooks 1 and 2.

783 Multi-Sequenced Speed Drills for Fluency Multi-Sequenced Speed Drills for Fluency in Decoding
Oxton House Publishers
PO Box 209
Farmington, ME 04938 207-779-1923
800-539-7323
FAX 207-779-0623
http://www.oxtonhouse.com
e-mail: info@oxtonhouse.com

William Burlinghoff PhD, Owner
Bobby Brown, Marketing Director
Dr. Phyllis Fischer, Author
This 179-page set of reading speed drills are carefully constructed to promote decoding automaticity and the fluent recognition of words. They follow the traditional Orton-Gillingham spelling and sound sequences. The set also includes eight pages of teaching advice and a master chart fro tracking student programs. *$29.95*
195 pages
ISBN 1-881929-14-0

784 Next Stop
Educators Publishing Service
PO Box 9031
Cambridge, MA 02139-9031 617-547-6706
800-225-5750
FAX 617-547-3805
http://www.epsbooks.com
e-mail: CustomerService.EPS@schoolspecialty.com
Tanya Auger, Author
Kathryn Hansen, Key Accounts Coordinator
Jeff Belanger, Regional Sales Manager
Increase reading and language skills while exploring different literacy genres. This series is intended for students who are ready to move beyond phonetically controlled readers to the nest stop-real chapter books that will help prepare them for the more challenging literature they will encounter in later grades.

785 Patterns of English Spelling
AVKO Educational Research Foundation
3084 Willard Rd
Birch Run, MI 48415-9404 810-686-9283
866-285-6612
FAX 810-686-1101
http://www.avko.org
e-mail: webmaster@avko.org
Don Mc Cabe, Research Director/Author
Barry Chute, President
Julie Guyette, Vice President
Use the index to locate the page upon which you can find all the words that share the same patterns. If you look up the word cat, you will find all the pages where all the words are located. If you look up the word precious you will find all the words ending in cious. There are ten volumes which can be purchased all together or separately. *$119.95*
Whole set

786 Phonemic Awareness: The Sounds of Reading
Corwin Press
2455 Teller Rd
Thousand Oaks, CA 91320-2218 805-499-9734
800-233-9936
FAX 805-499-5323
http://www.corwinpress.com
e-mail: order@corwin.com
Victoria Groves Scott, Author
Mike Soules, President
Lisa Shaw, Executive Director Editorial
In this dynamic new video, Dr. Scott demonstrates the principal components of phonemic awareness: identification; comparison; segmentation; blending and rhyming. This video will help you to better understand phonemic awareness training and will show you how to apply these components not only to the reading curriculum but to all subjects through the school day. Filmed in actual classroom settings. *$69.95*
25 minute video
ISBN 1-890455-29-6

787 Polar Express
Houghton Mifflin
215 Park Ave S
New York, NY 10003-1603 212-420-5846
FAX 212-420-5850
http://www.houghtonmifflinbooks.com
e-mail: trade_publicity@hmco.com

Chris Van Allsburg, Author

Share the magic and enchantment of the holiday season with this CD-ROM version of the Caldecott-winning picture book.

788 Prehistoric Creaures Then & Now
HMH Supplemental Publishers
6277 Sea Harbor Dr
5th Floor
Orlando, FL 32887

800-531-5015
FAX 800-699-9459
http://www.harcourtachieve.com
e-mail: greatservice@hmhpub.com

K S Rodriguez, Author
Linda K. Zecher, President and CEO
Eric Shuman, Chief Financial Officer

When reading is a struggle, academic success is even harder to achieve. Now you can put social studies and science curriculum content within reach of every students with Steadwell Books — the series designed specifically for limited readers. Attention-getting photos and informative illustrations, maps, and time lines communicate the social studies and science concepts found in the text.

ISBN 0-739821-47-4

789 Primary Phonics
Educators Publishing Service
PO Box 9031
Cambridge, MA 02139-9031

617-547-6706
800-225-5750
FAX 617-547-3805
http://www.epsbooks.com
e-mail: CustomerService.EPS@schoolspecialty.com

Barbara W Makar, Author
Kathryn Hansen, Key Accounts Coordinator
Jeff Belanger, Regional Sales Manager

This revised program of storybooks and coordinated workbooks teaches reading for grades K-2. There is a set of ten storybooks to go with each of the first five workbooks. A Primary Phonics Picture Dictionary contains 2,500 commonly used words, including most of the words in the series. This series' individualized nature permits students to progress at their own speed. Teacher's manual available.

790 Read On! Plus
Sunburst Technology
1550 Executive Dr
Elgin, IL 60123-9311

800-321-7511
FAX 888-608-0344
http://store.sunburst.com
e-mail: service@sunburst.com

Michael Guillory, Channel Sales/Marketing Manager

Promote skills and strategies that improve reading comprehension, and build appreciation for literature and the written word.

791 Reader's Quest I
Sunburst Technology
1550 Executive Dr
Elgin, IL 60123-9311

800-321-7511
FAX 888-608-0344
http://store.sunburst.com
e-mail: service@sunburst.com

Michael Guillory, Channel Sales/Marketing Manager

These reading workshops provide students with direct reading instruction, interactive practice activities, and practical strategies to ensure reading success.

792 Reader's Quest II
Sunburst Technology
1550 Executive Dr
Elgin, IL 60123-9311

800-321-7511
FAX 888-608-0344
http://store.sunburst.com
e-mail: service@sunburst.com

Michael Guillory, Channel Sales/Marketing Manager

These reading workshops provide students with direct reading instruction, interactive practice activities, and practical strategies to ensure reading success.

793 Reading Comprehension Bundle
Sunburst Technology
1550 Executive Dr
Elgin, IL 60123-9311

800-321-7511
FAX 888-608-0344
http://store.sunburst.com
e-mail: service@sunburst.com

Michael Guillory, Channel Sales/Marketing Manager

This collection for the intermediate-level classroom develops the skills students need to read for meaning and understanding.

794 Reading Comprehension in Varied Subject Matter
Educators Publishing Service
PO Box 9031
Cambridge, MA 02139-9031

617-547-6706
800-225-5750
FAX 617-547-3805
http://www.epsbooks.com
e-mail: CustomerService.EPS@schoolspecialty.com

Jane Ervin, Author
Kathryn Hansen, Key Accounts Coordinator
Jeff Belanger, Regional Sales Manager

Ten workbooks that present a wide range of people and situations with new reading selections, new vocabulary, and a new writing exercise. Each book contains 31 selections in the subject areas of social studies, science, literature, mathematics, philosophy, logic, language, and the arts.

795 Reading Pen
Wizcom Technologies
20 Haganan St.
Einav Industrial Park

073-290-6131
http://www.wizcomtech.com
e-mail: customer_service@wizcomtech.com

Isaac Soibelman, President

Portable assitive reading device that reads words aloud and can be used anywhere. Scans a word from printed text, displays the word in large characters, reads the word aloud from built-in speaker or ear phones and defines the word with the press of a button. Displays syllables, keeps a history of scanned words, adjustable for left or right-handed use. Includes a tutorial video and audio cassette. Not recommended for persons with low vision or impaired fine motor control. *$279.00*

796 Reading Who? Reading You!
Sunburst Technology
1550 Executive Dr
Elgin, IL 60123-9311

800-321-7511
FAX 888-608-0344
http://store.sunburst.com
e-mail: service@sunburst.com

Michael Guillory, Channel Sales/Marketing Manager

Teach beginning reading skills effectively with phonics instruction built into engaging games and puzzles that have children asking for more.

797 Reading for Content
Educators Publishing Service
PO Box 9031
Cambridge, MA 02139-9031 617-547-6706
800-225-5750
FAX 617-547-3805
http://www.epsbooks.com
e-mail: CustomerService.EPS@schoolspecialty.com
Carol Einstein, Author
Kathryn Hansen, Key Accounts Coordinator
Jeff Belanger, Regional Sales Manager
Reading for Content is a series of 4 books designed to help students improve their reading comprehension skills. Each book contains 43 pasages followed by 4 questions. Two questions ask for a recall of main ideas, and two ask the student to draw conclusions from what they have just read.

798 Reading for Job and Personal Use
5910 Rice Creek Parkway
Shoreview, MN 55126 651-287-7608
800-328-2560
FAX 651-287-7227
http://www.agsnet.com
e-mail: agsmail@agsnet.com
Kevin Brueggeman, President
Matt Keller, Marketing Manager
Joyce Hing-McGowan, Author
The practical, real-life exercises in these texts teach students how to read and comprehend catalogs, training manuals, letters and memos, signs, reports, charts, and more.

799 Reasoning & Reading Series
Educators Publishing Service
PO Box 9031
Cambridge, MA 02139-9031 617-547-6706
800-225-5750
FAX 617-547-3805
http://www.epsbooks.com
e-mail: CustomerService.EPS@schoolspecialty.com
Joanne Carlisle, Author
Kathryn Hansen, Key Accounts Coordinator
Jeff Belanger, Regional Sales Manager
These workbooks develop basic language and thinking skills that build the foundation for reading comprehension. Exercises reinforce reading as a critical reasoning activity. Many exercises encourage students to come up with their own response in instances where there is no single correct answer. In other cases, exercises lend themselves to students working collaboratively to see how many different answers satisfy a question.

800 Right into Reading: A Phonics-Based Reading and Comprehension Program
Educators Publishing Service
PO Box 9031
Cambridge, MA 02139-9031 617-547-6706
800-225-5750
FAX 617-547-3805
http://www.epsbooks.com
e-mail: CustomerService.EPS@schoolspecialty.com
Jane Ervin, Author
Kathryn Hansen, Key Accounts Coordinator
Jeff Belanger, Regional Sales Manager
Right into Reading introduces phonics skills in a carefully ordered sequence of bite-size lessons so that students can progress easily and successfully from one reading level to the next. The stories and selections are unusually diverse and interactive.

801 See Me Add
Teddy Bear Press
3703 S Edmunds St
Ste 67
Seattle, WA 98118 206-402-6947
FAX 866-870-7323
http://www.teddybearpress.com
e-mail: fparker@teddybearpress.net
Fran Parker, Author

Introduces the concept of addition using simple story problems and the basic sight word vocabulary found in the I Can Read and Reading Is Fun programs. *$25.00*

802 See Me Subtract
Teddy Bear Press
3703 S Edmunds St
Ste 67
Seattle, WA 98118 206-402-6947
FAX 866-870-7323
http://www.teddybearpress.com
e-mail: fparker@teddybearpress.net
Fran Parker, Author

Introduces the concept of subtraction using simple story problems. *$25.00*

803 Sounds and Spelling Patterns for English
Oxton House Publishers
PO Box 209
Farmington, ME 04938 207-779-1923
800-539-7323
FAX 207-779-0623
http://www.oxtonhouse.com
e-mail: info@oxtonhouse.com
William Burlinghoff PhD, Owner
Bobby Brown, Marketing Director
Dr. Phyllis Fischer, Author
This book is a clear, concise, practical, jargon-free overview of the sounds that make up the English languate and the symbols that we use to represent them in writing. It includes an explanatory chapter on phonological and phonemic awareness and a broad range of strategies for helping beginning readers develop fluent decoding skills. *$24.95*
140 pages
ISBN 1-881929-01-9

804 Specialized Program Individualizing Reading Excellence (SPIRE)
Educators Publishing Service
PO Box 9031
Cambridge, MA 02139-9031 617-547-6706
800-225-5750
FAX 617-547-3805
http://www.epsbooks.com
e-mail: CustomerService.EPS@schoolspecialty.com
Sheila Clark Edmands, Author
Kathryn Hansen, Key Accounts Coordinator
Jeff Belanger, Regional Sales Manager
SPIRE is a comprehensive multisensory reading and language arts program for students with learning differences.

805 Starting Comprehension
Educators Publishing Service
PO Box 9031
Cambridge, MA 02139-9031 617-547-6706
800-225-5750
FAX 617-547-3805
http://www.epsbooks.com
e-mail: CustomerService.EPS@schoolspecialty.com
Ann L Staman, Author
Kathryn Hansen, Key Accounts Coordinator
Jeff Belanger, Regional Sales Manager

A reading series of 12 workbooks that develops essential comprehension skills at the earliest reading level. It is divided into two different strands, one for students who have a strong visual sense, the other for those who learn sounds easily. Vocabulary introduced within context of exercises, using most of the words in the books. Student relates the details of the passage to the main idea.

806 Stories and More: Animal Friends
Riverdeep, Inc.
100 Pine Street
Suite 1900
San Francisco, CA 94111-5205   415-659-2000
                                             FAX 415-659-2020
                                    http://www.web.riverdeep.net
                                        e-mail: info@riverdeep.net
Barry O'Callaghan, Executive Chairman

Stories and More: Animal Friends features three well-known stories — The Gunnywolf, The Trek, and Owl and the Moon — with engaging activities that strengthen students reading comprehension. A scaffolding of pre-reading, reading, and post-reading activities for each story helps kindergarten and 1st grade students practice prediction and sequencing skills; appreciate the importance of character and setting; and respond to literature through writing, drawing, and speaking. *$ 69.95*

807 Stories and More: Time and Place
Riverdeep, Inc.
100 Pine Street
Suite 1900
San Francisco, CA 94111-5205   415-659-2000
                                             FAX 415-659-2020
                                    http://www.web.riverdeep.net
                                        e-mail: info@riverdeep.net
Barry O'Callaghan, Executive Chairman

Stories and More: Time and Place combines three well-loved stories — The House on Maple Street, Roxaboxen, and Galimoto — with — angaging activities that strengthen students' reading comprehension. In these books, the setting plays a primary role. Second and third grade students learn the importance of time, culture, and place in our lives.

808 Stories from Somerville
Oxton House Publishers
PO Box 209
Farmington, ME 04938   207-779-1923
                                             800-539-7323
                                             FAX 207-779-0623
                                    http://www.oxtonhouse.com
                                        e-mail: info@oxtonhouse.com
William Berlinghoff PhD, Managing Editor
Bobby Brown, Marketing Director
Kim Ramsey, Author
This set of two readers and three workbooks contains a total of 75 separate but interconnected, phonetically-controlled stories that follow a careful pattern of skill development. They are compatible with most phonics-based reading programs. The realistic personal interactions of the characters also provide opportunities for rich class discussion about various social skills that may be troublesome for many students, including those with learning disabilities. *$69.95*

> ISBN 1-881929-40-4

809 Take Me Home Pair-It Books
Harcourt Achieve
6277 Sea Harbor Dr
5th Floor
Orlando, FL 32887
                                             800-531-5015
                                             FAX 800-699-9459
                                    http://www.harcourtachieve.com
                                        e-mail: greatservice@hmhpub.com

Linda K. Zecher, President and CEO
Eric Shuman, Chief Financial Officer
John K. Dragoon, EVP
Make reading time a family favorite. Our most popular Pair-It Book titles in convenient take-home packages make it easy to get parents involved in reinforcing reading. *$346.10*

810 Taking Your Camera To...Steadwell
Harcourt Achieve
6277 Sea Harbor Dr
5th Floor
Orlando, FL 32887
                                             800-531-5015
                                             FAX 800-699-9459
                                    http://www.harcourtachieve.com
                                        e-mail: greatservice@hmhpub.com
Linda K. Zecher, President, CEO
Eric Shuman, Chief Financial Officer
John K. Dragoon, Executive Vice President
Give limited readers unlimited access to major countries! Each title devotes a spread to the land, the people, major cities, lifestyles, places to visit, government and religion, earning a living, sports and school, food and holidays, quick facts, statistics and maps, and the future. *$7.80*

811 Teaching Comprehension: Strategies for Stories
Oxton House Publishers
PO Box 209
Farmington, ME 04938   207-779-1923
                                             800-539-7323
                                             FAX 207-779-0623
                                    http://www.oxtonhouse.com
                                        e-mail: info@oxtonhouse.com
William Burlinghoff PhD, Managing Editor
Bobby Brown, Marketing Director
Dr. Phyllis Fischer, Author
This handbook gives teachers a richly detailed roadmap for providing students with effective strategies for comprehending and remembering stories. It inlcudes story-line masters for helping students to organize their thinking about a story and to accurately depict characters and sequence events. *$24.95*

> 62 pages
> ISBN 1-881929-27-2

812 Tenth Planet: Roots, Suffixes, Prefixes
Sunburst Technology
1550 Executive Dr
Elgin, IL 60123-9311
                                             800-321-7511
                                             FAX 888-608-0344
                                    http://store.sunburst.com
                                        e-mail: service@sunburst.com
Michael Guillory, Channel Sales/Marketing Manager

Students learn to decode difficult and more complex words as they engage in six activities where they construct and dissect words with roots, prefixes and suffixes.

813 Transition Stage 2-3
Harcourt Achieve
6277 Sea Harbor Dr
5th Floor
Orlando, FL 32887
                                             800-531-5015
                                             FAX 800-699-9459
                                    http://www.harcourtachieve.com
                                        e-mail: greatservice@hmhpub.com
Linda K. Zecher, President and CEO
Eric Shuman, Chief Financial Officer
John K. Dragoon, EVP
A series of 20 books, each containing 16 pages, that provide readers with a gradual transition into early fluency. All stories are available on audio cassette, and four are available in big book format. *$951.80*

814   **Vowels: Short & Long**
Sunburst Technology
1550 Executive Dr
Elgin, IL 60123-9311

800-321-7511
FAX 888-608-0344
http://store.sunburst.com
e-mail: service@sunburst.com
Michael Guillory, Channel Sales/Marketing Manager

Introduce students to vowels and the role they play in the structure of words. By engaging in word building activities, students learn to identify short and long vowels and regular spelling patterns.

815   **Wilson Language Training**
47 Old Webster Rd
Oxford, MA 01540-2705

508-368-2399
800-899-8454
FAX 508-368-2300
http://www.wilsonlanguage.com
e-mail: info@wilsonlanguage.com
Barbara A Wilson, Co-Founder/President
Ed Wilson, Co-Founder/Publisher

Dedicated to providing educators with the resources they need to help their students become fluent, independent readers. Provides professional development and research-based reading and spelling curricula for all ages.

816   **Wordly Wise 3000 ABC 1-9**
Educators Publishing Service
PO Box 9031
Cambridge, MA 02139-9031

617-547-6706
800-225-5750
FAX 617-547-3805
http://www.epsbooks.com
e-mail: CustomerService.EPS@schoolspecialty.com
Kenneth Hodkinson, Author
Sandra Adams, Co-Author
Kathryn Hansen, Key Accounts Coordinator
Three thousand new and carefully selected words taken from literature, textbooks and SAT-prep books, are the basis of this new series that teaches vocabulary through reading, writing, and a variety of exercises for grades 4-12.

817   **Wordly Wise ABC 1-9**
Educators Publishing Service
PO Box 9031
Cambridge, MA 02139-9031

617-547-6706
800-225-5750
FAX 617-547-3805
http://www.epsbooks.com
e-mail: CustomerService.EPS@schoolspecialty.com
Kenneth Hodkinson, Author
Sandra Adams, Co-Author
Kathryn Hansen, Key Accounts Coordinator
Vocabulary workbook series employs crossword puzzles, riddles, word games and a sense of humor to make the learning of new words an interesting experience.

Science

818   **Learn About Life Science: Animals**
Sunburst Technology
1550 Executive Dr
Elgin, IL 60123-9311

800-321-7511
FAX 888-608-0344
http://store.sunburst.com
e-mail: service@sunburst.com
Michael Guillory, Channel Sales/Marketing Manager

Learn about animal classification, adaptation to climate, domestication and special relationships between humans and animals.

819   **Learn About Life Science: Plants**
Sunburst Technology
1550 Executive Dr
Elgin, IL 60123-9311

800-321-7511
FAX 888-608-0344
http://store.sunburst.com
e-mail: service@sunburst.com
Michael Guillory, Channel Sales/Marketing Manager

Students explore the world of plants. From small seeds to tall trees students learn what plants are and what they need to grow.

820   **Learn About Physical Science: Simple Machines**
Sunburst Technology
1550 Executive Dr
Elgin, IL 60123-9311

800-321-7511
FAX 888-608-0344
http://store.sunburst.com
e-mail: service@sunburst.com
Michael Guillory, Channel Sales/Marketing Manager

Students delve into the mechanical world learning about the ways simple machines make our work easier.

821   **Life Cycles Beaver**
HMH Supplemental Publishers
6277 Sea Harbor Dr
5th Floor
Orlando, FL 32887

800-531-5015
FAX 800-699-9459
http://www.harcourtachieve.com
e-mail: greatservice@hmhpub.com
Sabrina Crewe, Author
Linda K. Zecher, President and CEO
Eric Shuman, Chief Financial Officer
Dramatic photos tell the story of animal growth and development. This softcover series enriches any classroom science curriculum. Animal development is a complex subject but this series makes it understandable for young readers with simple text and informative images that follow each animal from birth to maturity. *$8.80*

822   **Maps & Navigation**
Sunburst Technology
1550 Executive Dr
Elgin, IL 60123-9311

800-321-7511
FAX 888-608-0344
http://store.sunburst.com
e-mail: service@sunburst.com
Michael Guillory, Channel Sales/Marketing Manager

This exciting nautical simulation provides students with opportunities to use their math and science skills.

823   **Our Universe**
HMH Supplemental Publishers
6277 Sea Harbor Drive
5th Floor
 rlando, FL 32887

800-531-5015
FAX 800-699-9459
http://www.harcourtachieve.com
e-mail: greatservice@hmhpub.com
Gregory Vogt, Author
Linda K. Zecher, President and CEO
Eric Shuman, Chief Financial Officer

Unravel the mysteries of space! A complex universe becomes amazingly clear in these easy-to-read titles. *$96.00*

ISBN 0-739833-55-3

824   Prehistoric Creatures Then & Now
HMH Supplemental Publishers
6277 Sea Harbor Dr
5th Floor
Orlando, FL 32887

800-531-5015
FAX 800-699-9459
http://www.harcourtachieve.com
e-mail: greatservice@hmhpub.com

K S Rodriguez, Author
Linda K. Zecher, President and CEO
Eric Shuman, Chief Financial Officer
Now limited readers can dig into the details of dinosaurs! Each information-packed title includes a special spread with a project, a profile of a dinosaur expert, or a description of a recent dinosaur discovery.

ISBN 0-739821-47-4

825   Space Academy GX-1
Riverdeep
222 Berkeley Street
Boston, MA 02116

617-351-5000
888-242-6747
FAX 877-892-9820
http://www.riverdeep.net
e-mail: IIEcustomerservice@hmhpub.com

Linda K. Zecher, President and CEO
Eric Shuman, Chief Financial Officer
John K. Dragoon, EVP
Explore the solar system with Space Academy GX-1! Fully aligned with national science standards and state curricula, Space Academy GX-1, students investigate the astronomical basis for seasons, phases of the moon, gravity, orbits, and more. As students succeed, Grow Slides adjust to offer more advanced topics and problems.

826   Talking Walls
Riverdeep
222 Berkeley Street
Boston, MA 02116

617-351-5000
888-242-6747
FAX 877-892-9820
http://www.riverdeep.net
e-mail: IIEcustomerservice@hmhpub.com

Linda K. Zecher, President
Eric Shuman, Chief Financial Officer
John K. Dragoon, Executive Vice President
The Talking Walls Software Series is a wonderful springboard for a student's journey of exploration and discovery. This comprehensive collection of researched resources and materials enables students to focus on learning while conducting a guided search for information.

827   Talking Walls: The Stories Continue
Riverdeep
222 Berkeley Street
Boston, MA 02116

617-351-5000
888-242-6747
FAX 877-892-9820
http://www.riverdeep.net
e-mail: IIEcustomerservice@hmhpub.com

Linda K. Zecher, President and CEO
Eric Shuman, Chief Financial Officer
John K. Dragoon, EVP
Using the Talking Walls Software Series, students discover the stories behind some of the world's most fascinating walls. The award-winning books, interactive software, carefully chosen Web sites, and suggested classroom activities build upon each other, providing a rich learning experience that includes text, video, and hands-on projects.

828   ThemeWeavers: Nature Activity Kit
Riverdeep
222 Berkeley Street
Boston, MA 02116

617-351-5000
888-242-6747
FAX 877-892-9820
http://www.riverdeep.net
e-mail: IIEcustomerservice@hmhpub.com

Linda K. Zecher, President and CEO
Eric Shuman, Chief Financial Officer
John K. Dragoon, EVP
ThemeWeavers: Nature Activity Kit is an all-in-one solution for theme-based teaching. In just a few minutes, you can select from dozens of ready-to-use activities centering on the seasons and weather and be ready for the next day's lesson! Interactive and engaging activities cover multiple subject areas such as language arts, math, science, social studies and art.

829   Thinkin' Science
Sunburst Technology
1550 Executive Dr
Elgin, IL 60123-9311

800-321-7511
FAX 888-608-0344
http://store.sunburst.com
e-mail: service@sunburst.com

Michael Guillory, Channel Sales/Marketing Manager

Five environments introduce students to the scientific methods and concepts needed to understand basic earth, life and physical sciences. Students learn to think like scientists as they solve problems using hypothesis, experimentation, observation and deduction.

830   Thinkin' Science ZAP!
Sunburst Technology
1550 Executive Dr
Elgin, IL 60123-9311

800-321-7511
FAX 888-608-0344
http://store.sunburst.com
e-mail: service@sunburst.com

Michael Guillory, Channel Sales/Marketing Manager

Working with laser beams, electrical circuits, and visible sound waves, students practice valuable thinking skills, observation, prediction, deductive reasoning, conceptual modeling, theory building and hypothesis testing while experimenting within scientifically accurate learning environment.

831   True Tales
HMH Supplemental Publishers
6277 Sea Harbor Dr
5th Floor
Orlando, FL 32887

800-531-5015
FAX 800-699-9459
http://www.harcourtachieve.com
e-mail: greatservice@hmhpub.com

Henry Billings, Author
Linda K. Zecher, President and CEO
Eric Shuman, Chief Financial Officer
If you have been looking for reading comprehension materials for limited readers, your search is over. True Tales presents powerful real-lfe events with direct connections to geography and science at reading level 3. Gripping accounts of personal triumph and tragedy put geography and science in a very real context. Accompanying activities develop reading and language arts, science, and geography skills students need to boost test scores. *$205.00*

ISBN 0-739834-49-5

832 **Virtual Labs: Electricity**
Riverdeep
222 Berkeley Street
Boston, MA 02116   617-351-5000
                                            888-242-6747
                                        FAX 877-892-9820
                                     http://www.riverdeep.net
                        e-mail: IIEcustomerservice@hmhpub.com
Linda K. Zecher, President, CEO
Eric Shuman, Chief Financial Officer
John K. Dragoon, Executive Vice President
Five environments introduce students to the scientific methods and conepts needed to understand basic Earth, life, and physical sciences. Students will learn to think like scientists as they solve problems using hypothesis, experimentation, observation, and deduction. *$69.95*

Social Skills

833 **Activities Unlimited**
Therapro
225 Arlington St
Framingham, MA 01702-8773   508-872-9494
                                            800-257-5376
                                        FAX 508-875-2062
                                  http://www.theraproducts.com
                               e-mail: info@theraproducts.com
A Cleveland, Author
B Caton, Co-Author
L Adler, Co-Author
Helps young children develop fine and gross motor skills, increase their language, become self-reliant and play cooperatively. An innovative resource that immediately attracts and engages children. Short of time? Need a good idea? Count on Activites Unlimited. *$17.95*

834 **Activity Schedules for Children with Autism: Teaching Independent Behavior**
Therapro
225 Arlington St
Framingham, MA 01702-8773   508-872-9494
                                            800-257-5376
                                        FAX 508-875-2062
                                  http://www.theraproducts.com
                               e-mail: info@theraproducts.com
Lynn McClannahan PhD, Author
Patricia Krantz PhD, Co-Author
Karen Conrad, President
An activity schedule is a set of pictures or words that cue a child to follow a sequence of activities. When mastered, the children are more self-directed and purposeful at home, school and leisure activites. In this book, parents and professionals can find detailed instructions and examples, assess a child's readiness to use activity schedules, and understand graduated guidance and progress monitoring. Great for promoting independence in children with autism. *$16.95*
117 pages

835 **Alert Program with Songs for Self-Regulation**
Therapro
225 Arlington St
Framingham, MA 01702-8773   508-872-9494
                                            800-257-5376
                                        FAX 508-875-2062
                                  http://www.theraproducts.com
                               e-mail: info@theraproducts.com
Mary Sue Williams OTR, Author
Sherry Shellenberger OTR, Co-Author
Karen Conrad, President
This program compares the body to an engine, running either high, low, or just right. Side A is an overview, Side B has 15 songs for self-regulation. Extremely successful in helping kids recognize and change their own engine speeds. *$23.95*
Audio Tape

836 **An Introduction to How Does Your Engine Run?**
Therapro
225 Arlington St
Framingham, MA 01702-8773   508-872-9494
                                            800-257-5376
                                        FAX 508-875-2062
                                  http://www.theraproducts.com
                               e-mail: info@theraproducts.com
Mary Sue Williams OTR, Author
Sherry Shellenberger OTR, Co-Author
Karen Conrad, President
Introduces the entire Alert Program, which explains how we regulate our arousal states. Describes the use of sensorimotor strategies to manage levels of alertness. This program is fun for students and the adults working with them, and translates easily into real life. *$7.95*

837 **Andy and His Yellow Frisbee**
Woodbine House
6510 Bells Mill Rd
Bethesda, MD 20817-1636   301-897-3570
                                            800-843-7323
                                        FAX 301-897-5838
                                  http://www.woodbinehouse.com
                               e-mail: info@woodbinehouse.com
Mary Thompson, Author

A heartwarming story about Andy, a boy with autism. Like many children with autism, Andy has a fascination with objects in motion. His talent for spinning his Frisbee and a new classmate's curiosity set this story in motion. Rosie, the watchful and protective sister, supplies backround on Andy and autism, as well as a sibling's perspective. *$14.95*
24 pages

838 **Breakthroughs Manual: How to Reach Students with Autism**
Therapro
225 Arlington St
Framingham, MA 01702-8773   508-872-9494
                                            800-257-5376
                                        FAX 508-875-2062
                                  http://www.theraproducts.com
                               e-mail: info@theraproducts.com
Karen Sewell, Author
Karen Conrad, President

This manual features practical suggestions for everyday use with preschool through high school students. Covers communication, behavior, academics, self-help, life and social skills. Includes reproducible lesson plans and up to date listing of classroom materials and catalog supply companies. *$49.50*
243 pages

839 **Busy Kids Movement**
Therapro
225 Arlington St
Framingham, MA 01702-8773   508-872-9494
                                            800-257-5376
                                        FAX 508-875-2062
                                  http://www.theraproducts.com
                               e-mail: info@theraproducts.com
Karen Conrad, President

Full of ideas for developing youngsters' gross motor skills. Games, dramatics, action songs, music and rythm activities. *$9.95*
64 pages

840 **Calm Down and Play**
Childswork
PO Box 1246
Wilkes-Barre, PA 18703-1246
                                            800-962-1141
                                        FAX 800-262-1886
                                    http://www.childswork.com

Sally Germain, Editor
Loretta Oleck Berger, Author

Filled with fun and effective activities to help children: calm down and control their impulses; focus, concentrate, and organize their thoughts; identify and verbalize feelings; channel and release excess energy appropriately; and build self-esteem and confidence. *$17.95*

841 **Courageous Pacers Classroom Chart**
Therapro
225 Arlington St
Framingham, MA 01702-8773

508-872-9494
800-257-5376
FAX 508-875-2062
http://www.theraproducts.com
e-mail: info@theraproducts.com

Karen Conrad, President
Tim Erson, Author

Highly recommended to accompany the Courageous Pacers Program. Assists in keeping record of 12 students' progress in walking and lifting. A great visual tool to view progress.

842 **Courageous Pacers Program**
Therapro
225 Arlington St
Framingham, MA 01702-8773

508-872-9494
800-257-5376
FAX 508-875-2062
http://www.theraproducts.com
e-mail: info@theraproducts.com

Karen Conrad, President
Tim Erson, Author

This fun and easy program was developed to help students become more active. Research shows that students who are more active, do better in school. The goal of the program is simple: get students to walk 100 miles and lift 10,000 pounds in a year.
92 pages

843 **Face to Face: Resolving Conflict Without Giving in or Giving Up**
1959 South Power Road
Ste 103-279
Mesa, AZ 85206

602-633-4213
FAX 202-667-8629
http://www.nafcm.org
e-mail: admin@nafcm.org

Mary Ellen Bowen
Jan Bellard, Author
Jilda Gutierrez, Co-Author
Modular curriculum for training program for AmeriCorps members. Addresses conflict at the personal level, interpersonal level, and group collaboration. Includes workbook.

844 **Forms for Helping the ADHD Child**
Childswork
PO Box 1246
Wilkes-Barre, PA 18703-1246

800-962-1141
FAX 800-262-1886
http://www.childswork.com

Sally Germain, Editor
Lawrence E. Shapiro, Author

Forms, charts, and checklists for treating children with Attention Deficit Hyperactivity Disorder cover a wide range of approaches. Includes effective aids in assessing, treating, and monitoring the progress of the ADHD child. *$ 31.95*
100 pages

845 **Funsical Fitness With Silly-cise CD: Motor Development Activities**
Therapro
225 Arlington St
Framingham, MA 01702-8773

508-872-9494
800-257-5376
FAX 508-875-2062
http://www.theraproducts.com
e-mail: info@theraproducts.com

Karen Conrad, President

This unique blending of developmentally appropriate gross motor, sensory integration, and aerobic activities is guaranteed to build children's strength, balance endurance, coordination, and self confidence. Leads children through four 15-minute classes of Wacky Walking, Grinnastics, Brain Gym, Warm Ups, Adventurobics, and Chill Out activities. *$15.00*

846 **Games we Should Play in School**
Therapro
225 Arlington St
Framingham, MA 01702-8773

508-872-9494
800-257-5376
FAX 508-875-2062
http://www.theraproducts.com
e-mail: info@theraproducts.com

Frank Aycox, Author
Karen Conrad, President

Includes over 75 interactive, fun, social games; describes how to effectively lead Social Play sessions in the classroom. Students become more cooperative, less antagonistic and more capable of increased attentiveness. Contains the secrets to enriching the entire school environment. *$16.50*
154 pages

847 **Jarvis Clutch: Social Spy**
Educators Publishing Service
PO Box 9031
Cambridge, MA 02139-9031

617-547-6706
800-225-5750
FAX 617-547-3805
http://www.epsbooks.com
e-mail: CustomerService.EPS@schoolspecialty.com

Melvin D Levine MD FAAP, Author
Kathryn Hansen, Key Accounts Coordinator
Jeff Belanger, Regional Sales Manager
In Jarvis Clutch social spy, Dr. Mel Levine teams up with eight grader Jarvis Clutch for an insider's look at life on the middle school social scene. Jarvis's wry and insightful observations of student interactions at Eastern Middle School bring to light the myriad social challenges that adolescents face every day, including peer pressure, the need to seem cool, the perils of dating., Include the commentary in Jarivs' Spy Notes!

848 **Learning in Motion**
Therapro
225 Arlington St
Framingham, MA 01702-8773

508-872-9494
800-257-5376
FAX 508-875-2062
http://www.theraproducts.com
e-mail: info@theraproducts.com

Patricia Angermeir OTR BCP, Author
Joan Krzyzanowski OTR MS, Co-Author
Kristina Keller Moir OTR BCP, Co-Author
Written by 3 OTs, this book is for the busy therapist or teacher of preschoolers to second graders. Provides group activities using gross, fine andsensory motor skills in theme based curricula. Every lesson plan contains goals, objectives, materials and adaptations to facilitate inclusion and multilevel instructions. Includes 130 lesson plans with corresponding parent letters that explain the lesson and provide home follow-up activities. *$39.95*
379 pages

849 New Language of Toys: Teaching Communication Skills to Children with Special Needs
Therapro
225 Arlington St
Framingham, MA 01702-8773   508-872-9494
                                  800-257-5376
                              FAX 508-875-2062
                        http://www.theraproducts.com
                        e-mail: info@theraproducts.com
Karen Conrad, President
Sue Schwarz PhD, Author
Joan Heller Miller EdM, Co-Author
Play time becomes a fun and educational experience with this revised hands-on approach for developing communication skills using everyday toys. Includes a fresh assortment of toys, books and new chapters on computer technology, language learning, videotapes and television. *$18.95*
289 pages

850 Reaching Out, Joining In: Teaching Social Skills to Young Children with Autism
Therapro
225 Arlington St
Framingham, MA 01702-8773   508-872-9494
                                  800-257-5376
                              FAX 508-875-2062
                        http://www.theraproducts.com
                        e-mail: info@theraproducts.com
Mary Jane Weiss PhD BCBA, Author
Sandra Harris PhD, Co-Author
Karen Conrad, President
Describes how to help young children diagnosed within the autism spectrum with one of their most challenging areas of development, social behavior. Focuses on four broad topics: play skills; the language of social skills; undestanding another person's perspective; and using these skills in an inclusive classroon. The authors present concrete strategies to teach basic play skills, how to play with others, to recognize social cues and engage in social conversation. Practical and accessible. *$16.95*
215 pages

851 Right from the Start: Behavioral Intervention for Young Children with Autism
Therapro
225 Arlington St
Framingham, MA 01702-8773   508-872-9494
                                  800-257-5376
                              FAX 508-875-2062
                        http://www.theraproducts.com
                        e-mail: info@theraproducts.com
Mary Jane Weiss PhD BCBA, Author
Sandra L Harris PhD, Co-Author
Karen Conrad, President
This informative and user-friendly guide helps parents and service providers explore programs that use early intensive behavioral intervention for young children with autism and related disorders. Within these programs, many children improve in intellectual, social and adaptive functioning, enabling them to move on to regular elementary and preschools. Benefits all children, but primarily useful for children age five and younger. *$16.95*
215 pages

852 S'Cool Moves for Learning: A Program Designed to Enhance Learning Through Body-Mind
Therapro
225 Arlington St
Framingham, MA 01702-8773   508-872-9494
                                  800-257-5376
                              FAX 508-875-2062
                        http://www.theraproducts.com
                        e-mail: info@theraproducts.com
Debra M Heiberger MA, Author
Margot C Heiniger White MA OTR, Co-Author
Karen Conrad, President

The movement activities described in this book are organized in a way that is easy to integrate into the class routine throughout the day. The Minute Moves for the Classroom included in several chapters is a handy reference of movement activities which help make the transition from one activity to another fun and smooth. *$35.00*

853 Simple Steps: Developmental Activities for Infants, Toddlers & Two Year Olds
Therapro
225 Arlington St
Framingham, MA 01702-8773   508-872-9494
                                  800-257-5376
                              FAX 508-875-2062
                        http://www.theraproducts.com
                        e-mail: info@theraproducts.com
Karen Miller, Author
Karen Conrad, President

Three hundred activities linked to the latest research in brain development. Outlines a typical developmental sequence in 10 domains: social/emotional, fine motor; gross motor; language; cognition; sensory; nature; music and movement; creativity and dramatic play. Chapters on curriculum development and learning environment also included. *$24.95*
293 pages

854 Solutions Kit for ADHD
Childswork
PO Box 1246
Wilkes-Barre, PA 18703-1246
                                  800-962-1141
                              FAX 800-262-1886
                        http://www.childswork.com
Sally Germain, Editor
Dana Regan, Author
Lawrence E Shapiro, Co-Author
This comprehensive kit is packed with hands-on materials for a multi-modal approach to working with ADHD kids aged 5 through 12. *$105.00*

855 Song Games for Sensory Integration
Therapro
225 Arlington St
Framingham, MA 01702-8773   508-872-9494
                                  800-257-5376
                              FAX 508-875-2062
                        http://www.theraproducts.com
                        e-mail: info@theraproducts.com
Karen Conrad, President
Aubrey Carton, Author
Lois Hickman, Co-Author
For young children with sensory processing challenges, 15 play-along routines help remediate everything from bilateral skills to vestibular dysfunction. Narrative is helpful for parents. Includes an 81 page book filled with ideas for extending therapeutic value of these activites. 87 minute CD. *$21.00*
Audio Tape

856 Start to Finish: Developmentally Sequenced Fine Motor Activities for Preschool Children
Therapro
225 Arlington St
Framingham, MA 01702-8773   508-872-9494
                                  800-257-5376
                              FAX 508-875-2062
                        http://www.theraproducts.com
                        e-mail: info@theraproducts.com
Nory Marsh, Author
Karen Conrad, President

Seventy stimulating activities target 4 areas of fine motor development normally acquired between 3 and 5: hand manipulation, pencil grasp, scissors skill and grasp, and visual motor skills. Each 30 minute activity has skills, projected goal, supplies needed, instructions and modifications provided and needs limited preparation time. *$59.50*

857 Stop, Relax and Think
Childswork
PO Box 1246
Wilkes Barre, PA 18703-1246

800-962-1141
FAX 800-262-1886
http://www.childswork.com

Sally Germain, Editor

In this board game, active impulsive children learn motor control, relaxation skills, how to express their feelings, and how to problem-solve. Can be used both as a diagnostic and a treatment tool, and behaviors learned in the game can be generalized into the home or classroom. *$52.00*

858 Stop, Relax and Think Ball
Childswork
PO Box 1246
Wilkes-Barre, PA 18703-1246

800-962-1141
FAX 800-262-1886
http://www.childswork.com

Sally Germain, Editor

This ball teaches children to control their impulsivity by helping them understand and control their actions. *$22.00*

859 Stop, Relax and Think Card Game
Childswork
PO Box 1246
Wilkes-Barre, PA 18703-1246

800-962-1141
FAX 800-262-1886
http://www.childswork.com

Sally Germain, Editor
Becky Bridges, Author

Players are dealt Stop, Relax and Think cards and also Stressed Out, Confused, and Discouraged cards. As they acquire more cards, they must choose different self-control skills, and they learn the value of patience and cooperating with others to achieve a goal. *$21.95*

860 Stop, Relax and Think Scriptbook
Childswork
PO Box 1246
Wilkes-Barre, PA 18703-1246

800-962-1141
FAX 800-262-1886
http://www.childswork.com

Sally Germain, Editor
Hennie Shore, Author

In this uniquely designed book, children can practice what to say and how to act in eight different scenarios common to children with behavioral problems. The counselor and the child sit across from each other and read the scripts. *$24.95*

861 Stop, Relax and Think Workbook
Childswork
PO Box 1246
Wilkes-Barre, PA 18703-1246

800-962-1141
FAX 800-262-1886
http://www.childswork.com

Sally Germain, Editor
Lisa M. Schab, LCSW, Author

This new workbook contains more than 60 paper and pencil activities that teach children such important skills as: thinking about consequences, staying focused and completing a task, engaging in quiet activities without disturbing others, and more. *$19.95*

862 Successful Movement Challenges
Therapro
225 Arlington St
Framingham, MA 01702-8773

508-872-9494
800-257-5376
FAX 508-875-2062
http://www.theraproducts.com
e-mail: info@theraproducts.com

Jack Capon, Author
Karen Conrad, President

Extensive and exciting movement activities for children in preschool, elementary and special education. Includes movement exploration challenges using parachutes, balls, hoops, ropes, bean bags, rythm sticks, scarves and much more. This popular publication also includes body conditioning, mat activities and playground apparatus activities. Everyone enjoys the creative and carefully designed movement experiences. *$14.25*
   127 pages

863 Teaching Kids with Mental Health and Learning Disorders in the Regular Classroom
Free Spirit Publishing
Ste 200
217 5th Ave N
Minneapolis, MN 55401-1260

800-735-7323
866-703-7322
FAX 866-419-5199
http://www.freespirit.com
e-mail: help4kids@freespirit.com

Judy Galbraith, Founder/President
Myles L. Cooley, Author

Generalized Anxiety Disorder (GAD), depression, Asperger's Syndrome, and ADHD. Many students have these and other mental health issues and learning problems. Written by a clinical psychologist, this guide describes mental health and learning disorders often observed in school children, explains how each might be exhibited in the classroom, and offers expert suggestions on what to do (and sometimes what not to do). *$34.95*
   256 pages
   ISBN 1-575420-89-9

864 Understanding Argumentative Communication: How Many Ways Can You Ask for a Cookie?
Therapro
225 Arlington St
Framingham, MA 01702-8773

508-872-9494
800-257-5376
FAX 508-875-2062
http://www.theraproducts.com
e-mail: info@theraproducts.com

Christine Derse MEd, Author
Janice Lopes MSEd, Co-Author
Karen Conrad, President

Ten uncomplicated lesson plans for classroom use. Teach a complete overview of all that Argumentative Communication encompasses or give students a brief awareness lesson about just one type of communication. Lessons can be used either consecutively or singly. Includes defining communication, gestures, sign language, object boards, picture boards, headsticks, eye pointing, scanning with picture boards, picture boards in sentence format and computers for argumentative communication. *$18.95*
   142 pages

865 Updown Chair
R.E.A.L. Design
187 S Main St
Dolgeville, NY 13329-1455

315-429-3071
800-696-7041
FAX 315-429-3071
http://www.realdesigninc.com
e-mail: rdesign@twcny.rr.com

Kris Wohnsen, Co-Owner
Sam Camarello, Co-Owner

The updown chair is designed for children from 43-63 in height. It combines optimal positioning and sitting comfort with ease of adjustment. Changing the seat height can be done quickly and safely with our exclusive foot lever activation which uses a pneumatic cylinder assist. Children can be elevated to just the right position for floor or table top activities.

866   Wikki Stix Hands On-Learning Activity Book
Therapro
225 Arlington St
Framingham, MA   01702-8773   508-872-9494
                                            800-257-5376
                                        FAX 508-875-2062
                            http://www.theraproducts.com
                            e-mail: info@theraproducts.com
Karen Conrad, President

Loaded with great ideas for using Wikki Stix. For all ages and curriculums. *$3.50*

867   Workbook for Verbal Expression
PO Box 1579
Appleton, WI   54912-1579
                                            888-388-3224
                                        FAX 888-388-6344
                             http://www.speechbin.com
                      e-mail: customercare@schoolspecialty.com
Michael P. Lavelle, President and CEO
Beth M Kennedy, Author
Rick Holden, EVP of Education
A book of 100s of excercises from simple naming, automatic speech sequences, and repetition exercises to complex tasks in sentence formulation and abstract verbal reasoning. Item number 1435.

Social Studies

868   American Government Today
HMH Supplemental Publishers
6277 Sea Harbor Dr
5th Floor
Orlando, FL   32887
                                            800-531-5015
                                        FAX 800-699-9459
                            http://www.harcourtachieve.com
                            e-mail: greatservice@hmhpub.com
Mark Sanders, Author
Linda K. Zecher, President and CEO
Eric Shuman, Chief Financial Officer
Give limited readers unlimited access to social studies and citizenship topics! Whether applying for citizenship or studying for GED Test, learners need to know about our nation's capital and the democracy it hosts. In this series, even limited readers can get a clear picture of a complex system. *$52.00*

ISBN 0-139822-03-9

869   Calliope
Cobblestone Publishing
Ste C
30 Grove St
Peterborough, NH   03458-1453   603-924-7209
                                            800-821-0115
                                        FAX 603-924-7380
                            http://www.cobblestonepub.com
                            e-mail: customerservice@caruspub.com
Rosalie Baker, Editor

Kid's world history magazine written for kids ages 9 to 14, goes beyond the facts to explore provocative issues. *$33.95*
       9x/year

870   Discoveries: Explore the Desert Ecosystem
Sunburst Technology
1550 Executive Dr
Elgin, IL   60123-9311
                                            800-321-7511
                                        FAX 888-608-0344
                             http://store.sunburst.com
                             e-mail: service@sunburst.com
Michael Guillory, Channel Sales/Marketing Manager

This program invites students to explore the plants, animals, culture and georgraphy of the Sonoran Desert by day and by night.

871   Discoveries: Explore the Everglades Ecosystem
Sunburst Technology
1550 Executive Dr
Elgin, IL   60123-9311
                                            800-321-7511
                                        FAX 888-608-0344
                             http://store.sunburst.com
                             e-mail: service@sunburst.com
Michael Guillory, Channel Sales/Marketing Manager

This multi curricular research program takes students to the Everglades where they anchor their exploration photo realistic panaramas of the habitiat.

872   Discoveries: Explore the Forest Ecosystem
Sunburst Technology
1550 Executive Dr
Elgin, IL   60123-9311
                                            800-321-7511
                                        FAX 888-608-0344
                             http://store.sunburst.com
                             e-mail: service@sunburst.com
Michael Guillory, Channel Sales/Marketing Manager

This theme based CD-ROM enables students of all abilities to actively research a multitude of different forest ecosystems in the Appalachian National Park.

873   Easybook Deluxe Writing Workshop: Colonial Times
Sunburst Technology
1550 Executive Dr
Elgin, IL   60123-9311
                                            800-321-7511
                                        FAX 888-608-0344
                             http://store.sunburst.com
                             e-mail: service@sunburst.com
Michael Guillory, Channel Sales/Marketing Manager

Writing workshops combine theme-based activities with the award-winning EasyBook Deluxe.

874   Easybook Deluxe Writing Workshop: Immigration
Sunburst Technology
1550 Executive Dr
Elgin, IL   60123-9311
                                            800-321-7511
                                        FAX 888-608-0344
                             http://store.sunburst.com
                             e-mail: service@sunburst.com
Michael Guillory, Channel Sales/Marketing Manager

Writing workshops combine theme-based activities with the award-winning EasyBook Deluxe.

875   Easybook Deluxe Writing Workshop: Rainforest & Astronomy
Sunburst Technology
1550 Executive Dr
Elgin, IL 60123-9311

800-321-7511
FAX 888-608-0344
http://store.sunburst.com
e-mail: service@sunburst.com
Michael Guillory, Channel Sales/Marketing Manager

Writing workshops combine theme-based activities with the award-winning EasyBook Deluxe.

876   Explorers & Exploration: Steadwell
HMH Supplemental Publishers
6277 Sea Harbor Dr
5th Floor
Orlando, FL 32887

800-531-5015
FAX 800-699-9459
http://www.harcourtachieve.com
e-mail: greatservice@hmhpub.com
Linda K. Zecher, President and CEO
Eric Shuman, Chief Financial Officer

Long ago adventures are still a thrill in these vividly illustrated titles. Maps, diagrams, and contemporary prints lend an authenic air. A time line and list of events in the appropriate century put history in perspective. *$44.40*

ISBN 0-739822-05-5

877   First Biographies
HMH Supplemental Publishers
6277 Sea Harbor Dr
5th Floor
Orlando, FL 32887

800-531-5015
FAX 800-699-9459
http://www.harcourtachieve.com
e-mail: greatservice@hmhpub.com
Linda K. Zecher, President, CEO
Eric Shuman, CFO

True stories of true legends! Legendary figures triumph over tough challenges in these brief biographies. Beginning readers learn about favorite heroes and heroines in books they can read for themselves. *$98.80*

ISBN 0-817268-91-X

878   Imagination Express Destination Time Trip USA
Sunburst Technology
1550 Executive Dr
Elgin, IL 60123-9311

800-321-7511
FAX 888-608-0344
http://store.sunburst.com
e-mail: service@sunburst.com
Michael Guillory, Channel Sales/Marketing Manager

Student's travel through time to explore the history and development of a fictional New England town. An online scrapbook lets them learn about architecture, fashion, entertainment and events of the six major periods in U.S. history.

879   Make-a-Map 3D
Sunburst Technology
1550 Executive Dr
Elgin, IL 60123-9311

800-321-7511
FAX 888-608-0344
http://store.sunburst.com
e-mail: service@sunburst.com
Michael Guillory, Channel Sales/Marketing Manager

Students learn basic mapping, geography and navigation skills. Students design maps of their immediate surroundings by dragging and dropping roads and buildings and adding landmarks, land forms and traffic signs.

880   Maps & Navigation
Sunburst Technology
1550 Executive Dr
Elgin, IL 60123-9311

800-321-7511
FAX 888-608-0344
http://store.sunburst.com
e-mail: service@sunburst.com
Michael Guillory, Channel Sales/Marketing Manager

This exciting nautical simulation provides students with opportunities to use their math and science skills.

881   Prehistoric Creaures Then & Now
HMH Supplemental Publishers
6277 Sea Harbor Dr
5th Floor
Orlando, FL 32887

800-531-5015
FAX 800-699-9459
http://www.harcourtachieve.com
e-mail: greatservice@hmhpub.com
K S Rodiguez, Author
Linda K. Zecher, President and CEO
Eric Shuman, Chief Financial Officer
Now limited readers can dig into the details of dinosaurs! Each information-packed title includes a special spread with a project, a profile of a dinosaur expert, or a description of a recent dinosaur discovery.

ISBN 0-739821-47-4

882   Story of the USA
Educators Publishing Service
PO Box 9031
Cambridge, MA 02139-9031

617-547-6706
800-225-5750
FAX 617-547-3805
http://www.epsbooks.com
e-mail: CustomerService.EPS@schoolspecialty.com
Franklin Escher Jr, Author
Kathryn Hansen, Key Accounts Coordinator
Jeff Belanger, Regional Sales Manager
A series of four workbooks for grades 4-8 which presents basic topics in American History: Book 1, Explorers and Settlers - Book 2, A Young Nation Solves Its Problems - Book 3, America Becomes A Giant - and Book 4, Modern America. A list of vocabulary words introduces each chapter and study questions test students' knowledge.

883   Talking Walls Bundle
Sunburst Technology
1550 Executive Dr
Elgin, IL 60123-9311

800-321-7511
FAX 888-608-0344
http://store.sunburst.com
e-mail: service@sunburst.com
Michael Guillory, Channel Sales/Marketing Manager

Broaden students' perspective of cultures around the world with this two program CD-ROM bundle. From the Great Wall of China to the Berlin Wall to the Vietnam Memorial, students explore 28 walls that represent examples of the greatest human achievements to the most intimate expressions of individuality.

884   Test Practice Success: American History
HMH Supplemental Publishers
6277 Sea Harbor Dr
5th Floor
Orlando, FL 32887

800-531-5015
FAX 800-699-9459
http://www.harcourtachieve.com
e-mail: greatservice@hmhpub.com
Linda K. Zecher, President and CEO
Eric Shuman, Chief Financial Officer

When you are trying to meet history standards, standardized test preparation is hard to schedule. Now you can do both at the same time. Steck-Vaughn/Berrent Test Practice Success: American History refreshes basic skills, familiarizes students with test formats and directions, and teaches test-taking strategies, while drawing on the material students are studying in class. *$16.30*

ISBN 0-739831-31-3

885   True Tales
HMH Supplemental Publishers
6277 Sea Harbor Dr
5th Floor
Orlando, FL 32877

800-531-5015
FAX 800-699-9459
http://www.harcourtachieve.com
e-mail: greatservice@hmhpub.com
Henry Billings, Author
Linda K. Zecher, President and CEO
Eric Shuman, Chief Financial Officer
If you have been looking for reading comprehension materials for limiteed readers, your search is over. True Tales presents powerful real-lfe events with direct connections to geography and science at reading level 3. Gripping accounts of personal triumph and tragedy put geography and science in a very real context. Accompanying activities develop reading and language arts, science, and geography skills students need to boost test scores. *$205.00*

ISBN 0-739834-49-5

Study Skills

886   Experiences with Writing Styles
Harcourt Achieve
6277 Sea Harbor Dr
5th Floor
Orlando, FL 32887

800-531-5015
FAX 800-699-9459
http://www.harcourtachieve.com
e-mail: greatservice@hmhpub.com
Linda K. Zecher, President and CEO
Eric Shuman, Chief Financial Officer

Give your students experience applying the writing process in nine relevant situations, from personal narratives to persuasive paragraphs to research reports. Units provide a clear definition of each genre and plenty of practice with prewriting, writing, revising, proofreading, and publishing. *$11.99*

887   Keyboarding Skills
Educators Publishing Service
PO Box 9031
Cambridge, MA 02139-9031

617-547-6706
800-225-5750
FAX 617-547-3805
http://www.epsbooks.com
e-mail: CustomerService.EPS@schoolspecialty.com
Diana Hanbury King, Author
Kathryn Hansen, Key Accounts Coordinator
Jeff Belanger, Regional Sales Manager

This innovative touch typing method enables students of all ages to learn to type quickly and easily. After learning the alphabet, students can practice words, phrases, numbers, symbols and punctuation.

888   Learning Strategies Curriculum
Edge Enterprises
Ste 107
708 W 9th St
Lawrence, KS 66044-2846

785-749-1473
877-767-1487
FAX 785-749-0207
http://www.edgeenterprisesinc.com
e-mail: eeinfo@edgeenterprisesinc.com
Jean B. Schumaker Ph.D., President
Jacqueline Schafer, Editor

A learning strategy is an individual's approach to a learning task. It includes how a person thinks and acts when planning, executing and evaluating performance on the task and its outcomes. In short, learning strategy instruction focuses on how to learn and how to effectively use what has been learned. Manuals range from sentence writing to test taking. All require training. For information, contact the Kansas Center for Research on Learning, 3061 Dole Center, Lawrence 66045 (785-864-4780)

889   Super Study Wheel: Homework Helper
Therapro
225 Arlington St
Framingham, MA 01702-8773

508-872-9494
800-257-5376
FAX 508-875-2062
http://www.theraproducts.com
e-mail: info@theraproducts.com
Karen Conrad, President

The fun and simple way to find study tips. Developed by learning specialists and an occupational therapist, the Super Study Wheel is an idea-packed resource (with 101 tips) to improve study skills in 13 areas. As a visual, motor and kinesthetic tool, it is very helpful to students with unique learning styles. *$6.95*

Toys & Games, Catalogs

890   Maxi Aids
42 Executive Blvd
Farmingdale, NY 11735-4710

631-752-0521
800-522-6294
FAX 631-752-0689
TTY: 631-752-0738
http://www.maxiaids.com
Elliot Zaretsky, President

Aids and appliances for independent living with products designed especially for the visually impaired, blind, hard of hearing, deaf, deaf-blind, arthritic and the physically challenged. New educational games and toys section.

891   PCI Educational Publishing
Suite 100
4560 Lockhill Rd
San Antonio, TX 78249-2075

210-377-1999
800-594-4263
FAX 888-259-8284
http://www.pcieducation.com
e-mail: jberger@pcieducation.com
Lee Wilson, President and CEO
Janie Haugen-McLane, Founder
Randy Pennington, Executive Vice President

Offers 14 programs in a gameboard format to improve life and social skills including Cooking Class, Community Skills, Looking Good, Eating Skills, Workplace Skills, Behavior Skills, Time Skills, Money Skills, Safety Skills, Household Skills, Social Skills, Health Skills, Survival Skills and Recreation Skills. Also offers a Life Skills catalog with over 140 additional products.

Toys & Games, Products

892   Beads and Baubles
Therapro
225 Arlington St
Framingham, MA 01702-8773   508-872-9494
                                    800-257-5376
                              FAX 508-875-2062
                     http://www.theraproducts.com
                     e-mail: info@theraproducts.com
Karen Conrad, President

A basic stringing activity great for developing fine motor skills. Over 100 pieces in various shapes, colors, and sizes to string on a lace. Three laces included. *$7.99*

893   Beads and Pattern Cards
Therapro
225 Arlington St
Framingham, MA 01702-8773   508-872-9494
                                    800-257-5376
                              FAX 508-875-2062
                     http://www.theraproducts.com
                     e-mail: info@theraproducts.com
Karen Conrad, President

Colorful wooden sphers, cubes, cylinders and laces provide pre-reading/early math practice and help develop shape/color sorting and recognition skills. *$27.95*

894   Big Little Pegboard Set
Therapro
225 Arlington St
Framingham, MA 01702-8773   508-872-9494
                                    800-257-5376
                              FAX 508-875-2062
                     http://www.theraproducts.com
                     e-mail: info@theraproducts.com
Karen Conrad, President

Kids love to play with this set of 25 safe, brightly colored hardwood pegs and a durable foam rubber board. *$18.95*

895   Busy Box Activity Centers
Enabling Devices
50 Broadway
Hawthorne, NY 10532   914-747-3070
                              800-832-8697
                        FAX 914-747-3480
                http://www.enablingdevices.com
          e-mail: customer_support@enablingdevices.com
Steven E. Kanor, President

With their bright colors and exciting variety of textures and shapes that are designed to invite exploration that results in rewards including buzzers, music box melodies, radio, vibrations, puffs of air, flashing lights, and even a model that talks. Encourages hand-eye coordination, fine motor skills, gross arm movement. A full line of activity centers are available to meet the needs of the learning disabled, hearing impaired, visually impaired and multisensory impaired. *$163.95*

896   Colored Wooden Counting Cubes
Therapro
225 Arlington St
Framingham, MA 01702-8723   508-872-9494
                                    800-257-5376
                              FAX 508-875-2062
                     http://www.theraproducts.com
                     e-mail: info@therapro.com
Karen Conrad, President

100 cubes in 6 colors are perfect for counting, patterning, and building activities. Activity Guide included. *$19.95*

897   Disc-O-Bocce
Therapro
225 Arlington St
Framingham, MA 01702-8723   508-872-9494
                                    800-257-5376
                              FAX 508-875-2062
                     http://www.theraproducts.com
                     e-mail: info@therapro.com
Karen Conrad, President

Requested by therapists working with adults, this item is also great for children. Hundreds of uses include tossing the discs onto the ground and stepping on them to follow their path, tossing and trying to hit the same color disc on the floor, or using the discs to toss in a game of tic-tac-toe on the floor. Includes 12 colorful bocce discs in a storage box with handle. *$29.95*

898   Earobics® Clinic Version
Abilitations Speech Bin
PO Box 1579
Appleton, W 54912-1579
                                    800-850-8602
                              FAX 888-388-6344
                        http://www.abilitations.com
            e-mail: customercare@schoolspecialty.com
Ilana Dannerman PT, Therapist

Earobics features: Tasks and Level Counter with real time display, adaptive training technology for individualized programs and reporting to track and evaluate each individual's progress. Step 2 teaches critical language comprehension skills and trains the critical auditory skills children need for success in learning. Item number C484. *$298.99*

899   Earobics® Home Version
Abilitations Speech Bin
PO Box 1579
Appleton, W 54912-1579
                                    800-850-8602
                              FAX 888-388-6344
                        http://www.abilitations.com
            e-mail: customercare@schoolspecialty.com
Ilana Dannerman PT, Therapist

Step 2 teaches critical language comprehension skills and trains the critical auditory skills children need for success in learning. It offers hundreds of levels of play, appealing graphics, and entertaining music to train the critical auditory skills young children need for success in learning. Item number C483. *$58.99*

900   Earobics® Step 1 Home Version
School Specialty
PO Box 1579
Appleton, WI 54912-1579
                                    888-388-3224
                              FAX 888-388-6344
                        http://www.schoolspecialty.com
            e-mail: customercare@schoolspecialty.com
Step 1 offers hundreds of levels of play, appealing graphics, and entertaining music to train the critical auditory skills young children need for success in learning. Item number C481. *$58.99*

901   Eye-Hand Coordination Boosters
Therapro
225 Arlington St
Framingham, MA 01702-8723   508-872-9494
                                           800-257-5376
                                     FAX 508-875-2062
                          http://www.theraproducts.com
                            e-mail: info@therapro.com
Karen Conrad, President
L. Jay Lev, Author

A book of 92 masters that can be used over and over again
with work sheets that are appropriate for all ages. These are
perceptual motor activities that involve copying and tracing
in the areas of visual tracking, discrimination and spatial relationships. *$21.50*

902   Familiar Things
Therapro
225 Arlington St
Framingham, MA 01702-8723   508-872-9494
                                           800-257-5376
                                     FAX 508-875-2062
                          http://www.theraproducts.com
                            e-mail: info@therapro.com
Karen Conrad, President

Identify and match shapes of common objects with these
large square, rubber pieces. *$19.99*

903   Flagship Carpets
PO Box 1008
Chatsworth, GA 30705
                                           800-848-4055
                       http://www.flagshipcarpets.com
                       e-mail: info@flagshipcarpets.com
Offers a variety of carpet games like hopscotch, the alpha-
bet, geography maps, custom logo mats and more.

904   GeoSafari Wonder World USA
Educational Insights
152 W. Walnut St
Suite 201
Gardena, CA 90248
                                           800-955-4436
                                     FAX 888-892-8731
                       http://www.educationalinsights.com
                       e-mail: CS@educationalinsights.com
Navigate the United States in a thrilling, interactive tour
across this giant, beautifully detailed 4' x 6' cloth map embroidered with state boundaries. As children learn about
American geography, they will love attaching the 78
self-stick felt pieces that identify the states and their unique
features. *$199.99*

905   Geoboard Colored Plastic
Therapro
225 Arlington St
Framingham, MA 01702-8723   508-872-9494
                                           800-257-5376
                                     FAX 508-875-2062
                          http://www.theraproducts.com
                            e-mail: info@therapro.com
Karen Conrad, President

Teach eye/hand coordination skills while strengthening
pincher grasp with rubber bands. *$3.25*

906   Geometrical Design Coloring Book
Therapro
225 Arlington St
Framingham, MA 01702-8723   508-872-9494
                                           800-257-5376
                                     FAX 508-875-2062
                          http://www.theraproducts.com
                            e-mail: info@therapro.com

Karen Conrad, President
Spyros Horemis, Author

Color these 46 original designs of pure patterns and abstract
shapes for a striking and beautiful result, regardless of skill
level. Most designs are made of a combination of small and
large areas. *$3.95*

907   Get in Shape to Write
Therapro
225 Arlington St
Framingham, MA 01702-8723   508-872-9494
                                           800-257-5376
                                     FAX 508-875-2062
                          http://www.theraproducts.com
                            e-mail: info@therapro.com
Karen Conrad, President
Phillip Bongiorno MA OTR, Author
Lorette Konezny, Editor
Practice the visual perceptual motor skills needed for writing with these colorful, fun, and engaging activities. The 23
reusuable activities will keep a student's interest while they
learn to process auditory, visual, and motoor movement patterns. In addition, learn concepts of matching and sorting
colors, shapes and familiar objects. *$12.95*

908   Half 'n' Half Design and Color Book
Therapro
225 Arlington St
Framingham, MA 01702-8723   508-872-9494
                                           800-257-5376
                                     FAX 508-875-2062
                          http://www.theraproducts.com
                            e-mail: info@therapro.com
Karen Conrad, President
Elaine Heller, Author

Geometric designs appropriate for all ages. The client draws
over dotted lines to finish the other half of the printed design.
$15.00

909   Link N' Learn Activity Book
Therapro
225 Arlington St
Framingham, MA 01702-8723   508-872-9494
                                           800-257-5376
                                     FAX 508-875-2062
                          http://www.theraproducts.com
                            e-mail: info@therapro.com
Karen Conrad, President
Carol A. Thornton, Author

A nice accompaniment to the color rings. There are great
cognitive activities included. *$9.99*

910   Link N' Learn Activity Cards
Therapro
225 Arlington St
Framingham, MA 01702-8723   508-872-9494
                                           800-257-5376
                                     FAX 508-875-2062
                          http://www.theraproducts.com
                            e-mail: info@therapro.com
Karen Conrad, President

Learn patterning, sequencing and color discrimination and
logic skills with this set of 20 cards that show life-sized
links. An instructor's guide is included. *$7.99*

911   Link N' Learn Color Rings
Therapro
225 Arlington St
Framingham, MA 01702-8723   508-872-9494
                                           800-257-5376
                                     FAX 508-875-2062
                          http://www.theraproducts.com
                            e-mail: info@therapro.com

Karen Conrad, President

These easy to hook and separate colorful 1-1/2 inch plastic rings can be used in color sorting, counting, sequencing, and other perceptual/cognitive activities. *$5.99*

912 Magicatch Set
Therapro
225 Arlington St
Framingham, MA 01702-8723   508-872-9494
                                   800-257-5376
                              FAX 508-875-2062
                   http://www.theraproducts.com
                      e-mail: info@therapro.com

Karen Conrad, President

This Velcro catch game offers a much higher degree of success and feeling of security than traditional ball tossing games. 7 1/2 inch neon catching paddles and 2 1/2 inch ball, in a mesh bag. No latex. *$7.50*

913 Magnetic Fun
Therapro
225 Arlington St
Framingham, MA 01702-8723   508-872-9494
                                   800-257-5376
                              FAX 508-875-2062
                   http://www.theraproducts.com
                      e-mail: info@therapro.com

Karen Conrad, President

One swipe of the magic wand can pick up small objects without the need for a refined pincher grasp. *$13.95*

914 Maze Book
Therapro
225 Arlington St
Framingham, MA 01702-8723   508-872-9494
                                   800-257-5376
                              FAX 508-875-2062
                   http://www.theraproducts.com
                      e-mail: info@therapro.com

Karen Conrad, President
Paul McCreary, Author

Significantly more challenging than the ABC Mazes; rich in perceptual activities. *$10.95*
                    32 pages

915 Opposites Game
Therapro
225 Arlington St
Framingham, MA 01702-8723   508-872-9494
                                   800-257-5376
                              FAX 508-875-2062
                   http://www.theraproducts.com
                      e-mail: info@therapro.com

Karen Conrad, President

Children can explore the concept of opposites by matching and then joining these tiles. Self correcting feature allows for both independent and supervised play. Helps build observation and recognition skills. *$8.50*

916 Parquetry Blocks & Pattern Cards
Therapro
225 Arlington St
Framingham, MA 01702-8723   508-872-9494
                                   800-257-5376
                              FAX 508-875-2062
                   http://www.theraproducts.com
                      e-mail: info@therapro.com

Karen Conrad, President

Encourages visual perceptual skills and challenges a person's sense of design and color with squares, triangles, and rhombuses in six colors. *$28.90*

917 Pegboard Set
Therapro
225 Arlington St
Framingham, MA 01702-8723   508-872-9494
                                   800-257-5376
                              FAX 508-875-2062
                   http://www.theraproducts.com
                      e-mail: info@therapro.com

Karen Conrad, President

Encourage development of fine motor skills while teaching color, sorting, patterning and counting! Pegboard is 10.75 inches square and made of durable plastic featuring 100 holes in a 10 x 10 array. *$10.50*

918 Plastic Cones
Therapro
225 Arlington St
Framingham, MA 01702-8723   508-872-9494
                                   800-257-5376
                              FAX 508-875-2062
                   http://www.theraproducts.com
                      e-mail: info@therapro.com

Karen Conrad, President

The 12-inch versions of the construction project cones are bright orange and made of lightweigth vinyl. Hole in top. *$8.25*

919 Primer Pak
Therapro
225 Arlington St
Framingham, MA 01702-8723   508-872-9494
                                   800-257-5376
                              FAX 508-875-2062
                   http://www.theraproducts.com
                      e-mail: info@therapro.com

Karen Conrad, President

A challenging sampler of manipulatives. Four Fit-A-Space disk puzzles with basic shapes, an 8x8 Alphabet Puzzle, three Lacing Shapes for primary lacing, and 24 Locktagons to form structures. *$14.99*

920 Rhyming Sounds Game
Therapro
225 Arlington St
Framingham, MA 01702-8723   508-872-9494
                                   800-257-5376
                              FAX 508-875-2062
                   http://www.theraproducts.com
                      e-mail: info@therapro.com

Karen Conrad, President

Introduces 32 different rhyming sounds as players match the ending sound of the picture tile to the corresponding object on the category boards. Includes sorting/storage tray, 56 picture tiles, and 4 category cards with self-checking feature. No reading required. *$9.99*

921 Shape and Color Sorter
Therapro
225 Arlington St
Framingham, MA 01702-8723   508-872-9494
                                   800-257-5376
                              FAX 508-875-2062
                   http://www.theraproducts.com
                      e-mail: info@therapro.com

Karen Conrad, President

This simple and safe task of perception includes 25 crepe foam rubber pieces to sort by shape or color. Comes in five bright colors, each color representing a shape. Shapes fit nicely onto five large pegs. *$14.99*

922 **Shapes**
Therapro
225 Arlington St
Framingham, MA 01702-8723   508-872-9494
                                    800-257-5376
                                FAX 508-875-2062
                    http://www.theraproducts.com
                        e-mail: info@therapro.com

Karen Conrad, President
Muncie Hendler, Author

This 8 1/2 x 11 inch high quality coloring book will help children learn to recognize shapes while improving their fine motor and perceptual skills. *$1.50*
30 pages

923 **Snail's Pace Race Game**
Therapro
225 Arlington St
Framingham, MA 01702-8723   508-872-9494
                                    800-257-5376
                                FAX 508-875-2062
                    http://www.theraproducts.com
                        e-mail: info@therapro.com

Karen Conrad, President

This classic, easy color game is back and is fun for all to play. Roll the colored dice to see which wooden snail will move closer to the finish line. Promotes color recognition, understanding of taking turns, and sharing. *$ 19.95*

924 **Speak & Learn Communicator**
Enabling Devices
50 Broadway
Hawthorne, NY 10532   914-747-3070
                                    800-832-8697
                                FAX 914-747-3480
                    http://www.enablingdevices.com

Steven Kanor PhD, Founder

Memory game! Have fun individualizing this matching memory game. Pre-record your questions and answers and you're ready to play. This is an exciting way to reinforce identification and matching numbers, letters, shapes, and words. *$390.95*

925 **Spider Ball**
Therapro
225 Arlington St
Framingham, MA 01702-8723   508-872-9494
                                    800-257-5376
                                FAX 508-875-2062
                    http://www.theraproducts.com
                        e-mail: info@therapro.com

Karen Conrad, President

Easy to catch, won't roll away! This foam rubber ball has rubber legs that make it incredibly easy to catch. Invented by a PE teacher to help children improve their ball playing skills. The Spiderball's legs act as brakes bringing it to a stop when rolled and minimizing the time needed to chase a missed ball. 2 1/4 inch diameter. *$4.50*

926 **Squidgie Flying Disc**
Therapro
225 Arlington St
Framingham, MA 01702-8723   508-872-9494
                                    800-257-5376
                                FAX 508-875-2062
                    http://www.theraproducts.com
                        e-mail: info@therapro.com

Karen Conrad, President

This is a great flexible flying disc that is amazingly easy to throw and travels over long distances. It is soft and easy to catch. It will even float in the pool! *$5.50*

927 **String A Long Lacing Kit**
Therapro
225 Arlington St
Framingham, MA 01702-8723   508-872-9494
                                    800-257-5376
                                FAX 508-875-2062
                    http://www.theraproducts.com
                        e-mail: info@therapro.com

Karen Conrad, President

A lacing activity that develops hand eye coordination and concentration as children create 2 colorful bead buddies. Each buddy has 4 laces attached to its painted heal now build the body with 23 beads! *$15.00*

928 **Things in My House: Picture Matching Game**
Therapro
225 Arlington St
Framingham, MA 01702-8723   508-872-9494
                                    800-257-5376
                                FAX 508-875-2062
                    http://www.theraproducts.com
                        e-mail: info@therapro.com

Karen Conrad, President

Strengthen visual discrimination, sorting, and organizing skills. Young children enjoy finding correct matches in this fun first game. The colorful graphics depicting familiar household objects and activities encourage verbalization and imaginative play. *$9.99*

929 **Toddler Tote**
Therapro
225 Arlington St
Framingham, MA 01702-8723   508-872-9494
                                    800-257-5376
                                FAX 508-875-2062
                    http://www.theraproducts.com
                        e-mail: info@therapro.com

Karen Conrad, President

Offers one Junior Fit-A-Space panel that has large geometric shapes; 4 Shape Squares providing basic shapes in a more challenging size; 2 Peg Play Vehicles and Pegs introducing early peg board skills; 3 Familiar Things and 2 piece puzzles and a handy take-along bag. *$14.99*

930 **Whistle Kit**
Therapro
225 Arlington St
Framingham, MA 01702-8723   508-872-9494
                                    800-257-5376
                                FAX 508-875-2062
                    http://www.theraproducts.com
                        e-mail: info@therapro.com

Karen Conrad, President

The whistles in this collection are colorful and sturdy. Most feature moving parts as well as noise-makers to stimulate both ocular and oral motor skills. Includes nine whistles. Respiratory demand ranges from easy to difficult. *$18.95*

931 **Wikki Stix**
Therapro
225 Arlington St
Framingham, MA 01702-8723   508-872-9494
                                    800-257-5376
                                FAX 508-875-2062
                    http://www.theraproducts.com
                        e-mail: info@therapro.com

Karen Conrad, President

Colorful, nontoxic waxed strings which are easily molded to create various forms, shapes and letters. Combine motor planning skill with fine motor skill by following simple shapes with Wikki Stix and then coloring in the shape. *$5.99*

932 Windup Fishing Game
Therapro
225 Arlington St
Framingham, MA 01702-8723   508-872-9494
                                    800-257-5376
                                 FAX 508-875-2062
                        http://www.theraproducts.com
                           e-mail: info@therapro.com
Karen Conrad, President

Encourages eye-hand coordination. Rubber hook safely catches velcro on chipboard fish. *$3.99*

933 Wonder Ball
Therapro
225 Arlington St
Framingham, MA 01702-8723   508-872-9494
                                    800-257-5376
                                 FAX 508-875-2062
                        http://www.theraproducts.com
                           e-mail: info@therapro.com
Karen Conrad, President

This 3 inch ball made of many small suction cups feels good in the palm of the hand and, when thrown against a smooth surface, will firmly stick. Pulling it from the surface requires strength, resulting in proprioceptive stimulation. *$5.99*

Writing

934 ABC's, Numbers & Shapes
Therapro
225 Arlington St
Framingham, MA 01702-8723   508-872-9494
                                    800-257-5376
                                 FAX 508-875-2062
                        http://www.theraproducts.com
                           e-mail: info@therapro.com
Karen Conrad, President

Do-A-Dot Activity Books are great for pre-writing skill books, printed on heavy paper stock, with each page perforated for easy removal. They promote eye-hand coordination and visual recognition. *$4.95*

935 Author's Toolkit
Sunburst Technology
1550 Executive Dr
Elgin, IL 60123-9311
                                    800-321-7511
                                 FAX 888-608-0344
                        http://store.sunburst.com
                         e-mail: service@sunburst.com
Students can use this comprehensive tool to organize ideas, make outlines, rough drafts, edit and print all their written work.

936 Callirobics: Advanced Exercises
Therapro
225 Arlington St
Framingham, MA 01702-8723   508-872-9494
                                    800-257-5376
                                 FAX 508-875-2062
                        http://www.theraproducts.com
                           e-mail: info@therapro.com
Karen Conrad, President
Liora Laufer, Author

Allows those who have finished earlier Callirobics programs to continue improving their handwriting in a fun and creative way. Callirobics Advanced lets one create shapes to popular music from around the world. *$29.95*
        Book and CD

937 Callirobics: Exercises for Adults
Therapro
225 Arlington St
Framingham, MA 01702-8723   508-872-9494
                                    800-257-5376
                                 FAX 508-875-2062
                        http://www.theraproducts.com
                           e-mail: info@therapro.com
Karen Conrad, President
Liora Laufer, Author

Callirobics-for-Adults is a program designed to help adults regain handwriting skills to music. The music assists as an auditory cue in initiating writing movements, and will help develop a sense of rhythm in writing. The program consists of two sections: exercises of simple graphical shapes that help adults gain fluency in the writing movement, and exercises of various combinations of cursive letters. *$35.95*

938 Callirobics: Handwriting Exercises to Music
Therapro
225 Arlington St
Framingham, MA 01702-8723   508-872-9494
                                    800-257-5376
                                 FAX 508-875-2062
                        http://www.theraproducts.com
                           e-mail: info@therapro.com
Karen Conrad, President
Liora Laufer, Author

Ten structured sessions, each with 2 exercises and 2 pieces of music. Includes stickers and a certificate book. *$29.95*
        Book and CD

939 Callirobics: Prewriting Skills with Music
Therapro
225 Arlington St
Framingham, MA 01702-8723   508-872-9494
                                    800-257-5376
                                 FAX 508-875-2062
                        http://www.theraproducts.com
                           e-mail: info@therapro.com
Karen Conrad, President
Liora Laufer, Author

These 11 handwriting exercises are a series of simple and enjoyable graphical patterns to be traced by the child while listening to popular melodies. *$29.95*
        Book and CD

940 Caps, Commas and Other Things
Academic Therapy Publications
20 Commercial Blvd
Novato, CA 94949-6120   415-883-3314
                                    800-422-7249
                                 FAX 888-287-9975
                        http://www.academictherapy.com
                       e-mail: sales@academictherapy.com
Jim Arena, President
Joanne Urban, Manager
Sheryl Pastorek, Author
A writing program for regular, remedial and ESL students in grades 3 through 12 and adults in basic education classes remedial ESL. Six levels on capitalization and punctuation, four levels on written expression. Specific lesson plans with reproducible worksheets. *$20.00*
        264 pages
        ISBN 0-878793-25-9

941 Dysgraphia: Why Johnny Can't Write
Therapro
225 Arlington St
Framingham, MA 01702-8723   508-872-9494
                                    800-257-5376
                                 FAX 508-875-2062
                        http://www.theraproducts.com
                           e-mail: info@therapro.com
Karen Conrad, President
Diane Walton Cavey, Author

Dysgraphia is a serious writing difficulty. This book provides guidelines for recognizing dysgraphic children and explains their special writing needs. Offers valuable tips, ideas and methods to promote success and self regard. *$13.95*

942   Easybook Deluxe
Sunburst Technology
1550 Executive Dr
Elgin, IL 60123-9311

800-321-7511
FAX 888-608-0344
http://store.sunburst.com
e-mail: service@sunburst.com

Designed to support the needs of a wide range of writers, this book publishing tool provides students with a creative environment to write, design and illustrate stories and reports, and to print their work in book formats.

943   Easybook Deluxe Writing Workshop: Colonial Times
Sunburst Technology
1550 Executive Dr
Elgin, IL 60123-9311

800-321-7511
FAX 888-608-0344
http://store.sunburst.com
e-mail: service@sunburst.com

Writing workshops combine theme-based activities with the award-winning EasyBook Deluxe.

944   Easybook Deluxe Writing Workshop: Immigration
Sunburst Technology
1550 Executive Dr
Elgin, IL 60123-9311

800-321-7511
FAX 888-608-0344
http://store.sunburst.com
e-mail: service@sunburst.com

Writing workshops combine theme-based activities with the award-winning EasyBook Deluxe.

945   Easybook Deluxe Writing Workshop: Rainforest & Astronomy
Sunburst Technology
1550 Executive Dr
Elgin, IL 60123-9311

800-321-7511
FAX 888-608-0344
http://store.sunburst.com
e-mail: service@sunburst.com

Writing workshops combine theme-based activities with the award-winning EasyBook Deluxe.

946   Easybook Deluxe Writing Workshop: Whales & Oceans

Sunburst Technology
1550 Executive Dr
Elgin, IL 60123-9311

800-321-7511
FAX 888-608-0344
http://store.sunburst.com
e-mail: service@sunburst.com

Writing workshops combine theme-based activities with the award-winning EasyBook Deluxe.

947   Fonts 4 Teachers
Therapro
225 Arlington St
Framingham, MA 01702-8723

508-872-9494
800-257-5376
FAX 508-875-2062
http://www.theraproducts.com
e-mail: info@therapro.com

Karen Conrad, President

A software collection of 31 True Type fonts for teachers, parents and students. Fonts include Tracing, lined and unlined Traditional Manuscript and Cursive (similar to Zaner Blouser and D'Nealian), math, clip art, decorative, time, American Sign Language symbols and more. The included manual is very informative, with great examples of lesson plans and educational goals. *$39.95*
Windows/Mac

948   From Scribbling to Writing
Therapro
225 Arlington St
Framingham, MA 01702-8723

508-872-9494
800-257-5376
FAX 508-875-2062
http://www.theraproducts.com
e-mail: info@therapro.com

Karen Conrad, President

Ideas, exercises and practice pages for all children preparing to write. Contains line drawing exercises, forms to complete, and forms for encouraging good flow of movement during writing. *$32.50*
99 pages

949   Fun with Handwriting
Therapro
225 Arlington St
Framingham, MA 01702-8723

508-872-9494
800-257-5376
FAX 508-875-2062
http://www.theraproducts.com
e-mail: info@therapro.com

Karen Conrad, President

One hundred and one ways to improve handwriting. Includes key to writing legibly, chalkboard activities, evaluation tips, and real world handwriting projects. *$16.00*
160 pages Spiral-bound

950   Getting Ready to Write: Preschool-K
Therapro
225 Arlington St
Framingham, MA 01702-8723

508-872-9494
800-257-5376
FAX 508-875-2062
http://www.theraproducts.com
e-mail: info@therapro.com

Karen Conrad, President

A wonderful little book for any handwriting program. Includes many basic skills needed for beginning writing such as matching like objects, finding differences, writing basic strokes, left to right sequence, etc. *$6.50*
97 pages

951   Getting it Write
Therapro
225 Arlington St
Framingham, MA 01702-8723

508-872-9494
800-257-5376
FAX 508-875-2062
http://www.theraproducts.com
e-mail: info@therapro.com

Karen Conrad, President

A 6-week course for individuals or groups of 4-10 children, 6-12 years. Weekly, 1/2 hour classes begin with a short orientation followed by 25 minutes of games and sensory motor activities, from prewriting to writing practice, from basic strokes to letter formation. Reproducible manuscript and cursive worksheets are included along with homework assignments. *$58.95*
215 pages

952 Handwriting Without Tears
8001 Macarthur Blvd
Cabin John, MD 20818   301-263-2700
                                          FAX 301-263-2707
                                          http://www.hwtears.com
                                          e-mail: info@hwtears.com
Jan Z Olsen, Founder and Developer

An easy and fun method for children of all abilities to learn
printing and cursive.

953 Handwriting: Manuscript ABC Book
Therapro
225 Arlington St
Framingham, MA 01702-8723   508-872-9494
                                           800-257-5376
                                           FAX 508-875-2062
                                     http://www.theraproducts.com
                                           e-mail: info@therapro.com
Karen Conrad, President

Illustrated rhymes, practice letters and words, coloring and
tear out alphabet cards teach letter formation. *$11.95*
          56 pages

954 Home/School Activities Manuscript Practice
Therapro
225 Arlington St
Framingham, MA 01702-8723   508-872-9494
                                           800-257-5376
                                           FAX 508-875-2062
                                     http://www.theraproducts.com
                                           e-mail: info@therapro.com
Karen Conrad, President

Directions for forming lower and upper case letters, and
numbers, with space for practice. Activities use letters in
words and sentences. *$11.95*
          64 pages

955 Let's Write Right: Teacher's Edition
AVKO Educational Research Foundation
3084 Willard Rd
Birch Run, MI 48415-9404   810-686-9283
                                           866-285-6612
                                           FAX 810-686-1101
                                           http://www.avko.org
                                       e-mail: webmaster@avko.org
Don Mc Cabe, Research Director/Author
Barry Chute, President
Clifford Schroeder, Treasurer
This is a teacher's lesson plan book which uses an approach
designed specifically for dyslexics to teach reading and
spelling skills through the side door of penmanship exercises with an empasis on legibility. Student books are handy
but are not required. *$19.95*

956 Let's-Do-It-Write: Writing Readiness Workbook
Therapro
225 Arlington St
Framingham, MA 01702-8723   508-872-9494
                                           800-257-5376
                                           FAX 508-875-2062
                                     http://www.theraproducts.com
                                           e-mail: info@therapro.com
Karen Conrad, President

A great variety of prewriting activities and exercises focusing on development of eye-hand coordination and motor,
sensory and cognitive skills. Also, helps improve sitting
posture, cutting skills, pencil grasp, spatial orientation and
problem-solving. Written by an occupational therapist who
is a special educator. *$19.95*
          112 pages

957 Making Handwriting Flow
Oxton House Publishers
PO Box 209
Farmington, ME 04938   207-779-1923
                                            800-539-7323
                                       FAX 207-779-0623
                                       http://www.oxtonhouse.com
                                       e-mail: info@oxtonhouse.com
William Burlinghoff PhD, Owner

This packet inlcudes a 16-page booklet, 'Using Models and
Drills for Fluency,' and 28 pages of tracing models of nu-
merals, whole words, phrases, and sentences for both manuscript and cursive handwriting, along with a chart for
tracking student progress. *$24.95*

          ISBN 1-881929-15-9

958 Media Weaver 3.5
Sunburst Technology
1550 Executive Dr
Elgin, IL 60123-9311
                                            800-321-7511
                                       FAX 888-608-0344
                                       http://store.sunburst.com
                                       e-mail: service@sunburst.com
Publishing becomes a multimedia event with this dynamic
word processor that contains hundreds of media elements
and effective process writing resources.

959 Middle School Writing: Expository Writing
HMH Supplemental Publishers
6277 Sea Harbor Dr
5th Floor
Orlando, FL 32887
                                            800-225-5425
                                       FAX 800-269-5232
                                       http://www.harcourtachieve.com
An effective comprehensive review and reinforcement of
the writing and research skills students will need. Effectively used in both school and home setting. Ideal for junior
high or high school students in need of remediation. *$7.99*

          ISBN 0-739829-28-9

**960 PAF Handwriting Programs for Print, Cursive (Right
or Left-Handed)**
Educators Publishing Service
PO Box 9031
Cambridge, MA 02139-9031   617-547-6706
                                           800-435-7728
                                       FAX 888-440-2665
                                       http://www.epsbooks.com
Eileen Perlman, Co-Author

These workbooks can be used in conjunction with the PAF
curriculum or independently as a classroom penmanship
program. They were specifically designed to accommodate
all students including those with fine-motor, visual-motor
and graphomotor weaknesses. The workbooks contain both
large models for introducing motor patterns and smaller
models to facilitate the transition to primary and loose-leaf
papers. A detailed instruction booklet accompanies each
workbook. *$25.00*

961 StartWrite
Therapro
225 Arlington St
Framingham, MA 01702-8723   508-872-9494
                                           800-257-5376
                                       FAX 508-875-2062
                                     http://www.theraproducts.com
                                           e-mail: info@therapro.com
Karen Conrad, President

With this easy-to-use software package, you can make papers and handwriting worksheets to meet individual student's needs. Type letters, words, or numbers and they appear in a dot format on the triple line guide. Change letter size, add shading, turn on or off guide lines and arrow strokes and place provided clipart. Fonts include Manuscript and Cursive, Modern Manuscript and Cursive and Italic Manuscript and Cursive. Useful manual included. *$42.50*
Windows/Mac

962   Strategies for Success in Writing
HMH Supplemental Publishers
6277 Sea Harbor Dr
5th Floor
Orlando, FL 32887
800225-5425
FAX 800-269-5232
http://www.harcourtachieve.com
Help your students gain success and master all the steps in writing through essay-writing strategies and exercises in proofreading, editing, and revising written work. This program also helps students approach tests strategically. *$16.60*

ISBN 0-739810-47-2

963   Sunbuddy Writer
Sunburst Technology
1550 Executive Dr
Elgin, IL 60123-9311
800-321-7511
FAX 888-608-0344
http://store.sunburst.com
e-mail: service@sunburst.com
An easy-to-use picture and word processor designed especially for young writers.

964   Tool Chest: For Teachers, Parents and Students
Therapro
225 Arlington St
Framingham, MA 01702-8723
508-872-9494
800-257-5376
FAX 508-875-2062
http://www.theraproducts.com
e-mail: info@therapro.com
Karen Conrad, President
Diana A. Henry, Author

Ideas for self-regulation and handwriting skills. 26+ activities, each on its own page, with rationale, supplies needed, instructions and related projects. Provides a fast way to prepare for OT activities. Supports the videotapes Tools for Teachers and Tools for Students. *$19.95*

965   Type-It
Educators Publishing Service
PO Box 9031
Cambridge, MA 02139-9031
617-547-6706
800-435-7728
FAX 888-440-2666
http://www.epsbooks.com
A linguistically oriented beginning 'touch-system' typing manual. A progress chart allows students to pace their progress in short, easily attainable units, often enabling them to proceed with little or no supervision.

966   Write On! Plus: Beginning Writing Skills
Sunburst Technology
1550 Executive Dr
Elgin, IL 60123-9311
800-321-7511
FAX 888-608-0344
http://store.sunburst.com
e-mail: service@sunburst.com
This classic process writing series teaches a wide range of core writing and literature skills through hundreds of motivating and challenging activities.

967   Write On! Plus: Elementary Writing Skills
Sunburst Technology
1550 Executive Dr
Elgin, IL 60123-9311
800-321-7511
FAX 888-608-0344
http://store.sunburst.com
e-mail: service@sunburst.com
This classic process writing series teaches a wide range of core writing and literature skills through hundreds of motivating and challenging activities.

968   Write On! Plus: Essential Writing
Sunburst Technology
1550 Executive Dr
Elgin, IL 60123-9311
800-321-7511
FAX 888-608-0344
http://store.sunburst.com
e-mail: service@sunburst.com
This classic process writing series teaches a wide range of core writing and literature skills through hundreds of motivating and challenging activities.

969   Write On! Plus: Growing as a Writer
Sunburst Technology
1550 Executive Dr
Elgin, IL 60123-9311
800-321-7511
FAX 888-608-0344
http://store.sunburst.com
e-mail: service@sunburst.com
This classic process writing series teaches a wide range of core writing and literature skills through hundreds of motivating and challenging activities.

970   Write On! Plus: High School Writing Skills
Sunburst Technology
1550 Executive Dr
Elgin, IL 60123-9311
800-321-7511
FAX 888-608-0344
http://store.sunburst.com
e-mail: service@sunburst.com
This classic process writing series teaches a wide range of core writing and literature skills through hundreds of motivating and challenging activities.

971   Write On! Plus: Literature Studies
Sunburst Technology
1550 Executive Dr
Elgin, IL 60123-9311
800-321-7511
FAX 888-608-0344
http://store.sunburst.com
e-mail: service@sunburst.com
This classic process writing series teaches a wide range of core writing and literature skills through hundreds of motivating and challenging activities.

972   Write On! Plus: Middle School Writing Skills
Sunburst Technology
1550 Executive Dr
Elgin, IL 60123-9311
800-321-7511
FAX 888-608-0344
http://store.sunburst.com
e-mail: service@sunburst.com
This classic process writing series teaches a wide range of core writing and literature skills through hundreds of motivating and challenging activities.

973 **Write On! Plus: Responding to Great Literature**
Sunburst Technology
1550 Executive Dr
Elgin, IL 60123-9311

800-321-7511
FAX 888-608-0344
http://store.sunburst.com
e-mail: service@sunburst.com

This classic process writing series teaches a wide range of core writing and literature skills through hundreds of motivating and challenging activities.

974 **Write On! Plus: Spanish/ English Literacy Series**
Sunburst Technology
1550 Executive Dr
Elgin, IL 60123-9311

800-321-7511
FAX 888-608-0344
http://store.sunburst.com
e-mail: service@sunburst.com

This classic process writing series teaches a wide range of core writing and literature skills through hundreds of motivating and challenging activities.

975 **Write On! Plus: Steps to Better Writing**
Sunburst Technology
1550 Executive Dr
Elgin, IL 60123-9311

800-321-7511
FAX 888-608-0344
http://store.sunburst.com
e-mail: service@sunburst.com

This classic process writing series teaches a wide range of core writing and literature skills through hundreds of motivating and challenging activities.

976 **Write On! Plus: Writing with Picture Books**
Sunburst Technology
1550 Executive Dr
Elgin, IL 60123-9311

800-321-7511
FAX 888-608-0344
http://store.sunburst.com
e-mail: service@sunburst.com

This classic process writing series teaches a wide range of core writing and literature skills through hundreds of motivating and challenging activities.

977 **Writer's Resources Library 2.0**
Sunburst Technology
1550 Executive Dr
Elgin, IL 60123-9311

800-321-7511
FAX 888-608-0344
http://store.sunburst.com
e-mail: service@sunburst.com

Students quickly access seven reference resources with this indispensable writing tool.

978 **Writing Trek Grades 4-6**
Sunburst Technology
1550 Executive Dr
Elgin, IL 60123-9311

800-321-7511
FAX 888-608-0344
http://store.sunburst.com
e-mail: service@sunburst.com

Enhance your students' experience in your English language arts classroom with twelve authentic writing projects that build students' competence while encouraging creativity.

979 **Writing Trek Grades 6-8**
Sunburst Technology
1550 Executive Dr
Elgin, IL 60123-9311

800-321-7511
FAX 888-608-0344
http://store.sunburst.com
e-mail: service@sunburst.com

Twelve authentic language arts projects, activities, and assignments develop your students' writing confidence and ability.

980 **Writing Trek Grades 8-10**
Sunburst Technology
1550 Executive Dr
Elgin, IL 60123-9311

800-321-7511
FAX 888-800-3028
http://store.sunburst.com
e-mail: service@sunburst.com
Michael Guillory, Channel Sales/Marketing Manager

Help your students develop a concept of genre as they become familiar with the writing elements and characteristics of a variety of writing forms.

Learning Disabilities

981 ACA Charlotte
ACA Membership Division
5999 Stevenson Ave
Alexandria, VA 22304-3304

800-347-6647
FAX 800-473-2329
http://www.counseling.org
e-mail: membership@counseling.org
Marcheta Evans, President

Keynote speakers and workshops as well as exhibits are offered.
March

982 ACRES -American Council on Rural Special Education Conference
Montana Center On Disabilities/MSU-Billings
1500 University Drive
Billings, MT 59101

406-657-2312
888-866-3822
FAX 406-657-2313
http://www.acressped.org
e-mail: inquiries@acres-sped.org
Ben Lignugaris-Kra, Manager

Conference of special educators, teachers and professors working with exceptional needs students. Keynote speakers, silent auction.
March

983 AR-CEC Annual Conference
Arkansas Council for Exceptional Children
P.O.Box 928
Russellville, AR 72811-0928

479-967-6025
FAX 479-967-6056
http://www.cec.k12.ar.us
e-mail: chris.foley@rsdmail.k12.ar.us
Chris Foley, President
Becky Watkins, Vice President

The council is dedicated to meeting the needs of it's members through serving as an effective advocate, fostering involvement of the membership and advancing the professional and ethical growth of it's members. The conference is held annually at the Hot Springs Convention Center in Hot Springs, AR.
November

984 ASHA Convention
American Speech-Language-Hearing Association
2200 Research Blvd
Rockville, MD 20850-3289

301-296-5700
http://www.asha.org
e-mail: convention@asha.org
Catherine H Gottfried, President
Arlene Pietranton, PhD, CAE, Executive Director

ASHA is the nation's leading organization for speech-language pathologists, speech/language/hearing scientists and audiologists. Topics addressed include hearing impairments, special education and speech communication. 10,000 attendees.
November

985 Active Parenting Publishers
1955 Vaughn Rd NW
Ste 108
Kennesaw, GA 30144-7808

770-429-0565
800-825-0060
FAX 770-429-0334
http://www.activeparenting.com
e-mail: cservice@activeparenting.com
Michael Popkin PhD, President

Provides parenting education curricula, including one for parents of ADD/ADHD children.

986 Annual Postsecondary Disability Training Institute
University of Connecticut
249 Glenbrook Rd
Unit 2064
Storrs Mansfield, CT 06269-2064

860-486-3321
FAX 860-486-5799
http://www.cped.uconn.edu
e-mail: carrol.waite@uconn.edu
Joseph Madaus, Institute Coordinator
Carroll Waite, Program Assistant

Assists concerned professionals to meet the unique needs of college students with disabilities.
June

987 Assessing Learning Problems Workshop
Learning Disabilities Resources
2775 S. Quincy St.
Arlington, VA 22206

FAX 703-998-2060
http://www.ldonline.org
Noel Gunther, Executive Director
Christian Lindstrom, Director, Learning Media
Shalini Anand, Senior Manager, Web Development
This workshop includes behavioral manifestations of information processing problems and how to relate these to learning processes.

988 Assistive Technology Training Program
Calfornia State University, Northridge
Cntr On Disabilities Training Prog.
18111 Nordhoff St., Bayramian Hall 110
Northridge, CA 91330-8340

818-677-2578
FAX 818-677-4929
TTY: 818-677-2684
http://www.csun.edu
Sonya Hernandez, Conference Coordinator

Sponsor of national and international assistive technology training programs. The programs help to expand the knowledge of professionals and also introduces newcomers to the field. Participants learn about all forms of assistive technology and their potential areas of application.

989 Association Book Exhibit: Brain Research
Association Book Exhibit
9423 Old Mount Vernon Rd
Alexandria, VA 22309-2716

703-619-5030
FAX 703-619-5035
http://www.bookexhibit.com
e-mail: info@bookexhibit.com
Mark Terotchi, President

Attendence is 800-1,000. Every serious publisher of Neuroscience material represented.

990 Behavioral Institute for Children and Adolescents
1711 County Rd B W
Ste 110S
Roseville, MN 55113

651-484-5510
FAX 651-483-3879
http://www.behavioralinstitute.org
e-mail: mknoll@behavioralinstitute.org
Melissa Knoll, Managing Director

Promoting improved services for troubled children and youths. Provides a wide variety of supporting services to professionals and parents who work with children with emotional and behavioral challenges. Services include professional development, discounted publications and materials, conferences, workshops, consultation, program design and evaluation, a professional library and scholarship program.

991 **CACLD Spring & Fall Conferences**
Connecticut Assoc for Children and Adults with LD
25 Van Zant Street
Suite 15-5
East Norwalk, CT 06855-1719   203-838-5010
                                FAX 203-866-6108
                              http://www.CACLD.org
                          e-mail: cacld@optonline.net
Beryl Kaufman, Executive Director
Elaine Eckenrode, Conference Coordinator

Offers speakers, workshops, presentations and more for professionals and parents of individuals with a learning disability or attention deficit disorder. CACLD has also donated hundreds of books and tapes to libraries, schools, and parent centers which help in training teachers and paraprofessionals.

992 **CASE Conference**
Council Of Administrators Of Special Education
Osigian Office Centre
101 Katelyn Circle, Suite E
Warner Robbins, GA 31088   478-333-6892
                                FAX 478-333-2453
                              http://www.casecec.org
                          e-mail: lpurcell@casecec.org
Dr Emily Collins, President
Luann Purcell, Executive Director

International educational organization dedicated to the enhancement of worth, dignity, and the potential of each individual in society.
                    January

993 **CEC Federation Conference: Virginia**
Council for Exceptional Children
1110 N. Glebe Road
Suite 300
Arlington, VA 22201   888-232-7733
                          FAX 703-264-9494
                          TDD:866-915-5000
                      http://www.cec.sped.org
                   e-mail: victore@cec.sped.org
Anmarie Kallason, Senior Director
Ebony Montgomery, Conventions/Meetings Assistant
Bruce Ramirez, Manager
Find a wealth of information targeted just for educators. Choose from more than 600 workshops, lectures, demonstrations, mini workshops, panels and poster sessions.
                    April

994 **CEC/KASP Federation Conference: Kansas**
Council for Exceptional Children

                          http://www.kansascec.org
Joy Fuqua, President
Janette Stuart, Constitution Chair
Frances Strieby, Treasurer/Finance
Exhibits and workshop sessions for educators building a brighter tomorrow.
                    October

995 **CSUN Conference**
California State University, Northridge
18111 Nordhoff St
Northridge, CA 91330-8200   818-677-1200
                              http://www.csun.edu
                          e-mail: conference@csun.edu
Wayne Fernandes, Manager

Comprehensive, international conference, where all technologies across all ages, disabilities, levels of education and training, employment and independent living are addressed. It is the largest conference of its kind with exhibit halls open free to public.

996 **Center on Disabilities Conference**
California State University, Northridge
18111 Nordhoff St
Bayramian Hall 110
Northridge, CA 91330-8340   818-677-2578
                                FAX 818-677-4929
                              http://www.csun.edu
                          e-mail: conference@csun.edu
Sandy Plotin, Managing Director

Focuses on issues pertaining to the disabled learner and gifted education. 2,000 attendees.

997 **Closing the Gap Conference**
526 Main Street
P.O. Box 68
Henderson, MN 56044-0068   507-248-3294
                                FAX 507-248-3810
                          http://www.closingthegap.com
                        e-mail: info@closingthegap.com
Budd Hagen, President
Connie Kneipe, Vice President/General Manager
Jan Latzke, Subscriptions/Conference Reg.
Annual international conference with over 100 exhibitors concerned with the use of assistive technology in special education and rehabilitation.
                    October

998 **College Students with Learning Disabilities Workshop**
Learning Disabilities Resources
2775 S. Quincy St.
Arlington, VA 22206
                              FAX 703-998-2060
                          http://www.ldonline.org
Noel Gunther, Executive Director
Christian Lindstrom, Director, Learning Media
Shalini Anand, Senior Manager, Web Development
This workshop is designed to provide both information and motivation to both students and college personnel.

999 **ConnSENSE Conference**
University of Connecticut
Unit 4171
233 Glenbrook Rd
Storrs Mansfield, CT 06269-4174   860-486-2020
                                    FAX 860-486-4412
                                    TDD:860-486-2077
                              http://www.csd.uconn.edu
                              e-mail: csd@uconn.edu
Donna Korbel, Director
Jennifer H. Lucia, Associate Director
Christine M. Wenzel, Assistant Director
Annual conference on technology for people with special needs.

1000 **Creative Mind: Building Foundations that will Last Forever**
P Buckley Moss Foundation for Children's Education
152 P. Buckley Moss Drive
Waynesboro, VA 22980-7485   540-932-1728
                                FAX 540-941-8865
                          http://www.mossfoundation.org
                      e-mail: foundation@mossfoundation.org
Patty Moss, President

The mission of the foundation is to integrate art into all educational programs, with a special focus on children who learn in different ways.

1001 **EDU Therapeutics Annual Conference**
2100 Garden Rd
Bldg B, Ste 6-D
Monterey, CA 93940-5334   831-484-0994
                                FAX 831-484-0998
                          http://www.edu-therapeutics.com
                      e-mail: joan_smith@comcast.net
Joan Smith, Director

Provides diagnositc assessment for LD, ADD, head-trauma (Cognitive), and dyslexia. Provides teacher/clinical training in LD, ADD, dyslexia with EDU-therapeutics.

1002 Eden Family of Services
Eden Services
One Eden Way
Princeton, NJ 08540-5711   609-987-0099
                               FAX 609-987-0243
                          http://www.edenservices.org
                          e-mail: info@edenservices.org
Tom Mc Cool, President

Provides year-round educational services, early intervention, parent training and workshops, respite care, outreach services, community based residential services and employment opportunities for individuals with autism.

1003 Educating Children Summer Training Institute (ECSTI)
Muskingum College-Graduate & Continuing Studies
117 Montgomery Hall
163 Stormont Street
New Concord, OH 43762-1118   740-826-8038
                               FAX 740-826-6038
                          http://www.muskingum.edu
                          e-mail: ecsti@muskingum.edu
Bonnie Callahan, Director

ECSIT offers graduate teacher education and continuing professional development through a series of week long courses. An innovative immersion program, ECSTI offers over 40 course options.

1004 Educational Options for Students with Learning Disabilities and LD/HD
Connecticut Assoc for Children and Adults with LD
25 Van Zant St
Norwalk, CT 06855-0719   203-838-5010
                               FAX 203-866-6108
                          http://www.cacld.org
                          e-mail: cacld@optonline.net
Beryl Kaufman, Executive Director

Annual conference held for parents, students and professionals. Features workshops, panels, exhibitors and a bookstore.
Spring

1005 IDA Conference
International Dyslexia Association
40 York Road
4th Floor
Baltimore, MD 21204-5243   410-296-0232
                               FAX 410-321-5069
                          http://www.interdys.org
                          e-mail: info@interdys.org
Mark S Cohen, Executive Director

The conference promotes effective teaching approaches and strives to pursue and provide the most comprehensive range of information and services that address dyslexia and related difficulties with learning to read and write.
November

1006 Inclusion of Learning Disabled Students in Regular Classrooms Workshop
Learning Disabilities Resources
2775 S. Quincy St.
Arlington, VA 22206
                               FAX 703-998-2060
                          http://www.ldonline.org
Noel Gunther, Executive Director
Christian Lindstrom, Director, Learning Media
Shalini Anand, Senior Manager, Web Development
This workshop provides teachers with practical suggestions and techniques for including students with learning problems.

1007 Interest Driven Learning Master Class Workshop
199 NE Burr Oak Ct
Lees Summit, MO 64064-1962   816-478-4824
                               800-245-5733
                          FAX 816-478-4824
                          http://www.drpeet.com
                          e-mail: drpeet@drpeet.com
Bill Peet MD, President

Provides master classes or workshops on how to use talking word processors and interactive fiction to create highly effective supplemental reading and writing activities for learners of varying abilities aged three to eight. Assistive technology access channels provided for all disabilities. All strategies taught reference the results of 25 years or research.

1008 International Conference on Learning Disabilities
Council for Learning Disabilities
11184 Antioch Road
P.O. Box 405
Overland Park, KS 66210-0405   913-491-1011
                               FAX 913-491-1012
                          http://www.cldinternational.org
                          e-mail: CLDinfo@ie-events.com
Mary Provost, Conference Director

Focuses on all aspects pertaining to learning disabled individuals from a teaching and research perspective.
October

1009 LDA Annual International Conference
Learning Disabilities Association of America
4156 Library Rd
Pittsburgh, PA 15234-1349   412-341-1515
                               FAX 412-344-0224
                          http://www.LDAAmerica.org
                          e-mail: info@ldaamerica.org
Mary-Clare Reynolds, Executive Director

Topics addressed at the conference include advocacy, adult literacy and classroom for individuals with learning disabilities..
March

1010 LDAT Annual State Conference
1011 West 31st Street
Austin, TX 78705-2099   512-458-8234
                               800-604-7500
                          FAX 512-458-3826
                          http://www.ldat.org
                          e-mail: contact@ldat.org
Jean Kueker, President

Promotes the education and general welfare of individuals with learning disabilities.

1011 LDR Workshop: What Are Learning Disabilities, Problems and Differences?
Learning Disabilities Resources
2775 S. Quincy St.
Arlington, VA 22206
                               FAX 703-998-2060
                          http://www.ldonline.org
Noel Gunther, Executive Director
Christian Lindstrom, Director, Learning Media
Shalini Anand, Senior Manager, Web Development
In this workshop, Dr. Cooper draws on personal experiences with a learning disability and on his clinical work with thousands of individuals with a wide variety of learning problems to provide the participants with an understanding of the positive and negative aspects of being, living and learning differently.

1012 Landmark School Outreach Program
Landmark School
429 Hale Street
P.O. Box 227
Prides Crossing, MA 01965-0227   978-236-3216
FAX 978-927-7268
http://www.landmarkoutreach.org
e-mail: outreach@landmarkschool.org
Dan Ahearn, Director

Provides consultation and professional development to
schools, professional organizations, parent groups, and
businesses on topics related to individuals with learning disabilities. Services are individually designed to meet the client's specific needs and can range from a two-hour
workshop to a year-long collaboration. Options include: annual Professional Development Institute at Landmark
School; on-site professional development programs at
schools; online professional development program.

1013 Learning Disabilities and the World of Work Workshop

Learning Disabilities Resources
2775 S. Quincy St.
Arlington, VA 22206
FAX 703-998-2060
http://www.ldonline.org
Noel Gunther, Executive Director
Christian Lindstrom, Director, Learning Media
Shalini Anand, Senior Manager, Web Development
This workshop is designed for employers, parents or profes-
sionals working with individuals with learning disabilities.

**1014 Learning Problems and Adult Basic Education Work-
shop**
Learning Disabilities Resources
2775 S. Quincy St.
Arlington, VA 22206
FAX 703-998-2060
http://www.ldonline.org
Noel Gunther, Executive Director
Christian Lindstrom, Director, Learning Media
Shalini Anand, Senior Manager, Web Development
This workshop for adult educators discusses the manifesta-
tions of learning problems in adults.

**1015 Lindamood-Bell Learning Processes Professional Devel-
opment**
416 Higuera St
San Luis Obispo, CA 93401-3833   805-541-3836
800-233-1819
FAX 805-541-8756
http://www.lindamoodbell.com
Nanci Bell, Co-founder and the Director

Offers workshops nationwide for educators in the internationally acclaimed Lindamood-Bell teaching methods. Approximately 40 workshops hosted annually across the
United State and Internationally. Inservices also available.

1016 NCFL Conference
National Center For Family Literacy
325 W. Main Street
Suite 300
Louisville, KY 40202-4237   502-584-1133
FAX 502-584-0172
http://www.famlit.org
e-mail: ncfl@famlit.org
Sharon Darling, President

Comprehensive conference serving family literacy professionals and practitioners who are in the field of improving
literacy skills and the lives of the parents and children. Attendees will learn about the latest research in the education
industry, and hear from celebrity advocates and authors.
March

1017 National Head Start Association
1651 Prince St
Alexandria, VA 22314-2818   703-739-0875
FAX 703-739-0878
http://www.nhsa.org
e-mail: yvinci@nhsa.org
Yasmina Vinci, Executive Director

Both Adminstrator and Mid-Manager credentials are offered
in a six day, institute style setting, workshop. Family Services and Health credentials are offered through a self study
format.
September

1018 National Head Start Association Parent Conference
1651 Prince St
Alexandria, VA 22314-2818   703-739-0875
FAX 703-739-0878
http://www.nhsa.org
e-mail: asmith@nhsa.orgrg
Yasmina Vinci, Executive Director
Angela Smith, Conferences

Newest information on enhancing parent involvement, child
development, and sharpening parenting skills. More than
100 workshops.

**1019 North American Montessori Teachers' Association Con-
ference**
13693 Butternut Rd
Burton, OH 44021-9571   440-834-4011
FAX 440-834-4016
http://www.montessori-namta.org
e-mail: staff@montessori-namta.org
David Kahn, Director

Montessori method of teaching is discussed as well as topics
pertaining to all levels of special education. This and other
conferences are held in different locations and months
throughout the year. Please contact us for more information.

Quarterly

1020 Pacific Rim Conference on Disabilities
University of Hawaii Center on Disability Studies
1776 University Ave
UA 4-6
Honolulu, HI 96822-2447   808-956-7539
FAX 808-956-7878
http://www.pacrim.hawaii.edu
e-mail: prinfo@hawaii.edu
Valerie Shearer, Director
Charmaine Crockett, Conference Organizer

Participants from the US and other Pacific Rim nations study
such topics in disabilities as lifelong inclusion in education
and community, new technology, family support, employment and adult services.
March

**1021 Pennsylvania Training and Technical Assistance Net-
work Workshops**
PaTTAN
6340 Flank Drive
Suite 600
Harrisburg, PA 17112-2764   717-541-4960
800-360-7282
FAX 717-541-4968
http://www.pattan.net
e-mail: askpattan@pattan.net
Angela Kirby-Wehr, Director
Victor Rodriguez-Diaz, Ph.D., Assistant Director

Supports the Department of Education's efforts to lead and serve the educational community by offering professional development that builds the capacity of loacl educational agencies to meet students' needs. PaTTAN's primary focus is special education. However, services are also provided to support Early Intervention, student assessment, tutoring and other partnership efforts, all designed to help students succeed.

1022 Social Skills Workshop
Learning Disabilities Resources
2775 S. Quincy St.
Arlington, VA 22206

FAX 703-998-2060
http://www.ldonline.org
Noel Gunther, Executive Director
Christian Lindstrom, Director, Learning Media
Shalini Anand, Senior Manager, Web Development
This workshop is relevant for individuals with learning disabilities, parents or professionals.

1023 Son-Rise Program
Autism Treatment Center of America

413-229-2100
877-766-7473
http://www.autismtreatment.com
e-mail: autism@option.org
Since 1983, the Autism Treatment Center of America has provided innovative training programs for parents and professionals caring for children challenged by Autism, Autism Spectrum Disorders, Pervasive Developmental Disorder (PDD) and other developmental difficulties. The Son-Rise Program teaches a specific yet comprehensive system of treatment and education designed to help families and caregivers enable their children to dramatically improve in all areas of learning.

1024 TASH Annual Conference Social Justice inthe 21st Century
Fl 7
1025 Vermont Ave NW
Washington, DC 20005-3577

202-467-4410
888-221-9425
FAX 202-857-0368
http://www.tash.org
e-mail: info@tash.org
Howard Weiss, Executive Director

Progressive international conference that focuses on strategies for achieving full inclusion for people with disabilities. This invigorating conference, which brings together the best hearts and minds in the disability movement, features over 450 breakout sessions, exhibits, roundtable discussions, poster sessions and much more.
December

1025 Teaching Math Workshop
Learning Disabilities Resources
2775 S. Quincy St.
Arlington, VA 22206

FAX 703-998-2060
http://www.ldonline.org
Noel Gunther, Executive Director
Christian Lindstrom, Director, Learning Media
Shalini Anand, Senior Manager, Web Development
A workshop for teachers on how to teach math to individuals with learning problems.

1026 Teaching Reading Workshop
LD OnLine/Learning Disabilities Resource
WETA Public Television
2775 S. Quincy Street
Arlington, VA 22206

FAX 703-998-2060
http://www.ldonline.org
This workshop explains how to teach individuals with reading problems, dyslexia, ADD, and specific learning disabilities.

1027 Teaching Spelling Workshop
LD OnLine/Learing Disabilities Resource
WETA Public Television
2775 S. Quincy Street
Arlington, VA 22206

FAX 703-998-2060
http://www.ldonline.org
A workshop that focuses on how to spell, which directly affects an individual's ability to write.

1028 Technology & Persons with Disabilities Conference
California State University Northridge
18111 Nordhoff St
BH 110
Northridge, CA 91330-8340

818-677-2578
FAX 818-677-4929
http://www.csun.edu
e-mail: conference@csun.edu
Jolene Koester, President

A major training venue held yearly for professionals from around the world who are involved in the field of disabilities and assistive technology that helps disabled individuals in the fields of education, employment and independent living.

March

1029 Wilson Language Training
47 Old Webster Rd
Oxford, MA 01540-2705

508-368-2399
800-899-8454
FAX 508-368-2300
http://www.wilsonlanguage.com
e-mail: info@wilsonlanguage.com
Barbara Wilson, Director

Our workshops instruct teachers, or other professionals in a related field, how to succeed with students who have not learned to read, write and spell despite great effort. Established in order to provide training in the Wilson Reading System, the Wilson staff provides Two-Day Overview Workshops as well as certified Level I and II training.

1030 Young Adult Institute Conference on Developmental Disabilities
460 W 34th St
New York, NY 10001-2382

212-273-6100
FAX 212-268-1083
http://www.yai.org
Stephen E. Freeman, L.C.S.W., Chief Executive Officer
Thomas A. Dern, L.C.S.W., Chief Operating Officer
Sanjay Dutt, Chief Financial Officer
Annual conference of developmental disabilities. In-depth sessions on the keys to success in developmental and learning disabilities.
May

Assistive Devices

1031 AbleData
USDE National Institution on Disability
8630 Fenton St
Ste 930
Silver Spring, MD 20910-3820   301-608-8998
800-227-0216
FAX 301-608-8958
TTY: 301-608-8912
http://www.abledata.com
e-mail: abledata@macrointernational.com
Katherine Belknap, Project Director
Juanita Hardy, Information Specialist
David Johnson, Publications Director
Database contains descriptions of more than 35,000 commercially available, one-of-a-kind, and do-it-yourself products for rehabilitation and independent living. A wealth of information on assistive technology.

1032 Ablenet
2625 Patton Road
Roseville, MN 55113-1308   651-294-2200
800-322-0956
FAX 651-294-2259
http://www.ablenetinc.com
e-mail: customerservice@ablenetinc.com
Jennifer Thalhuber, President/CEO
Bill Sproull, Chairman
Paul Sugden, Vice President of Finance
Dedicated to making a difference in the lives of people with disabilities.

1033 Adaptive Device Locator System (ADLS)
Academic Software
3504 Tates Creek Rd
Lexington, KY 40517-2601   859-552-1020
http://www.acsw.com
e-mail: asistaff@acsw.com
Warren E Lacefield, President
Penelope D Ellis, COO/Dir Sales/Marketing

System describes thousands of devices, cross references over 1000 vendors and illustrates devices graphically. The ADLS databases include a full spectrum of living aids, products ranging from specialized eating utensils to dressing aids, electronic switches, computer hardware and software, adapted physical education devices and much more. Now accessible on the internet through Adaptworld.com and Acsw.com *$195.00*

1034 Alliance for Technology Access
1304 Southpoint Blvd.
Suite 240
Petaluma, CA 94954-7464
800-914-3017
FAX 707-765-2080
http://www.ataccess.org
Sharon Hall, President

The mission of the Alliance for Technology Access (ATA) is to increase the use of technology by children and adults with disabilities and functional limitations.

1035 Braille Keyboard Sticker Overlay Label Kit
Hooleon Corporation
PO Box 589
Melrose, NM 88124   575-253-4503
800-937-1337
FAX 505-253-4299
http://www.hooleon.com
e-mail: sales@hooleon.com
Joan Crozier, Founder
Bob Crozier, Founder

Transparent with raised braille allows both sighted and nonsighted users to use same keyboard.

1036 Connect Outloud
Freedom Scientific
11800 31st Ct N
St Petersburg, FL 33716-1805   727-803-8000
800-444-4443
FAX 727-803-8001
http://www.freedomscientific.com
e-mail: info@freedomscientific.com
Lee Hamilton, President, CEO, and Chairman

Designed to allow beginners through experienced blind or low vision computer users to access the Internet through speech and Braille output. Based on our JAWS for Windows technology, and offers additional access to Windows XP. *$249.00*

1037 Controlpad 24
Genovation
17741 Mitchell N
Irvine, CA 92614-6028   949-833-3355
800-822-4333
FAX 949-833-0322
http://www.genovation.com
e-mail: max@genovation.com
Fully programmable 24 key pad. Its principal purpose is to provide single keystroke macros.

1038 Dyna Vox Technologies
Ste 400
2100 Wharton St
Pittsburgh, PA 15203-1942   412-381-4883
866-396-2869
FAX 412-381-5241
http://www.dynavoxtech.com
Sherry Bertner, Managing Director

DynaVox Technologies develops, manufactures, distributes and supports a variety of speech-output devices that allow individuals challenged by speech, lanugage and learning disabilities to make meaningful connections with their world. The company's products allow individuals of all ages and abilities to initiate and participate in conversations at home, work, in school and throughout the community. *$4500.00*

1039 EZ Keys XP
Words+
42505 10th St W
Lancaster, CA 93534-7059   661-723-7723
800-869-8521
FAX 661-723-2114
http://www.words-plus.com
e-mail: info@word-plus.com
Assistance program that provides keyboard control, dual word prediction, abbreviation-expansion and speech output while running standard software. *$695.00*

1040 Enabling Devices
50 Broadway
Hawthorne, NY 10532   914-747-3070
800-832-8697
FAX 914-747-3480
http://www.enablingdevices.com
Steven Kanor PhD, President

A designer, manufacturer and distributor of unique and affordable assitive and adaptive technologies for the physically and mentally challenged, ED/TFSC's products are sought by parents, teachers, and professionals alike.

1041 Genie Color TV
TeleSensory
650 Vaqueros Ave
Suite F
Sunnyvale, CA 94085-3525   408-616-8700
800-804-8004
FAX 408-616-8720
http://www.telesensory.com
e-mail: info@telesensory.com

Brings clarity and comfort to reading and writing. Since many people with low vision find that specific color combinations enhance legibility, VersiColor offers 24 customized foreground and background color combinations to choose from in addition to a full color mode. Genie can also connect to a computer for use with Telesensory's Vista screen magnification system. *$2995.00*

1042 **Genovation**
17741 Mitchell N
Irvine, CA 92614-6028   949-833-3355
                                       800-822-4333
                                    FAX 949-833-0322
                          http://www.genovation.com
                          e-mail: max@genovation.com
Produces a wide variety of computer input devices for data-entry, and custom applications. Produces the Function Keypad 682 for people with limited dexterity. It is programmable, allowing the user to store macros (selected patterns of key strokes) into memory, and relegendable keys allow easy labeling of user-programmed functions. Additional options such as larger keys (1x2), allow reconfiguration to meet the user's needs. Call toll-free for pricing and availability.

1043 **Handbook of Adaptive Switches and Augmentative Communication Devices, 3rd Ed**
3504 Tates Creek Road
Lexington, KY 40517   895-552-1020
                               http://www.acsw.com
                          e-mail: asistaff@acsw.com
Warren E Lacefield, President

An essential sourcebook for assistive technology specialists, teacheers, therapists, and others who select adaptive swicthes and augmentative communication devices for persons with disabilities.

1044 **Home Row Indicators**
Hooleon Corporation
PO Box 589
Melrose, NM 88124   575-253-4503
                                       800-937-1337
                                    FAX 505-253-4299
                             http://www.hooleon.com
                          e-mail: sales@hooleon.com
Joan Crozier, Founder
Bob Crozier, Founder

Plastic adhesive labels with a raised bump in the center allowing the user to designate home row keys, or any other key, for quick recognition.

1045 **IntelliKeys**
IntelliTools
24 Prime Parkway
Natick, MA 01760
                                       800-547-6747
                             http://www.intellitools.com
                 e-mail: customerservice@cambiumtech.com
Arjan Khalsa, CEO

Alternative, touch-sensitive keyboard. Plugs into any MAC, APPLE, or IBM compatible computer, no interface needed. *$395.00*

1046 **JAWS Screen Reading Software**
Freedom Scientific
11800 31st Ct N
St Petersburg, FL 33716-1805   727-803-800
                                       800-444-4443
                                    FAX 727-803-8001
                          http://www.freedomscientific.com
                          e-mail: info@freedomscientific.com
Lee Hamilton, President, CEO, and Chairman

JAWS is a powerful accessibility solution for the blind & people with low vision that reads information from computer screens using synthesised speech. This advanced & versitile software was specifically designed to meet the needs of blind and visually impaired computer users. WIth JAWS, users can access their computer applications and the Internet via text-to-speech technology. Through the use of a refreshable braille display, JAWS can provide braille output in addition to or instead of speech

1047 **JAWS for Windows**
Freedom Scientific
11800 31st Ct N
St Petersburg, FL 33716-1805   727-803-8000
                                       800-444-4443
                                    FAX 727-803-8001
                          http://www.freedomscientific.com
                          e-mail: info@freedomscientific.com
Lee Hamilton, President, CEO, and Chairman

Works with your PC to provide access to today's software applications and the internet. With its internal software speech synthesizer and the computer's sound card, information from the screen is read aloud, providing technology to access a wide variety of information, education and job related applications.

1048 **Large Print Keyboard**
Hooleon Corporation
PO Box 589
Melrose, NM 88124   575-253-4503
                                       800-937-1337
                                    FAX 505-253-4299
                             http://www.hooleon.com
                          e-mail: sales@hooleon.com
Joan Crozier, Founder
Bob Crozier, Founder

Keyboard with 104 keys features large print on all the keys. *$49.95*

1049 **Large Print Lower Case Key Label Stickers**
Hooleon Corporation
PO Box 589
Melrose, NM 88124   575-253-4503
                                       800-937-1337
                                    FAX 505-253-4299
                             http://www.hooleon.com
                          e-mail: sales@hooleon.com
Joan Crozier, Founder
Bob Crozier, Founder

For children learning the keyboard. Made of durable rigid plastic and are die cut to fit exactly.

1050 **Lekotek of Georgia Shareware**
Lekotek of Georgia
Ste 102
1955 Cliff Valley Way NE
Atlanta, GA 30329-2437   404-633-3430
                                    FAX 404-633-1242
                             http://www.lekotekga.org
                          e-mail: info@lekotekga.org
Helene Prokesch, Executive Director and Founder
Peggy McWilliams, Director of Technology Services
Ellen Lindemann, Assistant Director
Software created by our staff using Intellipics, Intellipics Studio or Hyperstudio. Players are included to run this shareware. Color overlays for intellemusic are included. Input methods are mouse, switch, touch window, head mouse and intellikeys if applicable. Subjects are colors and emotions, early childhood music in English and Spanish, shapes and sounds, pictures and letters.

1051 Open Book
Freedom Scientific
11800 31st Ct N
St Petersburg, FL 33716-1805   727-803-8000
     800-444-4443
     FAX 727-803-8001
     http://www.freedomscientific.com
     e-mail: info@freedomscientific.com
Lee Hamilton, President, CEO, and Chairman

Allows you to convert printed documents or graphic based text into an electronic text format using accurate optical character recognition and quality speech. The many powerful low vision tools allow you to customize how the document appears on your screen, while other features provide portability. *$995.00*

1052 Phonic Ear Auditory Trainers
Phonic Ear
2080 Lakeville Hwy
Petaluma, CA 94954-6713   707-769-1110
     800-227-0735
     FAX 707-769-9624
     http://www.phonicear.com
     e-mail: mail@phonicear.com
Paul Hickey, Director

A line of learning disabled communication equipment.

1053 QuicKeys
Startly Technologies
PO Box 65580
West Des Moines, IA 50265   515-221-1801
     800-523-7638
     FAX 515-221-1806
     http://www.startly.com
Assigns Macintosh & Windows functions to one keystroke.

1054 Reading Pen
Wizcom Technologies
Boston Post Rd W 33
Ste 320
Marlborough, MA 01752-1829   508-251-5388
     888-777-0552
     FAX 508-251-5394
     http://www.wizcomtech.com
     e-mail: usa.info@wizcomtech.com
Michael Kenan, President

Portable assistive reading device that reads words aloud and can be used anywhere. Scans a word from printed text, displays the word in large characters, reads the word aloud from built-in speaker or ear phones and defines the word with the press of a button. Displays syllables, keeps a history of scanned words, adjustable for left or right-handed use. Includes a tutorial video and audio cassette. Not recommended for persons with low vision or impaired fine motor control.

1055 Switch Accessible Trackball
Lekotek of Georgia
Ste 102
1955 Cliff Valley Way NE
Atlanta, GA 30329-2437   404-633-3430
     FAX 404-633-1242
     http://www.lekotekga.org
     e-mail: info@lekotekga.org
Helene Prokesch, Executive Director and Founder
Peggy McWilliams, Director of Technology Services
Ellen Lindemann, Assistant Director
Universal to Mac or Windows, this device aids computer navigation where traditional devices are not used. Trackball guards available. *$125.00*

1056 Unicorn Expanded Keyboard
1720 Corporate Cir
Natick, MA 01760
     800-547-6747
     http://www.intellitools.com
     e-mail: customerservice@cambiumtech.com
Arjan Khalsa, CEO

Alternative keyboard with large, user-defined keys, requires interface. Smaller version is also available.

1057 Unicorn Smart Keyboard
Ste 9
Natick, MA 01760
     800-547-6747
     http://www.intellitools.com
     e-mail: customerservice@cambiumtech.com
Arjan Khlasa, CEO

Works with any standard keyboard and offers seven overlays and a cable for one type of computer.

1058 Universal Numeric Keypad
Genovation
17741 Mitchell N
Irvine, CA 92614-6028   949-833-3355
     800-822-4333
     FAX 949-833-0322
     http://www.genovation.com
     e-mail: max@genovation.com
A 21 key numeric keypad that works with any laptop or portable computer.

1059 Up and Running
IntelliTools
1720 Corporate Cir
Natick, MA 01760
     800-547-6747
     http://www.intellitools.com
     e-mail: customerservice@cambiumtech.com
Arjan Khalsa, CEO

A custom overlay kit for the IntelliKeys Keyboard that provides instant access to a wide range of software including over 60 popular educational programs. *$69.95*

1060 VISTA
TeleSensory
650 Vaqueros Ave
Suite F
Sunnyvale, CA 94085-3525   408-616-8700
     800-8048004
     FAX 408-616-8720
     http://www.telesensory.com
     e-mail: info@telesensory.com
Image enlarging system that magnifies the print and graphics on the screen from three to 16 times. *$2495.00*

1061 VisagraphIII Eye-Movement Recording System& Reading Plus
Taylor Associated Communications
110 West Canal Street
Suite 301
Winooski, VT 05404   802-735-1942
     800-732-3758
     FAX 802-419-4786
     http://www.readingplus.com
     e-mail: info@readingplus.com
Mark Taylor, Chief Executive Officer
Kelly Scannell, Chief Operating Officer
Stan Taylor, Founder/Chairman
Measures reading performance efficiency, visual and functional proficiency, perceptual development, and information processing competence.

1062 Window-Eyes
GW Micro
725 Airport North Office Park
Fort Wayne, IN 46825-6707
260-489-3671
FAX 260-489-2608
http://www.gwmicro.com
e-mail: support@gwmicro.com
Erik Deckers, Director of Sales and Marketing

Screen reader that is adaptable to your specific needs and preferances. Works automatically so you can focus on your application program, not so much on operating the screen reader.

Books & Periodicals

1063 AppleWorks Education
AACE
PO Box 1545
Chesapeake, VA 23327-1545
757-366-5606
FAX 703-997-8760
http://www.aace.org
e-mail: info@aace.org
Gary Marks, Publisher
Tracy Jacobs, Office Manager

Covers educational uses of AppleWorks software. *$25.00*

1064 Bibliography of Journal Articles on Microcomputers & Special Education
Special Education Resource Center
25 Industrial Park Rd
Middletown, CT 06457-1516
860-632-1485
800-842-8678
FAX 860-632-8870
http://www.ctserc.org
e-mail: info@ctserc.org
Marianne Kirner, Executive Director
Ingrid Canady, Assistant Director for Program
John Mercier, Assistant Director
This pamphlet offers information on a wide variety of professional journals in the fields of microcomputers and special education.

1065 Closing the Gap Newsletter
Closing the Gap Solutions
PO Box 68
Henderson, MN 56044
507-248-3294
FAX 507-248-3810
http://www.closingthegap.com
e-mail: info@closingthegap.com
Megan Turek, Managing Editor
Becky Hagen, Advertising and Exhibit sales
Sarah Anderson, Administrative Assistant
Bimonthly newsletter on the use of computer technology in special education and rehabilitation. CTG also sponsors an annual international conference. *$34.00*
40 pages
ISSN 0886-1935

1066 Computer Access-Computer Learning
Special Needs Project
818-718-9900
FAX 818-349-2027
http://www.specialneeds.com
Hod Gray, Editor
Ginny LaVine, Author
A resource manual in adaptive technology. *$22.50*
226 pages

1067 MACcessories: Guide to Peripherals
Western Illinois University: Macomb Projects
1 University Cir
Macomb, IL 61455-1367
309-298-1414
FAX 309-298-2305
http://www.wiu.edu
e-mail: info@wiu.edu

Amanda Silberer, Hearing Clinic Coordinator
Joyce Johanson, Associate Director
Beverly Stuckwisch, Secretary
Designed to help the Macintosh user understand peripheral devices. Includes descriptions of each device, advantages and disadvantages of each, procedures for installation, troubleshooting tips, suggested software and company resources. *$15.00*
41 pages

1068 Switch to Turn Kids On
Western Illinois University: Macomb Projects
Horrabin Hall 71b 1 University Cir
Macomb, IL 61455-1390
800-322-3905
http://www.wiu.edu/users/micpc
e-mail: ML-Frederick@wiu.edu
Susan Schoonover, Chief Clerk

Guide to homemade switches gives information on conducting a switch workshop and constructing a battery interrupter as well as various kinds of switches (tread switches, ribbon switches, mercury switches, pillow switches). Contains illustrations and step-by-step instructions. *$12.00*
47 pages

Centers & Organizations

1069 American Foundation for the Blind
2 Penn Plaza
Suite 1102
New York, NY 10121
212-502-7600
800-232-5463
FAX 888-545-8331
http://www.afb.org
e-mail: afbinfo@afb.net
Carl R. Augusto, President/CEO
Sylvia Simpson, Executive Assistant
Rick Bozeman, Director, Finance
Is a national nonprofit that expands possibilities for people with vision loss. AFB's priorities include broadening access to technology; elevating the quality of information and tools for the professionals who serve people with vision loss; and promoting independent and healthy living for people with vision loss by providing them and their families with relevant and timely resources.

1070 Artificial Language Laboratory
Michigan State University
405 Computer Ctr
East Lansing, MI 48824-1042
517-353-0870
FAX 517-353-4766
http://www.msu.edu
John Eulenberg PhD, Director

Multidisciplinary teaching and research center involved in basic and applied research concerning the computer processing of formal linguistic structures.

1071 Association for Educational Communications and Technology
Ste 2
1800 N Stonelake Dr
Bloomington, IN 47404-2447
812-335-7675
877-677-2328
FAX 812-335-7678
http://www.aect.org
e-mail: aect@aect.org
Phillip Harris MD, Executive Director
Larry Vernon, Director of Electronic Services

Provides leadership in educational communications and technology by linking professionals holding a common interest in the use of educational technology and its application to the learning process.

1072 Birmingham Alliance for Technology Access Center
Birmingham Independent Living Center
206 13th St S
Birmingham, AL 35233-1317   205-251-2223
                                   FAX 205-251-0605
                                   TTY: 205-251-2223
                                   http://www.ilrgb.org
                                   e-mail: bilc@bellsouth.net
Daniel G Kessler, Executive Director

Information dissemination, network, referral service, support services, and training. Disabilities served are cognitive, hearing, learning, physical, speech and vision.

1073 Bluegrass Technology Center
409 Southland Drive
Lexington, KY 40503   859-294-4343
                                   800-209-7767
                                   FAX 866-576-9625
                                   http://www.bluegrass-tech.org
                                   e-mail: office@bluegrass-tech.org
Debbie Sharon, Acting Executive Director
Carol Moffett, EdS, ATP, Assistive Technology Consultant
Linnie Lee, Assistive Technology Consultant
Provides support to all persons with disabilities in their efforts to access technology and to increase awareness and understanding of how that technology can enhance their abilities to participate more fully in their community, assisting individuals directly or indirectly by working with their caregivers, therapists, vocational counselors, case managers, educators, employers, and community members.

1074 CAST
Center for Applied Special Technology
Ste 3
40 Harvard Mill Sq
Wakefield, MA 01880-3233   781-245-2212
                                   FAX 781-245-5212
                                   TDD:781-245-9320
                                   http://www.cast.org
                                   e-mail: cast@cast.org
David Rose, President

A nonprofit organization that works to expand learning opportunities for all individuals, especially those with disabilities, through the research and development of innovative, technology-based educational resources and strategies.

1075 Center for Accessible Technology
3075 Adeline
Suite 220
Berkeley, CA 97403   510-841-3224
                                   FAX 510-841-7956
                                   http://www.cforat.org
                                   e-mail: info@cforat.org
Carol Cody, Executive Director
Josh Kirschenbaum, Associate Director
Judith Rogers, Occupational Therapist
Resource center for parents, professionals, developers and individuals with disabilities, filled with computers, software, adapted toys and adaptive technology.

1076 Center for Enabling Technology
College of New Jersey
PO Box 7718
2000 Pennington Road
Ewing, NJ 08628   609-771-3016
                                   FAX 609-637-5172
                                   TTY: 609-771-2309
                                   http://www.tcnj.edu
William Behre, Dean
Christine Schindler, Assistive Technology Specialist
Amy Dell, Program Coordinator
Ongoing projects that match assistive devices to the children who need them. Training and educational workshops.

1077 Comprehensive Services for the Disabled
PO Box 1605
Wall, NJ 07719-1605   732-681-5632
                                   800-784-2919
                                   FAX 732-681-5632
Donald DeSanto, Executive Director

Helps special students realize their potential and bring college admission a step closer. Program designed to meet the needs and maximize the unique talents of each individual. The staff consists of highly qualified teachers who see beyond labels and reach the person inside. By pacing scholastics to each student's ability, the college increases understanding and makes learning a positive experience. Instruction is tailored to each individual.

1078 Computer Access Center
Empowertech
1705 Five Points Rd SW
Albuquerque, NM   505-242-9588
                                   http://www.cac.org
                                   e-mail: info@cacradicalgrace.org
Richard Rohr, Founder

Computer resource center serving primarily as a place where people with all types of disabilities can preview equipment. Workshops, seminars, after school clubs for children and individual consultations are provided.

1079 Council for Exceptional Children Annual Convention & Expo
Council for Exceptional Children
2900 Crystal Drive
Suite 1000
Arlington, VA 22202   703-264-9454
                                   800-224-6830
                                   FAX 703-620-2521
                                   TTY: 866-915-5000
                                   http://www.cec.sped.org
                                   e-mail: victore@cec.sped.org
Anmarie Kallas, Senior Director/Conventions
Victor Erickson, Director Advertising/Exhibits

This database contains citations and abstracts of print and nonprint materials dealing with exceptional children, those who have disabilities and those who are gifted. Resources in all areas of special education and related services (including services provided by audiologists, speech therapists, occupational therapists, physical therapists, and educational psychologists) are covered in ECER.

1080 Dialog Information Services
2250 Perimeter Park Drive
Suite 300
Morrisville, NC 27560   919-804-6400
                                   800-334-2564
                                   FAX 919-804-6410
                                   http://www.dialog.com
Roy Martin, President
Tim Wahlberg, General Manager
Tim Hall, Director
Offers access to over 390 data bases containing information on various aspects of disabling conditions and services to disabled individuals.

1081 HEATH Resource Center
2134 G St NW
Washington, DC 20052
                                   http://www.heath.gwu.edu
                                   e-mail: AskHEATH@gwu.edu
Juliana Taymans, Faculty Advisory Board
Dr Lynda West, Principal Investigator
Dr Joel Gomez, Principal Investigator

The HEATH Resource Center is an online clearinghouse on postsecondary education for individuals with disabilities. The HEATH Resource Center Clearinghouse has information for students with disabilities on educational disability support services, policies, procedures, adaptations, accessing college or university campuses, career-technical schools, and other postsecondary training entities.

1082   **High Tech Center Training Unit**
21050 McClellan Rd
Cupertino, CA 95014-4276   408-996-4636
                                         800-411-8954
                                     FAX 408-996-6042
                                    TTY: 408-252-4938
                               http://www.htctu.fhda.edu
                                   e-mail: info@htctu.net
Gaeir Dietrich, Director
Michael Fosnaugh, Administrative Assistant
Dale Kan, Network Specialist
Provides training for faculty and staff of the California community colleges in access technologies.

1083   **Iowa Program for Assistive Technology**
IA University Assistive Technology
100 Hawkins Dr
Iowa City, IA 52242-1011
                                         800-779-2001
                                  http://http://iowaat.org
                                  e-mail: IPAT@uiowa.edu
Jane Gay, Director
Gary Johnson, Coordinator, Community Program
Marlene Phipps, Office Clerk
Computer accesssed solutions for physically challenged students.

1084   **Learning Independence through Computers**
LINC
2301 Argonne Drive
Baltimore, MD 21218-4325   410-554-9134
                                     FAX 410-261-2907
                                    http://www.linc.org
Theo Pinette, Executive Director
Jessica Robles, Volunteer Services Manager
Justin Creamer, Sr. Assistive Technology
Resource center that offers specially adapted computer technology to children and adults with a variety of disabilities. State-of-the-art systems allow consumers to achieve their potential for productivity and independence at home, school, work and in the community. Also offers a quarterly newsletter called Connections.

1085   **Lighthouse Central Florida**
215 E New Hampshire St
Orlando, FL 32804-6403   407-898-2483
                                     FAX 407-895-5255
                       http://www.lighthousecentralflorida.org
                               e-mail: lighthouse@lcf-fl.org
Lee Nasehi, President/CEO
Donna Esbensen, VP/CFO

Provides life-changing services for children and adults who are blind and sight-impaired. Offers a comprehensive array of professional vision rehabilitation services in the Central Florida area.
                                              1976

1086   **Project TECH**
Massachusetts Easter Seal Society
6th Fl
484 Main St
Worcester, MA 01608-1893
                                         800-244-2756
                                     FAX 508-831-9768
                                    TTY: 800-564-9700
                               http://www.eastersealsma.org
                             e-mail: info@eastersealsma.org
David S. Hoffman, Vice Chair
Harry E. Salerno, Chairman
Anthony A. Tambone, Treasurer

Assistive technology services, suited to an individual's needs. Transition from school to work, employment planning, occupational skills and more are coached here.

1087   **RESNA Technical Assistance Project**
Ste 1540
1700 N Moore St
Arlington, VA 22209-1917   703-524-6686
                                     FAX 703-524-6639
                                    http://www.resna.org
                            e-mail: membership@resna.org
Nell Bailey, Executive Director
Alex Mihailidis, PhD, P.Eng, President
Paul J. Schwartz, MSIE, ATP, R, Treasurer
Provides technical assistance to states in the development and implementation of consumer responsive statewide programs of technology-related assistance under the Technology Related Assistance for Individuals with Disabilities Act of 1988.

1088   **Ruth Eason School**
648 Old Mill Rd
Millersville, MD 21108-1373   410-222-3815
                                     FAX 410-222-3817
                                    http://www.aacps.org
                             e-mail: schoolsite@aacps.org
Cathy Larner, Principal
Linda Abey, Principal
Tracy D' Angelo, Secretary

1089   **Star Center**
1119 Old Humboldt Rd
Jackson, TN 38305-1752   731-668-3888
                                         800-464-5619
                                     FAX 731-668-1666
                                    TTY: 731-668-9664
                                http://www.starcenter.tn.org
                           e-mail: information@starcenter.tn.org
Margaret Doumitt, Executive Director

Technology center for people with disabilities. Some of the services are: music therapy, art therapy, augmentative communication evaluation and training, vocational evaluation, job placement, vision department, environmental controls.

1090   **Tech-Able**
1451 Klondike Road
Suite D
Conyers, GA 30094-5982   770-922-6768
                                     FAX 770-992-6769
                                    http://www.techable.org
                            e-mail: c.b.wright@techable.org
Cassandra Baker-Wright, Executive Director
Patricia Hanus, Program Assistant
Erika Ruffin-Mosley, Assistive Technology Trainer
Assistive technology demonstration and information center. Provides demonstrations of computer hardware and software specially designed to assist people with disabilities. Serves a wide range of disabilities and virtually all age groups. Also custom fabrication of key guards and switches.

1091   **Technology Access Center**
475 Metroplex Dr
Ste 301
Nashville, TN 37211-3142   615-248-6733
                                         800-368-4651
                                     FAX 615-259-2536
                                    TDD:615-248-6733
                               http://www.tacnashville.org
                            e-mail: techaccess@tacnashville.org
Bob Kibler, Director
Lynn Magner, Service Coordinator

Serves the community as a resource center and carries out specific projects related to assistive technology.

1092 Technology Access Foundation
4436 Rainier Ave S
Seattle, WA 98118-1373   206-725-9095
                              FAX 206-725-9097
                         http://www.techaccess.org
                         e-mail: taf@techaccess.org
Trish Millines, Executive Director

Provides information, consultation and technical assistance
on assistive technology for people with disabilities, including computer hardware and software technology, and adaptive and assistive equipment.

1093 Technology Assistance for Special Consumers
1856 Keats Dr NW
Huntsville, AL 35810-4465   256-859-8300
                              FAX 256-859-4332
                         http://www.ucptasc.org
                         e-mail: tasc@ucphuntsville.org
Laura Parks, M.Ed., Assistive Technology Specialist
Julie Yockel, M.S., CCC-SLP, AAC Specialist
Mark Pepper, STAR Reutilization Specialist
Offers a computer resource center which has both computers
and software for use at the center or for short-term.

1094 Technology Utilization Program
National Aeronautics and Space Administration
Suite 5K39
Washington, DC 20546   202-358-0000
                              FAX 202-358-4338
                         http://www.hq.nasa.gov
                         e-mail: public-inquiries@hq.nasa.gov.
Charles F. Bolden, Jr., Administrator
Michael Griffin, Administrator
Lori B. Garver, Deputy Administrator
Adapts aerospace technology to the development of equip-
ment for the disabled, sick and elderly persons.

1095 Technology for Language and Learning
PO Box 327
East Rockaway, NY 11518   516-625-4550
                              FAX 516-621-3321
                         e-mail: ForTLL@aol.com
Joan Tanenhaus, Executive Director

An organization dedicated to advancing the use of computers and technology for children and adults with special language and learning needs. Public domain computer software
for special education.

Games

1096 A Day at Play
Don Johnston
26799 W Commerce Dr
Volo, IL 60073-9675   847-740-0749
                              800-999-4660
                         FAX 847-740-7326
                         http://www.donjohnston.com
                         e-mail: info@donjohnston.com
Ruth Ziolkowski, President

A Day at Play and Out and About, programs in the UKanDu
Little Books Series, are early literacy programs that consist
of several create-your-own four-page animated stories that
help build language experience for early readers. Students
fill in the blanks to complete a sentence on each page and
then watch the page come alive with animation and sound.
After completing the story, students can print it out to make a
book which can be read over and over again.

1097 Academic Drill Builders: Wiz Works
SRA Order Services
PO Box 182605
Columbus, OH 43218   800-334-7344
                              FAX 614-860-1877
                         http://www.sraonline.com
                         e-mail: SEG_CustomerService@mcgraw-hill.com
The McGraw-Hill Education Urban Advisory Resource
works with large urban districts across the country to help
them provide better quality instruction, curriculum, and as-
sessment to their students. *$49.00*

1098 Adaptive Physical Education Program
2 Merwick Road
Princeton, NJ 08540-5711   609-987-0099
                         http://www.edenservices.org
Tom Mc Cool, Executive Director
Anne Holmes, Outreach/Support Director
This volume contains teaching programs in the area of sen-
sory integration and adaptive physical education for stu-
dents with autism. *$50.00*

1099 Alpine Tram Ride
Merit Software
Ste 603
121 W 27th St
New York, NY 10011-6262   212-675-8567
                              800-753-6488
                         FAX 212-675-8607
                         http://www.meritsoftware.com
                         e-mail: sales@meritsoftware.com
Ben Weintraub, CEO

Teaches cognitive redevelopment skills. *$12.95*

1100 Blocks in Motion
Don Johnston
26799 W Commerce Dr
Volo, IL 60073-9675   847-740-0749
                              800-999-4660
                         FAX 847-740-7326
                         http://www.donjohnston.com
                         e-mail: info@donjohnston.com
Ruth Ziolkowski, President

An art and motion program that makes drawing, creating and
animating fun and educational for all users. Based on the
Piagetian theory for motor-sensory development, this program promotes the concept that the process is as educational
and as much fun as the end result. Good fine motor skills are
not required for students to be successful and practice critical thinking. *$99.00*

1101 CONCENTRATE! On Words and Concepts
Laureate Learning Systems
110 E Spring St
Winooski, VT 05404-1898   802-655-4755
                              800-562-6801
                         FAX 802-655-4757
                         http://www.laureatelearning.com
                         e-mail: laureate-webmaster@laureatelearning.com
Mary Sweig Wilson Ph.D., President/CEO/Author
Bernard J. Fox, Vice President/Author
Marion Blank, Ph.D, Developmental Psychologist
A series of educational games that reinforces the lessons of
the Words and Concepts Series while developing short term
memory skills. *$105.00*

1102 Camp Frog Hollow
Don Johnston
26799 W Commerce Dr
Volo, IL 60073-9675   847-740-0749
                              800-999-4660
                         FAX 847-740-7326
                         http://www.donjohnston.com
                         e-mail: info@donjohnston.com

Ruth Ziolkowski, President

Camp Frog Hollow chronicles the further adventures of K.C. and Clyde as they head off to summer camp. This entertaining approach to reading, literacy and learning can be beneficial for individual reading lessons or large group activities. The journaling feature provides students the opportunity to record their thoughts and feelings while the tracking feature provides a record of progress for the teacher/parent.

1103 Create with Garfield
SRA Order Services
PO Box 182605
Columbus, OH 43218

800-843-8855
FAX 972-228-1982
http://www.sraonline.com
e-mail: SEG_CustomerService@mcgraw-hill.com
The McGraw-Hill Education Urban Advisory Resource works with large urban districts across the country to help them provide better quality instruction, curriculum, and assessment to their students.

1104 Create with Garfield: Deluxe Edition
SRA Order Services
PO Box 182605
Columbus, OH 43218

800-843-8855
FAX 972-228-1982
http://www.sraonline.com
e-mail: SEG_CustomerService@mcgraw-hill.com
The McGraw-Hill Education Urban Advisory Resource works with large urban districts across the country to help them provide better quality instruction, curriculum, and assessment to their students.

1105 Dino-Games
Academic Software
3504 Tates Creek Rd
Lexington, KY 40517-2601

859-552-1020
FAX 253-799-4012
http://www.acsw.com
e-mail: asistaff@acsw.com
Dr Warren E Lacefield, President

Single switch software programs designed for early switch practice. CD-ROM for Mac or PC. Visit web site for demonstrations. *$39.00*

1106 Early Games for Young Children
Software to Go-Gallaudet University
800 Florida Ave NE
Washington, DC 20002-3600

202-651-5220
FAX 202-651-5109
http://http://clerccenter.gallaudet.edu
e-mail: clerc.center@gallaudet.edu
Ken Kurlychek, Information Specialist
Ed Bosso, Vice President

1107 Garfield Trivia Game
SRA Order Services
PO Box 182605
Columbus, OH 43218

800-843-8855
FAX 972-228-1982
http://www.sraonline.com
e-mail: SEG_CustomerService@mcgraw-hill.com
The McGraw-Hill Education Urban Advisory Resource works with large urban districts across the country to help them provide better quality instruction, curriculum, and assessment to their students.

1108 KC & Clyde in Fly Ball
Don Johnston
26799 W Commerce Dr
Volo, IL 60073-9675

847-740-0749
800-999-4660
FAX 847-740-7326
http://www.donjohnston.com
e-mail: info@donjohnston.com
Ruth Ziolkowski, President

In the UKanDu Series of interactive software which is designed to promote learning, independence, and accommodate special needs. Word interaction and context are stressed as students progress through the story and make decisions on how the storyline will advance. Active interaction at the word level is encouraged by UKanDu the wordbird, the tour guide to language in this story. *$95.00*

1109 Mind Over Matter
World Class Learning
PO Box 639
Candler, NC 28715

800-638-6470
FAX 800-638-6499
http://www.wclm.com
e-mail: dealers@wclm.com
A game program that challenges students to solve 185 visual word puzzles or create their own puzzles, using symbols and graphics.

1110 Monkey Business
Merit Software
Ste 603
121 W 27th St
New York, NY 10001-6262

212-675-8567
800-753-6488
FAX 212-675-8607
http://www.meritsoftware.com
e-mail: sales@meritsoftware.com
Ben Weintraub, CEO

Choose one of the three levels of difficulty and play until a minimum score is reached. *$10.95*

1111 Multi-Scan
Academic Software
3504 Tates Creek Rd
Lexington, KY 40517-2601

859-552-1020
http://www.acsw.com
e-mail: asistaff@acsw.com
Warren E Lacefield, President

Single switch activity center containing educational games such as numerical dot to dot, concentration, mazes, and matching, for PCs and Macintosh CD-ROM. Handbook for adaptive switches available. *$149.00*

1112 On a Green Bus
Don Johnston
26799 W Commerce Dr
Volo, IL 60073-9675

847-740-0749
800-999-4660
FAX 847-740-7326
http://www.donjohnston.com
e-mail: info@donjohnston.com
Ruth Ziolkowski, President

An early literacy program in the UKandDu Little Books Series consisting of several create-your-own four-page animated stories that help build language experience for early readers. Students fill in the blanks, completing sentences on each page. After completing the story, students can print it out to make a book which can be read over and over again.

1113 Teddy Barrels of Fun
SRA Order Services
PO Box 182605
Columbus, OH 43218

1-888-772-45
FAX 972-228-1982
http://www.sraonline.com
e-mail: SEG_CustomerService@mcgraw-hill.com
The McGraw-Hill Education Urban Advisory Resource works with large urban districts across the country to help them provide better quality instruction, curriculum, and assessment to their students. *$42.00*

Language Arts

1114 Alphabet Circus
SRA Order Services
PO Box 182605
Columbus, OH 43218

1-888-772-45
FAX 972-228-1982
http://www.sraonline.com
e-mail: SEG_CustomerService@mcgraw-hill.com
The McGraw-Hill Education Urban Advisory Resource works with large urban districts across the country to help them provide better quality instruction, curriculum, and assessment to their students. *$35.00*

1115 American Sign Language Dictionary: Software
Speech Bin
PO Box 1579
Appleton, WI 54912-1579

888-388-3224
FAX 888-388-6344
http://www.speechbin.com
e-mail: customercare@schoolspecialty.com
The CD includes captivating video clips that show 2,500+ words, phrases, and idioms in sign language. The videos may be played at normal speed, slow motion, and stop action. Animations explain origins of selected signs; drills and games are provided to reinforce learning. Item number M545 for Windows $24.95 Item number M540 for MAC. *$29.95*

1116 American Sign Language Video Dictionary & Inflection Guide
Harris Communications
15155 Technology Dr
Eden Prairie, MN 55344-2273

952-906-1180
800-825-6758
FAX 952-906-1099
TTY: 800-825-9187
http://www.harriscomm.com
e-mail: info@harriscomm.com
Robert Harris, President

Combines text, video, and animation to create a leading interactive reference tool that makes learning ASL easy and fun. Contains 2700 signs, searching capabilities in 5 languages, new learning games, and expanded sections in fingerspelling. Part #CD 144. *$49.95*
448 pages Video

1117 AtoZap!
Sunburst Technology
3150 W Higgins Rd
Suite 140
Hoffman Estates, IL 60619

800-321-7511
http://www.sunburst.com
e-mail: Service@sunburst.com
When users select an A, little airplanes that fly madly about appear. Users select T and students have their own telephone to talk to any one of nine animated friends. This program for prereaders has an activity for every letter.

1118 Auditory Skills
Psychological Software Services
6555 Carrollton Ave
Indianapolis, IN 46220-1664

317-257-9672
FAX 317-257-9674
http://www.neuroscience.cnter.com
e-mail: nsc@neuroscience.cnter.com
Odie L Bracy, Clinical Neuropsychologist
Nancy Bracy, Office Manager
Andrea Oakes, Clinical Assistant
Four computer programs designed to aid in the remediation of auditory discrimination problems. *$50.00*

1119 Basic Skills Products
EDCON Publishing Group
30 Montauk Blvd
Oakdale, NY 11769-1490

631-567-7227
888-553-3266
FAX 631-567-8745
http://www.edconpublishing.com
Deals with basic math and language arts. Free catalog available.

1120 Challenging Our Minds
Psychological Software Services
6555 Carrollton Ave
Indianapolis, IN 46220-1664

317-257-9672
FAX 317-257-9674
http://www.challenging-our-minds.com
e-mail: info@challenging-our-minds.com
Odie L Bracy, President
Nancy Bracy, Office Manager

Challenging our Minds (COM) is a cognitive enhancement system designed by a neuropsychologist to develop and enhance cognitive functions across the domains of attention, executive skills, memory, visuospatial skills, problem solving skills, communication and psychosocial skills. COM is a subscription website provididn online cognitive enhancement applications for all children.

1121 Character Education:Life Skills Online Education
Phillip Roy Inc.
13064 Indian Rocks Rd
Largo, FL 33774-2001

727-593-2700
800-255-9085
FAX 727-595-2685
http://www.philliproy.com
e-mail: info@philliproy.com
Ruth Bragman, President

Includes 77 CDs, 77 books and unlimited interactive online access, per purchasing site. All print materials are also available to be Brailled and all CDs come with complete audio components along with interactive graphics. Pre/post tests included along with teacher's guide and lesson plans. All materials can be duplicated at purchasing site. No yearly fees. *$3950.00*

1122 Cognitive Rehabilitation
Technology for Language and Learning
PO Box 327
East Rockaway, NY 11518

516-625-4550
FAX 516-621-3321
A series of public domain programs that strengthen cognitive skills, memory, language and visual motor skills. *$20.00*

1123 Construct-A-Word I & II
SRA Order Services
PO Box 182605
Columbus, OH 43218

800-843-8855
FAX 1-972-228-19
http://www.sraonline.com
e-mail: SEG_CustomerService@mcgraw-hill.com

The McGraw-Hill Education Urban Advisory Resource works with large urban districts across the country to help them provide better quality instruction, curriculum, and assessment to their students. *$99.00*

1124 Crypto Cube
Software to Go-Gallaudet University
800 Florida Ave NE
Washington, DC 20002-3695 202-651-5031
FAX 202-651-5109
http://http://clerccenter.gallaudet.edu
e-mail: clerc.center@gallaudet.edu
Ken Kurlychek, Electronic Information
Ed Bosso, Vice President

1125 Curious George Pre-K ABCs
Sunburst Technology
3150 W Higgins Rd
Suite 140
Hoffman Estates, IL 60619
800-321-7511
http://www.sunburst.com
e-mail: service@sunburst.com
Children go on a lively adventure with Curious George visiting six multi level activities that provide an animated introduction to letters and their sounds. Students discover letter names and shapes, initial letter sounds, letter pronunciations, the order of the alphabet and new vocabulary words during the fun exursions with Curious George. Mac/Win CD-ROM

1126 Eden Institute Curriculum: Classroom
2 Merwick Road
Princeton, NJ 08540-5711 609-987-0099
http://www.edenservices.org
Tom Mc Cool, President
Anne Holmes, Outreach/Support Director
This volume is geered toward students with autism who have mastered some basic academic skills and are able to learn in a small group setting. Teaching programs include academics, domestic and social skills. *$100.00*

1127 Elephant Ears: English with Speech
Ballard & Tighe
PO Box 219
Brea, CA 92822 714-990-433
800-321-4332
FAX 714-255-9828
http://www.ballard-tighe.com
e-mail: info@ballard-tighe.com
Dorothy Roberts, Chairperson
Sari Luoma, Vice President, Assessment
Mark Espinola, CEO
Features instruction and assessment of prepositions in a 3-part diskette. *$49.00*

1128 Emerging Literacy
Technology for Language and Learning
PO Box 327
East Rockaway, NY 11518 516-625-4550
FAX 516-621-3321
A five-volume set of stories. *$25.00*

1129 Essential Learning Systems
Creative Education Institute
PO Box 7306
Waco, TX 76714-7306 254-751-1188
800-234-7319
FAX 888-475-2402
http://www.ceilearning.com
e-mail: info@ceilearning.com
Enables special education, learning disabled and dyslexic students to develop the skills they need to learn. Using computer exercises to appropriately stimulate the brain's language areas, the lagging learning skills can be developed and patterns of correct language taught.

1130 First Phonics
Sunburst Technology
3150 W Higgins Rd
Suite 140
Hoffman Estates, IL 60619
800-321-7511
http://www.sunburst.com
e-mail: service@sunburst.com
Targets the phonics skills that all children need to develop, sounding out the first letter of a word. This program offers four different engaging activities that you can customize to match each child's specific need.

1131 Gremlin Hunt
Merit Software
Ste 603
121 W 27th St
New York, NY 10001-6262 212-675-8567
800-753-6488
FAX 212-675-8607
http://www.meritsoftware.com
e-mail: sales@meritsoftware.com
Ben Weintraub, CEO

Gremlins test visual discrimination and memory skills at three levels. *$9.95*

1132 High Frequency Vocabulary
Technology for Language and Learning
PO Box 327
East Rockaway, NY 11518 516-625-4550
FAX 516-621-3321
Each volume of the series has 10 stories that teach specific vocabulary. *$35.00*

1133 Hint and Hunt I & II
SRA Order Services
PO Box 182605
Columbus, OH 43218
800-843-8855
FAX 972-228-1982
http://www.sraonline.com
e-mail: SEG_CustomerService@mcgraw-hill.com
The McGraw-Hill Education Urban Advisory Resource works with large urban districts across the country to help them provide better quality instruction, curriculum, and assessment to their students. *$99.00*

1134 HyperStudio Stacks
Technology for Language and Learning
PO Box 327
East Rockaway, NY 11518 516-625-4550
FAX 516-621-3321
Offers various volumes in language arts, social studies and reading. *$10.00*

1135 IDEA Cat I, II and III
Ballard & Tighe
PO Box 219
Brea, CA 92822 714-990-4332
800-321-4332
FAX 714-255-9828
http://www.ballard-tighe.com
e-mail: info@ballard-tighe.com
Dorothy Roberts, Chairperson
Sari Luoma, Vice President, Assessment
Mark Espinola, CEO
Computer-assisted teaching of English language lessons reinforces skills of Level I, II, and III of the IDEA Oral Program. *$142.00*

1136 Improving Reading/Spelling Skills via Keyboarding
AVKO Educational Research Foundation
3084 Willard Rd
Birch Run, MI 48415-9404 810-686-9283
866-285-6612
FAX 810-686-1101
http://www.avko.org
e-mail: webmaster@avko.org

Don Mc Cabe, Research Director/Author
Barry Chute, President
Clifford Schroeder, Treasurer
Students learn spelling patterns and acquire important word recognition skills as they slowly and methodically learn proper fingering and keystrokes on a typewriter or computer keyboard. *$12.95*

ISBN 1-564004-01-5

1137 Katie's Farm
Lawrence Productions
25 Ottawa Avenue SW
Suite 204
Galesburg, MI 49053-9688
800-421-4157
http://www.lpi.com
e-mail: sales@lpi.com Karen Morehouse, Operations
Manager
Designed to encourage exploration and language development. *$29.95*

1138 Kid Pix
Riverdeep
222 Berkeley Street
Boston, MA 02116
617-351-5000
888-242-6747
FAX 877-892-9820
http://www.riverdeep.net
e-mail: IIEcustomerservice@hmhpub.com
Eric Shuman, Chief Financial Officer
John K. Dragoon, EVP & Chairman
William Bayers, EVP
Houghton Mifflin Harcourt offers a wide array of technology-driven pre-k-12 solutions that inspire excellence and innovation in education, and raise student achievement. *$59.95*

1139 Kids Media Magic 2.0
Sunburst Technology
3150 W Higgins Rd
Suite 140
Hoffman Estates, IL 60619
800-321-7511
http://www.sunburst.com
e-mail: service@sunburst.com
The first multimedia word processor designed for young children. Help your child become a fluent reader and writer. The Rebus Bar automatically scrolls over 45 vocabulary words as students type.

1140 Language Carnival I
SRA Order Services
PO Box 182605
Columbus, OH 43218
800-843-8855
FAX 972-228-1982
http://www.sraonline.com
e-mail: SEG_CustomerService@mcgraw-hill.com
The McGraw-Hill Education Urban Advisory Resource works with large urban districts across the country to help them provide better quality instruction, curriculum, and assessment to their students.

1141 Language Carnival II
SRA Order Services
PO Box 182605
Columbus, OH 43218
800-843-8855
FAX 972-228-1982
http://www.sraonline.com
e-mail: SEG_CustomerService@mcgraw-hill.com
The McGraw-Hill Education Urban Advisory Resource works with large urban districts across the country to help them provide better quality instruction, curriculum, and assessment to their students.

1142 Language Master
Franklin Learning Resources
1 Franklin Plz
Burlington, NJ 08016-4907
609-386-2500
800-266-5626
FAX 609-387-2666
http://www.franklin.com
e-mail: service@franklin.com
A language master without speech defining over 83,000 words, spelling correction capability, pick/edit feature, vocabulary enrichment activities and advanced word list. *$79.95*

1143 Learn to Match
Technology for Language and Learning
PO Box 327
East Rockaway, NY 11518
516-625-4550
FAX 516-621-3321
Joan Tanenhaus, Founder

Ten volume set of picture-matching disks. *$50.00*

1144 Letter Sounds
Sunburst Technology
3150 W Higgins Rd
Suite 140
Hoffman Estates, IL 60619
800-321-7511
http://www.sunburst.com
e-mail: service@sunburst.com
Students develop phonemic awareness skills as they make the connection between consonant letters and their sounds.

1145 Letters and First Words
C&C Software
5713 Kentford Cir
Wichita, KS 67220-3131
316-683-6056
800-752-2086
Carol Clark, President

Helps children learn to identify letters and recognize their associated sounds. *$30.00*

1146 Lexia Phonics Based Reading
Lexia Learning Systems
200 Baker Avenue Ext
Concord, MA 01742
978-405-6200
800-435-3942
FAX 781-287-0062
http://www.lexialearning.com
e-mail: info@lexialearning.com
Nicholas C Gaehde, President and CEO

Five activity areas with 64 branching units and practice with 535 one-syllable words and 90 two-syllable words, sentences and stories. *$250.00*

1147 Look! Listen! & Learn Language!
Abilitations Speech Bin
PO Box 1579
Appleton, WI 54912-1579
888-388-3224
FAX 888-388-6344
http://www.speechbin.com
e-mail: customercare@schoolspecialty.com
Interactive activities for children with autism, PDD, Down syndrome, language delay, or apraxia include: hello; Match Same to Same; Quack; Let's talk About It; visual scanning/attention and match ups! Item number L177. *$98.99*

1148 M-ss-ng L-nks Single Educational Software
Sunburst Technology
3150 W Higgins Rd
Suite 140
Hoffman Estates, IL 60619
800-321-7511
http://www.sunburst.com
e-mail: service@sunburst.com

This award-winning program is an engrossing language puzzle. A passage appears with letters or words missing. Students complete it based on their knowledge of word structure, spelling, grammar, meaning in context, and literary style.

1149 Max's Attic: Long & Short Vowels
Sunburst Technology
3150 W Higgins Rd
Suite 140
Hoffman Estates, IL 60619

800-321-7511
http://www.sunburst.com
e-mail: service@sunburst.com

Filled to the rafters with phonics fun, this animated program builds your students' vowel recognition skills.

1150 Memory I
Psychological Software Services
6555 Carrollton Ave
Indianapolis, IN 46220-1664

317-257-9672
FAX 317-257-9674
http://www.neuroscience.cnter.com
e-mail: nsc@neuroscience.cnter.com

Odie L Bracy, Clinical Neuropsychologist
Nancy Bracy, Office Manager
Andrea Oakes, Clinical Assistant

Consists of four computer programs designed to provide verbal and nonverbal memory exercises. *$110.00*

1151 Memory II
Psychological Software Services
6555 Carrollton Ave
Indianapolis, IN 46220-1664

317-257-9672
FAX 317-257-9674
http://www.neuroscience.cnter.com
e-mail: nsc@neuroscience.cnter.com

Odie L Bracy, Clinical Neuropsychologist
Nancy Bracy, Office Manager
Andrea Oakes, Clinical Assistant

These programs allow for work with encoding, categorizing and organizing skills. *$150.00*

1152 Microcomputer Language Assessment and Development System
Laureate Learning Systems
110 E Spring St
Winooski, VT 05404-1898

802-655-4755
800-562-6801
FAX 802-655-4757
http://www.laureatelearning.com
e-mail: laureate-webmaster@laureatelearning.com

Mary Sweig Wilson Ph.D., President/CEO
Bernard J. Fox, Vice President
Marion Blank, Ph.D, Developmental Psychologist

A series of seven diskettes designed to teach over 45 fundamental syntactic rules. Students are presented two or three pictures, depending on the grammatical construction being trained with optional speech and/or text and asked to select the picture which represents the correct construction. *$775.00*

1153 Mike Mulligan & His Steam Shovel
Sunburst Technology
3150 W Higgins Rd
Suite 140
Hoffman Estates, IL 60619

800-321-7511
http://www.sunburst.com
e-mail: service@sunburst.com

This CD-ROM version of the Caldecott classic lets students experience interactive book reading and participate in four skills-based extension activities that promote memory, matching, sequencing, listening, pattern recognition and map reading skills.

1154 My Own Bookshelf
Soft Touch
12301 Central Ave NE
Ste 205
Blaine, MN 55434

763-755-1402
888-755-1402
FAX 763-862-2920
http://www.softtouch.com
e-mail: sales@marblesoft.com

Mark Fulton, President

Research indicates that when students select their own books to read, their literacy levels improve. My Own Bookshelf gives students the ability to select their own books and to read them as often as they wish. *$30.00*

1155 Optimum Resource
1 Mathews Drive
Suite 107
Hilton Head Island, SC 29926-3667

843-689-8000
888-784-2592
FAX 843-689-8008
http://www.stickybear.com
e-mail: info@stickybear.com

An educational software publishing company for grades K-12. Our software titles are available in Consumer, School, Labpack or Site License versions. Please call for further details. Prices range from $59.95 for Consumer to $699.95 for Site Licenses.

1156 Phonology: Software
Abilitations Speech Bin
PO Box 1579
Appleton, WI 54912-1579

888-388-3224
FAX 888-388-6344
http://www.speechbin.com
e-mail: customercare@schoolspecialty.com

This unique software gives you six entertaining games to treat children's phonological disorders. The program uses target patterns in a pattern cycling approach to phonological processess. Item number L183. *$98.99*

1157 Python Path Phonics Word Families
Sunburst Technology
3150 W Higgins Rd
Suite 140
Hoffman Estates, IL 60619

800-321-7511
http://www.sunburst.com
e-mail: service@sunburst.com

Your child improves their word-building skills by playing three fun strategy games that involve linking one-or two-letter consonant beginnings to basic word endings.

1158 Read, Write and Type! Learning System
Talking Fingers
830 Rincon Way
San Rafael, CA 94903-2924

415-472-3103
800-674-9126
http://www.readwritetype.com
e-mail: contact@talkingfingers.com

Jeannine Herron, Developer

This 40-lesson adventure is a powerful tool for 6-8 year-olds just learning to read, for children of other cultures learning to read and write in English, and for students of any age who are struggling to become successful readers and writers.

1159 Same or Different
Merit Software
Ste 603
121 W 27th St
New York, NY 10001-6262

212-675-8567
800-753-6488
FAX 212-675-8607
http://www.meritsoftware.com
e-mail: sales@meritsoftware.com

Ben Weintraub, CEO

Requires students to make important visual discriminations which involve shape, color and whole/part relationships. *$9.95*

1160   Sequencing Fun!
Sunburst Technology
3150 W Higgins Rd
Suite 140
Hoffman Estates, IL 60619
800-321-7511
http://www.sunburst.com
e-mail: service@sunburst.com
Text, pictures, animation and video clips provide a fun filled program that encourages critical thinking skills.

1161   Show Time
Software to Go-Gallaudet University
800 Florida Ave NE
Washington, DC 20002-3695
202-651-5220
FAX 202-651-5109
http://http://clerccenter.gallaudet.edu
e-mail: clerc.center@gallaudet.edu
Ken Kurlychek, EI Specialist
Ed Bosso, Vice President

1162   Soft Tools
Psychological Software Services
6555 Carrollton Ave
Indianapolis, IN 46220-1664
317-257-9672
FAX 317-257-9674
http://www.neuroscience.cnter.com
e-mail: nsc@neuroscience.cnter.com
Odie L Bracy, Clinical Neuropsychologist
Nancy Bracy, Office Manager
Andrea Oakes, Clinical Assistant
Menu-driven disk versions of the computer programs published in the Cognitive Rehabilitation Journal. *$50.00*

1163   Sound Match
Enable/Schneier Communication Unit
1603 Court St
Syracuse, NY 13208-1834
315-455-7591
FAX 315-455-7591
http://www.enablecny.org
e-mail: info@enablecny.orgÿÿ
Prudence York, Executive Director/CEO
Earleen Foulk, Liaison
Marvin Reed, President
Presents a variety of sounds/noises requiring gross levels of auditory discrimination and matching. *$25.00*

1164   Speaking Language Master Special Edition
Franklin Learning Resources
1 Franklin Plz
Burlington, NJ 08016-4907
609-386-2500
800-525-9673
FAX 609-387-2666
http://www.franklin.com
e-mail: service@franklin.com
A language master with speech defining over 110,000 words, spelling correction capability, pick/edit feature, vocabulary enrichment activities and advanced word list. *$79.95*

1165   Spell-a-Word
RJ Cooper & Associates
Ste 39
27601 Forbes Rd
Laguna Niguel, CA 92677-1241
949-582-2572
800-752-6673
FAX 949-582-3169
http://www.rjcooper.com
e-mail: infoRJ@rjcooper.com
R J Cooper, Owner

A large print, talking, spelling program. It uses an errorless learning method. It has both a drill and test mode, which a supervisor can set. Letters, words or phrases are entered by a supervisor and recorded by supervisor, peer, or sibling. Available for Mac, Windows. *$99.00*

1166   Spellagraph
Software to Go-Gallaudet University
800 Florida Ave NE
Washington, DC 20002-3695
202-651-5220
FAX 202-651-5109
http://http://clerccenter.gallaudet.edu
e-mail: clerc.center@gallaudet.edu
Ken Kurlychek, EI Specialist
Ed Bosso, Vice President

1167   Spelling Ace
Franklin Learning Resources
1 Franklin Plz
Burlington, NJ 08016-4907
609-386-2500
800-525-9673
FAX 609-239-5948
http://www.franklin.com
e-mail: service@franklin.com
The basic spelling corrector with 80,000 words. Sound-Alikes feature identifies commonly confused words. *$25.00*

1168   Spelling Mastery
SRA/McGraw-Hill
PO Box 182605
Columbus, OH 43218
800-843-8855
FAX 972-228-1892
http://www.sraonline.com
e-mail: SEG_CustomerService@mcgraw-hill.com
The McGraw-Hill Education Urban Advisory Resource works with large urban districts across the country to help them provide better quality instruction, curriculum, and assessment to their students.

1169   Stanley Sticker Stories
Riverdeep
222 Berkeley Street
Boston, MA 02116
617-351-5000
888-242-6747
FAX 877-892-9820
http://www.riverdeep.net
e-mail: IIEcustomerservice@hmhpub.com
Eric Shuman, Chief Financial Officer
John K. Dragoon, EVP & Chairman
William Bayers, EVP
Houghton Mifflin Harcourt offers a wide array of technology-driven pre-k-12 solutions that inspire excellence and innovation in education, and raise student achievement. *$59.95*

1170   Sunken Treasure Adventure: Beginning Blends
Sunburst Technology
3150 W Higgins Rd
Suite 140
Hoffman Estates, IL 60619
800-321-7511
http://www.sunburst.com
e-mail: service@sunburst.com
Focus on beginning blends sounds and concepts with three high-spirited games that invite students to use two letter consonant blends as they build words.

1171 Syllasearch I, II, III, IV
SRA Order Services
PO Box 182605
Columbus, OH 43218

800-843-8855
FAX 972-228-1982
http://www.sraonline.com
e-mail: SEG_CustomerService@mcgraw-hill.com
The McGraw-Hill Education Urban Advisory Resource
works with large urban districts across the country to help
them provide better quality instruction, curriculum, and assessment to their students. *$99.00*

1172 Talking Nouns II: Sterling Edition
Laureate Learning Systems
110 E Spring St
Winooski, VT 05404-1898   802-655-4755
800-562-6801
FAX 802-655-4757
http://www.laureatelearning.com
e-mail: laureate-webmaster@laureatelearning.com
Mary Sweig Wilson Ph.D., President/CEO
Bernard J. Fox, Vice President
Marion Blank, Ph.D, Developmental Psychologist
Designed to build expressive language and augmentative
communication skills. *$130.00*

1173 Talking Nouns: Sterling Edition
Laureate Learning Systems
110 E Spring St
Winooski, VT 05404-1898   802-655-4755
800-562-6801
FAX 802-655-4757
http://www.laureatelearning.com
e-mail: laureate-webmaster@laureatelearning.com
Mary Sweig Wilson Ph.D., President/CEO
Bernard J. Fox, Vice President
Marion Blank, Ph.D, Developmental Psychologist
An interactive communication product that helps build ex-
pressive language and augmentative communication skills.
$130.00

1174 Talking Verbs Sterling Edition
Laureate Learning Systems
110 E Spring St
Winooski, VT 05404-1898   802-655-4755
800-562-6801
FAX 802-655-4757
http://www.laureatelearning.com
e-mail: laureate-webmaster@laureatelearning.com
Mary Sweig Wilson Ph.D., President/CEO
Bernard J. Fox, Vice President
Marion Blank, Ph.D, Developmental Psychologist
Builds expressive language and augmentative communica-
tion skills. *$130.00*

1175 Twenty Categories
Laureate Learning Systems
110 E Spring St
Winooski, VT 05404-1898   802-655-4755
800-562-6801
FAX 802-655-4757
http://www.laureatelearning.com
e-mail: laureate-webmaster@laureatelearning.com
Mary Sweig Wilson Ph.D., President/CEO/Author
Bernard J. Fox, Vice President/Author
Marion Blank, Ph.D, Developmental Psychologist
Designed to use with children and adults, these two diskettes
provide instruction in both abstracting the correct category
for a noun and placing a noun in the appropriate category.
$100.00

1176 Type to Learn 3
Sunburst Technology
3150 W Higgins Rd
Suite 140
Hoffman Estates, IL 60619

800-321-7511
http://www.sunburst.com
e-mail: service@sunburst.com
With the 25 lessons in this animated update of Type to Learn,
students embark on time travel missions to learn
keyboarding skills.

1177 Type to Learn Jr
Sunburst Technology
3150 W Higgins Rd
Suite 140
Hoffman Estates, IL 60619

800-321-7511
http://www.sunburst.com
e-mail: service@sunburst.com
One of the first steps to literacy is learning how to use the
keyboard. Age appropriate instruction and three practice activities help students use the computer with greater ease.

1178 Type to Learn Jr New Keys for Kids
Sunburst Technology
3150 W Higgins Rd
Suite 140
Hoffman Estates, IL 60619

800-321-7511
http://www.sunburst.com
e-mail: service@sunburst.com
With new keys to learn, your early keyboarders focus on using the letter and number keys, the shift key, home row and
are introduced to selected internet symbols.

1179 Vowel Patterns
Sunburst Technology
3150 W Higgins Rd
Suite 140
Hoffman Estates, IL 60619

800-321-7511
http://www.sunburst.com
e-mail: service@sunburst.com
Some vowels are neither long nor short. In this investigation,
students explore and learn to use abstract vowels.

**1180 Word Invasion: Academic Skill Builders in Language
Arts**
SRA Order Services
PO Box 182605
Columbus, OH 43218

800-843-8855
FAX 972-228-1982
http://www.sraonline.com
e-mail: SEG_CustomerService@mcgraw-hill.com
The McGraw-Hill Education Urban Advisory Resource
works with large urban districts across the country to help
them provide better quality instruction, curriculum, and assessment to their students. *$49.00*

**1181 Word Master: Academic Skill Builders in Language
Arts**
SRA Order Services
PO Box 182605
Columbus, OH 43218

800-843-8855
FAX 972-228-1982
http://www.sraonline.com
e-mail: SEG_CustomerService@mcgraw-hill.com

The McGraw-Hill Education Urban Advisory Resource works with large urban districts across the country to help them provide better quality instruction, curriculum, and assessment to their students. *$49.00*

1182 Word Wise I and II: Better Comprehension Through Vocabulary
SRA Order Services
PO Box 182605
Columbus, OH 43218

800-843-8855
FAX 972-228-1982
http://www.sraonline.com
e-mail: SEG_CustomerService@mcgraw-hill.com
The McGraw-Hill Education Urban Advisory Resource works with large urban districts across the country to help them provide better quality instruction, curriculum, and assessment to their students.

Life Skills

1183 Bozons' Quest
110 E Spring St
Winooski, VT 05404-1898

802-655-4755
800-562-6801
FAX 802-655-4757
http://www.laureatelearning.com
e-mail: laureate-webmaster@laureatelearning.com
Mary Sweig Wilson Ph.D., President/CEO
Bernard J. Fox, Vice President
Marion Blank, Ph.D, Developmental Psychologist
A computer game designed to teach cognitive skills and strategies and left/right discrimination skills.

1184 Calendar Fun with Lollipop Dragon
SVE & Churchill Media
PO Box 2284
South Burlington, VT 05407-2284

888-892-3484
FAX 877-324-6830
http://www.clearvue.com
e-mail: education_info@discovery.com
Young students learn the calendar basics. *$84.00*

1185 Comparison Kitchen
SRA Order Services
PO Box 182605
Columbus, OH 43218

800-843-8855
FAX 1-972-228-19
http://www.sraonline.com
e-mail: SEG_CustomerService@mcgraw-hill.com
The McGraw-Hill Education Urban Advisory Resource works with large urban districts across the country to help them provide better quality instruction, curriculum, and assessment to their students. *$35.00*

1186 Early Learning: Preparing Children for School, Phillip Roy, Inc.
13064 Indian Rocks Rd
Largo, FL 33774-2001

727-593-2700
800-255-9085
FAX 727-595-2685
http://www.philliproy.com
e-mail: info@philliproy.com

Ruth Bragman, President

This program includes unlimited online access to 42 interactive lessons per individual. This pre-kindergarten curriculum has over 250 activities which include: Math, Problem-Solving, Reading, Language Development, Physical Skills, Self-Esteem, Your Community, and Healthy Habits. Includes audio and interactive graphics. Allows parents to work with their children at home or any place. Can be duplicated at the purcasing school. No yearly fees.

1187 Electric Crayon
Merit Software
Ste 603
121 W 27th St
New York, NY 10001-6262

212-675-8567
800-753-6488
FAX 212-675-8607
http://www.meritsoftware.com
e-mail: sales@meritsoftware.com

Ben Weintraub, CEO

A tool to help preschool and primary aged children learn about and enjoy the computer. *$14.95*

1188 First Categories Sterling Edition
Laureate Learning Systems
110 E Spring St
Winooski, VT 05404-1898

802-655-4755
800-562-6801
FAX 802-655-4757
http://www.laureatelearning.com
e-mail: laureate-webmaster@laureatelearning.com
Mary Sweig Wilson Ph.D., President/CEO
Bernard J. Fox, Vice President
Marion Blank, Ph.D, Developmental Psychologist
A computer program that trains 6 early categories using 60 nouns. Eleven innovative, activities, hundreds of drawings, and photographs and exciting 3-D animation make this program fun and effective. *$230.00*

1189 First R
Milliken Publishing
501 East Third Street
Box 802
Dayton, OH 45401

937-228-6118
800-444-1144
FAX 937-223-2042
http://www.millikenpub.com
e-mail: lep@lorenz.com

Thomas Moore, President

A phonetically-based word recognition program with emphasis on comprehension. *$325.00*

1190 First Verbs Sterling Edition
Laureate Learning Systems
110 E Spring St
Winooski, VT 05404-1898

802-655-4755
800-562-6801
FAX 802-655-4757
http://www.laureatelearning.com
e-mail: laureate-webmaster@laureatelearning.com
Mary Sweig Wilson Ph.D., President/CEO
Bernard J. Fox, Vice President
Marion Blank, Ph.D, Developmental Psychologist
A computer program that trains and tests 40 early developing verbs using animated pictures and a natural sounding female voice. *$225.00*

1191 First Words II Sterling Edition
Laureate Learning Systems
110 E Spring St
Winooski, VT 05404-1898

802-655-4755
800-562-6801
FAX 802-655-4757
http://www.laureatelearning.com
e-mail: laureate-webmaster@laureatelearning.com
Mary Sweig Wilson Ph.D., President/CEO
Bernard J. Fox, Vice President
Marion Blank, Ph.D, Developmental Psychologist
Continues the training of First Words with training and testing of an additional 50 early developing nouns presented within the same 10 categories as used in First Words. *$235.00*

1192   **First Words Sterling Edition**
Laureate Learning Systems
110 E Spring St
Winooski, VT 05404-1898   802-655-4755
         800-562-6801
         FAX 802-655-4757
http://www.laureatelearning.com
e-mail: laureate-webmaster@laureatelearning.com
Mary Sweig Wilson Ph.D., President/CEO
Bernard J. Fox, Vice President
Marion Blank, Ph.D, Developmental Psychologist
A talking program that trains and tests 50 early developing nouns presented within 10 categories. *$235.00*

1193   **Fish Scales**
SRA Order Services
PO Box 182605
Columbus, OH 43218
         800-843-8855
         FAX 1-972-228-19
http://www.sraonline.com
e-mail: SEG_CustomerService@mcgraw-hill.com
The McGraw-Hill Education Urban Advisory Resource works with large urban districts across the country to help them provide better quality instruction, curriculum, and assessment to their students. *$35.00*

1194   **Following Directions: Left and Right**
Laureate Learning Systems
110 E Spring St
Winooski, VT 05404-1898   802-655-4755
         800-562-6801
         FAX 802-655-4757
http://www.laureatelearning.com
e-mail: laureate-webmaster@laureatelearning.com
Mary Sweig Wilson Ph.D., President/CEO
Eleanor Semel, Ed.D., Author
Bernard J. Fox, Vice President
This computer program uses ten activities to improve your ability to follow directions and develop left/right discrimination skills. *$125.00*

1195   **Following Directions: One and Two-Level Commands**
Laureate Learning Systems
110 E Spring St
Winooski, VT 05404-1898   802-655-4755
         800-562-6801
         FAX 802-655-4757
http://www.laureatelearning.com
e-mail: laureate-webmaster@laureatelearning.com
Mary Sweig Wilson Ph.D., President/CEO
Bernard J. Fox, Vice President
Marion Blank, Ph.D, Developmental Psychologist
Designed for a broad range of students experiencing difficulty in processing, remembering and following oral commands, a program of exercises on short and long-term memory highlighting specific spatial, directional and ordinary terms. *$175.00*

1196   **Functional Skills System and MECA**
Conover Company
4 Brookwood Ct
Appleton, WI 54914-8618
         800-933-1933
         FAX 800-933-1943
http://www.conovercompany.com
e-mail: sales@conovercompany.com
Functional Skills System software assists in the transition from school to the community and workplace. Functional literary, functional life skills, functional social skills, functional work skills. MECA - The system for creating post-secondary transition outcomes and the instructional services to support them. *$2535.00*

1197   **Information Station**
SVE & Churchill Media
PO Box 2284
South Burlington, VT 05407-2284
         888-892-3484
         FAX 877-324-6830
http://www.clearvue.com
e-mail: education_info@discovery.com
Students who boot up this software will find themselves floating miles above the earth orbiting the planet in an information station satellite. *$144.00*

1198   **Lion's Workshop**
Merit Software
Ste 603
121 W 27th St
New York, NY 10001-6262   212-675-8567
         800-753-6488
         FAX 212-675-8607
http://www.meritsoftware.com
e-mail: sales@meritsoftware.com
Ben Weintraub, CEO

Presents various objects with parts missing or with like objects to be matched. *$9.95*

1199   **Marsh Media**
Marshware
PO Box 8082
Shawnee Mission, KS 66208
         800-821-3303
         FAX 866-333-7421
http://www.marshmedia.com
e-mail: info@marshmedia.com
Joan K Marsh, President

Marsh Media publishes closed captioned health and guidance videos for the classroom and school library. Catalog available.

1200   **Math Spending and Saving**
World Class Learning
PO Box 639
Candler, NC 28715
         800-638-6470
         FAX 800-638-6499
http://www.wclm.com
e-mail: jdash@wclm.com
Designed for secondary students and adults, this program focuses on personal financial management, comparison shopping and calculation of essential banking transactions.

1201   **Money Skills**
MarbleSoft
Ste 205
12301 Central Ave NE
Blaine, MN 55434-1417   763-755-1402
         888-755-1402
         FAX 763-755-0440
http://www.marblesoft.com
e-mail: mail@marblesoft.com
Vicki Larson, Sales

Money Skills 2.0 includes five activities that teach counting money and making change: Coins and Bills; Counting Money; Making Change; how much change? and the Marblesoft Store. Teaches American, Canadian and European money using clear, realistic pictures of the money. Single and dual-switch scanning options on all difficulty levels. Runs on Macintosh and Windows computers. *$60.00*

1202   **My House: Language Activities of Daily Living**
Laureate Learning Systems
110 E Spring St
Winooski, VT 05404-1898   802-655-4755
         800-562-6801
         FAX 802-655-4757
http://www.laureatelearning.com
e-mail: laureate-webmaster@laureatelearning.com

Mary Sweig Wilson Ph.D., President/CEO
Barbara Couse Adams, M.S., Author
Bernard J. Fox, Vice President
Train over 300 functional vocabulary items, increase understanding of objects and their functions while building independence in the home, community, and school. *$150.00*

1203 Optimum Resource
1 Mathews Drive
Suite 107
Hilton Head Island, SC 29926-3667   843-689-8000
                                             888-784-2592
                                        FAX 843-689-8008
                              http://www.stickybear.com
                              e-mail: info@stickybear.com
An educational software publishing company for grades K-12. Our software titles are available in Consumer, School, Labpack or Site License versions. Please call for further details. Prices range from $59.95 for Consumer to $699.95 for Site Licenses.

1204 PAVE: Perceptual Accuracy/Visual Efficiency
Software to Go-Gallaudet University
800 Florida Ave NE
Washington, DC 20002-3600   202-651-5220
                                    FAX 202-651-5109
                     http://http://clerccenter.gallaudet.edu
                     e-mail: clerc.center@gallaudet.edu
Ken Kurlychek, EI Specialist
Ed Bosso, Vice President

1205 Print Shop Deluxe
Riverdeep
222 Berkeley Street
Boston, MA 02116   617-351-5000
                                         888-242-6747
                                    FAX 877-892-9820
                              http://www.riverdeep.net
                     e-mail: IIEcustomerservice@hmhpub.com
Eric Shuman, Chief Financial Officer
John K. Dragoon, EVP & Chairman
William Bayers, EVP
Houghton Mifflin Harcourt offers a wide array of technology-driven pre-k-12 solutions that inspire excellence and innovation in education, and raise student achievement.

1206 Quiz Castle
Software to Go-Gallaudet University
800 Florida Ave NE
Washington, DC 20002-3600   202-651-5220
                                    FAX 202-651-5109
                     http://http://clerccenter.gallaudet.edu
                     e-mail: clerc.center@gallaudet.edu
Ken Kurlychek, Information Specialist
Ed Bosso, Vice President

1207 Secondary Print Pack
Failure Free
140 Cabarrus Ave W
Concord, NC 28025-5150   704-786-7838
                                         800-542-2170
                                    FAX 704-785-8940
                              http://www.failurefree.com
                              e-mail: info@failurefree.com
Joseph Lockavitch, President

Thousands of independent activities teaching over 750 words. *$1929.00*

1208 Stickybear Software
Optimum Resource
1 Mathews Drive
Suite 107
Hilton Head Island, SC 29926-3667   843-689-8000
                                         888-784-2592
                                    FAX 843-689-8008
                              http://www.stickybear.com
                              e-mail: info@stickybear.com
An educational software publishing company for grades K-12. Our software titles are available in Consumer, School, Labpack or Site License versions. Please call for further details. Prices range from $59.95 for Consumer to $699.95 for Site Licenses.

1209 Teenage Switch Progressions
RJ Cooper & Associates
Ste 39
27601 Forbes Rd
Laguna Niguel, CA 92677-1241   949-582-2572
                                         800-752-6673
                                    FAX 949-582-3169
                              http://www.rjcooper.com
                              e-mail: info@rjcooper.com
R J Cooper, Owner

Five activities for teenage persons working on switch training, attention training, life skills simulation and following directions. *$75.00*

1210 TeleSensory
650 Vaqueros Ave
Suite F
Sunnyvale, CA 94085-3525   408-616-8700
                                         800-804-8004
                                    FAX 408-616-8720
                              http://www.telesensory.com
                              e-mail: info@telesensory.com
Helps visually impaired people become more independent with the most comprehensive products available anywhere for reading, writing, taking notes and using computers.

Math

1211 2+2
RJ Cooper & Associates
Ste 39
27601 Forbes Rd
Laguna Niguel, CA 92677-1241   949-582-2572
                                         800-752-6673
                                    FAX 949-582-3169
                              http://www.rjcooper.com
                              e-mail: info@rjcooper.com
R J Cooper, Owner

This large print, talking, early academic program is for drilling math facts, including addition, subtraction, multiplication and division. It uses an errorless learning method. Available for Mac, Windows. *$89.00*

1212 Access to Math
Don Johnston
26799 W Commerce Dr
Volo, IL 60073-9675   847-740-0749
                                         800-999-4660
                                    FAX 847-740-7326
                              http://www.donjohnston.com
                              e-mail: info@donjohnston.com
Ruth Ziolkowski, President

The Macintosh talking math worksheet program that's two products in one. For teachers, it makes customized worksheets in a snap. For students who struggle, it provides individualized on-screen lessons.

1213 Algebra Stars
Sunburst Technology
3150 W Higgins Rd
Suite 140
Hoffman Estates, IL 60619

800-321-7511
http://www.sunburst.com
e-mail: service@sunburst.com

Students build their understanding of algebra by constructing, categorizing, and solving equations and classifying polynomial expressions using algebra tiles.

1214 Alien Addition: Academic Skill Builders in Math
SRA Order Services
PO Box 182605
Columbus, OH 43218

FAX 972-228-1982
http://www.sraonline.com
e-mail: SEG_CustomerService@mcgraw-hill.com

The McGraw-Hill Education Urban Advisory Resource works with large urban districts across the country to help them provide better quality instruction, curriculum, and assessment to their students. *$49.00*

1215 Awesome Animated Monster Maker Math
Sunburst Technology
3150 W Higgins Rd
Suite 140
Hoffman Estates, IL 60619

800-321-7511
http://www.sunburst.com
e-mail: service@sunburst.com

With an emphasis on building core math skills, this humorous program incorporates the monstrous and the ridiculous into a structured learning environment. Students choose from six skill levels tailored to the 3rd to 8th grade.

1216 Awesome Animated Monster Maker Math and Monster Workshop
Sunburst Technology
3150 W Higgins Rd
Suite 140
Hoffman Estates, IL 60619

800-321-7511
http://www.sunburst.com
e-mail: service@sunburst.com

Students develop money and strategic thinking skills with this irresistable game that has them tinker about making monsters.

1217 Awesome Animated Monster Maker Number Drop
Sunburst Technology
3150 W Higgins Rd
Suite 140
Hoffman Estates, IL 60619

800-321-7511
http://www.sunburst.com
e-mail: service@sunburst.com

Your students will think on their mathematical feet estimating and solving thousands of number problems in an arcade-style game designed to improve their performance in numeration, money, fractions, and decimals.

1218 Basic Math Competency Skill Building
Educational Activities Software
PO Box 220790
Saint Louis, MO 63122

866-243-8464
FAX 239-225-9299
http://www.ea-software.com
e-mail: jwest@siboneylg.com

Jan West, Sales Director
Michael Conlon, Author

An interactive, tutorial and practice program to teach competency with arithmetic operations, decimals, fractions, graphs, measurement and geometric concepts. (stand alone version) MA02 *$369.00*

1219 Basic Skills Products
EDCON Publishing Group
30 Montauk Blvd
Oakdale, NY 11769-1490

631-567-7227
888-553-3266
FAX 631-567-8745
http://www.edconpublishing.com

Deals with basic math and language arts. Free catalog available.

1220 Building Perspective
Sunburst Technology
3150 W Higgins Rd
Suite 140
Hoffman Estates, IL 60619

800-321-7511
http://www.sunburst.com
e-mail: service@sunburst.com

Develop spatial perception and reasoning skills with this award-winning program that will sharpen your students' problem-solving abilities.

1221 Building Perspective Deluxe
Sunburst Technology
3150 W Higgins Rd
Suite 140
Hoffman Estates, IL 60619

800-321-7511
http://www.sunburst.com
e-mail: service@sunburst.com

New visual thinking challenges await your students as they engage in three spacial reasoning activities that develop their 3D thinking, deductive reasoning and problem solving skills

1222 Combining Shapes
Sunburst Technology
3150 W Higgins Rd
Suite 140
Hoffman Estates, IL 60619

800-321-7511
http://www.sunburst.com
e-mail: service@sunburst.com

Students discover the properties of simple geometric figures through concrete experience combining shapes. Measurements, estimating and operation skills are part of this fun program.

1223 Conceptual Skills
Psychological Software Services
6555 Carrollton Ave
Indianapolis, IN 46220-1664

317-257-9672
FAX 317-257-9674
http://www.neuroscience.cnter.com
e-mail: nsc@neuroscience.cnter.com

Odie L Bracy, Clinical Neuropsychologist
Nancy Bracy, Office Manager
Andrea Oakes, Clinical Assistant

Twelve programs designed to enhance skills involved in relationships, comparisons and number concepts. *$50.00*

1224 Concert Tour Entrepreneur
Sunburst Technology
3150 W Higgins Rd
Suite 140
Hoffman Estates, IL 60619

800-321-7511
http://www.sunburst.com
e-mail: service@sunburst.com

Your students improve math, planning and problem solving skills as they manage a band in this music management business simulation.

1225   Counters
Software to Go-Gallaudet University
800 Florida Ave NE
Washington, DC 20002-3695   202-651-5231
                                              FAX 202-651-5109
                http://http://clerccenter.gallaudet.edu
                e-mail: clerc.center@gallaudet.edu
Ken Kurlychek, EI Specialist
Ed Bosso, Vice President

1226   Counting Critters
Software to Go-Gallaudet University
800 Florida Ave NE
Washington, DC 20002-3695   202-651-5231
                                              FAX 202-651-5109
                http://http://clerccenter.gallaudet.edu
                e-mail: clerc.center@gallaudet.edu
Ken Kurlychek, Information Specialist
Ed Bosso, Vice President

1227   DLM Math Fluency Program: Addition Facts
SRA Order Services
PO Box 182605
Columbus, OH 43218
                                              888-772-4543
                                              FAX 972-228-1982
                http://www.sraonline.com
                e-mail: SEG_CustomerService@mcgraw-hill.com
The McGraw-Hill Education Urban Advisory Resource works with large urban districts across the country to help them provide better quality instruction, curriculum, and assessment to their students. *$32.00*

1228   DLM Math Fluency Program: Division Facts
SRA Order Services
PO Box 182605
Columbus, OH 43218
                                              888-772-4543
                                              FAX 972-228-1982
                http://www.sraonline.com
                e-mail: SEG_CustomerService@mcgraw-hill.com
The McGraw-Hill Education Urban Advisory Resource works with large urban districts across the country to help them provide better quality instruction, curriculum, and assessment to their students.

1229   DLM Math Fluency Program: Multiplication Facts
SRA Order Services
PO Box 182605
Columbus, OH 43218
                                              888-772-4543
                                              FAX 972-228-1982
                http://www.sraonline.com
                e-mail: SEG_CustomerService@mcgraw-hill.com
The McGraw-Hill Education Urban Advisory Resource works with large urban districts across the country to help them provide better quality instruction, curriculum, and assessment to their students. *$32.00*

1230   DLM Math Fluency Program: Subtraction Facts
SRA Order Services
PO Box 182605
Columbus, OH 43218
                                              888-772-4543
                                              FAX 972-228-1982
                http://www.sraonline.com
                e-mail: SEG_CustomerService@mcgraw-hill.com

The McGraw-Hill Education Urban Advisory Resource works with large urban districts across the country to help them provide better quality instruction, curriculum, and assessment to their students. *$32.00*

1231   Data Explorer
Sunburst Technology
3150 W Higgins Rd
Suite 140
Hoffman Estates, IL 60619
                                              800-321-7511
                http://www.sunburst.com
                e-mail: service@sunburst.com
This easy-to-use CD-ROM provides the flexibility needed for eleven different graph types including tools for long-term data analysis projects.

1232   Dragon Mix: Academic Skill Builders in Math
SRA Order Services
PO Box 182605
Columbus, OH 43218
                                              888-772-4543
                                              FAX 1-972-228-19
                http://www.sraonline.com
                e-mail: SEG_CustomerService@mcgraw-hill.com
The McGraw-Hill Education Urban Advisory Resource works with large urban districts across the country to help them provide better quality instruction, curriculum, and assessment to their students. *$49.00*

1233   Elementary Math Bundle
Sunburst Technology
3150 W Higgins Rd
Suite 140
Hoffman Estates, IL 60619
                                              800-321-7511
                http://www.sunburst.com
                e-mail: service@sunburst.com
Number sense and operations are the focus of the Elementary Math Bundle. Students engage in activities that reinforce basic addition and subtraction skills. This product comes with Splish Splash Math, Ten Tricky Tiles and Numbers Undercover.

1234   Equation Tile Teasers
Sunburst Technology
3150 W Higgins Rd
Suite 140
Hoffman Estates, IL 60619
                                              800-321-7511
                http://www.sunburst.com
                e-mail: service@sunburst.com
Students develop logic thinking and pre-algebra skills solving sets of numbers equations in three challenging problem-solving activities.

1235   Equations
Software to Go-Gallaudet University
800 Florida Ave NE
Washington, DC 20002-3600   202-651-5877
                                              FAX 202-651-5109
                http://http://clerccenter.gallaudet.edu
                e-mail: clerc.center@gallaudet.edu
Ken Kurlychek, Information Specialist
Ed Bosso, Vice President

1236   Factory Deluxe
Sunburst Technology
3150 W Higgins Rd
Suite 140
Hoffman Estates, IL 60619
                                              800-321-7511
                http://www.sunburst.com
                e-mail: service@sunburst.com

Five activities explore shapes, rotation, angles, geometric attributes, area formulas, and computation. Includes journal, record keeping, and on-screen help. This program helps sharpen geometry, visual thinking and problem solving skills.

1237 Fast-Track Fractions
SRA Order Services
PO Box 182605
Columbus, OH 43218

888-772-4543
FAX 972-228-1982
http://www.sraonline.com
e-mail: SEG_CustomerService@mcgraw-hill.com
The McGraw-Hill Education Urban Advisory Resource works with large urban districts across the country to help them provide better quality instruction, curriculum, and assessment to their students. *$46.00*

1238 Fraction Attraction
Sunburst Technology
3150 W Higgins Rd
Suite 140
Hoffman Estates, IL 60619

800-321-7511
http://www.sunburst.com
e-mail: service@sunburst.com
Build the fraction skills of ordering, equivalence, relative sizes and multiple representations with four, multi-level, carnival style games.

1239 Fraction Fuel-Up
SRA Order Services
PO Box 182605
Columbus, OH 43218

888-772-4543
FAX 972-228-1982
http://www.sraonline.com
e-mail: SEG_CustomerService@mcgraw-hill.com
The McGraw-Hill Education Urban Advisory Resource works with large urban districts across the country to help them provide better quality instruction, curriculum, and assessment to their students. *$46.00*

1240 Get Up and Go!
Sunburst Technology
3150 W Higgins Rd
Suite 140
Hoffman Estates, IL 60619

800-321-7511
http://www.sunburst.com
e-mail: service@sunburst.com
Students interpret and construct timelines through three descriptive activities in the animated program. Students are introduced to timelines as they participate in an interactive story.

1241 Learning About Numbers
C&C Software
5713 Kentford Cir
Wichita, KS 67220-3131

316-683-6056
800-752-2086

Carol Clark, President

Three segments use computer graphics to provide students with an experience in working with numbers. *$25.00*

1242 Math Machine
Software to Go-Gallaudet University
800 Florida Ave NE
Washington, DC 20002-3695

202-651-5220
FAX 202-651-5109
http://http://clerccenter.gallaudet.edu
e-mail: clerc.center@gallaudet.edu

Ken Kurlychek, EI Specialist
Ed Bosso, Vice President

1243 Math Masters: Addition and Subtraction
SRA Order Services
PO Box 182605
Columbus, OH 43218

800-843-8855
FAX 972-228-1982
http://www.sraonline.com
e-mail: SEG_CustomerService@mcgraw-hill.com
The McGraw-Hill Education Urban Advisory Resource works with large urban districts across the country to help them provide better quality instruction, curriculum, and assessment to their students.

1244 Math Masters: Multiplication and Division
SRA Order Services
PO Box 182605
Columbus, OH 43218

800-843-8855
FAX 972-228-1982
http://www.sraonline.com
e-mail: SEG_CustomerService@mcgraw-hill.com
The McGraw-Hill Education Urban Advisory Resource works with large urban districts across the country to help them provide better quality instruction, curriculum, and assessment to their students.

1245 Math Shop
Software to Go-Gallaudet University
800 Florida Ave NE
Washington, DC 20002-3695

202-651-5220
FAX 202-651-5109
http://http://clerccenter.gallaudet.edu
e-mail: clerc.center@gallaudet.edu

Ken Kurlychek, EI Specialist
Ed Bosso, Vice President

1246 Math Skill Games
Software to Go-Gallaudet University
800 Florida Ave NE
Washington, DC 20002-3695

202-651-5220
FAX 202-651-5109
http://http://clerccenter.gallaudet.edu
e-mail: clerc.center@gallaudet.edu

Ken Kurlychek, EI Specialist
Ed Bosso, Vice President

1247 Math for Everyday Living
Educational Activities Software
PO Box 87
Baldwin, NY 11510

800-797-3223
FAX 516-623-9282
http://www.edact.com
e-mail: learn@edact.com

Rose Falco, Educational Activities

Designed for secondary students, a tutorial and practice program with simulated activities for applying math skills in making change, working with sales slips, unit pricing, computing gas mileage and sales tax. *$89.00*

1248 Mighty Math Astro Algebra
Riverdeep
222 Berkeley Street
Boston, MA 02116 617-351-5000
888-242-6747
FAX 877-892-9820
http://www.riverdeep.net
e-mail: IIEcustomerservice@hmhpub.com
Eric Shuman, Chief Financial Officer
John K. Dragoon, EVP & Chairman
William Bayers, EVP
Houghton Mifflin Harcourt offers a wide array of technology-driven pre-k-12 solutions that inspire excellence and innovation in education, and raise student achievement.
$59.95

1249 Mighty Math Calculating Crew
Riverdeep
222 Berkeley Street
Boston, MA 02116 617-351-5000
888-242-6747
FAX 877-892-9820
http://www.riverdeep.net
e-mail: IIEcustomerservice@hmhpub.com
Eric Shuman, Chief Financial Officer
John K. Dragoon, EVP & Chairman
William Bayers, EVP
Houghton Mifflin Harcourt offers a wide array of technology-driven pre-k-12 solutions that inspire excellence and innovation in education, and raise student achievement.
$59.95

1250 Mighty Math Carnival Countdown
Riverdeep
222 Berkeley Street
Boston, MA 02116 617-351-5000
888-242-6747
FAX 877-892-9820
http://www.riverdeep.net
e-mail: IIEcustomerservice@hmhpub.com
Eric Shuman, Chief Financial Officer
John K. Dragoon, EVP & Chairman
William Bayers, EVP
Houghton Mifflin Harcourt offers a wide array of technology-driven pre-k-12 solutions that inspire excellence and innovation in education, and raise student achievement.
$59.95

1251 Mighty Math Cosmic Geometry
Riverdeep
222 Berkeley Street
Boston, MA 02116 617-351-5000
888-242-6747
FAX 877-892-9820
http://www.riverdeep.net
e-mail: IIEcustomerservice@hmhpub.com
Eric Shuman, Chief Financial Officer
John K. Dragoon, EVP & Chairman
William Bayers, EVP
Houghton Mifflin Harcourt offers a wide array of technology-driven pre-k-12 solutions that inspire excellence and innovation in education, and raise student achievement.
$59.95

1252 Mighty Math Number Heroes
Riverdeep
222 Berkeley Street
Boston, MA 02116 617-351-5000
888-242-6747
FAX 877-892-9820
http://www.riverdeep.net
e-mail: IIEcustomerservice@hmhpub.com
Eric Shuman, Chief Financial Officer
John K. Dragoon, EVP & Chairman
William Bayers, EVP
Houghton Mifflin Harcourt offers a wide array of technology-driven pre-k-12 solutions that inspire excellence and innovation in education, and raise student achievement.
$59.95

1253 Mighty Math Zoo Zillions
Riverdeep
222 Berkeley Street
Boston, MA 02116 617-351-5000
888-242-6747
FAX 877-892-9820
http://www.riverdeep.net
e-mail: IIEcustomerservice@hmhpub.com
Eric Shuman, Chief Financial Officer
John K. Dragoon, EVP & Chairman
William Bayers, EVP
Houghton Mifflin Harcourt offers a wide array of technology-driven pre-k-12 solutions that inspire excellence and innovation in education, and raise student achievement.
$59.95

1254 Millie's Math House
Riverdeep
222 Berkeley Street
Boston, MA 02116 617-351-5000
888-242-6747
FAX 877-892-9820
http://www.riverdeep.net
e-mail: IIEcustomerservice@hmhpub.com
Eric Shuman, Chief Financial Officer
John K. Dragoon, EVP & Chairman
William Bayers, EVP
Houghton Mifflin Harcourt offers a wide array of technology-driven pre-k-12 solutions that inspire excellence and innovation in education, and raise student achievement.
$59.95

1255 Number Farm
Software to Go-Gallaudet University
800 Florida Ave NE
Washington, DC 20002-3695 202-651-5220
FAX 202-651-5109
http://http://clerccenter.gallaudet.edu
e-mail: clerc.center@gallaudet.edu
Ken Kurlychek, EIS
Ed Bosso, Vice President

1256 Number Please
Merit Software
Ste 603
121 W 27th St
New York, NY 10001-6262 212-675-8567
800-753-6488
FAX 212-675-8607
http://www.meritsoftware.com
e-mail: sales@meritsoftware.com
Ben Weintraub, CEO

Students are challenged to remember combinations of 4, 7 and 10 digit numbers. *$9.95*

1257 Number Sense and Problem Solving
Sunburst Technology
3150 W Higgins Rd
Suite 140
Hoffman Estates, IL 60619
800-321-7511
http://www.sunburst.com
e-mail: service@sunburst.com
Build number and operation skills with these three programs: How the West Was One + Three x Four, Divide and Conquer and Puzzle Tank.

1258 Number Stumper
Software to Go-Gallaudet University
800 Florida Ave NE
Washington, DC 20002-3600 202-651-5220
FAX 202-651-5109
http://http://clerccenter.gallaudet.edu
e-mail: clerc.center@gallaudet.edu

Ken Kurlychek, EI Specialist
Ed Bosso, Vice President

1259 Race Car 'rithmetic
Software to Go-Gallaudet University
800 Florida Ave NE
Washington, DC 20002-3600   202-651-5220
                                    FAX 202-651-5109
          http://http://clerccenter.gallaudet.edu
          e-mail: clerc.center@gallaudet.edu
Ken Kurlychek, EI Specialist
Ed Bosso, Vice President

1260 Read and Solve Math Problems #1
Educational Activities
PO Box 87
Baldwin, NY 11510
                                    800-797-3223
                                    FAX 516-623-9282
                          http://www.edact.com
                          e-mail: learn@edact.com
Rose Falco, Educational Activities

A tutorial and practice program for students which focuses
on recognition of key words in solving arithmetic word problems, writing equations and solving word problems. *$109.00*

1261 Read and Solve Math Problems #2
Educational Activities
PO Box 87
Baldwin, NY 11510
                                    800-797-3223
                                    FAX 516-623-9282
                          http://www.edact.com
                          e-mail: learn@edact.com
Rose Falco, Educational Activities

A tutorial and practice program for students which focuses
on recognition of key words in solving two-step arithmetic
problems, writing equations and solving two-step word
problems. *$109.00*

1262 Read and Solve Math Problems #3
Educational Activities
PO Box 87
Baldwin, NY 11510
                                    800-797-3223
                                    FAX 516-623-9282
                          http://www.edact.com
                          e-mail: learn@edact.com
Rose Falco, Educational Activities

Designed for students, this tutorial and practice program
provides initial instruction and experience in critical thinking and problem-solving using fractions and mixed numbers. *$109.00*

1263 Shape Up!
Sunburst Technology
3150 W Higgins Rd
Suite 140
Hoffman Estates, IL 60619
                                    800-321-7511
                          http://www.sunburst.com
                          e-mail: service@sunburst.com
Students actively create and manipulate shapes to discover
important ideas about mathematics in an electronic play-
ground of two and three dimensional shapes.

1264 Spatial Relationships
Sunburst Technology
3150 W Higgins Rd
Suite 140
Hoffman Estates, IL 60619
                                    800-321-7511
                          http://www.sunburst.com
                          e-mail: service@sunburst.com
Your students will strenghten their spatial perception, spa-
tial reasoning and problem-solving skills with three great
programs now on one CD-ROM.

1265 Splish Splash Math
Sunburst Technology
3150 W Higgins Rd
Suite 140
Hoffman Estates, IL 60619
                                    800-321-7511
                          http://www.sunburst.com
                          e-mail: service@sunburst.com
Students learn and practice basic operation skills as they engage in this high interest program that keeps them motivated. Great visual rewards and three levels of difficulty
keep students challanged.

1266 Tenth Planet: Combining & Breaking Apart Numbers
Sunburst Technology
3150 W Higgins Rd
Suite 140
Hoffman Estates, IL 60619
                                    800-321-7511
                          http://www.sunburst.com
                          e-mail: service@sunburst.com
Students explore part-whole relationships and develop num-
ber sense by combining and breaking apart numbers in a va-
riety of problem-solving situations.

1267 Tenth Planet: Comparing with Ratios
Sunburst Technology
3150 W Higgins Rd
Suite 140
Hoffman Estates, IL 60619
                                    800-321-7511
                          http://www.sunburst.com
                          e-mail: service@sunburst.com
Students learn that ratio is a way to compare amounts by using multiplication and division. Through five engaging activities, students recognize and describe ratios, develop
proportional thinking skills, estimate ratios, determine
equivalent ratios, and use ratios to analyze data.

1268 Tenth Planet: Equivalent Fractions
Sunburst Technology
3150 W Higgins Rd
Suite 140
Hoffman Estates, IL 60619
                                    800-321-7511
                          http://www.sunburst.com
                          e-mail: service@sunburst.com
This exciting investigation develops students' conceptual
understanding that every fraction can be named in many dif-
ferent but equivalent ways.

1269 Tenth Planet: Fraction Operations
Sunburst Technology
3150 W Higgins Rd
Suite 140
Hoffman Estates, IL 60619
                                    800-321-7511
                          http://www.sunburst.com
                          e-mail: service@sunburst.com

Students build on their concepts of fraction meaning and equivalence as they learn how to perform operations with fractions.

1270 World Class Learning Materials
World Class Learning
PO Box 639
Candler, NC 28715

800-638-6470
FAX 800-638-6499
http://www.wclm.com
e-mail: jdash@wclm.com

Designed for secondary students and adults, this program focuses on personal financial management, comparison shopping and calculation of essential banking transactions.

1271 Zap! Around Town
Sunburst Technology
3150 W Higgins Rd
Suite 140
Hoffman Estates, IL 60619

800-638-6470
http://www.sunburst.com
e-mail: service@sunburst.com

Students develop mapping and direction skills in this easy-to-use, animated program featuring Shelby, your friendly Sunbuddy guide.

Preschool

1272 Creature Series
Laureate Learning Systems
110 E Spring St
Winooski, VT 05404-1898

802-655-4755
800-562-6801
FAX 802-655-4757
http://www.laureatelearning.com
e-mail: laureate-webmaster@laureatelearning.com
Mary Sweig Wilson Ph.D., President/CEO
Bernard J. Fox, Vice President
Marion Blank, Ph.D, Developmental Psychologist
Six different computer programs designed to improve visual and auditory attention and teach cause and effect, turn taking, and switch use. *$95.00*

1273 Curious George Visits the Library
Software to Go-Gallaudet University
800 Florida Ave NE
Washington, DC 20002-3600

202-651-5220
FAX 202-651-5109
http://http://clerccenter.gallaudet.edu
e-mail: clerc.center@gallaudet.edu
Ken Kurlychek, EI Specialist
Ed Bosso, Vice President

1274 Early Discoveries: Size and Logic
Software to Go-Gallaudet University
800 Florida Ave NE
Washington, DC 20002-3600

202-651-5220
FAX 202-651-5109
http://http://clerccenter.gallaudet.edu
e-mail: clerc.center@gallaudet.edu
Ken Kurlychek, EI Specialist
Ed Bosso, Vice President

1275 Early Emerging Rules Series
Laureate Learning Systems
110 E Spring St
Winooski, VT 05404-1898

802-655-4755
800-562-6801
FAX 802-655-4757
http://www.laureatelearning.com
e-mail: laureate-webmaster@laureatelearning.com
Mary Sweig Wilson Ph.D., President/CEO
Bernard J. Fox, Vice President
Marion Blank, Ph.D, Developmental Psychologist
Three programs that introduce early developing grammatical constructions and facilitate the transition from single words to word combinations. *$175.00*

1276 Early Learning I
MarbleSoft
Ste 205
12301 Central Ave NE
Blaine, MN 55434-1417

763-755-1402
888-755-1402
FAX 763-755-0440
http://www.marblesoft.com
e-mail: mail@marblesoft.com
Vicki Larson, Sales

Early Learning 2.0 includes four activities that teach prereading skills. Single and dual-switch scanning are built in and special prompts allow blind students to use all levels of difficulty. Includes Matching Colors, Learning Shapes, Counting Numbers and Letter Match. Runs on Macintosh and Windows computers. *$70.00*

1277 Early and Advanced Switch Games
RJ Cooper & Associates
Ste 39
27601 Forbes Rd
Laguna Niguel, CA 92677-1241

949-582-2572
800-752-6673
FAX 949-582-3169
http://www.rjcooper.com
e-mail: info@rjcooper.com
R J Cooper, Owner

Thirteen single switch games that start at cause/effect, work through timing and selection and graduate with matching and manipulation tasks. *$75.00*

1278 Edustar's Early Childhood Special Education Programs

Edustar America
Ste 186
6220 S Orange Blossom Trl
Orlando, FL 32809-4627

561-638-8733
800-952-3041
FAX 561-330-0849
David Zeldin, Marketing Manager
Stewart Holtz, Curriculum Director

Integrated software program that incorporates manipulatives and special tables for learning early childhood subjects. Features include an illuminated six key keyboard. A special U-shaped touch table for the physically challenged and changeable mats and keys for different subject areas.

1279 Joystick Games
Technology for Language and Learning
PO Box 327
East Rockaway, NY 11518

516-625-4550
FAX 516-621-3321
Joan Tanenhaus, Founder

Five volumes of public domain joystick programs. *$28.50*

1280 Kindercomp Gold
Software to Go-Gallaudet University
800 Florida Ave NE
Washington, DC 20002-3600   202-651-5220
                                    FAX 202-651-5109
http://http://clerccenter.gallaudet.edu
e-mail: clerc.center@gallaudet.edu
Ken Kurlychek, EI Specialist
Ed Bosso, Vice President

1281 Old MacDonald's Farm Deluxe
KidTECH
12301 Central Ave NE
Ste 205
Blaine, MN 55434   763-755-1402
                                    888-755-1402
                                    FAX 763-862-2920
http://www.softtouch.com
e-mail: sales@marblesoft.com
Mark Fulton, President

Utilizes the all-time favorite children's song to teach vocabulary and animal sounds to young children. *$30.00*

1282 Shape and Color Rodeo
SRA Order Services
PO Box 182605
Columbus, OH 43218   800-843-8855
                                    FAX 972-228-1892
http://www.sraonline.com
e-mail: SEG_CustomerService@mcgraw-hill.com
The McGraw-Hill Education Urban Advisory Resource works with large urban districts across the country to help them provide better quality instruction, curriculum, and assessment to their students. *$35.00*

1283 Trudy's Time and Place House
Riverdeep
222 Berkeley Street
Boston, MA 02116   617-351-5000
                                    888-242-6747
                                    FAX 877-892-9820
http://www.riverdeep.net
e-mail: IIEcustomerservice@hmhpub.com
Eric Shuman, Chief Financial Officer
John K. Dragoon, EVP & Chairman
William Bayers, EVP
Houghton Mifflin Harcourt offers a wide array of technology-driven pre-k-12 solutions that inspire excellence and innovation in education, and raise student achievement. *$59.95*

1284 Word Pieces
Software to Go-Gallaudet University
800 Florida Ave NE
Washington, DC 20002-3600   202-651-5220
                                    FAX 202-651-5109
http://http://clerccenter.gallaudet.edu
e-mail: clerc.center@gallaudet.edu
Ken Kurlychek, EI Specialist
Ed Bosso, Vice President

Problem Solving

1285 Captain's Log
BrainTrain
727 Twinridge Ln
North Chesterfield, VA 23235-5270 804-320-0105
                                    800-822-0538
                                    FAX 804-320-0242
http://www.braintrain.com
e-mail: info@braintrain.com

Joseph A Sandford, Founder

A comprehensive, multilevel computerized mental gym to help people with brain injuries, learning disabilities, developmental disabilities, ADD, ADHD and psychiatric disorders improve their cognitive skills. *$2695.00*

ISBN 3-490019-95-0

1286 Changes Around Us CD-ROM
5th Floor
6277 Sea Harbor Dr
Orlando, FL 32887   800-531-5015
                                    FAX 800-699-9459
http://www.harcourtachieve.com
e-mail: greatservice@hmhpub.com
Linda K. Zecher, President and CEO
Eric Shuman, Chief Financial Officer
John K. Dragoon, EVP
Nature is the natural choice for observing change. By observing and researching dramatic visual sequences such as the stages of development of a butterfly, children develop a broad understanding of the concept of change. As they search this multimedia database for images and information about plant and animal life cycles and seasonal change, students strengthen their abilities in research, analysis, problem-solving, critical thinking and communication.

1287 Factory Deluxe: Grades 4 to 8
Sunburst Technology
3150 W Higgins Rd
Suite 140
Hoffman Estates, IL 60619   800-321-7511
http://www.sunburst.com
e-mail: Service@sunburst.com
Five activities explore shapes, rotation, angles, geometric attributes, area formulas, and computation. Includes journal, record keeping, and on-screen help. This program helps sharpen geometry, visual thinking and problem solving skills.

1288 Freddy's Puzzling Adventures
SRA Order Services
PO Box 182605
Columbus, OH 43218   800-843-8855
                                    FAX 972-228-1892
http://www.sraonline.com
e-mail: SEG_CustomerService@mcgraw-hill.com
The McGraw-Hill Education Urban Advisory Resource works with large urban districts across the country to help them provide better quality instruction, curriculum, and assessment to their students. *$34.00*

1289 Guessing and Thinking
Software to Go-Gallaudet University
800 Florida Ave NE
Washington, DC 20002-3695   202-651-5231
                                    FAX 202-651-5109
http://http://clerccenter.gallaudet.edu
e-mail: clerc.center@gallaudet.edu
Ken Kurlychek, EI Specialist
Ed Bosso, Vice President

1290 High School Math Bundle
Sunburst Technology
3150 W Higgins Rd
Suite 140
Hoffman Estates, IL 60619   800-321-7511
http://www.sunburst.com
e-mail: service@sunburst.com

Each program in this bundle focuses on a specific area to ensure that your students master the math skills they need. This bundle allows students to master basics of Algebra, explore equations and graphs, practice learning with algebra graphs, use trigonometric functions, apply math concepts to practical situations and improve problem solving and data analysis skills.

1291 Ice Cream Truck
Sunburst Technology
3150 W Higgins Rd
Suite 140
Hoffman Estates, IL 60619

800-321-7511
http://www.sunburst.com
e-mail: service@sunburst.com
Elementary students learn important problem solving, strategic planning and math operation skills, as they become owners of a busy ice cream truck.

1292 Memory Match
Software to Go-Gallaudet University
800 Florida Ave NE
Washington, DC 20002-3695

202-651-5231
FAX 202-651-5109
http://http://clerccenter.gallaudet.edu
e-mail: clerc.center@gallaudet.edu
Ken Kurlychek, EI Specialist
Ed Bosso, Vice President

1293 Memory: A First Step in Problem Solving
Software to Go-Gallaudet University
800 Florida Ave NE
Washington, DC 20002-3600

202-651-5220
FAX 202-651-5109
http://http://clerccenter.gallaudet.edu
e-mail: clerc.center@gallaudet.edu
Ken Kurlychek, EI Specialist
Ed Bosso, Vice President

1294 Merit Software
Merit Software
Ste 603
121 W 27th St
New York, NY 10001-6262

212-675-8567
800-753-6488
FAX 212-675-8607
http://www.meritsoftware.com
e-mail: sales@meritsoftware.com
Bob Weintraub, CEO

Deductive logic and problem solving are the primary skills developed in the variation of the game MASTERMIND. *$9.95*

1295 Middle School Math Bundle
Sunburst Technology
3150 W Higgins Rd
Suite 140
Hoffman Estates, IL 60619

800-321-7511
http://www.sunburst.com
e-mail: Service@sunburst.com
This bundle helps improve student's logical thinking, number sense and operation skills. This product comes with Math Arena, Building Perspective Deluxe, Equation Tile Teasers and Easy Sheet.

1296 Nordic Software

800-306-6502
FAX 402-489-1560
http://www.nordicsoftware.com

Develops and publishes entertaining, educational software. Children ages three and up can build math skills, expand their vocabulary and increase proficiency in spelling, among other subjects. *$59.95*

1297 Number Sense & Problem Solving CD-ROM
Sunburst Technology
3150 W Higgins Rd
Suite 140
Hoffman Estates, IL 60619

800-321-7511
http://www.sunburst.com
e-mail: service@sunburst.com
Build number and operation skills with these three programs: How the West Was One + Three x Four, Divide and Conquer and Puzzle Tank.

1298 Problem Solving
Psychological Software Services
6555 Carrollton Ave
Indianapolis, IN 46220-1664

317-257-9672
FAX 317-257-9674
http://www.neuroscience.cnter.com
e-mail: nsc@neuroscience.cnter.com
Odie L Bracy, Clinical Neuropsychologist
Nancy Bracy, Office Manager
Andrea Oakes, Clinical Assistant
Nine computer programs designed to challenge high functioning patients/students with tasks requiring logic. *$150.00*

1299 Single Switch Games
MarbleSoft
Ste 205
12301 Central Ave NE
Blaine, MN 55434-1417

763-755-1402
888-755-1402
FAX 763-755-0440
http://www.marblesoft.com
e-mail: mail@marblesoft.com
Vicki Larson, Sales

There's a lot of educational software for single switch users, but how about something that's just for fun? We've taken some games similar to the ones you enjoyed as a kid and made them work just right for single switch users. Includes Single Switch Maze, A Frog's Life, Switching Lanes, Switch Invaders, Slingshot Gallery and Scurry. Runs on Macintosh and Windows computers. *$30.00*

1300 Sliding Block
Merit Software
Ste 603
121 W 27th St
New York, NY 10001-6262

212-675-8567
800-753-6488
FAX 212-675-8607
http://www.meritsoftware.com
e-mail: sales@meritsoftware.com
Ben Weintraub, CEO

Learners rearrange one of the four pictures which can be scrambled at five separate levels to test visual discrimination and problem solving skills. *$9.95*

1301 SmartDriver
BrainTrain
727 Twinridge Ln
North Chesterfield, VA 23235-5270

804-320-0105
800-822-0538
FAX 804-320-0242
http://www.braintrain.com
e-mail: info@braintrain.com

Joseph A Sandford, Founder

Visual attention building software where you 'win' by driving defensively and following the rules of the road. Children love this driving game that teaches visual attention, visual tracking, patience, following the rules, planning, and hand-eye coordination.

1302   SoundSmart
BrainTrain
727 Twinridge Ln
North Chesterfield, VA 23235-5270   804-320-0105
                                            800-822-0538
                                       FAX 804-320-0242
                                http://www.braintrain.com
                                e-mail: info@braintrain.com
Joseph A Sandford, Founder

Auditory Attention Building software to help improve phonenic awareness, listening skills, working memory, mental processing speech and self-control. *$549.00*

1303   Strategy Challenges Collection: 1
Riverdeep
222 Berkeley Street
Boston, MA 02116   617-351-5000
                                            888-242-6747
                                       FAX 877-892-9820
                                 http://www.riverdeep.net
                         e-mail: IIEcustomerservice@hmhpub.com
Eric Shuman, Chief Financial Officer
John K. Dragoon, EVP & Chairman
William Bayers, EVP
Houghton Mifflin Harcourt offers a wide array of technology-driven pre-k-12 solutions that inspire excellence and innovation in education, and raise student achievement. *$39.95*

1304   Strategy Challenges Collection: 2
Riverdeep
222 Berkeley Street
Boston, MA 02116   617-351-5000
                                            888-242-6747
                                       FAX 877-892-9820
                                 http://www.riverdeep.net
                         e-mail: IIEcustomerservice@hmhpub.com
Eric Shuman, Chief Financial Officer
John K. Dragoon, EVP & Chairman
William Bayers, EVP
Houghton Mifflin Harcourt offers a wide array of technology-driven pre-k-12 solutions that inspire excellence and innovation in education, and raise student achievement. *$39.95*

1305   Thinkin' Things Collection: 3
Riverdeep
222 Berkeley Street
Boston, MA 02116   617-351-5000
                                            888-242-6747
                                       FAX 877-892-9820
                                 http://www.riverdeep.net
                         e-mail: IIEcustomerservice@hmhpub.com
Eric Shuman, Chief Financial Officer
John K. Dragoon, EVP & Chairman
William Bayers, EVP
Houghton Mifflin Harcourt offers a wide array of technology-driven pre-k-12 solutions that inspire excellence and innovation in education, and raise student achievement.

1306   Thinkin' Things: All Around Frippletown
Riverdeep
222 Berkeley Street
Boston, MA 02116   617-351-5000
                                            888-242-6747
                                       FAX 877-892-9820
                                 http://www.riverdeep.net
                         e-mail: IIEcustomerservice@hmhpub.com
Eric Shuman, Chief Financial Officer
John K. Dragoon, EVP & Chairman
William Bayers, EVP

Houghton Mifflin Harcourt offers a wide array of technology-driven pre-k-12 solutions that inspire excellence and innovation in education, and raise student achievement.

1307   Thinkin' Things: Collection 1
Riverdeep
222 Berkeley Street
Boston, MA 02116   617-351-5000
                                            888-242-6747
                                       FAX 877-892-9820
                                 http://www.riverdeep.net
                         e-mail: IIEcustomerservice@hmhpub.com
Eric Shuman, Chief Financial Officer
John K. Dragoon, EVP & Chairman
William Bayers, EVP
Houghton Mifflin Harcourt offers a wide array of technology-driven pre-k-12 solutions that inspire excellence and innovation in education, and raise student achievement.

1308   Thinkin' Things: Collection 2
Riverdeep
222 Berkeley Street
Boston, MA 02116   617-351-5000
                                            888-242-6747
                                       FAX 877-892-9820
                                 http://www.riverdeep.net
                         e-mail: IIEcustomerservice@hmhpub.com
Eric Shuman, Chief Financial Officer
John K. Dragoon, EVP & Chairman
William Bayers, EVP
Houghton Mifflin Harcourt offers a wide array of technology-driven pre-k-12 solutions that inspire excellence and innovation in education, and raise student achievement.

1309   Thinkin' Things: Sky Island Mysteries
Riverdeep
222 Berkeley Street
Boston, MA 02116   617-351-5000
                                            888-242-6747
                                       FAX 877-892-9820
                                 http://www.riverdeep.net
                         e-mail: IIEcustomerservice@hmhpub.com
Eric Shuman, Chief Financial Officer
John K. Dragoon, EVP & Chairman
William Bayers, EVP
Houghton Mifflin Harcourt offers a wide array of technology-driven pre-k-12 solutions that inspire excellence and innovation in education, and raise student achievement.

Professional Resources

1310   Accurate Assessments
1016 Leavenworth St
Omaha, NE 68102-2944   402-341-8880
                                            800-324-7966
                                       FAX 402-341-8911
                               http://www.myaccucare.com
                            e-mail: info@orionhealthcare.com
Accurate Assessments offers a full range of superior innovative technological services and expertise to the behavioral health industry. Our premier product, AccuCare Behavioral Healthcare System, was developed by teams of experts in their respective fields, insuring our products are truly useful to clinicians and are easy to use. This innovative software program is a comprehensive and adaptable approach to the behavioral health practice environment.

1311   Beyond Drill and Practice: Expanding the Computer Mainstream
Council for Exceptional Children
Suite 500
655 Tyee Road
Victoria, BC   250-412-3258
                                 http://www.abebooks.com/sell
                             e-mail: sellbooks@abebooks.com
Susan Jo Russell, Author
Rebecca Corwin, Author
Janice R. Mokros, Author

Provides informative guidelines and examples for teachers who want to expand the use of the computer as a learning tool. *$10.00*
120 pages

1312 CE Software
PO Box 65580
West Des Moines, IA 50265   515-221-1801
                                 800-523-7638
                                 FAX 515-221-1806
                          http://www.cesoft.com
International software developer. Many products for adaptive technology.

1313 Compass Learning
203 Colorado St
Austin, TX 78701-3922   512-478-9600
                                 800-678-1412
                                 FAX 512-492-6193
                  http://www.compasslearning.com
              e-mail: lkrauss@compasslearning.com
Eric Loeffel, Chief Executive Officer
Rebecca Tongsinoon, Vice President
Trey Chambers, Chief Financial Officer
Educational software for teachers of K-12.

1314 Computer Retrieval of Information on Scientific Project (CRISP)
National Institute of Health
9000 Rockville Pike
Bethesda, MD 20892   301-402-7469
                                 866-504-9552
                           TTY: 301-451-5939
                   http://www.crisp.cit.nih.gov
                    e-mail: commons@od.nih.gov
Caryn G Morse, Manager
Dorrette Finch, Research Documentation Div. Dir.

A major scientific information system containing data on the research programs supported by the US Public Health Service.

1315 Conover Company
4 Brookwood Ct
Appleton, WI 54914-8618   920-882-1272
                                 800-933-1933
                                 FAX 920-231-4809
                  http://www.conovercompany.com
                 e-mail: sales@conovercompany.com
Becky Schmitz, President
Mike Schmitz, Vice President of Operations

Provides off-the-shelf as well as custom sales and marketing, training, presentation, and application programs that connect learning to the workplace. Delivery platforms include workshops, print, custom software, CD-ROM, multimedia, internet, and intranet.

1316 Developmental Profile
Western Psychological Services
625 Alaska Avenue
Torrance, CA 90503-5124   424-201-8800
                                 800-648-8857
                                 FAX 424-201-6950
                   http://www.wpspublish.com
            e-mail: customerservice@wpspublish.com
Jeffrey Manson, President

This computer program substantially reduces the time educators spend on preparing Individualized Educational Plans (IEPs). The system allows the user to use any IEP format. Simply type the format into the computer, and the program will customize the system to your district's specifications. *$115.00*

1317 FileMaker Inc.
5201 Patrick Henry Dr
Santa Clara, CA 95054-1164   408-987-7000
                                 800-725-2747
                                 FAX 408-987-3002
                       http://www.filemaker.com
Dominique P Goupil, President
Bill Epling, Senior Vice President of Finance
Simon Thornhill, Vice President of Engineering
Company that produces a variety of Macintosh Documentation.

1318 International Society for Technology in Education (ISTE)
University of Oregon
Ste 300
180 W 8th Ave
Eugene, OR 97401-2916   541-302-3777
                                 800-366-5191
                                 FAX 541-302-3778
                            http://www.iste.org
                       e-mail: iste@iste.org
Holly Jobe, President
Ric Wiltse, Treasurer
Ben Smith, Secretary
A nonprofit professional organization dedicated to promoting appropriate uses of information technology to support and improve learning, teaching, and administration in K-12 education and teacher education.

1319 KidDesk
Riverdeep
222 3rd Ave SE
Suite 4
Cedar Rapids, IA 52401-1542   319-395-9626
                                 800-825-4420
                                 FAX 319-395-0217
          http://http://web.riverdeep.net/portal/page?_pa
                       e-mail: info@riverdeep.net
Barry O'Callaghan, Executive Chairman & CEO
Jim Ruddy, Chief Revenue Officer
Tony Mulderry, Executive Vice President
A hard disk security program, KidDesk makes it easy for kids to launch their programs, but impossible for them to access adult programs. Includes interactive desktop accessories including desktop-to-desktop electronic mail, and voice mail. *$24.95*

1320 KidDesk: Family Edition
Riverdeep
222 3rd Ave SE
Suite 4
Cedar Rapids, IA 52401-1542   319-395-9626
                                 800-825-4420
                                 FAX 319-395-0217
          http://http://web.riverdeep.net/portal/page?_pa
                       e-mail: info@riverdeep.net
Barry O'Callaghan, Executive Chairman & CEO
Jim Ruddy, Chief Revenue Officer
Tony Mulderry, Executive Vice President
Now kids can launch their programs, but can't access yours! With KidDesk Family Edition, you can give your children the keys to the computer without putting your programs and files at risk! The auto-start option provides constant hard drive security — any time your computer is turned on, KidDesk will appear. *$24.95*

1321 Laureate Learning Systems
110 E Spring St
Winooski, VT 05404-1898   802-655-4755
                                 800-652-6801
                                 FAX 802-655-4757
                   http://www.laureatelearning.com
        e-mail: laureate-customer-service@laureatelearning.co
Dr. Mary Sweig Wilson, Co-Founder
Bernard J. Fox, Co-Founder

Provides resources for people with learning disabilities.

1322 Learning Company
Riverdeep
100 Pine St
Suite 1900
San Francisco, CA 94111-5205   415-659-2000
                                                                   800-825-4420
                                                       FAX 415-659-2020
http://http://web.riverdeep.net/portal/page?_pa
                        e-mail: info@riverdeep.net
Barry O'Callaghan, Executive Chairman & CEO
Jim Ruddy, Chief Revenue Officer
Tony Mulderry, Executive Vice President

1323 Microsoft Corporation
1 Microsoft Way
Redmond, WA 98052-6399   425-882-8080
                                                                   800-642-7676
                                                       FAX 425-936-7329
                        http://www.microsoft.com
Steve Ballmer, CEO
Lisa Brummel, Chief People Officer
Tony Bates, President
Our mission is to enable people and businesses throughout
the world to realize their full potential.

1324 Print Module
Failure Free
140 Cabarrus Ave W
Concord, NC 28025-5150   704-786-7838
                                                                   888-233-READ
                                                       FAX 704-785-8940
                        http://www.failurefree.com
                        e-mail: info@failurefree.com
Joe Lockavitch, VP Sales and Marketing

Includes teacher's manual, instructional readers, flashcards,
independent activities and illustrated independent reading
booklets. *$499.00*

1325 PsycINFO Database
American Psychological Association
750 1st St NE
Washington, DC 20002-4242   202-336-5500
                                                                   800-374-2721
                                                       FAX 202-336-5997
                                                       TDD:202-336-6123
                                                       TTY: 202-336-6123
                                                       http://www.apa.org
                                                       e-mail: mis@apa.org
Suzanne Bennett Johnson, PhD, President
Norman B. Anderson, PhD, Chief Executive Officer
Bonnie Markham, PhD, PsyD, Treasurer
An online abstract database that provides access to citations
to the international serial literature in psychology and re-
lated disciplines from 1887 to present. Available via
PsycINFO Direct at www.psycinfo.com.

1326 Public Domain Software
Kentucky Special Ed TechTraining Center
229 Taylor Education Building
University of Kentucky
Lexington, KY 40506   859-257-4713
                                                       FAX 859-257-1325
                                                       TDD:859-257-4714
http://http://education.uky.edu/EDSRC/
                        e-mail: bcoll01@uky.edu
Mary John O'Hair, Dean and Professor
Parker Fawson, Associate Dean
Steve R. Parker, Associate Professor
Entire collections of Macintosh, MS-DOS or Apple II soft-
ware.

1327 Riverdeep
100 Pine St
Suite 1900
San Francisco, CA 94111-5205   415-659-2000
                                                                   800-825-4420
                                                       FAX 415-659-2020
http://http://web.riverdeep.net/portal/page?_pa
                        e-mail: info@riverdeep.net
Barry O'Callaghan, Executive Chairman & CEO
Jim Ruddy, Chief Revenue Officer
Tony Mulderry, Executive Vice President
Developer of educational software, including software for
mathematics instruction.

1328 Scholastic
2931 E McCarty St
Jefferson City, MO 65101-4468   573-636-5271
                                                                   800-724-6527
                                                       FAX 573-636-0549
                                       http://www.scholastic.com
                        e-mail: custserv@scholastic.com
Faye Edwards, Executive VP/CAO/CEO
Larry Holland, Human Resources Director
Dick Robinson, President & CEO
For more than 90 years, Scholastic has been delivering outstanding books, magazines and educational programs directly to schools and families through channels that have
become childhood traditions - Scholastic Book Fairs,
monthly Book Clubs, and Scholastic News classroom
magazines.

1329 Speech Bin Abilitations
PO Box 1579
Appleton, WI 54912-1579
                                                       888-388-3224
                                                       FAX 888-388-6344
                                       http://www.speechbin.com
            e-mail: customercare@schoolspecialty.com
Tobi Isaacs MEd, Director

The Speech Bin offers materials to help persons of all ages
who have special needs. We specialize in products for children and adults who have communication disorders.

1330 Sunburst
1550 Executive Dr
Elgin, IL 60123-9311
                                                       800-321-7511
                                                       FAX 888-800-3028
                                       http://www.sunburst.com
                        e-mail: service@sunburst.com
Dan Figurski, President
Michael Guillroy, Channel Sales/Marketing Manager

Reading

1331 Adaptive Technology Tools
Freedom Scientific
11800 31st Ct N
St Petersburg, FL 33716-1805   727-803-8000
                                                                   800-444-4443
                                                       FAX 727-803-8001
                                       http://www.freedomscientific.com
                        e-mail: info@FreedomScientific.com
Dr. Lee Hamilton, President
Peggy Dalton, Director, Professional Services
Bryan Carver, Inside Sales Director
A wide variety of adaptive technology tools for the visually
or reading impaired person.

1332 An Open Book
Freedom Scientific
11800 31st Ct N
St Petersburg, FL 33716-1805 727-803-8000
800-444-4443
FAX 727-803-8001
http://www.freedomscientific.com
e-mail: info@FreedomScientific.com
Dr. Lee Hamilton, President
Peggy Dalton, Director, Professional Services
Bryan Carver, Inside Sales Director
The stand-alone reading machine, An Open Book, is an
easy-to-use appliance for noncomputer users that comes
equipped with a Hewlett Packard ScanJet IIP scanner,
DECtalk PC speech synthesizer and a 17 key keypad. An
Open Book uses Calera WordScan optical character recognition (OCR) to convert pages into text, then reads it aloud
with a speech synthesizer.

1333 An Open Book Unbound
Freedom Scientific
11800 31st Ct N
St Petersburg, FL 33716-1805 727-803-8000
800-444-4443
FAX 727-803-8001
http://www.freedomscientific.com
e-mail: info@Freedomscientific.com
Dr. Lee Hamilton, President
Peggy Dalton, Director, Professional Services
Bryan Carver, Inside Sales Director
PC-based OCR and reading software. Together with a scanner and a speech synthesizer, this software provides everything needed to make an IBM-compatible PC into a talking
reading machine. The system includes automatic page orientation, automatic contrast control, decolumnization of
multicolumn documents and recognition of a wide variety of
type fonts and sizes. *$995.00*

1334 Bailey's Book House
Riverdeep
222 3rd Ave SE
Suite 4
Cedar Rapids, IA 52401-1542 319-395-9626
800-825-4420
FAX 319-395-0217
http://http://web.riverdeep.net/portal/page?_pa
e-mail: info@riverdeep.net
Barry O'Callaghan, Executive Chairman & CEO
Jim Ruddy, Chief Revenue Officer
Tony Mulderry, Executive Vice President
The award-winning Bailey's Book House now features 2
new activities! Bailey and his friends encourage young children to build important literacy skills while developing a
love for reading. In seven activities, kids explore the sounds
and meanings of letters, words, sentences, rhymes and stories. No reading skills are required: all directions and written
words are spoken. *$59.95*

1335 Comprehension Connection
Milliken Publishing
501 East Third Street
Box 802
Dayton, OH 45401 937-228-6118
800-444-1144
FAX 937-223-2042
http://www.millikenpub.com
e-mail: lep@lorenz.com
Thomas Moore, President

Comprehension Connection improves reading comprehension by stressing basic skills that combine the reading process with relevant activities and interesting,
thought-provoking stories. This award-winning software
package spans six reading levels that increase in difficulty.
Passages range from 150-300 words. *$150.00*

1336 Cosmic Reading Journey
Sunburst Technology
1550 Executive Dr
Elgin, IL 60123-9311
888-321-7511
FAX 888-800-3028
http://www.sunburst.com
e-mail: service@sunburst.com
Michael Guillroy, Channel Sales/Marketing Manager
Dan Figurski, President

This reading comprehension program provides meaningful
summary and writing activities for the 100 books that early
readers and their teachers love most.

1337 Don Johnston Reading
Don Johnston
26799 W Commerce Dr
Volo, IL 60073-9675 847-740-0749
800-999-4660
FAX 847-740-7326
http://www.donjohnston.com
e-mail: info@donjohnston.com
Ruth Ziolkowski, President
Mindy Brown, Marketing Director

Don Johnston Inc. is a provider of quality products and services that enable people with special needs to discover their
potential and experience success. Products are developed
for the areas of computer access and for those who struggle
with reading and writing.

1338 Failure Free Reading
140 Cabarrus Ave W
Concord, NC 28025-5150 704-786-7838
888-233-READ
FAX 704-785-8940
http://www.failurefree.com
e-mail: info@failurefree.com
Joe Lockavitch, VP Sales/Marketing

Curriculum areas covered: reading for those with learning
disabilities and moderate mentally disabled/emotionally
disabled.

1339 Judy Lynn Software
PO Box 373
East Brunswick, NJ 08816 732-390-8845
FAX 732-390-8845
http://www.judylynn.com
e-mail: techsupt@judylynn.com
Elliot Pludwinski, Founder/President

Offers switch computer programs for windows. The programs are geared towards students with a cognitive age level
from 9 months and up. Programs are reasonably priced from
$39-$79. Recipient of a Parents' Choice Honor.

1340 Kurzweil 3000
Kurzweil Educational Systems
Ste 302
100 Crosby Dr
Bedford, MA 01730-1438 781-276-0600
800-547-6747
FAX 781-276-0650
http://www.kurzweiledu.com
e-mail: info@kurzweiledu.cc
Mike Sokol, President/CEO

Kurzweil Educational's flagship product for struggling
readers and writers. It is widely recognized as the most comprehensive and integrated solution for addressing language
and literacy difficulties. The software uses a multisensory
approach — presenting printed or electronic text on the computer screen with added visual and audible accessibility. The
product incorporates a host of dynamic features including
powerful decoding, study skills tools and test taking tools.

1341   Lexia Cross-Trainer
Lexia Learning Systems
200 Baker Avenue Ext
Concord, MA 01742   978-405-6200
                                          800-435-3942
                                     FAX 978-287-0062
                           http://www.lexialearning.com
                           e-mail: info@lexialearning.com
Nick Gaehde, President
Joel Brown, Vice President, Sales
Collin Earnst, Vice President of Marketing
Interactive software with an engaging video-gme interface
that is designed to strengthen cognitive skills. Activities that
advance visual-spatial and logical reasoning skills are designed to improve the memory, critical thinking, and problem solving abilities necessary for academic success in all
subjects. *$250.00*

1342   Lexia Early Reading
Lexia Learning Systems
200 Baker Avenue Ext
Concord, MA 01742   978-405-6200
                                          800-435-3942
                                     FAX 978-287-0062
                           http://www.lexialearning.com
                           e-mail: info@lexialearning.com
Nicholas C Gaehde, President
Joel Brown, Vice President, Sales
Collin Earnst, Vice President of Marketing
Engaging, interactive software fochildren aged four to six
that introduces and develops proficiency with phonological
principles and the alphabet - both proven indicators of later
reading success.

1343   Lexia Primary Reading
Lexia Learning Systems
200 Baker Avenue Ext
Concord, MA 01742   978-405-6200
                                          800-435-3942
                                     FAX 978-287-0062
                           http://www.lexialearning.com
                           e-mail: info@lexialearning.com
Nicholas C Gaehde, President
Joel Brown, Vice President, Sales
Collin Earnst, Vice President of Marketing
Interactive software designed to ensure mastery of basic
phonological skills and introduce more advanced phonics
priciples. five levels of engaging activities deliver practice
in phonemic awareness, sight-word recognition, word attack
strategies, sound-symbol correspondence, listening and
reading comprehension. *$50.00*

1344   Lexia Strategies for Older Students
Lexia Learning Systems
200 Baker Avenue Ext
Concord, MA 01742   978-405-6200
                                          800-435-3942
                                     FAX 978-287-0062
                           http://www.lexialearning.com
                           e-mail: info@lexialearning.com
Nicholas C Gaehde, President
Joel Brown, Vice President, Sales
Collin Earnst, Vice President of Marketing
Reading skills software program specifically designed for
ages 9-adult. Five levels of activities provide extensive practice in everything from basic phonological awareness to advanced word attack strategy and vocabulary development
based on Greek and Laitn word roots. *$250.00*

1345   Mike Mulligan & His Steam Shovel
Sunburst Technology
1550 Executive Dr
Elgin, IL 60123-9311
                                          888-321-7511
                                     FAX 888-800-3028
                               http://www.sunburst.com
                           e-mail: service@sunburst.com

Michael Guillory, Channel Sales/Marketing Manager
Dan Figurski, President

This CD-ROM version of the Caldecott classic lets students
experience interactive book reading and participate in four
skills-based extension activities that promote memory,
matching, sequencing, listening, pattern recognition and
map reading skills.

1346   Optimum Resource
1 Mathews Drive
Suite 107
Hilton Head Island, SC 29926-3667   843-689-8000
                                          888-784-2592
                                     FAX 843-689-8008
                               http://www.stickybear.com
                           e-mail: stickyb@stickybear.com
Richard Hefter, President

An educational software publishing company for grades
K-12. Our software titles are available in Consumer, School,
Labpack or Site License versions. Please call for further de-
tails. Prices range from $59.95 for Consumer to $699.95 for
Site Licenses.

1347   Polar Express
Sunburst Technology
1550 Executive Dr
Elgin, IL 60123-9311
                                          888-321-7511
                                     FAX 888-800-3028
                               http://www.sunburst.com
                           e-mail: service@sunburst.com
Michael Guillory, Channel Sales/Marketing Manager
Dan Figurski, President

Share the magic and enchantment of the holiday season with
this CD-ROM version of Chris Van Allsburg's
Caldecott-winning picture book.

1348   Prolexia
4726 13th Ave NW
Rochester, MN 55901-2631   507-780-1859
                                          888-776-5394
                                     FAX 507-252-0131
                               http://www.prolexia.com
                           e-mail: info@prolexia.com
John Rylander, President

UltraPhonics Tutor software teaches reading, spelling,
handwriting, & pronunciation to beginners and those with
dyslexia via multisensory structured phonics.

1349   Read On! Plus
Sunburst Technology
1550 Executive Dr
Elgin, IL 60123-9311
                                          888-321-7511
                                     FAX 888-800-3028
                               http://www.sunburst.com
                           e-mail: service@sunburst.com
Michael Guillory, Channel Sales/Marketing Manager
Dan Figurski, President

Promote skills and strategies that improve reading comprehension, and build appreciation for literature and the written
word.

1350   **Read, Write and Type! Learning Systems**
Talking Fingers
830 Rincon Way
San Rafael, CA 94903-2924   415-472-3103
     800-674-9126
     FAX 415-472-7812
     TDD:415-472-3106
http://www.readwritetype.com
e-mail: contact@talkingfingers.com
Jeannine Herron, Co-Founder
Dr. Leslie Grimm, Co-Founder

A 40-level software adventure providing highly motivating instruction and practice in phonics, reading, writing, spelling and typing. This multisensory program includes 9 levels of assessment and reports. Classroom packs available.

1351   **Reading Power Modules Books**
Steck-Vaughn Company
6277 Sea Harbor Dr
5th Floor
Orlando, FL 32887   800-531-5015
     800-225-5425
     FAX 800-699-9459
http://www.steck-vaughn.com
e-mail: info@steck-vaughn.com
Connie Alden, Vice President of HR
Michael Ruecker, Vice President of HR

Supplementary reading based on 4 decades of reading research. Companion books give students and teachers a choice of formats. High interest stories reinforce reading comprehension skills while building vocabulary, spelling skills, reading fluency, and speed.

1352   **Reading Skills Bundle**
Sunburst Technology
1550 Executive Dr
Elgin, IL 60123-9311
     888-321-7511
     FAX 888-800-3028
http://www.sunburst.com
e-mail: service@sunburst.com
Michael Guillory, Channel Sales/Marketing Manager
Dan Figurski, President

Teach beginning reading with teacher-developed programs that sequentially present phonics, phonemic awareness, word recognition, and reading comprehension concepts.

1353   **Reading Who? Reading You!**
Sunburst Technology
1550 Executive Dr
Elgin, IL 60123-9311
     888-321-7511
     FAX 888-800-3028
http://www.sunburst.com
e-mail: service@sunburst.com
Michael Guillory, Channel Sales/Marketing Manager
Dan Figurski, President

Teach beginning reading skills effectively with phonics instruction built into engaging games and puzzles that have children asking for more.

1354   **Sentence Master: Level 1, 2, 3, 4**
Laureate Learning Systems
110 E Spring St
Winooski, VT 05404-1898   802-655-4755
     800-562-6801
     FAX 802-655-4757
http://www.laureatelearning.com
e-mail: info@laureatelearning.com
Dr. Mary Sweig Wilson, Co-Founder
Bernard J. Fox, Co-Founder

A revolutionary way to teach beginning reading. Avoiding the confusing rules of phonics and the complexity of whole language, The Sentence Master focuses on the most frequently-used words of our language; i.e. the, is, but, and, etc., by truly teaching these little words, The Sentence Master gives students control over the majority of text they will ever encounter. *$495.00*

1355   **Simon Sounds It Out**
Don Johnston
26799 W Commerce Dr
Volo, IL 60073-9675   847-740-0749
     800-999-4660
     FAX 847-740-7326
http://www.donjohnston.com
e-mail: info@donjohnston.com
Ruth Ziolkowski, President
Mindy Brown, Marketing Director

Struggling students who can recite the alphabet and recognize letters on a page may still have trouble making connections between letters and sounds. This creates a barrier to recognizing and learning words which prevents your students from reading and writing successfully. Simon Sounds It Out provides the vital practice and repetition they need to overcome the letter-to-sound barrier. *$59.00*

1356   **Stickybear Software**
Optimum Resource
1 Mathews Drive
Suite 107
Hilton Head Island, SC 29926-3667   843-689-8000
     888-784-2592
     FAX 843-689-8008
http://www.stickybear.com
e-mail: stickyb@stickybear.com
Richard Hefter, President

An educational software publishing company for grades K-12. Our software titles are available in Consumer, School, Labpack or Site License versions. Please call for further details. Prices range from $59.95 for Consumer to $699.95 for Site Licenses.

1357   **Tenth Planet Roots, Prefixes & Suffixes**
Sunburst Technology
1550 Executive Dr
Elgin, IL 60123-9311
     888-321-7511
     FAX 888-800-3028
http://www.sunburst.com
e-mail: service@sunburst.com
Michael Guillory, Channel Sales/Marketing Manager
Dan Figurski, President

Students learn to decode difficult and more complex words as they engage in six activities where they construct and dissect words with roots, prefixes and suffixes.

1358   **Time for Teachers Online**
Stern Center for Language and Learning
135 Allen Brook Ln
Williston, VT 05495-9209   802-878-2332
     800-544-4863
     FAX 802-878-0230
http://www.sterncenter.org
e-mail: learning@sterncenter.org
Blanche Podhajski, Ph.D., President
John Connell, M.B.A., Chief Operating Officer
Jane Nathan, Ph.D., Research Director
A 45 hour course completed entirely on the internet, designed to help teachers implement research-based best practices in reading instruction. *$525.00*

Science

1359 Changes Around Us CD-ROM
5th Floor
6277 Sea Harbor Dr
Orlando, FL 32887

800-531-5015
FAX 800-699-9459
http://www.harcourtachieve.com
e-mail: greatservice@hmhpub.com
Linda K. Zecher, President and CEO
Eric Shuman, Chief Financial Officer
John K. Dragoon, EVP
Nature is the natural choice for observing change. By observing and researching dramatic visual sequences such as the stages of development of a butterfly, children develop a broad understanding of the concept of change. As they search this multimedia database for images and information about plant and animal life cycles and seasonal change, students strengthen their abilities in research, analysis, problem-solving, critical thinking and communication.

1360 Exploring Heat
TERC
2067 Massachusetts Ave
Cambridge, MA 02140-1340   617-873-9600
FAX 617-873-9601
http://www.terc.edu
e-mail: communications@terc.edu
Frank E. Davis Ed.D., President
Laurie Brennan, Chief Operating Officer
Carol Lumm, Director of Human Resources
A combination of lessons, software, temperature probes and activity sheets, specifically designed for the learning disabled child. *$160.00*

1361 Field Trip Into the Sea
Sunburst Technology
1550 Executive Dr
Elgin, IL 60123-9311

888-321-7511
FAX 888-800-3028
http://www.sunburst.com
e-mail: service@sunburst.com
Michael Guillory, Channel Sales/Marketing Manager
Dan Figurski, President

Visit a kelp forest and the rocky shore with this information packed guide that lets your students learn about the plants, animals and habitats of coastal environments.

1362 Field Trip to the Rain Forest
Sunburst Technology
1550 Executive Dr
Elgin, IL 60123-9311

888-321-7511
FAX 888-800-3028
http://www.sunburst.com
e-mail: service@sunburst.com
Michael Guillory, Channel Sales/Marketing Manager
Dan Figurski, President

Visit a Central American rainforest to learn more about its plants and animals with this dynamic research program that includes a useful information management tool.

1363 Learn About Life Science: Animals
Sunburst Technology
1550 Executive Dr
Elgin, IL 60123-9311

888-321-7511
FAX 888-800-3028
http://www.sunburst.com
e-mail: service@sunburst.com
Michael Guillory, Channel Sales/Marketing Manager
Dan Figurski, President

Learn about animal classification, adaptation to climate, domestication and special relationships between humans and animals.

1364 Learn About Life Science: Plants
Sunburst Technology
1550 Executive Dr
Elgin, IL 60123-9311

888-321-7511
FAX 888-800-3028
http://www.sunburst.com
e-mail: service@sunburst.com
Michael Guillory, Channel Sales/Marketing Manager
Dan Figurski, President

Students explore the world of plants. From small seeds to tall trees students learn what plants are and what they need to grow.

1365 Milliken Science Series: Circulation and Digestion
Milliken Publishing
501 East Third Street
Box 802
Dayton, OH 45401   937-228-6118
800-444-1144
FAX 937-223-2042
http://www.millikenpub.com
e-mail: lep@lorenz.com
Thomas Moore, President
Delores Boufard, Author

A program designed to introduce students to two subsystems of the human body. Provides practice using the correct terms for the various organs that make up each system, illustrating how the parts of each subsystem work together, and ensuring that students can explain the functions of the subsystems and their parts.

1366 Sammy's Science House
Riverdeep
222 3rd Ave SE
Suite 4
Cedar Rapids, IA 52401-1542   319-395-9626
800-825-4420
FAX 319-395-0217
http://http://web.riverdeep.net/portal/page?_pa
e-mail: info@riverdeep.net
Barry O'Callaghan, Executive Chairman & CEO
Jim Ruddy, Chief Revenue Officer
Tony Mulderry, EVP
Developed by early learning experts, the award-winning Sammy's Science House builds important early science skills, encourages wonder and joy as children discover the world of science around them. Five engaging activities help children practice sorting, sequencing, observing, predicting and constructing. They'll learn about plants, animals, minerals, fun seasons and weather, too! *$59.95*

1367 Talking Walls
Riverdeep
222 3rd Ave SE
Suite 4
Cedar Rapids, IA 52401-1509   319-395-9626
800-825-4420
FAX 319-395-0217
http://http://web.riverdeep.net/portal/page?_pa
e-mail: info@riverdeep.net
Barry O'Callaghan, Executive Chairman & CEO
Jim Ruddy, Chief Revenue Officer
Tony Mulderry, EVP
The Talking Walls Software Series is a wonderful springboard for a student's journey of exploration and discovery. This comprehensive collection of researched resources and materials enables students to focus on learning while conducting a guided search for information.

1368   Talking Walls: The Stories Continue
Riverdeep
222 3rd Ave SE
Suite 4
Cedar Rapids, IA 52401-1509   319-395-9626
                                           800-825-4420
                                      FAX 319-395-0217
          http://http://web.riverdeep.net/portal/page?_pa
                         e-mail: info@riverdeep.net
Barry O'Callaghan, Executive Chairman & CEO
Jim Ruddy, Chief Revenue Officer
Tony Mulderry, EVP
Using the Talking Walls Software Series, students discover
the stories behind some of the world's most fascinating
walls. The award-winning books, interactive software, carefully chosen Web sites, and suggested classroom activities
build upon each other, providing a rich learning experience
that includes text, video, and hands-on projects.

Social Studies

1369   Discoveries: Explore the Desert Ecosystem
Sunburst Technology
1550 Executive Dr
Elgin, IL 60123-9311
                                           800-321-7511
                                      FAX 888-800-3028
                              http://www.sunburst.com
                         e-mail: service@sunburst.com
Michael Guillory, Channel Sales/Marketing Manager
Dan Figurski, President

This program invites students to explore the plants, animals,
culture and georgraphy of the Sonoran Desert by day and by
night.

1370   Discoveries: Explore the Everglades Ecosystem
Sunburst Technology
1550 Executive Dr
Elgin, IL 60123-9311
                                           800-321-7511
                                      FAX 888-800-3028
                              http://www.sunburst.com
                         e-mail: service@sunburst.com
Michael Guillory, Channel Sales/Marketing Manager
Dan Figurski, President

This multi curricular research program takes students to the
Everglades where they anchor their exploration photo realistic panaramas of the habitiat.

1371   Discoveries: Explore the Forest Ecosystem
Sunburst Technology
1550 Executive Dr
Elgin, IL 60123-9311
                                           800-321-7511
                                      FAX 888-800-3028
                              http://www.sunburst.com
                         e-mail: service@sunburst.com
Michael Guillory, Channel Sales/Marketing Manager
Dan Figurski, President

This theme based CD-ROM enables students of all abilities
to actively research a multitude of different forest ecosystems in the Appalachian National Park.

1372   Imagination Express Destination: Castle
Riverdeep
222 3rd Ave SE
Suite 4
Cedar Rapids, IA 52401-1542   319-395-9626
                                           800-825-4420
                                      FAX 319-395-0217
          http://http://web.riverdeep.net/portal/page?_pa
                         e-mail: info@riverdeep.net
Barry O'Callaghan, Executive Chairman & CEO
Jim Ruddy, Chief Revenue Officer
Tony Mulderry, EVP
Kids enter a medieval kingdom where knights, jesters, wild
boars and falconers become actors in their own interactive
stories. As kids cast characters, develop plots, narrate and
write and record dialogue, they become enthusiastic writers,
editors, producers and publishers! *$59.95*

1373   Imagination Express Destination: Neighborhood
Riverdeep
222 3rd Ave SE
Suite 4
Cedar Rapids, IA 52401-1542   319-395-9626
                                           800-825-4420
                                      FAX 319-395-0217
          http://http://web.riverdeep.net/portal/page?_pa
                         e-mail: info@riverdeep.net
Barry O'Callaghan, Executive Chairman & CEO
Jim Ruddy, Chief Revenue Officer
Tony Mulderry, EVP
In Destination: Neighborhood, familiar settings and characters encourage kids to write about actual or imagined adventures. Kids enjoy developing creativity, writing and
communication skills as they explore the neighborhood and
all the people who live there. As kids select scenes, choose
and animate stickers, write, narrate, add music and record dialogue, their stories, journals, letters and poems come alive!
$59.95

1374   Imagination Express Destination: Ocean
Riverdeep
222 3rd Ave SE
Suite 4
Cedar Rapids, IA 52401-1542   319-395-9626
                                           800-825-4420
                                      FAX 319-395-0217
          http://http://web.riverdeep.net/portal/page?_pa
                         e-mail: info@riverdeep.net
Barry O'Callaghan, Executive Chairman & CEO
Jim Ruddy, Chief Revenue Officer
Tony Mulderry, EVP
The fascinating shores and depths of Destination: Ocean in-
spire kids to create interactive stories and movies. Using exciting new technology, kids make stickers move across each
scene: sharks swim through the sea kelp while dolphins leap
above waves! With Destination: Ocean, your child's writing
and creativity will soar! *$59.95*

1375   Imagination Express Destination: Pyramids
Riverdeep
222 3rd Ave SE
Suite 4
Cedar Rapids, IA 52401-1542   319-395-9626
                                           800-825-4420
                                      FAX 319-395-0217
          http://http://web.riverdeep.net/portal/page?_pa
                         e-mail: info@riverdeep.net
Barry O'Callaghan, Executive Chairman & CEO
Jim Ruddy, Chief Revenue Officer
Tony Mulderry, EVP
Kids can create interactive electronic books and movies featuring pharaohs, mummies and life on the Nile. Builds writing, creativity and communication skills as they learn about
and explore this captivating destination. Kids select scenes,
choose and animate characters, plan plots, write stories, narrate pages and add music, dialogue and sound effects to
make their own adventures. *$59.95*

1376 Imagination Express Destination: Rain Forest
Riverdeep
222 3rd Ave SE
Suite 4
Cedar Rapids, IA 52401-1542   319-365-6108
                                     800-825-4420
                              FAX 319-395-0217
http://http://web.riverdeep.net/portal/page?_pa
e-mail: info@riverdeep.net
Barry O'Callaghan, Executive Chairman & CEO
Jim Ruddy, Chief Revenue Officer
Tony Mulderry, EVP
Rain Forest invites kids to step into a Panamanian rain forest, where they craft exciting, interactive adventures filled with exotic plants, insects, waterfalls and Kuna Indians. Kids build essential communication skills as they select scenes and characters, plan plots, write, narrate, animate and record dialogue to create remarkable adventures! *$59.95*

1377 Imagination Express Destination: Time Trip USA
Riverdeep
222 3rd Ave SE
Suite 4
Cedar Rapids, IA 52401-1542   319-395-9626
                                     800-825-4420
                              FAX 319-395-0217
http://http://web.riverdeep.net/portal/page?_pa
e-mail: info@riverdeep.net
Barry O'Callaghan, Executive Chairman & CEO
Jim Ruddy, Chief Revenue Officer
Tony Mulderry, EVP
Children will love traveling through time to create interactive electronic books and movies set in a fictional New England town. As students select scenes, cast charcters, develop plots, narrate, write and record dialogue, they'll bring the town's history to life through their own exciting adventures. *$59.95*

Speech

1378 Eden Institute Curriculum: Speech and Language
2 Merwick Road
Princeton, NJ 08540-5711   609-987-0099
                              FAX 609-987-0243
http://www.edenservices.org
e-mail: info@edenservices.org
Dr. Tom Mc Cool, President/CEO
Melinda McAleer, Chief Development Officer
Anne Holmes, M.S., C.C.C.,, Chief Clinical Officer
Peceptive, expressive and pragmatic language skills programs for students with autism. *$170.00*

1379 Spectral Speech Analysis: Software
Speech Bin
PO Box 1579
Appleton, WI 54912-1579
                                     888-388-3224
                              FAX 888-388-6344
http://www.speechbin.com
e-mail: customercare@schoolspecialty.com
Tobi Isaacs MEd, Director

This exciting new software uses visual feedback as an effective speech treatment tool. Speech-language pathologists can record speech and corresponding visual displays for clients who then try to match either auditory or visual targets. These built-in visual patterns can be displayed as either sophisticated spectrograms or real-time waveforms. Item number P227. *$159.95*

Word Processors

1380 Dr. Peet's TalkWriter
Interest Driven Learning
Apt 303
446 Bouchelle Dr
New Smyrna Beach, FL 32169-5429   816-478-4824
                                     800-245-5733
                              FAX 816-478-4824
http://www.drpeet.com
e-mail: lpeet@drpeet.com
Bill William Peet, PhD, CEO
Libby Peet EdD, Adaptive Access Specialist

A talking, singing word processor designed to meet the needs of young learners from three to eight. Runs on Windows.

1381 Kids Media Magic 2.0
Sunburst Technology
1550 Executive Dr
Elgin, IL 60123-9311
                                     800-321-7511
                              FAX 888-800-3028
http://www.sunburst.com
e-mail: service@sunburst.com
Michael Guillory, Channel Sales/Marketing Manager
Dan Figurski, President

The first multimedia word processor designed for young children. Help your child become a fluent reader and writer. The Rebus Bar automatically scrolls over 45 vocabulary words as students type.

1382 Media Weaver 3.5
Sunburst Technology
1550 Executive Dr
Elgin, IL 60123-9311
                                     800-321-7511
                              FAX 888-800-3028
http://www.sunburst.com
e-mail: service@sunburst.com
Michael Guillory, Channel Sales/Marketing Manager
Dan Figurski, President

Publishing becomes a multimedia event with this dynamic word processor that contains hundreds of media elements and effective process writing resources.

1383 Sunbuddy Writer
Sunburst Technology
1550 Executive Dr
Elgin, IL 60123-9311
                                     800-321-7511
                              FAX 888-800-3028
http://www.sunburst.com
e-mail: service@sunburst.com
Michael Guillory, Channel Sales/Marketing Manager
Dan Figurski, President

An easy-to-use picture and word processor designed especially for young writers.

1384 Write: Outloud to Go
Don Johnston
26799 W Commerce Dr
Volo, IL 60073-9675   847-740-0749
                                     800-999-4660
                              FAX 847-740-7326
http://www.donjohnston.com
e-mail: info@donjohnston.com
Ruth Ziolkowski, President
Mindy Brown, Marketing Director

A flexible and user-friendly talking word processor that offers multisensory learning and positive reinforcement for writers of all ages and ability levels. Powerful features include a talking spell checker, on-screen speech and file management and color capabilities that allow for customization to meet individual needs or preferences. Requires Macintosh computer. Voted Best Special Needs Product by the Software Publishers Association. *$99.00*

Writing

1385 **Abbreviation/Expansion**
Zygo Industries
48834 Kato Road
Suite 101-A
Fremont, CA 94538   510-249-9660
                                     800-234-6006
                                 FAX 510-770-4930
                        http://www.zygo-usa.com
                     e-mail: zygo@zygo-usa.com
Lawrence H. Weiss, President

Allows the individual to define and store word/phrase abbreviations to achieve efficiency and accelerated entry rate of text. *$95.00*

1386 **Author's Toolkit**
Sunburst Technology
1550 Executive Dr
Elgin, IL 60123-9311
                                     800-321-7511
                                 FAX 888-800-3028
                        http://www.sunburst.com
                    e-mail: service@sunburst.com
Michael Guillory, Channel Sales/Marketing Manager
Dan Figurski, President

Students can use this comprehensive tool to organize ideas, make outlines, rough drafts, edit and print all their written work.

1387 **Dr. Peet's Picture Writer**
Interest Driven Learning
Apt 303
446 Bouchelle Dr
New Smyrna Beach, FL 32169-5429   386-427-4473
                                     800-245-5733
                                 FAX 816-478-4824
                          http://www.drpeet.com
                      e-mail: lpeet@drpeet.com
Bill William Peet, PhD, CEO
Libby Peet EdD, Adaptive Access Specialist

A talking picture-writer. It guides novice writers, regardless of age, motivation or ability, in creating simple talking picture sentences about things that are interesting and important to them. *$500.00*

1388 **Easybook Deluxe**
Sunburst Technology
1550 Executive Dr
Elgin, IL 60123-9311
                                     800-321-7511
                                 FAX 888-800-3028
                        http://www.sunburst.com
                    e-mail: service@sunburst.com
Michael Guillory, Channel Sales/Marketing Manager
Dan Figurski, President

Designed to support the needs of a wide range of writers, this book publishing tool provides students with a creative environment to write, design and illustrate stories and reports, and to print their work in book formats.

1389 **Fonts4Teachers**
Therapro
225 Arlington St
Framingham, MA 01702-8723   508-872-9494
                                     800-257-5376
                                 FAX 508-875-2062
                     http://www.theraproducts.com
                  e-mail: info@theraproducts.com
Karen Conrad, President

A software collection of 31 True Type fonts for teachers, parents and students. Fonts include Tracing, lined and unlined Traditional Manuscript and Cursive (similar to Zaner Blouser and D'Nealian), math, clip art, decorative, time, American Sign Language symbols and more. The included manual is very informative, with great examples of lesson plans and educational goals. *$39.95*
             Windows/Mac

1390 **Great Beginnings**
Teacher Support Software
5600 W 83rd Street
Suite 300, 8200 Tower
Bloomington, MN 55437   888-351-4199
                                     800-351-1404
                                 FAX 800-896-1760
                          http://www.gamco.com
                  e-mail: support@orchardlng.com
Robin Tinker, VP Marketing

From a broad selection of topics and descriptive words, students may create their own stories and illustrate them with colorful graphics. *$69.95*

1391 **Language Experience Recorder Plus**
Teacher Support Software
5600 W 83rd Street
Suite 300, 8200 Tower
Bloomington, MN 55437   888-351-4199
                                     800-351-1404
                                 FAX 800-896-1760
                          http://www.gamco.com
                  e-mail: support@orchardlng.com
Robin Tinker, VP Marketing

This program provides students with the opportunity to read, write and hear their own experience stories. Analyzes student writing. Cumulative word list, word and sentence counts and readability estimate. *$99.95*

1392 **Mega Dots 2.3**
Duxbury Systems
Unit 6
270 Littleton Rd
Westford, MA 01886-3523   978-692-3000
                                 FAX 978-692-7912
                     http://www.duxburysystems.com
                      e-mail: info@duxsys.com
Joe Sullivan, President
Peter Sullivan, VP of Software Development
Anne Ronco, Executive Assistant
MegaDots is a mature DOS braille translator with powerful features for the volume transcriber and producer. Its straightforward, style based system and automated features let you create great braille with only a few keystrokes, yet it is sophisticated enough to please the fussiest braille producers. You can control each step MegaDots follows to format, translate and produce braille documents. *$540.00*

1393 **Once Upon a Time Volume I: Passport to Discovery**
Compu-Teach
16541 Redmond Way
Suite C
Redmond, WA 98052-4463   425-885-0517
                                     800-448-3224
                                 FAX 425-883-9169
                       http://www.compu-teach.com
                  e-mail: info@compu-teach.com
David Urban, President

Features familiar objects associated with three unique themes. These graphic images offer limitless possibilities for new stories and illustrations. As children author books from one to hundreds of pages, they can either display them on screen or print them out. Themes: Farm Life; Down Main Street; and On Safari. *$59.95*

1394 Once Upon a Time Volume II: Worlds of Enchantment
Compu-Teach
16541 Redmond Way
Suite C
Redmond, WA 98052-4463   425-885-0517
                                                          800-448-3224
                                            FAX 425-883-9169
                                http://www.compu-teach.com
                                e-mail: info@compu-teach.com
David Urban, President

Makes writing, reading and vocabulary skills easy to learn. While building their illustrations, children experiment with perspective and other spatial relationships. This volume features familiar objects associated with three unique themes: Underwater; Dinosaur Age; and Forest Friends. *$59.95*

1395 Once Upon a Time Volume III: Journey Through Time
Compu-Teach
16541 Redmond Way
Suite C
Redmond, WA 98052-4463   425-885-0517
                                                          800-448-3224
                                            FAX 425-883-9169
                                http://www.compu-teach.com
                                e-mail: info@compu-teach.com
David Urban, President

Makes writing, reading and vocabulary skills easy to learn. With imagination as a youngster's only guide, the important concepts of story creation and illustration are naturally discovered. Themes: Medieval Times, Wild West and Outer Space. *$59.95*

1396 Once Upon a Time Volume IV: Exploring Nature
Compu-Teach
16541 Redmond Way
Suite C
Redmond, WA 98052-4463   425-885-0517
                                                          800-448-3224
                                            FAX 425-883-9169
                                http://www.compu-teach.com
                                e-mail: info@compu-teach.com
David Urban, President

The latest in award-winning creative writing series. Kids just hear, click and draw as the state of the art graphics and digitized voice make writing, reading and vocabulary skills easy to learn. Themes: Rain Forest; African Grasslands; Ocean; Desert; and Forest. *$59.95*

1397 Read, Write and Type Learning System
Talking Fingers, California Neuropsych Services
830 Rincon Way
San Rafael, CA 94903-2924   415-472-3103
                                                          800-674-9126
                                            FAX 415-472-7812
                                            TDD:415-472-3106
                                http://www.readwritetype.com
                                e-mail: contact@talkingfingers.com

Jeannine Herron, Co-Founder
Dr. Leslie Grimm, Co-Founder

A 40-level software adventure providing highly motivating instruction and practice in phonics, reading, writing, spelling and typing. This multisensory program includes 9 levels of assessment and reports. Classroom packs available.

1398 StartWrite Handwriting Software
Therapro
225 Arlington St
Framingham, MA 01702-8723   508-872-9494
                                                          800-257-5376
                                            FAX 508-875-2062
                                http://www.theraproducts.com
                                e-mail: info@theraproducts.com
Karen Conrad, President

With this easy-to-use software package, you can make papers and handwriting worksheets to meet individual student's needs. Type letters, words, or numbers and they appear in a dot format on the triple line guide. Change letter size, add shading, turn on or off guide lines and arrow strokes and place provided clipart. Fonts include Manuscript and Cursive, Modern Manuscript and Cursive and Italic Manuscript and Cursive. Useful manual included. *$39.95*
                            Windows/Mac

1399 Writing Trek Grades 4-6
Sunburst Technology
1550 Executive Dr
Elgin, IL 60123-9311
                                                          800-321-7511
                                            FAX 888-800-3028
                                http://www.sunburst.com
                                e-mail: service@sunburst.com
Michael Guillory, Channel Sales/Marketing Manager
Dan Figurski, President

Enhance your students' experience in your English language arts classroom with twelve authentic writing projects that build students' competence while encouraging creativity.

1400 Writing Trek Grades 6-8
Sunburst Technology
1550 Executive Dr
Elgin, IL 60123-9311
                                                          800-321-7511
                                            FAX 888-800-3028
                                http://www.sunburst.com
                                e-mail: service@sunburst.com
Michael Guillory, Channel Sales/Marketing Manager

Twelve authentic language arts projects, activities, and assignments develop your students' writing confidence and ability.

1401 Writing Trek Grades 8-10
Sunburst Technology
1550 Executive Dr
Elgin, IL 60123-9311
                                                          800-321-7511
                                            FAX 888-800-3028
                                http://www.sunburst.com
                                e-mail: service@sunburst.com
Michael Guillory, Channel Sales/Marketing Manager
Dan Figurski, President

Help your students develop a concept of genre as they become familiar with the writing elements and characteristics of a variety of writing forms.

General

1402   American Institute for Foreign Study
9 W Broad Street
Stamford, CT 06902   203-399-5000
                                        866-906-2437
                                    FAX 203-399-5590
                                http://www.aifs.com
                                e-mail: info@aifs.com
Sir Cyril Taylor, Founder and Chairman
Bill Gertz, President and CEO

Organizes cultural exchange programs throughout the world
for more than 50,000 students each year, and arranges insurance coverage for our own participants as well as those of
other organizations. Also provides summer travel programs
overseas and in the U.S. ranging from 1 week to a full
academic year.

1403   American-Scandinavian Foundation
58 Park Avenue
New York, NY 10016   212-879-9779
                                    FAX 212-686-1157
                            http://www.scandinaviahouse.org
                                e-mail: info@amscan.org
Edward Gallagher, President

Promotes international understanding through educational
and cultural exchange between the United States and Denmark, Finalnd, Iceland, Norway and Sweden.

1404   Andeo International Homestays
620 SW 5th Avenue
Suite 625
Portland, OR 97204-1421   503-274-1776
                                        800-274-6007
                                    FAX 503-274-9004
                                http://www.andeo.org
                                e-mail: info@andeo.org
Kellie Irish, Outbound Programs Coordinator
Helen Lawrence, Program Coordinator

Formerly International Summerstays, an international network of families, students, teachers, independent travelers
and homestay specialists who are dedicated to exploring
cross-cultural friendship and understanding.

1405   Arcadia University, College of Global Studies
450 South Easton Road
Glenside, PA 19038-3295   215-572-2901
                                        866-927-2234
                                    FAX 215-572-2174
                            http://www.arcadia.edu/abroad
                        e-mail: educationabroad@arcadia.edu
Dr Nicolette Deville Christensen, VP, College of Global
Studies
Timothy Barton, Director of Student Services

The College offers study abroad programs for undergraduate
and graduate students, internship and research opportunities, student and faculty exchanges and service learning programs, all ranging in length from semester, year, and
short-term study/research abroad programs.

1406   Army & Air Force Exchange Services
PO Box 660202
Dallas, TX 75266   214-465-6690
                                        800-527-2345
                                    FAX 214-312-3674
                                http://www.aafes.com
Thomas C. Shull, Director/Chief Executive Officer
Brig. Gen. C Blake, Deputy Director
Michael P. Howard, Chief Operating Officer
Brings tradition of value, service and support to its 11.5 mil-
lion authorized customers at military installations in the
United States, Europe and in the Pacific.

1407   Association for International Practical Training
10400 Little Patuxent Parkway
Suite 250
Columbia, MD 21044-3519   410-997-2200
                                        800-994-2443
                                    FAX 410-992-3924
                                http://www.aipt.org
                                e-mail: aipt@aipt.org
Elizabeth Chazottes, President and CEO
Karen Krug, Chief Financial Officer

Nonprofit organization dedicated to encouraging and facilitating the exchange of qualified individuals between the US
and other countries so they may gain practical work experience and improve international understanding.

1408   Basic Facts on Study Abroad
International Education
809 United Nations Plaza
New York, NY 10017-3580   212-883-8200
                                    FAX 212-984-5452
                                http://www.iie.org
                            e-mail: publications@un.org
Allen E Goodman, President and CEO
Peggy Blumenthal, Executive Vice President and COO
Jaye Chen, Executive Vice President
Information book including foreign study planning, educa-
tional choices, finances, and study abroad programs.

1409   Council on International Educational Exchange
300 Fore Street
Portland, ME 04101   207-553-4000
                                    FAX 207-553-4299
                                http://www.ciee.org
                                e-mail: contact@ciee.org
Michael Stohl, Board Chair

CIEE creates and administers programs that allow high
school and university students and educators to study and
teach abroad. Programs and literature address participants
with disabilities.

1410   Earthstewards Network
PO Box 10697
Bainbridge Island, WA 98110   206-842-7986
                                        800-561-2909
                                    FAX 206-842-8918
                            http://www.earthstewards.org
                        e-mail: outreach@earthstewards.org
Jerilyn Brusseau, Director
Bruce Haley, Director
Charlie Olson, Director
Hundreds of active, caring people in the US, Canada and
other countries. Puts North American teenagers working
alongside Northern Irish teenagers and more.

1411   Educational Foundation for Foreign Study
1 Education St
Cambridge, MA 02141-1805
                                        800-447-4273
                                    FAX 617-619-1401
                                http://www.effoundation.org
                                e-mail: foundation@ef.com
Offers an opportunity to study and live for a year in a foreign
country for students between the ages of 15 and 18.

**1412   High School Student's Guide To Study, Travel and Ad-
venture Abroad**
Council on International Education Exchange
300 Fore Street
Portland, ME 04101   207-553-4000
                                        800-407-8839
                                    FAX 207-553-4299
                                http://www.ciee.org
                                e-mail: contact@ciee.org
James P. Pellow, CEO and President
Robert E. Fallon, Chair of Board of Directors
Kenton Keith, Vice Chair/Secretary

This guide provides high school students with all the information they need for a successful trip abroad. Included are sections to help students find out if they're ready for a trip abroad, make the necessary preparations, and get the most rom their experience. Over 200 programs are described including language study, summer camps, homestays, study tours, and work camps. The program descriptions include information for people with disabilities.

1413 Higher Education Consortium for Urban Affairs

2233 University Ave W
Suite 210
Saint Paul, MN 55114-1698

651-287-3300
FAX 651-659-9421
http://www.hecua.org
e-mail: hecua@hecua.org

Jenny Keyser, Executive Director
Patrick Mulvihill, Director of Operations
Sarah Pradt, Director of Programs
Consortium of 15 Midwest colleges and universities offering undergraduate, academic programs, both international and domestic that incorporate field study and internships in the examination of urban and global issues.

1414 International Cultural Youth Exchange (ICYE)

134 W 26th Street
New York, NY 10001

212-206-7307
FAX 212-633-9085
http://www.icye.org
e-mail: icye@icye.org

A nonprofit youth exchange promoting youth mobility, intercultural learning and international voluntary service. ICYE organizes long- and short-term exchanges combining home stays with voluntary service in 34 countries around the world.

1415 International Partnership for Service-Learning and Leadership

1515 SW 5th Ave.
Suite 606
Portland, OR 97201

503-954-1812
FAX 503-954-1881
http://www.ipsl.org
e-mail: info@ipsl.org

Thomas Winston Morgan, President
Arianne Newton, Director of Programs

A not-for-profit educational organization incorporated in NYS serving students, collegs, universities, service agencies and related organizations around the world by fostering programs that link volunteer service to the community and academic study.

1416 Lions Club International

300 W 22nd Street
Oak Brook, IL 60523-8842

630-571-5466
FAX 630-571-8890
http://www.lionsclub.org
e-mail: districtadministration@lionsclub.org

Wayne A. Madden, International President
Barry J. Palmer, First Vice President
Joseph Preston, Second Vice President
Over 46,000 individual clubs in over 190 countries and geographical areas, providing community service and promoting improved international relations. Clubs work with local communities to provide needed and useful programs for sight, diabetes and hearing, and aid in study abroad.

1417 Lisle

900 County Road 269
Leander, TX 78641-1633

512-259-4404
800-477-1538
http://www.lisleinternational.org
e-mail: lisle2@io.com

Mark Kinney, Executive Director
Lori Bratton, Secretary
Barbara Bratton, Treasurer/Operations Mgr

Educational organization which works toward world peace and a better quality of human life through increased understanding between persons of similar and different cultures.

1418 Mobility International (MIUSA)

132 E Broadway
Suite 343
Eugene, OR 97401

541-323-1284
FAX 541-343-6812
TTY: 541-343-1284
http://www.miusa.org

Susan Sygall, CEO

MIUSA offers short-term international exchange programs in the US and abroad for people with and without disabilities, including non-apparent disabilities.

1419 National Society for Experimental Education

19 Mantua Rd
Mount Royal, NJ 08061-1006

856-423-3427
FAX 856-423-3420
http://www.nsee.org
e-mail: nsee@talley.com

James Walters, President
Pam Brumbaugh, President Elect
Haley Brust, Executive Director
A nonprofit membership association of educators, businesses, and community leaders. Also serves as a national resource center for the development and improvement of experimental education programs nationwide.

1420 No Barriers to Study

Lock Haven University
401 N Fairview St
Lock Haven, PA 17745-2342

570-484-2053
http://http://www.lhup.edu/
e-mail: honors_program@lhup.edu

Dr. Jackie Whitling, Program Director
Joanie Walker, Program Secretary
Brent Barge, Student Associate
A regional consortium committed to facilitating study abroad for college students with disabilities.

1421 People to People International

911 Main St
Suite 2110
Kansas City, MO 64105-5305

816-531-4701
FAX 816-561-7502
http://www.ptpi.org
e-mail: ptpi@ptpi.org

Mary Eisenhower, President, CEO
Brian Hueben, Vice President, Finance
Rosanne Rosen, SVP
Nonpolitical, nonprofit organization working outside the government to advance the cause of international understanding through international contact.

1422 SUNY Buffalo Office of International Education

1300 Elmwood Avenue
South Wing 410
Buffalo, NY 14222

716-878-4620
FAX 716-878-3054
http://www.buffalostate.edu/studyabroad
e-mail: intleduc@buffalostate.edu

Lee Ann Grace, Director
Hal D. Payne, Vice President, Student Affairs

1423 Sister Cities International

915 15th Street, NW
4th Floor
Washington, DC 20005

202-347-8630
FAX 202-393-6524
http://www.sister-cities.org
e-mail: info@sister-cities.org

Patrick Madden, President
Launa Kowalski, Chair
Nancy Eidam, Operating Officer

A nonprofit citizen diplomacy network; creating and strengthening partnerships between the US and international communities in an effort to increase global cooperation at the municipal level, to promote cultural understanding, and to stimulate economic development. Encourages local community development and volunteer action by motivating and empowering private citizens, municipal officials and business leaders to conduct long-term programs of mutual benefit, including exchange situations.

1424   Study Abroad
Davidson College
Box 7155
Davidson, NC 28035   704-894-2250
                                       FAX 704-894-2120
http://http://www3.davidson.edu/cms/x12.xml?deb
                          e-mail: abroad@davidson.edu
Jill Gremmels, Director of the Library
Jill Gremmels, Director of the Library
Lisa Smith, Staff Assistant to the Director

1425   World Experience
2440 S Hacienda Blvd
Suite 116
Hacienda Heights, CA 91745-4763   626-330-5719
                                           800-633-6653
                                       FAX 626-333-4914
http://www.worldexperience.org
e-mail: info@worldexperience.org

Kerry Gonzales, President
Marge Archambault, President

Offers a quality and affordable program for over three decades and continues to provide students and host families a youth exchange program based on individual attention, with the help of an international network of overseas directors and USA coordinators

1426   Youth for Understanding USA
6400 Goldsboro Rd
Suite 100
Bethesda, MD 20817-5841   240-235-2100
                                           800-833-6243
                                       FAX 240-235-2104
http://www.yfu-usa.org
e-mail: admissions@yfu.org

Mike Finnell, President
David Barber, Director Admissions/Registration

Nonprofit international exchange program, prepares young people for their responsibilities and opportunities in todays changing, interdependent world through homestay exchange programs. Offers year, semester, and summer study abroad and scholarship opportunities in 40 countries worldwide.

Federal

1427 ABLE DATA
USDE National Institution on Disability/Rehab
Ste 930
8630 Fenton St
Silver Spring, MD 20910-3820   301-608-8998
800-227-0216
FAX 301-608-8958
TDD:301-608-8912
http://www.abledata.com
e-mail: abledata@macrointernational.com
Katherine Belknap, Project Director
Juanita Hardy, Information Specialist
David Johnson, Publications Director
Sponsored by the National Institute on Disability and Reha-
bilitation Research (NIDRR) of the US Department of Edu-
cation; provides information on more than 34,000 assistive
technology products, including detailed descriptions of each
product, price and company information.

1428 ADA Information Line
US Department of Justice
950 Pennsylvania Ave NW
Washington, DC 20530-0009   800-514-0301
FAX 202-307-1197
TTY: 800-514-0383
http://www.ada.gov
John L Wodatch, Chief

Answers questions about Title II (public services) and Title
III (public accommodations) of the Americans with Disabilities Act (ADA). Provides materials and technical assistance
on the provisions of the ADA.

1429 ADA Technical Assistance Programs
US Department of Justice
950 Pennsylvania Ave NW
Washington, DC 20530-0001   202-514-2000
800-514-0301
TTY: 800-514-0383
http://www.usdoj.gov
e-mail: AskDOJ@usdoj.gov
Federally funded regional resource centers that provide information and referral, technical assistance, public awareness, and training on all aspects of the Americans with
Disabilities Act (ADA).

1430 Americans with Disabilities Act (ADA) Resource Center

National Center for State Courts
300 Newport Ave
Williamsburg, VA 23185-4147   757-259-1819
800-616-6164
FAX 757-220-0449
http://www.ncsconline.org
e-mail: webmaster@ncsc.dni.us
Mary McQueen, President
Robert Baldwin, Exec. VP and General Counsl.

Disseminates information on ADA compliance to state and
local court systems. Will develop a diagnostic checklist and
strategies for compliance specifically relevant to the state
and local courts.

1431 Civil Rights Division: US Department of Justice
Office of the Assistant Attorney General
950 Pennsylvania Ave NW
Washington, DC 20530-0001   202-514-2000
FAX 202-514-0293
TDD:202-514-0716
http://www.usdoj.gov
e-mail: AskDOJ@usdoj.gov
Eric Holder, Attorney General

The program institution within the federal government responsible for enforcing federal statutes prohibiting discrimination on the basis of race, sex, disability, religion, and
national origin.

1432 Clearinghouse on Adult Education and Literacy
US Department of Education
400 Maryland Ave SW
Washington, DC 20202-0001   800-872-5327
FAX 202-401-0689
TTY: 800-437-0833
http://www.ed.gov
Arne Duncan, Secretary of Education

The Clearinghouse was established in 1981 to link the adult
education community with existing resources in adult education, provide information which deals with state administered adult education programs funded under the Adult
Education and Family Literacy Act, and provide resources
that support adult education activities.

1433 Clearinghouse on Disability Information
Office of Special Education/Rehabilitative Service
400 Maryland Ave SW
550 12th St SW
Washington, DC 20202   202-245-7307
FAX 202-245-7636
TDD:202-205-5637
http://www.ed.gov
Carolyn Corlett, Contact

Provides information to people with disabilities, or anyone
requesting information, by doing research and providing
documents in response to inquiries. Information provided
includes areas of federal funding for disability-related programs. Staff is trained to refer requests to other sources of
disability-related information, if necessary.

**1434 Employment and Training Administration: US Depart-
ment of Labor**
Frances Perkins Building
200 Constitution Ave NW
Washington, DC 20210-0001   202-693-2700
877-872-5627
FAX 202-693-2726
TTY: 877-889-5627
http://www.doleta.gov
e-mail: etapagemaster@dol.gov
Jane Oates, Asst Secretary, ETA

Administers federal government job training and worker
dislocation programs, federal grants to states for public employment service programs, and unemployment insurance
benefits. These services are primarily provided through
state and local workforce development systems.

1435 Equal Employment Opportunity Commission
131 M Street, NE
Washington, DC 20507-0001   202-663-4900
800-669-4000
TTY: 202-663-4494
http://www.eeoc.gov
e-mail: info@eeoc.gov
Stuart Ishimaru, Acting Chair

Enforces Section 501 which prohibits discrimination on the
basis of disability in Federal employment, and requires that
all Federal agencies establish and implement affirmative action programs for hiring, placing and advancing individuals
with disabilities. Also oversees Federal sector equal employment opportunity complaint processing system.

1436 Eunice Kennedy Shriver National Institute of Child Health and Human Development (NICHD)
National Institutes of Health
PO Box 3006
Rockville, MD 20847-0001
800-370-2943
FAX 866-760-5947
TTY: 888-320-6942
http://www.nichd.nih.gov
e-mail: NICHDInformationResourceCenter@mail.nih.gov

Alan E Guttmacher, MD, Acting Director

The mission of the Eunice Kennedy Shriver National Institute of Child Health and Human Development (NICHD) is to ensure that every person is born healthy and wanted, that women suffer no harmful effects from the reproductive process, that all children have the chance to fulfill their potential to live healthy and productive lives free from disease or disability, and to ensure the health, productivity, independence and well-being of all people through optimal rehabilitation.

1437 National Council on Disability
Ste 850
1331 F St NW
Washington, DC 20004-1138
202-272-2004
FAX 202-272-2022
TTY: 202-272-2074
http://www.ncd.gov
e-mail: executivedirector@ncd.gov
Mike Collins, Executive Director
Joan M Durocher, Executive Director (Interim)

An independent federal agency comprised of 15 members appointed by the President and confirmed by the Senate.

1438 National Institute of Mental Health
Science Writing, Press & Dissemination Branch
6001 Executive Blvd
Room 8184, MSC 9663
Bethesda, MD 20892-9663
301-443-4513
866-615-6464
FAX 301-443-4279
TTY: 301-443-8431
http://www.nimh.nih.gov
e-mail: nimhinfo@nih.gov
Dr Thomas R Insel MD, Director

Mission is to diminish the burden of mental illness through research. This public health mandate demands that we harness powerful scientific tools to achieve better understanding, treatment and eventually prevention of mental illness.

1439 National Institute on Disability and Rehabilitation Research
US Department of Education
400 Maryland Ave SW
Washington, DC 20202-0001
202-245-7640
FAX 202-245-7323
http://www.ed.gov
Andrew Pepin, Executive Administrator

Provides leadership and support for a comprehensive program of research related to the rehabilitation of individuals with disabilities. All of the programmatic efforts are aimed to improving the lives of individuals with disabilities from birth through adulthood.

1440 National Library Services for the Blind and Physically Handicapped
1291 Taylor St NW
Washington, DC 20011
202-707-5100
888-657-7323
FAX 202-707-0712
TDD:202-707-0744
http://www.loc.gov/nls
e-mail: nls@loc.gov

Frank Cylke, Director

Administers a national library service that provdies braille and recorded books and magazines on free loan to anyone who cannot read standard print becuase of visual or physical disabilities.

1441 National Technical Information Service: US Department of Commerce
5301 Shawnee Rd
Alexandria, VA 22312
703-605-6000
800-553-6847
FAX 703-605-6900
http://www.ntis.gov
e-mail: info@ntis.gov

Ellen Herbst, Director

Serves the nation as the largest central resource for government-funded scientific, technical, engineering, and business related information available today.

1442 Office for Civil Rights: US Department of Health and Human Services
200 Independence Ave SW
Rm 509F, HHH Bldg
Washington, DC 20201
877-696-6775
TDD:800-537-7697
http://www.hhs.gov/ocr
e-mail: www.hhs.gov/ocr

Winston Wilkinson, Director

Promotes and ensures that people have equal access to an dopportunity to participate in and receive services from all HHS programs without facing unlawful discrimination, and that the privacy of their health information is protectec while ensuring access to care.

1443 Office for Civil Rights: US Department of Education
400 Maryland Ave SW
Washington, DC 20202-1100
800-421-3481
FAX 202-453-6012
TDD:877-521-2172
http://www.ed.gov/ocr
e-mail: ocr@ed.gov
Russlynn Ali, Asst Secretary for Civil Rights

To ensure equal access to education and to promote educational excellence throughout the nation through vigourous enforcement of civil rights.

1444 Office of Disability Employment Policy: US Department of Labor
200 Constitution Ave SW
Washington, DC 20210-0001
866-487-2365
FAX 202-693-7888
TTY: 877-889-5627
http://www.dol.gov
Provides national leadership by developing and influencing disability-related employment policy as well as practice affecting the employment of people with disabilities.

1445 Office of Federal Contract Compliance Programs: US Department of Labor
200 Constitution Ave SW
Washington, DC 20210-0001
866-487-2365
TTY: 877-889-5627
http://www.dol.gov
e-mail: ofccp-public@dol.gov
Kathleen Martinez, Assistant Secretary

Responsible for ensuring that employers doing business with the Federal government comply with the laws and regulations requiring nondiscrimination and affirmative action in employment.

1446 Office of Personnel Management
1900 E St NW
Washington, DC 20415   202-606-1800
                              TTY: 202-606-2532
                              http://www.opm.gov
                              e-mail: general@opm.gov
Linda M Springer, Director

The central personnel agency of the federal government. Provides information on the selective placement program for persons with disabilities.

1447 Rehabilitation Services Administration State Vocational Program
US Department of Education
400 Maryland Ave SW
Washington, DC 20202-0001   202-245-7488
                                   http://www.ed.gov
Edward Anthony, Deputy Commissioner

State and local vocational rehabilitation agencies provide comprehensive services of rehabilitation, training and job-related assistance to people with disabilities and assist employers in recruiting, training, placing, accommodating and meeting other employment-related needs of people with disabilities.

1448 Social Security Administration
Office of Public Inquiries
6401 Security Blvd
Baltimore, MD 21235-6401   410-965-6114
                                  800-772-1213
                                  FAX 410-966-2027
                                  TTY: 800-325-0778
                                  http://www.socialsecurity.gov
Bill Vitek, Commissioner

Provides financial assistance to those with disabilities who meet eligibility requirements.

1449 US Bureau of the Census
4600 Silver Hill Rd
Washington, DC 20233-0002   301-763-3030
                                   FAX 301-457-3670
                                   http://www.census.gov
                                   e-mail: pio@census.gov
Thomas E Zebelsky, Director

The principal statistical agency of the federal government. It publishes data on persons with disabilities, as well as other demographic data derived from censuses and surveys.

1450 US Department of Health & Human Services
200 Independence Ave SW
Washington, DC 20201-0004   202-690-7650
                                   877-696-6775
                                   http://www.hhs.gov
Mike Leavitt, Secretary

Councils in each state provide training and technical assistance to local and state agencies, employers and the public, improving services to people with developmental disabilities.

Alabama

1451 Alabama Council for Developmental Disabilities
P.O.Box 301410
100 North Union St
Montgomery, AL 36130-1410   334-242-3973
                                   800-232-2158
                                   FAX 334-242-0797
                                   http://www.acdd.org
                                   e-mail: debra.florea@mh.alabama.gov
Elmyra Jones, Executive Director

Serves as an advocate for Alabama's citizens with developmental disabilities and their families; to empower them with the knowledge and opportunity to make informed choices and exercise control over their own lives; and to create a climate for positive social change to enable them to be respected, independent and productive integrated members of society.

1452 Alabama Department of Industrial Relations
649 Monroe St
Montgomery, AL 36131-0099   334-242-8990
                                   FAX 334-242-3960
                                   http://dir.alabama.gov
                                   e-mail: director@dir.alabama.gov
Tom Surtees, Director

To effectively use tax dollars to provide state and federal mandated workforce protection programs promoting a positive economic environment for Alabama employers and workers and to produce and disseminate information on the Alabama economy.

1453 Alabama Disabilities Advocacy Program
P.O.Box 870395
Tuscaloosa, AL 35487-0001   205-348-4928
                                   800-826-1675
                                   FAX 205-348-3909
                                   http://www.adap.net
                                   e-mail: adap@adap.ua.edu
Ellen Gillespie, Director

To provide quality, legally-based advocacy services to Alabamians with disabilities in order to protect, promote and expand their rights.

1454 Employment Service Division: Alabama
Department of Industrial Relations
649 Monroe St
Montgomery, AL 36131-0001   334-242-8003
                                   FAX 334-242-8012
                                   http://dir.alabama.gov
                                   e-mail: es@dir.alabama.gov
Bob Brantley, Director

Alaska

1455 Alaska State Commission for Human Rights
800 A St
Ste 204
Anchorage, AK 99501-7500   907-274-4692
                                  800-478-4692
                                  FAX 907-278-8588
                                  TDD:907-276-3177
                                  http://www.gov.state.ak.us
Paula Haley, Executive Director
Anne Keene, Administrative Officer

The state agency which enforces the Alaska Human Rights Law. Consists of seven persons appointed by the governor and confirmed by the legislature.

1456 Assistive Technology of Alaska (ATLA)
Ste 4
2217 E Tudor Rd
Anchorage, AK 99507-1068   907-563-2599
                                  800-723-2852
                                  FAX 907-563-0699
                                  http://atlaak.com
                                  e-mail: atla@atlaak.org
Kathy Privratsky, Executive Director

To enhance the quality of life for Alaskans through education, demonstration, consultation, acquisition and implementation of assistive technologies. ATLA is Alaska's only assistive technology project for the Tech Act.

1457 Center for Community
Ste B
700 Katlian St
Sitka, AK 99835-7359

907-747-6960
800-478-6970
FAX 907-747-4868
http://www.ptialaska.net/~cfcsitka
Connie Sipe, Executive Director
Margaret Andrews, Deputy Executive Director

Center for Community is a multiservice agency that provides early intervention, respite, futures planning, functional skills training, and vocational assistance and personal care for people with disabilities.

1458 Correctional Education Division: Alaska
Department of Corrections/Division of Institutions
Ste 601
550 W 7th Ave
Anchorage, AK 99501

907-269-7397
FAX 907-269-7390
http://www.correct.state.ak.us/
e-mail: anna.herzberger@alaska.gov
Anna Herberger, Criminal Justice Planner
Leslie Houston, Director

1459 Disability Law Center of Alaska
Ste 103
3330 Arctic Blvd
Anchorage, AK 99503-4580

907-565-1002
800-478-1234
FAX 907-565-1000
http://www.dlcak.org
e-mail: akpa@dlcak.org
David Fleurant, Executive Director

An independent non-profit organization that provides legal advocacyservices for people with disabilities anywhere in Alaska. To promote and protect the legal and human rights of individuals with physical and/or mental disabilities.

1460 Employment Security Division
Alaska Department of Labor & Workforce Development
P.O.Box 115509
Juneau, AK 99811-5509

907-465-2712
FAX 907-465-4537
http://labor.state.ak.us
e-mail: esd.director@alaska.gov
Tom Nelson, Director

Promotes employment, economic stability, and growth by operating a no-fee labor exchange that meets the needs of employers, job seekers, and veterans.

1461 State Department of Education & Early Development
State of Alaska
PO Box 110500
Juneau, AK 99811-0500

907-465-2800
FAX 907-465-4156
http://www.eed.state.ak.us
Larry LeDoux, Commissioner
Esther J Cox, State Board of Education Chair

State education agency

1462 State GED Administration: GED Testing Program
Alaska Department of Education
Ste 200
801 W 10th St
Juneau, AK 99811-0500

907-465-2880
FAX 907-465-4156
TTY: 907-465-2815
http://www.eed.state.ak.us/
e-mail: eed.webmaster@alaska.gov

Roger Samson, Commissioner
Karen Rehfeld, Executive Director
Barbara Thompson, TLS Director

Arizona

1463 Arizona Center for Disability Law
Ste 202
5025 E Washington St
Phoenix, AZ 85034

602-274-6287
800-927-2260
FAX 602-274-6779
TTY: 602-274-6287
http://www.azdisabilitylaw.org
e-mail: center@azdisabilitylaw.org
Lorraine Freyer, Executive Director

Advocates for the leagl rights of persons with disabilities to be free from abuse, neglect and discrimination; and to have access to education, healthcare, housing and jobs, and other services in order to maximize independence and achieve equality.

1464 Arizona Center for Law in the Public Interest
2205 E Speedway
Tucson, AZ 85719-4728

520-529-1798
FAX 520-529-2927
http://www.aclpi.org
e-mail: jherrcardillo@aclpi.org
Bruce Samuels, President
Timothy M Hogan, Executive Director

A non-profit law firm dedicated to ensuring government accountability and protecting the legal rights of Arizonans.

1465 Arizona Department of Economic Security
Rehabilitation Services Administration
Suite 200
3221 N 16th St
Phoenix, AZ 85016-7159

602-266-6752
800-563-1221
FAX 602-241-7158
TTY: 602-241-1048
http://www.azdes.gov/rsa
e-mail: (email from) www.azdes.gov
Tracy Wareing, Director
Sharon Sergent, Deputy Director

Promotes the safety, well-being, and self sufficiency of children, asults and families.

1466 Arizona Department of Education
1535 W Jefferson St
Phoenix, AZ 85007

602-542-5393
800-352-4558
http://www.ade.az.gov
Tom Horne, Public Instruction Supt

To ensure academic excellence for all students.

1467 Arizona Governor's Committee on Employment of the Handicapped
ALS Association Arizona Chapter
Ste 1
4643 E Thomas Rd
Phoenix, AZ 85018-7740

602-297-3800
866-350-2572
FAX 602-297-3804
http://www.alsaz.org
e-mail: ken@alsaz.org

Ken Brissa, President & CEO

To lead the fight to cure and treat ALS through global, cutting-edge research, and to empower people with Lou Gehrig's disease and their families to live fuller lives by providing them with compassionate care and support.

1468 Correctional Education
Arizona Department of Corrections
1601 W Jefferson St
Phoenix, AZ 85007-3002   602-542-1160
                              FAX 602-364-0259
                    e-mail: bkilian@adc.state.az.us

Dora Schriro, Manager

1469 Division of Adult Education
Arizona Department of Education
P.O.Box 26
Phoenix, AZ 85001-0026   602-258-2410
                              FAX 602-258-4977
                        http://www.ade.az.gov

Karen Liersch, Director

To ensure that learners 16 years of age and older have access
to quality educational opportunities.

1470 Fair Employment Practice Agency
Office of the Arizona Attorney General
1275 W Washington St
Phoenix, AZ 85007-2926   602-542-5025
                                800-352-8431
                              FAX 602-542-4085
                              TDD:602-542-5002
                              TTY: 602-542-5002
                        http://www.azag.gov
                    e-mail: civilrightsinfo@azag.gov

Terry Goddard, Attorney General

1471 GED Testing Services
Arizona Department of Education
P.O.Box 26
Phoenix, AZ 85001-0026   602-258-2410
                              FAX 602-258-4977
                        http://www.ade.az.gov
                    e-mail: phxged@ade.az.gov

Karen Liersch, Director

1472 Governor's Council on Developmental Disabilities
Ste 201
1740 West Adams
Phoenix, AZ 85007   602-542-8970
                                877-665-3176
                              FAX 602-542-8978
                              TTY: 602-542-8979
                        http://www.azgcdd.org
                    e-mail: djohnson@azdes.gov

Stephen W Tully, Chairman
Karla Phillips, Vice Chairman

To work in partnership with individuals with developmental
disabilities and their families through systems change, advocacy and capacity building activities that promote
indpendence, choice and the ability to pursue their own
dreams.

Arkansas

1473 Arkansas Department of Corrections
PO Box 8707
Pine Bluff, AR 71611-8707   870-267-6999
                              FAX 870-267-6244
                        http://www.arkansas.gov

Ray Hobbs, Director

To provide public safety by carrying out the mandates of the
courts; provide a safe humane environment for staff and inmates; provide programs to strengthen the work ethic; and
provide opportunities for spiritual, mental, and physical
growth.

1474 Arkansas Department of Education
4 Capitol Mall
Little Rock, AR 72201-1019   501-682-4475
                              FAX 501-682-1079
                        http://arkansased.org

Tom Kimbrell, Commissioner

Strives to ensure that all children in the state have acess to a
quality education by providing educators, administrators
anad staff with leadership, resources and training.

1475 Arkansas Department of Special Education
1401 W Capitol Ave
Victory Bldg., Suite 450
Little Rock, AR 72201-2936   501-682-4221
                              FAX 501-682-5159
                              TTY: 501-682-4222
                        http://arksped.k12.ar.us
                    e-mail: spedsupport@arkansas.gov

Marcia Harding, Associate Director

1476 Arkansas Department of Workforce Education
3 Capitol Mall
Luther Hardin Bldg.
Little Rock, AR 72201-1005   501-682-1500
                              FAX 501-682-1509
                        http://dwe.arkansas.gov

Bill Walker, Director

To provide the leadership and contribute resources to serve
the diverse and changing workforce training needs of the
youth and adults in Arkansas.

1477 Arkansas Department of Workforce Services
P.O.Box 2981
#2 Capitol Mall
Little Rock, AR 72201-2981   501-682-3106
                              FAX 501-682-3748
                              TDD:501-296-1669
                        http://www.dws.arkansas.gov
                    e-mail: artee.williamson@arkansas.gov

Freddy Jacobs, Equal Opportunity Manager

**1478 Arkansas Governor's Developmental Disabilities
Council**
Ste 805
5800 W 10th St
Little Rock, AR 72204-1763   501-661-2589
                                800-462-0599
                              FAX 501-661-2399
                        http://www.ddcouncil.org
                    e-mail: mary.edwards@arkansas.gov

Mary Edwards, Council Coordinator

Supports people with developmental disabilities in the
achievement of independence, productivity, integration and
inclusion in the community.

1479 Assistive Technology Project
Increasing Capabilities Access Network (ICAN)
26 Corporate Hill Dr
Little Rock, AR 72205-4538   501-666-8868
                                800-828-2799
                              FAX 501-666-5319
                        http://www.arkansas-ican.org

A consumer responsive statewide program promoting
assistive technology devices and resources for persons of all
ages and all disabilities.

1480 Client Assistance Program (CAP) Disability Rights Center of Arkansas
1100 N University Ave
Suite 201
Little Rock, AR 72207-6343
501-296-1775
800-482-1174
FAX 501-296-1779
http://www.arkdisabilityrights.org
e-mail: panda@arkdisabilityrights.org
Nan Ellen East, Executive Director
Eddie Miller, CAP Director

The purpose of CAP is to protect the rights of persons receiving or seeking services funded under the federal Rehabilitation Act. According to thise law, CAP services are available for all clients or applicants of the following services: Vocational Rehabilitation Services, Independent Living Services, Supported Employment, Independent Living Centers, and Projects with Industry.

1481 Increasing Capabilities Access Network
26 Corporate Hill Dr
Little Rock, AR 72205-4538
501-666-8868
800-828-2799
FAX 501-666-5319
TDD:501-666-8868
http://www.arkansas-ican.org
e-mail: info@ar-ican.org
Linda Morgan, Project Administrator

A federally funded program of Arkansas Rehabilitation Services, is designed to make technology available and accessible for all who need it. ICAN is a funding information resource and provides information on new and existing technology free to any person regardless of age or disability.

1482 Office of the Governor
State Capitol Room 250
Little Rock, AR 72201
501-682-2345
FAX 501-682-1382
http://www.governor.arkansas.gov
Mike Beebe, Governor

1483 Protection & Advocacy Agency
Disability Rights Center
1100 N University Ave
Little Rock, AR 72207-6343
501-296-1775
800-482-1174
FAX 501-296-1779
TTY: 302-575-0696
http://www.arkdisabilityrights.org
e-mail: panda@arkdisabilityrights.org
Nan Ellen East, Executive Director

Carry out activities under several Federal programs to provide a range of services to adocate for and protect the rights of persons with disabilities throughout the state

1484 State GED Administration
Arkansas Department of Workforce Education
Rm 305
3 Capitol Mall
Little Rock, AR 72201-1013
501-682-1980
FAX 501-682-1982
http://dwe.arkansas.gov
e-mail: tambra.nicholson@mail.state.ar.us
Janice Hanlon, GED Test Administrator

Serves all Arkansans who are 16 years or older, not enrolled in or graduated from high school, and who meet other state requirements regarding residency and testing eligibility.

California

1485 California Department of Fair Employment and Housing
2218 Kausen Dr
Ste 100
Elk Grove, CA 95758
916-478-7251
FAX 916-478-7329
http://www.dfeh.ca.gov
Phyllis W Cheng, Director

To protect the people of California from unlawful discrimination in employment, housing and public accomodations, and from the perpetration of acts of hate violence.

1486 California Department of Rehabilitation
P.O.Box 944222
721 Capitol Mall
Sacramento, CA 94244-2220
916-324-1313
TTY: 916-558-5807
http://www.rehab.cahwnet.gov
e-mail: externalaffairs@dor.ca.gov
Tony Sauer, Director

Works in partnership with consumers and other stakeholders to provide services and advocacy resulting in employment, independent living and equality for individuals with disabilities.

1487 California Department of Special Education
1430 N St
Sacramento, CA 95814-5901
916-319-0800
TTY: 916-445-4556
http://www.cde.ca.gov
e-mail: scheduler@cde.ca.gov
Mary Hudler, Director

Information and reesources to serve the unique needs of persons with disabilities so that each person will meet or exceed high standards of achivement in academic and nonacademic skills.

1488 California Employment Development Department
800 Capitol Mall, MIC 83
Sacramento, CA 95814-4807
916-654-8210
FAX 916-657-5294
http://www.edd.ca.gov
Patrick Henning, Director

Promotes California's economic growth by providing services to keep employers, employees, and job seekers competitive.

1489 California State Board of Education
Ste 5111
1430 N St
Sacramento, CA 95814-5901
916-319-0827
FAX 916-319-0175
http://www.cde.ca.gov
Debra Merle, Executive Director

The State Board of Education (SBE) is the governing and policy making body of the California Department of Education. The SBE sets K-12 education policy in the areas of standards, instructional materials, accessment, and accountability.

1490 California State Council on Developmental Disabilities
Ste 210
1507 21st St
Sacramento, CA 95811-5297
916-322-8481
866-802-0514
FAX 916-443-4957
http://www.scdd.ca.gov
e-mail: council@dss.ca.gov
Alan Kerzin, Executive Director

Advocates, promotes and implements policies and practices that achieve self-determination, independence, productivity and inclusion in all aspects of community life for Californians with developmental disabilities and their families.

1491 Career Assessment and Placement Center Whittier Union High School District
9401 Painter Ave
Whittier, CA 90605-2729   562-698-8121
                                        FAX 562-693-5354
Daniel Hubert

Provides job placement programs, remunerative work services and work adjustment training programs.

1492 Clearinghouse for Specialized Media
California Department of Education
1430 N St
Ste 3207
Sacramento, CA 95814-5901   916-455-5103
                                       FAX 916-323-9732
                            http://www.cde.ca.gov/re/pn/sm
                                  e-mail: cgmt@cde.ca.gov
Thomas Adams, Director
Jonn Paris-Salb, Education Administrator I

Provides accessible formats of adopted curriculum to qualified students with disabilities in California.

1493 DBTAC: Pacific ADA Center
Ste 1030
555 12th St
Oakland, CA 94607-4046   510-285-5600
                                       800-949-4232
                                       FAX 510-285-5614
                            http://www.adapacific.org
Erica Jones, Director

To build a partnership between the disability and business communities and to promote full and unrestricted participation in society for persons with disabilities through education and technical assistance.

1494 Disability Rights California (California's Protection and Advocacy System)
100 Howe Ave
Ste 135N
Sacramento, CA 95825   916-488-9950
                                       800-776-5746
                                       FAX 916-488-9960
                                       TTY: 800-719-5798
                       http://www.disabilityrightsca.org
               e-mail: legalmail@disabilityrightsca.org
Catherine Blakemore, Executive Director
Andrew Mudryk, Deputy Director
Stuart Seaborn, Managing Attorney
A private, nonprofit organization that protects the legal, civil and service rights of Californians with disabilities.
1978

1495 Education & Inmate Programs Unit
P.O.Box 942883
Sacramento, CA 94283-0001   916-445-8035
                                       800-952-5544
                                       FAX 916-324-1416
                            http://www.corr.ca.gov
Jan Stuter, Manager
Gary Sutherland, Federal Grand Administrator
Adrianne Johnson, Secretary

1496 Employment Development Department: Employment Services Woodland
800 Capitol Mall
Sacramento, CA 95814-4807   530-661-2600
                                       FAX 530-668-3152
                            http://www.edd.ca.gov

Bill Burke, Contact

The Employment Development Department promote's California's economic growth by providing services to keep employers, employees, and job seekers competitive.

1497 Employment Development Department: Employment Services W Sacramento
California Health & Human Services Agency
500 Jefferson Blvd
W Sacramento, CA 95605-2350   916-375-6288
                                       FAX 916-375-6310
                                       http://www.edd.ca.gov

Bill Burke, Contact

1498 Office of Civil Rights: California
US Department of Education
Ste 7200
50 Beale St
San Francisco, CA 94105-1813   415-486-5555
                                       800-949-4232
                                       FAX 510-285-5614
                                       TDD:877-521-2172
                                       http://www.ed.gov
                       e-mail: ocr.sanfrancisco@ed.gov

1499 Region IX: US Department of Education
US Department of Education
Rm 205
50 United Nations Plz
San Francisco, CA 94102-4912   415-556-4120
                                       FAX 415-437-7540
                                       http://www.ed.gov
The Office of Federal Contract Compliance Programs is part of the US Department of Labor's Employment Standards Administration. It has a national network of six regional offices, each with district and area offices in major metropolitan centers.

1500 Region IX: US Department of Health and Human Services
90 7th St
San Francisco, CA 94103-6701   415-437-8500
                                       FAX 415-437-8505
                                       http://www.hhs.gov
                       e-mail: thomas.lorentzen@hhs.gov
Tom Lorentzen, Regional Director

1501 Sacramento County Office of Education
P.O.Box 269003
Sacramento, CA 95826-9003   916-228-2500
                                       FAX 916-228-2403
                                       http://www.scoe.net
David Gordon, Superintendent

A customer-driven educational leader and agent got change in the country, region and state, is to support the preparation of students for a changing and global 21st century society, through a continuously improving system of aprtnerships and coordinated services for our diverse community.

Colorado

1502 Assistive Technology Partners
Ste 130
601 E 18th Ave
Denver, CO 80203-1493   303-315-1280
                                       800-255-3477
                                       FAX 303-837-1208
                                       TTY: 303-837-8964
                                       http://www.uchsc.edu
Cathy Bodine, Executive Director

Designed to support capacity building and advocacy activities, and to assist states in maintaining permanent, comprehensive statewide programs of technology related assistance for all people with disabilities living in Colorado.

1503 **Colorado Civil Rights Division**
Ste 1050
1560 Broadway
Denver, CO 80202-4941   303-894-7855
                                     800-886-7675
                                 FAX 303-894-7885
                        http://www.dora.state.co.us
                        e-mail: ccrd@dora.state.co.us
Steven Chavez, Executive Director

1504 **Colorado Department of Labor and Employment**
Ste 201
633 17th St
Denver, CO 80202-3660   303-318-8000
                          http://www.coworkforce.com
Brian Aggeler, Executive Director

1505 **Colorado Developmental Disabilities**
Colorado Department of Human Services
4055 S Lowell Blvd
Denver, CO 80236-3120   303-866-7450
                                 FAX 303-866-7470
                 http://www.cdhs.state.co.us/ddd/
Sharon Jacksi, Director

Provides leadership for the direction, funding, and operation of services to persons with developmental disabilities within Colorado.

1506 **Correctional Education Division**
Colorado Department of Corrections
Ste 400
2862 S Circle Dr
Colorado Springs, CO 80906-4101   719-579-9580
                                 FAX 719-226-4755
                http://www.doc.state.co.us/programs.htm
            e-mail: executive.director@doc.state.co.us
Joe Ortiz, Executive Director
Dr Anthony Romero, Asst Director, Educational Serv

To meet the diverse educational needs of inmates through the provision of quality academic, vocational, life skills, and transitional services whereby inmates can successfully integrate into society, gain and maintain employment and become responsible, productive individuals.

1507 **Legal Center for People with Disabilities and Older People**
455 Sherman Ste
Suite 130
Denver, CO 80203-4403   303-722-0300
                                     800-288-1376
                                 FAX 303-722-0720
                                 TTY: 303-722-3619
                        http://www.thelegalcenter.org
                    e-mail: tlcmail@thelegalcenter.org
Mary Anne Harvey, Executive Director
Randy Chapman, Director of Legal Services

The Legal Center protects and promotes the rights of people with disabilities and older people in Colorado through direct legal representation, advocacy, education and legislative analysis.

1508 **Region VIII: US Department of Education**
Office of Civil Rights
Cesar E Chavez Memorial Buil
Denver, CO 80204   303-844-5695
                                 FAX 303-844-4303
                                 http://www.ed.gov
                        e-mail: ocr.denver@ed.gov
Mary Lou Mobley, Civil Rights Director
Nancy Haberkorn, Program Manager

This office covers the states of Arizona, Colorado, New Mexico, Utah, and Wyoming.

1509 **Region VIII: US Department of Health and Human Services**
1961 Stout St
Ste 1456
Denver, CO 80294-1961   303-844-3372
                                 FAX 303-844-4545
                                 http://www.hhs.gov
                        e-mail: joe.nunez@hhs.gov
Margaret Salazar, Regional Director
Tony Salters, Executive Officer

1510 **Region VIII: US Department of Labor-Office of Federal Contract Compliance**
US Department of Labor
Ste 950
1809 California St
Denver, CO 80202   303-844-1600
                                 FAX 303-844-1616
These regional offices of agencies enforce laws prohibiting employment discrimination on the basis of disability.

1511 **State Department of Education**
201 E Colfax Ave
Denver, CO 80203-1704   303-866-6600
                                 FAX 303-830-0793
                        http://www.cde.state.co.us
                e-mail: commissioner@cde.state.co.us
Dwight D Jones, Commissioner

The administrative arm of the Colorado Board of Education. CDE serves colorado's 178 local school districts, providing them with leadership, consultation and administrative services on a statewide and regional basis.

Connecticut

1512 **Bureau of Special Education & Pupil Services**
Department of Education
Po Box 2219
Room 360
Hartford, CT 06145-2219   860-713-6912
                                 FAX 860-713-7014
                        http://www.state.ct.us/sde/
                e-mail: annelouise.thompson@ct.gov
George Coleman, Manager
Anne Louise Thompson, Bureau Chief

Offers information on educational programs and services. The Complaint Resolution Process Office answers and processes parent complaints regarding procedural violations by local educational agencies and facilities. The Due Process Office is responsible for the management of special education and due process proceedings which are available to parents and school districts.

1513 **CHILD FIND of Connecticut**
25 Industrial Park Rd
Middletown, CT 06457-1516   860-632-1485
                                     800-445-2722
                                 FAX 860-632-8870
                                 http://www.ctserc.org
                        e-mail: info@ctserc.org

Mary Ann Kirner, Director
Carol Sullivan, Assistant Director
Sarah Barzee, Assistant Director
A service under the direction of The Connecticut State Department of Education and operated by the Special Education Resource Center. The primary goal is the identification, diagnosis and programming of all unserved disabled children.

1514 Connecticut Bureau of Rehabilitation Services
Department of Social Services
25 Sigourney St
Hartford, CT 06106-5041
860-424-4844
800-537-2549
FAX 860-424-4850
TDD:860-424-4839
http://www.ct.gov/brs
e-mail: brs.dss@ct.gov
Michael P Starkowski, Commissioner
Amy Porter, Bureau Director

Creates opportunities that enable individuals with significant disabilities to work competitively and live independently. Strive to provide appropriate, individualized services, develop effective partnerships, and share sufficient information so that consumers and their families may make informed choices about the rehabilitation process and employment options.

1515 Connecticut Department of Social Services
25 Sigourney St
Hartford, CT 06106-5041
860-424-4908
800-842-1508
TDD:800-842-4524
TTY: 800-842-4524
http://www.ct.gov
e-mail: pgr.dss@ct.gov
Michael P Starkowski, Commissioner

Provides a broad range of services to the elderly, disabled, families and individuals who need assistance in maintaining or achieving their full potential for self-director, self-reliance and independent living.

1516 Connecticut Office of Protection and Advocacy for Persons with Disabilities
60-B Weston St
Hartford, CT 06120-1551
860-297-4300
800-842-7303
FAX 860-566-8714
TDD:860-297-4380
TTY: 860-297-4380
http://www.ct.gov
James Mc Gaughey, Executive Director

Supports families and individuals who are affected by developmental disabilities.

1517 Connecticut State Department of Education
165 Capitol Ave
Hartford, CT 06106-1659
860-713-6543
FAX 860-713-7011
http://www.sde.ct.gov
Mark McQuillan, Commissioner

The adminstrative arm of the Connecticut State Board of Education. Through leadership, curriculum, research, planning, evaluation, assessment, data analyses and other assistance, the Department helps to ensure equal opportunity and excellence in education for all Connecticut students.

1518 Connecticut Tech Act Project
Dept of Social Services/Bureau of Rehab Services
11th Fl
25 Sigourney St
Hartford, CT 06106-5041
860-424-4881
800-537-2549
FAX 860-424-4850
TTY: 860-424-4839
http://www.cttechact.com
Arlene Lugo, Program Coordinator

Increasing independence and improve the lives of individuals with disabilities through increased access to Assistive Technology for work, school and community living.

1519 Correctional Education Division: Connecticut
Unified School District #1
24 Wolcott Hill Rd
Wethersfield, CT 06109-1152
860-692-7536
FAX 860-692-7538
http://www.state.ct.us/doc/
e-mail: angela.jalbert@po.state.ct.us
Angela J Jalbert, Superintendent
Leo Amone, Commissioner

Education continues to be one of the Department's more valuable assets in providing opportunities that will support an offender's successful community reintegration. Education programming is available to inmates through the Unified School District (USD)#l, a legally vested school district within the Department of Correction (DOC).

1520 Protection & Advocacy Agency
Office of P&A for Persons with Disabilities
Ste B
60 Weston St
Hartford, CT 06120-1551
860-297-4300
800-842-7303
FAX 860-566-8714
TTY: 860-297-4380
http://www.ct.gov/opapd
James Mc Gaughey, Executive Director

To advnace the cause of equal rights for persons with disabilities and their families.

1521 State GED Administration
Bureau of Adult Education and Training
25 Industrial Park Rd
Middletown, CT 06457-1516
860-807-2110
FAX 860-807-2112
e-mail: ged@ct.govwloski@po.state.ct.us
Paul F Flinter, Bureau Chief
Ajit Gopalakrishnan, GED Administrator

The primary aid of the GED testing program in Connecticut is to provide a second opportunity for individuals to obtain their high school diplomas.

1522 State of Connecticut Board of Education & Services for the Blind
184 Windsor Ave
Windsor, CT 06095-4536
860-602-4000
FAX 860-602-4020
TDD:860-602-4002
http://www.ct.go
e-mail: besb@po.state.ct.us
Brian S Sigman, Executive Director

Provide quality educational and rehabilitative service to all people who are legally blind or deaf-blind and children who are visually impaired at no cost to our clients or their families.

Delaware

1523 Client Assistance Program (CAP)
254 E Camden Wyoming Ave
Camden, DE 19934-1303
302-698-9336
800-640-9336
FAX 302-698-9338
http://www.manta.com/c/mmpgrv5/client-assistanc
e-mail: charlesdmoore@comcast.net
Melissa Shahan, Executive Director

Provides free services to consumers and applicants for projects, programs and facilities funded under the Rehabilitation Act.

1524 Community Legal Aid Society
100 W 10th St
Wilmington, DE 19801-6603
302-575-0660
FAX 302-575-0840
TDD:302-575-0696
TTY: 302-575-0696
http://www.declasi.org
e-mail: clasincc@declasi.org
Christopher White, Executive Director

Community Legal Aid Society is a private, non-profit law firm dedicated to equal justice for all. Prodive civil legal services to assist clients in becoming self sufficient and meeting basic needs with dignity. Clients include members of the community who have low incomes, who have disabilities, or who are age 60 and over.

1525 Correctional Education Division
Department of Corrections
245 McKee Rd
Dover, DE 19901-2232
302-739-5601
FAX 302-739-8220
http://www.state.de.us
e-mail: Gail.Stallings@state.de.us
Carl Danberg, Commissioner
Lori Quinney, Contact Person
John Ryan, Associate

1526 Delaware Assistive Technology Initiative(DATI)
University of Delaware
P.O.Box 269
Wilmington, DE 19899-0269
302-651-6790
800-870-3284
FAX 302-651-6793
TDD:302-651-6794
http://www.dati.org
e-mail: dati@asel.udel.edu
Beth Mineo, Director

DATI connects Delawareans who have disabilities with the tools they need in order to learn, work, play, and participate in community life safely and independently. DATI also operates Assistive Technology Resource Centers that offer training as well as no-cost equipment demonstrations and loans. DATI also provides funding information, develops partnerships with state agencies and organizations, and publishes resource materials and event calendars.

1527 Delaware Department of Education
Ste 2
401 Federal St
Dover, DE 19901-3639
302-735-4000
FAX 302-739-4654
http://www.doe.k12.de.us
e-mail: dedoe@doe.k12.de.us
Valerie Woodruff, Secretary

Committed to promoting the highest quality education for every Delaware student by providing visionary leadership and superior service.

1528 Delaware Department of Labor
4425 N Market St
Wilmington, DE 19802-1307
302-761-8085
FAX 302-761-6634
http://www.delawareworks.com
e-mail: dlabor@state.de.us
Thomas Sharp, Secretary

Connects people to jobs, resources, monetary benefits, workplace protections and labor market information to promote financial independence, workplace justice and a strong economy.

1529 State GED Administration: Delaware
Department of Education
Ste 1
35 Commerce Way
Dover, DE 19904-5747
302-857-3340
FAX 302-739-1770
http://www.doe.k12.de.us
e-mail: mwhelan@doe.k12.de.us
Maureen Whelan, Director

The primary aid of the GED testing program in Delaware is to provide a second opportunity for individuals to obtain their high school diplomas.

District of Columbia

1530 Client Assistance Program (CAP): District of Columbia
University Legal Services
Suite 130
220 I St NE
Washington, DC 20002-4364
202-547-4747
FAX 202-547-2083
http://www.uls-dc.org
e-mail: jcooney@uls-dc.org
Jane Brown, Program Director

A federally funded program authorized under the amended Rehabilitation Act of 1973. University Legal Services administers the CAP program i the District of Columbig under contract with the District of Columbia Rehabilitation Services Administration. The goal of CAP is to identify, explain, and resolve the problems residents of the District of Columbia may be having with the rehabilitation program as quickly as possible.

1531 DC Department of Employment Services
Government of the District of Columbia
Ste 3000
64 New York Ave NE
Washington, DC 20002-3320
202-724-7000
FAX 202-673-6993
TDD:202-673-6994
TTY: 202-673-6994
http://www.does.dc.gov
e-mail: does@dc.gov
Summer Spencer, Director

The mission of the Department of Employment Services is to plan, develop and administer employment-related services to all segments of the Washington, DC metropolitan population. We achieve our mission through empowering and sstaining a diverse workforce, which enables all sectors of the community to achieve economic and social stability.

1532 District of Columbia Department of Corrections
Government of the District of Columbia
Room 203 N
1923 Vermont Ave NW
Washington, DC 20001-4125
202-673-7316
FAX 202-671-2043
http://doc.dc.gov
e-mail: doc@dc.gov
Devon Brown, Director

Provides public safety by ensuring the safe, secure, and human confinement of pertrial detainees and sentenced misdemeanant prisoners.

1533 District of Columbia Fair Employment Practice Agencies
DC Office of Human Rights
Suite 570 N
414 4th St NW
Washington, DC 20001
202-727-4559
FAX 202-727-9589
TTY: 202-727-8673
http://www.ohr.dc.gov
e-mail: ohr@dc.gov

Gustavo F Velasquez, Director

The DC Office of Human Rights is an agency of the District of Columbia government that seeks to eradicate discrimination, increase equal opportunity, and protect human rights in the city. The Office is also the advocate for the practice of good human relations and mutual understanding among the various racial ethnic and religious groups in the District of Columbia.

1534 Office of Civil Rights: District of Columbia
US Department of Education
P.O.Box 14620
Washington, DC 20044-4620
202-786-0500
FAX 202-208-7797
TDD:877-521-2172
http://www.ed.gov.ocr
e-mail: ocr.dc@ed.gov

Stephanie J Monroe, Assistant Secretary

This office covers the states of District of Columbia, North Carolina, South Carolina and Virginia.

1535 Office of Human Rights: District of Columbia
Government of the District of Columbia
Ste 570 N
441 4th St NW
Washington, DC 20001-2714
202-727-4559
FAX 202-724-3786
http://ohr.dc.gov
e-mail: ohr@dc.gov

Gustavo Velasques, Director

The DC Office of Human Rights is an agency of the District of Columbia government that seeks to eradicate discrimination, increase equal opportunity, and protect human rights in the city.

1536 Protection and Advocacy Program: Districtof Columbia

University Legal Services
Ste 300
3220 Pennsylvania Ave SE
Washington, DC 20020-3712
202-645-7175
FAX 202-645-7178
http://www.uls-dc.org
e-mail: jbrown@uls-dc.org

Anne Tyson, Executive Director

A program authorized by federal law to help the District of Columbia residents with developemntal disabilities exercise their full rights as citizens.

Florida

1537 Client Assistance Program (CAP): Advocacy Center for Persons with Disabilities
Ste 102
2728 Centerview Dr
Tallahassee, FL 32301-6200
850-488-9071
800-342-0823
FAX 850-488-8640
TDD:800-346-4127
http://www.advocacycenter.org

Gary Weston, Executive Director

Assists anyone with a disability that is interested in applying for and receiving services from rehabilitation programs, projects or facilities funded under the Rehabilitation Act.

1538 Florida Department of Labor and Employment Security

2571 Executive Center Dr
Tallahassee, FL 32301
850-414-4615
FAX 850-921-1459

Sandra Bell, Manager

1539 Florida Fair Employment Practice Agency
Florida Commission on Human Relations
2009 Apalachee Pkwy
Suite 100
Tallahassee, FL 32301-4830
850-488-7082
800-342-8170
FAX 850-488-5291
http://fchr.state.fl.us
e-mail: fchrinfo@fchr.myflorida.com
Derick Daniel, Executive Director

To prevent unlawful discrimination by ensuring people in Florida are treated fairly and are given access to opportunities in employment, housing, and certain public accommodations; and to promote mutual respect among groups through education and partnerships.

Georgia

1540 Client Assistance Program (CAP): Georgia Division of Persons with Disabilities
123 N McDonough St
Decatur, GA 30030-3317
404-373-3116
800-822-9727
FAX 404-373-4110
http://www.georgiacap.com
e-mail: acarraway@georgiacap.com
Charles L Martin, Director
Ashley Carraway, Assistant Director
Jennifer Page, Counselor
Advocacy counseling and other services for persons with disabilities.

1541 Georgia Advocacy Office
Ste 430
150 Ponce De Leon Ave NE
Decatur, GA 30030-1942
404-885-1234
800-537-2329
FAX 404-378-0031
http://www.thegao.org
e-mail: info@thegao.org

Ruby Moore, Executive Director

Our mission is to work with and for oppressed and vulnerable individuals in Georgia who are labeled as disabled of mentally ill of secure their protection and advocacy.

1542 Georgia Department of Technical & Adult Education
Technical College System of Georgia
Ste 400
1800 Century Pl NE
Atlanta, GA 30345-4304
404-679-1625
FAX 404-679-1630
http://www.dtae.org

Ron Jackson, Commissioner

The Georgia Department of Technical and Adult Education oversees the state's system of technical colleges, the adult literacy program, and a host of economic and workforce development programs

1543 Governor's Council on Developmental Disabilities
Ste 26-246
2 Peachtree St NW
Atlanta, GA 30303-3141   404-657-2126
                                           888-275-4233
                                       FAX 404-657-2132
                                       TDD:404-657-2133
                                       http://www.gcdd.org
                    e-mail: eejacobson@dhr.state.ga.us
Eric Jacobson, Executive Director

To collaborate with Georgia citizens, public and private advocacy organizations, and policy makers to positively influence ppublic policies that enhance the quality of life for people with developmental disabilities and their families.

1544 Office of Civil Rights: Georgia
US Department of Education
Ste 19t70
61 Forsyth St SW
Atlanta, GA 30303-8927   404-562-6350
                                       FAX 404-562-6455
                                       TDD:877-521-2172
                                       http://www.ed.gov
                        e-mail: ocr.atlanta@ed.gov
This office covers the states of Florida, Georgia and Tennessee

1545 Region IV: Office of Civil Rights
Sam Nun Atlanta Federal Center
Rm 5b95
61 Forsyth St SW
Atlanta, GA 30303-8931   404-562-7888
                                       FAX 404-562-7899
                                       http://www.hhs.gov
                    e-mail: chris.downing@hhs.gov
Christopher Downing, Regional Manager

1546 State Department of Education
Department of Technical and Adult Education
2051 Twin Towers E
Atlanta, GA 30334   404-657-7410
                                           800-331-3627
                                       FAX 404-657-6978
                                   http://www.doe.k12.ga.us
                    e-mail: stateboard@doe.k12.ga.us
Jean DeVard-Kem MD, Assistant Commissioner

1547 State GED Administration: Georgia
GA Department of Technical and Adult Education
Ste 555
1800 Century Pl NE
Atlanta, GA 30345-4311   404-679-1621
                                       FAX 404-679-4911
                                   http://www.dtae.tec.ga.us
                            e-mail: klee@dtae.org
Kimberly Lee, Director GED

The primary aid of the GED testign program in Georgia is to provide a second opportunity for individuals to obtain their high school diplomas.

1548 Tools for Life, the Georgia Assistive Technology Act Program
Georgia Institute of Technology/AMAC
512 Means Street
Suite 250
Atlanta, GA 30318   404-894-0541
                                           800-497-8665
                                       TDD:866-373-7778
                                       http://www.gatfl.org
                            e-mail: info@gatfl.org
Carolyn P Phillips M.Ed., ATP, Director
Liz Persaud, Coordinator

The Tools for Life lists local and national training opportunities coming to Georgia.

Hawaii

1549 Correctional Education
Department of Public Safety
Ste 405
919 Ala Moana Blvd
Honolulu, HI 96814-4920   808-587-1288
                                       FAX 808-587-1280
                            e-mail: maureen@smsii.com
Maureen Tito, Program Manager

1550 Hawaii Disability Rights Center
Ste 1040
900 Fort Street Mall
Honolulu, HI 96813-3701   808-949-2922
                                           800-882-1057
                                       FAX 808-949-2928
                        http://www.hawaiidisabilityrights.org
                    e-mail: gary@hawaiidisabilityrights.org
Gary Smith, President

1551 Hawaii State Council on Developmental Disabilities
Ste 113
919 Ala Moana Blvd
Honolulu, HI 96814-4920   808-586-8100
                                       FAX 808-586-7543
                                       http://www.hiddc.org
                        e-mail: council@hiddc.org
Waynette Cabral, Executive Administrator

To support people with developmental disabilities to control their own destiny and determine the quality of life they desire.

1552 State GED Administration: Hawaii
Community Education Section
Bldg 302
475 22nd Ave
Honolulu, HI 96816-4400
                                       FAX 808-5863234
Annette Young-Ogata, Educational Specialist

Idaho

1553 Disability Rights Idaho
Comprehensive Advocacy (Co-Ad)
Ste B-100
4477 Emerald St
Boise, ID 83706-2066   208-336-5353
                                           800-632-5125
                                       FAX 208-336-5396
                                       TDD:208-336-5353
                        http://www.disabilityrightsidaho.org
                    e-mail: info@disabilityrightsidaho.org
James R Baugh, Executive Director

Comprehensive Advocacy, Inc is the designated Protection and Advocacy System for Idaho. Co-Ad provides advocacy for people with disabilities who have been abused/neglected; denied services or benefits; have experienced rights violations or discrimination because of their disability; or have voting accessibility problems. Co-Ad provides information & referral; negotitation & mediation; short term & technical assistance; legal advice/representation.

1554 Idaho Assistive Technology Project
121 West Sweet Ave
Moscow, ID 83843-2268   208-885-3557
                                          800-432-8324
                                      FAX 208-885-3628
                              http://www.idahoat.org
                              e-mail: rseiler@uidaho.edu
Ron Seiler, Project Director

The Idaho Assistive Technology Project)IATP) is a federally funded program managed by the Center on Disabilities
and Human Development at the University of Idaho. The
goal of IATP is to increase the availability of assistive technology devices and services for Idahoans with disabilities.
The IATP offers free trainings and technical assistance, a
low-interest loan program, assistive technology assessments for children and agriculture workers, and free
informational materials.

1555 Idaho Department of Education
P.O.Box 83720
650 W State St
Boise, ID 83720-0027   208-332-6800
                                          800-432-4601
                                      FAX 208-334-2228
                              http://www.sde.state.id.us
Tom Luna, Superintendent

Determined to create a customer-driven education system
that meets the needs of every student in Idaho and prepares
them to live, work and succeed in the 21st century.

1556 Idaho Division of Vocational Rehabilitation
Room 150
650 W State St
Boise, ID 83720-0001   208-334-3390
                                      FAX 208-334-5305
                              http://www.vr.idaho.gov
                              e-mail: department.info@vr.idaho.gov
Dr Michael Graham, Administrator

A state-federal program whose goal is to assist people with
disabilities to prepare for, secure, retain or regain employment.

1557 Idaho Fair Employment Practice Agency
Idaho Human Rights Commission
1109 Main St
Boise, ID 83720-0001   208-334-2873
                                          888-249-7025
                                      FAX 208-334-2664
                              http://www.humanrights.idaho.gov
Leslie L Goddard, Director

1558 Idaho Human Rights Commission
317 West Main St
Second Floor
Boise, ID 83735-0660   208-334-2873
                                          888-249-7025
                                      FAX 208-334-2664
                                      TDD:208-334-4751
                                      TTY: 208-334-4751
                              http://www.state.id.us
                              e-mail: inquiry@ihrc.idaho.gov
Leslie L Goddard, Director

To administer state and federal andti-discrimination laws in
Idaho in a manner that is fair, accurate, and timely; and to
work towards ensuring that all people within the state are
treated with dignity and respect in their places of employment, housing, education and public accommodations.

1559 Idaho Professional Technical Education
650 W State Street
Len B Jordan Bldg., Room 324
Boise, ID 83720-0095   208-334-3216
                                      FAX 208-334-2365
                              http://www.pte.idaho.gov
                              e-mail: csengel@pte.idaho.gov
Cheryl Engel, GED Administrator
Jennifer Provencio, GED Transcripts/Information

The primary aid of the GED testing program in Idaho is to
provide a second opportunity for individuals to obtain their
high school equivalency certificate.

1560 State Department of Education: Special Education
P.O.Box 83720
650 W State St
Boise, ID 83720-0003   208-332-6800
                                          800-432-4601
                                      FAX 208-332-2228
                              http://www.sde.idaho.gov
                              e-mail: jetaylor@sde.idaho.gov
Jean Taylor, Director
Jacque Hyatt, Director

Our mission is to enable all students to achieve high academic standards and quality of life. The Special Education
Team works collaboratively with districts, agencies, and
parents to ensure students receive quality, meaningful, and
needed services.

Illinois

1561 Chicago Board of Education
Office of the Board of Education
Fl 6
125 S Clark St
Chicago, IL 60603-4016   773-553-1000
                                      FAX 773-553-1502
                              http://www.cps.edu/Pages/home.aspx
                              e-mail: kmartin@cps.k12.il.us
Rufus Williams, President

Offers instruction and information services, curriculum information and government relations advocacy.

**1562 Client Assistance Program (CAP): Illinois Department
of Human Services**
100 South Grand Ave East
Springfield, IL 62702-5042   217-557-1601
                                          800-641-3929
                                      TTY: 217-557-2134
                              http://www.dhs.state.il.us
                              e-mail: dhscap@dhs.state.il.us
Carol L Adams PhD, Secretary

Provides free services to consumers and applicants for projects, programs and facilities funded under the Rehabilitation Act.

1563 Correctional Education
Illinois Department of Corrections
1301 Concordia Ct
PO Box 19277
Springfield, IL 62794-9277   217-558-2200
                                          800-546-0844
                                      FAX 217-522-0355
                              http://www.idoc.state.il.us/
                              e-mail: info@doc.illinois.gov
Roger E Walker Jr, Director

1564 DBTAC: Great Lakes ADA Center
University of Illinois at Chicago
Rm 405
1640 W Roosevelt Rd
Chicago, IL 60608-1316

312-413-1407
800-949-4232
FAX 312-413-1856
TTY: 312-413-1407
http://www.adagreatlakes.org
e-mail: adata@adagreatlakes.org

Robin Jones, Project Director
Peter Berg, Technical Assistance Coordinator

Increases awareness and knowledge with the ultimate goal of achieving voluntary compliance with the Americans with Disabilities Act. This is accomplished within targeted audiences through provision of customized training, expert assistance, and dissemination of information developed by various sources, including the federal agencies responsible for enforcement of the ADA.

1565 Illinois Affiliation of Private Schools for Exceptional Children
Lawrence Hall Youth Services
Lawrence Hall Youth Services
4833 N. Francisco Ave.
Chicago, IL 60625-3640

773-769-3500
FAX 773-769-0106
http://www.lawrencehall.org
e-mail: info@lawrencehall.org

Mary Hollie, CEO
Sharri Demitrowicz, Education Vice President

1566 Illinois Assistive Technology
Ste 100
1 W Old State Capitol Plz
Springfield, IL 62701-1224

217-522-7985
800-852-5110
FAX 217-522-8067
TTY: 212-522-9966
http://www.iltech.org
e-mail: iatp@iltech.org

Wilhelmina Gunther, Executive Director

The primary focus is on education, employment, community living, information technology and telecommunications. The mission is to enable people iwth disabilities so they can fully participate in all aspects of life.

1567 Illinois Council on Developmental Disabilities
830 S Spring St
Springfield, IL 62704-2618

217-782-9696
FAX 217-524-5339
http://www.state.il.us
e-mail: sheila.romano@illinois.gov

Sheila Romano, Director

Dedicated to improving the lives of people with developmental disabilities through advocacy, systemic change and capacity building. Focuses its efforts across a person's life span so that people with developmental disabilities can enjoy life as any other Illinoisan. The Council completes its work through a variety of methods including grant awards, technical assistance and collaboration.

1568 Illinois Department of Commerce and Community Affairs
JTPA Programs Division
500 E Monroe
Springfield, IL 62701-1316

217-525-9308
800-785-6055
FAX 800-785-6055
TDD:800-785-6055
http://www.commerce.state.il.us

Patty Ambrose, Director
Pam Donough, Manager

1569 Illinois Department of Employment Security
33 S State St
Chicago, IL 60603-2808

312-793-5280
800-244-5631
FAX 312-793-9834
TTY: 866-322-8357
http://www.ides.state.il.us

James P Sledge, Director

IDES helps job seekers find jobs and employers find workers. We also analyze and publish a gold mine of information on careers and the Illinois economy.

1570 Illinois Department of Human Rights
100 W Randolph St
Ste 10-100
Chicago, IL 60601-3391

312-814-4320
FAX 312-814-6251
TDD:312-263-1579
http://www.state.il.us/dhr
e-mail: susan.allen@illinois.gov

Rocco Claps, Director

Civil rights enforcement agency covering employment, housing, financial credit, public accomodation, sexual harassment in education in the State of Illinois.

1571 Illinois Department of Rehabilitation Services
1026 E Jackson St
Macomb, IL 61455-2520

309-833-4573
888-337-5267
FAX 309-837-1659
TDD:888-261-2867
TTY: 866-376-8446
http://www.dhs.state.il.us
e-mail: dhs.ors@illinois.gov

Karen Engstrom, Manager

1572 Illinois Office of Rehabilitation Services
Illinois Department of Human Services
100 S Grand Ave E
Springfield, IL 62762-0001

217-557-1601
FAX 217-557-1647
TTY: 217-557-2134

Michelle Saddler, Secretary

DHS' Office of Rehabilitation Services is the state's lead agency serving individuals with disabilities.

1573 Illinois State Board of Education
100 N 1st St
Springfield, IL 62777-0001

217-782-4321
866-262-6663
FAX 217-782-9224
http://www.isbe.net

Christopher Koch EdD, State Superintendent, Education
Elizabeth Hanselman, Asst Superintendent, Special Ed

Sets educational policies and guidelines for public and private schools, preschool through grade 12, as well as vocational education. Analyzes the aims, needs and requirements of edcuation and recommends legislation to the General Assembly and Governor for the benefit of the more than 2 million school children in Illinois.

1574 Office of Civil Rights: Illinois
US Department of Education
Ste 1475
500 W Madison St
Chicago, IL 60661-4544   312-730-1560
                          FAX 312-730-1576
                          TDD:877-521-2172
                          http://www.ed.gov
                  e-mail: ocr.chicago@ed.gov
This office covers the states of Illinois, Indiana, Iowa, Minnesota, North Dakota, and Wisconsin.

1575 Protection & Advocacy Agency
Equip for Equality
Ste 300
20 N Michigan Ave
Chicago, IL 60602-4861   312-341-0022
                                   800-537-2632
                          FAX 312-341-0295
                          TTY: 800-610-2779
              http://www.equipforequality.org
        e-mail: contactus@equipforequality.org
Zena Naiditch, President

The mission of Equip for Equality is to advance the human and civil rights of children and adults with physical and mental disabilities. The only state-wide cross-disability, comprehensive advocacy organization providing self-advocacy assistance, legal services, and disability rights education while also engaging in publi policy and legislative advocacy and conducting abuse investigation and other oversight activities.

1576 Region V: Civil Rights Office
US Department of Health & Human Services
Ste 240
233 N Michigan Ave
Chicago, IL 60601-5521   312-886-2359
                          FAX 312-886-1807
                          TDD:312-353-5693
                          http://www.hhs.gov
            e-mail: valarie.alston@hhs.gov
Valarie Morgan-Alston, Regional Manager

1577 Region V: US Department of Labor: Office of Federal Contract Compliance
US Department of Labor
Ste 570
230 S Dearborn St
Chicago, IL 60604-1520   312-596-7010
                          FAX 312-596-7044
                          http://www.dol.gov
        e-mail: ofccp-mw-preaward@dol.gov
Sandra S Zeigler, Regional Director

These regional offices of agencies enforce laws prohibiting employment discrimination on the basis of disability.

1578 Region V: US Small Business Administration
Ste 1150
500 W Madison St
Chicago, IL 60661-2511   312-353-4528
                          FAX 312-886-5688
                          http://www.sba.gov
Judith A Roussel, District Director

These regional offices of agencies enforce laws prohibiting employment discrimination on the basis of disability.

Indiana

1579 Assistive Technology
Ste G
5333 Commerce Square Dr
Indianapolis, IN 46237-8627
                                   800-528-8246
                          http://www.attaininc.org
            e-mail: attaininfo@attaininc.org
Gary Hand, Executive Director
Mary Duffer, Executive Assistant

Provide direct service programs and creates structural change in the public and private sectors to promote the availability and use of Assistive Technology.

1580 Indiana ATTAIN Project
Indiana Family and Social Services Administration
P.O.Box 7083
Indianapolis, IN 46207-7083   317-233-0800
                          http://www.in.gov/fssa
Mitch Robb, Director
John Clark, Secretary
Rita Anderson, Executive Director

1581 Indiana Department of Correction
Rm E334
302 W Washington St
Indianapolis, IN 46204-2762   317-232-1746
                          FAX 317-233-4948
                          http://www.in.gov
              e-mail: rkoester@idoc.in.gov
Kevin Moore, Commissioner

To maintain public safety and provide offenders with self improvement programs, job skills and family values in an efficient and cost effective manner for a successful return to the community as law-abiding citizens.

1582 Indiana Department of Workforce Development Disability Program Navigator
10 N Senate Ave
Indianapolis, IN 46204-2277   317-232-6702
                                   800-891-6499
                          FAX 317-233-4793
                          http://www.in.gov/dwd
              e-mail: bcarvin@dwd.in.gov
Brianna Morse, Project Director

Provides guideance to employers on the hiring of individuals with disabilities as well as additional tax credits and assistance for their employers. Also provide assistance to schools on transition to work needs of students with disabilities. Guides individuals with disabilities through the career services available in our WorkOne Centers as they obtain employment.

1583 Indiana Protection & Advocacy Services
Ste 222
4701 N Keystone Ave
Indianapolis, IN 46205-1561   317-722-5555
                                   800-622-4845
                          FAX 317-722-5564
                          TTY: 800-838-1131
                          http://www.in.gov
              e-mail: kpedevilla@ipas.IN.gov
Thomas Gallagher, Executive Director

Created to protect and advocate the rights of people with disabilities and is Indiana's federally designated Protection and Advocacy system and client assistance program. An independent state agency, which recieves no state funding and is independent from all service providers, as required by federal and state law.

1584 State Department of Education
151 W Ohio St
Indianapolis, IN 46204-2798
317-232-6610
800-527-4931
FAX 317-232-8004
http://www.doe.state.in.us
e-mail: webmaster@doe.in.gov
Suellen Reed, Superintendent

Mission is to fulfill its statutory responsibilty by establishing policies that promote excellence in learning for all students.

1585 State GED Administration
Office of Adult Education
151 W Ohio St
Indianapolis, IN 46204-1905
317-232-0528
FAX 317-233-0859
http://www.doe.state.in.us
e-mail: lwarner@doe.in.gov
Linda Warner, Adult Education Director

Iowa

1586 Client Assistance Program (CAP): Iowa Division of Persons with Disabilities
2nd Floor
Lucas State Office Building
Des Moines, IA 50319
888-219-0471
FAX 515-242-6119
TTY: 888-219-0471
http://www.iowa.gov
e-mail: dhr.disabilities@iowa.gov
Jill Fulitano-Avery, Administrator

Exists to promote the employment of Iowans with disabilities and reduce barriers to employment by providing information, referral, assessment and guidance, training and negotiation services to employers and citizens with disabilities.

1587 Governor's Council on Developmental Disabilities
617 E 2nd St
Des Moines, IA 50309-1831
515-281-9082
800-452-1936
FAX 515-281-9087
http://idaction.com
e-mail: fmorris@dhs.state.ia.us
Becky Harker, Executive Director

Identifies, develops and promotes public policy and support practices through capacity building, advocacy, and systems change activities. The purpose is to ensure that people with developmental disabilities and their families are included in planning, decision making, and development of policy related to services and supports that affect their quality of life and full participation in communities of their choice.

1588 Iowa Department of Education
400 E 14th St
Des Moines, IA 50319-0146
515-281-5293
FAX 515-242-5988
http://www.iowa.gov/educate
e-mail: judy.jeffrey@iowa.gov
Kevin Fangman, Acting Director

Champion excellence in education through superior leadership and services. Committed to high levels of learning, achievement and performance for all students, so they will become successful members of their community and the workforce.

1589 Iowa Employment Service
1000 E Grand Ave
Des Moines, IA 50319-1020
515-281-5387
TTY: 800-562-4692
http://www.iowajobs.gov
e-mail: iwd.customerservice@iwd.iowa.gov

1590 Iowa Welfare Programs
Iowa Department of Human Services
5th Floor
Hoover State Building
Des Moines, IA 50319
515-281-5452
FAX 515-281-4940
TDD:800-735-2942
http://www.dhs.state.ia.us
e-mail: kconcan@dhs.state.ia.us
Kevin Concannon, Executive Director
Sally Cunningham, Deputy Director
Dan Gilbert, Administrator
To provide assistance to families in need in the Des Moines area.

1591 Iowa Workforce Investment Act
Department of Economic Development
200 E Grand Ave
Des Moines, IA 50309-1856
515-725-3000
FAX 515-725-3010
TDD:800-735-2934
http://www.iowalifechanging.com
e-mail: info@iowa.gov
David Lyons, Executive Director
Mike Blouin, Director
Deb Townsend, Web Specialist
Job placement and training services. Especially for those workers who have been laid off, or have other barriers to steady employment.

1592 Learning Disabilities Association of Iowa
321 E 6th St
Des Moines, IA 50329-0001
515-280-8558
888-690-5324
FAX 515-243-1902
http://www.lda-ia.org
e-mail: kathylda@askresource.org
Dr Richard Owens, President
Kathy Specketer, Coordinator

Dedicated to identifying causes and promoting prevention of learning disabilities and to enhancing the quality of life for all individuals with learning disabilities and their families.

1593 Protection & Advocacy Services
Ste 300
400 East Court Ave
Des Moines, IA 50309-2548
515-278-2502
800-779-2502
FAX 515-278-0539
TTY: 515-278-0571
http://www.ipna.org
e-mail: info@ipna.org
Sylvia Piper, President

A federally funded program that will protect and advocate for the human and legal rights that ensure individuals with disabilities and/or mental illness a free, appropriate public education, employment opportunities and residence or treatment in the least restricitve environment or method and for freedom from stigma.

Kansas

1594 Disability Rights Center of Kansas
Ste 100
635 SW Harrison St
Topeka, KS 66603-3726

785-273-9661
877-776-1541
FAX 785-273-9414
TDD:877-335-3725
http://www.drckansas.org

Rocky Nichols, Executive Director

Provides free services to consumers and applicants for projects, programs and facilities funded under the rehabilitation act.

1595 Kansas Adult Education Association
Barton County Community College
245 NE 30th Rd
Great Bend, KS 67530

620-792-2701
800-748-7594
http://www.barton.cc.ks.us

Veldon Law, President
Todd Moore, Director for Admission
Cassandra Montoya, Student Work Services
The Kansas Adult Education Association has been the professional association for adult educators at community colleges, school districts, and non-profit organizations.

1596 Kansas Department of Labor
401 SW Topeka Blvd
Topeka, KS 66603-3182

785-296-5000
FAX 785-296-0179
http://www.dol.ks.gov

Jim Garner, Secretary

Formerly the Kansas Department of Human Resources, advances the economic well being of all Kansans through responsive workforce services.

1597 Kansas Department of Social and Rehabilitation Services
500 SW VanBuren
Topeka, KS 66603-1505

785-296-2500
FAX 785-296-5895
TDD:785-296-4026
TTY: 785-296-4026
http://www.srskansas.org

Robbie Berry, Secretary

To protect children and promote adult self-sufficiency.

1598 Kansas Human Rights Commission
Rm 568 S
900 SW Jackson St
Topeka, KS 66612-1258

785-296-3206
888-793-6874
FAX 785-296-0589
TTY: 785-296-0245
http://www.khrc.net
e-mail: khrc@ink.org

William V Minner, Director

To prevent and eliminate discrimination and assure equal opportunities in all employment relations, to eliminate profiling in conjunction with traffic stops, to eliminate and prevent discrimination, segregation or separation, and assure equal opportunities in all places of public accommodations an in housing.

1599 Kansas State Department of Education
120 SE 10th Ave
Topeka, KS 66612-1182

785-291-3097
FAX 785-296-6715
http://www.ksde.org
e-mail: contact@ksde.org

Alexa Posney, Commissioner

Promotes the mission of the Kansas State Board of Education through leadership and support for student learning in Kansas.

1600 Kansas State GED Administration
Kansas Board of Regents
Ste 520
1000 SW Jackson St
Topeka, KS 66612-1368

785-296-3421
FAX 785-296-0983
http://www.kansasregents.org
e-mail: cpuderbaugh@ksbor.org

Reginald L Robinson, President/CEO
Crystal Puderbaugh, State GED Administrator

Promotes adult education.

1601 Office of Disability Services
Wichita State University
1845 Fairmount St
Wichita, KS 67260-0132

316-978-3309
FAX 316-978-3114
TDD:316-978-3391
http://webs.wichita.edu/?u=disserv
e-mail: webmaster@wichita.edu

Grady Landrum, Director

To enable students, staff, faculty and guests of Wichita State University to achieve their educational goals, both personal and academic, to the fullest of their abilities by providing and coordinating accessibility services which afford individuals with learning, mental or physical disabilities the equal opportunity to attain these goals.

1602 State Literacy Resource Center
Kansas Board of Regents Adult Education
Ste 520
1000 SW Jackson St
Topeka, KS 66612-1368

785-296-0175
FAX 785-296-4526
http://www.kansasregents.org
e-mail: dglass@ksbor.org

Dianne Glass, Director
Michelle Carson, Associate Director
Reginald Robinson, President/CEO

Kentucky

1603 Assistive Technology Office
8412 Westport Rd
Louisville, KY 40242-3044

502-429-4484
800-327-5287
FAX 502-429-7114
http://www.katsnet.org
e-mail: chase.forrester@ky.gov

Derrick Cox, Director

To make assistive technology information, devices and services easily obtainable for people of any age and/or disability.

1604 Kentucky Adult Education
Council on Postsecondary Education
Ste 250
1024 Capital Center Dr
Frankfort, KY 40601-7514

502-573-5114
800-928-7323
FAX 502-573-5436
http://www.kyae.ky.gov
e-mail: ginny.sullivan@ky.gov

Ginny Sullivan, Executive Secretary

To provide a responsive and innovative adult education system that enables students to acheive and prosper.

1605   Kentucky Client Assistance Program
5th Fl
209 Saint Clair St
Frankfort, KY 40601-1817   502-564-8035
                                             800-633-6283
                                      FAX 502-564-1566
                                      http://kycap.ky.gov
                               e-mail: vickil.staggs@ky.gov
Vicki Staggs, Contact

Provides advocacy for persons with disabilities who are clients or applicants of the Office of Vocational Rehabilitation or the Office for the Blind and are having problems receiving services.

1606   Kentucky Department of Corrections
Health Services Building
P.O.Box 2400
275 East Main St
Frankfort, KY 40602-2400   502-564-4726
                                      FAX 502-564-5037
                               http://www.corrections.ky.gov
Ladonna Thompson, Commissioner

To protect the citizens of the Commonwealth and to provide a safe, secure and human environment for staff and offenders in carrying out the mandates of the legislative and judicial processes; and to provide opportunities for offenders to acquire skills which facilitate non-criminal behavior.

1607   Kentucky Department of Education
500 Mero St
Frankfort, KY 40601-1987   502-564-4770
                                      FAX 502-564-7749
                                      TTY: 502-564-4970
                               http://www.education.ky.gov
                   e-mail: melissa.terrell@education.ky.gov
Ken Draut, Commissioner

1608   Kentucky Protection and Advocacy
100 Fair Oaks Ln 3rd Floor
Frankfort, KY 40601-1108   502-564-2967
                                             800-372-2988
                                      FAX 502-564-0848
                                      http://www.kypa.net
Marsha Hockensmith, Executive Director

An independent state agency that was designated by the Governor as the protection and advocacy agency for Kentucky. To protect and promote the rights of Kentuckians with disabilities through legally based individuals and systemic advocacy, and education.

1609   Learning Disabilities Association of Kentucky
118
2210 Goldsmith Ln
Louisville, KY 40218-1070   502-473-1256
                                             877-587-1256
                                      FAX 502-473-4695
                                      http://www.ldaofky.org
                               e-mail: Info@LDAofKy.org
Tim Woods, Executive Director

Louisiana

1610   Client Assistance Program (CAP): Louisiana HDQS Division of Persons with Disabilities
Advocacy Center
Ste 2600
1010 Common St
New Orleans, LA 70112-2429   504-237-2337
                                             800-960-7705
                                      FAX 504-522-5507
                                      TTY: 866-935-7348
                               http://www.advocacyla.org
                   e-mail: advocacycenter@advocacyala.org
Lois Simpson, Executive Director

Advocacy services to applicants and clients of Louisiana Rehabilitation Services (LRS) and American Indian Rehabilitation Services (AIRS). No fee. Committed to the belief in the dignity of every life and the freedom of everyone to experience the highest degree of self-determination. Exists to protect and advocate for human and legal rights of the elderly and disabled. Umbrella organization for Advocacy Centers in Baton Rouge, Lafayette, Shreveport, Monroe, Pineville, Jackson, and Mandeville.

1611   Client Assistance Program (CAP): Shreveport Division of Persons with Disabilities
Advocacy Center
Bldg 2 Suite 248
2620 Centenary Blvd
Shreveport, LA 71104-3356   318-227-6186
                                             800-839-7688
                                      FAX 318-227-1841
                                      http://www.advocacyla.org
                               e-mail: dmirvis@advocacyla.org
Diane Mirvis, Executive Director

Advocacy services for applicants and clients of Louisiana Rehabilitation Services (LRS) and American Indian Rehabilitation Services (AIRS). No fee.

1612   Correctional Education
Louisiana Department of Education
P.O.Box 94064
Baton Rouge, LA 70804-9064   225-383-4761
                                             877-453-2721
                                      FAX 225-342-0193
                                      http://www.doe.state.la.us
Cosby Joiner, Director
George Nelson, President

Promotes quality correctional education.

1613   Louisiana Assistive Technology Access Network
3042 Old Forge Dr Suite D
PO Box 14115
Baton Rouge, LA 70898-3181   225-925-9500
                                             800-270-6185
                                      FAX 225-925-9560
                                      http://www.latan.org
                               e-mail: cpourciau@latan.org
Julie Nesbit, President/CEO
Clara Pourciau, Assistant Director
Maria Yiannopoulos, Public Information Officer
Assists individuals with disabilities to achieve a higher quality of life and greater independence through increased access to assistive technology as part of their daily lives.

1614   State Department of Education
Department of Education
P.O.Box 94064
Baton Rouge, LA 70804-9064
                                             877-453-2721
                                      FAX 225-219-4439
                                      http://www.louisianaschools.net
                               e-mail: customerservice@la.gov

Paul G Pastorek, Superintendent
Patrick Dobard, Confidential Assistant

1615 State GED Administration
Louisiana Department of Education
P.O.Box 94604
Baton Rouge, LA 70804

877-453-2721
FAX 225-219-4439
http://www.doe.state.la.us

Debi K Faucette, Director

Promotes quality education.

Maine

1616 Adult Education Team
Maine Department of Education
23 State House Sta
Augusta, ME 04333-0023

207-624-6752
FAX 207-624-6821
http://www.maine.gov
e-mail: jeff.fantine@maine.gov
Jeffrey A Fantine, Adult Education State Director

1617 Bureau of Rehabilitation Services
Department of Labor
150 State House Sta
Augusta, ME 04333-0150

800-698-4440
FAX 207-287-5292
TTY: 888-755-0023
http://www.maine.gov

Laura Fortman, Commissioner

Works to bring about full access to employment, independence and community integration for people with disabilities.

1618 Client Assistance Program (CAP) C.A.R.E.S., Inc.
CARES
134 Main St
Suite 2 C
Winthrop, ME 04364-1400

207-377-7055
800-773-7055
FAX 207-377-7057
http://www.caresinc.org
e-mail: steve.beam@caresinc.com
Dean Crocker, Executive Director

A federally funded program that provides information, assistance and advocacy to people with disabilities who are applying for or receiving services under the Rehabilitation Act.

1619 Developmental Disabilities Council
139 State House Sta
Augusta, ME 04333-0139

207-287-4213
800-244-3990
FAX 207-287-8001
http://www.maineddc.org
e-mail: jbell@maineddc.org
Julia Bell, Executive Director

A partnership of people with developmental disabilities, family memebers, and state and local agencies and organizations. The purpose is to assure that individuals with disabilities and their families participate in the design of, and have access to needed community services, individualized supports, and other forms of assistance thqat promote-self determination, independence, productivity, integration, and inclusion in all facets of family and community life.

1620 Maine Human Rights Commission
51 State House Sta
Augusta, ME 04333-0051

207-624-6050
FAX 207-624-6063
TTY: 888-577-6690
http://www.maine.gov/mhrc
Patricia Ryan, Executtive Director

Holds the responsibility of enforcing Maine's anti-discrimination laws. The Commission investigates complaints of unlawful discrimination in employmen, housing, education, access to public accommodatoins, extension of credit, and offensive names.

1621 Protection & Advocacy Agency
Disability Rights Center
P.O.Box 2007
Augusta, ME 04338-2007

207-626-2774
800-452-1948
FAX 207-621-1419
TTY: 800-452-1948
http://www.drcme.org
e-mail: advocate@drcme.org
Kim Moody, Executive Director
Leeann Mosley, Operations Director

The Disability Rights Center is Maine's protection and advocacy agency for people with disabilities. To enhance and promote the equality, self-determination, independence, productivity, integratio, and inclusion of people with disabilities through education, strategoc advocacy and legal intervention.

1622 Security and Employment Service Center
Dept of Administrative and Financial Services
108 State House Sta
Augusta, ME 04333-0108

207-623-6700
FAX 207-287-8394
TTY: 800-794-1110
http://www.maine.gov

Dennis Corliss, Director

Provides financial and human resource services to the Departments of Defense, Veterans, and Emergency Management; Labor; Professional and Financial REgulation; and, Public Safety.

Maryland

1623 Client Assistance Program (CAP) Maryland Division of Rehabilitation Services
2301 Argonne Dr
Baltimore, MD 21218-1628

410-554-9361
800-638-6243
FAX 410-554-9362
http://www.dors.state.md.us
e-mail: cap@dors.state.md.us
Thomas Laverty, Director

Helps individuals who have concerns or difficulties when applying or receiving rehabiliation services funded under the Rehabilitation Act.

1624 Correctional Education
Division of Career Technology & Adult Learning
200 W Baltimore St
Baltimore, MD 21201-2549

410-767-0500
800-358-3010
FAX 410-333-6033
http://www.marylandpublicschools.org
e-mail: mmechlinski@msde.state.md.us
Mark Mechlinski, Director

Provides educational programs and library services to residents of the Division of Correction and the Patuxent Institution.

1625 Disability Law Center
Ste 400
1800 N Charles St
Baltimore, MD 21201-5909   410-727-6352
                                  800-233-7201
                                  FAX 410-727-6389
                                  TTY: 410-727-6387
                                  http://www.mdlclaw.org
                                  e-mail: feedback@mdlclaw.org
Virginia Knowlton, Executive Director

A provate, non-profit organization staffed by attorneys and paralegals. MDLC is the Protection and Advocacy organization for Maryland. MDLC's mission is to endure that people with disabilities are accorded the full rights and entitlements afforded to them by state and federal law.

1626 Maryland Developmental Disabilities Council
Ste 1300
217 E Redwood St
Baltimore, MD 21202-3313   410-767-3670
                                  800-305-6441
                                  FAX 410-333-3686
                                  http://www.md-council.org
                                  e-mail: brianc@md-council.org
Brian Cox, Executive Director

A public policy organization comprised of people with disabilities and family memebers who are joined by state officials, service providers an dother designated partners. Also an independent, self-governing organization that represents the interests of people with developmental disabilities and their families.

1627 Maryland Technology Assistance Program
Rm T-17
2301 Argonne Dr
Baltimore, MD 21218-1628   410-554-9361
                                  800-832-4827
                                  FAX 410-554-9237
                                  TTY: 866-881-7488
                                  http://www.mdtap.org
                                  e-mail: mdtap@mdtap.org
Beth Lash, Executive Director

Provides tools to help people who are disabled or elderly enjoy the same rights and opportunities as other citizens.

1628 State Department of Education
200 W Baltimore St
Baltimore, MD 21201-2595   410-767-0100
                                  888-246-0016
                                  FAX 410-333-2275
                                  TDD:410-333-6442
                                  http://www.marylandpublicschools.org
Nancy Grasmick, State Superintendent

To provide leadership, support, and accountability for effective systems of public education, library services, and rehabilitation services.

Massachusetts

1629 Autism Support Center: Northshore Arc
6 Southside Rd
Danvers, MA 01923-1409   978-777-9135
                                 800-728-8476
                                 FAX 978-762-3980
                                 http://www2.shore.net/~nsarc
                                 e-mail: asc@ne-arc.org
Susan Gilroy, Director
Jerry Carthy, Executive Director

Created to support parents and professionals who expressed a need for assistance finding information and support about autism, pervasive developmental disorder (PDD) and Asperger's Disorder. Empowers families who have a member with autism or related disorder by providing current, accurate, and unbiased information about autism, services, referrals, resources and research trends.

1630 Department of Corrections
Ste 3
50 Maple St
Milford, MA 01757-3680   508-422-3300
                                 FAX 508-422-3383
                                 http://www.mass.gov

Harold Clark, Commissioner

Promote public safety by incarcerating offenders while providing opportunities for participation in effective programs.

1631 Massachusetts Commission Against Discrimination
1 Ashburton Pl
6th Floor, Room 601
Boston, MA 02108-1599   617-994-6000
                                 FAX 617-994-6000
                                 TTY: 617-994-6196
                                 http://www.mass.gov
                                 e-mail: mcadfeedback@mass.gov
Malcolm Medley, Chairman

The state's chief civil rights agency that works to eliminate discrimination on a variety of bases and areas, and strives to advance the civil rights of the people of the Commonwealth through law enforcement, outreach and training.

1632 Massachusetts General Education Development (GED)
MA Department of Elementary & Secondary Education
350 Main St
Malden, MA 02148-5089   781-338-6621
                                 http://www.doe.mass.edu
                                 e-mail: rmechem@doe.mass.edu
Tom Mechem, State GED Chief Examiner

Thirty-two test centers operate state-wide to serve the needs of the adult population in need of a high school credential.

1633 Massachusetts Office on Disability
Rm 1305
1 Ashburton Pl
Boston, MA 02108-1518   617-727-7440
                                 800-322-2020
                                 FAX 617-727-0965
                                 http://www.mass.gov

Myra Berloff, Director

To bring about full and equal participation of people with disabilities in all aspects of life. It works to assure the advancement of legal rights and for the promotion of maximum opportunities, supportive services, accommodations and accessibility in a manner which fosters dignity and self determination.

1634 Massachusetts Rehabilitation Commission
600 Washington Street
Boston, MA 02211-1616   617-204-3600
                                 800-245-6543
                                 FAX 617-727-1354
                                 http://www.mass.gov/mrc
                                 e-mail: commissioner@mrc.state.ma.us
Charles Carr, Commissioner

Promotes dignity for individuals with disabilities through employment and independent living in the community.

1635 Office of Civil Rights: Massachusetts
US Department of Education
Ste 900
33 Arch St
Boston, MA 02110-1453   617-289-0111
                                                   FAX 617-289-0150
                                                   TDD:877-521-2172
                                                   http://www.ed.gov
                                           e-mail: ocr.boston@ed.gov
This office covers the states of Connecticut, Maine, Massachusetts, New Hampshire, Rhode Island and Vermont.

1636 Office of Federal Contract Compliance: Boston District Office
US Department of Labor
Room E235
E235 Jfk Federal Building
Boston, MA 02203   617-565-7000
                                                   FAX 617-624-6702
                                                   TDD:617-565-9869
                                                   http://www.dol.gov
                                       e-mail: beatty.reba@dol.gov
Reba Beatty, District Director
Rhonda Aubn-Smith, Assistant Director

Enforces laws prohibiting employment discrimination on the basis of disability.

1637 Protection & Advocacy Agency
Disability Law Center
Ste 925
11 Beacon St
Boston, MA 02108-3051   617-723-8455
                                                        800-872-9992
                                                   FAX 617-723-9125
                                                   TTY: 617-227-9464
                                              http://www.dlc-ma.org
                                          e-mail: mail@dlc-ma.org
Robert Whitney, President

A private, non-profit organization responsible for providing protection and advocacy for the rights of Massachusetts residents with disabilities. Provides legal advocacy on disability issues that promote the fundamental rights of all pepole with disabilities to participate fully and equally in the social and economic life of Massachusetts.

1638 Region I: Office for Civil Rights
US Department Health & Human Services
Government Center
Boston, MA 02203   617-565-1500
                                                   FAX 617-565-1491
                                                   http://www.hhs.gov
                                      e-mail: brian.golden@hhs.gov
Brian Golden, Regional Director

1639 Region I: US Small Business Administration
Massachusetts District Office
Rm 265
10 Causeway St
Boston, MA 02222-1093   617-565-5590
                                                   http://www.sba.gov
Robert H Nelson, District Director

These regional offices of agencies enforce laws prohibiting employment discrimination on the basis of disability.

1640 State Department of Adult Education
Adult and Community Learning Services
4th Fl
350 Main St
Malden, MA 02148-5089   781-388-3300
                                                   FAX 781-388-3394
                                       http://www.doe.mass.edu/acls/#
                                        e-mail: acls@doe.mass.edu

Adult and Community Learning Services, a unit at the MA Department of Education, oversees and improves no-cost basic educational services (ABE) for adults in Masssachusetts. ACLS's mission is to provide each and every adult with opportunities to develop literacy skills needed to qualify for further education, job training, and better employment, and to reach his/her full potential as a family member, productive worker, and citizen.

Michigan

1641 Client Assistance Program (CAP): Michigan Department of Persons with Disabilities
Suite 500
409 Legacy Pkwy
Lansing, MI 48911   517-487-1755
                                                        800-288-5923
                                                   FAX 517-487-0827
                                                   TTY: 800-292-5896
                                                   http://www.mpas.org
                                         e-mail: molson@mpas.org
Manuela Kress-Shull, Executive Director
Manuela Kress-Shull, Manager

Assists people who are seeking or receiving services from Michigan Rehabilitation Services, Consumer Choice Programs, Michigan Commission for the Blind, Centers for Independent Living, and Supported Employment and Transition Programs.

1642 Michigan Correctional Educational Division
Department of Corrections: Prisoner Education Prog
PO Box 30003
206 E Michigan Ave
Lansing, MI 48909-7503   517-335-1426
                                                   FAX 517-335-0045
                                       http://www.michigan.gov/corrections
                                      e-mail: spencede@state.mi.us
Diane Spence, Director

The goal of the Michigan Department of Corrections is to provide the greatest amount of protection while making the most efficient use of the State's resources.

1643 Michigan Department of Community Health
201 Townsend St
Lansing, MI 48913   517-373-3740
                                                        877-932-6424
                                                   http://www.michigan.gov
                                       e-mail: adulted@michigan.gov
Janet Olszewski, Director

An advocacy organization that engages in advocacy, capacity building and systemic change activities that promote self-determination, independence, productivity, integration and inclusion in all facets of community life for people with developmental disabilities.

1644 Michigan Protection and Advocacy Service
4095 Legacy Pkwy
Suite 500
Lansing, MI 48911-4264   517-487-1755
                                                        800-288-5923
                                                   FAX 517-487-0827
                                                   http://www.mpas.org
                                         e-mail: molson@mpas.org
Michelle Huerta, President
Kate Pew Wolters, First Vice President
Thomas Landry, Second Vice President
Advocates for people with disabilities and gives information and advice about their rights as a person with disabilities.

1645 State Department of Adult Education
Michigan Department of Labor & Economic Growth
3rd Floor
201 N Washington Sq
Lansing, MI 48913

517-373-8800
877-932-6424
FAX 517-335-3630
http://www.michigan.gov
e-mail: adulted@michigan.gov

Dianne Duthie, Director

Promotes quality adult education.

1646 State GED Administration
DELEG
201 N Washington Sq
Victor Bldg, 2nd Fl
Lansing, MI 48913-0001

517-373-1692
FAX 517-335-3461
http://www.michigan.gov
e-mail: heckmana@michigan.gov

Dianne Duthie, GED State Administrator
Amy Heckman, Department Analyst
Jeannie Flak, Department Technician
Promotes adult education.

Minnesota

1647 Health Services Minneapolis
University of St Thomas
Ste 110
1000 Lasalle Ave
Minneapolis, MN 55403-2025

651-962-4763
http://www.stthomas.edu
e-mail: lifework@stthomas.edu

Brian D Dusbiber, Director
Steve Fritz, Athletic Director
Gene McGivern, Sports Information Director
Provides special services and resources to meet the unique needs of graduate students, education students (both graduate and undergraduate), and alumni/ae.

1648 Minnesota Department of Children, Families & Learning
Department of Education
1500 Highway 36 W
Roseville, MN 55113-4035

651-582-8200
FAX 651-582-8202
http://www.education.state.mn.us
e-mail: alice.seagren@state.mn.us

Alice Seagren, Commissioner
Chas Anderson, Deputy Commissioner

To improve educational achievement by establishing clear standards, measuring performance, assisting educators and increasing opportunities for life long learning.

1649 Minnesota Department of Human Rights
Freeman Building
625 Robert Street North
Saint Paul, MN 55155

651-539-1100
800-657-3704
FAX 651-296-9042
TTY: 651-296-1283
http://www.humanrights.state.mn.us
e-mail: velma.korbel@state.mn.us

Kevin M. Lindsey, Commissioner
Jeff Holman, Director of Communications
Kristi Streff, Human Resources
To make Minnesota discrimination free.

1650 Minnesota Governor's Council on Developmental Disabilities
370 Centennial Office Building
658 Cedar Street
Saint Paul, MN 55155-1603

651-296-4018
877-348-0505
FAX 651-297-7200
TTY: 800-627-3529
http://www.mncdd.org or www.mnddc.org
e-mail: admin.dd@state.mn.us

Colleen Wieck PhD, Executive Director

To provide information, education, and training to build knowledge, develop skills, and change attitudes that will lead to increased independence, productivit, self determination, integration and inclusion for all people with developmental disabilities and their families.

1651 Minnesota's Assistive Technology Act Program
Minnesota STAR Program
358 Centennial Office Building
658 Cedar St
Saint Paul, MN 55155-1603

651-201-2640
888-234-1267
FAX 651-282-6671
http://www.starprogram.state.mn.us
e-mail: star.program@state.mn.us

Jo Erbes, Executive Director
Jennie Delisi, Program Staff
Joan Gillum, Program Staff
STAR's mission is to help all Minnesotans with disabilities gain access to and acquire the assistive technology they need to live, learn, work and play. The Minnesota STAR Program is federally funded by the Rehabilitation Services Administration in assordance with the Assistive Technology Act of 1998.

1652 Protection & Advocacy Agency
Minnesota Disability Law Center
430 1st Ave N
Suite 300
Minneapolis, MN 55401-1742

612-332-1441
800-292-4150
FAX 612-334-5755
TDD:612-332-4668
http://www.mndlc.org
e-mail: mndlc@midmnlegal.org

Margaret Russell, Director
Cathy Haukedahl, Executive Director
Andrea Kaufman, Director of Development
To advance the dignity, self-determination and equality of individuals with disabilities.

1653 State Department of Adult Basic Education
Department of Education
1500 Highway 36 W
Roseville, MN 55113-4035

651-582-8200
http://education.state.mn.us
e-mail: mde.abe@state.mn.us

Becky Leschner, Director

Offered through Minnesota's public school system, provides opportunities to obtain academic, interpersonal and problem-solving skills necessary to live self-sufficient lives.

Mississippi

1654 Mississippi Department of Corrections
723 N President St
Jackson, MS 39202-3021

601-359-5600
FAX 601-359-5680
http://www.mdoc.state.ms.us
e-mail: cepps@mdoc.state.ms.us

Christopher Epps, Commissioner
Phil Bryant, Governor
Emmitt L. Sparkman, Deputy Commissioner

To provide and promote public safety through efficient and effective offender custody, care, control and treatment consistent with sound correctional prinicipals and constitutional standards.

1655 Mississippi Department of Employment Security
PO Box 1699
Jackson, MS 39215-1699   601-321-6000
http://www.mdes.ms.gov
e-mail: comments@mdes.ms.gov
Tommye Dale Favre, Executive Director

Brings people and jobs together.

1656 Mississippi Project START
2550 Peachtree Street
Jackson, MS 39216   601-987-4872
800-852-8328
FAX 601-364-2349
http://www.msprojectstart.org
e-mail: contactus@msprojectstart.org
Dorothy Young, Project Director
Kacee Mott, Administrative Assistant
Jason Bates, Repair Specialist
To ensure the provision of appropriate Technology-Related services for Mississippians with disabilities by increasing the awareness of and access to Assistive Technology and by helping the existing service systems to become more consumer repsonsive so that all Mississippians with disabilities will receive appropriate Technology-related services and devices.

1657 State Department of Adult Education
359 North West St
P.O. Box 771, Suite 301
Jackson, MS 39205-0771   601-359-3498
FAX 601-359-2198
http://www.mde.k12.s.us/special_education
e-mail: eburnham@mdek12.state.ms.us
Ann Moore, State Director
Ellen Davis Burnham, Bureau Director, Data/Fiscal Mgt

Promotes adult education.

1658 State Department of Education
PO Box 771
Jackson, MS 39205   601-359-3513
http://www.mde.k12.ms.us
Dr. O. Wayne Gann, Chair
Howell Gage, Vice-Chair
Kami Bumgarner, Board of Director
Promotes quality education.

Missouri

1659 Assistive Technology
1501 NW Jefferson Street
Blue Springs, MO 64015   816-655-6700
800-647-8557
FAX 816-655-6710
TTY: 816-655-6711
http://www.at.mo.gov
e-mail: MoAT1501@att.net
C. Marty Exline, Director
David Baker, Program Coordinator
Eileen Belton, Program Coordinator
To increase access to assistive technology for Missourians with all types of disabilities, of all ages.

1660 Assistive Technology Project
University of Missouri-Kansas City
5100 Rockhill Rd
Kansas City, MO 64110-2446   816-235-1000
FAX 816-235-2662
http://www.umkc.edu

Dr. Elson S. Floyd, President
Carol Hintz, Assoc. Vice Chancellor
Curt Crespino, Vice Chancellor - Advancement
Promotes independent living through technology.

1661 EEOC St. Louis District Office
Robert A Young Federal Building
Rm 8.100
1222 Spruce St
Saint Louis, MO 63103-2828
800-669-4000
FAX 314-539-7894
TTY: 800-669-6820
http://www.eeoc.gov
James R Neely Jr, Director
Jacqueline A Berrien, Chair
Constance S. Barker, Commissioner
These regional offices of agencies enforce laws prohibiting employment discrimination on the basis of disability.

1662 Great Plains Disability and Business Technical Assistance Center (DBTAC)
100 Corporate Lake Dr
Columbia, MO 65203-7170   573-882-3600
800-949-4232
FAX 573-884-4925
TTY: 573-882-3600
http://www.adaproject.org
e-mail: ada@missouri.edu
Jim De Jong, Director
Julie Brinkhoff, Assistant Director
Troy Balthazor, Information Specialist
To provide information, materials and technical assistance to individuals and entities that are covered by the Americans with Disabilities Act. In addition to the ADA, Great Plains ADA Center provides the ADA and disability-related legislation such as the Family Medical Leave Act, Workforce Investment Act and the Telecommunications Act.

1663 Missouri Protection & Advocacy Services
925 S Country Club Dr
Jefferson City, MO 65109-4510   573-893-3333
866-777-7199
FAX 573-893-4231
http://www.moadvocacy.org
e-mail: mopasjc@embarqmail.com
Larry Opinsky, Chair
Joel Wrinkle, Vice Chair
Michele Ohmes, Secretary/Treasurer
A federally mandated system in the state of Missouri which provides protection of the rights of persons with disabilities through leagally-based avocacy

1664 Office of Civil Rights: Missouri
US Department of Education
Ste 2037
8930 Ward Pkwy
Kansas City, MO 64114-3302   816-268-0550
FAX 816-823-1404
TDD:877-521-2172
http://www.ed.gov
e-mail: ocr.kansascity@ed.gov
Lisa Robinson, Assistant Regional IG for Audit
Tony Miller, Deputy Secretary
Russlynn Ali, Assistant Secretary
This office covers the states of Kansas, Missouri, Nebraska, Oklahoma and South Dakota.

1665 Protection & Advocacy Agency
925 S Country Club Dr
Jefferson City, MO 65109-4510   573-893-3333
800-392-8667
FAX 573-893-4231
http://www.moadvocacy.org
e-mail: mopasjc@embarqmail.com
Larry Opinsky, Chair
Joel Wrinkle, Vice Chair
Michele Ohmes, Secretary/Treasurer

Protects the rights of individuals with disabilities by providing advocacy and legal services.

1666 Region VII: US Department of Health and Human Services
Office For Civil Rights
Bolling Federal Building
601 E 12th St
Kansas City, MO 64106-2817
816-426-7278
FAX 816-426-3686
TDD:816-426-7065
http://www.hhs.gov/region7
e-mail: frank.campbell@hhs.gov
Jay Angoff, Regional Manager
Leon Rodriguez, Director
William B. Schultz, Acting General Counsel

Montana

1667 Assistive Technology Project
University of Montana Rural Institute
52 Corbin Hall
Missoula, MT 59812
406-243-5467
800-732-0323
FAX 406-243-4730
TTY: 800-732-0323
http://www.ruralinstitute.umt.edu
e-mail: rural@ruralinstitute.umt.edu
Perry J. Brown, Ph.D., Provost
R. Timm Vogelsberg, Ph.D., Executive Director
R. Timm Vogelsberg, Ph.D., Administration & Technology

This statewide program at the University of Montana promotes assistive devices and services for persons of all ages with disabilities.

1668 Correctional Education
Montana Department of Corrections
PO Box 201301
Helena, MT 59620-1301
406-444-3930
FAX 406-444-4920
http://http://mt.gov/statejobs/pocontacts.mcpx
Mike Ferriter, Director

1669 Montana Council on Developmental Disabilities (MCDD)
2714 Billings Ave
Helena, MT 59601-9767
406-443-4332
866-443-4332
FAX 406-443-4192
http://www.mtcdd.org
e-mail: deborah@mtcdd.org
Deborah Swingley, CEO

The goal of the Council is to increase the indpendence, productivity, inclusion and integration into the community of people with developmental disabilities through systemic change, capacity building and advocacy activities.

1670 Montana Department of Labor & Industry
PO Box 1728
Helena, MT 59624-1728
406-444-2840
FAX 406-444-1394
TTY: 406-444-1394
http://dli.mt.gov
e-mail: dliquestion@mt.gov
Keith Kelly, Commissioner
Leisa Smith, Program Director
Kali Wicks, Program Specialist
Promotes the well-being of Montana's workers, employers, an dcitixens, and upholds their rights and responsibilities. Committed to being responsive to communities and businesses at the local level.

1671 Montana Office of Public Instruction
PO Box 202501
Helena, MT 59620-2501
406-444-3095
888-231-9393
http://http://opi.mt.gov/
e-mail: opisupt@mt.gov
Denise Juneau, Superintendent

Supports schools so that students acheive high standards.

1672 Office of Adult Basic and Literacy Education
Montana Office of Public Instruction
PO Box 202501
Helena, MT 59620-2501
406-444-3095
888-231-9393
http://http://opi.mt.gov/
Denise Juneau, Superintendent

Adult education programs include basic literacy, workplace literacy, family literacy, preparation for GED, English as a Second Language and other services that provide adults and out of school youth opportunities at enhancing skills, improving parenting, and youth assistance related to employment and self-sufficiency.

1673 University of Montana's Rural Institute - MonTECH
700 SW Higgins Ave.
Suite 250
Missoula, MT 59803
406-243-5751
877-243-5511
http://montech.ruralinstitute.umt.edu
e-mail: montech@ruralinstitute.umt.edu
Kathy Laurin PhD, Program Director

A program of the University of Montana Rural Institute: Center for Excellence in Disability, Education, Research and Service. Specialize in Assistive Technology and oversee a variety of AT related grants and contracts. The overall goal is to develop a comprehensive, statewide system of assistive technology related assistance.

Nebraska

1674 Answers4Families: Center on Children, Families and the Law
PO Box 880227
Lincoln, NE 68588
402-472-0844
800-746-8420
http://www.answers4families.org
e-mail: jwilliam@answers4families.org
Charlotte Lewis, Director

A project of the Center on Children, Families and Law at University of Nebraska. Mission is to provide info, opportunities, education and support to Nebraskans through Internet resources. The Center serves individuals with special needs and mental health disorders, foster families, caregivers, assisted living, and school nurses.

1675 Assistive Technology Partnership
3901 N 27th St
Suite 5
Lincoln, NE 68521-4177
402-471-0734
888-806-6287
FAX 402-471-6052
http://atp.ne.gov
e-mail: mark.schultz@atp.state.ne.us
Leslie Novacek, Director

Dedicated to helping Nebraskan's with disabilities, their families and professionals obtain assistive technology devices and services.

1676 Client Assistance Program (CAP): Nebraska Division of Persons with Disabilities
Nebraska Department of Education
301 Centennial Mall South
Box 94987
Lincoln, NE 68509
402-471-3656
800-742-7594
FAX 402-471-0117
http://www.cap.state.ne.us
e-mail: victoria.rasmussen@cap.ne.gov
Frank Lloyd, Executive Director

The Client Assistance Program helps individuals who have concerns or difficulties when applying for or receiving rehabilitation services funded under the Rehabilitation Act.

1677 Nebraska Advocacy Services
Center for Disability Rights, Law & Advocacy
134 South 13th Street
Suite 600
Lincoln, NE 68508-1930
402-474-3183
800-422-6691
FAX 402-474-3274
http://www.nebraskaadvocacyservices.org
e-mail: info@nebraskaadvocacyservices.org
Timothy F Shaw, CEO
Eric Evans, Chief Operating Officer
Patricia Nichelson, Legal Secretary
Created to assist individuals with disabilities and their families in protecting and advocating for their rights. From its beginning, NAS has promoted the principles of equality, self-determination, and dignity of persons with disabilities.

1678 Nebraska Department of Labor
550 S 16th St
Lincoln, NE 58508
402-471-9000
800-833-7352
FAX 402-471-2318
http://www.dol.nebraska.gov
e-mail: lmi_ne@nebraska.gov
Phillip Baker, Administrator

1679 Nebraska Equal Opportunity Commission
301 Centennial Mall S
5th Fl
Lincoln, NE 68509-4934
402-471-2024
800-642-6112
FAX 402-471-4059
http://www.neoc.ne.gov.
Barbara Albers, Executive Director

A state agency that investigates complaints of discrimination in employment, housing and public accomodations.

1680 State Department of Education
PO Box 94987
Lincoln, NE 68509-4987
402-471-2295
FAX 402-471-8127
http://www.nde.state.ne.us
e-mail: vicki.l.bauer@nebraska.gov
Douglas D Christensen, Commissioner
Vicki L Bauer, Director

Organized into teams that interact to operate the agency and carry out the duties assigned by state and federal statutes and the policy directions of the State Board of Education.

1681 State GED Administration: Nebraska
Nebraska Department of Education
PO Box 94987
Lincoln, NE 68509-4987
402-471-4807
FAX 402-471-8127
http://www.nde.state.ne.us
e-mail: vicki.l.bauer@nebraska.gov
Vicki L Bauer, Director
Douglas D Christensen, Commissioner

To provide educational opportunities for adults to improve their literacy skills to a level requisite for effective citizenship and productive employment. This includes preparation for and successful completion of the high school equivalency program.

1682 Vocational Rehabilitation
Nebraska Department of Education
203 E Stolley Park Rd
Suite B
Grand Island, NE 68801
308-385-6200
800-632-3382
FAX 308-385-6104
http://www.vocrehab.state.ne.us
e-mail: vr.grandisland@vr.ne.gov
Frank C Lloyd, Asst Commissioner of Education

The Nebraska Rehabilitation Program has people with disabilities join the workforce. Our team of experts provides direct services for employers and people with disabilities that lead to employment.

Nevada

1683 Assistive Technology
Office of Disability Services
3656 Research Way
Suite 32
Carson City, NV 89706-7932
775-687-4452
FAX 775-687-3292
TTY: 775-687-3388
http://www.dhhs.nv.gov
e-mail: jrosenlund@dhhs.nv.gov
John Rosenlund, NV Asst Tech Coll Proj Dir
Todd Butterworth, Bureau Chief

Promotes independent living through technology.

1684 Client Assistance Program (CAP): Nevada Division of Persons with Disability
Dpt of Employment, Training and Rehabilitation
2800 E. St. Louis Ave. Las Vegas
Las Vegas, NV 89104-2829
702-486-6688
800-633-9879
FAX 702-486-6691
TTY: 702-486-1018
http://www.detr.state.nv.us
e-mail: detrcap@nvdetr.org
Robin Hall-Walker, Program Assistant
Kate Osti, Counselor
Kathy Treants, Training & Information Counselor
To assist and advocate for clients and applicants in their relationships with projects, programs, and community rehabilitation programs that provide services under the Act. The program is also responsible for informing individuals with disabilities in Nevada, of the services and benefits available to them.

1685 Correctional Education and Vocational Training
Bldg 17
5500 Snyder Ave
Carson City, NV 89701-6752
775-887-3285
FAX 775-687-6715
http://www.doc.nc.gov
e-mail: mhall@doc.nv.gov
Jackie Crawford, Director
Marta Hall, Education Coordinator

To continue and expand an educational training program which contains literacy, ESL, numeracy, community outreach, and vocational training that will provide long-term benefits to both inmates and the Nevada community in general.

1686 Department of Employment, Training and Rehabilitation

500 E 3rd St
Carson City, NV 89713

702-486-6688
800-633-9879
FAX 702-486-6691
TTY: 702-486-1018
http://www.detr.state.nv.us

Robin Hall-Walker, Client Assistance Rep
Kate Osti, Counselor
Kathy Treants, Training & Information Counselor
Comprised of four divisions with numerous bureaus programs, and services housed in offices throughout Nevada to provide citizens the state's premier source of employment, training, and rehabilitative programs.

1687 Nevada Bureau of Disability Adjudication

Ste 300
1050 E William St
Carson City, NV 89701-3102

775-687-4430
FAX 775-886-0101
http://detr.state.nv.us/rehab
e-mail: detrvr@nvdetr.org

Sandra Kelley, Manager

Evaluates applications from individuals with permanent disabilities to determine if they are eligible for federal Supplemental Security Income or Social Security Disability Insurance (SSDI).

1688 Nevada Disability and Law Center

6039 Eldora Ave
Ste C
Las Vegas, NV 89146-5611

702-257-8150
888-349-3843
FAX 702-257-8170
TTY: 702-257-8160
http://www.ndalc.org
e-mail: ndalc@ndalclv.org

Jack Mayes, Executive Director
William Heaivilin, Supervising Rights Attorney

A private, nonprofit organization and serves as Nevada's federally mandated protection and advocacy system for the human, legal, and service rights of individuals with disabilities.

1689 Nevada Equal Rights Commission

1515 E Tropicana Ave
Las Vegas, NV 89119-6517

702-486-7161
FAX 702-486-7054
TDD:702-486-7164
http://www.nvdetr.org
e-mail: detrnerc@nvdetr.org

Robin Hall-Walker, Client Assistance Rep
Kate Osti, State Independent Living Council
Kathy Treants, Parents Training & Information
To foster the rights of all persons to seek, obtain and maintain employment, and to access services in places of public accomodation without discrimination, distinction, exclusion or restriction because of race, religion creed, color, age, sex (gender and/or orientation), disability, national origin, or ancestry.

1690 Nevada Governor's Council on Developmental Disabilities

896 W. Nye Ln.
Suite 202
Carson City, NV 89703

775-684-8619
FAX 775-684-8626
http://www.nevadaddcouncil.org
e-mail: smanning@dhhs.nv.gov

Sherry Manning, DD Council Director
Lisa Antram, Chair
Filiberto Ontiveros, Vice chair

Tp provide resources at the community level which promote equal opportunity and life choices for people with disabilities through which they may positively contribute to Nevada society.

1691 Nevada State Rehabilitation Council

Nevada Rehabilitation Division
1370 S Curry St
Carson City, NV 89703-5146

775-684-3200
FAX 775-684-4186
http://www.detr.state.nv.su
e-mail: pjjune@nvdetr.org

Robin Hall-Walker, Client Assistance Rep
Kate Osti, State Independent Living Council
Kathy Treants, Parents Training & Information
To help insure vocational rehabilitation programs are consumer oriented, driven and result in employment outcomes for Nevadans with disabilities. Funding for innovation and expansions grants

1692 State Department of Adult Education

Nevada Department of Education
755 N Roop St
Suite 201
Carson City, NV 89701-3113

775-687-7300
FAX 775-687-8636
http://nde.doe.nv.gov
e-mail: mailto:rfitzpatrick@doe.nv.gov

Rorie Fitzpatrick, Deputy Superintendent
James Guthrie, Superintendent
Christina Harper, Administrative Assistant III
To provide leadership and resources to enable all learners to gain knowledge and skills needed to achieve career and employment goals, meet civic duties and accomplish educational objective.

1693 State Department of Education

700 E Fifth St
Carson City, NV 89701-5096

775-687-9217
FAX 775-687-9101
http://www.doe.nv.gov

Keith Rheault, Superintendent

The Nevada State Board of Education acts as an advocate and visionary for all children and sets the policy that allows every child equal access to educational services, provides the vision for a premier educational system and works in partnership with other stakeholders to ensure high levels of success for all in terms of job readiness, graduation, ability to be lifelong learners, problem solvers, citizens able to adapt to a changing world and contributing members of a society.

New Hampshire

1694 Disability Rights Center

18 Low Ave
Concord, NH 03301-4971

603-228-0432
800-834-1721
FAX 603-225-2077
TTY: 800-834-1721
http://www.drcnh.org
e-mail: advocacy@drcnh.org

Richard Cohen, Executive Director
James Fox, Staff Attorney
Julia Freeman-Woolpert, Outreach Advocacy Director
Dedicated to eliminating barriers existing in New Hampshire to the full an dequal enjoyment of civil and other legal rights by people with disabilities.

1695 Granite State Independent Living

21 Chenell Dr
Concord, NH 03301-8539

603-228-9680
800-826-3700
FAX 603-225-3304
TTY: 888-396-3459
http://www.gsil.org
e-mail: info@gsil.org

Clyde E. Terry, JD, Chief Executive Officer
Debora Krider, Ed.D, Chief Operating Officer
Kecin Walsh, Vice President of Finance/IT
A statewide non-profit, service and advocacy organization that provides tools for living life on your terms. To promote life with independence for people with disabilities through the four core services of advocacy, information, education and support.

1696   Institute on Disability
University of New Hampshire
10 W Edge Dr
Suite 101
Durham, NH 03824-3513   603-862-4320
                                        FAX 603-862-0555
                                    http://www.iod.unh.edu
                            e-mail: contact.iod@unh.edu
Charles E. Drum, Director & Professor
Susan Fox, Associate Director
Andrew Houtenville, Director of Research
Established to provide a coherent university-based focus for the improvement of knowledge, policies, and practices related to the lives of persons with disabilities and their families. Also advances policies and systems changes, promising practices, education, and research that strengthen communities and ensure full access, equal opportunities, and participation for all persons.

1697   New Hampshire Commission for Human Rights
2 Chenell Dr
Unit 2
Concord, NH 03301-8501   603-271-2767
                                        FAX 603-271-6339
                                        TDD:800-735-2964
                                    http://www.nh.gov/hrc
                        e-mail: humanrights@nhsa.state.nh.us
Joni Esperian, Executive Director
Roxanne Juliano, Assistant Executive Director

Enforcement of RSA 354-A, the Law Against Discrimination and the ADA Title I, Employment, and Housing. Private School/Pre-and After School program enrollees, not public school. All employees covered regardless of public/private distinction if 6 or more employees (NH) 15 or more (Federal).

1698   New Hampshire Developmental Disabilities Council
21 South Fruit St
Suite 22
Concord, NH 03301-2451   603-271-3236
                                        800-852-3345
                                        FAX 603-271-1156
                                        TDD:800-735-2964
                                    http://www.nhddc.org
                        e-mail: Carol.M.Stamatakis@ddc.nh.gov
Carol Stamatakis, Executive Director
David Ouellette, Project Manager
Shirley Wood, Accountant
A federally funded agency that supports public policies and initiative that remoce barriers and promote opportunities in all areas of life.

1699   New Hampshire Employment Security
32 S Main St
Concord, NH 03301-4857   603-224-3311
                                        800-852-3400
                                        FAX 603-228-4145
                                        TDD:800-852-3400
                                    http://www.nh.gov
                        e-mail: webmaster@nhes.state.nh.us
Tara Reardon, Commissioner
Darrell Gates, Deputy Commissioner

Refers individuals with disabilities to organizations and agencies that assist people with disabilities without charge.

1700   New Hampshire Governor's Commission on Disability
57 Regional Dr
Concord, NH 03301-8518   603-271-2773
                                        800-852-3405
                                        FAX 603-271-2837
                                        TTY: 603-271-2774
                                    http://www.nh.gov
                            e-mail: Disability@nh.gov
John Richards, Executive Director
Jillian Shedd, Accessibility Coordinator
Gayle Baird, Accountant I
To remove barriers, architectural or attitudinal, which bar persons with disabilities from participating in the mainstream of society.

1701   Parent Information Center
P.O. Box 2405
Concord, NH 03302   603-224-7005
                                        800-947-7005
                                    FAX 603-224-4365
                            http://www.parentinformationcenter.org
Kevin Lew-Hanson, Executive Director

A recognized leader in building strong family/school partnerships. PIC provides information, support, and educational programs for parents, family members, educators, and the community. PIC is a pioneer in promoting effective parent involvment in the special education process.

1702   ServiceLink
555 Auburn St
Manchester, NH 03103-4803   603-644-2240
                                        866-634-9412
                                        FAX 603-644-2361
                                    http://www.nh.gov
                            e-mail: Disability@nh.gov
John Richards, Executive Director
Jillian Shedd, Accessibility Coordinator
Gayle Baird, Accountant I
Provides community supportive information and referral assistance to Edlers, their families and Adults with Disabilities in accessing services for caregivee support, financial and legal concerns, home care services, housing information and assistance, recreational and social events, information about applying for Medicaid and Medicaid programs such as Choices For Independence program.

1703   State Department of Education: Division of Career Technology & Adult Learning-Vocational Rehab
101 Pleasant Street
Concord, NH 03301-3860   603-271-3471
                                        800-299-1647
                                        FAX 603-271-1953
                                    http://www.ed.state.nh.us
                            e-mail: Lori.Temple@doe.nh.gov
Paul K Leather, Deputy Commissioner
Lisa Danley, CTE State Director
Judy Fillion, Director
Provides services to both individuals with disabilities and employers. People with disabilities can work and take advantage of the opportunities available to the citizens of New Hampshire. A joint State/Federal program that seeks to empower people to make informed choices, build viable careers, and live more independently in the community.

New Jersey

1704   Assistive Technology Center (ATAC)
Disability Rights New Jersey
210 S Broad St
Ste 3
Trenton, NJ 08608-2407   609-292-9742
                                        800-922-7233
                                        FAX 609-777-0187
                                        TTY: 609-633-7106
                                    http://www.drnj.org
                            e-mail: advocate@njpanda.org

Curtis Edmonds, Director

Assists individuals in overcoming barriers in the system and making assistive technology more accessible to individuals with disabilities throughout the state.

1705 New Jersey Department of Law and Public Safety
New Jersey Division on Civil Rights
PO Box 46001
Newark, NJ 07101-8003   973-648-2700
                                            FAX 973-648-4405
                                            TTY: 973-648-4678
                                            http://www.nj.gov/
J Frank Vespa-Papaleo Esq, Director

The Division on Civil Rights enforces the New Jersey Law Against Discrimination which prohibits discrimination in employment, housing and public accommodations because of race, creed, color, national origin, ancestry, sex, affectional and sexual orientation, marital status, nationality or handicap.

1706 New Jersey Department of Special Education
New Jersey Department of Education
PO Box 500
Trenton, NJ 08625   609-292-0147
                                            FAX 609-984-8422
                                            http://www.state.nj.us
Roberta Wohle, Director

The office is resonsible for administering all federal funds received for educating people with disabilities ages 3 through 21. Also monitors the delivery of special education programs operated under state authority, provides mediation services to parents and school districts, processes hearings and conducts complaint investigations. Also funds four learning resource centers (LRCs) that provide information, circulate materials, offer technical assistance/consultation and production services.

1707 New Jersey Programs for Infants and Toddlers with Disabilities: Early Intervention System
New Jersey Department of Health
50 E State St
P.O. Box 364
Trenton, NJ 08625-0364   609-777-7734
                                                 888-653-4463
                                            FAX 609-777-7739
          http://www.state.nj.us/health/fhs/eiphome.htm
               e-mail: terry.harrison@ddn.state.nj.us
Terri Harrison, Part C Coordinator

The New Jersey Early Intervention System provides a comprehensive system of services for children, birth to age three, with developmental delays or disabilities and their families.

1708 Protection & Advocacy Agency (NJP&A)
Ste 3
210 S Broad St
Trenton, NJ 08608-2407   609-292-9742
                                                 800-922-7233
                                            FAX 609-777-0187
                                            TTY: 609-633-7106
                                            http://www.njpanda.org
                              e-mail: advocate@njpanda.org
Sarah Mitchell, Executive Director
Joseph Young, Deputy Director
Marie Davis, Office Manager
To protect, advocate for and advance the rights of persons with disabilites in pursuit of a society in which persons with disabilities exercise self-determination and choice, and are treated with dignity.

1709 State Department of Adult Education
Department of Education
PO Box 500
Trenton, NJ 08625   609-984-5593
                                            FAX 609-633-9825
                                            http://www.state.nj.us/education

Arlene Roth, Director Adult Education
Alfred Murray, Executive Director

1710 State GED Administration: Office of Specialized Populations
New Jersey Department of Education
PO Box 500
Trenton, NJ 08625   609-292-8853
                                            FAX 609-633-9825
                              http://www.state.nj.us/education
Arlene Roth, Director Adult Education
Alfred Murray, Executive Director

New Mexico

1711 Client Assistance Program (CAP): New Mexico Protection and Advocacy System
1720 Louisiana Blvd. NE
Suite 204
Albuquerque, NM 87110-7070   505-256-3100
                                                 800-432-4682
                                            FAX 505-256-3184
                                            TTY: 505-256-3100
                                            http://http://www.drnm.org
                                            e-mail: info@drnm.org
Michael J. Rourke, President
Adam Carrasco, Vice President
Jonathan Toledo, Secretary Treasurer
Helps persons with disabilities who have concerns about agencies in New Mexico that provide rehabilitation or independent living services. The kind of help may be information or advocacy. For questions about Division of Vocational Rehabilitation, Commission for the Blind, Independent Living Centers and Preojects With Industsry CAP can help.

1712 New Mexico Department of Workforce Solutions: Workforce Transition Services Division
401 Broadway NE
Albuquerque, NM 87102   505-841-8405
                                            FAX 505-841-8491
                                            http://www.dws.state.nm.us
Currently composed of two bureaus and under the supervision of a Division Director responsible for the design, administration, management and implementation of the Workforce Investment Act in New Mexico and any successor legislation. Within this capacity, the Division serves on behalf of the Governor with respect to statewide oversight and compliance, and as the principle support staff to the State Workforce Development Board.

1713 New Mexico Human Rights Commission Education Bureau
Ste 103
1596 Pacheco St
Santa Fe, NM 87505-3960   505-827-6817
                                            FAX 505-827-9676
          http://http://www.dws.state.nm.us/LaborRelation
Francie Cordova, Executive Director

1714 New Mexico Public Education Department
300 Don Gaspar Ave
Santa Fe, NM 87501-2744   505-827-5800
                                            http://www.sde.state.nm.us
                              e-mail: join.ped@state.nm.us
Dr Veronica Garcia, Secretary
Lisa G Salazar, GED Administrator
Andrew Winnegar, Project Director
To provide leadership, technical assistance and quality assurance to improve student performance and close the achievement gap.

1715 New Mexico State GED Testing Program
New Mexico Public Education Department
300 Don Gaspar Ave
Santa Fe, NM 87501-2744   505-827-5800
http://www.ped.state.nm.us
e-mail: join.ped@state.nm.us
Lisa G Salazar, GED Administrator
Dr Veronica Garcia, Secretary
Andrew Winnegar, Project Director
The primary aid of the GED testing program in New Mexico
is to proive a second opportunity for individuals to obtain
their high school diplomas.

1716 New Mexico Technology-Related Assistance Program
Department of Education
300 Don Gaspar Ave
Santa Fe, NM 87503   505-827-5800
http://www.ped.state.nm.us
e-mail: join.ped@state.nm.us
Andrew Winnegar, Project Director
Lisa G Salazar, GED Administrator
Dr Veronica Garcia, Secretary

1717 State Department of Adult Education
Department of Education
300 Don Gaspar Ave
Santa Fe, NM 87501-2744   505-827-5800
http://www.sde.state.nm.us
e-mail: join.ped@state.nm.us
Patricia Chavez, Contact
Lisa G Salazar, GED Administrator
Dr Veronica Garcia, Secretary

New York

1718 DBTAC: Northeast ADA Center
Cornell University
201 Dolgen Hall
Ithaca, NY 14853   607-255-6686
800-949-4232
FAX 607-255-2763
http://www.ilr.cornell.edu
e-mail: dbtacnortheast@cornell.edu
Wendy Strobel, Project Director
Susanne Bruyere, Principal Investigator

Provides information, referrals, resources, and raining on
equal opportunity for people with disabilities and on the
Americans with Disabilities Act. Serve businesses, employers, government entities, individuals with disabilities, and
the media in NY, NJ, PR, and the US Virgin Islands.

1719 Department of Correctional Services
Bldg 2
1220 Washington Ave
Albany, NY 12226-2050   518-457-8126
http://http://www.doccs.ny.gov
Brian Fischer, Commissioner
Andrew M. Cuomo, Governor

To provide for public protection by administering a network
of correctional facilities that: retain inmates in safe custody
until released by law; offer inmates an opportunity to improve their rmployment potential and their ability to function in a non-criminal fashion; offer staff a variety of
opportunities for career enrichment and advancement; and,
offer stable and humane community environments in which
all participants, staff anf inmates can perform their required
tasks.

1720 NYS Commission on Quality of Care/TRAID Program
401 State St
Schenectady, NY 12305-2303   518-388-2892
800-624-4143
FAX 518-388-2890
TTY: 800-624-4143
http://www.cqcapd.state.ny.us
e-mail: lisa.rosano@cqcapd.state.ny.us
Andrew M. Cuomo, Governor
Roger Bearden, Chair
Bruce Blower, Member
A statewide systems advocacy program promoting assistive
technology devices and services to persons of all ages with
all disabilities.

1721 NYS Developmental Disabilities Planning Council
99 Washington Avenue, 12th Floor
Suite 1230
Albany, NY 12210-2329   518-486-7505
800-395-3372
FAX 518-402-3505
http://http://ddpc.ny.gov/
e-mail: ddpc@ddpc.state.ny.us
Shiela M. Carey, Executive Director
Thomas F. Lee, Public Information Officer
Thomas A. Meyers, Chief Information Officer
In partnership with individuals with developmental disabili-
ties, their families and communities provides leadership by
promoting policies, plans and practices.

**1722 New York Department of Labor: Division of Employ-
ment and Workforce Solutions**
Building 12
W.A. Harriman Campus
Albany, NY 12240   518-457-9000
888-469-7365
FAX 518-457-9526
TDD:800-662-1220
http://www.labor.ny.gov
e-mail: nysdol@labor.state.ny.us
Leo Rosales, Director Communications
Ruth Pillittere, Assistant Director Communication
Karen Coleman, Division Director

**1723 New York State Commission on Quality Care and Ad-
vocacy for Persons with Disabilities (CQCAPD)**
401 State St
Schenectady, NY 12305-2303   518-388-2892
800-624-4143
FAX 518-388-2890
TTY: 800-624-4143
http://www.cqcapd.state.ny.us
e-mail: rosemary.lamb@cqcapd.state.ny.us
Andrew M. Cuomo, Governor
Roger Bearden, Chair
Bruce Blower, Member
Our mission is to improve the quality of life for persons with
disabilities, to protect their rights, and to advocate needed
changes by promoting the development of laws, policies and
practices that advance the inclusion of all persons with disabilities into the rich fabric of our society.

**1724 New York State Office of Vocational & Educational Ser-
vices for Individuals with Disabilities**
1 Commerce Plaza
Rm 1609
Albany, NY 12234-1000   518-465-2492
800-222-5627
http://www.vesid.nysed.gov
e-mail: accesadm@mail.nysed.gov
Philip Larocque, Deputy Commissioner

To promote educational equity and excellence for students with disabilities while ensuring that they receive the rights and protection to which they are entitles; assure appropriate continuity between the child and adult services systems; and provide the highest quality vocational rehabilitation and independent living services to all eligible persons as quickly as those services are required to enable them to work and live independent, self-directed lives.

1725 Office of Civil Rights: New York
US Department of Education
Fl 26
1 Financial Sq
New York, NY 10005-3534   646-428-3900
FAX 646-428-3843
TDD:877-521-2172
http://www.ed.gov.
e-mail: ocr.newyork@ed.gov
Daniel Schultz, Regional IG for Audit
Brian Hickey, Special Agent In Charge
Russlynn Ali, Assistant Secretary
This office covers the states of New Jersey and New York.

1726 Office of Curriculum & Instructional Support
New York State Department of Education
Rm 319
89 Washington Ave
Albany, NY 12234-1000   518-474-8892
FAX 518-474-0319
http://www.emsc.nysed.gov
e-mail: hgoldsmi@mail.nysed.gov
Howard J Goldsmith, Executive Coordinator

Support quality curriculum, instruction, career and technical education, adult and famiy literacy, middle-level education, professional development for teachers, and promote workforce development.

1727 Programs for Children with Special Health Care Needs
Bureau of Child & Adolescent Health Dept of Health
Room 208
Corning Tower Building
Albany, NY 12237   518-474-2084
FAX 518-474-5445
http://www.health.state.ny.us
e-mail: cak03@health.state.ny.us
Nirav R. Shah, M.D., M.P.H., Commissioner
Andrew M. Cuomo, Governor

Our mission is to achieve a statewide system of care for CSHCN and their families that links them to appropriate health and related services, identifies gaps and barriers and assists in their resolution, and assures access to quality health care.

1728 Programs for Infants and Toddlers with Disabilities
Bureau of Early Intervention
Room 287
Corning Tower Building
Albany, NY 12237   518-473-7016
800-577-2229
FAX 518-486-1090
http://www.health.state.ny.us
e-mail: blm01@health.state.ny.us
Nirav R. Shah, M.D., M.P.H., Commissioner
Andrew M. Cuomo, Governor

The Early Intervention Program offers a variety of therapeutic and support services to eligible infants and toddlers with disabilities and their families.

1729 Protection & Advocacy Agency
NY Commission on Quality of Care
Ste 1002
99 Washington Ave
Albany, NY 12210-2822   518-487-7708
FAX 518-487-7777
http://http://ddpc.ny.gov/

Shiela M. Carey, Executive Director
Thomas F. Lee, Public Information Officer
Thomas A. Meyers, Chief Information Officer

1730 Region II: US Department of Health and Human Services
26 Federal Plz
New York, NY 10278-0004   212-264-4600
FAX 212-264-3620
http://www.hhs.gov
e-mail: jaime.torres@hhs.gov
Jaime R Torres, Regional Director
Dennis E Gonzalez, Executive Officer

The United States government's principal agency for protecting the health of all Americans and providing essential human services, especially for those who are least able to help themselves.

1731 State GED Administration
State Department of Education
PO Box 7348
Albany, NY 12224   518-474-5906
FAX 518-474-3041
http://www.emsc.nysed.gov
e-mail: ged@mail.nysed.gov
Pat Mooney, GED Administrator

Instruction and testing for those over the age of 16 to earn the General Educational Development diploma.

North Carolina

1732 Assistive Technology Program
1110 Navaho Dr
Raleigh, NC 27609-7352   919-872-2298
FAX 919-850-2792
TTY: 919-850-2787
http://www.ncatp.org
e-mail: ldeese@ncatp.org
A Lynne Deese MA ATP, Assistive Technologist

A state and federally funded program that provides assistive technology services statewide to people of all ages and abilities.

1733 Client Assistance Program (CAP): North Carolina Division of Vocational Rehabilitation Services
2806 Mail Service Ctr
Raleigh, NC 27699-2800   919-855-3600
800-215-7227
FAX 919-715-2456
http://http://www.ncdhhs.gov/dvrs/
e-mail: kathy.brack@ncmail.net
Gloria Sims, Director
Tami Andrews, Administrative Assistant

The Client Assistance Program helps people understand and use rehabilitation services.

1734 North Carolina Council on Developmental Disabilities
3125 Poplarwood Court
Suite 200
Raleigh, NC 27604   919-850-2901
800-357-6916
FAX 919-850-2915
TTY: 919-850-2901
http://www.nc-ddc.org
e-mail: info@nccdd.org
Holly Riddle, J.D., M.Ed., Executive Director
Ronald Reeve, Council Chairperson
Kelly Bohlander, Assistant Director
To ensure that people with developmental disabilities and their families participate in the design of and have access to culturally competent services and supports, as well as other assistance and opportunities, which promote inclusive communities.

1735 **North Carolina Division of Vocational Rehabilitation**
2801 Mail Service Ctr
Raleigh, NC 27699-2801
919-324-1500
800-689-9090
FAX 919-733-7968
TTY: 919-855-3579
http://dvr.dhhs.state.nc.us
e-mail: dvr.info@ncmail.net
Linda Harrington, Director

To promote employment and independence for people with disabilities through customer partnership and community leadership.

1736 **North Carolina Division of Workforce Services**
Ste 12
4316 Mail Service Ctr
Raleigh, NC 27699-4301
919-733-4151
800-228-8443
FAX 919-662-4770
http://www.nccommerce.com
J. Keith Crisco, Secretary of Commerce
Dale Carroll, Deputy Secretary and COO
Scott R. Daugherty, Commissioner for Small Business

1737 **North Carolina Employment Security Commission**
700 Wade Avenue
Raleigh, NC 27605
919-733-7522
888-737-0259
FAX 919-707-1060
http://www.ncesc.com
e-mail: esc.ui.customerservice@ncesc.gov
Harry Payne, Chairman
Tom Whitaker, Chief Legal Counsel
Manfred Emmrich, Director, Employment Services

1738 **North Carolina Office of Administrative Hearings: Civil Rights Division**
200 West Jones Street
Raleigh, NC 27603
919-807-7100
FAX 919-733-4866
http://www.oah.state.nc.us
Julian Mann, III, Director
Camille Winston, Deputy Director

Responsible for charges alleging discrimination in the basis of race, color, sex, religion, age, national origin or disability in employment, or charges alleging retaliation for opposition to such discrimination brought by previous and current state employees or applicants for employment for positions covered by the State Personnel Act, including county government employees.

1739 **State Department of Adult Education**
North Carolina Community College
200 West Jones Street
Raleigh, NC 27603
919-807-7100
FAX 919-807-7164
http://www.nccommunitycolleges.edu
e-mail: whitfieldr@nccommunitycolleges.edu
Hilda Pinnix-Ragland, Chair
Dr. Stuart Fountain, Vice Chair

North Dakota

1740 **Client Assistance Program (CAP): North Dakota**
Wells Fargo Bank Building, 400 East
Suite 409
Bismarck, ND 58501-4071
701-328-2950
800-472-2670
FAX 701-328-3934
http://www.nd.gov/cap
e-mail: panda@nd.gov

David Boeck, Director of Legal Services
Corinne Hofmann, Director of Policy and Operation
Teresa Larsen, Executive Director
Assists clients and client applicants of North Dakota Vocational Rehabilitation services, Tribal Vocational Rehabilitation, or Independent Living services.

1741 **North Dakota Department of Human Services**
600 E Boulevard Ave
Bismarck, ND 58505
701-328-2310
800-472-2622
FAX 701-328-2359
TTY: 800-366-6888
http://www.nd.gov.dhs
e-mail: dhseo@nd.gov
Maggie Anderson, Interim Executive Director

To provide quality, efficient, and effective human services, which improve the lives of people.

1742 **North Dakota Department of Labor: Fair Employment Practice Agency**
600 E Boulevard Ave
Department 406
Bismarck, ND 58505
701-328-2660
800-582-8032
FAX 701-328-2031
TTY: 800-366-6888
http://www.nd.gov/labor
e-mail: labor@nd.gov; humanrights@nd.gov
Tony Weiler, Commissioner of Labor
Kathy Kulesa, Human Rights Director
Robin Bosch, Business Manager
Provides information and enforces laws related to labor standards and discrimination in employment, housing, public services, public accommodations and lending. The department also issues sub minimum wage certificates, verifies independent contractor status and licenses employment agencies.

1743 **North Dakota Department of Public Instruction**
600 E Boulevard Ave
Department 201
Bismarck, ND 58505
701-328-2660
FAX 701-328-1717
http://www.dpi.state.nd.us
Jerry Coleman, Director - School Finance
Valerie Fischer, Director - Coordinated School
Greg Gallagher, Director - Standards
To ensure a uniform, statewide system for effective learning.

1744 **North Dakota State Council on Developmental Disabilities**
ND Department of Human Services
600 E Boulevard Ave
Bismarck, ND 58505
701-328-2372
FAX 701-328-4727
http://http://www.ndhealth.gov/
e-mail: asmith@nd.gov
Arvy Smith, Deputy State Health Officer
Darin Meschke, Director
Terry Dwelle, M.D., M.P.H.T., State Health Officer

Ohio

1745 **Assistive Technology**
Martha Morehouse Pavilion, 2050 Ken
Suite 3300, Rm 3308
Columbus, OH 43220
614-293-9134
800-784-3425
TTY: 614-293-0767
http://www.atohio.org
e-mail: atohio@osu.edu

William T Darling PhD, Director
Eric Rathburn, Distributor

To help Ohioans with disabilities acquire assistive technology. Offer several programs and services to achieve that goal. Also keep up with current legislative activity that affects persons with disabilities.

1746 Client Assistance Program (CAP)
Ohio Legal Rights Service
50 W Broad St
Suite 1400
Columbus, OH 43215-5923   614-466-7264
                                            800-282-9181
                                        FAX 614-728-3749
                                        TTY: 614-728-2553
                                    http://www.olrs.ohio.gov
                            e-mail: webmaster@olrs.state.oh.us
Kalpana Yalamanchili, Chair
William Crum, Member
Elena Lidrbauch, Member
Advocates for and protects the rights of individuals with disabilities who are applying for or receiving rehabilitation services from the Ohio BUreau of Vocational Rehabilitation (BVR) or the Ohio Bureau of Services for the Visually Impaired (BSVI).

1747 Correctional Education
Department of Rehabilitation & Correction
770 W Broad St
Columbus, OH 43222-1419   614-752-1159
                                        FAX 614-752-0900
                                    http://www.drc.ohio.gov
                        e-mail: drc.publicinfo@odrc.state.oh.us
Gary C. Mohr, Director
Stephen J. Huffman, Assistant Director
Linda Janes, Chief of Staff
Protects and supports Ohioans by ensuring that adult felony offenders are effectively supervised in environments that are safe, humane, and appropriately secure.

1748 Office of Civil Rights: Ohio
US Department of Education
Ste 750
600 Superior Ave E
Cleveland, OH 44114-2602   216-522-4970
                                        FAX 216-522-2573
                                        TDD:877-521-2172
                                    http://www.ed.gov
                            e-mail: ocr.cleveland@ed.gov
Arne Duncan, Secretary of Education
Tony Miller, Deputy Secretary
Russlynn Ali, Assistant Secretary
This office covers the states of Michigan and Ohio.

1749 Ohio Adult Basic and Literacy Education
25 S Front St
Columbus, OH 43215-4183   614-995-1545
                                            877-644-6338
                                        FAX 614-728-8470
                                        TTY: 888-886-0181
                                    http://www.ode.state.oh.us
                        e-mail: denise.pottmeyer@ode.state.oh.us
Michael Sawyers, Acting Superintendent
John Childs, Chief Operating Officer
James Herrholtz, Associate Superintendent
Provides quality leadership for the establishment, improvement an dexpansion of lifelong learning opportunities for adults in their family, community and work roles.

1750 Ohio Civil Rights Commission
Fl 5
30 E Broad St
Columbus, OH 43215-3414   614-466-2785
                                            888-278-7101
                                        FAX 614-644-8776
                                    http://crc.ohio.gov
                            e-mail: paytonm@ocrc.state.oh.us

Leonard Hubert, Chairman
Eddie Harrell, Jr., Commissioner
Rashmi Yajnik, Commissioner
To enforce state laws against discrimination. OCRC receives and investigates charges of discrimination in employment, public accommodations, housing, credit and higher education on the bases of race, colo, religion, sex, national origin, disability, age, ancestry or familial status.

1751 Ohio Developmental Disabilities Council
899 E Broad St
Ste 203
Columbus, OH 43205   614-466-5205
                                            800-766-7426
                                        FAX 614-466-0298
                                    http://ddc.ohio.gov
                        e-mail: carolyn.knight@dodd.ohio.gov
Carolyn Knight, Executive Director

To create change that improves independence, productivity and inclusion for people with developmental disabilities and their families in community life.

1752 Ohio Office of Workforce Development
Ohio Department of Job & Family Services
Fl 32
30 E Broad St
Columbus, OH 43215-3414   614-752-3091
                                        FAX 614-995-1298
                                    http://jfs.ohio.gov
                            e-mail: workforce@jfs.ohio.gov
Michael B. Colbert, Director
Roxanne Ward, Executive Assistant
Sonnetta Sturkey, Chief Operations Officer
The role of OWD is to work in partnership with the U.S. Department of Labor, Governor's Office and a variety of stakeholders in order to provide administration and operational management for several federal programs and to offer specific services in support of the programs. OWD's primary responsibility is to promote job creation and to advance Ohio's workforce.

1753 Protection & Advocacy Agency
Ohio Legal Rights Service
50 W Broad St
Suite 1400
Columbus, OH 43215-5923   614-466-7264
                                            800-282-9181
                                        FAX 614-728-3749
                                        TTY: 614-728-2553
                                    http://olrs.ohio.gov
                            e-mail: webmaster@olrs.state.oh.us
Michael B. Colbert, Director
Roxanne Ward, Executive Assistant
Sonnetta Sturkey, Chief Operations Officer
To protect and advocate, in partnership with people with disabilities, for their human, civil and legal rights.

1754 State Department of Education
25 S Front St
Columbus, OH 43215-4183   614-995-1545
                                            877-644-6338
                                        FAX 614-728-8470
                                        TTY: 888-886-0181
                                    http://www.ode.state.oh.us
                        e-mail: denise.pottmeyer@ode.state.oh.us
Michael Sawyers, Acting Superintendent
John Childs, Chief Operating Officer
James Herrholtz, Associate Superintendent

1755 State GED Administration
State Department of Education
Rm 309
25 S Front St
Columbus, OH 43215-4176   614-466-8872
                                        FAX 614-995-7544
                                http://http://www.education.ohio.gov
                            e-mail: edchoice@education.ohio.gov

John R. Kasich, Governor
Michael L. Sawyers, Acting Superintendent of Public

Oklahoma

1756 **Assistive Technology**
Seretean OSU-Wellness Center
1514 W Hall of Fame
Stillwater, OK 74078   405-744-9748
                                               800-257-1705
                                          FAX 405-744-2487
                                          TDD:888-885-5588
                              http://okabletech.okstate.edu
                              e-mail: linda.jaco@okstate.edu
Linda Jaco, Director of Sponsored Programs
Milissa Gofourth, Program Manager
Brenda Dawes, Program Manager

1757 **Client Assistance Program (CAP): Oklahoma Division**
Office of Handicapped Concerns
2401 NW 23rd St
Suite 90
Oklahoma City, OK 73107-2431   405-521-3756
                                              800-522-8224
                                         FAX 405-522-6695
                                         TDD:405-522-6706
                               http://www.ohc.state.ok.us
                        e-mail: steven.stokes@ohc.state.ok.us
Steve Stokes, Director

The purpose of this program is to advise and inform clients and client applicants of all services and benefits available to them through programs authorized under the Rehabilitation Act of 1973. Assist and advocates for clients and client applicants in their relationships with projects, programs, and community rehabilitation programs providing services under the Act.

1758 **Correctional Education**
Department of Corrections
PO Box 11400
Oklahoma City, OK 73136   405-425-2500
                                         FAX 405-425-2500
                               http://www.doc.state.ok.us
                        e-mail: justin.jones@doc.state.ok.us
Justin Jones, Director
Ed Evans, Associate Director
Linda Parrish, Deputy Director, Administrative

1759 **Oklahoma State Department of Education**
2500 N Lincoln Blvd
Oklahoma City, OK 73105-4596   405-521-3301
                                         FAX 405-521-6205
                                http://www.sde.state.ok.us
                       e-mail: linda_young@mail.sde.state.ok.us
Janet Barresi, State Superintendent

Improve student success through: service to schools, parents and students; leadership for education reform; and regulation/deregulation of state and federal laws to provide accountability while removing any barriers to student success.

1760 **Protection & Advocacy Agency**
Disability Law Center
300 Cameron Building
Oklahoma City, OK 73106   405-525-7755
                                              800-880-7755
                                         FAX 405-525-7759
                      http://http://www.redlands-partners.org
                              e-mail: kayla@okdlc.org
Kayla Bower, Executive Director
Valerie Williams, Director
Anne Trudgeon, Director

Helps people with disabilities achieve equality, inclusion in society and personal independence without regard to disabling conditions.

1761 **State Department of Adult Education**
Department of Education
2500 N Lincoln Blvd
Oklahoma City, OK 73105-4596   405-521-3301
                                              800-405-0355
                                         FAX 405-521-6205
                                http://www.sde.state.ok.us
                       e-mail: linda_young@mail.sde.state.ok.us
Joyce DeFehr, Executive Director
Sandy Garrett, State Superintendent

1762 **State GED Administration**
State Department of Education
2500 N Lincoln Blvd
Oklahoma City, OK 73105-4596   405-521-3301
                                              800-405-0355
                                         FAX 405-521-6205
                                http://www.sde.state.ok.us
                       e-mail: linda_young@mail.sde.state.ok.us
Joyce DeFehr, Executive Director
Sandy Garrett, State Superintendent

Oregon

1763 **Assistive Technology Program**
Access Technologies
2225 Lancaster Drive NE
Salem, OR 97305-1396   503-361-1201
                                              800-677-7512
                                         FAX 503-370-4530
                         http://www.accesstechnologiesinc.org
                         e-mail: info@accesstechnologiesinc.org
Laurie Brooks, President
Phyllis Petteys, Center Director
Davey Hulse, Chair
A statewide program promoting services and assistive devices for people with disabilities.

1764 **Department of Community Colleges and Workforce Development**
255 Capitol St NE
Salem, OR 97310-1300   503-378-8648
                                         FAX 503-378-8434
                                        http://www.oregon.gov
                        e-mail: ccwd.info@odccwd.state.or.us
Camille Preus, Commissioner

Contribute leadership and resources to increase skills, knowledge and carrier opportunities.

1765 **Disability Rights Oregon**
610 SW Broadway
Suite 200
Portland, OR 97205   503-243-2081
                                              800-452-1694
                                         FAX 503-243-1738
                                 http://www.oradvocacy.org
Bob Joondeph, Executive Director
Jan Campbell, Chair
Michael Bailey, Vice Chair
An independent non-profit organization which provides legal advocacy services for people with disabilities anywhere in Oregon. OAC offers free legal assistance and other advocacy services to individuals who are considered to have physical or mental disabilities. OAC works only on legal problems which relate directly to the disability.

1766 Office of Vocational Rehabilitation Services
Department of Human Services
500 Summer St NE E-87
Salem, OR 97301-1120   503-945-5880
                                        866-801-0130
                                    FAX 503-947-5010
                                    TTY: 866-801-0130
                                http://www.oregon.gov
                            e-mail: info.vr@#state.or.us
Stephanie Taylor, Administrator

Helps Oregonians with disabilities to prepare for, finad and retain jobs.

1767 Oregon Bureau of Labor and Industry: Fair Employment Practice Agency
800 NE Oregon St
Suite 1045
Portland, OR 97232-2162   971-673-0761
                                    FAX 971-673-0762
                                http://www.boli.state.or.us
                            e-mail: BOLI.mail@state.or.us
Brad Avakian, Commissioner

1768 Oregon Council on Developmental Disabilities
540 24th Pl NE
Salem, OR 97301-4517   503-945-9941
                                        800-292-4154
                                    FAX 503-945-9947
                                http://www.ocdd.org
                            e-mail: ocdd@ocdd.org
Bill Lynch, Executive Director

To create change that improves the lives of Oregonians with developmental disabilities.

1769 Oregon Department of Education: School-to-Work
255 Capitol St NE
Salem, OR 97310   503-947-5600
                                    FAX 503-378-5156
                                    TDD:503-378-3825
                                http://www.ode.state.or.us
                            e-mail: ode.frontdesk@ode.state.or.us
Katy Coba, Executive Director
Patrick Burk, Education Policy Deputy Director

School-to-Work is a federally funded initiative that provides funding for state and local implementation of the Oregon Educational Act for the 21st Century.

1770 Oregon Department of Human Services: Children, Adults & Families Division
E15
500 Summer St NE
Salem, OR 97301-1097   503-945-5600
                                    FAX 503-378-2897
                                http://www.dhs.state.or.us
                            e-mail: dhs.info@state.or.us
Bruce Goldberg, Interim Director

This group is responsible for administering self-sufficiency and child-protective programs. These include Jobs, Temporary Assistance for Needy Families, Employment Related Day Care, Food Stamps, child-abuse investigation and intervention, foster care and adoptions.

1771 Oregon Employment Department
875 Union St NE
Salem, OR 97311   877-517-5627
                                        800-237-3710
                                    FAX 503-947-1472
                                http://www.employment.oregon.gov
                            e-mail: findit.emp.state.or.us/write-us/
Laurie Warner, Director

Supports economic stability for Oregonians and communities during times of unemployment through the payment of unemployment benefits. Serves businesses by recruiting and referring the best qualified applicants to jobs, and provides resources to diverse job seekers in support of their employment needs.

Pennsylvania

1772 Bureau of Adult Basic & Literacy Education
12th Floor
333 Market St
Harrisburg, PA 17126   717-772-3737
                                    FAX 717-783-0583
                http://http://www1.whsd.net/admin/Special_Educa
                            e-mail: rosbrandt@state.pa.us
Cheryl Keenan, Director
Pedro Cortes, Manager

1773 Client Assistance Program (CAP): Pennsylvania Division
1515 Market Street
Suite 1300
Philadelphia, PA 19102   215-557-7112
                                        888-745-2357
                                    FAX 215-557-7602
                                    TDD:215-577-7112
                                http://www.equalemployment.org
                            e-mail: info@equalemployment.org
Stephen S. Pennington, Executive Director
Jamie C. Ray-Leonetti, Co-Director
Margaret Passio-McKenna, Senior Advocate
CAP is an advocacy program for people with disabilities administered by the Center for Disability Law and Policy. CAP helps people who are seeking services from the Office of Vocational Rehabilitation, Blindness and Visual Services, Centers for Independent Living and other programs funded under federal law. CAP services are provided at no charge.

1774 Disability Rights Network of Pennsylvania
1414 N Cameron St
Second Floor
Harrisburg, PA 17103-1049   717-236-8110
                                        800-692-7443
                                    FAX 717-236-0192
                                    TDD:877-375-7139
                                    TTY: 800-692-7443
                                http://drnpa.org
                            e-mail: ldo@drnpa.org
Shelley Moore, Administrator

A statewide, non-profit corporation designated as the federally-mandated organization to advance and protect the civil rights of adults and children with disabilities. DRN works with people with disabilities and their families, their organizations, and their advocates to ensure their rights to live in their communities with the services they need, to receive a full and inclusive education, to live free of discrimination, abuse and neglect.

1775 Office of Civil Rights: Pennsylvania
US Department of Education
Ste 515
100 Penn Sq E
Philadelphia, PA 19107   215-656-8541
                                    FAX 215-656-8605
                                    TDD:877-521-2172
                                http://www.ed.gov
                            e-mail: ocr_philadelphia@ed.gov
Bernard Tadley, Regional IG for Audit
Steven Anderson, Special Agent In Charge
Russlynn Ali, Assistant Secretary
This office covers the states of Delaware, Kentucky, Maryland, Pennsylvania and West Virginia.

1776 **Pennsylvania Department of Corrections**
1920 Technology Parkway
Mechanicsburg, PA 17050　　　　　717-728-2573
FAX 717-975-2242
http://www.cor.state.pa.us
e-mail: ra-contactdoc@pa.gov
John E. Wetzel, Secretary
Tom Corbett, Governor

To protect the public by confining persons committed to our custody in safe, secure facilities, and to provide opportunities for inmates to acquire the skills and values necessary to become productive law-abiding citizens; while respecting the rights of crime victims.

1777 **Pennsylvania Developmental Disabilities Council**
605 South Dr
Room 561 Forum Building
Harrisburg, PA 17120　　　　　717-787-6057
877-685-4452
TTY: 717-705-0819
http://www.paddc.org
Graham Mulholland, Executive Director
Tom Corbett, Governor
Jeff Parker, Council Chairperson
Engages in advocacy, systems change and capacity building for people with disabilities and their families in order to: support people with disabilities in taking control of their own lives; ensure access to goods, services, and supports; build inclusive communities; pursue a cross-disability agenda; and to change negative societal attitudes towards people with disabilities.

1778 **Pennsylvania Human Rights Commission**
301 Chestnut St
Ste 300
Harrisburg, PA 17101-2702　　　　717-787-4412
FAX 717-787-0420
TTY: 717-787-4087
http://hfloyd@state.pa.us
Homer Floyd, Executive Director

To administer and enforce the PHRAct and the PFEOA of the Commonwealth of the Pennsylvania for the identification and elimination of discrimination and the providing of equal opportunity for all persons.

1779 **Pennsylvania's Initiative on Assistive Technology**
1755 N 13th St
Student Center, Rm 411 S
Philadelphia, PA 19122-6024
800-204-7428
FAX 215-204-6336
TTY: 866-268-0579
http://disabilities.temple.edu
e-mail: atinfo@temple.edu
Sandra McNally, Public Awareness Coordinator

Strives to enhance the lives of Pennsylvanians with disabilities, older Pennsylvanians, and their families, through access to and acquisition of assistive technology devices and services, which allow for choice, control and independence at home, work, school, play and in their neighborhoods.

1780 **Region III: US Department of Health and Human Services Civil Rights Office**
US Department of Health & Human Services
Suite 436
105 S Independence Mall W
Philadelphia, PA 19106　　　　　215-861-4633
FAX 215-861-4625
http://www.hhs.gov
e-mail: gordon.woodrow@hhs.gov
Gordon Woodrow, Regional Manager
Bill Corr, Deputy Secretary
Kathleen Sebelius, Secretary

1781 **State Department of Education**
333 Market St
Harrisburg, PA 17126　　　　　717-783-6788
TTY: 717-783-8445
http://www.pdeinfo.state.pa.us
Ron Tomalis, Secretary
Tom Corbett, Governor

To lead and serve the educational community to enable each individual to grow into an inspired, productive, fulfilled lifelong learner.

1782 **State GED Administration**
Pennsylvania Department of Education
333 Market St
Harrisburg, PA 17126　　　　　717-787-5532
FAX 717-783-0583
http://http://www1.whsd.net/admin/Special_Educa
Janice Wessell, Director

Rhode Island

1783 **Correctional Education**
Rhode Island Department of Corrections
PO Box 8312
Cranston, RI 02920　　　　　401-462-1000
FAX 401-464-2509
TTY: 401-462-5180
http://http://www.doc.ri.gov
e-mail: director@doc.ri.gov
Ashbel T. Wall, II, Director
Susan Lamkins, Programming Services Officer
Kathleen Kelly, Chief Legal Counsel

1784 **Protection & Advocacy Agency**
Rhode Island Disability Law Center
275 Westminster St
Suite 401
Providence, RI 02903-3434　　　　401-831-3150
800-733-5332
FAX 401-274-5568
TTY: 401-831-5335
http://www.ridlc.org
e-mail: info@ridlc.org
Raymond Bandusky, Executive Director

To assist people with differing abilities in their efforts to achieve full inclusion in society and to exercise their civil and human rights through the provision of legal advocacy.

1785 **Rhode Island Commission for Human Rights**
180 Westminster St
3rd Floor
Providence, RI 02903-1918　　　　401-222-2661
FAX 401-222-2616
TTY: 402-222-2664
http://www.richr.ri.gov
Michael Evora, Executive Director
John B. Susa, Ph.D., Chairperson
Cynthia Hiatt, Legal Counsel
A state agency that enforces civil rights law.

1786 **Rhode Island Department of Elementary and Secondary Education**
Rhode Island Department of Education
255 Westminster St
Providence, RI 02903-3400　　　　401-222-4600
FAX 401-222-5106
http://www.ride.ri.gov

Deborah A. Gist, Commissioner

1787 Rhode Island Department of Labor & Training
1511 Pontiac Ave
Cranston, RI 02920-4407   401-462-8000
                                    FAX 401-462-8872
                                    TDD:401-462-8006
                                http://www.dlt.state.ri.us
                            e-mail: mmadonna@dlt.ri.gov
Sandra Powell, Director

Providing workforce protection and development services
with courtesy, responsiveness and effectiveness.

1788 Rhode Island Developmental Disabilities Council
400 Bald Hill Rd
Suite 515
Warwick, RI 02886-1692   401-737-1238
                                    FAX 401-737-3395
                                    TDD:401-732-1238
                                  http://www.riddc.org
                              e-mail: riddc@riddc.org
Mary Okero, Executive Director
John Susa, Ph.D., Chairperson

Promotes the ideas that will enhance the lives of people with
developmental disabilities.

1789 State Department of Adult Education
255 Westminster St
Providence, RI 02903-3400   401-222-4600
                                    FAX 401-222-5106
                                  http://www.ride.ri.gov
Deborah A. Gist, Commissioner

Administer grant funded programs in Adult Basic Education, GED, and English for Speakers of Other Languages.
Promote stronger families, upward mobility, and active citizenship through effective adult basic education services.
The classes support adults who wish to advance their education towards a high school credential, training, and/or post
secondary degrees.

South Carolina

1790 Assistive Technology Program
South Carolina Developmental Disabilities Council
1205 Pendleton St
Suite 450
Columbia, SC 29201-3756   803-734-0465
                                    TTY: 803-734-1147
                                http://www.scddc.state.sc.us
                            e-mail: vbishop@oepp.sc.gov
Valarie Bishop, Executive Director
Jennifer Van Cleave, Program Information Coordinator
Esther Williams, Administrative Support Specialis
A statewide project established to provide an opportunity for
individuals with disabilities to lead the fullest, most produc-
tive lives possible.

1791 Protection & Advocacy for People with Disabilities
3710 Landmark Dr
Ste 208
Columbia, SC 29204-4034   803-782-0639
                                    866-275-7273
                                    FAX 803-790-1946
                                    TTY: 866-232-4525
                                  http://www.pandasc.org
                            e-mail: info@pandasc.org
Gloria Prevost, Executive Director

To protect the legal, civil, and human rights of people with
disabilities in South Carolina by enabling individuals to advocate for themselves, speaking in their behalf when they
have been discriminated against or denied a services to
which they are entitled, and promoting policies and services
which respect their choices.

1792 South Carolina Developmental Disabilities Council
1205 Pendleton St
Suite 450
Columbia, SC 29201-3756   803-734-0465
                                    TTY: 803-734-1147
                                http://www.scddc.state.sc.us
                            e-mail: vbishop@oepp.sc.gov
Valarie Bishop, Executive Director
Jennifer Van Cleave, Program Information Coordinator
Esther Williams, Administrative Support
To provide leadership in advocating, funding and imple-
menting initiatives which recognize the inherent dignity of
each individual, and promote independence, productivity,
respect and inclusion for all persons with disabilities and
their families.

1793 South Carolina Employment Security Commission
PO Box 995
Columbia, SC 29202   803-737-2400
                                    800-436-8190
                                    FAX 803-737-0140
                                  http://www.sces.org
                            e-mail: aturner@dew.sc.gov
Major Genera Turner, Executive Director
Joseph Lowder, Chief of Staff
Laura W. Robinson, Assistant Executive Director

**1794 South Carolina Employment Services and Job Training
Services**
PO Box 995
Columbia, SC 29202   803-737-2400
                                    800-436-8190
                                    FAX 803-737-0140
                                  http://www.sces.org
                            e-mail: aturner@dew.sc.gov
Major Genera Turner, Executive Director
Joseph Lowder, Chief of Staff
Laura W. Robinson, Assistant Executive Director

1795 South Carolina Human Affairs Commission
2611 Forest Dr
Suite 200
Columbia, SC 29204-2379   803-737-7800
                                    800-521-0725
                                    FAX 803-253-4191
                                    TDD:803-253-4125
                        http://http://www.state.sc.us/schac/
                        e-mail: information@schac.state.sc.us
Raymond Buxton, Commissioner
John A. Oakland, Chair
Rev. Willie Albert Thompson, Vice Chair
To eliminate and prevent unlawful discrimination in: em-
ployment on the basis of race, color, national origin, religion, sex, age and disability; housing on the basis of race,
color, national origin, religion, sex, familial status and disability; and public accommodations on the basis of race,
color, national origin and religion.

1796 State Department of Adult Education
South Carolina Department of Education
Ste 402
1429 Senate St
Columbia, SC 29201-3730   803-734-8500
                                    FAX 803-734-3643
                                    http://ed.sc.gov
                            e-mail: dstout@ed.sc.gov
John Cooley, CFO
Don Cantrell, CIO
Scott English, COO
Provides the opportunity for adults with low literacy skills
(less than eighth grade level), to work with materials to be
taught in an environment conducive to their level, and to im-
prove their reading, math, and writing skills.

1797 State GED Administration
South Carolina Department of Education
Ste 105
1429 Senate St
Columbia, SC 29201-3730
803-734-8500
FAX 803-734-8336
http://ed.sc.gov
e-mail: clclark@ed.sc.gov
John Cooley, CFO
Don Cantrell, CIO
Scott English, COO

South Dakota

1798 Client Assistance Program (CAP): South Dakota Division
South Dakota Advocacy Services
221 S Central Ave
Suite 38
Pierre, SD 57501-2479
605-224-8294
800-658-4782
FAX 605-224-5125
TTY: 800-658-4782
http://www.sdadvocacy.com
e-mail: sdas@sdadvocacy.com
Robert J. Kean, Executive Director

Provides free services to eligible consumers and applicants for projects, programs and facilities funded under the rehabilitation act.

1799 Department of Correction: Education Coordinator
4904 S Quail Run Ave
Sioux Falls, SD 57108-2962
605-332-8335
FAX 605-332-8335
http://www.state.sd.us
Tim Reisch, Secretary
Dennis Daugaard, Governor

To protect the citizens of South Dakota by providing safe and secure facilities for juvenile and adult offenders committed to our custody by the courts, to provide effective community supervision upon their release.

1800 Easter Seals South Dakota
1351 N Harrison Ave
Pierre, SD 57501-2373
605-224-5879
FAX 605-224-133
http://sd.easterseals.com
Creates solutions that change the lives of children, adults and families with disabilities or other needs; to promote disability prevention and awareness.

1801 South Dakota Advocacy Services
221 S Central Ave
Suite 38
Pierre, SD 57501-2479
605-224-8294
800-658-4782
FAX 605-224-5125
TTY: 800-658-4782
http://www.sdadvocacy.com
e-mail: sdas@sdadvocacy.com
Robert J. Kean, Executive Director

To protect and advocate the rights of South Dakotans with disabilities through legal, administrative, and other remedies.

1802 South Dakota Council on Developmental Disabilities
Department of Human Services
500 E Capitol Ave
Pierre, SD 57501-5007
605-773-6369
800-265-9684
FAX 605-773-5483
http://dhs.sd.gov
e-mail: infoddc@state.sd.us

Arlene Poncelet, Director

The SD Council is authorized under federal law to address the unmet needs of people with developmental disabilities through advocacy, capacity building and systems change activities. The mission is to assist people with developmental disabilities and their families in achieving the quality of life they desire.

1803 South Dakota Department of Labor: Employment Services & Job Training
700 Governors Dr
Pierre, SD 57501-2291
605-773-5422
FAX 605-773-4211
TTY: 605-773-3101
http://www.state.sd.us
e-mail: miker@dol.pr.state.sd.us
Mike Ryan, Administrator
Dorothy Leigl, Manager

Job training programs provide an important framework for developing public-private sector partnerships. We help prepare South Dakotans of all ages for entry or re-entry into the labor force.

1804 South Dakota Division of Human Rights
700 Governors Dr
Pierre, SD 57501-2291
605-773-3681
FAX 605-773-4211
http://www.state.sd.us
e-mail: james.marsh@state.sd.us
James Marsh, Director

To promote equal opportunity through the administration and enforcement of the Human Relations Act of 1972. The act is designed to protect the public from discrimination because of race, color, creed, religion, sex, disability, ancestry or national origin.

1805 South Dakota Division of Special Education
Department of Education
700 Governors Dr
Pierre, SD 57501-2291
605-773-3678
FAX 605-773-3782
http://www.state.sd.us
Ann Larsen, Special Education Programs Dir

The Office of Special Education advocates for the availability of the full range of personnel, programming, and placement options, including early intervention and transition services, required to assure that all individuals with disabilities are able to achieve maximum independence upon exiting from school.

1806 State GED Administration
Department of Labor
700 Governors Dr
Pierre, SD 57501-2291
605-773-3101
FAX 605-773-6184
http://www.sdjobs.org
e-mail: barb.unruh@state.sd.us
Pam Roberts, Labor Secretary
Barb Unruh, Adult Education/Literacy/GED Adm

Tennessee

1807 Department of Human Services: Division of Rehabilitation Services
400 Deaderick St
15th Floor
Nashville, TN 37243-1403
615-313-4700
FAX 615-741-4165
http://www.tennessee.gov/humanserv
e-mail: human-services.webmaster@state.tn.us

Virginia Lodge, Commissioner
Bill Haslam, Governor

To improve the well-being of economically disadvantaged, disabled or vulnerable Tennesseans through a network of financial, employment, rehabilitative and protective services.

1808 State Department of Education
6th Floor
Andrew Johnson Tower
Nashville, TN 37243
615-532-1617
http://www.state.tn.us
e-mail: education.comments@state.tn.us
John Sharp, Director
Amy Sharp, Director
Debbie Crews, Supervisor
The department provides many services, and it is our responsibility to ensure equal, safe, and quality learning opportunities for all students, pre-kindergartern through 12th grade.

1809 State GED Administration
TDLWFD/Adult Education
220 French Landing Dr
Nashville, TN 37243
615-741-2731
800-531-1515
FAX 615-532-4899
http://www.state.tn.us

Phil White, Administrator

1810 Tennessee Council on Developmental Disabilities
404 James Robertson Pkwy
Ste 130
Nashville, TN 37243-0001
615-532-6615
FAX 615-532-6964
TTY: 615-741-4562
http://www.tn.gov/cdd
e-mail: tnddc@tn.gov
Wanda Willis, Executive Director

A State office that promotes public policies to increase and support the inclusion of individuals with developmental disabilities in their communities.

1811 Tennessee Technology Access Project
4th Floor
400 Deadrick St
Nashville, TN 37248
615-313-5183
800-732-5059
TTY: 615-313-5695
http://www.state.tn.us
e-mail: tn.ttap@state.tn.us
Kevin Wright, Executive Director

A statewide program designed to increase access to, and acquisition of, assisitve technology devices and services.

Texas

1812 Advocacy
7800 Shoal Creek Blvd
Ste 171E
Austin, TX 78757-1097
512-454-4816
800-252-9108
FAX 512-323-0902
http://www.advocacyinc.org
e-mail: infoai@advocacyinc.org
Mary Faithful, Executive Director

Nonprofit legal organization that provides services and advances the rights of people with disabilities.

1813 Learning Disabilities Association
PO Box 831392
Richardson, TX 75083-1392
512-458-8234
800-604-7500
FAX 512-458-3826
http://www.ldat.org
e-mail: contact@ldat.org
Jean Kueker, President
Ann Robinson, State Coordinator

Promotes the educational and general welfare of individuals with learning disabilities.

1814 Office of Civil Rights: Texas
US Department of Education
Ste 1620
1999 Bryan St
Dallas, TX 75201-6817
214-661-9540
FAX 214-661-9587
TDD:877-521-2172
http://www.ed.gov
e-mail: ocr.dallas@ed.gov
Keith M. Maddox, Regional IG for Audit
Thomas Utz Jr., Special Agent In Charge
Russlynn Ali, Assistant Secretary
The Dallas office covers the states of Alabama, Arkansas, Louisiana, Mississippi and Texas.

1815 Southwest Texas Disability & Business Technical Assistance Center: Region VI
2323 S Shepherd Dr
#1000
Houston, TX 77019-7019
713-520-0232
800-949-4232
FAX 713-520-5785
TTY: 713-520-0232
http://www.swdbtac.org
e-mail: swdbtac@ilru.org
Wendy Wilkinson, Project Director
Laurie Redd, Executive Director

One of ten DBTACs funded by the National Institute on Disability and Rehabilitation Research. The DBTAC serves a wide range of audiences who are interested in or impacted by these laws, including employers, businesses, government agencies, schools and people with disabilities.

1816 State GED Administration
Texas Education Agency
1701 Congress Ave
Austin, TX 78701-1402
512-463-9292
FAX 512-305-9493
http://www.tea.state.tx.us
e-mail: ged@tea.state.tx.us
G Paris Ealy, GED State Program Administrator

To build capacity for consistent testing services throughout the state in order that all eligible candidates may have an pooportunity to earn high school equivalency credentials based on the General Educational Development (GED) Tests.

1817 Texas Council for Developmental Disabilities
6201 E Oltorf St
Suite 600
Austin, TX 78741-7509
512-437-5432
800-262-0334
FAX 512-437-5434
http://www.txddc.state.tx.us
e-mail: tcdd@tcdd.state.tx.us
Roger Webb, Executive Director

To create change so that all people with disabilities are fully included in their communities and exercise control over their own lives.

1818 Texas Department of Assistive and Rehabilitative Services
4800 N Lamar Blvd
Austin, TX 78756-3106
512-377-0500
800-628-5115
TTY: 866-581-9328
http://www.dars.state.tx.us
e-mail: dars.inquiries@dars.state.tx.us
Terry Murphy, Commissioner

To work in partnership with Texans with disabilities and families with children who have developmental delays to improve the quality of their lives and to enable their full participation in society.

1819 Texas Department of Criminal Justice
PO Box 99
Huntsville, TX 77342
512-475-3250
FAX 512-305-9398
http://www.tdcj.state.tx.us
Brad Livingston, Executive Director

To provide public safety, promote positive change in offender behavior, reintegrate offenders into society, and assist victims of crime.

1820 Texas Education Agency
1701 N Congress Ave
Austin, TX 78701-1494
512-463-9734
FAX 512-463-9838
http://www.tea.state.tx.us
e-mail: commissioner@tea.state.tx.us
David A. Anderson, General Counsel
Joanie Allen, General Counsel
Andrew Allen, General Counsel
To provide leadership, guidance, and resources to help schools meet the educational needs of all students.

1821 Texas Workforce Commission: Civil Rights Division
101 E 15th St
Rm 1440
Austin, TX 78778-0001
512-463-2642
888-452-4778
FAX 512-463-2643
TTY: 512-371-7473
http://www.twc.state.tx.us
e-mail: robert.gomez@twc.state.tx.us
Robert Gomez, Director

Enforces the Texas Commission on Human Rights Act and the Texas Fair Housing Act. The Human Rights Act prohibits employment discrimination based on race, color, religion, sex, age, national origin, disability and retaliation. The Fair Housing Act prohibits housing discrimination based on race, color, religion, sex, national origin, mental or physical disability, familial status and retaliation.

1822 Texas Workforce Commission: Workforce Development Division
PO Box 12728
Austin, TX 78711-2728
512-936-0697
http://www.twc.state.tx.us
e-mail: larry.jones@twc.state.tx.us
Larry Jones, Director

Provides oversight, coordination, guidance, planning, technical assistance and implementation of employment and training activities with a focus on meeting the needs of employers throughout the state of Texas. Also supports work conducted in local workforce development areas, provides assistance to boards in the achievement of performance goals, evaluates education and training providers, and promotes and develops partnerships with other agencies and institutions.

Utah

1823 Assistive Technology Center
1595 W 500 S
Salt Lake City, UT 84104-5238
801-887-9380
800-866-5550
http://www.usor.utah.gov/ucat
Kent Remund, Director
Lynn Marcoux, Executive Secretary
Craig Boogaard, Manager
To enhance human potential through facilitating the application of assistive technologies for persons with disabilities.

1824 Assistive Technology Program
6588 Old Main Hill
6855 Old Main Hill
Logan, UT 84322-6855
435-797-3824
800-524-5152
FAX 435-797-2355
http://www.uatpat.org
Martin Blair, Director
Marilyn Hammond, UATF Director
Alma Burgess, Create Program Coordinator
Serve individuals with disabilities of all ages in Utah and the intermountain region. Provide AT devices and services, and train university students, parents, children with disabilities and professional services providers about AT. Also coordinate the services with community organizations and others who provide independence-related support to individuals with disabilities.

1825 Center for Persons with Disabilities
Utah State University
6800 Old Main Hl
Logan, UT 84322-6800
435-797-1981
866-284-2821
FAX 435-797-3944
http://www.cpdusu.org
M Bryce Fifield PhD, Executive Director
Cynthia Rowland, Associate Director

Utah's University Center for excellence in developmental disabilities education, research, and services. We collaborate with partners to strengthen families and individuals across the lifespan through education, policy, research and services.

1826 Department of Workforce Services
PO Box 45249
Salt Lake City, UT 84145
801-526-9675
FAX 801-526-9211
http://jobs.utah.gov
e-mail: dwscontactus@utah.gov
Kristen Cox, Executive Director

Provides employment and support services for our customers to improve their economic opportunities.

1827 Disability Law Center
205 N 400 W
Salt Lake City, UT 84103-1125
801-363-1347
800-662-9080
FAX 801-363-1437
TTY: 800-500-4182
http://www.disabilitylawcenter.org
e-mail: mattknotts@disabilitylawcenter.org
Barbara M. Campbell,, Treasurer
Joshua Cannon, Board of Trustee
Mike Chidester, Board of Trustee
A private non-profit organization designated as the Protection and Advocacy agency for the state of Utah to protect the rights of people with disabilities in Utah. To enforce and strengthen laws that protect the opportunities, choices and legal rights of people with disabilities in Utah.

1828 Utah Antidiscrimination and Labor Division
Utah Labor Commission
PO Box 146630
Salt Lake City, UT 84114-6630   801-530-6801
                                       800-222-1238
                                   FAX 801-530-7609
        http://www.laborcommission.utah.gov
                      e-mail: uald@utah.gov
Sherrie M Hayashi, Commissioner

Investigates and resolves employment and housing discrimination complaints and enforces Utah's minimum wage, wage payment requirements, laws which protect youth in employment and the requirement that private employemnt agencies be licensed. The Division also conducts public awareness and educational presentations.

1829 Utah Developmental Disabilities Council
155 S 300 W
Suite 100
Salt Lake City, UT 84101-1288   801-533-3965
                                   FAX 801-533-3968
        http://www.utahddcouncil.org
Sherri Dial, Chair
Eric Stoker, Vice Chair
Clarissa Crisp, Treasurer
The mission of the Utah DD council is to be the states leading source of critical innovative and progressive knowledge, advocacy, leadership and collaboration to enhance the life of individuals with developmental disabilities.

1830 Utah State Office of Education
PO Box 144200
Salt Lake City, UT 84114-4200   801-538-7870
                                   FAX 801-538-7868
        http://www.utahged.org
        e-mail: marty.kelly@schools.utah.gov
Marty Kelly, State GED Administrator

Promotes adult education and GED Testing in Utah.

Vermont

1831 Vermont Department of Children & Families
103 South Main Street
2 & 3 North
Waterbury, VT 05671-5500   802-241-3110
                                  800-649-2642
        http://http://dcf.vermont.gov/
        e-mail: kim.keiser@ahs.state.vt.us
Dave Yacovone, Commissioner

To promote the social, emotional, physical and economic well being and the safety of Vermont's children and families.

1832 Vermont Department of Education
120 State St
Montpelier, VT 05620-2501   802-828-3135
        http://www.education.vermont.gov
        e-mail: doe-edinfo@state.vt.us
Kate Nicolet, Director of Adult Education
Sharon Parker, Assistant Director
Donna McAllister, Health Education Consultant
Provide leadership and support to help all Vermont students achieve excellence.

1833 Vermont Department of Labor
PO Box 488
Montpelier, VT 05601   802-828-4000
                          FAX 802-828-4022
                          TDD:802-828-4203
        http://www.labor.vermont.gov
        e-mail: pat.moulton.powden@state.vt.us
Annie Noonan, Commissioner
Rose Lucenti, Director
Steve Monahan, Director of Workers' Comp

To improve and enhance services to the public by combining under one department: employment security, employment-related services, labor market information, safety and training for Vermont workers, and employers, workers compensation, and wage and hour.

1834 Vermont Developmental Disabilities Council
103 S Main St
Waterbury, VT 05671-9800   802-241-2612
                                  888-317-2006
                              FAX 802-241-2989
        http://www.ddc.vermont.gov
        e-mail: karen.schwartz@ahs.state.vt.us
Karen Schwartz, Executive Director

Statewide board that works to increase public awareness about critical issues affecting Vermonters with developmental disabilities and their families. 13 of the 21 board members are people with developmental disabilities or family members.

1835 Vermont Governor's Office
109 State St
Montpelier, VT 05609   802-828-3333
                          FAX 802-828-3339
                          TTY: 800-649-6825
        http://www.governor.vermont.gov
Peter Shumlin, Governor
Jeb Spaulding, Secretary
Chuck Ross, Secretary

1836 Vermont Protection and Advocacy Agency
Ste 7
141 Main St
Montpelier, VT 05602-2916   802-229-1355
                                   800-834-7890
                               FAX 802-229-1359
        http://www.vtpa.org
        e-mail: ed.paquin@vtpa.org
Ed Paquin, Executive Director

Dedicated to addressing problems, questions and complaints brought to it by Vermonters with disabilities. Mission is to promote the equality, dignity, and self-determination of people with disabilities. Provides information, referral and advocacy services, in cluding legal representation when appropriate, to individuals with disabilities throughout Vermont. Also advocates to promote positive systematic responses to issues affecting people with disabilities.

1837 Vermont Special Education
Vermont Department of Education
120 State St
Montpelier, VT 05620-2501   802-828-3135
        http://education.vermont.gov
        e-mail: doe-edinfo@state.vt.us
Kate Nicolet, Director of Adult Education
Sharon Parker, Assistant Director
Donna McAllister, Health Education Consultant
Provides technical assistance to schols and other organization to help ensure that schools understand and comply with federal and state laws and regulations related to providing special education services.

Virginia

1838 Assistive Technology System
8004 Franklin Farms Dr
Richmond, VA 23229   804-662-9990
                            800-435-8490
                        FAX 804-622-9478
        http://www.vats.org
        e-mail: kathryn.hayfield@drs.virginia.gov
Kathryn Hayfield, Director
Elizabeth Flaherty, Chairperson
Matthew Deans, Vice-Chair

To ensure that Virginians of all ages and abilities can acquire the appropriate, affordable assistive and information technologies and services they need to participate in society as active citizens.

1839 Department of Correctional Education
PO Box 26963
Richmond, VA 23261-6963
804-674-3000
FAX 804-225-3255
TDD:804-371-8647
http://dce.virginia.gov
e-mail: docmail@vadoc.virginia.gov
Debra Gardner, Chief Deputy Director
Harold W. Clarke, Director
A. David Robinson, Chief of Corrections Operations
Provides quality educational programs that enable incarcerated youth and adults to become responsible, productive, tax-paying members of their community.

1840 Office of Adult Education and Literacy
Virginia Department of Education
PO Box 2120
Richmond, VA 23218-2120
804-225-2075
FAX 804-225-3352
http://www.doe.virginia.gov
Bob McDonnell, Governor
Dr. Patricia Wright, Superintendent
Marie G. Williams, Director
Operates as the designated agency to coordinate all secondary adult education and literacy services in the commonwealth.

1841 State Department of Education
Office of Adult Education and Literacy
PO Box 2120
Richmond, VA 23218-2120
804-225-2075
FAX 804-225-3352
http://www.doe.virginia.gov
Bob McDonnell, Governor
Dr. Patricia Wright, Superintendent
Marie G. Williams, Director
Promotes quality education.

1842 State GED Administration
Office of Adult Education and Literacy
PO Box 2120
Richmond, VA 23218-2120
804-225-2075
FAX 804-225-3352
http://www.doe.virginia.gov
Bob McDonnell, Governor
Dr. Patricia Wright, Superintendent
Marie G. Williams, Director
Promotes quality education for adults.

1843 Virginia Board for People with Disabilities
1100 Bank Street
7th Floor
Richmond, VA 23219
804-786-0016
800-845-4464
FAX 804-786-1118
TTY: 800-845-4464
http://www.vaboard.org
e-mail: katherine.lawson@vbpd.virginia.gov
Heidi Lawyer, Executive Director
John Kelly, Chair
Charles Meacham, Vice Chair
To enrich the lives of Virginians with disabilities by providing a voice for their concerns.

1844 Virginia Office for Protection & Advocacy Agency
1910 Byrd Ave
Suite 5
Richmond, VA 23230-3034
804-225-2042
800-552-3962
FAX 804-662-7057
TTY: 800-552-3962
http://www.vopa.state.va.us
e-mail: general.vopa@vopa.virginia.gov

V Coleen Miller, Executive Director
Sherry Confer, Deputy Director
Lisa McGee, Executive Assistant
Through zealous and effective advocacy and legal representation to: protect and advance legal, human, and civil rights of persons with disabilities; combat and prevent abuse, neglect, and discrimination; and to promote independence, choice, and self determination by persons with disabilities.

Washington

1845 Correctional Education
Department of Corrections
PO Box 41100
Olympia, WA 98504-1100
360-725-8213
FAX 360-586-6582
http://www.doc.wa.gov
e-mail: doccorrespondence@doc1.wa.gov
Harold Clarke, Secretary of Department

The Department of Corrections, in collaboration with its criminal justice partners, will contribute to staff and community safety and hold offenders accountable through administration of criminal sanctions and effective re-entry programs.

1846 Department of Personnel & Human Services
614 Division St
Port Orchard, WA 98366-4614
360-337-7150
FAX 360-337-7187
http://www.kitsapgov.com
e-mail: appserv@co.kitsap.wa.us
Robert Gelder, Commissioner
Charlotte Garrido, Commissioner
Josh Brown, Commissioner
Exists to serve the needs of elected County Officials, appointed department heads, County employees and the entire community through a variety of programs and processes. The employees of this department perform work in a wide variety of specialized areas, providing programs and services vital to the community and to Kitsap County as a unit of local government.

1847 Disability Rights Washington
315 5th Ave S
Suite 850
Seattle, WA 98104-2679
206-324-1521
800-562-2702
FAX 206-957-0729
TTY: 206-957-0728
http://www.disabilityrightswa.org
e-mail: info@dr-wa.org
Mark Stroh, Executive Director

A private non-profit organization that protects the rights of people with disabilities statewide. To advance the dignity, equality, and self-determination of people with disabilities. Also work to pursue justice on matters related to human and legal rights.

1848 Region X: Office of Federal Contract Compliance
US Department of Labor
90 7th St
Ste 18300
San Francisco, CA 94103
415-625-7800
FAX 415-625-7799
http://www.dol.gov/ofccp
e-mail: ofccp-pa-preaward@dol.gov
William D Smitherman, Regional Director

Administers Federal Law requiring recipients of Federal Contract dollars to uphold affirmative action and equal employment pooprtunity for all workers, including but not limited to minorities, women, veterans and disabled employees.

1849 Region X: US Department of Education Office for Civil Rights
US Department of Education
Room 3362
915 2nd Ave
Seattle, WA 98174-1009   206-220-7900
                                    FAX 206-220-7887
                                    TDD:877-521-2172
                                    http://www.ed.gov
                              e-mail: ocr.seattle@ed.gov
Arne Duncan, Secretary of Education
Tony Miller, Deputy Secretary
Russlynn Ali, Assistant Secretary
This office covers the states of Alaska, Hawaii, Idaho, Montana, Nevada, Oregon, and Washington.

1850 Region X: US Department of Health and Human Services, Office of Civil Rights
US Department of Health & Human Services
2201 6th Ave
Seattle, WA 98121-1857   206-615-2010
                                    FAX 206-615-2087
                                    http://www.hhs.gov
                              e-mail: susan.johnson@hhs.gov
Susan Johnson, Regional Director

1851 WA State Board for Community and Technical Colleges

PO Box 42495
1300 Quince Street SE
Olympia, WA 98504-2495   360-704-4309
                                    FAX 360-704-4415
                              http://www.sbctc.ctc.edu
                              e-mail: bgordon@sbctc.edu
Beth Gordon, Contact
John Boesenberg, Deputy Executive Director

Promotes adult education.

1852 Washington Human Rights Commission
PO Box 42490
711 S. Capitol Way, Suite 402
Olympia, WA 98504-2490   360-753-6770
                                    1-800-233-32
                                    FAX 360-586-2282
                                    TTY: 1 8-0 3-0 75
                              http://www.hum.wa.gov
Sharon Ortiz, Executive Director
Steve Hunt, Commission Chair
Deborah Siou Lee, Commissioner
The Washington State Human Rights Commission enforces the Washington Law Against Discrimination, the broadest civil rights statute in the United States. It provides technical assistance and training. It also does studies and writes white papers on issues of social justice.

1853 Washington State Board for Community and Technical Colleges
Office of Adult Basic Education
PO Box 42495
Olympia, WA 98504-2495   360-704-4326
                                    FAX 360-704-4419
                        http://www.sbctc.edu/college/e_index
                              e-mail: imendoza@sbctc.edu
Israel David Mendoza, Director, Adult Basic Education

Promotes the quality of adult education.

1854 Washington State Client Assistance Program
2531 Rainier Avenue South
Seattle, WA 98144   206-721-5999
                                    1-800-544-21
                                    FAX 206-721-4537
                                    TTY: 1 8-0 7-1 60
                              http://www.washingtoncap.org
                              e-mail: info@washingtoncap.org

Jerry Johnsen, Director
Bob Huven, Rehabilitation Coordinator

Provides information and advocacy for persons seeking services from the Department of Services for the Blind and the Division of Vocational Rehabilitation. Approximately 25 percent of cases involve assistive technology issues.

1855 Washington State Developmental Disabilities Council
PO Box 48314
Olympia, WA 98504-8314   360-586-3560
                                    800-634-4473
                                    FAX 360-586-2424
                              http://www.ddc.wa.gov
                              e-mail: Ed.Holen@ddc.wa.gov
Ed Holen, Executive Director
Sieng Bonham, Budget & Fiscal Director
Donna Patrick, Public Policy Director
Holds that individuals with developmental disabilities, including those with the most severe disabilities, have the right to achieve independence, productivity, integration and inclusion into the community.

1856 Washington State Governor's Committee on Disability Issues & Employment
PO Box 9046
Olympia, WA 98507-9046   360-902-9500
                                    800-318-6022
                                    FAX 866-610-9225
                                    TTY: 800-365-8969
                              http://www.esd.wa.gov
                              e-mail: Uitelecenters@Esd.wa.gov
Sheryl Hutchison, Communications Director
Bill Tarrow, Deputy Communications Director
Joe Elling, Chief Labor Economist
Information about disability rights programs and services.

West Virginia

1857 Client Assistance Program (CAP): West Virginia Division
West Virginia Advocates
1207 Quarrier St
Litton Building, Suite 400
Charleston, WV 25301-1826   304-346-0847
                                    800-950-5250
                                    FAX 304-346-0867
                              http://www.wvadvocates.org
                              e-mail: contact@wvadvocates.org
Robert Hardesty, President
Clifton Clark, Treasurer
Cathy Reed, Secretary
Mandated in 1984, to provide advocacy to individuals seeking services under the federal Rehabilitation Act (such as services from the West Virginia Division of Rehabilitation Services, Centers for Independent Living, supported employment programs and sheltered workshops).

1858 Office of Institutional Education
State Department of Education
Building 6, Room 728
1900 Kanawha Blvd East
Charleston, WV 25305-0330   304-558-7881
                                    FAX 304-558-5042
                              http://wvde.state.wv.us/institutional/
                              e-mail: fwarsing@access.k12.wv.us
Dr Fran Warsing, Superintendent
Rhonda Mahan, Secretary
Jacob C. Green, Assistant Director
Provides educational services to over 6,000 institutionalized juveniles and adults. It protects the constitutional rights of institutionalized persons by providing programs and services that help change their lives.

1859 State Department of Education
1900 Kanawha Blvd E
Building 6
Charleston, WV 25305-0330   304-558-2681
FAX 304-558-0048
http://wvde.state.wv.us
e-mail: dvermill@access.k12.wv.us
Jorea M Marple, State Superintendent
Charles Heinlein, Deputy Superintendant

Promotes quality education.

1860 State GED Administration
1900 Kanawha Blvd E
Charleston, WV 25305-0009   304-558-6315
FAX 304-558-4874
http://www.wvabe.org/ged/
e-mail: dkimbler@access.k12.wv.us
Debra Kimbler, GED Administrator

Our organization's goal is to provide reasonable accommodations to qualifying GED candidates.

1861 West Virginia Adult Basic Education
West Virginia Department of Education
1900 Kanawha Blvd E
Rm 6
Charleston, WV 25305-0001   304-558-0280
800-642-2670
FAX 304-558-3946
http://wvde.state.wv.us
e-mail: dvarner@access.k12.wv.us
Dr Debra L Frazier Varner, Executive Director

To enable adult learners to be literate, productive, and successful in the workplace, home and community by delivering responsive adult education programs and services.

1862 West Virginia Assistive Technology System
959 Hartman Run Rd
Morgantown, WV 26505-7701   304-293-4692
800-841-8436
FAX 304-293-7294
TTY: 800-518-1448
http://wvats.cedwvu.org
e-mail: wvats@hsc.wvu.edu
Jessica Wright, AT Coordinator

Provides access to Assistive Technology through information and referral, technical assistance training, device demonstration, loan & exchange.

Wisconsin

1863 Correctional Education
Department of Corrections
PO Box 7925
3099 East Washington Avenue
Madison, WI 53707-7925   608-240-5000
FAX 608-240-3300
http://www.wi-doc.com
e-mail: docweb@wi.gov
Gary Hamblin, Secretary
Charles Cole, Deputy Secretary
Dennis Schuh, Executive Assistant

1864 Department of Public Instruction
PO Box 7841
125 S. Webster Street
Madison, WI 53707-7841   608-266-3390
800-441-4563
http://dpi.wi.gov
e-mail: webadmin@dpi.wi.gov
Tony Evers, State Superintendent

Promotes quality education.

1865 Disability Rights Wisconsin
Suite 700
131 W Wilson Street
Madison, WI 53703-3263   608-267-0214
800-928-8778
FAX 608-267-0368
TTY: 888-758-6049
http://www.disabilityrightswi.org
Tom Masseau, Executive Director

DRW challenges systems and society to achieve positive changes in the lives of people with disabilities and their families.

1866 State GED Administration
Department of Public Instruction
PO Box 7841
125 S. Webster Street
Madison, WI 53707-7841   608-267-1062
800-768-8886
FAX 608-267-9275
http://dpi.wi.gov
e-mail: beth.lewis@dpi.wi.gov
Beth Lewis, GED/HSED Administrator
Judith Stowell, Office Operations Associate

Promotes quality adult education.

1867 Wisconsin Board for People with Developmental Disabilities
201 W Washington Ave
Ste 110
Madison, WI 53703-2796   608-266-7826
888-332-1677
FAX 608-267-3906
TDD:608-266-6660
TTY: 602-266-6660
http://www.wi-bpdd.org
e-mail: bpddhelp@wi-bpdd.org
Jennifer Ondrejka, Executive Director

Established to advocate on behalf of individuals with developmental disabilities, foster welcoming and inclusive communities, and improve the disability service system. To help people with developmental disabilities become independent, productive, and included in all facets of community life.

1868 Wisconsin Department of Workforce Development
PO Box 7946
Madison, WI 53707-7946   608-266-3131
FAX 608-266-1784
TTY: 608-267-0477
http://www.dwd.state.wi.us
e-mail: reggie.newson@dwd.wisconsin.gov
Reggie Newson, Department Secretary
Jonathan Barry, Deputy Secretary
Georgia Maxwell, Executive Assistant
A state agency charged with building and strengthening Wisconsin's workforce in the 21st century and beyond. The Departmen's primary responsibilities include providing job services, training and employment assistance to people looking for work, at the same time as itworks with employers on finding the necessary workers to fill current job openings.

1869 Wisconsin Equal Rights Division
PO Box 8928
201 E. Washington Ave, Room A300
Madison, WI 53708-8928   608-266-6860
FAX 608-267-4592
TTY: 608-264-8752
http://www.dwd.wisconsin.gov/er
e-mail: Jim Chiolino@dwd. wisconsin.gov
Jim Chiolino, Acting Division Administrator
Marlene Duffield, Supervisor
Julie Babler, Office Manager

To protect the rights of all people in Wisconsin under the civil rights and labor standards laws we administer; to achieve compliance through education, outreach, and enforcement by empowered and committed employees; and to perform our responsibilities with reasonableness, efficiency, and fairness.

1870 Wisconsin Governor's Committee for People with Disabilities
PO Box 7851
1 W. Wilson Street, Room 437
Madison, WI 53703-7851   608-261-7816
                                FAX 608-266-3386
                                TTY: 888-701-1251
                                http://dhs.wisconsin.gov
                   e-mail: DennisG.Smith@dhs.wisconsin.gov
Dennis G. Smith, Secretary
Christopher Craggs, Area Administrator
Kitty Rhoades, Deputy Secretary
Established to improve employment opportunities for people with disabilities.

Wyoming

1871 Adult Basic Education
Wyoming Community College Commission
2020 Carey Ave
8th Fl
Cheyenne, WY 82002-0001   307-777-7763
                                 FAX 307-777-6567
                      http://communitycolleges.wy.edu
                      e-mail: mhess@commission.wu.edu
Marcia Hess, Program Manager

Focuses on strengthening basic reading, writing, and math skills for adults.

1872 Client Assistance Program (CAP): Wyoming
7344 Stockmann Street
Cheyenne, WY 82009   307-638-7668
                                 FAX 307-638-0815
                      http://www.wypanda.com
                      e-mail: wypanda@wypanda.com
Tori Rosenthal, President
Jeanne Thobro, CEO

Provides free services to consumers and applicants for projects, programs and facilities funded under the rehabilitation act.

1873 Correctional Education: Wyoming Women's Center
PO Box 300
1000 West Griffith
Lusk, WY 82225-0220   307-334-3693
                                 FAX 307-334-2254
          http://corrections.wy.gov/institutions/wwc/inde
                      e-mail: chris.thayer@wyo.gov

Phil Myer, Warden
Martha Decker, Associate Warden

The Wyoming Women's Center is a full service, secure correctional facility for female offenders and the sole adult female facility in the State of Wyoming. In October 2000, WWC opened a self-contained 16 bed intensive addiction treatment unit, a is highly structured long term 7-9 month program based upon the therapeutic community treatment model. It is tailored to provide gender specific services and is funded with a combination of state and federal resources.

1874 Protection & Advocacy System
7344 Stockmann Street
Cheyenne, WY 82009   307-632-3496
                                 FAX 307-638-0815
                      http://www.wypanda.com
                      e-mail: wypanda@wypanda.com
Tori Rosenthal, President
Jeanne Thobro, CEO

It is the goal of Wyoming's Protection & Advocacy System, Inc. to ensure that all of its web resources are accessible to all who use this website. The pages reflect this process.

1875 State Department of Education
2300 Capitol Ave
2nd Fl
Cheyenne, WY 82002-0001   307-777-7673
                                 FAX 307-777-6234
                      http://www.k12.wy.us

Jim Mc Bride, Superintendent

1876 State GED Administration
State Department of Education
2300 Capitol Ave
Hathaway Building, 2nd Floor
Cheyenne, WY 82002-0050   307-777-7690
                                 FAX 307-777-6234
                                 TTY: 307-777-7744
                      http://www.k12.wy.us

Cindy Hill, State Superintendant
Rita Watson, Executive Assistant

Promotes quality adult education.

1877 Wyoming Department of Workforce Services
1510 East Pershing Blvd
Cheyenne, WY 82002   307-777-3700
                                 866-804-3678
                                 FAX 307-777-5870
                http://www.wyomingworkforce.org
                      e-mail: joan.evans@wyo.gov
Joan K. Evans, Director
Lisa M. Osvold, Deputy Director

Employment training for persons working in Wyoming.

National Programs

1878 Academic Institute
13400 NE 20th St
Ste 47
Bellevue, WA 98005   425-401-6844
                                   FAX 425-401-6323
                       http://www.academicinstitute.com
                   e-mail: sherrill@academicinstitute.com
Sherrill O'Shaughnessy, Founder/Executive Director

To prepare students for success in college and their lives beyond by helping them cultivate: a sense of capability, determination, resilience, self-advocacy and a love of learning.

1879 American Association for Adult and Continuing Education
10111 Martin Luther King Jr Hwy
Ste 200C
Bowie, MD 20720   301-459-6261
                                   FAX 301-459-6241
                             http://www.aaace.org
                         e-mail: aaace10@aol.com
Cle Anderson, Manager

Provides leadership for the field of adult and continuing education by expanding opportunities for adult growth and development; unifying adult educators; fostering the development and dissemination of theory, research, informaiton and best practices; promoting identity and standards for the profession; and advocating relevant public policy and social change initiatives.

1880 American Literacy Council
PO Box 3010
Cedar City, UT 84721-3010   914-271-3294
                       http://www.americanliteracy.com
              e-mail: presidentalc3@americanliteracy.com
Robert Alan Mole, President

Conveys information on new solutions, innovative technologies and tools for engaging more boldly in the battle for literacy.

1881 Association of Educational Therapists
11300 W Olympic Blvd
Ste 600
Los Angeles, CA 90064   310-909-1490
                                       800-286-4267
                                   FAX 310-437-0585
                             http://www.aetonline.org
                         e-mail: aet@aetonline.org
Risa Graff, President

Dedicated to defining the professional practice of educational therapy, setting standards for ethical practice, and promoting state-of-the-art service delivery through on-going professional development and training programs.

1882 Association on Higher Education and Disability
107 Commerce Center Drive
Ste 204
Huntersville, NC 28078   704-947-7779
                                   FAX 704-948-7779
                                   TTY: 617-287-3882
                             http://www.ahead.org
                         e-mail: ahead@ahead.org
Stephan J Smith, Executive Director
Oanh Huynh, Associate Executive Director

A professional membership organization for individuals involved in the development of policy and in the provision of quality services to meet the needs of persons with disabilities involved in all areas of higher education.

1883 Career College Association (CCA)
1101 Connecticut Ave NW
Ste 900
Washington, DC 20036   202-336-6700
                                       866-711-8574
                                   FAX 202-336-6828
                             http://www.career.org
                         e-mail: cca@career.org
A voluntary membership organization of accredited, private, postsecondary schools, institutes, colleges and universities that provide career-specific educational programs.
1,400 members

1884 Center for the Improvement of Early Reading Achievement (CIERA)
University of Michigan School of Education
610 E University Ave
Rm 2002 SEB
Ann Arbor, MI 48109-1259   734-647-6940
                                   FAX 734-615-4858
                             http://www.ciera.org
                         e-mail: ciera@umich.edu
Karen Wixon, Former Director
Joanne Carlisle, Former Co-Director
Deanna Birdyshaw, Former Associate Director
To improve the reading achievement of America's youth by generating and disseminating theoretical, empirical, and practical solutions to the learning and teaching of beginning reading.

1885 Council for Educational Diagnostic Services
Council for Exceptional Children
1110 N Glebe Rd
Ste 300
Arlington, VA 22201-5704   888-232-7733
                                   FAX 703-264-9494
                                   TTY: 866-915-5000
                             http://www.cec.sped.org
Bruce Ramirez, Director

Ensures the highest quality of diagnostic and prescriptive procedures involved in the education of individuals with disabilities and/or who are gifted.

1886 Distance Education and Training Council (DETC)
1601 18th St NW
Ste 2
Washington, DC 20009   202-234-5100
                                   FAX 202-332-1386
                             http://www.detc.org
                         e-mail: detc@detc.org
Michael P Lambert, Executive Director/Secretary

A voluntary, non-governmental, educational organization that operates a nationally recognized accrediting association. Fosters and preserves high quality, educationally sound and widely accepted distance education and independent learning solutions.
1926

1887 Division for Children's Communication Development
Council for Exceptional Children
2900 Crystal Drive
Suite 1000
Arlington, VA 22202-3557   888-232-7733
                                       888-232-7733
                                   FAX 703-265-9494
                                   TTY: 866-915-5000
                             http://www.cec.sped.org
                         e-mail: service@cec.sped.org
Margaret J. McLaughlin, President
James P. Heiden, Treasurer

Dedicated to improving the education of children with communication delays and disorders and hearing loss. Members include professionals serving individuals with hearing, speech and language disorders in the areas of receptive and expressive, verbal and nonverbal spoken, written and sign communication. Members receive a quarterly journal and newsletter three times a year.

1888   Division for Culturally and Linguistically Diverse Learners
Council for Exceptional Children
1110 N Glebe Rd
Ste 300
Arlington, VA 22201-5704   703-264-9454
                                             888-232-7733
                                        FAX 703-264-9494
                                        TTY: 866-915-5000
                                   http://www.cec.sped.org
Sandra Cooley-Nichols, President

Advances educational opportunities for culturally and linguistically diverse learners with disabilities and/or who are gifted, their families and the professionals who serve them.

1889   Division for Research
Council for Exceptional Children
1110 N Glebe Rd
Ste 300
Arlington, VA 22201-5704   703-264-9454
                                             888-232-7733
                                        FAX 703-264-9494
                                        TTY: 866-915-5000
                                   http://www.cec.sped.org
Timothy J Landrum, President

Devoted to the advancement of research related to the education of individuals with disabilities and/or who are gifted.

1890   Educational Advisory Group
2222 Eastlake Ave E
Seattle, WA 98102-3419   206-323-1838
                                        FAX 206-267-1325
                                http://www.eduadvisory.com
Yvonne Jones, Director

Specializes in matching children with the learning environments that are best for them and works with families to help them identify concerns and establish priorities about their child's education.

1891   Institute for Educational Leadership
4455 Connecticut Ave NW
Ste 310
Washington, DC 20008   202-822-8405
                                        FAX 202-872-4050
                                        http://www.iel.org
                                        e-mail: iel@iel.org
Martin J Blank, President

To improve education and the lives of children and their families through positive and visionary change.

1892   Institute for Human Centered Design
200 Portland St
Ste 1
Boston, MA 02114   617-695-1225
                                             800-949-4232
                                        FAX 617-482-8099
                                        TTY: 617-695-1225
                         http://www.adaptiveenvironments.org
                    e-mail: info@humancentereddesign.com
Valerie Fletcher, Executive Director

Founded as Adaptive Environments, committed to advancing the role of design in expanding opportunity and enhancing experience for people of all ages and abilities through excellence in design.

1893   Institute for the Study of Adult Literacy
Pennsylvania State Univ. College of Education
405 Keller Bldg
University Park, PA 16802-3202   814-863-3777
                                        FAX 814-863-6108
                                   http://www.ed.psu.edu/isal
                                        e-mail: isal@psu.edu
Barbara Van Horn, Co-Director

Experienced staff assista providers with: program design and delivery; customized instructional materials and assessment development; professional development (including distance learning); and program evaluations.

1894   International Dyslexia Association
40 York Rd
4th Fl
Baltimore, MD 21204   410-296-0232
                                        FAX 410-321-5069
                                   http://www.interdys.org
                          e-mail: speregoy@interdys.org
Stephen M Peregoy, Executive Director

Nonprofit, scientific and educational organization dedicated to the study and treatment of dyslexia.

1895   Learning Resource Network
PO Box 9
River Falls, WI 54022   715-426-9777
                                             800-678-5376
                                        FAX 888-234-8633
                                        http://www.lern.org
                                        e-mail: info@lern.org
William A Draves, President
Tammy Peterson, Information Specialist

An international association of lifelong learning programming, offering information and resources to providers of lifelong learning programs.

1896   National Adult Education Professional Development Consortium
444 N Capital St NW
Ste 422
Washington, DC 20001   202-624-5250
                                        FAX 202-624-8826
                                   http://www.naepdc.org
                          e-mail: lmclendon@naepdc.org
Dr Lennox McLendon, Executive Director

Advances the leadership of state staff in adult education throughout the states and territories so that every program will be of quality and excellence as we together increase literacy and prepare adults for success as contributing members of the society through work, community and family; and, will be the leading voice in adult education for the nation.

1897   National Adult Literacy & Learning Disabilities Center (NALLD)
Academy for Educational Development
1825 Connecticut Ave NW
Washington, DC 20009-5708   202-884-8000
                                        FAX 202-884-8400
                                   http://www.fhi360.org
                          e-mail: media@fhi360.org
Albert J. Siemens, Chief Executive Officer
Torrey C. Brown, Chairman
Peter W. McClean, Managing Director
The center is a national resource for information on learning disabilities in adults and on the relationship between learning disabilities and low-level literacy skills.

1898 National Association for Adults with Special Learning Needs

KOC Member Services
1143 Tidewater Court
Westerville, OH 43082

888-562-2756
FAX 614-392-1559
http://www.naasln.org

Joan Hudson-Miller, Co-President
Richard Cooper PhD, Co-President

An association for those who serve adults with special learning needs. Members include educators, trainers, employers and human service providers. The goal is to ensure that adults with special learning needs have opportunities necessary to become successful lifelong learners.

1899 National Association of Private Special Education Centers

601 Pennsylvania Ave NW
Ste 900, South Bldg
Washington, DC 20004

202-434-8225
FAX 202-434-8224
http://www.napsec.org
e-mail: napsec@aol.com

The indispensable voice and premier resource for the private special education community. Represents early intervention services, school, residential therapeutic centers, postsecondary college experience programs and adult living services.
1971

1900 National Center for Family Literacy

325 W Main St
Ste 300
Louisville, KY 40202

502-584-1133
FAX 502-584-0172
http://www.famlit.org
e-mail: ncfl@famlit.org

Mission is to not only provide every family with the opportunity to learn, but the ability to learn anf grow together. Ensures the cycle of learning and progress passes from generation to generation.

1901 National Center for Learning Disabilities (NCLD)

381 Park Ave S
Suite 1401
New York, NY 10016

212-545-7510
888-575-7373
FAX 212-545-9665
http://www.ncld.org

James H Wendorf, Executive Director

To ensure that the nation's 15 million children, adolescents, and adults with learning disabilities have every opportunity to succeed in school, work and life.

1902 National Center for the Study of Adult Learning & Literacy

Harvard Graduate School of Education
7 Appian Way
Cambridge, MA 02138

617-495-5828
FAX 617-495-4811
http://www.gse.harvard.edu
e-mail: webeditor@gse.harvard.edu

John P Comings MD, Director

The National Center for the Study of Adult Learning & Literacy both informs and learns from practice. Its rigorous, high quality research increases knowledge and gives those teaching, managing, and setting policy in adult literacy education a sound basis for making decisions.

1903 National Center on Adult Literacy (NCAL)

University of Pennsylvania
3910 Chestnut St
Philadelphia, PA 19104-3111

215-898-3283
FAX 215-898-9804
http://www.literacyonline.org

NCAL's mission incorporates three primary goals: to improve understanding of youth and adult learning; to foster innovation and increase effectiveness in youth and adult basic education and literacy work; and to expand access to information and build capacity for literacy and basic skills service.
1990

1904 National Education Association (NEA)

1201 16th St NW
Washington, DC 20036-3290

202-833-4000
FAX 202-822-7974
http://www.nea.org

Dennis Van Roekel, President
John I Wilson, Executive Director

Adovcates for education professionals and to unite members and the nation to fulfill the promise of public education to prepare every student to succeed in a diverse and interdependent world.

1905 National Lekotek Center

2001 N Clybourn
Chicago, IL 60614

773-528-5766
FAX 773-537-2992
http://www.lekotek.org
e-mail: lekotek@lekotek.org

The central source on toys and play for children with special needs.

1906 Office of Special Education Programs

US Department of Education
330 C St SW
Washington, DC 20202-0001

202-208-5815
http://www2.ed.gov

Melody Musgrove, Director

Dedicated to improving results for infants, toddlers, children and youth with disabilities ages birth through 21 by providing leadership and financial support to assist states and local districts.

1907 ProLiteracy

1320 Jamesville Ave
Syracuse, NY 13210

315-422-9121
888-528-2224
FAX 315-422-6369
http://www.proliteracy.org
e-mail: info@proliteracy.org

David C Harvey, President/CEO

Champions the power of literacy to improve the lives of adults and their families, communities, and societies. Works with its members and partners, and the adult learners they serve, along with local, national, and international organizations. Helps build the capacity and quality of programs that are teaching adults to read, write, compute, use technology and learn English as a new language.

1908 Thinking and Learning Connection

Parents Helping Parents
239 Whitclem Ct
Palo Alto, CA 94306

650-493-3497
FAX 650-494-3499
http://www.php.com

Mary Ellen Peterson, Executive Director/CEO, PHP

A group of independent associates committed to teaching learning different students. The primary focus is working with dyslexia and dyscalculia. The individualized education programs utilize extensive multisensory approaches to teach reading, spelling, handwriting, composition, comprehension and mathematics.

Alabama

1909 Alabama Commission on Higher Education
PO Box 302000
Montgomery, AL 36130-2000   334-242-1998
                                    FAX 334-242-0268
                         http://www.ache.state.al.us
Gregory G Fitch PhD, Executive Director

Ths state agency responsible for the overall statewide planning and coordination of higher education in Alabama. Seeks to provide reasonable access to quality collegiate and university education for the citizens of Alabama.

1910 South Baldwin Literacy Council
PO Box 1973
Foley, AL 36536   251-943-7323
                                    FAX 251-970-3578
                         http://baldwinliteracy.com
                         e-mail: literacy@gulftel.com
Tracy Walter, Executive Director

Provides instruction by trained volunteer tutors in a one-on-one or small group setting to residents of South Baldwin County. Instruction is centered around the learners' individual goals and capabilities and is designed to improve basic reading, writing and life skills.

1911 The Literacy Council
2301 1st Ave N
Ste 102
Birmingham, AL 35203   205-326-1925
                                    888-448-7323
                         http://www.literacy-council.org
                         e-mail: info@literacy-council.org
Steve Hannum, Interim Executive Director

A non-profit organization which serves a five-county area, is dedicated to reducing literacy. Efforts include providing resources and referrals by maintaining a toll-free literacy helpline which serves as a primary point of contact for individuals seeking literacy assistance.

Alaska

1912 Alaska Adult Basic Education
SERRC
210 Ferry Eay
Juneau, AK 99801-1390   907-586-6806
                                    FAX 907-463-3811
                         http://www.serrc.org
                         e-mail: info@serrc.org
Sheryl Weinberg, Executive Director

The mission of the Adult Basic Education program is to provide instruction in the basic skills of reading, writing, and mathematics to adult learners in order to prepare them for transitioning into the labor market or higher academic or vocational training.

1913 Anchorage Literacy Project
Ste 104
1345 Rudakof Cir
Anchorage, AK 99508-6104   907-337-1981
                                    FAX 907-338-3105
                         http://www.alaskaliteracyprogram.org
                         e-mail: akliteracy@alaskaliteracyprogram.org
Jim Parker, President
Anne Newell, Secretary
Mary Gibbs, Treasurer
Dedicated to improving the lives of adults and their families by helping to build their literacy skills. Offer direct literacy skills for adults-native born citizens and recent immigrants alike-through on-site classes and one-on-one tutoring.

1914 Literacy Council of Alaska
517 Gaffney Rd
Fairbanks, AK 99701   907-456-6212
                                    FAX 907-456-4302
                         http://www.literacycouncilofalaska.org
                         e-mail: lca@literacycouncilofalaska.org
Promotes literacy for people of all ages in Fairbanks and the Interior. The goals are to help community members achieve individual educational goals and to raise public awareness about literacy.

Arizona

1915 Chandler Public Library Adult Basic Education
PO Box 4008
Mail Stop 601
Chandler, AZ 85244-4008   480-782-2800
                         http://www.chandlerlibrary.org
                         e-mail: marybeth.gardner@chandleraz.gov
Dolly Franco, President
Chris Loschiavo, Secretary
Marybeth Gardner, Library Development
Provides adult basic education classes for learners who need to improve their basic skills in reading, writing, and math. Gives GED preparation classes to help students prepare to take the GED exam.

1916 Literacy Volunteers of Maricopa County
1500 E Thomas Rd
Ste 102
Phoenix, AZ 85014   602-274-3430
                                    FAX 602-274-5983
                         http://www.literacyvolunteers-maricopa.org
                         e-mail: lvmc@lvmc.net
Lynn Reed, Executive Director

A non-profit organization dedicated to teaching adults 16 years and older how to read, write, speak English and prepare for the GED. Also offer computer literacy which inclues the basics of using a computer, accessing the Internet and using basic Microsoft programs.

1917 Literacy Volunteers of Tucson A Program of Literacy Connects
2850 E Speedway Blvd
Tucson, AZ 85716   520-882-8006
                         http://www.literacyconnects.org
                         e-mail: info@literacyconnects.org
Edie Lantz-Leppert, Basic Literacy Program Manager

Recruits, trains and matches tutors with adults (age 16 and up) in need of basic literacy (reading and writing) skills and/or English Language Acquisition for Adults (ELAA). Provides a friendly non-threatening environment that appeals to adult learners in all walks of life.

1918 Yuma Reading Council
2951 S. 21st Dr.
Yuma, AZ 85364-3846   928-782-1871
                                    FAX 928-782-9420
                         http://www.yumalibrary.org
                         e-mail: greg.ferguson@yumacountyaz.go
Gregory Ferguson, Chairman

Provides one to one tutoring for basic literacy and english as a second language, and converstaion classes for beginning, intermediate and advanced levels for English as a second language students.

Arkansas

1919 Arkansas Adult Learning Resource Center

3905 Cooperative Way
Ste D
Little Rock, AR 72209

877-963-4433
FAX 501-907-2492
http://www.aalrc.org
e-mail: info@aalrc.org

Marsha Talyor, Director

The Arkansas Adult Learning Resource Center was established in 1990 to provide a source for identification, evaluation, and dissemination of materials and information to adult education/literacy programs within the state.

1920 Arkansas Literacy Council

525 W Capitol Ave
Little Rock, AR 72201

501-907-2490
800-264-7323
FAX 501-907-2492
http://www.arkansasliteracy.org
e-mail: info@arkansasliteracy.org

Marie C Bruno, Executive Director

Provides structure to a network of local literacy councils. These councils recruit and train volunteers to tutor adults who either need help with basic reading, writing, and math skills, or who want to learn English as a Second Language

1921 Drew County Literacy Council

PO Box 534
Monticello, AR 71657

870-367-7007
800-264-7323
FAX 870-367-7007
http://www.arkansasliteracy.org
e-mail: mkjarrett71655@yahoo.com

Margaret Jarrett, Director

Formed by citizens that were concerned about the adult illiteracy rate reported in the 1980 census. Strives to recruit, train and match volunteer tutors with illiterate adults in the county using The Laubach Way to Reading and Laubach Way to English.

1922 Faulkner County Literacy Council

615 E Robins St
PO Box 2106
Conway, AR 72033

501-329-7323
http://www.faulknercoliteracy.org
e-mail: fclc@conwaycorp.net

Emily Maggion, Executive Director

Provides free instruction through trained volunteers to adults in Faulkner County who lack basic reading, writing, mathematics, English as a second language and life skills.

1923 Literacy Action of Central Arkansas

100 Rock St
Ste 403
Little Rock, AR 72201

501-372-7323
FAX 501-371-9888
http://www.literacylittlerock.org
e-mail: info@literacylittlerock.org

Samantha Friedman, President

A non-profit organization that teaches reading skills to adults and English skills to non-native adults.
1986

1924 Literacy Council Of Lonoke County

306 N Center
PO Box 234
Lonoke, AR 72086

501-676-7478
FAX 501-676-7478
http://www.arkansasliteracy.org
e-mail: lonokeliteracy@sbcglobal.net

Claire Rogers, Director

1925 Literacy Council of Arkansas County

116 W 3rd St, Ste A
PO Box 94
Stuttgart, AR 72160

870-673-4551
FAX 870-673-3800
http://www.arkansasliteracy.org
e-mail: litarco@centurytel.net

Eddye Kay Hansen, Director

1926 Literacy Council of Benton County

205 NW A St
Bentonville, AR 72712

479-273-3486
FAX 479-273-7545
http://goliteracy.org
e-mail: readlcbc@sbcgloabl.net

Vicki Ronald, Director

A non-profit agency that increases Adult English literacy by developing volunteer tutors to teach students because Literacy Changes Lives. Empowers people to improve their wuality of lives within the community we all share by increasing adult English Literacy.

1927 Literacy Council of Crittenden County

2000 W Broadway St
West Memphis, AR 72301

870-733-6760
FAX 870-733-6737
http://www.arkansasliteracy.org
e-mail: jkfluker@midsouthcc.edu

Kim Fluker, Director

1928 Literacy Council of Garland County

119 Hobson Ave
Hot Springs, AR 71901

501-624-7323
FAX 501-624-2994
http://www.arkansasliteracy.org
e-mail: literacylady@sbcglobal.net

Pat McClaran, Director

1929 Literacy Council of Grant County

201 S Rose St
PO Box 432
Sheridan, AR 72150

870-942-5711
FAX 870-942-7228
http://www.arkansasliteracy.org
e-mail: literacy@windstream.net

Jo Ann Click, Director

1930 Literacy Council of Hot Spring County

122 E Page
PO Box 1485
Malvern, AR 72104

501-332-4039
FAX 501-332-4043
http://www.readhelp.com
e-mail: readhelp@sbcglobal.net

Jane Goodwin, Director

Offers a variety of educational services at no charge that range from literacy for adults to peer-tutoring for children; English as a second language to Learning Differences screening.

1931   Literacy Council of Jefferson County
402 E 5th
PO Box 7066
Pine Bluff, AR 71611   870-536-7323
                                            FAX 870-850-0984
                        http://www.arkansasliteracy.org
                e-mail: clarenceburnettjr@yahoo.com
Clarenece Burnett Jr, Director

1932   Literacy Council of Monroe County
234 W Cedar St
Brinkley, AR 72021   870-734-3333
                                            FAX 870-734-3333
                        http://www.arkansasliteracy.org
                        e-mail: lcmc1992@gmail.com
Martha Pineda, Director

1933   Literacy Council of North Central Arkansas
PO Box 187
Leslie, AR 72645   870-447-3241
                                                800-264-7323
                                            FAX 870-447-3241
                        http://www.arkansasliteracy.org
                e-mail: pogocatwoman26@gmail.com
Susan Vorwald, Director

1934   Literacy Council of Western Arkansas
PO Box 423
Fort Smith, AR 72902   479-783-2665
                                            FAX 479-783-5332
                        http://www.arkansasliteracy.org
                e-mail: helptoread@sbcglobal.net
Bruce Singleton, Director

1935   Literacy League of Craighead County
324 W Huntington Ave
PO Box 9251
Jonesboro, AR 72403   870-910-6511
                                            FAX 870-910-0552
                        http://www.arkansasliteracy.org
                e-mail: acbutts2006@yahoo.com
Amy Butts, Director

1936   Ozark Literacy Council
2596 Keystone Crossing
Fayetteville, AR 72703   479-521-8250
                                            FAX 479-582-0846
                        http://www.ozarkliteracy.org
Wendy Poole, Executive Director

Provides quality basic literacy and language instruction enabling people to learn and communicate effectively.

1937   Pope County Literacy Council
1000 S Arkansas Ave
PO Box 1276
Russellville, AR 72811   479-967-7323
                                            FAX 479-968-6248
                        http://www.arkansasliteracy.org
                e-mail: popecoliteracy@centurytel.net
Jennifer Merkey, Director

1938   St. John's ESL Program
583 W Grand Ave
Hot Springs, AR 71901-3937   501-624-3171
                                            FAX 501-624-3171
                            http://www.sjshs.org
                        e-mail: aisaacs@sjshs.org

Angela Issacs, Principal
David Myers, President
Patty Owens, Secretary

1939   Twin Lakes Literacy Council
1318 Bradley Dr
Ste 14
Mountain Home, AR 72653   870-425-7323
                                            FAX 870-424-3646
                http://www.twinlakesliteracycouncil.org
                    e-mail: twinlakeslc@yahoo.com
Nancy Tester, Executive Director

To promote and enhance literacy efforts and to encourage volunteers to participate in all phases of this endeavor.

1940   Van Buren County Literacy Council
Clinton, AR 72031   501-745-6440
                                            FAX 501-745-6440
                        http://www.arkansasliteracy.org
                    e-mail: dogwood@artelco.com
Brenda Wood, Director

California

1941   Butte County Library Adult Reading Program
1820 Mitchell Ave
Oroville, CA 95966-5333   530-538-7641
                                                888-538-7198
                                            FAX 530-538-7235
                            http://www.buttecounty.net
                e-mail: literacy@buttecounty.net
Bill Connelly, Supervisor
Paul Hahn, Chief Administrative Officer

Tutoring at no charge in reading, writing and math. Participants will learn the basics and more with one-on-one tutoring. A volunteer tutor will meet with participants at any branch library in Butte County.

1942   California Association of Special Education & Services
CASES Executive Office
1722 J St
Ste 3
Sacramento, CA 95814   916-447-7061
                                            FAX 916-447-1320
                            http://www.capses.com
                        e-mail: info@capses.com
Wayne K Miyamoto MEd, Public/Governmental Affairs Dir
Janeth Rodriguez MA, Communications/Operations Dir

A statewide professional association of nonpublic schools, agencies, organizations and individuals who specialize in the delivery of quality special education programs to students with special education needs.

1943   California Department of Education
Office of the Secretary for Education
1121 L St
Ste 600
Sacramento, CA 95814-3943   916-323-0611
                                            FAX 916-323-3753
                            http://www.ose.ca.gov
Bonnie Reiss, Secretary of Education

The Office of the Secretary for Education is responsible for advising and making policy recommendations to the Governor on education issues.

1944   California Literacy
PO Box 70916
Pasadena, CA 91117-7916   626-395-9989
                                            FAX 626-356-9327
                            http://www.caliteracy.org
                        e-mail: office@caliteracy.org

Archana Carey, Director

California Literacy was founded in 1956 and is the nation's oldest and largest statewide adult volunteer literacy organization. Its purpose is to establish literacy programs and to support them through tutor training, consulting, and ongoing education.

1945 Lake County Literacy Coalition
1425 N High St
Lakeport, CA 95453 707-263-8817
FAX 707-263-6796
http://www.co.lake.ca.us
A non-profit volunteer organization that sponsors and supports the Adult Literacy Program of Lake County Library. Also offer special training sessions on specific topics, such as ESL, learning disabilities and teaching grammar.

1946 Literacy Program: County of Los Angeles Public Library
Rm 208
7400 E. Imperial Hwy
Downey, CA 90242-3375 562-940-8400
http://www.colapublib.org
e-mail: mdtodd@library.lacounty.gov
Margaret Don Todd, County Librarian

The Literacy Centers of the County of Los Angeles Public Library offer a variety of literacy services for adults and families at no charge. Literacy services include one-to-one basic literacy tutoring, English as a Second Language group instruction, Family Literacy and self-help instruction on audio cassettes, videocassettes and computer-based training. The literacy program is an affiliate of Literacy Volunteers of America, Inc.

1947 Literacy Volunteers of America: Willits Public Library
390 E Commercial St
Willits, CA 95490-3202 707-459-5908
http://www.mendolibrary.org
e-mail: lvawillits@pacific.net
Donna Kerr, Branch Librarian

The Literacy program offers one-on-one reading, writing and tutoring for adults in the area.

1948 Marin Literacy Program
San Rafael Public Library
1100 E St
San Rafael, CA 94901 415-485-3318
FAX 415-485-3112
http://www.marinliteracy.org
e-mail: readandwrite@marinliteracy.org
Susan Charltong, Literacy Program Supervisor

Provides Marin County adults with free student-centered instruction in reading, writing, and speaking to help them reach their full potential at work, at home, and in the community.

1949 Merced Adult School
50 E 20th St
Merced, CA 95340 209-385-6524
FAX 209-385-6430
http://www.muhsd.k12.ca.us
e-mail: dglass@muhsd.k12.ca.us
Debra L Glass, Principal

To empower adult students to discover their own unique, productive places in our dynamic world and encourage them to be lifelong learners.

1950 Metropolitan Adult Education Program
760 Hillsdale Ave
San Jose, CA 95136 408-723-6400
http://www.metroed.net
Sylvia Karp, Director

A unit of the Metropolitan Education and offers adult education classes for free or at a very low-cost. Classes are convenient, accessible, and have flexible schedules to meet the family and work needs of adults. Courses range from basic skills in math, reading and writing, ESL Citizenship, 50+ Program to Career Technical (Vocational) certificate programs.

1951 Mid City Adult Learning Center
Belmont Community Adult School
1510 Cambria St
Los Angeles, CA 90017-4307 213-483-8689
FAX 213-413-1356
http://www.literacynet.org/slrc/la/home.html
e-mail: midcity@otan.dni.us
Judy Griffin, Resource Manager
Fernando Dejo, Technical Assistant

Provides adult education on ESL, basic reading, language and literacy programs.

1952 Newport Beach Public Library Literacy Services
1000 Avocado Ave
Newport Beach, CA 92660 949-717-3800
FAX 949-640-5681
http://www.newport-beach.ca.us
Provides free literacy instruction to adults who live or work in the Newport Beach area.

1953 Pomona Public Library Literacy Services
625 S Garey Ave
PO Box 2271
Pomona, CA 91769 909-620-2035
FAX 909-620-3713
http://www.youseemore.com
e-mail: library@ci.pomona.ca.us
The Pomona Literacy Service provides free adult literacy services to the City of Pomona. Volunteers provide tutorial programs to adults (16 years and older) who do not have basic literacy skills or whose literacy skills are so limited that they are not able to function independently in daily life or acquire employment or higher education.

1954 Recording for the Blind & Dyslexic: Los Angeles
5022 Hollywood Blvd
Los Angeles, CA 90027-6104 323-664-5525
800-732-8398
FAX 323-664-1881
http://www.rfbda.org
e-mail: los_angeles@rfbda.org
A national, nonprofit organization providing recorded textbooks, library services and other educational materials to students who cannot read standard print because of a visual, physical or learning disability. $50.00 registration fee and a $25.00 annual renewal fee. No fee for students whose schools are members.

1955 Recording for the Blind and Dyslexic: Inland Empire-Orange County Unit
Orange County Studio
2021 E 4th St
Studio 114
Santa Ana, CA 92705-3912 909-949-4316
FAX 714-547-4241
http://www.rfbd.org/ieoc
e-mail: kcowen@rfbd.org
Mike Davis, Executive Director

Volunteers record texts on audio cassettes and computer disks for the visually, physically and perceptually disabled.

1956 Sacramento Public Library Literacy Service
828 I St
Sacramento, CA 95814 916-264-2700
800-209-4627
http://www.saclibrary.org
e-mail: director@saclibrary.org
Rivkah Sass, Library Director

The Literacy Service is committed to helping adults attain the skills they need to achieve their goals and develop their knowledge and potential. Free one-on-one tutoring is provided to English speaking adults who want to improve their basic reading and writing skills.

1957   Sweetwater State Literacy Regional Resource Center
Adult Resource Center
458 Moss St
Chula Vista, CA 91911-1726   619-691-5791
                                    FAX 619-425-8728
http://www.literacynet.org/slrc/sweetwater/home
                        e-mail: hurley@otan.dni.us
Alice Hurley, Director

The Sweetwater State Literacy Resource Center is located at the Adult and Continuing Education Division of the Sweetwater Union High School District. The Division is the fourth largest adult education program in the State of California, serving over 32,000 adult learners yearly.

1958   Vision Literacy of California
Pro Literacy Worldwide
540 Valley Way
Bldg 4
Milpitas, CA 95035-4106   408-676-7323
                                 FAX 408-956-9384
                    http://www.visionliteracy.org
                    e-mail: info@visionliteracy.org
Patricia Lawson-North, Director
Steven C. Toy, President
Kathleen Campbell, Treasurer
Vision Literacy is dedicated to enriching the community in which we live by helping adults improve their literacy skills.

Colorado

1959   Adult Literacy Program
PO Box 4856
Basalt, CO 81621-4856   970-963-9200
                    http://www.englishinaction.org
                    e-mail: lara@englishinaction.org
Julie Fox-Rubin, Founder
Lara Beaulieu, Executive Director
Shinta Damayanti, Administrative Assistant
Building community through language and leadership development.

1960   Archuleta County Education Center
P.O.Box 1079
Pagosa Springs, CO 81147-1079   970-264-2835
          http://www.archuletacountyeducationcenter.com
Lynell Wiggers, Adult Education Program Director

A non-profit organization, that through fundraising, grants and strategic partnerships with other organizations and agencies, provides a wide variety of learning experiences and services for children, youth and adults as well as providing a fundamental infrastructure asset that supports the economic development priorities of the communities it serves.

1961   Colorado Adult Education and Family Literacy
Colorado Department of Education
201 E Colfax Ave
Denver, CO 80203   303-866-6600
                          FAX 303-866-6599
                    http://www.cde.state.co.us
Margaret Kirkpatrick, State Director

To assist adults to become literate in English and obtain the knowledge and skills necessary for employment and self-sufficiency.

1962   Durango Adult Education Center
701 Camino del Rio
Ste 301
Durango, CO 81301-5254   970-385-4354
                                 FAX 970-385-7968
                        http://www.durangoaec.org
                        e-mail: info@durangoaec.org
Bob Harrington, President
Paulette Church, Executive Director

A private, non-profit organization that has been dedicated to providing educational resources for adults, seniors and youth in the duragno area.

1963   Learning Source
455 S Pierce St
Lakewood, CO 80226   303-922-4683
                            FAX 303-742-9929
                    http://www.coloradoliteracy.org
                    e-mail: info@coloradoliteracy.org
Susan Lythgoe, Executive Director

Provides opportunities for motivated adult learners and families to attain their educational goals through adult and family literacy, GED preparation and English Language instruction.

1964   Pine River Community Learning Center
535 Candelaria Dr
Ignacio, CO 81137   970-563-0681
                    http://www.prclc.org
                    e-mail: lowen@prclc.org
Susan Visser, Executive Director

A nonprofit educational organization dedicated to the principle that life is learning, to the unparalleled welath of cultures in the rural Southwest and the unique gifts of its people.

Connecticut

1965   Connecticut Literacy Resource Center
111 Charter Oak Ave
Hartford, CT 06106-1912   860-247-2732
                                 FAX 860-246-3304
                        http://www.crec.org
                    e-mail: communications@crec.org
Dr. Bruce E. Douglas, Executive Director

The Literacy Center offers services that foster literacy development from early childhood to adult. Technical assistance and training are available in the following areas: School Readiness; k-12; and Family Literacy.

1966   LEARN: Regional Educational Service Center
44 Hatchetts Hill Rd
Old Lyme, CT 06371-1512   860-434-4800
                                 FAX 860-434-4837
                        http://www.learn.k12.ct.us
                    e-mail: director@learn.k12.ct.us
Eileen Howley, Executive Director

LEARN initiates, supports and provides a wide range of programs and services that enhance the quality and expand the opportunities for learning in the educational community.

1967   Literacy Center of Milford
Fannie Beach Community Center
16 Dixon St
Milford, CT 06460   203-878-4800
                http://www.literacycenterofmilford.com
                    e-mail: literacycenter@optimum.net
Tami Jackson, Executive Director

Serves people from other countries who want to learn the English language and it helps people in need of mastering basic reading, writing and math skills. Provides a quality program where people can find the help and support they require to meet their basic literacy needs.

1968 Literacy Volunteers of Central Connecticut

20 High St
New Britain, CT 06051-2206   860-229-7323
FAX 860-223-6729
http://www.literacycentral.org
e-mail: lvccoffice@gmail.com
Darlene Hurtado, Executive Director

Provides small group and one-on-one literacy tutoring to over 350 adults with flexible hours, individual attention, student centered learning, and high quality, caring volunteer tutors. Provide free, high quality training to adults who would like to become Literacy Volunteers.

1969 Literacy Volunteers of Eastern Connecticut

106 Truman St
New London, CT 06320-5632   860-443-4800
http://www.englishhelp.org
e-mail: office@englishhelp.org
Susan Townsley, Executive Director

A not-for-profit, volunteer-based organization whose mission is to help people communicate in English and thrive in American culture, as consumers and as workers.

1970 Literacy Volunteers of Greater Hartford

30 Arbor St
Hartford, CT 06106   860-233-3853
FAX 860-236-1640
http://www.lvgh.org
e-mail: cj.hauss@lvgh.org
Carol Hauss, Executive Director

Improves the ability of Greater Hartford adults to read, write and speak English. Trains volunteers to provide English literacy instruction to over 600 Hartford area adults per year.

1971 Literacy Volunteers of Greater New Haven

4 Science Park
New Haven, CT 06511   203-865-3867
FAX 203-562-7833
http://www.lvagnh.org
e-mail: info@lvagnh.org
Nancy Fryer, President
Doss Venema, Executive Director

A non-profit educational organization that trains and supports volunteer tutors who provide free literacy tutoring for adults who need to improve their reading, writing, and oral communication skills.

1972 Literacy Volunteers of Northern Connecticut

Asnuntuck CC B-131
1010 Enfield Street
Enfield, CT 06082-3873   860-253-3038
http://connecticut.networkofcare.org
Brain J Mc Cartney, Executive Director

1973 Literacy Volunteers-Valley Shore

25 Middlesex Turnpike
PO Box 1006
Westbrook, CT 06498   860-399-0280
FAX 860-767-1038
http://www.vsliteracy.org
e-mail: info@vsliteracy.org
Michael A Noto, Director

1974 Literacy Volunteers: Stamford/Greenwich

141 Franklin St
Stamford, CT 06901   203-324-5214
FAX 203-348-8917
http://www.lvsg.org
e-mail: djr@lvsg.org
Diane Rosenthal, Executive Director

A community-based organization that utilizes the services of trained volunteers to provide free, high-quality reading, writing and English language programs to adults, both American and foreign born, for the purpose of enabling them to acquire the literacy skills necessary to achieve personal and occupational goals.

1975 Mercy Learning Center

637 Park Ave
Bridgeport, CT 06604-4611   203-334-6699
FAX 203-332-6852
http://www.mercylearningcenter.org
e-mail: mercy.learning.cntr@snet.net
Jane E Ferreira, President/CEO

Provides basic literacy and life skills training to low-income women using a holistic approach within a compassionate, supportive environment.

Delaware

1976 Delaware Department of Education: Adult Community Education

Department of Public Instruction
401 Federal Street
John G. Townsend Building
Dover, DE 19901   302-735-4000
FAX 302-739-4654
http://www.doe.k12.de.us

Mark Murphy, Secretary

Provides students with opportunities to develop skills needed to qualify for further education, job training, and better employment.

1977 Literacy Volunteers Serving Adults: Northern Delaware

PO Box 2083
Wilmington, DE 19899   302-658-5624
FAX 302-654-9132
http://www.litvolunteers.org
e-mail: litvolunteers@verizon.net
Cynthia E Shermeyer, Executive Director

Helps adults improve literacy skills and thereby realize their potential to be confident, self sufficient and productive employees and community members. Deliver services and programs in reading, writing, English language, math, workplace and computer skills.

1978 Literacy Volunteers of America: Wilmington Library

704 King St.
3rd Floor, One Customs House Buliding
Wilmington, DE 19801   302-571-7400
FAX 302-654-9132
http://www.wilmlib.org
e-mail: wilmweb@lib.de.us
David Burdash, Executive Director

An organization of volunteers that provide a variety of services locally to enable people to achieve personal goals through literacy programs.

1979 NEW START Adult Learning Program
115 High St
PO Box 128
Odessa, DE 19730-0128   302-378-3444
                                       FAX 302-378-7803
                                    http://corbitlibrary.org
                              e-mail: suemenei@gmail.com
Susan Menei, Coordinator

A non-profit educational organization whose mission is to enable adults to acquire the listening, speaking, reading, writing, mathematics and technology skills they need to solve problems they encounter in daily life.

1980 State of Delaware Adult and Community Education Network
PO Box 639
516 W. Loockerman St.
Dover, DE 19904   302-739-7080
                                          800-464-4357
                                       FAX 302-739-5565
                                    http://www.acenetwork.org
Joanne Heaphy, Director

The ACE Network is a service agency that supports adult education and literacy providers through training and resource development.

District of Columbia

1981 Academy of Hope
601 Edgewood St NE
Ste 25
Washington, DC 20017   202-269-6623
                                       FAX 202-269-6632
                                    http://www.aohdc.org
Lecester Johnson, Executive Director

Changes lives and improves community by providing high-quality adult education in a supportive and empowering environment.

1982 Carlos Rosario International Public Charter School
1100 Harvard St NW
Washington, DC 20009   202-797-4700
                                       FAX 202-232-6442
                                http://www.carlosrosario.org
                              e-mail: info@carlosrosario.org
Offers an array of classes integrated within award-winning adult education programs which are considered models at the national and international level.

1983 District of Columbia Public Schools
1200 First St NE
Washington, DC 20002   202-442-5885
                                       FAX 202-442-5517
                                    http://dcps.dc.gov
Michelle Rhee, Chancellor

The public school system is committed to constant improvements in the achievement of all students today in preparation for their world tomorrow.

1984 Literacy Volunteers of the National Capital Area
635 Edgewood St NE
Washington, DC 20017   202-387-1772
                                       FAX 202-588-0714
                                    http://www.lvanca.org
                              e-mail: info@lvanca.org
Rita Daniels, Executive Director

Empowers adults and families by providing literacy instruction and skills-based education, thereby enriching all aspects of their personal and professional lives.

1985 U.S. Department Of Education
LBJ, Dept Of Education Building
400 Maryland Avenue, Southwest
Washington, DC 20202-0001   202-842-0973
                                          800-872-5327
                                       FAX 202-205-8748
                                    http://www.ed.gov
                              e-mail: ovae@ed.gov
Tassie Thompson, Director

To help all people achieve the knowledge and skills to be lifelong learners, to be successful in their chosen careers, and to be effective citizens.

1986 Washington Literacy Council
1918 18th St NW
Ste B2
Washington, DC 20009-1794   202-387-9029
                                       FAX 202-387-0271
                        http://www.washingtonliteracycouncil.org
                              e-mail: info@washlit.org
Terry Algire, Executive Director

The Washinton Literacy Council trains volunteers to use reading redmediation approaches when tutoring and leading small groups.

Florida

1987 Adult Literacy League
345 W Michigan St
Ste 100
Orlando, FL 32806   407-422-1540
                                       FAX 407-422-1529
                                http://www.adultliteracyleague.org
                              e-mail: info@adultliteracyleague.org
Joyce Whidden, Executive Director

Develops readers to build a strong and literate community. Serves as the premier literacy resource providing education, training and information in Central Florida.

1988 Advocacy Center for Persons with Disabilities
National Disability Rights Network
2728 Centerview Drive
Ste 102
Tallahassee, FL 32301   850-488-9071
                                          800-342-0823
                                       FAX 850-488-8640
                                    TDD:800-346-4127
                                http://www.advocacycenter.org
Hubert Grissom, President

To advance the quality of life, dignity, equality, and freedom of choice of persons with disabilities through collaboration, education, advocacy, as well as legal and legislative strategies.

1989 Florida Coalition
250 N Orange Ave
Ste 1110
Orlando, FL 32801   407-246-7110
                                          800-237-5113
                                       FAX 407-246-7104
                                http://www.floridaliteracy.org
                              e-mail: info@floridaliteracy.org
Greg Smith, Executive Director

A nonprofit organization funded through private and corporate donations, state of Florida grants, and a diverse membership.

1990 Florida Literacy Resource Center
283 Trojan Trail
Tallahassee, FL 32311
850-922-5343
FAX 850-922-5352
http://www.ace-leon.org
e-mail: info@ACE-Leon.org
Barbara Van Camp, Principal

As part of the State Library, the State Resource Center provides electronic and print resources.

1991 Florida Vocational Rehabilitation Agency: Division of Vocational Rehabilitation
2002 Old Saint Augustine Rd
Bldg A
Tallahassee, FL 32301-4862
850-245-3399
TDD:800-451-4327
http://www.rehabworks.org
Bill Palmer, Director

A federal state program that works with people who have physical or mental disabilities to prepare for, gain or retain employment.

1992 Learn to Read
3802 Baymeadows Rd
Ste 12 PMB #146
Jacksonville, FL 32256
904-399-8894
FAX 904-399-2508
http://www.learntoreadinc.org
Dedicated to improving adult literacy in Duval County. Serves adults 16 years of age and older in Northeats Florida who want to improve reading skills or learn to read.

1993 Learning Disabilities Association of Florida
Bridges Academy
894 Gary Hillery Drive
Winter Springs, FL 32708
941-637-8957
FAX 941-637-0617
http://www.lda-fl.com
The Learning Disabilities Association of Florida is a non-profit volunteer organization of parents, professionals and LD adults.

1994 Literacy Florida
2981 S Lookout Blvd
Port St Lucie, FL 34984
http://www.literacyflorida.org
e-mail: havenpsl@adelphia.net
Jim Wilder, President

Supports Florida's adult literacy volunteers and their programs. Provides information and services to literacy volunteers and providers in communications and networking, technical assistance and training, public affairs, advocacy, and student leadership.

Georgia

1995 Gainesville Hall County Alliance for Literacy
4-1/2 Stallworth St
Gainesville, GA 30501
770-531-4337
FAX 770-531-6406
http://allianceforliteracy.org
e-mail: all4lit@bellsouth.net
Serves as the Umbrella agency for all literacy concerns in the community. Provides free educational programs for adults 16 years and older who have not graduated from high school or whose native language is not English.

1996 Georgia Department of Education
Department of Technical & Adult Education
Ste 400
1800 Century Pl NE
Atlanta, GA 30345-4304
404-679-1625
FAX 404-679-1630
http://www.dtae.org
e-mail: mdelaney@dtae.org
Ron Jackson, Director

To oversee the state's system of technical colleges, the adult literacy program, and a host of economic workforce development programs.

1997 Georgia Department of Technical & Adult Education
Ste 400
1800 Century Pl NE
Atlanta, GA 30345-4304
404-679-1625
FAX 404-679-1630
http://www.dtae.org
e-mail: mdelaney@dtae.org
Ron Jackson, Director

The Georgia Department of Technical and Adult Education oversees the state's system of technical colleges, the adult literacy program, and a host of economic and workforce development programs

1998 Georgia Literacy Resource Center: Office of Adult Literacy
Ste 400
1800 Century Pl NE
Atlanta, GA 30345-4304
404-679-1625
FAX 404-679-1630
http://www.dtae.org
e-mail: mdelaney@dtae.org
Ron Jackson, Director

The mission of the adult literacy programs is to enable every adult learner in Georgia to acquire the necessary basic skills in reading, writing, computation, speaking, and listening to compete successfully in today's workplace, strengthen family foundations, and exercise full citizenship.

1999 Literacy Volunteers of America: Forsyth County
PO Box 1097
Cumming, GA 30028-1097
770-887-0074
http://www.litreacyforsyth.org
e-mail: focolit@sellsouth.net
Eddith DeVeau, Executive Director
Dianne Anth, Director

Dedicated to teaching adults to read in the Forsyth County region.

2000 Literacy Volunteers of Atlanta
246 Sycamore St
Ste 110
Decatur, GA 30030
404-377-7323
FAX 404-377-8662
http://www.lvama.org
e-mail: vkingsland@lvama.org
Michele Henry, Executive Director

To increase adult and family literacy primarily through volunteer tutoring. The goal is to provide all of the literacy skills crucial for more productive, prosperous and confident lives, thus improving the quality of life of all Georgians.

2001 Newton County Reads
8134 Geiger St
Box 5
Covington, GA 30014
678-342-7943
FAX 678-342-7964
http://www.newtonreads.org
e-mail: newtoncountyreads@earthlink.net
Renee' Jones, Director

Helps adults improve their literacy skills and/or earn a GED certificate through an active volunteer tutoring program; maintain an ever-expanding list of literacy resources available in Newton County; helps adults find and get started in the literacy programs that most effectively meet their needs.

2002 North Georgia Technical College Adult Education
1500 Hwy 197 N
PO Box 65
Clarkesville, GA 30523   706-754-7700
                                FAX 706-754-7777
          http://www.northgatech.edu/adulted
                e-mail: info@northgatech.edu
Steve Dougherty, President

Designed for adults who have different needs, backgrounds, and skill levels. Provide a full range of services for adults who need to acquire or improve basic reading, math, and/or written communication skills in order to prepare them to enter or succeed in the workplace or postsecondary educational programs.

2003 Okefenokee Regional Library System
401 Lee Ave
Waycross, GA 31501-3010   912-287-4978
                                 FAX 912-284-2533
                http://www.okrls.org
                e-mail: ikeaton@okrls.org
Lace Keaton, Director

Public library

2004 Toccoa/Stephens County Literacy Council
P.O.Box 63
Toccoa, GA 30577-1400   706-886-6082
                               FAX 706-282-7633
          e-mail: mwalters3@yahoo.com
Michelle Austin, Director

2005 Volunteers for Literacy of Habersham County
PO Box 351
Cornelia, GA 30531   706-776-4063
          http://www.habershamga.com

Hawaii

2006 CALC/Hilo Public Library
300 Waianuenue Ave
Hilo, HI 96720-2447   808-933-8893
                              FAX 808-933-8895
                http://literacynet.org
                e-mail: calchilo@gte.net
Kit Holz, Project Manager

Mission is to provide access to learning resources and tutoring services to help adults acquire and/or improve their skills in reading, writing, math, English as a Second Language and computer use.

2007 Hawaii Literacy
200 N Vineyard Blvd
Ste 320
Honolulu, HI 96817-3938   808-537-6706
                                  FAX 808-528-1690
          http://www.hawaiiliteracy.org
          e-mail: info@hawaiiliteracy.org
Suzanne Skojold, Executive Director

Helps people gain knowledge and skills by providing literacy and lifelong learning services.

2008 Hui Malama Learning Center
375 Mahalani St
Wailuku, HI 96793   808-244-5911
                            FAX 808-242-0762
                http://www.mauihui.org
          e-mail: huimalama@mauihui.org
Pualani Enos, Executive Director

Provides middle school, high-school, and GED-preparation programs, as well as tutoring and educational enrichment programs to public and private school students grades K-12.

Idaho

2009 ABE:College of Southern Idaho
Adult Basic Education
315 Falls Ave
P.O. Box 1238
Twin Falls, ID 83303-1238   208-732-6221
                                    800-680-0274
                                FAX 208-736-4705
                http://www.csi.edu
                e-mail: info@csi.edu
Jerry Beck, President
Dr. Jeff Fox, EVP
Dr. Cindy Bond, Instructional Dean
Designed to improve the educational level of adults, out-of-school youth and non-English speaking persons in our eight-county service area.

2010 Idaho Adult Education Office
PO Box 83720
650 W. State Street
Boise, ID 83720-0027   208-332-6800
                               800-432-4601
                           FAX 208-334-2228
                http://www.sde.idaho.gov
          e-mail: MRMcGrath@sde.idaho.gov
Tom Luna, State Superintendant
Luci Willits, Chief of Staff
Melissa McGrath, Public Information officer

2011 Idaho Coalition for Adult Literacy
325 W State St
Boise, ID 83702-6055   208-334-2150
                               800-458-3271
                           FAX 208-334-4016
                http://www.lili.org
          e-mail: lili@libraries.idaho.gov
Ann Joslin, Coordinator

An nonprofit organization which raise public awareness about the importance of a literate society.

2012 Idaho State Library
325 W State St
Boise, ID 83702-6055   208-334-2150
                               800-458-3271
                           FAX 208-334-4016
                http://www.lili.org
          e-mail: lili@isl.state.id.us
Ann Joslin, Director

Offers a history of pioneering new frontiers in library services.

2013 Learning Lab
308 E 36th St
Garden City, ID 83714   208-344-1335
                                FAX 208-344-1171
          http://www.learninglabinc.org
          e-mail: info@learninglabinc.org
Ann Heilman, Executive Director

A computer-assisted learning center for adults and families with birth to six-year-old children. Students receive basic skills instruction including mathematics, reading, writing, spelling, GED preparation and workplace skills in a comfortable, confidential environment.

Illinois

2014 Adult Literacy at People's Resource Center

201 S Naperville Rd
Wheaton, IL 60187   630-682-5402
                            FAX 630-682-5412
                  http://www.peoplesrc.org
Thomas Okarma, President

Exists to respond to basic human needs, promote dignity and justice, and create a future of hope and opportunity for the residents of DuPage County, IL through discovering and sharing personal and community resources.

2015 Aquinas Literacy Center

3540 S Hermitage Ave
Chicago, IL 60609   773-927-0512
         http://www.aquinasliteracycenter.org
               e-mail: aquinaslit@aol.com
Alison Altmeyer, Executive Director

A nonprofit, community-based literacy center serving the residents of McKinley Park and other south and southwest side Chicago neighborhoods. Offers individualized English language instruction, group conversation classes, and group computer classes at not cost to students.

2016 C.E.F.S. Literacy Program

1805 S Banker
PO Box 928
Effingham, IL 62401-0928   217-342-2193
                                FAX 217-342-4701
               http://www.cefseoc.org
         e-mail: learningcenter@cefseoc.org
Helps adults and families meet their literacy goals in reading, writing, math and English language skills and to promote education and lifelong learning as the key to personal, economic, and social success.

2017 Carl Sandburg College Literacy Coalition

1150 West Carl Sandburg Drive
Galesburg, IL 61401-9576   309-344-1631
                                FAX 309-344-1626
               http://www.sandburg.edu
         e-mail: kavalos@sandburg.edu
Improves the reading and basic math skills of adults and their families by offering one-on-one and small group tutoring services.

2018 Common Place Family Learning Center

514 S Shelley St
Peoria, IL 61605-1837   309-674-3315
                                FAX 309-674-0627
               http://www.commonplacepeoria.org
               e-mail: cvoss04@sbcglobal.net
Connie Voss, Director
Kathryn Lambert, Adult Programs Director
Linda Hoskins, Adult Services Coordinator
A non-profit, social service agency located on the south side of Peoria, IL. Strive to eliminate poverty and injustice through education. The youth and adult programs are based on education and literacy.

2019 Dominican Literacy Center

260 Vermont Ave
Aurora, IL 60505-3100   630-898-4636
                                FAX 630-898-4636
         http://www.dominicanliteracycenter.org
               e-mail: domlitctr@sbcglobal.net
Helps women learn to read, write and speak English within an atmosphere of mutual respect and dignity.

2020 Equip for Equality

20 N Michigan Ave
Ste 300
Chicago, IL 60603-6303   312-341-0022
                                800-537-2632
                          FAX 312-341-0295
                       TTY: 800-610-2779
               http://www.equipforequality.org
         e-mail: contactus@equipforequality.org
Zena Naiditch, President/CEO

Advances the human and civil rights of children and adults with physical and mental disabilities in Illinois. The only statewide, cross-disability, comprehensive advocacy organization prodiving self-advocacy assistance, legal services, and disability rights education while also engaging in public policy and legislative advocacy and conducting abuse investigations and other oversight activities.

2021 Equip for Equality: Carbondale

300 East Main Street
Suite 18
Carbondale, IL 62901   618-457-7930
                                800-758-0559
                          FAX 618-457-7985
                       TTY: 800-610-2779
               http://www.equipforequality.org
         e-mail: contactus@equipforequality.org
Zena Naiditch, President/CEO
Duane C. Quaini, Chairperson
Pamela A. Hansen, Treasurer
Independent, private, not-for-profit organization that provides free legal services and self advocacy assistance to people with disabilities in the areas of discrimination, assistive technology, special education, guardianship defense, abuse and neglect, and community integration.

2022 Equip for Equality: Moline

1515 Fifth Avenue
Suite 420
Moline, IL 61265   309-786-6868
                                800-758-6869
                          FAX 309-797-8710
                       TTY: 800-610-2779
               http://www.equipforequality.org
         e-mail: contactus@equipforequality.org
Zena Naiditch, President/CEO
Duane C. Quaini, Chairperson
Pamela A. Hansen, Treasurer
Independent, private, not-for-profit organization that provides free legal services and self advocacy assistance to people with disabilities in the areas of discrimination, assistive technology, special education, guardianship defense, abuse and neglect, and community integration.

2023 Equip for Equality: Springfield

1 West Old State Capitol Plaza
Suite 816
Springfield, IL 62701   217-544-0464
                                800-758-0464
                          FAX 217-523-0720
                       TTY: 800-610-2779
               http://www.equipforequality.org
         e-mail: contactus@equipforequality.org
Zena Naiditch, President/CEO
Duane C. Quaini, Chairperson
Pamela A. Hansen, Treasurer
Independent, private, not-for-profit organization that provides free legal services and self advocacy assistance to people with disabilities in the areas of discrimination, assistive technology, special education, guardianship defense, abuse and neglect, and community integration.

2024 Illinois Library Association

33 W Grand Ave
Ste 301
Chicago, IL 60654 312-644-1896
FAX 312-644-1899
http://www.ila.org
e-mail: ila@ila.org

The Illinois Library Association is the voice for Illinois Libraries and the millions who depend on them. It provides leadership for the development, promotion, and improvement of library services in Illinois and for the library community.

2025 Illinois Literacy Resource Development Center

209 W Clark St
Ste 15
Champaign, IL 61820-4640 217-355-6068
FAX 217-355-6347
http://www.champaign.illinoiscircle.com/c-15597
Suzanne Knell, Executive Director

The Illinois Literacy Resource Development Center is dedicated to improving literacy policy and practice at the local, state, and national levels. It is a nonprofit organization supporting literacy and adult education efforts throughout Illinois and the nation. One key to its success has been its ability to build partnerships among the organizations, individuals and agencies working in the literacy arena from the local to the national level.

2026 Illinois Office of Rehabilitation Services

Illinois Department of Human Services
100 S Grand Ave E
Springfield, IL 62762 217-557-1601
800-843-6154
TTY: 800-447-6404
http://www.dhs.state.il.us
Michelle R. Saddler, Secreary
Matthew Hammoudeh, Assistant Secretary of Operation
Grace Hong Duffin, Chief of Staff
DHS' Office of Rehabilitation Services is the state's lead agency serving individuals with disabilities.

2027 Literacy Chicago

17 N State St
Ste 1010
Chicago, IL 60602 312-870-1100
FAX 312-870-4488
http://www.literacychicago.org
e-mail: info@literacychicago.org
Barry Benson, Executive Director

A nonprofit organization that empowers individuals to achieve greater self sufficiency through language and literacy instruction.

2028 Literacy Connection

270 N Grove Ave
Elgin, IL 60120 847-742-6565
FAX 847-742-6599
http://www.elginliteracy.org
e-mail: info@elginliteracy.org
Karen Oswald, Executive Director

A non-profit, community-based organization helping individuals acquire fundamental literacy skills and learn to read, write, speak and understand English.

2029 Literacy Council

982 N Main St
Rockford, IL 61103 815-963-7323
FAX 815-963-7347
http://www.theliteracycouncil.org
e-mail: read@theliteracycouncil.org
John Hurley, Executive Director

Provides literacy instruction to individuals and families to strengthen communities.

2030 Literacy Volunteers of America: Illinois

30 E Adams St
Ste 1130
Chicago, IL 60603 312-857-1582
FAX 312-857-1586
http://www.literacyvolunteersillinois.org
e-mail: info@lvillinois.org
Dorothy M Miaso, Executive Director

A statewide organization committed to developing and supporting volunteer literacy programs that help families, adults and out-of-school teens increase their literacy skills.

2031 Literacy Volunteers of DuPage

24W500 Maple Ave
Ste 217
Naperville, IL 60540-6057 630-416-6699
FAX 630-416-9465
http://www.literacyvolunteersdupage.org
e-mail: info@literacydupage.org
Tana Tatnall, Executive Director

A nonprofit, community-based organization that provides accessible and customized tutoring in reading, writing, speaking, and understanding English to help adults achieve independence.

2032 Literacy Volunteers of Fox Valley

One S Sixth Ave
Saint Charles, IL 60174 630-584-2811
FAX 630-584-3448
http://www.lvfv.org
e-mail: info@lvfv.org

Peg Coker, Executive Director

Helps individuals in the region acquire and validate the literacy skills that they need to function more effectively in contemporary U.S. society.

2034 Literacy Volunteers of Lake County

128 N County St
Waukegan, IL 60085 847-623-2041
FAX 847-623-2092
http://www.adultlearningconnection.org
Mission is to extend educational opportunities to Lake COunty adult students and their families.

2033 Literacy Volunteers of Western Cook County

125 N Marion St
Ste 301
Oak Park, IL 60301 708-848-8499
FAX 708-848-9564
http://www.lvwcc.org
e-mail: info@lvwcc.org
Tiffany Morgan, Executive Director

Helps adults reach their literacy goals through customized one-on-one tutoring by trained volunteers.

2035 Project CARE

Morton College
3801 S Central Ave
Cicero, IL 60804-4300 708-656-8000
FAX 708-656-3186
http://www.morton.edu
e-mail: projectcare@morton.edu
Maria Beltran, Program Support Specialist

A volunteer adult literacy program that uses trained tutors to teach adult students seeking assistance with reading and writing, and/or adults who are learning English as a second language.

2036 Project READ
Benjamin Godfrey Campus, Rm 2405
5800 Godfrey Rd
Godfrey, IL 62035-2426   618-468-7000
                                              800-YES-LCCC
                                        FAX 618-468-7820
                                    http://www.lc.cc.il.us
                                   e-mail: lartis@lc.edu
Dennis Krieb, Director
Lori Artis, Vice President

Goal is to increase literacy throughout the area with
one-on-one tutoring. Project READ Community Service Coordinators are available to provide information to community groups, arrange free training for volunteers and
distribute materials and support to tutor-learner pairs.

Indiana

2037 Adult Literacy Program of Gibson County
232 W Broadway
Princeton, IN 47670   812-386-9100
                           http://www.gibsonadultliteracy.org
                       e-mail: literacy@gibsoncounty.net
Sharon Buyher, President

Provides an opportunity for any adult in Gibson County to
attain basic English Language literacy skills.

**2038 Indy Reads: Indianapolis/Marion County Public Li-
brary**
PO Box 211
Indianapolis, IN 46206-0211   317-275-4100
                                     http://www.imcpl.org
              e-mail: jimlingenfelter@five2fivedesign.com
Jim Lingenfelter, President
Robert J. Bonner, Secretary

Indy Reads, a nationally recognized not-for-profit affiliate
of the Indianapolis-Marion County Public Library, exists to
improve the reading and writing skills of adults in Marion
County who read at or below the sixth grade level.

2039 Literacy Alliance
709 Clay St
Ste 100
Fort Wayne, IN 46802-2019   260-426-7323
                                        FAX 260-424-0371
                                     http://www.tria.org
                              e-mail: trlafw@yahoo.com
Judith Stabelli, Executive Director

Adult education

2040 Morrisson/Reeves Library Literacy Resource Center
80 N 6th St
Richmond, IN 47374-3079   765-966-8291
                                        FAX 765-962-1318
                                    http://www.mrlinfo.org
                              e-mail: library@mrlinfo.org
Carol B McKey, Library Director

The Literacy Resource Center provides free training for volunteers to tutor adults in Wayne County who want to learn to
read, write and do basic math.

2041 Steuben County Literacy Coalition
1208 S Wayne St
Angola, IN 46703   260-665-1414
                                        FAX 260-665-3357
                               http://www.steubenliteracy.org
Kathleen Armstrong, Executive Director

Mission shall be to foster lifelong leraning and improved literacy through high quality and accessible educational opportunities for children and adults in Steuben County.

Iowa

2042 Adult Basic Education and Adult Literacy Program
Kirkwood Community College
6301 Kirkwood Blvd SW
Cedar Rapids, IA 52404   319-398-5517
                                              800-363-2220
                                   http://www.kirkwood.edu
                              e-mail: info@kirkwood.edu
Provides instruction to enable adults to increase self-sufficiency, improve employability, prepare for continued learning and better meet their responsibilities. Recruits
volunteers, trains them in literacy teaching techniques and
matches them with adults wanting instruction in reading
skills development.

**2043 Iowa Department of Education: Iowa Literacy Council
Programs**
400 E 14th St
Grimes State Office Buliding
Des Moines, IA 50319-0146   515-281-3436
                                        FAX 515-242-5988
                                  http://www.educateiowa.gov
                         e-mail: jason.glass@iowa.gov
Jason Glass, Director
Gail Sullivan, Chief of Staff

Helps adults and families develop their potential through improved literacy, education, and training.

2044 Iowa Literacy Resource Center
415 Commercial St
Waterloo, IA 50701-1317   319-233-1200
                                              800-772-2023
                                        FAX 319-233-1964
                                    http://www.readiowa.org
                            e-mail: riesberg@neilsa.org
Eunice Riefberg, Director

The Center provides a link to resource materials in Iowa and
at a regional and national level for adult literacy practitioners and students. These resources are available in many formats: including print, audio, video and online.

2045 Iowa Vocational Rehabilitation Agency
Department of Education
510 E 12th Street
Des Moines, IA 50319   515-281-4211
                                        FAX 515-281-7645
                                       TTY: 1 8-0 5-2 14
                                   http://www.ivrs.iowa.gov
                       e-mail: David.Mitchell@iowa.gov
David Mitchell, Administrator

2046 Iowa Workforce Investment Act
200 E Grand Ave
Des Moines, IA 50309-1856   515-725-3000
                                        FAX 515-725-3010
                    http://www.iowaeconomicdevelopment.com/
                              e-mail: info@iowa.gov
Debi Durham, Director

Job placement and training services. Especially for those
workers who have been laid off, or have other barriers to
steady employment.

2047 Learning Disabilities Association of Iowa
5665 Greendale Rd
Ste D
Johnston, IA 50131   515-280-8558
                                              888-690-5324
                                        FAX 515-243-1902
                                     http://www.lda-ia.org
                           e-mail: kathylda@askresource.org
Kathy Specketer MAT, State Coordinator

Dedicated to identifying causes and promoting prevention of learning disabilities and to enhancing the quality of life for all individuals with learning disabilities and their families.

2048 Library Literacy Programs: State Library of Iowa
1112 E Grand Ave
Miller Building
Des Moines, IA 50319-9002
515-281-4105
800-248-4483
FAX 515-281-6191
http://www.statelibraryofiowa.org
e-mail: helpdesk@silo.lib.ia.us
Mary Wegner, Director/State Librarian

2049 Southeastern Community College:Literacy Program
200 N Main St
Mt Pleasant, IA 52641-2027
319-385-8012
http://www.scciowa.edu
e-mail: jcrull@scciowa.edu
Jennifer Crull, Director

Provides information to students who need to get their GED, and helps them to read and write.

2050 Western Iowa Tech Community College
PO Box 5199
4647 Stone Avenue
Sioux City, IA 51102-5199
712-274-6400
800-352-4649
http://www.witcc.edu
e-mail: info@witcc.edu
Beverly S. Simone, President

Recruits volunteer mentors and adult learners throughout the year, and arranges for them to meet and work together.

Kansas

2051 Arkansas City Literacy Council
Arkansas City Public Library
120 E 5th Ave
Arkansas City, KS 67005
620-442-1280
http://www.arkcity.org
e-mail: literacy@acpl.org
Lianne Flax, Adult Services Director

A non-profit, volunteer organization that provides literacy and English language tutoring to adults and older youth so they may gain the listening, speaking, and reading skills needed to be successful in life.

2052 Butler Community College Adult Education
131 N Haverhill Rd
El Dorado, KS 67042-3225
316-321-4030
FAX 316-322-8450
http://www.butlercc.edu
e-mail: schoens@butlercc.edu
Cue Choens, Director/GED Examiner

Mission is to produce students who make measurable gains in educational skill, workplace readiness, and technology skills.

2053 Emporia Literacy Program
3301 W. 18th Ave
Flint Hills Technical College
Emporia, KS 66801-2847
620-343-4600
800-711-6947
FAX 620-343-4610
http://www.fhtc.edu
e-mail: mcrouch@fhtc.edu
Mike Crouch, Executive Director

2054 Hutchinson Public Library: Literacy Resources
901 N Main St
Hutchinson, KS 67501-4401
620-663-5441
FAX 620-663-1583
http://www.hutchpl.org
e-mail: sgustaf@hutchpl.org
Sandra Gustafson, Coordinator

Provides staff to help adults improve their reading, writing and language skills.

2055 Kansas Adult Education Association
Barton County Community College
245 NE 30th Rd
Barton Community College
Great Bend, KS 67530
620-792-2701
800-748-7594
http://www.barton.cc.ks.us
e-mail: shirers@bartonccc.eduÿ
Sarah Shirer, Secretary
Dr. Penny Quinn, Vice President

The Kansas Adult Education Association has been the professional association for adult educators at community colleges, school districts, and non-profit organizations.

2056 Kansas Correctional Education
4th Floor
900 SW Jackson St
Topeka, KS 66612-1284
785-296-3317
888-317-8204
http://www.kdoc.dc.state.ks.us
e-mail: kdocpub@doc.ks.gov
Ray Roberts, Secretary
Jan Clausing, Director of Human Resources

The provision of correctional education programming to inmates.

2057 Kansas Department of Corrections
Landon State Office Building
900 SW Jackson St, 4th Fl
Topeka, KS 66612
785-296-3317
888-317-8204
FAX 785-296-0014
http://www.doc.ks.gov
e-mail: kdocpub@doc.ks.gov
Roger Werholtz, Secretary of Corrections

State corrections agency/department.

2058 Kansas Department of Social & Rehabilitation Services
915 SW Harrison St
Topeka, KS 66612-1505
785-296-3959
888-369-4777
FAX 785-296-2173
TTY: 785-296-1491
http://www.dcf.ks.gov
Phyllis Gilmore, Secretary
Wm. Jeff Kahrs, Chief of Staff
Angela de Rocha, Communications Director
To assist people with disabilities achieve suitable employment and independence.

2059 Kansas Literacy Resource Center
1000 SW Jackson St
Ste 520
Topeka, KS 66612-1368
785-296-3421
FAX 785-296-0983
http://www.kansasregents.org
e-mail: dglass@ksbor.org
Dianne S Glass, State Director, Adult Education

Enhances systems, both public and private, which provide basic skills education across Kansas. The Center serves as the catalyst for collaborative efforts that address the needs of undereducated adults in Kansas.

2060 Kansas State Department of Adult Education
120 SE 10th Ave
Topeka, KS 66612-1182
785-296-3201
FAX 785-296-7933
http://www.ksde.org
e-mail: ddebacker@ksde.org
Dr. Diane DeBacker, Commisioner
Cheryl Whelan, General Councel
Karen Watney, Director, HR
To assist adults to become literate and obtain the knowledge and skills necessary for employment and self-sufficiency.

2061 Kansas State Literacy Resource Center: Kansas State Department of Education
Ste 520
1000 SW Jackson St
Topeka, KS 66612-1368
785-296-3421
FAX 785-296-0983
http://www.kansasregents.org
Tim Emert, Chairman
Andy Tompkins, President/CEO

The State Literacy Resource Center can assist adult education practitioners across the nation in locating and accessing the most current materials in their issue area.

2062 Preparing for the Future: Adult Learning Services
230 W 7th St
Junction City, KS 66441-3097
785-238-4311
FAX 785-238-7873
http://www.jclib.org
e-mail: jclibrary@jclib.org
Susan Moyer, Director

Kentucky

2063 Ashland Adult Education
Ashland Community & Technical College
1400 College Drive
Ashland, KY 41101-3617
606-326-2000
800-928-4256
http://ashland.kctcs.edu
e-mail: joan.flanery@kctcs.edu
Joan Flanery, Program Director

Provides education services that prepare adults with the essential skills they need to function as workers, citizens and family members of the 21st century. The program enables them to develop essential skills for living and wage earning and to better their self-concepts.

2064 Kentucky Laubach Literacy Action
Ste 250
1024 Capital Center Dr
Frankfort, KY 40601-7514
502-573-5114
800-928-7323
FAX 502-573-5436
TTY: 800-928-7323
http://kyae.ky.gov
e-mail: dvislisel@mail.state.ky.us
Reecie Stagnolia, Vice President

Dedicated to helping adults of all ages improve their lives and their communities by learning reading, writing, match and problem-solving skills.

2065 Kentucky Literacy Volunteers of America
Ste 250
1024 Capital Center Dr
Frankfort, KY 40601-7514
502-573-5114
FAX 502-573-5436
TTY: 800-928-7323
http://kyae.ky.gov
e-mail: dvislsel@mail.state.ky.us
Reecie Stagnolia, Vice President

Promotes literacy for people of all ages.

2066 Operation Read
251 W 2nd St
Lexington, KY 40507-1135
859-254-9964
866-774-4872
FAX 859-254-5834
http://bluegrass.kctcs.edu
e-mail: opread@gx.net
Nicholas Mueller, Executive Director

Helping adults learn to read to help imrove their lives, the lives of their children and the lives in their community.

2067 Simpson County Literacy Council
231 S College St
Franklin, KY 42134-1809
270-586-7234
FAX 270-598-0906
http://www.readtobefree.org
e-mail: read@readtobefree.org
Debra Thompson, Director

A private, non-profit organization that provides a variety of services to enable people to achieve personal goals through literacy, basic reading & math, GED prep, computer classes, math & reading for college and more.

2068 Winchester Adult Education Center
52 N Maple St
Winchester, KY 40391
859-744-1975
FAX 859-744-1424
http://www.winchesteradulteducation.org
e-mail: mwells_cae@roadrunner.com
Jim Porter, Executive Director

For those 16 years of age and older and out of school, provides facilities, materials, and services in order to improve lifelong learning skills leading to economic independence and quality of life.

Louisiana

2069 Adult Literacy Advocates of Baton Rouge
1427 Main Street
Baton Rouge, LA 70802-4607
225-383-1090
FAX 225-387-5999
http://www.adultliteracyadvocates.org
e-mail: info@adultliteracyadvocates.org
Pam Creighton, Executive Director

2070 Literacy Council of Southwest Louisiana
Central School Arts & Humanities Center
809 Kirby St
Ste 126
Lake Charles, LA 70601
337-494-7000
FAX 337-494-7915
http://www.literacyswla.org
e-mail: ndemarest@literacyswla.org
Delma Porter, President

A community-based, non-profit organization that provides instructional programs to improve educational skill levels in Southwest Louisiana and works to increase public awareness of literacy-related issues.

2071 Literacy Volunteers Centenary College
PO Box 41188
Shreveport, LA 71134-1188
318-869-2411
FAX 318-869-2474
e-mail: lvecent@bellsouth.net
Sue Lee, Executive Director

2072 VITA (Volunteer Instructors Teaching Adults)

Ste 404
905 Jefferson St
Lafayette, LA 70501-7913   337-234-4600
                                        FAX 337-264-7672
                                        http://www.vitalaf.org
                                        e-mail: vitala@bellsouth.net
Dr. Huey McCauley, President

Specially trained volunteers learn to teach reading and writing using easy to follow manuals and to also provide goal-oriented, one on one or in small group. VITA provides the professional training, materials, and support that enable the volunteers to assist adults in acquiring basic reading and writing skills.

Maine

2073 Biddeford Adult Education

18 Maplewood Ave
Biddeford, ME 04005   207-282-3883
                                        FAX 207-286-9581
                                        http://www.biddschools.org
                                        e-mail: adulted@biddschools.org
Janet Kalman, Director

2074 Center for Adult Learning and Literacy: University of Maine

Pro Literacy Worldwide
5749 Merrill Hall
Orono, ME 04469-5749   207-581-1865
                                        877-486-2364
                                        FAX 207-581-1517
                                        http://www.umaine.edu
                                        e-mail: president@umaine.edu
Paul W. Ferguson, President

The Center for Adult Learning and Literacy offers quality, research-based professional development and resources, based on funded initiatives to improve the quality of services within the Maine Adult Education System.

2075 Literacy Volunteers of Androscoggin

15 Sacred Heart Place
Auburn, ME 04210   207-333-4785
                                        http://www.literacyvolunteersandro.org
                                        e-mail: info@literacyvolunteersandro.org
Tahlia Chamberlain, Executive Director

Providing free one-on-one tutoring and other educational services to help adults in Androscoggin County acquire the basic reading, writing and math skills they need to enhance their lives and achieve their personal goals.

2076 Literacy Volunteers of Aroostook County

Caribou Learning Center
75 Bennett Drive
Caribou, ME 04736   207-325-3490
                                        FAX 207-325-8916
Barbara Sutton, Executive Director

Provides free, confidential services to any Aroostokk COunty adult with the desire to increase their literacy skill.

2077 Literacy Volunteers of Bangor

200 Hogan Rd
Bangor, ME 04401-5604   207-947-8451
                                        FAX 207-942-1391
                                        http://lvbangor.org
                                        e-mail: marylyon@lvbangor.org
Mary Marin Lyon, Executive Director

A group of people who are dedicated to improving literacy in the community one person at a time. Many of the volunteers choose to become a tutor and teach another adult to read or speak English.

2078 Literacy Volunteers of Greater Augusta

12 Spruce St
Ste 2
Augusta, ME 04330   207-626-3440
                                        FAX 207-626-3440
                                        http://www.lva-augusta.org
                                        e-mail: info@lva-augusta.org
Jen Small, Affiliate Director

Promote and foster increased literacy for adults who have low literacy skills or those for whom English is not their native language through volunteer tutoring.

2079 Literacy Volunteers of Greater Portland

PO Box 8585
Portland, ME 04104   207-775-0105
                                        FAX 207-780-1701
                                        http://www.lvaportland.org
                                        e-mail: lvportland@learningworks.me
Kristen Stevens, Executive Director

Offers, free, confidential, student-centered, individual and small group tutoring to adults seeking to develop the literacy skills they need to reach important life goals like reading their first books, obtaining citizenship, helping their children with homework, taking care of personal bills and finding employment.

2080 Literacy Volunteers of Greater Saco/Biddeford

PO Box 467
Saco, ME 04072   207-283-2954
                                        http://lvsaco-biddeford.maineadulted.org
                                        e-mail: lvasaco@gwi.net
Kathy Kilrain del Rio, Executive Director

Trains volunteers to provide educational programs and services that improve reading, writing and related literacy skills, and to empower adults by enhancing their life skills in the area of family, work, health and community.

2081 Literacy Volunteers of Greater Sanford

883 Main St
Ste 4
Sanford, ME 04073   207-324-2486
                                        FAX 207-324-2486
                                        http://www.sanfordliteracy.org
                                        e-mail: kmoran@sandfordliteracy.org
Kimberley Moran, Executive Director

Supports the literacy needs of local adults with free, confidential, one-on-one tutoring and small group instruction in reading, math, computers, studying for the GED, licenses, and other life skills by trained adult volunteers.

2082 Literacy Volunteers of Maine

142 High St
Ste 526
Portland, ME 04101   207-773-3191
                                        FAX 207-221-1123
                                        http://www.lvmaine.org
                                        e-mail: info@lvmaine.org
Chip Brewer, Co-President
Benjamin Smith, Co-President

Dedicated to providing increased access to literacy services for Maine adults who wish to acquire or improve their literacy skills.

2083 Literacy Volunteers of Mid-Coast Maine

28 Lincoln St
Rockland, ME 04841   207-594-5154
                                        FAX 207-594-5154
                                        http://lvmidcoast.maineadulted.org
                                        e-mail: bgifford@msad5.org
Beth A Gifford, Program Director

Dedicated to improving the literacy skills of adults in our community. Deliver instruction using a dedicated corps of well trained volunteer tutors.

2084 Literacy Volunteers of Waldo County
5 Stephenson Ln
Belfast, ME 04915   207-338-2200
FAX 207-338-1652
http://www.broadreachmaine.org
Ruth H Southworth MEd, Executive Director

Helps children and families to develop the skills they need to lead healthy and productive lives. Share the knowledge and experience with child-and-family serving organizations across the state and nation.

2085 Maine Literacy Resource Center
University of Maine
5749 Merrill Hall
Orono, ME 04469-5749   207-581-1865
877-486-2364
FAX 207-581-1517
http://www.umaine.edu
e-mail: president@umaine.edu
Paul W. Ferguson, President

As part of the State Library, the State Resource Center provides electronic and print resources.

2086 Tri-County Literacy
2 Sheridan Rd
Bath, ME 04530   207-443-6384
877-885-7441
http://www.tricountyliteracy.org
e-mail: tricountyliteracy@tricountyliteracy.org
Darlene Marciniak, Executive Director

A non-profit organization dedicated to improving people's lives through three literacy programs; Adult Literacy, Read With Me (Family Literacy), and Reading For Better Business.

Maryland

2087 Anne Arundel County Literacy Council
80 W St
Ste A
Annapolis, MD 21401-2401   410-269-4465
FAX 410-974-2023
http://www.icanread.org
e-mail: programdirector@aaclc.org
Lisa Vernon, President

A volunteer, non-profit organization dedicated to serving the needs of functionally illiterate adults in Anne Arundel County. Provides free, personalized one-on-one training to adults who read at a 5th grade level or lower.

2088 Calvert County Literacy Council
PO Box 2508
Prince Frederick, MD 20678-2508   410-535-3233
http://www.somd.lib.md.us
e-mail: calvertliteracy@somd.lib.md.us
Maria Isle Birnkammer, Director

Provides volunteers to help with one-on-one tutoring or small group tutoring.

2089 Center for Adult and Family Literacy: Community College of Baltimore County
7200 Sollers Point Rd
Building E, Ste 104
Baltimore, MD 21222-4649   443-840-3692
http://www.ccbcmd.edu
e-mail: abonner@ccbcmd.edu
Sandra Kurtinitis, President

Classes to provide training and instruction for adults with literacy problems.

2090 Charles County Literacy Council
United Way Bldg
10250 La Plata Rd
La Plata, MD 20646   301-934-6488
FAX 301-392-9286
http://www.charlescountyliteracy.org
e-mail: charlescountyliteracy@comcast.net
Sonja L Scharles, President

A not-for-profit organization, provides free community-based one-on-one adult literacy tutoring to ensure that all adults have the access to quality education needed to fully realize their potential as individuals, parents and citizens

2091 Howard University School of Continuing Education
Ste 100
1100 Wayne Ave
Silver Spring, MD 20910-5603   301-585-2296
FAX 301-585-8911
http://www.howard.edu
e-mail: csnell@howard.edu
Cudore L. Snell, Dean

Howard University Continuing Education was established in April 1986 to meet the education and training needs of professionals, administrators, entrepreneurs, technical personnel, paraprofessionals and other adults on an individual or group basis.

2092 Literacy Council of Frederick County
110 E Patrick St
Frederick, MD 21701   301-600-2066
http://www.frederickliteracy.org
e-mail: info@frederickliteracy.org
Caroline Gaver, President

A non-profit, non-secretarian, educational organization dedicated to helping non-literate and semi-literate adult residents in the county improve their language skills through one-on-one tutoring.

2093 Literacy Council of Montgomery County
21 Maryland Ave
Ste 320
Rockville, MD 20850   301-610-0030
FAX 301-610-0034
http://www.literacycouncilmcmd.org
e-mail: info@literacycouncilmcmd.org
Martha E. Stephens, Executive Director

A non-profit organization founded to help adults living or working in the county who want to achieve functional levels of reading, writing, and speaking English so that they may improve the quality of their life and their ability to participate in the community.

2094 Literacy Council of Prince George's County
6352 Adelphi Rd
Ste 101
Hyattsville, MD 20782   301-699-9770
FAX 301-699-9707
http://www.literacycouncil.org
e-mail: info@literacycouncil.org
The primary non-profit organization for the advocacy and implementation of literacy programs in the county. Provides services for adult learners in acquiring, improving and applying basic literacy skills includinf reading, writing, math and oral communication.

2095 Maryland Adult Literacy Resource Center
UMBC, Department of Education
1000 Hilltop Circle
Baltimore, MD 21250-2029   410-455-6725
                     888-464-3346
             FAX 410-455-1139
          http://www.umbc.edu
          e-mail: ira@umbc.edu

Katherine Ira, Director

As part of the State Library, the State Resource Center provides resources and information for adult literacy providers and students in Maryland.

Massachusetts

2096 A Legacy for Literacy
330 Homer St
Newton Center, MA 02459   617-796-1360
             TTY: 617-552-7154
    http://www.newtonfreelibrary.net
  e-mail: legacyforliteracy@yahoo.com
Susan Becam, Literacy Program Coordinator

Provides free tutoring services for adults of limited English proficiency.

2097 Adult Center at PAL
Curry College
1071 Blue Hill Ave
Milton, MA 02186   617-333-0500
            FAX 617-333-2114
          http://www.curry.edu
     e-mail: lhubbard@curry.edu
Laura Hubbard, Coordinator

Offers adults with learning disabilities or attention deficits a safe, supportive place to work on developing their strengths. Serves adult students enrolled in courses at Curry College or at other institutions of higher education.

2098 ESL Center
43 Amity St
Amherst, MA 01002   413-259-3090
            FAX 413-256-4096
     http://www.joneslibrary.org
     e-mail: esl@joneslibrary.org
Lynne Weintraub, Coordinator

Provides volunteer tutors, tutoring space, study materials, computer-assisted instruction, citizenship classes, English classes and referrals to adult immigrants in the Amherst area.

2099 Eastern Massachusetts Literacy Council
English at Large
400 High St
Medford, MA 02155-3608   781-395-2374
            TTY: 781-395-2374
     http://www.englishatlarge.org
  e-mail: volunteer@englishatlarge.org
Stephen Reny, President
Andrew Chesterton, Chairman

The Eastern Massachusetts Literacy Council is a private non-profit affiliate of ProLiteracy Worldwide, the largest nonprofit volunteer adult literacy organization in the world. The EMLC trains volunteers to assist adults who are learning English as another language and adults who wish to strengthen their basic reading skills.

2100 JOBS Program: Massachusetts Employment Services Program
19 Staniford St
Charles F. Hurley Building
Boston, MA 02114-1704   617-626-5300
            FAX 617-348-5191
          http://www.mass.gov
  e-mail: DCSCustomerfeedback@detma.org
John Wagnar, Director

The Employment Services Program is a joint federal and state funded program whose primary goal is to provide a way to self-sufficiency for TAFDC families ESP is an employment-oriented program that is based on a work-first approach.

2101 Literacy Network of South Berkshire
100 Main St
Lee, MA 01238-1614   413-243-0471
            FAX 413-243-6754
       http://www.litnetsb.org
     e-mail: info@litnetsb.org
Pam Kittredge, Executive Director

Serving the 15 towns of Southern Berkshire County in Massachusetts. Providing free one-on-one tutoring to adults in reading, GED preparation, ESL, and citizenship preparation.

2102 Literacy Volunteers of Greater Worcester
3 Salem Sq
Rm 332
Worcester, MA 01608   508-754-8056
            FAX 508-754-8056
          http://www.lvgw.org
     e-mail: litvolworc@gmail.com
Laurie D'Amico, Director
Paris Baillie, ESL Coordinator

Provides confidential, free, individualized, year-round tutoring in either basic reading or English for speakers of other languages.

2103 Literacy Volunteers of Massachusetts
15 Court Square
Ste 540
Boston, MA 02108   617-367-1313
            FAX 617-367-8894
          TTY: 888-466-1313
          http://www.lvm.org
     e-mail: kgriffiths@lvm.org
Kristin Griffiths, Director

Literacy Volunteers of Massachusetts helps adults learn to read and write or speak English by matching them with trained volunteer tutors.

2104 Literacy Volunteers of Methuen
305 Broadway
Methuen, MA 01844-6806   978-686-4080
            FAX 978-686-8669
       http://www.nevinslibrary.org
     e-mail: litvolmeth@gmail.com
Sue Jefferson, Coordinator

Brings free, private, flexible, individualized instruction to adults in the community who are struggling everyday with basic reading and language problems.

2105 Literacy Volunteers of the Montachusett Area
610 Main St
Fitchburg, MA 01420   978-343-8184
            FAX 978-343-4680
http://www.literacyvolunteersmontachusett.org
     e-mail: literacy26@aol.com
Gloria Maybury, Program Coordinator

Promotes and fosters increased literacy in the Montachusett Area through trained volunteer tutoring and to empower adults for whom English is a second language. Encourage and aid individuals, groups or organizations desiring to increase literacy through voluntary programs.

2106 Massachusetts Correctional Education: Inmate Training & Education
PO Box 71
Hodder House, Two Merchant Road
Framingham, MA 01704 508-935-0901
FAX 508-935-0907
http://www.state.ma.us/doc/
e-mail: cvicari@doc.state.ma.us
Carolyn J. Vicari, Director

To establish departmental policy regarding inmates' involvement in academic and vocational training programs.

2107 Massachusetts Family Literacy Consortium
MA Dept of Elementary & Secondary Education
75 Pleasant St
Malden, MA 02148
FAX 781-338-3394
http://www.doe.mass.edu
e-mail: MFLC@doe.mass.edu
Kathy Rodriguez, Coordinator

A statewide initiative with the mission of forging effective partnerships among state agencies, community organizations, and other interested parties to expand and strengthen family literacy and support.

2108 Massachusetts GED Administration: Massachusetts Department of Education
75 Pleasant St
Malden, MA 02148 781-338-6604
http://www.doe.mass.edu
e-mail: rderfler@doe.mass.edu
Ruth Derfler, Director

Thirty-three test centers operate state-wide to serve the needs of the adult population in need of a high school credential.

2109 Massachusetts Job Training Partnership Act: Department of Employment & Training
19 Staniford St
Boston, MA 02114-2502 617-626-5400
FAX 617-570-8581
http://www.detma.org
e-mail: mstonge@detma.org
Edward Malmberg, Executive Director

Supplies information on the local labor market and assists companies in locating employees.

2110 Pollard Memorial Library Adult Literacy Program
401 Merrimack St
Lowell, MA 01852-5999 978-970-4120
FAX 978-970-4117
TDD:978-970-4129
http://www.pollardml.org
Victoria Woodley, Director

Offers free, confidential, private and flexibly scheduled tutoring to adults with little or no reading or writing skills, and those who wish to become more fluent English speakers, readers or writers.

Michigan

2111 Capital Area Literacy Coalition
1028 E Saginaw
Lansing, MI 48906-5518 517-485-4949
FAX 517-485-1924
http://www.thereadingpeople.org
e-mail: mail@thereadingpeople.org
Lois Bader, Executive Director

The Capital Area Literacy Coalition helps children and adults learn to read, write and speak English with an ultimate goal of helping individuals achieve self-sufficiency.

2112 Kent County Literacy Council
111 Library St NE
Grand Rapids, MI 49503-3268 616-459-5151
FAX 616-245-8069
http://www.kentliteracy.org
e-mail: info@kentliteracy.org
Susan Ledy, Executive Director

A non-profit organization founded in 1986 that provides literacy services to over 1,000 adults in reading and english communication. In addition to the adult tutoring programs, we also serve area counties through the Customized Workplace English Program providing fee-based customized Workplace English Language, accent modification, and multicultrual training to area companies; and the Family Literacy Program which offers literacy and ESL instruction, workshops, and events.

2113 Michigan Assistive Technology: Michigan Rehabilitation Services
119 Pere Marquette Dr
Suite 1C
Lansing, MI 48912-1231 517-485-4477
FAX 517-485-4488
http://www.publicpolicy.com
e-mail: ppa@publicpolicy.com
Jeffrey D. Padden, President
Nancy Hewat, Executive Director

Solves information and policy-development problems for clients.

2114 Michigan Libraries and Adult Literacy
PO Box 30007
702 W. Kalamazoo St.
Lansing, MI 48909-7507 517-373-1300
877-479-0021
FAX 517-373-5700
TDD:517-373-1592
http://www.michigan.gov
e-mail: librarian@michigan.gov
Nancy Robertson, Director

2115 Michigan Workforce Investment Act
119 Pere Marquette Dr
Suite 1C
Lansing, MI 48912-1231 517-485-4477
FAX 517-485-4488
http://www.publicpolicy.com
e-mail: ppa@publicpolicy.com
Jeff Padden, President

Minnesota

2116 Adult Basic Education
Minnesota Department of Education
1500 Highway 36 W
Roseville, MN 55113 651-582-8442
FAX 651-634-5154
http://www.education.state.mn.us

Alice Seagren, Commissioner
Barry Shaffer, Director

Available statewide at no cost to adult learners and is administered through the Minnesota Department of Education. To be eligible for ABE services, a person must be 16 years old or older, not enrolled in K-12 public or private school and lack basic academic skills in one or more of the following areas: reading, writing, speaking and mathematics.

2117   Alexandria Literacy Project
1204 Hwy 27 W
Alexandria, MN 56308   320-762-3312
                                    FAX 320-762-3313
                              http://www.thealp.org
                 e-mail: sschroep@alexandria.k12.mn.us
Sandy Schroepfer, Coordinator

Purpose is to recruit and tutor adults who want to improve their basic reading, writing, spelling and/or math skills; to tutor adults originally from other countries who want to improve their English listening, speaking, reading and writing skills; to train volunteer tutors and literacy leaders; to promote and encourage this teaching and training.

2118   English Learning Center
Our Saviour's Outreach Ministries
2315 Chicago Ave S
Minneapolis, MN 55404   612-871-5900
                                    FAX 612-871-0017
                              http://www.osom-mn.org
Sandy Aslaksen, Executive Director

Educationally empowering immigrant and refugee adults and their families towards self-determination.

2119   LDA Minnesota Learning Disability Association
6100 Golden Valley Rd
Golden Valley, MN 55422   952-582-6000
                                    FAX 952-922-8102
                           http://www.ldaminnesota.org
                       e-mail: info@ldaminnesota.org
Kitty Christiansen, Executive Director
Arty Dorman, Programs Director
Susan Freivalds, Resource Development Director
A non-profit agency providing programs and services for learners of all ages, specializing in learning disabilities or other learning difficulties such as ADHD.

2120   Minnesota Department of Employment and Economic Development
Minnesota Workforce Center
332 Minnesota St
Suite E-200
Saint Paul, MN 55101-1351   651-259-7114
                                          800-657-3858
                                    TTY: 651-296-3900
                     http://www.positivelyminnesota.com
              e-mail: DEED.CustomerService@state.mn.us
Mark R. Phillips, Commisioner
Bonnie Elsey, Director

The Department of Employment and Economic Development is Minnesota's principal economic development agency, with programs promoting business expansion and retention, workforce development, international trade, community development and tourism.

2121   Minnesota LINCS: Literacy Council
700 Raymond Avenue
Suite 180
Saint Paul, MN 55114   651-645-2277
                                          800-225-7323
                                    FAX 651-645-2272
                            http://www.mnliteracy.org
                         e-mail: email@mnliteracy.org
Tracy E. Tracy, President
Jewelie Grape, Chairman

Makes information available to literacy and other educators throughout Minnesota. The system is a result of cooperation between numerous agencies and organizations in Minnesota that realize the benefit of using the internet to provide information to the public. The system allows literacy and other educators to locate information at one central site or follow links to connect to wherever the information resides.

2122   Minnesota Life Work Center
University of St Thomas
1000 LaSalle Ave
Ste 110
Minneapolis, MN 55403   651-962-4763
                    http://www.stthomas.edu/lifeworkcenter
                        e-mail: lifework@stthomas.edu
Provides special services and resources to meet the needs of all students, especially those on the Minneapolis campus.

2123   Minnesota Literacy Training Network
University of St Thomas
1000 Lasalle Ave
Minneapolis, MN 55403-2025   651-962-4000
                                          800-328-6819
                                    FAX 651-962-4014
                              http://www.stthomas.edu
Sharon Ficher, Executive Director
Deborah Simmons, Director

Literacy Training Network offers noncredit learning opportunities for adult basic education and literacy training staff in Minnesota.

2124   Minnesota Vocational Rehabilitation Services
332 Minnesota St
Ste E-200
Saint Paul, MN 55101-1805   651-259-7366
                                          800-328-9095
                                    FAX 651-297-5159
                                    TTY: 651-296-3900
                           http://www.deed.state.mn.us
                      e-mail: kim.peck@state.mn.us
Kimberley Pack, Director

Provides basic vocational rehabilitation services to consumers including vocational counseling, planning, guidance and placement, as well as certain special services based on individual circumstances.

Mississippi

2125   Corinth-Alcorn Literacy Council
1023 N Fillmore St
Corinth, MS 38834-4100   662-286-9759
                                    FAX 662-286-8010
                           http://www.alcornliteracy.com
                      e-mail: literacy38834@yahoo.com
Cheryl Meints, President
Tommy Hardwick, Treasurer
Becky Williams, Secretary

Missouri

2126   Joplin NALA Read
ProLiteracy America
PO Box 447
Joplin, MO 64802-0447   417-782-2646
                                    FAX 417-782-2648
                              http://www.joplinnala.org
                       e-mail: joplinnala@123mail.org
Marj Boudreaux, Director
Joan Doner, Program Coordinator

An adult literacy council, serving adults 17 years and older in the areas of Math, ESL, and reading. Trains volunteers to tutor and furnish all books for the tutors and students. A not-for-profit organization, that receives funding from United Way and the state Adult Education & Literacy department.

2127 **LIFT: St. Louis**
815 Olive St
Ste 22
Saint Louis, MO 63101   314-678-4443
800-729-4443
FAX 314-678-2938
http://www.lift-missouri.org
e-mail: todea@webster.edu
Tim O'Dea, Executive Director

Serves as Missouri's Literacy Resource Center, provides training, technical assistance, and materials for educators and family literacy programs.

2128 **Literacy Kansas City**
211 W Armour Blvd
Third Fl
Kansas City, MO 64111   816-333-9332
FAX 816-444-6628
http://www.literacykc.org
e-mail: volunteer@literacykc.org
Mike Bertrand, Executive Director

To advance literacy through direct services, advocacy and collaboration.

2129 **Literacy Roundtable**
YMCA Literacy Council
2635 Gravois Ave
Saint Louis, MO 63118   314-776-7102
FAX 314-776-6872
http://www.literacyroundtable.org
e-mail: cmithcell@ymcastlouis.org
Caroline Mitchell, Coordinator

A consortium of literacy providers throughout the St. Louis-Metro East area whose mission is to support literacy efforts in the Missouri and Illinois bi-state region.

2130 **MVCAA Adult/Family Literacy**
1415 S Odell Ave
Marshall, MO 65340-3144   660-886-7476
FAX 660-886-5868
http://www.mvcaa.net
e-mail: info@mvcaa.net
Pam LaFrenz, Executive Director
Peggy McGaugh, Vice-Chairman

2131 **Parkway Area Adult Education and Literacy**
13157 N Olive Spur
Saint Louis, MO 63146   314-415-4940
FAX 314-415-4938
http://www.pkwy.k12.mo.us/ael
e-mail: pkwyael@yahoo.com
Sally Sandy, Director

Adult basic skills, literacy, GED prep, work readiness, transition to post-secondary, ESL, citizenship, TOFEL prep for those 17 years of age and no longer enrolled in school.

2132 **St Louis Public Schools Adult Education and Literacy**
801 N. 11th Street
Saint Louis, MO 63101   314-231-3720
FAX 314-367-3057
http://www.slps.org
e-mail: Supt@slps.org
Dr. Kevin Adams, Superintendent
Dr. Nicole Williams, Chief Academics Officer

Provides opportunities for adults to participate in the GED; ESOL; Workforce Development; Life Skills; Literacy Enhancement and Family Literacy programs.

Montana

2133 **LVA Richland County**
121 3rd Ave NW
Sidney, MT 59270   406-480-1971
http://www.richlandlva.org
e-mail: info@richlandlva.org
Sue Zimmerman, Program Coordinator

A non-profit, community-based organization working to help adults improve their basic literacy skills, and learn other skills needed for today's modern life.

2134 **Montana Literacy Resource Center**
PO Box 201800
1515 E 6th Avenue
Helena, MT 59620-1800   406-444-3115
FAX 406-444-0266
TDD:406-444-4799
TTY: 406-444-4799
http://www.msl.mt.gov
e-mail: msl@mt.gov
Jennie Stapp, State Librarian

A state-wide literacy support network.

Nebraska

2135 **Answers4Families: Center on Children, Families, Law**
206 S 13th St
Ste 1000
Lincoln, NE 68508-0227   402-472-0844
800-746-8420
FAX 402-472-8412
http://www.answers4families.org
A project of the Center on Children, Families and Law at University of Nebraska. Mission is to provide info, opportunities, education and support to Nebraskans through Internet resources. The Center serves individuals with special needs and mental health disorders, foster families, caregivers, assisted living, and school nurses.

2136 **Client Assistance Program (CAP): Nebraska Division of Persons with Disabilities**
301 Centennial Mall S
Box 94987
Lincoln, NE 68509   402-471-3656
800-742-7594
FAX 402-471-0117
http://www.cap.state.ne.us
e-mail: victoria.rasmussen@nebraska.gov
Frank Lloyd, Executive Director

The Client Assistance Program helps individuals who have concerns or difficulties when applying for or receiving rehabilitation services funded under the Rehabilitation Act.

2137 **Lincoln Literacy Council**
745 S 9th St
Lincoln, NE 68508   402-476-7323
FAX 402-476-2122
http://www.lincolnliteracy.org
e-mail: info@lincolnliteracy.org
Clayton Nass, Executive Director

To assist people of all cultures and strengthen the community by teaching English language and literacy skills.

2138 Literacy Center for the Midlands
1823 Harney St
Ste 204
Omaha, NE 68102 402-342-7323
FAX 402-345-9045
http://www.midlandsliteracy.org
e-mail: btodd@midlandsliteracy.org
Beverly Todd, Executive Director

To empower adults and families by helping them acquire the literacy skills and practices to be active and contributing members of their communities.

2139 Platte Valley Literacy Association
2504 14th St
Columbus, NE 68601 402-564-5196
FAX 402-563-3378
http://www.megavision.net
e-mail: literacy@megavision.com
Jolene Hake, Executive Director

Organization that collaborates with Central Community College Adult Basic Education to respond to the educational needs of our community.

Nevada

2140 Nevada Department of Adult Education
755 N Roop St
Carson City, NV 89701 775-687-7289
FAX 775-687-8636
http://nde.doe.nv.gov
Brad Deeds, ABE/ESL/GED Programs

provides adult basic education and literacy services in order to assist adults to become literate and obtain the knowledge and skills necessary for employment and self-sufficiency; to assist adults who are parents to obtain the educational skills necessary to become full partners in the education of their children; and to assist adults in the completion of a secondary school education.

2141 Nevada Economic Opportunity Board: Community Action Partnership
330 W. Washington Ave
Suite 7
Las Vegas, NV 89106 702-647-3307
FAX 702-647-3125
http://www.eobccnv.org
e-mail: contact@eobccnv.org
Linda Harris, Secretary

Located in one of the fastest growing and most diverse communities in the United States, the Economic Opportunity Board of Clark County is a highly innovative Community Action Agency. Our mission is to eliminate poverty by providing programs, resources, services, and advocacy for self-sufficiency and economic empowerment.

2142 Nevada Literacy Coalition: State Literacy Resource Center
100 N Stewart St
Carson City, NV 89701-4285 775-885-1010
800-445-9673
FAX 775-684-3344
http://www.nevadaculture.org
e-mail: sfgraf@clan.lib.nv.us
Marilyn Brandvold, Coordinator

The Nevada State Literacy Resource Center has books, newsletters and a wide variety of multi-media resources such as videos, audiotapes and games for literacy instruction and programs for literacy students, trainers and tutors.

2143 Northern Nevada Literacy Council
1400 Wedekind Rd
Reno, NV 89512-2465 775-356-1007
FAX 775-356-1009
http://www.nnlc.org
e-mail: director@nnlc.org
Vickie Newell, Executive Director

Provides English as a second language, adult basic skills, and GED preparatory instructions for adults, 18 years of age and over, who lack a high school diploma or GED or essential basic skills to function successfully in the workplace.

New Hampshire

2144 New Hampshire Literacy Volunteers of America
405 Pine St
Manchester, NH 03104-6106 603-624-6550
FAX 603-624-6559
http://www.manchesternh.gov
Denise Van Zanten, Library Director
Sarah Basbas, Branch Manager

This program is the only nationally accredited adult literacy program in New Hampshire. Provides free confidential one-to-one tutoring for adults who want to learn to write and read for lifelong learning.

2145 New Hampshire Second Start Adult Education
17 Knight St
Concord, NH 03301 603-228-1341
FAX 603-228-3852
http://www.second-start.org
e-mail: abe@second-start.org
James Snodgrass, Director

Provides instruction in basic reading, writing and math.

New Jersey

2146 Jersey City Library Literacy Program
472 Jersey Ave
Jersey City, NJ 07302-3456 201-547-4518
FAX 201-435-5746
http://www.jclibrary.org
e-mail: literacy@jclibrary.org
Nancy G Sambul, Executive Director
Darnelle Richardson, Program Coordinator

Provides free one-on-one basic reading instruction for Jersey City residents aged sixteen and older. Work with students ranging from non-readers through the fifth grade level. Offers small conversation group classes for immigrants striving to learn to speak, read and write English.

2147 Literacy Volunteers in Mercer County
3535 Quakerbridge Rd
Ste 104
Hamilton, NJ 08619 609-587-6027
FAX 609-587-6137
http://www.mercerliteracy.org
e-mail: lvmercer@verizon.net
Cheryl Kirton, Executive Director

Trains, coordinates and supports the efforts of a dedicated group of volunteer literacy tutors. Volunteers provide free, confidential literacy tutoring services to adult residents in Mercer COunty at a variety of locations including the public libraries, workplace sites, churches and retirement homes.

2148 Literacy Volunteers of America Essex/Passaic County
Passaic Public Library
195 Gregory Ave
Passaic, NJ 07005   973-470-0039
                                FAX 973-470-0098
                        http://www.lvanewark.org
                    e-mail: lvanewark@verizon.net
Dr Robert Dicker, Executive Director

Provides free literacy services to adults who have been identified as needing instruction in reading and/or English conversation; and to families who are experiencing literacy
and/or learning difficulties.

2149 Literacy Volunteers of Camden County
203 Laurel Rd
Voorhees, NJ 08043-2349   856-772-1636
                                FAX 856-772-2761
                        http://lva.camden.lib.nj.us
                    e-mail: literacy@camden.lib.nj.us
Denise Weinberg, Director

An adult literacy organization that tutors Camden County,
NJ adults (18 years or over) residents who are at the lowest
levels of literacy and who need help speaking or understanding English (ESL) or who need help with elementary reading
or math skills.

2150 Literacy Volunteers of Cape-Atlantic
743 N Main St
Pleasantville, NJ 08232-1541   609-383-3377
                                FAX 609-383-0234
                        http://www.lvacapeatlantic.com
                    e-mail: literacyvolunteers@comcast.net
Sheila McLaughlin, Executive Director

Helps individuals in Atlantic and Cape May Counties improve their English language skills so they can participate
more fully in family, workplace and community life.

2151 Literacy Volunteers of Englewood Library
31 Engle St
Englewood, NJ 07631-2903   201-568-2215
                                FAX 201-568-6895
                        http://www.englewoodlibrary.org
                            e-mail: ctaylor@bccls.org
Charlene Taylor, Library Director
Grace Colaneri, Head of Literacy

Offers three tutor-training workshops each year with an extensive collection of books, workbooks, and cassettes for tutors and students to borrow with a current library card.

2152 Literacy Volunteers of Gloucester County
PO Box 1106
Turnersville, NJ 08012   856-218-4743
                        http://www.literacyvgc.org
                    e-mail: info@literacyvgc.org
Trudy Lawrence, Executive Director

Providing free, one-on-one adult tutoring to those with the
lowest level of literacy - below a 5th grade level.

2153 Literacy Volunteers of Middlesex
Suite F
380 Washington Road
Sayreville, NJ 08872   732-432-8000
                                FAX 732-432-8189
                            http://www.lpnj.org
                        e-mail: info@lpnj.org

Mary Ellen Firestone, President
Christine Sienkielewski, Director

Trained volunteers that provide free tutoring services to
adults with limited literacy skills, enabling them to achieve
their personal goals and to enhance their contributions to the
community.

2154 Literacy Volunteers of Monmouth County
213 Broadway
Long Branch, NJ 07740   732-571-0209
                                FAX 732-571-2474
                        http://www.lvmonmouthnj.org
                    e-mail: lvmonmouth@brookdalecc.edu
Mission is to promote increased literacy for adults in
Monmouth County through the effetive use of volunteers
and in collaboration with individuals, groups and organizations desiring to foster increased literacy.

2155 Literacy Volunteers of Morris County
10 Pine St
Morristown, NJ 07960   973-984-1998
                                FAX 973-971-0291
                        http://www.lvamorris.org
                    e-mail: lvamorris@yahoo.com
Debbie Leon, Director

Promotes increased literacy and fluency in English for adult
learners in this area through the effective use of volunteers,
the provisions of support services for volunteers and learners, and through collaboration with individuals, groups and
any organization desirous of fostering increased literacy.

2156 Literacy Volunteers of Plainfield Public Library
800 Park Ave
Plainfield, NJ 07060-2517   908-757-1111
                                FAX 908-754-0063
                        http://www.plainfieldlibrary.info
                    e-mail: literacy@plfdpl.info
Stella Segura, Coordinator

Mission is to develop the literacy skills of adults with minimum reading skills.

2157 Literacy Volunteers of Somerset County
120 Finderne Ave
Box 7
Bridgewater, NJ 08807   908-725-5430
                                FAX 908-707-2077
                        http://www.literacysomerset.org
Alan Karmin, Executive Director

Promotes literacy through a network of community volunteers.

2158 Literacy Volunteers of Union County
800 Park Avenue
Plainfield, NJ 07060   908-755-7998
                                FAX 908-518-0601
                        http://www.lvaunion.org
                    e-mail: literacyinfo@lvaunion.org
Elizabeth Gloeggler, Executive Director

A non-profit organization that improves the lives of adults in
the county by teaching them to read, write and speak English
so they can participate more fully in family, workplace and
community life.

2159 People Care Center
120 Finderne Ave
Bridgewater, NJ 08807   908-725-2299
                                FAX 908-725-2607
                        http://www.peoplecarecenter.org
                    e-mail: info@peoplecarecenter.org
Elissa Director, Executive Director

New Mexico

2160 Adult Basic Education Division of Dona Ana Community College
2800 N. Sonoma Ranch Blvd
Las Cruces, NM 88011-8001
505-527-7540
800-903-7503
FAX 575-528-7300
http://dabcc-www.nmsu.edu
e-mail: sdegiuli@nmsu.edu
Margie C. Huerta, President
Stephen DeGiulio, Coordinator, Literacy Program

2161 Carlsbad Literacy Program
Ann Wood Literacy Center
511 N 12th St
Carlsbad, NM 88220
575-885-1752
FAX 505-885-7980
http://www.carlsbadliteracy.com
e-mail: literacy1@valornet.com
Delora Elizondo, Coordinator

Provides opportunities for adult community members to learn to read and to improve their reading and writing abilities.

2162 Curry County Literacy Council
Clovis Community College
417 Schepps Blvd
Rm 171
Clovis, NM 88101
505-769-4095
http://www.clovis.edu
e-mail: curry.literacy@clovis.edu
B J Williams, Program Coordinator

Goal is to provide one with a sense of security to gain employment, have life skills, and assist in language development.

2163 Deming Literacy Program
PO Box 1932
2301 South Tin St.
Deming, NM 88031-1932
575-546-7571
FAX 505-546-1356
http://www.centerfornonprofitexcellence.org
e-mail: dlpdeming@gmail.com
Marisol D. Perez, Director

The Literacy Home Mentoring and After School Project will encourage parents to read to their children at home, as well as provide mentors to help children with their reading skills after school.

2164 Literacy Volunteers of America: Dona Ana County
PO Box 30001
MSC 3DA
Las Cruces, NM 88003-8001
575-527-7544
800-903-7540
FAX 575-528-7065
http://www.readwritenow.org
e-mail: sdegiuli@nmsu.edu
Abel Chavarria, Chairman
Linda Coshenet, Secretary

The Literacy Volunteers of America is designed to help people who cannot read or write the English language. This program gives adults a new opportunity to learn reading through the sixth-grade level.

2165 Literacy Volunteers of America: Las Vegas, San Miguel
Box 9000
Las Vegas, NM 87701
505-454-8043
http://www.nmhu.edu
e-mail: president_office@nmhu.edu
James Fries, President
Gilbert D. Rivera, Vice President

Las Vegas/San Miquel Literacy Volunteers are a part of the national non-profit organization Literacy Volunteers of America, which is dedicated to promoting literacy throughout the country.

2166 Literacy Volunteers of America: Socorro County
PO Box 1431
Socorro, NM 87801-1431
505-835-4659
FAX 505-835-1182
http://www.volunteermatch.org
e-mail: lva_socorro@hotmail.com
Joyce Aguilar, Executive Director

Promotes literacy for people of Socorro County.

2167 Literacy Volunteers of Santa Fe
6401 Richards Ave
Santa Fe, NM 87508-4887
505-428-1353
FAX 505-428-1338
http://www.lvsf.org
e-mail: letty.naranjo@spcc.edu
Letty Naranjo, Executive Director

Dedicated to providing free tutoring and encouragement for adults and their families who want to read, write and speak English.

2168 New Mexico Coalition for Literacy
3209 Mercantile Ct
Ste B
Santa Fe, NM 87507
505-982-3997
800-233-7587
FAX 505-982-4095
http://www.nmcl.org
e-mail: info@nmcl.org
Heather Heunermund, Executive Director

Encourages and supports community-based literacy programs and is the New Mexico affiliate and coordinator for the national program of ProLiteracy America, overseeing certification and coordination of its volunteer, tutor trainers.

2169 Read West
2900 Grande Blvd
PO Box 44508
Rio Rancho, NM 87174-4508
505-892-1131
FAX 505-896-3780
http://www.readwest.org
e-mail: readwest@earthlink.net
Willard Steinsick, Executive Director
Muncie Hansen, Program Coordinator

Targets adults with low literacy or whose first language is not English. Provides free, customized, one-to-one, tutoring to help adults improve. their reading, writing and English language.
1989

2170 Roswell Literacy Council
609 W 10th St
Roswell, NM 88201
575-625-1369
FAX 575-622-8280
http://www.roswell-literacy.org
e-mail: literacy@dfn.com
Andrae England, Director

Dedicated to adult learning in Chaves County.

2171 Valencia County Literacy Council
280 La Entrada
Los Lunas, NM 87031-7633
505-925-8926
FAX 505-925-8924
http://www.valencialiteracy.org
e-mail: joglesby@valencialiteracy.org
Jill Oglesby, Executive Director

To enable adults to achieve personal goals and very young children to achieve pre-literacy skills through literacy services provided to families free of charge.

New York

2172 Literacy Volunteers of America: Middletown
70 Fulton St
Middletown, NY 10940-5251　　　845-341-5460
　　　　　　　　　　　　　　　FAX 845-343-7191
　　　　　　　　　http://www.literacyorangeny.org
　　　　　　　　　e-mail: divlitorange@warwick.net
Christine Rolando, Executive Director

An organization of volunteers that provides a variety of services to enable people to achieve personal goals through literacy. Their belief is that the ability to read is critical to personal freedom and maintenance of a democratic society. These beliefs have led to the following commitments: the personal growth of their students; the effective use of their volunteers; the improvement of society and strengthening and improving the organization.

2173 Literacy Volunteers of Oswego County
34 E Bridge St
Ste 301
Oswego, NY 13126　　　　　　　315-342-8839
　　　　　　　　　　　http://www.lvoswego.org
　　　　　　　　　　　e-mail: info@lvoswego.org
Jane Murphy, Executive Director

A non-profit community-based educational organization that provides quality tutoring in basic literacy skills and conversational English.

2174 Literacy Volunteers of Otsego & Delaware Counties
Oneonta Adult Education
189 Main St
Oneonta, NY 13820-3510　　　　607-433-3645
　　　　　　　　　　　　　　　800-782-3858
　　　　　　　　　http://www.oneontaadulted.org
　　　　　　　　　　e-mail: lvodc@oneonta.edu
To change lives of courageous, motivated adults who do not possess functional skills needed to perform ordinary, everyday tasks in an ever-changing global society.

2175 New York Literacy Assistance Center
32 Broadway
10th Fl
New York, NY 10004　　　　　　212-803-3300
　　　　　　　　　　　　　　　FAX 212-785-3685
　　　　　　　　　　　　http://www.lacnyc.org
　　　　　　　　　　　e-mail: elyser@lacnyc.org
Elyse Barbell, Executive Director

A nonprofit organization dedicated to supporting and promoting the expansion of quality literacy services in New York.

2176 New York Literacy Resource Center
State University of New York
1400 Washington Ave
Albany, NY 12222　　　　　　　518-442-3300
　　　　　　　　　　　　　　　800-331-0931
　　　　　　　　　　　　　FAX 518-442-5383
　　　　　　　　　　　　http://www.albany.edu
Maritza Ramirez-Vallinas, Director

State Literacy Resource Center is a statewide literacy information network throughout the state.

2177 New York Literacy Volunteers of America
777 Maryvale Dr
Buffalo, NY 14225-2712　　　　716-631-5282
　　　　　　　　　　　　　　　FAX 716-631-0657
　　　　　　　　　　　　http://www.lvanys.org
　　　　　　　　　e-mail: buffalo@literacynewyork.org

Kevin G Smith, Executive Director

Provides technical program, and training assistance and workshops to a network of 36 local, community-based affiliates who annually provide over 400,000 hours of reading and basic skills instruction to adult learners.

2178 Resources for Children with Special Needs
116 E 16th St
5th Fl
New York, NY 10003-2112　　　　212-677-4650
　　　　　　　　　　　　　　　FAX 212-254-4070
　　　　　　　　　　　http://www.resourcesnyc.org
　　　　　　　　　　e-mail: info@resourcesnyc.org
Rachel Howard, Executive Director

Independent nonprofit organization that works for families and children with all special needs, across all boroughs, to understand, navigate, and access the services needed to ensure that all children have the opportunity to develop their full potential.

North Carolina

2179 Blue Ridge Literacy Council
PO Box 1728
Hendersonville, NC 28793-1728　　828-696-3811
　　　　　　　　　　　　　　　FAX 828-696-3887
　　　　　　　　　　　http://www.litcouncil.org
　　　　　　　　　　e-mail: brlcdb@yahoo.com
Diane Bowers, Executive Director

Provides adults in Henderson County the English communication and literacy skills they need to reach their full potential as individuals, parents, workers and citizens.

2180 Durham Literacy Center
PO Box 52209
Durham, NC 27717　　　　　　　919-489-8383
　　　　　　　　　　　　　　　FAX 919-489-7637
　　　　　　　　　　　http://www.durhamliteracy.org
　　　　　　　　　　e-mail: info@durhamliteracy.org
Reginald Hodges, Executive Director

Works to assist Durham County teenagers and adults achieve personal goals and experience positive life change through increased literacy. Helps teenagers and adults gain the reading and writing skills, English language skills, and educational credentials (GED) needed to earn a living wage.

2181 Gaston Literacy Council
116 S Marietta St
Gastonia, NC 28052　　　　　　704-868-4815
　　　　　　　　　　　　　　　FAX 704-867-7796
　　　　　　　　　　　http://www.gastonliteracy.org
　　　　　　　　　　e-mail: literacy@gaston.org
Kaye Gribble, Executive Director

A progressive organization dedicated to helping individuals improve their reading, writing, mathematics, listening, speaking, and technology skills.

2182 Literacy Council Of Buncombe County
31 College Place, Building B
Suite 221
Asheville, NC 28801-2705　　　　828-254-3442
　　　　　　　　　　　　　　　FAX 828-254-1742
　　　　　　　　　　　http://www.litcouncil.com
　　　　　　　　　　e-mail: literacybc@litcouncil.com
Amanda Edwards, Executive Director
Becca Loli, Adult Education Program

Promotes increased adult literacy in Buncombe County through effective use of trained tutors; to provide support services for tutors and learners; and to collaborate with individuals, groups, or other community organizations desiring to foster increased adult literacy.

2183 Literacy Volunteers of America: Pitt County
105-A E Arlington Blvd
Greenville, NC 27858   252-353-6578
                              FAX 252-353-6868
                        http://www.pittliteracy.org
                        e-mail: info@pittliteracy.org
To promote literacy in Pitt County through trained volunteer tutors who provide one on one and small group tutoring to adults with limited reading, writing or English speaking/literacy skills.

2184 North Carolina Literacy Resource Center
North Carolina Community College
217 W Jones St
Raleigh, NC 27603   919-707-8125
                              FAX 919-715-5161
                        http://www.ncccs.cc.nc.us
                        e-mail: allenb@ncccs.cc.nc.us
Lisa Tolley, Program Manager

North Carolina Community College Literacy Resource Center collects and disseminates information about literacy resources and organizations.

2185 Reading Connections of North Carolina
122 N Elm St
Ste 520
Greensboro, NC   336-230-2223
                              FAX 336-230-2203
                      http://www.readingconnections.org
                      e-mail: info@readingconnections.org
Jennifer Gore, Executive Director

To provide and advocate for free, individualized adult literacy services to promote life changes for Guilford County residents and surrounding communities.

North Dakota

2186 North Dakota Adult Education and Literacy Resource Center
1609 4th Ave NW
Minot, ND 58703-2911   701-328-2393
                              FAX 701-328-4770
                        http://www.dpi.state.nd.us
Valerie Fischer, State Director
Jolli Marcellais, Administrative Assistant

Promotes and supports free programs that help adults over the age of 16 obtain the basic academic and educational skills they need to be productive workers, family members, and citizens.

2187 North Dakota Department of Career and Technical Education
State Capitol 15th Floor
600 E Boulevard Ave
Bismarck, ND 58505   701-328-3180
                              FAX 701-328-1255
                              http://www.nd.gov
                              e-mail: cte@nd.us
Wayne Kutzer, Director

The mission of the Board for Vocational and Technical Education is to work with others to provide all North Dakota citizens with the technical skills, knowledge, and attitudes necessary for successful performance in a globally competitive workplace.

2188 North Dakota Department of Human Services: Welfare & Public Assistance
600 E Boulevard Ave
Sept 325, ND 58505-0602   701-328-2310
                              800-472-2622
                              FAX 701-328-2359
                              TTY: 800-366-6888
                              http://www.nd.gov/dhs
                              e-mail: dhseo@nd.gov
Carol K Olson, Executive Director

To provide services and support for poor, disabled, ill, elderly or juvenile clients in North Dakota.

2189 North Dakota Department of Public Instruction
600 E Blvd Ave
Dept 201, Fls 9, 10 & 11
Bismarck, ND 58505   701-328-2260
                              FAX 701-328-2461
                        http://www.dpi.state.nd.us
                        e-mail: wsanstead@nd.gov
Wayne Sanstead, State Superintendent

This unit provides funding and technical assistance to local programs and monitors progress of each funded project. This unit is also responsible for the administration of the GED Testing Program.

2190 North Dakota Reading Association
2420 2nd Ave SW
Minot, ND 58701-3332   701-857-4642
                              FAX 701-857-8761
                        http://ndreadon.utma.com
                        e-mail: Paula.Rogers@sendit.nodak.edu
Joyce Hinman, State Coordinator

To provide a variety of professional development opportunities; to increase the building of partnerships with other organizations; to actively promote literacy locally and globally; to assist in the strengthening of local councils and their services to members; and to promote writing with young authors.

2191 North Dakota Workforce Development Council
1600 E Century Ave
Suite 2
Bismarck, ND 58503   701-328-5300
                              FAX 701-328-5320
                              TTY: 800-366-6888
                              http://www.ndcommerce.com
                              e-mail: commerce@nd.gov
Paul Govig, Director

The role of the North Dakota Workforce Development Council is to advise the Governor and the Public concerning the nature and extent of workforce development in the context of North Dakota's economic development needs, and how to meet these needs effectively while maximizing the efficient use of available resources and avoiding unnecessary duplication of effort.

Ohio

2192 Central/Southeast ABLE Resource Center
Ohio University
338 McCracken Hall
Athens, OH 45701   740-593-4419
                              800-753-1519
                              FAX 740-593-2834
                        http://www.ouliteracycenter.org
                        e-mail: literacy@ohio.edu
Sharon Reynolds, Director

Committed to the development of literacy in southeastern Ohio and to research in all areas of literacy.

2193 Clark County Literacy Coalition
137 E High St
Springfield, OH 45502-1215   937-323-8617
                                          FAX 937-328-6911
              http://www.clarkcountyliteracy.org
       e-mail: david.smiddy@clarkcountyliteracy.org
Lisa Holmes, President

Dedicated to increasing the level of functional literacy and
self-sufficiency among the people in Clark County.

2194 Columbus Literacy Council
195 N Grant Ave
Columbus, OH 43215-2607   614-221-5013
                                          FAX 614-221-5892
                http://www.columbusliteracy.com
          e-mail: jwatson@columbusliteracy.org
Joy D Watson, Executive Director

A volunteer-based organization dedicated to increasing the
level of functional literacy of adults in Central Ohio through
teaching the English language skills of listening, speaking,
reading and writing.

2195 Literacy Council of Clermont/Brown Counties
756 Cincinnati Batavia Pike
Cincinnati, OH 45245   513-943-3741
                                          FAX 513-943-3002
              http://www.clermontbrownliteracy.org
       e-mail: susan.vilardo@clermontbrownliteracy.org
Susan Vilardo, Executive Director

Offers one-on-one volunteer tutor education in reading,
writing, spelling and comprehension to adults 19 years of
age and older who cannot read and adults who are
ESL/ESOL.

2196 Miami Valley Literacy Council
333 W First St
Ste 130
Dayton, OH 45402   937-223-4922
                                          FAX 937-223-0271
                http://www.discoverliteracy.org
          e-mail: rgilmore@discoverliteracy.org
Russ Gilmore, Executive Director

Offers classes, one-to-one tutoring, and independent study
options to adults in the Miami Valley who have low-level literacy of English language skills. Also works with
school-aged children and teens below grade level in reading
and math in the after-school program The Learning Club.

2197 Ohio Literacy Network
6161 Busch Blvd
Ste 84
Columbus, OH 43229   614-505-0716
                                            800-228-7323
                                          FAX 614-505-0718
               http://www.ohioliteracynetwork.org
        e-mail: atoops@ohioliteracynetworking.org
Allen Toops, Executive Director

Mission is to build Ohio's workforce by strengthening adult
and family literacy education accomplished by connecting
learners, educators and volunteers to a wide variety of educational resources.

2198 Ohio Literacy Resource Center
Kent State University
Research 1-1100 Summit St
PO Box 5190
Kent, OH 44242-0001   330-672-2007
                                            800-765-2897
                                          FAX 330-672-4841
                 http://literacy.kent.edu
             e-mail: olrc@literacy.kent.edu

Marty Ropog, Director

The OLRC Mission is to stimulate joint planning and coordination of literacy services at the local, regional and state levels, and to enhance the capacity of state and local
organizations and services delivery systems.

2199 Project LEARN of Summit County
60 S High St
Akron, OH 44326-1000   330-434-9461
                                            866-866-7323
                                          FAX 330-643-9195
               http://www.projectlearnsummit.org
            e-mail: info@projectlearnsummit.org
Rick Mc Intosh, Executive Director
Marquita Mitchell, Developemtn/Workforce Solutions
Eileen Chou, Community Relations Manager
Project LEARN is a nonprofit, community-based organization providing Summit County's nonreading adult population with free, confidential, small group classes and
tutoring. Helps adults reach their goals of self-sufficiency,
independence and job retention.

2200 Project LITE
6th And Reid Ave
Lorain, OH 44052   440-244-1192
                                            800-322-READ
                                          FAX 440-244-1733
                http://www.lorain.lib.oh.us
          e-mail: contact-lite@lorain.lib.oh.us
Linda Pierce, Director

2201 Project: LEARN
105 W Liberty St
Medina, OH 44256   330-723-1314
               http://www.projectlearnmedina.org
Linda Smalley, Executive Director

Provides one-on-one tutoring to adults in reading, math and
English as a second language.

**2202 Seeds of Literacy Project: St Colman Family Learning
Center**
3104 West 25th St
Cleveland, OH 44109   216-661-7952
                                          FAX 216-661-7952
                http://www.seedsofliteracy.org
          e-mail: bonnieentler@seedsofliteracy.org
Bonnie Entler, Executive Director

Helping adults in need of assistance in reading, writing and
mathematical skills and to improve their ability to function,
compete, and advance in society in an atmosphere of Christian care and compassion.

Oklahoma

2203 Center for Study of Literacy
Northeastern State University
2400 Shawnee
PO Box 549
Muskogee, OK 74402-0549   918-444-5250
                                          FAX 918-781-5425
                   http://www.nsuok.edu
              e-mail: mcelroyt@nsuok.edu
Dr Tim McElroy, Dean/Director

Provides the illiterate or undereducated adult with training;
provides instructional support for the Northeastern State
University's faculty and pre-service teachers participate in
computer literacy training to gain an understanding of computer assisted instruction; to serve as a reesource unit for
other social agencies, teachers, administrators and public
school students; to serve as the clearinghouse for literacy for
the state of Oklahoma; to initiate research on literacy.

2204   Community Literacy Center
PO Box 60687
Oklahoma City, OK 73146-0687   405-524-7323
                                       FAX 405-631-4218
            http://www.communityliteracy.com
            e-mail: okcread@communityliteracy.com
Becky O'Dell, Executive Director

A private, non-profit organization dedicated to teaching adults to read.

2205   Creek County Literacy Program
27 W Dewey Ave
Sapulpa, OK 74066-3909   918-224-9647
                                 FAX 918-224-3546
            http://www.creeklit.okpls.org
            e-mail: creeklit@yahoo.com
Barbara Belk, Executive Director

Provides free reading instruction to functionally illiterate adults who live or work in Creek County, to prepare families to manage their health care needs and to be effectively involved in the education of their children, to tutor children/youth who may have different learning styles, and to provide reading improvement programs county-wide

2206   Great Plains Literacy Council
Southern Prairie Library System
421 N Hudson St
Altus, OK 73521-3654   580-477-2890
                               FAX 580-477-3626
            http://www.spls.lib.ok.us
            e-mail: literacy1@spls.lib.ok.us
Ida Fay Winters, Director

Helps to increase the awareness of the illiteracy problem and offers a viable solution. Recruits dedicated, tutors who help to motivate those who are considered illiterate and give them the opportunity to become contributing members of the community.

2207   Guthrie Literacy Program
201 N Division St
Guthrie, OK 73044   405-227-6209
            http://www.guthrie.okpls.org
            e-mail: guthrieliteracy@email.com
Linda Gens, Library Services Director

Utilizes curriculum that focuses on the individual student's interests and needs, then tutors help the student set the goals and work with them to achieve those goals.

2208   Junior League of Oklahoma City
1001 NW Grand Blvd
Oklahoma City, OK 73118-6039   405-843-5668
                                       FAX 405-843-0994
            http://www.jloc.org
            e-mail: info@jloc.org
Jill Greene, President

Organization of women committed to promoting volunteerism, developing the potential of women and to improving the community through the effective action and leadership of trained volunteers. The purpose is exclusively educational and charitable.

2209   Literacy & Evangelism International
1800 S Jackson Ave
Tulsa, OK 74107-1897   918-585-3826
                               FAX 918-585-3224
            http://www.literacyevangelism.org
            e-mail: general@literacyevangelism.org
A missionary fellowship desiring to see the Church in every nation effectively reaching the illiterate, bringing them the Living Word Jesus Christ, through enabling them to read the written Word of God.

2210   Literacy Volunteers of America: Tulsa City County Library
400 Civic Contry library
400 Civic Center
Tulsa, OK 74103   918-549-7323
                          FAX 918-596-7907
            http://www.tulsalibrary.org
            e-mail: jgreb@tccl.lib.ok.us
Linda Saferite, Executive Director

We offer one-on-one tutoring to adults and young adults who wish to improve their reading and writing skills.

2211   Muskogee Area Literacy Council
801 W Okmulgee St
Muskogee, OK 74401   918-682-6657
                             FAX 918-682-9466
            http://www.eok.lib.ok.us
            e-mail: muskpublib@eok.lib.ok.us
Penny Chastain, Coordinator

2212   Northwest Oklahoma Literacy Council
1500 Main St
Woodward, OK 73801-3044   580-254-8582
                                  FAX 580-254-8546
            e-mail: nwoklitcouncil@woodward.lib.ok.us
Cathy Johnson, Director

Mission is to break the intergenerational cycle of illiteracy by broadening the learner and service base to include family members. Services include literacy and parenting instruction, as a compliment to ESL, adult basic education, and learning disabilities programs.

2213   Oklahoma Literacy Council
300 Park Ave
Oklahoma City, OK 73102-3600   405-232-3780
                                       FAX 405-606-3722
            http://www.literacyokc.org
            e-mail: director@literacyokc.org
Millonn Lamb, Executive Director

Promotes literacy in adults who are in need of improving literacy skills to function successfully in society.

2214   Oklahoma Literacy Resource Center
200 NE 18th St
Oklahoma City, OK 73105-3205   405-522-3205
                                       FAX 405-525-7804
            http://www.odl.state.ok.us
            e-mail: lgelders@oltn.state.ok.us
Leslie Gelders, Literacy Administrator

Provides leadership, resources, training, and information to Oklahoma;s library and community-based literacy network.

2215   Opportunities Industrialization Center of Oklahoma County
400 N Walnut Ave
Oklahoma City, OK 73104-2207   405-235-2651
                                       FAX 405-235-2653
            http://oicofoklahomacounty.org
            e-mail: oicoc@sbcglobal.net
Patricia Kelly, Executive Director

Empowers individuals through Academic and Career education to become more productive citizens in the community.

Oregon

2216 Oregon Department of Human Resource Adult & Family Services Division
500 Summer St NE
Salem, OR 97301

503-945-5944
FAX 503-378-2897
TTY: 503-945-6214
http://www.oregon.gov
e-mail: dhr.info@state.or.us

Carolyn Ross, Director

This group combines programs from the former Adult & Family Services Division and the State Office for Services to Children and Families.

2217 Oregon Employment Department
875 Union St NE
Salem, OR 97311

877-517-5627
800-237-3710
FAX 503-947-1472
http://www.workinginoregon.org

Laurie Warner, Director

Supports economic stability for Oregonians and communities during times of unemployment through the payment of unemployment benefits. Serves businesses by recruiting and referring the best qualified applicants to jobs, and provides resources to diverse job seekers in support of their employment needs.

2218 Oregon GED Administrator: Office of Community College Services
255 Capitol St NE
Salem, OR 97310-1300

503-378-8648
FAX 503-378-3365
http://www.oregon.gov
e-mail: sharlene.walker@state.or.us

Deborah Lares, Director

Mission is to contribute leadership and resources to increase the skills, knowledge and career opportunities of Oregonians.

2219 Oregon State Library
250 Winter St NE
Salem, OR 97301-3950

503-378-4243
FAX 503-585-8059
http://www.oregon.gov
e-mail: leann.bromeland@state.or.us

MaryKay Dahlgreen, Director

Mission is to provide quality information services to Oregon state government, to provide reading materials to blind and print-disabled Oregonians, and to provide leadership, grants, and other assistance to improve local library service for all Oregonians.

Pennsylvania

2220 Delaware County Literacy Council
2217 Providence Ave
Chester, PA 19013-5218

610-876-4811
FAX 610-876-5414
http://www.delcoliteracy.org
e-mail: delco@delcoliteracy.org

Madeline Bialecki, Executive Director

Dedicated to providing free, individual and small group literacy instruction to non-and low-reading adults residing in Delaware County, through a county-wide network of trained volunteer tutors and instructors.

2221 Learning Disabilities Association of Pennsylvania
4751 Lindle Rd
Ste 114
Harrisburg, PA 17111

717-939-3731
888-775-3272
http://www.ldapa.org
e-mail: ldapaininfo@aol.com

Deborah Rodes, President

An advocacy organization dedicated to helping children and adults with learning disabilities and other related neurological disorders.

2222 Literacy Council of Lancaster/Lebanon
38 W King St
Lancaster, PA 17603-3809

717-295-5523
FAX 717-295-5342
http://www.adultlit.org
e-mail: info@adultlit.org

Sean Frederick, President

A private, non-profit education agency that provides high quality basic education to adults in Lancaster and Lebanon Counties. Promotes literacy and help adults reach their reading, writing, math and English communication goalsthrough personalized instruction.

2223 Pennsylvania Literacy Resource Center
12th Floor
333 Market St
Harrisburg, PA 17126

717-783-6788
800-992-2283
FAX 717-783-5420
TTY: 717-783-8445
http://www.portal.state.pa.us
e-mail: alubrecht@pa.gov

Alice Lubrecht, Director

As part of the State Library, the State Resource Center provides electronic and print resources.

2224 York County Literacy Council
800 E King St
York, PA 17403

717-845-8719
FAX 717-699-5620
http://www.yorkliteracy.org
e-mail: exec.dir@yorkliteracy.org

Bobbi Anne Cavanaugh, Executive Director

Dedicated to advancing adult literacy in York County. Client services are provided confidentially and free of charge to York County residents

Rhode Island

2225 Literacy Volunteers of America: Rhode Island
Ste 106
260 W Exchange St
Providence, RI 02903

401-861-0815
FAX 401-861-0863
http://www.literacyvolunteers.org
e-mail: lvaricindy@aol.com

Yvette Kenner, Executive Director

The mission of LVA-RI is to advance adult literacy in Rhode Island by: providing training and support services to local LVA-RI affiliates, volunteer tutors and adult literacy services; providing the state with information about adult literacy and with appropriate referral services; collaborating with other organizations to promote adult literacy in Rhode Island.

2226 Literacy Volunteers of Kent County
1672 Flat River Rd
Coventry, RI 02816-8909 401-822-9103
FAX 401-822-9133
http://www.coventrylibrary.org
e-mail: lvkc@coventrylibrary.org
Receive intensive tutor training through a series of workshops that will prepare you to teach one-on-one or in small groups.

2227 Literacy Volunteers of Providence County
P.O.Box 72611
Providence, RI 02907-0611 401-351-0511
http://www.lvari.org
e-mail: chris@lvari.org
Christine Hedenberg, Executive Director

Provides critical support services to local literacy volunteer affiliates, volunteer tutors and adult literacy students; collaborating with organizations to promote adult literacy in Rhode Island; partnering with companies and employers to improve workforce literacy skills; and acting as a state-wide resource for awareness and information about adult literacy, and for adult learner referrals to educational programs.

2228 Literacy Volunteers of South County
1935 Kingstown Rd
Wakefield, RI 02879 401-225-1068
http://www.211ri.org
e-mail: ionag_2002@yahoo.com
David Henley, President

Volunteer-based literacy agent that provides services in Narragansett, North Kingstown and South Kingstown. Provides free, one-on-one tutoring to sdults who request Basic English Skills or English as a Second Language.

2229 Literacy Volunteers of Washington County
93 Tower St
Units 25 & 26
Westerly, RI 02891 401-596-9411
http://www.literacywashingtoncounty.org
e-mail: litwashcty@verizon.net
Ramon Garcia, President
Mary Lou Gentz, Executive Director

Assists adults interested in improving their literacy skills through free programs based on a participant's individual goals.

2230 Literary Resources Rhode Island
Brown University
PO Box 1974
Providence, RI 02912 401-863-1000
FAX 401-863-3094
http://www.brown.edu
e-mail: president@brown.edu
Christina Paxon, President
Heather Goode, Office Assistant

Literacy Resources Rhode Island was established in 1997. Its goals include: expand existing professional capacity within the state's adult education community; increase educator and learner capacity to use and interact with online technology; and assist in improving delivery of services to adult learners, thereby strengthening adult education provision across the state.

2231 Rhode Island Human Resource Investment Council
1511 Pontiac Ave
Building 72-2
Cranston, RI 02920 401-462-8782
FAX 401-462-8865
http://www.rihric.com
e-mail: rbrooks@dlt.ri.gov
Rick Brooks, Executive Director
Maureen Mooney, Office Manager

2232 Rhode Island Vocational and Rehabilitation Agency
40 Fountain St
Providence, RI 02903-1898 401-421-7005
FAX 401-421-9259
TDD:401-421-7016
http://www.ors.ri.gov
e-mail: rcarroll@ors.state.ri.us
Raymond A Carroll, Administrator

Assists people with disabilities to become employed and to live independently in the community. In order to achieve this goal, we work in partnership with the State Rehabilitation Council, our customers, staff and community.

2233 Rhode Island Workforce Literacy Collaborative
260 W Exchange St
Ste 201
Providence, RI 02903-1047 401-861-0815
FAX 401-861-0863
http://www.riwlc.org
Yvette Kenner, Executive Director

A group of non-profit agencies and other companies funded by the Human Resource Investment Council to provide workforce or worksite literacy services to adults in Rhode Island. These services are designed to upgrade the skills of those who are employed or seeking employment, in order to help Rhode Island achieve a high-performance workforce.

South Carolina

2234 Greater Columbia Literacy Council Turning Pages Adult Literacy
4840 Forest Dr
Ste 6-B, PMB 267
Columbia, SC 29206-2412 803-240-2441
FAX 803-782-1210
http://www.literacycolumbia.org
e-mail: literacycolumbia@earthlink.net
Deborah W Yoho, Executive Director

Mission is to enable adults, through customized learning programs, to improve English language and reading skills.

2235 Greenville Literacy Association
225 S Pleasantburg Dr
Ste C-10
Greenville, SC 29607-2533 864-467-3456
FAX 864-467-3558
http://www.greenvilleliteracy.org
e-mail: thomas@greenvilleliteracy.org
Jane Thomas, Executive Director

To empower adults to participate more effectively in the community by providing quality instruction in reading, writing, math and speaking English

2236 Greenwood Literacy Council
PO Box 1467
Greenwood, SC 29648-1467 864-223-1303
FAX 864-223-0475
http://www.gwd50.org
e-mail: kjennings12@gwd50.org
Kathy Jennings, Director

Provides ongoing, comprehensive adult literacy programs in Greenwood, for illiterate adults and their families.

2237 Literacy Volunteers of the Lowcountry
Pro Literacy America
1-B Kittie's Landing Way
Bluffton, SC 29910-3725 843-815-6616
FAX 843-686-6949
http://www.lowcountryliteracy.org
e-mail: nwilliams@lowcountryliteracy.org
Nancy Williams, Executive Director

To increase adult literacy in the greater Beaufort County area by providing leadership, creating awareness, and offering quality instructional services.

2238 Oconee Adult Education

315 Holland Ave
Seneca, SC 29678   864-886-4429
                                   FAX 864-886-4430
                          http://www.oconee.k12.sc.us
                       e-mail: swillis@oconee.k12.sc.us
Steve Williams, Director

To assist adults in becoming literate, to assist adults in the completion of a secondary school education, and to assist adults in improving their knowledge and skills relating to employment and parenting.

2239 South Carolina Adult Literacy Educators

297, Pascallas Street
Blackville, SC 29817   803-284-5605
                                   FAX 803-284-4417
                          http://www.barnwell19.k12.sc.us
Teresa L. Pope, Superintendent

2240 South Carolina Department of Education

1429 Senate St
Columbia, SC 29201-3730   803-734-8500
                                   FAX 803-734-4426
                            http://www.ed.sc.gov
                        e-mail: sc.supfed@ed.sc.gov
Jim Rex, Superintendent

Provides people of all ages and backgrounds who are blind, visually impaired or reading disabled with free books, magazines, and special publications in Braille, Large Print and Audio formats.

2241 South Carolina Literacy Resource Center

1722 Main St.
Suite 104
Columbia, SC 29201   803-929-2563
                                     800-277-7323
                                   FAX 803-929-2571
        http://www2.ed.gov/pubs/TeachersGuide/slrc.html
                          e-mail: SCLRC@aol.com
Peggy May, Director

The mission of the South Carolina Resource Center is to provide leadership in literacy to South Carolina's adults and their families, in conjunction with state and local public and private nonprofit efforts. The Center serves as a site for training for adult literacy providers, as a reciprocal link with the National Institute for Literacy for the purpose of sharing information to service providers, and as a clearinghouse for state-of-the-art literacy materials and technology.

2242 Trident Literacy Association

5416-B Rivers Ave
North Charleston, SC 29406   843-747-2223
                                   FAX 843-744-2970
                          http://www.tridentlit.org
                       e-mail: echepenik@tridentlit.org
Eileen Chepenik, Executive Director

To increase literacy in Charleston, Berkeley, and Dorchester counties by offering instruction, using a self-paced, individualized curriculum in reading, writing, mathematics, English as a second language, GED preparation, and basic computer use.

South Dakota

2243 Adult Education and Literacy Program

South Dakota Department of Labor
Kneip Bldg
700 Governors Dr
Pierre, SD 57501   605-773-3101
                                   FAX 605-773-6185
                            http://www.state.sd.us
                       e-mail: marcia.hess@state.sd.us
Marcia Hess, State Administrator

Adult Education & Literacy instruction is designed to teach persons 16 years of age or older to read and write English and to substantially raise their educational level. The purpose of the program is to expand the educational opportunities for adults and to establish programs that will enable all adults to acquire basic skills necessary to function in society and allow them to continue their education to at least the level of completion of secondary school.

2244 South Dakota Literacy Council

816 Samara Ave
Volga, SD 57071   605-627-5138
                                   FAX 605-627-5138
                            http://www.readsd.org
                     e-mail: jberglund@blackhills.com
John Berglund, President

Goal is to help people receive educational help in a confidential setting.

2245 South Dakota Literacy Resource Center

700 Governors Drive
Pierre, SD 57501   605-773-3101
                                     800-423-6665
                                   FAX 605-773-6184
        http://wdcrobcolp01.ed.gov/programs/EROD
                       e-mail: marcia.hess@state.sd.us
Marcia Hess, State Administrator

The mission of the SD Literary Resource Center is to establish a state wide on-line computer catalog of all existing literacy materials within South Dakota and a South Dakota Literacy Resource Center home page with links to other literacy sites within South Dakota, regionally and nationally.

Tennessee

2246 Adult Education Foundation of Blount County

1500 Jett Rd
Maryville, TN 37804-3359   865-982-8998
                                   FAX 865-983-8848
        http://www.blountk12.org/adult_ed/index.htm
                     e-mail: blountliteracy@gmail.com
Carol Ergenbright, Coordinator

Serving as an advocate for adult literacy by partnering with Adult Education programs and staff; promoting community involvement and providing assistance with funding.

2247 Center for Literary Studies

University of Tennessee
600 Henley St
Ste 312
Knoxville, TN 37996-0001   865-974-4109
                                   FAX 865-974-3857
                            http://www.cls.utk.edu
Geri Mulligan, Director

To support and advance literacy education across the lifespan. Works with providers of literacy edcuation to strengthen their capacity to help individuals build knowledge and improve skills needed to be life-long learners and active members of families, communities, and workplaces.

229

2248 Claiborne County Adult Reading Experience
Claiborne County Schools
PO Box 179
1403 Tazewell Rd
Tazewell, TN 37879   423-626-2273
                                               FAX 423-626-5945
                   http://www.claibornecountyschools.com
                   e-mail: swilliams3@k12tn.net
Sandra Williams, Supervisor
Donna Lewis, Program Coordinator

2249 Collierville Literacy Council
167 Washington St
Collierville, TN 38017-2697   901-854-0288
                   http://www.colliervilleliteracy.org
                   e-mail: colliervilleliteracy@earthlink.net
A non-profit organization dedicated to providing opportunities for adults to attain educational goals that enhance individual growth and benefit families, the work place and the community.

2250 Learning Center for Adults and Families
833 N Ocoee St
Cleveland, TN 37311-2254   423-478-1117
                                               FAX 423-478-1153
                   http://www.learningcenter.ws
                   e-mail: clewis@learningcenter.ws
Candace Lewis, Executive Director

2251 Literacy Council of Kingsport
326 Commerce St
Kingsport, TN 37660-4321   423-392-4643
                   http://www.literacycouncilofkingsport.org
                   e-mail: ltrcy@yahoo.com
Nada Weekley, Executive Director
Pat Mattingly, Program/Volunteer Coordinator

A non-profit organization dedicated to serving citizens in Kingsport and Sullivan County. Offers free, one-on-one tutoring for adults and qualified children who want to learn to read or to improve their reading skills.

2252 Literacy Council of Sumner County
260 W Main St
Hendersonville, TN 37075   615-822-8112
                                               FAX 615-822-3665
                   http://www.literacysumner.org
                   e-mail: info@literacysumner.org
Margie Anderson, Director

To provide resources, counseling, and tutoring to children, youth, and adults to enhance their skills in all academic areas.

2253 Literacy Mid-South
902 S Cooper St
Memphis, TN 38104-5603   901-327-6000
                                               FAX 901-458-4969
                   http://www.literacymidsouth.org

2254 Nashville Adult Literacy Council
Cohn Adult Learning Center
4805 Park Ave
Rm 211
Nashville, TN 37209   615-298-8060
                                               FAX 615-298-8444
                   http://www.nashvilleliteracy.org
                   e-mail: mnugent@nashvilleliteracy.org
Meg Nugent, Director

Teaches reading to U.S.-born adults and English skills to adult immigrants.

2255 Read To Succeed
PO Box 12161
Murfreesboro, TN 37129   615-738-7323
                   http://www.readtosucceed.org
Ronni Shaw, Executive Director

The community literacy collaborative in Rutherford County, will promote reading, with an emphasis on family literacy. This non-profit initiative supports literacy programs and fosters awareness of the importance of reading.

2256 Tennessee Department of Education
710 James Robertson Parkway
Andrew Johnson Tower, 6th Floor
Nashville, TN 37243-0382   615-741-2731
                                                     800-531-1515
                   http://www.state.tn.us
                   e-mail: education.comments@tn.gov
Timothy K Webb, Commissioner

Mission is to take Tennessee to the top in education. Guides administration of the state's K-12 public schools.

2257 Tennessee School-to-Work Office
14th Floor, Citizens Plaza State Of
400 Deaderick Street
Nashville, TN 37243   615-313-4981
                   http://www.state.tn.us
                   e-mail: maryjane.ware@tn.gov
Bill Haslam, Governor

Texas

2258 Commerce Library Literacy Program
1210 Park Street
Commerce, TX 75428   903-886-6858
                                               FAX 903-886-7239
                   http://www.reocities.com/Athens/academy/6919/cl
                   e-mail: commerce@koyote.com
Pricilla Donovan, Director

2259 Greater Orange Area Literacy Services
PO Box 221
520 W Decatur Ave
Orange, TX 77631   409-886-4311
                                               FAX 409-886-0149
                   e-mail: goalsliteracy@sbcglobal.net
Sharon LeBlanc, Executive Director

Adult literacy program

2260 Irving Public Library Literacy Program
825 W Irving Blvd
Irving, TX 75060   972-721-2691
                   http://cityofirving.org
                   e-mail: tbearden@cityofirving.org
Tracy Bearden, Manager

Promotes literacy among people of all ages.

2261 Literacy Austin
2222 Rosewood Ave
Austin, TX 78702   512-478-7323
                                               FAX 512-479-7323
                                               TDD:512-478-7323
                   http://www.literacyaustin.org
                   e-mail: info@literacyaustin.org
Gail Harmon, Program Director
Melinda Mitchiner, Program Services Coordinator

Mission is to provide instruction for basic literacy and English as a Second Language (ESL) to adults, age 17 and older, who read below the fifth-grade leve. Vision is to improve the quality of an adult's life through improved literacy skills.

2262 Literacy Center of Marshall: Harrison County
PO Box 148
Marshall, TX 75671   903-935-0962
http://www.marshallliteracy.org
e-mail: kdeluca23@gmail.com
Karla DeLuca, Executive Director

2263 Literacy Volunteers of America: Bastrop
1201 Church St
Bastrop, TX 78602-2909   512-321-6686
http://www.main.org/lva-bastrop/
e-mail: suemunster@aol.com
Sue Steinbring, Director

Provides literacy training and pre-GED for students, English as a Second Language, tutoring and tutor training.

2264 Literacy Volunteers of America: Bay City Matagorda County
PO Box 1596
Bay City, TX 77404-1596   979-244-9544
FAX 979-244-9566
http://www.literacymc.org
e-mail: lva_mc@yahoo.com
Linda Brown, Director

Promotes literacy for people of all ages.

2265 Literacy Volunteers of America: Laredo
P 10 Fort McIntosh
LCC Main Campus
Laredo, TX 78040   956-724-5207
FAX 956-725-4253
http://www.lvalaredo.org
e-mail: lvlaredo@grandecom.net
Doroteo Sandoval, Executive Director

Promotes literacy for people of all ages.

2266 Literacy Volunteers of America: Montgomery County
PO Box 2704
Conroe, TX 77305-2704   936-494-0635
888-878-9400
http://lvamc.org
e-mail: literacymc@yahoo.com
Linda Ricketts, Director

As part of the national literacy organization, combats illiteracy in Montgomery County through volunteer tutoring.

2267 Literacy Volunteers of America: Port Arthur Literacy Support
4615 9th Ave
Port Arthur, TX 77642   409-985-8838
FAX 409-985-5969
http://www.pap.lib.tx.us
e-mail: jmartine@pap.lib.tx.us
Jose Martinez, Director
Marilyn Moseley, Administrative Secretary

A library based umbrella group which works with three primary programs: ono-on-one tutoring for those who cannot read or read at a very low level; GED Computer Lab assistance for adults who are striving to get their General Equivalency Diploma - in cooperation with Port Arthur Independent School District; and English-as-a-Second Language (ESL) in cooperation with the Port Arthur Independent School District.

2268 Literacy Volunteers of America: Wimberley Area
PO Box 135
Wimberley, TX 78701   512-847-8953
FAX 701-254-4313
http://www.wimberley.org
e-mail: trailsend@anvilcom.com

Linda Mueller, Director

Nonprofit, volunteer organization which exists to improve the reading, writing, speaking, cultural and life skills of adults reading at or below the sixth grade level and/or those for whom English is not their native language. Provides GED instruction. All services are free.

2269 Texas Families and Literacy
1006 C.
Junction Hwy
Kerrville, TX 78028   830-896-8787
FAX 830-896-3639
http://www.familiesandliteracy.org
e-mail: famandlit1@hctc.net
Mike Hunter, Executive Director
Paula Wilson, Operations Coordinator
Kathy Wike, Administrative Assistant

2270 Texas Family Literacy Center
EDU Room 2112
601 University Drive
San Marcos, TX 78666   512-245-9600
FAX 512-245-8151
http://www.tei.education.txstate.edu/famlit
e-mail: yr01@txstate.edu
Ysabel Ramirez, Grant Directror
Gloria Rodriguez, Grant Secretary

Mission is to strengthen family literacy programs and enhance the knowledge skills, instructional practices and resources available to family literacy educators statewide.

2271 Victoria Adult Literacy
802 E Crestwood Dr
Victoria, TX 77901   361-582-4273
FAX 361-582-4348
http://www.victorialiteracycouncil.org
e-mail: valcsm@yahoo.com
Stacey Milberger, Executive Director
Donna Bentley, Development Coordinator

2272 Weslaco Public Library
525 S Kansas Ave
Weslaco, TX 78596   956-968-4533
FAX 956-969-8922
http://www.weslaco.lib.tx.us
e-mail: webmaster@weslaco.lib.tx.us
Michael Fisher, Executive Director

Utah

2273 Bridgerland Literacy
255 N Main St
Logan, UT 84321   435-716-9141
http://www.bridgerlandliteracy.org
e-mail: danielle.bird@loganutah.org
Danielle Bird, Director

2274 Project Read
550 N University Avenue
Suite 215
Provo, UT 84601   801-852-6654
FAX 801-852-7663
http://www.project-read.com
e-mail: projectreadutah@gmail.com
Shauna K Brown, Director
Chelsea Hansen, Program Coordinator

Seeks to prevent and alleviate adult illiteracy in Utah County. Provides one-on-one tutoring services to help improve reading and writing skills sufficiently to meet personal goals, function well in society, and become more productive citizens.

2275 Utah Literacy Action Center
3595 S Main St
Salt Lake City, UT 84115-4434   801-265-9081
                                    FAX 801-265-9643
                            http://www.literacyactioncenter.org
                               e-mail: lac@netutah.net
Deborah Young, Executive Director

Transforms English-speaking adults, who enter the program
with limited reading, writing, or math skills, into skilled,
passionate, habitual, critical readers, writers, and mathema-
ticians.

Vermont

**2276 ABE Career and Lifelong Learning: Vermont Depart-
ment of Education**
120 State St
Montpelier, VT 05620-2501   802-828-3135
                                    FAX 802-828-3146
                    http://women.vermont.gov/resource-directory/edu
                            e-mail: srobinson@doe.state.vt.us
Sandra Robinson, Director

Promotes quality education.

2277 Central Vermont Adult Basic Education
46 Washington St
Ste 100
Barre, VT 05641   802-476-4588
                                    FAX 802-476-5860
                            http://www.cvabe.org
                               e-mail: info@cvabe.org
Provides free adult education and literacy instruction for
adults, out of school youth, and immigrants and refugees in
the belief that a person who is literate has the essential key
for self understanding and for full and active membership in
the world.

2278 Tutorial Center
208 Pleasant St
Bennington, VT 05201-2526   802-447-0111
                                    FAX 802-447-7607
                            http://tutoringvermont.org
Jack Glade, Executive Director

Provides tutoring to improve success for 200 children; prevents 20 teenagers at risk of dropping out from doing so;
helps 80 high school dropouts to earn a high school diploma
or GED; builds literacy skills of 400 adults; helps 20 adults
transition into college or post-secondary career paths; and
transforms 50 computer-illiterate adults into competent
computer users.

**2279 Vermont Assistive Technology Project: Dept of Aging
and Disabilities**
103 S Main St
Weeks Bldg
Waterbury, VT 05671-2305   802-241-2620
                                   800-750-6355
                                   FAX 802-241-2174
                                   TTY: 802-241-1464
                            http://dail.vermont.gov
                        e-mail: julie.tucker@ahs.state.vt.us
Julie L Tucker, Program Director

Provides information and referrals, training for service providers and others, equipment and software demonstrations,
tryouts, and technical assistance.

2280 Vermont Division of Vocational Rehabilitation
VocRehab Of Vermont
103 S Main Street
Weeks 1A Building
Waterbury, VT 05671-2303
                                    866-879-6757
                            TTY: 802-241-1455
                        http://www.vocrehab.vermont.gov
                        e-mail: jana.sherman@ahs.state.vt.us
Diane Dalmasse, Director of VocRehab Division

VocRehab's mission is to assist Vermonters with disabilities, find and maintain meaningful employment in their communities. VocRehab Vermont works in close partnership
with the Vermont Association of Business, Industry and Rehabilitation.   Contact local VocRehab office for
information about services.

2281 Vermont Literacy Resource Center: Dept of Education
120 State St
Montpelier, VT 05602-2703   802-828-5148
                                    FAX 802-828-0573
                            http://www.state.vt.us
                               e-mail: wross@doe.state.vt.us
Wendy Ross, Director

The Vermont Literacy Resource Center links Vermont to national, regional, and state literacy organizations, provides
staff development and serves as a clearinghouse for the literacy community. The Vermont Literacy Resource Center is
located at the Vermont Department of Education.

Virginia

2282 Adult Learning Center
4160 Virginia Beach Blvd
Virginia Beach, VA 23452   757-648-6050
                                   FAX 757-306-0999
                        http://www.adultlearning.vbschools.com
                            e-mail: alchs@vbschools.com
Bonnie C Mizenko, Director

To respond to the needs of the adult population by offering a
comprehensive educational program to the community.

2283 Charlotte County Literacy Program
395 Thomas Jefferson Hwy
Suite B
Charlotte Court House, VA 23923   434-542-5782
                        http://www.charlotte-learning.org/
                            e-mail: charlit@pure.net
Tonya Pulliam, Director

Offers basic and family literacy programs, ESL and computer, parenting and work skills.

2284 Citizens for Adult Literacy & Learning
PO Box 123
Monroe, VA 24574   434-929-2630
                            http://www.callamherst.org
                        e-mail: marcia.swain@callamherst.org
Marcia Swain, Program Coordinator

Aim is to help adults improve their quality of life by mastering basic reading, writing and math skills.

2285 Eastern Shore Literacy Council
36282 Lankford Hwy
Suite 13-D
Belle Haven, VA 23306   757-442-6637
                                      FAX 757-442-6517
                            http://www.shoreliteracy.org
                               e-mail: esliteracy@verizon.net

Janet Booth, Director
Laura Chuquin-Naylor, Program Coordinator

Providing literacy tutoring without charge to adult residents of the Eastern Shore so they may acquire the skills needed to improve their participaption in society and enrich their lives.

2286 Highlands Educational Literacy Program
13168 Meadowview Square
Meadowview, VA
376-944-5144
FAX 276-676-0677
http://www.helpliteracyofwc.org
e-mail: helplit2@gmail.com
Christy Hicks, Chairperson

To provide basic literacy instruction for adults in Washington County, changing lives one word at a time.

2287 Literacy Council of Northern Virginia
2855 Annandale Rd
Falls Church, VA 22042
703-237-0866
FAX 703-237-2863
http://www.lcnv.org
e-mail: info@lcnv.org
Patricia Donnelly, Executive Director

To teach adults the basic skills of reading, writing, speaking and understanding English in order to empower them to participate more fully and confidently in their communities.

2288 Literacy Volunteers of America: Nelson County
PO Box 422
Lovingston, VA 22949
434-996-0485
http://www.nelsoncountyliteracy.org
e-mail: nanamump@aol.com
Charles Strauss, Director

2289 Literacy Volunteers of America: New River Valley
195 W Main St
Christiansburg, VA 24073
540-382-7262
FAX 540-382-7262
http://www.lvnrv.org/
e-mail: lvnrv@verizon.net
Nia Indelicato, Executive Director
Dr. Toni Cox, President

The empowerment of every adult in the New River Valley through the provision of opportunities to achieve independence through literacy.

2290 Literacy Volunteers of America: Prince William
4326 Dale Blvd
Ste 2
Woodbridge, VA 22193
703-670-5702
FAX 703-583-0703
http://www.lvapw.org
e-mail: lvapw@aol.com
Kim Sells, Executive Director

Mission is to teach adults to read. Takes volunteers from the community, train them to be tutors and then match them with adults with low literacy skills. Provides the professional training, materials, and support that enable the volunteers to be effective tutors.

2291 Literacy Volunteers of America: Shenandoah County
PO Box 303
Woodstock, VA 22664
540-459-2446
http://www.lv-sc.org
e-mail: pagould@adelphia.net
Paula Gould, Director

2292 Literacy Volunteers of Charlottesville/Albemarle
418 7th St NE
PO Box 1156
Charlottesville, VA 22902
434-977-3838
http://literacyforall.org
e-mail: info@literacyforall.org

Jackie Bright, Executive Director

Provides one-on-one, confidential tutoring in basic literacy and English as a second language to adults living ot working in Charlottesville and Albemarle County.

2293 Literacy Volunteers of Roanoke Valley
706 S Jefferson St
Roanoke, VA 24016-5104
540-265-9339
877-582-7323
FAX 540-265-4814
http://www.lvarv.org
e-mail: info@lvarv.org
Annette Loschert, Executive Director

To teach English literacy skills to adults and to raise literacy awareness throughout the Roanoke Valley.

2294 Literacy Volunteers: Campbell County Public Library
PO Box 310
Rustburg, VA 24588-0310
434-332-9561
FAX 434-332-9697
http://www.campbellcountylibraries.org
e-mail: lpwheeler@co.campbell.va.us
Nan Carmack, Program Manager

Provides free, confidential instruction for adults who live or work in Campbell COunty, VA. Adult Basic Education and English for Speakers of other languages.

2295 Loudoun Literacy Council
P.O.Box 1932
Leesburg, VA 20177-1932
703-777-2205
FAX 703-777-7260
http://www.loudounliteracy.org
e-mail: info@loudounliteracy.org
Candace Olin Kroehl, Executive Director

A community-based, nonprofit, educational organization dedicated to improving literacy throughout Loudoun County. Recruit and train volunteers to teach adults, both native-speakers and speakers of other languages, to read, speak, write and understand English. Also provides early literacy enrichment for at-risk preschool children and children who reside in local homeless shelters, while supporting their parents as their child's first teacher.

2296 READ Center Reading & Education for Adult Development
2000 Bremo Rd
Ste 102
Richmond, VA 23226
804-288-9930
FAX 804-288-9915
http://www.readcenter.org
e-mail: read@readcenter.org
Helps low-level reading adults develop basic reading and communication skills through one-to-one tutoring so they can fulfill their goals and their roles as citizens, workers and family members.

2297 Skyline Literacy Coalition
975 S High St
Harrisonburg, VA 22801-1636
540-433-0505
FAX 540-879-2517
http://skylineliteracy.org
e-mail: skylitlee@comcast.net
Lee Smith Osina, Executive Director

A nonprofit organization dedicated to promoting learning and literacy throughout the Shenandoah Valley.

2298 Virginia Adult Learning Resource Center

3600 W Broad St, Ste 669
PO Box 842037
Richmond, VA 23230-4930   804-828-6521
                                 800-237-0178
                                 FAX 804-828-7539
                                 http://www.valrc.org
                                 e-mail: vdesk@vcu.edu

Barbara Gibson, Manager

To equip the field of adult education and literacy with essential skills and resources by delivering innovative and effective training, publications, curriculum design, and prgram development.

2299 Virginia Council of Administrators of Special Education

1110 N Glebe Rd
Ste 300
Arlington, VA 22201-5704   703-264-9454
                                  800-224-6830
                                  FAX 703-264-9494
                                  http://www.vcase.org
                                  e-mail: marylwall@aol.com

Marylou Wall, Manager

A professional organization that promotes professional leadership through the provision of collegial support and current information on recommended instructional practices as well as local, state and national trends in Special Education for professionals who serve students with disabilities in order to improve the quality and delivery of special education services in Virginia's public schools.

2300 Virginia Literacy Foundation

413 Stuart Circle
Executive Suite 303
Richmond, VA 23220   804-237-8909
                                 FAX 804-237-8901
                                 http://www.virginialiteracy.org
                                 e-mail: contact@virginialiteracy.org

Mark E Emblidge PhD, Executive Director

Provides funding and technical cupport to private, volunteer literacy organizations throughout Virginia via challenge grants, training and direct consulting.

Washington

2301 Division of Vocational Rehabilitation

PO Box 45340
Olympia, WA 98504-5340   360-725-3636
                                 800-367-5621
                                 FAX 360-407-8007
                                 http://www.dshs.wa.gov

Serves people with disabilities who want to work but face a substantial barrier to finding or keeping a job. Provides individualized employment services and counseling to people with disabilites and also provides technical assistance and training to employers about the employment of people with disabilities.

2302 Literacy Council of Kitsap

612 5th St
Bremerton, WA 98337-1416   360-373-1539
                                 FAX 360-373-6859
                                 http://www.kitsapliteracy.org
                                 e-mail: info@kitsapliteracy.org

Olga Fedorovski, Executive Director

Dedicated to Adult Basic Education (ABE) and GED testing preparation, along with English as a Second Language. Promote and provide literacy services to the residents of Kitsap County.

2303 Literacy Council of Seattle

8500 14th Ave NW
Crown Hill UMC
Seattle, WA 98117   206-233-9720
                                 http://www.literacyseattle.org
                                 e-mail: info@literacyseattle.org

Sharon S Victor, President

Volunteers teach adults the English skills they need to be successful in their jobs, families, and the community.

2304 Literacy Source: Community Learning Center

720 N 35th St
Seattle, WA 98103   206-782-2050
                                 FAX 206-781-2583
                                 http://www.literacy-source.org
                                 e-mail: info@literacy-source.org

Anne Helmholz, Executive Director

Builds a literate community and promote self-sufficiency by providing learner-centered instruction to adults in English literacy and basic life skills.

2305 Mason County Literacy Council

133 W Railroad Ave
PO 2529
Shelton, WA 98584   360-426-9733
                                 FAX 360-426-9789
                                 http://www.masoncountyliteracy.org

Kris Smock, Executive Director

Provides free instruction to adults to improve reading, writing and math skills, study for a GED, or learn English as a second language.

2306 St. James ESL Program

St. James Cathedral
804 9th Ave
Seattle, WA 98104-1265   206-382-4511
                                 FAX 206-622-5303
                                 http://www.stjames-cathedral.org
                                 e-mail: esl@stjames-catherdral.org

Chris Koehler, Director

Helping adult refugees and immigrants learn English and become U.S. citizens.

2307 Whatcom Literacy Council

PO Box 1292
220 Elm St
Bellingham, WA 98225   360-647-3264
                                 FAX 360-752-6770
                                 http://www.whatcomliteracy.org
                                 e-mail: gina@whatcomliteracy.org

Gina Barrieau-Gonzales, Interim Executive Director

Helping adults in Whatcom County improve their literacy skills or learn to use English as a second language. Through customized, individual tutoring, students learn critical skills needed to become self-sufficient.

West Virginia

2308 Division of Technical & Adult Education Services: West Virginia

1900 Kanawha Blvd E
Charleston, WV 25305   304-558-2000
                                 FAX 304-342-7025
                                 http://careertech.k12.wv.us
                                 e-mail: gparsons@access.k12.wv.us

Kathy D'Antoni EdD, Asst State Superintendent
Gigi Parsons, Division Secretary

Better prepare students for the world of work and higher education through education programs and training offered at the career and technical education sites throughout the state.

2309 W Virginia Regional Education Services

501 22nd St
Dunbar, WV 25064-1711   304-766-7655
                                       800-642-2670
                                       FAX 304-766-2824
Chuck Nichols, Executive Director

Offers services for literacy and adult basic education including literacy hotline, networks newsletter, resources for English as a second language, beginning literacy, learning disabilities and other special learning needs.

2310 West Virginia Department of Education

1900 Kanawha Blvd E
Bldg 6, Rm 351
Charleston, WV 25305-0330   304-558-3660
                                       800-642-2670
                                       FAX 304-558-0198
                                       http://wvde.state.wv.us

Wisconsin

2311 ADVOCAP Literacy Services

W911 State Highway 44
Markesan, WI 53946   920-398-3907
                                       800-631-6617
                                       FAX 920-398-2103
                                       http://www.advocap.org
                                       e-mail: mikeb@advocap.org
Michael Bonertz, Executive Director

2312 Fox Valley Literacy Coalition

103 E Washington St
Appleton, WI 54911   920-991-9840
                                       FAX 920-991-1012
                                       http://wwwfvlc.net
                                       e-mail: foxvalleylit@tds.net
Christine Cheevers, Executive Director

Provides English literacy education to adults with the help of trained volunteers. To improve people's lives and build community by providing and coordinating literacy services.

2313 Jefferson County Literacy Council

112 S Main St
Jefferson, WI 53549   920-675-0500
                                       FAX 920-675-0510
                                       http://www.jclc.us
                                       e-mail: jottow@jclc.us
Jill Ottow, Executive Director

Committed to building communities that are strong in literacy, language and cultural understandings through information and resource sharing, referral, assessment and instructional services.

2314 Literacy Council of Greater Waukesha

217 Wisconsin Ave
Ste 16
Waukesha, WI 53186   262-547-7323
                                       http://www.waukeshaliteracy.org
                                       e-mail: drunning@waukeshaliteracy.org
Debra Running, Executive Director

Provides, confidential, one-on-one tutoring and mentoring services to individuals who need help with reading, writing, spelling, math and English as a second language.

2315 Literacy Network

1118 S Park St
Madison, WI 53715-1755   608-244-3911
                                       FAX 608-244-3899
                                       http://www.madisonarealiteracy.org
                                       e-mail: info@litnetwork.org

Jeff Burkhart, Executive Director

Teaches reading, writing, and speaking skills to Dane County adults and families so they can achieve financial independence, good health and greater involvement in the community.

2316 Literacy Services of Wisconsin

2724 W Wells St
Milwaukee, WI 53208-3597   414-344-5878
                                       FAX 414-344-1061
                                       http://www.literacyservices.org
                                       e-mail: india@literacyservices.org
India McCanse, Executive Director

Provides literacy education motivated adults through the efforts of dedicated volunteers, the support of th ecommunity and the use of specialized curriculum to meet the individual and community needs.

2317 Literacy Volunteers of America: Chippewa Valley

770 Scheidler Rd
Chippewa Falls, WI 54729   715-738-3857
                                       FAX 715-967-2445
                                       http://www.lvcv.org
A community-based literacy program that trains and supports volunteers to educate adults and their families, helping them acquire the skills necessary to achieve economic self-sufficiency and function effectively in their roles as citizens, workers, and family members.

2318 Literacy Volunteers of America: Eau Claire

800 Wisconsin St #70
Bldg D02, Ste 301
Eau Claire, WI 54703   715-834-0222
                                       FAX 715-834-2546
                                       http://www.lvcv.org
A community-based literacy program that trains and supports volunteers to educate adults and their families, helping them acquire the skills necessary to achieve economic self-sufficiency and function effectively in their roles as citizens, workers, and family members.

2319 Literacy Volunteers of America: Marquette County

PO Box 671
Montello, WI 53949-0671   608-297-8900
                                       FAX 608-297-2673
                                       e-mail: literacyvmc@yahoo.com
Vicki Huffman, Treasurer

Promotes literacy for people of all ages.

2320 Marathon County Literacy Council

300 1st St
Wausau, WI 54403   715-261-7292
                                       FAX 715-261-7232
                                       http://wvls.lib.wi.us
                                       e-mail: info@mcliteracy.us
A nonprofit organization dedicated to improving literacy throughout Marathon County. Offers tutoring services for all Marathon County adults in need of assistance.

2321 Milwaukee Achiever Literacy Services

5566 N 69th St
Milwaukee, WI 53218   414-463-7389
                                       http://milwaukeeachiever.org
Peg Palmer, Executive Director

Provides education, life skills training and workforce development instruction for adult learners in an atmosphere of mutual acceptance and respect.

2322 Racine Literacy Council

734 Lake Ave
Racine, WI 53403   262-632-9495
                                       FAX 262-632-9502
                                       http://www.racineliteracy.com
                                       e-mail: kgregor@racineliteracy.com

Kay Gregor, Executive Director

A volunteer-based organization whose mission is to provide adult literacy programs in Racine County and to bring awareness to the community about the importance and impact of literacy.

2323   Walworth County Literacy Council
1000 E Centralia St
Elkhorn, WI 53121   262-957-0142
                                      FAX 262-741-5275
                    http://www.walworthcoliteracy.com
                 e-mail: wclc@walworthcoliteracy.com
Abby Baker, Coordinator

Provides student-centered instruction in basic literacy skills and English as a second language. Promotes awareness of literacy issues and seeks support from the community to develop literacy programs.

2324   Winnebago County Literacy Council
106 Washington Ave
Oshkosh, WI 54901-4985   920-236-5185
                                      FAX 920-236-5227
                            http://www.winlit.org
                       e-mail: traska@winlit.org
Susan Traska, Executive Director

To increase literacy skills of adults and families so they can make informed decisions in order to function effectively in society.

2325   Wisconsin Literacy Resource Center
211 S Paterson St
Ste 310
Madison, WI 53703   608-257-1655
                                      FAX 608-661-0208
                    http://www.wisconsinliteracy.orgs
                 e-mail: info@wisconsinliteracy.org
Michele Erikson, Executive Director

A statewide agency that was formed as a coalition of adult, family and workplace literacy providers for the purpose of supporting one another through resource development, information and referrals, training and advocacy.

Wyoming

2326   Teton Literacy Program
1715 High School Rd, Ste 260
PO Box 465
Jackson, WY 83001   307-733-9242
                                      FAX 307-733-9086
                          http://www.tetonliteracy.org
                 e-mail: info@tetonliteracy.org
Valley Peters-Bradley, Interim Executive Director

Serves Teton County with educational resources to better reading, writing, and language skills of the diverse community.

Adults

2327

A Mind At A Time
Simon & Schuster
1230 Avenue of the Americas
New York, NY 10020-1513   212-698-7000
http://www.simonandschuster.biz
e-mail: shop.feedback@simonsays.com
Melvin Levine, Author

Written by Melvin Levine, and published in 2003. It shows parents and others how to identify the individual learning patterns, explaining how to strenghten a child's abilities and either bypasss or overcome the child's weakness, producing positive results instead of reapeated frustration and failure. *$15.00*
352 pages
ISBN 0-743202-23-6

2328

A Miracle to Believe In
Option Indigo Press
2080 S Undermountain Rd
Sheffield, MA 01257-9643   413-229-8727
800-562-7171
FAX 413-229-8727
http://www.optionindigo.com
e-mail: indigo@bcn.net
Barry Kausman, Author

A group of people from all walks of life come together and are transformed as they reach out, under the direction of Kaufman, to help a little boy the medical world had given up as hopeless. This heartwarming journey of loving a child back to life will not only inspire, but presents a compelling new way to deal with life's traumas and difficulties. *$7.99*
388 pages Yearly

2329

All Kinds of Minds: Young Student's Book About Learning Disabilities & Disorders
Educators Publishing Service
PO Box 9031
Cambridge, MA 02139-9031   617-547-6706
800-225-5750
FAX 888-440-2665
http://eps.schoolspecialty.com/
e-mail: CustomerService.EPS@schoolspecialty.com
Melvin Levine, Author

Written by Melvin Levine, and published in 1992. Helps children with learning disabilities to come to terms with it. Shows them how to get around or just work out any problems with their disabilities.
283 pages paperback
ISBN 0-838820-90-5

2330

Closer Look: Perspectives & Reflections on College Students with LD
Curry College Bookstore
1071 Blue Hill Ave
Milton, MA 02186-2302   617-333-0500
FAX 617-333-6860
http://www.curry.edu
e-mail: dgoss@curry.edu
Diane Goss, Editor/Author
Jane Adelizzi, Co-Author

This book is a collection of personal accounts by teachers and learners. It's a sensitive portrayal of the real world of teaching and learning, particularly as it impacts on those with learning differences. Topics include connections between theory and practice, emotions and learning disabilities, classroom trauma, learning disabilities and social deficits, metacognitive development, ESL and learning disabilities, models for inclusion and practical strategies. *$24.95*
241 pages paperback
ISBN 0-964975-20-3

2331

Diverse Learners in the Mainstream Classroom: Strategies for Supporting ALL Students Across Areas
Heinemann
PO Box 6926
Portsmouth, NH 03802-6926   800-225-5800
800-541-2086
FAX 877-231-6980
http://www.heinemann.com
e-mail: custserv@heinemann.com
Yvonne S Freeman, Author
Davide E Freeman, Co-Author
Reynaldo Ramirez, Co-Author
A comprehensive book offering strategies and practices teachers can use from PreK-through high school. Provides everything from the big picture to the everyday details teachers want. *$27.00*
272 pages
ISBN 0-325013-13-8

2332

Dyslexia in Adults: Taking Charge of Your Life
Taylor Publishing
7211 Circle S Road
Austin, TX 78745   512-444-0571
800-225-3687
FAX 512-440-2160
http://www.balfour.com
Kathleen Nosek, Author

Adult dyslexics are experts at hiding reading, writing, and spelling difficulties long after high school. Dyslexia in Adults is a perfect guidebook for adult dyslexias to use in coping with day-to-day problems that are complicated by their learning disability. *$12.95*
206 pages Paperback
ISBN 0-878339-48-5

2333

Faking It: A Look into the Mind of a Creative Learner
Heinemann
PO Box 6926
Portsmouth, NH 03802-6926   800-225-5800
800-541-2086
FAX 877-231-6980
http://www.heinemann.com
e-mail: custserv@heinemann.com
Christopher Lee, Author
Rosemary Jackson, Co-Author

Engage in professional dialog with Heinemann's celebrated authors and colleagues! *$17.95*
200 pages paperback
ISBN 0-867092-96-3

2334

From Disability to Possibility: The Powerof Inclusive Classrooms
Heinemann
PO Box 6926
Portsmouth, NH 03802-6926   800-225-5800
800-541-2086
FAX 877-231-6980
http://www.heinemann.com
e-mail: custserv@heinemann.com
Patrick Schwarz, Author

Offers a meaningful, practical and doable alternative to traditional special education practice both during the school years and after. *$15.00*
112 pages
ISBN 0-325009-93-3

2335

How to Get Services by Being Assertive
Family Resource Center on Disabilities
Room 300
20 E Jackson Blvd
Chicago, IL 60604-2265   312-939-3513
800-952-4199
FAX 312-854-8980
TDD:312-939-3519
http://www.frcd.org
e-mail: info@frcd.org

Charlotte Jardins, Executive Director
Myra Christian, Contact
Gloria Mikucki, Contact
A 100 page manual that demonstrates positive assertiveness techniques. Price includes postage and handling. *$12.00*
  100 pages

2336 Inclusion-Classroom Problem Solver; Structures and Supports to Serve ALL Learners
Heinemann
PO Box 6926
Portsmouth, NH 03802-6926   800-225-5800
                                    800-541-2086
                               FAX 877-231-6980
                          http://www.heinemann.com
                    e-mail: custserv@heinemann.com
Constance McGrath, Author

Provides proven ways to create a classroom that replaces frustrating temporary accommodations with and inclusive, joyous environment designed to work for every student. *$17.50*
  144 pages
  ISBN 0-325012-70-4

2337 Kids Behind the Label: An Inside at ADHD for Classroom Teachers
Heinemann
PO Box 6926
Portsmouth, NH 03802-6926   800-225-5800
                                    800-541-2086
                               FAX 877-231-6980
                          http://www.heinemann.com
                    e-mail: custserv@heinemann.com
Trudy Knowles, Author

Students with Attention-Deficit/Hyperactivity Disorder (ADHD) tell you what they experience coming to class each day. Their descriptions will forever change how you approach ADHD students, allowing you to contrast their frustrating in-school behavior with the frustration they feel trying to complete their work and make sense of their world. *$18.50*
  160 pages
  ISBN 0-325009-67-4

2338 Myth of Laziness
Simon & Schuster
1230 Avenue of the Americas
New York, NY 10020-1513   212-698-7000
                         http://www.simonandschuster.biz
                    e-mail: shop.feedback@simonsays.com
Melvin Levine, Author

Written by Melvin Levine and published in 2003. It shows parents how to nurture their children's strength's and improve their classroom productivity. Also, it shows how correcting these problems early will help children live a fulfilling and productive adult life.
  288 pages
  ISBN 0-743213-68-8

2339 New Horizons Information for the Air Traveler with a Disability
Office of Aviation Enforcement and Proceedings
1200 New Jersey Ave SE
Washington, DC 20590
                        http://airconsumer.ost.dot.gov
This guide is designed to offer travelers with disabilities a brief but authoritative source of information about Air Carrier Access rules; the accommodations, facilities, and services that are now required to be available.

2340 No Easy Answer
Bantam Partners
1745 Broadway
New York, NY 10019-4305   212-782-9000
                          http://www.randomhouse.com
                 e-mail: bdpublicity@randomhouse.com

Sally Smith, Author

Parents and teachers of learning disabled children have turned to No Easy Answer for information, advice, and comfort. This completely updated edition contains new chapters on Attention Deficit Disorder and Attention Deficit Hyperactivity Disorder, and on the public laws that guarantee an equal education for learning disabled children. *$23.00*
  416 pages paperback
  ISBN 0-553354-50-7

2341 Out of Darkness
Connecticut Assoc for Children and Adults with LD
Ste 15-5
25 Van Zant St
Norwalk, CT 06855-1729   203-838-5010
                            FAX 203-866-6108
                          http://www.cacld.org
                  e-mail: cacld@optonline.net
Beryl Kaufman, Executive Director

Article by an adult who discovers at age 30 that he has ADD. *$1.00*
  4 pages

2342 Painting the Joy of the Soul
Learning Disabilities Association of America
4156 Library Rd
Pittsburgh, PA 15234-1349   412-341-1515
                               FAX 412-344-0224
                          http://www.ldanatl.org
                    e-mail: ldanatl@usaor.net
Peter Rippe, Author
P Buckley Moss, Co-Author

The first comprehensively researched and written book on the art and life of America's beloved artist, P. Buckley Moss, whose passion for painting is equal only to her passion for people, especially those with learning disabilities. Inspirational book about a woman who succeeded not in spite of her disability, but because of it. Contains 168 full color pages, over 100 art images. *$50.00*
  168 pages
  ISBN 0-964687-09-7

2343 Rethinking the Education of Deaf Students: Theory and Practice from a Teacher's Perspective
Heinemann
PO Box 6926
Portsmouth, NH 03802-6926   800-225-5800
                                    800-541-2086
                               FAX 877-231-6980
                          http://www.heinemann.com
                    e-mail: custserv@heinemann.com
Sue Livingston, Author

Offers alternatives and demonstrates how American Sign Language (ASL) and English can coexist in the same classroom, embedded in the context of what is being taught. *$23.00*
  180 pages
  ISBN 0-435072-36-0

2344 Son-Rise: The Miracle Continues
Option Indigo Press
2080 S Undermountain Rd
Sheffield, MA 01257-9643   413-229-2100
                                   800-562-7171
                              FAX 413-229-8727
                          http://www.optionindigo.com
                       e-mail: indigo@bcn.net
Barry Neil Kaufman, Author
Raun Kaufman, Co-Author

This book documents Raun Kaufman's astonishing development from a lifeless, autistic, retarded child into a highly verbal, lovable youngster with no traces of his former condition. It includes details of Raun's extraordinary progress from the age of four into young adulthood. It also shares moving accounts of five families that successfully used the Son-Rise Program to reach their own special children. An awe-inspiring reminder that love moves mountains. *$14.95*
372 pages
ISBN 0-915811-61-8

2345   The Eight Ball Club: Ocean of Fire
ESOL Publishing LLC
10305 Colony View Dr
Fairfax, VA 22032-3222   703-250-7097
                http://www.theeightballclub.com
e-mail: esolpublishing@cox.net; mcpuginrodas@aol.com
Melanie Rodas, President
MC Pugin-Rodas, Author

Publisher of novels designed for Special Ed and ESL students and activity books that go with the novel. These novels can be enjoyed by mainstream students as well. The Eight Ball Club: Ocean of Fire has vocab words in bold print, photographic illustrations, academic science terms, and a glossary. It's a teen-interest, easy reading adventure. *$18.95*
144 pages

2346   What About Me? Strategies for Teaching Misunderstood Learners
Heinemann
PO Box 6926
Portsmouth, NH 03802-6926   800-225-5800
                                            800-541-2086
                        FAX 877-231-6980
                    http://www.heinemann.com
                e-mail: custserv@heinemann.com
Christopher Lee, Author
Rosemary Jackson, Co-Author

A practical yet personal book on how to help special learners grow into self-sufficient responsible adults who can recognize their strengths and manage their weeknesses. *$19.50*
166 pages
ISBN 0-325003-48-1

2347   You're Welcome: 30 Innovative Ideas for the Inclusive Classroom
Heinemann
PO Box 6926
Portsmouth, NH 03802-6926   800-225-5800
                                            800-541-2086
                        FAX 877-231-6980
                    http://www.heinemann.com
                e-mail: custserv@heinemann.com
Patrick Schwarz, Author
Paula Kluth, Co-Author

Three handbooks; 30 key ideas-all the information you need to start making inclusion work effectively. *$18.00*

ISBN 0-325012-04-9

Children

2348   An Alphabet of Animal Signs
Harris Communications
15155 Technology Dr
Eden Prairie, MN 55344-2273   952-906-1180
                                            800-825-6758
                        FAX 952-906-1099
                        TDD:952-906-1198
                        TTY: 800-825-9187
                    http://www.harriscomm.com
                e-mail: info@harriscomm.com
S Harold Collins, Author
Darla Hudson, Customer Service

A fun sign language starter book that presents an animal sign for each letter of the alphabet. Part #B816. *$4.95*
16 pages Paperback
ISBN 0-931993-65-2

2349   Basic Vocabulary: American Sign Language Basic Vocabulary: American Sign Language for Parents
Harris Communications
15155 Technology Dr
Eden Prairie, MN 55344-2273   952-906-1180
                                            800-825-6758
                        FAX 952-906-1099
                        TDD:952-906-1198
                        TTY: 800-825-9187
                    http://www.harriscomm.com
                e-mail: info@harriscomm.com
Terrance K O'Rourke, Author
Darla Hudson, Customer Service

A child's first dictionary of signs. Arranged alphabetically, this book incorporates developmental lists helpful to both deaf and hearing children with over 1,000 clear illustrations. Part #B294. *$8.95*
228 pages Paperback
ISBN 0-932666-00-0

2350   Beginning Signing Primer
Harris Communications
15155 Technology Dr
Eden Prairie, MN 55344-2273   952-906-1180
                                            800-825-6758
                        FAX 952-906-1099
                        TDD:952-906-1198
                        TTY: 800-825-9187
                    http://www.harriscomm.com
                e-mail: info@harriscomm.com
Darla Hudson, Customer Service

A set of 100 cards designed especially for beginning signers. The cards present seven topics with words and signs. The topics: Color; Creatures; Family; Months; Days; Time and Weather. Part #B398. *$7.95*

2351   Christmas Bear
Teddy Bear Press
Suite 67
3703 S. Edmunds Street
Seattle, WA 98118   206-402-6947
                                            866-870-7323
                        FAX 858-874-0423
                    http://www.teddybearpress.net
                e-mail: fparker@teddybearpress.net
Fran Parker, President/Author

An 11x17 big book with color illustrations and a large print format uses the same simple sentence structure fount in I Can Read and Reading Is Fun programs. This story adds seasonal words to the developing sight vocabulary found in our reading programs. *$19.95*
12 pages
ISBN 1-928876-11-0

2352   Don't Give Up Kid
Verbal Images Press
46 Duncott Rd.
Fairport, NY 14450-8602   585-746-7239
                        FAX 585-264-1448
                    http://verbalimagespress.com
                e-mail: jeanne@verbalimagespress.com
Victoria Harmison, Marketing Director
Jeanne Gehret MA, Author

Like a river overflowing its banks, Ben wreaks havoc until he learns to recognize his Attention Deficit Disorder (ADD). By the end of this tale, Ben's family wonders how they could have gotten along without his specia way of seeing the world. *$9.95*
40 pages Paperback
ISBN 1-884281-10-9

2353 Fischer Decoding Mastery Test
Oxton House Publishers
124 Main Street
Suite 203
Farmington, ME 04938

207-779-1923
800-539-7323
FAX 207-779-0623
http://www.oxtonhouse.com
e-mail: info@oxtonhouse.com

William Berlinghoff PhD, Managing Editor
Cheryl Martin, Marketing
Debra Richards, Office Manager
This powerful, flexible diagnostic tool tells you precisely which decoding skills have been mastered (don't need to be taught), which skills are in transition (need some attention), and which skills need to be taught from scratch. Based on more than 40 years of clinical experience, it is a highly reliable way to pinpoint each beginning reader's exact needs and to measure progress against previous performance.

2354 Fundamentals of Autism
Slosson Educational Publications
PO Box 280
538 Buffalo Road
East Aurora, NY 14052

888-756-7766
FAX 800-655-3840
http://www.slosson.com
e-mail: slosson@slosson.com

Steven Slosson, President
Georgina Moynihan, TTFM

A handbook for those who work with children diagnosed as autistic.

2355 Funny Bunny and Sunny Bunny
Teddy Bear Press
Suite 67
3703 S. Edmunds Street
Seattle, WA 98118

206-402-6947
866-870-7323
FAX 858-874-0423
http://www.teddybearpress.net
e-mail: fparker@teddybearpress.net

Fran Parker, President/Author

An 11x17 big book with color illustrations and a large print format uses the same simple sentence structure fount in I Can Read and Reading Is Fun programs. This story adds seasonal words to the developing sight vocabulary found in our reading programs. *$19.95*
17 pages
ISBN 1-928876-14-5

2356 Halloween Bear
Teddy Bear Press
Suite 67
3703 S. Edmunds Street
Seattle, WA 98118

206-402-6947
866-870-7323
FAX 858-874-0423
http://www.teddybearpress.net
e-mail: fparker@teddybearpress.net

Fran Parker, President/Author

An 11x17 big book with color illustrations and a large print format uses the same simple sentence structure fount in I Can Read and Reading Is Fun programs. This story adds seasonal words to the developing sight vocabulary found in our reading programs. *$19.95*
13 pages
ISBN 1-928876-15-3

2357 Handmade Alphabet
Harris Communications
15155 Technology Dr
Eden Prairie, MN 55344-2273

952-906-1180
800-825-6758
FAX 952-906-1099
TDD:952-906-1198
TTY: 800-825-9187
http://www.harriscomm.com
e-mail: info@harriscomm.com

Laura Rankin, Author
Darla Hudson, Customer Service

An alphabet book which celebrates the beauty of the manual alphabet. Each illustration consists of the manual representation of the letter linked with an item beginning with that letter. Part #B310SC. *$6.99*
32 pages Paperback
ISBN 0-803709-74-9

2358 I Can Read Charts
Teddy Bear Press
Suite 67
3703 S. Edmunds Street
Seattle, WA 98118

206-402-6947
866-870-7323
FAX 858-874-0423
http://www.teddybearpress.net
e-mail: fparker@teddybearpress.net

Frank Babaloni, President/Author

Designed to accompany the I Can Read program is an 11x17 big book containing 54 charts which can be used to assist in introducing new words to students. These charts also provide review for previously taught words with either individual student or a small group. *$59.95*
54 pages

2359 I Can Sign My ABC's
Harris Communications
15155 Technology Dr
Eden Prairie, MN 55344-2273

952-906-1180
800-825-6758
FAX 952-906-1099
TDD:952-906-1198
TTY: 800-825-9187
http://www.harriscomm.com
e-mail: info@harriscomm.com

Darla Hudson, Customer Service

The Sign with Me alphabet book is a book for all children. It is designed to teach the 26 letters of the alphabet and the corresponding manual alphabet in sign language. The book provides early exposure to letter recognition plus a unique opportunity to introduce sign language to young children. Part #B132. *$11.95*
52 pages Hardcover
ISBN 0-939849-00-3

2360 Jumpin' Johnny Get Back to Work: A Child's Guide to ADHD/Hyperactivity
Connecticut Assoc for Children and Adults with LD
Ste 15-5
25 Van Zant St
Norwalk, CT 06855-1729

203-838-5010
FAX 203-866-6108
http://www.CACLD.org
e-mail: cacld@juno.com

Michael Gordon PhD, Author

Written primarily for elementary age youngsters with ADHD, this book helps them to understand their disability. Also valuable as an educational tool for parents, siblings, friends and classmates. The author's text reflects his sensitivity toward children with ADHD. *$12.50*
24 pages

2361 Leo the Late Bloomer
Connecticut Assoc for Children and Adults with LD
Ste 15-5
25 Van Zant St
Norwalk, CT 06855-1729   203-838-5010
                                 FAX 203-866-6108
                          http://www.CACLD.org
                         e-mail: cacld@juno.com
Beryl Kaufman, Executive Director
Robert Kraus, Author

A wonderful book for the young child who is having problems learning. Children follow along with Leo as he finally blooms. *$6.50*

2362 My First Book of Sign
Harris Communications
15155 Technology Dr
Eden Prairie, MN 55344-2273   952-906-1180
                                    800-825-6758
                                 FAX 952-906-1099
                                 TDD:952-906-1198
                                 TTY: 800-825-9187
                          http://www.harriscomm.com
                          e-mail: info@harriscomm.com
Pamela J Baker, Author
Darla Hudson, Customer Service

This book is an excellent source to teach children and even adults sign language. The illustrations are accurate in their representation of sign. It is colorful and visually attractive which makes it easy to read. The black and white manual alphabet, the fingerspelling, and aspects of sign provide exellent directions and pointers to signing correctly. The sign descriptions are a great supplement to the illustrations. Part #B147. *$22.95*
        76 pages Hardcover
        ISBN 0-930323-20-3

2363 My Signing Book of Numbers
Harris Communications
15155 Technology Dr
Eden Prairie, MN 55344-2273   952-906-1180
                                    800-825-6758
                                 FAX 952-906-1099
                                 TDD:952-906-1198
                                 TTY: 800-825-9187
                          http://www.harriscomm.com
                          e-mail: info@harriscomm.com
Patricia Bellan Gillen, Author
Darla Hudson, Customer Service

Learn signs for numbers 0 through 20, and 30 through 100 by tens. *$22.95*
        56 pages Hardcover
        ISBN 0-930323-37-8

2364 Rosey: The Imperfect Angel
Special Needs Project
Ste H
324 State St
Santa Barbara, CA 93101-2364   805-962-8087
                                    800-333-6867
                                 FAX 805-962-5087
                          http://www.specialneeds.com
                          e-mail: books@specialneeds.com
Sandra Lee Peckinpah, Author

Rosie, an angel with a cleft palate, works hard in her heavenly garden after the Boss Angel declares her disfigured mouth as lovely as a rose petal. Her reward is to be born on earth, as a baby with a cleft. *$15.95*
        28 pages
        ISBN 0-962780-60-8

2365 Scare Bear
Teddy Bear Press
Suite 67
3703 S. Edmunds Street
Seattle, WA 98118   206-402-6947
                                    866-870-7323
                                 FAX 858-874-0423
                          http://www.teddybearpress.net
                          e-mail: fparker@teddybearpress.net
Fran Parker, President/Author

An 11x17 big book with color illustrations and a large print format uses the same simple sentence structure fount in I Can Read and Reading Is Fun programs. This story adds seasonal words to the developing sight vocabulary found in our reading programs. *$19.95*
        13 pages
        ISBN 1-928876-16-1

2366 Signing is Fun: A Child's Introduction to the Basics of Sign Language
Harris Communications
15155 Technology Dr
Eden Prairie, MN 55344-2273   952-906-1180
                                    800-825-6758
                                 FAX 952-906-1099
                                 TDD:952-906-1198
                                 TTY: 800-825-9187
                          http://www.harriscomm.com
                          e-mail: info@harriscomm.com
Mickey Flodin, Author
Darla Hudson, Customer Service

The author of Signing for Kids offers children their first glimpse at a whole new world. Starting with the alphabet and working up to everyday phrases, this volume uses clear instructions on how to begin using American Sign Language and features an informative introduction to signing and its importance. One hundred and fifty illustrations. Part #B496 *$9.00*
        95 pages Paperback
        ISBN 0-613720-18-0

2367 Sixth Grade Can Really Kill You
Penquin Putnam Publishing Group
375 Hudson St
New York, NY 10014-3658   212-366-2000
                                    800-847-5515
                                 FAX 212-366-2666
                          http://www.penguingroup.com
                   e-mail: ÿecommerce@us.penguingroup.com
Barthe DeClements, Author

Helen's learning difficulties cause her to act up and are threatening to keep her from passing sixth grade.
        160 pages Paperback
        ISBN 0-142413-80-1

2368 Snowbear
Teddy Bear Press
Suite 67
3703 S. Edmunds Street
Seattle, WA 98118   206-402-6947
                                    866-870-7323
                                 FAX 858-874-0423
                          http://www.teddybearpress.net
                          e-mail: fparker@teddybearpress.net
Fran Parker, President/Author

An 11x17 big book with color illustrations and a large print format uses the same simple sentence structure fount in I Can Read and Reading Is Fun programs. This story adds seasonal words to the developing sight vocabulary found in our reading programs. *$19.95*
        13 pages
        ISBN 1-928876-12-9

2369 **Someone Special, Just Like You**
Special Needs Project
Ste H
324 State St
Santa Barbara, CA 93101-2364   805-962-8087
                                       800-333-6867
                                   FAX 805-962-5087
                        http://www.specialneeds.com
                        e-mail: books@specialneeds.com
Tricia Brown, Author

A handsome photo-essay including a range of youngsters
with disabilities at four preschools in the San Francisco Bay
area. *$7.95*
                64 pages

2370 **Study Skills: A Landmark School Student Guide**
429 Hale St
Prides Crossing
Prides Crossing, MA 01965   978-236-3216
                                   FAX 978-927-7268
                        http://www.landmarkoutreach.org
                        e-mail: outreach@landmarkschool.org
Robert Broudo, Principal

2371 **Unicorns Are Real!**
Learning Disabilities Association of America
4156 Library Rd
Pittsburgh, PA 15234-1349   412-341-1515
                                   FAX 412-344-0224
                        http://www.ldanatl.org
                        e-mail: ldanatl@usaor.net
Barbara Meister Vitale, Author

This mega best-seller provides 65 practical, easy-to fol-
low-lessons to develop the much ignored right brain tenden-
cies of children. These simple yet dramatically effective
ideas and activities have helped thousands with learning difficulties. Includes an easy-to-administer screening checklist
to determine hemisphere dominance, engaging instructional
activities that draw on the intuitive, nonverbal abilities of
the right brain, a list of skills associated with each brain
hemisphere and more. *$14.95*
                174 pages
                ISBN 0-446323-40-3

2372 **Valentine Bear**
Teddy Bear Press
Suite 67
3703 S. Edmunds Street
Seattle, WA 98118   206-402-6947
                                       866-870-7323
                                   FAX 858-874-0423
                        http://www.teddybearpress.net
                        e-mail: fparker@teddybearpress.net
Fran Parker, President/Author

An 11x17 big book with color illustrations and a large print
format uses the same simple sentence structure fount in I Can
Read and Reading Is Fun programs. This story adds seasonal
words to the developing sight vocabulary found in our reading programs. *$19.95*
                13 pages
                ISBN 1-928876-13-7

2373 **Visual Perception and Attention Workbook**
Therapro
225 Arlington St
Framingham, MA 01702-8723   508-872-9494
                                       800-257-5376
                                   FAX 508-875-2062
                        http://www.therapro.com
                        e-mail: info@therapro.com
Karen Conrad, Owner
Kathleen Anderson MS CCC-SP, Author
Pamela Crow Miller, Co-Author
Simple mazes, visual discrimination and visual form con-
stancy task, telling time and much more.

Law

2374 **ADA Quiz Book**
DBTAC: Rocky Mountain ADA Center
Ste 103
3630 Sinton Rd
Colorado Springs, CO 80907-5072   719-444-0268
                                       800-949-4232
                                   FAX 719-444-0269
                                   TTY: 719-444-0268
                        http://www.adainformation.org
                        e-mail: publications@mtc-inc.com
Jana Copeland, Editor
Bob Cook, Religious Leader
Candice Brandt, Training Coordinator
A collection of puzzles, quizzes, questions and case studies
on the Americans with Disabilities Act of 1990 and accessible information technology. Features sections on ADA basics, employment, state and local governments, public
accommodations, architectural accessibility, disability eti-
quette, effective communication, and electronic and information technology. *$9.95*
                81 pages 4.00 shipping

2375 **Discipline**
Special Education Resource Center
25 Industrial Park Rd
Middletown, CT 06457-1516   860-632-1485
                                   FAX 860-632-8870
                        http://www.ctserc.org
                        e-mail: info@ctserc.org
Mary Ann Kirner, Executive Director

A general analysis of the problems encountered in the discipline of students with disabilities. Discussion of the legal
principles of discipline that have evolved pursuant to Public
Law 94-142.

2376 **Dispute Resolution Journal**
American Arbitration Association
Fl 10
1633 Broadway
New York, NY 10019-6708   212-716-5800
                                       800-778-7879
                                   FAX 212-716-5905
                        http://www.adr.org
                        e-mail: zuckermans@adr.org
William K Slate Ii, CEO
Susan Zuckerman, Author

Provides information on mediation, arbitration and other
dispute resolution alternatives. *$150.00*
                96 pages Quarterly

2377 **Education of the Handicapped: Laws**
William Hein & Company
1285 Main St
Buffalo, NY 14209-1987   716-882-2600
                                       800-828-7571
                                   FAX 716-883-8100
                        http://www.wshein.com
                        e-mail: mail@wshein.com
Kevin Marmion, President
Bernard D Reams Jr, Author

Focuses on elementary and secondary Education Act of
1965 and its amendment, Education For All Handicapped
Children Act of 1975 and its amendments and acts providing
services for the disabled.

                ISBN 0-899411-57-6

2378 Ethical and Legal Issues in School Counseling
American School Counselor Association
Ste 625
1101 King St
Alexandria, VA 22314-2957　　　　703-683-2722
　　　　　　　　　　　　　　　　800-306-4722
　　　　　　　　　　　　　　FAX 703-683-1619
　　　　　　　　http://www.schoolcounselor.org
　　　　　　　　e-mail: asca@schoolcounselor.org
Wayne C Huey, Author
Theodore Phant Remley, Editor

Perhaps the increase in litigation involving educators and mental health practitioners is a factor. Certainly the laws are changing or at least are being interpreted differently, requiring counselors to stay up-to-date. The process of decision-making and some of the more complex issues in ethical and legal areas are summarized in this digest. *$40.50*
　　341 pages
　　ISBN 1-556200-55-2

2379 Individuals with Disabilities: Implementing the Newest Laws
Corwin Press
2455 Teller Rd
Thousand Oaks, CA 91320-2218　　　805-499-9734
　　　　　　　　　　　　　　　　800-233-9936
　　　　　　　　　　　　　　FAX 805-499-5323
　　　　　　　　　　　http://www.corwin.com
　　　　　　　　　e-mail: order@corwin.com
Joan L Curcio, Author
Patricia F First, Co-Author

Aimed at school administrators, this highly readable book covers the three major pieces of legislation: Americans with Disabilities Act of 1990; Individuals with Disabilities Education Act; and the Rehabilitation Act of 1973. Suitable for lay public use, anyone needing an overview of the laws affecting education and disabilities. *$12.95*
　　64 pages
　　ISBN 0-803960-55-7

2380 Learning Disabilities and the Law in Higher Education and Employment
JKL Communications
Ste 707
2700 Virginia Ave NW
Washington, DC 20037-1909　　　　202-321-4100
　　　　　　　　　　　　　　FAX 850-233-3350
　　　　　　　　　e-mail: lathamlaw@gmail.com
Peter S Latham JD, Director
Patricia Horan Latham JD, Director

Deals with issues in education and employment. Covers: Section 504, the IDEA, and ADA. Reviews court cases. *$15.00*

　　ISBN 1-883560-13-6

2381 Least Restrictive Environment
Special Education Resource Center
25 Industrial Park Rd
Middletown, CT 06457-1516　　　　860-632-1485
　　　　　　　　　　　　　　FAX 860-632-8870
　　　　　　　　　　　http://www.ctserc.org
　　　　　　　　　e-mail: info@ctserc.org
Mary Ann Kirner, Executive Director

A general discussion and analysis of the mandate to educate students with disabilities to the maximum extent appropriate with nondisabled students.

2382 Legal Notes for Education
Oakstone Business Publishing
136 Madison Avenue
8th Floor
New York, NY 10016　　　　　　212-209-0500
　　　　　　　　　　　　　FAX 212-209-0501
　　　　　　　　　http://www.haightscross.com
　　　　　　　　e-mail: info@haightscross.com
Steven B. Epstein, Chairman

Summaries of court decisions dealing with education law. *$122.00*

2383 Legal Rights of Persons with Disabilities: An Analysis of Federal Law
LRP Publications
360 Hiatt Drive
Palm Beach Gardens
Florida, FL 33418
　　　　　　　　　　　　　　　800-341-7874
　　　　　　　　　　　　　FAX 561-622-2423
　　　　　　　　　　　http://www.lrp.com
　　　　　　　　e-mail: custserv@lrp.com
Bonnie P Tucker, Author

This book will provide professionals working with the disabled a comprehensive analysis of the rights accorded individuals with disabilities under federal law. *$185.00*
　　2226 pages
　　ISBN 0-934753-46-6

2384 New Directions
Association of State Mental Health Program Direct
113 Oronoco St
Alexandria, VA 22314-2015　　　　703-683-4202
　　　　　　　　　　　　　　FAX 703-683-8773
　　　　　　　　　　　http://www.nasddds.org
　　　　　　　　e-mail: ksnyder@nasddds.org
Robert Glover, Executive Director

A newsletter offering information on laws, amendments, and legislation affecting the disabled. *$55.00*

2385 New IDEA Amendments: Assistive Technology Devices and Services
Special Education Resource Center
25 Industrial Park Rd
Middletown, CT 06457-1516　　　　860-632-1485
　　　　　　　　　　　　　　FAX 860-632-8870
　　　　　　　　　　　http://www.ctserc.org
　　　　　　　　　e-mail: info@ctserc.org
Mary Ann Kirner, Executive Director

A discussion of new mandates created by the 1990 Amendments to Public Law 94-142. An overview of the requirement for the provision of assistive technology devices and services as well as a discussion on the transition services that are to be provided to disabled adolescents.

2386 Numbers that add up to Educational Rights for Children with Disabilities
Children's Defense Fund
25 E Street N.W.
Washington, DC 20001-1522　　　　202-628-8787
　　　　　　　　　　　　　　　800-233-1200
　　　　　　　　http://www.childrensdefense.org
　　　　　　　e-mail: cdfinfo@childrensdefense.org
Ellen Mancuso, Author

Information on the laws 94-142 and 504. *$4.75*
　　68 pages
　　ISBN 0-938008-73-0

2387 Parent's Guide to the Social Security Administration
The Eden Family of Services
2 Merwick Rd
Princeton, NJ 08540-5711   609-987-0099
                                             FAX 609-987-0243
                                    http://www.edenautism.org
                                   e-mail: info@edenau.orgtism

Tom Mc Cool, President

A parents' guide to the Social Security Administration and
Social Security Work Incentive Programs. *$16.00*

2388 Procedural Due Process
Special Education Resource Center
25 Industrial Park Rd
Middletown, CT 06457-1516   860-632-1485
                                             FAX 860-632-8870
                                       http://www.ctserc.org
                                     e-mail: www.ctserc.org

Mary Ann Kirner, Executive Director

Analyzes the importance of the procedural safeguards afforded to parents and their children with disabilities by the
Public Law 94-142. Safeguards are discussed and possible
legal implications are addressed.

2389 Public Law 94-142: An Overview
Special Education Resource Center
25 Industrial Park Rd
Middletown, CT 06457-1516   860-632-1485
                                             FAX 860-632-8870
                                       http://www.ctserc.org
                                     e-mail: info@ctserc.org

Mary Ann Kirner, Executive Director

An overview of the general provisions of the Individuals
with Disabilities Education Act, commonly referred to as
Public Law 94-142. Designed to provide the less-experi-
enced viewer with a fundamental understanding of the Public Law and its significance.

2390 Purposeful Integration: Inherently Equal
Federation for Children with Special Needs
Suite 1102
529 Main Street
Boston, MA 02109   617-236-7210
                                             800-331-0688
                                             FAX 617-241-0330
                                         http://www.fcsn.org
                                     e-mail: fcsninfo@fcsn.org

James F. Whalen, President
Michael Weiner, Treasurer

This publication covers integration, mainstreaming, and
least restrictive environments. *$8.00*
        55 pages

2391 Section 504 of the Rehabilitation Act
Special Education Resource Center
25 Industrial Park Rd
Middletown, CT 06457-1516   860-632-1485
                                             FAX 860-632-8870
                                       http://www.ctserc.org
                                     e-mail: info@ctserc.org

Mary Ann Kirner, Executive Director

A general overview of the legal implications of the Rehabilitation Act and its implementing regulations, a law that is often forgotten in the process of appropriately educating
children with disabilities.

**2392 Section 504: Help for the Learning Disabled College
Student**
Connecticut Assoc for Children and Adults with LD
Ste 15-5
25 Van Zant St
Norwalk, CT 06855-1729   203-838-5010
                                             FAX 203-866-6108
                                       http://www.cacld.org
                                     e-mail: cacld@juno.com

Beryl Kaufman, Executive Director
Joan Sedita, Author

Provides a review of Section 504 of the Vocational Rehabilitation Act as it relates specifically to the learning disabled.
$3.25

**2393 So You're Going to a Hearing: Preparing for Public
Law 94-142**
Learning Disabilities Association of America
4156 Library Rd
Pittsburgh, PA 15234-1349   412-341-1515
                                             FAX 412-344-0224
                                       http://www.ldanatl.org
                                     e-mail: ldanatl@usaor.net

A public informational source offering legal advice to children and youth with learning disabilities. *$5.50*

2394 Special Education Law Update
Data Research
Ste 3100
4635 Nicols Rd
Eagan, MN 55122-3337   651-452-8267
                                             800-365-4900
                                             FAX 651-452-8694
                                http://www.dataresearchinc.com

Monthly newsletter service. Cases, legislation, administrative regulations and law review articles dealing with special
education law. Annual index and binder included. *$159.00*

2395 Special Education in Juvenile Corrections
Council for Exceptional Children
Suite 1000
2900 Crystal Drive
Arlington, VA 22202-3557   703-620-3660
                                             866-509-0218
                                             FAX 703-264-9494
                                             TTY: 866-915-5000
                                       http://www.cec.sped.org
                                     e-mail: service@cec.sped.org

Margaret J. McLaughin, President
James P. Heiden, Treasurer

This topic is of increasing concern. This book describes the
demographics of incarcerated youth and suggests some
promising practices that are being used. *$8.90*
        25 pages
        ISBN 0-865862-03-6

2396 Special Law for Special People
Gray,Rust, St. Amand, Moffett & Brieske LLP
950 E Paces Ferry Rd NE
1700 Atlanta Plaza
Atlanta, GA 30326-1180   404-870-7373
                                             FAX 404-870-7374
                                       http://www.grsmb.com

A ten-tape video series that is designed to assist in educating
regular education personnel as to the legal requirements of
IDEA and Section 504. *$5.95*

2397 Statutes, Regulations and Case Law
Center for Education and Employment Law
PO Box 3008
Malvern, PA 19355
                                             800-365-4900
                                             FAX 610-647-8089
                                       http://www.ceelonline.com

Curt Brown Esq, Group Publisher
Steve McEllistrem Esq, Senior Editor

Provides summaries of recent court cases impacting disability issues as well as reports on legislation and administrative regulations that are of importance to you. *$259.00*
Monthly

2398   Stories Behind Special Education Case Law
Special Needs Project
Ste H
324 State St
Santa Barbara, CA 93101-2364   805-962-8087
                                       800-333-6867
                                  FAX 805-962-5087
                       http://www.specialneeds.com
                    e-mail: books@specialneeds.com

Reed Martin, Author

The personal stories behind ten leading court cases that shaped the basic principles of special education law. *$12.95*
119 pages Paperback
ISBN 0-878223-32-0

2399   Students with Disabilities and Special Education
Center for Education and Employment Law
PO Box 3008
Malvern, PA 19355
                                       800-365-4900
                                  FAX 610-647-8089
                        http://www.ceelonline.com
Curt Brown Esq, Group Publisher
Steve McEllistrem Esq, Senior Editor

A desk reference that helps you determine if your program conforms to IDEA statutes and regulations in a comprehensive and concise format. We bring you analyses of recent court cases across the country that will help you safeguard your legal rights, and educate your colleagues in the law so they too are better qualified to identify and deal with developing legal issues. *$294.00*
500+ pages
ISBN 0-939675-44-7

2400   Technology, Curriculum, and Professional Development

Corwin Press
2455 Teller Rd
Thousand Oaks, CA 91320-2218   805-499-9734
                                       800-233-9936
                                  FAX 805-499-5323
                          http://www.corwin.com
                     e-mail: order@corwin.com
John Woodward, Author/Editor
Larry Cuban, Co-Author/Editor

Adapting schools to meet the needs of students with disabilities. The history of special education technologies, the requirements of IDEA'97, and the successes and obstacles for special education technology implementation. *$76.95*
264 pages
ISBN 0-761977-42-2

2401   Testing Students with Disabilities
Corwin Press
2455 Teller Rd
Thousand Oaks, CA 91320-2218   805-499-9734
                                       800-233-9936
                                  FAX 805-499-5323
                          http://www.corwin.com
                     e-mail: order@corwin.com
Martha Thurlow, Author
James Ysseldyke, Co-Author
Judy Elliot, Co-Author
Practical strategies for complying with district and state requirements. Helps translate the issues surrounding state and district testing of students with disabilities, including IDEA, into what educators need to know and do. *$ 80.95*
344 pages
ISBN 0-761938-08-7

2402   US Department of Justice: Disabilities Rights Section
950 Pennsylvania Ave NW
Washington, DC 20530   202-307-0663
                                       800-514-0301
                                  FAX 202-307-1197
                                  TTY: 800-514-0383
                              http://www.ada.gov
                        e-mail: askdoj@usdoj.gov

Gregory B. Friel, Chief
Zita Jhonson Betts, Deputy Chief
Roberta Kirkendall, Special Council
Information concerning the rights people with learning disabilities have under the Americans with Disabilities Act.

2403   US Department of Justice: Disability Rights Section
950 Pennsylvania Ave NW
Washington, DC 20530   202-307-0663
                                       800-514-0301
                                  FAX 202-307-1197
                                  TTY: 800-514-0383
                              http://www.ada.gov
                        e-mail: askdoj@usdoj.gov

Gregory B. Friel, Chief
Zita Jhonson Betts, Deputy Chief
Roberta Kirkendall, Special Councel
The primary goal of the Disability Rights Section is to achieve equal opportunity for people with disabilities in the United States by implementing the Americans with Disabilities Act (ADA).

Parents & Professionals

2404   125 Brain Games for Babies
Therapro
225 Arlington St
Framingham, MA 01702-8723   508-872-9494
                                       800-257-5376
                                  FAX 508-875-2062
                          http://www.therapro.com
                     e-mail: info@therapro.com

Jackie Silberg, uthor

Packed with everyday opportunities to enhance brain development of children from birth to 12 months. Each game includes notes on recent brain research in practical terms. *$14.95*
143 pages
ISBN 0-876591-99-3

2405   A Miracle to Believe In
Option Indigo Press
2080 S Undermountain Rd
Sheffield, MA 01257-9643   413-229-8727
                                       800-562-7171
                                  FAX 413-229-8727
                        http://www.optionindigo.com
                      e-mail: indigo@bcn.net

Barry Kausman, Author

A group of people from all walks of life come together and are transformed as they reach out, under the direction of Kaufman, to help a little boy the medical world had given up as hopeless. This heartwarming journey of loving a child back to life will not only inspire, but presents a compelling new way to deal with life's traumas and difficulties. *$7.99*
388 pages
ISBN 0-449201-08-2

2406   A Practical Parent's Handbook on Teaching Children with Learning Disabilities
Charles C Thomas
2600 S 1st St
Springfield, IL 62704-4730   217-789-8980
                                       800-258-8980
                                  FAX 217-789-9130
                          http://www.ccthomas.com
                     e-mail: books@ccthomas.com

Shelby Holley, Author

Publisher of Education and Special Education books.
308 pages
ISBN 0-398061-50-5

2407   ADHD in Adolescents: Diagnosis and Treatment
Guilford Publications
72 Spring St
New York, NY 10012-4019   212-431-9800
                                              800-365-7006
                                        FAX 212-966-6708
                                  http://www.guilford.com
                                  e-mail: info@guilford.com
Arthur L Robin, Author

Here Dr. Robin teaches us not only about the facts of the disorder, but also about its nature and the proper means of clinically evaluating it. Includes numerous reproducible forms for clinicians and clients, among them rating scales and detailed checklists for psychological testing, interviewing, treatment planning, and school and family interventions. *$35.00*
461 pages Paperback
ISBN 1-572303-91-3

2408   About Dyslexia: Unraveling the Myth
Connecticut Assoc for Children and Adults with LD
Ste 15-5
25 Van Zant St
Norwalk, CT 06855-1729   203-838-5010
                                        FAX 203-866-6108
                                   http://www.cacld.org
                             e-mail: cacld@optonline.net
Beryl Kaufman, Executive Director
Priscilla Vail, Author

This book focuses on the communication patterns of strength and weaknesses in dyslexic people from early childhood through adulthood. *$7.95*
49 pages
ISBN 1-864010-55-8

2409   Absurdities of Special Education: The Best of Ants...Flying...and Logs
Corwin Press
2455 Teller Rd
Thousand Oaks, CA 91320-2218   805-499-9734
                                              800-233-9936
                                        FAX 805-499-5323
                                   http://www.corwin.com
                                  e-mail: order@corwin.com
Kevin Ruelle, Editor
Michael F Giangreco, Author

Now available in this full color edition. Create beautiful transperances or use in PowerPoint presentations for staff development. Also a great gift for parents of educators. *$30.95*
114 pages Paperback
ISBN 1-890455-40-7

2410   Access Aware: Extending Your Reach to People with Disabilities
Alliance for Technology Access
1119 Old Humboldt Road
Jackson, TN 38305   731-554-5282
                                              1-800-914-30
                                        FAX 731-554-5283
                                      TTY: 731-554-5284
                                   http://www.ataccess.org
                             e-mail: atainfo@ataccess.org
Allegra Wilson, Administrative Assistant
Todd Plummer, Development Manager

This easy-to-use manual is designed to help any organization become more accessible for people with disabilities. *$45.00*
219 pages
ISBN 0-897933-00-1

2411   Activities for a Diverse Classroom
PEAK Parent Center
Ste 200
611 N Weber St
Colorado Springs, CO 80903-1072   719-531-9400
                                              800-284-0251
                                        FAX 719-531-9452
                                http://www.peakparent.org
                             e-mail: info@peakparent.org
Leah Katz, Author
Caren Sax, Co-Author
Douglas Fisher, Co-Author
A valuable resource for elementary teachers, this book helps begin the sometimes difficult conversation about diversity in the classroom. With the 18 fun, enriching, and do-it-tomorrow activities outlined in this text, teachers can help create a sense of community in the classroom as they introduce students to new ways of thinking about the need for friendships and the acceptance of others. *$11.00*
68 pages
ISBN 1-884720-07-2

2412   Activity Schedules for Children with Autism: A Guide for Parents and Professionals
Woodbine House
6510 Bells Mill Rd
Bethesda, MD 20817-1636   301-897-3570
                                              800-843-7323
                                        FAX 301-897-5838
                              http://www.woodbinehouse.com
                           e-mail: info@woodbinehouse.com
Lynn E McClannahan PhD, Author
Patricia J Krantz PhD, Author

Detailed instructions and examples help parents prepare their child's first activity schedule, then progress to more varied and sophisticated schedules. The goal of this system is for children with autism to make effective use of unstructured time, handle changes in routine, and help them choose among an established set of home, school, and leisure activities independently. *$14.95*
117 pages Paperback
ISBN 0-933149-93-X

2413   Alternate Assessments for Students with Disabilities
Corwin Press
2455 Teller Rd
Thousand Oaks, CA 91320-2218   805-499-9734
                                              800-233-9936
                                        FAX 805-499-5323
                                   http://www.corwin.com
                                  e-mail: order@corwin.com
Robb Clouse, Editorial Director
Sandra Thompson, Author
Martha Lurlow, Co-Author
Distinguished group of experts in a landmark book, co-published with the Council for Exceptional Children show you how to shift to high expectations for all learners, improve schooling for all. *$30.95*
168 pages Paperback
ISBN 0-761977-74-0

2414   American Sign Language Concise Dictionary
Harris Communications
15155 Technology Dr
Eden Prairie, MN 55344-2273   952-906-1180
                                              800-825-6758
                                        FAX 952-906-1099
                                      TDD:952-906-1198
                                      TTY: 800-825-9187
                                  http://www.harriscomm.com
                              e-mail: info@harriscomm.com

Martin Sternberg, Author
Darla Hudson, Customer Service

A portable version containing 2,000 of the most commonly used words and phrases in ASL. Illustrated with easy-to-follow hand, arm and facial movements. Part #B104. *$11.95*
  737 pages Paperback

2415 American Sign Language Dictionary: A Comprehensive Abridgement
Harris Communications
15155 Technology Dr
Eden Prairie, MN 55344-2273   952-906-1180
                                                800-825-6758
                                           FAX 952-906-1099
                                          TDD:952-906-1198
                                          TTY: 800-825-9187
                                  http://www.harriscomm.com
                                 e-mail: info@harriscomm.com
Martin Sternberg, Author
Darla Hudson, Customer Service

An abridged version of American Sign Language. A comprehensive dictionary with 4,400 illustrated signs. It has 500 new signs and 1,500 new illustrations. Third edition. Part #B103HC, and B103SC. *$24.00*
  772 pages Paperback

2416 Another Door to Learning
Independent Publishers Group
814 N Franklin St
Chicago, IL 60610-3813   312-337-0747
                                                800-888-4741
                                           FAX 312-337-5985
                                    http://www.ipgbook.com
                                 e-mail: frontdesk@ipgbook.com
Judy Schwartz, Author

Stories of eleven atypical learners who got the help they needed to make a lasting difference in their lives.

  ISBN 0-824513-85-1

2417 Ants in His Pants: Absurdities and Realities of Special Education
Corwin Press
2455 Teller Rd
Thousand Oaks, CA 91320-2218   805-499-9734
                                                800-233-9936
                                           FAX 805-499-5323
                                     http://www.corwin.com
                                 e-mail: order@corwin.com
Michael F Giangreco, Author
Kevin Ruelle, Editor

With wit, humor, and profound one liners, this book will transform your thinking as you take a lighter look at the often comical and occcasionally harsh truth in the field of special education. This carefully crafted collection of 101 cartoons can be made into transparencies for staff development and training. *$20.95*
  128 pages
  ISBN 1-890455-42-3

2418 Attention-Deficit Hyperactivity Disorder
slosson Educational Publications
PO Box 544
538 Buffalo Road
East Aurora, NY 14052   716-652-0930
                                                888-756-7766
                                           FAX 800-655-3840
                                     http://www.slosson.com
                                 e-mail: slosson@slosson.com
Steve Slosson, President
Sue Larson, Author

The book addresses issues of theory and practice quickly, with compassion and practicality and, most importantly, is very effective. Well-grounded answers and suggestions which would facilitate behavior, learning, social-emotional functioning, and other factors in preschool and adolescence are discussed.

2419 Attention-Deficit Hyperactivity Disorder: A Handbook for Diagnosis and Treatment
Guilford Publications
72 Spring St
New York, NY 10012-4019   212-431-9800
                                                800-365-7006
                                           FAX 212-966-6708
                                    http://www.guilford.com
                                 e-mail: info@guilford.com
Russell A Barkely, Author

Incorporates the latest findings on the nature, diagnosis, assessment, and treatment of ADHD. Clinicians, researchers, and students will find practical and richly referenced information on nearly every aspect of the disorder. *$ 55.00*
  628 pages

2420 Autism and the Family: Problems, Prospects and Coping with the Disorder
Charles C Thomas Publisher
PO Box 19265
Springfield, IL 62794-9265   217-789-8980
                                                800-258-8980
                                           FAX 217-789-9130
                                    http://www.ccthomas.com
                                 e-mail: books@ccthomas.com
David E Gray, Author

Publisher of Education and Special Education books. *$52.95*

  198 pages Hardcover
  ISBN 0-398068-43-7

2421 Backyards & Butterflies: Ways to Include Children with Disabilities
Brookline Books
Suite B-001
8 Trumbull Rd
Northampton, MA 01060   413-584-0184
                                                800-666-2665
                                           FAX 413-5846184
                                 http://www.brooklinebooks.com
                                 e-mail: brbooks@yahoo.com
Doreen Greenstein PhD, Author

This colorful, profusely illustrated book shows parents and others who work with disabled children how to design and build simple, inexpensive assistive technology devices that open up the world of outdoor experiences for these children. *$14.95*
  72 pages Paperback
  ISBN 1-571290-11-7

2422 Behavior Technology Guide Book
The Eden Family of Services
2 Merwick Rd
Princeton, NJ 08540-5711   609-987-0099
                                           FAX 609-987-0243
                                    http://www.edenautism.org
                                 e-mail: info@edenau.orgtism
Tom Mc Cool, President

Techniques for increasing and decreasing behavior using the principles of applied behavior analysis and related teaching strategies — discrete trial, shaping, task analysis and chaining.

2423   Children with Cerebral Palsy: A Parent's Guide
Therapro
225 Arlington St
Framingham, MA 01702-8723   508-872-9494
                                   800-257-5376
                              FAX 508-875-2062
                          http://www.therapro.com
                          e-mail: info@therapro.com
Elaine Geralis, Editor

This book explains what cerebral palsy is, and discusses its
diagnosis and treatment. It also offers information and advice concerning daily care, early intervention, therapy, educational options and family life. *$18.95*
    481 pages
    ISBN 0-933149-82-4

**2424   Children with Special Needs: A Resource Guide for Par-
ents, Educators, Social Worker**
Charles C Thomas
PO Box 19265
Springfield, IL 62794-9265   217-789-8980
                                   800-258-8980
                              FAX 217-789-9130
                          http://www.ccthomas.com
                          e-mail: books@ccthomas.com
Michael P Thomas, President

Publisher of Education and Special Education books. *$57.95*

    234 pages Cloth
    ISBN 0-398069-33-6

2425   Children with Tourette Syndrome
Woodbine House
6510 Bells Mill Rd
Bethesda, MD 20817-1636   301-897-3570
                                   800-843-7323
                              FAX 301-897-5838
                      http://www.woodbinehouse.com
                      e-mail: info@Woodbinehouse.com
Tracy Haerle, Editor

A guide for parents of children and teenagers with Tourette
syndrome. Covers medical, educational, legal, family life,
daily care, and emotional issues, as well as explanations of
related conditions. *$14.95*
    352 pages Paperback
    ISBN 0-933149-39-5

2426   Classroom Success for the LD and ADHD Child
Therapro
225 Arlington St
Framingham, MA 01702-8723   508-872-9494
                                   800-257-5376
                              FAX 508-875-2062
                          http://www.therapro.com
                          e-mail: info@therapro.com
Suzanne H Stevens, Author

Helpful book for parents and therapists who work with children with learning disabilities. It addresses specific issues
such as organization, homework and concentration. Stevens
offers practical suggestions on adjusting teaching techniques, adapting texts, adjusting classroom management
procedures and testing and grading fairly. *$13.95*
    342 pages Revised
    ISBN 0-895871-59-9

**2427   Common Ground: Whole Language & Phonics Work-
ing Together**
Educators Publishing Service
PO Box 9031
Cambridge, MA 02139-9031
                                   800-225-5750
                              FAX 888-440-2665
                      http://eps.schoolspecialty.com
                      e-mail: customer_service@epsbooks.com

Priscilla L Vail, Author

Offers guidelines for reading instruction in the primary
grades that combines whole language with multisensory
phonics instruction. *$8.95*
    88 pages
    ISBN 0-838852-11-4

2428   Common Sense About Dyslexia
Special Needs Project
Ste H
324 State St
Santa Barbara, CA 93101-2364   805-962-8087
                                      800-333-6867
                                 FAX 805-962-5087
                          http://www.specialneeds.com
                          e-mail: books@specialneeds.com
Ann Marshall Huston, Author

Offers important, need-to-know information about dyslexia.
$26.50
    284 pages Hardcover
    ISBN 0-819163-23-6

**2429   Complete IEP Guide: How to Advocate for Your Special
Ed Child**
NOLO
950 Parker St
Berkeley, CA 94710-2524   800-728-3555
                                   FAX 800-645-0895
                              http://www.nolo.com
Lawrence M Siegel, Author

This book has all the plain-English suggestions, strategies,
resources and forms to develop an effective IEP. *$34.99*
    402 pages paperback
    ISBN 1-413305-10-5

2430   Complete Learning Disabilities Resource Library
Slosson Educational Publications
PO Box 544
538 Buffalo Road
East Aurora, NY 14052   716-652-0930
                                   888-756-7766
                              FAX 800-655-3840
                          http://www.slosson.com
                          e-mail: slosson@slosson.com
Joan M Harwell, Author

These volumes provide easy-to-use tips, techniques, and activities to help students with learning disabilities at all grade
levels. *$29.95*
    320 pages Paperback
    ISBN 0-787972-32-0

**2431   Computer & Web Resources for People with Disabili-
ties: A Guide to...**
Alliance for Technology Access
1119 Old Humboldt Road
Jackson, TN 38305   731-554-5282
                                   800-914-3017
                              FAX 731-554-5283
                              TTY: 731-554-5284
                          http://www.ataccess.org
                          e-mail: atainfo@ataccess.org
Allegra Wilson, Administrative Assistant
Todd Plummer, Development Manager

This highly acclaimed book includes detailed descriptions
of software, hardware and communication aids, plus a gold
mine of published and online resources. *$20.75*
    364 pages

2432 Conducting Individualized Education Program Meetings that Withstand Due Process
Charles C Thomas Publisher
PO Box 19265
Springfield, IL 62794-9265
217-789-8980
800-258-8980
FAX 217-789-9130
http://www.ccthomas.com
e-mail: books@ccthomas.com
James N Hollis, Author

Publisher of Education and Special Education books. *$41.95*

171 pages Hardcover
ISBN 0-398068-46-1

2433 Connecting Students: A Guide to Thoughtful Friendship Facilitation
PEAK Parent Center
Ste 200
611 N Weber St
Colorado Springs, CO 80903-1072
719-531-9400
800-284-0251
FAX 719-531-9452
http://www.peakparent.org
e-mail: info@peakparent.org
C Beth Schaffner, Author
Barbara Buswell, Co-Author

Offers real-life examples of how friendship facilitation can be implemented in natural ways in schools, neighborhoods, and communities. Perfect for anyone working to build classrooms and schools that ensure caring, acceptance and belonging for ALL students. *$11.00*
48 pages Paperback
ISBN 1-884720-01-3

2434 Contemporary Intellectual Assessment: Theories, Tests and Issues
Guilford Publications
72 Spring St
New York, NY 10012-4019
212-431-9800
800-365-7006
FAX 212-966-6708
http://www.guilford.com
e-mail: info@guilford.com
Patti L Harrison, Editor
Judy L Genshaft, Editor

This unique volume provides a comprehensive conceptual and practical overview of the current state of the art of intellectual assessment. The book covers major theories of intelligence, methods of assessing human cognitive abilities, and issues related to the validity of current intelligence test batteries. *$75.00*
667 pages Hardcover
ISBN 1-593851-25-1

2435 Deciding What to Teach and How to Teach It Connecting Students through Curriculum and Instruction
PEAK Parent Center
Ste 200
611 N Weber St
Colorado Springs, CO 80903-1072
719-531-9400
800-284-0251
FAX 719-531-9452
http://www.peakparent.org
e-mail: info@peakparent.org
Elizabeth Castagnera, Author
Douglas Fisher, Co-Author
Karen Rodifer, Co-Author

Provides exciting and practical resource tips to ensure that all students participate and learn successfully in secondary general education classrooms. Leads the reader through a step-by-step process for accessing general curriculum, making accommodations and modifications, and providing appropriate supports. Planning grids and concrete strategies make this an essential tool for both secondary educators and families. Support strategies are enhanced in this second edition *$ 14.00*
48 pages
ISBN 1-884720-19-6

2436 Defiant Children
Guilford Publications
72 Spring St
New York, NY 10012-4019
212-431-9800
800-365-7006
FAX 212-966-6708
http://www.guilford.com
e-mail: info@guilford.com
Russell A Barkley, Author
Christine M Benton, Co-Author

This book is written expressly for parents who are struggling with an unyielding or combative child, helping them understand what causes defiance, when it becomes a problem, and how it can be resolved. Its clear eight-step program stresses consistency and cooperation, promoting changes through a system of praise, rewards, and mild punishment. Filled with helpful sidebars, charts, and checklists. *$39.00*
264 pages Paperback
ISBN 1-572301-23-6

2437 Developing Fine and Gross Motor Skills
Therapro
225 Arlington St
Framingham, MA 01702-8723
508-872-9494
800-257-5376
FAX 508-875-2062
http://www.therapro.com
e-mail: info@therapro.com
Donna Staisiunas Hurley, Author

This new home exercise program has dozens of beautifully illustrated, reproducible handouts for the parent, therapists, health care and child care workers. Each interval of 3 to 6 months in the child's development is divided into a fine motor and a gross motor section. Each section has several exercise sheets that guide parents in ways to develop specific motor skills that typically occur at that age level. Also includes practical information on how to guide parents when doing the exercises.
157 pages
ISBN 0-890799-43-1

2438 Diamonds in the Rough
Slosson Educational Publications
PO Box 544
538 Buffalo Road
East Aurora, NY 14052
716-652-0930
888-756-7766
FAX 800-655-3840
http://www.slosson.com
e-mail: slosson@slosson.com
Peggy Strass Dias, Author

An invaluable multidisciplinary reference guide to learning disabilities. It is an indispensable resource for educators, health specialists, parents and librarians. The author has printed a clear picture of the archetypical learner with a step-by-step view of the learning disabled child. *$53.00*
156 pages Spiral-Bound
ISBN 0-970379-90-0

2439 Dictionary of Special Education & Rehabilitation
Love Publishing Company
Ste 2200
9101 E Kenyon Ave
Denver, CO 80237-1854
303-221-7333
FAX 303-221-7444
http://www.lovepublishing.com
e-mail: lpc@lovepublishing.com
Glenn A Vergason, Author
M L Anderegg, Co-Author

This updated edition of one of the most valuable resources in the field is over six years in the making incorporates hundreds of additions. It provides clear, understandable definitions of more than 2,000 terms unique to special education and rehabilitation. *$34.95*
210 pages Paperback
ISBN 0-891082-43-3

2440 Early Childhood Special Education: Birth to Three
Connecticut Assoc for Children and Adults with LD
Ste 15-5
25 Van Zant St
Norwalk, CT 06855-1729
203-838-5010
FAX 203-866-6108
http://www.cacld.org
e-mail: cacld@optonline.net
J B Jordan, Author
Beryl Kaufman, Executive Director

Resources on early childhood education. *$34.00*
262 pages Paperback
ISBN 0-865861-79-X

2441 Educating Deaf Children Bilingually
Harris Communications
15155 Technology Dr
Eden Prairie, MN 55344-2273
952-906-1180
800-825-9187
FAX 952-906-1099
TDD:952-906-1198
TTY: 800-825-9187
http://www.harriscomm.com
e-mail: info@harriscomm.com
Darla Hudson, Customer Service
Shawn Neal Mahshie, Author

Perspectives and practices in educating deaf children with the goal of grade-level achievement in fluency in the languages of the deaf community, general society and of the home are discussed in this book. Part #B442. *$16.95*
262 pages

2442 Educating Students Who Have Visual Impairments with Other Disabilities
Brookes Publishing Company
PO Box 10624
Baltimore, MD 21285
410-337-9580
800-638-3775
FAX 410-337-8539
http://www.brookespublishing.com
e-mail: custserv@brookespublishing.com
Sharon Z Sacks PhD, Editor
Rosanne K Silberman EdD, Editor

This text provides techniques for facilitating functional learning in students with a wide range of visual impairments and multiple disabilities. *$49.95*
552 pages Paperback
ISBN 1-557662-80-0

2443 Effective Teaching Methods for Autistic Children
Charles C Thomas
PO Box 19265
Springfield, IL 62794-9265
217-789-8980
800-258-8980
FAX 217-789-9130
http://www.ccthomas.com
e-mail: books@ccthomas.com

Rosalind C Oppenheim, Author

Publisher of Education and Special Education books. *$21.25*

116 pages Hardcover
ISBN 0-398028-58-3

2444 Emergence: Labeled Autistic
Academic Therapy Publications
20 Commercial Blvd
Novato, CA 94949-6120
415-883-3314
800-422-7249
FAX 888-287-9975
http://www.academictherapy.com
e-mail: books@ccthomas.com
Jim Arena, President
Joanne Urban, Manager

An autistic individual shares her history, and includes her own suggestions for parents and professionals. Technical Appendix, which overviews recent treatment methods and more.

2445 Essential ASL: The Fun, Fast, and Simple Way to Learn American Sign Language
Harris Communications
15155 Technology Dr
Eden Prairie, MN 55344-2273
952-906-1180
800-825-6758
FAX 952-906-1099
TDD:952-906-1198
TTY: 800-825-9187
http://www.harriscomm.com
e-mail: info@harriscomm.com
Darla Hudson, Customer Service

This pocket version contains more than 700 frequently used signs with 2,000 easy-to-follow illustrations. Also, 50 common phrases. Part #B511. *$7.95*
322 pages Paperback

2446 Family Guide to Assistive Technology
Federation for Children with Special Needs
Suite 1102
529 Main Street
Boston, MA 02109
617-236-7210
800-331-0688
FAX 617-241-0330
http://www.fcsn.org
e-mail: fcsninfo@fcsn.org
Katherine A Kelker, Author
Roger Holt, Co-Author
John Sullivan, Co-Author
This guide is intended to help parents learn more about assistive technology and how it can help their children. Includes tips for getting started, ideas about how and where to look for funding and contact information for software and equipment. *$15.95*
160 pages Paperback
ISBN 1-571290-74-5

2447 Family Place in Cyberspace
Alliance for Technology Access
1119 Old Humboldt Road
Jackson, TN 38305
731-554-5282
800-914-3017
FAX 731-554-5283
TTY: 731-554-5284
http://www.ataccess.org
e-mail: atainfo@ataccess.org
Allegra Wilson, Administrative Assistant
Todd Plummer, Development Manager

Includes We Can Play, a variety of suggestions and ideas for making play activities accessible to all. Available in English and Spanish. Access in Transition. Information and resources for students with disabilities who are facing the transition from public school to the next stage in life. Includes links and resources. Assistive Technology in K-12 Schools gives a range of information about integrating assistive technology into schools.

2448   Fine Motor Skills in Children with Downs Syndrome: A Guide for Parents and Professionals
Therapro
225 Arlington St
Framingham, MA 01702-8773   508-872-9494
                                              800-257-5376
                                         FAX 508-875-2062
                                http://www.theraproducts.com
                                e-mail: info@theraproducts.com
Maryanne Bruni, Author

Fine motor skills are the hand skills that allow us to do the things like hold a pencil, cut with scissors, eat with a fork, and use a computer. This practical guide shows parents and professionals how to help children with Downs syndrome from infancy to 12 years improve fine motor functioning. Includes many age appropriate activities for home or school, with step by step instructions and photos. Invaluable for families and professionals. *$19.95*
241 pages Paperback
ISBN 1-890627-67-4

2449   Fine Motor Skills in the Classroom: Screening & Remediation Strategies
Therapro
225 Arlington St
Framingham, MA 01702-8773   508-620-0022
                                              800-257-5376
                                         FAX 508-620-0023
                                http://www.theraproducts.com
                                e-mail: info@theraproducts.com
Arthur Berry, Author

The Give Yourself a Hand program, revised. Developed as a tool to facilitate consultation in the classroom. The manual consists of training modules, a screening to administer to an entire class, report formats for teachers and parents, and classroom and home remediation activities. The program is designed to include everyone involved in the education process and to make them aware of the opportunites offered by occupational therapy in the classroom.
96 pages

2450   Flying By the Seat of Your Pants: More Absurdities and Realities of Special Education
Corwin Press
2455 Teller Rd
Thousand Oaks, CA 91320-2218   805-499-9734
                                              800-233-9936
                                         FAX 805-499-5323
                                     http://www.corwin.com
                                  e-mail: order@corwin.com
Michael F Giangreco, Author
Kevin Ruelle, Co-Author

In the sequel to Ants in His Pants, Giangreco continues to stimulate the reader to think differently about some of our current educational practices and raise questions about specific issues surrounding special education. Whether an educator, parent or advocate for persons with disabilities, you will smile, laugh aloud and ponder the hidden truths playfully captured in these carefully crafted cartoons. Transparencies may be created directly from the book. *$20.95*
112 pages Paperback
ISBN 1-890455-41-5

2451   Gross Motor Skills Children with Down Syndrome: A Guide For Parents and Professionals
Therapro
225 Arlington St
Framingham, MA 01702-8723   508-872-9494
                                              800-257-5376
                                         FAX 508-875-2062
                                     http://www.therapro.com
                                  e-mail: info@therapro.com
Patricia C Winders, Author

Children with Down syndrome master basic gross motor skills, everything from rolling over to running, just as their peers do, but may need additional help. This guide describes and illustrates more than 100 easy to follow activities for parents and professionals to practice with infants and children from birth to age six. Checklists and statistics allow readers to track, plan and maximize a child's progress. *$18.95*
236 pages
ISBN 0-933149-81-6

2452   Guide for Parents on Hyperactivity in Children Fact Sheet
Learning Disabilities Association of America
4156 Library Rd
Pittsburgh, PA 15234-1349   412-341-1515
                                         FAX 412-344-0224
                                     http://www.ldanatl.org
                                  e-mail: ldanatl@usaor.net
Klaus K Minde, Author

Describes difficulties faced by a child with ADHD. Elaborates on types of management and ends with a section called 'A Day With a Hyperactive Child: Possible Problems'. *$2.00*
23 pages

2453   Guide to Private Special Education
Porter Sargent Handbooks
2 LAN Drive
Suite 100
Westford, MA 01886   978-692-9708
                                         FAX 978-692-2304
                                http://www.portersargent.com
                                e-mail: info@portersargent.com
Daniel P. McKeever, Senior Editor
Leslie Weston, Manager

Lists and describes educational programs for families and consultants looking to place elementary and secondary students with special needs in the best possible learning environments. *$75.00*
1152 pages Triannual
ISBN 0-875581-50-1

2454   Guidelines and Recommended Practices for Individualized Family Service Plan
Education Resources Information Center
Suite 500
655 15th St. NW
Washington, DC 20005
                                              800-538-3742
                                     http://www.eric.ed.gov
Mary J McGonigel, Author

Presents a growing consensus about best practices for comprehensive family-centered early intervention services as required by Part H of the Individuals with Disabilities Education Act. *$15.00*
208 pages

2455 Handbook for Implementing Workshops for Siblings of Special Needs Children
Special Needs Project
Ste H
324 State St
Santa Barbara, CA 93101-2364   805-962-8087
                                      800-333-6867
                                 FAX 805-962-5087
                        http://www.specialneeds.com
                        e-mail: books@specialneeds.com
Donald Meyer, Author

Based on three years of professional experience working with siblings ages 8 through 13 and their parents, this handbook provides guidelines and technologies for those who wish to start and conduct workshops for siblings. *$40.00*
65 pages

2456 Handbook of Research in Emotional and Behavioral Disorders
Guilford Publications
72 Spring St
New York, NY 10012-4019   212-431-9800
                                 800-365-7006
                            FAX 212-966-6708
                        http://www.guilford.com
                        e-mail: info@guilford.com
Robert B Rutherford Jr, Author
Mary Magee Quinn, Co-Author
Sarup R Mathur, Editor
Integrates current knowledge on emotional and behavioral disorders in the school setting. Also, emphasizes the importance of interdisciplinary collaboration in service provision and delineates best-practice guidelines for research. *$38.00*
622 pages Paperback
ISBN 1-593854-71-4

2457 Handling the Young Child with Cerebral Palsy at Home

Therapro
225 Arlington St
Framingham, MA 01702-8723   508-872-9494
                                   800-257-5376
                              FAX 508-875-2062
                        http://www.therapro.com
                        e-mail: info@therapro.com
Nancie R Finnie, Author

This guide for parents remains a classic book on handling their cerebral palsied child during all activities of daily living. It has been said that its message is so important that it should be read by all those caring for such children including doctors, therapists, teachers and nurses. Many simple line drawings illustrate handling problems and solutions. *$55.95*

320 pages paperback
ISBN 0-750605-79-0

2458 Help Build a Brighter Future: Children at Risk for LD in Child Care Centers
Learning Disabilities Association of America
4156 Library Rd
Pittsburgh, PA 15234-1349   412-341-1515
                              FAX 412-344-0224
                        http://www.ldanatl.org
                        e-mail: ldanatl@usaor.net
Offers information for parents and professionals caring for the learning disabled child. *$3.00*

2459 Help Me to Help My Child
Hachette Book Group
3 Center Plz
Boston, MA 02108-2003
                                   800-759-0190
                              FAX 800-331-1664
                        http://www.hachettebookgroup.com
                        e-mail: customer.service@hbgusa.com
Jill Bloom, Author

Contains nontechnical information on testing, advocacy, legal issues, instructional practices, and social-emotional development, as well as a resource list and bibliography.
324 pages Hardcover
ISBN 0-316099-81-3

2460 Help for the Hyperactive Child: A Good Sense Guide for Parents
Learning Disabilities Association of America
4156 Library Rd
Pittsburgh, PA 15234-1349   412-341-1515
                              FAX 412-344-0224
                        http://www.ldanatl.org
                        e-mail: ldanatl@usaor.net
William G Crook, Author

A practical guide; offering parents of ADHD children alternatives to Ritalin. *$16.95*
245 pages
ISBN 0-933478-18-6

2461 Help for the Learning Disabled Child
Slosson Educational Publications
PO Box 544
538 Buffalo Road
East Aurora, NY 14052   716-652-0930
                               888-756-7766
                          FAX 800-655-3840
                        http://www.slosson.com
                        e-mail: slosson@slosson.com
Lou Stewart, Author

An easy-to-read text describes observable behaviors, offers remediation techniques, materials, and specific test to assist in further diagnosis.

2462 Helping Your Child with Attention-Deficit Hyperactivity Disorder
Learning Disabilities Association of America
4156 Library Rd
Pittsburgh, PA 15234-1349   412-341-1515
                              FAX 412-344-0224
                        http://www.ldanatl.org
                        e-mail: ldanatl@usaor.net
M Fowler, Author

2463 Helping Your Hyperactive Child
Connecticut Assoc for Children and Adults with LD
Ste 15-5
25 Van Zant St
Norwalk, CT 06855-1729   203-838-5010
                           FAX 203-866-6108
                        http://www.cacld.org
                        e-mail: cacld@optonline.net
Beryl Kaufman, Executive Director
John Taylor, Author

A large, comprehensive book for parents, covering everything from techniques pertaining to sibling rivalry to coping with marital stresses. Contains thorough discussions of various treatments: nutritional, medical and educational. Also is an excellent source of advice and information for parents of kids with ADHD.
496 pages Hardcover
ISBN 1-559580-13-5

2464 How the Special Needs Brain Learns
Corwin Press
2455 Teller Rd
Thousand Oaks, CA 91320-2218   805-499-9734
                                      800-233-9936
                                 FAX 805-499-5323
                        http://www.corwin.com
                        e-mail: order@corwin.com
David A Sousa, Author

Research on the brain function of students with various learning challenges. Practical classroom activities and strategies, such as how to build self-esteem, how to work in groups, and strategies for engagement and retention. Focuses on the most common challenges to learning for many students. *$35.95*
248 pages Paperback
ISBN 1-412949-87-4

2465   How to Get Services by Being Assertive
Family Resource Center on Disabilities
Room 300
20 E Jackson Blvd
Chicago, IL 60604-2265   312-939-3513
                                            800-952-4199
                                        FAX 312-854-8980
                                        TDD:312-939-3519
                                        http://www.frcd.org
                                        e-mail: info@frcd.org
Charlotte Jardins, Executive Director
Myra Christian, Contact
Gloria Mikucki, Contact
A 100 page manual that demonstrates positive assertiveness techniques. Price includes postage and handling. *$12.00*

2466   How to Organize Your Child and Save Your Sanity
Learning Disabilities Association of America
4156 Library Rd
Pittsburgh, PA 15234-1349   412-341-1515
                                        FAX 412-344-0224
                                        http://www.ldanatl.org
                                        e-mail: ldanatl@usaor.net
Ruth Brown, Author

13 pages $3.00

2467   How to Organize an Effective Parent-Advocacy Group and Move Bureaucracies
Family Resource Center on Disabilities
Room 300
20 E Jackson Blvd
Chicago, IL 60604-2265   312-939-3513
                                            800-952-4199
                                        FAX 312-854-8980
                                        TDD:312-939-3519
                                        http://www.frcd.org
                                        e-mail: info@frcd.org
Charlotte Jardins, Executive Director
Myra Christian, Contact
Gloria Mikucki, Contact
A 100-page handbook that gives step-by-step directions for organizing parent support groups from scratch. *$12.00*

2468   How to Own and Operate an Attention Deficit Disorder
Learning Disabilities Association of America
4156 Library Rd
Pittsburgh, PA 15234-1349   412-341-1515
                                        FAX 412-344-0224
                                        http://www.ldanatl.org
                                        e-mail: ldanatl@usaor.net
Debra W Maxey, Author

Clear, informative and sensitive introduction to ADHD. Packed with practical things to do at home and school, the author offers her insight as a professional and mother of a son with ADHD. *$8.95*
43 pages

2469   Hyperactive Children Grown Up
Guilford Publications
72 Spring St
New York, NY 10012-4019   212-431-9800
                                            800-365-7006
                                        FAX 212-966-6708
                                        http://www.guilford.com
                                        e-mail: info@guilford.com
Gabrielle Weiss, Author

Long considered a standard in the field, this book explores what happens to hyperactive children when they grow into adulthood. Updated and expanded, this second edition describes new developments in ADHD, current psychological treatments of ADHD, contemporary perspectives on the use of medications, and assessment, diagnosis and treatment of ADHD adults. *$35.00*
473 pages Paperback
ISBN 0-898625-96-3

2470   If it is to Be, It is Up to Me to Do it!
AVKO Educational Research Foundation
Ste W
3084 Willard Rd
Birch Run, MI 48415-9404   810-686-9283
                                            866-285-6612
                                        FAX 810-686-1101
                                        http://www.avko.org
                                        e-mail: webmaster@avko.orgÿ
Don Mc Cabe, Research Director/Author

This is a tutors' book that can be used by anyone who can read this paragraph. It also contains the student's response pages. It is especially good to use to help an older child or adult. It uses the same basic format as Sequential Spelling I except it has the sentences to be read along with the word to be spelled. The students get to correct their own mistakes immediately. This way they quickly learn that mistakes are opportunities to learn. *$19.95*
96 pages
ISBN 1-564007-42-1

2471   In Their Own Way: Discovering and Encouraging Your Child's Learning
Special Needs Project
Ste H
324 State St
Santa Barbara, CA 93101-2364   805-962-8087
                                            800-333-6867
                                        FAX 805-962-5087
                                        http://www.specialneeds.com
                                        e-mail: books@specialneeds.com
Dr Thomas Armstrong, Author

An unconventional teacher has written a very popular book for a wide audience. It's customary to be categorical about youngsters who learn conventionally/are normal/are OK — and those who don't/who need special ed/are learning disabled. *$8.37*
224 pages Paperback
ISBN 0-791716-67-8

2472   In Time and with Love
Special Needs Project
Ste H
324 State St
Santa Barbara, CA 93101-2364   805-962-8087
                                            800-333-6867
                                        FAX 805-962-5087
                                        http://www.specialneeds.com
                                        e-mail: books@specialneeds.com
Marilyn Segal, Author
Wendy Masi, Co-Author
Roni Leiderman, Co-Author
Play and parenting techniques for children with disabilities. *$18.95*
256 pages Paperback

2473   In the Mind's Eye
Prometheus Books
59 John Glenn Drive
Amherst, NY 14228-2197   716-691-0133
                                            800-421-0351
                                        FAX 716-691-0137
                                        http://www.prometheusbooks.com
                                        e-mail: marketing@prometheusbooks.com
Thomas West, Author

The second edition will review a number of recent developments, which support and extend the ideas and perspectives originally set forth in the first edition. Among these will be brief profiles of two dyslexic scientists known for their ability to generate, in quite different fields, powerful but unexpected innovations and discoveries. *$25.98*

> *440 pages*
> *ISBN 1-591027-00-3*

2474 **Inclusion: A Practical Guide for Parents**
Corwin Press
2455 Teller Rd
Thousand Oaks, CA 91320-2218 805-499-9734
800-233-9936
FAX 805-499-5323
http://www.corwin.com
e-mail: order@corwin.com

Lorraine O Moore, Author

This comprehensive resource answers parent questions related to inclusive education and provides the tools to promote and enhance their child's learning. This publication includes practical strategies, exercises, questionnaires and do-it-yourself graphs to assist parents with their child's learning. Beneficial for parents, psychologists, social workers, and educators. *$28.95*

> *152 pages*
> *ISBN 1-890455-44-6*

2475 **Inclusion: Strategies for Working with Young Children**
Corwin Press
2455 Teller Rd
Thousand Oaks, CA 91320-2218 805-499-9734
800-233-9936
FAX 805-499-5323
http://www.corwin.com
e-mail: order@corwin.com

Lorraine O Moore, Author

Developed for early childhood through grade two educators and parents, this comprehensive developmentally focused publication focuses on the whole child. Hundreds of developmentally-based strategies help young children learn about feelings, empathy, resolving conflicts, communication, large/small motor development, prereading, writing and math strategies are included, plus much more. Excellent training tool. *$28.95*

> *146 pages*
> *ISBN 1-890455-33-4*

2476 **Inclusive Elementary Schools**
PEAK Parent Center
Ste 200
611 N Weber St
Colorado Springs, CO 80903-1072 719-531-9400
800-284-0251
FAX 719-531-9452
http://www.peakparent.org
e-mail: info@peakparent.org

Douglas Fisher, Author
Nancy Frey, Co-Author
Caren Sax, Co-Author
Walks readers through a state of the art, step-by-step process to determine what and how to teach elementary school students with disabilities in general education classrooms. Highlights strategies for accommodating and modifying assignments and activities by using core curriculum. Complete with user-friendly sample forms and creative support strategies, this is an essential text for elementary educators and parents. *$13.00*

> *45 pages Paperback*
> *ISBN 1-884720-21-8*

2477 **Innovations in Family Support for People with Learning Disabilities**
Brookes Publishing Company
PO Box 10624
Baltimore, MD 21285 410-337-9580
800-638-3775
FAX 410-337-8539
http://www.brookespublishing.com
e-mail: custserv@pbrookes.com

Barbara Coyne Cutler, Author

> *272 pages Paperback $22.00*
> *ISBN 1-870335-15-5*

2478 **Interventions for ADHD: Treatment in Developmental Context**
Guilford Publications
72 Spring St
New York, NY 10012-4019 212-431-9800
800-365-7006
FAX 212-966-6708
http://www.guilford.com
e-mail: info@guilford.com

Phyllis Anne Teeter, Author

This book takes a lifespan perspective on ADHD, dispelling the notion that it is only a disorder of childhood and enabling clinicians to develop effective and appropriate interventions for preschoolers, school-age children, adolescents, and adults. The author reviews empirically-and clinically-based treatment interventions including psychopharmacology, behavior management, parent/teacher training, and self-management techniques. *$40.00*

> *378 pages Hardcover*
> *ISBN 1-572303-84-0*

2479 **Invisible Disability: Understanding Learning Disabilities in the Context of Health & Edu.**
Learning Disabilities Association of America
4156 Library Rd
Pittsburgh, PA 15234-1349 412-341-1515
FAX 412-344-0224
http://www.ldanatl.org
e-mail: ldanatl@usaor.net

Pasquale Accardo, Author

> *50 pages Paperback $9.00*
> *ISBN 0-937846-39-2*

2480 **It's Your Turn Now**
Harris Communications
15155 Technology Dr
Eden Prairie, MN 55344-2273 952-906-1180
800-825-6758
FAX 952-906-1099
TDD:952-906-1198
TTY: 800-825-9187
http://www.harriscomm.com
e-mail: info@harriscomm.com

Darla Hudson, Customer Service

Using dialogue journals with deaf students help the students learn to enjoy communicating ideas, information, and feelings through reading and writing. The book reviews teacher's questions and answers, frustrations and successes. Part #B584. *$14.95*

> *130 pages*

2481 **Key Concepts in Personal Development**
Marsh Media
PO Box 8082
Shawnee Mission
Kansas City, MO 66208 800-821-3303
FAX 866-333-7421
http://www.marshmedia.com
e-mail: info@marshmedia.com

Puberty Education for Students with Special Needs. Comprehensive, gender-specific kits and supplemental parent packets address human sexuality education for children with mild to moderate developmental disabilities. *$19.95*

2482   Ladders to Literacy: A Kindergarten Activity Book
Brookes Publishing Company
PO Box 10624
Baltimore, MD 21285   410-337-9580
                                                   800-638-3775
                                               FAX 410-337-8539
                          http://www.brookespublishing.com
                          e-mail: custserv@brookspublishing.com
Rollanda E O'Connor, Author
Angela Notari Syverson, Co-Author
Patricia F Vadasy, Co-Author
The kindergarten activities are designed for higher developmental levels, focusing on preacademic skills, early literacy development, and early reading development. Goals and scaffolding are more intense as children learn to recognize letters, match sounds with letters, and develop phonological awareness and the alphabetic principle. *$49.95*
         337 pages Spiral bound
         ISBN 1-557668-32-9

2483   Ladders to Literacy: A Preschool Activity Book
Brookes Publishing Company
PO Box 10624
Baltimore, MD 21285   410-337-9580
                                                   800-638-3775
                                               FAX 410-337-8539
                          http://www.brookespublishing.com
                          e-mail: custserv@brookespublishing.com
Rollanda E O'Connor, Author
Angela Notari Syverson, Co-Author

The preschool activity book targets basic preliteracy skills such as orienting children toward printed materials and teaching letter sounds. It also provides professionals (and parents) with developmentally appropriate and ecologically valid assessment procedures — informal observation guidelines, structured performance samples, and a checklist — for measuring children's learning. *$49.95*
         486 pages Spiral bound
         ISBN 1-557669-13-9

2484   Landmark School's Language-Based Teaching Guides
Landmark School
429 Hale St
PO Box 227
Prides Crossing, MA 01965   978-236-3216
                                               FAX 978-927-7268
                          http://www.landmarkoutreach.org
                          e-mail: outreach@landmarkschool.org
Robert Broudo, Author

Landmark School's Language-Based Teaching Guides provide research-based practical teaching strategies for teachers and parents working with students who have learning disabilities. Topics inlcude study skills, expressive langage skills, writing, mathematics. *$30.00*
         104 pages Paperback
         ISBN 0-962411-96-5

2485   Language and Literacy Learning in Schools
Guilford Publications
72 Spring St
New York, NY 10012-4019   212-431-9800
                                                   800-365-7006
                                               FAX 212-966-6708
                          http://www.guilford.com
                          e-mail: info@guilford.com
Elaine R Stillman, Author
Louise C Wilkinson, Co-Author

Interweaves the voices of classroom teachers, speech-language pathologists whos children learning to become literate in English as a first or second language, and researchers from multiple disciplines. *$27.00*
         366 pages Hardcover
         ISBN 1-593854-69-2

2486   Language-Related Learning Disabilities
Brookes Publishing Company
PO Box 10624
Baltimore, MD 21285   410-337-9580
                                                   800-638-3775
                                               FAX 410-337-8539
                          http://www.brookespublishing.com
                          e-mail: custserv@pbrookes.com
Adele Gerber, Author

         416 pages Hardcover $47.00
         ISBN 1-557660-53-0

2487   Learning Disabilities & ADHD: A Family Guide to Living and Learning Together
John Wiley & Sons Inc
111 River Street
Hoboken, NJ 07030-5774   201-748-6000
                                               FAX 201-748-6088
                          http://www.wiley.com
                          e-mail: info@wiley.com
Betty Osman, Author

         228 pages paperback $14.95
         ISBN 0-471155-10-1

2488   Learning Disabilities A to Z
Simon and Schuster
1230 Avenue of the Americas
New York, NY 10020-1513   212-698-7000
                          http://www.simonandschuster.biz
                          e-mail: shop.feedback@simonsays.com
Corinne Smith, Author
Lisa Strick, Co-Author

Brings the best of recent research and educational experience to parents, teachers and caregivers who are responsible for children with information processing problems. Corinne Smith and Lisa Strick provide a comprehensive guide to the causes, indentification and treatment of learning disabilities. You will learn how these subtle neurological disorders can have a major impact on a child's development, both in and out of school. *$17.00*
         416 pages Paperback
         ISBN 0-684844-68-0

2489   Learning Disabilities: Lifelong Issues
Brookes Publishing Company
PO Box 10624
Baltimore, MD 21285   410-337-9580
                                                   800-638-3775
                                               FAX 410-337-8539
                          http://www.brookespublishing.com
                          e-mail: custserv@brookespublishing.com
Shirley C Cramer, Author
William Ellis, Editor

Based on the diverse, representative viewpoints of educators, practitioners, policy makers, and adults with learning disabilities, this volume sets forth an agenda for improving the educational and ultimately, social and economic, futures of people with learning disabilities. *$36.00*
         319 pages Paperback
         ISBN 1-557662-40-1

2490   Learning Disabilities: Literacy, and Adult Education
Brookes Publishing Company
PO Box 10624
Baltimore, MD 21285   410-337-9580
                                        800-638-3775
                                 FAX 410-337-8539
                http://www.brookespublishing.com
                e-mail: custserv@pbrookes.com
Susan A Vogel PhD, Author
Stephen Reder PhD, Editor

This book focuses on adults with severe learning disabilities
and the educators who work with them. *$49.95*
        377 pages Paperback
        ISBN 1-557663-47-5

**2491   Learning Disabilities: Theories, Diagnosis and Teaching
Strategies**
Houghton Mifflin
222 Berkeley St
Boston, MA 02116-3748   617-351-5000
                                 FAX 617-351-1119
                http://www.houghtonmifflinbooks.com
                e-mail: TradeCustomerService@hmhpub.com
J Lerner, Author

Theories on learning disabilities.

        ISBN 0-395794-86-2

**2492   Learning Outside The Lines: Two Ivy League Students
with Learning Disabilities and ADHD**
Fireside
1230 Avenue of the Americas
New York, NY 10020-1513   212-698-7000
                http://www.simonandschuster.biz
                e-mail: shop.feedback@simonsays.com
Edward M Hallowell, Author
Jonathan Mooney, Co-Author
David Cole, Co-Author
Takes you on a personal empowerment and profound educa-
tional change, proving once again that rules sometimes need
to be broken. *$14.00*
        288 pages
        ISBN 0-684865-98-X

**2493   Legacy of the Blue Heron: Living with Learning Dis-
abilities**
Oxton House Publishers
124 Main Street
Suite 203
Farmington, ME 04938   207-779-1923
                                        800-539-7323
                                 FAX 207-779-0623
                http://www.oxtonhouse.com
                e-mail: info@oxtonhouse.com
William Berlinghoff PhD, Managing Editor
Cheryl Martin, Marketing
Debra Richards, Office Manager
This book is available in soft cover or as a six-cassette
audiobook. It is an engaging personal account by a severe
dyslexic who became a successful engineer, business man,
boat builder, and president of the Learning Disabilities Association of America. Drawing on his life experiences, the
author presents a rich array of wise, common-sense advice
for dealing with learning disabilities.
        256 pages Paperback
        ISBN 1-881929-20-5

2494   Let's Learn About Deafness
Harris Communications
15155 Technology Dr
Eden Prairie, MN 55344-2273   952-906-1180
                                        800-825-6758
                                 FAX 952-906-1099
                                 TDD:952-906-1198
                                 TTY: 800-825-9187
                http://www.harriscomm.com
                e-mail: info@harriscomm.com

Darla Hudson, Customer Service

Hands-on activities, games, bulletin board displays, surveys, quizzes, craft projects, and skits used to help teachers
and their students become more aware of deafness and its implications are included in this book. Part #B253. *$ 16.95*
        82 pages

**2495   Life Beyond the Classroom: Transition Strategies for
Young People with Disabilities**
Brookes Publishing Company
PO Box 10624
Baltimore, MD 21285   410-337-9580
                                        800-638-3775
                                 FAX 410-337-8539
                http://www.brookespublishing.com
                e-mail: custserv@brookespublishing.com
Paul Wehman, Author

Community living, leisure activities, personal relationships
as well as employment. Planning with community, individualized, state and local governments, curriculum for transition, job development and placement, independent living
plans for people with mild MR, severe disabilities, LD,
physical and health impairments, and traumatic brain injury.
$74.95
        719 pages Hardcover
        ISBN 1-557667-52-7

2496   Living with a Learning Disability
Southern Illinois University Press
1915 University Press Dr
Carbondale, IL 62901-4323   618-453-2281
                                        800-621-2736
                                 FAX 800-453-1221
                http://www.siupress.com
                e-mail: custserv@press.uchicago.edu
Barbara Martin, Director
Amy Etcheson, Marketing and Sales Manager

This book presents the kinds of adaptations needed for educating, communicating with, and parenting the child, the adolescent, and the young adult with learning disabilities.
Deals with such issues as relationships, the legal process,
implications for the professional, juvenile delinquency, and
the future.
        17.5 pages
        ISBN 0-809316-68-4

**2497   Making the Writing Process Work: Strategies for Com-
position & Self-Regulation**
Brookline Books
Suite B-001
8 Trumbull Rd
Northampton, MA 01060   413-584-0184
                                        800-666-2665
                                 FAX 413-5846184
                http://www.brooklinebooks.com
                e-mail: brbooks@yahoo.com
Karen R Harris, Author
Steve Graham, Co-Author

Presents cognitive strategies for writing sequences of specific steps which make the writing process clearer and enable students to organize their thoughts about the writing
task. *$24.95*
        239 pages Paperback
        ISBN 1-571290-10-9

2498   McGraw Hill Companies
PO Box 182604
Columbus, OH 43272-2604   877-833-5524
                                 FAX 614-759-3749
                http://www.mcgraw-hill.com
                e-mail: customer.service@mcgraw-hill.com
Henry Hirschberg, President

Corrective reading program, helps students master the essential decoding and comprehension skills.

2499 Me! A Curriculum for Teaching Self-Esteem Through an Interest Center
Connecticut Assoc for Children and Adults with LD
Ste 15-5
25 Van Zant St
Norwalk, CT 06855-1729
203-838-5010
FAX 203-866-6108
http://www.cacld.org
e-mail: cacld@optonline.com
Beryl Kaufman, Executive Director

A curriculum for the professional. *$18.50*

2500 Meeting the Needs of Students of ALL Abilities
Corwin Press
2455 Teller Rd
Thousand Oaks, CA 91320-2218
805-499-9734
800-233-9936
FAX 805-499-5323
http://www.corwin.com
e-mail: order@corwin.com
Colleen Capper, Author
Elise Fattura, Co-Author
Maureen Keyes, Co-Author
Step-by-step handbook offers practical strategies for administrators, teachers, policymakers and parents who want to shift from costly special learning programs for a few students, to excellent educational services for all students and teachers, and adapting curriculum and instruction. *$75.95*
224 pages Hardcover
ISBN 0-761975-00-4

2501 Misunderstood Child
Connecticut Assoc for Children and Adults with LD
Ste 15-5
25 Van Zant St
Norwalk, CT 06855-1729
203-838-5010
FAX 203-866-6108
http://www.cacld.org
e-mail: cacld@optonline.net
Beryl Kaufman, Executive Director

A guide for parents of learning disabled children. *$14.95*
448 pages Paperback
ISBN 0-307338-63-0

2502 Negotiating the Special Education Maze
Woodbine House
6510 Bells Mill Rd
Bethesda, MD 20817-1636
301-897-3570
800-843-7323
FAX 301-897-5838
http://www.woodbinehouse.com
e-mail: info@woodbinehouse.com
Stephen Chitwood, Author
Deidre Hayden, Co-Author

Now in its fourth edition, Negotiating the Special Education Maze isone of the best tools available to parents and teachers for developing an effective special education program for their child or student. Every step is explained, from eligibility and evaluation to the Individualized Education Program and beyond. *$16.95*
264 pages Paperback
ISBN 0-933149-72-7

2503 New Language of Toys
Woodbine House
6510 Bells Mill Rd
Bethesda, MD 20817-1636
301-897-3570
800-843-7323
FAX 301-897-5838
http://www.woodbinehouse.com
e-mail: info@woodbinehouse.com
Sue Schwartz PhD, Author

This revised and updated edition presents a fun, hands-on approach to developing communication skills in children with disabilities using everyday toys. There's a fresh assortment of toys and books, as well as newe chapters on computer technology and language learning, videotapes and television. *$16.95*
289 pages Paperback 7x10
ISBN 0-933149-73-5

2504 No One to Play with: The Social Side of Learning Disabilities
Connecticut Assoc for Children and Adults with LD
Ste 15-5
25 Van Zant St
Norwalk, CT 06855-1729
203-838-4353
FAX 203-866-6108
http://www.cacld.org
e-mail: cacld@juno.com
Marie Armstrong, Information Specialist
Beryl Kaufman, Executive Director

Your child suffers from a learning disability and you have read reams on how to improve on her academic skills and now want to address his or her social needs. *$13.00*

2505 Nobody's Perfect: Living and Growing with Children who Have Special Needs
Brookes Publishing Company
PO Box 10624
Baltimore, MD 21285
410-337-9580
800-638-3775
FAX 410-337-8539
http://www.brookespublishing.com
e-mail: custserv@brookespublishing.com
Paul H Brookes, President
Melissa A Behm, VP

Study of four families with children who have special needs. How they all adapted in surviving, how they care for the child, family, parents and siblings. How families react and relate. What it is like in community and extended family? Basic issues dicussed: self-esteem, separating parent from the adult with special needs and other issues. *$23.00*
352 pages Paperback
ISBN 1-557661-43-X

2506 Opening Doors: Connecting Students to Curriculum, Classmate, and Learning, Second Edition
PEAK Parent Center
Ste 200
611 N Weber St
Colorado Springs, CO 80903-1072
719-531-9400
800-284-0251
FAX 719-531-9452
http://www.peakparent.org
e-mail: info@peakparent.org
Barbara Buswell, Author
Beth Schaffner, Co-Author
Alison B Seyler, Co-Author
This innovative text contains practical how-to's for inculding and supporting students with disabilities in the general education classroom. It explores the processes, thinking, and approaches that successful implementers of inclusion have used. Written for educators and parents of both elementary and secondary students, topics include instructional strategies, curriculum modifications, behavior, standards, literacy, and providing support. *$13.00*

ISBN 0-884720-12-9

2507 Optimizing Special Education: How Parents Can Make a Difference
Insight Books
233 Spring St
New York, NY 10013-1522
212-460-1500
800-221-9369
FAX 212-647-1898
http://www.springer.com
e-mail: info@springer.com

Rudiger Gebauer, Owner

The author shows families how to use education laws to increase services or change services to suit a child's needs. Book contains personal anecdotes and balanced viewpoint of parent and professional relationships. *$26.50*
300 pages
ISBN 0-306443-23-6

2508 Out of Sync Child: Recognizing and Coping with Sensory Integration Dysfunction
Therapro
225 Arlington St
Framingham, MA 01702-8723   508-872-9494
                                              800-257-5376
                                         FAX 508-875-2062
                                  http://www.therapro.com
                                  e-mail: info@therapro.com

Karen Conrad, Owner

Finally, a parent-friendly book about sensory integration (SI) clearly written to explain SI dysfunction from the perspective of a teacher who has worked extensively with an OT. Part I deals with recognizing SI dysfunction. Part II addresses coping with SI dysfunction.

2509 Out of the Mouths of Babes: Discovering the Developmental Significance of the Mouth
Therapro
225 Arlington St
Framingham, MA 01702-8723   508-872-9494
                                              800-257-5376
                                         FAX 508-875-2062
                                  http://www.therapro.com
                                  e-mail: info@therapro.com

Karen Conrad, Owner

Help children who have difficulty with focusing, staying alert, or being calm with these simple techniqes and activities. Learn how behavior is affected by suck/swallow/breathe (SSB) synchrony with suggestions for correcting specific problems. This informal writing style and many illustrations make it a great resource for parents, teachers and therapists.

2510 Parent Manual
Federation for Children with Special Needs
Suite 1102
529 Main Street
Boston, MA 02109   617-236-7210
                                              800-331-0688
                                         FAX 617-241-0330
                                         TDD:617-236-7210
                                    http://www.fcsn.org
                                  e-mail: fcsninfo@fcsn.org

Rich Robison, President

Outlines parents' and children's rights in special education as guaranteed by Chapter 766, the Massachusetts special education law, and the Individuals with Disabilities Education Act (IDEA), the federal special education law *$ 25.00*
75 pages

2511 Play Therapy
Books on Special Children
PO Box 3378
Amherst, MA 01004-3378   413-256-8164
                                         FAX 413-256-8896
                                  http://www.boscbooks.com
                                  e-mail: irene@boscbooks.com

Irene Slovak, Founder
Kevin John O'Connor, Author

Leading authorities present various theoretical models of play therapy treatment and application. Case studies on how various treatments are applied. *$44.95*
350 pages Hardcover
ISBN 0-471106-38-0

2512 Positive Self-Talk for Children
PO Box 305
Congers, NY 10920   845-638-1236
                                         FAX 845-638-0847
                                  http://www.boscbooks.com/
                                  e-mail: irene@boscbooks.com

D Bloch, Author

This book teaches positive talk and ideas to achieve positive self-esteem. Use this as a refererence in specific situations: ie: fears on 1st day of school, doctor's visit. Covers cases, includes specific dialogue.

2513 Practical Parent's Handbook on Teaching Children with Learning Disabilities
Charles C Thomas
PO Box 19265
Springfield, IL 62794-9265   217-789-8980
                                              800-258-8980
                                         FAX 217-789-9130
                                  http://www.ccthomas.com
                                  e-mail: books@ccthomas.com

Michael P Thomas, President

Publisher of Education and Special Education books. *$65.95*

308 pages Cloth
ISBN 0-398059-03-9

2514 Raising Your Child to be Gifted: Successful Parents
Brookline Books
Suite B-001
8 Trumbull Rd
Northampton, MA 01060   413-584-0184
                                              800-666-2665
                                         FAX 413-5846184
                                  http://www.brooklinebooks.com
                                  e-mail: brbooks@yahoo.com

James R Campbell PhD, Author

Moving beyond the usual genetic eplanations for giftedness, Dr. James Campbell presents powerful evidence that it is parental involvement- very specific methods of working with and nurturing a child which increases the child's chances of being gifted. *$21.95*
275 pages Paperback
ISBN 1-571290-94-X

2515 Right from the Start: Behavioral Intervention for Young Children with Autism: A Guide
Therapro
225 Arlington St
Framingham, MA 01702-8723   508-872-9494
                                              800-257-5376
                                         FAX 508-875-2062
                                  http://www.therapro.com
                                  e-mail: info@therapro.com

Karen Conrad, Owner

This informative and user-friendly guide helps parents and service providers explore programs that use early intensive behavioral intervention for young children with autism and related disorders. Within these programs, many children improve in intellectual, social and adaptive functioning, enabling them to move on to regular elementary and preschools. Benefits all children, but primarily useful for children age five and younger.
215 pages

2516 SMARTS: A Study Skills Resource Guide
Connecticut Assoc. for Children and Adults with LD
Ste 15-5
25 Van Zant St
Norwalk, CT 06855-1729   203-838-5010
                                         FAX 203-866-6108
                                    http://www.cacld.org
                                  e-mail: cacld@juno.com

Marie Armstrong, Information Specialist
Beryl Kaufman, Executive Director

A comprehensive teachers handbook of activities to help students develop study skills. *$20.50*

2517   School-Based Home Developmental PE Program
Therapro
225 Arlington St
Framingham, MA 01702-8723   508-872-9494
                                    800-257-5376
                              FAX 508-875-2062
                        http://www.therapro.com
                        e-mail: info@therapro.com

Karen Conrad, Owner

A wire bound flip book. Comprehensive developmental physical education program indentifies and improves motor ability right down to the specific sensory and perceptual motor areas for children. Has what you need: assessment; parent involvement; understandable directions; examples; and sample letters to parents. Includes fun sheets that parents/professionals can use with children. Activities are for vestibular integration, body awareness, eye-hand coordination, and fine motor manipulation.

2518   Seeing Clearly
Therapro
225 Arlington St
Framingham, MA 01702-8773   508-872-9494
                                    800-257-5376
                              FAX 508-875-2062
                     http://www.theraproducts.com
                     e-mail: info@theraproducts.com

Karen Conrad, Owner

This booklet is chock-full of great information regarding vision and visual perceptual problems and activities designed to improve visual skills of both adults and children. Begins with an overview of the development of vision with a checklist of warning signs of vision problems. 25 eye game activities are divided into those for Eye Movements, Suspended Ball, Chalkboard and Visualization (e.g. Pictures in your Mind, Spelling Comprehension, etc.)

2519   Self-Perception: Organizing Functional Information Workbook
Therapro
225 Arlington St
Framingham, MA 01702-8773   508-872-9494
                                    800-257-5376
                              FAX 508-875-2062
                     http://www.theraproducts.com
                     e-mail: info@theraproducts.com

Karen Conrad, Owner
Kathleen Anderson MS CCC-SP, Author
Pamela Crow Miller, Co-Author
Recognizing human and animal body parts, discriminating between right and left, and exploring attitudes, emotions, humor and personal problem-solving.

2520   Sensory Integration and the Child: Understanding Hidden Sensory Challenges
Therapro
225 Arlington St
Framingham, MA 01702-8773   508-872-9494
                                    800-257-5376
                              FAX 508-875-2062
                     http://www.theraproducts.com
                     e-mail: info@theraproducts.com

Karen Conrad, Owner

Designed to educate parents, students, and beginning therapists in sensory integration treatment.

2521   Sensory Integration: Theory and Practice
Therapro
225 Arlington St
Framingham, MA 01702-8773   508-872-9494
                                    800-257-5376
                              FAX 508-875-2062
                     http://www.theraproducts.com
                     e-mail: info@theraproducts.com

Karen Conrad, Owner

This is the very latest in sensory integration theory and practice. The entire volume achieves an admirable balance between theory and practice, covering sensory integration theory, various kinds of sensory integrative dysfunction and comprehensive discussions of assessment, direct treatment, consultation and continuing research issues.

2522   Siblings of Children with Autism: A Guide for Families
Therapro
225 Arlington St
Framingham, MA 01702-8773   508-872-9494
                                    800-257-5376
                              FAX 508-875-2062
                     http://www.theraproducts.com
                     e-mail: info@theraproducts.com

Karen Conrad, Owner

An invaluable guide to understanding sibling relationships, how they are affected by autism, and what families can do to support their other children while coping with the intensive needs of the child with autism.

2523   Simple Steps: Developmental Activities for Infants, Toddlers & Two Year Olds
Therapro
225 Arlington St
Framingham, MA 01702-8773   508-872-9494
                                    800-257-5376
                              FAX 508-875-2062
                     http://www.theraproducts.com
                     e-mail: info@theraproducts.com

Karen Conrad, Owner

300 activites linked to the latest research in brain development. Outlines a typical developmental sequence in 10 domains: social/emotional, fine motor, gross motor, language, cognition, sensory, nature, music & movement, creativity and dramatic play. Chapters on curriculum development and learning environment also included.

2524   Social Perception of People with Disabilities in History
4156 Library Rd
Pittsburgh, PA 15234-1349   412-341-1515
                              FAX 412-344-0224
                         http://www.ldanatl.org
                       e-mail: ldanatl@usaor.net

Herbert C Covey, Author
Patrica H. Latham, President
Sharon Bloechle, Secretary
Shows how historical factors shape some of our current perceptions about disability. Of interest to special educators, historians, students of the humanities and social scientists.

2525   Son Rise: The Miracle Continues
Option Indigo Press
2080 S Undermountain Rd
Sheffield, MA 01257-9643   413-229-2100
                                   800-562-7171
                              FAX 413-229-8727
                       http://www.optionindio.com
                        e-mail: indigo@bcn.net

Barry Neil Kaufman, Author

This book documents Raun Kaufman's astonishing development from a lifeless, autistic, retarded child into a highly verbal, lovable youngster with no traces of his former condition. It details Raun's extraordinary progress from the age of four into young adulthood. It also shares moving accounts of five families that successfully used the Son-Rise Program to reach their own special children. An awe-inspiring reminder that love moves mountains. A must for any parent, professional or teacher.-OUT OF *$14.95*
346 pages Bi-Annually
ISBN 0-915811-61-8

2526 Study Skills: A Landmark School Teaching Guide
Landmark School
429 Hale St
Prides Crossing, MA 01965   978-236-3216
                              FAX 978-927-7268
                    http://www.landmarkoutreach.org
                    e-mail: outreach@landmarkschool.org
Dan Ahearn, Program Director
Trish Newhall, Associate Director

Designed to help all students learn to comprehend and organize the information they must learn in school, Study Skills: A Landmark School Student Guide offers instruction in how to apply specific comprehension and study skills including multiple exercises to practice each skill. Intended for reading levels of middle school and beyond. *$25.00*
104 pages
ISBN 0-962411-96-5

2527 Stuttering and Your Child: Questions and Answers
Stuttering Foundation of America
PO Box 11749
Memphis, TN 38111   901-452-7343
                              800-992-9392
                          FAX 901-761-0484
                    http://www.stutteringhelp.org
                    e-mail: info@stutteringhelp.org
Jane Fraser, President

Provides help, information, and resources to those who stutter, their families, schools day care centers, and all others who need help for a stuttering problem. *$2.00*
64 pages
ISBN 0-933388-43-8

2528 Substance Use Among Children and Adolescents
John Wiley & Sons Inc
10475 Crosspoint Blvd
Indianapolis, IN 46256-3386
                              877-762-2974
                          FAX 800-597-3299
                    http://www.wiley.com
William J Pesce, President/CEO
Anne Marie Pagliaro, Author
Peter B. Wiley, Chairman
Exposure and use among infants, children and adolescents. Impact on mental and physical health. Ingestion of substances during pregnancy and effects on fetus and neonate. Drug abuse effects on learning, memory.. Preventing and treating children and adolescents. Available only as a print on demand title. *$132.00*
416 pages Hardcover
ISBN 0-471580-42-2

2529 Success with Struggling Readers: The Benchmark School Approach
Guilford Publications
72 Spring St
New York, NY 10012-4019   212-431-9800
                              800-365-7006
                          FAX 212-966-6708
                    http://www.guilford.com
                    e-mail: info@guilford.com
Irene West Gaskins, Author

Presents a proven approach for helping struggling students become fully engaged readers, learners, thinkers, and problem solvers. Demonstrates ways to teach effective strategies for decoding words and understanding concepts, and to give students the skills to apply these strategies across the curriculum based on their individual cognitive styles and the specific demands of the task at hand. *$30.00*
264 pages
ISBN 1-593851-69-3

2530 Supporting Children with Communication Difficulties In Inclusive Settings
Special Needs Project
Ste H
324 State St
Santa Barbara, CA 93101-2364   805-962-8087
                              800-333-6867
                          FAX 805-962-5087
                    http://www.specialneeds.com
                    e-mail: editor@specialneeds.com
Hod Gray, Founder/President
Linda McCormick, Author
Diane Frome Loeb, Co-Author
A collaboration of professionals and parents can achieve language communication competence in classroom and other settings. Essential background material, assessment and intervention and needs of special populations are discussed. Contains sectional headings and marginal comments, chapter summary. *$75.00*
530 pages Paperback
ISBN 0-023792-72-8

2531 Tactics for Improving Parenting Skills (TIPS)
Sopris West
4093 Specialty Pl
Longmont, CO 80504-5400   303-651-2829
                              800-547-6747
                          FAX 303-776-5934
                    http://www.soprislearning.com.
Bob Algozzine, Author
Jim Ysseldyke, Author

Perhaps best described as a compliation of one-page parenting brochures, this helpful resource represents volumes of ideas and suggestions on topics of concern in today's families.OUT OF BUSINESS
202 pages
ISBN 1-570350-35-3

2532 Teach Me Language
Slosson Educational Publications
PO Box 280
East Aurora, NY 14052   716-652-0930
                              800-828-4800
                          FAX 800-655-3840
                    http://www.slosson.com
                    e-mail: slosson@slosson.com
Steven Slosson, President

Teach Me Language is designed for teachers, therapists, and parents, and includes a step-by-step how to manual with 400 pages of instructions, explanations, examples, and games and cards to attack language weaknesses common to children with pervasive developmental disorders. *$29.95*

2533 Teaching Developmentally Disabled Children
Slosson Educational Publications
PO Box 280
East Aurora, NY 14052   716-652-0930
                              800-828-4800
                          FAX 800-655-3840
                    http://www.slosson.com
                    e-mail: slosson@slosson.com
Steven Slosson, President

This instructional program for teachers, nurses, and parents is clear and concisely shows how to help children who are developmentally disabled function more normally at home, in school, and in the community. *$34.00*
250 pages

2534 Teaching Reading to Children with Down Syndrome
Woodbine House
6510 Bells Mill Rd
Bethesda, MD 20817-1636   301-897-3570
                                800-843-7323
                             FAX 301-897-5838
               http://www.woodbinehouse.com
               e-mail: info@woodbinehouse.com
Teach your child with Down syndrome to read using the author's nationally recognized, proven method. From introducing the alphabet to writing and spelling, the lessons are easy to follow. The many pictures and flash cards included appeal to visual learners and are easy to photocopy! *$16.95*
392 pages Paperback
ISBN 0-933149-55-7

2535 Teaching of Reading: A Continuum from Kindergarten through College
AVKO Educational Research Foundation
Ste W
3084 Willard Rd
Birch Run, MI 48415-9404   810-686-9283
                                866-285-6612
                             FAX 810-686-1101
                       http://www.avko.org
                  e-mail: avkoemail@aol.com
Don Mc Cabe, Research Director/Author
Barry Chute, President
Gloria Goldsmith, Secretary
This book covers concepts, techniques, and practical diagnostic tests not normally taught in regular college courses on reading. It is designed to be used by teachers, parents, tutors, and college reading instructors willing to try new approaches to old problems. *$49.95*
364 pages
ISBN 1-564006-50-6

2536 Teaching the Dyslexic Child
Slosson Educational Publications
PO Box 280
East Aurora, NY 14052   716-652-0930
                              800-828-4800
                           FAX 800-655-3840
                     http://www.slosson.com
                e-mail: slosson@slosson.com
Steven Slosson, President

Teaching the Dyslexic Child talks about the frustrations that the dyslexic youngsters and their parents encounter in the day to day collisions with life's demand. *$12.00*
128 pages

2537 Understanding Learning Disabilities: A Parent Guide and Workbook, Third Edition
York Press
P.O.Box 504
Timonium, MD 21094-0504   410-560-1557
                                800-962-2763
                             FAX 410-560-6758
                     http://www.yorkpress.com
                      e-mail: york@abs.net
Elinor Hartwig, President

An invaluable resource for parents who are new to the field of learning disabilities. Easy to read and overflowing with helpful information and advice. *$25.00*
380 pages
ISBN 0-912752-67-X

2538 Understanding and Teaching Children with Autism
John Wiley & Sons Inc
10475 Crosspoint Blvd
Indianapolis, IN 46256-3386   317-572-3000
                                  FAX 317-572-4000
                                http://www.wiley.com
William J Pesce, President/CEO
Rita Jordan, Author
Stuart Powell, Co-Author
The triad of impairment: social, language and communication and thought behavior aspects of development discussed. Difficulties in interacting, transfer of learning and bizarre behaviors are syndome. Many LD are associated with autism. *$175.00*
188 pages Hardcover
ISBN 0-471958-88-3

2539 What to Expect: The Toddler Years
Workman Publishing
225 Varick St
New York, NY 10014-4304   212-254-5900
                                800-722-7202
                             FAX 212-254-8098
                     http://www.workman.com
                   e-mail: Info@workman.com
Peter Workman, President
Jenny Mandel, Special Markets Director

They guided you through pregnancy, they guided you through baby's first year, and now they'll guide you through the toddler years. In a direct continuation of What to Expect When You're Expecting and What to Expect the Frist Year, American's bestselling pregnancy and childcare authors turn their uniquely comprehensive, lively, and reassuring coverage to years two and three. *$15.95*
928 pages Paperback

Young Adults

2540 Assertive Option: Your Rights and Responsibilities
Research Press
PO Box 9177
Champaign, IL 61826-9177   217-352-3273
                                800-519-2707
                             FAX 217-352-1221
                http://www.researchpress.com
                e-mail: rp@researchpress.com
Russell Pence, President
Albert Ellis, Author

A self instructional assertiveness book, with many exercises and self tests. *$24.95*
348 pages
ISBN 0-878221-92-1

2541 Behavior Survival Guide for Kids
Free Spirit Publishing
Ste 200
217 5th Ave N
Minneapolis, MN 55401-1299   612-338-2068
                                 866-703-7322
                              FAX 612-337-5050
                     http://www.freespirit.com
                e-mail: help4kids@freespirit.com
Judy Galbraith, President

Offers up-to-date information, practical strategies, and sound advice for kids with diagnosed behavior problems (BD, ED, EBD) and those with general behavior problems so they can help themselves. *$14.95*
176 pages
ISBN 1-575421-32-1

2542 **Delivered form Distraction: Getting the Most out of Life with Attention Deficit Disorder**
Ballantine Books
1745 Broad way
New york, NY 10019
FAX 212-572-6066
http://www.randomhouse.com
e-mail: BBDPublicity@randomhouse.com
Edward M Hallowell, Author
John J Ratey, Co-Author

Random House has long been committed to publishing the best literature by writers both in the United States and abroad. In addition to their commercial success, books published by Random House, Inc. have won an unrivalled number of Nobel and Pulitzer Prizes. *$25.95*
416 pages
ISBN 0-345442-30-X

2543 **Education of Students with Disabilities: Where Do We Stand?**
National Council on Disability
Suite 1050
1331 F St NW
Washington, DC 20004
202-272-2004
FAX 202-272-2022
TTY: 202-272-2074
http://www.ncd.gov
e-mail: mquigley@ncd.ogv
Ethel D Briggs, Acting Executive Director
Brenda Bratton, Executive Secretary

The council reviews the education of students with disabilities as a critical priority. Success in education is a predictor of success in adult life. For students with disabilities, a good education can be the difference between a life of dependence and nonproductivity and a life of independence and productivity.

2544 **HEATH Resource Directory: Clearinghouseon Postsecondary Edu for Individuals with Disabilities**
George Washington University
2134 G St NW
Washington, DC 20052
202-973-0904
800-544-3284
FAX 202-973-0908
http://www.heath.gwu.edu
e-mail: askheath@gwu.edu
Donna Martinez, Director
Dr Lynda West, Principal Investigator
Dr Joel Gomez, Principal Investigator
The HEATH Resource Center is an online clearinghouse on postsecondary education for individuals with disabilities. The HEATH Resource Center Clearinghouse has information for students with disabilities on educational disability support services, policies, procedures, adaptations, accessing college or university campuses, career-technical schools, and other postsecondary training entities.

2545 **Keeping Ahead in School: A Students Book About Learning Disabilities & Learning Disorders**
Educators Publishing Service
PO Box 9031
Cambridge, MA 02139-9031
617-547-6706
800-225-5750
FAX 617-547-0412
http://www.epsbooks.com
e-mail: eps@epsbooks.com
Gunnar Voltz, President
Alana Trisler, Author

Written for students 9 to 15 years of age with learning disorders. This book helps students gain important insights into their problems by combining realism with justifiable optimism. *$24.75*

ISBN 0-838820-09-7

2546 **Modern Consumer Education: You and the Law**
Triumph Learning
PO Box 1270
Northborough, MA 01460-4270
800-338-6519
FAX 866-805-5723
http://www.triumphlearning.com
e-mail: customerservice@triumphlearning.com
Buz Traugot, Sales Representative

An instructional program to teach independent living, with emphasis on legal resources and survival skills. *$59.00*

2547 **Phonemic Awareness: Lessons, Activities & Games**
Sage/Corwin Press
2455 Teller Rd
Thousand Oaks, CA 91320-2218
805-499-9734
FAX 805-499-5323
http://www.corwinpress.com
e-mail: order@corwin.com
Peggy Hammeken, President
Kevin Ruelle, Illustrator

Help struggling readers with Phonemic Awareness training. This all inclusive book iuncludes 48 scripted lessons. May be used as a prerequisite to reading or for stuggling students. Includes 49 reproductible masters. May be used with individual students or with groups. *$27.95*
176 pages

2548 **Reading Is Fun**
Teddy Bear Press
3703 S. Edmunds Street
Suite B-182
Seattle, WA 98118
858-560-8718
FAX 866-870-7323
http://www.teddybearpress.net
e-mail: fparker@teddybearpress.net
Fran Parker, President

Introduces 55 primer level words in six reading books and accompanting activity sheets. This easy to use reading program provides repition, visual motor, visual discrimination and word comprehension excersies. The manual and placement test. *$85.00*

ISBN 1-928876-01-3

2549 **Reading and Writing Workbook**
Therapro
225 Arlington St
Framingham, MA 01702-8773
508-872-9494
800-257-5376
FAX 508-875-2062
http://www.theraproducts.com
e-mail: info@theraproducts.com
Karen Conrad, Owner
Kathleen Anderson MS CCC-SP, Author
Pamela Crow Miller, Co-Author
Writing checks and balancing a checkbook, copying words and sentences, and writing messages and notes. Helps with recognition and understanding of calenders, phone books and much more.

2550 **Survival Guide for Kids with ADD or ADHD**
Free Spirit Publishing
Ste 200
217 5th Ave N
Minneapolis, MN 55401-1299
612-338-2068
866-703-7322
FAX 612-337-5050
http://www.freespirit.com
e-mail: help4kids@freespirit.com
Judy Galbraith, President

Explains how kids diagnosed with ADD and ADHD can help themselves succeed in school, get along better at home, and form healthy, enjoyable relationships with peers. In kid-friendly language and a format that welcomes reluctant and easily distracted readers, this book helps kids know they're not alone and offers practical strategies for taking care or oneself, modifying behavior, enjoying school, having fun, and dealing with doctos, counselors, and medication. Includes scenarios and quizzes. *$13.95*
>*128 pages*
>*ISBN 1-575421-95-X*

2551   **Survival Guide for Kids with LD Learning Differences**
Free Spirit Publishing
Ste 200
217 5th Ave N
Minneapolis, MN 55401-1299   612-338-2068
                                                 866-703-7322
                                           FAX 612-337-5050
                              http://www.freespirit.com
                        e-mail: help4kids@freespirit.com
Judy Galbraith, President

Answers the many questions young people have, like 'Why is it hard for kids with LD to learn?' and 'What happens when you grow up?' It explains what LD means (and doesn't mean); defines different kinds of LD; describes what happens in LD programs; helps kids deal with sad, hurt, and angry feelings; suggests ways to get along better in school and at home; and inspires young people to set goals and plan for the future. Also includes resources for parents and teachers. *$10.95*
>*112 pages*
>*ISBN 1-575421-19-4*

2552   **Survival Guide for Teenagers with LD Learning Differences**
Free Spirit Publishing
Ste 200
217 5th Ave N
Minneapolis, MN 55401-1299   612-338-2068
                                                 866-703-7322
                                           FAX 612-337-5050
                              http://www.freespirit.com
                        e-mail: help4kids@freespirit.com
Judy Galbraith, President

This guide helps young people with LD succeed in school and prepare for life as adults. It explains what LD is and how kids get into LD programs, clarifies readers' legal rights and responsibilities, and covers other vital topics including assertiveness, jobs, friends, dating, self-sufficiency, and responsible citizenship. *$12.95*
>*200 pages*
>*ISBN 0-915793-51-2*

2553   **Who I Can Be Is Up To Me: Lessons in Self-Exploration and Self-Determination**
Research Press
2612 N. Mattis Ave PO Box 9177
Champaign, IL 61822-9177   217-352-3273
                                                 800-519-2707
                                           FAX 217-352-1221
                          http://www.researchpress.com
                         e-mail: rp@researchpress.com
Gloria D Campbell-Whatley, Author
Robert W. Parkinson, Founder

>*127 pages $24.95*
>*ISBN 0-878224-84-X*

2554   **Winning at Math: Your Guide to Learning Mathematics Through Successful Study Skills**
Academic Success Press
6023 26th St W
Bradenton, FL 34207-4402   941-746-1645
                                                 800-444-2524
                                           FAX 941-753-2882
                          http://www.academicsuccess.com
                              e-mail: pnolting@ad.com
Paul Nolting, Owner

A guide that helps people with learning disabilities learn math easier. *$24.95*

2555   **Winning the Study Game**
Sage/Corwin Press
2455 Teller Rd
Thousand Oaks, CA 91320-2218   805-499-9734
                                           FAX 805-499-9734
                              http://www.corwinpress.com
                          e-mail: order@corwin.com
Peggy Hammeken, President
Kevin Ruelle, Illustrator

A comprehensive study skills program for students with learning differences in grades 6-11. The student book has 16 units which will help students learn to study better, take notes, advance their thinking skills while stregthening their reading and writing. The student version is available in a reproducible or consumable format. Teachers guide sold separately. *$34.95*
>*2500 pages*
>*ISBN 1-890455-48-2*

General

2556 **A Student's Guide to Jobs**
NICHCY
1825 Connecticut Ave NW c/o FHI360
Suite 700
Washington, DC 20009   202-884-8200
                               800-695-0285
                          FAX 202-884-8441
                           TDD:800-695-0285
                          http://www.nichcy.org
                        e-mail: nichcy@fhi360.org

Susan Ripley, Director

Young people with intellectual and developmental disabilities speak freely about their job-related experiences. *$2.00*
          8 pages

2557 **A Student's Guide to the IEP**
NICHCY
1825 Connecticut Ave
Washington, DC 20009   202-884-8200
                               800-695-0285
                          FAX 202-884-8441
                          http://www.nichcy.org
                        e-mail: nichcy@fhi360.org

Susan Ripley, Director

A guide for students that features other students discussing their experiences as active members on their IEP team. *$2.00*

          12 pages

2558 **Accessing Parent Groups**
NICHCY
1825 Connecticut Ave NW
Suite 700
Washington, DC 20009   202-884-8200
                               800-695-0285
                          FAX 202-884-8441
                          http://www.nichcy.org
                        e-mail: nichcy@fhi360.org

Susan Ripley, Director

Helps parents locate support groups where they can share information, give and receive emotional support, and address common concerns. *$2.00*
          12 pages

2559 **Accessing Programs for Infants, Toddlers and Pre-schoolers**
NICHCY
1825 Connecticut Ave NW
Suite 700
Washington, DC 20009   202-884-8200
                               800-695-0285
                          FAX 202-884-8441
                          http://www.nichcy.org
                        e-mail: nichcy@fhi360.org

Susan Ripley, Director

This guide helps locate intervention services for infants and toddlers with disabilities. Also answers questions about educational programs for preschoolers. *$2.00*
          20 pages

2560 **Advocacy Services for Families of Children in Special Education**
Arizona Department of Education
1535 W Jefferson St
Phoenix, AZ 85007-3209   1-800-352-45
                                 800-352-4558
                            FAX 602-542-5440
                          http://www.ade.state.az.us
                         e-mail: ADE@ade.az.gov

Robert Plummer, Manager
Art Heikkila, Auditor

Information provided to families that have children in special education.

2561 **Assessing Children for the Presence of a Disability**
NICHCY
1825 Connecticut Ave NW
Suite 700
Washington, DC 20009   202-884-8200
                               800-695-0285
                          FAX 202-884-8441
                          http://www.nichcy.org
                        e-mail: nichcy@fhi360.org

Susan Ripley, Director

Describes the criteria and process preformed by school systems to determine if a child has a learning disabilty. *$4.00*
          28 pages

2562 **Assessing the ERIC Resource Collection**
NICHCY
1825 Connecticut Ave NW
Suite 700
Washington, DC 20009   202-884-8200
                               800-695-0285
                          FAX 202-884-8441
                          http://www.nichcy.org
                        e-mail: nichcy@fhi360.org

Susan Ripley, Director

A nationwide network that gives access to education literature, this document explains how to search and retrieve documents from ERIC. Also explains how to find information about children with disabilites. *$2.00*
          8 pages

2563 **Complete Set of State Resource Sheets**
NICHCY
1825 Connecticut Ave NW
Suite 700
Washington, DC 20009   202-884-8200
                               800-695-0285
                          FAX 202-884-8441
                          http://www.nichcy.org
                        e-mail: nichcy@fhi360.org

Susan Ripley, Director

Provides a sheet for every state and territory in the United States. *$10.00*
          200 pages

2564 **Directory of Organizations**
NICHCY
1825 Connecticut Ave NW
Suite 700
Washington, DC 20009   202-884-8200
                               800-695-0285
                          FAX 202-884-8441
                          http://www.nichcy.org
                        e-mail: nichcy@fhi360.org

Susan Ripley, Director

Lists many organizations and services *$4.00*
          28 pages

2565 **Education of Children and Youth with Special Needs: What do the Laws Say?**
NICHCY
1825 Connecticut Ave NW
Suite 700
Washington, DC 20009   202-884-8200
                               800-695-0285
                          FAX 202-884-8441
                          http://www.nichcy.org
                        e-mail: nichcy@fhi360.org

Susan Ripley, Director

Provides an overview of 3 laws that aid disabled children; 1. Section 504 of the Rehabilitation Act of 1973, 2. the Individuals with Disabilities Education Act, and 3. the Carl P. Perkins Vocational Educational Act. *$4.00*
16 pages

2566   Ethical and Legal Issues in School Counseling
American School Counselor Association
Ste 625
1101 King St
Alexandria, VA 22314-2957   703-683-2722
                                             800-306-4722
                                       FAX 703-683-1619
                          http://www.schoolcounselor.org
                          e-mail: asca@schoolcounselor.org
Richard Wong, Executive Director
Stephanie Will, Office Manager
Jill Cook, Assistant Director
Contains answers to many of the most controversial and challenging questions school counselors face every day. *$40.50*

ISBN 1-556200-55-2

2567   Fact Sheet: Attention Deficit Hyperactivity Disorder
Learning Disabilities Association of America
4156 Library Rd
Pittsburgh, PA 15234-1349   412-341-1515
                                       FAX 412-344-0224
                                   http://www.ldanatl.org
                          e-mail: ldanatl@usaor.net
Patrica H. Latham, President
Sharon Bloechle, Secretary
Ed Schlitt, Treasurer
A pamphlet offering factual information on ADHD.

2568   Fundamentals of Autism
Slosson Educational Publications
PO Box 280
East Aurora, NY 14052   716-652-0930
                                    800-828-4800
                                FAX 800-655-3840
                             http://www.slosson.com
                          e-mail: slosson@slosson.com
Steven Slosson, President
John Slosson, Vice President

Provides a quick, user friendly effective and accurate approach to help in identifying and developing educationally related program objectives for children diagnosed as Autistic. These materials have been designed to be easily and functionally used by teachers, therapists, special education/learning disability resource specialists, psychologists, and others who work with children diagnosed with similar disabilites.

2569   General Information about Autism
NICHCY
1825 Connecticut Ave NW
Suite 700
Washington, DC 20009   202-884-8200
                                   800-695-0285
                               FAX 202-884-8441
                             http://www.nichcy.org
                          e-mail: nichcy@fhi360.org
Susan Ripley, Director

Offers information about autism.

2570   General Information about Disabilities
NICHCY
1825 Connecticut Ave NW
Suite 700
Washington, DC 20009   202-884-8200
                                   800-695-0285
                               FAX 202-884-8441
                             http://www.nichcy.org
                          e-mail: nichcy@fhi360.org
Susan Ripley, Director

A fact sheet offering information on the Education of the Handicapped Act.
2 pages

2571   General Information about Speech and Language Disorders
NICHCY
1825 Connecticut Ave NW
Suite 700
Washington, DC 20009   202-884-8200
                                   800-695-0285
                               FAX 202-884-8441
                             http://www.nichcy.org
                          e-mail: nichcy@fhi360.org
Susan Ripley, Director

Offers characteristics, educational implications and associations in the area of speech and language disorders.

2572   IDEA Amendments
NICHCY
1825 Connecticut Ave NW
Suite 700
Washington, DC 20009   202-884-8200
                                   800-695-0285
                               FAX 202-884-8441
                             http://www.nichcy.org
                          e-mail: nichcy@fhi360.org
Susan Ripley, Director

Examines the important changes that have occured in the Individuals Education Act, amended in June of 1997. *$4.00*
40 pages

2573   If Your Child Stutters: A Guide for Parents
Stuttering Foundation of America
PO Box 11749
Memphis, TN 38111   901-452-7343
                                800-992-9392
                            FAX 901-452-3931
                         http://www.stutteringhelp.org
                      e-mail: info@stutteringhelp.org
Jane Fraser, President

A guide that enables parents to provide appropriate help to children who stutter. *$1.00*

2574   Individualized Education Programs
NICHCY
1825 Connecticut Ave NW
Suite 700
Washington, DC 20009   202-884-8200
                                   800-695-0285
                               FAX 202-884-8441
                             http://www.nichcy.org
                          e-mail: nichcy@fhi360.org
Susan Ripley, Director

Provides guidance regarding the legal requirement for beginning a student's IEP. *$2.00*
32 pages

2575   Interventions for Students with Learning Disabilities
NICHCY
1825 Connecticut Ave NW
Suite 700
Washington, DC 20009   202-884-8200
                                   800-695-0285
                               FAX 202-884-8441
                             http://www.nichcy.org
                          e-mail: nichcy@fhi360.org
Susan Ripley, Director

A document that examines 2 different interventions for students who have learning disabilities; the first deals with strategies and the second with phonological awareness. *$4.00*
16 pages

2576 **National Resources**
NICHCY
1825 Connecticut Ave NW
Suite 700
Washington, DC 20009
202-884-8200
800-695-0285
FAX 202-884-8441
http://www.nichcy.org
e-mail: nichcy@fhi360.org
Susan Ripley, Director

Lists different organizations that provide information about different disabilities.
6 pages

2577 **National Toll-free Numbers**
NICHCY
1825 Connecticut Ave NW
Suite 700
Washington, DC 20009
202-884-8200
800-695-0285
FAX 202-884-8441
http://www.nichcy.org
e-mail: nichcy@fhi360.org
Susan Ripley, Director

Gives the names of organizations with toll-free numbers who specialize in different disabilities.
6 pages

2578 **Parenting a Child with Special Needs: A Guide to Reading and Resources**
NICHCY
1825 Connecticut Ave NW
Suite 700
Washington, DC 20009
202-884-8200
800-695-0285
FAX 202-884-8441
http://www.nichcy.org
e-mail: nichcy@fhi360.org
Susan Ripley, Director

Provides information to families whose child has been diagnosed with a disability. Also gives insight on how disabilities can in turn affect the family. *$4.00*
24 pages

2579 **Parents Guide**
NICHCY
1825 Connecticut Ave NW
Suite 700
Washington, DC 20009
202-884-8200
800-695-0285
FAX 202-884-8441
http://www.nichcy.org
e-mail: nichcy@fhi360.org
Lisa Kupper, Editor
Susan Ripley, Manager

Talks directly to parents about specific disability issues.

2580 **Planning a Move: Mapping Your Strategy**
NICHCY
1825 Connecticut Ave NW
Suite 700
Washington, DC 20009
202-884-8200
800-695-0285
FAX 202-884-8441
http://www.nichcy.org
e-mail: nichcy@fhi360.org
Susan Ripley, Director

This guide helps to make moving to a new place easier for parents and their children by listing available services in the new area and compiling educational and medical records. *$2.00*
12 pages

2581 **Planning for Inclusion: News Digest**
NICHCY
1825 Connecticut Ave NW
Suite 700
Washington, DC 20009
202-884-8200
800-695-0285
FAX 202-884-8441
http://www.nichcy.org
e-mail: nichcy@fhi360.org
Susan Ripley, Director

Provides a general guide to raising children with learning disabilities in an educational setting. *$4.00*
32 pages

2582 **Promising Practices and Future Directions for Special Education**
NICHCY
1825 Connecticut Ave NW
Suite 700
Washington, DC 20009
202-884-8200
800-695-0285
FAX 202-884-8441
http://www.nichcy.org
e-mail: nichcy@fhi360.org
Susan Ripley, Director

Examines different research regarding the educational methods for children with learning disabilities. *$4.00*
24 pages

2583 **Public Agencies Fact Sheet**
NICHCY
1825 Connecticut Ave NW
Suite 700
Washington, DC 20009
202-884-8200
800-695-0285
FAX 202-884-8441
http://www.nichcy.org
e-mail: nichcy@fhi360.org
Susan Ripley, Director

General information on public agencies that serve the disabled individual.
2 pages

2584 **Questions Often Asked about Special Education Services**
NICHCY
1825 Connecticut Ave NW
Suite 700
Washington, DC 20009
202-884-8200
800-695-0285
FAX 202-884-8441
http://www.nichcy.org
e-mail: nichcy@fhi360.org
Susan Ripley, Director

Offers information regarding special education.

2585 **Questions Often Asked by Parents About Special Education Services**
NICHCY
1825 Connecticut Ave NW
Suite 700
Washington, DC 20009
202-884-8200
800-695-0285
FAX 202-884-8441
http://www.nichcy.org
e-mail: nichcy@fhi360.org
Susan Ripley, Director

A publication to help parents learn about the Individuals with Disabilities Education Act. Also discusses how student access special education and other related services.
12 pages

2586 Questions and Answers About the IDEA News Digest
NICHCY
1825 Connecticut Ave NW
Suite 700
Washington, DC 20009   202-884-8200
                                        800-695-0285
                                    FAX 202-884-8441
                                    http://www.nichcy.org
                                e-mail: nichcy@fhi360.org

Susan Ripley, Director

Covers the more commonly asked questions from families
and professionals about the IDEA. *$4.00*
            28 pages

**2587 Related Services for School-Aged Children with Disabil-
ities**
NICHCY
1825 Connecticut Ave NW
Suite 700
Washington, DC 20009   202-884-8200
                                        800-695-0285
                                    FAX 202-884-8441
                                    http://www.nichcy.org
                                e-mail: nichcy@fhi360.org

Susan Ripley, Director

Examines the different services offered to children with disabilities such as speech-language pathology, transportation,
occupational and physical therapy and special health services. *$4.00*
            24 pages

2588 Resources for Adults with Disabilities
NICHCY
1825 Connecticut Ave NW
Suite 700
Washington, DC 20009   202-884-8200
                                        800-695-0285
                                    FAX 202-884-8441
                                    http://www.nichcy.org
                                e-mail: nichcy@fhi360.org

Susan Ripley, Director

Helps adults with disabilities find organizations that will
help them find employment, education, recreation and independent living. *$2.00*
            16 pages

2589 Serving on Boards and Committees
NICHCY
1825 Connecticut Ave NW
Suite 700
Washington, DC 20009   202-884-8200
                                        800-695-0285
                                    FAX 202-884-8441
                                    http://www.nichcy.org
                                e-mail: nichcy@fhi360.org

Susan Ripley, Director

Part of the Parent's Guide series, this publication examines
the different boards and committees on which parents of
children with disabilities often serve. Also suggests ways to
go about becoming involved with such organizations. *$2.00*
            8 pages

**2590 Special Education and Related Services: Communicat-
ing Through Letterwriting**
NICHCY
1825 Connecticut Ave NW
Suite 700
Washington, DC 20009   202-884-8200
                                        800-695-0285
                                    FAX 202-884-8441
                                    http://www.nichcy.org
                                e-mail: nichcy@fhi360.org

Susan Ripley, Director

Identifies the rights of parents and their children with disabilities and explains when and how to notify the school in
writing about such conditions. *$2.00*
            20 pages

2591 State Resource Sheet
NICHCY
1825 Connecticut Ave NW
Suite 700
Washington, DC 20009-1492   202-884-8200
                                        800-695-0285
                                    FAX 202-884-8441
                                    http://www.nichcy.org
                                e-mail: nichcy@fhi360.org

Susan Ripley, Director

List numbers of different organizations that deal with disabilities by state.

2592 Underachieving Gifted
Council for Exceptional Children
2900 Crystal drive
Suite 1000
Arlington, VA 22202-3557   703-264-9454
                                        888-232-7733
                                    FAX 703-264-9494
                                    TTY: 866-915-5000
                                    http://www.cec.sped.org/
                                e-mail: service@cec.sped.org

Michael George, Director

A collection of annotated references from the ERIC and Exceptional Child Evaluation Resources (171 abstracts). Note:
Abstracts only. Not the complete research. *$1.00*

**2593 What Every Parent Should Know about Learning Dis-
abilities**
Connecticut Assoc. for Children and Adults with LD
Ste 15-5
25 Van Zant St
Norwalk, CT 06855-1729   203-838-5010
                                    FAX 203-866-6108
                                    http://www.CACLD.org
Beryl Kaufman, Executive Director

What to do with a child with a learning disability.

2594 Who's Teaching Our Children with Disabilities?
NICHCY
1825 Connecticut Ave NW
Suite 700
Washington, DC 20009-1492   202-884-8200
                                        800-695-0285
                                    FAX 202-884-8441
                                    http://www.nichcy.org
                                e-mail: nichcy@fhi360.org

Susan Ripley, Director

Takes a detailed look at the people who are teaching children with disabilities. *$4.00*
            24 pages

2595 Your Child's Evaluation
NICHCY
1825 Connecticut Ave NW
Suite 700
Washington, DC 20009-1492   202-884-8200
                                        800-695-0285
                                    FAX 202-884-8441
                                    http://www.nichcy.org
                                e-mail: nichcy@fhi360.org

Susan Ripley, Director

This document describes the steps that the school system
will use to determine if you child has a learning disability.
$2.00
            4 pages

Adults

2596 International Dyslexia Association: Illinois Branch Newsletter
Bldg 7
751 Roosevelt Rd
Glen Ellyn, IL 60137-5904
630-469-6900
FAX 630-469-6810
http://www.readibida.org
e-mail: info@readibida.org.
Jo Ann Paldo, President
Kathleen L Wagner, Executive Director

2597 NICHCY News Digest
NICHCY
1825 Connecticut Ave NW
Suite 700
Washington, DC 20009-1492
202-884-8200
800-695-0285
FAX 202-884-8441
http://www.nichcy.org
e-mail: nichcy@fhi360.org
Lisa Kupper, Editor
Susan Ripley, Director

Addresses a single disability issue in depth.

2598 Volta Voices
Alexander Graham Bell Association
3417 Volta Pl NW
Washington, DC 20007-2737
202-337-5220
FAX 202-337-8314
TTY: 202-337-5221
http://www.agbell.org
e-mail: info@agbell.org
Melody Felzein, Production/Editing Manager
Harrison Judy, Director

Covers a wide variety of topics, including hearing aid and cochlear implants, early intervention and education, professional guidance, legislative updates and perspectives from individuals from across the United States and around the world.

Children

2599 Calliope
Cobblestone Publishing
Ste C
30 Grove St
Peterborough, NH 03458-1453
603-924-7209
800-821-0115
FAX 603-924-7380
http://www.cobblestonepub.com
e-mail: cobbfeedback@caruspub.com
Rosalie Baker, Editor

Kid's world history magazine, written for kids ages 9 to 14, goes beyond the facts to explore provoactive issues. *$29.95*
52 pages 9 times anually
ISSN 1050-7086

2600 KIND News
NAHEE
Washington, DC 02000
202-452-1100
FAX 860-434-9579
http://www.kidsnews.org
e-mail: membership@humanesociety.org
Lesia Winiarskyj, Director Publications
Janet D. Frake, Secretary
Lona Williams, Director

Four-page color newspaper with games, puzzles and entertaining, informative articles designed to install kindness to people, animals, and the enviroment and to make reading fun. *$30.00*
4 pages 9x school year
ISSN 1050-9542

2601 KIND News Jr: Kids in Nature's Defense
Kind News
2100 L St., NW
Washington, DC 02000
202-452-1101
FAX 860-434-6282
http://www.kindnews.org
e-mail: membership@humanesociety.org
Lesia Winiarsky, Director Publications
Janet D. Frake, Secretary
Lona Williams, Director
Short, easy-to-read items on the environment and animal world with puzzles, contests and cartoons. Many illustrations, pictures.

2602 KIND News Primary: Kids in Nature's Defense
Kind News
2101 L St., NW
Washington, DC 02000
202-452-1102
FAX 860-434-6282
http://www.kindnews.org
e-mail: membership@humanesociety.org
Lesia Winiarsky, Director Publications
Janet D. Frake, Secretary
Lona Williams, Director
Short, easy-to-read items on the environment and animal world with puzzles, pictures to color and cartoons. Many illustrations, pictures.

2603 KIND News Sr: Kids in Nature's Defense
NAHEE
2102 L St., NW
Washington, DC 02000
202-452-1103
FAX 860-434-6282
http://www.kindnews.org
e-mail: membership@humanesociety.org
Lesia Winiarsky, Director Publications
Janet D. Frake, Secretary
Lona Williams, Director
Publication put out by the National Association for Humane and Environmental Education, KIND News Sr. is intended for children between grades 5 through 6. The magazine covers different pet issues such as how to care for,feed and play with pets.

2604 Let's Find Out
Scholastic
555 Broadway
New York, NY 10012-3919
212-625-0778
Jamie Martillo, Editor
Richard Robinson, CEO

Get your PreK and K classes off to a great start with Free-trail copies of Let's Find Out, and bring all this to your teaching program: monthly seasonal themes in 32 colorful weekly issues, activity pages to develop early reading and math skills. *$4.25*

2605 National Association for Humane and Environmental Education
2100L St.,NW
Washington, DC 02000
202-452-1100
FAX 860-434-6282
http://www.kidsnews.org
e-mail: membership@humanesociety.org
Lesia Winiarsky, Director Publications
Janet D. Frake, Secretary
Lona Williams, Director

2606 Ranger Rick
National Wildlife Foundation/Membership Services
989 Avenue of Americans
Suite 400
New York, NY 10018   212-730-1700
                            800-822-9919
                        FAX 212-730-1823
                        http://www.nuf.org
                        e-mail: info@nuf.com
Gerry Bishop, Editor
Mark Putten, CEO
Anthony Winn, Director,PSLDI
A magazine for children ages 6-12 that is dedicated to helping students gain a greater understanding and appreciation of nature. *$15.00*

2607 Stone Soup, The Magazine by Young Writers& Artists
Children's Art Foundation
PO Box 83
Santa Cruz, CA 95063   831-426-5557
                              800-447-4569
                        http://www.stonesoup.com
                        e-mail: editor@stonesoup.com
Gerry Mandel, Editor
William Rubel, Editor

A literary magazine publishing fiction, poetry, book reviews and art by children through age 13. ISSN: 0094 579X. *$34.00*

48 pages 6x/year

Parents & Professionals

2608 Association of Higher Education Facilities Officers Newsletter
1643 Prince St
Alexandria, VA 22314-2818   703-684-1446
                              FAX 703-549-2772
                        http://www.appa.org
E L Medlin, Executive VP
John F. Bernhards, Assosiate vice President
Anita Dosik, Publication Manager
A newsletter whose purpose is to promote excellence in the administration, care, operation, planning, and development of higher education facilities.

2609 Children and Families
National Head Start Association
1651 Prince St
Alexandria, VA 22314-2818   703-739-0875
                              FAX 703-739-0878
                        http://www.nhsa.org
                        e-mail: mmcgrady@nhsa.com
Michael McGrady, Executive Director

The magazine of the National Head Start Association.

2610 Connections: A Journal of Adult Literacy
Adult Literacy Resource Institute
100 William T Morrissey Blvd
Dorchester, MA 02125-3300   617-782-8956
                              FAX 617-782-9011
                              TTY: 617-782-9011
                        http://www.alri.org
Connections is primarily intended to provide an opportunity for adult educators in the Boston area to communicate with colleagues.

2611 Council for Exceptional Children
Ste 300
1110 N Glebe Rd
Arlington, VA 22201-5704   703-243-0446
                              888-232-7733
                        FAX 703-264-9494
                        TTY: 703-264-9446
                        http://www.cec.sped.org
                        e-mail: cathym@cec.sped.org
Bruce Ramirez, Manager
Dave Edyburn, Editor
Nancy Safer, Executive Director
The Council for Exceptional Children (CEC) is the largest international professional organization dedicated to improving the educational success of individuals with disabilities and/or gifts and talents. CEC advocates for appropriate governmental policies, sets professional standards, provides professional development, advocates for individuals with exceptionalities, and helps professionals obtain conditions and resources necessary for effective professional practice.

2612 Education Funding News
Education Funding Research Council
1725 K St NW
Washington, DC 20006-1401   202-872-4000
                              800-876-0226
                        FAX 800-926-2012
                        http://www.grantsandfunding.com
Emily Lechy, Editor
Phil Gabel, CEO

Provides the latest details on funding opportunities in education. *$298.00*
50 pages

2613 Exceptional Children
Council for Exceptional Children
1110 N Glebe Rd
Ste 300
Arlington, VA 22201-5704   703-264-9454
                              888-232-7733
                        FAX 703-264-9494
                        TTY: 703-264-9446
                        http://www.cec.sped.org
Bruce Ramirez, Manager

Peer review journal publishing original research on the education and development of toddlers, infants, children and youth with exceptionality and articles on professional issues of concern to special educators. Published quarterly.

2614 Exceptional Parent Magazine
551 Main St
Johnstown, PA 15901-2032
                              877-372-7368
                        http://www.eparent.com
                        e-mail: epar@kable.com
Rick Rader, Editor-in-Chief
Nikki Prevenslik, Managing Editor
Joseph M Valenzano Jr, President/CEO/Publisher
EP is the magazine for exceptional parents with exceptional children. Each month EP provides a forum to network with others who are providing a richer life for themselves and for their children. ISSN: 0046-9157. *$39.95*
92 pages Monthly

2615 Federation for Children with Special Needs Newsletter
Ste 420
1135 Tremont St
Roxbury Crossing, MA 02120-2199   617-236-7210
                              FAX 617-572-2094
                        http://www.fcsn.org
                        e-mail: fcsninfo@fcsn.org
Richard Robison, Executive Director
Sara Miranda, Associate Executive Director

The mission of the Federation is to provide information, support, and assistance to parents of children with disabilities, their professional partners, and their communities. Major services are information and referrals and parent and professional training.

2616   International Dyslexia Association Quarterly Newsletter: Perspectives
4th Fl
40 York Rd
Baltimore, MD 21204-5243   410-296-0232
                                             800-ABC-D123
                                         FAX 410-321-5069
                                 http://www.interdys.org
                          e-mail: jdallam@interdys.org
Rob Hott, Information & Referral
Lee Grossманÿ, Executive Director

Leading resource for individuals with dyslexia, their families, teachers, and educational professionals around the world. A non-profit organization dedicates to the study and treatment of dyslexia, we encourage you to join our mission and become a member. You will receive regular information about managing dyslexia, access to an international network of professionals in the field, discounts on conference fees and publications, quarterly and biannual publications
50-56 pages Free to Members

2617   International Dyslexia Association: Illinois Branch Newsletter
Bldg 7
751 Roosevelt Rd
Glen Ellyn, IL 60137-5904   630-469-6900
                                         FAX 630-469-6810
                                 http://www.readibida.org
                          e-mail: info@readibida.org
Jo Ann Paldo, President
Kathleen L Wagner, Executive Director

The Illinois Branch, serving the entire state of Illinois and founded in 1978, is dedicated to the study and remediation of dyslexia and to the support and encouragement of individuals with dyslexia and their families.

2618   International Dyslexia Association: Philadelphia Branch Newsletter
P.O.Box 251
Bryn Mawr, PA 19010-0251   610-527-1548
                                         FAX 610-527-5011
Jann Glider, President
Amy Ress, Manager

An international 501(c)(3) nonprofit, scientific and educational organization dedicated to the study and treatment of dyslexia. All branches hold at least one public meeting, workshop or conference per year.

2619   International Reading Association Newspaper: Reading Today
PO Box 8139
Newark, DE 19714-8139   302-731-1600
                                          800-336-7323
                                      FAX 302-731-1057
                              http://www.reading.org
                    e-mail: customerservice@reading.org
Alan Farstrup, Executive Director

The International Reading Association is a professional membership organization dedicated to promoting high levels of literacy for all by improving the quality of reading instruction, disseminating research and information about reading, and encouraging the lifetime reading habit. Our members include classroom teachers, reading specialistsss, consultants, administrators, supervisors, university faculty, researchers, psychologists, librarians, media specialists, and parents.
Bi-monthly

2620   Journal of Physical Education, Recreation and Dance
1900 Association Dr
Reston, VA 20191-1502   703-476-3400
                                      FAX 703-476-9537
                              http://www.aahperd.org
Michael T Shoemaker, Editor
Courtney Schmidt, Associate Editor
Irene Cucina, President
Most frequently published, and most wide-ranging periodical reaching over 20,000 members and providing information on a greater variety of HPERD issues than any other publication. ISSN NUMBER: 0730-3084 *$9.00*
80 pages monthly

2621   LDA Alabama Newsletter
Learning Disabilities Association Alabama
P.O.Box 11588
Montgomery, AL 36111-0588   334-277-9151
                                          FAX 334-284-9357
                                  http://www.ldaal.org
                          e-mail: alabama@ldaal.org
Debbie Gibson, President

Educational, support, and advocacy group for individuals with learning disabilities and ADD.

2622   LDA Illinois Newsletter
Learning Disabilities Association Illinois
Ste 106
10101 S Roberts Rd
Palos Hills, IL 60465-1556   708-430-7532
                                          FAX 708-430-7592
                              http://www.idanatl.org/illinois
Sharon Schussler, Manager

A non profit organization dedicated to the advancement of the education and general welfare of children and youth of normal or potentially normal intelligence who have perceptual, conceptual, coordinative or related learning disabilities.

2623   Link Newsletter
Parent Information Center of Delaware
5570 Kirkwood Hwy
Wilmington, DE 19808-5002   302-366-0152
                                          888-547-4412
                                      FAX 302-999-7637
                              http://www.glrppr.org
                          e-mail: picofdel@picofdel.org
Marie-Anne Aghazadian, Executive Director
Kathie Herel, Assistant Director

GLRPPR is a professional organization dedicated to promoting information exchange and networking to P2 professionals in the Great Lakes regions of the United States and Canada. *$12.00*
20 pages quarterly

2624   OSERS Magazine
Office of Special Education & Rehabilitative Svcs.
303 C St SW
Washington, DC 20202   202-727-6436
                                          800-433-3243
                                      TTY: 202-205-8241
                              http://www.ed.gov
Provides information, research and resources in the area of special learning needs.
Quarterly

2625   Resources in Education
US Government Printing Office
710 N Capitol St NW
Washington, DC 20401   202-512-0132
                                      FAX 202-512-1355
                              http://www.access.gpo.gov
                          e-mail: www.admine@gpo.gov
Patricia Simmons, Manager

A monthly publication announcing education related documents.

2626 **TESOL Journal**
Teachers of English to Speakers of Other Languages
Ste 200
706 S Washington St
Alexandria, VA 22314   703-836-0774
                                    FAX 703-836-7864
                                    http://www.tesol.org
                                    e-mail: info@tesol.org
Rosa Amorosino, Executive Director

TESOL Journal articles focus on teaching and classroom research for classroom practitioners. The journal includes articles about adult education and literacy in every volume year. Subscriptions available to members only.

2627 **TESOL Newsletter**
Teachers of English to Speakers of Other Languages
Ste 200
700 S Washington St
Alexandria, VA 22314-4287   703-836-0774
                                    FAX 703-836-7864
                                    http://www.tesol.org
                                    e-mail: info@tesol.org
Rosa Amorosino, Executive Director

TESOL produces the Adult Education Interest Section Newsletter and the Refugee Concerns Interest Section Newsletter. They provide news, ideas, and activities for ESL instructors. Subscriptions are available to members only.

2628 **TESOL Quarterly**
Teachers of English to Speakers of Other Languages
Ste 200
700 S Washington St
Alexandria, VA 22314-4287   703-836-0774
                                    FAX 703-836-7864
                                    http://www.tesol.edu
                                    e-mail: info@tesol.org
Rosa Amorosino, Executive Director

TESOL Quarterly is a referred interdisciplinary journal teachers of English to speakers of other languages. Subscriptions available to members.

Young Adults

2629 **Get Ready to Read!**
National Center for Learning Disabilities
381 Park Ave S
New York, NY 10016-8806   212-545-7510
                                         888-575-7373
                                    FAX 212-545-9665
                                    http://www.ld.org
                                    e-mail: help@ncld.org

Amber Eden, Assistant Director Online Comm.
Hal Stucker, Managing Editor

The National Center for Learning Disabilities (NCLD) works to ensure that the nation's 15 million children, adolescents, and adults with learning disabilities have every opportunity to succeed in school, work, and life.
Quarterly

2630 **LD Advocate**
National Center for Learning Disabilities
381 Park Ave S
New York, NY 10016-8806   212-545-7510
                                         888-575-7373
                                    FAX 212-545-9665
                                    http://www.ld.org
                                    e-mail: help@ncld.org
Marcia Griffith, Marketing Executive
Hal Stucker, Managing Editor

The National Center for Learning Disabilities (NCLD) works to ensure that the nation's 15 million children, adolescents, and adults with learning disabilities have every opportunity to succeed in school, work, and life.
Monthly

2631 **LD News**
National Center for Learning Disabilities
381 Park Ave S
New York, NY 10016-8806   212-545-7510
                                         888-575-7373
                                    FAX 212-545-9665
                                    http://www.ld.org
                                    e-mail: help@ncld.org
Marcia Griffith, Marketing Executive
Hal Stucker, Managing Editor

The National Center for Learning Disabilities (NCLD) works to ensure that the nation's 15 million children, adolescents, and adults with learning disabilities have every opportunity to succeed in school, work, and life.
Monthly

2632 **Our World**
National Center for Learning Disabilities
381 Park Ave S
New York, NY 10016-8806   212-545-7510
                                         888-575-7373
                                    FAX 212-545-9665
                                    http://www.ld.org
                                    e-mail: help@ncld.org
Marcia Griffith, Marketing Executive
Hal Stucker, Managing Editor

The National Center for Learning Disabilities (NCLD) works to ensure that the nation's 15 million children, adolescents, and adults with learning disabilities have every opportunity to succeed in school, work, and life.
Quarterly

General

2633 Academic Communication Associates
Educational Book Division
PO Box 4279
Oceanside, CA 92052-4279
760-758-9593
888-758-9558
FAX 760-758-1604
http://www.acadcom.com
e-mail: acom@acadcom.com
Larry Mattes, Founder/President

Publishes hundreds of speech and language products, educational books and assessment materials for children and adults with speech, language, and hearing disorders, learning disabilities, developmental disabilities, and special learning needs. Products include books, software programs, learning games, augmentative communication materials, bilingual/multicultural materials, and special education resources.

2634 Academic Success Press
6023 26th Street W
PO Box 132
Bradenton, FL 34206
888-822-6657
http://www.academicsuccess.com
e-mail: info@academicsuccess.com
Paul D Nolting PhD, Learning Specialist
Kimberly Nolting, VP of Marketing & Research

Publishes books and materials in the interest of making the classroom learning experience less difficult, while improving student learning, to transform the classroom into a more successful environment where educators and students can use inventive learning techniques based on sound academic research.

2635 Academic Therapy Publications
20 Commercial Blvd
Novato, CA 94949-6191
415-883-3314
800-422-7249
FAX 415-883-3720
http://www.academictherapy.com
e-mail: sales@academictherapy.com
Jim Arena, President

Publishes supplementary education materials for people with reading, learning and communication disabilities; features professional texts and reference books, curriculum materials, teacher/parent resources, and visual/perceptual training aids.

2636 Active Parenting Publishers
1955 Vaughn Rd NW
Ste 108
Kennesaw, GA 30144-7808
770-429-0565
800-825-0060
FAX 770-429-0334
http://www.activeparenting.com
e-mail: cservice@activeparenting.com
Michael Popkin PhD, President

Provides parenting education curricula, including one for parents of ADD/ADHD children.

2637 Alexander Graham Bell Association for the Deaf and Hard of Hearing
3417 Volta Pl NW
Washington, DC 20007-2737
202-337-5220
866-37-5226
FAX 202-337-8314
TTY: 202-337-5221
http://www.agbell.org
e-mail: publications@agbell.org

Jessica Ripper, Executive Director
Jennifer Vernon, Coordinator Production/Editing

Publishes and distributes books, brochures, instructional materials, videos, CDs and audiocassettes relating to hearing loss. *$62.00*
64 pages Bimonthly

2638 American Guidance Service
PO Box 99
Circle Pines, MN 55014
651-287-7220
800-328-2560
FAX 800-471-8457
http://www.agsnet.com
e-mail: agsmail@agsnet.com
Produces assessments, textbooks, and instructional materials for people with a wide range of needs; publishes individually administered tests to measure cognitive ability, achievement, behavior, speech and language skills, and personal and social adjustment.

2639 American Printing House for the Blind
PO Box 6085
Louisville, KY 40206
502-895-2405
800-233-1839
FAX 502-899-2274
http://www.aph.org
e-mail: info@aph.org
Tuck Tinsley, President
Fred Gissoni, Customer Support
Tony Grantz, Business Development Manager
Promotes independence of blind and visually impaired persons by providing specialized materials, products, and services needed for education and life.

2640 American Psychological Association
750 1st St NE
Washington, DC 20002-4242
202-336-5500
800-374-2722
FAX 202-336-5518
http://www.apa.org/psycinfo
e-mail: psycinfo@apa.org
Norman B Anderson, CEO

Publishes periodicals, including PsycSCAN, a quarterly print abstract that provides citations to the journal literature on Learning Disorders and Mental Retardation, including theories, research, assessment, treatment, rehabilitation, and educational issues. Also publishes Psychological Abstracts, a monthly print reference tool containing summaries of journal articles, book chapters and books in the field of psychology and related disciplines.

2641 Associated Services for the Blind
919 Walnut St
Philadelphia, PA 19107-5287
215-627-5930
FAX 215-922-0692
http://www.asb.org
e-mail: asbinfo@asb.org
Patricia C Johnson, CEO
Lauren Scarpa, Public Relations Officer

Promotes self-esteem, independence, and self determination in people who are blind or visually impaired. ASB accomplishes this by providing support through education, training and resources, as well as through community action and public education, serving as a voice for the rights of all people who are blind or visually impaired.

2642 Association on Higher Education and Disability
Ste 204
107 Commerce Centre Dr
Huntersville, NC 28078-5870
704-947-7779
FAX 704-948-7779
http://www.ahead.org
e-mail: information@ahead.org
Stephen J Smith, Executive Director

A professional membership organization for individuals in volved in the development of policy and in the provision of quality services to meet the needs of persons with disabilities involved in all areas of higher education.

2643 At-Risk Youth Resources
Sunburst Visual Media
303 Crossways Park Drive
Woodbury, NY 11797
FAX 800-262-1886
http://www.at-risk.com
e-mail: customerservice@guidance-group.com
Publisher of life-skills educational media for the K-12 market. In addition, we also produce science and social studies programs for students in grades K-8
78 pages

2644 Bethany House Publishers
6030 East Fulton Road
Ada, MI 49301
952-829-2500
800-877-2665
FAX 952-829-2572
http://www.bethanyhouse.com
e-mail: orders@bakerbooks.com
Gary Johnson, President
Teresa Fogarty, General Publicist

Publishes books in large-print format for the learning disabled.

2645 Blackwell Publishing
350 Main St
Malden, MA 02148-5020
781-870-1200
FAX 781-388-8255
http://www.blackwellpublishing.com
e-mail: dpeters@bos.blackwellpublishing.com
Lisa Bybee, President
Rene Olivieri, Chief Executive
Dawn Peters, Media Contact
Publishes books and journals for the higher education, research and professional markets, including several journals on topics relating to learning disabilities.

2646 Brookes Publishing Company
PO Box 10624
Baltimore, MD 21285
410-337-9580
800-638-3775
FAX 410-337-8539
http://www.brookespublishing.com
e-mail: custserv@brookespublishing.com
Paul Brooks, Owner
Melissa Behm, Vice President

Publishes books, texts, curricula, videos, tools and a newsletter based on research in disabilities, education and child development, including learning disabilities, ADHD, communication and language, reading and literacy, and special education.

2647 Brookline Books/Lumen Editions
34 University Rd
Brookline, MA 02445-4533
617-734-6772
800-666-2665
FAX 617-734-3952
http://www.brooklinebooks.com
e-mail: brbooks@yahoo.com
Milton Budoff, Executive Director

Publishes books on education, learning and topics relating to disabilities.

2648 Charles C Thomas, Publisher, Ltd.
2600 S 1st St
Springfield, IL 62704-4730
217-789-8980
800-258-8980
FAX 217-789-9130
http://www.ccthomas.com
e-mail: books@ccthomas.com

Michael P Thomas, President

Publisher of titles in Criminal Justice and Police Science, the Behavioral Sciences, Education and Special Education, Biomedical Sciences.

2649 City Creek Press
PO Box 8415
Minneapolis, MN 55408
612-823-2500
800-585-6059
FAX 612-823-5380
http://www.citycreek.com
Judy Liautaud, Owner

Publishes books and products offering a literature-based method of learning, such as books, clue cards, posters, magnetic math story boards, workbooks and audio tapes; the program is multisensory, interactive, and appeals to the visual, auditory and tactile learning styles.

2650 Concept Phonics
Oxton House Publishers
P.O.Box 209
Farmington, ME 04938-0209
207-779-1923
800-539-7323
FAX 207-779-0623
http://www.oxtonhouse.com
e-mail: info@oxtonhouse.com
William Burlinghoff, Owner
Bobby Brown, Marketing Director

Publisher of effective, economical educational materials for early reading and math. We pay special attention to materials that work well for students with dyslexia and other learning disabilities.

2651 Corwin Press
Sage Publications
2455 Teller Rd
Woodbury
Thousand Oaks, CA 91320-2218
805-499-0721
800-818-7243
FAX 805-499-9774
http://www.corwinpress.com
e-mail: webmaster@sagepub.com
Blaise Simqu, CEO

Publishes books and products for all learners of all ages and their educators, including subjects such as classroom management, early childhood education, guidance and counseling, higher/adult education, inclusive education, exceptional students, student assessment, as well as behavior, motivation and discipline.

2652 Educators Publishing Service
PO Box 9031
Cambridge, MA 02139-9031
617-547-6706
800-435-7728
FAX 617-547-0285
http://www.epsbooks.com
e-mail: epsbooks@epsbooks.com
Gunnar Voltz, President

Publishes vocabulary, grammar and language arts materials for students from kindergarten through high school, and specializes in phonics and reading comprehension as well as materials for students with learning differences.

2653 Federation for Children with Special Needs
529 Main Street
Suite 1102
Boston, MA 02120-2199
617-236-7210
800-331-0688
FAX 617-572-2094
http://www.fcsn.org
e-mail: fcsinfo@fcsn.org
Rich Robison, Executive Director
Emanuel Alves, Vice President
James F. Whalen, President

The mission of the Federation is to provide information, support, and assistance to parents of children with disabilities, their professional partners, and their communities. Major services are information and referrals and parent and professional training.

2654 Free Spirit Publishing
217 5th Ave N
Ste 200
Minneapolis, MN 55401-1299   612-338-2068
                                     800-735-7323
                                     FAX 866-419-5199
                          http://www.freespirit.com
                          e-mail: help4kids@freespirit.com
Judy Galbraith, Owner

Publishes non-fiction materials which empower young people and promote self-esteem through improved social and learning skills. Topics include self-awareness, stress management, school success, creativity, friends and family, and special needs such as gifted and talented learners and children with learning differences.

2655 Gander Publishing
450 Front St
Avila Beach, CA 93424   805-541-5523
                                     800-554-1819
                                     FAX 805-782-0488
                          http://www.ganderpub.com
Wendy Cook, Sales Director

Publisher and distributor of Lindamood-Bell Programs; Seeing Stars, Visualizing and Verbalizing, On Cloud Nine and Talkies.

2656 Gordon Systems & GSI Publications
PO Box 746
Syracuse, NY 13214-0746   315-446-4849
                                     800-550-2343
                                     FAX 315-446-2012
                          http://www.gsi-add.com
                          e-mail: info@gsi-add.com
Michael Gordon PhD, Founder

Books and videos for parents, teachers, children, siblings and adults re: ADHD and foster care. Gordon Diagnostic System is and FDA approved objective measure for use in evaluations of ADHD anf traumatic brain injury. Attention Training System is used in classroom with ADHD children.

2657 Grey House Publishing
4919 Route 22
Amenia, NY 12501   518-789-8700
                                     800-562-2139
                                     FAX 845-373-6360
                          http://www.greyhouse.com
                          e-mail: customerservice@greyhouse.com
Richard Gottlieb, President
Leslie Mackenzie, Publisher
Laura Mars, Vice President, Editorial
Publisher of reference materials, especially directories and encyclopedias. Other Health titles include: The Complete Directory for People with Disabilities; The Complete Directory of Pediatric Disorders; The Chronic Illness Directory; The Mental Health Directory; Older Americans Information Directory; The Directory of Hospital Personnel; The HMO/PPO Directory; and The Medical Device Register.

2658 Guilford Publications
72 Spring St
New York, NY 10012-4068   212-431-9800
                                     800-365-7006
                                     FAX 212-966-6708
                          http://www.guilford.com
                          e-mail: info@guilford.com
Bob Matloff, President
Chris Jennison, Senior Editor Education

Publishes books for education on the subjects of literacy, general education, school psychology and special education. Also offers books, videos, audio cassettes and software, as well as journals, newsletters, and AD/HD resources.

2659 Hazelden Publishing
PO Box 11
Center City, MN 55012   651-213-4200
                                     800-257-7810
                                     FAX 651-213-4411
                          http://www.hazelden.org
                          e-mail: info@hazelden.org
Nick Motu, VP/Publisher
Christine Anderson, Public Relations

Hazelden a national nonprofit organization founded in 1949,helps people reclaim their lives from the disease of addiction.Built on decades of knowledge and exsperience,Hazelden offers a comprehensive approach to addiction that addresses the full range of patient,family, and professional needs, including treatment and continuing care for youth and adults,research,higher education, piblic education and advocacy,and publishing.

2660 Heinemann-Boynton/Cook
361 Hanover St
Portsmouth, NH 03802-6926   603-431-7894
                                     800-225-5800
                                     FAX 603-431-7840
                          http://www.boyntoncook.com
                          e-mail: custserv@heinemann.com
Lesa Scott, VP Human Resources

Publishes professional resources and provides educational services for teachers, and offers nearly 100 titles related to learning disabilities.

2661 High Noon Books
20 Commercial Blvd
Novato, CA 94949-6120   800-422-7249
                                     FAX 888-287-9975
                          http://www.academictherapy.com
                          e-mail: sales@academictherapy.com
Jim Arena, President

Features over 35 sets of high-interest, low-level books written on a first through fourth grade reading level, for people with reading difficulties, ages nine and up.

2662 JKL Communications
Ste 707
2700 Virginia Ave NW
Washington, DC 20037-1909   202-333-1713
                                     FAX 202-333-1735
                          http://www.lathamlaw.org
                          e-mail: lathamlaw@gmail.com
Peter S Latham JD, Director
Patricia Horan Latham JD, Director

Publishes books and videos on learning disabilities and ADD with a focus on legal issues in school, higher education and employment.

2663 Jewish Braille Institute of America
110 E 30th St
New York, NY 10016-7393   212-889-2525
                                     800-433-1531
                                     FAX 212-689-3692
                          http://www.jewishbraille.org
                          e-mail: eisler@jbilibrary.org
Dr. Ellen Isler, President
Israel Taub, Associate Director
Sandra Radinsky, Director of Development

Publishes magazines, a newsletter, and special resources available to the reading disabled who are themselves print-handicapped in varying degrees. Seeks the integration of Jews who are blind, visually impaired and reading disabled into the Jewish community and society.

2664   Learning Disabilities Association of America

4156 Library Rd
Pittsburgh, PA 15234-1349   412-341-1515
                                    FAX 412-344-0224
                              http://www.ldanatl.org
                              e-mail: info@ldaamerica.org

Sheila Buckley, President
Suzanne Fornaro, First VP
Connie Parr, Second VP

Maintains a large inventory of publications, videos and other materials related to learning disabilities, and publishes two periodicals available by subscription as well as various books, booklets, brochures, papers and pamphlets on topics related to learning disabilities.

2665   Learning Disabilities Resources

6 E Eagle Rd
Havertown, PA 19083-1424   610-446-6126
                                          800-869-8336
                                    FAX 610-446-6129
                          http://www.learningdifferences.com
                              e-mail: rcooper-ldr@comcast.net

Rich Cooper, Owner

Offers a variety of resources to help teach the learning disabled, including alternative ways to teach math, language, spelling, vocabulary, and also how to organize and study. Available in books, videos, and audio tapes.

2666   Library Reproduction Service

14214 S Figueroa St
Los Angeles, CA 90061-1034   310-354-2610
                                          800-255-5002
                                    FAX 310-354-2601
                          http://www.lrs-largeprint.com
                              e-mail: lrsprint@aol.com

Peter Jones, Owner

Offers large print reproductions to special needs students in first grade through post-secondary, as well as adult basic and continuing education programs; also produces an extensive collection of large print classics for all ages as well as children's literature.

2667   LinguiSystems

3100 4th Ave
East Moline, IL 61244-9700   309-755-2300
                                          800-776-4332
                                    FAX 309-755-2377
                                    TDD:800-933-8331
                          http://www.linguisystems.com
                              e-mail: service@linguisystems.com

Linda Bowers, CEO
Rosemary Huisingh, Co-Owner

Publishes a newsletter and speech-language materials for learning disabilities, ADD/ADHD, auditory processing and listening, language skills, fluency and voice, reading and comprehension, social skills and pragmatics, vocabulary and concepts, writing, spelling, punctuation and other specialized subjects.

2668   Love Publishing Company

Ste 2200
9101 E Kenyon Ave
Denver, CO 80237-1854   303-221-7333
                                    FAX 303-221-7444
                          http://www.lovepublishing.com
                              e-mail: lpc@lovepublishing.com

Stan Love, Owner

Publishes titles for use in special education, counseling, social work, and individuals with learning differences.

2669   Magination Press

750 1st St NE
Washington, DC 20002-4241   202-336-5510
                                          800-374-2721
                                    FAX 202-336-5500
                          http://www.maginationpress.com
                              e-mail: magination@apa.org

Publishes special books for children's special concerns, including starting school, learning disabilities, and other topics in psychology, development and mental health.

2670   Marsh Media

8025 Ward Parkway Plz
Kansas City, MO 64114-2131   816-523-1059
                                          800-821-3303
                                    FAX 816-333-7421
                          http://www.marshmedia.com
                              e-mail: info@marshmedia.com

Joan Marsh, President

Puberty education for students with special needs curriculum. DVDs on personal safety and social skills.
1969

2671   Mindworks Press

4019 Westerly Pl
Ste 100
Newport Beach, CA 92660-2333   949-266-3700
                                    FAX 949-266-3770
                          http://www.amenclinics.com
                              e-mail: contact@amenclinic.com

Daniel G Amen, Medical Director & CEO

Features books, audio, video, and CD-ROMs addressing a range of disorders, including anxiety, depression, obsessive-compulsiveness and ADD.

2672   National Association for Visually Handicapped

111 E 59th St
New York, NY 10022-1202   212-889-3141
                                    FAX 212-727-2931
                          http://www.lighthouse.org
                              e-mail: staff@navh.org

Lorianie Marchi, CEO

Publishes information about sight and sight problems for adults and children. Offers a product line of low-vision aids, a collection of articles about eye conditions, causes and treatment modalities, and a newsletter issued four times a year with information to assist people in dealing with low vision.

2673   National Bible Association

405 Lexington Avenue
New York, NY 10174   212-765-0847
                                          212-907-6427
                                    FAX 212-408-1360
                          http://www.nationalbible.org
                              e-mail: nba@nationalbible.org

Eugene B Habecker, President
Tamara Collins, VP Reading Program

Publishes Read it! A Journal for Bible Readers, which is issued three times a year. Also offers many versions of the Bible, including large-print editions and the easy-to-read Contemporary English Version.

2674   Northwest Media

326 W 12th Ave
Eugene, OR 97401-3449   541-343-6636
                                          800-777-6636
                                    FAX 541-343-0177
                          http://www.sociallearning.com
                              e-mail: nwm@northwestmedia.com

Lee White, President
Susan Larson, Marketing Director

Publishes material with a focus on independent living and foster care products. Training resources for parents: www.fosterparentcollege.com and for teens: www.vstreet.com.

2675 PEAK Parent Center
Ste 200
611 N Weber St
Colorado Springs, CO 80903-1072   719-531-9400
                                          800-284-0251
                                     FAX 719-531-9452
                            http://www.peakparent.org
                            e-mail: info@peakparent.org
Barbara Buswell, Executive Director
Kent Willis, President, Board of Directors

A federally-designated Parent Traning and Information Center (PTI). As a PTI, PEAK supports and empowers parents, providing them with information and strategies to use when advocating for their children with disabilities by expanding knowledge of special education and offering new strategies for success.

2676 Performance Resource Press
Ste F
1270 Rankin Dr
Troy, MI 48083-2843   248-588-7733
                                          800-453-7733
                                     FAX 248-588-6633
                            http://www.prponline.net
                    e-mail: customerservice@prponline.net
George Watkins, President

Publishes over 600 products, including catalogs, journals, digests, newsletters, books, videos, posters and pamplets with a focus on behavioral health.

2677 Peytral Publications
PO Box 1162
Minnetonka, MN 55345   952-949-8707
                                          877-739-8725
                                     FAX 952-906-9777
                            http://www.peytral.com
                            e-mail: help@peytral.com
Peggy Hammeken, President

Publishes and distributes special education materials which promote success for all learners.

2678 Phillip Roy Catalog
Phillip Roy
13064 Indian Rocks Rd
Largo, FL 33774-2001   727-593-2700
                                          800-255-9085
                                     FAX 727-595-2685
                            http://www.philliproy.com
                            e-mail: info@philliproy.com
Phillip Roy, Owner
Ruth Bragman, President

Publishes educational materials written for students of any age with different learning abilities. Offers an alternative approach to traditional education. Free catalog upon request.

2679 Reader's Digest Partners for Sight Foundation
Reader's Digest Rd
Pleasantville, NY 10570   914-244-4900
                                          800-877-5293
                                     http://www.rd.com
                            e-mail: partnersforsight@rd.com
Susan Olivo, VP/General Manager
Dianna Kelly-Naghizadeh, Program Manager
Thomas Ryder, CEO

Offers large type editions of select books and large print editions of Readers Digest Magazines, as well as a foundation newsletter, Sightlines, which is published in large format with large type.

2680 Research Press Publisher
PO Box 9177
Champaign, IL 61826-9177   217-352-3273
                                          800-519-2707
                                     FAX 217-352-1221
                            http://www.researchpress.com
                            e-mail: orders@researchpress.com
Gail ll Salyards, President
Dennis Wiziecki, Marketing

Research Press provides user-friendly research-based prevention and intervention materials.

2681 Riggs Institute
21106 479th Ave
White, SD 57276-6605   503-646-9459
                                          800-200-4840
                                     FAX 503-644-5191
                            http://www.riggsinst.org
                            e-mail: riggs@riggsinst.org
Myrna McCulloch, Founder/Director/Author

Publishes materials to help remedial students using the Orton method, a multisensory approach to learning. Offers a catalog of products, including teacher's editions, phonogram cards, audio CDs for students, student materials and classroom materials.

2682 Scholastic
557 Broadway
New York, NY 10012-3999   212-343-6100
                                          800-246-2986
                                     FAX 212-343-6934
                            http://www.scholastic.com
Richard Robinson, CEO
Barbara A Marcus, VP/President Children's Books
Richard M Spaulding, Executive VP Marketing
Produces educational materials to assist and inspire students of all ages, including a range of special education books, software, and other products.

2683 Schwab Learning
21 Mission Street
San Francisco, CA 94105   415-795-4920
                                          800-230-0988
                                     FAX 415-795-4921
                            http://www.schwabfoundation.org
                            e-mail: info@schwabfoundation.org
Nancy Beachtle, Director
Helan O. Schwab, President

Provides information, guidance, support and materials that address the emotional, social, practical and academic needs and concerns of children with learning difficulties, and their parents.

2684 Slosson Educational Publications
PO Box 280
East Aurora, NY 14052-0280   716-652-0930
                                          888-756-7766
                                     FAX 716-655-3840
                            http://www.slosson.com
                            e-mail: slosson@slosson.com
Steven Slosson, President

Publishes and distributes educational materials in the areas of intelligence, aptitude, developmental disabilities, school screening and achievement, speech-language and assessment therapy, emotional/behavior, and special needs. Offers a product line of testing and assessment materials, books, games, videos, cassettes and computer software intended for use by professionals, psychologists, teachers, counselors, students and parents.

2685 **Teddy Bear Press**
3703 S. Edmunds Street
Suite 67
Seattle, MA 98118   206-402-6947
                                               FAX 866-870-7323
                                    http://www.teddybearpress.net
                              e-mail: fparker@teddybearpress.net
Fran Parker, Author

Publishes books and reading materials designed with the beginning reader in mind, written and illustrated by a special
education teacher specializing in elementary education,
learning disabilities, and education for the emotionally and
mentally challenged.

2686 **Therapro**
225 Arlington St
Framingham, MA 01702-8773   508-872-9494
                                               800-257-5376
                                           FAX 508-875-2062
                                 http://www.theraproducts.com
                              e-mail: info@theraproducts.com
Karen Conrad, Owner

Offers specialty products and publications for all ages in the
field of occupational therapy, including assistive technology, evaluations, handwriting programs, sensory-motor
awareness and alerting products, oral motor products, early
learning products, and perception, cognition and language
resources.

2687 **Thomas Nelson Publishers**
PO Box 141000
Nashville, TN 37214-1000   615-248-2110
                                               800-889-9000
                                           FAX 615-391-5225
                                 http://www.thomasnelson.com
                              e-mail: publicity@thomasnelson.com
Thomas Lewis Nelson, Owner
Michael S Hyatt, Executive VP/Group Publisher
Phil Stoner, Executive VP/Group Publisher
Publishes books and other resources for the learning dis-
abled.

2688 **Thorndike Press**
295 Kennedy Memorial Dr
Waterville, ME 04901-4539   207-859-1000
                                               800-223-1244
                                           FAX 207-859-1008
                           http://www.galegroup.com/thorndike
                              e-mail: gale.printorders@cengage.com
Jamie Knobloch, Director Marketing
Jill Leckta, Publisher

Publishes and distributes over 900 new large-print editions
per year, with an emphasis on bestsellers and genre fiction,
as well as nonfiction titles.

2689 **Ulverscroft Large Print Books**
PO Box 1230
West Seneca, NY 14224-8230   716-674-4270
                                               800-955-9659
                                           FAX 716-674-4195
                                      http://www.ulverscroft.com
                              e-mail: enquiries@ulverscroft.co.uk
Janice Gowan, Executive Director

Publishes large print books and audio products for people
hard of seeing.

2690 **Wadsworth Publishing Company**
10 Davis Dr
Belmont, CA 94002-3002   650-598-9757
                                               800-354-9706
                                           FAX 650-637-7544
                                      http://www.wadworth.com
                              e-mail: brian.joyner@cangage.com
Susan Badger, Acquisitions Editor

Publishes books on a wide range of topics in special education, including behavior modification, language disorders
and development, and learning disabilities.

2691 **Woodbine House**
6510 Bells Mill Rd
Bethesda, MD 20817-1636   301-897-3570
                                               800-843-7323
                                           FAX 301-897-5838
                                 http://www.woodbinehouse.com
                              e-mail: info@woodbinehouse.com
Irv Shapell, Owner

Specializes in books about children with special needs; publishes sixty-five titles within the Special Needs Collection,
covering AD/HD, learning disabilities, special education,
communication skills, and other disabilities, for use by parents, children, therapists, health care providers and teachers.

2692 **Xavier Society for the Blind**
154 E 23rd St
New York, NY 10010-4595   212-473-7800
                              http://www.xaviersocietyfortheblind.org
                              e-mail: info@xaviersocietyfortheblind.org
Kathleen Lynch, Manager
Gina Ballero, Secretary to Director

Provides resources for the visually impaired, including
large-print, braille, and audio products.

Classroom Resources

2693 Collaboration in the Schools: The Problem-Solving Process
Pro-Ed
8700 Shoal Creek Blvd
Austin, TX 78757-6897
512-451-3246
800-897-3202
FAX 512-451-8542
http://www.proedinc.com
e-mail: info@proedinc.com
Donald D Hammill, Owner

An inservice/preservice video that demonstrates the stages of the consultative/collaborative process, as well as many of the various communicative/interactive skills and collaborative problem solving skills. *$106.00*

2694 Educational Evaluation
Stern Center for Language and Learning
135 Allen Brook Ln
Williston, VT 05495-9209
802-878-2332
800-544-4863
FAX 802-878-0230
http://www.sterncenter.org
e-mail: learning@sterncenter.org
Blanche Podhajski, President

The evaluation is an assessment of intelligence, academic achievement, language, and emotional and behavioral issues related to learning and includes pre- and post- evaluation conferences with parents and/ or students as well as an extensive written report detailing results and recommendations.

2695 Fundamentals of Reading Success
Educators Publishing Service
PO Box 9031
Cambridge, MA 02139-9031
617-547-6706
800-225-5750
FAX 617-547-0412
http://www.epsbooks.com
e-mail: eps@epsbooks.com
Arlene W Sonday, Author

This Orton-Gillingham-based video series teaches a phonic or code-emphasis approach to reading, spelling, and handwriting, and provides the foundation for a multisensory phonics curriculum. May be used by teachers and tutors. *$480.00*

ISBN 0-838872-52-2

2696 Individual Instruction
Stern Center for Language and Learning
135 Allen Brook Ln
Williston, VT 05495-9209
802-878-2332
800-544-4863
FAX 802-878-0230
http://www.sterncenter.org
e-mail: learning@sterncenter.org
Blanche Podhajski, President

Individualized instruction to help students develop literacy skills and achieve academic success, building on learning strengths and compensating for areas of difficulty.

2697 Instructional Strategies for Learning Disabled Community College Students
Graduate School and University Center
365 5th Ave
New York, NY 10016-4309
212-817-7000
FAX 212-817-1503
http://www.gc.cuny.edu
Frances Degenhorowitz, President

For working with a cross-section of types of individuals with learning problems. *$47.50*

2698 Key Concepts in Personal Development
Marsh Media
8025 Ward Parkway Plz
Kansas City, MO 64114-2131
816-523-1059
800-821-3303
FAX 816-333-7421
http://www.marshmedia.com
e-mail: info@marshmedia.com
Joan Marsh, President

Puberty Education for Children with Special Needs. Comprehensive, gender-specific kits and supplemental parent packets address human sexuality for children with miild to moderate developmental disabilities.

2699 Living With Attention Deficit Disorder
Aquarius Health Care Media
30 Forest Road
Millis, MA 20054
508-376-1244
888-440-2963
FAX 508-376-1245
http://www.aquariusproductions.com
e-mail: aquarius@aquariusproductions.com
Leslie Kussmann, President
Anne Baker, Billing and Accounting

This video presents tips for teachers and students how to deal with ADD, including how to adapt school structures and classes. *$125.00*
Video, 22 mins

2700 New Room Arrangement as a Teaching Strategy
Teaching Strategies
PO Box 42243
Washington, DC 20015
301-634-0818
800-637-3652
FAX 301-657-0250
http://www.teachingstrategies.com
e-mail: info@teachingstrategies.com
Diane Trister-Dodge, President

A manual and video present the impact of the early childhood classroom environment on how children learn, how they relate to others and how teachers teach. *$35.00*

2701 Now You're Talking: Extend Conversation
Educational Productions
Ste 700
7101 Wisconsin Ave
Bethesda, MD 20814-4814
800-950-4949
FAX 301-634-0826
http://www.edpro.com
e-mail: custserv@edpro.com
Linda Freedman, President

Video. Teachers in a language-based preschool and speech-language pathologists model effective techniques that focus and extend conversations of young children. *$295.00*

2702 Phonemic Awareness: Lessons, Activities and Games
Sage/Corwin Press
2455 Teller Rd
Thousand Oaks, CA 91320-2218
805-410-7408
FAX 805-499-2692
http://www.corwinpress.com
Peggy Hammeken, President

Exceptional field tested guide to help educators who want to reach phonemic awareness as a prerequisite to reading, and/or to supplement the current curriculum. Special educators and speech clinicians will find this practical guide especially helpful as research indicates that deficits in phonemic awareness is often a major contributor to reading disabilities. This book or video contains fifty-eight scripted lessons, forty-nine reproducible blackline master and progress charts.

2703 Professional Development
Stern Center for Language and Learning
135 Allen Brook Ln
Williston, VT 05495-9209
802-878-2332
800-544-4863
FAX 802-878-0230
http://www.sterncenter.org
e-mail: learning@sterncenter.org
Blanche Podhajski, President

Staff development programs for preschool through grade 12 designed in response to requests from teachers and administrators for cutting-edge information about different kinds of learners and the teaching strategies most successful for them.

2704 Purdue University Speech-Language Clinic
100 N University St
West Lafayette, IN 47907-2098
765-494-3663
800-359-2968
FAX 765-494-3660
http://www.cla.purdue.edu
LuAnn Keyton, Director

The Speech-Language Clinic provides opportunities for individuals with communication problems to receive individual and group diagnostic evaluations, screenings and therapy services. The clinic provide services for children and adults with mild to severe speech sound problems and/or impaired oral-motor control, language problems associated with autism, language-learning disabilities, hearing impairment, stuttering, and voice problems. *$81.00*

2705 Restructuring America's Schools
Association for Supervision/Curriculum Development
1703 N Beauregard St
Alexandria, VA 22311-1746
703-578-9600
FAX 703-549-3891
http://www.ascd.org
Gene Carter, Executive Director

A leader's guide and videotape designed for administrators, teachers, parents, school board members, and community leaders.

2706 Skillstreaming Video: How to Teach Students Prosocial Skills
Research Press
PO Box 9177
Champaign, IL 61826-9177
217-352-3273
800-519-2707
FAX 217-352-1221
http://www.researchpress.com
e-mail: rp@researchpress.com
Russell Pence, President

A video and two books providing an overview of a training procedure for teaching elementary and secondary level students the skills they need for coping with typical social and interpersonal problems. *$365.00*

2707 Spelling Workbook Video
Learning Disabilities Resources
PO Box 716
Arlington, VA 22206
610-525-8336
800-869-8336
FAX 703-998-2060
http://www.ldonline.org
An instructional video which works through the spelling workbooks for teachers and students. *$16.00*

2708 Strategic Planning and Leadership
Association for Supervision/Curriculum Development
1703 N Beauregard St
Alexandria, VA 22311-1714
703-578-9600
800-933-2723
FAX 703-575-5400
http://www.ascd.org

Gene Carter, Executive Director

Designed to explain and illustrate effective approaches to dealing with change through strategic planning.

2709 Teaching Adults with Learning Disabilities
Stern Center for Language and Learning
135 Allen Brook Ln
Williston, VT 05495-9209
802-878-2332
800-544-4863
FAX 802-878-0230
http://www.sterncenter.org
e-mail: bpodhajski@sterncenter.org
Blanche Podhajski, President

A videotape training program and companion guide designed to help adult literacy teachers identify and instruct adults with learning disabilities. The focus of this five hour video series is on teaching basic reading and spelling skills. *$199.95*

2710 Teaching Math
Learning Disabilities Resources
PO Box 716
Bryn Mawr, PA 19010
610-525-8336
800-869-8336
FAX 610-525-8337
http://www.ldonline.org
Neol Gunther, Executive Director
Susannah Harris, Senior Manager

A video for educational professionals teaching math to disabled children. *$12.00*

2711 Teaching People with Developmental Disabilities
Research Press
PO Box 9177
Champaign, IL 61826-9177
217-352-3273
800-519-2707
FAX 217-352-1221
http://www.researchpress.com
e-mail: rp@researchpress.com
Russell Pence, President

A set of four videotapes and accompanying participant workbooks designed to help teachers, staff, volunteers, or family members master task analysis, prompting, reinforcement and error correction. *$595.00*

2712 Teaching Strategies Library: Research Based Strategies for Teachers
Association for Supervision/Curriculum Development
1703 N Beauregard St
Alexandria, VA 22311-1714
703-548-9600
FAX 703-575-5400
http://www.ascd.org
HF Silver, Author
Gene Carter, Executive Director

A trainer's manual and five videotapes designed for inservice education of teachers K-12 focusing on four different types of learning expected of students: mastery, understanding, synthesis and involvement.

2713 Teaching Students Through Their Individual Learning Styles
St. John's University, Learning Styles Network
PO Box 417
Henrietta, NY 14467
888-887-7552
FAX 256-740-0310
http://www.learningstyles.net
James Benson, Executive Director

A set of six videotapes introducing the Dunn and Dunn learning styles model. Explains the environmental, emotional, sociological, physical and psychological elements of style.

2714 Telling Tales
KET, The Kentucky Network Enterprise Division
600 Cooper Dr
Lexington, KY 40502-1669   859-258-7000
800-354-9067
FAX 859-258-7396
http://www.tellingtales.org
e-mail: info@tellingtales.org
Susan Jasper, Founder

Resource for teachers,librarians and drama departments at all levels of instruction. Telling Tales can be used to encourage creativity and self expression and help students understand their cultural and language arts skills, and develop openess to diverse cultures, build self confidence and leadership skills, improve communication and language arts skills and develop oral history projects. *$30.00*

2715 Word Feathers
KET, The Kentucky Network Enterprise Division
600 Cooper Dr
Lexington, KY 40502-1669   859-258-7000
800-354-9067
FAX 859-258-7396
http://www.tellingtales.org
e-mail: info@tellingtales.org
Susan Jasper, Founder

An activity-oriented language arts video series.

Parents & Professionals

2716 3 R'S for Special Education: Rights, Resources, Results
Brookes Publishing Company
PO Box 10624
Baltimore, MD 21285   410-337-9580
800-638-3775
FAX 410-337-8539
http://www.pbrookes.com
e-mail: custserv@pbrookes.com
Paul H Brooks, Owner

This video helps parents navigate the steps of the special education system and work towards securing the best education and services for their children. *$49.95*
Video

2717 A Child's First Words
Orange County Learning Disabilities Association
PO Box 25772
Santa Ana, CA 92799-5772   714-547-4206
http://www.oclda.org
e-mail: info@oclda.org
Shows the importance of not waiting until your child is older to worry about their speech. *$20.00*
Catalog #7353

2718 A Culture Undiscovered
Fanlight Productions
Ste 2
4196 Washington St
Boston, MA 02131-1731   617-469-4999
FAX 617-469-3379
http://www.fanlight.com
e-mail: fanlight@fanlight.com
Ben Achtenberg, Owner
Nicole Johnson, Publicity Coordinator

Explores the needs and experiences of college students, from diverse racial and/or ethnic backgrounds, who have learning disabilities.
Video, 36 min

2719 A Mind of Your Own
Fanlight Productions
Ste 2a
4196 Washington St
Boston, MA 02131-1731   617-469-4999
800-937-4113
FAX 617-469-3379
http://www.fanlight.com
e-mail: fanlight@fanlight.com
Ben Achtenberg, Owner
Nicole Johnson, Publicity Coordinator

New video on learning disabilities from the National Film Board of Canada, follows four learning disabled students through their struggles academically and socially as well as their successes in learning to cope with their disabilities and develop their own unique talents. Amtec Award of Merit. 37 minutes. *$199.00*
Rental $60/day
ISSN DD29-0

2720 ABC's of Learning Disabilities
American Federation of Teachers
555 New Jersey Ave NW
Washington, DC 20001-2029   202-879-4400
FAX 202-879-4597
http://www.aft.org
e-mail: online@aft.org
Sandra Feldman, President

This film illustrates the case histories of four learning disabled students with various learning disabilities.

2721 ADHD
Brookes Publishing Company
PO Box 10624
Baltimore, MD 21285   800-638-3775
FAX 410-337-8539
http://www.pbrookes.com
e-mail: custserv@pbrookes.com
Paul H Brooks, President
Melissa A Behm, Executive Vice President
George Stamathis, Vice President/Publisher
This video shows methods for helping students who have ADHD increase attention to tasks, improve listening skills, become better organized, and boost work production. *$99.00*

Video
ISBN 1-557661-15-4

2722 ADHD in Adults
Guilford Publications
72 Spring St
New York, NY 10012-4019   212-431-9800
800-365-7006
FAX 212-966-6708
http://www.guilford.com
e-mail: info@guilford.com
Bob Matloff, President
Jody Falco, Editor in Chief

This program integrates information on ADHD with the actual experiences of four adults who suffer from the disorder. Representing a range of professions, from a lawyer to a mother working at home, each candidly discusses the impact of ADHD on his or her daily life. These interviews are qugmented by comments from family members and other clinicians who treat adults with ADHD *$95.00*
36-min VHS

2723 ADHD in the Classroom: Strategies for Teachers
Guilford Publications
72 Spring St
New York, NY 10012-4019   212-431-9800
800-365-7006
FAX 212-966-6708
http://www.guilford.com
e-mail: info@guilford.com

Bob Matloff, President
Jody Falco, Editor in Chief

Viewers see the problems teachers encounter with children who suffer with ADHD, as well as instructive demonstrations of effective behavior management techbiques including color charts and signs, point system, token economy, and turtle-control technique. Also includes a Leader's Guide and a 42-page Manual. *$95.00*
36-min. VHS

2724 ADHD: What Can We Do?
Guilford Publications
72 Spring St
New York, NY 10012-4019   212-431-9800
                                  800-365-7006
                             FAX 212-966-6708
                        http://www.guilford.com
                         e-mail: info@guilford.com

Bob Matloff, President
Jody Falco, Editor in Chief

A video program that introduces teachers and parents to a variety of the most effective techniques for managing ADHD in the classroom, at home, and on gamily outings. Includes Leader's Guide and 30-page Manual. *$95.00*

ISBN 0-898629-72-1

2725 ADHD: What Do We Know?
Guilford Publications
72 Spring St
New York, NY 10012-4019   212-431-9800
                                  800-365-7006
                             FAX 212-966-6708
                        http://www.guilford.com
                         e-mail: info@guilford.com

Bob Matloff, President
Jody Falco, Editor in Chief

An introduction for teachers and special education practitioners, school psychologists and parents of ADHD children. Topics outlined in this videoinclude the causes and prevalence of ADHD, ways children with ADHD behave, otherconditions that may accompany ADHD and long-term prospects for children with ADHD. *$95.00*
Video

2726 Adapting to Your Child's Personality
Aquarius Health Media Care
30 Forest Road
Millis, MA 20054-1066   508-376-1244
                                  888-440-2963
                             FAX 508-376-1245
                     http://www.aquarisproductions.com
                  e-mail: aquarius@aquarisproductions.com
Leslie Kussmann, President
Anne Baker, Billing and Accounting

Join a child behavioral specialist, two moms and their toddlers (with different personalities!) to find out how to mold your own responses so that you can more effectively influence your child. VHS: A-KIDSPERSONAL also on DVD. *$ 145.00*
Video, 30 mins

2727 Adults with Learning Problems
Learning Disabilities Resources
2775 S. Quincy St
Arlington, VA 22206   610-525-8336
                                 800-869-8336
                            FAX 703-998-2060
                        http://www.ldonline.org
Neol Gunther, Executive Director
Susannah Harris, Senior Manager

Educational materials for adults with a learning disability.

2728 All Children Learn Differently
Orange County Learning Disabilities Association
PO Box 25772
Santa Ana, CA 92799-5772   714-547-7206
                         http://www.oclda.org
                          e-mail: info@oclda.org
Covers cognitive, perceptual, nutritional, optometric, speech and language motor aspects. *$29.95*
Catalog #6812

2729 American Sign Language Phrase Book Videotape Series
Harris Communications
15155 Technology Dr
Eden Prairie, MN 55344-2273   952-906-1180
                                  800-825-6758
                             FAX 952-906-1099
                            TDD:952-906-1198
                             TTY: 800-825-9187
                        http://www.harriscomm.com
                         e-mail: info@harriscomm.com
Darla Hudson, Customer Service

Includes book and three videotapes, each 60 minutes long. In Volume 1 you will find everyday expressions, signing and deafness, getting acquainted, health and water; in Volume 2 you will find family, school, food and drink, clothing, sports and recreation; and in Volume 3 you will find travel, animal, colors, civics, religion, numbers, time, dates and money. Set of books and videos. Part #BVT141. *$134.95*

2730 Andreas: Outcomes of Inclusion
Center on Disability and Community Inclusion
499c Waterman Building
Burlington, VT 05401   802-651-9050
                             FAX 802-656-1357
                             TTY: 802-656-4031
                    http://www.uvm.edu/zvapvt/timfox
                       e-mail: syuan@zoo.uvm.edu
Mitch Cantor, Executive Director

Video portrays the academic, occupational, and social inclusion of a high school student with severe disabilities. Includes commentary of parents, administrators, teachers, support personnel, classmates.

2731 Around the Clock: Parenting the Delayed ADHD Child
Guilford Publications
72 Spring St
New York, NY 10012-4019   212-431-9800
                                  800-365-7006
                             FAX 212-966-6708
                        http://www.guilford.com
                         e-mail: info@guilford.com
Bob Matloff, President
Jody Falco, Editor in Chief

This videotape provides both professionals and parents a helpful look at how the difficulties facing parents of ADHD children can be handled. *$150.00*
45-min. VHS

2732 Art of Communication
United Learning
Ste 100
1560 Sherman Ave
Evanston, IL 60201-4817   847-328-6700
                                  800-424-0362
                             FAX 847-328-6706
                        http://www.unitedlearning.com
                         e-mail: info@unitedlearning.com
Ronald Reed, Vice President

Designed for parents and professionals, this video focuses on: effective parent-child communication; nonverbal communication in children; effective listening; effects of negative and critical messages; and deterrents limiting child/parent communication. *$99.00*

2733 Attention Deficit Disorder
Pro-Ed
8700 Shoal Creek Blvd
Austin, TX 78757-6816

512-451-3246
800-897-3202
FAX 512-451-8542
http://www.proedinc.com

Donald D Hammill, Owner
DR Jordan, Author

A video and book providing helpful suggestions for both home and classroom management of students with attention deficit disorder. *$60.00*
Yearly

2734 Augmentative Communication Without Limitations
Prentke Romich Company (PRC)
1022 Heyl Rd
Wooster, OH 44691-9786

330-262-1984
800-262-1984
FAX 330-263-4829
http://www.prentrom.com

David L Moffatt, President
Cherie Weaver, Marketing Coordinator

Prentke Romich Company (PRC) is a worldwide leader in the development and manufacture of augmentative communication devices, computer access products, and other assistive technology for people with severe disabilities.

2735 Autism
Aquarius Health Media Care
30 Forest Road
Millis, MA 20054-1066

508-376-1244
888-440-2963
FAX 508-376-1245
http://www.aquariusproductions.com
e-mail: orders@aquariusproductions.com

Leslie Kussmann, President/Producer

Through therapeutic horseback riding a young boy emerges from his isolated world. He finds a connection with his horse when he isn't able to talk to adults. A teenage girl gains social confidence as she leads her llama at a local fair. This film explores the power animals can have on helping someone with autism to connect. This film is great for anyone working the autistic and their families. VHS: A-DISHWAA also on DVD. *$125.00*
Video, 30 mins

2736 Behind the Glass Door: Hannah's Story
Ste 2a
4196 Washington St
Boston, MA 02131-1731

617-469-4999
800-937-4113
FAX 617-469-3379
http://www.fanlight.com
e-mail: fanlight@fanlight.com

Karen Pascal, Producer
Ben Achtenberg, Owner

New video, produced in association with Vision TV, follows the Shepard family through five years of struggle, hardship and bittersweet success in raising their child, Hannah, who was diagnosed with autism. Offers insight into the stress families and educators face as they tackle this mysterious disorder. Offers hope and inspiration to parents. Recipient of Silver Screen Award; US International Film and Video Festival.

2737 Beyond the ADD Myth
Brookes Publishing Company
PO Box 10624
Baltimore, MD 21285

410-337-9580
800-638-3775
FAX 410-337-8539
http://www.pbrookes.com
e-mail: custerv@pbrookes.com

Paul H Brooks, President
Melissa A Behm, Executive VP
George Stamthis, VP/Publisher
This video builds on the theory that many of the behaviors associated with attention deficit disorder are not solely due to neurological dysfunction but actually result from a wide range of social, psychological, and educational causes. *$22.00*
Video
ISBN 1-557661-15-4

2738 Child Who Appears Aloof: Module 5
Educational Productions
PO Box 957
Hillsboro, OR 97123

503-297-6393
800-950-4949
FAX 503-297-6395
http://www.edpro.com
e-mail: custserv@edpro.com

Linda Freedman, Owner

A 30 minute video and 60 page facilitation packet focusing on children who pull back, who avoid social contact. Teaches strategies to understand and support these children. Part of the Hand-in-Hand Series. *$295.00*

2739 Child Who Appears Anxious: Module 4
Educational Productions
PO Box 957
Hillsboro, OR 97123

503-297-6393
800-950-4949
FAX 503-297-6395
http://www.edpro.com
e-mail: custserv@edpro.com

Linda Freedman, Owner

A 35 minute video and 60 page training facilitation packet examining the issues of anxious children and how a supporting adult can help bring them into play. Part of the Hand-in-Hand Series. *$295.00*

2740 Child Who Dabbles: Module 3
Educational Productions
PO Box 957
Hillsboro, OR 97123

503-297-6393
800-950-4949
FAX 503-297-6395
http://www.edpro.com
e-mail: custserv@edpro.com

Linda Freedman, Owner

A 30-minute video and 60-page training facilitation guide that compares dabbling to quality, invested play and offers various strategies for adultsto help children build play skills. Part of Hand-in-Hand Series. *$295.00*

2741 Child Who Wanders: Module 2
Educational Productions
PO Box 957
Hillsboro, OR 97123

503-297-6393
800-950-4949
FAX 503-297-6395
http://www.edpro.com
e-mail: custserv@edpro.com

Linda Freedman, Owner

A 30-minute video and 67-page training facilitation packet showing how to identify children who cannot engage in play so wander about the room. Shows creative interventions to help teach new skills. Part of Hand-in-Hand Series.

2742 Child Who is Ignored: Module 6
Educational Productions
9000 SW Gemini Dr
Beaverton, OR 97008-7151

503-644-7000
800-950-4949
FAX 503-350-7000
http://www.edpro.vom

Linda Freedman, Owner
Molly Krumm, Marketing Director

A 30 minute video and 60 page facilitation guide illustrating the children who are ignored by others and offering several interventions for them to learn social skills. Part of the Hand-in-Hand Series. *$295.00*

2743   Child Who is Rejected: Module 7
Educational Productions
PO Box 957
Hillsboro, OR 97123   503-297-6393
                                           800-950-4949
                                           FAX 503-297-6395
                                           http://www.edpro.com
                                           e-mail: custserv@edpro.com
Linda Freedman, Owner

A 35-minute video and 60-page facilitation packet with strategies to help children whose behavior and/or appearance causes them to be rejected by other children. Part of Hand-in-Hand Series.

2744   Concentration Video
Center for Alternative Learning
6 E Eagle Rd
Havertown, PA 19083-1424   610-446-6126
                                           800-204-7667
                                           FAX 610-446-6129
                                           http://www.learningdifferences.com
                                           e-mail: rcooper-ldr@comcast.net
Rich Cooper, Director/Founder/Author

A 53 minute instructional video provides an optimistic perspective about attention problems ADD. Dr. Cooper discusses different types of attention problems causes and solutions. The second part of the video contains concentration exercises to help children and adults with attention problems. *$16.00*
53 Mins/Video

2745   Degrees of Success: Conversations with College Students with LD
4th Fl
240 Greene St
New York, NY 10003-6675   212-387-8205
                                           FAX 212-995-4114
                                           http://www.nyu.edu/osl/csd
A new video which features college students with learning disabilities speaking in their own words about: making the decision to attend college, developing effective learning strategies, coping with frustrations and utilizing college support services. Includes resource packet with suggested discussion questions and list of other resources.

2746   Developing Minds: Parent's Pack
Learning Disabilities Resources
PO Box 2284
South Burlington, VT 05407-2284
                                           800-542-9714
                                           FAX 802-864-9846
                                           http://www.ldonline.org
                                           e-mail: ldonline@weta.com
Dr. Mel Levine, Author
Lia Salza, Editorial Associate

Created especially for parents, this video set provides an overview of why some children struggle with learning. The programs offer strategies for supporting kids' learning differences, based on the work of Dr. Mel Levin and his neurodevelopmental view on how to help children and adolescents become successful learners. *$59.90*
2 Videos

2747   Developing Minds: Teacher's Pack
Learning Disabilities Resources
PO Box 2284
South Burlington, VT 05407-2284
                                           800-542-9714
                                           FAX 802-864-9846
                                           http://www.ldonline.org
                                           e-mail: ldonline@weta.com
Dr. Mel Levine, Author
Lia Salza, Editorial Associate

Created especially for educators, this video set provides an overview of why some children struggle with learning. The programs offer strategies for supporting kids' learning differences, based on the work of Dr. Mel Levin and his neurodevelopmental view on how to help children and adolescents become successful learners. *$59.90*
2 Videos

2748   Dyslexia: A Different Kind of Learning
Aquarius Health Media Care
18 N Main St
Millis, MA 20054-1066   508-376-1244
                                           888-440-2963
                                           FAX 508-376-1245
                                           http://www.aquarisproductions.com
                                           e-mail: aquarius@aquarisproductions.com
Leslie Kussmann, President

Part of the Prescription for Learning Series. This programs shows us what it's like to grow up with dyslexia and the challenge people with dyslexia face in school. The video presents tips for teachers and students on how to deal with it, including how to adapt school structures and classes. VHS: A-TISDYSLEXIA *$125.00*
Video, 24 mins

2749   FAT City
Connecticut Assoc. for Children and Adults with LD
Ste 15-5
25 Van Zant St
Norwalk, CT 06855-1713   203-838-5010
                                           FAX 203-866-6108
                                           http://www.CACLD.org
                                           e-mail: cacld@juno.com
Beryl Kaufman, Executive Director
Marie Armstrong, Information Specialist

Nationally acclaimed video designed to sensitize adults to the frustration, anxiety and tension that the learning disabled child experiences daily. Add $5.00 for shipping and handling. *$49.95*

2750   First Steps Series: Supporting Early Language Development
Educational Productions
PO Box 957
Hillsboro, OR 97123   503-297-6393
                                           800-950-4949
                                           FAX 503-297-6395
                                           http://www.edpro.com
                                           e-mail: custserv@edpro.com
Linda Freedman, Owner

Four 20-minute videos used in early intervention efforts for training staff and parents. Teach how to support language acquisition and model responsive, connected adult-child relationships foundational for all development and learning

2751   Getting Started With Facilitated Communication
Syracuse Univ./Facilitated Communication Institute
370 Huntington Hall
Syracuse, NY 13244-2324   315-443-9379
                                           FAX 315-443-9218
                                           http://www.soeweb.syr.edu/thefci
                                           e-mail: fcstaff@syr.edu

Annegret Schubert, Author
Douglas Biklen, Ph.D.ÿ, Director

Details on the getting started process, including discussion of candidacy, facilitator attitude, materials and equipment, and the components involved in a first session. Several first sessions are excerpted, showing a child, a teenager, a person with challenging behavior, and a child with significant but not fully functional speech.

14-min/Video

2752   Getting Started with Facilitated Communication
Syracuse University, Institute on Communication
370 Huntington Hall
Syracuse, NY 13244   315-443-9657
                                         FAX 315-443-2274
                          http://www.soeweb.syr.edu/thefci
                                 e-mail: fcstaff@syr.edu
Annegret Schubert, Author
Douglas Biklen, Ph.D.ÿ, Director

This videotape describes the details of the getting started process, including discussion of candidacy, facilitator attitude, materials and equipment, and the components involved in a first session.

2753   Help! This Kid's Driving Me Crazy!
Pro-Ed
8700 Shoal Creek Blvd
Austin, TX 78757-6816   512-451-3246
                                             800-897-3202
                                         FAX 512-451-8542
                             http://www.proedinc.com
Donald D Hammill, Owner

Designed for parents and professionals working with children up to five years old, this videotape and booklet offers information about the nature, special needs, and typical behavioral characteristics for young children with attention deficit disorder. *$5.00*

2754   How Difficult Can This Be?
Learning Disabilities Resources
PO Box 2284
South Burlington, VT 05407-2284
                                             800-542-9714
                                         FAX 802-864-9846
                                 http://www.ldonline.org
                              e-mail: ldonline@weta.com
Richard Lavoie, Author
Lia Salza, Editorial Associate

This program looks at the world through the eyes of a child with learning disabilities by taking you to a unique workshop attended by parents, educators, psychologists, and social workers. There they join in a series of classroom activities that cause frustration, anxiety and tension - emotions all too familiar to the student with a learning disability. *$49.95*

70 mins/Video

2755   I Want My Little Boy Back
BBC - Autism Treatment Center of America
2080 S Undermountain Rd
Sheffield, MA 01257-9643   413-229-2100
                                             800-714-2779
                                         FAX 413-229-8931
                          http://www.autismtreatment.com
                             e-mail: autism@option.org
Tracy Baisden, Marketing Associate

This BBC documentary follows an English family with a child with autism before, during, and after their time at the Son-Rise Program. It uniquely captures the heart of the Son-Rise Program and is extremely useful in understanding its techniques. *$20.00*

2756   I'm Not Stupid
Learning Disabilities Association of America
4156 Library Rd
Pittsburgh, PA 15234-1349   412-341-1515
                                         FAX 412-344-0224
                                 http://www.ldanatl.org
                          e-mail: ldanatl@usaor.net
This video depicts the constant battle of the learning disabled child in school. *$22.00*

2757   Identifying Learning Problems
Center for Alternative Learning
6 E Eagle Rd
Havertown, PA 19083-1424   610-446-6126
                                             800-204-7667
                                         FAX 610-446-6129
                     http://www.learningdifferences.com
                        e-mail: rcooper-ldr@comcast.net
Rich Cooper, Director/Founder/Author

A presentation made to adult educators and volunteer tutors discusses what to look for in a student who has difficulty learning. The red flags (common behaviors and errors) are described. *$16.00*

1hr 40mins

2758   Inclusion Series
Comforty Mediaconcepts
2145 Pioneer Rd
Evanston, IL 60201-2564   847-475-0791
                                         FAX 847-475-0793
                        e-mail: comforty@comforty.com
Jacky Comforty, Owner

A series of video programs on inclusive education and community life. Titles include: Choices, providing instruction for all audiences to the inclusion process; Inclusion: Issues for Educators, focusing on particular teachers and administrators in Illinois schools; Families, Friends, Futures, emphasizing the need for early inclusion; and Together We're Better, providing an overview of this comprehensive program. Videos available separately or as a set.

2759   International Professional Development Training Catalog
Center for Alternative Learning
6 E Eagle Rd
Havertown, PA 19083-1424   610-446-6126
                                             800-204-7667
                                         FAX 610-446-6129
                     http://www.learningdifferences.com
                        e-mail: scooper-ldr@comcast.net
Rich Cooper, Director

Training session details how individuals with learning differences, problems and disabilities think and learn.

2760   Latest Technology for Young Children
Western Illinois University: Macomb Projects
27 Horrabin Hall
Macomb, IL 61455   309-298-1955
                                         FAX 309-298-2305
                             http://www.mprojects.wiu.edu
                          e-mail: PL-Hutinger@wiu.edu
Patricia Hutinger EdD, Director
Joyce Johanson, Coordinator
Amanda Silberer, Manager
This 25 minute videotape focuses on the Macintosh LC and adaptations for young children and includes a discussion of the features and advantages of the Macintosh LC, software demonstrations, footage of child applications, and ideas for off-computer activities. Videotape and written materials available.OUT OF BUSINESS *$40.00*

16-20 pages

2761 **Learning Disabilities and Discipline: Rick Lavoie's Guide to Improving Children's Behavior**
Connecticut Assoc. for Children and Adults with LD
Ste 15-5
25 Van Zant St
Norwalk, CT 06855-1713 203-838-5010
FAX 203-866-6108
http://www.CACLD.org
e-mail: cacld@juno.com
Beryl Kaufman, Executive Director

In this video, Richard Lavoie, a nationally known expert on learning disabilities, offers practical advice on dealing with behavioral problems quickly and effectively. Shows how preventive discipline can anticipate many problems before they start. Explains how teachers and parents can create stable, predictable environments in which children with learning disabilities can flourish. 62 minutes. *$49.95*

2762 **Learning Disabilities and Self-Esteem**
Connecticut Assoc. for Children and Adults with LD
Ste 15-5
25 Van Zant St
Norwalk, CT 06855-1713 203-838-5010
FAX 203-866-6108
http://www.CACLD.org
e-mail: cacld@juno.com
Beryl Kaufman, Executive Director

The 60 minute Teacher video contains program material for building self-esteem in the classroom. The 60 minute Parent video contains program material for building self-esteem in the home. A 16 page Program Guide accompanies each video. Dr. Robert Brooks, a clinical psychologist, renowned speaker and nationally known expert on learning disabilities, is on the faculty at Harvard Medical School and is the author of The Self-Esteem Teacher. *$49.95*

2763 **Learning Disabilities and Social Skills: Last One Picked..First One Picked On**
Connecticut Assoc. for Children and Adults with LD
Ste 15-5
25 Van Zant St
Norwalk, CT 06855-1713 203-838-5010
FAX 203-866-6108
http://www.CACLD.org
e-mail: cacld@juno.com
Beryl Kaufman, Executive Director

Nationally recognized expert on learning disabilities, Richard Lavoie, gives examples on how to help LD children succeed in everyday social situations. Lavoie helps students dissect their social errors to learn correct behavior. Mistakes are seen as opportunities for learning. Available in parent (62 min.) or teacher (68 min.) version. *$49.95*

2764 **Learning Disabilities: A Complex Journey**
Aquarius Health Media Care
18 N Main St
Millis, MA 20054-2324 508-376-1244
888-440-2963
FAX 508-376-1245
http://www.aquariusproductions.com
e-mail: orders@aquariusproductions.com
Leslie Kussmann, President/Producer

Does your child have trouble reading? Does your daughter seem to have more difficulty with schoolwork than you would expect, even though she's trying her hardest? Is your son avoiding school, claiming illness a little to often, insisitng that he's stupid when you know that's not really true? If so, your child may have a learning disability— a neurological problem processing information that he's actually smart enough to understand. How do you find out? VHS: A-KIDSLD also on DVD. *$125.00*
Video, 26 mins

2765 **Learning Problems in Language**
Center for Alternative
6 E Eagle Rd
Havertown, PA 19083-1424 610-446-6126
800-204-7667
FAX 610-446-6129
http://www.learningdifferences.com
e-mail: rcooper-ldr@comcast.net
Rich Cooper, Founder/Director/Author

This video was recorded at the National Laubach Conference in 1992 for reading tutors and teachers. In the video, Dr. Cooper discusses ideas for teaching reading and other academic skills to adults. *$16.00*
2hr, 50 mins

2766 **Legacy of the Blue Heron: Living with Learning Disabilities**
Oxton House Publishers
PO Box 209
Farmington, ME 04938 207-779-1923
800-539-7323
FAX 207-779-0623
http://www.oxtonhouse.com
e-mail: info@oxtonhouse.com
William Berlinghoff PhD, Managing Editor
Cheryl Martin, Marketing
Debra Richards, Office Manager
Thi book is available in soft cover or as a six-cassette audiobook. It is an engaging personal account by a servere dyslexic who became a successful engineer, business man, boat builder, and president of the Learning Disabilities Association of America. Drawing on his life experiences, the author presents a rich array of wise, common-sense advice for dealing with learning disabilities.

2767 **Letting Go: Views on Integration**
Iowa University Affiliated Programs
100 Hawkins Dr
Iowa City, IA 52242-1016 319-353-6390
800-272-7713
FAX 319-356-8284
http://www.healthcare.uiowa.edu
e-mail: disability-library@uiowa.edu
Three parents share their thoughts regarding the struggle between protecting their children with disabilities verses allowing the same freedom as other children. *$25.00*
19 mins/Video

2768 **Lily Videos : A Longitudinel View of Lily with Down Syndrome**
Davidson Films
Ste 210
735 Tank Farm Rd
San Luis Obispo, CA 93401-7073 805-594-0422
888-437-4200
FAX 805-594-0532
http://www.davidsonfilms.com
e-mail: dfi@davidsonfilms.com
Elaine Taunt, Manager
Fran Davidson, Owner

1. Lily: A Story About a Girl Like Me 2. Lily: A Sequal 3. Lily: At Thirty.

2769 **Making Sense of Sensory Integration**
Therapro
225 Arlington St
Framingham, MA 01702-8773 508-872-9494
800-257-5376
FAX 508-875-2062
http://www.theraproducts.com
e-mail: info@theraproducts.com
Karen Conrad, Owner

A discussion for parents and caregivers about sensory integration (SI), how it affects children throughout their lives, how diagnosis is made, appropriate treatment, recognizing red flags, and how SI difficulties affect child and family in their everyday lives. Informative 33 page book included. 75 minute CD. *$17.95*
31 pages Audio CD
ISBN 1-931615-14-4

2770 Motivation to Learn: How Parents and Teachers Can Help
Association for Supervision/Curriculum Development
1703 N Beauregard St
Alexandria, VA 22311-1746   703-578-9600
                                          800-933-2723
                                     FAX 703-575-5400
                                     http://www.ascd.org
Gene Carter, Executive Director

Two videos intended for all those concerned about how educators and families can develop student motivation to learn, solve motivational problems, and effectively participate in parent-teacher conferences.

2771 Normal Growth and Development: Performance Prediction
Love Publishing Company
PO Box 22353
Denver, CO 80237   303-221-7333
                                     FAX 303-221-7444
                        http://www.lovepublishing.com
                  e-mail: lovepublishing@compuserve.com
Dan Love, Director
Stan Love, Owner

Teaches the age at which skills are normally achieved by children ages 0 to 48 months. *$140.00*
Video

2772 Oh Say What They See: Language Stimulation
Educational Productions
9000 SW Gemini Dr
Beaverton, OR 97008-7151   503-644-7000
                                          800-950-4949
                                     FAX 503-350-7000
                                     http://www.edpro.com
                             e-mail: custserv@edpro.com
Linda Freedman, Owner
Molly Krumm, Marketing Director

A complete video training program illustrating indirect language stimulation techniques to teachers, parents, students, child care staff, and other adult caregivers working with children.

2773 Parent Teacher Meeting
Learning Disabilities Resources
PO Box 716
Bryn Mawr, PA 19010   610-525-8336
                                          800-869-8336
                                     FAX 610-525-8337
                             http://www.ldonline.org
Discusses learning differences and instructional techniques.
$12.00

2774 Phonemic Awareness: The Sounds of Reading
Sage/Corwin Press
2455 Teller Rd
Thousand Oaks, CA 91320-2218   805-410-7408
                                     FAX 805-499-2692
                        http://www.corwinpress.com
                             e-mail: order@corwin.com
Peggy Hammeken, President
Victoria Groves Scott, Author

This staff development video may be used with paraprofessionals and teachers to learn the techniques of teaching pnomemic awareness. *$59.95*
Video
ISBN 1-890455-29-6

2775 Puberty Education for Students with Special Needs
Marsh Media
PO Box 8082
Shawnee Mission, KS 66208   802-821-3303
                                     FAX 866-333-7421
                             http://www.marshmedia.com
                             e-mail: info@marshmedia.com
Liz Smith, Author
Liz Sweeney, Co-Author

Two gender-specific kits include an instructional video, a comprehensive teaching guide and packets of 10 student booklets. These reassuring titles are clear, practical and positive and are intended for the following special populations: Students with developmental disabilities or delays, Intrusive behavior or mental illness, Down Syndrome, Autism Spectrum Disorder, Learning disabilities, Behavioral disabilities, Communicative disorders.
36 pages

2776 Regular Lives
WETA-TV, Department of Educational Activities
Ste 440
2775 S Quincy St
Arlington, VA 22206-2269   703-998-2600
                                     FAX 703-998-3401
                                     http://www.weta.com
                             e-mail: info@weta.com
Sharon P Rockefeller, President

Designed to show the successful integration of handicapped students in school, work and community settings. Demonstrates that sharing the ordinary routines of learning and living is essential for people with disabilities.

2777 STEP/Teen: Systematic Training for Effective Parenting of Teens
AGS
PO Box 99
Circle Pines, MN 55014   763-786-4343
                                          800-328-2560
                                     FAX 763-786-9077
                                     http://www.agsnet.com
                             e-mail: agsmail@agsnet.com
Kevin Brueggeman, Manager

A parent training program designed to help parents of teenagers in the following areas: understanding misbehavior; improving communication and family relationships; understanding and expressing emotions and feelings and discipline. *$229.50*

2778 Speech Therapy: Look Who's Not Talking
Aquarius Health Media Care
18 N Main St
Sherborn, MA 01770-1066   508-650-1616
                                          888-440-2963
                                     FAX 508-650-1665
                        http://www.aquariusproductions.com
                  e-mail: aquarius@aquarisproductions.com
Leslie Kussmann, President

A Keeping Kids Healthy Series. Your child is old enough to be talking - other children are by this age - but for some reason, your child just can't put the words together. When should you step in to help? And what, exactly, can you do? VHS: A-KIDSPEECH. Also available on DVD. *$125.00*
Video, 14 mins

2779 Student Directed Learning: Teaching Self Determination Skills
Beech Center on Disability, University of Kansas
1200 Sunnyside Ave
Lawrence, KS 00000   785-864-7600
                              FAX 785-864-7605
                    http://www.beachcenter.org
                    e-mail: wehmeyer@ku.edu
Mike Wehmeyer, Associate Director

Written for educators and service providers who seek a comprehensive understanding of the process of helping students develop self-determination skills. The text follows academic principles and clearly is geared to professionals rather than to families. An educator seeking to understand technical self-determination concepts will find this organizational structure effective. *$73.00*

ISBN 0-534159-42-7

2780 Study Skills: How to Manage Your Time
Guidance Associates
100 S Bedford Rd
Mount Kisco, NY 10549-3425   914-244-1055
                                800-431-1242
                           FAX 914-244-1056
              http://www.guidanceassociates.com
              e-mail: info@guidanceassociates.com
Fred Gaston Jr, Owner

Describes how to create a personal schedule that will help users get more accomplished each day and waste less time. *$61.00*
   Video

2781 The Power of Positive Communication
Educational Productions
PO Box 957
Hillsboro, OR 97123   503-297-6393
                              800-950-4949
                         FAX 503-297-6395
                    http://www.edpro.com
                    e-mail: custserv@edpro.com
Linda Freedman, Owner

A complete three-session training on CD-ROM teaches how and why to use clear, positive language to help children to follow expectations and learn. Emphasizes strategies that assist both children with special needs and English language learners.

2782 Time Together: Adults Supporting Play
Educational Productions
PO Box 957
Hillsboro, OR 97123   503-297-6393
                              800-950-4949
                         FAX 503-297-6395
                    http://www.edpro.com
                    e-mail: custserv@edpro.com
Linda Freedman, Owner

A complete video training program for beginning childhood teachers,aides and parents illustrating when to join a child's play, how to enhance and extend the play, and when to step back.

2783 Tools for Students
Therapro
225 Arlington St
Framingham, MA 01702-8773   508-872-9494
                               800-257-5376
                          FAX 508-875-2062
                    http://www.theraproducts.com
                    e-mail: info@theraproducts.com
Karen Conrad, Owner

This is a 30 minute fun and participatory 'how-to' presentation which provides solutions to the problems indentified in the Tools for Teachers Video. It can be used by teachers in the classroom and by parents at home. There are 25 sensory tools for movement, proprioception, mouth and hand fidgets, calming and recess. Pencil-holding and hand games to develop hand manipulation skills are also demonstrated. *$25.95*
   Video

2784 Tools for Teachers
Therapro
225 Arlington St
Framingham, MA 01702-8773   508-872-9494
                               800-257-5376
                          FAX 508-875-2062
                    http://www.theraproducts.com
                    e-mail: info@theraproducts.com
Karen Conrad, Owner

Provides a logical approach to sensory integration and hand skill strategies for anyone to use, is ideal for in-services. Within 20 minutes, you'll learn how to help students calm down, focus, and increase their self-awareness. This is a great tool for teachers and therapists (it shows how to inplement sensory diet, into classroom), administrators and parents. *$25.95*
   Video

2785 TrainerVision: Inclusion, Focus on Toddlers and Pre-K
Educational Productions
PO Box 957
Hillsboro, OR 97123   503-297-6393
                              800-950-4949
                         FAX 503-297-6395
                    http://www.edpro.com
                    e-mail: custserv@edpro.com
Linda Freedman, Owner

Instructive video clips focus on non-typically developing toddlers and pre-K children. Shows how to gently support skill building, independence and social competence. The clips are ideal to enrich training, classes and online courses.

2786 Treatment of Children's Grammatical Impairments in Naturalistic Context
Purdue University Continuing Education
1586 Stewart Ctr
West Lafayette, IN 47907   765-494-7231
                               800-830-0269
                          FAX 765-494-0567
       http://www.continuinged.purdue.edu/media/speech
Marc Fey, Presenter

The basic assumption is challenged that language intervention which takes place in naturalistic settings will be more effective than intervention that occurs in settings that are more heavily constrained by a clinician or other intervention agent. The concept of naturalness will be described as a continuum that is influenced by a number of factors that can be manipulated by clinicians. Several effective intervention approaches that reflect different levels of naturalness are presented. *$50.00*
   1hr:42 mins

2787 Understanding Attention Deficit Disorder
Connecticut Assoc. for Children and Adults with LD
Ste 15-5
25 Van Zant St
Norwalk, CT 06855-1713   203-838-5010
                          FAX 203-866-6108
                    http://www.CACLD.org
                    e-mail: cacld@juno.com
Beryl Kaufman, Executive Director

A video in an interview format for parents and professionals providing the history, symptoms, methods of diagnosis and three approaches used to ease the effects of attention deficit disorder. A comprehensive general introduction to ADHD. 45 minutes. *$20.00*

Video

2788 United Learning
Ste 100
1560 Sherman Ave
Evanston, IL 60201-4817   847-328-6700
                                        888-892-3494
                                    FAX 847-328-6706
            http://www.unitedlearning.com
        e-mail: crechner@unitedlearning.com
Ronald Reed, President
Joel Altschul, Vice President
Coni Rechner, Vice President
United Learning is a provider of audio-visual materials that inform and educate people of all ages. It helps teachers teach more effectively and to help students learn more efficiently. Offering videos, cd's, dvd's, and now delivery of video clips and text via the internet.

2789 What Every Teacher Should Know About ADD
United Learning
Ste 100
1560 Sherman Ave
Evanston, IL 60201-4817   847-328-6700
                                        888-892-3484
                                    FAX 847-328-6706
            http://www.unitedlearning.com
            e-mail: info@unitedlearning.com
Ronald Reed, President
Mark Zinselmeier, Operations VP/General Manager
Coni Rechner, Marketing VP
This program is for teachers, paraprofessionals, administrators, and special educators because it separates clearly fact from fiction and is written specifically for and about educators who deal with disruptive, inattentive, and hyperactive pre-school and elementary age children on a daily basis. *$79.00*

28-min. video

2790 When a Child Doesn't Play: Module 1
Educational Productions
PO Box 957
Hillsboro, OR 97123   5.03E+11
                                        800-950-4949
                                    FAX 503-297-6395
              http://www.edpro.com
            e-mail: custserv@edpro.com
Linda Freedman, Owner

A 30 minute video with 100 pages of facilitation materials presentsdramatic footage of children with play problems and how they miss critical opportunities to learn. Illustrates supportive strategies for adults. Foundation program for Hand-in-Hand Series. *$350.00*

Vocational

2791 Different Way of Learning
Brookes Publishing Company
PO Box 10624
Baltimore, MD 21285
                                        800-638-3775
                                    FAX 410-337-8539
              http://www.pbrookes.com
          e-mail: custserv@pbrookes.com
Paul H Brooks, President
Melissa A Behn, Executive Vice President
George Stamthis, Vice President/Publisher
This video prepares students with learning disabilities for the transition from school to the workplace. *$49.00*

Video
ISBN 1-557663-49-1

2792 Employment Initiatives Model: Job Coach Training Manual and Tape
Young Adult Institute
460 W 34th St
New York, NY 10001-2320   212-273-6100
                                    FAX 212-268-1083
                http://www.yai.org
            e-mail: ahorowitz@yai.org
Philip Levy, Manager
Thomas A Dern, Assoc. Executive Director
Aimee Horowitz, Project Specialist
Video and manual providing an overview and orientation for staff members involved in transition services to ensure that they are well-grounded inthe concepts, responsibilities, and activities that are required to provide quality supported employment services.

2793 First Jobs: Entering the Job World
Triumph Learning
PO Box 1270
Littleton, MA 01460-4270
                                        800-338-6519
                                    FAX 212-675-8922
            http://www.triumphlearning.com
    e-mail: customerservice@triumphlearning.com
Career/vocational education with emphasis on job search skills, job interviews and survival skills. *$139.00*

2794 How Not to Contact Employers
Nat'l Clearinghouse of Rehab. Training Materials
6524 Old Main Hil
Logan, UT 84322-6524   435-797-7537
                                    FAX 866-821-5355
              http://https://ncrtm.org/
              e-mail: ncrtm@usu.edu
Sara P. Johnston, M.S, Director
Jennifer Robinson, Official Assistant

A single vignette of what not to do when visiting perspective employers to secure positions for clients. *$10.00*

2795 KET Basic Skills Series
KET, The Kentucky Network Enterprise Division
600 Cooper Dr
Lexington, KY 40502-2296   859-258-7000
                                        800-354-9067
                                    FAX 859-258-7399
                http://www.ket.org
Barbra Ledford, President

Offers an independent learning system for workers who need retraining or help with basic skills

2796 KET Foundation Series
KET, The Kentucky Network Enterprise Division
600 Cooper Dr
Lexington, KY 40502-2296   859-258-7000
                                        800-354-9067
                                    FAX 859-258-7399
                http://www.ket.org
Barbra Ledford, President

A highly effective basic skills series that is tailor-made for the needs of proprietary and vocational schools.

2797 KET/GED Series
KET, The Kentucky Network Enterprise Division
600 Cooper Dr
Lexington, KY 40502-1669   859-258-7000
                                        800-354-9067
                                    FAX 859-258-7399
                http://www.ket.org
Barbra Ledford, President

This nationally acclaimed instructional series helps adults prepare for the GED test.

2798   KET/GED Series Transitional Spanish Edition
KET, The Kentucky Network Enterprise Division
600 Cooper Dr
Lexington, KY 40502-1669   859-258-7000
                                            800-354-9067
                                   FAX 859-258-7399
                                   http://www.ket.org

Barbra Ledford, President

This award-winning series offers ESL students effective preparation for the GED test.

2799   Life After High School for Students with Moderate and Severe Disabilities
Beech Center on Disability, University of Kansas
3111 Haworth Hall
Lawrence, MA 00000   785-864-7600
                                   FAX 785-864-7605
                          http://www.beachcenter.org

A set of three videotapes and a participant handbook document, and a teleconference in which family members, people with disabilities, teachers, rehabilitation specialists, program administrators and policy makers focus on improving the quality of services in high school and supported employment programs.

2800   On Our Own Transition Series
Young Adult Institute
460 W 34th St
New York, NY 10001-2320   212-273-6100
                                   FAX 212-268-1083
                                   http://www.yai.org
                          e-mail: ahorowitz@yai.org
Thomas A Dern, Assoc. Executive Director
Aimee Horowitz, Project Specialist
Designed for parents and professionals, this series of 15 videotapes examines innovative transitional approaches that help create marketable skills, instill self-esteem and facilitate successful transition for individuals with developmental disabilities.

General

2801 www.HealthCentral.com
Former Surgeon-General Dr. C Everett Koop

Information on health and conditions that affect learning, particularly heavy on the ADHD side.

2802 www.ala.org
American Library Association

Run by the American Library Association, this site works to raise public awareness about learning disabilities.

2803 www.allaboutvision.com
All About Vision

Vision information and resources, including articles on learning-related vision problems.

2804 www.apa.org/psycinfo
American Psychological Association

An online abstract database that provides access to citations to the international serial literature in psychology and related disciplines from 1887 to present. Available via PsycINFO Direct at www.psycinfo.com.

2805 www.autismtreatment.com
Autism Treatment Center of America

Since 1983, the Autism Treatment Center of America, has provided innovative training programs for parents and professionals caring for children challenged by Autism, Autism Spectrum Disorders, Pervasive Developmental Disorders (PDD) and other developmental difficulties. The Son-Rise Program teaches a specific yet comprehensive system of treatment and education designed to help families and caregivers enable their children to dramatically improve in all areas of learning.

2806 www.childdevelopmentinfo.com
Child Development Institute

Provides online information on child development, psychology, parenting, learning, health and safety as well as childhood disorders such as attention deficit disorder, dyslexia and autism. Provides comprehensive resources and practical suggestions for parents.

2807 www.disabilityinfo.gov
DisabilityInfo.gov

Provides one-stop online access to resources, services, and information available throughout the federal government to Americans with disabilities, their families, employers and service providers; also promotes awareness of disability issues to the general public.

2808 www.disabilityresources.org
Disability Resources

A guide to internet resources available with information and recommendations for disability assistance.

2809 www.doleta.gov/programs/
O'Net: Department of Labor's Occ. Information

Employment assistance, descriptions, and articles about learning disabled employees and government resources.

2810 www.dyslexia.com
Davis Dyslexia Association International

Links to internet resources for learning. Includes dyslexia, Autism and Asperger's Syndrome, ADD/ADHD and other learning disabilities.

2811 www.familyvillage.wisc.edu
University of Wisconsin-Madison

A global community that integrates information, resources and communication opportunities on the Internet for all those involved with cognitive and other disabilities.

2812 www.funbrain.com
Quiz Lab

Internet education site for teachers and kids. Access thousands of assessment quizzes online. Assign paperless quizzes that are graded automatically by email. Teaching tools are free and easy to use.

2813 www.health.disovery.com
Discovery Health

Information on conditions that impact learning.

2814 www.healthanswers.com
Health Answers Education

Health information, including learning disabilities, etc.

2815 www.healthatoz.com
Medical Network

Health information, including ADD, ADHD, etc.

2816 www.healthcentral.com
HealthCentral Network

Information and products for a healthier life. Includes conditions that impact learning.

2817 www.healthymind.com
HealthyMind.com

Information on ADD and learning disabilities.

2818 www.hood.edu/seri/serihome.htm
Special Education Resources on the Internet

Contains links to information about definitions, legal issues, and teaching and learning related to learning disabilities.

2819 www.icpac.indiana.edu/infoseries/is-50.htm
Finding Your Career: Holland Interest Inventory

Includes information on self-assessing one's skills and matching them to careers.

2820 www.intelihealth.com
Aetna InteliHealth

Includes information on learning disabilities.

2821 www.irsc.org
Internet Research for Special Children

Attention deficit and hyperactivity disorder help website, created so information, support and ADD coaching are available without having to pour over all 531,136 links that come up on a net search.

2822 www.jobhunt.org/slocareers/resources.html
Online Career Resources

Contains assessment tools, tutorials, labor market information, etc.

2823 **www.ld-add.com**
Attention Deficit Disorder (ADD or ADHD)

Do you think that you or your child has ADHD with or without learning disabilities? If the answer is yes, this webpage is for you.

2824 **www.ldonline.org**
Learning Project at WETA

Learning disabilities information and resources.

2825 **www.ldpride.net**
LD Pride Online

Inspired by Deaf Pride, a site developed as an interactive community resource for youth and adults with learning disabilities and ADD.

2826 **www.ldteens.org**
Study Skills Web Site

Run by the New York State Chapter of the International Dyslexia Association; a site for students, created by students; provides helpful tips and links.

2827 **www.marriottfoundation.org**
Marriott Foundation

Provides information on job opportunities for teenagers and young adults with disabilities.

2828 **www.my.webmd.com**
Web MD Health

Medical website with information which includes learning disabilities, ADD/ADHD, etc.

2829 **www.ntis.gov**
National Techinical Information Service

A worldwide database for research, development and engineering reports on a range of topics, including architectural barrier removal, employing individuals with disabilities, alternative testing formats, job accommodations, school-to-work transition for students with disabilities, rehabilitation engineering, disability law and transportation.

2830 **www.ocde.K12.ca.us/PAL/index2.html**
Peer Assistance Leadership (PAL)

A California-based outreach program for elementary, intermediate and high school students.

2831 **www.oneaddplace.com**
One A D D Place

A virtual neighborhood of information and resources relating to ADD, ADHD and learning disorders.

2832 **www.optimums.com**
JR Mills, MS, MEd

Information on learning disabilities.

2833 **www.pacer.org**
Does My Child Have An Emotional Disorder

Our mission is to expand opportunities and enhance the quality of life of children and young adults with disabilities and their families, based on the concept of parents helping parents.

2834 **www.parentpals.com**
Ameri-Corp Speech and Hearing

Offers parents and professionals special education support, teaching ideas and tips, special education continuing education, disability-specific information and more.

2835 **www.peer.ca/peer.html**
Peer Resources Network

A Canadian organization that offers training, educational resources, and consultation to those interested in peer helping and education. Their resources section has information on books, articles and videos.

2836 **www.petersons.com**
Peterson's Education and Career Center

Contains postings for full-and part-time jobs as well as summer job opportunities.

2837 **www.specialchild.com**
Resource Foundation for Children with Challenges

Variety of information for parents of children with disabilities, including actual stories, family and legal issues, diagnosis search, etc.

2838 **www.specialneeds.com**
Special Needs Project

A place to get books about disabilities.

2839 **www.wrightlaw.com**
Wrightslaw

Provides information about advocacy.

Counseling & Psychology

2840 American Psychologist
American Psychological Association
750 1st St NE
Washington, DC 20002-4242

202-336-5500
800-374-2721
FAX 202-336-5518
TDD:202-336-6123
TTY: 202-336-6123
http://www.apa.org
e-mail: journals@apa.org

Norman B Anderson, Editor

Contains archivel documents and articles covering current issues in psychology, the science and practice of psychology, and psychology's contribution to public policy.
9 times x year
ISSN 0003-066X

2841 Educational Therapist Journal
Association of Educational Therapists
7044 S. 13th Street
Oak Creek, WI 53154

414-908-4949
FAX 414-768-8001
http://www.aetonline.org
e-mail: aet@aetonline.org

Jeanette Rivera, President

A multidisciplinary publication, that publishes articles and reviews on clinical practice, research, and theory. In addition, it serves to inform the reader of AET activities and business and presents issues relevant to the practice of educational therapy. *$40.00*
Quarterly

2842 Journal of Social and Clinical Psychology
Guilford Press
72 Spring Street
New York, NY 10012-4019

800-365-7006
FAX 212-966-6708
http://www.guilford.com
e-mail: info@guilford.com

Thomas E Joiner PhD, Editor

Discusses theory, research and research methodology from personality and social psychology toward the goal of enhancing the understanding of human well-being and adjustment. Also covers a wide range of areas, including intimate relationships, attributions, stereotyping, social skills, depression research, coping strategies, and more. It fosters interdisciplinary communication and scholarship among students and practitioners of social/personality and clinical/counseling/health psychology. *$165.00*
128 pages 10x a year
ISSN 0736-7236

2843 Learning Disabilities Research & Practice
Blackwell Publishing
350 Main St
Malden, MA 02148-5089

781-388-8200
FAX 781-388-8210
http://www.blackwellpublishing.com

Charles Hughes, Editor

Because learning disabilities is a multidisciplinary field of study, this important journal publishes articles addressing the nature and characteristics of learning disabled students, promising research, program development, assessment practices, and teaching methodologies from different disciplines. In so doing, LDRP provides information of great value to professionals involved in a variety of different disciplines including school psychology, counseling, reading and medicine. *$68.00*
Quarterly
ISSN 0938-8982

2844 School Psychology Quarterly
American Psychological Association
750 1st St NE
Washington, DC 20002-4241

202-336-5500
800-374-2721
FAX 202-336-5518
TDD:202-336-6123
TTY: 202-336-6123
http://www.apa.org
e-mail: journals@apa.org

Norman B Anderson, Editor

This journal advances the latest research, theory, and practice and features a new book review section. Strengthening the relationship between school psychology and broad-based psychological science. *$57.00*
Quarterly
ISSN 1045-3830

General

2845 ASCD Express
Association for Supervision/Curriculum Development
1703 N Beauregard St
Alexandria, VA 22311-1714

703-578-9600
800-933-2723
FAX 703-575-5400
http://www.ascd.org
e-mail: express@ascd.org

Rick Allen, Editor
Willona Sloan, Editor

This newsletter highlights articles on research-based teaching practices and provides you with quick links to these articles, relevant resources, and multimedia clips. *$29.00*
Bi-weekly

2846 American Journal of Occupational Therapy
American Occupational Therapy Association
4720 Montgomery Lane
Bethesda, MD 20814

301-652-2682
FAX 301-652-7711
TDD:800-377-8555
http://www.aota.org
e-mail: ajoteditor@cox.net

Mary A Corcoran PhD, Editor

An official publication of the American Occupational Therapy Association, inc. This peer reviewed journal focuses on research, practice, and health care issues in the field of occupational therapy. Also publishes articles that are theoretical and conceptual and that represent theory-based research, research reviews, and applied research realted to innovative program approaches, educational activities, and professional trends. *$50.00*
6x a year

2847 American School Board Journal
National School Boards Association
1680 Duke St
Alexandria, VA 22314-3474

703-838-6722
703-838-6722
FAX 703-549-6719
http://www.asbj.com

Marilee C Rist, Publisher
Glenn Cook, Editor

American School Board Journal chronicles change, interprets issues, and offers readers — some 40,000 school board members and school administrators — practical advice on a broad range of topics pertinent to school go9vernance and management, policy making, student achievement, and the art of school leadership. In addition, regular departments cover education news, school law, research, and new books. *$54.00*
Monthly

2848 Annals of Otology, Rhinology and Laryngology
Annals Publishing Company
4507 Laclede Ave
Saint Louis, MO 63108-2103   314-367-4987
                                  FAX 314-367-4988
                              http://www.annals.com
                          e-mail: manager@annals.com
Ken Cooper, President
Richard J. H Smith, Managing Director

Offers original manuscripts of clinical and research importance in otolaryngology - head and neck surgery, audiology, speech pathology, head and neck oncology and surgery, and related specialties. All papers are peer-reviewed *$ 179.00*
  112 pages Monthly
  ISSN 0003-4894

2849 Autism Research Review International
Autism Research Institute
4182 Adams Ave
San Diego, CA 92116-2599   619-281-7165
                                  FAX 619-563-6840
                              http://www.autism.com
Steve Edelson, Editor
Janet Johnson, Managing Director

Covering biomedical and educational advances in autism research. *$18.00*
  Quarterly

2850 CABE Journal
Connecticut Association of Boards of Education
81 Wolcott Hill Rd
Wethersfield, CT 06109-1286   860-571-7446
                                     800-317-0033
                                  FAX 860-571-7452
                              http://www.cabe.org
                          e-mail: bcarney@cabe.org
Robert Rader, Executive Director
Patrice McCarthy, Deputy Director

Reaches virtually all board members, superintendents and business managers in Connecticut. It's the only publication which does so on a regular basis. It is designed to encompass all material in an easy-to-read fashion. Readers if the journal find a wide range of topics covered in each issue.
  11x a year

2851 CEC Today
Council for Exceptional Children
Ste 300
1110 N Glebe Rd
Arlington, VA 22201-5704   703-245-0600
                                  888-232-7733
                              FAX 703-264-9494
                              TTY: 866-915-5000
                          http://www.cec.sped.org
                      e-mail: service@cec.sped.org
Lynda Voyles, Editor
Drew Albritten M.D., President
Bruce Ramirez, Manager
An online member newsletter that keeps you up-to-date on professional and legal developments.
  4x per year

2852 Disability Compliance for Higher Education
LRP Publications
360 Hiatt Dr
Palm Beach Gardens, FL 33418-7106   561-622-6520
                                       800-341-7874
                                   FAX 561-622-0757
                               http://www.lrp.com
                           e-mail: webmaster@lrp.com
Kenneth Kahn, CEO
Virginia Charleston, Product Group Manager
Cynthia Gomez, Author
Combines insightful analyses of disability laws with details of innovative accomodations for your students and staff. *$198.00*
  12 issues/yr

2853 Education Digest
Prakken Publications
PO Box 8623
Ann Arbor, MI 48107-8623   734-975-2800
                                  FAX 734-975-2787
                              http://www.eddigest.com
                          e-mail: pam@eddigest.com
Pam Moore, Editor

The Education Digest reviews recent periodicals and reports on education to produce 12 or more condensations for quick, easy reading, along with the regular monthly columns and features. *$32.00*
  9 Issues

2854 Education Week
Editorial Projects in Education
Ste 100
6935 Arlington Rd
Bethesda, MD 20814-5287   301-280-3100
                                 800-346-1834
                             FAX 301-280-3200
                             http://www.edweek.org
Virginia Edwards, Editor

Offers articles of interest to educators, teachers, professionals and special educators on the latest developments, laws, issues and more in the various fields of education. *$74.94*

2855 Educational Leadership
Association for Supervision/Curriculum Development
1703 N Beauregard St
Alexandria, VA 22311-1746   703-578-9600
                                   800-933-2722
                               FAX 703-575-5400
                               http://www.ascd.org
                        e-mail: edleadership@ascd.org
Marge Scherer, Editor

RICHARD J. H. SMITH
  8x a year

2856 Educational Researcher
American Educational Research Association
1430 17th St NW
Washington, DC 20036   202-238-3200
                              FAX 202-238-3250
                              http://www.aera.net
                          e-mail: pubs@aera.net
Patricia B Elmore, Editor
Gregory Camilli, Editor

Received by all members of AERA, contains scholarly articles that come from a wide range of dosciplines and are of general significance to the education research community.
  9x a year
  ISSN 0013-189X

2857 Educational Technology
Educational Technology Publications
700 E Palisade Ave
Englewood Cliffs, NJ 07632-3060   201-871-4007
                                     800-952-BOOK
                                 FAX 201-871-4009
                     http://www.asianvu.com/bookstoread/etp
                         e-mail: edtecpubs@aol.com
Lawrence Lipsitz, Editor

The world's leading periodical publication covering the entire field of educational technology, an area pioneered by the magazine's editors in the early 1960s. *$179.00*
  6x annually

2858 Gifted Child Today
Prufrock Press
Ste 220
5926 Balcones Dr
Austin, TX 78731-4263   512-300-2220
                                FAX 512-300-2221
                          http://www.prufrock.com
                          e-mail: info@prufrock.com
Susan K Johnsen PhD, Editor
Sarah Morrison, Editor

Offers teachers information about teaching gifted children.
Offers parents information about raising a gifted child, how
to tell if your child is gofted, and effective strategies for
parenting a gifted child. *$40.00*
     Quarterly

2859 Journal of Learning Disabilities
Sage Publications
2455 Teller Rd
Thousand Oaks, CA 91320-2218   805-499-9774
                                    800-818-7243
                              FAX 805-499-0871
                          http://www.sagepub.com
                          e-mail: journals@sagepub.com
H Lee Swanson, Editor

Recognized internationally as the oldest and most authoritative journal in the area of learning disabilities. The editorial
board reflects the international, multidisciplinary nature of
JLD, comprising researchers and practitioners in numerous
fields, including education, psychology, neurology, medicine, law and counseling. *$69.00*
     Bimonthly
     ISSN 0022-2194

2860 Journal of Postsecondary Education and Disability
Association on Higher Education and Disability
Ste 204
107 Commerce Centre Dr
Huntersville, NC 28078-5870   704-947-7779
                              FAX 704-948-7779
                          http://www.ahead.org
                          e-mail: ahead@ahead.org
James Martin PhD, Editor

Serves as a resource to members and other professionals dedicated to the advancement of full participation in higher education for persons with disabilities. Is also the leading forum
for scholarship in the field of postsecondary disability
support services.

2861 Journal of Rehabilitation
National Rehabilitation Association
633 S Washington St
Alexandria, VA 22314-4109   703-836-0850
                                    888-258-4295
                              FAX 703-836-0848
                          http://www.nationalrehab.org
                          e-mail: info@nationalrehab.org
Daniel C Lustig, Editor
David R Strauser, Editor
Sara Sundeen, President
The Journal of Rehabilitation publishes articles by leaders in
the fields of rehabilitation. The articles are written for reha-
bilitation professionals and students studying in the fields of
rehabilitation *$65.00*
     Quarterly
     ISSN 0022-4154

2862 Journal of School Health
Blackwell Publishing
350 Main St
Malden, MA 02148-5089   781-388-8200
                              FAX 781-388-8210
                  http://www.blackwellpublishing.com
          e-mail: customerservices@blackwellpublishing.com
James H Price, Editor

Committed to communicating information regarding the
role of schools and school personnel in facilitating the development and growth of healthy youth and healthy school
environments.
     Monthly
     ISSN 0022-4391

2863 Journal of Special Education Technology
Council for Exceptional Children
Ste 300
1110 N Glebe Rd
Arlington, VA 22201-5704   703-245-0600
                                    888-232-7733
                              FAX 703-264-9494
                          http://www.cec.sped.org
J Emmett Gardner, Editor

The Journal of Special Education Technology (JSET) is a
refereed professional journal that presents up-to-date information and opinions about issues, research, policy, and practice related to the use of technology in the field of special
education. The publication is sent to subscribers and members of the Technology and Media Division of the Council
for Exceptional Children. *$60.00*
     Quarterly

2864 LDA Alabama Newsletter
Learning Disabilities Association of Alabama
PO Box 11588
Montgomery, AL 36111   334-277-9151
                              FAX 334-284-9357
                          http://www.ldaal.org
Debbie Gibson, President
Dr. Jendia Grissett, Secretary

Educational support and advocacy for those with learning
disabilities and Attention Deficit Disorder.

2865 LDA Rhode Island Newsletter
Learning Disabilities Association of Rhode Island
4156 Library Road
Pittsburgh, PA 15234-1349   412-341-1515
                              FAX 412-344-0224
                              TDD:401-946-6968
                          http://www.ldanatl.org
                          e-mail: info@ldaamerica.org
Mary Clare Reynolds, Interim Executive Director
Frank Kline PhD, Editor

A nonprofit, volunteer organization whose members give
their time and support to children with learning disabilities
as well as share information with other parents, professionals and individuals with learning disabilities.

2866 Learning Disabilities Quarterly
Council for Learning Disabilities
PO Box 405
Overland Park, KS 66201   913-491-1011
                              FAX 913-941-1012
                          http://www.cldinternational.org
                          e-mail: ldq@bc.edu
David Scanlon, Editor

Presents scientifically-based research, and includes articles
by nationally known authors.
     4x a year

2867 Learning Disabilities: A Multidisciplinary Journal
Learning Disabilities Association of America
4156 Library Rd
Pittsburgh, PA 15234-1349   412-341-1515
                              FAX 412-344-0224
                          http://www.LDAAmerica.org
                          e-mail: info@ldaamerica.org
Steve Russell, Editor

A technical publication oriented toward professionals in the
field of learning disabilities. *$30.00*
     Quarterly

2868   Learning and Individual Differences
Elsevier
6277 Sea Harbor Dr
Orlando, FL 32887   407-563-6022
                                                          877-839-7126
                                                      FAX 407-363-1354
                                                      TDD:301-657-4155
                                                   http://www.elsevier.com
              e-mail: journalcustomerservice-usa@elsevier.com
E L Grigorenko, Editor

A multidisciplinary journal in education.

ISSN 1041-6080

2869   National Organization on Disability
5 East 86th Street
Ste 400
New York, NY 10028   646-505-1191
                                                          800-248-2253
                                                      FAX 202-293-7999
                                                      TTY: 202-293-5968
                                                      http://www.nod.org
                                                   e-mail: info@nod.org
H.W. Bush, President

Website offering information and articles on the organization.

2870   OT Practice
American Occupational Therapy Association
PO Box 31220
Bethesda, MD 20824-1220   301-652-2682
                                                          800-SAY-AOTA
                                                      FAX 301-652-7711
                                                      TDD:800-377-8555
                                                      http://www.aota.org
                                               e-mail: otpractice@aota.org
Laura Collins, Editor
Frederick P Somers, Executive Director

The clinical and professional magazone of the AOTA. It serves as a comprehensive, authoritative source for practical information to help occupational therapists and occupational therapy assistants to succeed professionally. Provides professional news and information on all aspects of practice and encourages a dialogue among AOTA members on professional concerns and views.
64 pages

2871   Occupational Outlook Quarterly
US Department of Labor
200 Constitution Ave
Washington, DC 20212   202-693-5000
                                                      FAX 202-693-6111
                                                      http://www.dol.gov
Olivia Crosby, Editor

Information on new educational and training opportunities, emerging jobs, prospects for change in the work world and the latest research findings.

2872   Publications from HEATH
HEATH Resource Center
2134 G St NW
Washington, DC 20052   202-973-0904
                                                      FAX 202-994-3365
                                                   http://www.heath.gwu.edu
                                                e-mail: askheath@gwu.edu
Donna Martinez, Director
Dr. Lynda West, Principal Investigator

A newsletter offering information on postsecondary education for individuals with disabilities.

2873   Teaching Exceptional Children
Council for Exceptional Children
Ste 300
1110 N Glebe Rd
Arlington, VA 22201-5704
                                                          888-232-7733
                                                      FAX 703-264-9494
                                                      TTY: 866-915-5000
                                                   http://www.cec.sped.org/
                                                e-mail: service@cec.sped.org
Drew Albritten MD, President
Bruce Ramirez, Manager

Published specifically for teachers and administrators of children who are gifted. Features practical articles that present methods and materials for classroom use as well as current issues in special education teaching and learning. Brings together its readers the latest data on technology, assistive technology, and procedures and techniques with applications to students with exceptionalities. The focus of its practical content is on immediate application.
6x per year

2874   Texas Key
Learning Disabilities Association of Texas
PO Box 831392
Richardson, TX 75083-1392   512-458-8234
                                                          800-604-7500
                                                      FAX 512-458-3826
                                                      http://www.ldat.org
                                                e-mail: contact@ldat.org
Ann Robinson, Editor
Jean Kueker, President

Quarterly newsletter providing information of intrest to parents and professionals in the field of learning.
16-24 pages

Language Arts

2875   ASHA Leader
American Speech-Language-Hearing Association
2200 Research Blvd
Rockville, MD 20850-3289   301-296-5700
                                                          800-498-2071
                                                      FAX 301-296-8580
                                                      http://www.asha.org
                                                e-mail: leader@asha.org
Susan Boswell, Editor

Pertains to the professional and administrative activities in the fields of speech-language pathology, audiology and the American Speech-Language-Hearing Association.
16X/year

2876   American Journal of Speech-Language Pathology: A Journal of Clinical Practice
American Speech-Language-Hearing Association
2200 Research Blvd
Rockville, MD 20850-3289   301-296-5700
                                                          800-498-2071
                                                      FAX 301-296-8580
                                                      http://www.asha.org
                                                e-mail: subscribe@asha.org
Laura Justice, Editor

The journal pertains to all aspects of clinical practice in speech-language pathology. Articles address screening, assessment, and treatment techniques; prevention; professional issues; supervision; and administration, and may appear in the form of clinical forums, clinical reviews, letters to the editor, or research reports that emphasize clinical practice.
Quarterly
ISSN 1058-0360

2877 Communication Outlook
Michigan State University Artificial Language Lab
405 Computer Ctr
East Lansing, MI 48824-1042   517-353-0870
                                     FAX 517-353-4766
                                     http://www.msu.edu
                                     e-mail: artlang@pilot.msu.edu
Rebecca Ann Baird, Editor

Quarterly journal which focuses on communication aids and techniques. Provides information also for blind and visually impaired persons. *$18.00*
        Quarterly

2878 Journal of Speech, Language, and Hearing Research
American Speech-Language-Hearing Association
2200 Research Blvd
Rockville, MD 20850-3289   301-296-5700
                                  888-498-2071
                                  FAX 301-296-8580
                                  http://www.asha.org
                                  e-mail: subscribe@asha.org
Katherine Verdolini, Editor
Karla K McGregor, Editor
Robert Slauch, Editor
Pertains broadly to the studies of the processes and disorders of hearing, language, and speech and to the diagnosis and treatment of such disorders. Articles may take any of the following forms: reports of original research, including single-study experiments; theoretical, tutorial, or review pieces; research notes; and letters to the editor.
        Bi-Monthly
        ISSN 1092-4388

2879 Kaleidoscope, Exploring the Experience of Disability Through Literature and Fine Arts
United Disability Services
701 S Main St
Akron, OH 44311-1019   330-762-9755
                              FAX 330-762-0912
                              http://www.udsakron.org
                              e-mail: kaleidoscope@udsakron.org
Gail Willmott, Editor

Creatively focuses on the experience of disability through diverse forms of literature and the fine arts. An award-winning magazine unique to the field of disability studies, it is open to writers with or without disabilities. KALEIDO-SCOPE strives to express how disability does or does not affect society and individuals feelings and reactions to disability. Its portrayals of disability reflect a conscious effort to challenge and overcome stereotypical and patronizing attitudes. *$6.00*
        64 pages $10.00/year

2880 Language Arts
National Council of Teachers of English
1111 W Kenyon Rd
Urbana, IL 61801-1010   217-328-3870
                               877-369-6283
                               FAX 217-328-9645
                               http://www.ncte.org
                               e-mail: public_info@ncte.org
Patricia Enciso, Editor
Laurie Katz, Editor
Barbara Kiefer, Editor
Language Arts provides a forum for discussions on all aspects of language arts learning and teaching, primarily as they relate to children in pre-kindergarten through the eighth grade. Articles discuss both theory and classroom practice, highlight current research, and review children's and young adolescent literature, as well as classroom and professional resources of interest to language arts educators. *$25.00*
        Bi-monthly

College Guides

2881 NACE Journal
National Association of Colleges and Employers
62 Highland Ave
Bethlehem, PA 18017-9481   610-868-1421
                                           800-544-5272
                                           FAX 610-868-0208
                                           http://www.naceweb.org
                                           e-mail: callen@naceweb.org
Marilyn Mackes, Editor

Gives hard data on practitioners, budgets, the college relations and recruitment function, entry-level hiring, on-campus recruitment, new hires and much much more. *$70.00*
100+ pages Quarterly

Counseling & Psychology

2882 Accommodations in Higher Education under the Americans with Disabilities Act (ADA)
Guilford Press
72 Spring St
New York, NY 10012-4019
                                           800-365-7006
                                           FAX 212-966-6708
                                           http://www.guilford.com
                                           e-mail: info@guilford.com
Michael Gordon, Editor
Shelby Keiser, Editor

This practical manual offers essential information and guidance for anyone involved with ADA issues in higher education settings. Fundamental principals and actual clinical and administrative procedures are outlined for evaluating, documenting, and accommodating a wide range of mental and physical impairments. *$29.00*
245 pages
ISBN 1-572303-23-9

2883 Affect and Creativity
Routledge
270 Madison Ave
New York, NY 10016-601   212-216-7800
                                           800-634-7064
                                           FAX 212-563-2269
                                           http://www.routledge.com
Sandra Walker Russ, Author

This volume offers information on the role of affect and play in the creative process. Designed as a required or supplemental text in graduate level courses in creativity, children's play, child development, affective/cognitive development and psychodynamic theory. *$39.95*
160 pages
ISBN 0-805809-86-4

2884 Best Practice Occupational Therapy: In Community Service with Children and Families
Therapro
225 Arlington St
Framingham, MA 01702-8773   508-872-9494
                                           800-257-5376
                                           FAX 508-875-2062
                                           http://www.theraproducts.com
                                           e-mail: info@theraproducts.com
Winnie Dunn PhD OTR FAOTA, Author

An invaluable resource for sudents and practitioners interested in working with children and families in early intervention programs and public schools. Includes screening, pre-assessment, the referral process, best practice assessments, designing best paractice services and examples of IEPs and IFSPs. Many of the forms (screenings, checklists for teachers, referral forms assessment planning guide, etc.) are reproducible. The case studies give good examples of reports. *$55.00*

2885 Cognitive-Behavioral Therapy for Impulsive Children
Guilford Press
72 Spring St
New York, NY 10012-4019
                                           800-365-7006
                                           FAX 212-966-6708
                                           http://www.guilford.com
                                           e-mail: info@guilford.com
Philip C Kendall, Author
Lauren Braswell, Co-Author

The first edition of this book has been used successfully by thousands of clinicians to help children reduce impulsivity and improve their self-control. Building on the procedures reviewers call powerful tools and of great value to professionals who work with children. This second edition includes treatments, assessment issues and procedures and information on working with parents, teachers and groups of children. *$39.00*
239 pages
ISBN 0-898620-13-9

2886 Curriculum Based Activities in Occupational Therapy: An Inclusion Resource
Therapro
225 Arlington St
Framingham, MA 01702-8773   508-872-9494
                                           800-257-5376
                                           FAX 508-875-2062
                                           http://www.theraproducts.com
                                           e-mail: info@theraproducts.com
Lisa Loiselle, Author
Susan Shea, Co-Author

This book is a comprehensive guide to classroom based occupational therapy. The authors have compiled over 162 classroom activities developed to provide a strong linkage between educational and therapeutic goals. Each structured activity is categorized into standard curriculum subsections (reading, math, written language, etc.). Designed for a 3rd and 4th grade classroom, it can be modified for use in lower grades. *$35.00*
225 pages

2887 Emotional Disorders & Learning Disabilities in the Elementary Classroom
Corwin Press
2455 Teller Rd
Thousand Oaks, CA 91320-2218   805-499-9734
                                           800-233-9936
                                           FAX 805-499-5323
                                           http://www.corwinpress.com
                                           e-mail: order@corwinpress.com
Jean Cheng Gorman, Author

This unique book focuses on the interaction between learning disabilities and emotional disorders, fostering an understanding of how learning problems affect emotional well-being and vice-versa. This resource and practical classroom guide for all elementary school teachers includes an overview of common learning disabilities and emotional problems and a classroom-tested, research-based list of classroom interactions and interventions. *$30.95*
160 pages
ISBN 0-761976-20-2

2888 Emotionally Abused & Neglected Child: Identification, Assessment & Intervention
John Wiley & Sons Inc
111 River St
Hoboken, NJ 07030-5773   201-748-6000
                                        FAX 201-748-6088
                                        http://www.wiley.com
                                        e-mail: info@wiley.com
Dorota Iwaniec, Author

Describes emotional abuse and neglect and how it affects child's growth, development and well-being. Diagnosis, assessment and issues that should be addressed. *$60.00*
        424 pages Paperback
        ISBN 0-470011-01-7

2889 Ethical Principles of Psychologists and Code of Conduct

American Psychological Association
750 1st St NE
Washington, DC 20002-4241   202-336-5500
                                       800-374-2722
                                       FAX 202-336-5633
                                       TDD:202-336-6123
                                       http://www.apa.org
                                       e-mail: psycinfo@apa.org
Marion Harrell, Deport Manager
Norman Anderson, CEO

General ethical principles of psychologists and enforceable ethical standards.

2890 General Guidelines for Providers of Psychological Services
American Psychological Association
750 1st St NE
Washington, DC 20002-4241   202-336-5500
                                       800-374-2722
                                       FAX 202-336-5633
                                       TDD:202-336-6123
                                       http://www.apa.org
                                       e-mail: psycinfo@apa.org
Marion Harrell, Deport Manager
Norman Anderson, CEO

Offers information for the professional in the area of psychology.

2891 HELP...at Home
Therapro
225 Arlington St
Framingham, MA 01702-8773   508-872-9494
                                       800-257-5376
                                       FAX 508-875-2062
                                       http://www.theraproducts.com
                                       e-mail: info@theraproducts.com
Stephanie Parks MA, Author

Practical and convenient format covers the 650 assesment skills from the Hawaii Early Learning Profile, with each page formatted as a separate, reproducible activity sheet. Therapist annotates, copies and hands out directly to parents to facilitate their involvement. *$112.50*

2892 Handbook of Psychological and Educational Assessment of Children
Guilford Press
72 Spring St
New York, NY 10012-4019
                                       800-365-7006
                                       FAX 212-966-6708
                                       http://www.guilford.com
                                       e-mail: info@guilford.com
Cecil R Reynolds, Editor
Randy W Kamphaus, Editor

Provides practitioners, researchers, professors, and students with an invaluable resource, this unique volume covers assessment of intelligence, learning styles, learning strategies, academic skills, and special populations, and discusses special topics in mental testing. Chapter contributions are by eminent psychologists and educators in the field of assessment with special expertise in research or practice in their topic areas. *$89.00*
        718 pages

2893 Helping Students Become Strategic Learners: Guidelines for Teaching
Brookline Books
8 Trumbull Rd
 Suite B-001
Northampton, MA 01060   413 584 0184
                                       FAX 413-584-6184
                                       http://www.brooklinebooks.com
                                       e-mail: brbooks@yahoo.com
Karen Schneid, Author

A practical book that helps the beginning or experienced teacher translate skill-specific strategy methods into their classroom teaching. The author demonstrates how teachers can implement cognitive strategy instruction in their own classrooms. Each chapter includes an introduction to the principles of a given teaching strategy and a review of the skill area in question—namely reading, writing and mathematics. *$27.95*
        Paperback
        ISBN 0-914797-85-9

2894 Overcoming Dyslexia in Children, Adolescents and Adults
Pro-Ed
8700 Shoal Creek Blvd
Austin, TX 78757-6897   512-451-3246
                                       800-397-7633
                                       FAX 512-451-8542
                                       http://www.proedinc.com
                                       e-mail: info@proedinc.com
Dale R Jordan, Author

This book describes some forms of dyslexia in detail and then relates those problems to the social, emotional and personal development of dyslexic individuals. *$42.00*
        417 pages

2895 Pathways to Change: Brief Therapy Solutions with Difficult Adolescents
Guilford Press
72 Spring St
New York, NY 10012-4019
                                       800-365-7006
                                       FAX 212-966-6708
                                       http://www.guilford.com
                                       e-mail: info@guilford.com
Matthew D Selekman, Author

This innovative, practical guide presents an effective brief therapy model for working with challenging adolescents and their families. The solution-oriented techniques and strategies so skillfullly presented in the original volume are now augmented by ideas and findings from other therapeutics traditions, with a heightened focus on engagement and relationship building. *$44.00*
        292 pages
        ISBN 1-572309-59-8

2896 Practitioner's Guide to Dynamic Assessment
Guilford Press
72 Spring St
New York, NY 10012-4019
                                       800-365-7006
                                       FAX 212-966-6708
                                       http://www.guilford.com
                                       e-mail: info@guilford.com
Carol S Lidz, Author

A hands-on guide that is degined specifically for practitioners who engage in diagnostic assessment related to the functioning of children in school. It reviews and critiques current models of dynamic assessment and presents the research available on these existing models. *$25.00*

210 pages Paperback
ISBN 0-898622-42-5

2897 Reading and Learning Disability: A Neuropsychological Approach to Evaluation & Instruction
Charles C Thomas
2600 S 1st St
Springfield, IL 62704-4730   217-789-8980
800-258-8980
FAX 217-789-9130
http://www.ccthomas.com
e-mail: books@ccthomas.com

Estelle L Fryburg, Author

Publisher of Education and Special Education books. *$74.95*

398 pages Paper
ISBN 0-398067-45-8

2898 Revels in Madness: Insanity in Medicine and Literature
University of Michigan Press
839 Greene St
Ann Arbor, MI 48104-3209   734-764-4388
FAX 734-615-1540
http://www.press.umich.edu

Allen Thiher, Author
Karen Hill, Interim Director
Kelly Sippell, Assistant Director
Revels in Madness offers a history of western culture's shifting understanding of insanity as evidenced in its literature and as influenced by medical knowledge. *$75.00*
368 pages Cloth
ISBN 0-472110-35-3

2899 Teaching Students with Learning and Behavior Problems
Pro-Ed
8700 Shoal Creek Blvd
Austin, TX 78757-6816   512-451-3246
800-897-3202
FAX 512-451-8542
http://www.proedinc.com
e-mail: info@proedinc.com

Donald D Hammill, Author
Nettie R Bartel, Co-Author

Provides teachers with a comprehensive overview of the best practices in informal assessment and adaptive instruction. With the current trend both regular and exceptional students will find this text a useful resource. *$63.00*

2900 Treating Troubled Children and Their Families
Guilford Press
72 Spring St
New York, NY 10012-4019
800-365-7006
FAX 212-966-6708
http://www.guilford.com
e-mail: info@guilford.com

Ellen F Wachtel, Author

Integrating systemic, psychodynamic, and cognitive-behavioral perspectives, this acclaimed book presents an innovative framework for therapeutic work. Shows how parents and children all too often get entangled in patterns that cause grief to both generations, and demonstrates ho to help being about change with a combinations of family-focused interventions. *$30.00*
320 pages Paperback
ISBN 1-593850-72-7

General

2901 A History of Disability
University of Michigan Press
839 Greene St
Ann Arbor, MI 48104-3209   734-764-4388
FAX 734-615-1540
http://www.press.umich.edu
e-mail: ump.webmaster@umich.edu

Henri Jacques Stiker, Author

A bold analysis of the evolution of western attitudes toward disability. The book traces the history of western cultural responses to disability, from ancient times to the present. *$23.95*

264 pages Paper
ISBN 0-472086-26-9

2902 A Human Development View of Learning Disabilities: From Theory to Practice
Charles C Thomas, 2nd Ed.
2600 S 1st St
Springfield, IL 62704-4730   217-789-8980
800-258-8980
FAX 217-789-9130
http://www.ccthomas.com
e-mail: books@ccthomas.com

Corraine E Kass, Author
Cleborne D Maddux, Co-Author

Publisher of Education and Special Education books. 252 pp (7x10), 5 tables, ISBN 978-0-398-07565-1 (paper) $39.95 Published 2005 *$35.95*
252 pages Paper
ISBN 0-398075-65-1

2903 Academic Skills Problems Workbook
Guilford Press
72 Spring St
New York, NY 10012-4019
800-365-7006
FAX 212-966-6708
http://www.guilford.com
e-mail: info@guilford.com

Edward S Shapiro, Author

This user-friendly workbook offers numerous opportunities for practicing and mastering direct assessment and intervention procedures. The workbook also includes teacher and student interview forms; a complete guide to using the Behavioral Observation of Students in Schools (BOSS) Observation code, exercises on administering assessments and scoring, interpreting, and graphing the results; and much more. *$30.00*
147 pages
ISBN 1-572309-68-7

2904 Academic Skills Problems: Direct Assessment and Intervention
Guilford Press
72 Spring St
New York, NY 10012-4019
800-365-7006
FAX 212-966-6708
http://www.guilford.com
e-mail: info@guilford.com

Edward S Shapiro, Author

Provides comprehensive framework for the direct assessment of academic skills. Presented is a readily applicable, four-step approach for working with students experiencing a range of difficulties with reading, spelling, written language, or math. *$45.00*
370 pages
ISBN 1-572309-77-6

2905   Adapted Physical Education for Students with Autism
Charles C Thomas, Publisher, Ltd.
2600 S 1st St
Springfield, IL 62704-4730   217-789-8980
                                               800-258-8980
                                          FAX 217-789-9130
                          http://www.ccthomas.com
                          e-mail: books@ccthomas.com
Kimberly Davis, Author

Publisher of Education and Special Education books. 142
pp. (7x10), 10 il. ISBN 978-0-398-06085-5 (paper) $29.95.
Published 1990. *$27.95*
        142 pages Paper
        ISBN 0-398060-85-5

**2906   Adapting Curriculum & Instruction in Inclusive Early
Childhood Settings**
Indiana Institute on Disability and Community
2853 E 10th St
Bloomington, IN 47408-2601   812-855-9396
                                          FAX 812-855-9630
                                          TTY: 812-855-9396
                          http://www.iidc.indiana.edu
                          e-mail: iidc@indiana.edu
David Mank, Director

Offers ideas and strategies that will be beneficial to all
young children, including children with identified disabilities, children who are at risk, and students who need enriched curricular options. This is also an excellent resource
for preservice training as well as inservice training for independent child care providers, center, and schools. *$11.00*

2907   Annals of Dyslexia
International Dyslexia Association
4th Fl
40 York Rd
Baltimore, MD 21204-5243   410-296-0232
                                          FAX 410-321-5069
                          http://www.interdys.org
                          e-mail: subscriptions@springer.com
Rob Hott, Editor
Chris Schatschneider PhD, Editor
Lee Grossmanÿ, Executive Director
The Society's scholarly journal contains updates on current
research and selected proceedings from talks given at each
ODS international conference. Issues of Annals are avail-
able from 1982 through the present year. *$15.00*
        2X / year

**2908   Art for All the Children: Approaches to Art Therapy
for Children with Disabilities, 2nd Ed.**
Charles C Thomas, Publisher, Ltd.
2600 S 1st St
Springfield, IL 62704-4730   217-789-8980
                                               800-258-8980
                                          FAX 217-789-9130
                          http://www.ccthomas.com
                          e-mail: books@ccthomas.com
Frances E Anderson, Author

Publisher of Education and Special Education books. *$56.95*

        398 pages Paper
        ISBN 0-398060-07-7

**2909   Art-Centered Education & Therapy for Children with
Disabilities**
Charles C Thomas, Publisher, Ltd.
2600 S 1st St
Springfield, IL 62704-4730   217-789-8980
                                               800-258-8980
                                          FAX 217-789-9130
                          http://www.ccthomas.com
                          e-mail: books@ccthomas.com
Frances E Anderson, Author

Publisher of Education and Special Education books. 284 pp
(6-3/4x9), 100 il, 14 tables. ISBN 978-0-398-06006-0 (paper) $42.95. Published 1994. *$41.95*
        284 pages Cloth
        ISBN 0-398058-96-2

**2910   Atypical Cognitive Deficits in Developmental Disorders:
Implications for Brain Function**
Routledge
270 Madison Ave
New York, NY 10016-601   212-216-7800
                                          FAX 212-563-2269
                          http://www.routledge.com
Sarah H Broman, Editor
Jordan Grafman, Editor

This volume is based on a conference held to examine what
was known about cognitive behaviors and brain structure
and function in three syndromes. *$99.95*
        360 pages
        ISBN 0-805811-80-0

2911   Auditory Processes
Academic Therapy Publications
20 Commercial Blvd
Novato, CA 94949-6120   415-883-3314
                                               800-422-7249
                                          FAX 888-287-9975
                          http://www.academictherapy.com
                          e-mail: sales@academictherapy.com
Jim Arena, President
Joanne Urban, Manager
Pamela Gillet PhD, Author
Explains how teachers, educational consultants and parents
can identify auditory processing problems, understand their
impact and implement appropriate instructional strategies to
enhance learning. *$15.00*
        120 pages
        ISBN 0-878790-94-2

2912   Body and Physical Difference: Discourses of Disability
University of Michigan Press
839 Greene St
Ann Arbor, MI 48104-3209   734-764-4388
                                          FAX 734-615-1540
                          http://www.press.umich.edu
                          e-mail: ump.webmaster@umich.edu
David T Mitchell, Editor
Sharon L Synder, Editor
Karen Hill, Executive Director
For years the subject of human disability has engaged those
in the biological, social and cognitive sciences, while at the
same time, it has been curiously neglected within the
humanites. The Body and Physical Difference seeks to introduce the field of disability studies into the humanities by
exploring the fantasies and fictons that have crystallized
around conceptions of physical and cognitive difference.
$65.00
        320 pages cloth
        ISBN 0-472066-59-9

**2913   Brief Intervention for School Problems: Outcome-In-
formed Strategies**
Guilford Press
72 Spring St
New York, NY 10012-4019
                                               800-365-7006
                                          FAX 212-966-6708
                          http://www.guilford.com
                          e-mail: info@guilford.com
John J Murphy, Author
Barry L Duncan, Co-Author

This practical guide provides innovative strategies for resolving academic and behavioral difficulties by enlisting the
strengths and resources of students, parents, and teachers.
$30.00
        210 pages
        ISBN 1-593854-92-7

2914   Cognitive Strategy Instruction That Really Improves Children's Performance
Brookline Books
PO Box 1209
Brookline, MA   02446
617-734-6772
800-666-2665
FAX 413-584-6184
http://www.brooklinebooks.com
e-mail: brbooks@yahoo.com

Michael Pressley, Author

A concise and focused work that summarily presents the few procedures for teaching strategies that aid academic subject matter learning that are empirically validated and fit well with the elementary school curriculum. *$27.95*
        203 pages
        ISBN 0-914797-66-2

2915   Competencies for Teachers of Students with Learning Disabilities
Council for Exceptional Children
Ste 300
1110 N Glebe Rd
Arlington, VA 22201-5704
703-245-0600
888-232-7733
FAX 703-264-9494
TTY: 703-264-9446
http://www.cec.sped.org/
e-mail: service@cec.sped.org

Amme Graves, Author
Mary Landers, Author
Bruce Ramirez, Manager
Lists 209 specific professional competencies needed by teachers of students with learning disabilities and provides a conceptual framework for the ten areas in which the competencies are organized. *$5.00*
        25 pages

2916   Cooperative Learning and Strategies for Inclusion
Brookes Publishing Company
PO Box 10624
Baltimore, MD 21285
410-337-9580
800-638-3775
FAX 410-337-8539
http://www.brookspublishing.com
e-mail: custserv@brookespublishing.com

JoAnne Putnam PhD, Editor

This book supplies educators, classroom support personnel, and administrators with numerous tools for creating positive, inclusive classroom environments for students from preschool through high school. *$32.95*
        288 pages Paperback
        ISBN 1-557663-46-7

2917   Creative Curriculum for Preschool
Teaching Strategies
PO Box 42243
Washington, DC 20015
301-634-0818
800-637-3652
FAX 301-657-0250
http://www.teachingstrategies.com
e-mail: customerrelations@teachingstrategies.com

Diane Trister-Dodge, Author
Laura Colker, Co-Author
Cate Heroman, Co-Author
Focuses on the developmentally appropriate program in early childhood education. Illustrates how preschool and kindergarten teachers set the stage for learning, and how children and teachers interact and learn in various interest areas. *$44.95*
        540 pages
        ISBN 1-879537-43-5

2918   Curriculum Development for Students with Mild Disabilities
Charles C Thomas, Publisher, Ltd.
2600 S 1st St
Springfield, IL 62704-4730
217-789-8980
800-258-8980
FAX 217-789-9130
http://www.ccthomas.com
e-mail: books@ccthomas.com

Carroll J Jones, Author

Publisher of Education and Special Education books. 454 pp. ISBN 978-0-398-079911-6, $69.95. Published 2010. *$38.95*
        258 pages Spiral (paper)
        ISBN 0-398707-18-2

2919   Curriculum-Based Assessment: A Primer, 3rd Ed.
Charles C Thomas
2600 S 1st St
Springfield, IL 62704-4730
217-789-8980
800-258-8980
FAX 217-789-9130
http://www.ccthomas.com
e-mail: books@ccthomas.com

Charles H Hargis, Author

Publisher of Education and Special Education books. 210 pp (8-1/2x11), 59 tables, ISBN 978-0-398-07815-7 (spiral) $39.95. Published 2008. *$33.95*
        174 pages Paperback
        ISBN 0-398075-52-1

2920   Curriculum-Based Assessment: The Easy Way to Determine Response-to-Intervention, 2nd Ed.
Charles C Thomas
2600 S 1st St
Springfield, IL 62704-4730
217-789-8980
800-258-8980
FAX 217-789-9130
http://www.ccthomas.com
e-mail: books@ccthomas.com

Carroll J Jones, Author

Publisher of Education and Special Education books. 210 pp, (8-1/2x11), 59 tables, ISBN 978-0-398-07815-7 (spiral) $39.95. Published 2008. *$33.95*
        174 pages Spiral (paper)

2921   Defects: Engendering the Modern Body
University of Michigan Press
839 Greene St
Ann Arbor, MI 48104-3209
734-764-4388
FAX 734-615-1540
http://www.press.umich.edu
e-mail: ump.webmaster@umich.edu

Helen Deutsch, Editor
Felicity Nussbaum, Editor

Defects brings together essays on the emergence of the concept of monstrosity in the eighteenth century and the ways it paralleled the emergence of notions of sexual difference. *$27.95*
        344 pages Paper
        ISBN 0-472066-98-8

2922   Developmental Variation and Learning Disorders
Educators Publishing Service
PO Box 9031
Cambridge, MA 02139-9031
800-435-7228
FAX 888-440-2665
http://www.epsbooks.com
e-mail: eps@epsbooks.com

Melvin D Levine MD FAAP, Author

The Second Edition of this useful reference includes completely revised on attention, memory, and language, with significant modifications of the remaining chapters. Sections on educational skills have been expanded and updated; the chapter on causes and complications of learning disorders has been updated to include recent references and ongoing reserach efforts. *$61.80*

ISBN 0-838819-92-3

2923 **Dictionary of Special Education and Rehabilitation**
Love Publishing Company
Ste 2200
9101 E Kenyon Ave
Denver, CO 80237-1854　　　　　303-221-7333
　　　　　　　　　　　　　　　FAX 303-221-7444
　　　　　　　http://www.lovepublishing.com
　　　　　　　e-mail: lpc@lovepublishing.com
Glenn A Vergason, Author
M L Anderegg, Co-Author

This updated edition of one of the most valuable resources in the field is over six years in the making and incorporates hundreds of additions. It provides clear, understandable definitions of more than 2,000 terms unique to special education and rehabilitation. It also provides listing of professional organizations and resources, includes latest terms, and is a critical reference for anyone in the special education field. *$34.95*
210 pages　Paperback
ISBN 0-891802-43-3

2924 **Directory for Exceptional Children**
Porter Sargent Handbooks
2 Lan Drive Ste 100 Westford
Boston, MA 01886　　　　　　978-842-2812
　　　　　　　　　　　　　　800-342-7870
　　　　　　　　　　　FAX 978-692-2304
　　　　　　　http://www.portersargent.com
　　　　　　　e-mail: info@portersargent.com
Daniel McKeever, Editor
John Yonce, Director
Leslie Weston, Production Editor
A comprehensive survey of 3000 schools, facilities, and organizations across the USA. Serving children and yound adults with developmental, physical, medical, and emotional disabilities. Aide to parents, consultants, educators, and other professionals. *$75.00*
1152 pages
ISBN 0-875581-31-5

2925 **Eden Family of Services Curriculum Series:**
Eden Services
One Eden Way
Princeton, NJ 08540-5711　　　609-987-0099
　　　　　　　　　　　　　　FAX 609-987-0243
　　　　　　　http://www.edenservices.org
　　　　　　　e-mail: info@edenservices.org
Tom Mc Cool, President

This volume contains teaching programs for students ages three through adult in the area of cognitive skills; self-care and domestics; vocational skills; speech and languages and physcial education, recreation and leisure. Complete series $700; individual volumes $150-200

2926 **Educating All Students Together**
Corwin Press
2455 Teller Rd
Thousand Oaks, CA 91320-2218　　805-499-9734
　　　　　　　　　　　　　　　　800-233-9936
　　　　　　　　　　　　FAX 805-499-5323
　　　　　　　http://www.corwinpress.com
　　　　　　　e-mail: order@corwinpress.com
Leonard C Burrello, Author
Carl A Lashley, Co-Author
Edith E Beatty, Co-Author

A plan for unifying the separate and parallel systems of special and general education. Key concepts include: schools embracing special services personnel; the role of the community; program evaluation and incentives; brain and holographic design; collaboration between school administrators and teachers; and adapting curriculum; and instruction. *$33.95*
264 pages
ISBN 0-761976-98-1

2927 **Educating Children with Multiple Disabilities: A Collaborative Approach**
Brookes Publishing Company
PO Box 10624
Baltimore, MD 21285　　　　　410-337-9580
　　　　　　　　　　　　　　800-638-3775
　　　　　　　　　　　FAX 410-337-8539
　　　　　　　http://www.brookespublishing.com
　　　　　　　e-mail: custserv@brookespublishing.com
Fred P Orelove PhD, Editor
Dick Sobsey EdD, Editor
Rosanne K Silberman EdD, Editor
Gives undergraduate and graduate students up-to-the-minute research and strategies for educating children with severe and multiple disabilities. *$49.00*
672 pages　Paperback
ISBN 1-557667-10-1

2928 **Ending Discrimination in Special Education**
Charles C Thomas
2600 S 1st St
Springfield, IL 62704-4730　　　217-789-8980
　　　　　　　　　　　　　　　800-258-8980
　　　　　　　　　　　　FAX 217-789-9130
　　　　　　　http://www.ccthomas.com
　　　　　　　e-mail: books@ccthomas.com
Herbert Grossman, Author

Publisher of Education and Special Education books. *$23.95*

142 pages　Paper
ISBN 0-398073-04-6

2929 **Exceptional Teacher's Handbook: First Year Special Education Teacher's Guide for Success**
Corwin Press
2455 Teller Rd
Thousand Oaks, CA 91320-2218　　805-499-9734
　　　　　　　　　　　　　　　　800-233-9936
　　　　　　　　　　　　FAX 805-499-5323
　　　　　　　http://www.corwinpress.com
　　　　　　　e-mail: order@corwinpress.com
Carla F Shelton, Author
Alice B Pollingue, Co-Author
Mike Soules, President
Provides a step-by-step management approach complete with planning checklists and other ready-to-use forms. Arranged sequentially, the book guides new teachers through the entire school year, from preplanning to post planning. *$35.95*
240 pages
ISBN 0-761931-96-6

2930 **Focus on Exceptional Children**
Love Publishing Company
Ste 2200
9101 E Kenyon Ave
Denver, CO 80237-1854　　　　　303-221-7333
　　　　　　　　　　　　　　　FAX 303-221-7444
　　　　　　　http://www.lovepublishing.com
　　　　　　　e-mail: lpc@lovepublishing.com
Edwin S Ellis, Editor
Timothy J Lewis, Editor
Chriss S Thomas, Editor

Published monthly except June, July, and August, get a constant flow of fresh teaching ideas-and keep up with the latest research- with this monthly newsletter that translates theory into strategies for action. Each issue focuses in depth on a single topic, such as assessment, cooperative learning, attention deficit disorders, inclusion, classroom management, discipline, and ohter timely issues. *$36.00*

ISSN 0015-511X

2931 Frames of Reference for the Assessment of Learning Disabilities
Brookes Publishing Company
PO Box 10624
Baltimore, MD 21285
410-337-9580
800-638-3775
FAX 410-337-8539
http://www.brookespublishing.com
e-mail: custserv@brookespublishing.com
G Reid Lyon PhD, Editor

This valuable reference offers an in-depth look at the fundamental concerns facing those who work with children with learning disabilities — assessment and identification. *$59.95*
672 pages Hardcover
ISBN 1-557661-38-3

2932 HELP Activity Guide
Therapro
225 Arlington St
Framingham, MA 01702-8773
508-872-9494
800-257-5376
FAX 508-875-2062
http://www.theraproducts.com
e-mail: info@theraproducts.com
Karen Conrad, Owner
Setan Furuns PhD, Author

Takes you easily beyond assesment to offer the important next step, thousands of practical, task-analyzed curriculum activities and intervention strategies indexed by the 650 HELP skills. With up to ten activities and strategies per skill, this valuable resource includes definitions for each skill, illustrations, cross-references to skills in other developmental areas and a glossary. *$40.00*
190 pages

2933 HELP for Preschoolers Assessment and Curriculum Guide
Therapro
225 Arlington St
Framingham, MA 01702-8773
508-872-9494
800-257-5376
FAX 508-875-2062
http://www.theraproducts.com
e-mail: info@theraproducts.com
Karen Conrad, Owner
Setan Furuns PhD, Author

Assessment procedure and instructional activities in one easy to use reference. Offers 6 sections of key information for each of the 622 skills: Definition, Materials, Assesment Procedures, Adaptions, Instructional Materials, and Instructional Activities.

2934 Hidden Youth: Dropouts from Special Education
Council for Exceptional Children
2900 Crystal Drive
Suite 1000
Arlington, VA 22202-3557
888-232-7733
FAX 703-264-9494
TTY: 866-915-5000
http://www.cec.sped.org/
e-mail: service@cec.sped.org

Donald L MacMillan, Author
James P. Heiden, Treasurer
Bruce Ramirez, Manager
Margaret J. McLaughlin, President
Examines the characteristics of students and schools that place students at risk for early school leaving. Discusses the accounting procedures used by different agencies for estimating graduation and dropout rates and cautions educators about using these rates as indicators of educational quality. *$8.90*
37 pages
ISBN 0-865862-11-7

2935 How Difficult Can This Be?
CT Association for Children and Adults with LD
Ste 15-5
25 Van Zant St
Norwalk, CT 06855-1713
203-838-5010
FAX 203-866-6108
http://www.cacld.org
e-mail: caccld@optonline.net
Richard Lavoie, Producer

FAT City Workshop video and discussion guide. Looks at the world through the eyes of a learning disabled child. Features a unique workshop attended by educators, psychologists, social workers, parents, siblings and a student with LD. They participate in a series of classroom activities which cause Frustration, Anxiety, and Tension-emotions all too familiar to the student with a learning disability. A discussion of topics ranging from school/home communication to social skills follows. *$49.95*

2936 How Does Your Engine Run? A Leaders Guide to the Alert Program for Self Regulation
Therapro
225 Arlington St
Framingham, MA 01702-8773
508-872-9494
800-257-5376
FAX 508-875-2062
http://www.theraproducts.com
e-mail: info@theraproducts.com
Karen Conrad, Owner
Mary Sue Williams OTR, Author
Sherry Schellenberge OTR, Co-Author
Introduces the entire Alert Program. Explains how we regulate our arousal states and describes the use of sensorimotor strategies to manage levels of alertness. This program is fun for students and the adults working with them, and translates easily into real life.

2937 How to Write an IEP
Academic Therapy Publications
20 Commercial Blvd
Novato, CA 94949-6120
415-883-3314
800-422-7249
FAX 888-287-9975
http://www.academictherapy.com
e-mail: sales@academictherapy.com
Jim Arena, President
Joanne Urban, Manager

This practical guide for teachers and parents contains the latest updates to the 2004 Individuals with Disabilities Education Act (IDEA). *$19.00*
168 pages
ISBN 1-571284-43-5

2938 IEP Success Video
Sopris West
4185 Salazar Way
Frederick, CO 80504-3520
303-651-2829
800-547-6747
http://www.sopriswest.com
e-mail: customerservice@sopriswest.com
Barbara D Baterman JD PhD, Author

Explains the five underlying principles of the individualized education program (IEP) process: evaluation and identification, IEPs and related services, placement, funding, and procedural safeguards. *$98.95*

2939 Implementing Cognitive Strategy Instruction Across the School: The Benchmark Manual for Teachers
Brookline Books
PO Box 1209
Brookline, MA 02446   617-734-6772
                             800-666-2665
                        FAX 413-584-6184
             http://www.brooklinebooks.com
                  e-mail: brbooks@yahoo.com
Irene Gaskins, Author
Thorne Elliot, Author

Describes a classroom based program planned and executed by teachers to focus and guide students with serious reading problems to be goal oriented, planful, strategic and self-assessing. *$24.95*
> *Paperback*
> *ISBN 0-914797-75-1*

2940 Improving Test Performance of Students with Disabilities in the Classroom
Corwin Press
2455 Teller Rd
Thousand Oaks, CA 91320-2218   805-499-9734
                                  800-233-9936
                             FAX 805-499-5323
                http://www.corwinpress.com
                 e-mail: order@corwinpress.com
Judy L Elliott, Author
Martha L Thurlow, Co-Author

Elliott and Thurlow, long-time colleagues at the National Center on Educational Outcomes build on their highly respected work in accountability and assessment of students with disabilities to focus now on improving test performance — with an emphasis throughout on practical application. Common learning disabilities and emotional problems and a classroom-tested, research-based list of classroom interventions. *$35.95*
> *232 pages Paperback*
> *ISBN 1-412917-28-X*

2941 Including Students with Severe and Multiple Disabilities in Typical Classrooms
Brookes Publishing Company
PO Box 10624
Baltimore, MD 21285   410-337-9580
                             800-638-3775
                        FAX 410-337-8539
             http://www.brookespublishing.com
          e-mail: custserv@brookespublishing.com
June Downing PhD, Author

This straightforward and jargon-free resource gives instructors the guidance needed to educate learners who have one or more sensory impairments in addition to cognitive and physical disabilities. *$44.95*
> *352 pages Paperback*
> *ISBN 1-557669-08-2*

2942 Inclusion: 450 Strategies for Success
Corwin Press
2455 Teller Rd
Thousand Oaks, CA 91320-2218   805-499-9734
                                  800-233-9936
                             FAX 805-499-5323
                http://www.corwinpress.com
Peggy A Hammeken, Author
Carl A Lashley, Co-Author

Commences with step-by-step guidelines to help develop, expand and improve the existing inclusive education setting. Hundreds of practical teacher tested ideas and accommodations are conveniently listed by topic and numbered for quick, easy reference. *$33.95*
> *192 pages Educators*
> *ISBN 1-890455-25-3*

2943 Inclusion: An Essential Guide for the Paraprofessional
Corwin Press
2455 Teller Rd
Thousand Oaks, CA 91320-2218   805-499-9734
                                  800-233-9936
                             FAX 805-499-5323
                http://www.corwinpress.com
Peggy A Hammeken, Author
Carl A Lashley, Co-Author

This best-selling publication is developed specifically for paraprofessionals and classroom assistants. The book commences with a simplified introduction to inclusive education, handicapping conditions, due process, communication, collaboration, confidentiality and types of adaptations. Used by many schools and universities as a training tool for staff development. *$35.95*
> *224 pages*
> *ISBN 1-890455-34-2*

2944 Inclusive Elementary Schools
PEAK Parent Center
Ste 200
611 N Weber St
Colorado Springs, CO 80903-1072   719-531-9400
                                     800-284-0251
                                FAX 719-531-9452
                   http://www.peakparent.org
                 e-mail: info@peakparent.org
Douglas Fisher, Author
Nancy Frey, Co-Author
Caren Sax, Co-Author
Walks readers through a state of the art, step-by-step process to determine what and how to teach elementary school students with disabilities in general education classrooms. Highlights strategies for accommodating and modifying assignments and activities by using core curriculum. Complete with user-friendly sample forms and creative support strategies, this is an essential text for elementary educators and parents. *$13.00*

2945 Instructional Methods for Secondary Students with Learning & Behavior Problems
Allyn & Bacon
Ste 300
75 Arlington St
Boston, MA 02116-3988
                             800-848-9500
                        FAX 877-260-2530
             http://www.ablongman.com
Patrick J Schloss, Author
Maureen A Schloss, Co-Author
Cynthia N Schloss, Co-Author
This book presents teaching principles useful to general high school educators and special educators working with students demonstrating a variety of academic, behavioral, and social needs in secondary schools. *$120.00*
> *432 pages*
> *ISBN 0-205442-36-6*

2946 Intervention in School and Clinic
Sage Publications
2455 Teller Rd
Thousand Oaks, CA 91320-2218   805-499-0721
                                  800-818-7243
                             FAX 805-499-8096
                http://www.sagepub.com
                 e-mail: journals@sagepub.com
Randall Boone PhD, Editor
Kyle Higgins PhD, Editor

Equips teachers and clinicians with hands-on tips, techniques, methods and ideas for improving assessment, instruction, and management for individuals with learning disabilities or behavior disorders. Articles focus on curricular, instructional, social, behavioral, assessment, and vocational strategies and techniques that have a direct application to the classroom setting. This innovative and readable periodical provides educational information ready for immediate implementation

5 times a year
ISSN 1053-4512

2947 KDES Health Curriculum Guide
Harris Communications
15155 Technology Dr
Eden Prairie, MN 55344-2273   800-825-6758
                                    FAX 952-906-1099
                                    TTY: 952-825-1198
                          http://www.harriscomm.com
                          e-mail: info@harriscomm.com
Sara Gillespie, Author
Doris Schwartz, Co-Author
Darla Hudson, Customer Service
This guide provides students with the information they need to make wise choices for healthy living. Divided into age-appropriate sections; preschool through middle school; the units cover four main areas: Health and Fitness, Safety and First Aid, Drugs, and Life. Asspendices provide resource lists and information on topics such as hygiene, street safety, teaching health. Part #B568. *$9.95*
125 pages

2948 Making School Inclusion Work: A Guide to Everyday Practices
Brookline Books
PO Box 1209
Brookline, MA 02446   617-734-6772
                              800-666-2665
                          FAX 617-734-3952
                   http://www.brooklinebooks.com
                   e-mail: brbooks@yahoo.com
Katie Blenk, Author
Doris Fine, Author

Tells the reader how to conduct a truly inclusive school program that educates a diverse student body together, regardless of ethnic or racial background, economic level, or physical or cognitive ability. Indication given on what is ment by true inclusion, what inclusion is not, and who should not be conducting an inclusive program. *$24.95*
264 pages Paperback
ISBN 0-914797-96-4

2949 Mentoring Students at Risk: An Underutilized Alternative Education Strategy for K-12 Teachers
Charles C Thomas
2600 S 1st St
Springfield, IL 62704-4730   217-789-8980
                                    800-258-8980
                                FAX 217-789-9130
                          http://www.ccthomas.com
                          e-mail: books@ccthomas.com
Gary Reglin, Author
Charles C. Thomas, Publisher

Publisher of Education and Special Education books. *$20.95*

110 pages Paper
ISBN 0-398068-33-2

2950 Myofascial Release and Its Application to Neuro-Developmental Treatment
Therapro
225 Arlington St
Framingham, MA 01702-8773   508-872-9494
                                    800-257-5376
                                FAX 508-875-2062
                          http://www.theraproducts.com
                          e-mail: info@theraproducts.com

Karen Conrad, Owner
Regi Boehme OTF, Author

This fully illustrated resource provides the therapist with techniques to approach myofascial restrictions which are secondary to tonal dysfunction in children and adults with neurological deficits. The Neuro-Developmental Treatment approach is included in the illustrated treatment rationale.

2951 Narrative Prosthesis: Disability and the Dependencies of Discourse
University of Michigan Press
839 Greene St
Ann Arbor, MI 48104-3209   734-764-4388
                                FAX 734-615-1540
                          http://www.press.umich.edu
                          e-mail: ump.webmaster@umich.edu
David T Mitchell, Author
Sharon L Snyder, Co-Author

This book develops a narrative theory of the pervasive use of disability as a device of characterization in literature and film. It argues that, while other marginalized identities have suffered cultural exclusion due to dearth of images reflecting their experience, the marginality of disabled people has occurred in the midst of the perpetual circulation of images of disability in print and visual media. *$65.00*
264 pages Cloth
ISBN 0-472097-48-7

2952 Points of Contact: Disability, Art, and Culture
University of Michigan Press
839 Greene St
Ann Arbor, MI 48104-3209   734-764-4388
                                FAX 734-615-1540
                          http://www.press.umich.edu
                          e-mail: ump.webmaster@umich.edu
Susan Crutchfield, Editor
Marcy Epstein, Editor

A richly diverse collection of essays, memoir, poetry and photography on aspects of disability and its representation in art. Brings together contributions by leading writers, artists, scholars, and critics to provide a remarkably broad and consistently engaging look at the intersection of disability and the arts. *$60.00*
312 pages Cloth
ISBN 0-472097-11-1

2953 Prescriptions for Children with Learning and Adjustment Problems: A Consultant's Desk Reference
Charles C Thomas
2600 S 1st St
Springfield, IL 62704-4730   217-789-8980
                                    800-258-8980
                                FAX 217-789-9130
                          http://www.ccthomas.com
                          e-mail: books@ccthomas.com
Ralph F Blanco, Author
Charles C. Thomas, Publisher

Publisher of Education and Special Education books. *$35.95*

264 pages Paper

2954 Preventing Academic Failure
Educators Publishing Service
PO Box 9031
Cambridge, MA 02139-9031   617-547-6706
                                    800-435-7728
                                FAX 888-440-2665
                          http://www.epsbooks.com
                          e-mail: feedback@epsbooks.com
Phyllis Bertin, Author
Eileen Perlman, Co-Author

This multisensory curriculum meets the needs of children with learning disabilities in regular classrooms by providing a four-year sequence of written language skills (reading, writing and spelling). PAF has a handwriting and numerical program. *$42.00*

ISBN 0-838852-71-8

2955 Resourcing: Handbook for Special Education RES Teachers
Council for Exceptional Children
Ste 300
1110 N Glebe Rd
Arlington, VA 22201-5704

888-232-7733
FAX 703-264-9494
TTY: 866-915-5000
http://www.cec.sped.org
e-mail: service@cec.sped.org

Mary Yeomans Jackson, Author
Drew Albritten MD, President
Bruce Ramirez, Manager

Be prepared to function at your best as a member of a school-based team. Resourcing wil help you take a leadership role as you work in collaboration with general classroom teachers and other practitioners. Assess your personal readiness for being a resource professional within your school. Includes many useful forms and checklists for conducting meetings and organizing your workday. *$12.00*

64 pages
ISBN 0-865862-19-2

2956 School-Home Notes: Promoting Children's Classroom Success
Guilford Press
72 Spring St
New York, NY 10012-4019

800-365-7006
FAX 212-966-6708
http://www.guilford.com
e-mail: info@guilford.com

Mary Lou Kelley, Author

Describes common obstacles to parent and teacher communication and clearly explicates how these obstacles can be overcome. It provides a critical appraisal of the relevant literature on parent-and-teacher managed contingency systems and factors influencing the efficacy of the procedure. *$28.00*

198 pages Paperback
ISBN 0-898622-35-2

2957 Segregated and Second-Rate: Special Education in New York
Advocates for Children of New York
Fl 5
151 W 30th St
New York, NY 10001-4024

212-947-9779
866-427-6033
FAX 212-947-9790
http://www.advocatesforchildren.org
e-mail: info@advocatesforchildren.org

Diane Autin, Author
Emily Dentzer, Co-Author
Briar McNutt, Co-Author
Highlights the fact that New York rates last among all states in inclusive education.

2958 Sensory Integration: Theory and Practice
Therapro
225 Arlington St
Framingham, MA 01702-8773

508-872-9494
800-257-5376
FAX 508-875-2062
http://www.theraproducts.com
e-mail: info@theraproducts.com

Karen Conrad, Owner
Anne Fisher, Author
Elizabeth Murray, Co-Author
The very latest in sensory integration theory and practice. *$60.00*

481 pages

2959 Strangest Song: One Father's Quest to Help His Daughter Find Her Voice
Prometheus Books
59 John Glenn Dr
Amherst, NY 14228-2119

716-691-0133
800-421-0351
FAX 716-691-0137
http://www.prometheusbooks.com
e-mail: marketing@prometheusbooks.com

Teri Sforza, Author
Howard Lenhoff, Co-Author
Sylvia Lenhoff, Co-Author
The first book to tell the story of Williams syndrome and the extraordinary musicality of many of the people who have it. An inspiring blend of human interest and breakthrough science, offers startling insights into the mysteries of the brain and hope that science can find new ways to help the handicapped. *$24.00*

296 pages
ISBN 1-591024-78-1

2960 Take Part Art
CT Association for Children and Adults with LD
Ste 15-5
25 Van Zant St
Norwalk, CT 06855-1713

203-838-5010
http://www.cacld.org
e-mail: cacld@optonline.net

Bob Gregson, Author

Offers information on art therapies and their inclusion in learning disabled environments. *$19.50*

2961 Teachers Ask About Sensory Integration
Therapro
225 Arlington St
Framingham, MA 01702-8773

508-872-9494
800-257-5376
FAX 508-875-2062
http://www.theraproducts.com
e-mail: info@theraproducts.com

Karen Conrad, Owner
Carol Kranowitz, Author
Stacey Szkult, Co-Author
A narration and discussion for teachers and school professionals about how to teach children with sensory integration problems. 60 page book included, filled with checklists, idea sheets, sensory profiles and resorces. 86 minute audio tape.

Audio Tape

2962 Teaching Gifted Kids in the Regular Classroom CD-ROM
Free Spirit Publishing
Ste 200
217 5th Ave N
Minneapolis, MN 55401-1260

612-338-2068
866-703-7322
FAX 612-337-5050
http://www.freespirit.com
e-mail: help4kids@freespirit.com

Judy Galbraith, President
Judy Galbrai

Includes all of the forms from the book, plus many additional extension menus, ready to customize and print for classroom use. Macintosh and Windows compatible. *$17.95*

ISBN 1-575421-01-4

2963 Teaching Gifted Kids in the Regular Classroom
Free Spirit Publishing
Ste 200
217 5th Ave N
Minneapolis, MN 55401-1260   612-338-2068
                                     866-703-7322
                              FAX 612-337-5050
                       http://www.freespirit.com
                 e-mail: help4kids@freespirit.com
Judy Galbraith, President

The definitive guide to meeting the learning needs of gifted students, as well as those labeled slow, remedial, or LD, in the mixed-abilities classroom, without losing control, causing resentment, or spending hours preparing extra materials. The updated edition includes more than 50 reproducible forms and handouts for all grades. *$34.95*
   256 pages
   ISBN 1-575420-89-9

2964 Teaching Students Ways to Remember: Strategies for Learning Mnemonically
Brookline Books
PO Box 1209
Brookline, MA 02446   617-734-6772
                              800-666-2665
                       FAX 617-734-3952
                http://www.brooklinebooks.com
                 e-mail: brbooks@yahoo.com
Margo Mastropieri MD, Author

This book was written in response to the enormous interest in mnemonic instruction by teachers and administrators, telling them how it can be used with their students. *$21.95*

   ISBN 0-398074-77-7

2965 Teaching Visually Impaired Children, 3rd Ed.
Charles C Thomas
2600 S 1st St
Springfield, IL 62704-4730   217-789-8980
                                     800-258-8980
                              FAX 217-789-9130
                       http://www.ccthomas.com
                 e-mail: books@ccthomas.com
Virginia E Bishop, Author

Publisher of Education and Special Education books. *$49.95*

   352 pages Paper
   ISBN 0-398065-95-0

2966 To Teach a Dyslexic
AVKO Educational Research Foundation
Ste W
3084 Willard Rd
Birch Run, MI 48415-9404   810-686-9283
                                   866-285-6612
                            FAX 810-686-1101
                       http://www.avko.org
                 e-mail: avkoemail@aol.com
Don Mc Cabe, Research Director/Author

Just as it takes a thief to catch a thief, this is an autobiography of a dyslexic who discovered how to teach dyslexics. Common sense, logical approach, valuable to all who teach in our nation's classrooms. *$14.95*
   288 pages
   ISBN 1-564000-04-4

2967 Understanding & Management of Health Problems in Schools: Resource Manual
Temeron Books
PO Box 896
Bellingham, WA 98227
                              FAX 360-738-4016
                  http://www.temerondetselig.com
                 e-mail: temeron@telusplanet.net

H Moghadam, Author

Intended as a supplement to information given by parents and physicians, this book is a valuable aid to teachers and other school personnel in regards to some of the primary health issues that affect children and adolescents. *$ 13.95*
   152 pages
   ISBN 1-550591-21-5

2968 Understanding and Managing Vision Deficits
Therapro
225 Arlington St
Framingham, MA 01702-8773   508-872-9494
                                    800-257-5376
                             FAX 508-875-2062
                      http://www.theraproducts.com
                 e-mail: info@theraproducts.com
Mitchell Scheiman, OD, Author
Karen Conrad, Owner

This book is a unique and comprehensive collaboration from OT's and optometrists developed to increase the understanding of vision. Learn to screen for common visual deficits and effectively manage patients with vision disorders. Provides recommendations for direct intervention techniques for a variety of vision problems and supportive and compensatory stratagies for visual field deficits and visual neglect.

2969 Working with Visually Impaired Young Students: A Curriculum Guide for 3 to 5 Year-Olds
Charles C Thomas
2600 S 1st St
Springfield, IL 62704-4730   217-789-8980
                                     800-258-8980
                              FAX 217-789-9130
                       http://www.ccthomas.com
                 e-mail: books@ccthomas.com
Ellen Trief, Editor
Charles C Thomas, Publisher

Publisher of Education and Special Education books. *$42.95*

   208 pages Spiral Paper
   ISBN 0-398068-75-2

Language Arts

2970 Communication Skills for Visually Impaired Learners, 2nd Ed.
Charles C Thomas, Publisher, Ltd.
2600 S 1st St
Springfield, IL 62704-4730   217-789-8980
                                     800-258-8980
                              FAX 217-789-9130
                       http://www.ccthomas.com
                 e-mail: books@ccthomas.com
Randall K Harley, Author
Charles C Thomas, Publisher
LaRhea D Sanford, Co-Author
Publisher of Education and Special Education books. 322 pp. (7x10), 39 il, $59.95 (paper) ISBN 978-0-398-06693-2 *$57.95*
   322 pages Paper
   ISBN 0-398066-93-2

2971 First Start in Sign Language
Harris Communications
15155 Technology Dr
Eden Prairie, MN 55344-2273   952-906-1180
                                      800-825-6758
                               FAX 952-906-1099
                               TTY: 950-906-1198
                       http://www.harriscomm.com
                 e-mail: info@harriscomm.com
Amy J Strommer, Author
Darla Hudson, Customer Service

Fun pictures, stories, and activities are all included in this introduction to American Sign Language. Students first learn to sign words for people, animals, objects and actions. Then they learn to produce simple sentences and to sign stories. Reproducible activity pages are included throughout the book. For students in kindergarten through sixth grade. Part #B469. *$32.00*
190 pages Paperback

2972 From Talking to Writing: Strategies for Scaffolding Expository Expression
Landmark School
PO Box 227
Prides Crossing, MA 01965   978-236-3000
FAX 978-927-7268
http://www.landmarkoutreach.org
e-mail: outreach@landmarkschool.org
Terrill M Jennings, Author
Charles W Haynes, Co-Author

Designed for teachers who work with students who have difficulty with writing and/or expressive language skills, this book provides practical strategies for teaching expository expression at the word, sentence, paragraph, and short essay levels. *$25.00*
191 pages

2973 Language Learning Everywhere We Go
Academic Communication Associates
PO Box 4279
Oceanside, CA 92052-4279   760-722-9593
888-758-9558
FAX 760-722-1625
TDD:952-906-1198
TTY: 800-825-9187
http://www.acadcom.com
e-mail: acom@acadcom.com
Cecilia Casas, Author
Patricia Portillo, Co-Author

Students learn the vocabulary associated with each situation that they encounter on their travels with Bernardo Bear. Questions and vocabulary lists are included in English and Spanish for each picture. The 103 situational pictures may all be reproduced. *$34.00*
209 pages Paperback

2974 Making the Writing Process Work: Strategies for Composition & Self-Regulation
Brookline Books
PO Box 1209
Brookline, MA 02446   617-734-6772
800-666-2665
FAX 617-734-3952
http://www.brooklinebooks.com
e-mail: brbooks@yahoo.com
Karen R Harris, Author
Steve Graham, Co-Author

Presents cognitive strategies for writing sequences of specific steps which make the writing process clearer and enable students to organize their thoughts about the writing task. The strategies help students know how to turn thoughts into writing products. This is especially important for students having difficulty producing acceptable writing products, but all students benefit from learning these procedures. *$24.95*

ISBN 1-571290-10-9

2975 Multisensory Teaching Approach
MTS Publications
415 N McGraw St
Forney, TX 75126-8661   972-564-6960
877-552-1090
FAX 972-552-9889
http://www.mtsedmar.com
e-mail: msmith@mtsedmar.com

Margaret Smith, Author
Margaret T. Smith, Executive Director

MTA is a comprehensive, multisensory program in reading, spelling, cursive handwriting, and alphabet and dictionary skills for both regular and remedial instruction. Ungraded, MTA is based on the Orton-Gillingham techniques and Alphabetic Phonics. *$192.99*

2976 Signs of the Times
Harris Communications
15155 Technology Dr
Eden Prairie, MN 55344-2273   800-825-6758
800-825-9187
FAX 952-906-1099
TTY: 800-825-9187
http://www.harriscomm.com
e-mail: info@harriscomm.com
Edgar H Shroyer, Author
Darla Hudson, Customer Service

Containing 1,185 signs in 41 lessons, this classroom text is an excellent beginning Pidgin or Contact Sign English book that fills the gap between sign language dictionaries and American Sign Language texts. Each lesson contains clearly illustrated vocabulary, English glosses and synonyms, sample sentences to defice vocabulary context, and sentences for practice. Part #B202. *$34.95*
433 pages Softcover

2977 Slingerland Multisensory Approach to Language Arts
Slingerland Institute for Literacy
Ste 1
12729 Northup Way
Bellevue, WA 98005-1935   425-453-1190
FAX 425-635-7762
http://www.slingerland.org
e-mail: mail@slingerland.com
Bonnie Meyer, Author
Beth H. Slingerland, Founder

This adaptation of the Orton-Gillingham approach for classroom teachers provides a phonetically structured introduction to reading, writing and spelling. Books 1 and 2 are for first and second grade, Book 3 for primary classrooms and older students. Numerous supplementary materials are available.

2978 Teaching Language Deficient Children: Theory and Application of the Association Method
Pro-Ed
8700 Shoal Creek Blvd
Austin, TX 78757-6816   512-451-3246
800-897-3202
FAX 512-451-8542
http://www.proedinc.com
N Etoile DuBard, Author
Maureen K Martin, Co-Author

This revised and expanded edition of Teaching Aphasics and Other Language Deficient Children offers information on its theory, implementation of the method and sample curriculum. *$52.00*
360 pages
ISBN 0-838823-40-8

2979 Visualizing and Verbalizing for Language Comprehension and Thinking
Lindamood Bell
416 Higuera St
San Luis Obispo, CA 93401-3833   805-541-3836
800-233-1819
FAX 805-541-8756
http://www.lindamoodbell.com
Nanci Bell, Author

This book identifies the important sensory connection that imagery provides and teaches specific techniques. Specific steps and sample dialog are presented. Summary pages after each step make it easy to implement the program in the classroom.
284 pages
ISBN 0-945856-01-6

2980 **Writing: A Landmark School Teaching Guide**
Landmark School
PO Box 227
Prides Crossing, MA 01965   978-236-3216
                                    FAX 978-927-7268
                    http://www.landmarkoutreach.org
                    e-mail: outreach@landmarkschool.org
Jean Gudaitis Tarricone, Author

This book offers strategies for teaching writing at the paragraph and short essay levels. It emphasizees the integration of language and critical thinking skills within a five-step writing process. Sample templates and graphic organizers as well as exercises that teachers can use in their classrooms are included. *$25.00*
92 pages

Math

2981 **Landmark Method for Teaching Arithmetic**
Landmark School
PO Box 227
Prides Crossing, MA 01965   978-236-3000
                                    FAX 978-927-7268
                    http://www.landmarkoutreach.org
                    e-mail: outreach@landmarkschool.org
Christopher Woodin, Author

This book is written for teachers who work with students having difficulty learning math. It includes practical strategies for teaching multiplication, division, word problems, and math facts. It also introduces the reader to two learning tools developed at Landmark — Woodin Ladders and Woodmark Icons. Sample templates and exercises are included. *$25.00*
145 pages

2982 **Math and the Learning Disabled Student: A Practical Guide for Accommodations**
Academic Success Press
6023 26th St W
Bradenton, FL 34207-4402   941-746-1645
                                   888-822-6657
                             FAX 941-753-2882
                    http://www.academicsuccess.com
                    e-mail: info@academicsuccess.com
Paul D Nolting PhD, Author
Kim Ruble, Editor

More and more learning disabled students are experiencing difficulty passing mathematics. The book is especially written for counselors and mathematics instructors of learning disabled students, and provides information on accommodations for students with different types of learning disabilities. *$49.95*
256 pages
ISBN 0-940287-23-4

2983 **Teaching Mathematics to Students with Learning Disabilities**
Pro-Ed
8700 Shoal Creek Blvd
Austin, TX 78757-6816   512-451-3246
                                800-897-3202
                          FAX 512-451-8542
                    http://www.proedinc.com
                    e-mail: info@proedinc.com
Nancy S Bley, Author
Carol A Thornton, Co-Author

Offers information on problem-solving, estimation and the use of computers in teaching mathematics to the child with learning disabilities. *$49.00*

Preschool

2984 **Access for All: Integrating Deaf, Hard of Hearing, and Hearing Preschoolers**
Harris Communications
15155 Technology Dr
Eden Prairie, MN 55344-2273   800-825-6758
                                      800-825-9168
                                FAX 952-906-1198
                                TTY: 800-825-9187
                    http://www.harriscomm.com
                    e-mail: info@harriscomm.com
Gail Solit, Author
Maral Taylor, Co-Author
Darla Hudson, Customer Service
Covers basic information needed to establish a successful preschool program for deaf and hearing children; interagency cooperation, staff training, and parental involvement. Part #BUT103. *$29.95*
169 pages Video-90 min.

2985 **When Slow Is Fast Enough: Educating the Delayed Preschool Child**
Guilford Press
72 Spring St
New York, NY 10012-4019   800-365-7006
                                  FAX 212-966-6708
                    http://www.guilford.com
                    e-mail: info@guilford.com
Joan F Goodman, Author

This bold and controversial book asks what we are accomplishing in early intervention programs that attempt to accelerate development in delayed young children. She questions the value of such programs on educational, psychological, and moral grounds, suggesting that in pressuring these children to perform more, and sooner, we undermine their capacity for independent development and deprive them of the freedom we insist upon for the nondelayed. *$29.00*
306 pages Paperback
ISBN 0-898624-91-6

Reading

2986 **Gillingham Manual**
Educators Publishing Service
PO Box 9031
Cambridge, MA 02139-9031   617-547-6706
                                   800-225-5750
                             FAX 617-547-0412
                    http://www.epsbooks.com
                    e-mail: eps@epsbooks.com
Anna Gillingham, Author
Bessie W Stillman, Co-Author

This classic in the field of specific language disability has now been completely revised and updated. The manual covers reading, spelling, writing and dictionary technique. It may be used with individuals or small groups. *$74.15*
352 pages
ISBN 0-838802-00-1

2987 **Phonology and Reading Disability**
University of Michigan Press
839 Greene St
Ann Arbor, MI 48104-3209   734-764-4388
                                   FAX 734-615-1540
                    http://www.press.umich.edu
Donald Shankweiler, Editor
Isabelle Y Liberman, Editor
Karen Hill, Executive Director

Discusses the importance to the learning process of the phonological structures of words. *$52.50*
184 pages Cloth
ISBN 0-472101-33-7

2988 Preventing Reading Difficulties in Young Children
National Academies Press
500 Fifth St NW
Washington, DC 20001　　　　　202-334-3313
888-624-8373
FAX 202-334-2451
http://www.nap.edu

Catherine E Snow, Editor
Susan Burns, Editor
Michael Keho Griffin, Editor
Explores how to prevent reading difficulties in the context of social, historical, cultural, and biological factors. *$34.16*
448 pages Hardback
ISBN 0-309064-18-X

2989 Readability Revisited: The New Dale-Chall Readability Formula
Brookline Books
8 Trumbull Rd,
Suite B-001
Northampton, MA 01060　　　　617-734-6772
800-666-2665
FAX 413-584-6184
http://www.brooklinebooks.com
e-mail: brbooks@yahoo.com

Jeanne Chall, Author
Edgar Dale, Co-Author

Information is given on reading difficulties in children with learning disabilities and how to overcome them. *$29.95*
168 pages
ISBN 1-571290-08-7

2990 Reading Problems: Consultation and Remediation
Guilford Press
72 Spring St
New York, NY 10012-4019
800-365-7006
FAX 212-966-6708
http://www.guilford.com
e-mail: info@guilford.com

P G Aaron, Author
R Malatesha Joshi, Co-Author
Bob Matloff, President
Designed to both help school psychologists and reading specialists effectively assume the consultation role, this volume provides an overview of reading problems while serving as a guide to effective practice. *$42.00*
285 pages

2991 Reading Programs that Work: A Review of Programs from Pre-K to 4th Grade
Milken Family Foundation
1250 4th St
Santa Monica, CA 90401-1366　　　310-570-4800
FAX 310-570-4801
http://www.mff.org
e-mail: media@mff.org

John Schacter PhD, Author

This publication tackles two questions, joining the research behind why children fail to read with research on effective solutions to reverse this failure. Included in the reading report are analyses of 35 different reading programs and their impact on student achievement.
72 pages

2992 Reading and Learning Disabilities: A Resource Guide
NICHCY
1825 Connecticut Ave NW
Suite 700
Washington, DC 20009　　　　　202-884-8200
800-695-0285
FAX 202-884-8441
TDD:800-695-0285
http://www.nichcy.org
e-mail: nichcy@aed.org

Lisa Kupper, Editor

This publication describes some of the most common learning disabilities that can cause reading problems and provides information on organizations that can provide needed assistance.

2993 Reading and Learning Disability: A Neuropsychological Approach to Evaluation & Instruction
Charles C Thomas
2600 S 1st St
Springfield, IL 62704-4730　　　217-789-8980
800-258-8980
FAX 217-789-9130
http://www.ccthomas.com
e-mail: books@ccthomas.com

Estelle L Fryburg, Author

Publisher of Education and Special Education books. *$74.95*

398 pages Paper
ISBN 0-398067-45-8

2994 Starting Out Right: A Guide to Promoting Children's Reading Success
National Academies Press
500 Fifth St NW
Washington, DC 20055　　　　　202-334-3313
888-624-8373
FAX 202-334-2451
http://www.nap.edu

Susan Burns, Editor
Peg Griffin, Editor
Catherine Snow, Editor
This book discusses how best to help children succeed in reading. This book also includes 55 activities yo do with children to help them become successful readers, a list of recommended children's books, and a guide to CD-ROMs and websites. A must read for specialists in primary education as well as pediatricians, childcare providers, tutors, literacy advocates, and parents. *$13.46*
192 pages
ISBN 0-309064-10-4

2995 Teaching Reading to Disabled and Handicapped Learners
Charles C Thomas
2600 S 1st St
Springfield, IL 62704-4730　　　217-789-8980
800-258-8980
FAX 217-789-9130
http://www.ccthomas.com
e-mail: books@ccthomas.com

Harold D Love, Author

Publisher of Education and Special Education books. *$43.95*

260 pages Paperback
ISBN 0-398062-48-4

2996 Textbooks and the Students Who Can't Read Them
Brookline Books
PO Box 1209
Brookline, MA 02446　　　　　617-734-6772
800-666-2665
FAX 617-734-3952
http://www.brooklinebooks.com
e-mail: brbooks@yahoo.com

Jean Ciborowski, Author

This book proposes how to involve low readers more effectively in textbook learning. It presents instructional techniques to improve students' willingness to work in mainstream textbooks. *$21.95*
Paperback
ISBN 0-914797-57-3

Social Skills

2997   ADHD in the Schools: Assessment and Intervention Strategies
Guilford Press
72 Spring St
New York, NY 10012-4019

800-365-7006
FAX 212-966-6708
http://www.guilford.com
e-mail: info@guilford.com

George J DuPaul, Author
Gary Stoner, Co-Author

This popular reference and text provides essential guidance for school-based professionals meeting the challenges of ADHD at any grade level. Comprehensive and practical, the book includes several reproducible assessment tools and handouts. *$30.00*
330 pages
ISBN 1-593850-89-1

2998   Behavior Change in the Classroom: Self-Management Interventions
Guilford Press
72 Spring St
New York, NY 10012-4019

800-365-7006
FAX 212-966-6708
http://www.guilford.com
e-mail: info@guilford.com

Edward S Shapiro, Author
Christine Cole, Co-Author

This book presents practical approaches for designing and implementing self-management interventions in school settings. Rich with detailed instruction, the volume covers the conceptual foundation for the development of self-management from both contingency management and cognitive-behavioral perspectives. *$35.00*
204 pages
ISBN 0-898623-66-9

2999   Group Activities to Include Students with Special Needs
Corwin Press
2400 Conejo Spectrum Drive
Thousand Oaks, CA 91320-2218

805-499-9734
800-233-9936
FAX 805-499-5323
http://www.corwin.com
e-mail: order@corwin.com

Julia Wilkins, Author

This hands-on resource offers 120 group activities emphasizing participation, cooperation, teamwork, mutual support, and improved self-esteem. This practical guide provides instant activities that can be used without preparation and incorporated into the daily routine with ease and confidence. Classroom games, gym and outdoor games, and ball games are designed to help your students gain the valuable skills they need to interact appropriately within the school setting. *$35.95*
240 pages
ISBN 0-761977-26-1

Publications

3000 **Campus Opportunities for Students with Learning Differences**
Octameron Associates
PO Box 2748
Alexandria, VA 22301-748
703-836-5480
FAX 703-836-5650
http://www.octameron.com

Judith Crooker, Author
Stephen Crooker, Co-Author

A book about going to college for young adults with various learning disabilities. Details questions to ask in selecting a college and teaches how to be a self-advocate. *$5.00*
36 pages
ISBN 1-575090-52-X

3001 **Career College and Technology School Databook**
Chronicle Guidance Publications
66 Aurora St
Moravia, NY 13118-3569
315-497-0330
800-622-7284
FAX 315-497-0339
http://www.chronicleguidance.com
e-mail: janet@chronicleguidance.com

Janet Seemann, Editor
Cheryl Fickeisen, President ,CEO

Offers information on occupational education programs currently available in the United States, Guam, and Puerto Rico. Programs consist of study or training leading to definite occupations. Prepares people for employment in recognized occupations, helps people make educated occupational choices, and upgrade and update their occupational skills. Includes data on vocational schools offering postsecondary occupational education. Accrediting associations are listed with contact information. *$25.46*
171 pages Annual
ISBN 1-556313-39-4

3002 **Chronicle Financial Aid Guide**
Chronicle Guidance Publications
66 Aurora St
Moravia, NY 13118-3569
800-622-7285
FAX 315-497-0339
http://www.chronicleguidance.com
e-mail: janet@chronicleguidance.com

Janet Seemann, Editor
Cheryl Fickeisen, President ,CEO

Offers information on more than 1,950 financial aid programs, offering over 400,000 awards from current, verified sources. *$25.49*
434 pages Annual
ISBN 1-556313-40-0

3003 **Colleges for Students with Learning Disabilities or ADD**

Peterson's
2000 Lenox Drive
Lawrenceville, NJ 08648-2314
609-896-1800
800-338-3282
FAX 609-896-4531
http://www.petersons.com
e-mail: custsvce@petersons.com

Charles Mangrum II, Author

Directs special-needs students to educational programs and services at 1,000 two-and four-year colleges and universities in the US and Canada. *$29.95*
560 pages Paperback
ISBN 0-768904-55-2

3004 **Disabled Faculty and Staff in a Disabling Society: Multiple Identities in Higher Education**
Association on Higher Education and Disability
Ste 204
107 Commerce Centre Dr
Huntersville, NC 28078-5870
704-947-7779
FAX 704-948-7779
http://www.ahead.org

Mary Lee Vance PhD, Editor
Scott Lissner, President

In this compelling anthology, 33 higher education professionals share personal stories, as well as relevant research associated with how they juggled both professional and personal needs. *$28.95*
300 pages

3005 **Four-Year College Databook**
Chronicle Guidance Publications
66 Aurora St
Moravia, NY 13118-3569
315-497-0330
800-622-7285
FAX 315-497-0339
http://www.chronicleguidance.com
e-mail: janet@chronicleguidance.com

Janet Seemann, Editor
Cheryl Fickeisen, President

Contains 2,160 institutions offering 790 four-year graduate and professional majors. *$25.48*
626 pages Annual
ISBN 1-556313-42-4

3006 **From Legal Principle to Informed Practice**
Association on Higher Education and Disability
Ste 204
107 Commerce Centre Dr
Huntersville, NC 28078-5870
704-947-7779
FAX 704-948-7779
http://www.ahead.org

Jane E Jarrow, Author
L Scott Lissner, Co-Author

This must have resource for disability service providers in higher education demystifies the legal underpinnings of the work you do; offering valuable insight, discussion, and instruction on understanding the principles and premises of the legal framework that support the full participation of students with disabilities in higher education. *$75.00*
118 pages

3007 **Going to College: Expanding Opportunities for People with Disabilities**
Association on Higher Education and Disability
Ste 204
107 Commerce Centre Dr
Huntersville, NC 28078-5870
704-947-7779
FAX 704-948-7779
http://www.ahead.org

Elizabeth Evans Getzel MA, Author
Paul Wehmann PhD eds, Co-Author

An important textbook for DSS and other college professionals engaged in the transitoin of students with disabilities to college. *$34.95*
336 pages

3008 **ISS Directory of International Schools**
International Schools Services
PO Box 5910
Princeton, NJ 08543-5910
609-452-0990
FAX 609-452-2690
http://www.iss.edu
e-mail: iss@iss.edu

Dan Scinto, President
David Cobb, Executive Director

Comprehensive guide to over 550 American and international schools worldwide. *$49.95*
550 pages
ISBN 0-913663-24-7

3009 Learning Disabilities in Higher Educationand Beyond: An International Perspective
Association on Higher Education and Disability
Ste 204
107 Commerce Centre Dr
Huntersville, NC 28078-5870   704-947-7779
                                     FAX 704-948-7779
                                     http://www.ahead.org
Jane E Jarrow, Author
L Scott Lissner, Co-Author
Scott Fickeisen, President
Builds upon an examination of the legal rights of people with learning disabilities in the United States, Canada, the United Kingdom, and Israel, then moves on to discuss assessment and diagnosis, programs, and support services, the social-emotional impact of learning disabilities, and how adults with learning disabilities fared after college. *$30.00*
384 pages

3010 Member Directory
NAPSEC
601 Pennsylvania Avenue
Suite 1032
Washington, DC 20004-1202   202-434-8225
                                     FAX 202-434-8224
                                     http://www.napsec.org
                                     e-mail: napsec@aol.com
Sherry Kolbe, Executive Director

A membership directory listing NAPSEC'S members, disabilities served, program descriptions, school profiles, admissions procedures and funding approval. *$32.00*
300 pages Bi-Annual

3011 Navigating College College Manual for Teaching the Portfolio
Association on Higher Education and Disability
Ste 204
107 Commerce Centre Dr
Huntersville, NC 28078-5870   704-947-7779
                                     FAX 704-948-7779
                                     http://www.ahead.org
Kimberly Nolting, Author
Scott Fickeisen, President,CEO

Provides in-class activity ideas for each chapter. As well, it provides suggestions to help students master the out of class assignments along with suggested grading rubrics. *$19.95*

3012 Navigating College: Strategy Manual for a Successful Voyage
Association on Higher Education and Disability
Ste 204
107 Commerce Centre Dr
Huntersville, NC 28078-5870   704-947-7779
                                     FAX 704-948-7779
                                     http://www.ahead.org
Kimberly Nolting, Author
Scott Fickeisen, President,CEO

A portfolio of readings and activities for new college students, all based in student persistance research. *$24.95*
131 pages

3013 Schoolsearch Guide to Colleges with Programs & Services for Students with LD
Schoolsearch
Ste 1851
381 Elliot St
Newton Upper Falls, MA 02464-1146   617-559-3666
                                         FAX 617-559-3665
                                         http://www.schoolsearch.com
                                         e-mail: mlipkin@schoolsearch.com

Midge Lipkin, Author
Midge Lipkin, Founder

Lists more than 600 colleges and universities that offer programs and services to high school graduates with learning disabilities. *$29.95*
706 pages
ISBN 0-962032-63-8

3014 Two-Year College Databook
Chronicle Guidance Publications
66 Aurora St
Moravia, NY 13118-3569   315-497-0330
                                     800-899-0454
                                     FAX 315-497-0339
                                     http://www.chronicleguidance.com
                                     e-mail: janet@chronicleguidance.com
Janet Seemann, Editor
Cheryl Fickeisen, President

Contains information on college majors, and on 2,432 institutions offering 760 occupational-career, associate, and transfer programs. *$25.47*
476 pages Annual
ISBN 1-556313-41-7

Alabama

3015 Auburn University
Program for Students with Disabilities
1244 Haley Ctr
Auburn, AL 36849   334-844-4000
                                     FAX 334-844-2099
                                     http://www.auburn.edu
                                     e-mail: psd@auburn.edu
Sarah Colby Weaver PhD, Director

Provides reasonable accommodations and services for qualified students with documented disabilities who are attending Auburn University, enrolled in distance learning classes, or participating in programs sponsored by Auburn University.

3016 Auburn University at Montgomery
Center for Disability Services
PO Box 244023
Montgomery, AL 36124-4023   334-244-3000
                                     800-227-2649
                                     FAX 334-244-3762
                                     TDD:334-244-3754
                                     http://www.aum.edu
                                     e-mail: tmassey2@mail.aum.edu
Tamara Massey-Garrett MS, Director
Jay Gogue, President
Lovvorn Caro, Representative
Offers a variety of services to students with disabilities including equipment, extended testing time, interpreting services, counseling services, and special accommodations.

3017 Birmingham-Southern College
900 Arkadelphia Rd
Birmingham, AL 35254-0002   205-226-4960
                                     800-523-5793
                                     FAX 205-226-4627
                                     http://www.bsc.edu
Sara Hoover, Director, Counselith/Health Svcs

Offers a variety of services to students with disabilities including notetakers, extended testing time, counseling services, and special accommodations.

3018 Chattahoochee Valley State Community College
2602 College Dr
Phenix City, AL 36869-7917   334-291-4900
                                     FAX 334-291-4944
                                     http://www.cvcc.cc.al.us
Laurel M Blackwell, President
Jacquie Thacker, ADA Coordinator

Offers a variety of services to students with disabilities including note takers, extended testing time, counseling services and special accommodations.

3019 Churchill Academy
395 Ray Thorington Rd
Montgomery, AL 36117-8486 334-270-4225
FAX 334-270-7805
http://www.churchillacademymontgomery.com
e-mail: info@churchillacademymontgomery.com
Lisa Schroeder, Director
Judy Hall, Service Co-ordinator

A one-of-a-kind school for bright children with unique learning differences.

3020 Enterprise Ozark Community College
600 Plaza Drive
Enterprise, AL 36330-1300 334-347-2623
800-624-3438
FAX 334-774-6399
http://www.escc.edu
Lizz Barton, Assistant
Dr. Nancy W. Chandler, President

A public two-year college with 15 special education students out of a total of 600. Certified by the Federal Aviation Administration, and offers the only comprehensive aviation maintenance training program in the state of Alabama, with instruction in airframe, powerplant and avionics.

3021 Horizons School
2018 15th Ave S
Birmingham, AL 35205-3812 205-322-6606
800-822-6242
FAX 205-322-6605
http://www.horizonsschool.org
e-mail: jcarter@horizonsschool.org
Jade Carter, Director
Marie H McElheny, Assistant Director
Student White, Student Recruiter
Offers a non-degree transition program specifically designed to facilitate personal, social and career independence for students with specific learning disabilities and other handicapping conditions.

3022 Jacksonville State University
Disability Support Services
700 Pelham Rd N
Jacksonville, AL 36265-1623 256-782-5781
FAX 256-782-5291
http://www.jsu.edu
e-mail: dss@jsu.edu
William A Meehan, Director
Bibb Graves Hall, President

Offers a variety of services to students with disabilities including notetakers, extended testing time, counseling services, and special accommodations.

3023 James H Faulkner State Community College
1900 S Us Highway 31
Bay Minette, AL 36507-2698 251-580-2100
800-231-3752
FAX 251-580-2236
http://www.faulknerstate.edu
e-mail: bkennedy@faulknerstate.edu
Gary L Branch, Dean Student Development
Adams Kenneth G, Director

A public two-year community college with approximately 125 students with disabilities out of a total student population of 4,350. Committed to the professional and cultural growth of each student without regard to race, color, qualified disability, gender, religion, creed, national origin, or age. Attempts to provide an educational environment that promotes development and learning through a wide variety of educational programs, adequate and comfortable facilities, and flexible scheduling.

3024 Troy State University Dothan
500 University Drive
Dothan, AL 36303 334-983-6556
FAX 334-983-6322
TTY: 800-414-5756
http://www.troy.edu
e-mail: academicsupport@troy.edu
Barbara Alford, President
Keith Seagle, Counseling Services Director

Offers a variety of services to students with disabilities including notetakers, extended testing time, counseling services, and special accommodations.

3025 University of Alabama
Office of Disability Services
PO Box 870132
Tuscaloosa, AL 35487 205-348-6010
FAX 205-348-8377
http://www.ua.edu
e-mail: intergradapply@aalan.ua.edu
Robert E Witt, President
Dr. Judy Bonner, Interim President
C. Ray Hayes, Vice-Cancellor
A public four-year college with approximately 650 students identified with disabilities out of a total of 19,200.

3026 University of Montevallo
Office of Disability Services
Station 6250
Montevallo, AL 35115 205-665-6000
FAX 205-665-6080
http://www.montevallo.edu
e-mail: mccuned@montevallo.edu
Deborah McCune, Director
Mark Bolton, Human Resource
Guy Bailey, President
Offers a variety of services to students with disabilities including notetakers, extended testing time, counseling services, and special accommodations.

3027 University of North Alabama
Office of Developmental Services
PO Box 5008
Florence, AL 35632 256-765-4608
800-825-5862
FAX 256-765-6016
http://www.una.edu
e-mail: jadams@unanov.una.edu
Jennifer S Adams, Director

Developmental services of UNA provides accommodation and supportive services to assist students with disabilities throughout their college expirence.

3028 University of South Alabama
Disabled Student Services
307 N University Blvd
Mobile, AL 36688 251-460-6101
FAX 251-460-6080
http://www.usouthal.edu
e-mail: aagnew@usouthal.edu
V Gordon Moulton, President
Dr. John W. Smith, Special Assistant

Offers a variety of services to students with disabilities including note takers, extended testing time, counseling services, and special accommodations.

3029 Wallace Community College Selma
3000 Earl Goodwin Pkwy
Selma, AL 36703-2808

334-876-9227
FAX 334-876-9250
http://www.wccs.edu
e-mail: info@wccs.edu

James Mitchell, President
Olivia Acoff, Councellor

Offers a variety of services to students with disabilities including note takers, extended testing time, counseling services and special accommodations.

Alaska

3030 Alaska Pacific University
Disabled Student Services
4101 University Dr
Anchorage, AK 99508-4647

907-564-8317
FAX 907-562-8248
TTY: 800-252-7528
http://www.alaskapacific.edu
e-mail: admissions@alaskapacific.edu

Douglas M North, Coordinator Disability Support
Bantz President
Four-year college offering special services to students that are learning disabled.

3031 Gateway School and Learning Center
900 W.Fireweed Lane
P.O.Box 113149
Anchorage, AK 99511-3149

907-522-2240
FAX 907-344-0304
http://www.gatewayschoolak.com
e-mail: learning@gatewayschoolak.com

Beverly Lau, Principal

Provides specialized educational services for students grades 1-12 with dyslexia and other language-processing disorders.

3032 Juneau Campus: University of Alaska Southeast
11120 Glacier Hwy
Juneau, AK 99801-8699

907-796-6000
877-465-4827
FAX 907-465-6365
http://www.uas.alaska.edu
e-mail: uas.info@uas.alaska.edu

Patrick Gamble, President
Joel Milsat, Director
Fuller A. Cowell, Founder
Offers a variety of services to students with disabilities including notetakers, extended testing time, counseling services, and special accommodations.

3033 Ketchikan Campus: University of Alaska Southeast
2600 7th Ave
Ketchikan, AK 99901-5728

907-225-6177
TTY: 888-550-6177
http://www.ketch.alaska.edu
e-mail: info@uas.alaska.edu

Kathleen Wiechelman, Assistant Professor
Founder
Offers a variety of services to students with disabilities including note takers, extended testing time, counseling services and special accommodations.

3034 University of Alaska Anchorage
Office of Disability Services
3211 Providence Dr
Anchorage, AK 99508-4645

907-786-1800
FAX 907-786-6123
http://www.uaa.alaska.edu
e-mail: aydss@uaa.alaska.edu

Fran Ulmer, Director
Patrick Gamble, President

Provides equal opportunites for students who experience disabilities.

Arizona

3035 New Way Learning Academy
1300 N 77th St
Scottsdale, AZ 85257-3776

480-946-9112
FAX 480-946-2657
http://www.newwayacademy.org
e-mail: dawn@newwayacademy.org

Dawn Gutierrez, Head of School
Tom Jones, Chairman
Kerry Wangberg, Vice Chairman
Non-profit, private K-12 day school specializing in children with learning differences. We proudly and passionately serve students with dyslexia, AD/HD and other learning differences.

3036 SALT Center
University of Arizona
1010 N Highland Ave
PO Box 210136
Tucson, AZ 85721-0001

520-621-8493
FAX 520-626-3260
http://www.salt.arizona.edu
e-mail: saltctr@email.arizona.edu

Jeff Orgera, Director
Nancy Singer, Asst Director Admissions

An academic support program that provides a comprehensive range of fee-based services to University of Arizona students with learning and attention challenges.

3037 Turning Point School
8780 National Blvd
Culver City, CA 90232

310-841-2505
FAX 310-841-5420
http://www.turningpointschool.com
e-mail: info@turningpointschool.org

Nancy Von Wald, Director
Deborah Richman, Head of the School

A private, non profit school providing education for those with specific learning disabilities, Dyslexia.

3038 Upward Foundation
Special Education Program
6306 N 7th St
Phoenix, AZ 85014-1549

602-279-5801
FAX 602-279-0033
http://www.upwardfoundation.org
e-mail: info@upwardfoundation.org

Sharon Graham, Executive Director

Improving the lives of children with severe disabilities and other special needs.

Arkansas

3039 Jones Learning Center
University of the Ozarks
415 N College Ave
Clarksville, AR 72830-2880

479-979-1403
800-264-8636
FAX 479-979-1429
http://www.ozarks.edu
e-mail: jlc@ozarks.edu

Julia Frost, Director
Dodi Pelts, Assistant Director

Offers enhanced services to students who show potential for success in a competitive academic environment.

3040 Philander Smith College
Student Support Program (SPARK)
900 Trudie Kibbe Reed Dr
Little Rock, AR 72202-3717   501-370-5221
                                           800-446-6772
                                        FAX 501-370-5277
                              http://www.philander.edu
                    e-mail: administrator@philander.edu
Walter M Kimbrough, President
Adrian Tharpe, Co-ordinator

Offers a variety of services to students with disabilities including notetakers, extended testing time, counseling services, and special accommodations.

3041 Southern Arkansas University
Disabled Student Programs and Services
100 East UniversityÿÿÿMagnolia
Magnolia, AR 71753-5000   870-235-5000
                                        FAX 870-235-4133
                                  http://www.saumag.edu
                           e-mail: eewalker@saumag.edu
Eunice Walker, Director
David F.Rankin, President

Offers a variety of services to students with disabilities including notetakers, extended testing time, counseling services, and special accommodations.

3042 University of Arkansas
Center for Educational Access
Room 104 Arkansas Union
Fayetteville, AR 72701   479-575-2000
                                           800-377-8632
                                        FAX 479-575-7445
                                    http://www.uark.edu
                                  e-mail: ada@uark.edu
Annie Jannarone, Director
Sen. J. William Fulbright

Offers a variety of services to students with disabilities including note takers, extended testing time, counseling services, and special accommodations.

California

3043 ACCESS Program
Moorpark College
7075 Campus Rd
Moorpark, CA 93021-1605   805-378-1400
                                        FAX 805-378-1594
                                        TDD:805-378-1461
                         http://www.moorparkcollege.edu
                            e-mail: sdattile@vcccd.edu
Sherry D'Attile, Director

A public two-year college with 154 special education students out of a total of 12,414.

3044 Allan Hancock College
800 S College Dr
Santa Maria, CA 93454-6399   805-922-6966
                                        FAX 805-928-7905
                             http://www.hancockcollege.edu
                        e-mail: lap@hancockcollege.edu
Robert Parisi, Director

Students with mobility, visual, hearing and speech impairments, learning disabilities, acquired brain injury, developmental disabilities, psychological and other disabilities are eligible to receive special services which enable them to fully participate in the community college experience at Allan Hancock College.

3045 Antelope Valley College
Disabled Student Services Program
3041 W Avenue K
Lancaster, CA 93536-5426   661-722-6300
                                        FAX 661-722-6361
                                     http://www.avc.edu
                                 e-mail: llucero@avc.edu
Louis Lucero, Director

A public two-year college with 228 learning disabled students out of a total of 11,105.

3046 Aspen Education Group
Ste 300
17777 Center Court Dr N
Cerritos, CA 90703-9328   888-972-7736
                                        FAX 562-402-7036
                          http://www.aspeneducation.com
Elliot A Sainer, President

Provider of education programs for the struggling or underachieving young people. Offers professionals and families the opportunity to choose a setting that best meets a student's unique academic and emotional needs.

3047 Bakersfield College
Disabled Student Programs and Services
1801 Panorama Dr
Bakersfield, CA 93305-1299   661-395-4011
                                        FAX 661-395-4079
                                        TTY: 661-395-4334
                        http://www.2.bakersfieldcollege.edu
                    e-mail: anegome@bakersfieldcollege.edu
Greg A Chamberlain, Director

A public two-year college with 207 special education students out of a total of 12,312.

3048 Barstow Community College
Disabled Student Programs and Services
2700 Barstow Rd
Barstow, CA 92311-6608   760-252-2411
                                        FAX 760-252-1875
                                        TDD:760-252-6759
                                        TTY: 760-252-6759
                            http://www.barstow.cc.ca.us
                        e-mail: dsps@barstow.cc.ca.us
Richard Jones, Assistant Coordinator
Robert Pacheco, LD Specialist Coordinator
Thom M. Armstrong, Ph.D, President
Educational support program for disabled students including special classes and support services for all disabled students.

3049 Bridge School
Educational Program
545 Eucalyptus Ave
Hillsborough, CA 94010-6404   650-696-7295
                                        FAX 650-342-7598
                                http://www.bridgeschool.org
Vicki Casella, Executive Director
President
Our program is based on the principle of providing access to and participation in an age-appropriate curriculum adapted to the special needs of children with motor, sensory and speech impairments.

3050 Butte College
Disabled Student Programs and Services
3536 Butte Campus Dr
Oroville, CA 95965-8399   530-895-2511
                                        FAX 530-895-2345
                                        TDD:530-895-2308
                                    http://www.butte.edu
                                e-mail: dsps@butte.edu
Diana J Van Der Ploeg, Coordinator
Carol Oba-Winslow, Disabilities Specialist
Kimberly Perry, President
A public two-year college with 223 special education students out of a total of 12,848.

3051 Cabrillo College
Disabled Student Programs and Services
Room 800
3500 Soquel Dr
Aptos, CA 95003
831-479-6100
FAX 831-477-5687
TTY: 831-479-6421
http://www.cabrillo.cc.ca.us
e-mail: jonapoli@cabrillo.edu
Brian King, President

A two-year college that offers services and programs to disabled students.

3052 California State University: East Bay
25800 Carlos Bee Blvd
Hayward, CA 94542-3001
510-885-3000
FAX 510-885-2049
http://www.csuhayward.edu
e-mail: sdrc@csueastbay.edu
Linda Dobb, Learning Resources Counselor

Students with documented disabilities and functional limitations are eligible for accomodations designed to provide equivalent access to general campus and classroom programs and activities. The campus provides an SDRC - Student Disability Resource Center - with assistive technology and testing accomodations. They also offer Project Impact and the EXCEL Program, both of which serve their disabled student body.

3053 California State University: Fullerton
Disabled Student Services
PO Box 6830
Fullerton, CA 92834-6830
657-278-4444
FAX 714-278-2408
TDD:714-278-2786
http://www.fullerton.edu
e-mail: dliverpool@fullerton.edu
Doug Liverpool, LD/Mental Heath Specialist
Mildred Garc¡a, President

A public four-year college with 800 special education students out of a total of 75,000. The Office of Disabled Student Services aims to increase access and retention for students with permanent and temporary disabilities by ensuring equitable treatment in all aspects of campus life. Provides co-curricular and academically related services which empower students with disabilities to achieve academic and personal self-determination.

3054 California State University: Long Beach-Stephen Benson Program
Disabled Student Services
1250 N Bellflower Blvd
Long Beach, CA 90840-0004
562-985-4430
FAX 562-985-4529
http://www.csulb.edu/sbp
e-mail: bcarey@csulb.edu
Brian Carey, Coordinator

Four-year college offers a program for the learning disabled.

3055 Chaffey Community College District
Disability Programs and Services
5885 Haven Ave
Rancho Cucamonga, CA 91737-3002
909-652-8000
FAX 909-652-6386
TTY: 909-466-2829
http://www.chaffey.edu
e-mail: joe.jondreau@chaffey.edu
Joe Jondreau, Director
Lizza Napoli, Assistant

Chaffey College's Disabled Student Programs and Services (DSP&S) offer instruction and support services to students with developmental, learning, physical, psychological disabilities or aquired brain injury. Students can recieve a variety of services such as: test facilitation, note taking, tutoring, adaptive physical education, pre-vocational training, career preparation, and job placement.

3056 Charles Armstrong School
1405 Solana Dr
Belmont, CA 94002-3653
650-592-7570
FAX 650-592-0780
http://www.charlesarmstrong.org
e-mail: dvielbaum@charlesarmstrong.org
Rosalie Whitlock, Head of School

Serves students with language-based learning differences, such as dyslexia, by providing an appropriate educational experience which enables the students to acquire language skills, while instilling a joy of learning, enhancing self-worth, and allowing each student the right to identify, understand and fulfill personal potential.

3057 Chartwell School: Seaside
2511 Numa Watson Rd
Seaside, CA 93955-6774
831-394-3468
FAX 831-394-6809
http://www.chartwell.org
e-mail: information@chartwell.org
Nora Lee, Head of School
Executive Di
Our mission is to educate children with a wide range of language-related visual and auditory learning challenges in a way that provides them with the learning skills and self-esteem necessary to return successfully to mainstream education. Chartwell also helps individuals with specific learning challenges access their full potential by providing leading-edge education, research and community outreach.

3058 College of Alameda
Disabled Student Services
555 Ralph Appezzato Memorial Pkwy
Alameda, CA 94501-2109
510-522-7221
FAX 510-748-2339
TTY: 510-748-2330
http://www.alameda.peralta.edu
e-mail: hmaxwell@peralta.edu
George Herring, Coordinator
Lynn Rex, LD Specialist
Dr. Jannett N. Jackson, Ph.D, President
Accommodations, assessment and special classes are provided for learning disabled students enrolled at College Alameda, a 2 year college located by San Francisco Bay.

3059 College of Marin
Disabled Students Program
835 College Ave
Kentfield, CA 94904-2590
415-457-8811
FAX 415-457-4791
http://www.marin.cc.ca.us
e-mail: chris.schultz@marin.edu
Frances L White, Coordinator
Ellen Tollen, LD Specialist
Diana Conte, President
Offers a variety of services to students with disabilities including note takers, extended testing time, counseling services, and special accommodations. Also offers diagnostic testing and remedial classes for learning disabled students.

3060 College of the Canyons
Disabled Student Programs and Services
26455 Rockwell Canyon Rd
Santa Clarita, CA 91355-1899
661-259-7800
FAX 661-259-8302
TTY: 661-255-7967
http://www.coc.cc.ca.us
e-mail: jane.feuerhelm@canyons.edu

Dianne G Van Hook, President

A public two-year college with 45 special education students out of a total of 6,255.

3061 College of the Redwoods
Disabled Student Programs and Services
7351 Tompkins Hill Rd
Eureka, CA 95501-9300
707-476-4100
800-641-0400
FAX 707-476-4421
TTY: 707-476-4284
http://www.redwoods.edu
e-mail: tracey-thomas@redwoods.edu
Jeff Marsee, Director
Trish Blair, LD Specialist

Mission is to assist individual students in the development of a realistic self-concept, assist in the development of educational interests and employment goals, provide the advice, counseling, and equipment necessary to facilitate success, starting with specialized assistance in the registration process.

3062 College of the Sequoias
Disability Resource Center
Instructional Media Center
Visalia, CA 93277
559-730-3805
FAX 559-730-3803
TDD:559-730-3913
TTY: 559-730-3913
http://www.cos.edu
e-mail: sharmeenl@cos.edu
David Maciel, Director
Stan Carrizosa, President

A public two-year college with approximately 600 special education students out of a total of 10,300.

3063 College of the Siskiyous
800 College Ave
Weed, CA 96094-2899
530-938-5297
FAX 530-938-5378
http://www.siskiyous.edu
e-mail: dsps@siskiyous.edu
Sunny Greene, DSPS Director

Offers services to learning and physically disabled students throught the DSPS - Disabled Students Programs & Services.

3064 Columbia College
11600 Columbia College Dr
Sonora, CA 95370-8580
209-588-5130
FAX 209-588-5058
http://www.gocolumbia.edu
e-mail: rodtsk@yosemite.edu
Karin Rodts, DSPS Coordinator/LD Specialist

Offers a variety of services to students with disabilities including note takers, extended testing time, counseling services and special accommodations.

3065 Cuesta College
3300 Building
1st Fl
San Luis Obispo, CA 93403
805-546-3148
FAX 805-546-3930
http://www.academic.cuesta.edu
e-mail: dspsinfo@cuesta.edu
Patrick Schwab EdD, Director

A public, two-year community college, offering instruction and services to students with learning disabilities since 1973. A comprehensive set of services and special classes are available. Contact the program for further information.

3066 Disabled Students Programs & Services
Laney College
900 Fallon St
Oakland, CA 94607-4893
510-834-5740
FAX 510-986-6913
TTY: 510-464-3400
http://www.laney.peralta.edu
e-mail: rpruitt@peralta.edu
Elnora Webb, President

Provides services and instructional programs for students with disabilities.

3067 East Los Angeles College
1301 Avenida Cesar Chavez
Monterey Park, CA 91754-6099
323-265-8650
FAX 323-265-8759
http://www.elac.cc.ca.us
Philip A. Cohen, CEO
Ram Gust, Librarian
Kareem Ahmad, President
A public two-year college with 44 special education students out of a total of 14587. There is a an additional fee for the special education program in addition to the regular tuition.

3068 Evergreen Valley College
Disabilities Support Programs
East Fifth Street
Greenville, NC 27858-4353
252-328-6131
FAX 408-223-6341
TDD:408-238-8722
http://www.euc.edu
e-mail: bonnie.clark@euc.edu
David W Coon, LD Specialist
John D. Messick, President

A public two-year college with 82 learning disabled students out of a total of 9,000.

3069 Excelsior Academy
Disabled Student Programs
7202 Princess View Dr
San Diego, CA 92120-1332
619-583-6762
FAX 619-583-6764
http://www.excelsioracademy.com
e-mail: cchapman@excelsioracademy.com
Frank Maguire, Executive Director
Karina Arana, Director

Provide a safe and nurturing environment wherein students become literate, thinking, independent, and productive citizens. Serving students in Grade 3-12 with unique learning profiles.

3070 Fresno City College
Disabled Student Programs and Services
1101 E University Ave
Fresno, CA 93741
559-442-4600
559-489-2281
FAX 559-265-5777
TDD:559-442-8237
http://www.fresnocitycollege.edu
e-mail: janice.emerzian@fresnocitycollege.edu
Cynthia Azari, District Director
Toni Cantu, President
Dr.Chris Willa, Vice President
A public two-year college with 259 special education students out of a total of 17,949.

3071 Frostig Center
Marianne Frostig Center of Educational Therapy
971 N Altadena Dr
Pasadena, CA 91107-1870
626-791-1255
FAX 626-798-1801
http://www.frostig.org
e-mail: center@frostig.org
Bennett Ross, Principal
Linda Moore, Chairman
Phyllis Kochavi, Vice-Chairman

Dedicated to providing children with learning disabilities a quality academic program that also promotes their language, motor, social-emotional, and creative growth.

3072 Gavilan College
Disabled Student Programs and Services
5055 Santa Teresa Blvd
Gilroy, CA 95020-9599
408-852-2861
FAX 408-848-4801
TTY: 408-846-4924
http://www.gavilan.edu
e-mail: drc@gavilan.edu
Steven M Kinsella, Associate Dean
Vice-Preside
Offers a variety of services to students with disabilities including note takers, extended testing time, counseling services and special accommodations.

3073 Hartnell College
Disabled Student Programs and Services
411 Central Ave
Salinas, CA 93901-1688
831-755-6700
FAX 831-755-6751
TDD:831-770-6199
http://www.hartnell.edu
Phoebe K Helm, LD Specialist

A public two-year college with 72 special education students out of a total of 7,593.

3074 Institute for the Redesign of Learning
Transition and Adult Services
211 Pasadena Ave
South Pasadena, CA 91030-2919
323-341-5580
FAX 323-257-3101
http://www.redesignlearning.org
Nancy Lavelle, President
Jason D. Rubin, Managing Diredtor

A full day school serving 100 boys and girls, at-risk infants and children. Vocational Program serves adults and includes Supported Employment Services and an Independent Living Program.

3075 Irvine Valley College
Disabled Student Programs and Services
Rm Sc171
5500 Irvine Center Dr
Irvine, CA 92618-300
949-451-5100
TTY: 949-451-5785
http://www.ivc.edu
e-mail: ivcdsps@ivc.edu
Andrea Richard, LD Specialist
Richard Morley, Executive Director

The goal is to effectivly provide assistance to all students with disabilities to achieve academic success while at Irvine Valley. The primary function is to accommodate a student's disability, whether it is a physical, communication, learning or psychological disability.

3076 Kayne Eras Center
Exceptional Children's Foundation
8740 Washington Boulevard
Culver City, CA 90232-8800
310-204-3300
FAX 310-845-8001
http://www.kayneeras.org
e-mail: jraffle@kayneeras.org
Scott Bowling, President
Philip G. Miller, Chairperson

Operates a state certified, non-public school for youth ages 5 to 22 who are having difficulty functioning in the public school system due to developmental delays, learning disabilities, emotional or behavior challenges, and/or health impairments.

3077 Long Beach City College: Liberal Arts Campus
Disabled Student Programs and Services
Rm A119
4901 E Carson St
Long Beach, CA 90808-1706
562-938-4111
FAX 562-938-4651
TDD:562-938-4833
http://www.dsps.lbcc.cc.ca.us
e-mail: mmatsui@lbcc.edu
Eloy Oakley, President
Jeffrey Kellog, Vice President

Disabled Student Services (DSPS) is a program within Student Services at LBCC. DSPS provides many support services that enable students with disability related limitations to participate in the college's programs and activities. DSPS offers a wide range of services that compensate for a students limitations, like note taking assistance, interpretive services, alternative media, etc.

3078 Los Angeles Mission College
Disabled Student Programs and Services
Rm 1018
13356 Eldridge Ave
Sylmar, CA 91342-3245
818-364-7600
FAX 818-364-7755
TDD:818-364-7861
http://www.lamission.edu
e-mail: scuderi@lamission.edu
Judith Valles, Director

A support system that enables students to fully participate in the college's regular programs and activities. We provide a variety of services from academic and vocational support to assistance with finacial aid. All services are individulalized according to specific needs. They do not replace regular programs, but rather, accommodate students special requirements.

3079 Los Angeles Pierce College
Disabled Student Programs and Services
6201 Winnetka Ave
Woodland Hills, CA 91371
818-719-6404
FAX 818-710-9844
TTY: 818-719-6430
http://www.piercecollege.edu
e-mail: special_services@piercecollege.edu
Robert M Garber, Director
Dr. Kathleen Burke, President

A public two-year college with 257 special education students out of a total of 19,207.

3080 Los Angeles Valley College Services for Students with Disabilities (SSD)
5800 Fulton Ave
Van Nuys, CA 91401-4096
818-947-2681
FAX 818-778-5775
TDD:818-947-2680
TTY: 818-947-2680
http://www.lavc.edu
e-mail: ssd@lavc.edu
Dave Green, Associate Dean, SSD

Provides specialized support services to students with disabilities which are in addition to the regular services provided to all students. Special accommodations and services are determined by the nature and extent of the disability related educational limitations of the student and are provided based upon the recommendation of DSPS.

3081 Monterey Peninsula College
Disabled Student Programs and Services
980 Fremont St
Monterey, CA 93940-4799
831-646-4070
FAX 831-646-4171
http://www.mpc.edu
e-mail: ssandi@mpc.edu

Dr Douglas Garrison, Superintendent/President
Carsbia Anderson, VP Student Services
Terria Odom-Wolfer, Faculty Coordinator
Supportive Services & Instruction program provides services and specialized instruction for enrolled students with disabilities.

3082   Mount San Antonio Community College
Disabled Student Programs and Services
Bldg 9b
1100 N Grand Ave
Walnut, CA 91789-1399   909-274-7500
                                          FAX 909-594-7661
                                          TTY: 909-594-3447
                                   http://http://www.mtsac.edu/
                                   e-mail: ghanson@mtsac.edu
John S Nixon, Director
Dr. George H . Bell, President

A public two-year college with 1,500 students with disabilities who receive special services. Total population of students is approximately 40,000.

3083   Napa Valley College
Disabled Student Programs and Services
2277 Napa Vallejo Hwy
Napa, CA 94558-7555   707-253-3000
                                              800-826-1077
                                          FAX 707-259-8010
                                          TTY: 707-253-3084
                                   http://www.napavalley.edu
                              e-mail: wmartinez@napavalley.edu
Christopher Mc Carthy, Dean of Program
Dr. Ronald Kraft, President

Offers a variety of services to students with disabilities including note takers, extended testing time, counseling services and special accommodations.

3084   Ohlone College
Disabled Student Programs and Services
43600 Mission Blvd
Fremont, CA 94539-5847   510-659-6000
                                          FAX 510-659-6058
                                          TTY: 510-659-6269
                                     http://www.ohlone.edu
                               e-mail: deafcenter@ohlone.edu
Gari Browning, Dean
President

Special services are provided to meet the unique needs of Deaf, Hard of Hearing, and Disabled students and help them achieve a successful college career.

3085   Orange Coast College
Special Programs and Services
2701 Fairview Rd
Costa Mesa, CA 92626-5561   714-432-5072
                                          FAX 714-432-5739
                               http://www.orangecoastcollege.edu
                                 e-mail: omartinez@occ.cccd.edu
Robert Dees, Supervisor
Margaret Gratton, President

A public two-year college with 350 special education students out of a total of 27,960. There is a an additional fee for the special education program in addition to the regular tuition.

3086   Park Century School
3939 Landmark St
Culver City, CA 90232-2315   310-840-0500
                                          FAX 310-840-0590
                               http://www.parkcenturyschool.org
A non-profit independent co-educational day school designed to meet the specific educational needs of bright children, ages 7 - 14 years, who have learning disabilities.

3087   Prentice School
18341 Lassen Dr
Santa Ana, CA 92705-2012   714-538-4511
                                              800-479-4711
                                          FAX 714-538-5004
                                     http://www.prentice.org
Carol Clark, Executive Director
Cheryl Cormier, Director Of Development

The Prentice School is an independent, nonprofit, coeducational day school for children ages pre-k through 8th grade with language learning differences.

3088   Raskob Learning Institute and Day School
3520 Mountain Blvd
Oakland, CA 94619-1627   510-436-1275
                                          FAX 510-436-1106
                                  http://www.raskobinstitute.org
                               e-mail: raskobinstitute@hnu.edu
Edith Gutterres, Executive Director

A co-educational school for students from diverse cultural and economic backgrounds with language-based learning disabilities. Raskob seeks to recognize and nurture the talents and strengths of each student while remediating areas of academic weakness.

3089   San Diego City College
Disabled Student Programs and Services
Rm A-115
1313 Park Blvd
San Diego, CA 92101-4787   619-388-3400
                                          FAX 619-388-3801
                                          TTY: 619-388-3313
                                     http://www.sdcity.edu
                                e-mail: bmason@sdccd.edu
Terrence Burgess, Coordinator
June E Richard, Co-Chairman

Offers a variety of services to students with disabilities including note takers, extended testing time, counseling services, and special accommodations.

3090   San Diego Miramar College
Disability Support Programs and Services
Rm C-304
10440 Black Mountain Rd
San Diego, CA 92126-2999   858-536-7800
                                          FAX 858-388-7901
                                          TDD:858-536-4301
                                   http://www.sdmiramar.edu
                            e-mail: kdoorly@sdccd.cc.ca.us
Patricia Hsieh, Coordinator
Martin High, Founder

A public two-year college with 500 learning disabled students. These students receive services and accommodations appropriate for their success in college. Individual counseling, class advising and LD assessments are also available. Special classes are offered to support college courses.

3091   San Diego State University
Student Disability Services
Suite 3101
Calpulli Center 5500 Campani Dr
San Diego, CA 92182   619-594-5200
                                          FAX 619-594-5642
                                          TDD:619-594-2929
                                          TTY: 619-594-2929
                                     http://www.sa.sdsu.edu
                               e-mail: mshojai@mail.sdsu.edu
Stephen L Weber, Director
Dr. James R Kitchen, Vice President

Program and Support services are available to students with certified visual limitations, hearing and communication impairments, learning disabilities, mobility, and other functional limitations.

3092 **Santa Monica College**
Center for Students with Disabilities
1900 Pico Blvd
Santa Monica, CA 90405-1644   310-434-4000
                                     FAX 310-434-4272
                                     TDD:310-434-4273
                              http://www.smc.edu
                       e-mail: schwartz_judy@smc.edu
Chui L Tsang, Coordinator

Offers guidance and counseling on admissions requirements
and procedures, as well as a number of special programs to
help students with their academic, vocational, and career
planning goals. In addition, the Center offers services such
as tutoring, specialized equipment, test proctoring, among
many other accommodations for students who are eligible.

3093 **Santa Rosa Junior College**
Adapted Physical Education
1501 Mendocino Ave
Santa Rosa, CA 95401-4395   707-527-4011
                                    FAX 707-527-4967
                             http://www.santarosa.edu
                       e-mail: disabilityinfo@santarosa.edu
Robert F Agrella, Coordinator
Frank Chong, Ed.D, President

Offers a variety of regular classes each semester for people
with disabilities.

3094 **Springall Academy**
Springall Program
6460 Boulder Lake Ave
San Diego, CA 92119-3142   619-460-5090
                                   FAX 619-490-5091
                            http://www.springall.org
                       e-mail: baker@springall.org
Arlene Baker, Executive Director

Offers a variety of services to students with disabilities including note takers, extended testing time, counseling services, and special accommodations. The academy is a
nonprofit school for learning and behaviorally challenged
students.

3095 **Stanbridge Academy**
515 E Poplar Ave
San Mateo, CA 94401-1715   650-375-5860
                                   FAX 650-375-5861
                          http://www.stanbridgeacademy.org
                       e-mail: mlynch@stanbridgeacademy.org
Marilyn Lynch, Admissions Director
Lanea Aquirela, Director

A private, non-profit school for students with mild to moderate learning differences, primary grades through high
school.

3096 **Stellar Academy for Dyslexics**
38325 Cedar Blvd
Newark, CA 94560-4801   510-797-2227
                                FAX 510-797-2207
                         http://www.stellaracademy.org
                       e-mail: stellaracademy@aol.com
Beth Mattsson-Boze, Director

To serve the needs of children with dyslexia using the
Slingerlandr approach.

3097 **Sterne School**
2690 Jackson St
San Francisco, CA 94115-1123   415-922-6081
                                       FAX 415-922-1598
                             http://www.sterneschool.org
                       e-mail: emcmanis@sterneschool.org
Lisa Graham, Head of School
Pasca Rigo, Founder

A private school serving students in 6-12 grade who have
specific learning disabilities.

3098 **Summit View School**
6455 Coldwater Canyon Ave
Valley Glen, CA 91606   818-623-6300
                                FAX 818-623-6390
                          http://www.summitview.org
                       e-mail: nnrosenfelt@thehelpgroup.org
Nancy Rosenfelt, Director

Serving students with specific learning disabilities.

3099 **Summit View School: Los Angeles**
12101 W Washington Blvd
Los Angeles, CA 90066   310-751-1100
                                FAX 818-623-6390
                          http://www.summitview.org
                       e-mail: nnrosenfelt@thehelpgroup.org
Nancy Rosenfelt, Director

Serving students with specific learning disabilities.

3100 **Tobinworld School: Glendale**
920 E Broadway
Glendale, CA 91205-1204   818-247-7474
                                  FAX 818-247-6516
                          http://www.tobinworld.org
                       e-mail: judyw@tobinworld.org
Charles Conrad, Principal

A non-profit school for children and young adults with behavior problems. Typically students have been classified as
severely emotionally disabled, autistic or developmentally
disabled.

3101 **University of California: Irvine**
Office for Disability Services
Building 313
100 Disability Services
Irvine, CA 92697   949-824-7494
                           FAX 949-824-3083
                           TDD:949-824-6272
                    http://www.disability.uci.edu
                       e-mail: dsc@uci.edu
Jan Serrantino EdD, Director
Gavin Keller, Assistant Director

Our mission is to provide effective and reasonable academic
accommodations and related disability services to UCI students, Extension and Summer Session students, and other
program participants. Consults with and educates faculty
about reasonable academic accommodations. Strives to improve access to UCI programs, activities, and facilities for
students with disabilities. Advises and educates academic
and administrative departments about access issues to
programs or facilities.

3102 **University of Redlands**
1200 E Colton Ave
PO Box 3080
Redlands, CA 92373-0999   909-748-8108
                                  FAX 909-335-5296
                          http://www.redlands.edu
                       e-mail: amy.wilms@redlands.edu
Amy Wilms ller, Asst Dean of Academics

Small, private 4-year, residential, liberal arts university.

3103 **Valley Oaks School: Turlock**
400 Oyster Point Boulevard
Francisco, CA 94080   650-866-4080
                              FAX 650-866-4081
                       http://www.aspiranet.org
                       e-mail: valleyoaks@charter.net

Siobhan Hanna, Principal

Focuses on specific learning techniques designed for students with learning disabilities and/or emotional disturbance.

3104 Ventura College
Mainstream Computer Program
4667 Telegraph Rd
Ventura, CA 93003-3899   805-654-6400
                                        FAX 805-648-8947
                            http://www.ventura.college.edu
                              e-mail: nlatham@vcccd.edu
Robin Calote, Coordinator

Implemented assistive technology for students with disabilities through the Mainstream Computer Program.

3105 Westmark School
After School Learning Center
5461 Louise Ave
Encino, CA 91316-2540   818-380-1365
                                        FAX 818-986-2605
                          http://www.westmarkschool.org
                       e-mail: dseaman@westmarkschool.org
Leslie Barnebey, Coordinator

Provides a caring environment where motivated students with learning differences discover their unique paths to personal and academic excellence in preparation for a successful college experience.

3106 Westview School
11801 Mississippi Ave
Los Angeles, CA 90025-6114   310-478-5544
                                        FAX 310-473-5235
                            http://www.westviewschool.com
                          e-mail: info@westviewschool.com
Jackie Strumwasser MA, Executive Director

A private, non-profit day school in Los Angeles for students with learning, attentional and/or mild emotional concerns in grades six through twelve.

Colorado

3107 Denver Academy
4400 E Iliff Ave
Denver, CO 80222-6019   303-777-5870
                                        FAX 303-777-5893
                             http://www.denveracademy.org
                        e-mail: ksmith@denveracademy.org
Kevin Smith, Headmaster

The only co-ed 1st-12th grade independent school in the Denver-metro area dedicated to teaching students with learning differences and unique learning profiles.

3108 Havern School
4000 S Wadsworth Blvd
Littleton, CO 80123-1308   303-986-4587
                                        FAX 303-986-0590
                                http://www.haverncenter.org
Cathy Pasquariello, Executive Director

Provides a specialized education program for elementary and middle school students with learning disabilities.

3109 Lamar Community College
2401 S Main St
Lamar, CO 81052-3999   719-336-2248
                                           800-968-6920
                                        FAX 719-336-5626
                                    http://www.lamarcc.edu
                             e-mail: admissions@lamarcc.edu

David Smith, Manager
Angela Woodward, Director Admissions
Becky Young, Special Populations Coordinator
Offers a variety of services to students with disabilities including notetakers, extended testing time, counseling services, and special accommodations.

3110 Regis University
Disability Services
3333 Regis Blvd
Denver, CO 80221-1099   303-458-4100
                                        FAX 303-964-5498
                                        TTY: 800-388-266
                                      http://www.regis.edu
                              e-mail: mbwillia@regis.edu
Michael J Sheeran, Director
John P. Fitzgibbons, President

A four-year private university with 110 students recieving disability services out of 1,600.

3111 University of Colorado: Boulder
Academic Resource Team (ART)
107 University of Colorado
Boulder, CO 80309-5001   303-492-8671
                                        FAX 303-492-5601
                                       TDD:303-492-8671
                                       TTY: 303-492-6106
                   http://www.colorado.edu/disabilityservices
                             e-mail: dsinfo@colorado.edu
Jim Cohn, Supervisor
Cindy Donahue, Director

Provides a variety of services to individuals with nonvisible disabilities, including individualized strategy sessions with a disability specialist, an assistive technology lab, and a career program for students with disabilities. Disability specialists also assist with obtaining reasonable accommodations if documentation meets disability services requirements and supports the need for them.

3112 University of Colorado: Denver
Autism and Developmental Disabilities Clinic
Ste C234
13121 E 17th Ave
Aurora, CO 80045-2535   303-724-5266
                                        FAX 303-724-7661
                                   http://www.jfkpartners.org
                          e-mail: bev.murdock@uchsc.edu
Cordelia Robinson, Director

The Autism and Developmental Disorders Clinic has provided a fall range of outpatient clinical services to individuals with autism spectrum disorders or other development disorders, and their families. Services are organized around consumer and family goals, Clinical activities available to clients include disciplinary and interdisciplinary evaluations for purposes of diagnostic clarification and for provision of recommendations for treatment.

3113 University of Denver
Learning Effectiveness Program
Suite 30
2050 E Evans Ave
Denver, CO 80208   303-871-4333
                                        FAX 303-871-3939
                                       http://www.du.edu
                                  e-mail: tmay@du.edu

Ted May, Director

A fee for service program offering comprehensive, individualized services to University of Denver Students with learning disabilities and or ADHD. The LEP is part of a larger organization called University Disability Services.

Connecticut

3114 Ben Bronz Academy
Learning Incentive
139 N Main St
West Hartford, CT 06107-1264   860-236-5807
FAX 860-233-9945
http://www.learningincentive.com
e-mail: tli@tli.com
Aileen Stan-Spence, Director

Ben Bronz Acadamy is a day school for bright disabled students. Guides 60 students through an intensive school day that includes writing, mathematics, literature, science and social studies. Oral language is developed and stressed in all classes.

3115 Connecticut College
Office of Disability Services
270 Mohegan Ave
New London, CT 06320-4150   860-447-1911
FAX 860-439-5065
http://www.conncoll.edu
e-mail: slduq@conncoll.edu
Leo Higdon, Director
Lee Coffin, Admissions Director

Offers a variety of services to students with disabilities including notetakers, extended testing time, counseling services, and special accommodations.

3116 Eagle Hill School
45 Glenville Rd
Greenwich, CT 06831-5392   203-622-9240
FAX 203-622-0914
http://www.eaglehillschool.org
e-mail: info411@eaglehill.com
Marjorie Castro, Head of School

A language based remedial program committed to educating children with learning disabilities.

3117 Forman School
12 Norfolk Rd
Litchfield, CT 06759-2537   860-567-8712
FAX 860-567-8317
http://www.formanschool.org
e-mail: admissions@formanschool.org
Adam Man, Principal
Julie Forman, Founder

Forman offers students with learning differences the opportunity to achieve academic excellence in a traditional college preparatory setting. A coeducational boarding school of 180 students, we maintain a 3:1 student:teacher ratio. Daily remedial instruction balanced with course offerings rich in content provide each student with a flexible program that is tailored to his or her unique learning style and needs.

3118 Marvelwood
Marvelwood School
PO Box 3001
Kent, CT 06757-3001   860-927-0047
800-440-9107
FAX 860-927-0021
http://www.marvelwood.org
e-mail: summer@marvelwood.org
Craig Ough, Director

A coeducational boarding and day school enrolling 150 students in grades 9-12. Provides an environment in which young people of varying abilities and learning needs can prepare for success in college and in life. In a nurturing, structured community, students who have not thrived academically in traditional settings are guided and motivated to reach and exceed their personal potential.

3119 Mitchell College
Learning Resource Center
437 Pequot Ave
New London, CT 06320-4498   860-701-5000
800-443-2811
FAX 860-701-5090
http://www.mitchell.edu
e-mail: love_p@mitchell.edu
Peter Love, Director

Small private college with comprehensive subject program for student with Learning Disabilities and/or ADHD.

3120 St. Joseph College
Academic Resource Center
1678 Asylum Ave
West Hartford, CT 06117-2791   860-231-5399
866-442-8752
FAX 860-232-4757
http://www.sjc.edu
e-mail: judyarzt@sjc.edu
Judy Arzt, Director
Pamela Trotman Reid, Ph.D, President

Offers a variety of services to students with disabilities including notetakers, extended testing time, counseling services, and special accommodations.

3121 University of Hartford
Learning Plus Program
200 Bloomfield Ave
Hartford, CT 06117-1599   860-768-4100
FAX 860-768-4183
http://www.hartford.edu
e-mail: ldsupport@hartford.edu
Lynne Golden, Director
Walter Harrison, President

Provides academic support to students with specific learning disabilities and/or attention deficit disorder. The support consists of one 45 minute appointment a week with an adult Learning Plus specialist presenting applicable learning strategies.

3122 Vocational and Life Skills Center
1356 Old Clinton Rd
Westbrook, CT 06498-1858   860-399-8080
FAX 860-399-3103
http://www.vistavocational.org
e-mail: hbosch@vistavocational.org
Helen Bosch, Executive Director
Robert B. Ostroff, M.D, President
Ryan Duques, Vice-President
Building self-esteem and confidence in the lives of adults with disabilities through work, independence and friendship. Offers a post-secondary program for young adults with learning disabilities providing individualized training and support in career development, independent living skills, social skills development and community involvement.

3123 Woodhall School
PO Box 550
Bethlehem, CT 06751-550   203-266-7788
FAX 203-266-5896
http://www.woodhallschool.org
e-mail: woodhallschool@woodhallschool.org
Sally Campbell Woodhall, Head of School
Patrica Burns, President
Sharon Pooley, Vice-President
Offers an opportunity to experience success for young men of above average intellectual ability in grades 9 -12 who have not achieved at a level commensurate with their ability in traditional school programs.

Delaware

3124 Centreville School
6201 Kennett Pike
Centreville, DE 19807-1017   302-571-0230
                                    FAX 302-571-0270
http://www.centrevilleschool.org
e-mail: centreville@centrevilleschool.org
Denise Orenstein, Head of School

Provides an educational program that produces academic success and social development for children with learning disabilities.

District of Columbia

3125 American University
Learning Services Program, Academic Support Center
4400 Massachusetts Ave NW
Washington, DC 20016-8200   202-885-3360
                                   FAX 202-885-1042
http://www.american.edu/asc
e-mail: asc@american.edu
Nancy Sydnor-Greenberg, Coordinator

Focuses on assisting students with their transition from high school to college during their freshman year. It is a small, mainstream program offering weekly individual meetings with the coordinator of the Learning Services Program throughout the student's first year. For additional information, see www.american.edu/asc.

3126 Catholic University of America
Disability Support Services
207 Pryzbyla Ctr
Washington, DC 20064   202-319-5211
                                   FAX 202-319-5126
                                   TTY: 202-319-5211
http://disabilityservices.cua.edu
e-mail: cua-disabilityservices@cua.edu
Emily Singer, Director

Four-year college that has support services for students with learning disabilities.

3127 Georgetown University
Disability Support Services/Learning Services
37th & O St NW
Washington, DC 20057   202-371-9019
                                   FAX 202-687-6158
http://www.georgetown.edu
e-mail: gwr@georgetown.edu
Marcia Fulk, Director
Chris Augostini, Vice President
John J. DeGioia, Ph.D., President
A four-year private university with a total enrollment of 6,418.

3128 Saint Coletta: Greater Washington
1901 Independence Ave SE
Washington, DC 20003-1733   202-350-8680
                                   FAX 202-350-8699
                                   TTY: 202-350-8695
http://www.stcoletta.org
Sharon B Raimo, Executive Director

Is a non-sectarian, non-profit organization that operates school and adult day programs for children and adults with mental retardation and autism.

3129 The Lab School of Washington
4759 Reservoir Rd NW
Washington, DC 20007-1921   202-965-6600
                                   TTY: 202-350-8695
http://www.labschool.org
e-mail: katherine.schantz@labschool.org
Katherine Schantz, Head Of School

An innovative, rigorous, arts-based program for intelligent students with moderate to severe learning disabilities.

Florida

3130 Barry University
Center for Advanced Learning
11300 NE 2nd Ave
Miami Shores, FL 33161-6695   305-899-3000
                                   800-756-6000
                                   FAX 305-899-3679
http://www.barry.edu
e-mail: webmaster@mail.barry.edu
Linda Bevilacqua, Director

A comprehensive support program for students with learning disabilities and attention deficit disorders.

3131 Beacon College
105 E Main St
Leesburg, FL 34748-5162   352-787-9731
                                   855-220-5376
                                   FAX 352-787-0796
http://www.beaconcollege.edu
e-mail: admissions@beaconcollege.edu
Brenda Meli, Director of Admisssions
Stephanie Knight, Asst. Director of Admissions
Andrew Marvin, Admissions Counselor
Offer academic degree programs to students with learning disabilities.

3132 Center Academy
470 W Central Pkwy
Ste 1001
Altamonte Springs, FL 32714   407-772-8727
                                   FAX 407-772-8747
http://www.centeracademy.com
e-mail: infoas@centeracademy.com
Virginia Brannan, Director

Private school, college prep, AD/HD, SLD, small classes, SACS & NIPSA accredited.

3133 DePaul School for Dyslexia
2747 Sunset Point Rd
Clearwater, FL 33759-1504   727-796-7679
                                   FAX 727-796-7927
http://www.thedepaulschool.org
e-mail: admin@thedepaulschool.org
Vicki Howell, Head of School

Provides an alternative educational experience for students K-8th grade with dyslexia, ADHD, ADD and other learning disabilities and attention deficits.

3134 Florida Community College: Jacksonville
Independent Living for Adult Blind
601 State St W
Jacksonville, FL 32202-4774   904-633-8498
                                   FAX 904-633-5979
http://www.fccj.org
e-mail: info@fccj.edu
Carol Spadling, President
Carolyn Krall, LD Specialist

An instructional program for adults who have vision loss to a degree that they experience some difficulty in their daily activities. Through guidance and specialized training offered through the ILAB program, individuals learn necessary skills for work and independence in their home and community.

3135   Jericho School for Children with Autism and Other Developmental Delays
1351 Sprinkle Dr
Jacksonville, FL 32211-5448   904-744-5110
                                             FAX 904-744-3443
                        http://www.thejerichoschool.org
                        e-mail: jerichoschool@yahoo.com
Angelo Martinez, Executive Director

Provides comprehensive, individualized science-based education not otherwise available in the community. Believes that those children with autism and other developmental delays deserve the opportunity to reach their full potential.

3136   Lynn University
Institute for Achievement and Learning
3601 N Military Trl
Boca Raton, FL 33431-5598   561-237-7000
                                          800-888-5966
                        http://www.lynn.edu
                        e-mail: dkendrick@lynn.edu
Kevin Ross, President

Provides a series of support services to students with learning differences through a series of programs designed to help the students to succeed in their academic endeavors.

3137   Morning Star School
4661 80th Ave
Pinellas Park, FL 33781-2496   727-544-6036
                                          FAX 727-546-9058
                        http://www.morningstarschool.org
                        e-mail: mschool2@tampabay.rr.com
Mary Lou Giacobbe, Principal

Students with special educational requirements need more care and attention than is offered in a traditional school setting.

3138   PACE-Brantley Hall School
3221 Sand Lake Rd
Longwood, FL 32779-5850   407-869-8882
                                          FAX 407-869-8717
                        http://www.mypbhs.org
                        e-mail: kshatlock@mypbhs.org
Kathleen Shatlock, Director

Specializes in teaching learning disabled children. Children that have been diagnosed with ADD, ADHD, and Dyslexia attend PACE.

3139   Paladin Academy
1250 Dykes Rd
Sunrise, FL 33326-1901   954-920-2008
                                          FAX 954-921-4657
Beth Cleary, Manager

3140   Tampa Bay Academy
Educational Program
12012 Boyette Rd
Riverview, FL 33569-5631   813-445-3125
                                          800-678-3838
                                          FAX 813-671-3145
                        http://www.tampabay-academy.com
                        e-mail: info@tampa.yfcs.com
Ed Hoefle, Executive Director
John Tracy, Founder

The curriculum is designed with academic goals that encompass both special and vocational education. Individual Educational Plans are developed to address the goals and learning styles of students.

3141   Tampa Day School
12606 Henderson Rd
Tampa, FL 33625-6548   813-269-2100
                                          FAX 813-490-2554
                        http://www.tampadayschool.com
Lois Delaney, Head of School

To provide a learning environment that promotes that individual feeling of success for each child, and to find the unique key that opens the door to optimize his/her learning potential. The purpose of our school is to meet each child's needs.

3142   The Vanguard School
22000 Hwy 27
Lake Wales, FL 33859-6858   863-676-6091
                                          FAX 863-676-8297
                        http://www.vanguardschool.org
                        e-mail: info@vanguardschool.org
Cathy Wooley-Brown, President
Derri Park, Principal
Melanie Brockmeir, Director of Admissions
The Vanguard School is a fully accredited (SCAS and FCIS) coeducational boarding school and day school educating students in grades 5-12 with learning differences such as attention issues, challenging reading disorder, dyslexia, and Asperger's Syndrome.

3143   Victory School
PO Box 630266
Miami, FL 33163-266   305-466-1142
                                          FAX 305-466-1143
                        http://www.thevictoryschool.org
                        e-mail: administrator@thevictoryschool.org
Judi Nelson, Executive Director
Richard Shan, Chairman

A Florida, non-secretarian, not-for-profit corporation that provides children with autism and smiliar disorders comprehensive individualized treatment with a 1:1 student/teacher ratio, in a classroom setting that is unique in Southeast Florida.

3144   Woodland Hall Academy
Dyslexia Research Institute
5746 Centerville Rd
Tallahassee, FL 32309-2893   850-893-2216
                                          FAX 850-893-2440
                        http://www.woodlandhallacademy.org
                        e-mail: dri@talstar.com
Pat Hardman, Director
Amber Mitchell, Principal
Robyn Rennick, Program Director
Designed to remediate and prevent the learning and behavior problems associated with the dyslexic and ADD/ADHD student.

Georgia

3145   Andrew College
FOCUS Program
501 College St
Cuthbert, GA 39840-5599   229-732-5908
                                          800-664-9250
                                          FAX 229-732-5905
                        http://www.andrewcollege.edu
                        e-mail: berniemattox@andrewcollege.edu
David Seyle, President

The FOCUS program offers an intensive level of academic support designed for and limited to documented learning disabilities or attention deficit disorder. While FOCUS supplements and complements the tutorial and advising to all students, the program also provides an additional level of professional assistance and mentoring. Those accepted into FOCUS are charged regular tuition andd fees, plus a FOCUS laboratory fee.

3146 Brandon Hall School
1701 Brandon Hall Dr
Atlanta, GA 30350-3799   770-394-8177
                                    FAX 770-804-8821
                        http://www.brandonhall.org
                    e-mail: jsingleton@brandonhall.org
Dr John L Singleton, President/Headmaster

College preparatory, co-ed day and boys' boarding school for students in grades 4-12. Designed for academic under-achievers and students with minor learning disabilities, attention deficit disorders and dyslexia.

3147 Cottage School
700 Grimes Bridge Rd
Roswell, GA 30075-4615   770-641-8688
                                    FAX 770-641-9026
                        http://www.cottageschool.org
                    e-mail: tcs@cottageschool.org
Jacque Digieso, Executive Director
Vinette Goodman, Executive Assistant

Building a sense of self for students with special learning needs through academic and experiential programming, The Cottage School prepares individuals for fulfillment of their true potential as confident, productive, and independent adults.

3148 Fort Valley State University
Differently Abled Services Center
1005 State University Dr
Fort Valley, GA 31030-3298   478-825-6211
                                    FAX 478-825-6266
                        http://www.fvsu.edu
                    e-mail: smitht0@fvsu.edu

Larry E Rivers, Director

Our mission is to increase retention for students with learning disorders by ensuring equal treatment, opportunity, and access for persons with impairments and/or disorders.

3149 Gables Academy
811 Gordon St
Stone Mountain, GA 30083-3533   770-465-7500
                                        877-465-7500
                                    FAX 770-465-7700
                        http://www.gablesacademy.com
                    e-mail: info@gablesacademy.com
James Meffen, Headmaster

A fully accredited non-profit learning center providing a full spectrum of educational services for students in the special needs population ages 9-18.

3150 Georgia State University
Margaret A Staton Office of Disability Services
Suite 230
New Student Center
Atlanta, GA 30303   404-413-1322
                                    FAX 404-413-1563
                        http://www.gsu.edu
                    e-mail: disrep@langate.gsu.edu
Rodney E Pennamon M Ed, Director

Works with any student who has a disability to ensure meaningful access to the goods and services offered by GSU. To achieve this goal, academic accommodations are often made on behalf of the student.

3151 Howard School
1192 Foster St NW
Atlanta, GA 30318-4329   404-377-7436
                                    FAX 404-377-0884
                        http://www.howardschool.org
                    e-mail: info@howardschool.org
Marifred Cilella, Head of School
Anne Beisel, Admissions Director

Educates students with language learning disabilitiesand learning differences. Instruction is personalized to complement individual learning styles, to address student needs and to help each student understand his or her learning process. The curriculum focuses on depth of understanding in order to make learning meaningful and therefore, maximize educational success.

3152 Mill Springs Academy
13660 New Providence Rd
Alpharetta, GA 30004-3413   770-360-1336
                                    FAX 770-360-1341
                        http://www.millsprings.org
                    e-mail: rmoore@millsprings.org
Robert Moore, President

Committed to a comprehensive, holistic program design that is multifaceted to meet the needs of the 'total child'.

3153 Schenck School
282 Mount Paran Rd NW
Atlanta, GA 30327-4698   404-252-2591
                                    FAX 404-252-7615
                        http://www.schenck.org
                    e-mail: office@schenck.org
Gena Calloway, Head of School

Offers a unique learning environment for children with dyslexia, as well as several auxiliary programs

3154 St. Francis School
9375 Willeo Rd
Roswell, GA 30075-4743   770-641-8257
                                    FAX 770-641-0283
                        http://www.stfranschool.com
Drew Buccellato, Headmaster

Providing an educational program of the highest quality that can meet the needs of students with diverse abilities who would profit from a smaller teacher-pupil ratio than is available in most public or private schools.

3155 Toccoa Falls College
PO Box 800777
Toccoa Falls, GA 30598-13   706-886-6831
                                        888-785-5624
                                    FAX 706-886-0210
                        http://www.tfc.edu
                    e-mail: wgardner@tfc.edu
Wayne Gardner, President
John Gailer, Admissions Director
Nancy Hyndman, Academic Success Director
Four-year college that provides services to the learning disabled.

3156 Wardlaw School
Atlanta Speech School
3160 Northside Pkwy NW
Atlanta, GA 30327-1598   404-233-5332
                                    FAX 404-266-2175
                        http://www.atlantaspeechschool.org
C Yates, Executive Director

For children ages 5 to 12 years old with average to very superior intelligence and mild to moderate language-based learning disabilities. The types of learning disabilities that are served include written language disorders, mathematical disabilities, ADD, dyslexia, and difficulty understanding and/or using spoken language.

Hawaii

3157   **University of Hawaii: Manoa**
Center on Disability Services
1776 University Ave
Honolulu, HI 96822-2447   808-956-9199
                                     FAX 808-956-7878
                               http://www.cds.hawaii.edu
                              e-mail: stodden@hawaii.edu

Robert Stodden, Director

Dedicated to supporting the quality of life, inclusion, and empowerment of all persons with disabilities and their families through partnerships in training, service, evaluation, research, dissemination, and technical assistance. Nurtures, sustains, and expands promising practices for people with disabilities.

Idaho

3158   **University of Idaho**
Center on Disabilities and Human Development
129 W 3rd St
Moscow, ID 83843-2268   208-364-9981
                                    800-393-7290
                               FAX 208-364-4035
                               TTY: 800-432-8324
                               http://www.idahocdhd.org
                             e-mail: idahocdhd@uidaho.edu

Julie Fodor, Director

Currently operates a variety of independent grant programs and carries out training, services, technical assistance, research and dissemination activities across the state and nation.

Illinois

3159   **Acacia Academy**
6425 Willow Springs Rd
La Grange Highlands, IL 60525-4468   708-579-9040
                                        FAX 708-579-5872
                              http://www.acaciaacademy.com
                             e-mail: info@acaciaacademy.com

Kathryn Fouks, Administrator

A school for grades K-12 for children with learning disabilities. NCA accredited and approved for out of district students in special education in the state of Illinois.

3160   **Brehm Preparatory School**
1245 E Grand Ave
Carbondale, IL 62901-3603   618-457-0371
                                        FAX 618-529-1248
                                   http://www.brehm.org
                            e-mail: admissionsinfo@brehm.org

Richard Collins, Executive Director

A coeducational boarding school for students with learning differences. Services are provided for students in grades 6-12. A post-secondary program, OPTIONS, is also available.

3161   **College of Dupage**
Vocational Skills Program
425 Fawell Blvd
Glen Ellyn, IL 60137-6599   630-790-1085
                                        FAX 630-942-2800
                                        TDD:630-858-9692
                                     http://www.cod.edu
                             e-mail: mullan@cdnet.cod.edu

Sunil Chand, Coordinator

Offers courses to students challenged with mild to moderate cognitive impairment. The courses are developmental-level, non-transferable credit courses designed to develop vocational skills that can lead to competitive, entry-level employment and enhance everyday living skills.

3162   **Cove School**
350 Lee Rd
Northbrook, IL 60062-1521   847-562-2100
                                        FAX 847-562-2112
                               http://www.coveschool.org
                             e-mail: ssover@coveschool.org

Sally Sover, Executive Director

For children and young adults in grades K-12 who are coping with a wide range of learning disabilities. The Cove School creates an exceptional environment for the children where they develop the emotional and social skills needed to reach their fullest potential.

3163   **DePaul University**
PLuS Program
2250 N Sheffield Ave
Chicago, IL 60604   773-325-7476
                                        FAX 773-325-2261
                           http://www.studentaffairs.depaul.edu
Stephanie Moye, Director

PLuS is a comprehensive program designed to assist students with specific learning disabilities and/or attention deficit disorders in experiencing academic success at DePaul University. Please visit PLuS' website for a description of services and application forms.

3164   **Hamel Elementary School**
P.O Box 250
Edwardsville, IL 62025   618-656-1182
                                        FAX 618-692-7493
                                   http://www.ecusd7.org
                             e-mail: bhutton@ecusd7.org

Barbara Hutton, Principal
Greg Roosevelt, President

Offer programs for students with learning disabilities, ADD and/or emotional difficulties.

3165   **Kaskaskia College**
27210 College Rd
Centralia, IL 62801-7878   618-545-3000
                                       800-642-0859
                                  FAX 618-545-3029
                               http://www.kaskaskia.edu
                            e-mail: cquick@kaskaskia.edu

James Underwood, Administrator
Cathy Quick, Executive Assistant to President
Cheryl Boehne, Coordinator of Partnership
Offers a variety of services to students with disabilities including note takers, extended testing time, counseling services, and special accommodations.

3166   **Lewis and Clark Community College**
College Life Program
5800 Godfrey Rd
Godfrey, IL 62035-2466   618-466-7000
                                       FAX 618-466-4044
                                       TTY: 618-466-4100
                                  http://www.lc.cc.il.us
                               e-mail: khaberer@lc.edu

327

Dale Chapman, Director

For those students with disabilities who have had few inclusive experiences in high school, the College for Life Program provides courses that continue the educational experience and also provides social growth opportunities on a college campus.

3167 Roosevelt University
Learning and Support Services Program
430 S Michigan Ave
Chicago, IL 60605-1394   312-341-3500
                                     FAX 312-341-2003
                              http://www.roosevelt.edu

Pamela Trotman Reid, Director

The Disabled Student Services office serves all students with special needs. The use of services is voluntary and confidential. This office is a resource for students and faculty. The goal of this office is to ensure educational opportunity for all students with special needs by providing access to full participation in all aspects of campus life and increase awareness of disability issues on campus.

3168 Saint Xavier University
Student Success Program
3700 W 103rd St
Chicago, IL 60655-3105   773-298-3000
                                     FAX 773-779-9061
                                  http://www.sxu.edu
                              e-mail: fuller@sxu.edu

Josiah Fuller, Director

Offers a variety of services to students with disabilities including notetakers, extended testing time, counseling services, and special accommodations.

3169 Southern Illinois University: Carbondale
Clinical Center Achieve Program
Mail Code 4602
Carbondale, IL 62901   618-453-2361
                                     FAX 618-453-6126
                                  http://www.siu.edu
                           e-mail: lukidawg@siu.edu

Sally DeDecker, Coordinator

The Achieve Program is a comprehensive academic support service for students with LD and/or ADHD. Students must apply to both Achieve and the University.

3170 University of Illinois: Chicago
Institute on Disability and Human Development
1640 W Roosevelt Rd
Chicago, IL 60608-1316   312-413-1647
                                     FAX 312-413-1630
                                  TTY: 361-241-0453
                                  http://www.uic.edu
                               e-mail: idhd@uic.edu

Tamar Heller, Director

Dedicated to promoting the independence, productivity and inclusion of people with disabilities into all aspects of society.

3171 University of Illinois: Urbana
Disability Resources and Educational Services
1207 S Oak St
Champaign, IL 61820-6901   217-333-8705
                                     FAX 217-333-0248
                                  TDD:217-333-4603
                         http://www.disability.uiuc.edu
                           e-mail: kwold2@illinois.edu

Karen Wold, Learning Disabilities Specialist

Provides comprehensive disability services to University of Illinois students with disabilities, including disabilities.

Indiana

3172 Ball State University
Disabled Student Development
2000 W University Ave
Muncie, IN 47306   765-289-1241
                                      800-382-8540
                                  FAX 765-285-4003
                                  http://www.bsu.edu
                             e-mail: rharris@bsu.edu

Peter Blume, Director
Rachel Perkins, Manager

Offers a variety of services to students with disabilities including note takers, extended testing time, counseling services, and special accommodations.

3173 Cathedral High School
5225 E 56th St
Indianapolis, IN 46226-1487   317-542-1481
                                     FAX 317-543-5050
                          http://www.cathedral-irish.org
                    e-mail: smatteson@cathedral-irish.org
Dave Worland, President

Provides, to a diverse group of students, opportunities for spiritual, intellectual, social, emotional and physical growth through service and academic excellence.

3174 Indiana Wesleyan University
TRIO Scholars Program
4201 S Washington St
Marion, IN 46953-4974   765-674-6901
                                     FAX 765-677-2499
                                http://www.indwes.edu
                    e-mail: aldersgatecenter@indwes.edu
Henry L Smith, Coordinator

To help students realize their full potential in relation to their academic pursuits at Indiana Wesleyan University. Benefits to TRIO Scholars include academic and cultural enrichment, disability services, mentoring, personal counseling, tutorial support, and the opportunity to apply for grant aid.

3175 Ivy Tech Community College
3501 N 1st Ave
Evansville, IN 47710-3398   812-426-2865
                                     FAX 812-492-0223
                                  TDD:812-429-9803
                                http://www.ivytech.edu
                           e-mail: ccates@ivytech.edu
Daniel L Schenk, Chancellor
Cyndi Cates, Disability Services Advisor
Shawna Garrett, Administrative Assistant
Provides reasonable and effective accommodations to qualified students with learning disabilities.

3176 Manchester College
Academic Development & Programming for Transition
604 E College Ave
North Manchester, IN 46962-1232   260-982-5000
                                     FAX 260-982-5042
                              http://www.manchester.edu
                    e-mail: bsoconnell@manchester.edu
Jo Young Switzer, Director

A specially designed academic advising program for students with disabilities.

3177 Pinnacle School
1503 W Arlington Rd
Bloomington, IN 47404   812-339-8141
                                     FAX 812-339-8390
                            http://www.pinnacleschool.org
                        e-mail: info@pinnacleschool.org
Denise Lessow EdD, Executive Director

Provides an independent, full-time specialized elementary (K-8) curriculum for children with dyslexia and other related specific learning disabilities.

3178   Saint Mary-of-the-Woods College
3301 Saint Mary-Of-The-Woods
Saint Mary of the Woods, IN 47876   812-535-5151
FAX 812-535-5169
http://www.smwc.edu
e-mail: smwc@smwc.edu
David Behrs, Vice President
Joan Lescinski, President

Offers a variety of services to students with disabilities including note takers, extended testing time, counseling services, and special accommodations.

3179   University of Indianapolis
BUILD Program
1400 E Hanna Ave
Indianapolis, IN 46227-3697   317-788-3336
800-232-8634
FAX 317-788-6152
http://www.build.uindy.edu
e-mail: mcavanaugh@uindy.edu
Mary L. Cavanaugh, Director
Sharon Fehnel, Administrative Assistant

Is a full support program at the University of Indianapolis designed to help the college students with specific learning disability earn an associate or baccalureate degree.

3180   Worthmore Academy
3535 Kessler Boulevard East Dr
Indianapolis, IN 46220-5154   317-251-6516
FAX 317-251-6516
http://www.worthmoreacademy.org
Brenda Jackson, Director

A place where children with learning differences may come and receive individualized instruction to help remediate his or her learning differences.

Iowa

3181   Clinton High School
817 8th Ave S
Clinton, IA 52732-5698   563-243-9600
FAX 563-243-5404
http://www.clinton.k12.ia.us
e-mail: ktharaldson@clintonia.org
Karinne Tharaldson, Principal

Provide services for individuals with special needs to achieve high levels of learning through equitable access to quality education for each student in an environment of mutual respect, trust, enthusiasm and cooperation.

3182   Des Moines Area Community College
2006 S Ankeny Blvd
Ankeny, IA 50023-3993   515-964-6200
800-362-2127
FAX 515-965-7316
TDD:964-381-1551
TTY: 515-964-6809
http://www.dmacc.edu
e-mail: webmaster@dmacc.cc.ia.us
Robert Denson, President

DMACC is committed to providing an accessible environment that supports students with disabilities in reaching their full potential. Support services are available for students with disabilities to ensure equal access to educational opportunities.

3183   Iowa Central Community College
330 Avenue M
Fort Dodge, IA 50501-5739   515-576-7201
800-362-2793
FAX 515-576-7206
http://www.iccc.cc.ia.us
e-mail: lundeen@triton.iccc.cc.ia.us
Bob Paxton, President

A public two-year college with approximately 50 special needs students out of a total of 3,003.

3184   Iowa Lakes Community College: Emmetsburg
Project Learning
3200 College Dr
Emmetsburg, IA 50536-1055   712-852-3554
800-242-5108
FAX 712-852-2152
http://www.iowalakes.edu
e-mail: info@iowalakes.edu
Tom Brotherton, Executive Dean
Colleen Peltz, Developmental Studies Professor

Developmentally disabled students learn basic independent living skills, which allow them to be integrated into the community. This program is conducted in conjunction with the local work activity center.

3185   Iowa Western Community College: Council Bluffs
Bridges for Learning in Applied Science & Tech
2700 College Rd
Council Bluffs, IA 51503-1057   712-325-3418
800-432-5852
FAX 712-325-3424
http://www.iwcc.cc.ia.us
e-mail: hirwin@iwcc.edu
Dan Kinney, Coordinator

The services are to assist studnts in participating in the vocational/technical training programs at IWCC by providing special education support and instructional services. This provides students with disabilities an opportunity to develop career or occupationaly specific skills.

3186   Loras College
Office of Disability Services
1450 Alta Vista St
Dubuque, IA 52001-4399   563-588-7100
FAX 563-588-7964
http://www.loras.edu
e-mail: ods@loras.edu
James Collins, Director

The Enhanced Program is a comprehensive program designed to provide additional support for students with a primary disability of learning disability or attention deficit disorder, however students with other disabilities will be considered. A fee is charged for the Enhanced Program.

3187   North Iowa Area Community College
On Track: Time Management Program
500 College Dr
Mason City, IA 50401-7299   641-423-1264
FAX 641-423-1711
http://www.niacc.edu
e-mail: vancelis@niacc.edu
Debra Derr, Coordinator
David Steffens, President

Our On Track Program is meant for students with disabilities who have realized they need a little extra help keeping track of assignments, due dates, and a busy schedule of activities. Balancing all these demands can be overwhelming, but you don't have to do it alone.

3188 SAVE Program
Iowa Lakes Community College: Emmetsburg
3200 College Dr
Emmetsburg, IA 50536-1055   712-362-2604
                                          800-521-5024
                                       FAX 712-852-2152
                               http://www.iowalakes.edu
Ann Petersen, Director

Provide special education secondary students with an option
where they will receive, based on their IEP goals, further education in the areas of life skills training, vocational/em-
ployability skills training, and transitional/self advocacy
skills training.

3189 Simpson College
Hawley Academic Resource Center
701 N C St
Indianola, IA 50125-1202   515-961-1682
                                          800-362-2454
                                       FAX 515-961-1363
                            http://www.simpson.edu/hawley
                                e-mail: little@simpson.edu
John Byrd, Director

Simpson College is a private, four-year liberal arts college
located south of Des Moines, Iowa. The Hawley Center offers services to students with disabilities including academic accommodations and other support services.

3190 University of Iowa
Realizing Educational and Career Hopes Program
N297 Lindquist Ctr
Iowa City, IA 52242-1529   319-335-5359
                                       FAX 319-384-2167
                                       TTY: 800-735-2942
                           http://www.education.uiowa.edu
                                 e-mail: reach@uiowa.edu
Dennis C Harper, Director

Specifically designed to meet the needs of young adults with
multiple learning and cognitive disabilities.

3191 Wartburg College
100 Wartburg Blvd
Waverly, IA 50677   319-352-8260
                                          800-772-2085
                                       FAX 319-352-8568
                                  http://www.wartburg.edu
                           e-mail: deb.lovers@wartburg.edu
Darrel Colson, President
Deborah Loers, VP Student Life
Vicki Edelnant, Pathways Center Director
Four year private, residential college

Kansas

3192 Baker University
Learning Resource Center
PO Box 65
Baldwin City, KS 66006-65   785-594-6451
                                          800-955-7747
                                   http://www.bakeru.edu
                         e-mail: marian@harvey.bakeru.edu
Kathy Marian, Director
Paige Illum, Admissions Director
Daniel Lambert, President
A private four-year college with a total of 923 students.

3193 Fort Scott Community College
2108 Horton St
Fort Scott, KS 66701-3141   620-223-2700
                                          800-874-3722
                                  http://www.fortscott.edu
                         e-mail: beckyw@ftscott.cc.ks.us
Becky Weddle, Director CE/ETC/Mill
Clayton Tatro, President

A public two-year college with 34 special education students out of a total of 1,928.

3194 Horizon Academy
4901 Reinhardt Drive
Roeland Park, KS 66205   913-789-9443
                                       FAX 913-789-8180
                            http://www.horizon-academy.org
                        e-mail: info@horizon-academy.com
Ann Cooling, President
Sharyl Kennedy, Executive Director

Private school for children with learning disabilities. Students learn word decoding skills in reading, oral and written
language comprehension and/or expression, math skills, organizational and social skills.

3195 Newman University
3100 W McCormick St
Wichita, KS 67213-2008   316-942-4291
                                       FAX 316-942-4483
                                  http://www.newmanu.edu
                          e-mail: niedensr@newmanu.edu
Noreen Carrocci, Dean of Students
Aidan Dunleavy, President
Mark Dresselhaus, Vice President
Offers a variety of services to students with disabilities in-
cluding notetakers, extended testing time, counseling ser-
vices, and special accommodations.

Kentucky

3196 Brescia University
717 Frederica St
Owensboro, KY 42301-3019   270-685-3131
                                          877-273-7242
                                       FAX 270-684-2507
                                   http://www.brescia.edu
                        e-mail: chris.houk@brescia.edu
Larry Hostetter, Dean of Enrollment
Dolores Kisler, Director Student Support
Judith Riney, Manager
Provides the following for students with learning disabili-
ties: developmental courses (English, mathematics and
study skills); individual tutoring for all areas; and academic
and career counseling.

3197 DePaul School
1925 Duker Ave
Louisville, KY 40205-1099   502-459-6131
                                       FAX 502-458-0827
                               http://www.depaulschool.org
                           e-mail: dpinfo@depaulschool.org
Anthony Kemper, Head of School

We teach a lot of bright kids who learn differently. And we
teach them the way they actually learn.

3198 Eastern Kentucky University
Project SUCCESS
521 Lancaster Ave
Richmond, KY 40475-3102   859-622-2933
                                       FAX 859-622-6794
                              http://www.disabilities.eku.edu
                         e-mail: teresa.belluscio@eku.edu
Michael Ballard, Director

Offers a comprehensive support program for college students with learning disabilities, attention deficit disorder
and other cognitive disorders. Upon admittance, Project
SUCCESS develops an individualized program of services
which serve to enhance the academic success of each
student.

Louisiana

3199 Louisiana College
Program to Assist Student Success
1140 College Dr
PO Box 545
Pineville, LA 71359-0001
318-487-7629
FAX 318-487-7285
http://www.lacollege.edu
e-mail: himel@lacollege.edu
Linda Himel, Director

This highly individualized program for students who have disabilities, provides support services and personal attention to students who may need special academic guidance, tutoring, and/or classroom assistance.

3200 Louisiana State University: Alexandria
8100 Highway 71 S
Alexandria, LA 71302-9119
318-445-3672
888-473-6417
FAX 318-473-6480
http://www.lsua.edu
David P Manuel, Director Student Services
Donna Roberts, Administrative Assistant
Robert Cavanaugh, Manager
Offers a variety of services to students with disabilities including extended testing time, counseling services, and special accommodations.

3201 Louisiana State University: Eunice
2048 Johnson Hwy
Eunice, LA 70535-6726
337-457-7311
888-367-5783
FAX 337-546-6620
http://www.lsue.edu
William Nunez, President

A public two-year college with 31 special education students out of a total of 2,595.

3202 Nicholls State University
Office of Disability
PO Box 2087
Thibodaux, LA 70310
985-448-4430
FAX 985-449-7009
http://www.nicholls.edu
e-mail: stacey.guidry@nicholls.edu
Stacey Guidry, Director

The Center provides assessments and remediation to students with Dyslexia and related learning disabilities. Programs are offered for college students as well as K-12 students.

3203 Northwestern State University
Learning Disabilities Association of Louisiana
Room 104-J
Teacher Education Center
Natchitoches, LA 71497
318-357-6011
FAX 318-357-3275
http://www.lacec.org
e-mail: duchardt@nsula.edu
Barbara Duchard MD, Associate Professor
Randy Webb, President

Northwestern State University is continuing the process of switching to new software to handle academic and financial records. ÿ On August 3, Northwestern State began implementation of student accounts receivable in the new software. By this fall, the university will be fully transitioned to the new software, and the migration will enhance services for students which include but are not limited to: extended hours for system access via the web for the purpose of applying for admission, registerin

3204 Southeastern Louisiana University
Slu 10496
Hammond, LA 70402
985-549-2185
FAX 985-549-2771
http://www.selu.edu
e-mail: mhall@selu.edu
Fawn Ukpolo, Director Institutional Research
Kay Mowrin, Director Disability Services
Dr. John Crain, President
Four-year college that offers programs for students whom are disabled.

Maine

3205 University of Maine
Disability Support Services
Onward Building
Orono, ME 04469
207-581-1865
1-877-486-23
FAX 207-581-2969
http://www.umaine.edu
e-mail: ann.smith@umit.maine.edu
Ann Smith, Director
Sara Henry, Disability Counselor

The primary goal of the University of Maine Disability Support Services is to create educational access for students with disabilities at UMaine by providing a point of coordination, information and education for those students and the campus community.

3206 University of New England: University Campus
Disability Services
11 Hills Beach Rd
Biddeford, ME 04005-9599
207-602-2815
FAX 207-602-5971
http://www.une.edu
e-mail: schurch@une.edu
Danielle Ripich, Director

Disability Services exists to ensure that the University fulfills the part of its mission that seeks to promote respect for individual differences and to ensure that no person who meets the academic and technical standards requisite for admission to, and continued enrollment at, the University is denied benefits or subjected to discrimination at UNE solely by reason of his or her disability.

Maryland

3207 Chelsea School
711 Pershing Dr
Silver Spring, MD 20910-4321
301-585-1430
FAX 301-585-9621
http://www.chelseaschool.edu
e-mail: information@chelseaschool.edu
T Messina, Head of School

To prepare students with language based learning disabilities for higher education by providing a world-class school which embeds literacy remediation and technology into all aspects of the curriculum.

3208 Harbour School
1277 Green Holly Drive
Annapolis, MD 21409
410-974-4248
FAX 410-757-3722
http://www.harbourschool.org
e-mail: info@harbourschool.org
Linda J Jacobs EdD, Executive Director

Our mission is to provide a supportive, caring and individualized education to students with learning disabilities, autism, speech language impairments, and other disabilities like ADD/ADHD in grades one through twelve by assisting each child to attain academic and personal achievement and success commensurate with the child's abilities. Personal achievement includes success in social, physical and vocational skills

3209 Highlands School
2409 Creswell Rd
Bel Air, MD 21015-6507   410-836-1415
                                FAX 410-412-1098
                    http://www.highlandsschool.net
                    e-mail: info@highlandsschool.net
Patricia Bonney, Executive Director
Richard Molinaro, President
Rowan C. Glidden, Viice-President
Offering a full academic program for students in grades k-8 with dyslexia, ADHD, and laguage based learning differences.

3210 Ivymont School
Autism Program
11614 Seven Locks Rd
Rockville, MD 20854-3261   301-469-0223
                                FAX 301-469-0778
                      http://www.ivymount.org
                    e-mail: lgladstone@ivymount.org
Rick Weintraub, President
Molly Meegan, Vice President

Provides a non-diploma functional life skills program for students ages 6-21 diagnosed with autism and offers a proactive generalization program which ensures student progress is generalized to their community and home.

3211 James E Duckworth School
11201 Evans Trl
Beltsville, MD 20705-3903   301-572-0620
                                FAX 301-572-0628
                      http://www.1.pgcps.org
                    e-mail: jedworth@pgcps.org
Lisa M. Wenzel, Principal

Is a public school in the Prince George's County Public School System., And serves students with moderate to severe disabilities ages 5 through 21.

3212 Jemicy School
11 Celadon Rd
Owings Mills, MD 21117-3099   410-653-2700
                                FAX 410-653-1972
                      http://www.jemicyschool.org
                    e-mail: mmcgowan@jemicyschool.org
Ben Shifrin, Head of School

Empowers students with dyslexia and language-based learning differences to realize their intellectual and social potential through a proven, multisensory curriculum.

3213 Jemicy School: Towson
12 Celadon Rd
Owings Mills, MD 21117-3099   410-653-2700
                                FAX 410-653-1972
                      http://www.jemicyschool.org
                    e-mail: mmcgowan@jemicyschool.org
Ben Shifrin, Head of School

Empowers students with dyslexia / language-based learning differences to realize their intellectual and social potential through a proven, multisensory curriculum.

3214 Margaret Brent School
5816 Lamont Ter
New Carrollton, MD 20784-3541   301-918-8780
                                FAX 301-918-8771
                      http://www.1.pgcps.org

Lisa M. Wenzel, Principal

Offers a language-based curriculum which infuses both language and literacy skills throughout the curriculum, utilizing 'picture communication symbols'.

3215 McDaniel College
Student Academic Support Services
2 College Hl
Westminster, MD 21157-4303   410-848-7000
                                     800-638-5005
                                FAX 410-386-4617
                      http://www.mcdaniel.edu
                    e-mail: sass@mcdaniel.edu
Karen Hamilton, Director
Melanie Conley, Associate Director

Is an optional service that is primarily for students with learning disabilities, ADD/HD, but there may be other students with disabilities who have a documented need for this service.

3216 Model Asperger Program
Ivymont School
11614 Seven Locks Rd
Rockville, MD 20854-3261   301-469-0223
                                FAX 301-469-0778
                      http://www.ivymount.org
                    e-mail: aspergerinfo@ivymount.org
Lennie Gladstone, Director

Students in this program have average to gifted cognitive abilities but struggle in mainstream learning environments due to difficulties with social skills, executive functioning, flexible thinking and self-regulation.

3217 Odyssey School
3257 Bridle Rdg
Stevenson, MD 21153-2034   410-580-5551
                                FAX 410-580-5352
                    http://www.theodysseyschool.org
                e-mail: msweeney@theodysseyschool.org
Martha Sweeney, Head of School
Martha Nesbitt, Admissions Director

Provides a warm and creative environment that balances a stimulating hands-on curriculum with a personalized approach to meet the needs of the individual child. Early intervention program, daily tutoring, visual arts/music/dance, leading edge technology, sports, character education and clubs.

3218 Summit School
Academic Program
664 Central Ave E
Edgewater, MD 21037-3429   410-798-0005
                                FAX 410-798-0008
                      http://www.thesummitschool.org
                    e-mail: jane.snider@thesummitschool.org
Jane R Snider EdD, Executive Director

Committed to providing a mainstream academic program that challenges intelligent young minds while addressing students with dyslexia and other learning differences.

3219 The Forbush School at Hunt Valley
Sheppard Pratt Health System
6501 N. Charles Street
Baltimore, MD 21285   410-938-3000
                                FAX 410-527-0329
                      http://www.sheppardpratt.org
                    e-mail: info@sheppardpratt.org
Tim Yearick, Educational Director

332

Special education classes for children and young adults ages 5-21 with autism, developmental delays, pervasive developmental disorder and multiple learning problems. Programs include motor skill development and sensory integration strategies, natural aided language stimulation, positive behavioral support and vocational programming.

3220 **The Forbush Therapeutic Preschool at Towson**
Sheppard Pratt Health System
6501 N. Charles Street
Gibson Building
Baltimore, MD 21285

410-938-3000
FAX 410-938-4412
http://www.sheppardpratt.org
e-mail: info@sheppardpratt.org

Tom Yearick, Executive Director

Provides special education and related services to children ages 3-7 with autism, pervasive developmental disorder, developmental delays, emotional and severe behavioral problems. Programs are designed to meet each students specific needs.

3221 **Towson University**
8000 York Rd
Towson, MD 21252

410-828-0622
800-225-5878
FAX 410-830-3030
TDD:410-704-2000
http://www.towson.edu
e-mail: swillemin@towson.edu

Robert L Caret, Director
Karen Oppenheimer, Associate Director
Ashley Meyers, Learning Disabilities Specialist
With more than 20,000 students, Towson University is the second largest public university in Maryland. Founded in 1866, the University offers more than 100 bachelor's, master's and doctoral degree programs in the liberal arts and sciences, and applied professional fields. Approximately 1,200 students are registered with the Disability Support Services office on campus.

Massachusetts

3222 **American International College**
Supportive Learning Services Program
1000 State St
Springfield, MA 01109-3155

413-737-7000
800-242-3142
FAX 413-205-3051
http://www.aic.edu
e-mail: inquiry@www.aic.edu

Vincent Maniaci, Coordinator

An independent four-year college with 95 special education students out of a total of 1,433. There is an additional fee for the special education program.

3223 **Berkshire Center**
18 Park St
Lee, MA 01238-1702

413-243-2576
877-566-9247
FAX 413-243-3351
http://www.cipberkshire.org
e-mail: knoel@cipberkshire.org

Karen Noel, Admissions Coordinator

Provides individualized social, academic, career & life skills instruction to young adults 18-26 with Aspergers, ADD and other learning differences. With our support and direction, students learn to realize & develop their potential.

3224 **Berkshire Meadows**
249 N Plain Rd
Housatonic, MA 01236-9736

413-528-2523
FAX 413-528-0293
http://www.berkshiremeadows.org
e-mail: berkshiremeadows@jri.org

Kathy Green, Director

Programs based on the philosophy that all people, no matter how severe their disabilities, should be given the opportunity to achieve their maximum potential.

3225 **Boston College**
140 Commonwealth Ave
Chestnut Hill, MA 02467-3858

617-552-8000
800-294-0294
FAX 617-552-8828
http://www.bc.edu
e-mail: ugadmis@bc.edu

Willaim P Leahy, Assistant Director
William P. Leahy, President

An independent four-year college with 195 special education students out of a total of 14,230. There is an additional fee for the special education program in addition to the regular tuition.

3226 **Boston University**
Office of Disability Services
2nd Fl
19 Deerfield St
Boston, MA 02215-1904

617-353-2000
FAX 617-353-9646
TDD:617-353-3658
TTY: 617-353-3658
http://www.bu.edu
e-mail: lwolf@bu.edu

Lorraine Wolf PhD, Director

Provides basic support services such as test taking accommodations, note taking assistance, etc. Provides comprehensive services that include learning strategies instruction for an additional fee. LDSS offers a six-week summer program, The Summer Transition Program, for high school graduates.

3227 **Bridgewater State College**
Pre-College Workshop for Students with Disabilitie
131 Summit St
Bridgewater, MA 02325

508-531-1000
FAX 508-531-1725
TTY: 508-531-6113
http://www.bridgew.edu
e-mail: p1connolly@bridgew.edu

Dana Mohler-Faria, President

A two-day program for new students with disabilities. Gives new students with disabilities an opportunity to talk about what BSC offers with upper-class students with disabilities.

3228 **Bristol Community College**
Program for Academic Support and Success
777 Elsbree St
Fall River, MA 02720-7399

508-678-2811
FAX 508-674-4315
http://www.bristolcc.edu

John J Sbrega, Coordinator

Provides an integrated program of early academic and career guidance for students with physical and/or learning disabilities.

3229 **Carroll School**
25 Baker Bridge Rd
Lincoln, MA 01773-3199

781-259-8342
FAX 781-259-8842
http://www.carrollschool.org

Stephen Wilkins, Head of School

A dynamic independent day school for elementary and middle school students who have been diagnosed with specific learning disabilities in reading and writing, such as dyslexia.

3230 Cotting School
453 Concord Ave
Lexington, MA 02421-8088
781-862-7323
FAX 781-861-1179
http://www.cotting.org
e-mail: admissions@cotting.org
David Manzo, President

Day school for children with a broad spectrum of learning and communication disabilities, physical challenges, and complex medical conditions.

3231 Curry College
Program for Advancement of Learning
1071 Blue Hill Ave
Milton, MA 02186-2395
617-333-0504
FAX 617-333-2114
http://www.curry.edu
e-mail: pal@curry.edu
Kenneth K Quigley Jr, President

PAL is a program within Curry College, a co-educational, four-year liberal arts institution serving 2,000 students and located in the Boston suburb of Milton, Massachusetts. For over 25 years, PAL has both shaped and been shaped by Curry's distinctive philosophy of education. Serves college age students with specific learning disabilities.

3232 Dearborn Academy
34 Winter St
Arlington, MA 02474-6920
781-641-5992
FAX 781-641-5997
http://www.dearbornacademy.org
e-mail: hrossman@sfcinc.org
Carol Core, Director

A program of psycho-educational day schools serving children in elementary, middle, and high school with emotional, behavioral, and learning difficulties. Students struggling to learn find a secure environment in which to thrive.

3233 Eagle Hill School
PO Box 16
Hardwick, MA 01037-0016
413-477-6000
FAX 413-477-6837
http://www.ehs1.org
e-mail: admission@ehs1.org
Dr PJ McDonald, Headmaster

Co-educational, college preparatory boarding and day school for students in grades 8-12 diagnosed with learning disabilities and ADD.

3234 Evergreen Center
Educational Programs and Services
345 Fortune Blvd
Milford, MA 01757-1723
508-478-5597
FAX 508-634-3251
http://www.evergreenctr.org
e-mail: services@evergreenctr.org
Robert Littleton Jr, Executive Director

Is a residential school serving children and adolescents with severe developmental disabilities.

3235 Harvard School of Public Health
Harvard University
677 Huntington Ave
Rm G29
Boston, MA 02115-6096
617-732-1036
FAX 617-432-3879
http://www.hsph.harvard.edu
e-mail: aeisenma@hsph.harvard.edu
Julio Frenk, Dean
Andrew Eisenmann, Student Affairs Director

An independent four-year college with 45 special education students out of a total of 6,621. Disabled students are encouraged to take advantage of opportunities available to help them achieve their educational goals.

3236 Hillside School
404 Robin Hill Road
Marlborough, MA 01752-1099
508-485-2824
FAX 508-485-4420
http://www.hillsideschool.net
e-mail: admissions@hillsideschool.net
David Beecher, Director

Hillside School is an independent boarding and day school for boys, grades 5-9. Hillside provides educational and residential services to boys needing to develop their academic and social skills while building self-confidence and maturity. The 200-acre school is located in a rural section of Marlborough and includes a working farm. Hillside accommodates both traditional learners who want a more personalized education, and those boys with learning difficulties and/or attention problems.

3237 Landmark Elementary and Middle School Program
Landmark School
PO Box 227
Prides Crossing, MA 01965
978-236-3010
FAX 978-926-1000
http://www.landmarkschool.org
e-mail: admission@landmarkschool.org
Robert Broudo, Head of School

Our mission is to enable and empower students with language-based learning disabilities to realize their educational and social potential through an exemplary school program complemented by outreach and training, diagnosis, and research.

3238 Landmark High School Program
Landmark School
PO Box 227
Prides Crossing, MA 01965
978-236-3010
FAX 978-926-1000
http://www.landmarkschool.org
e-mail: admission@landmarkschool.orgkschool.org
Robert Broudo, Head of School

Our mission is to transform lives by helping students with language-based learning disabilities realize their educational and social potential.

3239 Landmark School Outreach Program
Landmark School
429 Hale Street
P.O. Box 227
Prides Crossing, MA 01965-0227
978-236-3216
FAX 978-927-7268
http://www.landmarkoutreach.org
e-mail: outreach@landmarkschool.org
Robert Broudo, Head of School

Seeks to empower children with language-based learning disabilities by offering their teachers an exemplary program of applied research and professional development.

3240   Lesley University
Threshold Program
29 Everett St
Cambridge, MA 02138-2702   617-868-9600
                                    800-999-1959
                                    FAX 617-349-8544
                                    http://www.lesley.edu
                                    e-mail: threshld@lesley.edu
Jim Wilbur, Director
Helen McDonald, Admissions Director

The Threshold Program is a comprehensive, nondegree campus-based program at Lesley University for highly motivated young adults with diverse learning disabilities and other special needs.

3241   Linden Hill School
154 S Mountain Rd
Northfield, MA 01360-9701   413-498-2906
                                    FAX 413-498-2908
                                    http://www.lindenhs.org
                                    e-mail: office@lindenhs.org
James Mc Daniel, Headmaster

A middle school dedicated to helping boys with dyslexia or language-learning differences realize their full potential.

3242   Middlesex Community College
Transition Program
Enrollment Ctr 2nd Floor Spr
Bedford, MA 01730   781-280-3630
                                    FAX 781-275-7126
                                    http://www.middlesex.mass.edu
                                    e-mail: darceyd@middlesex.mass.edu
Susan Woods, Director

Designed expressly for students with significant learning disabilities. This two-year certificate program teaches consumer and business skills, independent living, and personal and social development.

3243   Northeastern University
Learning Disabilities Program
20 Dodge Hall 360 Huntington Ave
Boston, MA 02115   617-373-2000
                                    FAX 617-373-3758
                                    TTY: 617-373-2730
                                    http://www.northeastern.edu
                                    e-mail: m.barrows@neu.edu
Jim O'Shaughnessy, Director

Offers a variety of services to students with disabilities including note takers, extended testing time, counseling services, and special accommodations.

3244   Riverview School
551 Route 6a
East Sandwich, MA 02537-1494   508-888-0489
                                    FAX 508-833-7001
                                    http://www.riverviewschool.org
                                    e-mail: admissions@riverviewschool.org
Maureen Brenner, Director Admissions/Placement
Stephen L. Grinsell, Assistenty

An independent, residential school of international reputation and service enrolling 183 male and female students in its secondary and post-secondary programs. Students share a common history of lifelong difficulty with academic achievement and the development of friendships. On measures of intellectual ability, most students score within the 70-100 range and have a primary diagnosis of learning disability and/or complex language or learning disorder.

3245   Smith College
College Hall 104
Northampton, MA 01063-0001   413-585-2071
                                    FAX 413-585-4498
                                    TTY: 413-585-2071
                                    http://www.smith.edu
                                    e-mail: lrausche@email.smith.edu
Laura Rauscher, Director

Support services office for students, staff and faculty with disabilities.

3246   Springfield Technical Community College
PO Box 9000
Springfield, MA 01102-9000   413-755-6944
                                    413-755-6306
                                    FAX 413-781-6652
                                    http://www.stcc.edu
Ira H Rubenzahl, President

Springfield Technical Community College, a leader in technology and instructional innovation, transforms lives through educational opportunities that promote personal and professional success.

3247   The Kolburne School, Inc.
343 NM Southfield Rd
New Marlborough, MA 01230-2035   413-229-8787
                                    FAX 413-229-4165
                                    http://www.kolburne.net
                                    e-mail: info@kolburne.net
Jeane K Weinstein, Executive Director

A family operated residential treatment center located in the Berkshire Hills of Massachusetts. Through integrated treatment services, effective behavioral management, recreational programming, and positive staff relationships, our students develop the emotional stability, interpersonal skills and academic/vocational background necessary to return home with success.

3248   White Oake School
533 North Rd
Westfield, MA 01085-9774   413-562-9500
                                    FAX 413-562-9010
                                    http://www.whiteoakschool.org
                                    e-mail: ddrake@whiteoakschool.org
David Drake, Principal

Offer programs for students with learning disabilities, ADD and/or emotional difficulties.

3249   Willow Hill School
98 Haynes Rd
Sudbury, MA 01776-1343   978-443-2581
                                    FAX 978-443-7560
                                    http://www.willowhillschool.org
                                    e-mail: rtaft-farrell@willowhillschool.org
Stan Buckley, Head of School

Offers secondary level students with learning challenges opportunities to acquire academic and social skills needed to shape their own future. Ensuring that our students fulfill their potential is our priority. We are dedicated to attainment of academic excellence and a wide range of personal talents.

Michigan

3250   Andrews University
Old Us 31
Berrien Springs, MI 49104   269-471-7771
                                    800-253-2874
                                    FAX 269-471-6293
                                    http://www.andrews.edu

Niels-Erik Andreasen, President

Offers a variety of services to students with disabilities including notetakers, extended testing time, counseling services, and special accommodations.

3251 Aquinas College
1607 Robinson Rd SE
Grand Rapids, MI 49506-1799   616-632-8900
                                              800-678-9593
                                         FAX 616-459-2563
                                   http://www.aquinas.edu
                          e-mail: admissions@aquinas.edu
C Edward Balog, President
Tom Mikowski, Admissions Dean

An independent four-year college with 32 special education students out of a total of 2,300 students.

3252 Coaching Program
Calvin College
1845 Knollcrest Cir SE
Grand Rapids, MI 49546-4436   616-526-6113
                                              800-618-0122
                                         FAX 616-526-7066
                                     http://www.calvin.edu
                          e-mail: acadservices@calvin.edu
Todd Dornbos, Director

Provides the coaching program for students with learning disabilities, attention deficit disorders and other students who benefit from help with time management and study skills.

3253 Eastern Michigan University
Students with Disabilities Office
Suite 246
Student Center
Ypsilanti, MI 48197   734-487-2470
                                         FAX 734-487-5784
                                     http://www.emich.edu
                           e-mail: cbracke1@emich.edu
Caroline M Brackette PhD, Director

Four year college that offers students with learning disabilities support and services.

3254 Eton Academy
Academic Program
1755 E Melton Rd
Birmingham, MI 48009-7277   248-642-1150
                                         FAX 248-642-3670
                                http://www.etonacademy.org
Pete Pullen, Head of School

Our primary focus is to help students who learn differently achieve their fullest potential for academic excellence. Eton Academy offers a comprehensive curriculum that integrates the best available multi-sensory, hands-on and experiential learning methods to meet the individual needs of its students.

3255 Lake Michigan Academy
2428 Burton St SE
Grand Rapids, MI 49546-4806   616-464-3330
                                         FAX 616-285-1935
                                      http://www.wmldf.org
                                    e-mail: info@wmldf.org
Amy Barto, Executive Director

Lake Michigan academy provides academic excellence for students with specific learning disabilities and/or attention deficit disorder in grades 1-12

3256 Michigan Technological University
1400 Townsend Dr
Houghton, MI 49931-1200   906-487-2277
                                         FAX 906-487-3589
                                       http://www.mtu.edu
                             e-mail: gbmelton@mtu.edu
David Reed, President
Gloria Melton, Dean of Students
Debra Forsell, Senior Staff Assistant
A public undergraduate and graduate university with programs in engineering, sciences, business, technology, forestry, social sciences, and humanities. In 2005/06, there were requests for services from 70 individuals with physical or learning disabilities. Services include extended testing time, books on tape, and counseling. Total student enrollment 6,510.

3257 Montcalm Community College
2800 College Dr
Sidney, MI 48885-9723   989-328-2111
                                         FAX 989-328-2950
                                    http://www.montcalm.edu
                             e-mail: info@montcalm.edu
Robert Ferrentino, President
Jim Lantz, Vice President

Offers a variety of services to students with disabilities including note takers, extended testing time, counseling services, and special accommodations.

3258 Northwestern Michigan College
1701 E Front St
Traverse City, MI 49686-3061   231-995-1138
                                         FAX 231-995-1253
                                         TDD:231-995-1929
                                  http://www.nmc.edu/tss
                             e-mail: mpoertner@nmc.edu
Tim Nelson, President
Michelle Poertner, Tutoring Program Manager

Community college in Northern Michigan.

Minnesota

3259 Alexandria Technical and Community College
1601 Jefferson St
Alexandria, MN 56308-3799   320-762-0221
                                              888-234-1222
                                         FAX 320-762-4501
                                         TDD:320-762-4623
                                         TTY: 320-762-4623
                                     http://www.alextech.edu
                             e-mail: marya@alextech.edu
Kevin Kopischke, President
Mary Ackerman, Support Services Coordinator

Educational Institution

3260 Augsburg College
Center for Learning and Adaptive Student Services
2211 Riverside Ave
Minneapolis, MN 55454-1350   612-330-1000
                                         FAX 612-330-1443
                                         TDD:612-330-1748
                                         TTY: 612-330-1748
                                     http://www.augsburg.edu
                            e-mail: jonesk1@augsburg.edu
Paul Pribbenow, Director

The Center for Learning and Adaptive Student Services coordinates academics accommodations and services for students with learning, attentional and psychiatric disabilities.

3261 College of Saint Scholastica
1200 Kenwood Ave
Duluth, MN 55811-4199
218-723-6000
800-249-6412
FAX 218-723-6290
http://www.css.edu
e-mail: njewcomb@css.edu
Larry Goodwin, President

Offers a variety of services to students with disabilities including note takers, extended testing time, counseling services, and special accommodations.

3262 Groves Academy
3200 Highway 100 South
Saint Louis Park, MN 55416-2175
952-920-6377
FAX 952-920-2068
http://www.grovesacademy.org
e-mail: alexanderj@grovesacademy.org
John Alexander, Head of School
Kathy Boone, Director Of Education

A private, independent, day school for adults with langauge, learning and attentional disabilities.

3263 Institute on Community Integration
University of Minnesota
109 Pattee Hall
150 Pillsbury Dr SE
Minneapolis, MN 55455
612-624-4512
FAX 612-624-9344
http://ici.umn.edu
e-mail: icipub@umn.edu
David R Johnson PhD, Director

A federally designated University Center for Excellence in Developmental Disabilities, has over 400 print and electronic resources on topics relating to community living for persons with intellectual and developmental disabilities across the lifespan.

3264 Minnesota Life College
7501 Logan Ave S
Apt 2A
Richfield, MN 55423-3730
612-869-4008
FAX 612-869-0443
http://www.minnesotalifecollege.org
e-mail: info@minnesotalifecollege.org
Amy Gudmestad, Executive Director
Noah Gerding, Admissions/Development

Minnesota Life College is a not-for-profit, vocational and life skills training program for young adults with learning disabilities.

3265 Minnesota State Community and Technical College: Moorhead
1900 28th Ave S
Moorhead, MN 56560-4830
218-299-6500
800-426-5603
FAX 218-299-6810
TTY: 800-627-2539
http://www.minnesota.edu
e-mail: jerome.migler@minnesota.edu
Jerome Migler, Provost
John Centko, Dean of Academics
Richard Smestad, Vice President
Offers a variety of services to students with disabilities including notetakers, extended testing time, counseling services, and special accommodations.

3266 Student Disability Services
St. Cloud State University
720 4th Ave S
Saint Cloud, MN 56301-4498
320-308-4080
FAX 320-308-5100
http://www.stcloudstate.edu/sds
e-mail: sds@stcloudstate.edu
Earl Potter, President
Owen Zimpel, Disability Services Director

A public comprehensive university that provides services for students with learning disabilities and other needs: alternative testing, note taking, referrals to campus resources and advocacy/support.

3267 University of Minnesota: Morris
Student Disability Services
600 E 4th St
Morris, MN 56267-2134
320-589-2211
FAX 320-589-6035
TDD:320-589-6178
http://www.morris.umn.edu
e-mail: freyc@morris.umn.edu
Jacqueline Johnson, Coordinator

Offers a variety of services to students with disabilities including note takers, extended testing time, counseling services, and special accommodations.

Mississippi

3268 Mississippi State University
Adaptive Driving Program
PO Box 9736
Mississippi State, MS 39762-9736
662-325-2323
FAX 662-325-0896
TTY: 662-325-0520
http://www.msstate.edu
e-mail: jcirlotnew@tkmartin.msstate.edu
Janie Cirlot, Director

Specializes in the evaluation and training of persons with disabilities who wish to consider driving. Services may result in a recommendation for driving or further training, and when appropriate, will include specific recommendations regarding vehicle modifications and adaptive driving equipment. Also offers evaluation and training services for driving candidates using bioptic lenses.

3269 Project Art
Mississippi State University
PO Box 9736
Mississippi State, MS 39762-9736
662-325-2324
FAX 662-325-0896
TTY: 662-325-0520
http://www.msstate.edu
e-mail: jcirlotnew@tkmartin.msstate.edu
Janie Cirlot, Director

Provides recreational activities for students with and without disabilities in grades K-12. With the use of assistive technology and evnironmental adaptation, the program makes available recreational activities that have not traditionally been an option for children with disabilities.

3270 University of Southern Mississippi
PO Box 8586
Hattiesburg, MS 39406
601-266-1000
FAX 601-266-5756
TDD:601-266-6837
http://www.usm.edu
e-mail: latouisha.wilson@usm.edu
Shelby Thames, President

Four year college that provides students with support and resources whom are disabled.

Missouri

3271 Central Missouri State University
Office of Accessibility Services
Union 222
Warrensburg, MO 64093
660-543-4985
FAX 660-543-4658
TDD:660-543-4421
http://www.ucmo.edu
e-mail: mayfield@cmsu1.cmsu.edu
Teresa Alewel, Director ADA/504 Coordinator
Cathy Seeley MS, Coordinator

Provider of equal opportunity to education for students with disabilities through notetakers, extended testing time, interpreters and other accommodations.

3272 Churchill Center and School for Learning Disabilities
1021 Municipal Center Dr
Saint Louis, MO 63131-1133
314-997-4343
FAX 314-997-2760
http://www.churchillstl.org
e-mail: info@churchillstl.org
Sandra Gilligan, Director

Our mission is to give high potential children with learning disabilities the finest, individualized, remedial education and the support they need to achieve and return to a traditional classroom .

3273 Longivew Community College
ABLE Program
500 SW Longview Rd
Lees Summit, MO 64111
816-604-1000
FAX 816-672-2025
http://www.mcckc.edu
Fred Grogan, Director
Mark James, Cancellor

The program teaches students with neurological disabilities including, but not limited to, learning disabilities or brain injuries how to become independent learners.

3274 Missouri State University
Learning Diagnostic Clinic
300 S Jefferson
Springfield, MO 65897
417-836-6841
http://www.psychology.missouristate.edu
e-mail: stevecapps@missouristate.edu
Steve Capps, Director
Temonthy Bender, Faculty

Project Success is an academic support program for college students with a learning disability, ADHD, or other diagnosis who desire more comprehensive services. Those enrolled in Project Success will be offered a wide variety of services tailored for students with learning disabilities.

3275 North Central Missouri College
1301 Main St
Trenton, MO 64683-1824
660-359-3948
FAX 660-359-2211
http://www.nc.missouri.edu
Dr Neil Nuttall, President

Offers a variety of services to students with disabilities including note takers, extended testing time, counseling services, and special accommodations.

3276 St Louis Community College: Forest Park
Rm G329
5600 Oakland Ave
Saint Louis, MO 63110-1316
314-644-9100
FAX 314-644-9752
http://www.stlcc.edu
Morris Johnson, President

St. Louis Community College expands minds and changes lives every day. We create accessible, dynamic learning environments focused on the needs of our diverse communities.

3277 St Louis Community College: Meramec
11333 Big Bend Rd
Saint Louis, MO 63122-5799
314-984-7500
FAX 314-984-7166
http://www.stlcc.edu
Zerrie D Campbell, Interim President

St. Louis Community College expands minds and changes lives every day. We create accessible, dynamic learning environments focused on the needs of our diverse communities.

3278 University of Missouri: Kansas City
Department of Disability Services
5100 Rockhill Rd
Kansas City, MO 64110-2446
816-235-1000
FAX 816-235-6363
http://www.umkc.edu
e-mail: disability@umkc.edu
Scott Laurent, Coordinator

Offers a variety of services to students with disabilities including note takers, extended testing time, counseling services, and special accommodations.

Montana

3279 Western Montana College
710 S Atlantic St
Dillon, MT 59725-3598
406-683-7331
877-683-7331
http://www.umwestern.edu
Clarence Kostelecky, Special Services

A public four-year college with 6 special education students out of a total of 1,100.

Nebraska

3280 Midland Lutheran College
Academic Support Services
900 N Clarkson St
Fremont, NE 68025-4200
402-941-6501
800-642-8382
FAX 402-941-6513
http://www.midlandu.edu
e-mail: moseman@mlc.edu
Steven Titus, Director
Dr. Benjamin Sasse, President

Four-year college that provides academic support for students who have a learning disability.

3281 Southeast Community College: Beatrice Campus
Career and Advising Program
4771 W Scott Rd
Beatrice, NE 68310-7042
402-228-3468
800-233-5027
FAX 402-228-2218
http://www.southeast.edu
Dennis Headrick, Director

The Beatrice Campus offers the Academic Transfer program providing first and second year college coursees for students who wish to transfer credits to a four-year college.

3282 University of Nebraska: Omaha
6001 Dodge St
Omaha, NE 68182
402-554-2800
800-858-8648
FAX 402-554-3777
http://www.unomaha.edu
John Christensen, Manager
James B. Milliken, President

Offers a variety of services to students with disabilities including notetakers, extended testing time, counseling services, and special accommodations.

New Hampshire

3283 Dartmouth College
Student Accessibility Services
301 Collis Ctr
Hanover, NH 03755
603-646-1110
FAX 603-646-1629
TDD:603-646-1564
http://www.dartmouth.edu/~acskills/disability
e-mail: admissions.office@dartmouth.edu
Carl Thum, Ph.D, Direcror

The Student Accessibility Services (SAS) Office works with students, faculty and staff to ensure that the programs and activities of Dartmouth College are accessible, and students with disabilities receive reasonable accommodations in their curricular and co-curricular pursuits. Over 350 Dartmouth students are registered with SAS including students with learning disabilities, attentional or psychiatric disorders, and mobility, visual, hearing or chronic health conditions.

3284 Hampshire Country School
28 Patey Circle
Rindge, NH 03461-5950
603-899-3325
FAX 603-899-6521
http://www.hampshirecountryschool.org
e-mail: admissions@hampshirecountryschool.net
William Dickerman, Admissions Director
Bernd Foecking, Headmaster

Hampshire Country School is a boarding school for middle school boys with very high ability who need an unusual amount of adult attention and support, including boys with Asperger's, nonverbal learning disabilities and ADHD.

3285 Hunter School
PO Box 600
Rumney, NH 03266
603-786-3666
FAX 603-786-2221
http://www.hunterschool.org
e-mail: hunteradmissions@yahoo.com
Tim Tyler, Director

A small, non-profit school where young boys and girls with Attention Deficit Disorder (ADD), Attention Deficit/Hyperactivity Disorder (ADHD) or Asperger's Syndrome are nurtured, educated and celebrated. Offers both a residential program and a day school.

3286 Keene State College
229 Main St
Keene, NH 03435
603-352-1909
800-KSC-1909
FAX 603-358-2257
http://www.keene.edu
Dr. Helen F Giles-Gee, President

A public four-year college with 105 special education students out of a total of 3,800.

3287 Learning Skills Academy
PO Box 955
Rye, NH 03870-955
603-964-4903
FAX 603-964-3838
http://www.lsa.pvt.k12.nh.us
e-mail: marcus@lsa.pvt.k12.nh.us
Marcus Mann, Principal
Lisa McManus, Education Director

Our purpose is to ignite every potential in our students and since 1985 they have been successful both academically and socially. We prepare them for success in life by helping them to understand their learning profile: advocate for their needs; interact appropriately in scholastic and social situations; and bring their academic work to a level that matches their potential. When students reach these goals, our staff works with the student, parents and LEA to support successful transitions.

3288 New England College
98 Bridge St
Henniker, NH 03242-3292
603-428-2000
FAX 603-428-7230
http://www.nec.edu
Michelle Perkins, Academic Advising/Support
Paula Amato, Vice-President
Stephen Fritz, President
An independent four-year college with 140 students with learning differences out of a total undergraduate enrollment of 750.

3289 New Hampshire Vocational Technical College
379 Belmont Rd
Laconia, NH 03246-1364
603-524-3207
800-357-2992
FAX 603-524-8084
TDD:603-524-3207
http://www.laconia.nactc.edu
e-mail: laconow@nactc.edu
Maureen Baldwin-Lamper, Special Services
Don Morrissey, Vice President

Offers a variety of services to students with disabilities including notetakers, extended testing time, counseling services, and special accommodations.

3290 Rivier College
420 S Main St
Nashua, NH 03060-5086
603-888-1311
800-447-4843
FAX 603-897-8883
TDD:800-735-2964
http://www.rivier.edu
e-mail: kricci@rivier.edu
William Farrell, President

An independent four-year college with 17 special education students out of a total of 1,651.

3291 Southern New Hampshire University
Office of Disability Services
2500 N River Rd
Manchester, NH 03106-1018
603-626-9100
800-688-1249
FAX 603-626-9100
TTY: 603-645-4671
http://www.snhu.edu
e-mail: info@snhu.edu
Paul Leblanc, President
Hyla Jaffe, Disability Services Coordinator

Offers services to students with disabilities based on recommendations from documentaion supporting a disability. Accommodations are made for specific needs.

3292 University of New Hampshire
118 Memorial Union Building
Durham, NH 03824
603-862-1234
FAX 603-862-4043
TTY: 603-862-2607
http://www.unh.edu/disabilityservices
e-mail: disability.office@unh.edu
Maxine Little, Director
Janice Mutschler, Manager

Disability Services for Students provides services to students with documented disabilities to ensure that University activities and programs are accessible. It also promotes the development of student self-reliance and the personal independence necessary to succeed in a university climate.

New Jersey

3293 Banyan School
12 Hollywood Ave
Fairfield, NJ 07004-1101
973-439-1919
FAX 973-439-1396
http://www.banyanschool.com
e-mail: msaunders@banyanschool.com
Mary Jo Saunders, Director
Anna Rotonda, Plant Manager

3294 Caldwell College
Office of Disability Services
9 Ryerson Ave
Caldwell, NJ 07006-6195
973-618-3000
FAX 973-618-3358
http://www.caldwell.edu
e-mail: abenowitz@caldwell.edu
Patrice Werner, Coordinator

Four-year college that provides disability services to those students who are learnig disabled.

3295 Camden County College
PO Box 200
Blackwood, NJ 08012
856-227-7200
FAX 856-374-4975
http://www.camdencc.edu
e-mail: jkinzy@camdencc.edu
Joanne Kinzy, Coordinator
Phyllis Vecchia, President
Kevin G. Halpern, Chairman
A two-year college that provides services to the learning disabled.

3296 Centenary College
Office of Disabilities Services
400 Jefferson St
Hackettstown, NJ 07840-2100
908-852-1000
FAX 908-852-5410
http://www.centenarycollege.edu
e-mail: dso@centenarycollege.edu
Kenneth L Hoyt, Director

Offers two programs specifically designed to support students with mild emotional and learning disabilities: Project Able and Step Ahead. The goals of these programs are to provide a bridge between the structured and sometimes modified secondary-school setting to the predominantly self-directed college environment.

3297 Children's Center of Monmouth County
1115 Green Grove Rd
Neptune, NJ 07753-2571
732-922-0228
FAX 732-922-8133
http://www.ccprograms.com
George Scheer, Director

Offers educational services, training in adaptive living and pre-vocational skills for students, ages 3 to 21, with multiple disabilities or a diagnosis of autism and pervasive developmental delays.

3298 College of New Jersey
Office of Differing Disabilities
PO Box 7718
Ewing, NJ 08628
609-771-2571
FAX 609-637-5131
http://www.tcnj.edu/~wellness/disability/
e-mail: degennar@tcnj.edu
Ann DeGennaro, Director for Wellness
Terri Yamiolkowski, Coordinator

Four-year college provides services to students with disabilities.

3299 College of Saint Elizabeth
2 Convent Rd
Morristown, NJ 07960-6923
973-290-4000
http://www.cse.edu
Maria Cammarata, Dean Studies
Francis Raftery, President

Offers a variety of services to students with disabilities including notetakers, extended testing time, counseling services, and special accommodations.

3300 Community High School
PO Box 2118
Sunvalley, ID 83353
208-622-3962
FAX 208-622-3962
http://www.communityschool.org
e-mail: office@communityschool.us
Jim Steel, Education Director
Dennis Cohen, Program Director
John Swift, Chairman
Complete college prep HS program for LD/ADD adolescent grades 9-12.

3301 Community School
PO Box 2119
Sunvalley, ID 83353
208-622-3963
FAX 208-622-3963
http://www.communityschool.org
e-mail: office@communityschool.us
Isabel Shoukas, Executive Director
Dennis Cohen, Program Director
John Swift, Chairman
Comprehensive academic program for LD/ADD children grades K-8; NY and NJ funding available.

3302 Craig School
10 Tower Hill Rd
Mountain Lakes, NJ 07046-1210
973-334-1295
FAX 973-334-1299
http://www.craigschool.org
e-mail: kburke@craigschool.org
Katie Burke, Development Director
Eric Caparulo, Head of School

A school for children with learning differences such as dyslexia, auditory processing issues and ADD.

3303 Cumberland County College
Project Assist
PO Box 1500
Vineland, NJ 08362-1500
201-837-8071
FAX 856-690-0059
http://www.cccnj.net
e-mail: ssherd@cccnj.edu
Sandy Sherd, Director
Kenneth Ender, President

A two-year college that offers services to its learning disabled students.

3304 Fairleigh Dickinson University: Metropolitan Campus
1000 River Rd
Teaneck, NJ 07666-1914   201-692-2000
                                           800-338-8803
                                       FAX 201-692-2030
                                       http://www.fdu.edu
J Michael Adams, Campus Director
Grace Hottinger, Admissions Coordinator
Dr. Mary Farrell PhD, University Director
Comprehensive support services to students with language
based LD.

3305 Forum School
107 Wyckoff Ave
Waldwick, NJ 07463-1795   201-444-5882
                                       FAX 201-444-4003
                                http://www.theforumschool.com
e-mail: forum@ultradsl.net /info@theforumschool.com
Steven Krapes, Executive Director
Linda Oliver, Office Manager

Day school for children through age 16 who have neurologi-
cally based developmental disabilities, including autism,
ADHD, LD, and asperger syndrome. Services include extended year, speech, adaptive physical education, music, art
therapy, and parent program.

3306 Georgian Court University
The Learning Center (TLC)
900 Lakewood Ave
Lakewood, NJ 08701-2697   732-987-2659
                                           800-458-8422
                                       FAX 732-987-2026
                                       http://www.georgian.edu
                                   e-mail: fahrl@georgian.edu
Patricia A. Cohen, MSW, MA, Director
Luana Fahr, Deputy Director

The Learning Center is an assistance program designed to
provide an environment for students with mild to moderate
learning disabilities who desire a college education. The
program is not one of remediation, but it is an individualized
support program to assist candidates in becoming successful
college students. Emphasis is placed on developing
self-help strategies, study techniques, content tutoring, time
management, organization skills, and social skills all taught
by a certified professional.

3307 Gloucester County College
1400 Tanyard Rd
Sewell, NJ 08080-4249   856-468-5000
                                       FAX 856-468-9462
                                       TDD:856-468-8452
                                       http://www.gccnj.edu
                                   e-mail: dcook@gccnj.edu
William Anderson, Director Special Needs Services
Robert McErlane, Vice President
Daniel J. Ball III, CPA, President
The Office of Special Needs Services addresses supportive
needs toward academic achievement for those students with
documented disabilties such as learning disabled, visually
impaired, hard of hearing and mobility impaired
individuals.

3308 Hudson County Community College
25 Journal Sq
Jersey City, NJ 07306-4012   201-360-4360
                                           201-714-7100
                                       FAX 201-963-0789
                                   http://www.hudson.cc.nj.us
Ana Chapman, Execurive Director

Offers a variety of services to students with disabilities including note takers, extended testing time, counseling services, and special accommodations.

3309 Jersey City State College
2039 John F Kennedy Blvd
Jersey City, NJ 07305-1588   201-200-2000
                                           888-441-NJCU
                                       http://www.njcu.edu
Myrna Ehrlich MD, Director Project Mentor
President
Offers a variety of services to students with disabilities in-
cluding notetakers, extended testing time, counseling ser-
vices, and special accommodations.

3310 Kean University
Community Disabilities Services
1000 Morris Ave
Union, NJ 07083-7131   908-737-5326
                                       FAX 908-737-5235
                                       TDD:908-737-5156
                                       http://www.kean.edu
                                   e-mail: webmaster@kean.edu
Dawood Farahi, Director
Maria Pitts, Office Assistant

Provides services to disabled students.

3311 Middlesex County College
Project Connections
PO Box 3050
Edison, NJ 08818-3050   732-906-2561
                                       FAX 732-906-7767
                                   http://www.middlesex.cc.nj.us
                            e-mail: elizabeth_lowe@middlesex.edu
Elizabeth Lowe, Director LD Services
Elaine Weir-Daidone, Counselor
Lewis Ostar, Executive Director
Project Connections is a comprehensive academic and coun-
seling service for students with learning disabilities who are
enrolled in mainstream programs at Middlesex County
College.

3312 Morristown-Beard School
70 Whippany Rd
Morristown, NJ 07960-4523   973-539-3032
                                       FAX 973-539-1590
                                       http://www.mobeard.org
Alex Curtis, Headmaster
Debi Roath, President
John Adams, Vice President
Offer programs for students with learning disabilities, ADD
and/or emotional difficulties.

3313 New Jersey City University
2039 John F Kennedy Blvd
Jersey City, NJ 07305-1588   201-200-2000
                                           888-441-NJCU
                                       FAX 201-200-2044
                                       http://www.njcu.edu
Dr. Sue Henderson, President

Provides students with learning disabilities a mentor, a
teacher, advisor or a faculty member.

3314 Ocean County College
College Dr
Toms River, NJ 08754-2001   732-255-0400
                                       FAX 732-255-0444
                                       TDD:732-255-0424
                                       http://www.ocean.edu
                                   e-mail: mreustle@ocean.edu
Jon Larson, President
Anne Hammond, PASS Counselor

A regional resource center and comprehensive support center for college students with learning disabilities, offering a
range of services including psycho-educational assessments, faculty/staff in-service training, program development assistance and consultation, and technical support.
Individual and/or small group counseling is available, and
vocational/career counseling on transition issues is also
offered.

3315 Princeton University
303 W College
Princeton, NJ 08544　　　　　　609-258-3000
　　　　　　　　　　　　　　　FAX 609-258-1020
　　　　　　　　　　http://www.princeton.edu
Stephen Cochrane, Special Services
Christopher Eisgruber, CEO
Shirley M. Tilghman, President
Offers a variety of services to students with disabilities including note takers, extended testing time, counseling services, and special accommodations.

3316 Ramapo College of New Jersey
Office of Specialized Services
Ste C205
505 Ramapo Valley Rd
Mahwah, NJ 07430-1680　　　　201-684-7500
　　　　　　　　　　　　　　　FAX 201-684-7004
　　　http://www.ramapo.edu/content/student.resources
　　　　　　　　　　　　e-mail: oss@ramapo.edu
Peter P Mercer, President
Cathleen Davey, Vice President

Ramapo College demostated a strong commitment to providing equal access to all students through the removal of architectural and attitudinal barriers. Integration of qualified students with disabilities into college community has been the Ramapo way since the College opened in 1971.

3317 Raritan Valley Community College
PO Box 3300
Somerville, NJ 08876-1265　　　908-526-1200
　　　　　　　　　　　　　　　FAX 908-429-8589
　　　　　　　　　　http://www.raritanval.edu
Cathy Doyle, Disabilities Specialist
Jerry Ryan, Administrator

A public two-year college with 250 students with disabilities of a total of 6,000 per semster.

3318 Richard Stockton College of New Jersey
101 Vera King Farris Drive
Galloway, NJ 08205-9441　　　609-652-1776
　　　　　　　　　　　　　　　FAX 609-626-5550
　　　　　　　　　　http://www2.stockton.edu
　　　　　　　　e-mail: webmaster@stockton.edu
Dr. Richard Bjork, President
David Pinto, Manager

Offers a variety of services to students with disabilities including note takers, extended testing time, counseling services, and special accommodations.

3319 Rider University
2083 Lawrenceville Rd
Lawrenceville, NJ 08648-3099　　609-896-5000
　　　　　　　　　　　　　　　800-257-9026
　　　　　　　　　　　　　　　FAX 609-895-6645
　　　　　　　　　　http://www.rider.edu
　　　　　　　　e-mail: serv4dstu@rider.edu
Mordechai Rozanski, President
Dr. Barbara Blandford, SSD Director
Shirley Mersky, Assistant Director, SSD
Four-year college that provides resources, programs and support for students with learning disabilities through their SSD (Services for Students with Disabilities) center.

3320 Robert Wood Johnson Medical School
Elizabeth M Boggs Center on Dev. Disabilities
PO Box 2688
New Brunswick, NJ 08903-2688　　732-235-9300
　　　　　　　　　　　　　　　FAX 732-235-9330
　　　　　http://www.rwjms.umdnj.edu/boggscenter
Deborah Spitalink, Director

The Elizabeth M. Boggs Center, as a University Center for Excellence in Developmental Disabilities, values uniqueness and individuality and promotes the self-determination and full participation of people with disabilities and their families in all aspects of community life. The Boggs Center prepares students through interdisciplinary programs, provides community training and technical assistance, conducts research, and disseminates information and educational materials.

3321 Rutgers Center for Cognitive Science
152 Frelinghuysen Rd
Piscataway, NJ 08854-8020　　　732-445-0635
　　　　　　　　　　　　　　　FAX 732-445-6715
　　　　　　　　　　http://www.ruccs.rutgers.edu
　　　　　　　　e-mail: admin@ruccs.rutgers.edu
Rochel Gelman, Co-Director
Charles Gallistel, Co-Director

A public four-year college with 2 special education students out of a total of 437.

3322 Salem Community College
460 Hollywood Ave
Carneys Point, NJ 08069-2799　　856-299-2100
　　　　　　　　　　　　　　　FAX 856-351-2634
　　　　　　　　　　http://www.salemcc.org
　　　　　　　　e-mail: SCCinfo@salemcc.org
Peter Contini, President

Offers a variety of services to students with disabilities including extended testing time, counseling services, and special accommodations.

3323 Seton Hall University
400 S Orange Ave
South Orange, NJ 07079-2697　　973-761-9000
　　　　　　　　　　　　　　　FAX 973-761-7494
　　　　　　　　　　http://www.shu.edu
　　　　　　　　e-mail: fraziera@shu.edu
Robert T Sheeran, Director
Susan Lasker MD, President

Student Support Services is an academic program that addresses the needs of students with disabilities.

3324 Trenton State College
2000 Pennington Rd
Ewing, NJ 08628　　　　　　　609-771-3080
　　　　　　　　　　　　　　　FAX 609-637-5161
　　　　　　　　　　http://www.tcnj.edu
　　　　　　　　e-mail: webmaster@tcnj.edu
Juneau Gary MD, Special Services
R. Gitenstein, President

A public four-year college with 24 special education students out of a total of 6,118.

3325 William Paterson College of New Jersey
Special Education Services
300 Pompton Rd
Wayne, NJ 07470-2152　　　　　973-720-2000
　　　　　　　　　　　　　　　FAX 973-720-2090
　　　　　　　　　　http://www.wpunj.edu
　　　　　　　　e-mail: BOONES@wpunj.edu
Kathleen Woldrone, President
Sharon Lowry, Secretary

Offers a variety of services to students with disabilities including notetakers, extended testing time, counseling services, and special accommodations.

New Mexico

3326   **Albuquerque Technical Vocational Institute**
Special Services
525 Buena Vista Dr SE
Albuquerque, NM 87106-4023
505-224-3000
FAX 505-224-4684
TDD:505-224-3262
http://www.cnm.edu
e-mail: pauls@cnm.edu
Lisa McCulloch, Executive Director
Anna M. Sanchez, Director

Provides or coordinates services for students with all disabilities. For students with learning disabilities can arrange for special testing situations, notetaker/scribes, tape recorders, use of wordprocessors or other accommodations based on individual needs.

3327   **College of Santa Fe**
1600 Saint Michaels Dr
Santa Fe, NM 87508-7634
505-428-1000
FAX 505-428-1204
http://www.sfcc.edu
e-mail: theresa.garcia2@sfcc.edu
Sheila Ortego, Director
Chris Abeya, Chairman

Provides services to the learning disabled.

3328   **Eastern New Mexico University**
Special Programs and Services
1500 S Ave K
Portales, NM 88130
575-562-1011
800-243-6687
http://www.enmu.edu
e-mail: webmaster@enmu.edu
Steave Gamble, President

Four year college that provides programs for the learning disabled.

3329   **Eastern New Mexico University: Roswell**
PO Box 6000
Roswell, NM 88203
575-624-7000
FAX 505-624-7350
http://www.roswell.enmu.edu
e-mail: denise.mcghee@roswell.enmu.edu
Dr.John Madden, President
Lorinda Wilkins, Assistant Director

A public two-year college with a total of 2500 students. Has a one year certificate program designed to teach vocational and life skills to individuals with significant cognitive impairments.

3330   **Gateway School of New York**
Fl 6
211 W 61st St
New York, NY 10023-7952
212-777-5966
FAX 212-777-5794
http://www.gatewayschool.org
e-mail: info@gatewayschool.org
Robert Cunningham, Head of School
Hilary Woods Giuliano, Secretary

An ungraded lower school dedicated to helping children with learning disabilities develop the academic skills, learning strategies, social competence and self-confidence necessary to succeed.

3331   **Institute of American Indian Arts**
83 Avan Nu Po Rd
Santa Fe, NM 87508
505-424-2300
FAX 505-988-6446
http://www.iaia.edu

Dr. Robert Martin, President
Loren Kieve, Chairman

A public two-year college with 8 special education students out of a total of 237.

3332   **New Mexico Institute of Mining and Technology**
801 Leroy Pl
Socorro, NM 87801-4750
575-835-5011
800-428-8324
FAX 575-835-5655
http://www.nmt.edu
Daniel Lopez, President
Dal Symes, Executive Director

A public four-year college with 5 special education students out of a total of 1,128.

3333   **New Mexico Junior College**
1 Thunderbird Circle
Hobbs, NM 88240-9123
575-392-4510
800-657-6260
FAX 505-392-3668
http://www.nmjc.edu
Steve McCleery, President
Latima Kim, Secretary Administrator

A public two-year college with 170 special education students out of a total of 2,438.

3334   **New Mexico State University**
PO Box 30001
Las Cruces, NM 88003-8001
575-646-0111
800-662-6678
FAX 505-646-5222
http://www.nmsu.edu
e-mail: admissions@nmsu.edu
Dr.Wendy K. Williams, President
Michael Armendarez, Coordinator
Elizabeth Titus, Manager
A public four-year college with 230 registered students with disabilities out of a total of 12,922.

3335   **Northern New Mexico Community College**
1002 N Onate St
Espanola, NM 87532
505-747-2100
FAX 505-747-2180
http://www.nnmc.edu
Millie Lowry, Special Services
Jose Griego, President

If you have a learning disability, support services include: reading class, readers of tests, notetakers, taped texts, tutoring, math class, recorders for classroom use, library assistance, extra time for tests, self-esteem counseling, resume assistance and kurzweil reading computers.

3336   **San Juan College**
4601 College Blvd
Farmington, NM 87402-4699
505-326-3311
FAX 505-566-3790
http://www.sanjuancollege.edu
Toni Hopper Pendergrass, President
Dave Eppich, Vice President
Pamela Drake, Executive Director
A public two-year college with 28 special education students out of a total of 3,654.

3337   **University of New Mexico**
Main Campus
Albuquerque, NM 87131
505-277-0111
FAX 505-277-7224
http://www.unm.edu
e-mail: lssunm@unm.edu
Patricia Useem, Manager
Louis Caldera, CEO
Robert G. Frank, President

Offers a variety of services to students with disabilities including notetakers, extended testing time, counseling services, and special accommodations.

3338 University of New Mexico/School of Medicine
Center for Development and Disability
2300 Menaul Blvd NE
Albuquerque, NM 87107-1851
505-272-3000
FAX 505-272-5280
TDD:505-272-0321
http://www.cdd.unm.edu
e-mail: cdd@unm.edu

Cate McClain, Director
Melody Smith, Assistant Director
Elena Aguirre, Executive Director
The mission of the CDD is the full inclusion of people with disabilities and their families in their community by: engaging individuals in making life choices; partnering with communities to build resources; and improving systems of care.

3339 University of New Mexico: Los Alamos Branch
4000 University Dr
Los Alamos, NM 87544-2233
505-662-5919
800-894-5919
FAX 505-662-0344
http://www.la.unm.edu

Jay Ruybalid, Public Affairs Representative

Offers a variety of services to students with disabilities including notetakers, extended testing time, counseling services, and special accommodations.

3340 University of New Mexico: Valencia Campus
280 La Entrada Rd
Los Lunas, NM 87131
505-925-8500
FAX 505-925-8501
http://www.unm.edu/~vc

Sharon DiMaria, Coordinator
Alice Letteney, Executive Director
Robert G. Frank, President
A public two-year college with 57 special services students out of a total of 1,400.

3341 Western New Mexico University
PO Box 680
Silver City, NM 88062-680
1-575-538-63
800-872-9668
FAX 575-538-6278
http://www.wnmu.edu

Dr. Joseph Shepard, President
Faye Vowell, Vice President

Offers a variety of services to students with disabilities including notetakers, extended testing time, counseling services, and special accommodations.

New York

3342 Academic Resource Program
Long Island University/C.W. Post Campus
Learning Support Center
720 Northern Blvd
Brookville, NY 11548-1319
516-299-3057
FAX 516-299-2126
http://www.liv.edu/cwpost/learningsupport
e-mail: susan.rock@liu.edu

Susan Rock, Director
Marie Fatscher, Associate Director

A comprehensive, structured, fee-for-service, support program designed to teach undergraduate students with learning disabilities and/or ADHD skill and strategies that will help then achieve their academic potential in a university setting.

3343 Adelphi University
Disability Support Services
PO Box 701
Garden City, NY 11530-701
516-877-3145
FAX 516-877-3139
TTY: 516-877-3138
http://www.students.edu
e-mail: admissions@adelphi.edu

Dr. Robert A. Scott, President
Frank Angello, Secretary

The Bridges to Adelphi Project is designed to enhance college life for students with nonverbal learning disabilities by providing help with organizational skills, time management, independent living skills and social skills training.

3344 Adirondack Community College
640 Bay Rd
Queensbury, NY 12804-1498
518-743-2200
FAX 518-745-1433

Sara McKay, President

A two-year community college that provides services to the learning disabled.

3345 Albert Einstein College of Medicine
1165 Morris Park Ave
Bronx, NY 10461-1915
718-430-2801
FAX 718-430-3989
http://www.einstein.yu.edu
e-mail: helpdesk@yu.edu

Mary Kelly PhD, Director
Jerome Kleinman, Manager

Provides evaluation and psychoeducational treatment to children and adults of normal intelligence, 21 years or older, who have serious reading difficulties.

3346 Bank Street College: Graduate School of Education
610 W 1112th St
New York, NY 10025-1898
212-875-4400
FAX 212-875-4759
http://www.banksreet.edu
e-mail: GradCourses@bnkst.edu

Augusta Kappner, President
Frank Naura, Vice President

For learning disabled college students who are highly motivated to become teachers of children and youth with learning problems and who wish to earn a masters degree in Special Education.

3347 Binghamton University
PO Box 6000
Binghamton, NY 13902-6000
607-777-2000
FAX 607-777-6893
TDD:607-777-2686
http://ssd.binghamton.edu
e-mail: bjfairba@binghamton.edu

Andrew Cuomo, President
Andrea Snyder, LD Specialist

Provides assistance to BU students with physical, learning or other disabilities.

3348 Bramson Ort Technical Institute
6930 Austin St
Forest Hills, NY 11375-4222
718-261-5800
FAX 718-575-5118
http://www.bramsonort.org
e-mail: rbaskin@bramsonort.org

Ephraim Buhks, Executive Director
Rivka Burkos, Librarian
Dr. Ephraim Buhks, Director
Offers a variety of services to students with disabilities including notetakers, extended testing time, counseling services, and special accommodations.

3349 CUNY Queensborough Community College
22205 56th Ave
Oakland Gardens, NY 11364-1497   718-631-6262
                                   FAX 718-631-8539
                              http://www.qcc.cuny.edu
Dr. Diane Bova Call, Interim President
Susan Curtis, Marketing Executive

The Office of Services for Students with Disabilities (Science Building, Room 132) offers special assistance and couseling to students with specific needs. The services offered include academic, vocational, psychological and rehabilitation counseling, as well as liasion with community social agencies.

3350 Canisius College
Disability Support Service
2001 Main St
Buffalo, NY 14208-1098   716-883-7000
                                  FAX 716-888-2525
                                  TDD:716-888-3748
                             http://www.canisius.edu
                        e-mail: admissions@canisius.edu
Vincent Cooke, Director
Dan Norton, Graduate Assistant

Four-year college offering services to students with physical and cognitive disabilities.

3351 Cazenovia College
22 Sullivan St
Cazenovia, NY 13035-1085   315-655-3210
                                       800-654-3210
                                  FAX 315-655-4000
                             http://www.cazenovia.edu
                     e-mail: cazenovia@cazenovia.edu
Mark J Tierno, Special Services
Jesse Lott, Director

An independent college with a significant number of special education students.

3352 Center for Spectrum Services: Ellenville
4 Yankee Pl
Ellenville, NY 12428-1510   845-647-6464
                                  FAX 845-647-3456
                    http://www.centerforspectrumservices.org
            e-mail: mwerher@centerforspectrumservices.org
Mimi Werner, Coordinator

This center-based program is a school for preschool and school-age children who are 3 through 8 eight years old and have the educational classification of preschooler with a disability, autism, emotional disability or multiple disabilities.

3353 Center for the Advancement of Post Secondary Studies
Maplebrook School
5142 Route 22
Amenia, NY 12501-5357   845-373-9511
                                  FAX 845-373-7029
                          http://www.maplebrookschool.org
                   e-mail: admin@maplebrookschool.org
Donna Konkolics, Head of School
Mark J. Metzger, Chairman

A program based on students successfully completing the goals and objectives designed to prepare them for integration into today's world. Through small group and individualized instruction, the student will be assisted in reaching his/her academic, social, vocational, and physical potential.

3354 Churchill School and Center
Programs for Children
301 E 29th St
New York, NY 10016-8301   212-722-0610
                                  FAX 212-722-1387
                             http://www.churchillschool.com
                    e-mail: wfederico@churchillschool.com
Cynthia Wainwrigh, President
Lauri Kien Kotcher, Vice President

Offers educational programs, professional development in the field of learning disabilities, and advisory and referral services to students, parents, teachers of general and special education, and related service provides.

3355 Colgate University
Office Disabilities Services
13 Oak Dr
Hamilton, NY 13346-1386   315-228-7225
                                  FAX 315-228-7831
                              http://www.colgate.edu
                   e-mail: admission@mail.colgate.edu
Lynn Waldman, Director

Provides for a small body of liberal arts education that will expand individual potential and ability to particpate effectively in the society.

3356 College of New Rochelle: New Resources Division
Student Services
29 Castle Pl
New Rochelle, NY 10805-2339   914-654-5000
                                       800-933-5923
                                  FAX 914-654-5554
                                  http://www.cnr.edu
                              e-mail: info@cnr.edu

Stephen Sweeney, President

Offers a variety of services to students with disabilities including notetakers, extended testing time, counseling services, and special accommodations.

3357 College of Saint Rose
432 Western Ave
Albany, NY 12203-1419   518-454-5111
                                  FAX 518-438-3293
                                  TDD:1-800-637-85
                              http://www.strose.edu
                     e-mail: hermannk@strose.edu
R Mark Sullivan, Coordinator Special Services
Kimberly Lamparelli, Manager
David Szczerbacki, Ph.D, President
Four year college that provides disabled students with services and support.

3358 College of Staten Island of the City University of New York
2800 Victory Blvd
Staten Island, NY 10314-6600   718-982-4012
                                  FAX 718-982-4002
                                  TDD:718-982-2515
                              http://www.csi.cuny.edu
                   e-mail: venditti@postbox.csi.cuny.edu
Wilma Jones, Director

A public four-year college with 33 special education students out of a total of 11,136. Priority registration, test accommodations and tutoring.

3359 Columbia College
Disability Services
Ste 802
2920 Broadway
New York, NY 10027-7164   212-730-2522
                                  FAX 212-854-3448
                              http://www.columbia.edu
                     e-mail: disability@columbia.edu

Susan Cheer, Director
Colleen Lewis, Program Coordinator
Lee Bollinger, President
Four-year college that offers disability services to its students.

3360   Columbia-Greene Community College
4400 State Route 23
Hudson, NY 12534-4180   518-828-4181
                                        FAX 518-822-2015
                                   http://www.sunycgcc.edu

James Campion, President
Pat Nobes, Alternative Learning

A public two-year college in upstate New York with an enrollment of about 1,800. Services available to students with a documented learning disability include various academic accommodations, peer tutoring and academic counselling. Six developmental courses are offered in reading, math, English, and study skills.

3361   Concordia College: New York
Connections
171 White Plains Rd
Bronxville, NY 10708-1998   914-337-9300
                                        FAX 914-395-4500
                                   http://www.concordia-ny.edu
                                   e-mail: ghg@concordia-ny.edu

Viji George, president
Michael Weschler, Assistant Director
Kathleen Suss, Administrator

3362   Cornell University
Student Disability Services
420 C Cc Garden Avenue Ext
Ithaca, NY 14853   607-245-4636
                                        FAX 607-255-1562
                                        TDD:607-255-7665
                                   http://www.cornell.edu
                                   e-mail: info@cornell.edu

Helene Selco, Director
Nancy Jerabek, Office Manager

Cornell University is committed to ensuring that students with disabilities have equal access to all university programs and activities. Policy and procedures have been developed to provide students with as much independence as possible, to preserve confidentiality, and to provide students with disabilities the same exceptional opportunities available to all Cornell students.

3363   Corning Community College
1 Academic Dr
Corning, NY 14830-3299   607-936-3749
                                           800-358-7171
                                        FAX 607-962-9485
                                        TDD:607-962-9459
                                        TTY: 607-962-9459
                                   http://www.corning-cc.edu
                                   e-mail: northop@corning-cc.edu
Floyd Amann, Administrator
Dr. Katherin Douglas, President

A public two-year community college. There are approximately 100 LD students out of a student body of 4,500. A variety of services are available to students with LD, including specialized advising and registration, individualized tutoring, academic advising, and accommodations. Also on campus: Kurzweil reading machines, voice activated word processing, etc.

3364   Dowling College
Program for Potentially Gifted
150 Idle Hour Blvd
Oakdale, NY 11769-1999   631-244-3000
                                        FAX 631-563-7831
                                   http://www.dowling.edu
                                   e-mail: strached@dowling.edu

Drew Weidhorn, Vice Chairman
MK Schneid, Assistant Director
Michael P. Puorro, Chairman and President
Academic program to help college students with LD develop strategies for success. They work one-on-one with graduate students.

3365   Dutchess Community College
53 Pendell Rd
Poughkeepsie, NY 12601-1595   845-431-8000
                                           800-378-9707
                                        FAX 845-431-8981
                                   http://www.sunydutchess.edu
                                   e-mail: webmaster@sunydutchess.edu
D David Conklin, President

A public two-year college with 45 special education students out of a total of 7,511.

3366   Erie Community College: South Campus
Special Education Department
4041 Southwestern Blvd
Orchard Park, NY 14127-2199   716-851-1003
                                        FAX 716-851-1629
                                        TDD:716-851-1831
                                   http://www.ecc.edu
                                   e-mail: adamsjm@ecc.edu

Jack Quinn, Counselor
William Reuter, CEO

A public two-year college with 200 special education students out of a total of 3,455.

3367   Farmingdale State University
2350 Broadhollow Rd
Farmingdale, NY 11735-1021   631-420-2000
                                        FAX 631-420-2689
                                        TDD:631-420-2623
                                   http://www.farmingdale.edu
                                   e-mail: dss@farmingdale.edu

W Hubert Keen, Director
Kim Birnholz CRC, Counselor
Jonathan Gibralter, President
Our services are designed to meet the unique educational needs of currently enrolled students with documented permanent or temporary disabilities. The Office of Support Services is dedicated to the principle that equal opportunity be afforded each student to realize his/her fullest potential.

3368   Finger Lakes Community College
4355 Lakeshore Dr
Canandaigua, NY 14424-8395   585-394-3500
                                        FAX 585-394-5005
                                   http://www.fingerlakes.edu
                                   e-mail: admissions@flcc.edu
Daniel Hayes, President

Provides services such as pre-admission counseling, academic advisement, tutorials, computer assistance, workshops, peer counseling and support groups. The college does not offer a formal program but aids students in arranging appropriate accommodations.

3369   Fordham University
Disabled Student Services
Room 201
Keating Hall
Bronx, NY 10458   718-817-1000
                                        FAX 718-367-7598
                                        TDD:718-817-0655
                                   http://www.fordham.edu
                                   e-mail: disabilityservices@fordham.edu
Robert Gomprecht, Director
Stephen Freedman, Ph.D., Provost

The Office of Disability Services collaborates with students, faculty and staff to ensure appropriate services for students with disabilities. The University will make reasonable accommodations, and provide appropriate aids.

3370   **Fulton-Montgomery Community College**
2805 State Highway 67
Johnstown, NY 12095-3790   518-736-3622
                                       FAX 518-762-4334
                                    http://www.fmcc.suny.edu
                              e-mail: efosmire@fmcc.suny.edu
Ann Day, Coordinator
Dustin Swanger, Ed.D, President

A public two-year college with 76 special education students out of a total of 1,748.

3371   **Genesee Community College**
SUNY (State University of New York) Systems
1 College Rd
Batavia, NY 14020-9704   585-343-0055
                                       FAX 585-343-4541
                                    http://www.genessee.edu
                           e-mail: admissions@genessee.suny.edu
Stewart Steiner, President
Stephanie Smythe, Counselor
James M. Sunser, Ed.D., President
A public two-year college with 78 special education students out of a total of 3,212.

3372   **Hamilton College**
198 College Hill Rd
Clinton, NY 13323-1295   315-859-4011
                                       FAX 315-859-4083
                                       TDD:315-859-4294
                                    http://www.hamilton.edu
                              e-mail: rbellmay@hamilton.edu
Joan Stewart, President
Louise Peckingham, Compliance Officer

Four year college that offfers services for learning disabled students.

3373   **Harmony Heights**
PO Box 569
Oyster Bay, NY 11771-569   516-922-4060
                                       FAX 516-922-6126
                                 http://www.harmonyheights.org
                        e-mail: eb@harmonyheightsschool.com
Ellen Benson ACSW PD, Executive Director
Denis Garbo, president

A therapeutic residential and day school serving girls with emotional needs that cannot be adequately served in the standard high school setting.

3374   **Herkimer County Community College**
100 Reservoir Rd
Herkimer, NY 13350-1598   315-866-0300
                                       FAX 315-866-7253
                                       TDD:888-GO4HCCC
                                    http://www.hccc.ntcnet.com
                              e-mail: coylemf@hcc.suny.edu
Ravil Veli, LD Specialist
Suzanne Paddock, Counselor
Linda Veigh, Administrator
A public two-year college with approximately 200 documented disabled students. Tuition and fees: $2,450 (annual basis); overall enrollment 95-96: $2,445 (1,857 full time/588 part-time).

3375   **Hofstra University**
Program for Academic Learning Skills
212 Memorial Hall
Hempstead, NY 11549-1000   516-463-7075
                                       FAX 516-463-7070
                                    http://www.hofstra.edu
                              e-mail: pals@hofstra.edu
Robyn Weiss, Director
Stuart Rabinowitz, president
Herman A. Berliner, Ph.D., Vice President

Provides auxillary aids and compensatory services to certified learning disabled students who have been accepted to the University through regular admissions. These services are provided free of charge.

3376   **Houghton College**
Student Academic Services
1 Willard Ave
Houghton, NY 14744-8732   585-567-9200
                                       FAX 585-567-9572
                                    http://www.houghton.edu
                              e-mail: admission@houghton.edu
Shirley Mullen, Director
Irene Willis, Director

Four year college that provides academic support to disabled students.

3377   **Hudson Valley Community College**
Disabilities Resource Center
80 Vandenburgh Ave
Troy, NY 12180-6096   518-629-4822
                                       FAX 518-629-7586
                                       TDD:518-629-7596
                                       TTY: 1 8-7 3-5 48
                                    http://www.hvcc.edu
                              e-mail: editor@hvcc.edu
Andrew J Matonak, Director
Carolyn G. Cutis, Vice President

A public two-year college with 28 special education students out of a total of 10,106.

3378   **Hunter College of the City University of New York**
Office for Students with Disabilities
695 Park Ave
New York, NY 10045   212-772-4000
                                       FAX 212-650-3456
                                       TTY: 212-650-3230
                                    http://www.hunter.cuny.edu
                           e-mail: icitdir@hunter.cuny.edu
Sandra LaPorta, Director

Provides services to over 250 students with learning disabilities. A learning disability is a disorder in one or more of the basic psychological processes involved in understanding or in using spoken or written language.

3379   **Iona College**
College Assistance Program
715 North Ave
New Rochelle, NY 10801-1890   914-633-2077
                                            800-231-4662
                                       FAX 914-633-2642
                                    http://www.iona.edu
                              e-mail: lrobertello@iona.edu
James Liguori, Director
Joseph E. Nyre, PhD, President
Brian Nickerson, PhD, Provost
Offers a comprehensive support program for students with learning disabilities. CAP is designed to encourage success by providing instruction tailored to individual strenghts and needs.

3380   **Ithaca College**
110 Towers Concourse
Ithaca, NY 14850   607-274-1005
                                       FAX 607-274-3957
                                    http://www.ithaca.edu/sds
                              e-mail: sds@ithaca.edu
Linda Uhll, Acting Director
Tom Rochon, President

3381 **Ithaca College: Speech and Hearing Clinic**
953 Danby Road
Ithaca, NY 14850 607-274-3714
FAX 607-274-3237
http://www.ithaca.edu
e-mail: webmaster@ithaca.edu
Thomas R. Rochon, President

Offers a variety of services to students with disabilities including notetakers, extended testing time, counseling services, and special accommodations.

3382 **Jamestown Community College**
State University of New York Systems
PO Box 20
Jamestown, NY 14702-20 716-665-5220
800-388-8557
FAX 716-665-9110
http://www.sunyjcc.edu
e-mail: admissions@mail.sunyjcc.edu
Nancy Callahan, Disability Support
Gregory Cinque, President
Frank Berarducci, Assosiate Director
A public two-year college with 41 special education students out of a total of 4,541.

3383 **Jefferson Community College**
Jefferson Community College
Coffeen St
Watertown, NY 13601 315-786-2200
888-435-6522
FAX 315-786-0158
http://www.sunyjefferson.edu
e-mail: strainham@sunyjefferson.edu
Carol Mc Coy, Learning Skills/Disability
Joseph Olson, President

A public two-year college whose focus is teaching and learning. Thr ough educational excellence, innovative services and community partnerships. Jefferson advances the quality of life of our students and community.

3384 **John Jay College of Criminal Justice of the City University of New York**
Rm 30109n
445 W 59th St
New York, NY 10019-1104 212-237-8000
FAX 212-237-8901
TDD:212-237-8233
http://www.jjay.cuny.edu
e-mail: admiss@jjay.cuny.edu
Jeremy Travis, Coordinator
John Teravis, President

An independent two-year college with 67 special education students out of a total of 7,912.

3385 **Kildonan School**
425 Morse Hill Rd
Amenia, NY 12501-5209 845-373-8111
FAX 845-373-9793
http://www.kildonan.org
e-mail: admissions@kildonan.org
Benjamin Powers, Headmaster

Offers a fully accredited College Preparatory curriculum. The school is co-educational, enrolling boarding students in Grades 6-Postgraduate and day students in Grade 2-Postgraduate. Provides daily one-on-one Orton-Gillingham tutoring to build skills in reading, writing, and spelling. Daily independent reading and writing work reinforces skills and improves study habits. Interscholastic sports, horseback riding, clubs and community service enhance self-confidence.

3386 **Learning Disabilities Program**
ADELPHI UNIVERSITY
Adelphi University
Garden City, NY 11530 516-877-4710
800-233-5144
FAX 516-877-4711
http://academics.adelphi.edu/ldprog
e-mail: LDprogram@adelphi.edu
Susan Spencer Farinacci, Assistant Dean/Director
Janet Cohen, Assistant Director

The programs professional staff, all with advanced degrees, provide individual tutoring and counseling to learning disabled students who are completely mainstream in the University.

3387 **Manhattan College: Specialized Resource Center**
Room 300
Miguel Hall
Riverdale, NY 10471 718-862-8000
FAX 718-862-7808
http://www.manhattan.edu
William J Bisset Jr, VP Enrollment Management
Brennan O'Donnell, Ph.D, President
Thomas D. O'Malley, Chairman
The Specialized Resource Center serves all students with special needs including individuals with temporary disabilities, such as those resulting from injury or surgery. The mission of the center is to ensure educational opportunity for all students with special needs by providing access to full participation in all aspects of the campus life.

3388 **Maplebrook School**
Academic Program
5142 Route 22
Amenia, NY 12501-5357 845-373-8191
FAX 845-373-7029
http://www.maplebrookschool.org
e-mail: admin@maplebrookschool.org
Paul Scherer, Head of School
Mark J. Metzger, Chairman

The school offers several levels of academic achievement toward which a student may strive. Our curriculum follows the New York State guidelines, the teachers are trained in a multi-sensory approach and provide a small, nurturing classroom in which each student can reach their full potential.

3389 **Maria College**
700 New Scotland Ave
Albany, NY 12208-1798 518-482-3111
FAX 518-438-7170
http://www.mariacollege.edu
e-mail: laurieg@mariacollege.edu
Dr. Lea Johnson, President
Mary Riker, Contact

An independent two-year college with 13 special education students out of a total of 875.

3390 **Marist College**
Learning Disabilities Support Program
3399 North Rd
Poughkeepsie, NY 12601-1387 845-575-3000
FAX 845-471-6213
http://www.marist.edu
e-mail: specserv@marist.edu
Dennis J Murray, Director

Provides a comprehensive range of academic support services and accommodations which promote the full integration of students with disabilities into the mainstream college environment.

3391 Marymount Manhattan College
Academic Access and Learning Disabilities Program
221 E 71st St
New York, NY 10021-4597   212-517-0400
                                 FAX 212-517-0567
                              http://www.mmm.edu
                        e-mail: jbonomo@mmm.edu
Judson Shaver, Acting Director

The College's program for students with learning disabilities is designed to provide a structure that fosters academic success.

3392 Medaille College
Disability Services Department
18 Agassiz Cir
Buffalo, NY 14214-2695   716-880-2000
                                 800-292-1582
                                 FAX 716-884-0291
                              http://www.medaille.edu
                  e-mail: sageadmissions@medaille.edu
Joseph W Bascuas, President

Offers a variety of services to students with disabilities including notetakers, extended testing time, counseling services, and special accommodations.

3393 Mercy College
Star Program
555 Broadway
Dobbs Ferry, NY 10522-1189   914-674-7200
                                    FAX 914-674-7395
                              http://www.mercynet.edu
               e-mail: admissions@merlin.mercynet.edu
Kimberly Cline, President

Helps people with learning disabilities.

3394 Mohawk Valley Community College
1101 Sherman Dr
Utica, NY 13501-5394   315-792-5400
                              FAX 315-731-5858
                              TDD:315-792-5413
                              http://www.mvcc.edu
                        e-mail: dowsland@mvcc.edu
Randall Van Wagoner, Learning Disabilities Specialist
Elaine M. Falvo, Chairman
Michael Schafer, President
MVCC'S LD program is staffed by a half time LD specialist. Service provided to students with learning disabilities include advocacy, information and referral to on and off campus services, testing accommodations, taped materials, loaner tape recorders and note takers.

3395 Molloy College
1000 Hempstead Avenue
Rockville Centre, NY 11571-5002   516-678-5000
                                          888-4MALLOY
                                          FAX 516-678-2284
                              http://www.molloy.edu
                        e-mail: tforker@molloy.edu
Therese Forker, Director
Barbara Nirrengarten, Assistant Director
Drew Bogner, President
STEEP (Success Through Expanded Education), is a program specifically designed to assist students with learning disabilities and enable them to become successful students. The program offers the student the opportunities to learn techniques which alleviate some of their problems. Special emphasis is directed toward the development of positive self-esteem.

3396 Nassau Community College
Disabled Support Department
1 Education Dr
Garden City, NY 11530-6793   516-222-7501
                                     FAX 516-572-9874
                                     TTY: 513-572-7617
                              http://www.ncc.edu
                        e-mail: schimsj@ncc.edu
Janis Schimsky, Director Students w/Disabilities
Donald P. Astrab, President

Our goal is to help students achieve success while they are attending Nassau Community College by learning to become their own advocates through talking with their professors about their disability and the accommodations they need for the course.

3397 Nazareth College of Rochester
Disability Support Services
4245 East Ave
Rochester, NY 14618-3790   585-389-2525
                                   FAX 716-586-2452
                              http://www.naz.edu
                        e-mail: avhouse@naz.edu
Daan Braveman, President

Four-year college that offers students with a learning disablility support and services.

3398 New York City College of Technology
Student Support Services Program
Ste A-237
300 Jay St
Brooklyn, NY 11201-1909   718-260-5470
                                  FAX 718-260-5631
                                  TTY: 718-260-5443
          http://www.citytech.cuny.edu/students/support
                  e-mail: ffogelman@citytech.cuny.edu
Russell K. Hotzler,Phd, President

The Student Support Services Program, located in A-237, provides comprehensive services to students with disabilities. The array of interventions includes counseling, tutorials, workshops, use of computer lab with adaptive software, testing accommodations, sign-language interpreters, captioning, and implementation of accommodations as per documentation.

3399 New York Institute of Technology: Old Westbury
PO Box 8000
Old Westbury, NY 11568-8000   516-686-1000
                                      800-345-NYIT
                                      FAX 516-686-7789
                              http://www.nyit.edu
                        e-mail: eguillano@nyit.edu
Edward Guiliano, President
Alexandra Logue PhD, VP Academic Affairs

Offers the Vocational Independence Progran for students who have significant learning disabilities.

3400 New York University
Henry and Lucy Moses Center
70,WashingtonSquare South
New York, NY 10012   212-998-4980
                             FAX 212-995-4114
                              http://www.nyu.edu/csd
                        e-mail: lc83@nyu.edu
Lakshmi Clark MA, CSD Coordinator
Scott Hornack, Contact
John Sexton, President
The Henry and Lucy Moses Center for Students with Disabilities (CSD) functions to determine qualified disability status and to assist students in obtaining appropriate accommodations and services. CSD operates according to the Independent Living Philosophy, and thus strives in its policies and practices to empower each student to become an independent as possible. Our services are designed to encourage independence, backed by a strong system of supports.

3401 New York University Medical Center
Learning Diagnostic Program
550 First Avenue
New York, NY 10016-4901   212-263-7300
                                  FAX 212-263-7721
                    http://www.med.nyu.edu
Larry A Chinitz MD, President
Becky Chow, Assistant Professor

Assessment team, neurology, neuro-psychology, psychiatry services are offered.

3402 Niagara County Community College
3111 Saunders Settlement Rd
Sanborn, NY 14132-9460   716-614-6222
                                  FAX 716-614-5954
                    http://www.niagaracc.suny.edu
James Klyczek, President

The College provides reasonable accommodations for students with disabilties, including those with specific learning disabilities. Students with learning disabilities must provide documentation by a qualified professional that proves thry are eligible for accommodations.

3403 Niagara University
Support Services Department
1st Floor
Seton Hall
Niagara University, NY 14109   716-285-1212
                                  800-462-2111
                                  FAX 716-286-8063
                    http://www.niagara.edu
                    e-mail: ds@niagara.edu
Diane Stoelting, Specialized Support Services
Joseph L Levesque, C.M., President

Reasonable accommodations are provided to students with disabilities based on documentation of disability. Depending on how the disability impacts the individual, reasonable accommodations may include extended time on tests taken in a separate location with appropriate assistance, notetakes or use of a tape recorder in class, interpreter, textbooks and course materials in alternative format, as well as other academic and non-academic accommodations.

3404 Norman Howard School
Education Enterprise of New York
275 Pinnacle Rd
Rochester, NY 14623-4103   585-334-8010
                                  FAX 585-334-8073
                    http://www.normanhoward.org
                    e-mail: info@normanhoward.org
Rosemary Hodges, Co-Head of School
Linda Lawrence, Co-Head of School
Joseph M Martino, Executive Director
An independent co-educational day school for students with learning disabilities in grades 5-12. An approved special education program by the New York State Education Department and accredited by the New York Association of Independent Schools. Program supports many youngsters with various types of learning disabilities, including dyslexia, non-verbal LD, Asperger's Syndrome, anxiety and ADHD.

3405 North Country Community College
State University of New York
23 Santanoni Ave
Saranac Lake, NY 12983   518-891-2915
                                  888-879-6222
                                  FAX 518-891-2915
                    http://www.nccc.edu
                    e-mail: admissions@nccc.edu
Fred Smith, Learning Lab/Malone
Scott Lambert, Enrollment/Financial Aid Counsel
Gail Rodgers-Rice, President

Located in the Adirondack Olympic Region of northern New York, NCCC is committed to providing a challenging and supportive environment where the aspirations of all can be realized. The college provides a variety of services for students with special needs which includes: specialized advisement, tutors and supplemental instruction, specialized accommodations, technology and equipment to accommodate learning disabilities and other resources.

3406 Onondaga Community College
Disability Services Office
4585 W Seneca Turnpike
Syracuse, NY 13215-2099   315-498-2834
                                  FAX 315-498-2977
                    http://www.sunyocc.edu
                    e-mail: occinfo@sunyocc.edu
Nancy Carr, Director

A public two-year college with 650 students with disabilities.

3407 Orange County Community College
115 South St
Middletown, NY 10940-6437   845-341-4444
                                  FAX 845-341-4998
                    http://www.sunyorange.edu
Bill Richards, President
Melanie Bukovsky, Student Services Advocate

The Office of Special Services for the Disabled provides support services to meet the individual needs of students with disabilities. Such accommodations include oral testing, extended time testing, tape recorded textbooks, writing lab, note-takers and others. Pre-admission counseling ensures accessibility for the qualified student.

3408 Purchase College State University of New York
Special Services Office
735 Anderson Hill Rd
Purchase, NY 10577-1402   914-251-6000
                                  FAX 914-251-6064
                    http://www.purchase.edu
Thomas Schwarz, Coordinator Office Special Svcs
Donna Siegmann, Coordinator Supported Education
Dr. Steve Tyrell, President
Offers a variety of services to students with disabilities including note takers, extended testing time, counseling services, and special accommodations.

3409 Queens College City University of New York
Special Services Office
6530 Kissena Blvd
Flushing, NY 11367-1575   718-997-5000
                                  FAX 718-997-5895
                                  TDD:718-997-5870
                    http://www.qc.edu
                    e-mail: christopher_rosa@qc.edu
Christopher Rosa, Office Director
James L. Muyskens, President

Services include tutoring and notetaking, accommodating testing alternatives, counseling, academic and vocational advisement, as well as diagnostic assessments in order to pinpoint specific deficits.

3410 Readiness Program
New York Institute for Special Education
999 Pelham Pkwy N
Bronx, NY 10469-4905   718-519-7000
                                  FAX 718-231-9314
                    http://www.nyise.org
                    e-mail: bkappen@nyise.org
Bernadette M Kappen PhD, Executive Director

A pre-school that helps children who are developmentally delayed from ages 3 to 5. They have disabilities that include speech impairment, mild orthopedic impairment, or a learning or emotional disability. By providing specialized instruction, intensive therapies and early intervention many are able to be mainstreamed or are placed in a least restrictive educational environment when they reach the age of five.

3411   Rensselaer Polytechnic Institute
110 8th St
Troy, NY 12180-3590   518-276-6000
                                       800-448-6562
                                   FAX 518-276-4072
                                   http://www.rpi.edu
                               e-mail: hamild@rpi.edu
Shirley Ann Jackson, Disabled Student Services

An independent four-year college with 53 learning disabled students out of a total of 6,000.

3412   Rochester Business Institute
1630 Portland Ave
Rochester, NY 14621-3007   585-266-0430
                                       888-741-4271
                                   FAX 585-266-8243
                           http://www.rochester-institute.com
                               e-mail: dpfluke@cci.edu
Carl Silvio, President
Jim Rodriguez, Admissions Representative

An independent two-year college with 12 special education students out of a total of 528.

3413   Rochester Institute of Technology
Structured Monitoring Program
1 Lomb Memorial Drive
Rochester, NY 14623-5603   585-475-2411
                                   FAX 585-475-2215
                                   http://www.rit.edu
                               e-mail: smacst@rit.edu
Lisa Fraser, Chair Leraning Support Services
Pamela Lloyd, Disability Services Coordinator
Albert Simone, President
An independent four-year college offers a wide variety of accommodations and support services to students with documented disabilities.

3414   Rockland Community College
145 College Rd
Suffern, NY 10901-3699   845-574-4000
                                   FAX 845-574-4424
                           http://www.sunyrockland.edu
Xi Shi, Learning Disabilities Specialist
Cliff Wood, President

A public two-year college with 300 special education students out of a total of 5,500. The office of Disability Services provides a variety of support services tailored to meet the individual needs and learning styles of students with documented learning disabilities.

3415   Rose F Kennedy Center
Albert Einstein College of Medicine
1410 Pelham Pkwy S
Bronx, NY 10461-1116   718-430-8522
                                   FAX 718-904-1162
                           http://www.einstein.yu.edu.com
Robert Marion, Director

Mission is to help children with disabilities reach their full potential and to support parents in their efforts to get the best care, education, and treatment for their children.

3416   Ryken Educational Center
Xaverian High School
7100 Shore Rd
Brooklyn, NY 11209-1037   718-836-7100
                                   http://www.xaverian.org
                           e-mail: ctrasborg@xaverian.org
Carol Trasborg, Principal

Provides programs and services for high school students of average, or above-average intelligence who have specific learning disabilities. Its mission is to challenge and support learning disabled young men so that they achieve academically at their intellectual level. Our goal is to turn them into effective life-long learners who will go on to college.

3417   SUNY Canton
34 Cornell Dr
Campus Center 233
Canton, NY 13617-1098   315-386-7392
                                   FAX 315-379-3877
                                   TDD:315-386-7943
                                   http://www.canton.edu
                               e-mail: leev@canton.edu
Veigh Mehan Lee, Accomodative Services Director

Four year state college that provides resources and services to learning disabled students.

3418   SUNY Cobleskill
142 Schenectady Ave
Cobleskill, NY 12043   518-255-5282
                                       800-295-8988
                                   FAX 518-255-6430
                                   TDD:518-255-5454
                                   TTY: 518-255-6500
                           http://www.cobleskill.edu/dss
                           e-mail: dss@cobleskill.edu
Lynn Abarno, Disability Support Services Coor

A public two-year college with a Bachelor of Technology component in agriculture. Approximately 170 students identify themselves as having a learning disability out of the 2,000 total population. Tuition $3,500 in state/$8,300 out of state. Academic support services and accommodations for documented LD students.

3419   SUNY Institute of Technology: Utica/Rome
100 Seymour Road
Utica, NY 13502   315-792-7500
                                       866-278-6948
                                   FAX 315-792-7837
                                   http://www.sunyit.edu
                           e-mail: admissions@sunyit.edu
Marybeth Lyonsvan, Interim Director Admissions
Tat Saranr, Business Office Secretary

Upper division bachelor's degree in a variety of professional and technical majors; masters degree and continuing educational coursework is also available.

3420   Sage College
140 New Scotland Ave
Albany, NY 12208   518-292-8624
                                   FAX 578-292-1910
                                   http://www.sage.edu
                               e-mail: chowed@sage.edu
David Chowenhill, Director
Dr. Susan Scrimshaw, President

Four year college that offers services to students with a learning disability.

3421   Schenectady County Community College
Disability Services Department
78 Washington Ave
Schenectady, NY 12305-2294   518-381-1200
                                   FAX 518-346-0379
                                   http://www.sunysccc.edu

Gabriel Basil, Coordinator
Dr. Quintin Bullock, President

Access for All program is designed to make programs and facilities accessible to all students in pursuit of their academic goals. Disabled Student Services seeks to ensure accessible educational opportunities in accordance with individual needs. Offers general support services and program services such as: exam assistance, special scheduling, adaptive equipment, readers, taping assistance and more.

3422   Schermerhorn Program
New York Institute for Special Education
999 Pelham Pkwy N
Bronx, NY 10469-4905   718-519-7000
                                          FAX 718-231-9314
                                          http://www.nyise.org
                                          e-mail: bkappen@nyise.org
Bernadette M Kappen PhD, Executive Director

It offers diverse educational services to meet the needs of children who are legally blind, from the ages of 5 to 21. Students participate in individually designed academic and modified academic programs that emphasize independence.

3423   Siena College
515 Loudon Rd
Loudonville, NY 12211-1462   518-785-6537
                                          1-888-287-43
                                          FAX 518-783-4293
                                          http://www.siena.edu
                                          e-mail: jpellegrini@siena.edu
Richard Ives, Services for Student Director
Kevin Mackin, Administrator

Four year college that offers programs for the learning disabled.

3424   St. Bonaventure University
Teaching & Learning Center
3261 West State Road
St Bonaventure, NY 14778   716-375-2066
                                          800-462-5050
                                          FAX 716-375-2072
                                          http://www.sbu.edu
                                          e-mail: nmatthew@sbu.edu
Nancy Matthews, Coordinator
Margaret Carney, President

Catholic University in the Franciscan tradition. Independent coeducational institution offering programs through its schools of arts and sciences, business administration, education and journalism and mass communication. 2500 students, tuition $16,210, room and board $6,190.

3425   St. Lawrence University
23 Romoda Dr
Canton, NY 13617-1501   800-285-1856
                                          FAX 315-229-5502
                                          http://www.stlawu.edu
                                          e-mail: jmeagher@mail.stlawu.edu
Daniel F Sullivan, President
Liv Regosin, Director of Advising

The Office of Special Needs is here to ensure that all students with disabilities can freely and actively participate in all facets of University life, to coordinate support services and programs that enable students with disabilities to reach their educational potential, and to increase the level of awareness among all members of the University so that students with disabilites are able to perform at a level limited only by their abilities, not their disabilities.

3426   St. Thomas Aquinas College
Pathways
125 Route 340
Sparkill, NY 10976-1050   845-398-4100
                                          FAX 845-359-8136
                                          http://www.stac.edu
                                          e-mail: pathways@stac.edu
Margaret Fitzpatrick, Director
Amelia DeMarco MD, Associate Director
Sr. Margaret Carney, President
Comprehensive support program for selected college students with learning disabilites and/or ADHD. Services include individual professional mentoring, study groups, academic counseling, priority registration, assistive technology, and a specialized summer program prior to the first semester.

3427   State University of New York College Technology at Delhi
2 Main St
Delhi, NY 13753   607-746-4593
                                          800-96-DELHI
                                          FAX 607-746-4004
                                          http://www.delhi.edu
                                          e-mail: weinbell@delhi.edu
Linda Weinberg, Disabilities Coordinator

Provide services for students with disabilities. Alternate test-taking arrangements, adapted equipment, assistive technology, accessibility information, note taking services, reading services, tutorial assistance, interpreting services, accessble parking and elevators, sounseling, guidance and support, refferal information and advocacy services, workshops and support groups.

3428   State University of New York College at Brockport
State University of New York
350 New Campus Dr
Brockport, NY 14420-2914   585-395-5409
                                          800-382-8447
                                          FAX 585-395-5291
                                          TDD:585-395-5409
                                          http://www.brockport.edu
                                          e-mail: osdoffic@brockport.edu
Maryellen Post, Coordinator
John R. Halstead, PhDÿ, President

Provides support and assistance to students with medical, physical, emotional or learning disabilities, specially those experiencing problems in areas such as academic environment.

3429   State University of New York College of Agriculture and Technology
State Route 7
Cobleskill, NY 12043   518-255-5011
                                          800-295-8988
                                          FAX 518-255-6430
                                          TDD:518-255-5454
                                          TTY: 518-255-5454
                                          http://www.cobleskill.edu
                                          e-mail: labarno@cobleskill.edu
Lynn Abarno, Support Services Coordinator
Dr. Candace Vancko, President
Nancy Deusen, Executive Director
The primary objective is to develop and maintain a supportive campus environment that promotes academic achievement and personal growth for students with disabilities. Services provide by the office are based on each student's documentation and are tailored to each student's unique individual needs.

3430   State University of New York: Albany
1400 Washington Ave
Albany, NY 12222-0100   518-442-5490
                                          FAX 518-442-5400
                                          TDD:518-442-3366
                                          http://www.albany.edu

Carolyn Malloch, Asst Dir Disability Resource Ctr
Nancy Belowich-Negron, Director Disability Resource
Ctr

4-year public University.

3431   State University of New York: Buffalo
Special Services Department
1300 Elmwood Ave
Buffalo, NY 14222   716-878-4000
                                      FAX 716-645-3473
                                      TTY: 716-645-2616
                                http://www.buffalostate.edu
                            e-mail: savinomr@buffalostate.edu
Marianne Savino, Coordinator Special Services

The Office of Disability Services (ODS) is the University at
Buffalo's center for coordinating services and accommodations to ensure accessiblity and usability of all programs,
services and activities of UB by people with disabilities, and
is a resource for information and advocacy toward their full
participation in all aspects of campus life.

3432   State University of New York: Geneseo College
1 College Cir
Geneseo, NY 14454-1401   585-245-5112
                                      FAX 585-245-5032
                                 http://disability.geneseo.edu
                              e-mail: admissions@geneseo.edu
Tabitha Buggie-Hunt, Director Disability Services
Janet Jackson, Support Staff

To provide qualified students with disabilities, whether temporary or permanent, equal and comprehensive access to
college-wide programs, services, and campus facilities by
offering academic support, advisement, and removal of architectural and attitudinal barriers.

3433   State University of New York: Oswego
Disability Services Office
210 Swetman Hall
Oswego, NY 13126   315-312-3358
                                      FAX 315-312-2943
                                   http://www.oswego.edu
                               e-mail: dss@oswego.edu
Starr Knapp, Interim Coordinator

A public four-year college of arts and sciences currently
serving 140 students identified with disabling conditions.
Total enrollment is approximately 8,000. Full time coordinator of academic support services for students with disabilities works with students on an individual basis.

3434   State University of New York: Plattsburgh
Student Support Services
101 Broad St
Plattsburgh, NY 12901-2637   518-564-2000
                                      FAX 518-564-2807
                                  http://www.plattsburgh.edu
                        e-mail: michele.carpentier@plattsburgh.edu
John Ettling, President

Academic support program funded by the United States Department of Education. Staffed by caring and commited professional whose mission is to provide services for students
with disabilities.

3435   State University of New York: Potsdam
Sisson Hall
Potsdam, NY 13676   315-267-2000
                                      FAX 315-267-3268
                                      TDD:315-267-2071
                                      TTY: 315-267-2071
                                   http://www.potsdam.edu
                               e-mail: housese@potsdam.edu
Sharon House, Academic Coordinator
John F. Schwaller, president

A public four-year college with approximately 200 students
with disabilities out of a total of 4,000.

3436   Stony Brook University
Disability Support Services
128 Educational Communications Ctr
Stony Brook, NY 11794-0001   631-632-6748
                                      FAX 631-632-6747
                                      TTY: 631-632-6748
                                   http://www.sunysb.edu
                          e-mail: dss@notes.cc.sunysb.edu
Donna Molloy, Interim Director
Margaret Perno, Senior Counselor

The Office of Disability Support Services provides assistance for both students and employees. It coordinates advocacy and support services for students with disabilities in
their academic and student life activities. Assuring campus
accessibility, assisting with academic accommodations and
providing assistive devices are important components of the
programs.

3437   Suffolk County Community College: Ammerman
Special Services
533 College Rd
Selden, NY 11784-2899   631-451-4045
                                      FAX 631-451-4473
                                      TTY: 631-451-4041
                                   http://www.sunysuffolk.edu
Shaun L McKay, President
Marlene Boyce, Assistant Director
Arlene Zink, Office Manager
Office of services for students with disabilities.

3438   Suffolk County Community College: Eastern Campus
Speonk-Riverhead Rd
Riverhead, NY 11901   631-548-2500
                                      FAX 631-369-2641
                                   http://www.sunysuffolk.edu
Richard D Britton, Counselor
Dr. Shaun L. McKay, president

The Eastern Campus is an accessible, open admissions institution. Services are provided to learning disabled students to
allow them the same or equivalent educational experiences
as nondisabled students.

3439   Suffolk County Community College: Western Campus
Crooked Hill Rd
Brentwood, NY 11717   631-851-6700
                                      FAX 631-851-6509
                                   http://www.sunysuffolk.edu
ÿDr. Shirley Pippins, President

The goal of Suffolk Community College with regard to students with disabilities is to equalize educational opportunities by minimizing physical, psychological and learning
barriers. We attempt to provide as typical a college experience as is possible, encouraging students to achieve academically through the provision of special services, auxillary
aids, or reasonable program modifications.

3440   Sullivan County Community College
Learning & Student Development Services
112 College Rd
Loch Sheldrake, NY 12759-5723   845-434-5750
                                          800-577-5243
                                      FAX 845-434-4806
                                   http://www.sullivan.suny.edu
Mamie Howard-Gollardy, President

SCCC is fully committed to institutions accessability for individuals with disabilities. Students who wish to obtain particular services or accommodations should communicate their needs and concerns as early as possible. These may include, but are not limited to, extended time for tests, oral examinations, reader and notetaker services, campus maps, and elevator privileges. Books on tape may be ordered through recordings for the blind. Appropriate documentation needed.

3441 Syracuse University
Services For Students with Disabilities
Room 309
804 University Ave
Syracuse, NY 13244   315-443-1870
                                   FAX 315-443-4410
                                   TDD:315-443-1312
                                http://www.syracuse.edu
                             e-mail: dtwillia@syr.edu
James Shea, Coordinator Academic Services
Cesar Reyes, Administrative Assistant

The office of disability services provides and coordinates services for students with documented disabilities. Students must provide current documentation of their disability in order to receive disability services and reasonable accommodations.

3442 The Gow School
2491 Emery Road
P.O. Box 85
South Wales, NY 14139-0085   716-652-3450
                                   FAX 716-652-3457
                                   http://www.gow.org
M. Bradley Rogers, Jr., Headmaster

Boarding school for boys, grades 7-12, with dyslexia and other language based learning disabilities.

3443 Trocaire College
360 Choate Ave
Buffalo, NY 14220-2094   716-826-1200
                                   FAX 716-828-6107
                                http://www.trocaire.edu
Paul Hurley, President

An independent two-year college with 3 special education students out of a total of 1,056.

3444 Ulster County Community College
Student Support Services
Cottekill Rd
Stone Ridge, NY 12484   845-687-5000
                                       800-724-0833
                                   FAX 845-687-5292
                                http://www.sunyulster.edu
Donald C Katt, President

The Student Support Services program promotes student success for students who are academically disadvantaged, economically disadvantaged, first-generation college students, and or students with disabilities. The goals of the program are to increase the retention, graduation, and transfer rates of those enrolled.

3445 University of Albany
Campus Center 130
Albany, NY 12222   518-442-3300
                                   FAX 518-442-3583
                                   TDD:518-442-3366
                                http://www.albany.edu
                        e-mail: cmalloch@uamail.albany.edu
Carolyn Malloch, Learning Disability Specialist
George M. Philipÿ, President

Offers a full time Learning Disability Specialist to work with students that have learning disabilities and or attention deficit disorder. The specialist offers individual appointments to develop study and advocacy skills.

3446 Utica College
1600 Burrstone Rd
Utica, NY 13502-4857   315-792-3032
                                   FAX 315-223-2504
                                   http://www.utica.edu
                             e-mail: KHenkel@utica.edu
Kateri Henkel, Learning Services Director

Provides students with disabilities individualized learning accommodations designed to meet the academic needs of the student. Counseling support and the development of new strategies for the learning challenges posed by college level work are an integral part of the services offered through Academic Support Services.

3447 Van Cleve Program
The New York Institute for Special Education
999 Pelham Pkwy
Bronx, NY 10469-4905   718-519-7000
                                   FAX 718-231-9314
                                   http://www.nyise.org
Bernadette M Kappen PhD, Executive Director
Thomas Bergett, Ph.D, Assistant Executive Director

The children of this program have emotional or learning difficulties. Our goal is to reduce the behavioral and learning deficits of students by providing academic and social skills necessary to enter less restrictive programs.

3448 Vassar College
124 Raymond Ave
Poughkeepsie, NY 12604   845-437-7000
                                   FAX 845-437-7187
                                   TTY: 845-437-5458
                                   http://www.vassar.edu
                             e-mail: guthrie@vassar.edu
Frances D Fergusson, Director
Catharine Bond Hill, President

Offers a variety of services to students with disabilities including note takers, extended testing time, counseling services, and special accommodations.

3449 Wagner College
1 Campus Rd
Staten Island, NY 10301-4495   718-390-3100
                                       800-221-1010
                                   FAX 718-390-3467
                                   http://www.wagner.edu
Richard Guarasci, Director
Chris Davis, Administrative Assistant Counsel

An independent four-year college with 25 special education students out of a total of 1,272. There is an additional fee for the special education program in addition to the regular tuition.

3450 Westchester Community College
75 Grasslands Rd
Valhalla, NY 10595-1693   914-606-6600
                                   FAX 914-785-6540
                                   http://www.sunywcc.edu
Alan Seidman MD, Special Services
Gloria Leon, Director

Students with Disabilities parallels the mission of WCC to be accessable, community centered, comprehensive, adaptable and dedicated to lifelong learning for all students. Full participation for students with disabilities is encouraged.

3451 Xaverian High School
Legacy Program
7100 Shore Rd
Brooklyn, NY 11209-1098   718-491-0800
                                   http://www.xaverian.org
                             e-mail: ctrasborg@xaverian.org
Carol Trasborg, Principal

Our mission is to challenge and support learning disabled young men so that they achieve academically at their intellectual level. Our goal is to turn them into effective life-long learners who will go on to college.

North Carolina

3452 Appalachian State University
Learning Disability Program
PO Box 32158
Boone, NC 28608-2087 828-262-3056
FAX 828-262-7904
http://www.ods.appstate.edu
e-mail: wehnerst@appstate.edu
Maranda R. Maxey, Director Disability Services
Courtney K. McWhorter, Assistant Director

The Office of Disability Services (ODS) assists students with indentified disabilities by providing the support they need to become successful college graduates. ODS provides academic advising, alternative testing, assistance with technology, tutoring, practical solutions to learning problems, counseling, self-concept building and career exploration.

3453 Bennett College
900 E Washington St
Greensboro, NC 27401-3298 336-571-2100
800-413-5323
FAX 336-517-2228
http://www.bennett.edu
Linda Mack, Support Services
Johnnetta Cole, President

An independent four-year college with 10 special education students out of a total of 568.

3454 Brevard College
Office for Students with Special Needs & Disab
1 Brevard College Dr
Brevard, NC 28712-3497 800-527-9090
FAX 828-884-3790
http://www.brevard.edu
e-mail: admissions@brevard.edu
Drew Van Horn, President

Four year college provides services to special needs students.

3455 Caldwell Community College and Technical Institute
Basic Skills Department
2855 Hickory Blvd
Hudson, NC 28638-2626 828-726-2200
FAX 828-726-2216
http://www.cccti.edu
e-mail: ccrump@cccti.edu
Kenneth Boham, President
Cindy Richards, Administrative Assistant

A public two-year college with 18 special education students out of a total of 2,744.

3456 Catawba College
Learning Disability Department
2300 W Innes St
Salisbury, NC 28144-2488 704-637-4259
800-228-2922
FAX 704-637-4401
http://www.catawba.edu
e-mail: ekgross@catawba.edu
Emily Gross, Director
Julie Baranski, Office Assistant

An independent four-year liberal arts college with an enrollment of 1,400.

3457 Catawba Valley Community College
Student Services Office
2550 Us Highway 70 SE
Hickory, NC 28602-8302 828-327-7000
FAX 828-327-7276
http://www.cvcc.edu
e-mail: dulin@cvcc.edu
Garrett Hinshaw, Dean
Cuylar Dunbar, President

The following is a partial list of accommodations provided by the college: counseling services, tutors, note-takers and carbonless duplication paper, recorded textbooks, tape recorders for taping lecture classes, interpeters, computer with voice software, and extended time for texts. Catawba Valley Community College provides services for students with disabilities.

3458 Central Carolina Community College
1105 Kelly Dr
Sanford, NC 27330-9840 919-775-5401
FAX 919-718-7380
http://www.ccc.edu
Dr. T. Eston (Bud) Marchant, President

Adopted to guide its delivery of services to students with disabilities that states that no otherwise qualified individual shall by reason of disability be excluded from the participation in, be denied benefits of, or be subjected to discrimination under any program at Central Carolina Community College. The college will make program modification adjustments in instructional delivery and provide supplemental services.

3459 Central Piedmont Community College
Learning Disability Department
PO Box 35009
Charlotte, NC 28235-5009 704-542-0470
FAX 704-330-4020
TDD:704-330-5000
TTY: 704-330-4223
http://www.cpcc.cc.nc.us
e-mail: patricia.adams@cpcc.edu
Pat Goings-Adams, Learning Disabilities Counselor
Dr.Toni Zeiss, President
Ralph Pitts, Chairman
A public two-year college with 300 special education students out of a total of 60,000.

3460 Davidson County Community College
PO Box 1287
Lexington, NC 27293-1287 336-249-8186
FAX 336-249-0088
http://www.davidsonccc.edu
e-mail: emorse@davidsonccc.edu
Ed Morse MD, Dean
Mary Rittling, President

Offers a variety of services to students with disabilities including notetakers, extended testing time, counseling services, and special accommodations.

3461 Dore Academy
1727 Providence Rd
Charlotte, NC 28207-2631 704-365-5490
FAX 704-365-3240
http://www.doreacademy.org
e-mail: info@doreacademy.org
Roberta Smith, Founder
Erin Commendatore, Admissions Director

Dore Academy is Charlotte's oldest college-prep school for students with learning differences. A private, non-profit, independent day school for students in grades 1-12, it is approved by the state of North Carolina, Division of Exceptional children. All teachers are certified by the state and trained in the theory and treatment of dyslexia and attention disorders. With a maximum of 10 students per class (5 in reading classes), the teacher student ratio is 1 to 7.

3462   East Carolina University
Project STEPP
E 5th Street
Greenville, NC 27858   252-328-6131
                                                http://www.ecu.edu
                                        e-mail: williamssar@ecu.edu
ÿDr. Marilyn Sheerer, Vice Chancellor
Dr. Steve Ballard, Chancellor

The program offers comprehensive academic, social, and
life-skills support to a select number of students with identified Specific Learning Disabilities who have shown the potential to succeed in college.

3463   Fletcher Academy
400 Cedarview Ct
Raleigh, NC 27609-3819   919-782-5082
                                            FAX 919-782-5980
                              http://www.thefletcheracademy.com
                         e-mail: info@thefletcheracademy.com
Junell Blaylock, Headmaster
Tiffany Gregory, Admissions Director
Ruby Bugg, Dean of Students
A coeducational, independent day school serving students
from grades 1-12 with learning differences.

3464   Gardner-Webb University
Noel Program
PO Box 997
Boiling Springs, NC 28017-7201   704-406-4000
                                            FAX 704-406-3524
                                    http://www.gardner-webb.edu
                             e-mail: cpotter@gardner-webb.edu
Dr. A Frank Bonner, President
Dr. Ben Leslie, Provost

Four year college that provides a program for disabled students.

3465   Guilford Technical Community College
PO Box 309
Jamestown, NC 27282-309   336-334-4822
                                            FAX 336-841-2158
                                            TTY: 336-841-2158
                                    http://www.gtcc.cc.nc.us
                           e-mail: dcameron@gtcc.cc.nc.us
Donald Cameron, President
Sonny White, Vice President

The purpose of disability access services is to provide equal
access and comprehensive, quality services to all students
who experience barriers toacademic, personal and social
success.

3466   Hill Center
3200 Pickett Rd
Durham, NC 27705-6010   919-489-7464
                                            FAX 919-489-7466
                                        http://www.hillcenter.org
                                   e-mail: info@hillcenter.org
Sharon Maskel, Headmaster

Half day school and teacher training facility, established for
students with LD/ADHD.
                    1977

3467   Isothermal Community College
Department of Disability Services
PO Box 804
Spindale, NC 28160-804   828-286-3636
                                            FAX 828-286-8109
                                        TDD:828-286-3636
                                http://www.isothermal.cc.nc.us
                         e-mail: kharris@isothermal.cc.nc.us
Karen Harris, Director
Susan Vaughan, Manager
Dr. Myra B. Johnson, President

Isothermal Community College, in compliance with the
Americans with Disabilities Act, makes every effort to provide accommodations for students with disabilities. It is our
goal to integrate students with disabilities into the college
and help them participate and benefit from programs and activities enjoyed by all students. We at Isothermal are committed to improving life through learning.

3468   Johnson C Smith University
Disability Support Services Department
100 Beatties Ford Rd
Charlotte, NC 28216-5398   704-378-1010
                                            FAX 704-372-1242
                                            http://www.jcsu.edu
                                   e-mail: admissions@jcsu.edu
Dorothy C Yancy, Coordinator
James Saunders, Director

Four year college that provides support to those who are disabled.

3469   Key Learning Center
Carolina Day School
1345 Hendersonville Rd
Asheville, NC 28803-1923   828-274-0757
                                            FAX 828-274-0116
                                        http://www.cdschool.org
                                   e-mail: bsgro@cdschool.org
Diane Milner, Director

Provides students with learning differences the educational
opportunity to overcome their differences and to achieve
their maximum potential in school and life.

3470   Lenoir-Rhyne College
PO Box 7470
Hickory, NC 28603-7470   828-328-7315
                                            FAX 828-328-7329
                                            http://www.lr.edu
                                   e-mail: kirbydr@lrc.edu
Donavon Kirby, Coordinator
Wayne Powell, President

Four year college that provides services for those students
that are learning disabled.

3471   Mariposa School for Children with Autism
203 Gregson Dr
Cary, NC 27511-6495   919-461-0600
                                            FAX 919-461-0566
                                    http://www.mariposaschool.org
                             e-mail: info@mariposaschool.org
Jacqueline Gottlieb, Chairman
Cynthia Peters, President
Mark Stafford, MA, LPA, BCB, Executive Director
Provides year round one-on-one instruction to children with
autism, using innovative teaching techniques targeting multiple developmental areas in a single integrated setting. A
school of excellence choice for children with autism to maximize developemtn of their communication, social and
academic skills.

3472   Mars Hill College
100 Atletic Street
Mars Hill, NC 28754-9135   828-689-1307
                                                800-543-1514
                                            FAX 828-689-1478
                                            http://www.mhc.edu
                                   e-mail: ccain@mhc.edu
Dan Lunsford, President
Chris Cain, Director
Coorny Wood, Assistant Director
An independent four-year college with 15 special education
students out of a total of 1,321.

3473 **Mayland Community College**
Support Options for Achievement and Retention
PO Box 547
Spruce Pine, NC 28777-547   828-765-7351
                                   800-462-9526
                    http://www.mayland.edu
                    e-mail: dcagle@mayland.edu
Nancy Godwin, Director
Debra Cagle, Administrative Assistant

Offers a variety of services to students with disabilities including notetakers, extended testing time, counseling services, and special accommodations.

3474 **McDowell Technical Community College**
Student Enrichment Center
54 College Dr
Marion, NC 28752-8728   828-652-6021
                               FAX 828-652-1014
                    http://www.mcdowelltech.edu
                    e-mail: donnashort@cc.nc.us
Bryan Wilson, President
Joe Kaylor, Chairman

A public two-year college with 15 special education students out of a total of 857. Free auxiliary services for LD students include: tutors, books on tape, unlimited testing, oral testing, notetakers and counseling. All faculty are trained in working with the LD student.

3475 **Montgomery Community College: North Carolina**
1011 Page St
Troy, NC 27371-8387   910-576-6222
                             FAX 910-576-2176
                    http://www.montgomery.edu
Mary Kirk, President

Offers a variety of services to students with disabilities including note takers, extended testing time, counseling services, and special accommodations.

3476 **North Carolina State University**
Campus Box 7509
Raleigh, NC 27695-0001   919-515-7653
                                FAX 919-513-2840
                                TDD:919-515-8830
                                TTY: 919-515-8830
                    http://www.ncsu.edu/dso
                    e-mail: cheryl_branker@ncsu.edu
Cheryl Branker, Director

Academic accommodations and services are provided for students at the university who have documented learning disabilities. Admission to the university is based on academic qualifications and learning disabled students are considered in the same manner as any other student. Special assistance is available to accommodate the needs of these students, including courses in accessible locations when appropiate.

3477 **North Carolina Wesleyan College**
3400 N Wesleyan Blvd
Rocky Mount, NC 27804   252-985-5100
                               800-488-6292
                               FAX 252-985-5284
                    http://www.ncwc.edu
                    e-mail: albunn.infowc@edu
Elizabeth Lanchaster, Assistant Registrar
Cliff Sullivan, Registrar Director
Ian Newbold, President
The Center provides support to students interested in achieving academic success. The staff works to provide you with information about academic matters and serves as an advocate for you. Services focus on pre-major advising, tutoring, mentoring, skills enrichment, disabilities assistance, self-assessment and retention.

3478 **Piedmont Baptist College**
420 S Broad St
Winston Salem, NC 27101-5197   336-725-8344
                                      800-937-5097
                                      FAX 336-725-5522
                    http://www.pbc.edu
Charles W Petitt, President

Prepares men and women for Christian ministries, both lay and professional, through a rigorous program of biblical, general and professional studies.

3479 **Randolph Community College**
629 Industrial Park Ave
Asheboro, NC 27205-1009   336-626-0033
                                 FAX 336-629-4695
                    http://www.randolf.edu
                    e-mail: jbranch@randolf.edu
Joyce Branch, Special Services Director
Rebekah Megerian, Basic Skills
Diane Bell, Manager
A public two-year college with 23 special education students out of a total of 1,487. Applicants with disabilities who wish to request accommodations in compliance with the ADA must identify themselves to the admissions counselor before placement testing.

3480 **Rockingham Community College**
PO Box 38
Wentworth, NC 27375-38   336-342-4261
                                FAX 336-349-9986
                                TDD:336-634-0132
                    http://www.rockinghamcc.edu
                    e-mail: rkeys@rcc.cc.nc.us
Robert C Keys, President

Offers a variety of services to students with disabilities including notetakers, extended testing time, counseling services, and special accommodations.

3481 **Salem College**
S Church Street
Winston-Salem, NC 27108   336-721-2600
                                 FAX 336-917-5339
                    http://www.salem.edu
                    e-mail: smith@salem.edu
Susan Pauly, President

Offers a variety of services to students with disabilities including notetakers, extended testing time, counseling services, and special accommodations.

3482 **Sandhills Community College**
3395 Airport Rd
Pinehurst, NC 28374-8778   910-692-6185
                                  800-338-3944
                                  FAX 910-695-1823
                    http://www.sandhills.edu
John R Dempsey, President

Offers a variety of services to students with disabilities including notetakers, extended testing time, counseling services, and special accommodations.

3483 **Southwestern Community College: North Carolina**
447 College Dr
Sylva, NC 28779-8581   828-586-4000
                              800-447-4091
                              FAX 828-339-4613
                    http://www.southwesterncc.edu
                    e-mail: cheryl@southwest.cc.nc.us
Don Thomas, President
Janet Burnette, Executive Vice President

Southwestern Community College provides equal access to education for persons with disabilities. It is the responsibility of the student to make their disability known and to request academic adjustments. Requests should be made in a timely manner and submitted to the Director of Student Support Services. Every reasonable effort will be made to provide service, however, not requesting services prior to registration may delay implementation.

3484   St Andrews Presbyterian College

1700 Dogwood Mile St
Laurinburg, NC 28352-5521   910-277-5555
                                             FAX 910-277-5020
                                             http://www.sapc.edu
                                             e-mail: info@sapc.edu

John Deegan Jr, President

Four year college that supports and provides services to the learning disabled students.

3485   Stone Mountain School

126 Camp Elliott Rd
Black Mountain, NC 28711-9003   888-631-5994
                                             FAX 828-669-2521
                                http://www.stonemountainschool.org
                          e-mail: smoore@stonemountainschool.com
Sam Moore, Executive Director
Paige Thomas, Admissions Director

3486   Surry Community College

630 S Main St
Dobson, NC 27017-8432   336-386-3465
                                             FAX 336-386-8951
                                             http://www.surry.edu
                                             e-mail: riggsj@surry.edu
Deborah Friedman, Special Programs
Judy Riggs, Continuing Education Dean
Frank Sells, President
Offers a variety of services to students with disabilities including notetakers, extended testing time, counseling services, and special accommodations.

3487   Tri-County Community College

4460 E Us Highway 64 Alt
Murphy, NC 28906-6847   828-837-6810
                                             FAX 828-837-3266
                                             TDD:724-228-4028
                                             http://www.tccd.edu
Norman Oglesby, President
Erma C. John Hadley, M.Ed., Chancellor

Offers a variety of services to students with disabilities including notetakers, extended testing time, counseling services, and special accommodations.

3488   University of North Carolina Wilmington

Disability Resource Center
601 S College Rd
Wilmington, NC 28403-3201   910-962-7555
                                             FAX 910-962-7556
                                             TDD:800-735-2962
                                             TTY: 800-735-2962
                                http://www.uncw.edu/disability
                                e-mail: waybrantj@uncw.edu
Margaret N. Turner, Director
Jorja Waybrant, Assistant Director
Aimee Helmus, Disability Service Specialist
Offer accommodative services, consultation, counseling and advocacy for students with disabilities enrolled at UNCW.

3489   University of North Carolina: Chapel Hill

450 Ridge Rd
Ste 2109
Chapel Hill, NC 27599-5135   919-493-5362
                                             FAX 919-962-3674
                                http://learningcenter.unc.edu
                                e-mail: asp@email.unc.edu

Theresa Maitlan MD, LD Specialist/Coordinator

Promotes learning by providing academic support to meet the individual needs of students diagnosed with specific learning disabilities. Strives to ensure the independence of participating students so that they may succeed during and beyond their university years.

3490   University of North Carolina: Charlotte

Special Education Department
9201 University Blvd
Charlotte, NC 28223   704-687-8622
                                             FAX 704-547-3239
                                             http://www.uncc.edu
                                e-mail: abennett@email.uncc.edu
Philip L Dubois, Accounting Technician
Ann Bennett, Office Manager

Introduction to Students with Special Needs. Characteristics of students with special learning needs, including those who are gifted and those who experience academic, social, emotional, physical and developmental disabilities. Legal, historical and philosophical foudations of special education and current issues in providing appropriate educational services to students with special needs.

3491   University of North Carolina: Greensboro

Disability Services
215 Elliott University Ctr
Greensboro, NC 27402   336-334-5440
                                             FAX 336-334-4412
                                             http://www.uncg.edu
                                             e-mail: ods@uncg.edu

Mary Culkin, Director
Laura Ripplinger, Office Manager

A public four-year university with over 300 students with disabilities out of a total of 12,000.

3492   Wake Forest University

1834 Wake Forest Road
Winston Salem, NC 27106   336-758-5000
                                             FAX 336-758-6074
                                             http://www.wfu.edu

Thomas Hearn, President
John Anderson, Vice President
William Gordon, CEO
Offers a variety of services to students with disabilities including notetakers, extended testing time, counseling services, and special accommodations.

3493   Wake Technical Community College

Disabilities Support Department
9101 Fayetteville Rd
Raleigh, NC 27603-5696   919-866-5000
                                             FAX 919-779-3360
                                             TDD:919-779-0668
                                             http://www.waketech.edu
                                e-mail: jtkillen@waketech.edu
Stephen C Scott, Director
Elaine Sardi, Coordinator

If you are a person with a documented disability who requires accommodations to achieve equal access to Wake Tech facilities, academic programs or other activities, you may request reasonable accommodations.

3494   Western Carolina University

Student Support Services
137 Killian Anx
Cullowhee, NC 28723   828-227-7301
                                             FAX 828-227-7078
                                             http://www.wcu.edu
                                             e-mail: mellen@wcu.edu

Carol Mellen, Director
Suzanne Baker, Adviser

Students with a documented disability may be provided with appropriate academic accommodations such as, note takers, testing accomadations, books on tape, readers/scribes, use of adaptive equipment and priority registration.

3495 Wilkes Community College
Student Support Services
PO Box 120
Wilkesboro, NC 28697-120   336-838-6100
                                   FAX 336-838-6277
                     http://www.wilkescc.edu
          e-mail: nancy.sizemore@wilkescc.edu
Kim Faw, Director
Nancy Sizemore, Disability Coordinator

A public two-year community college. Special services include: testing and individualized education plans; oral and extended time testing; individual and small group tutoring; study skills; readers and proctors and specialized equipment.

3496 Wilson County Technical College
North Carolina Community College
PO Box 4305
Wilson, NC 27893   252-299-1195
                                   FAX 252-243-7148
                                   TDD:252-246-1362
                     http://www.wilsoncc.edu
William James, Student Support Services
Thelma McAllister, Secretary

Offers a variety of services to students with disabilities including notetakers, extended testing time, counseling services, and special accommodations.

3497 Wingate University
Disability Services Department
Post Office Box 159
Wingate, NC 28174   704-233-8000
                                   800-755-5550
                                   FAX 704-233-8014
                     http://www.wingate.edu
          e-mail: admit@wingate.edu
Jerry McGee, President

An independent four-year college with 50 special education students out of a total of 1,372. There is an additional fee for the special education program in addition to the regular tuition.

3498 Winston-Salem State University
601 S. Martin Luther King Jr. Drive
Winston Salem, NC 27110   336-750-2000
                                   FAX 336-750-2392
                     http://www.wssu.edu\fyc
Myra Watdell, Director
Donald J. Reaves, Ph.D, Chancellor

Offers a variety of services to students with disabilities including notetakers, extended testing time, counseling services, and special accommodations.

North Dakota

3499 Anne Carlsen Center for Children
701 3rd St NW
P.O. Box 8000
Jamestown, ND 58402-2963   701-252-3850
                                   800-568-5175
                                   FAX 701-952-5154
                     http://www.annecenter.org
Marcia Gums, President

Provides students a safe, secure and loving atmosphere to learn and grow. The program is filled with an array of sensory and literary enriched experiences and materials that allow each student to become an independent, freethinking being.

3500 Bismarck State College
1500 Edwards Ave
Bismarck, ND 58506   701-224-5450
                                   800-445-5073
                                   FAX 701-224-5550
                     http://www.bsc.nodak.edu
          e-mail: Ischlafm@gwmail.nodak.edu
Marlene Anderson, Executive Director
Dr. Larry C. Skogen, President
Dave Clark, Executive Vice President
Offers a variety of services to students with disabilities including notetakers, extended testing time, counseling services, and special accommodations.

3501 Dakota College at Bottineau
105 Simrall Blvd
Bottineau, ND 58318-1159   701-228-5400
                                   800-542-6866
                                   FAX 701-228-5614
                     http://www.dakotacollege.edu
          e-mail: jan.nahinurk@dakotacollege.edu
Jan Nahinurk, Director
Peggy Gregg, Disability Services Coordinator

Dakota College at Bottineau offers a variety of services to students with disabilities including note takers, extended testing time, academic advising, and special accommodations.

3502 Dickinson State University
Student Support Services
291 Campus Dr
Dickinson, ND 58601-4896   701-483-2507
                                   FAX 701-483-2006
                     http://www.dsu.nodak.edu
          e-mail: dsu.hawks@dickinsonstate.edu
Richard McCallum, Planner/Coordinator
Dr D. Coston, President

Four year college offers support services to learning disabled students.

3503 Fort Berthold Community College
PO Box 490
New Town, ND 58763-490   701-938-4230
                                   FAX 701-627-3609
                     http://www.spcc.bia.edu
          e-mail: lgwin@spcc.bia.edu
Susan Paulson, Academic Dean of Students
Russell Mason, President

An independent two-year college with 3 special education students out of a total of 279.

3504 Mayville State University
Learning Disabilities Department
330 3rd St NE
Mayville, ND 58257-1299   701-788-2301
                                   800-437-4104
                                   FAX 701-788-4748
                     http://www.mayvillestate.edu
          e-mail: kyllo@mayvillestate.edu
Gary Hagen, Academic Support Director
Pamela Balch, President

Offers a variety of services to students with disabilities including notetakers, extended testing time, counseling services, and special accommodations.

3505 Minot State University
North Dakota Center for Persons with Disabilities
500 University Ave W
Minot, ND 58707   701-858-3371
                                   800-777-0750
                                   FAX 701-858-3686
                                   TDD:701-858-3580
                     http://www.minotstateu.edu
          e-mail: ndcpd@minotstateu.edu

David Fuller, President
Susie Mack, Office Manager

NDCPD works with the disability community, university, faculty and researchers, policy makers and service providers to identify emerging needs in the disability community and how to obtain resources to address them.

3506 North Dakota State College of Science
Disability Support Services (DSS) Office
800 6th St N
Wahpeton, ND 58076
701-671-2401
800-342-4325
FAX 701-671-2499
http://www.ndscs.nodak.edu
e-mail: joy.eichhorn@ndscs.nodak.edu
Sharon Y Hart, Disability Services Coordinator

A public two-year comprehensive college with a student population of 2400. Students with disabilites comprise seven percent of the population. Tuition $2025.

3507 North Dakota State University
Disability Services
Post Office Box 6050
Fargo, ND 58108
701-231-8463
FAX 701-231-6318
TDD:800-366-6888
http://www.ndsu.edu
e-mail: bunnie.johnson-messelt@ndsu.edu
Jennifer Erickson, Disability Specialist
Bunnie Johnson-Messelt, Disability Services Coordinator
Dean L. Brescian, President
Students with permanent physical, psychological or learning disabilities may obtain accommodations. The Disability Services (DS) staff meet with the student to determine eligibility and identify reasonable accomodations. Accomodations are based on the functional limitations of the disability. DS staff assist in the implementation of approved accommodations. Referrals for disability diagnosis and for other support services such as tutoring are also provided by staff.

3508 Standing Rock College
1341 92nd St
Fort Yates, ND 58538-9721
701-854-8000
FAX 701-854-3403
http://www.sittingbull.edu

Linda Ivan, Special Services
Mark Holman, Manager

Offers a variety of services to students with disabilities including notetakers, extended testing time, counseling services, and special accommodations.

Ohio

3509 Art Academy of Cincinnati
1212 Jackson St
Cincinnati, OH 45202-7106
513-562-6262
800-323-5692
FAX 513-562-8778
http://www.artacadamy.edu
Gregory Smith, Dean of Students
Sarah Mulhauser, Student Services Director

Offers a variety of services to students with disabilities including notetakers, extended testing time, counseling services, and special accommodations.

3510 Baldwin-Wallace College
275 Eastland Rd
Berea, OH 44017-2088
440-826-2900
FAX 440-826-3777
http://www.bw.edu

Richard W Durst, President
Obobie Brender, Executive Assistant

Offers a variety of services to students with disabilities including notetakers, extended testing time, counseling services, and special accommodations.

3511 Bluffton College
Special Student Services
280 College Rd
Bluffton, OH 45817
419-358-3458
FAX 419-358-3323
http://www.bluffton.edu
e-mail: bergerd@bluffton.edu
Timothy Byers, Program Contact
James H. Harder, President

Four year college offers special programs to learninig disabled students.

3512 Bowling Green State University
413 S Hall
Bowling Green, OH 43403
419-372-2531
FAX 419-372-8496
http://www.bgsu.edu
e-mail: dss@bgsu.edu

Robert Cunningham, Director
Peggy Dennis, Associate Director
Lea Anne Kesler, Coordinator
The Disability Services Office is evidence of Bowling Green State University's commitment to provide a support system which assists in conquering obstacles that persons with disabilities may encounter as they pursue their educational goals and activities. Our hope is to facilitate mainstream mobility and recognize the diverse talents that persons with disabilities have to offer to our university and our community.

3513 Brown Mackie College: Akron
2791 Mogadore Rd
Akron, OH 44320
330-896-3600
FAX 330-733-5853
http://www.brownmackie.edu
Jannette Mason, Administrative Assistant
Fred Baldwin, Dean of Academic Services

Offers a variety of services to students with disabilities including notetakers, extended testing time, counseling services, and special accommodations.

3514 Case Western Reserve University
10900 Euclid Ave
Cleveland, OH 44106-4901
216-368-2000
FAX 216-368-8826
http://www.cwru.edu
Barbara Snyder, Disability Services Coordinator
Edward Hundert, President

While all students will have preferences for learning, students with physical or learning disabilities have different actual needs as well. Students with physical disabilities such as visual impairments, hearing impairments, or temporary or permanent motor impairments may need guide dogs, interpeters, note-takers, wheelchair accessible rooms, or other types of assistance to help them attend and participate in class. Also available, extra time or a separate room for exams, tutoring and more.

3515 Central Ohio Technical College
Developmental Education
1179 University Dr
Newark, OH 43055-1767
740-366-9494
800-963-9275
FAX 740-366-5047
http://www.cotc.edu

Bonnie Coe, President

Learning Assitance Center and Disability Services (LAC/DS) is the academic support unit in Student Support Services. LAC/DS provides FREE programs and services designed to help students sharpen skills necessary to succeed in college.

3516 Central State University
Office of Disability Services
1400 Brush Row Rd
Wilberforce, OH 45384-5800   937-376-6011
                              FAX 937-376-6245
                    http://www.centralstate.edu
        e-mail: publicrelations@centralstate.edu
John Garland, President
Carlos Vargas-Aburto, Vice President

Four year college that provides services for the learning disabled students.

3517 Cincinnati State Technical and Community College
3520 Central Pkwy
Cincinnati, OH 45223-2690   513-569-1500
                              FAX 513-569-1719
                    http://www.cincinnatistate.edu
            e-mail: dcover@cinstate.cc.oh.us
John Henderson, Administrator
O'Dell M. Owens, M.D., M.P.H, President

Services include assistance and support services for students with permanent and temporary disabilities, test proctoring, readers/scribes, taping, tape recording loan, reading machines, assistance with locating interpeters, mediating between student and faculty to overcome specific disability issues; also offers braille access.

3518 Clark State Community College
Disability Retention Center
570 E Leffel Ln
Springfield, OH 45505-4795   937-325-0691
                              FAX 937-328-6133
                    http://www.clarkstate.edu
Karen Rafinski, Counselor

In accordance with the Americans with Disabilities Act, it is the policy of Clark State Community College to provide reasonable accommodations to persons with disabilities. The office of disability services offers a variety of services to Clark State students who have documented physical, mental or learning disabilities.

3519 Cleveland Institute of Art
Academic Services
11141 East Blvd
Cleveland, OH 44106-1700   216-421-7000
                                     800-223-4700
                              FAX 216-421-7438
                    http://www.cia.edu
        e-mail: jmilenski@gate.cia.edu
David Deming, Associate Director
Rachel Browner, Director

No student should be discouraged from attending CIA because of a learning disability. A student working on their BFA degree at the Institute of Art can get academic support from the tutoring director in the Office of Academic Services. Services include books-on-tape, one-on-one tutoring, alternative curriculum advising, notetaking services, alternative test taking and assignment arrangements. Services outside the scope of the program can be arranged at the student's expense.

3520 Cleveland State University
1983 E 24th St
Cleveland, OH 44115-2440   216-687-2000
                                     888-278-6446
                              FAX 216-687-9366
                    http://www.csuohio.edu
        e-mail: m.zuccaro@csuohio.edu
Michael Schwartz, Disability Services
Ronald ÿM. Berkman, President

CSU aims to provide equal opportunity to all of its students. Services are available to those who might need some extra help because of a physical disability, communication impairment or learning disability. This program is designed to address the personal and academic issues of the physically handicapped students as they become oriented to campus. A full range of services is offered.

3521 College of Mount Saint Joseph
Project EXCEL
5701 Delhi Rd
Cincinnati, OH 45233-1669   513-244-4623
                                     800-654-9314
                              FAX 513-244-4629
                    http://www.msj.edu
        e-mail: debra_mato@mail.msj.edu
Anthony Aretz, President

Project EXCEL is a nationally recognized, comprehensive academic support system for students with specific learning disabilities and/or Attention Deficit/Attention Deficit Hyperactivity Disorder. Project EXCEL is a fee-for-service program. Students must be admitted to the College of Mount St. Joseph before applying for Project EXCEL.

3522 College of Wooster
1189 Beall Ave
Wooster, OH 44691-2363   330-263-2000
                              FAX 330-263-2427
                    http://www.wooster.edu
Grant H. Cornwell, President

Offers a variety of services to students with disabilities including notetakers, extended testing time, counseling services, and special accommodations.

3523 Columbus State Community College Disability Services
550 E Spring St
Columbus, OH 43215-1722   614-287-5353
                                     800-621-6407
                              FAX 614-287-3645
                              TDD:614-287-2570
                              TTY: 614-287-2570
                    http://www.cscc.edu
        e-mail: wcocchi@cscc.edu
Valeriana Moeller, President

A public two-year college serving qualified students with disabilities, including learning disabilities. Support services are provided based on disability documentation and can include, books, tapes, alternative testing, notetaking, counseling, equipment use, reader, scribe, and peer tutoring.

3524 Cuyahoga Community College: Eastern Campus
4250 Richmond Rd
Highland Hills, OH 44122-6195   800-954-8742
                                     866-933-5175
                              FAX 216-987-2054
                              TDD:866-933-5175
                    http://www.tri-c.edu
        e-mail: Maryann.Syarto@tri-c.cc.oh.us
Roland Chapdelaine, LD Director
Charlotte Burgin, Tutor
Jerry Sue Thornton, Ph.D, President
The ACCESS Programs strive to assist Tri-C students with disabilities to realize their learning potential, bring them into the mainstream of the College community, enhance their self-sufficiency, and enable them to achieve academic success. Services include tuoring, test proctoring, interpreters, adaptive equipment, readers and/or scribes for exams, alternative test taking arrangements, alternative format for printed materials and textbooks on tape.

3525 Cuyahoga Community College: Western Campus
1000 W Pleasant Valley Rd
Parma, OH 44134
216-987-5077
1-800-954-87
FAX 516-987-5050
TDD:216-987-5117
http://www.tri-c.edu
e-mail: rose.kolovrat@tri-c.edu

Rose Kolovrat, Director
ÿDr. Jerry Sue Thornton, President

The ACCESS programs strive to assist Tri-C students with disabilities to realize their learning potential, bring them into the mainstream of the College community, enhance their self-suffciency and enable them to achieve academic success. Services provided include tutoring, test proctoring, interpeters, adaptive equipment, readers/scribes for exams, alternative testing arrangements, alternative format for printed material and textbooks on tape.

3526 Defiance College
701 N Clinton St
Defiance, OH 43512-1695
419-784-4010
800-520-4632
FAX 419-784-0426
http://www.defiance.edu
e-mail: admissions@defiance.edu

Gerald Wood, President
Mark Thompson, Dean

Offers a variety of services to students with disabilities including notetakers, extended testing time, counseling services, and special accommodations.

3527 Denison University
104 Doane Hall
Granville, OH 43023
740-587-6666
800-336-4766
FAX 740-587-5629
http://www.denison.edu
e-mail: vestal@denison.edu

Jennifer Vestal, Associate Dean/Director
Heather Johnston Welliver, Associate Director

The Office of Academic Support (OAS) offers a wide range of services for students with disabilities. In supporting our students as they move forward toward graduation and the world of work beyond, we strongly encourage and promote self advocacy regarding disability related issues.

3528 FOCUS Program
Program for Students with Learning Disabilities
2550 Lander Rd
Pepper Pike, OH 44124-4318
440-449-4203
FAX 440-684-6138
http://www.ursuline.edu
e-mail: ekohut@ursuline.edu

Eileen Delaney Kohut, Director

A voluntary, comprehensive, fee-paid program for students with learning disabilities and ADHD. The goals of the FOCUS Program include providing a smooth transition for college life, helping students learn to apply the most appropriate learning strategies in college courses, and teaching students self-advocacy skills.

3529 Franklin University
201 S Grant Ave
Columbus, OH 43215-5399
614-797-4700
877-341-6300
FAX 614-224-8027
http://www.franklin.edu

Paul J Otte, President

Students who have disabilities may notify the University of their status by checking the appropriate space on the registration form each trimester. Then the Coordinator of Disability Services will help them file proper documentation so that accommodations can be made for their learning needs.

3530 Hiram College
PO Box 67
Hiram, OH 44234-67
330-569-3211
FAX 330-569-5398
http://www.hiram.edu

Lynn Taylor, Counseling Director
Tom Chema, President

Offers a variety of services to students with disabilities including notetakers, extended testing time, counseling services, and special accommodations.

3531 Hocking College
3301 Hocking Pkwy
Nelsonville, OH 45764-9588
740-753-3591
800-282-4163
FAX 740-753-7065
http://www.hocking.edu
e-mail: admissions@hocking.edu

John Light, President
Rosie Smith, Director

The Access Center Office of Disability Support Services is dedicated to serving the various needs of individuals with disabilities and promoting their participation in college life.

3532 ITT Technical Institute
1030 N Meridian Rd
Youngstown, OH 44509-4098
330-270-1600
800-832-5001
FAX 330-270-8333
http://www.itt-tech.edu

Frank Quartini, Manager

Offers a variety of services to students with disabilities including note takers, extended testing time, counseling services, and special accommodations.

3533 Julie Billiart School
4982 Clubside Rd
Lyndhurst, OH 44124-2596
216-381-1191
FAX 216-381-2216
http://www.juliebilliartschool.org
e-mail: jjohnston@jbschool.org

Agnesmarie Loporto, President
Jodi Johnston M Ed, Principal

Rooted in the educational vision of the Sisters of Notre Dame, Julie Billiart School is a Catholic, alternative K-8 school, which educates children of all faith traditions who experience special learning needs.

3534 Lorain County Community College
1005 Abbe Rd N
Elyria, OH 44035-1691
440-366-4100
800-955-5222
FAX 440-365-6519
http://www.lorainccc.edu

Roy Church, President

LCCC serves over 80 learning disabled students per year out of a total student population of about 7,000. Services include readers/testers, scribes, notetaking accommodations, assistive technology, advocacy training and personal counseling. Free tutoring is available to all students at the college. No diagnostic testing is available.

3535 Malone University
2600 Cleveland Ave NW
Canton, OH 44709-3308
330-471-8100
800-521-1146
FAX 330-471-8149
TDD:330-471-8496
http://www.malone.edu
e-mail: ameadows@malone.edu

Anna Meadows, Student Access Services Director
Dr Wil Friesen, President

An independent four-year college with about 40 special education students out of a total of almost 2,000.

3536 Marburn Academy
1860 Walden Dr
Columbus, OH 43229-3627   614-433-0822
FAX 614-433-0812
http://www.marburnacademy.org
e-mail: marburnadmission@marburnacademy.org
Earl B Oremus, Headmaster

A not-for-profit, independent, day school devoted to serving the educational needs of bright students with learning differences such as dyslexia and ADHD. The school programs are designed to help the student's learn strong work habits, teach values of persistance and courage in overcoming challenges and to build effective social interaction and problem solving patterns.

3537 Marietta College
Marietta College
215 5th St
Marietta, OH 45750-4047   740-376-4786
800-331-7896
FAX 740-376-4530
http://www.marietta.edu
e-mail: higgisd@marietta.edu

Walter Miller, Director
Jean Scott, President

An Independent four-year college that offers a variety of servies to students with disabilities including note takers, extended testing time, counseling services, and special accommodations. There is no separate fee for these services.

3538 Marion Technical College
1467 Mount Vernon Ave
Marion, OH 43302-5694   740-389-4636
FAX 740-389-6136
http://www.mtc.edu

J Richard Bryson, President
L. Douglas Boyer, vice President

The Student Resource Center also houses the Office of Disabilities. The SRC director will advocate on student's behalf for resonable accommodations for those with physical, mental and or emotional disabilities.

3539 Miami University Rinella Learning Center
Room 14
301 S Campus Avenue
Oxford, OH 45056-2481   513-529-1809
http://www.muohio.edu

David Hodge, President
Bobby Gempesaw, Provost

A public four-year college.

3540 Miami University: Middletown Campus
4200 N University Blvd
Middletown, OH 45042-3458   513-727-3200
800-662-2262
FAX 513-727-3223
TDD:513-727-3308
http://www.mid.muohio.edu
e-mail: nferguson@mid.muohio.edu
Kelly Cowan, Executive Director
Margir Perkins, Academic Services

Offers a variety of services to students with disabilities including notetakers, extended testing time, counseling services, and special accommodations.

3541 Mount Vernon Nazarene College
800 Martinsburg Rd
Mount Vernon, OH 43050-9500   740-392-6868
FAX 740-397-2769
http://www.mvnu.edu
e-mail: amy.stemen@mvnu.edu
Carol Matthews MD, Director
Amy Stemen, Office Manager

Four year college that provides programs for learning diabled students.

3542 Muskingum College
Center for Advancement of Learning
223 Montgomery Hall
New Concord, OH 43762   740-826-8211
FAX 740-826-8285
http://www.muskingum.edu
e-mail: ehenry@muskingum.edu
Eileen Henry EdD, Executive Director
President
The PLUS Program provides students identified as learning-disabled with individual and group learning strategies instruction embedded within course content.

3543 Northwest Technical College
1900 28th Ave S
Moorhead, MN 56560-4899   218-299-6500
800-426-5603
FAX 218-299-6810
http://www.minnesota.edu
e-mail: jerome.migler@minnesota.edu
Jerome Migler, President
John Centko, Dean of Academics
Richard Smestad, Vice President
Offers a variety of services to students with disabilities including notetakers, extended testing time, counseling services, and special accommodations.

3544 Oberlin College
Academic Support for Students with Disabilities
118 N Professor St
Oberlin, OH 44074   440-775-8121
FAX 440-775-8474
http://www.oberlin.edu
e-mail: communications@oberlin.edu
Nancy S Dye, Coordinator
Phyllis Hogan, Office Manager

An independent four-year college with small percentage of education students.

3545 Ohio State University Agricultural Technical Institute
1382 Dover Rd
Wooster, OH 44691-4000   330-264-1331
800-647-8283
FAX 330-202-3579
http://www.ati.ag.ohio-state.edu
e-mail: ati@osu.edu
Gerri Wolfe, LD Specialist
Chris Igodan, Executive Director

A public two-year college with nearly 10% special education students. There is no fee for the special education program in addition to the regular tuition.

3546 Ohio State University: Lima Campus
Disability Services
4240 Campus Dr
Lima, OH 45804-3576   419-995-8600
FAX 419-995-8483
http://www.lima.ohio-state.edu
e-mail: meyer.193@osu.edu
John Snyder, Coordinator/Disability Services
Gordon Gee, President

A public four-year college providing services to learning disabled students including extended test time, counseling, notetakers and other special accommodations.

3547 Ohio State University: Mansfield Campus
Disability Services
1760 University Dr
Mansfield, OH 44906-1547   419-755-4011
                                   FAX 419-755-4241
          http://www.mansfield.ohio-state.edu
                    e-mail: corso.1@osu.edu
Evelyn Freeman, President

A public four-year college providing services to learning disabled students including peer tutoring, extended test time, quiet rooms and other special accommodations.

3548 Ohio State University: Marion Campus

1465 Mount Vernon Ave
Marion, OH 43302-5628   740-389-6786
                                   FAX 740-292-5817
          http://www.osumarion.osu.edu
Gregory Rose, LD Specialist
Gregory Rose, Manager

A public four-year college providing a full range of services for students with disabilities.

3549 Ohio State University: Newark Campus

1179 University Dr
Newark, OH 43055-1797   740-364-3321
                                   FAX 740-364-9566
          http://www.newark.osu.edu
D Mac Donald, Learning Disability Specialist
Anne Federlein, President

A public four-year college providing services to learning disabled students including peer tutoring, extended test time, quiet rooms and other special accommodations. There is no separate fee for these services.

3550 Ohio State University: Nisonger Center

357 McKamball Hall
Columbus, OH 43210   614-685-3192
                                   FAX 614-366-6373
                                   TDD:614-688-8040
          http://www.nisonger.osu.edu
Stephen Rose, Executive Director
ÿJane Case-Smith, president

The Ohio State University Nisonger Center for Mental Retardation and Developmental Disabilities provides interdisciplinary training, research and exemplary services pertaining to people with developmental disabilities. The center, which is a part of a national network of activities called University Afffiliated Programs, was founded in 1968. Training is provided in medicine (pediatrics and psychiatry), dentistry, education, physical therapy, psychology and other relevant disciplines.

3551 Ohio University
Ohio University
101 Crewson House
Athens, OH 45701   740-593-4000
                                   FAX 740-593-2708
          http://www.ohiou.edu
William Smith, Director
Ruth Blickle, Administrative Associate
Dr.Rodrick J.McDavis, President
A public four-year college with a small percentage of special education students.

3552 Ohio University Chillicothe
PO Box 629
Chillicothe, OH 45601-629   740-774-7200
                                   877-462-6824
                                   FAX 740-774-7290
          http://www.ohiou.edu/~childept
                    e-mail: diekroge@ohio.edu
Diane Diekroger MD, Student Support Coordinator
Richard Bebee, Manager

Offers a variety of services to students with disabilities including note takers, extended testing time, counseling services, and special accommodations.

3553 Otterbein College
102 W College Ave
Westerville, OH 43081-1489   614-823-1618
                                   800-488-8144
                                   FAX 614-823-1983
          http://www.otterbein.edu
                    e-mail: lmonaghan@otterbein.edu
Ellen Kasulis, Director of Academic Support
Kathy Krendl, President

An independent four-year college with a small percentage of special education students.

3554 Owens Community College
Disability Resources Department
PO Box 10000
Toledo, OH 43699-1947   567-661-7000
                                   800-466-9367
                                   FAX 419-661-7607
          http://www.owens.edu
                    e-mail: bscheffert@owens.cc.oh.us
Beth Scheffert, Director
Dr. Mike Bower, president

A comprehensive Community College that offers educational programs in over 50 technical areas of study leading to the Associate of Applied Science, Associate of Applied Business or Associate of Technical Studies degree. Provides programs designed for college transfer and leads to the Associate of Arts or Associate of Science degree. Finally, a number of certificate programs as well as short term credit and non-credit programs are available.

3555 Shawnee State University
940 2nd St
Portsmouth, OH 45662-4347   740-351-3217
                                   800-959-4778
                                   FAX 740-351-3470
                                   TTY: 740-351-3159
          http://www.shawnee.edu
                    e-mail: jweaver@shawnee.edu
Rita Rice-Morris, Coordinator
Tess Midkiff, Executive Director
Rita Rice Morris, Ph.D., President
Offers a variety of services to students with disabilities including notetakers, extended testing time, counseling services, and special accommodations.

3556 Sinclair Community College
Learning Disability Support Services
Rm 11342
444 W 3rd St
Dayton, OH 45402-1453   937-512-2855
                                   800-315-3000
                                   FAX 937-512-4564
                                   TDD:937-512-3096
          http://www.sinclair.edu
Douglas Kaylor, Program Coordinator/Director
Robin More-Cooper, Counselor
Steven L. Johnson, President
Funded by the Federal Department of Education, Student Support Services is an organization devoted to helping students meet the challenges of college life. Our goals are to help students stay in school, then eventually graduate and/or transfer to a four-year college or university. We strive to develop new ways of helping students achieve their educational, career and professional goals.

3557 Southern State Community College
100 Hobart Dr
Hillsboro, OH 45133-9406   937-393-3431
                                   FAX 937-393-9831
          http://www.sscc.edu

Sherry Stout, Special Services
Lawrence Dukes, President

Offers a variety of services to students with disabilities including notetakers, extended testing time, counseling services, and special accommodations.

3558 Terra State Community College
Special Education Services
2830 Napoleon Rd
Fremont, OH 43420-9600   419-334-8400
                                 866-288-3772
                            FAX 419-334-3667
           http://www.terra.cc.us/terra2.html
               e-mail: info@terra.cc.oh.us
Richard Newman, Coordinator
Gina Staccone-Smeal, Coordinator
Mary Broestl, Manager
Provides quality learning experiences which are accessible and affordable. Terra is actively committed to excellence in learning and offers associate degrees in various technologies as well as in arts and sciences, applied business, and applied science. Our office of student support services works with students with learning disabilities and other disabilities.

3559 University of Cincinnati: Raymond Walters General and Technical College
9555 Plainfield Rd
Cincinnati, OH 45236-1007   513-745-5600
                            FAX 513-745-5780
                            TDD:513-745-8300
                http://www.ucblueash.edu
              e-mail: john.kraimer@uc.edu
Dolores Straker, Disability Services Director
Raymond Waltersÿ, president

Offers a variety of services to students with disabilities including notetakers, extended testing time, counseling services, and special accommodations.

3560 University of Findlay
Disability Services Office
1000 N Main St
Findlay, OH 45840-3653   419-422-8313
                                 800-472-9502
                            FAX 419-424-4822
                            TDD:419-434-5532
                 http://www.findlay.edu
            e-mail: ods@mail.findlay.edu
Debow Freed, Director Disability Services
Katherine Ro Fell, Ph.D, President

An independent four-year college with a small percentage of special needs students.

3561 University of Toledo
2801 W Bancroft St
Toledo, OH 43606-3390   419-530-2600
                            FAX 419-530-4505
                  http://www.utoledo.edu
Jeff Newton, Office Director
Joseph Hovey, Manager
Dr. Lloyd A. Jacob, President
A public four-year college whose mission is to provide the support services and accommodations necessary for all students to succeed.

3562 Urbana University
Student Affairs Office
597 College Way
Urbana, OH 43078   937-484-1400
                            FAX 937-484-1322
                   http://www.urbana.edu
             e-mail: webmaster@urbana.edu
Stephen Jones, Director
Steven J. Polsley, Chairman

An independent four-year college with a small percentage of special education students.

3563 Walsh University
2020 E Maple St
North Canton, OH 44720-3336   330-490-7090
                                 800-362-9846
                            FAX 330-499-7165
                     http://www.walsh.edu
             e-mail: bfreshour@walsh.edu
Richard Jusseaume, Director
Joni Hendricks, Secretary
Dan Suvak, Manager
An independent four-year college. The Office of Student Support Services maintains an early warning system for students in academic, financial, social and/or emtional difficulty. The Office proudly communicates regularly with students regarding their general well being, and assists in the students' academic and financial concerns with referals to appropriate offices.

3564 Washington State Community College
710 Colegate Dr
Marietta, OH 45750-9225   740-374-8716
                            FAX 740-374-9562
                    http://www.wscc.com
Charlotte Hatfield, President

A public two-year college with a small percentage of special education students.

3565 Wilmington College of Ohio
1870 Quaker Way
Wilmington, OH 45177-2499   937-382-6661
                                 800-341-9318
                            FAX 937-382-7077
                http://www.wilmington.edu
Jim Renoylds, President

Offers a variety of services to students with disabilities including notetakers, extended testing time, counseling services, and special accommodations.

Oklahoma

3566 Bacone College
2299 Old Bacone Rd
Muskogee, OK 74403-1568   918-683-4581
                                 888-682-5514
                            FAX 918-682-5514
                   http://www.bacone.edu
            e-mail: stewarta@bacone.edu
Rhonda Cambiano, Director
Ann Stewart, Coordinator
Dr. Robert J Duncan, President
Offers a variety of services to students with disabilities including notetakers, extended testing time, counseling services, and special accommodations.

3567 East Central University
1100 E 14th St
Ada, OK 74820-6999   580-332-8000
                            FAX 580-310-5654
                    http://www.ecok.edu/
Mary Huckleberry, Student Support Services
Pamela Armstrong, Registrar

A public four-year college with a small percentage of special education of students.

3568 Moore-Norman Technology Center
4701 12th Ave NW
Norman, OK 73069-8308   405-217-8201
                            FAX 405-364-1739
               http://www.mntechnology.com
         e-mail: sjohnson@mntechnology.com

John Hunter, Superintendent
Sande Johnson, Disability Coordinator

Offers a variety of services to students with disabilities including notetakers, extended testing time, counseling services, and special accommodations.

3569   Northeastern State University

600 N Grand Ave
Tahlequah, OK 74464-2301   918-456-5511
                                         FAX 918-458-2363
                                         http://www.nsuok.edu

David Wilcox, Assistant to Dean
Bela Foltin, Manager
Steve Turner, Ph.D, President
Four year college that offers programs and services to disabled students.

3570   Oklahoma City Community College

Department of Student Support Services
7777 S May Ave
Oklahoma City, OK 73159-4444   405-682-1611
                                         FAX 405-682-7585
                                         TDD:405-682-7520
                                         TTY: 405-682-7529
                                         http://www.okccc.edu
                                         e-mail: jhoward@okccc.edu
Barbara King, Students w/Disabilities Advisor
Pat Stowe, Director
Felix J. Aquino, Ph.D, Vice President
Comprehensive community college with individualized services and accommodations for students with disabilities arranged by the Office of Student Support Services. Services include Deaf Program, and accommodations as described by section 504 & ADA. Five tutoring labs are available on campus and assistive technology including voice synthesizers and voice recognition for computer based word processing.

3571   Oklahoma Panhandle State University

PO Box 430
Goodwell, OK 73939-430   580-349-2611
                                         FAX 580-349-2302
                                         TDD:580-349-1559
                                         http://www.opsu.edu
                                         e-mail: opsu@opsu.edu
David Bryan, President
Cheryl Ashpaugh, Director

Four year college that offers programs to the learning disabled.

3572   Oklahoma State University: Oklahoma City Technical School

900 N Portland Ave
Oklahoma City, OK 73107-6120   405-947-4421
                                         800-580-4099
                                         FAX 405-945-3289
                                         http://www.osuokc.edu
                                         e-mail: emilytc@osuokc.edu
Jerry D Carroll, President

Offers access to students with disabilities based upon the diagnostic documentation which is provided by the student and the functional impact of the disability.

3573   Oklahoma State University: Okmulgee Technical School

1801 E 4th St
Okmulgee, OK 74447-3942   918-293-4678
                                         800-722-4447
                                         FAX 918-756-6705
                                         http://www.osuit.edu
                                         e-mail: information@okstate.edu
Carol Been, Manager
ÿBill R. Path, President

Offers a variety of services to students with disabilities including notetakers, extended testing time, counseling services, and special accommodations.

3574   Oral Roberts University

7777 S Lewis Ave
Tulsa, OK 74171   918-495-6161
                                         FAX 918-495-7229
                                         http://www.oru.edu
                                         e-mail: droberson@oru.edu
Richard L Roberts, President
Jesse Pisors, DirectorÿDevelopment and Alumni

Four year college that offers resources to students with a learning disability.

3575   Rogers State University

1701 W Will Rogers Blvd
Claremore, OK 74017-3259   918-343-7579
                                         800-256-7511
                                         FAX 918-343-7712
                                         http://www.rsu.edu
                                         e-mail: msith@rsu.edu
Misty Smith, Director Of Student Development
Dr. Tobie Titsworth, VP For Student Affairs

A public four-year university with several special education students out of a total of approximately 3,300.

3576   Rose State College

Academic Support Department
6420 SE 15th St
Midwest City, OK 73110-2799   405-733-7311
                                         FAX 405-733-7399
                                         TDD:405-736-7308
                                         http://www.rose.edu
                                         e-mail: rjones@rose.edu
Terry Britton, President
Dr. Jeff Caldwell, Vice President

Services and facilities include academic advisement, referal and liaison with other community agencies, recorded textbooks and individual testing for qualified students.

3577   Southeastern Oklahoma State University

1405 N 4th Ave
Durant, OK 74701-609   580-745-2000
                                         800-435-1327
                                         FAX 580-745-2515
                                         TDD:580-745-2704
                                         http://www.se.edu
                                         e-mail: sdodson@sosu.edu
Michael Turner, Director
Glenn Johnson, President

Four year college that provides services to the learning disabled students.

3578   Southwestern Oklahoma State University

100 Campus Dr
Weatherford, OK 73096-3098   580-772-6611
                                         FAX 580-774-3795
                                         http://www.swosu.edu
                                         e-mail: cindy.dougherty@swosu.edu
John Hays, President

Offers a variety of services to students with disabilities including notetakers, extended testing time, counseling services, and special accommodations.

3579   St. Gregory's University

Partners in Learning
1900 W Macarthur St
Shawnee, OK 74804-2403   405-878-5100
                                         FAX 405-878-5198
                                         TDD:405-878-5103
                                         http://www.stgregorys.edu
                                         e-mail: hlwatson@stgregorys.edu
David Wagie, Coordinator Partners in Learning
Melody Harrington, Assistant Director for Partners

Four-year college offering assistive programs for students with learning disabilities.

3580 Tulsa Community College
Disabled Student Resource Center
909 South Boston Avenue
Tulsa, OK 74119-2095　　918-595-7000
FAX 918-595-7179
TDD:918-595-7287
http://www.tulsacc.edu
e-mail: info@tulsacc.edu

Thomas K Mc Keon, Director
Dr. Ric Baser, Vice President

Offers a variety of services to students with disabilities including note takers, extended testing time, counseling services, and special accommodations.

3581 Tulsa University
Center for Student Academic Support
800 Tucker Dr
Tulsa, OK 74104-9700　　918-631-2000
FAX 918-631-3459
TDD:918-631-3329
http://www.utulsa.edu
e-mail: jcorso@utulsa.edu

Jane Corso PhD, Director
Ruby Wile, Assistant Director
Geoffrey Orsak, President
The Center offers a comprehensive range of support services and accommodations for students with disabilities.

3582 University of Oklahoma
660 Parrington Oval
Norman, OK 73019-3142　　405-325-4357
800-522-0772
FAX 405-325-7545
TDD:405-325-4173
http://www.dsa.ou.edu/ods/
e-mail: sdyer@ou.edu

Suzette Dyer, Disability Services Director
Pam Sullivan, Manager

A public doctoral degree-granting research university. The University of Oklahoma is an equal opportunity institution.

Oregon

3583 Cascade College
PO Box 11000
Oklahoma City, OK 73136-1100　　405-425-5000
800-877-5010
FAX 503-257-1222
http://www.cascade.edu
e-mail: info@oc.edu

Dennis Lynn, President
Shawn Jones, Academic Dean

Offers a variety of services to students with disabilities including note takers, extended testing time, counseling services, and special accommodations.

3584 Central Oregon Community College
2600 NW College Way
Bend, OR 97701-5933　　541-383-7700
FAX 541-383-7506
http://www.cocc.edu

James Middleton, President
Jim Weaver, Director
Donald V. Reeder, Vice Chairman
Central Oregon Community College will be a leader in regionally and globally responsive adult, lifelong, postsecondary education for Central Oregon.

3585 Clackamas Community College
Disability Resource Center
19600 Molalla Ave
Oregon City, OR 97045　　503-594-3181
FAX 503-722-5865
TDD:503-650-6649
http://www.clackamas.edu
e-mail: betsyp@clackamas.edu

Joanne Truesdell, President
Lisabeth Pacheco, Disability Coordinator

A public two-year college. Special education services are designed to support student success by creating full access and providing appropriate accommodations for all students with disabilities.

3586 Corban College
500 Deer Park Dr
Salem, OR 97317　　503-581-8600
FAX 503-585-4316
http://www.corban.edu
e-mail: dmiliones@corban.edu

Reno Hoff, Director Career/Academics
Reno Hoff, President

Private four year Christian college offering assistance for learning disabled students.

3587 George Fox University
Disability Services Office
414 N Meridian St
Newberg, OR 97132-2697　　503-554-2314
800-765-4369
FAX 503-554-2339
http://ds.georgefox.edu
e-mail: rmuthiah@georgefox.edu

Rick Muthiah, Dean Of Learning Support Svcs.

An independent faith-based four-year college with a small percentagge of students with disabilities.

3588 Lane Community College
4000 E 30th Ave
Eugene, OR 97405-640　　541-463-3000
FAX 541-463-5201
TDD:541-463-3079
http://www.lanecc.edu
e-mail: moretd@lanecc.edu

Mary Spilde, President
Sonya Christian, Vice-President

We provide accommodations, technology, advising, support systems, training and education.

3589 Linfield College
900 SE Baker St
McMinnville, OR 97128-6894　　503-883-2200
FAX 503-883-2472
TDD:503-883-2396
TTY: 503-883-2396
http://www.linfield.edu
e-mail: chwhite@linfield.edu

Cheri E White, Asst Dir, Learning Support Svcs

An independent four-year college. Services include tutoring, extended time for testing, assistance with advising and counseling. Student needs are considered in customizing individual programs of support for documented special needs.

3590 Linn-Benton Community College Office of Disability Services
600 Pacific Blvd SW
Red Cedar Hall, Room 114
Albany, OR 97321　　541-917-4789
FAX 541-917-4328
TDD:541-917-4703
http://www.linnbenton.edu/go/ds
e-mail: ods@linnbenton.edu

Lynne Cox, Coordinator

A public two-year college. LBCC provides a number of services and programs for students with disabilities including classes, supportive services and aids.

3591 Mount Bachelor Academy
33051 NE Ochoco Hwy
Prineville, OR 97754-7990
541-462-3404
800-462-3404
FAX 541-462-3430
http://www.mtba.com/

Sharon Bitz, Executive Director

Aspen Education Group is recognized nationwide as the leading provider of education programs for struggling or underachieving young people. As the largest and most comprehensive network of therapeutic schools and programs, Aspen offers professionals and families the opportunity to choose a setting that best meets a student's unique academic and emotional needs.

3592 Mt. Hood Community College Disability Services Department
Learning Disabilities Department
26000 SE Stark St
Gresham, OR 97030-3300
503-491-6422
FAX 503-491-7389
TDD:503-491-7670
http://www.mhcc.edu
e-mail: dsoweb@mhcc.edu

John Sygielski, Coordinator
Laurie Clarke, Program Adviser
Michael Hay, President
A commitment to providing educational opportunities for all students forms the foundation of the disability services program. If you are a student with a disability, disability services will help you overcome potential obstacles so that you may be successful in your area of study. Disability services gives you the needed support to help you meet your goals without separating you and other students with disabilities from existing programs.

3593 Oregon Institute of Technology
Oregon State University Systems
3201 Campus Dr
Klamath Falls, OR 97601-8801
541-885-1000
800-422-2017
FAX 541-885-1777
TDD:541-885-1072
TTY: 541-885-1072
http://www.oit.edu
e-mail: access@oit.edu

Chris Maples, Acting President
Bob Nettles, VP Finance

A public four-year college enrolling about 3,000 students. Accommodations are tailored to the needs of individual students on a case-by-case basis for those self-identified as having learning disabilities.

3594 Oregon State University
Services for Students with Disabilities
A202 Kerr Administration Building
Corvallis, OR 97331
541-737-1000
FAX 541-737-7354
TDD:541-737-3666
http://www.oregonstate.edu
e-mail: disabilty.services@oregonstate.edu
Tracy Bentley-Towlin, Director
Dr. Edward Ray, President

A public four-year college with a small percentage of students.

3595 Portland Community College
PO Box 19000
Portland, OR 97280-990
503-244-6111
FAX 503-977-4882
TTY: 503-246-4072
http://www.pcc.edu

Carolee Schmeer, LD Specialist
Mary Ann Jarvis, President

Our team includes rehabilitation guidance counselors, learning disability specialists, sign language interpreters, a technology specialist, vocational progarm and special needs coordinatiors.

3596 Reed College
3203 SE Woodstock Blvd
Portland, OR 97202-8199
503-771-1112
FAX 503-777-7769
http://www.reed.edu
e-mail: admissions@reed.edu
John R. Kroger, President
Burel Clayton, Administrative Officer

Offers a variety of services to students with disabilities including notetakers, extended testing time, counseling services, and special accommodations.

3597 Southwestern Oregon Community College
1988 Newmark Ave
Coos Bay, OR 97420-2911
541-888-2525
800-962-2838
FAX 541-888-7285
http://www.socc.edu

Patty Scott, President

The college will provide reasonable accommodation for students with learning disabilities. Some instructors in academic skills have special training in working with learning disabled students.

3598 Treasure Valley Community College
650 College Blvd
Ontario, OR 97914-3423
541-881-8822
FAX 541-881-2717
http://www.tvcc.cc.or.us

Jim Sorensen, President

Offers a variety of services to students with disabilities including notetakers, extended testing time, counseling services, and special accommodations.

3599 Umpqua Community College
PO Box 967
Roseburg, OR 97470-226
541-440-4600
FAX 541-440-4612
http://www.umpqua.edu
Barbara Stoner, Disability Services Coordinator
David Beyer, Administrator

A public two-year college with a small percentage of special education students.

3600 University of Oregon
5278 University of Oregon
Eugene, OR 97403-5278
541-346-1155
FAX 541-346-6013
TTY: 541-346-1155
http://www.ds.uoregon.edu
Richard W Lariviere, President
Molly Sirois, Disability Services Advisor

A public four-year college with about 5% of students with disabilities.

3601 **Warner Pacific College**
2219 SE 68th Ave
Portland, OR 97215-4099   503-517-1020
                                         800-582-7885
                                    FAX 503-517-1350
                         http://www.warnerpacific.edu
               e-mail: webmaster@warnerpacific.edu
Jay Barber, President
Wayne Peterson, Vice President

Offers a variety of services to students with disabilities including notetakers, extended testing time, counseling services, and special accommodations.

3602 **Western Oregon University**
345 Monmouth Ave N
Monmouth, OR 97361-1371   503-838-8240
                                        877-877-1593
                                   FAX 503-838-8399
                              http://www.wou.edu
                      e-mail: webmaster@wou.edu
Allen Mc Kiel, Quality Services
Mark D. Weiss, President

A public four-year college. Strives to provide and promote a supportive, accessible, non-discriminatory learning and working environment for students, faculty, staff and community members with disabilities. These goals are realized through the provision of individualized support services, advocacy and the identification of current technology and information.

3603 **Willamette University**
Learning Disabilities Department
900 State St
Salem, OR 97301-3930   503-370-6300
                                   FAX 503-370-6148
                                   TDD:503-375-5383
         http://www.willamette.edu/dept/disability/main.
                        e-mail: jhill@willamette.edu
M Lee Pelton, Director Disability/Learning
Lynn Breen, Office Manager
Stephen E. Thorsett, President
Offers a variety of services to students with disabilities including notetakers, extended testing time, counseling services, and special accommodations. Provides services for all students on campus, including graduate schools.

Pennsylvania

3604 **Albright College**
13th & Bern Streets
P.O. Box 15234
Reading, PA 19612-5234   610-921-7662
                                   FAX 610-921-7530
                              http://www.albright.edu
                        e-mail: albright@alb.edu
Erin Evans, Asst. Dean & Director
Lex McMillan, IV, President

An independent four-year college with a small percentage of special education students. There is an additional fee for the education program in addition to the regular tuition.

3605 **Bloomsburg University**
400 E 2nd St
Bloomsburg, PA 17815-1301   570-389-4000
                                   FAX 570-389-3700
                              http://www.bloomu.edu
Jessica S Kozloff, Administrator
David L. Soltz, Ph.D, President

Offers a variety of services to students with disabilities including notetakers, extended testing time, counseling services, and special accommodations.

3606 **Bryn Mawr College**
Educational Support Services
101 N Merion Ave
Bryn Mawr, PA 19010-2899   610-526-5000
                                   FAX 610-525-7450
                              http://www.brynmawr.edu
                 e-mail: lmendez@brynmawr.edu
Jane McAuliffe, President
Tyler Garber, Vice President

Bryn Mawr is a private liberal arts college located in Bryn Mawr, Pennsylvania not far from Philadelphia. The College provides support services for qualified students with documented learning, physical, and psychological disabilities. For additional information visit www.brynmawr.edu/access_services .

3607 **Cabrini College**
Disability Support Services
610 King of Prussia Rd
Radnor, PA 19087-3698   610-902-8100
                                   FAX 610-902-8204
                                   TDD:610-902-8582
                              http://www.cabrini.edu
                 e-mail: ama722@cabrini.edu
Marie A George, Director
Roberta Jacquet, Manager
Marie Angelella George, President
Offers support services and appropriate accommodations to students with documented learning disabilities.

3608 **Carnegie Mellon University**
Equal Opportunity Services, Disability Resources
143 N Craig St
102 Whitfield Hall
Pittsburgh, PA 15213   412-268-2013
                                   FAX 412-268-1524
         http://www.cmu.edu/hr/eos/disability/index.html
                 e-mail: lpowell@andrew.cmu.edu
Larry Powell, Director

Four year college that offers its students services for the learning disabled.

3609 **College Misericordia**
Alternative Learners Project
301 Lake St
Dallas, PA 18612-1090   570-674-6400
                                        800-852-7675
                                   FAX 570-675-2441
                              http://www.misericordia.edu
                 e-mail: jrogan@miseri.edu
Michael Mc Dowell, President

An independent four-year college with about 5% special education students.

3610 **Community College of Allegheny County: College Center, North Campus**
Learning Disabilities Services
8701 Perry Hwy
Pittsburgh, PA 15237-5353   412-366-7000
                                   FAX 412-369-3624
                                   TDD:412-369-4110
                                   TTY: 412-369-4110
                              http://www.ccac.edu
                 e-mail: kwhite@ccac.edu
Donna Imhoff, Director

Support services for students with disabilities are provided according to individual needs. Services include assistance with testing, advisement, registration, classroom accommodations, professor and agency contact.

3611 Community College of Allegheny County: Boyce Campus
595 Beatty Rd
Monroeville, PA 15146-1348   724-325-6604
FAX 724-325-6733
TTY: 724-325-6733
http://www.ccac.edu
e-mail: mailto:Pflorent@ccac.edu
Patricia Florentine, Director

A 2 year community college campus in a suburban setting. Offers a variety of services to students with disabilities including notetakers, extended testing time, counseling services, and special accommodations.

3612 Community College of Philadelphia
Center on Disability
1700 Spring Garden St
Philadelphia, PA 19130-3991   215-751-8010
FAX 215-751-8762
http://www.ccp.edu
e-mail: fdirosa@ccp.edu
Stephen Curtis, President
Jackie Williams, Administrative Assistant
\
ÿWith more than 70 associate's degree, certification and continuing education programs, a lively campus near Center City, and a supportive, top-flight faculty,ÿCommunity College of Philadelphia is your path to possibilities.

3613 Delaware County Community College
901 Media Line Rd
Media, PA 19063-1027   610-359-5000
FAX 610-359-5055
TDD:610-359-5020
TTY: 610-359-5020
http://www.dccc.edu
e-mail: abinder@dccc.edu
Jerome Parker, Director Special Needs

Delaware County Community College, the ninth largest college in the Philadelphia metropolitan area, is a public, two year institution offering more than 60 programs of study. Its open-door policy, and affordable tuition make it accessible to all. Services to physically and learning disabled students include counseling services, tutoring, extended testing, tape recorded lectures, spelling allowances, assistive equipment, notes copied and study skills workshops.

3614 Delaware Valley College of Science and Agriculture
700 E Butler Ave
Doylestown, PA 18901-2698   215-345-1500
FAX 215-345-8916
http://www.delval.edu
e-mail: karen.kay@delval.edu
Dr Joseph S Brosnan, Counseling Director

Offers a variety of services to students with disabilities including notetakers, extended testing time, counseling services, and special accommodations.

3615 Delaware Valley Friends School
19 E Central Ave
Paoli, PA 19301-1345   610-640-4150
FAX 610-296-9970
http://www.dvfs.org
Katherine Schantz, Head of School

Our mission is to prepare students with learning differences for future work and study.

3616 Dickinson College
Services for Students with Disabilities
PO Box 1773
Carlisle, PA 17013-2896   717-243-5121
800-644-1773
FAX 717-245-1080
TTY: 717-245-1134
http://www.dickenson.edu
e-mail: jervis@dickinson.edu
Keith Jervis, Coordinator
William G. Durdenÿ, President

The Office of Counseling and Disability Services is dedicated to the enhancement of healthy student development. Professional and paraprofessional staff offer confidential individual and group counseling sessions and outreach services which help students with both general developmental issues and with specific personal or interpersonal difficulties.

3617 Drexel University
Office of Disability Services
3141 Chestnut St
Philadelphia, PA 19104-2875   215-895-2000
FAX 215-895-1414
http://www.drexel.edu
John A. Fry, President
Mark L. Greenberg, PhD, Provost and SVP

Drexel University's mission is to serve their students and society through comprehensive integrated academic offerings enhanced by technology, co-operative education, and clinical practice in an urban setting, with global outreach embracing research, scholarly activities, and community initiatives.

3618 East Stroudsburg University of Pennsylvania
200 Prospect St
East Stroudsburg, PA 18301-2999   570-422-3211
877-230-5547
FAX 570-422-3777
TDD:570-422-3543
http://www.esu.edu
e-mail: emiller@po-box.esu.edu
Robert J Dillman, Disability Services Director
Michelle Hoffman, Manager
Van Reidhead, Provost and Vice President
Four year college that offers services to disabled students.

3619 Gannon University
Program for Students with Learning Disabilities
109 University Sq
Erie, PA 16541   814-871-7000
814-426-6668
FAX 814-871-7338
http://www.gannon.edu
e-mail: kanter001@gannon.edu
Antoine Garibaldi, Director
Dr. Keith Taylor, President

Special Support Services are provided for students who have a diagnosed learning disability and choose to enroll in PSLO. Charge of $300.00 per semester special services include individual sessions with Educational Specialists, Kurzweil Reader, Copying Services, Advocacy Seminar Courses I and II, Reading Efficiency sessions, testing accommodations, etc.

3620 Gettysburg College
300 N Washington St
Gettysburg, PA 17325-1483   717-337-6300
800-431-0803
FAX 717-337-6008
http://www.gettysburg.edu
Janet Morgan Riggs, President

Offers a variety of services to students with disabilities including notetakers, extended testing time, counseling services, and special accommodations.

3621   **Gwynedd: Mercy College**
PO Box 901
Gwynedd Valley, PA 19437-901   215-646-7300
800-342-5462
FAX 215-641-5598
http://www.gmc.edu
e-mail: guido.r@gmc.edu
Rochelle Guido MS, Disability Support Svcs Coord.
Kathleen Mulroy, President

Recognizing the diversity of our student population and the challenges and needs this brings to the educational enterprise, Gwynedd-Mercy College, within the bounds of its resources, intends to provide reasonable accommodations for students with disabilities so that all students accepted into a program of study have equal access and subsequent opportunity to reach their academic and personal goals. Requests for specific accommodations are processed on an individual basis.

3622   **Harcum Junior College**

750 Montgomery Ave
Bryn Mawr, PA 19010-3476   610-525-4100
FAX 610-526-6086
http://www.harcum.edu

Ann Ranieri, Director
Charles Trout, President
ÿJon Jay DeTemple, PhDÿ, President
An independent two-year college. There is an additional fee for the special education program in addition to the regular tuition.

3623   **Harrisburg Area Community College**
Disability Services Office
1 Hacc Dr
Harrisburg, PA 17110-2999   717-780-2300
800-222-4222
FAX 717-780-2551
http://www.hacc.edu
e-mail: admit@hacc.edu
Edna V Baehre, Affairs/Enrollment Management
Carol Keeper, Director

A public two-year college with a small percentage of special needs students.

3624   **Hill Top Preparatory School**
737 S Ithan Ave
Bryn Mawr, PA 19010-1197   610-527-3230
FAX 610-527-7683
http://www.hilltopprep.org
Tom Needham, Head of School

Prepares students in grades 6-12 with diagnosed learning differences for higher education and successful futures. The school is d co-educational day school that offers an individually structures, rigorous curriculum that is complemented by a dynamic counseling support and menotoring program.

3625   **Indiana University of Pennsylvania**
201 Pratt Dr
Indiana, PA 15705-1003   724-357-4067
FAX 724-357-2889
TDD:724-357-4067
http://www.iup.edu/advisingtesting
e-mail: advising-testing@grove.iup.edu
Lawrence K Pettit, President
Todd Van Wieren, Assistant Director

Disability Support Services is a component of the Advising and Testing Center. The mission of DSS is to ensure that students with disabilities who attend Indiana University of Pennsylvainia receive an integrated, quality education.

3626   **Keystone Junior College**
P.O .Box 50
La Plume, PA 18440-1099   570-945-8000
877-4college
FAX 570-945-8962
http://www.keystone.edu
Edward G Boehm Jr, Manager

Offers a variety of services to students with disabilities including notetakers, extended testing time, counseling services, and special accommodations.

3627   **King's College**
Academic Skills Center
133 N River St
Wilkes Barre, PA 18711-801   570-208-5900
FAX 570-208-5967
http://www.kings.edu
e-mail: jaburke@kings.edu
Thomas O'Hara, Academic Skills Center Director
Thomas R. Smith, Chairman

First Year Academic Studies Program (FASP) - A proactive program to facilitate transition to college with intensive first-year programming with indivdual support in subsequent years. Students are enrolled as full-time students completing general education and major course requirements. Support includes regular meetings with a learning disability specialist, faculty tutorials/study groups, priority advisement, and development of self-advocacy skills. A fee charged for the first year.

3628   **Kutztown University of Pennsylvania**
15200 Kutztown Road
Kutztown, PA 19530   610-683-4060
FAX 610-683-1520
TDD:610-683-4499
http://www.kutztown.edu
e-mail: sutherla@kutztown.edu
Patricia Richter, Director

Kutztown University of Pennsylvania, a member of the Pennsylvania State System of Higher Education, was founded in 1856 as Keystone Normal School, and achieved University status in 1983. Today Kutztown University is a modern, comprehensive University. There are approximately 7,900 full and part time undergraduate and graduate students.

3629   **Lebanon Valley College**
101 N College Ave
Annville, PA 17003-1400   717-867-6275
FAX 717-867-6124
http://www.lvc.edu
e-mail: perry@lvc.edu
Stephen C MacDonald, President

Four year college that offers learning disabled students support and services.

3630   **Lehigh Carbon Community College**
4525 Education Park Dr
Schnecksville, PA 18078-2598   610-799-2121
FAX 610-799-1527
TTY: 610-799-1792
http://www.lccc.edu
e-mail: mmitchell@lccc.edu or lkelly@lccc.edu
Donald Snyder, President
Linda Kelly, Learning Specialist
Cathy Ahner, Office Assistant
Disability Support Services provides learning support to qualified students with disabilities in compliance with section 504 of the Rehabilitation Act and Americans with Disabilities Act, 1990. Requests for access and/or academic accommodations are reviewed on a case by case basis. Additional learning support is available through Educational Support Services.

3631   Lock Haven University of Pennsylvania
Learning Disabilities Office
401 N Fairview St
Lock Haven, PA 17745-2390   570-893-2011
                                          800-332-8900
                                     FAX 570-893-2432
                                  http://www.lhup.edu
                              e-mail: rjunco@lhup.edu
Keith T Miller, Director

A public four-year college with a small percentage of students with disabilities.

3632   Lycoming College
700 College Place
Williamsport, PA 17701   570-321-4000
                                          800-345-3920
                                     FAX 570-321-4337
                               http://www.lycoming.edu
Diane Bonner MD, Director
James Douthat, President

An independent four-year college with a small percentage of special education students.

3633   Manor Junior College
700 Fox Chase Rd
Jenkintown, PA 19046-3399   215-885-2360
                                     FAX 215-576-6564
                                 http://www.manor.edu
                           e-mail: ftadmiss@manor.edu
Sister Mary Cecilia, President
Sally Mydlowec, Vice President

Offers a variety of services to students with disabilities including notetakers, extended testing time, counseling services, and special accommodations.

3634   Mansfield University of Pennsylvania
Services for Students with Learning Disabilities
213 S Hall Academy St
Mansfield, PA 16933   570-662-4000
                                          800-577-6826
                                     FAX 570-662-4995
                              http://www.mansfield.edu
                         e-mail: wchabala@mansfield.edu
David Werner, Director
Dr. Allan Golden, President

Offers a variety of services to students with disabilities including, extended testing time, counseling services, and special accommodations.

3635   Marywood University
Special Education Department
2300 Adams Ave
Scranton, PA 18509-1598   570-348-6211
                                          866-279-9663
                                     FAX 570-961-4739
                               http://www.marywood.edu
Anne Munley, President
Alan M. . Levine, Vice President

Marywood challenges students to broaden their understanding of globale issues and to make decisions based on spiritual, ethical, and religious values.

3636   Mercyhurst College
Learning Differences Program
501 E 38th St
Erie, PA 16546   814-824-2000
                                          800-825-1926
                                     FAX 814-824-2438
                              http://www.mercyhurst.edu
                          e-mail: drogers@mercyhurst.edu
Tom Gamble, President

Mercyhurst provides a comprehensive program of academic accommodations and support services to students with documented learning disabilities. Accommodations may include audiotaped textbooks, extended time for tests, a test reader and use of a computer to complete essay tests.

3637   Messiah College
1 S College Ave
Grantham, PA 17027-9800   717-766-2511
                                          800-233-4220
                                     FAX 717-796-5217
                               http://www.messiah.edu
                   e-mail: disabilityservices@messiah.edu
Kim Phipps, President
Keith W Drahn PhD, Director
Carol Wickey, Assistant to Director
Private Christian college.

3638   Millersville University of Pennsylvania
Disability and Learning Services
1 South George St
Millersville, PA 17551   717-872-3011
                                     FAX 717-871-2129
                               http://www.millersv.edu
              e-mail: learning.services@millersville.edu
Sherlynn Bessick, Director
Terry Asche, Secretary
Vilas A. Prabhu, Provost and VP
Four year college that provides services to learning disabled students.

3639   Moravian College
1200 Main Street
Bethlehem, PA 18018   610-861-1300
                                          800-441-3191
                                     FAX 610-861-1577
                               http://www.moravian.edu
                          e-mail: memld02@moravian.edu
Debbie Hinkel, Secretary
Christopher Thomforde, President
Julie A. Del Giorno, Chief of Staff
Four year college that offers programs for the learning disabled.

3640   Northampton Community College
Disability Support Services
3835 Green Pond Rd
Bethlehem, PA 18020-7599   610-861-5300
                                     FAX 610-861-5373
                                     TDD:610-861-5351
          http://www.northampton.edu/disabilityservices
                   e-mail: LDemshock@northampton.edu
Art Scott, Disability Service Coordinator
Dr. Mark H. Erickson, President

Encourages academically qualified students with disabilities to take advantage of educational programs. Services and accommodations are offered to facilitate accessiblity to both college programs and facilities. Services provided to students with disabilities are based upon each student individual needs.

3641   Pace School
2432 Greensburg Pike
Pittsburgh, PA 15221-3611   412-244-1900
                                     FAX 412-244-0100
                              http://www.paceschool.org
                           e-mail: pace@paceschool.org
Karen Lamoureux, Chief Executive Officer
Gerri L. Sperling, Vice President
Robert Gold, Secretary
A placement option for school districts in Allegheny and surrounding counties that serves kids, K-9, with emotional challenges or Autism.

3642　**Pathway School**
162 Egypt Rd
Norristown, PA 19403-3090　　　　610-277-0660
　　　　　　　　　　　　　　　　FAX 610-539-1973
　　　　　　　　　　　http://www.pathwayschool.org
Bill O'Flanagan, Acting President
Diana Phifer, Director Of Admissions

Provides a comprehensive program of services for children
between the ages of 9 and 21 for whom mainstream public
and private school education is insufficient to meet their
needs. These youngsters display severe neuropsychiatric
disorders and complex learning issues necessitating focused
learning environments.

3643　**Pennsylvania Institute of Technology**
800 Manchester Ave
Media, PA 19063-4098　　　　　610-892-1000
　　　　　　　　　　　　　　　　800-422-0025
　　　　　　　　　　　　　　FAX 610-892-1510
　　　　　　　　　　　　http://www.pit.edu
Walter R Garrison, President

Offers a variety of services to students with disabilities including notetakers, extended testing time, counseling services, and special accommodations.

3644　**Pennsylvania State University**
Support Services for Students with Learning Disab
116 Boucke Bldg
University Park, PA 16802-5902　　　814-863-1807
　　　　　　　　　　　　　　　　FAX 814-863-3217
　　　　　　　　　　　　　　TDD:814-863-1807
　　　　　　　　　　http://www.equity.psu.edu/ods
　　　　e-mail: william.welsh@equity.psu.edu/ods
William Welsh, Director
Ann Ette, Secretary
Sanford Thatcher, Executive Director
Penn State provides academic accommodations and support
services to students with documented learning disabilities.
Accommodations may include audiotaped textbooks, ex-
tended time for tests, a test reader and use of a computer to
complete essay tests.

3645　**Pennsylvania State University: Mont Alto**
1 Campus Dr
Mont Alto, PA 17237-9799　　　　717-749-6000
　　　　　　　　　　　　　　　　FAX 717-749-6116
　　　　　　　　　　　　http://www.ma.psu.edu
　　　　　　　　　　　　e-mail: nmhz@psu.edu
Nanette Hatzef, Learning Center Director

It is the intention of Penn State University to provide equal
access to students with disabilities as mandated by the
Americans with Disabilities Act, and the Rehabilitiation
Act. Students with disabilities are encouraged to take advantage of the support services provided to help them successfully meet the high academic standards of the university.

3646　**Pennsylvania State University: Schuylkill Campus**
Disability Services
200 University Dr
Schuylkill Haven, PA 17972-2202　　570-385-6000
　　　　　　　　　　　　　　　　FAX 570-385-3672
　　　　　　　　　　　　http://www.sl.psu.edu
Cheryl Holland, Disability Services Coordinator
Keith Hillkirk, Administrator
Kelly M. Austin, Vice President
Offers a variety of services to students with disabilities in-
cluding notetakers, extended testing time, counseling ser-
vices, and special accommodations.

3647　**Pennsylvania State University: Shenango Valley Cam-
pus**
Office for Disability Services
105 Boucke Bldg
University Park, PA 16802-5902　　　814-863-1807
　　　　　　　　　　　　　　　　FAX 814-863-3217
　　　　　　　　　　　　　　TDD:814-863-1807
　　　　　　　　　　　　　　TTY: 814-863-1807
　　　　　　　　　　http://www.equity.psu.edu/ods
　　　　e-mail: william.welsh@equity.psu.edu/ods
William Welsh, Director
Karen Port, Exam Coordinator

Penn State encourages academically qualified students with
disabilities to take advantage of its educational programs.
To be eligible for disability related accommodations, individuals must have a documented disability as defined by the
Americans with Disabilities Act. A disability is defined by
the physical or mental impairment that substantially limits a
major life function. Individuals seeking accommodations
are required to provided documentation.

3648　**Pennsylvania State University: Worthington Scranton
Campus**
120 Ridgeview Dr
Dunmore, PA 18512-1602　　　　　570-963-2500
　　　　　　　　　　　　　　　　FAX 570-963-2535
　　　　　　　　　　　　http://www.sn.psu.edu
Michele Steele, Special Services
Marybeth Krogh-Jesperse, Manager
Dr. Alan Peslak, President
Penn State encourages academically qualified students with
disabilities to take advantage of its educational programs. It
is the policy of the university not to discriminate against per-
sons with disabilities in its admissions policies or proce-
dures or its educational programs, services and activities.

3649　**Point Park College**
Program for Academic Success
201 Wood St
Pittsburgh, PA 15222-1984　　　　412-391-4100
　　　　　　　　　　　　　　　　800-321-0129
　　　　　　　　　　　　　　FAX 412-392-3998
　　　　　　　　　　　http://www.pointpark.edu
　　　　　　　　e-mail: pboykin@pointpark.edu
Paul Hennigan, Director
Dr. Paul Hennigan, President

Provides appropriate, reasonable accommodations for students who are disabled in accordance with the Americans
with Disabilities Act. All campus accommodations are coordinated through the Program for Academic Success (PAS).

3650　**Reading Area Community College**
10 South Second Street
Reading, PA 19603-1706　　　　　610-372-4721
　　　　　　　　　　　　　　　　800-626-1665
　　　　　　　　　　　　　　FAX 610-607-6264
　　　　　　　　　　　　http://www.racc.edu
Dr. Anna Weitz, President
Mr. John C. Woodward, Chairman

A public two-year college with a small percentage of special
education students.

3651　**Seton Hill University**
Seton Hill Dr
Greensburg, PA 15601　　　　　　724-834-2200
　　　　　　　　　　　　　　　　800-826-6234
　　　　　　　　　　　　　　FAX 724-834-2752
　　　　　　　　　　　　　　TTY: 724-830-1151
　　　　　　　　　　　http://www.setonhill.edu
　　　　　　　　　e-mail: bassi@setonhill.edu
Joann Boyle, Director Counseling Center
Molly Robb Shimko, Associate Vice President

Offers programs to those who are eligible and learning disabled.

3652 Shippensburg University of Pennsylvania
1871 Old Main Dr
Shippensburg, PA 17257-2299   717-477-7447
                                 FAX 717-477-1273
                                 http://www.ship.edu
                                 e-mail: lawate@wharf.ship.edu
George F Harpster, President

Four year college that offers services to the learning disabled students.

3653 Solebury School
Learning Skills Program
6832 Phillips Mill Rd
New Hope, PA 18938-9682   215-862-5261
                              FAX 215-862-3366
                              http://www.solebury.org
Tom Wilschutz, Head of School

A special program for bright students who are hampered by specific learning differences. It is ideally suited for students who require specialized instruction to assist them in unlocking their potential.

3654 Stratford Friends School
2 Bishop Hollow Road
Newtown Square, PA 19073-5319   610-355-9580
                                    FAX 610-355-9585
                                    http://www.stratfordfriends.org
                                    e-mail: tmadigan@stratfordfriends.org
Tim Madigan, Ph.D., Head of School

Offer programs for students with language-based learning disabilities who have had difficulty learning in a traditional classroom.

3655 Summer Matters
1777 N Valley Rd
PO Box 730
Paoli, PA 19301   610-296-6725
                      FAX 610-640-0132
                      http://www.summermatters.org
                      e-mail: info@summermatters.org
Tim Lanshe, Director of Education

Represents a continuum of innovative summer enrichment and remedial experiences for youth and young adults. Offers 3 separate and unique programs for learning and fun.

3656 Temple University
1301 Cecil B Moore Ave
100 Ritter Annex
Philadelphia, PA 19122   215-204-1280
                             FAX 215-204-6794
                             TTY: 215-204-1786
                             http://www.temple.edu/disability
                             e-mail: drs@temple.edu
Vanessa Dash, LD Coordinator
John Bennett, Director

Offers a variety of services to students with disabilities including proctoring, interpreting and academic accommodations.

3657 Thaddeus Stevens College of Technology
750 E King St
Lancaster, PA 17602-3198   717-299-7408
                               800-842-3832
                               FAX 717-391-1360
                               http://www.stevenscollege.edu
                               e-mail: schuch@stevenscollege.edu
Deb Schuch, Counselor/Disabilities Coord.

A 2-year trade and technical college primarily serving socially and economically under-resourced students.

3658 Thiel College
Office of Special Needs
75 College Ave
Greenville, PA 16125-2181   724-589-2000
                                800-248-4435
                                FAX 724-589-2850
                                http://www.thiel.edu
                                e-mail: scowan@thiel.edu
Lance A Masters, Office Special Needs Coordinator
Mark Benninghoff, Vice President

Four year college that provides an Office of Special Needs for those students with disabilities.

3659 University of Pennsylvania
3451 Walnut Street
Philadelphia, PA 19104   215-898-5000
                             FAX 215-898-5756
                             http://www.upenn.edu
                             e-mail: lrcmail@pobox.upenn.edu
Susan Weaver, Special Services
Myrna Cohen, Director
Amy Gutmann, President
Services for People with Disabilities coordinates academic support services for students with disabilities; services include readers, notetakers, library research assistants, tutors or transcribers.

3660 University of Pittsburgh: Bradford
Learning Development Department
300 Campus Dr
Bradford, PA 16701-2898   814-362-7609
                              800-872-1787
                              FAX 814-362-7684
                              http://www.upb.pitt.edu
Gillian Boyce MD, Director
Kara Kennedy, Learning Development Specialist
Dr. Livingst Alexander, President
Offers a variety of services to students with disabilities including extended testing time, counseling services, and special accommodations.

3661 University of Pittsburgh: Greensburg
Disabilities Services Office
150 Finoli Drive
Greensburg, PA 15601   724-8367-704
                           FAX 724-836-7134
                           http://www.pitt.edu/~upg
                           e-mail: upgadmit@pitt.edu
Lou Ann Sears, Director Learning Resources Ctr
Gayle Pamerleau, Counselor
Sharon P. Smithÿ, President
The Learning Resources Center is an important place for students with disabilities at Pitt Greensburg. Students are encouraged to register with Lou Ann Sears to recieve any accommodations they are entitled to.

3662 University of Scranton
Memorial Hall
Scranton, PA 18510   570-941-7400
                         FAX 570-941-7899
                         http://http://matrix.scranton.edu
                         e-mail: addmissions@scranton.edu
Mary McAndrew, Assistant Director
Oliver Strickland, President
Meredith Lubas, Vice President
Four year college that offers programs for learning disabled students.

3663 University of the Arts
320 S Broad St
Philadelphia, PA 19102-4994   215-717-6000
                                  800-616-2787
                                  FAX 215-717-6045
                                  http://www.uarts.edu
Sean T. Buffington, President

Within this community of artists, the process of learning engages, refines, and articulates all of our creative capabilities; the Office of Educational Accessibility is here to assist students with disabilities in the pursuit of their personal, creative, artisitic and educational objectives.

3664 Ursinus College
PO Box 1000
Collegeville, PA 19426-1000 610-409-3000
FAX 610-489-0627
http://www.ursinus.edu
Winfield Guilmette, Vice President for Finance
Bobby Fong, President

Offers a variety of services to students with disabilities including notetakers, extended testing time, counseling services, and special accommodations.

3665 Valley Forge Educational Services
1777 N Valley Rd
PO Box 730
Paoli, PA 19301 610-296-6725
FAX 610-640-0132
http://www.vfes.net
e-mail: info@vfes.net
Tim Lanshe, Director of Education

Offers a wide variety of educational services focused on guiding 21st century learners to independence. Provides premier educational optoins for young children, adolescents and pre-21 adults ranging from school-based and summer programs to career planning to clinical and consulting services.

3666 Vanguard School
PO Box 730
Paoli, PA 19301-0730 610-296-6700
FAX 610-640-0132
http://www.vanguardschool-pa.org
e-mail: info@vanguardschool-pa.org
Tim Lanshe, Director of Education

Serves students whose exceptionalities include austism spectrum disorders, mild emotional disturbance and cognitive disabilities.

3667 Washington and Jefferson College
60 S Lincoln St
Washington, PA 15301-4801 724-222-4400
888-926-3529
FAX 724-223-6534
http://www.washjeff.edu
e-mail: info@washjeff.edu
Tori Haring-Smith, Assistant Dean
Denny Trelka, Dean

An independent four-year college with a small percentage of special education students.

3668 Westmoreland County Community College
145 Pavilion Lane
Youngwood, PA 15697 724-925-4000
800-262-2103
FAX 724-925-3823
TDD:724-925-4297
http://www.wccc.edu
e-mail: beresm@wccc-pa.edu
James N Falcon, Student Support Svcs Counselor
Sandra Zelenak, Student Development Director
Steven Ender, President
Offers a variety of services to students with disabilities including notetakers, extended testing time, counseling services, and special accommodations. All services are based on a review of a current evaluation presented by the student. Appropriate services are then arranged by the student support service counselor.

3669 Widener University
Disabilities Services
1 University Pl
Chester, PA 19013-5792 610-499-4000
FAX 610-499-4386
http://www.widener.edu
e-mail: csimonds@mail.widener.edu
James T Harris III, President
Cynthia Simonds PsyD, Director Disabilities Services

An independent four-year college with comprehensive support services, including disabilities services, academic coaching, tutoring services, a math center and writing center.

Rhode Island

3670 Brown University, Disability Support Services
20 Benevolent St
Box P
Providence, RI 02912-9012 401-863-9588
FAX 401-863-1444
TDD:401-863-9588
http://www.brown.edu
e-mail: dss@brown.edu
Catherine Axe, Director

Brown University has as its primary aim the education of a highly qualified and diverse student body and respects each student's dignity, capacity to contribute, and desire for personal growth and accomplishment. Brown's commitment to students with disabilities is based on awareness of what students require for success. The University desires to foster both intellectual and physical independence to the greatest extent possible in all of its students.

3671 Bryant College
Academic Services
1150 Douglas Pike
Smithfield, RI 02917-1287 401-232-6000
FAX 401-232-6319
http://www.bryant.edu
e-mail: lhazard@bryant.edu
Ronald Machtley, Director
Mary Moroney, Executive Director
Sharon Doyle, Office Manager
An independent four-year Business and Liberal Arts College. A learning specialist is on campus to provide services for students with learning disabilities.

3672 Community College of Rhode Island: Knight Campus
400 East Ave
Warwick, RI 02886-1805 401-825-1000
FAX 401-825-2365
http://www.ccri.edu
e-mail: webservices@ccri.edu
Ray M Dipasquale, Contact
Ray M. Di Pasquale, President

Academic accommodations are available to students with disabilities who demonstrate a documented need for the requested accommodation. Accommodations include but are not limited to adapted equipment, alternative testing, course accommodations, sign language interpreters, reader/audio taping services, scribes and peer note-takers.

3673 Disability Services for Students
University of Rhode Island
330 Memorial Union
Kingston, RI 02881 401-874-2098
FAX 401-874-5574
TTY: 800-745-5555
http://www.uri.edu
e-mail: dss@etal.uri.edu
Pamela Rohland, Director

Disability Service for Students fosters a barrier free environment to individuals with disabilities through education that focuses on inclusion, awareness, and knowledge of ADA/504 compliance. Our mission is two fold: 1. To encourage a sense of empowerment for students with disabilities by providing a process that involves the student. 2. To be an information resource to the University faculty and staff regarding disability awareness and academic services.

3674   Johnson & Wales University

8 Abbott Park Pl
Providence, RI 02903-3775   401-598-1000
                                          800-343-2565
                                          FAX 401-598-2880
                                          http://www.jwc.edu
                                          e-mail: mberstein@jwu.edu
John J Bowen, Center Academic Support Director

An independent four-year university servicing about 5% special education students. Accommodations are individualized to students presenting documentation and may include extended time testing, tape recorders in class, notetaking assistance, reduced course load, preferential scheduling and tutorial assistance.

3675   Providence College

Disability Support Services
1 Cunningham Square
Providence, RI 02918   401-865-1000
                                          FAX 401-865-2057
                                          TDD:401-865-2494
                                          http://www.providence.edu/oas
                                          e-mail: oas@providence.edu
Brian Shanley, Asst Dir Disability Support Svcs
Brian J. Shanley, President

Offers a variety of services to students with disabilities including note takers, extended testing time, counseling services, and special accommodations.

3676   Rhode Island College

Paul V Sherlock Center on Disabilities
600 Mount Pleasant Ave
Providence, RI 02908-1991   401-456-8072
                                          FAX 401-456-8773
                                          TDD:401-456-8150
                                          http://www.sherlockcenter.org
                                          e-mail: aantosh@ric.edu
Ellie O'Niell, Director
Erika Tuttle, Administrative Assistant

The University Affiliated Program (UAP) of Rhode Island is a member of a national network of UAPs. The UAP is charged with four core functions: 1. Providing pre-service training to prepare quality service providers. 2. Providing community outreach training and technical assistance. 3. Disseminating information about research and exemplary practice. 4. Research.

3677   Roger Williams University

One Old Ferry Road
Bristol, RI 02809   401-253-1040
                                          800-458-7144
                                          FAX 401-254-3185
                                          http://www.rwu.edu
Donald J. Farish, Ph.D., J.D., President

An independent comprehensive four-year university with about 5% special education students.

South Carolina

3678   Aiken Technical College

Student Services
PO Drawer 696
Aiken, SC 29802   803-593-9231
                                          FAX 803-593-6641
                                          http://www.atc.edu
                                          e-mail: weldon@atc.edu
Richard Weldon, Counselor
Jennifer Pinckney, Manager
Winsor Susan, President
A public two-year college offering services to the learning disabled.

3679   Camperdown Academy

501 Howell Rd
Greenville, SC 29615-2028   864-244-8899
                                          FAX 864-244-8936
                                          http://www.camperdown.org
Dan Blanch, Head of School

Our mission is to enable students with average to above average intelligence, who also experience learning difficulties in the areas of reading, organization, language processing, and written expression, to reach their maximum academic potential.

3680   Citadel-Military College of South Carolina

171 Moultrie St
Charleston, SC 29409   843-225-3294
                                          FAX 843-953-7036
                                          http://www.citadel.edu
John W. Rosa, President
Thomas J. Elzey, Vice President

Offers a variety of services to students with disabilities including notetakers, extended testing time, counseling services, and special accommodations.

3681   Clemson University

Student Development Services
707 University Under
Clemson, SC 29634   864-656-3311
                                          FAX 864-656-0514
                                          http://www.clemson.edu
                                          e-mail: bmartin@clemson.edu
Bonnie Martin, Director
Jim Barker, President

Four-year college offers services to learning disabled students.

3682   Coastal Carolina University

Disability Services Department
PO Box 261954
Conway, SC 29528-6054   843-347-3161
                                          FAX 843-349-2990
                                          http://www.coastal.edu
Monica Yates, Director
Vonna Gengo, Disability Services Coordinator
David A. DeCenzo, President
Coastal Carolina University provides a program of assistance to students with disabilities. Upon acceptance to the University, students will become eligible for support services by providing documentation of their disability. Accommodations include academic labs, tutorial referral, study skills, counseling, auxillary aids, coordination with other agencies and classroom accommodations.

3683   Erskine College

2 Washington St
Due West, SC 29639   864-359-4358
                                          FAX 864-379-2167
                                          http://www.erskine.edu
Dr. David A. Norman, President
Joe H. Patrick III, Chairman

Offers a variety of services to students with disabilities including notetakers, extended testing time, counseling services, and special accommodations.

3684 Francis Marion University

PO Box 100547
Florence, SC 29502-547

843-661-1362
800-368-7551
FAX 843-661-1202
http://www.fmarion.edu

Luther F Carter, President
Bradley R. Boles, Member

A public four-year college with services for special education students.

3685 Glenforest School

1041 Harbor Dr
West Columbia, SC 29169-3609

803-796-7622
FAX 803-796-1603
http://www.glenforest.org
e-mail: cwinkler@glenforest.org

Chris Winkler, Head of School
Shayna Simoneaux, Community Relations Director

A K-12 independent, SACS accredited, non-profit day school dedicated to educationg students who learn differently. Dedicated to serving children with learning differences and attention issues including: ADD/ADHD, Dyslexia, Dysgraphia and Autism Spectrum Disorders.

3686 Greenville Technical College

PO Box 5616
Greenville, SC 29606-5616

864-246-7282
800-922-1183
FAX 864-250-8580
http://www.greenvilletech.com

Owen Perkins, Associate Dean
Claire Carter, Executive Director

Committed to providing equal access for all students and assisting students in making their college experience successful in accordance with ADA/504 and the Rehabilitation Act. The Office of Special Needs for Students with Disabilities has counselors available to assist in the planning and implementation of appropriate accommodations.

3687 Limestone College

Program for Alternative Learning Styles
1115 College Dr
Gaffney, SC 29340-3799

864-489-7151
800-795-7151
FAX 864-487-8706
http://www.limestone.edu
e-mail: kkearse@limestone.edu

Walt Griffin, President
Nani Lou Cooper, Administrative Assistence

Independent four-year college with a program designed to serve students with learning disabilities. There is an additional fee for the first year in the program in addition to the regular tuition. However, that additional cost is reduced by 50% after the freshman year depending on the grade point average.

3688 Midlands Technical College

PO Box 2408
Columbia, SC 29202-2408

803-738-8324
FAX 803-738-7784
http://www.midlandstech.edu
e-mail: brussell@midland.tec.edu

Dr. Marshall White, Jr., President
Gina Mounsield, Vice President

Services to Students with Disabilities counselors support and assist students with disabilities in meeting their personal, educational and career goals. Services include academic and career planning, faculty/student liasion, assistive technology, readers, writers, interpeters, closed circuit television in libraries, TDD, testing services, orientation sessions and a support group.

3689 North Greenville College

Learning Disabilities Services
7801 N. Tigerville Rd
Tigerville, SC 29688-1892

864-977-7000
800-468-6642
FAX 864-977-2089
http://www.ngc.edu
e-mail: nisgett@ngc.edu

Nancy Isgett, Learning Disabilities Liaison
James Epting, President

Offers a variety of services to students with disabilities including notetakers, extended testing time, counseling services, and special accommodations.

3690 South Carolina State University

300 College Street NE
Orangeburg, SC 29115

803-536-7000
FAX 803-536-8702
http://www.scsu.edu
e-mail: gouveia@scsu.edu

Imogene Gouveia MD, Chief Psychologist
Andrew Hugine, President

Four-year college that provides information and resources for the learning disabled.

3691 Spartanburg Methodist College

1200 Textile Rd
Spartanburg, SC 29301

864-587-4000
800-772-7286
FAX 864-587-4355
http://www.smcsc.edu
e-mail: admiss@smcsc.edu

Sharon Porter, Student Support Director
Colleen Perry Keith, President
Steven Jeter, SSS Counselor
2-year educational institution, Junior College

3692 Technical College of Lowcountry: Beaufort

921 Ribaut Road
Beaufort, SC 29901-1288

843-525-8211
FAX 843-52-8285
http://www.tcl.edu

Carolyn Banner, Career Development
Dr. Thomas Leitzel, President

Offers a variety of services to students with disabilities including note takers, extended testing time, counseling services, and special accommodations.

3693 Trident Academy

1455 Wakendaw Rd
Mount Pleasant, SC 29464-9767

843-884-7046
FAX 843-881-8320
http://www.tridentacademy.com
e-mail: jferber@tridentacademy.com

Joe Ferber, Headmaster

An independent learning disabilities school for students in grades K-12 who have Dyslexia, Dysgraphia, Dyscalculia, Non-verbal Learning Disabilities, ADHD, CAPD and other learning differences.

3694 Trident Technical College

PO Box 118067
Charleston, SC 29423-8067

843-574-6111
877-349-7184
FAX 843-574-6682
http://www.tridenttec.edu

Mary Thornley, President

Recognizes its responsibility to identify and maintain the standards (academic, admissions, scores, etc.) that are necessary to provide quality academic programs while ensuring the rights of students with disabilities.

3695 **University of South Carolina**
Disability Services
106 Leconte
Columbia, SC 29208 803-777-7000
FAX 803-777-6741
TDD:803-777-6744
http://www.sc.edu
e-mail: kpettus@sc.edu

Karen Pettus, Director

The Office of Disability Services provides accommodations for students with documented physical, emotional, and learning disabilities. The professionally trained staff works toward accessiblity for all university programs, services, and activities in compliance with ADA/504. Services include orientation,priority registration, library access, classroom adaptions, interpeters, and access to adapted housing.

3696 **University of South Carolina: Aiken**
171 University Parkway
Aiken, SC 29801 803-648-6851
FAX 803-641-3362
http://www.usca.edu
e-mail: kayb@aiken.sc.edu
Randy Duckett, Special Services
Tom Hallman, Manager
Sandra Jordan, Chancellor
The mission of Disability Services (DS) is to facilitate the transition of students with disabilities into the University eniviroment and to provide appropriate accommodations for each student's special needs in order to ensure equal access to all programs, activities and services at USCA.

3697 **University of South Carolina: Beaufort**
801 Carteret St
Beaufort, SC 29902-4601 843-521-4100
FAX 843-521-4194
http://www.sc.edu/beaufort
Joan Lemoine MD, Associate Dean
Jane Upshaw, President

A public two-year college with services for special education students.

3698 **University of South Carolina: Lancaster**
Admissions Office
PO Box 889
Lancaster, SC 29721-889 803-313-7000
FAX 803-313-7106
http://www.lancaster.sc.edu
e-mail: ksaile@gwm.sc.edu
John Catalano, Administrator
Rebecca Parker, Director

Offers a variety of services to students with disabilities including notetakers, extended testing time, counseling services, and special accommodations.

3699 **Voorhees College**
PO Box 678
Denmark, SC 29042-678 803-780-1234
FAX 866-685-9904
http://www.voorhees.edu
e-mail: info@voorhees.edu
Adeleri Onisegu MD, Director
Curtiss Sumner, Manager

Four-year college that offers programs to learning disabled students.

3700 **Winthrop University**
Student Disabilities Department
701 Oakland Ave
Rock Hill, SC 29733-7001 803-323-2211
FAX 803-323-4861
TDD:803-323-2233
http://www.winthrop.edu
e-mail: smithg@winthrop.edu
Anthony Digiorio, Director
Rosanne Wallace, Administrator

Since each student has a unique set of special needs, the Counselor for Students with Disabilities makes every effort to provide the student with full access to programs and services. Reasonable accommodations are provided based on needs assessed through proper documentation and an intake interview with the couselor. The majority of buildings on campus are accessible.

South Dakota

3701 **Black Hills State College**
1200 University St
Unit 9078
Spearfish, SD 57799-0002 605-642-6011
800-255-2478
FAX 605-642-6099
http://www.bhsu.edu
e-mail: mike.mcneil@bhsu.edu
Kay Schallenkamp, Disability Services Coordinator

Provide the comprehensive supports necessary in meeting the individual needs of students with disabilities.

3702 **Children's Care Hospital and School**
Educational Program
2501 W 26th St
Sioux Falls, SD 57105-2498 605-782-2300
800-584-9294
FAX 605-336-0277
http://www.cchs.org
Lynn Clayton, President

Provides a variety of innovative educational services based on the individual learning, medical, and therapeutic needs of the child.

3703 **Northern State University**
1200 S Jay St
Aberdeen, SD 57401-7198 605-626-3011
FAX 605-626-2587
http://www.northern.edu
e-mail: admissions@northern.edu
Laurie Nichols, Director
James Smith, President

Four-year college that provides services to students with a learning disability.

3704 **South Dakota School of Mines & Technology**
501 E Saint Joseph St
Rapid City, SD 57701-3995 605-394-2511
800-544-8162
FAX 605-394-6131
http://www.sdsmt.edu
e-mail: fcampone@sdsmt.edu
Robert A. Wharton, Ph.D, President

Four-year college that offers support services to those students whom are disabled.

3705 **South Dakota State University**
PO Box 2201
Brookings, SD 57007   605-688-5907
                                            800-952-3541
                                        FAX 605-688-6891
                                        TDD:605-688-4394
                                    http://www.sdstate.edu
            e-mail: SDSU_Admissions@sdstate.edu
Nancy Hartenhoff-Crookf, Coordinator
Dana Dykhouse, President

Committed to providing equal opportunities for higher education for learning disabled students.

3706 **Yankton College**
PO Box 133
Yankton, SD 57078-133   605-665-3661
                                            866-665-3661
                                        FAX 605-665-3662
                                http://www.yanktoncollege.org
                                    e-mail: yc@byelectric
Jan Garrity, Executive Director

Offers a variety of services to students with disabilities including note takers, extended testing time, counseling services, and special accommodations.

Tennessee

3707 **Austin Peay State University**
Office of Disability Services
PO Box 4567
Clarksville, TN 37044   931-221-7011
                                        FAX 931-221-7102
                                        TDD:931-221-6278
                                        TTY: 931-221-6278
                                http://www.apsu.edu/disability
                                    e-mail: oldhamb@apsu.edu
Beulah Oldham, Director
Bryon Kluesner, Assistant Director
ÿLynette Taylor, Director
The Office of Disability Services is dedicated to providing academic assistance for students with disabilities enrolled at Austin Peay State University. We provide information to students, faculty, staff and administrators about the needs of students with disabilities. We ensure the accessiblity of programs, services, and activities to students having a disability. We are a resource of information pertaining to disability issues and advocate participation in campus life.

3708 **Bryan College: Dayton**
721 Bryan Drive
Dayton, TN 37321-7000   423-775-2041
                                            800-277-9522
                                        FAX 423-775-7199
                                    http://www.bryan.edu
                                    e-mail: info@bryan.edu
Mark Craver, Director of Admissions
Peter Held, VP Student Life

Committed to providing quality education for those who meet admission standards but learn differently from others. Modifications are made in the learning environment to enable LD students to succeed. Some of the modifications made require documentation of the specific disability while other adaptations do not. In addition to modifications the small teacher-student ratio allows the school to provide much individual attention to those with learning difficulties.

3709 **Carson-Newman College**
1646 Russell Ave
Jefferson City, TN 37760-2232   865-471-2000
                                            800-678-9061
                                        FAX 865-471-3502
                                    http://www.cn.edu

J Randall O'Brien, Associate Professor
James Netherton, President

An independent four-year college with support services for special education students.

3710 **East Tennessee State University**
Leap Program & Disability Services Office
PO Box 70267
Johnson City, TN 37614-1708   423-439-6268
                                        FAX 423-439-8489
                                        TDD:423-439-8370
                                        TTY: 423-439-8370
                                    http://www.etsu.edu
            e-mail: storey@mail.etsu.edu /gibson@etsu.edu
Linda Med, Disability Services Director
Martha Edde-Adams, Disability Services Asst. Dir.
Carolyn Hopson, Manager
The Learning Empowerment for Academic Performance Program is a grant funded program sponsored by Tennessee Department of Human Services, Division of Vocational Rehabilitation. The DSO works to provide services to give students with disabilities equal opportunities at ETSU.

3711 **Knoxville Business College**
720 N Hall of Fame Dr
Knoxville, TN 37917-6757   865-966-3869
                                        FAX 423-637-0127
                                    http://www.kbcollege.edu
Judy Ferguson, Dean Students

Offers a variety of services to students with disabilities including notetakers, extended testing time, counseling services, and special accommodations.

3712 **Middle Tennessee State University**
1301 E Main St
Murfreesboro, TN 37132   615-898-2300
                                        FAX 615-898-5444
                                    http://www.mtsu.edu
                                e-mail: dssemail@mtsu.edu
Sidney McPhee, President

We offer a wide variety of services to students with disabilities including testing accommodations, providing access to adaptive computer technologies and acting as a liaison to University departments.

3713 **Motlow State Community College**
PO Box 8500
Lynchburg, TN 37352-8500   931-393-1500
                                            800-654-4877
                                        FAX 931-393-1764
                                    http://www.mscc.edu
                            e-mail: asimmons@mscc.cc.tn.us
A. Simmons, Dean Student Development
Billy Soloman, Owner

A public two-year college with support services for special education students.

3714 **Northeast State Community College**
PO Box 246
Blountville, TN 37617-0246   423-354-2476
                                        FAX 423-279-7649
                                        TDD:423-279-7640
                                        TTY: 423-279-4649
                                http://www.northeaststate.edu
                            e-mail: memask@northeaststate.edu
Betty Mask, Coordinator
Roberta Dugger, Secretary

To assure equal educational opportunities for individuals with disabilities.

3715 Pellissippi State Technical Community College
PO Box 22990
Knoxville, TN 37933-990   865-694-6400
                                   FAX 865-539-7217
                              http://www.pstcc.edu
                   e-mail: semcmurray@pstcc.cc.tn.us
Joan Newman, Academic Assess Director
William Eanes, Manager
Dr.Anthony Wise, President
Services for Students with Disabilities develops individual
educational support plans, provides priority registration and
advisement, furnishes volunteer notetakers, provides read-
ers, scribes, tutor bank, provides interpeter services and publishes a newsletter. The office acts as a liaison, and assists
students in location of resources appropriate to their needs.

3716 Shelby State Community College
5983 Macon Cove
Memphis, TN 38134-3322   901-333-5000
                                   FAX 901-333-5711
                              http://www.sscc.cc.tn.us
Jimmy Wiley, Director
Mark Luttrell, Manager
Dr. Nathan Essex, President
A two-year college providing information and resources to
disabled students.

3717 Southern Adventist University
Academic Support
4841 University Drive
Collegedale, TN 37315-370   423-236-2000
                                     800-768-8437
                                   FAX 423-236-1000
                       http://www.ldpsych.southern.edu
                        e-mail: adossant@southern.edu
Alberto Santos, Dean
Mikhaile Spence, Graduate School Coordinator
Gordon Bietz, President
A private university offering undergraduate degrees in education designed for K-8, 1-8, 7-12, and K-12 certification
plus graduate degrees designed for inclusion (special needs
in the regular classroom), multiage/multigrade teaching,
outdoor education, and psychology and counseling of exceptional individuals. College age students with special needs
and those desiring to teach students with special needs are
welcome to apply.

3718 Southwest Tennessee Community College
5983 Macon Cove
Memphis, TN 38134   901-333-5000
                             877-717-7822
                           FAX 901-333-4788
                      http://www.southwest.tn.edu
                   e-mail: vesails@southwest.tn.edu
Nathan L Essex, Manager
Verties Sails III, Student Disability Svcs Coord

Offers a variety of services to students with disabilities including note takers, extended testing time, counseling services, and special accommodations.

3719 Tennessee State University
Office of Disabled Student Services
3500 John a Merritt Blvd
Nashville, TN 37209-1561   615-963-5000
                                    888-536-7655
                                  FAX 615-963-5027
                                  TDD:615-963-7440
                              http://www.tnstate.edu
                        e-mail: pscudder@tnstate.edu
Melvin Johnson, Director
Monique Mitchell, Secretary
Steven McCrary, Coordinator
Four year college offers services for learning disabled stu-
dents.

3720 University of Memphis
110 Wilder Tower N
Memphis, TN 38152   901-678-2911
                             FAX 901-678-5023
                             TDD:901-678-2880
                       http://www.saweb.memphis.edu
                         e-mail: sds@memphis.edu
Susan TePaske, Director
Jennifer Murchison, Asst Director
Phil Minyard, Coordinator
Emphasizes individual responsibility for learning by offering a developmentally oriented program of college survival
skills, learning strategies, and individualized planning and
counseling based on the student's strengths and weaknesses.
The program also coordinates comprehensive support services, including test accommodations, tutoring and learning
strategies, alternate format tests and assistive technology.
The program serves 400 to 500 students with learning
disabilities and ADHD per year.

3721 University of Tennessee
Boling Center for Developmental Disabilities
711 Jefferson Ave
Memphis, TN 38105-5003   901-448-6512
                                  888-572-2249
                                FAX 901-448-7097
                                TDD:901-448-4677
                            http://www.utmem.edu
Frederick B Palmer, Director

Interdisciplinary or focused evaluation of learning, behavioral and developmental problems in infants, toddlers, children and young adults. Treatment of some conditions
offered.

3722 University of Tennessee: Knoxville
Disability Services Office
2227 Dunford Hall
Knoxville, TN 37996-0001   865-974-6087
                                    FAX 865-974-9552
                                    TDD:865-974-6087
                                http://www.ods.utk.edu
                                  e-mail: ods@utk.edu
Annazette Houston, Director

The mission of the Office of Disability Services is to provide
each individual an equal opportunity to participate in the
University of Tennessee's programs and activities.

3723 University of Tennessee: Martin
209 Clement
Martin, TN 38238-0001   731-881-7723
                                 FAX 731-881-7702
                              http://www.utm.edu
                           e-mail: sroberts@utm.edu
Sharon Robertson, Assistant Coordinator
George Daniel, Director
Tom Rakes, Administrator
A four-year independent college that offers a program called
Program Access for College Enhancement for students with
learning disabilities.

3724 Vanderbilt University
Vanderbilt University
2301 Vanderbilt Pl
Nashville, TN 37203   615-322-7311
                               FAX 615-322-3762
                               TDD:615-322-4705
                           http://www.vanderbilt.edu
                 e-mail: melissa.a.smith@vanderbilt.edu
Madelyn Pullman, Director Disability Program
Nicholas Zeppos, Chancellor
Mark Dalton, Chairman
An independent four-year college with support services for
special education students.

3725 **William Jennings Bryan College**
HEATH Resource Center
Ste 220
2121 K St NW
Washington, DC 20037-1830

202-261-3594
800-544-3284
FAX 202-973-0908
http://www.heath.gwu.edu
e-mail: askheath@heath.gwu.edu

Palmer William, Publications Manager
Janine Heath, Manager

A public four-year college. The HEALTH Resource Center operates the national clearinghouse on postsecondary education for individuals with disabilities.

Texas

3726 **Alvin Community College**
Alvin Community College
3110 Mustang Rd
Alvin, TX 77511-4807

281-756-3500
FAX 281-756-3858
http://www.alvincollege.edu

Rodney Allbright, President
Alyssa Reeves, Admission Specialist

A public two-year college with support services for special education students.

3727 **Angelina College**
Student Services Office
PO Box 1768
Lufkin, TX 75902-1768

936-639-1301
FAX 936-639-4299
http://www.angelina.edu
e-mail: jtwohig@angelina.edu

James Twohig, Dean, Student Services
Larry Phillips, President
Karen Bowser, Special Student Services Coord
A public community college that offers two-year degrees in the arts and sciences designed to transfer to four-year colleges and universities as well as one and two year programs in technical and occupational fields.

3728 **Brookhaven College**
Special Services Office
3939 Valley View Ln
Farmers Branch, TX 75244-4997

972-860-4700
FAX 972-860-4897
http://www.dcccd.edu.bhc
Sharon Blackman, Grants Manager
Thom D. Chesney, Ph.D., President
Rodger Bennett, Vice President
Physically challenged and learning disabled special services office offers advisement, additional diagnostic evaluations, mobility assistance, note taking, textbook taping, interpreters for the deaf and assistance in test taking.

3729 **Cedar Valley College**
3030 N Dallas Ave
Lancaster, TX 75134-3799

972-860-8201
http://www.cedarvalleycollege.edu
Dr Jennifer Wimbish, President
Huan Luong, Vice President
Mickey Best, Executive Dean of Liberal Arts
The mission of Cedar Valley College is to provide quality learning that prepares students for success in a dynamic world.

3730 **Central Texas College**
PO Box 1800
Killeen, TX 76540-1800

254-526-7161
800-792-3348
FAX 254-526-1700
TDD:254-526-1378
http://www.ctcd.edu

Jose Apotte, Counselor
James Anderson, Manager
Mr. Howard Henslee, vice President of Sales
Offers a variety of services to students with disabilities including extended testing time, counseling services, and assistive technology.

3731 **Cisco College**
101 College Hts
Cisco, TX 76437

254-442-5000
FAX 254-442-5100
http://www.cisco.edu

Bobby Smith, Interim President
Dani Day, VP Learning Services
Amy Evans, Executive Director External Rel
Provides affordable, accessible education to more than 4,200 students through its two locations in Cisco and Abilene. Offers a variety of career and technical education programs and academic transfer options as well as many student support services like tutoring, academic intervention and counseling to ensure student success.

3732 **College of the Mainland**
Student Support Services
1200 N Amburn Rd
Texas City, TX 77591-2499

409-938-1211
888-258-8859
FAX 409-938-1306
http://www.com.edu
e-mail: kkimbark@com.edu

Larry Durrence, Director
Homer Hayes, President
Jennifer Johnson, Executive Assistant
Offers a variety of services to students with disabilities including notetakers, extended testing time, counseling services, and special accommodations. The mission of services for students with disabilities is to provide each student with the resources needed to register, enroll and complete their course work and/or degree plan.

3733 **Collin County Community College**
2200 W University Dr
McKinney, TX 75071-2999

972-548-6790
FAX 972-548-6716
http://www.collin.edu

Cary Israel, Director
Rex Parcells, Manager
Dr. Sherry Schumann, Vice President
A public two-year college. ACCESS provides resonable accommodations, individual attention and support for students with disabilities who need assistance with any aspect of their campus experience such as accessibility, academics and testing.

3734 **Dallas Academy**
950 Tiffany Way
Dallas, TX 75218-2743

214-324-1481
FAX 214-327-8537
http://www.dallas-academy.com
e-mail: mail@dallas-academy.com
Jim Richardson, Executive Director
Ronda Criss, Development Director
Jim Richardson, Executive Director
Offers a variety of services to students with disabilities including notetakers, extended testing time, counseling services, and special accommodations.

3735 **Dallas Academy: Coed High School**
950 Tiffany Way
Dallas, TX 75218-2743

214-324-1481
FAX 214-327-8537
http://www.dallas-academy.com
e-mail: mail@dallas-academy.com
Karen Kinsella, Assistant Director
Ronda Criss, Development Director
Jim Richardson, Executive Director

Coed Day School for bright children grades 7-12 with diagnosed learning differences. Curriculum includes sports, art, music, and photography programs.

3736 Dallas County Community College
3737 Motley Dr
Mesquite, TX 75150-2033

972-86+0-768
FAX 972-860-7227
http://www.dcccd.edu/

Jerry Prater, Chairman
Dr.ÿWright Lassiter, Chancellor

Offers a variety of services to students with disabilities including note takers, extended testing time, counseling services, and special accommodations.

3737 East Texas Baptist University
One Tiger Drive
Marshall, TX 75670-1498

903-935-7963
800-804-3828
FAX 903-938-7798
http://www.etbu.edu

Samuel Oliver, President

Offers a variety of services to students with disabilities including notetakers, extended testing time, counseling services, and special accommodations.

3738 East Texas State University
807 University Parkway
Johnson City, TN 37614-1700

423-439-1000
FAX 903-886-5702
http://www.etsu.edu

Tom Lynch, Contact

Offers a variety of services to students with disabilities including note takers, extended testing time, counseling services, and special accommodations.

3739 Eastfield College
3737 Motley Dr
Mesquite, TX 75150-2099

972-860-8348
FAX 972-860-7622
http://www.eastfieldcollege.edu
e-mail: efcdso@dcccd.edu
Dr Jean Conway, Interim President

Offers a variety of support services for students with disabilities and/or special requirements. Services are coordinated to fit the individual needs of the student and may include sign language interpreters, computer aided real-time translation services, notetaking services, tutoring referral, textbook taping, testing accomodations, and use of adaptive technology. Academic counseling, priority registration, and referral information are also available.

3740 El Centro College
801 Main Street
Dallas, TX 75202

214-860-2000
FAX 214-860-2440
http://www.elcentrocollege.edu
Norman Howden, Executive Dean
Karin Reed, Disability Services Coordinator
Paul McCarthy,ÿ, President
A public two-year college with support services for special education students.

3741 Fairhill School
16150 Preston Rd
Dallas, TX 75248-3558

972-233-1026
FAX 972-233-8205
http://www.fairhill.org

Jane Sego, Executive Director

A private, non-profit college preparatory school serving students in grades one through twelve. Fairhill's primary purpose is to provide a superior education for students of average and above intelligence who have been diagnosed with a learning difference such as Dyslexia, Dysgraphia, Dyscalculia, Auditory Processing Disorder, or Attention Deficit/Hyperactivity Disorder.

3742 Frank Phillips College
Special Populations Department
PO Box 5118
Borger, TX 79008-5118

806-457-4200
800-687-2056
FAX 806-457-4226
http://www.fpctx.edu
Karen Lane, Special Populations Coordinator
Erika Allen, Coordinator

Offers a variety of services to students with disabilities including notetakers, extended testing time, counseling services, and special accommodations.

3743 Galveston College
4015 Avenue Q
Galveston, TX 77550-7496

409-944-4242
FAX 409-944-1500
TDD:866-483-4242
http://www.gc.edu

W. Miles Shelton EdD, President
Jeff Engbrock, Director of Business Services

A public two-year college. A variety of services and programs are available to assist students with disabilities, those who are academically and/or economically disadvantaged and those with limited English proficiency.

3744 Great Lakes Academy
6000 Custer Rd
Ste 7
Plano, TX 75023-5100

972-517-7498
FAX 972-517-0133
http://www.greatlakesacademy.com
e-mail: admissions@greatlakesacademy.com
Marjolein Borsten, Executive Director

A full day non-profit private school that provides 1st-12th grade students with average to above-average intelligence, diagnosed with various Learning Differences, Asperger's Syndrome, ADD or AD/HD a stimulating environment and favorable atmosphere which affords each student opportunities to develop both socially and academically.

3745 Hill School
4817 Odessa Ave
Fort Worth, TX 76133-1640

817-923-9482
FAX 817-923-4894
http://www.hillschool.org
e-mail: hillschool@hillschool.org
Greg Owens, Headmaster
Laura Hutyra, Public Relations/Marketing Dir.

Hill School is a college preparatory, full-service school for bright students who learn differently. Our exceptional faculty emphasize intensive small-group instruction in core subject areas to ensure that all students have an opportunity to reach their full academic potential. Our students explore interests and affinities through athletics, fine arts (drama, visual arts, music, band) and a wide variety of community involvement activities. Also located in SW Ft. Worth and Grapevine.

3746 Jarvis Christian College
PO Box 1470
Hawkins, TX 75765-1470

903-769-5700
800-292-9517
FAX 903-769-5005
http://www.jarvis.edu
e-mail: florine_white@jarvis.edu

Florine White MD, Student Support Services Dir.
Dr. Lester Newman, President

Student Support Services is a federally funded program whose purpose is to improve the retention and graduate rate of program participants. Eligible program participants include low income, first generation college students and students with learning and physical disabilities. A variety of support services are provided.

3747   Lamar State College - Port Arthur
PO Box 310
Port Arthur, TX 77641-0310   409-983-4921
                                              800-477-5872
                                         FAX 409-984-6056
                                         TDD:409-984-6242
                                 http://www.pa.lamar.edu
                        e-mail: andrea.munoz@lamarpa.edu
Andrea Munoz, Special Populations Coordinator
Justin Montalvo, Administrative Assistant
Sam Monroe, President
A public two-year college with support services for special education students.

3748   Laredo Community College
Special Populations Office
W End Washington Street
Laredo, TX 78040   956-722-0521
                                         FAX 956-721-5367
                                   http://www.laredo.edu
                        e-mail: sylviat@laredo.cc.tx.us
Ramon H Dovalina, Counselor/Coordinator

Offers a variety of services to students with disabilities including notetakers, extended testing time, counseling services, and special accommodations.

3749   Lon Morris College
Disability Services: Cole Learning Enrichment Ctr
800 College Avenue
Jacksonville, TX 75766   903-589-4000
                                              800-259-5733
                                         FAX 903-589-4001
                             http://www.beabearcat.com
Sandra White, Director, Enrichment Center
Angela Jones, Assistant

A two-year liberal arts college that offers a learning support program (the Cole Learning Enrichment Center) for students with learning disabilities. Students work collaboratively with the director of the center to develop and achieve realistic career and education goals, determine educational needs based on testing data, and foster independence while developing and demonstrating their full potential and abilities.

3750   Lubbock Christian University
5601 19th St
Lubbock, TX 79407-2099   806-796-8800
                                              800-933-7601
                                         FAX 806-720-7255
                                      http://www.lcu.edu
                             e-mail: admissions@lcu.edu
Ken Jones, President
Rod Blackwood, Vice President

Offers a variety of services to students with disabilities including notetakers, extended testing time, counseling services, and special accommodations.

3751   McLennen Community College
1400 College Dr
Waco, TX 76708-1499   254-299-8622
                                         FAX 254-299-8654
                                  http://www.mclennan.edu
Dennis Michaelis, President
Mickey Reyes, Desktop Publishing Technician
Harry Harelik, Executive Director
A public two-year college with support services for special education students.

3752   Midwestern State University
Disability Counseling Office
3410 Taft Blvd
Wichita Falls, TX 76308-2096   940-397-4000
                                         FAX 940-397-4780
                                         TDD:940-397-4515
                                     http://www.mwsu.edu
                         e-mail: counselling@mwsu.edu
Jesse W Rogers, Director
ÿDr. Marilyn Fowle, Vice President

A public four-year college with support services for special education students.

3753   North Lake College
Disabilities Services Office
Rm A438
5001 N Macarthur Blvd
Irving, TX 75038-3899   972-273-3183
                                         FAX 972-273-3431
                                         TDD:972-273-3169
                                     http://www.dcccd.edu
Noni Kirk, Disability Services Coordinator
Sherry Beal, Office Manager
Thom D. Chesney, Ph.D., President
A public two-year college. Our mission is to provide a variety of support services to empower students, foster independence, promote achievement of realistic career and educational goals and assist students in discovering, developing and demonstrating full potential and abilities.

3754   Notre Dame School
2018 Allen St
Dallas, TX 75204-2604   214-720-3911
                                         FAX 214-720-3913
                             http://www.notredameschool.org
                        e-mail: tfrancis@notredameschool.org
Theresa Francis, Principal

Providing a quality education to children with developmental disabilities ages 6 to 21 and facilitating their intergration into society.

3755   Odyssey School
4407 Red River St
Austin, TX 78751-4039   512-472-2262
                                         FAX 512-236-9385
                             http://www.odysseyschool.com
                        e-mail: info@odysseyschool.com
Nancy Wolf, Head of School
Ed Schleicher, Vice President

Committed to the development of academic excellence and self-acceptance for students with learning and attentional differences. We believe all children can be successful in their intellectual, creative and social development. Our goal is to help each student discover his or her individual potential for greatness.

3756   Pan American University
Office of Disability Services
1201 W University Dr
Edinburg, TX 78539-2970   956-381-3306
                                         FAX 956-381-5196
                                         TDD:956-316-7092
                                     http://www.panam.edu
Farzaneh Razzaghi, Director
Esperanza Cavazos, Associate Director
Blandina Cardenas, President
Offers a variety of services to students with disabilities including note takers, extended testing time, counseling services, and special accommodations.

3757 Rawson-Saunders School
Soaring Eagles Program
2614-A Exposition Blvd
Austin, TX 78703-1702 512-476-8382
FAX 512-476-1132
http://www.rawson-saunders.org
e-mail: info@rawson-saunders.org
Laura Steinbach, Head of School

Developed to help learning disabled students, grades 1 to 8, maintain their language arts and math skills while increasing their self-esteem. Students participate in small group, hands-on activities in math, language arts, organized games/movement, keyboarding, sign language, and science or creative problem solving.

3758 Richland College
12800 Abrams Rd
Dallas, TX 75243-2199 972-238-6100
FAX 972-238-6346
http://www.rlc.dcccd.edu
Steve Mittelstet, President
Finney Varghese, Associate Vice President

Richland College's mission is teaching, learning, and community building.

3759 Sam Houston State University
1700 Sam Houston Ave
Huntsville, TX 77340 936-294-1111
FAX 936-294-1465
http://www.shsu.edu

James Gaertner, President
Dennis Culak, Manager

Offers a variety of services to students with disabilities including note takers, extended testing time, counseling services, and special accommodations.

3760 San Jacinto College: Central Campus
P.O.Box 2007
Pasadena, TX 77501-2007 281-476-1501
FAX 281-476-1892
http://www.sjcd.cc.tx.us
Catherine O'Brien, Special Populations
Dr. H. Neil Mathin, President

Offers a variety of services to students with disabilities including notetakers, extended testing time, counseling services, and special accommodations such as test readers and writers.

3761 San Jacinto College: South Campus
San Jacinto College: South Campus
13735 Beamer Rd
Houston, TX 77089-6099 281-998-6150
FAX 281-922-3401
http://www.sjcd.edu
e-mail: eeverett@sjcd.edu
Linda Watkins, President
Sherry Gray, Administrative Assistant

A public two-year college with support services for special education students.

3762 Schreiner University
2100 Memorial Blvd
Kerrville, TX 78028-5611 830-792-7256
800-343-4919
FAX 830-792-7294
http://www.schreiner.edu
e-mail: jgallik@schreiner.edu
Dr Jude Gallik, Learning Support Services Dir

Comprehensive support program for students with diagnosed specific learning disabilities with demonstrated potential for success at the college level.

3763 Shelton School
15720 Hillcrest Rd
Dallas, TX 75248-4161 972-774-1772
FAX 972-991-3977
http://www.shelton.org
Suzanne Stell, Executive Director

Primary emphasis is providing learning-different children (average or above intelligence) with full, effective curriculum through individualized, structured multisensory programs. Learning differences include dyslexia, attention deficit disorder (ADD), attention deficit hyperactivity disorder (ADHD), speech and language disorders.

3764 South Plains College
1401 College Ave
Levelland, TX 79336-6595 806-894-9611
FAX 806-897-2800
http://www.spc.cc.tx.us
Kelvin Sharp, President

Offers a variety of services to students with disabilities including notetakers, extended testing time, counseling services, and special accommodations.

3765 Southern Methodist University
Disability Accommodations & Success Strategies
PO Box 750201
Dallas, TX 75275 214-768-1470
FAX 214-768-1225
http://www.smu.edu/alec/dass.asp
e-mail: dass@smu.edu
Alexa Taylor, Associate Director
R Turner, President
Melinda Argentieri, Administrative Assistant
Provides access and accomodations to all SMU students with a disability. Also offers academic waching to undergraduates with learning and attention disorders.

3766 Southwestern Assemblies of God University
1200 Sycamore St
Waxahachie, TX 75165-2397 972-937-4010
888-YES-SAGU
FAX 972-923-0488
http://www.sagu.edu
e-mail: sagu@sagu.edu
Kermit S Bridges, President
Jay Trewern, Vice President
Katie White, Administrative Academic
Offers a variety of services to students with disabilities including notetakers, extended testing time, counseling services, and special accommodations.

3767 St. Edwards University
Learning Disabilities Services
3001 S Congress Ave
Austin, TX 78704-6489 512-448-8400
855-468-6738
FAX 512-448-8492
http://www.stedwards.edu
George Martin, President

An independent four-year college. Students with disabilities meet with a counselor from academic planning and support and they work together to ensure equal access to all academic services.

3768 St. Mary's University of San Antonio
1 Camino Santa Maria St
San Antonio, TX 78228-8500 210-436-3011
FAX 210-436-3782
http://www.stmarytx.edu
Barbara Biassiolli, Center Director
Lisa Seller, Assistant Director
Andre Hampton, Provost and VP
Offers a variety of services to students with disabilities including tutoring, extended testing time, and academic counseling services.

3769 Stephen F Austin State University
Office of Disability Services
1936 North St
Nacogdoches, TX 75962-3940   936-468-2504
                                 FAX 936-468-1104
                                 http://www.sfasu.edu

Baker Pattillo, Director
Tito Guerrero, President
Mr. James H. Dickerson, Secretary
Offers a variety of services to students with disabilities including note takers, extended testing time, counseling services, and special accommodations.

3770 Tarleton State University
PO Box T-0010
Stephenville, TX 76402   254-968-9000
                                 FAX 254-968-9703
                                 http://www.tarleton.edu

L. Dwayne Snider PhD, Associate VP
Lisa Howe, Assistant to the VP
F Dominic Dottavid, President
Four year college that provides students with learning disabilities support and services.

3771 Tarrant County College
Disability Support Services
1500 Houston Street Fort Worth
Hurst, TX 76102   817-515-8223
                                 FAX 817-515-6112
                                 TDD:817-515-6812
                                 http://www.tccd.edu
                                 e-mail: judy.kelly@tccd.edu

Larry Darlage, Director
Dorotha McDonnell, Secretary
Erma Johnson Hadley, TCC Chancellor
Offers a variety of support services to students with disabilities including notetakers, testing accommodations, as well as special accommodations, tutoring.

3772 Texas A&M University
1265 Tamu
College Station, TX 77843   979-845-3313
                                 FAX 979-845-2647
                                 http://www.tamu.edu
                                 e-mail: anne@stulife2.tamu.edu

Bob Wagoner, Coordinator
Charles Backus, Manager
R. Bowen Loftin, President
A public four-year college with support services for special education students.

3773 Texas A&M University: Commerce
PO Box 3011
Commerce, TX 75429-3011   903-886-5835
                                     888-868-2682
                                 FAX 903-468-3220
                                 http://www.tamu-commerce.edu
                                 e-mail: frank_perez@tamu-commerce.edu
Frank Perez, Assistant Director
Dan R. Jones, President
Sharon Johnson, Vice President
Four-year college that provides student support services and programs to those students who are learning disabled.

3774 Texas A&M University: Kingsville
1210 Retama Dr
Kingsville, TX 78363   361-592-4762
                                 FAX 361-593-2006
                                 http://www.tamuk.edu
                                 e-mail: kacjaol@tamuk.edu
Jeanie Alexander, Coordinator Disability Svcs
Dr. Steven Tallant, President

Four-year college that provides an academic support center for students who are disabled.

3775 Texas Southern University
3100 Cleburne St
Houston, TX 77004-4597   713-313-7011
                                 FAX 713-313-1092
                                 http://www.tsu.edu

John Rudley, Counselor
Priscilla Slade, President

A public four-year college with support services for special education students.

3776 Texas State Technical Institute: Sweetwater Campus
300 Homer K Taylor Dr
Sweetwater, TX 79556-4108   325-235-7300
                                 http://www.sweetwater.tstc.edu
Gail Lawrence, President

Offers a variety of services to students with disabilities including notetakers, extended testing time, counseling services, and special accommodations.

3777 Texas Tech University
AccessTECH & TECHniques Center
2500 Broadway
Lubbock, TX 79409   806-742-2011
                                 FAX 806-742-4837
                                 TDD:806-742-2092
                                 TTY: 806-742-4837
                                 http://www.accesstech.dsa.ttu.edu
                                 e-mail: accesstech@ttu.edu
Frank Silvas, Director
Larry Phillippe, Associate Director
Dr. Lawrence Schovanec, President
AccessTECH & TECHniques Center offer TTU students every opportunity to succeed in independence and education.

3778 Texas Woman's University
Disability Support Services
PO Box 425966
Denton, TX 76204-5966   940-898-3835
                                 FAX 940-898-3965
                                 TDD:940-898-3830
                                 http://www.twu.edu
                                 e-mail: dss@twu.edu
A public four-year college with support services for special education students.

3779 Tyler Junior College
PO Box 9020
Tyler, TX 75711-9020   903-510-2200
                                     800-687-5680
                                 FAX 903-510-2434
                                 http://www.tyler.cc.tx.us

Vickie Geisel, Special Services
Aubry Sharp, Manager
Dr. L. Michael Metke, President
Offers a variety of services to students with disabilities including note takers, extended testing time, counseling services, and special accommodations.

3780 University of Austin Texas
Texas Center for Disability Studies
1 University Station C1200
Austin, TX 78712   512-471-3434
                                     800-828-7839
                                 FAX 512-232-0761
                                 http://www.utexas.edu
                                 e-mail: txcds@uttcds.org
Penny Seay, Executive Director
John Moore, Assistant Director
William Powers Jr, President
The mission of the Texas Center for Disability Studies (TCDS) is to serve as a catalyst so that people with developmental and other disabilities are fully included in all levels of their communities and in control of their lives.

3781 **University of Houston**
Disability Support Services
4800 Calhoun Road
Houston, TX 77004
713-743-2255
FAX 713-743-5396
TDD:713-749-1527
TTY: 713-749-1527
http://www.uh.edu
e-mail: wscrain@mail.uhe.edu
Scott Crain, Counselor
Cheryl Amotuso, Director

A public four-year college with support services for students with disabilities.

3782 **University of North Texas**
Office of Disability Accommodation
PO Box 310770
Denton, TX 76203-770
940-565-4323
FAX 940-369-7969
TDD:940-369-8652
http://www.unt.edu/oda
e-mail: branding@unt.edu
Ron Venable, Director
Dr.Robert S. Nelson, President

The mission of the ODA is to provide reasonable accommodations to students and to apply appropriate adjustments to the classroom and associated learning environments. In order to facilitate this process, the ODA maintains all student diability-related medical and psychological documentation and the corresponding accommodation request records.

3783 **University of Texas at Dallas**
PO Box 830688
Richardson, TX 75083-0688
972-883-2111
FAX 972-883-2098
http://www.utdallas.edu
Kerry Tate, Asst Director Disability Service
David Daniel, President

Offers a variety of services to students with disabilities including notetakers, extended testing time, counseling services, and special accommodations.

3784 **University of Texas: Pan American**
1201 W University Dr
Edinburg, TX 78539-2909
956-381-2011
866-441-UTPA
FAX 956-381-2150
http://www.panam.edu
Charles Sorber, Assistant Director
Edna Luna, Administrator

Offers a variety of services to students with disabilities including notetakers, extended testing time, counseling services, and special accommodations.

3785 **University of the Incarnate Word**
4301 Broadway St
San Antonio, TX 78209-6318
210-829-6000
800-749-WORD
FAX 210-829-3847
http://www.uiw.edu
e-mail: uiwhr@universe.uiwtx.edu
Louis J Agnese Jr, President

Four year college that provides services to learning disabled students.

3786 **Wharton County Junior College**
911 E Boling Hwy
Wharton, TX 77488-3298
979-532-4560
800-561-9252
FAX 979-532-6545
http://www.wcjc.cc.tx.us/
Betty A Mc Crohan, Executive Director
John Milton Hodges, President

Offers a variety of services to students with disabilities including note takers, extended testing time, counseling services, and special accommodations.

3787 **Wiley College**
711 Wiley Ave
Marshall, TX 75670-5151
903-927-3300
800-658-6889
FAX 903-938-8100
http://www.wilec.edu
e-mail: vdavis@wileyc.edu
Haywood L Strickland, President
Dr. Glenda Carter, Executive Vice President
Dr. Ernest Plata, Vice President
Offers a variety of services to students with disabilities including notetakers, extended testing time, counseling services, and special accommodations.

3788 **Winston School**
5707 Royal Ln
Dallas, TX 75229-5500
214-691-6950
FAX 214-691-1509
http://www.winston-school.org
e-mail: info@winston-school.org
Polly Peterson, Head of School
Worsham Pamela, Manager

Our mission is to realize the extraordinary potential of bright students who learn differently through individualized learning strategies, and to aid in preparing graduates for college level work.

Utah

3789 **College of Eastern Utah**
451 E 400 N
Price, UT 84501-2699
435-613-5000
FAX 435-613-5112
http://www.ceu.edu
Michael King, DRC Director
Ryan Thomas, President

The DRC at CEU provides academic accommodations for the learning disabled.

3790 **Latter-Day Saints Business College**
411 E South Temple
Salt Lake City, UT 84111-1302
801-524-8100
FAX 801-524-1900
http://www.ldsbc.edu
Tina Orden, Dean Students
Stephen Woodhouse, President
Marjean Lake M.S, Director
Offers a variety of services to students with disabilities including notetakers, extended testing time, counseling services, and special accommodations.

3791 **Salt Lake Community College**
Disability Resource Center
4600 S Redwood Rd
Salt Lake City, UT 84123-3197
801-957-4111
FAX 801-957-4440
TDD:801-957-4646
TTY: 801-957-4646
http://www.slcc.edu
e-mail: linda.bennett@slcc.edu
Cynthia A Bioteau, President
Linda Bennett, Office Manager

A program to assist students with disabilities in obtaining equal access to college facilities and programs. The resource center serves all disabilities and provides services and accommodations such as testing, adaptive equipment, text on tape, readers, scribes, note takers, and interpreters for the deaf.

3792 Snow College
150 College Ave
Ephraim, UT 84627-1299
435-283-7000
800-848-3399
FAX 435-283-5259
http://www.snow.edu

Scott Wyatt, President
Michael Benson, Special Services

A public two-year college with support services for special education students.

3793 Southern Utah University
351 W Center St
Cedar City, UT 84720-2470
435-586-7700
FAX 435-865-8223
http://www.suu.edu
e-mail: thompson@suu.edu

Michael T Benson, Coordinator
Steven Bennion, President
Diana Graff, Manager
A public four-year University with support services for special education students.

3794 University Accessibility Center
Brigham Young University
2170 WSC
Provo, UT 84602
801-422-2767
FAX 801-422-0174
http://www.uac.byu.edu
e-mail: uac@byu.edu

Michael P Brooks, Director

REACH was established to assist students with disabilities to reach their full potential. It is our goal to provide an environment where the pursuit of excellence is expected, and students are strongly encouraged to make a contribution toward their own success.

3795 University of Utah
201 Presidents Cir
Salt Lake City, UT 84112-9049
801-581-7200
800-444-8638
FAX 801-585-5257
TDD:801-581-5020
http://www.utah.edu
e-mail: onadeau@saun.saff.utah.edu

Michael Young, Director
David Pershing, Plant Manager

A public four-year college. Services include admissions requirements modification, testing accommodations, priority registration, advisement on course selection and number, adaptive technology, support group. Documentation of learning disability is required.

3796 Utah State University
101 Old Main Hl
Logan, UT 84322-101
435-797-3852
FAX 435-797-0130
TDD:435-797-0740
http://www.usu.edu
e-mail: diane.baum@usu.edu

Dwight Davis, Director
Eric Olson, Manager

A public four-year college with support services for students with learning disabilities.

3797 Utah Valley State College
Accessibility Services Department
800 W University Pkwy
Orem, UT 84058
801-863-8105
FAX 801-863-7265
http://www.uvu.edu
e-mail: info@uvsc.edu

Terry Petrie, Disabled Services
Michelle Lundell, Department Director
Ann Lickey, Secretary

The mission for Accessibility Services at Utah Valley State College is to ensure, in compliance with federal and state laws, that no qualified individual with a disability be excluded from participation in or be denied the benefits of a quality education at UVSC or be subjected to discrimination by the college or its personnel. UVSC offers a large variety of support services, accommodative services and assistive technology for individuals with learning disabilities.

3798 Weber State University
Disabilities Support Office
3750 Harrison Blvd
Ogden, UT 84408
801-626-6000
FAX 801-626-6744
TDD:801-626-7283
http://www.weber.edu

Ann Millner, President

Offers a variety of services to students with disabilities including notetakers, extended testing time, counseling services, and special accommodations.

3799 Westminster College of Salt Lake City
Learning Disability Program
1840 S 1300 E
Salt Lake City, UT 84105-3697
801-484-7651
800-748-4753
FAX 801-468-0916
TDD:801-832-2286
http://www.westminstercollege.edu
e-mail: gdewitt@westminstercollege.edu

Michael S Bassis, Director
Amy Gordon, Office Manager
Dr.Brian Levin, President
Offers a variety of services to students with disabilities including notetakers, extended testing time, counseling services, and special accommodations.

Vermont

3800 Burlington College
95 North Ave
Burlington, VT 05401-2998
802-862-9616
800-862-9616
FAX 802-660-4331
http://www.burlington.edu
e-mail: jsanders@burlcol.edu

Jane O'Meara, President
Jillian McMahon, Office Manager

Education process vs test and grades. Small classes. Learning specialist available.

3801 Champlain College
Support Services
163 S Willard St
Burlington, VT 05401-3950
802-860-2700
800-570-5858
FAX 802-860-2750
http://www.champlain.edu
e-mail: peterson@champlain.edu

David F Finney, Coordinator
George H. Perry, President

Four year college that supports students with a learning disability.

3802 College of St. Joseph
71 Clement Rd
Rutland, VT 05701-3899
802-773-5900
877-270-9998
FAX 802-773-5900
http://www.csj.edu
e-mail: admissions@csj.edu

Frank G Miglorie Jr, President
Nancy Kline, Academic Dean
Susan Englese, Dean of Admissions

Offers a variety of services to students with disabilities including note takers, extended testing time, counseling services, and special accommodations.

3803 Community College of Vermont
Student Services Office
PO Box 489
Montpelier, VT 05601-489

802-228-6686
802-828-2800
FAX 802-241-3526
http://www.ccv.vsc.edu
e-mail: ccvinfo@ccv.vsc.edu

Mel Donovan, Student Services Director
Tim Donovan, President

A public two-year college offering courses, certificates and associate degrees.

3804 Green Mountain College
Calhoun Learning Center
1 Brennan Cir
Poultney, VT 05764-1078

802-776-6675
FAX 802-287-8099
http://www.greenmtn.edu
e-mail: admiss@greenmtn.edu

Paul Fonteyn, Director
Becky Eno, Assistant Director
Paul J. Fonteyn, President
Four-year college that offers support through the school's Calhoun Learning center to students with disabilities.

3805 Greenwood School
14 Greenwood Ln
Putney, VT 05346-8965

802-387-4545
FAX 802-387-5396
http://www.greenwood.org
e-mail: smiller@greenwood.org

Stewart Miller, Headmaster

A boarding school dedicated to taking bright and talented boys with learning differences and learning disabilities (LD) such as dyslexia, attentional difficulties (ADD / ADHD), or executive functioning deficits and empowering them with the skills and strategies necessary to bridge the gap between their outstanding promise and present abilities.

3806 Landmark College
River Rd S
Putney, VT 05346

802-387-4767
FAX 802-387-6880
http://www.landmark.edu

Peter Eden, President

Our programs are specially designed for a particular audience. designed exclusively for students with dyslexia, attention deficit hyperactivity disorder (AD/HD), or other specific learning disabilities.

3807 Norwich University
Learning Support Center
158 Harmon Dr
Northfield, VT 05663-1035

802-485-2000
800-468-6679
FAX 802-485-2032
http://www.norwich.edu
e-mail: gills@norwich.edu

Richard W Schneider, Special Services

The Learning Center offers an opportunity for individualized assistance with many aspects of academic life in a supportive, personalized atmosphere. Students may voluntarily choose from a wide variety of service options.

3808 Pine Ridge School
9505 Williston Rd
Williston, VT 05495-9598

802-434-2161
FAX 802-434-5512
http://www.pineridgeschool.com
e-mail: dkb3131@yahoo.com

Dana Blackhurst, Head of School

An educational community that is committed to empowering students with dyslexia and other language based learning disabilities, to define and achieve success throughout their lives.

3809 University of Vermont
ACCESS
A170 Living Learning Ctr
Burlington, VT 05405

802-656-3131
FAX 802-656-0739
TDD:802-656-3865
TTY: 802-656-7753
http://www.uvm.edu/access
e-mail: access@uvm.edu

Donna Panko, Learning Specialist
Nick Ogrizovich, Information Specialist
Joe Wilson, Learning Specialist
Provides accommodation, consultation, collaboration and educational support services as a means to foster opportunities for students with disabilities to participate in a barrier free learning environment.

3810 Vermont Technical College
Randolph Center
Randolph Center, VT 05061

802-728-1000
800-442-8821
FAX 802-728-1390
TDD:802-728-1278
http://www.vtc.vsc.edu
e-mail: rgoodall@vtc.edu

Robin Goodall, Learning Specialists
Eileen Haddon, Assistive Technology Project
Allen Rogers, President
Offers a variety of services to students with disabilities including individualized accommodations, counseling services, academic counseling.

Virginia

3811 Averett College
Support Services for Students
420 West Main
Danville, VA 24541

434-791-5600
FAX 804-791-4392
http://www.averett.edu
e-mail: priedel@averett.edu

Pamela Riedel MD, Support Services Coordinator
Bill Bradford, Assistant Professor of Aviation

Four-year college that offers services for the learning disabled.

3812 College of William and Mary
PO Box 8795
Williamsburg, VA 23187-8795

757-221-4000
TDD:757-221-1154
http://www.wm.edu

Carroll Hardy MD, Director
Gene Nichol, President

Offers a variety of services to students with disabilities including notetakers, extended testing time, counseling services, and special accommodations.

3813 Eastern Mennonite University
Academic Support Center - Student Disability Svcs.
1200 Park Rd
Harrisonburg, VA 22802-2462

540-432-4000
800-368-2665
FAX 540-432-4444
TDD:540-432-4631
TTY: 540-432-4599
http://www.emu.edu
e-mail: hedrickj@emu.edu

Loren E Swartzendruber, Coordinator
Dr. Loren Swartzendruber, President

EMU is committed to working out reasonable accommodations for students with documented disabilities to ensure equal access to the University and its related programs.

3814 Emory & Henry College
PO Box 947
Emory, VA 24327-0947
276-944-6144
800-848-5493
FAX 276-944-6180
http://www.ehc.edu
Jill Smeltzer, Director Counseling Services
Rosalind Reichard, President
Talmage Dobbins, Academic Support Services
A private four-year liberal arts college located in the foothills of southwest Virginia. Student enrollment of appox. 1,000, almost equally divided between men and women. The Paul Adrian Powell III resource center offers a variety of services to students with disabilities including extended testing time, counseling services, and special accommodations, as well as tutorial services.

3815 Ferrum College
PO Box 1000
Ferrum, VA 24088-9001
540-365-2121
800-868-9797
FAX 540-365-4203
http://www.ferrum.edu
Jennifer L Braaten, President
Dr. Leslie Lambert, Vice President

An independent four-year college with support services for special education students.

3816 GW Community School
9001 Braddock Rd
Springfield, VA 22151-1009
703-978-7208
FAX 703-978-7226
http://www.gwcommunityschool.com
e-mail: info@gwcommunityschool.com
Alexa Warden, Principal

The GW Community School is owned and operated by teachers who understand the learning process and the students' needs, and who genuinely enjoy teaching adolesents. They work closely with students and their families to maximize learning. The GW School for Divergent Learners embodies a vision shared by teachers, parents, and students. A school committed to developing and optimizing the giftedness and intellegence of each student and fostering a sense of social awareness and civic responsibility

3817 Hampden-Sydney College
1 College Road
Hampden Sydney, VA 23943-685
434-223-6000
FAX 434-223-6346
http://www.hsc.edu
Elizabeth Ford, Associate Dean
DR. Christop Howard, President

Offers a variety of services to students with disabilities including note takers, extended testing time, counseling services, and special accommodations.

3818 James Madison University
Office of Disabilities Services
Room 107
Wilson Learning Center
Harrisonburg, VA 22807
540-568-6705
FAX 540-568-7099
TDD:540-568-6705
TTY: 540-568-6705
http://www.jmu.edu/ods
e-mail: disability-svcs@jmu.edu
Valerie Schoolcraft, Program Manager

Offers Learning Strategies Instruction and Strategic Learning Course. Learning Resource Centers in writing, communication, math, science, and critical thinking. Assistive technology lab with various software and hardware include scanners, Kurzweil, etc. High speed scanner support alternate text accommodations. Students with learning disabilities of ADHD may participate in Learning Leaders program.

3819 John Tyler Community College
Office of Disability Services
13101 Jefferson Davis Hwy
Chester, VA 23831-5316
804-796-4000
800-552-3490
FAX 804-796-4362
http://www.jtcc.edu
Marshall Smith, Counselor
Dr. Marshall Smith, President

A public two-year college with support services for special education students.

3820 Liberty University
Office of Academic Disability Support
1971 University Blvd
Lynchburg, VA 24502-2213
434-582-2000
FAX 434-582-2976
TDD:434-522-0420
http://www.liberty.edu
e-mail: wdmchane@liberty.edu
Jerry Falwell, Academic Disability Support Dir.
Ron Godwin, President

Religiously oriented, private, coeducational, comprehensive four year institution. Students who have documented learning disabilities are eligible to receive support services. These would include academic advising, priority class registration, tutoring and testing accommodations.

3821 Little Keswick School
PO Box 24
Keswick, VA 22947-0024
434-295-0457
FAX 434-977-1892
http://www.littlekeswickschool.net
e-mail: tcolumbus@littlekeswickschool.net
Terry Columbus, Director
Marc Columbus, Headmaster

A therapeutic boarding school for 34 boys who have learning, emotional and behavioral difficulties.
1963

3822 Longwood College
201 High St
Farmville, VA 23919
434-395-2391
800-281-4677
FAX 434-395-2434
http://www.longwood.edu/disability
e-mail: disabilityresources@longwood.edu
Maggie Butler n, Director
Leah Mullins, Director

A public four-year college with support services for special education students.

3823 Lord Fairfax Community College
173 Skirmisher Ln
Middletown, VA 22645-1745
540-868-7000
800-906-5322
FAX 540-868-7100
http://www.lfcc.edu
John S Capps, Testing Center Coordinator
Dr. Cheryl Thompson-Stacy, President

A public two-year college. Students are encouraged to identify special needs during the admissions process and to request support services, such as individualized placement testing, developmental studies, learning assistance programs, and study skills. A 504 faculty team recommends accommodations to academic programs, and communicates with area service providers.

3824 Mary Washington College
University of Mary Washington Disability Services
1301 College Ave
Fredericksburg, VA 22401-5300   540-654-1000
                                        FAX 540-654-1073
                                        TDD:540-654-1102
                                        http://www.umw.edu
                                        e-mail: jhample@umw.edu
Judy G Hample, Director
Cathy Payne, Office Manager
William Anderson, President
A public four-year college with support services for special education students.

3825 New Community School
4211 Hermitage Rd
Richmond, VA 23227-3718   804-266-2494
                                      FAX 804-264-3281
                                      http://www.tncs.org
                                      e-mail: info@tncs.org
Julia Ann Greenwood, Head of School

Provides a program of college preparation for dyslexic (specific language learning disabled) students, grades 6-12. The program includes both remediation of language skills and academic challenge appropriate for students of average to above-average intellectual potential.

3826 New River Community College
PO Box 1127
Dublin, VA 24084-1127   540-674-3600
                                      866-462-6722
                                      FAX 540-674-3644
                                      TDD:540-674-3619
                                      http://www.nr.edu
                                      e-mail: nrdixoj@nr.ca.cc.va.us
Jeananne Dixon, Learning Disabilities Coord.
Bonnie Hall, Information Center
Jack Lewis, President
A public two-year college with support services for special education students.

3827 Norfolk State University
700 Park Ave
Norfolk, VA 23504-8090   757-823-8600
                                      FAX 757-823-2342
                                      http://www.nsu.edu
                                      e-mail: bbharris@nsu.du
Carolyn W Meyers, Disability Services Director
Tony Atwater, Ph.D., President
Marian Shepherd, Coordinator/SSDS
Four year university that offers programs for the students with learning disabilities.

3828 Northern Virginia Community College
Disability Support Department
8333 Little River Turnpike
Annandale, VA 22003-3724   703-323-7000
                                      FAX 703-323-3559
                                      http://www.nvcc.edu
Robert G Templon Jr, President
John T Denver, Executive Vice President

A public two-year college.

3829 Oakwood School
7210 Braddock Rd
Annandale, VA 22003-6068   703-941-5788
                                      FAX 703-941-4186
                                      http://www.oakwoodschool.com

Robert Mc Intyre, Head of School

A private, non-profit, co-educational day school for elementary and middle school students with mild to moderate learning differences.

3830 Old Dominion University
1525 Webb Ctr
Norfolk, VA 23529-0001   757-683-4655
                                      FAX 757-683-5356
                                      TDD:757-683-5356
                http://www.studentaffairs.odu.edu/disability
                       e-mail: disabilityservices@odu.edu
Kate Broderick, Office of Educational Access
John R Broderick, President
Tiosha Macklin, Manager
Providing accomodations for students admitted to Old Dominion University that have a documented disability.

3831 Patrick Henry Community College
Patrick Henry Community College 645
Martinsville, VA 24115-5311   276-638-8777
                                      800-232-7997
                                      FAX 276-656-0327
                                      TDD:276-638-2433
                                      http://www.ph.vccs.edu
                       e-mail: klandrum@patrickhenry.edu
Dr. Angeline Godwin, President
Kristen Bishop, Vice President
Gloria Amos, Senior Programmer
Offers a variety of services to students with disabilities including note takers, adaptive testing, counseling services, peer tutoring and adaptive equipment, and accessible transportation.

3832 Paul D Camp Community College
PO Box 737
Franklin, VA 23851-737   757-569-6700
                                      FAX 757-569-6795
                                      http://www.pdc.edu/

Douglas Boyce, Administrator

A public two-year institution with two campuses. Students with learning disabilities are eligible for special services provided by the Student Support Service Program. Learning-disabled students may take advantage of tutors (outside of class time and during class labs), notetakers, and taped textbooks. A counselor serves as student advocate and helps students arrange for classroom accommodations with instructors.

3833 Piedmont Virginia Community College
501 College Dr
Charlottesville, VA 22902-7589   434-977-3900
                                      FAX 434-971-8232
                                      http://www.pvcc.edu
                       e-mail: admissions@pvcc.edu
Frank Friedman, President
John R. Donnelly, Vice President
Malena L. Smith, Administrative Assistant
A two-year comprehensive community college dedicated to the belief that individuals should have equal opportunity to develop and extend their skills and knowledge. Consistent with this philosophy and in compliance with the Americans with Disabilities Act, we encourage persons with disabilities to apply.

3834 Randolph-Macon Woman's College
2500 Rivermont Ave
Lynchburg, VA 24503-1526   434-947-8000
                                      800-745-RMWC
                                      FAX 434-947-8139
                                      TDD:434-947-8608
                http://http://www.randolphcollege.edu
         e-mail: ADMISSIONS@RANDOLPHCOLLEGE.EDU
John Klein, President
Christopher Burnley, M.B.A., Treasurer
Wesley R. Fugate, Ph. D., Secretary

An independent four-year college with support services for students with disabilities.

3835 Rappahannock Community College
12745 College Dr
Glenns, VA 23149-2616   804-758-6700
                                     FAX 804-758-3852
                               http://www.rcc.vccs.edu
                        e-mail: mcralle@rappahannock.edu
Elizabeth Crowther, President
Kim.D McManus, Vice President, Finance & Admin
J. Marlene Cralle, Administrative Assistant
Offers a variety of services to students with disabilities including notetakers, extended testing time, counseling services, and special accommodations.

3836 Riverside School
2110 McRae Rd
Richmond, VA 23235-7533   804-320-3465
                                     FAX 804-320-6146
                               http://www.riversideschool.org
                          e-mail: info@riversideschool.org
Julia D Wingfield, Head of School

Provide remediation of the language skills of each of the at-risk students with dyslexia in grades 1-8, so that they can return to mainstream education fully prepared to realize their highest potential.

3837 Saint Coletta: Alexandria
Adult Programs
207 S Peyton St
Alexandria, VA 22314-2812   571-438-6940
                                     FAX 571-438-6949
                                     TTY: 202-350-8695
                               http://www.stcoletta.org
Jennifer Douglas, Co-Director
Melissa Davis, Co-Director

Offer adults age 18 and older opportunities to participate in vocational and pre-vocational training, life skills training, and community integration in order to achieve greater independence.

3838 Southern Virginia College
1 University Hill Dr
Buena Vista, VA 24416-3038   540-261-8400
                                          800-229-8420
                                     FAX 540-261-8451
                                 http://http://svu.edu/
                        e-mail: anthony.buchanan@svu.edu
Debbie Buchanan, President
Scott.Y Doxey, Operations
Michael Warren Greene, Information Technology Support

Offers a variety of services to students with disabilities including note takers, extended testing time, counseling services, and special accommodations.

3839 Southside Virginia Community College
109 Campus Dr
Alberta, VA 23821-2930   434-949-1000
                               http://www.sv.vccs.edu
                        e-mail: rhina.jones@southside.edu
John J Cavan, President
Linda G. Allen, IT Specialist
Jack Ancell, Dean of Information Services
Offers a variety of services to students with disabilities including notetakers, extended testing time, counseling services, and special accommodations.

3840 Southwest Virginia Community College
PO Box SVCC
Richlands, VA 24641   276-964-2555
                                     FAX 540-964-7259
                                     TDD:276-964-7235
                                  http://www.sw.edu
                          e-mail: admissions@sw.edu

Dr King, President
Michael Bales, Business Manager
Peggy Barber, Director
Offers a variety of services to students with disabilities including note takers, extended testing time, counseling services, and special accommodations.

3841 Thomas Nelson Community College
99 Thomas Nelson Dr
Hampton, VA 23666   757-825-2700
                                     FAX 757-825-2763
                                  http://www.tncc.edu
                               e-mail: info@TNCC.edu
Thomas Kellen, Admissions Advisor
Dr. John.T Dever, President
Howard Taylor, Administrator
A public two-year college with support services for students with disabilities.

3842 Tidewater Community College
300 Granby Street
Norfolk, VA 23510   757-822-1110
                                     TTY: 757-822-1248
                                  http://www.tcc.edu
                               e-mail: tcharro@tcc.edu
Edna Baehre-Kolovani, Ph.D., President
Mr. Franklin Dunn, Vice President
Ms. Lara M. S. Overy, Director ofÿDevelopment
This public two-year college offers transfer and occupational/technical degrees on four campuses and a visual arts center in the Hampton Roads area of Virginia. TCC offers students evaluations, all reasonable accommodations, and a wide array of assistive technology.

3843 University of Virginia
Learning Needs & Evaluation Cetner
400 Brandon Avenue,PO Box 800760
Charlottesville, VA 22908-760   434-924-5362
                                     FAX 434-982-3956
                          http://www.virginia.edu/studenthealth/
                        e-mail: studenthealth@virginia.edu
Patricia M. Lampkin, Vice President and Chief
James.C Turner, Director

Full range of support services for students admitted to any of the ten schools of the university, including graduate/professional schools. Including, but not limited to, alternate texts, exam accommodations, peer-notetakers, TTY and interpreters, assistive devices and housing and transportation accommodations.

3844 Virginia Commonwealth University
Services for Students with Disabilities
901 W Franklin St
Richmond, VA 23284-9066   804-828-0100
                                          800-841-3638
                                     FAX 804-828-1899
                                  http://www.vcu.edu
                        e-mail: vcuhsinternet@mcvh-vcu.edu
Sybil Halloran, Director
Amy.D Barnes, Director
Cathleen C. Burkeÿ, Director
Offers a variety of services to students with disabilities including note takers, extended testing time, counseling services, and special accommodations.

3845 Virginia Highlands Community College
PO Box 828
Abingdon, VA 24212-828   276-739-2400
                                          877-739-6115
                                     FAX 540-628-7576
                               http://http://www.vhcc.edu
                          e-mail: helpdesk@vhcc.edu
Chelsa Taylor, Purchasing Officer
Roger Spencer, Manager
Ron Proffitt, President
A public two-year college. Strives to assist students with disabilities in successfully responding to challenges of academic study and job training.

3846 Virginia Intermont College
1013 Moore St
Bristol, VA 24201-4298
276-669-6101
800-451-1842
FAX 276-466-7963
http://www.vic.edu
e-mail: bholbroo@vic.edu
E. Clorisa Phillips, President
Mary Anne Holbrook, Vice President
Linda C. Morgan, Vice President for Business and
Virginia Intermont College is a private, four-year Baptist affiliated liberal arts college located near the Appalachian
Mountains of Southwest Virginia. Intermont has an enrollment of 850 men and women students. Accommodations,
such as notetakers, extended time on tests, transcribers, oral
testing, tutors and other services, are provided based on
documentation of disabilities.

3847 Virginia Polytechnic Institute and State University
310 Lavery Hallÿ
Blacksburg, VA 24061
540-231-3788
FAX 540-231-3232
TTY: 540-231-0853
http://www.ssd.vt.edu
e-mail: ssd@vt.edu
Susan Angle MD, Director For Disability Services
Charles Steger, President
Robyn Hudson, Assistant Director
A public four-year college with support services for special
education students.

3848 Virginia Wesleyan College
Disabilities Services Office
1584 Wesleyan Dr
Norfolk, VA 23502-5599
757-455-3200
800-737-8684
FAX 757-466-8526
http://www.vwc.edu
e-mail: fpearson@vwc.edu
William T Greer Jr, President
Mr. Bruce Vaughan, Vice President of Operations
Mr. Cary A. Sawyer, Vice President of Finance
Four year college that offers support to students with a learn-
ing disability.

3849 Virginia Western Community College
PO Box 14007
Roanoke, VA 24038-4007
540-857-7231
FAX 540-857-6102
TDD:540-857-6351
http://http://www.virginiawestern.edu/
e-mail: helpdesk@virginiawestern.edu
Michael Henderson, Special Services
Dana Asciolla, Admissions Staff
Robert Sandel, President
A public two-year college with support services for special
education students.

Washington

3850 Bellevue Community College
3000 Landerholm Cir SE
Bellevue, WA 98007-6484
425-564-1000
FAX 425-649-3173
TTY: 425-564-4110
http://www.bcc.ctc.edu
e-mail: admissions@bellevuecollege.edu
Laura Saunders, Interim President
Carol Jones-Watkins, Coordinator

Disability Support Services provides accommodations for
people with disabilities to make their academic careers a
success. There is no separate fee for these services.

3851 Center for Disability Services
Central Washington University
400 E University Way
Ellensburg, WA 98926-7431
509-963-2171
FAX 509-963-3235
http://www.cwu.edu
e-mail: cdsrecept@cwu.edu
Rob Harden, Director
Pamela Wilson, Associate Director
Ian Campbell, Assistant Director
A public four-year college with disability support services
for students with disabilities.

3852 Centralia College
600 Centralia College Blvd
Centralia, WA 98531-4099
360-736-9391
FAX 360-330-7501
TTY: 360-807-6227
http://www.centralia.edu
e-mail: demerson@centralia.ctc.edu
James M Walton, President
Donna Emerson, Administrative Assistant
Michael Grubiak, Vice President
The Special Services Office offers a variety of services to
students with disabilities including notetakers, extended
testing time, counseling services, and special
accommodations.

3853 Children's Institute for Learning
4030 86th Ave SE
Mercer Island, WA 98040-4198
206-232-8680
FAX 206-232-9377
http://www.childrensinstitute.com
e-mail: shannonr@childrensInstitute.com
Trina Westerlund, Admissions Specialist

A full-day academic and therapeutic program for children
ages 3 to 17. Provides social, emotional, developmental and
neurological strategies for children with challenging learning differences and behavior disorders.

3854 Clark College
1800 E McLoughlin Blvd
Vancouver, WA 98663-3598
360-992-2314
FAX 360-992-2879
http://www.clark.edu/dss
e-mail: tjacobs@clark.edu
Kate Poffenroth, Office Assistant
Robert K. Knight, President
Bob Williamson, Vice President
Offers a variety of services to students with disabilities including note takers, extended testing time, counseling services, and special accommodations.

3855 Columbia Basin College, Resource Center Program
2600 N 20th Ave
Pasco, WA 99301-4108
509-542-4412
FAX 509-544-2032
TDD:509-547-0400
http://www.columbiabasin.edu
e-mail: pbuchmiller@columbiabasin.edu
Richard Cummins PhD, President
Peggy Buchmiller, Director
Pat Wright, Associate Director
Provides advocacy and Auxiliary aids and services to stu-
dents with a disability.

3856 Cornish College of the Arts
1000 Lenora St
Seattle, WA 98121-2718
800-726-ARTS
http://www.cornish.edu
e-mail: hello@cornish.edu
Dr. Nancy Uscher, President
Lois Harris, Ph.D., Provost and Vice President
Virginia Anderson, Chair
Through the Student Affairs Office, appropriate accommodations are provided for students with learning disabilities.

3857   Dartmoor School
13401 Bel Red Rd
Bellevue, WA 98005-2322   425-649-8976
                                          FAX 425-603-0038
                    http://http://www.dartmoorschool.org
Doris.J Bower, Founder and Executive Director
Andrew Wahl, President
Denise Leiby, Director of Special Education
A school where intellectual development and interest cre-
ates a mentorship between teacher and student, where stu-
dents call teachers by their first name, and where staff invest
actively in student achievement.

3858   ETC Preparatory Academy
9655 SE 36th St
Mercer Island, WA 98040-2911   206-236-1095
                                          FAX 206-236-0998
                                 http://www.etcinc.org
Ruth Hayes-Short, Director

Assessment, referral, tutorial, courses for credit, advocacy,
dissertation, adults and students that are school age.

3859   Eastern Washington University
124 Tawanka
Cheney, WA 99004   509-359-6871
                                          FAX 509-359-7458
                                  http://www.ewu.edu
                                  e-mail: dsss@ewu.edu
Kevin Hills, Director
Joetta Sieglock, Adaptive Technology Specialist
Pam McDermott, Program Assistant
Although the University does not offer a specialized pro-
gram specifically for learning disabled students, the disabil-
ity support services office works with students on a case by
case basis.

3860   Edmonds Community College
20000 68th Ave W
Lynnwood, WA 98036-5999   425-640-1320
                                          FAX 425-640-1622
                                          TDD:425-354-3113
                                          TTY: 425-774-8669
                                  http://www.edcc.edu/ssd
                                  e-mail: ssdmail@edcc.edu
Dee Olson, Director
Kaleb Cameron, Assistant Director
Ruben Alatorre, Coordinator-Sign Language
Offers a variety of services to students with disabilities in-
cluding notetakers, extended testing time, and special ac-
commodations.

3861   Epiphany School
3611 East Denny Way
Seattle, WA 98122-3471   206-323-9011
                                          FAX 206-324-2127
                    http://http://www.epiphanyschool.org
                    e-mail: office@epiphanyschool.orgÿ
J.D. Delafield, President
Michael Anderson, VP
Neen Koenigsbauer, Secretary
Now, with 233 students served by 43 faculty and staff,
Epiphany School and the Board of Trustees turn their attention to a new educational vision, examining the student
needs in a changing world, while staying true to the strengths
that have served them well for over 53 years. Epiphany has
proudly served more than 1,000 students, many of whom return to the School and increasingly bring their own children
to be educated here.

3862   Everett Community College
Center for Disabilities Services
2000 Tower St
Everett, WA 98201-1390   425-388-9100
                                          FAX 425-388-9129
                                          TDD:425-388-9438
                                  http://www.everettcc.edu
                                  e-mail: cds@everettcc.edu

David Beyer, Director
Kristine Grimsby, Program Assistant

Offers a variety of services to students with disabilities including notetakers, extended testing time, adaptive software
and individual accommodations.

3863   Evergreen State College
2700 Evergreen Pkwy NW
Olympia, WA 98505-5   360-867-6000
                                          FAX 360-867-6577
                                  http://www.evergreen.edu

Thomas L Purce, President

Evergreen's mission is to sustain a vibrant academic community and to offer students an education that will help them
excel in their intellectual, creative, professional and community service goals.

3864   Green River Community College
Rm 126
12401 SE 320th St
Auburn, WA 98092-3622   253-833-9111
                                          TDD:253-288-3359
                                  http://www.greenriver.edu
                            e-mail: rblosser@greenriver.edu
Dr. Eileen Ely, President
Jennifer Nelson, Program Assistant
Tom Campbell, Chair
Support services for students with disabilities to ensure that
our programs and facilities are accessible. Our campus is or-
ganized to provide reasonable accommodations, including
core services, to qualified students with dissabilities.

3865   Heritage Christian Academy
19527 104thÿAvenue NE
Bothell, WA 98011-2930   425-485-2585
                                          FAX 425-486-2895
                      http://http://www.hcabothell.org
                      e-mail: ÿInfo@hcabothell.org
Mr. Chris Butters, Facilities Manager
Carol Taylor, Principal
Wendy Chappell, Preschool Director
Heritage Christian Academy has had the opportunity to educate thousands of children in the Puget Sound region. The
school is well known throughout the region for its quality ac-
ademic program and it is becoming known for its unwaver-
ing dedication in equipping students with a Kingdom
Education that enables them to stand against a world view in
opposition to Christian values.

3866   Highline Community College
PO Box 98000
Des Moines, WA 98198-9800   206-878-3710
                                          FAX 206-870-3773
                                          TTY: 206-870-4853
                                  http://www.highline.edu
                            e-mail: cjones@highline.edu
Jini Allen, Human Resources Staff
Jack Bermingham, President
Debrena Jackson Gandy, Chair
Offers a variety of services to students with disabilities in-
cluding note takers, extended testing time, counseling ser-
vices, and special accommodations.

3867   Morningside Academy
201 Westlake Ave N
Seattle, WA 98109-5217   206-709-9500
                                          FAX 206-709-4611
                    http://www.morningsideacademy.org
                    e-mail: info@morningsideacademy.org
Beth Bartter, Director of Operations
Dr. Kent Johnson, Executive Director
Tim Smith, Administration and Facilities Di

Morningside Academy's school helps both elementary and middle school students to catch up and get ahead. Its students have not previously reached their potential; many have learning disabilities or ADD/ADHD diagnoses; all have average to well above average intelligence. Morningside is not a school for children with significant emotional problems, behavioral problems, or developmental delays.

3868 New Heights School
Children's Institute for Learning Differences
4030 86th Ave SE
Mercer Island, WA 98040-4198
206-232-8680
FAX 206-232-9377
http://www.childrensinstitute.com
e-mail: micheleg@childrensinstitute.com
Carrie Fannin, Managing Director
Trina Westerlund, Executive Director
Dominic Jimenezÿ, Director of Education
A Pre k-12 school based program serving children ages 3-18.

3869 North Seattle Community College
Educational Access Center
9600 College Way N
Seattle, WA 98103-3599
206-527-3600
FAX 206-527-3606
http://https://northseattle.edu/
Ronald H Lafayette, Manager

The Educational Access Center offers a variety of services to students with disabilities including notetakers, extended testing time, counseling services, and special accommodations.

3870 Northwest School
1415 Summit Ave
Seattle, WA 98122-3619
206-682-7309
FAX 206-467-7353
http://www.northwestschool.org
e-mail: admissions@northwestschool.org
Lisa Anderson, Vice President
Cory Carlson, President
Mike McGill, Head of School
The Northwest School is set in an urban campus that is housed in a historic landmark cared for by our students, we provide a curriculum for grades 6-12 that offers an international perspective and encourages independent and creative thinking in every class. They educate and shape their students into global citizens who will one day shape the community, nation, and world.

3871 Pacific Learning Solutions
314 N Olympic Ave
Arlington, WA 98223-9541
360-403-8885
FAX 360-403-7607
http://pacificlearningsolutions.com
e-mail: pacificlearningsolutions@gmail.com
Nola Smith, President

Tutoring for dyslexia; therapy for processing, memory recall and learning difficulties; LiFT (Listening is Fitness Training), Teacher consultant with Academy Northwest Private school helping home school families.

3872 Pierce Community College
9401 Farwest Dr SW
Lakewood, WA 98498-1999
253-964-6500
FAX 253-964-6599
http://www.pierce.ctc.edu
Jaqueline Rosenblatt, Chair
Linda Buzbee, Administrative Assistant
Brian Benedetti, Director, Marketing
A federally funded TRIO progrm providing academic support services to low income students, first generation college students and students with disabilities in order to improve their retention, academic proformance, graduation and transfer to four-year institutions.

3873 Seattle Academy of Arts and Sciences
1201 E Union St
Seattle, WA 98122-3925
206-323-6600
FAX 206-323-6618
http://www.seattleacademy.org
e-mail: admissions@seattleacademy.org
Jean Orvis, Administrator
Barbara Burk, Administrative Assistant
Joe Puggelli, Head of School
Seattle Academy prepares students to participate effectively in modern society. They seek a diversified student body and faculty.

3874 Seattle Central Community College
Seattle Community College District
1701 Broadway
Seattle, WA 98122-2400
206-587-3800
FAX 206-344-4390
TDD:206-934-5450
http://www.seattlecentral.org
e-mail: SCCCWCC@sccd.ctc.edu
Paul T. Killpatrick, Ph.D., President
Warren Brown, EVP
Adam Nance, Executive Director
Offers a variety of services to students with disabilities including notetakers, extended testing time, counseling services, and special accommodations.

3875 Seattle Christian Schools
18301 Military Rd S
Seatac, WA 98188-4684
206-246-8241
FAX 206-246-9066
http://http://www.seattlechristian.com
e-mail: ghunter@seattlechristian.org
Gloria Hunter, Superintendent
Bryan Peterson, Principal
Dave Steele, Administrator
Independent, interdenominational Christian Day School established in 1946, serving 750+ students.

3876 Seattle Pacific University
3307 3rd Ave W
Ste 214
Seattle, WA 98119-1997
206-281-2000
FAX 206-286-7348
TDD:206-281-2475
TTY: 206-281-2224
http://www.spu.edu/departs/cfl
e-mail: centerforlearning3@spu.edu
Heather Carlson, Program Coordinator
Niki Amarantides, Director
Mary Jayne Allen, Program Coordinator Learning Svc
Offers a variety of services to students with disabilities including notetakers, extended testing time, books on tape, interpreters and special accommodations.

3877 Shoreline Christian School
2400 NE 147th St
Shoreline, WA 98155-7395
206-364-7777
FAX 206-364-0349
http://www.shorelinechristian.org
e-mail: admin@shorelinechristian.org
Timothy Visser, Administrator
Rhonda Rasor, Office Staff
Laurie Dykstra, Director of Development
Shoreline Christian School educates students in preschool throughgrade 12, challenging them to grow academically, socially and spiritually.

3878 Snohomish County Christian
17931 64th Ave W
Lynnwood, WA 98037-7106
425-742-9518
FAX 425-745-9306
http://http://www.cpcsschools.com/lynnwood/
Euny Lee, Instructor
Gail Walker, Instructor
Heidy Berkey, Instructor

The Lynnwood Campus is focused on a Christ-centered education that prepares their students to authentically live for God while serving Him and others.

3879 South Puget Sound Community College

2011 Mottman Rd SW
Olympia, WA 98512-6292
360-754-7711
FAX 360-664-0780
http://www.spscc.ctc.edu
e-mail: advising@spscc.ctc.edu
Gerald Pumphrey, Disability Support Coordinator
Kenneth Minnaert, President
Marilyn Adair, Nursing/Director
Offers a variety of services to students with disabilities including notetakers, extended testing time, books on tape, readers, scribes, interpreters, assistance with registration.

3880 South Seattle Community College

6000 16th Ave SW
Seattle, WA 98106-1499
206-764-5300
FAX 206-764-5393
TDD:800-833-6388
http://www.sccd.ctc.edu/south
e-mail: rtillman@sccd.ctc.edu
Jill Wakefield, President

Offers a variety of services to students with disabilities including notetakers, extended testing time, counseling services and special accommodations.

3881 Spokane Community College

1810 N Greene St
Spokane, WA 99217-5399
509-533-7000
800-248-5644
TDD:509-533-7482
http://www.scc.spokane.edu
e-mail: shanson@scc.spokane.edu
Nancy Coffey, President
Claudia Parkins, Manager

Offers a variety of services to students with disabilities including notetakers, extended testing time, counseling services, and special accommodations.

3882 Spokane Falls Community College

3410 W Fort George Wright Dr
Spokane, WA 99224-5288
509-533-3500
888-509-7944
FAX 509-533-3237
TDD:509-533-3838
TTY: 509-533-3838
http://www.spokanefalls.edu
Janet Gullickson, President
Charlene Barkerÿ, Management Staff
Max Josquin, Information Systems Staff
Offers a variety of services to students with disabilities including notetakers, extended testing time, counseling services, and special accommodations.

3883 St. Alphonsus

5816 15th Ave NW
Seattle, WA 98107-3096
206-784-6464
FAX 206-789-5709
http://http://www.stalphonsus-sea.org
Lizzy Scholz, Pastoral Assistant
Timothy Simunds, Pastoral Assistant
Louie Van Hollebeke, Facilities Manager
The Society has assigned priests to serve the local Seattle area out of the parish rectory.The excellent relationship between the Archdiocese and the SOLT community has also afforded the assignment of dozens of SOLT sisters and novices to the convent located on St. Alphonsus parish grounds.

3884 St. Matthew's

1240 NE 127th St
Seattle, WA 98125-4021
206-363-6767
FAX 206-362-4863
http://http://stmatthewseattle.org
e-mail: parishoffice@stmatthewseattle.org
Fr. Jerry Burns, Priest
Jean Cooney, Administrative Assistant
Jon Rowley, Facilities Manager
St. Matthews believe in Jesus Christ and welcome all who seek God's Grace. Their compassionate community embraces many cultures. Through prayer, liturgy, our ministries and service to others, they cultivate a lifelong journey of faith.

3885 St. Thomas School

PO Box 124
Medina, WA 98039-124
425-454-5880
FAX 425-454-1921
http://www.stthomasschool.org
e-mail: info@stthomasschool.org
Bill Palmer, Director of Finance
Judi North, Director of Developmentÿ
St Thomas School aims to develop responsible citizens of a global society. In partnership with parents, they inspire and motivate intellectually curious students. Their small, nurturing environment supports the acquisition of a broad academic foundation with an emphasis on critical thinking, leadership skills, and the development of strong character and spiritual awareness.

3886 University Preparatory Academy

8000 25th Ave NE
Seattle, WA 98115-4600
206-525-2714
FAX 206-525-9659
http://www.universityprep.org
Erica Hamlin, Head of School
Susan Lansverk, Director of Finance
Lora Kolmer, Director of Communications
An independent school serving grades six through twelve, they offer an outstanding academic program guided by our mission statement:ÿUniversity Prep is committed to developing each student's potential to become an intellectually courageous, socially responsible citizen of the world. Their innovative teachers offer a collaborative journey of learning in a diverse community of talented students and involved families.ÿ

3887 University of Puget Sound

University of Puget Sound
1500 N Warner St
Tacoma, WA 98416-5
253-879-3211
FAX 253-879-3500
TDD:253-879-3399
TTY: 800-833-6388
http://www.ups.edu
e-mail: iwest@ups.edu
Sherry Kennedy, Administrative Assistant
Ivey West, Disability Services Coordinator
Barbara Racine, Manager
Support services and accommodations are individually tailored depending upon a student's disability, its severity, the students academic environment and courses, housing situation, activities, etc. Accommodations include instruction in study strategies, free tutoring, assistance in note taking, sign language and additional academic advising.

3888 University of Washington Disability Resources for Students

448 Schmitz Hall
Campus Mailbox 355889
Seattle, WA 98195-5839
206-543-8924
FAX 206-616-8379
TDD:206-543-8925
e-mail: uwdss@u.washington.edu

Provides services and academic accommodations to students with documented permanent and temporary disabilities to ensure equal access to the university's educational programs and facilities. Services may include but are not limited to exam accommodations, notetaking, audio-taped class texts/materials, sign language interpreters, auxilary aids (assistive listening devices, and accessible furniture).

3889   University of Washington: Center on Human Development and Disability
PO Box 357920
Seattle, WA 98195-7920   206-543-7701
                                 FAX 206-543-3417
              http://www.depts.washington.edu/chdd
                     e-mail: chdd@uw.edu
Michael Guralnick, Director
Richard Masse, M.P.H., Director of Administration
Elizabeth Aylward, Ph.D., Associate Director
The Center on Human Development and Disability (CHDD) at the University of Washington makes important contributions to the lives of people with developmental disabilities and their families, through a comprehensive array of research, clinical services, training, community outreach and dissemination activities.

3890   Walla Walla Community College
500 Tausick Way
Walla Walla, WA 99362-9267   509-522-4262
                                 877-992-9922
                                 FAX 509-527-4480
                                 TDD:509-527-4412
                     http://www.wwcc.edu
Claudia Angus, PhD., Coord.Disability Support Svcs.

The Special Services Office offers a variety of services to students with disabilities including notetakers, extended testing time, counseling services, and special accommodations.

3891   Washington State University
Disability Resource Center
217 Washington Building ÿPO Box 642
Pullman, WA 99164-2322   509-335-3417
                                 FAX 509-335-8511
                     http://www.drc.wsu.edu
                   e-mail: drc.frontdesk@ad.wsu.edu
Meredyth Goodwin, Director
Sheri Bain, Access Advisor
Jacqueline McCabe, Office Coordinator
Provide leadership in the development of an inclusive environment at WSU by eliminating barriers, whether they are physical, attitudinal, informational, or programmatic.

3892   Western Washington University
516 High St
Old Main 110
Bellingham, WA 98225-9019   360-650-3083
                                 FAX 360-650-3715
                     http://www.wwu.edu/depts/drs
                     e-mail: drs@wwu.edu
David Brunnemer, Director
Anna Talvi-Blick, disAbility Management & Accommod
Kim Thiessen, Accommodation Counselor & Deaf S
disAbility Resources for Students (DRS) offers a variety of services to students with disabilities including note takers, extended testing time, counseling services and special accommodations.

3893   Whatcom Community College
237 W Kellogg Rd
Bellingham, WA 98226-8003   360-383-3000
                                 FAX 360-676-2171
                     http://www.whatcom.ctc.edu
                     e-mail: advise@whatcom.ctc.edu
Kathi Hiyane-Brown, President
Anne Bowen, Executive Director
Patricia Onion, Vice President
A public two-year college with support services for special education students.

3894   Whitworth College
300 W Hawthorne Rd
Spokane, WA 99251   509-777-1000
                                 FAX 509-777-3725
                     http://www.whitworth.edu
                     e-mail: mhansen@whitworth.edu
Marianne Hanson, Director of Admissions
Aaron McMurray, Director
Garrett Riddle, Associate Director
Offers a variety of services to students with disabilities including note takers, extended testing time, counseling services, and special accommodations.

3895   Yakima Valley Community College
PO Box 22520
Yakima, WA 98907-2520   509-574-4600
                                 TDD:509-574-4600
                     http://http://www.yvcc.edu
Anthony Beebe, Vice President
Robert Ozuna, President
Ms. Patricia Whitefootÿ, Director
Offers a variety of services to students with disabilities including notetakers, extended testing time, counseling services, and special accommodations.

West Virginia

3896   Bethany College West Virginia
Special Advising Program
Room 4
Morlan Hall
Bethany, WV 26032   304-829-7000
                                 FAX 304-829-7580
                     http://www.bethanywv.edu
                     e-mail: alumni@bethanywv.edu
Dr. Scott D. Miller, President
Dr. Darin E. Fields, Vice President
William R. Kiefer, Executive Vice President
Bethany College is an academic community founded on the close interaction between students and faculty in the educational process. Bethany College values intellectual rigor and freedom, diversity of thought and lifestyle, personal growth within a community context, and responsible engagement with public issues.

3897   Davis & Elkins College
Learning Disability Program
100 Campus Dr
Elkins, WV 26241-3996   304-637-1900
                                 800-624-3157
                                 FAX 304-637-1413
                     http://http://www.dewv.edu/
                     e-mail: mccaulj@dne.wvnet.edu

G T Mann, Director

Offers a program to provide individual support to college students with specific learning disabilities. This comprehensive program includes regular sessions with one of the three full-time learning disabilities instructors and specialized assistance and technology not available elsewhere on campus.

3898   Fairmont State University
Student Disabilities Services
1201 Locust Ave
Fairmont, WV 26554-2470   304-367-4892
                                 800-641-5678
                                 FAX 304-367-1803
                                 TDD:304-367-4200
                     http://http://www.fairmontstate.edu/
Maria C. Bennett Rose, President
Ron Tucker, Chairman
Dixie Yann, Vice Chair
Four year college provides services to learning disabled students.

3899 Glenville State College
Student Disability Services
200 High St
Glenville, WV 26351-1200
304-462-7361
800-924-2010
FAX 304-462-4407
TDD:304-462-4136
http://http://www.glenville.edu/
e-mail: cottrill@GLENVILLE.WVNET.EDU
Peter B Barr, President
Teresa Sterns, Executive Assistant

Glenville State College, often referred to as the Lighthouse on the Hill, is West Virginia's only centrally located public college.With an enrollment of approximately 1,400 students, the college has a student to faculty ratio of 19 to 1. The college's enrollment is made up of many first generation students with approximately 90% of the students coming from West Virginia counties.

3900 Marshall University
Higher Education for Learning Problems
520 18th St
Huntington, WV 25755
800-642-3463
FAX 304-696-3231
http://www.marshall.edu
e-mail: weston@marshall.edu
Lynne Weston, Director
Diane Williams, Coordinator of College HELP
K Renna Moore, Administrative Assistant
Offers the following services: individual tutoring to assist with coursework, studying for tests, administration of oral tests when appropriate; assistance with improvement of memory, assistance with note taking; assistance to determine presence of learning problems.

3901 Salem International University
233 W Main St
Salem, WV 26426-1226
888-235-5024
FAX 304-326-1246
TDD:304-782-5011
http://http://www.salemu.edu
e-mail: admissions@salemiu.edu
John Reynolds, President

Student Support Services grant program funded by the US Dept of Education for 125 college students who are identified as disadvantaged and/or disabled. On staff are a counselor, a learning disabled specialist in math and science and a learning specialist in reading and writing.

3902 Southern West Virginia Community and Technical College
PO Box 2900
Mount Gay, WV 25637-2900
304-896-7432
FAX 304-792-7113
TTY: 304-792-7054
http://www.southern.wvnet.edu
e-mail: darrellt@southernwvnet.edu
Darrell Taylor, Dean of Student Development

Higher education

3903 West Virginia Northern Community College
1704 Market St
Wheeling, WV 26003-3643
304-233-5900
FAX 304-233-0272
http://http://www.wvncc.edu/
Martin Olshinsky, President
Dr. Darrell Cummings, Chair
Mary K. DeGarmo, Vice Chair
A public two-year college with support services for special education students.

3904 West Virginia State College
PO Box 1000
Institute, WV 25112-1000
304-766-3000
800-987-2112
FAX 304-766-4100
http://http://www.wvstateu.edu/
Kellie Dunlap, Disability Services
Dr.Brian.O Hemphill, President
Melvin Jones, Vice President
A public four-year college. Accommodations are individualized to meet student's needs.

3905 West Virginia University
Speech Pathology and Audiology
806 Allen Hall
PO Box 6122
Morgantown, WV 26506
304-293-4241
FAX 304-293-2905
http://www.wvu.edu/~speechpa
e-mail: robert.orlikoff@mail.wvu.edu
Lynn Cartwright, Manager
Cheryl Ridgway, Administrative Associate

Provides high-quality programs of instruction at the undergraduate, graduate, and prefessional level; to stimulate and foster both basic and applied research and scholarship; to engage in and encourage other creative and artistic work; and to bring the resources of the University to all segments of society through continuing education, extension, and public activities.

3906 West Virginia University at Parkersburg
300 Campus Dr
Parkersburg, WV 26104-8647
304-424-8378
FAX 304-424-8372
TDD:304-424-8337
http://www.wvup.edu/ada
e-mail: wvup_disabilitysv@mail.wvu.edu
Cathy Mutz, Director of Disability Services

Provides disability accomodations to qualified students based on appropriate documentation.

3907 West Virginia Wesleyan College
Mentor Advantage Program
59 College Ave
Buckhannon, WV 26201-2699
304-473-8000
800-722-9933
FAX 304-472-2571
http://www.wvwc.edu
e-mail: kuba_s@wvwc.edu
Pamela Balch, President

The mentoring program, developed from research on the transition and persistence of postsecondary students with learning disabilities and from self-regulated learning theory, is designed to create a bridge to academic regulation in the college environment.

Wisconsin

3908 Alverno College
3400 S 43rd St
Milwaukee, WI 53234
414-382-6026
800-933-3401
FAX 414-382-6354
http://www.alverno.edu
e-mail: colleen.barnett@alverno.edu
Nancy Bornstein, Instructional Services Director
Colleen Barnett, Student Accessibility Coord

An independent liberal arts college with 2,000 students in its weekday and weekend degree programs. Support services for students with learning disabilities include appropriate classroom accommodations, assistance in developing self advocacy skills, instructor assistance, peer tutoring, study groups, study strategies workshops, a communication resource center and math resource center.

3909   Beloit College
700 College St
Beloit, WI 53511-5595   608-363-2000
                                         FAX 608-363-2717
        http://www.beloit.edu/~stuaff/disability.html
Scott Bierman, President

Offers a variety of services to students with disabilities such as self advocacy training, study skills and time management guidance, couseling services, and special accommodations.

3910   Blackhawk Technical College
PO Box 5009
Janesville, WI 53547-5009   608-758-6900
                                         800-498-1282
                                         FAX 608-757-7740
                                         TDD:608-743-4422
                    http://www.blackhawk.edu
Dr Thomas Eckert, President
Christine Flottum, Project Manager

A public two-year college with support services for special education students.

3911   Cardinal Stritch University
Academic Support
6801 N Yates Rd
Milwaukee, WI 53217-3985   414-410-4166
                                         800-347-8822
                                         FAX 414-410-4239
                    http://www.stritch.edu
Marcia Laskey, Director Academic Support

An independent four-year college with support services for special education students.

3912   Carthage College
Academic Support Program
2001 Alford Park Dr
Kenosha, WI 53140-1994   262-551-8500
                                         FAX 262-551-6208
                    http://www.carthage.edu
F Gregory Campbell, President
William Abt, Senior Vice President
Gregory Baer, Director of Faculty Development
An independent four-year college with support services for special education students.

3913   Chippewa Valley Technical College
Chippewa Valley Technical College
620 W Clairemont Ave
Eau Claire, WI 54701-6162   715-833-6200
                                         800-547-2882
                                         FAX 715-833-6470
                    http://www.cvtc.edu
                    e-mail: infocenter@cvtc.edu
Bruce Barker, President
Joe Hegge, Vice President
Ronald Edwards, Manager
A public two-year college with support services for special education students.

3914   Edgewood College
1000 Edgewood College Dr
Madison, WI 53711-1997   608-663-4861
                                         800-444-4861
                                         FAX 608-663-3291
                    http://www.edgewood.edu
                    e-mail: admissions@edgewood.edu
Daniel Carey, President

An independent four-year college with support services for students with learning disabilities.

3915   Fox Valley Technical College
1825 N. Bluemound Drive, PO Box 227
Appleton, WI 54912-2277   920-735-5600
                                         800-735-3882
                                         FAX 920-831-4396
                    http://www.foxvalley.tec.wi.us
                    e-mail: helpdesk@fvtc.eduÿ
Anne Haberkorn, Dean
David Buettner, President
Mary Hansen, Manager
A public two-year college with support services for special education students.

3916   Gateway Technical College
3520 30th Ave
Kenosha, WI 53144-1690   262-564-2200
                                         FAX 262-564-2201
                                         TTY: 262-564-2206
                    http://www.gtc.edu

Bryan D Albrecht, President

In accordance with Section 504 of the Vocational Rehabilitation Act, Gateway provides a wide range of services that assist special needs students in developing independence and sel-reliance within the Gateway campus community. Reasonable accommodations will be made for students with learning disabilities or physical limitations.

3917   Lakeshore Technical College
Office For Special Needs
1290 North Ave
Cleveland, WI 53015-1414   920-693-1000
                                         FAX 920-693-1363
                                         TTY: 920-693-8956
                    http://www.gotoltc.edu
                    e-mail: rivi.hatt@qotoltc.edu
Michael Lanser, President
Karla Zahn, Student Success Manager
Rivi Hatt, ADA Learning Support Coordinator
A two-year college that provides comprehensive programs to students with learning disablities.

3918   Lawrence University
711 E. Boldt Way
Appleton, WI 54911   920-832-7000
                                         FAX 920-832-6884
                    http://www.lawrence.edu
                    e-mail: excel@lawrence.edu
Geoff Gajawski, Academic Services Assoc. Dean
Richard Warch, President

Four year college that offers services to the learning disabled.

3919   Maranatha Baptist Bible College
745 W Main St
Watertown, WI 53094-7600   920-261-9300
                                         800-622-2947
                                         FAX 920-261-9109
                    http://www.mbbc.edu
                    e-mail: cmidcalf@mbbc.edu
Larry R Oats, Director
David Jaspers, President

Four year college that offers programs for the learning disabled.

3920   Marian College of Fond Du Lac
45 S National Ave
Fond Du Lac, WI 54935-4699   920-923-7600
                                         800-2-MARIAN
                                         FAX 920-923-7154
          http://http://www.marianuniversity.edu
          e-mail: admission@marianuniversity.eduÿ

John.K Nelson, *Chair*
Steven R. DiSalvo, Ph.D.ÿ, President
Wayne.E Matzke, Vice Chair
Offers a variety of services to students with disabilities including note takers, extended testing time, counseling services, and special accommodations.

3921 Marquette University
Disability Services Department
PO Box 1881
Milwaukee, WI 53201-1881

414-288-7250
800-222-6544
FAX 414-288-3764
http://www.marquette.edu
e-mail: patriciaalmon@marquette.edu

Arthur F. Scheuber, Vice President
Rev. Scott R Pilarz, S.J.ÿ, President
Dr. Mary DiStanislaoÿ, Executive Vice President
An independent four-year university with support services for students with learning disabilities.

3922 Mid-State Technical College
500 32nd St N
Wisconsin Rapids, WI 54494-5512

715-422-5300
888-575-MSTC
FAX 715-422-5345
http://www.mstc.edu
e-mail: webmaster@midstate.tec.wi.us

Amanda Lang, Director
Dr. Sue Budjac, President
Carrie Becker, Technology Services Assistant
Offers a variety of services to students with disabilities including notetakers, extended testing time, counseling services, and special accommodations.

3923 Milwaukee Area Technical College
700 W State St
Milwaukee, WI 53233-1419

414-297-MATC
FAX 414-297-7990
http://www.matc.edu
e-mail: info@matc.edu

Dr. Michael Burke, President

A public two-year college with support services for disabled students.

3924 Nicolet Area Technical College
Disability Support Service
PO Box 518
Rhinelander, WI 54501-0518

715-365-4410
800-544-3039
FAX 715-365-4445
http://www.nicolet.tec.wi.us
e-mail: inquire@nicolet.tec.wi.us

Todd Allgood, Disability Support Services Dir
John Bates, Case Manager
Cindy Schmitz, Case Manager
In support of the Nicolet Area Technical College Student services mission, the Special Needs Support Program provides appropriate accommodations empowering students with disabilities to identify and develop abilities for successful educational and life experiences.

3925 Northcentral Technical College
1000 W Campus Dr
Wausau, WI 54401-1899

715-675-3331
FAX 715-675-9776
http://www.ntc.edu

Dr. Lori A. Weyers, President
Jeanne Worden, Vice President
Janel Kittel, Vice President - Finance, CFO
Offers a variety of services to students with disabilities including notetakers, extended testing time, counseling services, and special accommodations.

3926 Northeast Wisconsin Technical College
Special Services Program
2740 W Mason St, PO Box 19042
Green Bay, WI 54307-9042

920-498-5400
800-422-6982
FAX 920-498-6260
TTY: 920-498-6901
http://www.nwtc.edu
e-mail: more.info@nwtc.edu

H. Jeffrey Rafn, Ph.D., President
Jim Blumreich, CFO
Jennifer Canavera, Procurement Manager
The Special Needs Office of NWTC offers assistance to individuals with disabilities when choosing educational and vocational goals, building self-steem and increasing their occupational potential. We offer a wide range of support services and accommodations which increases the potential of individuals with exceptional education needs to successfully complete Associate Degree and Technical Diploma programs.

3927 Northland College
Northland College
1411 Ellis Ave
Ashland, WI 54806-3999

715-682-1699
FAX 715-682-1308
http://www.northland.edu
e-mail: admit@northland.edu

Karen I Halbersleben, President
Max Metz Jr., Associate Director of Admissions
Biagio Nigrelli, Admissions Counselor
Four year college that provides students with learning disabilities with support and services.

3928 Oconomowoc Developmental Training Center
36100 Genesee Lake Rd
Oconomowoc, WI 53066-9202

262-569-5515
FAX 262-569-6337
http://www.odtc-wi.com

Christie Ducklow, Director

Our mission is to provide comprehensive residential treatment, educational and vocational services to children, adolescents, and young adults with dually-diagnosed emotional disturbances and developmental disabilities.

3929 Ripon College
Student Support Services
300 Seward Street, PO Box 248ÿ
Ripon, WI 54971-248

920-748-8107
800-947-4766
http://www.ripon.edu
e-mail: adminfo@ripon.edu

Zach Messitte, President

Student Support Services (SSS) is a federally funded United States Department of Education TRIO program and provides a network of academic, personal and career services to hundreds of students on the Ripon campus who are first generation, lower income or physically or learning disabled.

3930 St. Norbert College
Academic Support Services
100 Grant St
De Pere, WI 54115-2099

920-337-3181
800-236-4878
FAX 920-403-4008
http://www.snc.edu
e-mail: karen.goode-bartholomew@snc.edu

Thomas Kunkel, President
Raechelle Clemmons, Chief Information Officer
Dr. Jeffrey Frick, Dean of the College and Academic
Provides reasonable accommodations for documented disabilities.

3931 University of Wisconsin Center: Marshfield Wood County
2000 W 5th St
Marshfield, WI 54449-3310   715-389-6530
http://www.marshfield.uwc.edu
Michelle Boernke, Director
Kimberly Kolstad, Academic Advisor
Matthew Lemmerman, Program Associate
A public two-year college with support services for special education students.

3932 University of Wisconsin-Madison
Waisman Center
1500 Highland Ave
Madison, WI 53705-2280   608-263-1656
FAX 608-263-0529
TDD:608-263-0802
http://www.waisman.wisc.edu
e-mail: webmaster@waisman.wisc.edu
Marsha Mailick Seltzer, PhD, Director
Qiang Chang, PhDÿ, Faculty Core Co-Director
Joe Egan, MPA, Associate Director
To advance knowledge about human development, developmental disabilities, and neurodegenerative diseases.

3933 University of Wisconsin: Eau Claire
105 Garfield Ave, P.O Box 4004
Eau Claire, WI 54702-4004   715-836-4636
FAX 715-836-3712
http://www.uwec.edu
e-mail: hansonbj@uwec.eduÿ
Pamela Gray, Director
Vickie Larson, President

Offers a variety of services to students with disabilities including note takers, extended testing time, counseling services, and special accommodations.

3934 University of Wisconsin: La Crosse
1725 State St
La Crosse, WI 54601-3742   608-785-8000
FAX 608-785-6868
TDD:608-785-6900
http://www.uwlax.edu
e-mail: reinert.june@uwlax.edu
Judith Albert, Executive Staff Asst
Robert Hetzel, Vice Chancellor
Joe Gow, Chancellor
Offers a variety of services to students with disabilities including note takers, extended testing time, counseling services, and special accommodations.

3935 University of Wisconsin: Madison
McBurney Disability Resource Center
702 W. Johnson Street
Suite 2104
Madison, WI 53715   608-263-2741
FAX 608-265-2998
TDD:608-263-6393
TTY: 608-263-6393
http://www.mcburney.wisc.edu
e-mail: mcburney@studentlife.wisc.edu
Cathleen Trueba, Director
B.A. Scheuers, Assistant Director
Barbara Lafferty, Office Manager
Offers a variety of services to students with disabilities including notetakers, extended testing time, counseling services, and special accommodations.

3936 University of Wisconsin: Milwaukee
Exceptional Education Department
PO Box 413
Milwaukee, WI 53201-413   414-229-4721
FAX 414-229-4705
http://www.exed.soe.uwm.edu
e-mail: oas@uwm.edu
Amy Otis Wilborn, Chairperson
Paul Ross, Director
Carol L. Colbeck, Dean

A public four-year college with support services for special education students.

3937 University of Wisconsin: Oshkosh
Project SUCCESS
800 Algoma Blvd
Oshkosh, WI 54901-8610   920-424-1234
TTY: 920-424-1319
http://www.uwosh.edu
e-mail: wegner@uwosh.edu
Tim Merrill, Facilities Manager
Richard H. Wells, Chancellor

A remedial program for students with language-based learning disabilities attending the University of Wisconsin Oshkosh.

3938 University of Wisconsin: Platteville
1 University Plaza
Platteville, WI 53818-3099   608-342-1491
800-362-5515
FAX 608-342-1122
http://www.uwplatte.edu
e-mail: wilsonj@uwplatt.edu
Dennis J. Shields, Chancellor
Joyce Burkholder, Administrative Assistant
Robert Cramer, Vice Chancellor
Coordinates academic accommodations, provides an advocacy resource center for students with disabilities.

3939 University of Wisconsin: River Falls
410 S. 3rd Street
River Falls, WI 54022   715-425-3911
FAX 715-425-3277
http://www.uwrf.edu
e-mail: dots@uwrf.edu
Mark Johnson, Coordinator
Ruth Taoford, Contract Manager
Van Galen, Dean
Offers a variety of services to students with disabilities including note takers, extended testing time, counseling services, and special accommodations.

3940 University of Wisconsin: Whitewater
Project ASSIST
800 W. Main Street
Whitewater, WI 53190-1790   262-472-1234
FAX 262-472-1518
http://www.uww.edu
e-mail: amachern@uww.edu
Richard J. Telfer, Chancellor

The program is based on the philosophy that students with learning disabilities can learn specific strategies that will enable them to become independent learners who can be successful in a college setting.

3941 Viterbo University
900 Viterbo Dr
La Crosse, WI 54601-8804   608-796-3000
800-VITERBO
FAX 608-796-3050
http://www.viterbo.edu
Dr. Richard Artman, Director
Barbara Gayle, Vice President
Todd Ericson, Vice President
An independent four-year college with special services for special education students.

3942 Walbridge School
7035 Old Sauk Rd
Madison, WI 53717-1010   608-833-1338
FAX 608-833-1338
http://www.walbridgeschool.com
e-mail: info@walbridgeschool.com
Steve Lien, Interim Head of School
Nancy Donahue, Director
Kristina Jasmine, Office Manager

Offers an alternative and comprehensive full day elementary through middle school program emphasizing multi-sensory teaching and individualization to address the learning differences of children. Specialized and personalized instruction is geared to children with learning disabilities including dyslexia and ADHD.

3943 Waukesha County Technical College
Special Services Department
800 Main St
Pewaukee, WI 53072-4696   262-691-5566
                                          877-892-9282
                                      FAX 262-691-5593
                                     http://www.wctc.edu
                                 e-mail: djilbert@wctc.edu
Barbara Prindiville, Director
Colleen Gonzalez, Transition Retention Specialist

Offers technical and associate degree programs. Services for students with a documented disability may include academic support services, transition services, assistance with the admissions process, testing accommodations, interpreting services, note taking and assistance with RFB&D.

3944 Western Wisconsin Technical College
400 Seventh Street North
La Crosse, WI 54601   608-785-9200
                                           800-322-9982
                            http://http://www.westerntc.edu/
Thomas.E Smith, Chair
Daniel.P Hanson, Vice Chair
Joanne.E Sandwick, Secretary
Offers a variety of services to students with disabilities including notetakers, extended testing time, counseling services, and special accommodations.

3945 Wisconsin Indianhead Tech College: Ashland Campus
505 Pine Ridge Driveÿ
Shell Lake, WI 54871-8727   715-468-2815
                                           800-243-WITC
                                      FAX 715-468-2819
                                     http://www.witc.edu
A public two-year college with support services for special education students.

3946 Wisconsin Indianhead Technical College: Rice Lake Campus
1900 College Drive
Rice Lake, WI 54868   715-234-7082
                                           800-243-WITC
                                      FAX 715-234-5172
                                     TTY: 888-261-8578
                                     http://www.witc.edu

Craig Fowler, Vice President

A public two-year college with support services for students with disabilities.

Wyoming

3947 Laramie County Community College: Disability Support Services
1400 E. College Drive
Education & Enrichment Cntr, Room 222
Cheyenne, WY 82007-3295   307-778-1359
                                           800-522-2993
                                      FAX 307-778-1262
                                      TTY: 307-778-1266
                                 http://www.lccc.wy.edu/dss
                               e-mail: tkeney@lccc.wy.edu
Dr. Joe Schaffer, President

Disability Support Services provides comprehensive, confidential services for LCCC students with documented disabilities. Services and adaptive equipment to reduce mobility, sensory and perceptual problems are available through the DRC, and all services are provided free of charge to LCCC students.

3948 University of Wyoming
1000 E. University Avenue
Laramie, WY 82071   307-766-1121
                                     http://www.uwyo.edu
An independent four-year college with support services for special education students.

3949 Wyoming Institute For Disabilities
University Of Wyoming
1000 E University Ave
Department 4298
Laramie, WY 82071-2000   307-766-2761
                                           888-898-9463
                                     http://www.uwyo.edu
                                 e-mail: wind.uw@uwyo.edu
Karen Williams, Executive Director WIND

Assists individuals with developmental disabilities and their families through early intervention, education, training and community services.

Alabama

3950   Good Will Easter Seals
2448 Gordon Smith Dr
Mobile, AL 36617-2319   251-471-1581
                                      800-411-0068
                                      FAX 251-476-4303
                        http://www.alabama.easterseals.com
Frank Harkins, Director

Children and adults with disabilities and special needs find
highest-quality services designed to meet their individual
needs.

3951   Parents As Partners In Education Of Alabama
Austism Society
576 Azalea Road, Suite 105
P.O. Box 161274
Mobile, AL 36616-2274   251-478-1208
                                      800-222-7322
                                      FAX 251-473-7877
                                      TTY: 251-478-1208
                        http://www.autism-society.org
Barbara Wheat MD, Director

Parent Training and Information Program views parents as
full partners in the educational process and a significant
source of support and assistance to each other. Funded by the
Division of Personnel Preparation, Office of Special Education Programs, these programs provide training and information to parents to enable such individuals to participate more
effectively with professionals in meeting the educational
needs of disabled children.

3952   Sequel TSI
Sequel Youth And Family Services
1131 Eagletree Ln SE
Huntsville, AL 35801-6478   256-880-3339
                                      888-758-4356
                                      FAX 256-880-7026
                        http://www.threesprings.com
                        e-mail: info@threesprings.com
John Ripleyÿ, Chairman
Steve Gilbert, Contact Person
Ed Irby, President
Formally known as Three Springs, Sequel TSI is a nationally
recognized leader in youth services, founded in 1985 to pro-
vide therapy and education to adolescents experiencing
emotional, behavioral and learning problems.

3953   Wiregrass Rehabilitation Center
WRC, Inc.
795 Ross Clark Circle
Dothan, AL 36303
                                      800-395-7044
                                      FAX 216-521-9460
                        http://www.wrcjobs.com
                        e-mail: info@wrcjobs.com
Dr. Jack Sasser, Administrator

Trains individuals to become employable and helps in assisting them to find jobs within their communities.

3954   Workshops
4244 3rd Ave S
Birmingham, AL 35222-2008   205-592-9683
                                      888-805-9683
                                      FAX 205-592-9687
                        http://www.workshopsinc.org
                        e-mail: susan.crow@workshopsinc.org
Susan C Crow, Executive Director
Kirsten Beauchamp, Program Services Director

Work adjustment and job development services for people
with disabilities.

Alaska

3955   Center for Community
700 Katlian
Suite B
Sitka, AK 99835-7359   907-747-6960
                                      800-478-6970
                                      FAX 907-747-4868
                        http://www.ptialaska.net
Connie Sipe, Executive Director

A state-wide provider of home and community-based services for people with disabilities, the elderly and others who
experience barriers to community living in Alaska.

3956   Gateway School and Learning Center
900 W. Fireweed Lane
P.O. Box 113149
Anchorage, AK 99511-3149   907-522-2240
                                      FAX 907-344-0304
                        http://www.gatewayschoolak.com
                        e-mail: learning@gatewayschoolak.com
Beverly Lau, Principal

Provides specialized educational services for students
grades 1-12 with dyslexia and other language-processing
disorders.

Arizona

**3957   Arizona Center Comprehensive Education and
Lifeskills**
10251 N 35th Ave
Phoenix, AZ 85051-1305   602-995-7366
                                      FAX 602-995-2636
                        http://www.accel.org
Connie F. Laird, Executive Director

A private, non-profit, special education school providing
therapeutic, educational, and behavioral services to over
200 students, ages 3-21, with cognitive, emotional, orthopedic, and/or behavioral disabilities.

3958   Devereux Arizona Treatment Network
11000 N Scottsdale Road
Suite 260
Scottsdale, AZ 85254   480-998-2920
                                      FAX 480-443-5587
                        http://www.devereux.org
Lane Barker, Executive Director

Provides a wide array of behavioral health and social welfare
services for persons with emotional and behavioral disorders or who are victims of physical or sexual abuse and
neglect.

3959   Life Development Institute (LDI)
18001 N. 79th Avenue
Building E-71
Glendale, AZ 85308-8396   623-773-2774
                                      FAX 623-773-2788
                        http://www.life-development-inst.org
                        e-mail: info@life-development-inst.org
Robert Crawford, President

Provides a supportive residential community that gives individuals the education, skills and training they need to live independently. By offering these programs in a residential
environment, the students are given a chance to learn independence, and instill in them a desire to succeed.

3960 Raising Special Kids

5025 E. Washington Street #204
Phoenix, AZ 85034-7439   602-242-4366
                                800-237-3007
                            FAX 602-242-4306
        http://www.raisingspecialkids.org
        e-mail: info@raisingspecialkids.org
Joyce Millard Hoie, Executive Director

A parent training and information center providing information, resources and support to families of children with disabilities and special needs in Arizona. Services are offered free of charge.

3961 Turning Point School

8780 National Blvd.
Culver City, CA 90232-3650   310-841-2505
                             FAX 310-841-5420
        http://www.turningpointschool.org
        e-mail: info@turningpointschool.org
Deborah Richman, Head Of School
Nancy Von Wald, Executive Director

A private, nonprofit school for children with dyslexia, attention deficit disorder and learning disabilities who have difficulties in reading, writing, spelling and math. Also offers camping, after-school classes and daycare.

Arkansas

3962 Arkansas Disability Coalition

1123 S. University Avenue
Suite 225
Little Rock, AR 72204-1605   501-614-7020
                                 800-223-1330
                             FAX 501-614-9082
                             TTY: 800-223-1330
                http://www.adcpti.org
        e-mail: adcoalition@earthlink.net
Wanda Stovall, Executive Director

Arkansas Disability Coalition's mission is to work for equal rights and opportunities for Arkansans with disabilities through public policy change, cross-disability collaboration, and empowerment of people with disabilities and their families.

California

3963 Almansor Transition & Adult Services

211 Pasadena Ave
South Pasadena, CA 91030-2919   323-341-5632
                                 877-837-4332
                             FAX 323-341-5644
        http://www.redesignlearning.org
        e-mail: info@resdesignlearning.org
Nancy Lavelle, Ph.D, Executive Director
Nita Moore, Program Director

A multi-service, community-based education and training facility for at-risk youth. Offering a range of professional services and support to the students and their parents.

3964 Ann Martin Children's Center

1250 Grand Ave
Piedmont, CA 94610-1070   510-655-7880
                             FAX 510-655-3379
            http://www.annmartin.org
David Theis, Executive Director
Betty Peterson MEd, Educational Therapist

A non-profit community agency, providing psychotherapy, educational therapy and diagnostic testing for children, adults and families. Also offer a monthly lecture series for educators and child mental health professionals.

3965 Brislain Learning Center

2545 Ceanothus Avenue
Suite 130
Chico, CA 95973-7717   530-342-2567
                                 800-791-6031
                             FAX 530-342-2573
        http://www.brislainlearningcenter.com
        e-mail: info@brislainlearningcenter.com
Judy Brislain, Director

Assists children of all ages who have learning disabilities. Offers a diagnostic program and tutoring program for ADD and learning disabilities. Provides counseling and support groups for children and adults.

3966 Center for Adaptive Learning

3227 Clayton Rd
Concord, CA 94519-2818   925-827-3863
                             FAX 925-827-4080
        http://www.centerforadaptivelearning.org
        e-mail: info@centerforadaptivelearning.org
Genevieve Stolarz, President

The center provides a comprehsive program that is designed to address many needs; physical, social, emotional and vocational. To empower adults with a developmental neurological disability to realize their own potential.

3967 Charles Armstrong School

1405 Solana Dr
Belmont, CA 94002-3693   650-592-7570
                             FAX 650-592-0780
        http://www.charlesarmstrong.org
        e-mail: info@charlesarmstrong.org
Rosalie Whitlock, Headmaster

The mission of the school is to serve the dyslexic learner by providing an appropriate educational experience which not only enables the students to acquire language skills, but also instills a joy of learning, enhances self-worth, and allows each the right to identify, understand and fulfill personal potential.

3968 Devereux California

P.O.Box 6784
Santa Barbara, CA 93160-6784   805-968-2525
                             FAX 805-968-3247
                http://www.devereux.org
        e-mail: info@devereux.org
Amy Evans, Executive Administrator

A treatment facility offering residential, educational and adult vocational or day activity programs to individuals ages 8-85 with multiple diagnoses such as; autistic spectrum disorders, emotional and/or behavioral disorders, mental retardation, developmental disabilities, and medical conditions.

3969 Dyslexia Awareness and Resource Center

928 Carpinteria St
Suite 2
Santa Barbara, CA 93103-3477   805-963-7339
                             FAX 805-963-6581
        http://www.dyslexiacenter.org
        e-mail: info@dyslexiacenter.org
Joan Esposito, Executive Director
Joan T. Esposito, Program Director
Sid Smith, Chairman

The center provides direct one-on-one services to adults and children affected with dyslexia, attention disorders and other learning disabilities. In addition the center conducts outreach and training seminars for public and private schools, for the juvenile court systems, for drug and alcohol programs, for family and social service programs, for literacy programs, and for homeless and mission programs.

3970 EDU-Therapeutics

14401 Roland Canyon Road
Salinas, CA 93908-5334   831-484-0994
FAX 861-484-0998
http://www.edu-therapeutics.com
e-mail: joan_smith@comcast.net
Dr Joan Smith, Director

EDU-Therapeutics is a unique learning system that offers effective solutions for overcoming dyslexia, attention deficit, learning disabilities and reading challenges. It succeeds because it changes how an individual uses his or her brain to learn. It is unique because it identifies the underlying cause of the learning inefficiency and eliminates the symptoms.

3971 Frostig Center

971 N Altadena Dr
Pasadena, CA 91107-1870   626-791-1255
FAX 626-798-1801
http://www.frostig.org
e-mail: helpline@frostig.org
Bennett Ross, Executive Director

A non profit organization that specializes in helping children who have learning disabilities. Offers parent training, consulting, school and tutoring services to learning disabled children.

3972 Full Circle Programs

70 Skyview Terrace
San Rafael, CA 94903-1845   415-499-3320
FAX 415-499-1542
http://www.marin.org
Full Circle has been actively caring for children and their families in need. Full Circle offers a continuum of care ranging from residential treatment for several emotionally disturbed boys, to outpatient counseling for children and their families.

3973 Help for Brain Injured Children

Cleta Harder Developmental School
981 N Euclid St
La Habra, CA 90631-2932   562-694-5655
FAX 562-694-5657
http://www.hbic.org
Cleta Harder, Executive Director

Help for brain-injured children. Long-term, low cost home rehabilitation programs. School programs, rehabilitation, academic, speech and physical therapy, as needed. Offer an after-school program for youngsters in regular school who are experiencing difficulties.

3974 Institute for the Redesign of Learning

Ste 200
1955 Fremont Avenue
South Pasadena, CA 91030-2694   323-257-3006
FAX 323-341-5642
http://www.redesignlearning.org
Al Hernandez, EdD, Education Director

A multi-service, community-based education and training facility for at-risk youth. Offering a range of professional services and support to the students and their parents.

3975 Kayne Eras Center

Exceptional Children's Foundation
5350 Machado Ln
Culver City, CA 90230-8800   310-737-9393
FAX 310-737-9344
http://www.kayneeras.org
e-mail: mjackson@kayneeras.org
Dwight Counsel, Principal

Kayne-Eras accomplishes its mission by offering educational resources, direct service, and a professional training center. Kayne-ERAS provides personalized programming to children and young adults from at risk conditions and those challenged by emotional, learning, developmental and/or chronic neurological and/or medical disabilities.

3976 Marina Psychological Services

4640 Admiralty Way
Ste 318
Marina Del Rey, CA 90292-6637   310-822-0109
FAX 310-822-1240
e-mail: marinapsych@hotmail.com
Stuart Shaffer PhD, Psychologist

Comprehensive psychological services for children and adults with learning disabilities and attention deficit disorders. Private, individualized assessment and treatment.

3977 Nawa Academy

17351 Trinity Mountain Rd
French Gulch, CA 96033-9709   530-359-2215
800-358-6292
FAX 530-359-2229
http://www.nawaacademy.org
e-mail: info@nawaacademy.org
David W Hull, Head of School
Jason Hull, Admissions Director

A boarding school located in a remote valley of the Trinity Alps that provides individual curriculum, theory and structure for 7-9 grade students, many of who have learning disabilities. ÆServices include individual counseling, small academic classes, and numerous after school activities.

3978 New Vistas Christian School

68 Morello Ave
Martinez, CA 94553-3042   925-370-7767
FAX 925-370-6395
http://www.newvistaschristian.com
e-mail: info@newvistaschristian.com
Correne Romeo, Director

A non-profit 1st-12th grade school for students of average or above average intelligence with learning disabilities offering a non-traditional approach to multiple learning styles.

3979 Newport Audiology Center

Newport Health Network
5990 Greenwood Plaza Blvd.
Suite 120
Greenwood Village, CO 80111   720-385-3700
http://www.newportaudiology.com
The aim is to enhance the quality of people's lives by improving their ability to communicate. We provide the highest level of audiological services possible, through our highly efficient staff, informative education programs, community services, high quality products, and true spirit of customer service.

3980 One To One Reading & Educational Tutoring

11971 Salem Dr
Granada Hills, CA 91344-2348   818-368-1801
FAX 818-368-9345
e-mail: drpakmanrains@aol.com
Paul Klinger, Director

Specialize in reading and math; reading grades 1-6, math through pre-algebra.

3981   Park Century School
3939 Landmark St
Culver City, CA 90232-2315   310-840-0500
                                        FAX 310-840-0590
                    http://www.parkcenturyschool.org
                    e-mail: nbley@parkcenturyschool.org
An independent school for average and above average intellect children with learning disabilities. The program emphasizes developing the skills and strategies necessary to return to a traditional program. With a 2:1 student-staff ratio.

3982   Pine Hill School
1325 Bouret Dr
San Jose, CA 95118-2408   408-979-8210
                                        FAX 408-979-8219
                    http://www.pinehillschool.com
                    e-mail: gregz@secondstart.org
Greg Zieman, Principal

A private school that provides special education and alternative services to students with a wide range of learning and behavior disabilities.

3983   Prentice School
Prentice School
18341 Lassen Dr
Santa Ana, CA 92705-2012   714-538-4511
                                           800-479-4711
                                        FAX 714-538-5004
                    http://www.prentice.org
Carol Clark, Executive Director
Cheryl Cormier, Director Of Development

The Prentice School is an independent, nonprofit, coeducational day school for children pre-k through 8th grade with language learning differences.

3984   Providence Speech and Hearing Center
1301 W Providence Ave
Orange, CA 92868-3892   714-923-1521
                                        FAX 714-639-2593
                    http://www.pshc.org
                    e-mail: pshc@pshc.org
Richard Van Dyke, Executive Vice President
Linda Smith, CEO
Raul Lopez, COO
Comprehensive services for testing and treatment of all speech, language and hearing problems. Individual and group therapy beginning with parent/infant programs.

3985   Raskob Learning Institute and Day School
3520 Mountain Blvd
Oakland, CA 94619-1627   510-436-1275
                                        FAX 510-436-1106
                    http://www.raskobinstitute.org
                    e-mail: raskobinstitute@hnu.edu
Edith Gutterres, Executive Director

A co-educational school for students from diverse cultural and economic backgrounds with language-based learning disabilities. Raskob seeks to recognize and nurture the talents and strengths of each student while remediating areas of academic weakness.

3986   Reading Center of Bruno
Ste 243
4952 Warner Ave
Huntington Beach, CA 92649-4423   714-377-7910
                                        FAX 562-436-4428
                    http://www.readingcenter.info
                    e-mail: readingct.@aol.com

Walt Waid, Director

Working with children, teens and adults with dyslexia, auditory and visual perceptual confusions through our specialized training program. Diagnostic testing is available, as well.

3987   Santa Cruz Learning Center
655 Capitola Road
Suite 200
Santa Cruz, CA 95062-1220   831-475-1354
                    http://www.santacruzlearningcenter.com
                    e-mail: malika@santacruzlearningcenter.com
Eleanor Stitt, Director

Individualized one-to-one tutoring for individuals aged 5 to adult. Specializes in dyslexia, learning difficulties and gifted persons. Includes test preparation, math, reading, self confidence, study skills, time organization and related services.

3988   Special Education Day School Program
Inst. for the Redesign of Learning/Almansor Center
1317 Huntington Drive
South Pasadena, CA 91030-4507   323-341-5580
                                        FAX 323-257-3101
                    http://www.redesignlearning.org
                    e-mail: info@resdesignlearning.org
Nancy Lavelle, Ph.D., President

Providing basic education and related services to children with language, learning, behavioral, developmental and emotional needs.

3989   Speech and Language Development Center
8699 Holder St
Buena Park, CA 90620-3699   714-821-3620
                                        FAX 714-821-5683
                                        TDD:714-821-3628
                    http://www.sldc.net
                    e-mail: info@sldc.net

Dawn O'Connor, President

A school and therapy center for children and young adults with language, learning, and behavior disorders (many have multiple handicapping conditions), resulting in complex educational needs.

3990   Stockdale Learning Center
Ste 104
1701 Westwind Dr
Bakersfield, CA 93301-3045   661-326-8084
                                        FAX 661-327-4752
                    http://www.stockdale-learning-center.com
                    e-mail: slc@igalaxy.net
Andrew J Barling, Executive Director

A professional State Certified Educational Therapy clinic designed to collaboratively diagnose and assess individuals 5 years of age through adult who have learning disabilities. Offering extensive services for dyslexia, ADD/HD, and other specific learning disabilities.

3991   Stowell Learning Center
15192 Central Ave
Chino, CA 91710   909-598-2482
                                        FAX 909-598-3442
                    http://www.learningdisability.com
                    e-mail: info@learningdisability.com
Jill Stowell, President

A diagnostic and teaching center for learning and attention disorders. Specializes in instruction for dyslexic or learning disabled children and adults. Our services include diagnostic evaluation, developmental evaluation, cognitive and educational therapy which is provided on a one-to-one basis, and a full day class for elementary age students with reading disabilities.

3992 Switzer Learning Center
2201 Amapola Ct
Torrance, CA 90501-1431
310-328-3611
FAX 310-328-5648
http://www.switzercenter.org
e-mail: drfoo@switzercenter.org
Rebecca Foo, Executive Director

Provides a personalized academic program in a therapeutic environment. Has one elementary, one middle school and six high school classrooms, plus two classrooms for middle and high school students with a moderate to severe autistic spectrum disorder.

3993 Team of Advocates for Special Kids
100 W Cerritos Ave
Anaheim, CA 92805-6546
714-533-8275
866-828-8275
FAX 714-533-2533
http://www.taskca.org
e-mail: taskca@yahoo.com
Marta Anchondo, Executive Director

A parent training and information center that parents and professionals can turn to for assistance in seeking and obtaining needed early intervention and educational, medical or therapeutic support service for children.

3994 The Almansor Center
Institute for the Redesign of Learning
1317 Huntington Dr
South Pasadena, CA 91030-4511
323-341-5580
FAX 323-257-3101
http://www.redesignlearning.org
e-mail: info@resdesignlearning.org
Nancy Lavelle Ph.D., President

A multi-service, community-based education and training facility for at-risk youth. Offering a range of professional services and support to the students and their parents.

3995 The Center For Educational Therapy
1264 Higuera Street
San Luis Obispo, CA 93401
805-801-9467
FAX 805-546-8700
http://www.center4edu-therapy.com
Dr. Dianne Olvera, Director

Provides educational assessment to determine learning style and document learning disabilities. Also provided are one-to-one remedial or tutorial services for individuals specializing in dyslexia.

3996 Vision Care Clinic
General, Preventive and Developmental Optometry
2730 Union Avenue
Suite A
San Jose, CA 95124-1496
408-377-1150
FAX 408-377-1152
http://www.visiondiva.com
V Liane Rice, Director

Diagnostic and training for those with visual disabilities.

Colorado

3997 Developmental Disabilities Resource Center
11177 West 7th Avenue
Suite 300
Lakewood, CO 80215-5520
303-233-3363
800-649-8815
FAX 303-233-4622
TDD:303-462-6606
http://www.ddrcco.com
e-mail: ahogling@ddrcco.com
Art Hogling, CEO

The mission is to provide leading-edge services that create opportunities for people with developmental disabilities and their families to participate fully in the community.

3998 Havern School
4000 S Wadsworth
Lakewood, CO 80123-1308
303-986-4587
FAX 303-986-0590
http://www.haverncenter.org
Cathy Pasquariello, Executive Director

School for children with learning disabilities. Educational programs, special language programs and occupational therapy is available.

Connecticut

3999 American School for the Deaf
139 N Main St
West Hartford, CT 06107-1269
860-570-2300
TTY: 860-570-2222
http://www.asd-1817.org
e-mail: ed.peltier@asd-1817.org
Ed Peltier, Executive Director

A residential/day program operating as a state-aided private school and governed by a board of directors. It is the oldest permanent school for the deaf in America, offering a comprehensive educational program for the deaf and hard of hearing students, infants, preschoolers, primary, elementary, junior high school, high school, and post-secondary students.

4000 Boys and Girls Village, Inc.
528 Wheelers Farms Rd
Milford, CT 06461-1847
203-877-0300
FAX 203-876-0076
http://www.boysvill.org
e-mail: fellenbaumk@boysvill.org
Steven Joffe, MSW, CEO
Catherine Murphy-Brooks, Director Of Education

The clients of Boys & Girls Village are children in crisis or children with learning difficulties who have experienced rejection, failure or abuse. Through the years, the agency has evolved into a leading therapeutic and learning facility offering residential shelter, clinical, after-school, counseling, special educational, foster & adoptive recruitment and training, family support services, and day programs for children and their families.

4001 Child Care Programs
Easter Seals Connecticut
85 Jones Street
P.O. Box 198
Hebron, CT 06248
860-228-9496
http://www.ct.easterseals.com
John Quinn, President

Meeting a growing need for high-quality child care for more than 20 million young children and their working parents, Easter Seals offers child care for children ages 6 months to 5 years. Young children are welcomed to a unique environment where children of all abilities learn together.

4002 Connecticut Institute for the Blind
The Oak Hill Cntr For Individual & Family Supports
120 Holcomb St
Hartford, CT 06112-1589
860-242-2274
TTY: 860-286-3113
http://www.ciboakhill.org
e-mail: info@ciboakhill.org

Patrick Johnson, Director

Largest private nonprofit community provider of services for people with disabilities in Connecticut.

4003 Devereux Glenholme School
81 Sabbaday Ln
Washington, CT 06793-1318   860-868-7377
                                    FAX 860-868-7894
                http://www.theglenholmeschool.org
                e-mail: info@theglenholmeschool.org
Gary L Fitzherbert, Director

The Glenholme School is a boarding school for students with social/emotional and/or learning disabilities. Glenholme is situated on 100 idyllic acres in the Connecticut countryside.

4004 Eagle Hill School
45 Glenville Rd
Greenwich, CT 06831-5392   203-622-9240
                                    FAX 203-622-0914
                http://www.eaglehillschool.org
                e-mail: info411@eaglehill.org
Mark Griffin, Director

Eagle Hill is a languaged-based, remedial program committed to educating children with learning disabilities. The curriculum is individualized, interdisciplinary, and transitional in nature.

4005 Focus Alternative Learning Center
P.O.Box 452
Canton, CT 06019-0452   860-693-8809
                                    FAX 860-693-0141
                http://www.focusalternative.org
                e-mail: info@focus-alternative.org
Donna Swanson, Director

FOCUS Alternative Learning Center is a private, licensed, non-profit, year-found clinical program committed to the treatment of children ages 6-18 diagnosed with Autism Spectrum disorders, attention and anxiety disorders, or who have processing and/or learning problems. Our Integral Model of Care™ focuses on the social, emotional and academic obstacles that impede a child's growth and success in school, at home and in the community.

4006 Forman School
Forman School
12 Norfolk Rd
P.O. Box 80
Litchfield, CT 06759-2537   860-567-8712
                                    FAX 860-567-8317
                http://www.formanschool.org
                e-mail: admissions@formanschool.org
Adam Man, Principal

Forman offers students with learning differences the opportunity to achieve academic excellence in a traditional college preparatory setting. A coeducational boarding school of 180 students, we maintain a 3:1 student:teacher ratio. Daily remedial instruction balanced with course offerings rich in content provide each student with a flexible program that is tailored to his or her unique learning style and needs.

4007 Founder's Cottage
Star, Lighting The Way
182 Wolfpit Ave
Norwalk, CT 06851-3436   203-846-9581
                                    FAX 203-847-0545
                http://www.starinc-lightingtheway.org
Katie Banzhaf, Executive Director

Facility-based respite care is provided by STAR at Founders Cottage. A lovely home, is co-ed, and can accomodate four individuals at a time. It is for people with development disabilities who are 16 years or older and who reside within the Southwest Region. All persons must be registered with the Connecticut Department of Mental Retardation and have a DMR number assigned.

4008 Gengras Center
Saint Joseph College
1678 Asylum Ave
West Hartford, CT 06117-2764   860-232-5616
                                    FAX 860-231-6795
                http://www.sjc.edu
                e-mail: blindauer@sjc.edu
Bernard Lindauer, Director

This state approved, private special education facility, provides a highly structured, intensive, self-contained special education program for elementary, middle and high school students. The program focuses on skill development in the core academic areas, functional application of skills, community life skills, work readiness skills, job training, social development and independent living skills. Special attention is given to the behavioral challenges of individual students.

4009 Intensive Education Academy
840 N Main St
West Hartford, CT 06117-2026   860-236-2049
                                    FAX 860-231-2843
                http://www.intensiveeducationacademy.org
                e-mail: iea_education@comcast.net
Jill O'Donnell, Principal

A state approved, non-profit, non sectarian special education facility for children 6 to 21 years with different learning styles. Individualized program with a 5:1 student teacher ratio. Program strives to help each student reach their potential by gaining confidence, recognizing their strengths and limitations, setting realistic goals and attaining satisfaction by achieving these goals. State approved. Full-day curriculum is offered.

4010 Klingberg Family Centers
370 Linwood St
New Britain, CT 06052-1998   860-224-9113
                                    FAX 860-832-8221
                http://www.klingberg.org
                e-mail: markj@klingberg.org
Mark Johnson, M.A., CFRE, Vice President
Lynn Roe, Director Of Intake

Provides structured programs for residential, day treatment and day school students in a therapeutic environment. We are a private, nonprofit organization serving children and families from across Connecticut.

4011 Learning Center
Children's Home
60 Hicksville Rd
Cromwell, CT 06416-2409   860-635-6010
                                    FAX 860-635-3708
                http://www.childhome.org
                e-mail: csarnowski@childhome.org
Cindy Sarnowski, Director of Education
Brandy Bunnell, Asst Director of Education
Garrett Mullaney, President/CEO
A private special education facility serving adolescents between the ages of 10 and 21. The flexibility of the program provides students with an opportunity to meet their academic needs. Technology is an important component of the program in addition to academics and an opportunity to participate in a vocational component.

4012 Lorraine D. Foster Day School
1861 Whitney Ave
Hamden, CT 06517-1406   203-230-4877
                              FAX 203-288-5749
                        http://www.ldfds.com
                        e-mail: ldfds@snet.net
Dominique Fontaine, Executive Director
Christine Kirschenbaum, Assistant Director

Teaches elementary grade children with special needs who have experienced difficulty learning in typical school settings.

4013 Mount Saint John
135 Kirtland St
Deep River, CT 06417-1816   860-343-1300
                              FAX 860-343-1392
                        http://www.mtstjohn.org
                        e-mail: info@mtstjohn.org
Douglas J. DeCerbo, Executive Director
Lee Farland, Director of Finance
Terre.C Daniels, Director of Human Resources
This is a residential treatment program that provides comprehensive and integrated treatment services to adolescent boys and young men who are not able to function in their home community due to combinations of behavioral, emotional, family and educational problems. The staff and Board of Mount Saint John are committed to providing a treatment program to meet the evolving and changing needs of the times and of the boys who come into our care.

4014 Natchaug Hospital School Program
189 Storrs Road
Mansfield Center, CT 06250-0260   860-456-1311
                                        800-426-7792
                                   FAX 860-423-6114
                              http://www.natchaug.org
Stephen Larcen, President

Natchaug Hospital operates three state approved K-12 special education programs for socially, emotionally disturbed youth. Natchaug Hospital also provides in patient and partial hospital programs at 9 Eastern Connecticut locations.

4015 Natchaug's Network of Care
Natchaug Hospital
189 Storrs Rd
Mansfield Center, CT 06250-0260   860-456-1311
                                        800-426-7792
                                   FAX 860-423-6114
                              http://www.natchaug.org
Stephen Larcen, President

The hospital's 54-bed facility in Mansfield Center, provides inpatient care for seriously emotionally disturbed children and adolescents as well as adults in crisis each year.

4016 Oak Hill Center
The Oak Hill Center for Individual/Family Support
120 Holcomb St
Hartford, CT 06112-1529   860-242-2274
                            TTY: 860-286-3113
                        http://www.ciboakhill.org
                        e-mail: info@ciboakhill.org
Patrick Johnson, Director

Offers many programs and services for children and adults with developmental, intellectual, physical disabilities and visual impairements.

4017 Saint Francis Home for Children, Inc.
651 Prospect St
New Haven, CT 06511-2003   203-777-5513
                              FAX 203-777-0644
                        http://www.stfrancishome.com
                        e-mail: info@stfrancishome.com

Paula Moody, Executive Director
Ivan Tate, Director

A psychological treatment facility for emotionally disturbed children. Clinical Services are provided by a full and part time theraputic staff. Each child receives weekly individual, small and large group therapy as well as weekly family therapy. Children attend St. Francis School, staffed by professional special ed teachers.

4018 Saint Francis Home for Children: Highland
651 Prospect St
New Haven, CT 06511-2003   203-777-5513
                              FAX 203-777-0644
                        http://www.stfrancishome.com
                        e-mail: info@stfrancishome.com
Paula Moody, Executive Director

4019 St. Vincent's Special Needs Center
St. Vincent's Medical Center
95 Merritt Blvd
Trumbull, CT 06611-5435   203-375-6400
                              FAX 203-380-1190
                  http://www.stvincentsspecialneeds.org
                  e-mail: feroleto.child.dev@snet.net
Barry Buxbaun, Director

Began as therapy treatment program for children with cerebral palsy, and have evolved into a provider of specialized lifelong education and therapeutic programs for children and adults with multiple developmental disabilities and special health care needs.

4020 The Children's Program
Connecticut College
Holmes Hall
75 Nameaug Avenue
New London, CT 06320-4150   860-439-2922
                              FAX 860-439-5317
                        http://www.conncoll.edu
                        e-mail: shrad@conncoll.edu
Lee Hisle, Program Director

The mission of the Connecticut College Children's Program is to provide, within a community context, a model child and family-focused early childhood program for infants and young children of diverse backgrounds and abilities in Southeastern Connecticut.

4021 The Foundation School
719 Derby Milford Rd
Orange, CT 06477-2299   203-795-6075
                           FAX 203-799-4797
Walter J Bell, Director

For students ages 3-21 with developmental needs, learning deficits, behavioral challenges and autism spectrum disorder. Basic developmental skills address speech/language and perceptual/motor areas. Academic skills are reading, writing and arithmetic with social studies, science and career studies.

4022 The Learning Clinic
P.O.Box 324
Brooklyn, CT 06234-0324   860-774-5619
                              FAX 860-774-1165
                        http://www.thelearningclinic.org
                        e-mail: admissions@thelearningclinic.org
Raymond Du Charme, Ph.D., Executive Director

A private, nonprofit educational program that provides day and residential school focused on ADHD and learning and emotional issues. The program is coeducational and serves seventy students. The aim is to assist students in meeting their academic goals and prepare for future experiences in educational, vocational, and community settings.

4023 VISTA Vocational & Life Skills Center
1356 Old Clinton Rd
Westbrook, CT 06498-1858   860-399-8080
FAX 860-399-3103
http://www.vistavocational.org
e-mail: info@vistavocational.org
Helen Bosch, President

Educational and support services for young adults with autism spectrum, ADD, learning disabilities, traumatic brain injuries, and developmental delays.

4024 Villa Maria Education Center
Villa Maria School
161 Skymeadow Dr
Stamford, CT 06903-3400   203-322-5886
FAX 203-322-0228
http://www.villamariaedu.org
e-mail: matyman@villamariaedu.org
Sister Carol Anne, Executive Director
Eileen Cassidy, Education Director
Mary Ann Tynan, Admissions Director
Dedicated to developing the full potential of students who are learning disabled, and does this by providing an education that will help children who learn differently acquire knowledge, develop skills, and increase the self-acceptance and self-esteem necessary to become responsible adults.

4025 Vocational Center for People who are Blind or Visually Impaired
Oak Hill Center
120 Holcomb St
Hartford, CT 06112-1529   860-242-2274
FAX 860-242-3103
http://www.ciboakhill.org
e-mail: info@ciboakhill.org
Bruce Stovall, Director

Providing children and adults with disabilities the opportunity to live, learn and work in the community.

4026 Waterford Country Schools
78 Hunts Brook Road
P.O. Box 408
Quaker Hill, CT 06375-0408   860-442-9454
FAX 860-442-2228
http://www.waterfordcountryschool.org
e-mail: info@waterfordcs.org
David Moorehead, Executive Director
Sharon Butcher, President

The school offers academic, prevocational, behavior management and life skills programs for children and young adults ages 8-18.

4027 Wheeler Clinic, Inc.
91 Northwest Dr
Plainville, CT 06062-1552   888-793-3500
800-793-3588
FAX 860-793-3520
http://www.wheelerclinic.org
e-mail: dberkowitz@wheelerclinic.org
Susan Walkama, President

A provider of behavioral health services for children, adolescents, adults and families that include mental health, substance abuse, special education, early childhood development, prevention, an employee assistance program and community education.

4028 Wilderness School
State of Connecticut Dept of Children & Families
240 N Hollow Rd
East Hartland, CT 06027-1002   860-653-8059
800-273-2293
FAX 860-653-8120
http://www.ct.gov
e-mail: dave.czaja@ct.gov
David Czaja, M.H.S.A., Director

A prevention, intervention, and transition program for troubled youth from Connecticut. The school offers high impact wilderness programs intended to foster positive youth development.

Delaware

4029 AdvoServ
4185 Kirkwood St Georges Rd
Bear, DE 19701-2272   302-834-7018
800-593-4959
FAX 302-836-2516
http://www.advoserv.com
e-mail: dusseaum@advoserv.com
M Dusseau, Admissions Director
R Katz, Education Director

Provides services to individuals whose challenges have defied all previous attempts at treatment. Through proven, positive and comprehensive strategies that teach individuals how to live problem-free, AdvoSer can help overcome the burdens and barriers associated with severe and intractable problems.

4030 Centreville School
6201 Kennett Pike
Centreville, DE 19807-1017   302-571-0230
FAX 302-571-0270
http://www.centrevilleschool.org
e-mail: centreville@centrevilleschool.org
Denise Orenstein, Director

Motivated by two fundamental goals; to provide learning disabled children a vibrant and challenging curriculum comparable to those found at any primary or intermediate level school, and to offer each student the specialized and focused support he or she needs.

4031 Parent Information Center of Delaware
5570 Kirkwood Hwy
Orchard Commons Business Center
Wilmington, DE 19808-5002   302-999-7394
888-547-4412
FAX 302-999-7637
http://www.picofdel.org
Marie-Anne Aghazadian, Executive Director

Assists individuals with disabilities and special needs and those who serve them; also provides information and referral to other agencies.

4032 Pilot School
100 Garden of Eden Rd
Wilmington, DE 19803-1599   302-478-1740
FAX 302-478-1746
http://www.pilotschool.org
e-mail: info@pilotschool.org

Kathleen Craven, Executive Director

Pilot School provides a creative, nurturing environment for children with special learning needs. The schools works with each child to give them the specific developmental tools, guidance and attention needed to learn and achieve in order to feel comfortable and successful.

District of Columbia

4033 Kingsbury Center
5000 14th St NW
Washington, DC 20011-6926   202-722-5555
                                 FAX 202-722-5533
                        http://www.kingsbury.org
                   e-mail: center@kingsbury.org
Peri-Anne Chobot, CEO/Head of School

DC's oldest non public school for children with learning disabilities.

4034 Paul Robeson School
Washington Department Of Mental Health
3700 10th St NW
Washington, DC 20010-1445   202-576-5151
                                 FAX 202-576-8804
                   http://www.mental.disorder.net
Harriet Crawley, Principal

The Department of Mental Health offers therapy and treatment at special education centers, such as The Paul Robeson School. The school offers individual, group and/or family psychotherapy or art therapy, play therapy, speech therapy, and recreational principles. They also provide physical education, adaptive physical education, and occupational therapy, if needed.

4035 The Lab School of Washington
4759 Reservoir Rd NW
Washington, DC 20007-1921   202-965-6600
                        http://www.labschool.org
          e-mail: katherine.schantz@labschool.org
Katherine Schantz, Head Of School

The Lab School is internationally recognized for its innovative programs for children and adults with learning disabilities. The Lab School offers individualized instruction to students in kindergarten through 12 grade.

Florida

4036 Academic Achievement Center
313 Pruett Rd
Seffner, FL 33584-3116   813-654-4198
                                 FAX 813-871-7468
                              http://www.iser.com
                     e-mail: ALSofAAC@aol.com
Lillian M Stark, Ph.D., Director
Arnold L. Stark, Ph.D., Educational Director

A private program for bright and gifted children with LD and/or ADD, offering multisensory-based instruction, remediation of basic skills, academic challenge in science, social science, and literature, plus award-winning art and drama, and curriculum-enhancing field trips and travel. Maximum student body is 22 and it is coeducational. After school tutoring and phonelogical awareness training are also available.

4037 Achievement Academy
716 E Bella Vista St
Lakeland, FL 33805-3009   863-683-6504
                                 FAX 863-688-9292
                   http://www.achievementacademy.com
                e-mail: paula@achievementacademy.com
Paula Sullivan, Executive Director

Serves children up to age 6 with autism, cerebral palsy, speech delays and down syndrome. The Birth to Three program offers services to children up to three years of age who may be at risk for developmental delays.
            'pages

4038 Atlantis Academy
Educational Services of America
1950 Prairie Rd
West Palm Beach, FL 33406-6764   561-642-3100
                                  FAX 561-969-1950
                   http://www.atlantisacademy.com
Dennis Kelley, Director

A small, private, highly individualized program, Pre K-12, for children with attention disorders, dyslexia and other academic learning problems. Day students only.

4039 Baudhuin Preschool
Nova SE University's Mailman Segal Institute
3301 College Ave
Fort Lauderdale-Davie, FL 33314-7796   954-262-7100
                                        800-541-6682
                                 FAX 954-262-3936
                   e-mail: baudhuin@nova.edu
Wendy Masi PhD, School Dean
Rachel Docekal, Executive Director
Nancy Lieberman, Director
For autistic children, the program supports the qualities and capabilities of each child. This therapeutic program focuses on cognitive, social-emotional, adaptive, behavioral, motor, and communication skill development within a relationship-based environment. Providing each child with choices, challenges, and opportunities that nurture feelings of competence, promote intellectual growth, and enable each child to achieve his or her potential.

4040 Children's Center for Development and Behavior
440 Sawgrass Corporate Parkway
Suite 106
Sunrise, FL 33325   954-745-1112
                                 866-290-6468
                                 FAX 954-745-1120
                   http://www.childpsych.org
          e-mail: administrative@childpsych.org
Shana Williams, Psy.D., Director - Psychological Service
David Lubin, Ph.D., BCBA-D, Vice President - Clinical Affair
Debbie White-Maynes, Ms. Ed,, Director of Academic Services
Dedicated to supporting the social, physical, emotional, intellectual and creative development in children with speech delays, general developmental disorders, Autism, and Down's Syndrome. Some of the programs include speech language pathology, behavior management, music therapy, occupational therapy and sibling support groups.

4041 Exceptional Student Education: Assistive Technology
Orange County Public School
445 W Amelia St
Orlando, FL 32801-1220   407-317-3504
                                 FAX 407-317-3526
                   e-mail: ruthie.rieder@ocps.net
Ruthie Rieder, Director

Services are provided for students who are mentally handicapped, emotionally handicapped, specific learning disabled, sensory impaired, speech and language impaired, physically impaired, hospital/homebound, autistic, gifted, and developmentally delayed. Services such as occupational/ physical therapy, assistive technology, and assistance for ESE bilingual students are also available.

4042 Kurtz Center
Complete Learning Center
1201 Louisiana Avenue
Suite C
Winter Park, FL 32789-2340   407-740-5678
FAX 407-629-6886
http://www.completelearningcenter.com
e-mail: ld-request@learningdisabilities.com
Sandy Dieringer, Director

A treatment facility and professional development provider, using scientifically based researched approaches in the treatment of those in need and in training other professionals, paraprofessionals and parents to use these approaches. Developed individualized programs for all ages that conquer all forms of learning disabilities/difficulties, including the various dyslexias and attention focus problems.

4043 McGlannan School
10770 SW 84th St
Miami, FL 33173-3898   305-274-2208
FAX 305-274-0337
TDD:305-274-2208
http://www.mcglannanschool.com
Frances K Mc Glannan, Director

A school that provides one-to-one learning for children with dyslexia and other learning disabilities. Diagnostic, multidisciplinary, prescriptive, research-based and individualized to reach the whole child.

4044 Morning Star School
Morning Star School
210 E Linebaugh Ave
Tampa, FL 33612-7405   813-935-0232
FAX 813-932-2321
http://www.morningstartampa.org
e-mail: edaly@tampa-morningstar.org
Eileen Daly, Principal
Brenda Budd, Assistant Principal
Paul Reed, Administrative Coordinator
A non-profit school for elementary and junior-high age children with learning disabilities and related learning differences.

4045 PACE-Brantley Hall School
3221 Sand Lake Rd
Longwood, FL 32779-5850   407-869-8882
FAX 407-869-8717
http://www.mypbhs.org
e-mail: bw@mypbhs.org
Kathleen Shatlock, Principal

An independent, nonprofit school for children with learning differences. The PACE program has been specifically designed for students who have been diagnosed with learning disabilities, attention deficit disorder, dyslexia and similar challenges.

4046 Reading Clinic
Tampa Day School
12606 Henderson Rd
Tampa, FL 33625-6548   813-269-2100
FAX 813-490-2554
http://www.tampadayschool.com
Lois Delaney, Director
Walt Karniski MD, Executive Director

Provides a learning environment that promotes that individual feeling of success for each child and to meet each child's needs. The Reading Clinic has been helping children become better readers for over 30 years. Once the problem is targeted, and provide the kind of help a child needs, the gains are immediate and long lasting.

4047 Renaissance Learning Center
5800 Corporate Way
West Palm Beach, FL 33407-2004   561-640-0270
FAX 561-640-0272
http://www.rlc2000.com
e-mail: renaissance@rlc2000.com
Debra Johnson, Principal/Director
Toby Honsberger, Asst Principal/Behavior Analyst

Develops and provides effective education and treatment programs for children ages 3-14 with autism.

4048 Summer Camp Program
Tampa Day School
12606 Henderson Road
Tampa, FL 33625-6548   813-269-2100
FAX 813-490-2554
http://www.tampadayschool.com
Lois Delaney, Head of School
Dee Dee Crooks, Office Manager
Linda Fedewa, Admissions Coordinator
Summer camp program for children in grades K-8. Camp is held in the Citrus Park area and children are encouraged to learn, play and grow while enjoying such activies as arts and crafts, sports, field trips and more.

4049 Susan Maynard Counseling
1501 Venera Avenue
Suite 225
Coral Gables, FL 33146-3032   305-667-5011
http://www.susanmaynardphd.com
e-mail: info@susanmaynardphd.com
Susan Maynard, Ph.D., School Psychologist

Serices include testing, evaluations and consultations for children who are exhibiting learning/behavior problems or physical and motor difficulties.

4050 Vanguard School
22000 Hwy 27
Lake Wales, FL 33859-6858   863-676-6091
FAX 863-676-8297
http://www.vanguardschool.org
e-mail: vanadmin@vanguardschool.org
Cathy Wooley-Brown, President
Robert Spellman, Principal

The Vanguard School program is designed for students age 10 through high school who are experiencing academic difficulties due to learning disability such as dyslexia or dyscalculia or an attention deficit.

Georgia

4051 Atlanta Speech School
3160 Northside Pkwy NW
Atlanta, GA 30327-1598   404-233-5332
FAX 404-266-2175
http://www.atlantaspeechschool.org
e-mail: cyates@atlspsch.org
C Yates, Executive Director

The Atlanta Speech School is one of the Southeast's oldest therapeutic educational centers for children and adults with hearing, speech, language, or learning disabilities. We help children and adults with communication disorders realize their full potential.

4052   Bedford School

5665 Milam Rd
Fairburn, GA 30213-2851   770-774-8001
FAX 770-774-8005
http://www.thebedfordschool.org
e-mail: bbox@thebedfordschool.org
Betsy Box, Executive Director

Serves children in grades 1-9 with learning disabilities. Students are grouped by skill levels in classes of 8-12. Students receive the proper academic remediation, as well as specific remedial help with physical skills, peer interaction and self-esteem.

4053   Brandon Hall School

1701 Brandon Hall Dr
Atlanta, GA 30350-3799   770-394-8177
FAX 770-804-8821
http://www.brandonhall.org
e-mail: jsingleton@brandonhall.org
Dr. John L. Singleton, President/Headmaster

Provides both one-on-one and small group college preparatory classes for students who, for a variety of reasons, have not been achieving their potential or who otherwise need a more intensive educational setting.

4054   Chatham Academy

4 Oglethorpe Professional Blvd
Savannah, GA 31406-3604   912-354-4047
FAX 912-354-4633
http://www.roycelearningcenter.com
e-mail: info@roycelearningcenter.com
Carolyn Hannaford, Principal

Providing a specialized curriculum and individualized instruction for students with diagnosed learning disabilities and/or attention deficit disorder. Chatham's goal is to improve students' functioning to levels commensurate with their potential in all areas so that they may return to and succeed in regular educational programs.

4055   Creative Community Services

4487 Park Drive
Suite A
Norcross, GA 30093   770-469-6226
866-618-2823
FAX 770-469-6210
http://www.ccsgeorgia.org
e-mail: info@ccsgeorgia.org
Sally Buchanan, Executive Director
Lois Moss, Program & Services Director

Therapeutic foster care services for children and home-based support for developmental disabled adults. CCS gives both kids and adults hope by encouraging independent living resulting in involved, engaged citizens and community members.

4056   Horizons School

1900 Dekalb Ave NE
Atlanta, GA 30307-2300   404-378-2219
800-822-6242
FAX 404-378-8946
http://www.horizonsschool.com
e-mail: HorizonsSchool@horizonschool.com
Les Garber, Director

The intent is to develop in students those values and skills which assure maximum opportunities. Students learn real-life skills through active participation in the classroom, as well as in other aspects of the school. They learn responsibility, decision-making, and problem-solving skills through active involvement in the management of the community. Such a leadership role empowers students, giving them the knowledge that they have control of personal decisions and interpersonal interactions.

4057   Jacob's Ladder Helping Children Succeed One Step at a Time

11705 Mountain Park Rd
Roswell, GA 30075-1820   770-998-1017
FAX 770-998-3258
http://www.jacobsladdercenter.com
e-mail: information@jacobsladdercenter.com
Amy O'Dell, Director

A neurodevelopmental learning center established to provide the child Autism, PDD, ADD/ADHD, Asperger's learning differences, Down or any developmental syndrome, the services they need in order to realize their full potential.

4058   Mill Springs Academy

13660 New Providence Rd
Alpharetta, GA 30004-3413   770-360-1336
FAX 770-360-1341
http://www.millsprings.org

Robert Moore, Headmaster

A value-based educational community dedicated to the academic, physical and social growth of those students who have not realized their full potential in traditional classroom settings. Learning strategies are generated from psycho-educational evaluations, previous school records, diagnostic skills assessment, observations and communication with other professionals involved with the student.

4059   Reading Success Plus, Inc.

4205 Columbia Rd
Martinez, GA 30907-1429   706-863-8173
800-997-3237
FAX 706-863-4523
http://www.readingsuccess.com
e-mail: readingsuccess@bellsouth.net
Roberta Hoehle, Director

Reading Success, Inc. is a locally owned and operated program, serving the CSRA for over 30 years and providing professional help to students with all kinds of learning problems. Our guarantee is; if one year of improvement has not been made in the 48 lessons, the student receives instruction free of charge for 18 lessons.

4060   The Howard School

1192 Foster Street NW
Atlanta, GA 30318   404-377-7436
FAX 404-377-0884
http://www.howardschool.org
e-mail: info@howardschool.org
Marifred Cilella, Head of School

The Howard School is an independent school for children ages K-12th grade who have learning differences and language learning disabilities. Instruction is personalized to complement individual learning styles, to address student needs and to help each student understand his or her learning process. The curriculum focuses on depth of understanding in order to make learning meaningful and therefore, maximize educational success.

4061 Wardlaw School
Atlanta Speech School
3160 Northside Pkwy NW
Atlanta, GA 30327-1555
404-233-5332
FAX 404-266-2175
http://www.atlantaspeechschool.org
e-mail: cyates@atlspsch.org
C Yates, Executive Director

Dedicated to serving children with average to very superior intelligence and mild to moderate learning disabilities. Children served in the Wardlaw School typically exhibit underlying auditory and/or visual processing problems that make it difficult for them to learn in their present educational setting.

Hawaii

4062 Center on Disability Studies
University of Hawaii at Manoa
1776 University Ave, UA4-6
Honolulu, HI 96822-2447
808-956-9142
FAX 808-956-5713
http://www.cds.hawaii.edu
e-mail: Robert.Stodden@cds.hawaii.edu
Robert Stodden, Director/Professor

The Center for Disability Studies is a Hawaii Unviersity Affiliated Program at the University of Hawaii at Manoa. The mission of the CDS is to support the quality of life, community inclusion, and self-determination of all persons with disabilities and their families.

4063 Learning Disabilities Association of Hawaii
Ste 205
245 N Kukui St
Honolulu, HI 96817-3921
808-536-9684
800-533-9684
FAX 808-537-6780
http://www.ldahawaii.org
e-mail: ldah@ldahawaiii.org
Michael Moore, Executive Director
Rosie Rowe, Education & Training Coordinator
Marge Neilson, Administrative Assistant
Serving families with children with learning disabilities and other special needs that interfere with learning by providing education advocacy, training and support in order to remove barriers and promote awareness and full educational opportunity. LDAH has several special projects that helps fulfill the mission of removing barriers and promoting awareness and full educational opportunity. The Parent Training and Information Center is one of these special projects that is offered.

4064 Variety School of Hawaii
710 Palekaua St
Honolulu, HI 96816-4755
808-732-2835
FAX 808-732-4334
http://www.varietyschool.org
e-mail: info@vatieryschool.org
Duane Yee, Executive Director

To identify and educate children with learning disabilities, to assist in achieving their maximum potential, through a multi-disciplinary approach.

Idaho

4065 Idaho Parents Unlimited, Inc.
1878 W. Overland Road
P.O. Box 50126
Boise, ID 83705
208-342-5884
800-242-4785
FAX 208-342-1408
http://www.ipulidaho.org
Evelyn Mason, Executive Director

A statewide organization founded to provide support, information and technical assistance to parents of children and youth with disabilities.

Illinois

4066 Acacia Academy
6425 South Willow Spring Road
La Grange Highlands, IL 60525-4468
708-579-9040
FAX 708-579-5872
http://www.acaciaacademy.com
Kathryn Fouks, Principal
Eileen Petzold, Assistant Principal

Offering personalized and exceptional educational instruction to each individual student in the development of his/her intellectual and academic potential.

4067 Allendale Association
P.O.Box 1088
Lake Villa, IL 60046-1088
847-356-2351
888-255-3631
FAX 847-356-0289
http://www.allendale4kids.org
e-mail: development@allendale4kids.org
Mary Shahbazian, President

A private, not-for-profit organization serving children and adolescents with moderate to profound emotional and behavioral disabilities. Allendaleis dedicated to excellence and innovation in the care, education, treatment and advocacy for troubled children, youth and their families.

4068 Associated Talmud Torahs of Chicago
2828 W Pratt Blvd
Chicago, IL 60645-4399
773-973-2828
FAX 773-973-6666
http://www.att.org
Harvey Well, Superintendent
Rabbi Schwartzman, Executive Director

Offers mainstreaming, independent skills, therapeutic swim classes and psychological services.

4069 Brehm Preparatory School
1245 E Grand Ave
Carbondale, IL 62901-3603
618-457-0371
FAX 618-529-1248
http://www.brehm.org
e-mail: admissionsinfo@brehm.org
Richard Collins, Executive Director

A boarding school specifically designed to meet the needs of students with complex learning disabilities and attention deficit disorder issues.

4070 Camelot Care Center: Illinois
1502 W Northwest Hwy
Palatine, IL 60067-1838
847-359-5600
http://www.camelotforkids.org

Todd Bock, Chief Executive Officer
Joe Carter, Chief Operating Officer
Phil Kane, Chief Financial Officer
Camelot's philosophy is to operate small facilities which allow their staff, at all levels, to build a relationship with each student and the families, school districts, and state agencies they serve. This partnership-oriented approach provides a high degree of accountability and accessibility, tracks and reports results, incorporates feedback, and shares success every step of the way.

4071 Camelot School: Palatine Campus

1502 N NW Hwy
Palatine, IL 60067 847-359-5600
FAX 847-359-2759
http://www.camelotforkids.org
Todd Bock, Chief Executive Officer
Joe Carter, Chief Operating Officer
Phil Kane, Chief Financial Officer
Programs offered by the center are the Residential Treatment Center and the Therapeutic Day School. These programs provide effective clinical treatment, and are highly successful in transitioning children back home to their families, or home school environment.

4072 Center for Speech and Language Disorders

606 N. Michigan
Elmhurst, IL 60126-1505 630-530-8551
FAX 630-530-5909
http://www.csld.org
e-mail: info@csld.org
Phyllis Kupperman, Executive Director

The mission is to help children with speech and language disorders reach their full potential. CSLD is an internationally recognized leader in the diagnosis and treatment of hyperlexia and other language disorders.

4073 Children's Center for Behavioral Development

353 N 88th St
East Saint Louis, IL 62203-2705 618-398-1152
FAX 618-398-6977
C P Birth, Executive Director

Special education programs for children and adults who are learning disabled, emotionally disturbed or have behavioral disorders. Some of the programs include vocational education classes, computer classes, art, and physical education.

4074 Cove School

350 Lee Rd
Northbrook, IL 60062-1521 847-562-2100
FAX 847-562-2112
http://www.coveschool.org
e-mail: ssover@coveschool.org
Sally Sover, Executive Director
Mr. John Stieper, Director of Education
Stacy Post, Director of Finance
The Cove School was established in 1947, to educate students with learning disabilities and to facilitate their return to their neighborhood schools in the shortest possible time. The heart of Cove's educational philosophy is to design a program that pulls out the child's skills.

4075 Educational Services of Glen Ellyn

364 Pennsylvania Ave
Glen Ellyn, IL 60137-4386 630-469-1479
FAX 630-469-1265
e-mail: educationalservices@juno.com
Megan Burke, Owner

Tutoring for all ages in all subject areas. Diagnostic testing, specializing in learning disabilities and career counseling for learning disabled adults.

4076 Elim Christian Services

13020 S Central Ave
Palos Heights, IL 60463-2698 708-389-0555
FAX 708-389-0671
http://www.elimcs.org
e-mail: info@elimcs.org
William Lodewyk, President

Elim Christian Services is a non-profit corporation that seeks to equip persons with special needs to achieve to their highest God-given potential.

4077 Esperanza Community Services

Esperanza School
520 N Marshfield Ave
Chicago, IL 60622-6392 312-243-6097
FAX 312-243-2076
TDD:800-526-0844
http://www.esperanzacommunityservices.org
e-mail: info@esperanzacommunity.org
Joseph Gorgol, Principal

Accredited by the Rehabilitation Accreditation Commission; Esperanza School is a private, therapeutic school serving students ages 5 to 21 with Autism, mild/moderate/severe cognitive disabilites, traumatic brain injuries and other health impairements.

4078 Family Resource Center on Disabilities

20 East Jackson Blvd.
Room 300
Chicago, IL 60604-2265 312-939-3513
800-952-4199
FAX 312-939-7297
TDD:312-939-3519
http://www.frcd.org
e-mail: info@frcd.ptiil.americom.net
Charlotte Des Jardins, Executive Director

FRCD was organized by parents, professionals, and volunteers who seek to improve services for all children with disabilities.

4079 Illinois Center for Autism

548 Ruby Ln
Fairview Heights, IL 62208-2614 618-398-7500
FAX 618-632-9094
http://www.illinoiscenterforautism.org
e-mail: info@illinoiscenterforautism.org
Sandra Rodenberg, Executive Director

A not-for-profit, community based, mental health treatment, and educational agency dedicated to serving people with autism. Referrals for possible student placement are made through local school districts, hospitals, regional special education centers, and doctors.

4080 Joseph Academy

1100 North 22nd Avenue
Melrose Park, IL 60160 708-345-4500
FAX 708-345-4516
http://www.josephacademy.org
e-mail: lcapparelli@josephacademy.org
Laura Capparelli, Principal

Founded in 1983, Joseph Academy provides a nurturing and challenging environment for young people. Our mission is to serve children and adolescents with behavioral, emotional and learning disorders by helping them develop the social, academic and vocational skills they need to function in society.

4081 Northwestern University Learning Clinic
2240 Campus Dr
Evanston, IL 60208-0895   847-491-3184
                                        FAX 847-467-7141
        http://www.communication.northwestern.edu
              e-mail: f-vansanten@northwestern.edu
Frank Van Santen, Clinic Director

A teaching clinic that provides diagnostic evaluations for
children and adults, remediation for children, and theory-based coursework for graduate steudents interested in
teaching people with learning disabilities.

4082 Professional Assistance Center for Education (PACE)
National-Louis University
5202 Old Orchard Road
Skokie, IL 60077   224-233-2670
                    http://www.nl.edu/pace
              e-mail: paceprogram@nl.edu
Carol Burns, Director
Barb Kite, Assistant Director

Founded in 1986, PACE is a two-year, noncredit
postsecondary certificate program located on the campus of
National-Louis University. The PACE program is designed
especially to meet the transitional needs of students with
multiple learning disabilities in a university setting.

4083 South Central Community Services
8316 S Ellis Ave
Chicago, IL 60619-5509   773-483-0900
                                        FAX 773-483-5701
                    http://www.sccsinc.org
Felicia Y Blasingame, President

A comprehensive human service agency committed to improving the quality of life for individuals and families by
providing mental health, educational, socio-economic, and
recreational programs and services throughout the State of
Illinois.

4084 Special Education Day School
Catholic Children's Home
1400 State St
Alton, IL 62002-3410   618-465-3594
                                        FAX 618-465-1083
        http://www.catholicchildrenshome.com
              e-mail: cch1400@ezl.com
Candace Hovey, Administrator
Steven Roach, Executive Director
Mike Montez, Associate Administrator
For children with learning disabilities, developmental and
behavioral disorders and through its comprehensive residential services for children in crisis. Providing year-round educational and therapuetic services to students who, due to a
variety of social, emotional and/or educational difficulties,
have been unsuccessful in public school programs.

4085 Summit School, Inc.
333 West River Road
Elgin, IL 60123   847-468-0490
                    http://www.summitinc.org
The Summit School offeres an array of services to children
and young adults with learning difficulties. The school provides the necessary academic and interpersonal skills
needed so that the students can live productive and meaningful lives.

4086 The Baby Fold
Hammit School
108 E Willow St
Normal, IL 61761-1694   309-452-1170
                                        FAX 309-862-2902
                    http://www.thebabyfold.org
              e-mail: info@thebabyfold.org
Dianne Schultz, Executive Director

A multi-service agency that provides Residential, Special
Education, Child Welfare, and Family Support Services to
children and families in central Illinois. Educational services are held at the Hammitt Elementary school and the
Hammitt Junior-Senior High School for children and adolescents with behavioral, learning, emotional and pervasive
developmental disabilities.

4087 The Early Achievement Center
Acacia Academy
6425 S. Willow Springs Rd
LaGrange Highlands, IL 60525-4468   708-579-9040
                                        FAX 708-579-5872
                    http://www.acaciaacademy.com
              e-mail: info@acaciaacademy.com
Kathryn Fouks, Principal

The Early Achievement Center Program encourages growth
of the total child in social, intellectual, physical, and emotional abilities.

4088 The Hope School Learning Center
The Hope Institute for Children and Families
50 East Hazel Dell Lane
Springfield, IL 62712   217-585-5437
                                        FAX 217-786-3356
                                        TDD:217-585-5105
                    http://www.thehopeschool.org
              e-mail: info@thehopeschool.org
Joseph Nyre, President

The Hope School is a private, not-for-profit eduational and
residential center that has been serving children with multiple disabilities and their families since 1957.

Indiana

**4089 Clearinghouse on Reading, English and Communica-
tions**
Indiana University of Bloomington
201 N. Rose Avenue
Bloomington, IN 47405-1006   812-856-8500
                    http://www.indiana.edu/~reading
                    e-mail: iuadmit@indiana.edu
Carl B. Smith, Director

Offers information on reading, English and communication
skills, preschool through college.

4090 IN*SOURCE
Indiana Resource Cntr -Families with Special Needs
1703 S Ironwood Dr
South Bend, IN 46613-3414   574-234-7101
                                       800-332-4433
                    http://www.insource.org
              e-mail: insource@insource.org
Richard Burden, Executive Director
Scott Carson, Assistant Director

The mission of IN*SOURCE is to provide parents, families
and service providers in Indiana the information and training
necessary to assure effective educational programs and appropriate services for children and young adults with
disabilities.

Kansas

4091 **Families Together**
501 SW Jackson St
Ste 400
Topeka, KS 66603-3300   785-233-4777
                                 888-815-6364
                            FAX 785-233-4787
                            TTY: 316-945-7747
http://www.familiestogetherinc.org
e-mail: wichita@familiestogetherinc.org
Lesli Girard, Center Director

Families Together is a statewide non-profit organization assisting Kansas families which include sons and/or daughters who have any form of disability.

4092 **Heartspring School**
8700 E 29th St N
Wichita, KS 67226-2169   316-634-8700
                                 800-835-1043
                            FAX 316-634-0555
http://www.heartspring.org
Jerry Stuart, Executive Director

Heartspring School has earned an international reputation for improving the lives of children. Heartspring is a not-for-profit private residential school that serves children 5-21. We serve children with disabilities such as autism, asperger's, communication disorders, developmental disabilities, dual diagnosed, behavoir disorders, hearing or vision impaired.

Kentucky

4093 **KY-SPIN, Inc.**
Kentucky Special Parent Involvement Network, Inc.
10301 Deering Rd
Ste B
Louisville, KY 40272-4000   502-937-6894
                                 800-525-7746
                            FAX 502-937-6464
                            TDD:502-937-6894
http://www.kyspin.com
e-mail: spininc@kyspin.com
Paulette Logsdon, Executive Director
Francis Edwards, Executive Assistant

Provides training, information and support to people with disabilities, their parents and families, and information on all types of disabilities and topics for all age groups.

4094 **Meredith-Dunn School**
3023 Melbourne Ave
Louisville, KY 40220-2067   502-456-5819
                            FAX 502-456-5953
http://www.meredithschool.org
e-mail: cbunnell@meredith-dunn-school.org
Kathy Beam, Principal
Cindy Bunnell, Admission Director

Meredith-Dunn School's instruction is designed to empower students with average or above-average abilities who learn differently in becoming accomplished learners and resilient indivıiduals. At Meredith-Dunn, labels no longer define our students; we honor the uniqueness of all learners, emphasizing their talents while addressing their difficulties. Grades 1-8.

4095 **Shedd Academy**
P.O.Box 493
Mayfield, KY 42066-0030   270-247-8007
                            FAX 270-247-0637
http://www.sheddacademy.org
e-mail: judy.brindley@sheddacademy.org

Paul Thompson, Executive Director

The mission of the Shedd Academy is to prepare dyslexia and ADD students for college or vocational training and for their future by helping them to understand their unique learning styles; fulfill their intellectual, academic, physical, artistic, creative, social, spiritual, and emotional potential; develop a sense of self responsibility; assume a value system so that they can become contributing members of society and increase their skills to ensure they are armed with a variety of abilities.

4096 **The de Paul School**
1925 Duker Ave
Louisville, KY 40205-1099   502-459-6131
                            FAX 502-458-0827
http://www.depaulschool.org
Anthony Kemper, Principal

Teaches students with specific learning differences how to: learn, be independent, and be successful. Co-ed, grades 1-8.

Louisiana

4097 **Project PROMPT**
Families Helping Families
201 Evans Road
Building 1, Suite 100
Harahan, LA 70123-5230   504-888-9111
                                 800-766-7736
                            FAX 504-888-0246
http://www.projectprompt.com
e-mail: info@projectprompt.com
Rose Gilbert, Executive Director

Parent Training and Information Program views parents as full partners in the educational process and a significant source of support and assistance to each other. Funded by the Division of Personnel Preparation, Office of Special Education Programs, these programs provide training and information to parents to enable such individuals to participate more effectively with professionals in meeting the educational needs of disabled children.

Maryland

4098 **Academic Resource Center**
Gunston Day School
P.O.Box 200
Centreville, MD 21617-0200   410-758-0620
                            FAX 410-758-0628
http://www.gunstondayschool.org
e-mail: info@gunstondayschool.org
Jeffrey Woodworth, Headmaster

Founded in 1911, the school provides tutoring for individuals K through adult. Also offers limited and brief educational testing.

4099 **Chelsea School**
711 Pershing Dr
Silver Spring, MD 20910-4321   301-585-1430
                            FAX 301-585-9621
http://www.chelseaschool.edu
e-mail: information@chelseaschool.edu
Anthony Messina, Jr., Head Of School
Katherine Fedalen, Assistant Head Of School

Committed to providing superior education to children with language-based learning disabilities.

4100   Children's Developmental Clinic
Prince George's Community College
301 Largo Rd
Largo, MD 20774-2109

301-336-6000
FAX 301-322-0519
TDD:301-322-0122
TTY: 301-322-0838
http://www.pgcc.edu
e-mail: advising@pgcc.edu

Ronald Williams, President

The Children's Development Clinic is a continuing education program conducted in cooperation with the Department of Health and Human Performance at Prince George's Community College. The clinic provides special services to children, birth and up, who are experiencing various development difficulties such as learning problems, developmental delays, physical fitness and coordination problems, brain injury, mental retardation, emotional problems, or orthopedic challenges.

4101   Frost Center
4915 Aspen Hill Rd
Rockville, MD 20853-3709

301-933-3452
FAX 301-933-0350
http://www.frostcenter.com
e-mail: chobbes@frostcenter.com

Sean McLaughlin, Director

The Frost school's programs and therapeutic day programs serve emotionally troubled and autistic children and adolescents and their families.

4102   Kennedy Krieger Institute
University Affiliated Program
707 N Broadway
Baltimore, MD 21205

443-923-9200
888-554-2080
FAX 443-923-2645
TTY: 443-923-2645
http://www.kennedykrieger.org

Gary W Goldstein, President

Internationally recognized for improving the lives of children and young adults with disorders of the brain, spinal cord and musculoskeletal system. Serves more than 14,000 individuals each year through inpatient and oupatient clinics; homes and community services; and school-based programs.

4103   Nora School
955 Sligo Ave
Silver Spring, MD 20910-4705

301-495-6672
FAX 301-495-7829
http://www.nora-school.org
e-mail: dave@nora-school.org

David Mullen, Head of School

A small, progressive, college preparatory high school that nurtures and empowers bright students who have been frustrated in larger, more traditional school settings.

4104   Phillips Programs for Children and Families
8920 Whiskey Bottom Rd
Laurel, MD 20723-1318

410-880-0730
FAX 301-470-1624
http://www.phillipsprograms.org
e-mail: karen.williams@phillipsprograms.org

Sally Sibley, President/CEO
Lisa Ott, Executive Director
Karen S Williams, Program Director

Phillips is a non-profit, private organization serving the needs of individuals with emotional and behavioral problems and their families through education, family support services, community education and advocacy.

4105   Ridge School of Montgomery County
Adventis Behavioral Health
14901 Broschart Rd
Rockville, MD 20850-3350

301-251-4500
800-204-8600
FAX 301-251-4588
http://www.adventisthealthcare.com

Craig Juengling, President

The school provides both a special education program and a general education program to meet the needs of the students who have difficulty learning in a traditional school environment.

4106   The Forbush School at Glyndon
Sheppard Pratt Health System
407 Central Avenue
Reisterstown, MD 21136

http://www.sheppardpratt.org

Jim Truscello, Director Of Education
Theresa Petrungaro, Principal
Vera Roth, Director

Provides educational and therapeutic services for children and young adults through 12th grade who have learning disabilities. Curriculum is designed to help the growth of each student in emotional and cognitive areas, and each student follows a program that is designed to meet their needs.

4107   The Parents' Place of Maryland
801 Cromwell Park Drive
Suite 103
Glen Burnie, MD 21061-2539

410-768-9100
FAX 410-768-0830
TDD:410-768-9100
http://www.ppmd.org
e-mail: info@ppmd.org

M J Thomas, Executive Director

Serving the parents of children with disabilities throughout Maryland, regardless of the nature of their child's disability or the age of their child. The staff helps families obtain the appropriate information on education, health care and services for their childs disabilities.

Massachusetts

4108   Adult Center at PAL: Program for Advancement of Learning
1071 Blue Hill Ave
Milton, MA 02186-2302

617-333-0500
800-668-0686
FAX 617-333-2018
TDD:617-333-2250
http://www.curry.edu/pal
e-mail: pal@curry.edu

Nancy Winbury PhD, Program Coordinator

The Adult Center at PAL (Program for Advancement of Learning) is the first program to offer academic and socio-emotional services to adults with LD/ADHD/Dyslexia in a college setting in the New England area. The ACD offers one-to-one academic tutorials; small support groups that meet weekly; and Saturday Seminars that explore issues that impact the lives of adults with LD/ADHD.

4109   Berkshire Meadows
249 N Plain Rd
Housatonic, MA 01236-9736

413-528-2523
FAX 413-528-0293
http://www.berkshiremeadows.org
e-mail: berkshiremeadows@jri.org

Kathy Green, Director

Berkshire Meadows is a year-round residential school that helps children and young adults with severe cognitive disabilities, autism and challenging behaviors.

4110 CAST
40 Harvard Mill Sq
Suite 3
Wakefield, MA 01880-3233

781-245-2212
888-858-9994
FAX 781-245-5212
TDD:781-245-9320
http://www.cast.org
e-mail: cast@cast.org

Ada Sullivan, President
David.H Rose, Chief Education Officer
Steve Borowick, Director of Design
A nonprofit organization that works to expand learning opportunities for all individuals, especially those with disabilities, through the research and development of innovative, technology-based educational resources and strategies.

4111 College Internship Program
The Berkshire Center
18 Park Street
Lee, MA 01238-1702

413-243-2576
FAX 413-243-3351
http://www.berkshirecenter.org
e-mail: admissions@berkshirecenter.org

Michael Mc Manmon, Executive Director
Lucy Gosselin, Program Director
Karen Noel, MSW, Admissions Coordinator
The College Internship Program provides individualized, post-secondary academic, internship and independent living experiences for young adults with learning differences. With the support and direction, students learn to realize and develop their potential.

4112 Commonwealth Learning Center
220 Reservoir St
Ste 6
Needham Heights, MA 02494-3133

781-444-5193
800-461-6671
FAX 781-444-6916
http://www.commlearn.com
e-mail: info@commlearn.com

Cecile Selwyn, Director

Offers individualized one-to-one instruction specializing in multisensory methodologies such as Orton-Gillingham. Work with students of all ages in academic support, organizational and study skills, and test preparation.

4113 Cotting School
453 Concord Ave
Lexington, MA 02421-8088

781-862-7323
FAX 781-861-1179
http://www.cotting.org.

David Manzo, President

Cotting School is for students with moderate to severe learning disabilities requiring assessment of learning style, remediation techniques and one-to-one instruction.

4114 Devereux Massachusetts
60 Miles Road
P.O. Box 219
Rutland, MA 01543-0219

508-886-4746
FAX 508-886-4773
http://www.devereux.org

Elizabeth Orcutt, Principal

A residential program for children, adolescents and young adults who have emotional, behavioral and substance abuse programs with developmental and learning disabilities.

4115 Educational Options
5 Suburban Road
503
Worchester, MA 01602-2079

508-304-9672
FAX 508-304-9257
http://www.optionsined.com
e-mail: info@optionsined.com

Renee Goldberg, Director
Neil Kalt, Ph.D., Staff
Gay Jackson, R.N., BS, Staff
Full-service educational consulting practice dedicated to assisting students plan their future. Work with students to identify their strengths and match these qualities with an academic setting that meets their educational, cultural and social and social aspirations.

4116 Evergreen Center
345 Fortune Blvd
Milford, MA 01757-1723

508-478-5597
FAX 508-634-3251
http://www.evergreenctr.org
e-mail: services@evergreenctr.org

Robert Littleton Jr, Executive Director

The Evergreen Center is a residential school serving children and adolescents with severe developmental disabilities.

4117 F.L. Chamberlain School
Frederick L. Chamberlain Center, Inc.
1 Pleasant Street
P.O. Box 778
Middleboro, MA 02346-0778

508-947-7825
FAX 508-947-0944
http://www.chamberlainschool.org
e-mail: rvonohlsen@chamberlainschool.org

William Doherty, Executive Director
Lucille Mutty, Program Director

The F. L. Chamberlain School offers a highly structured program for students ages 11-20 who having difficulties that effect learning and behavior. Students may either live on campus or attend day classes and academic programming is tailored to meet the specific needs of each student.

4118 Landmark School Outreach Program
Landmark School
429 Hale Street
P.O. Box 227
Prides Crossing, MA 01965-0227

978-236-3216
FAX 978-927-7268
http://www.landmarkoutreach.org
e-mail: outreach@landmarkschool.org

Robert Broudo, Headmaster

The Outreach Program provides professional development programs and publications that offer practical and effective strategies to help children learn. These strategies are based on Landmark's Six Teaching Principles and reflect Landmark's innovative instruction of students with language-based learning disabilites.

4119 Landmark School and Summer Programs
Landmark School
429 Hale Street
P.O. Box 227
Prides Crossing, MA 01965-0227

978-236-3216
FAX 978-927-7268
http://www.landmarkoutreach.org
e-mail: outreach@landmarkschool.org

Robert Broudo, Headmaster

Landmark is a coeducational boarding and day school for emotionally healthy students who have been diagnosed with a language based learning disability. We individualize instruction for each of our students, providing an intensive program emphasizing the development of language and learning skills within a highly structured environment. We also offer an intensive six-week summer program for students who wish to explore the benefits of short-term, skill-based learning.

4120 League School of Greater Boston

300 Boston Providence Turnpike
Walpole, MA 02032-1521   508-850-3900
FAX 617-964-3264
http://www.leagueschool.com
e-mail: info@leagueschool.com
Frank Gagliardi, Executive Director
Lisa Weeden, Principal

Providing social, academic, and vocational programs for children with Autism/Asperger Spectrum Disorders who need a specialized alternative to public school, preparing them to transfer into an environment offering greater independence.

4121 Learning Resource Center

Unity College
90 Quaker Hill Rd
Unity, ME 04988-3712   207-948-3131
800-624-1024
FAX 207-948-6277
http://www.unity.edu
e-mail: admissions@unity.edu
Jim Horan, Director
William Zoellick, Chair
Margot Kelley, Vice Chair
The Learning Resource Center provides instruction and supportive services to students with learning disabilities. A staff learning disabilites specialist works with students who have specific cognitive disabilites that interfers with learning.

4122 Linden Hill School

154 S Mountain Rd
Northfield, MA 01360-9701   413-498-2906
866-498-2906
FAX 413-498-2908
http://www.lindenhs.org
e-mail: office@lindenhs.org
James Mc Daniel, Headmaster
Gerald Shields, Principal

The Linden Hill School is a middle school for boys who come from around the world who have dyslexia or other language learning difficulties. Classes students attend are based on academic needs and the curriculum is designed to allow students to progress at their own pace.

4123 Living Independently Forever, Inc.

550 Lincoln Road Ext
Hyannis, MA 02601-6233   508-790-3600
FAX 508-778-4919
http://www.lifecapecod.org
e-mail: groupmashpee@lifecapecod.org
Mary Matthews, President
Barry Schwartz, Executive Director
Jim Godsill, Acting Director
Living Independently Forever, Inc. is dedicated to serving the life-long needs of adults with significant learning disabilities within our residential communities. LIFE is committed to providing these men and women with the adult education and the opportunities to develop their personal and vocational / occupational skills to their maximum potential, and to supporting them appropriately in independent and group living.

4124 May Institute

41 Pacella Park Dr
Randolph, MA 02368-1755   781-440-0400
800-778-7601
FAX 781-440-0401
TDD:781-440-0461
TTY: 781-440-0461
http://www.mayinstitute.org
e-mail: info@mayinstitute.org
Walter Christian, President

The May Institute provides educational and rehabilitative services for individuals with autism, developmental disabilities, neurological disorders and mental illness.

4125 Melmark New England

461 River Road
Andover, MA 01810   978-654-4300
FAX 978-654-4315
http://www.melmarkne.org
e-mail: newstudents@melmarkne.org
Joanne Gillis-Donovan, Ph.D., President and CEO
George P. Linke, Jr., Psy.D., EVP
Delyn M. Byerly, MBA, Chief Financial Officer
Serves children and adolescents within the autism spectrum disorders, and works to develop and enhance their abilities and confidence in a safe and nuturing environment.

4126 Riverbrook Residence

4 Ice Glen Rd
Stockbridge, MA 01262   413-298-4926
FAX 413-298-5166
http://www.riverbrook.org
e-mail: riverbro@berkshire.net
Joan Burkhard, Executive Director
Heather Murphy, Program Director

A residence in western Massachusetts, providing supported living to developmentally disabled women, with therapy and treatment focused on the arts.

4127 Riverview School

551 Route 6A East Sandwich
Cape Cod, MA 02537-1448   508-888-0489
FAX 508-833-7001
http://www.riverviewschool.org
e-mail: admissions@riverviewschool.org
Maureen Brenner, Principal

Riverview School is a coeducational residential school for adolescents and young adults with complex language, learning and cognitive disabilities.

4128 Seven Hills Academy at Groton

Seven Hills Foundation
81 Hope Avenue
Worcester, MA 01603-1284   508-755-2340
FAX 508-849-3882
TTY: 508-890-5584
http://www.sevenhills.org
Holly Jarek, President

Special education day programs for children and young adults with complex developmental and medical disabilities. Summer programs are also available.

4129 Son-Rise Program

The Option Inst./Autism Treatment Cntr Of America
2080 S Undermountain Rd
Sheffield, MA 01257-9643   413-229-2100
800-714-2779
FAX 413-229-3202
http://www.option.org
e-mail: correspondence@option.org
Barry Neil Kaufman, Program Coordinator

A worldwide teaching center for children and adults challenged by autism, autism spectrum disorders, pervasive developmental disorder, asperger's syndrome, and other developmental difficulties. The Son-Rise Program teaches specific and comprehensive system of treatment and education designed to help families and caregivers enable their children to dramatically improve in all areas of learning, development, communication and skill acquisition.

4130   The Learning Center School
The Protestant Guild for Human Services
411 Waverley Oaks Road
Waltham, MA 02452-8468   781-893-6000
                                     FAX 781-893-1171
                        http://www.protestantguild.org
Debrah Rosser, Executive Director

A private, 365-day community-based, educational program serving difficult to place students with a primary diagnosis of mild to severe mental retardation, autism, or other developmental disability. In addition, students may carry secondary diagnosis of hearing impairments and other communication disorders, traumatic brain injury, seizure disorders, Tourette's syndrome and emotional and psychiatric disorders.

4131   The New England Center for Children
33 Turnpike Rd
Southborough, MA 01772-2108   508-481-1015
                                     FAX 508-485-3421
                              http://www.necc.org
                              e-mail: info@necc.org
Vincent Strully, Executive Director

The New England Center for Children is a private, nonprofit organization serving children with autism and other related disabilities.

4132   The Perkins Day Treatment Program
Perkins
971 Main St
Lancaster, MA 01523-2569   978-365-7376
                                     FAX 978-368-8861
                                     TTY: 978-368-6437
                        http://www.perkinsprograms.org
Charles Conroy, Executive Director

The program offers comprehensive educational and clinical programs for children and adolescents with ADD, bi-polar disorder, depression, post traumatic stress disorder, asperger syndrom and thought disorders. Some of the academic programs are speech and language therapy, math, reading, arts, music and swimming.

4133   Willow Hill School
98 Haynes Rd
Sudbury, MA 01776-1343   978-443-2581
                                     FAX 978-443-7560
                         http://www.willowhillschool.org
Rhonda Taft-Farrell, Principal

Willow Hill School provides supportive and individualized educational programs for middle and high school students grades 6-12 who are capable of advancing along a strong academic curriculum, but have experienced frustration in earlier school settings.

Michigan

4134   Eton Academy
1755 E Melton Rd
Birmingham, MI 48009-7277   248-642-1150
                                     FAX 248-642-3670
                              http://www.etonacademy.org
Pete Pullen, Principal

The Eton Academy is a co-educational private day school dedicated to educating students with learning differences. The mission is to educate students who will understand their learning styles and practice strategies that will prepare them for responsible independence, life-long learning and participation in school, family and in their community.

4135   Lake Michigan Academy
2428 Burton St SE
Grand Rapids, MI 49546-4806   616-464-3330
                                     FAX 616-285-1935
                              http://www.wmldf.org
                              e-mail: abarto@wmldf.org
Andrea Goetz, Executive Director

Lake Michigan Academy is a state-certified, non-profit school for learning disabled children in grades 1 through 12 with average or above average intelligence. The learning disabilities of the children here vary. Some are dyslexic and have difficulty with decoding or comprehending written language. Some are dyscalculic and experience difficulty with mathematical computations and concepts. Many are dysgraphic and exhibit difficulties with writing skills. Our mission is to build self esteem.

4136   Specialized Language Development Center
3056 Walker Ridge Dr NW
Grand Rapids, MI 49544   616-361-1182
                                     888-271-8881
                                     FAX 616-361-3648
                              http://www.sldcenter.org
                              e-mail: info@sldcenter.org
Maura Race, Executive Director

A community resources of W Michigan committed to bringing the power of reading, writing, and spelling to all individuals with dyslexia or other learning styles, enabling them to reach their full potential.

Minnesota

4137   Groves Academy
3200 Highway 100 South
Saint Louis Park, MN 55416-2175   952-920-6377
                                     FAX 952-920-2068
                        http://www.grovesacademy.org
                        e-mail: alexanderj@grovesadacemy.org
John Alexander, Head Of School
Kathy Boone, Director Of Education

A day school for children who because of their learning disabilities have not been successful in a traditional school setting.

4138   LDA Learning Center
LDA Minnesota
6100 Golden Valley Road
Golden Valley, MN 55422   952-922-8374
                                     FAX 952-922-8102
                              http://www.ldaminnesota.org
                              e-mail: info@ldaminnesota.org
Kitty Christiansen, Executive Director
Victoria Weinberg, Program Director

Maximizes the potential of children, youths, adults and families, especially those with learning disabilities and other learning difficulties so that they can lead more productive and fulfilled lives. Provides consultations, tutoring, assessments, parent workshops, training and outreach on sliding fee scale.

Mississippi

4139 **Heritage School**
St. Columbus Episcopal Church
550 Sunnybrook Rd
Ridgeland, MS 39157-1810 601-853-7163
FAX 601-853-7163
http://www.stcolumbs.org/heritageschool
e-mail: heritageschool@stcolumbs.org
Jeanie Muirhead, Director
Fran Parks, Executive Director

Heritage School was establed in 1971 to provide an alternative learning environment for children with learning difficulties. A private, non-profit specialized school accredited through the State Department of Education to offer instruction for learning disabled and ADD/ADHD students from first through eighth grade.

Missouri

4140 **Churchill Center & School for Learning Disabilities**
1021 Municipal Center Drive
Town & Country, MO 63131-1596 314-997-4343
FAX 314-997-2760
http://www.churchillstl.org
e-mail: info@churchillstl.org
Sandra Gilligan, Director
Deborah Warden, Assistant Director - Operations

The Churchill School is a private, not-for-profit, coeducational day school. It is designed to serve children between the ages of 8-16 with diagnosed learning disabilities. The goal is to help each child reach his or her full potential and prepare for a successful return to a traditional classroom in as short a period of time as possible.

4141 **Gillis Center**
8150 Wornall Rd
Kansas City, MO 64114-5898 816-508-3500
FAX 816-508-3535
http://www.gillis.org
e-mail: geninfo@gillis.org
Linda Irick, Director

Gillis Center's mission is to help at-risk children and their families become contributing members of the community through education, counseling and social services.

4142 **MPACT - Missouri Parents Act**
8301 State Line Road
Suite 204
Kansas City, MO 64114
800-743-7634
FAX 816-531-4777
http://www.ptimpact.org
e-mail: info@ptimpact.org
Mary Kay Savage, Executive Director

MPACT assists parents to effectively advocate for their children's educational rights and services. MPACT is a statewide parent training and information center serving all disabilities. Our mission is to ensure that all children with special needs receive an education that allows them to achieve their personal goals.

4143 **Miriam School**
501 Bacon Ave
Saint Louis, MO 63119-1512 314-968-5225
FAX 314-968-7338
http://www.miriamschool.org
Joan Holland, Executive Director

A nonprofit day school for children between four and twelve years of age who are learning disabled and/or behaviorally disabled. Speech and language services and occupational therapy are integral components of the program. The focus of all the activities is to increase children's self-esteem and help them acquire the coping skills needed to successfully meet future challenges.

Montana

4144 **Parents Let's Unite for Kids**
516 N 32nd St
Billings, MT 59101-6003 406-255-0540
800-222-7585
FAX 406-255-0523
http://www.pluk.org
e-mail: info@pluk.org
Roger Holt, Executive Director

PLUK is a private, nonprofit organization formed in 1984 by parents and children with disabilities and chronic illnesses in the state of Montana for the purpose of information, support, training and assistance to aid their children at home, school and as adults.

Nebraska

4145 **Nebraska Parents Training and Information Center**
PTI (Parent Training & Information) Nebraska
3135 North 93rd Street
Omaha, NE 68134-4717 402-346-0525
800-284-8520
FAX 402-934-1479
TDD:800-284-8520
http://www.pti-nebraska.org
Glenda Davis, Executive Director

Parent Training and Information Program views parents as full partners in the educational process and a significant source of support and assistance to each other. Funded by the Division of Personnel Preparation, Office of Special Education Programs, these programs provide training and information to parents to enable such individuals to participate more effectively with professionals in meeting the educational needs of disabled children.

New Hampshire

4146 **Becket Family of Services**
P.O.Box 325
Orford, NH 03777-0325 603-353-9102
FAX 603-353-9412
http://www.becket.org
Jeff Caron, Executive Director

Becket guides and inspires adolescents having difficulties at home, in school or in the community.

4147 **Center for Children with Disabilities**
91 Maple Ave
Keene, NH 03431-1620 603-358-3384
FAX 603-358-6485
http://www.cedarcrest4kids.org
e-mail: info@cedarcrest4kids.org
Cathy Gray, President

provides long-term and short-term residential care, special education and therapy services for children with complex medical and developmental needs.

4148 Hampshire Country School
28 Patey Circle
Rindge, NH 03461-5950   603-899-3325
                               FAX 603-899-6521
http://www.hampshirecountryschool.org
e-mail: office@hampshirecountyschool.net
William Dickerman, Principal

Hampshire Country School is a small boarding school for middle-school students with Asperger's Syndrome, Nonverbal Learning Disabililties and Attention Deficit Hyperactivity Disorder. Faculty to student ratio is 2:3.

4149 Parent Information Center
151 Manchester St
Concord, NH 03301-5145   603-224-7005
                               800-947-7005
                          FAX 603-224-4365
                          TDD:603-224-7005
http://www.parentinformationcenter.org
e-mail: picinfo@parentinformationcenter.org
Kevin Lew-Hanson, Executive Director
Michelle Lewis, Project Director
Jennifer Cunha, Project Staff
Parent Training and Information Program views parents as full partners in the educational process and a significant source of support and assistance to each other. Funded by the Division of Personnel Preparation, Office of Special Education Programs, these programs provide training and information to parents to enable such individuals to participate more effectively with professionals in meeting the educational needs of children with disabilities.

New Jersey

4150 Bancroft
425 Kings Highway East
P.O. Box 20
Haddonfield, NJ 08033-0018   856-429-0010
                                    800-774-5516
                               FAX 856-429-1613
http://www.bancroftneurohealth.org
e-mail: adestefa@bnh.org
Toni Pergolin, President

Nonprofit organization offering educational/vocational programs, therapeutic support services and full range of community living opportunities for children and adults with brain injury in Maine, New Jersey, Delaware, and Louisiana. Residential options include community living supervised apartments, specialized supervised apartments, group homes and supported living models.

4151 Devereux Center for Autism
Devereux New Jersey
286 Mantua Grove Road
Building #4
West Deptford, NJ 08066   856-599-6400
                               FAX 856-423-8916
http://www.devereux.org
Pamela Cooper, President

Addressing the particular needs of children, adolescents and adults with Autism Spectrum Disorders, the center offers residential, educational and vocational programs. All programs are geared to reaching these individuals, helping them overcome challenging behaviors, and teaching them crucial life skills.

4152 ECLC of New Jersey
Ho-Ho-Kus Campus
302 North Franklin Turnpike
Ho-Ho-Kus, NJ 07423-1040   201-670-7880
                               FAX 201-670-6675
http://www.eclcofnj.org
e-mail: vlindorff@eclofnj.org
Vicki Lindorff, Principal

A private school for individuals with disabilities between the ages of 5-21. Our mission is to help disabled students discover how they fit into the world and guide them towards becoming independent and employed adults.

4153 Eden Autism Services
One Eden Way
Princeton, NJ 08540-5711   609-987-0099
                               FAX 609-987-0243
http://www.edenservices.org
Tom Mc Cool, President

Nonprofit organization founded in 1975 to provide a comprehensive continuum of lifespan services for individuals with autism and their families.

4154 Family Resource Associates, Inc.
35 Haddon Ave
Shrewsbury, NJ 07702-4007   732-747-5310
                               FAX 732-747-1896
http://www.frainc.org
e-mail: info@frainc.org
Nancy Phalanukorn, Executive Director

A New Jersey non-profit agency dedicated to helping individuals with disabilities and their families.

4155 Forum School
107 Wyckoff Ave
Waldwick, NJ 07463-1795   201-444-5882
                               FAX 201-444-4003
http://www.theforumschool.com
e-mail: info@theforumschool.com
Steven Krapes, Executive Director

Special education day school for developmentally children. The Forum School offers a therapeutic education environment for children who cannot be accommodated in a public school setting.

4156 Georgian Court University
The Learning Center (TLC)
900 Lakewood Ave
Lakewood, NJ 08701-2697   732-987-2659
                                 800-458-8422
                               FAX 732-987-2026
http://www.georgian.edu
Patricia A. Cohen, MSW, MA, Director

The Learning Center is an assistance program designed to provide an environment for students with mild to moderate learning disabilities who desire a college education. The program is not one of remediation, but it is an individualized support program to assist candidates in becoming successful college students. Emphasis is placed on developing self-help strategies, study techniques, content tutoring, time management, organization skills, and social skills all taught by a certified professional.

4157 Matheny Medical and Educational Center
65 Highland Avenue
P.O. Box 339
Peapack, NJ 07977-0339   908-234-0011
                               FAX 908-719-2137
http://www.matheny.org
e-mail: info@matheny.org
Steve Proctor, President

Matheny School and Hospital is a special educational facility and hospital for children and adults with medically complex developmental disabilities. The school provides comprehensive educational programs and functional life skills for children and young adults ages 3-21.

4158 Newgrange School

526 South Olden Avenue
Hamilton, NJ 08629-2101   609-584-1800
http://www.thenewgrange.org
Robert Hegedus, Executive Director

Newgrange is a non-profit organization established in 1977 to provide specialized educational programs for students with language based learning disabilities.

4159 SEARCH Day Program

73 Wickapecko Dr
Ocean, NJ 07712-4100   732-531-0454
FAX 732-531-5934
http://www.searchdayprogram.com
e-mail: info@searchdayprogram.com
Katherine Solana, Executive Director

SEARCH Day Program is a private, non-profit, New Jersey State certified agency serving children and adults with autism and their families.

4160 Statewide Parent Advocacy Network

Central Office
35 Halsey Street
Fourth Floor
Newark, NJ 07102-3000   973-642-8100
800-654-7726
FAX 973-642-8080
http://www.spannj.org
e-mail: span@spannj.org
Diane Autin, Executive Director

A nonprofit educational and advocacy center for parents of children from birth to 21 years of age. Assists families of infants, toddlers, children and youth with and without disabilities. Serves as a vehicle for the exchange of ideas, promoting awareness of the abilities and needs of the children and youth and improves services for children and families in the state of NJ.

4161 The Center School

319 North 3rd Avenue
Highland Park, NJ 08904-2495   732-249-3355
FAX 732-249-1928
http://www.thecenterschool.com
John Ryan, Director

A school designed for bright students in grades 1-12 with learning and behavioral difficulties. The Center School offers counseling, speech and language, and occupational therapy. Our school is committed to helping each student become as self-sufficient and successful as possible.

4162 The Children's Institute

1 Sunset Ave
Verona, NJ 07044-5118   973-509-3050
FAX 973-509-3060
http://www.tcischool.org
Bruce Ettinger, Principal

The Children's Institute is a private, non-profit school approved by the New Jersey State Board of Education, serving children facing learning, language and social challenges.

4163 The Craig School

200 Comly Road
Lincoln Park, NJ 07035-3050   973-305-8085
FAX 973-305-8086
http://www.craigschool.org
Eric M. Caparulo, D.Ed., Headmaster

The Craig School is an independent, nonprofit school serving children who have difficulty succeeding in the traditional classroom environment. We specialize in a language-based curriculum for children of average or above average intelligence with such disorders as dyslexia, auditory processing and attention deficit.

4164 The Lewis School and Clinic for Educational Therapy

53 Bayard Ln
Princeton, NJ 08540-3028   609-924-8858
FAX 609-924-5512
http://www.lewisschool.org
Marsha Lewis, Executive Director

The Clinic and School integrate teaching and diagnostic perspective of multisensory educational practices in the classrooms, and the perspective of clinical research into the brain's learning process.

4165 The Midland School

PO Box 5026
North Branch, NJ 08876   908-722-8222
FAX 908-722-6203
http://www.midlandschool.org
e-mail: info@midlandschool.org
Philip Gartlan, Executive Director
Barbara Barkan, Principal

A New Jersey approved non-profit school for children, ages 5-21 with developmental disabilities. Serving approx 210 students from public school districts throughout Northern and Central New Jersey. Midland provides a comprehensive special education program serving the individual social, emotional, academic and career education needs of its students.

4166 The Newgrange Education Center

407 Nassau Street at Cedar Lane
Princeton, NJ 08540   609-688-1280
FAX 609-430-3030
http://http://www.thenewgrange.org/
e-mail: info@thenewgrange.org
Gordon Sherman, Ph.D., Executive Director
Bob Hegedus, Principal
Deardra Rosenburg, Director of Education/Supervisor
Meets the educational and specialized needs of individuals with learning disabilities and their families. The center offers tutoring, educational evaluations and professional development opportunities.

New Mexico

4167 Designs for Learning Differences Sycamore School

8600 Academy Rd NE
Albuquerque, NM 87111-1107   505-822-0476
FAX 505-858-4427
http://www.dldsycamoreschool.com
e-mail: dldschool1@aol.com
Linda Murray, Principal

A private, non-profit school, serving children and young adults in grades 1-12 with learning difficulties.

4168 EPICS Parent Project
Abrazos Family Support Services
P.O.Box 788
Bernalillo, NM 87004-0788   505-867-3396
                                    FAX 505-867-3398
                                    http://www.swcr.org
                                    e-mail: info@abrazosnm.org
Martha Gorospe, Director
Norm Segel, Executive Director

Provides a variety of specialized educational programs, health, developmental and parent support programs for infants, children & adults with developmental delays or disabilities.

4169 Parents Reaching Out Network
1920 Columbia Drive Southeast
Albuquerque, NM 87106-3307   505-247-0192
                                    800-524-5176
                                    FAX 505-247-1345
                                    http://www.parentsreachingout.org
                                    e-mail: info@parentsreachingout.org
Sallie Van Curen, Executive Director

PRO views parents as full partners in the educational process and a significant source of support and assistance to each other. Programs provide training and information to parents to enable such individuals to participate more effectively with professionals in meeting the educational needs of disabled children.

New York

4170 Advocates for Children of New York
151 West 30th Street
5th Floor
New York, NY 10001-4197   212-947-9779
                                    FAX 212-947-9790
                                    http://www.advocatesforchildren.org
                                    e-mail: info@advocatesforchildren.org
Kim Sweet, Executive Director

Advocates for Children of New York, has worked in partnership with New York City's most impoverished and vulnerable families to secure quality and equal public education services. AFC works on behalf of children from infancy to age 21 who have disabilites, ethnic minorities, immigrants, homeless children, foster care children, limited English proficient children and those living in poverty.

4171 Anderson Center for Autism
4885 Route 9
P.O. Box 367
Staatsburg, NY 12580-0367   845-889-4034
                                    FAX 845-889-3104
                                    http://www.andersonschool.org
                                    e-mail: info@ACenterforAutism.org
Niel Pollack, Administrator

The Anderson Center for Autism provides the highest quality programs for children and adults with autism and other developmental disabilities.

4172 Andrus Children's Center
1156 N Broadway
Yonkers, NY 10701-1196   914-965-3700
                                    800-647-2301
                                    FAX 914-965-3883
                                    http://www.andruschildren.org
Tecla Critelli, President

For more than 75 years, Andrus has been a provider of programs and services for children and families with learning disabilities.

4173 Baker Victory Services
780 Ridge Rd
Lackawanna, NY 14218-1629   716-828-9500
                                    888-287-1160
                                    http://www.bakervictoryservices.org
                                    e-mail: ourladyofvictory.org
James J Casion, Executive Director

BVS offers a wide range of services for individuals with physical, developmental, and/or behavorial challenges. In addition, programming which supplies a lifetime of care; from infancy to late adulthood.

4174 Center for Spectrum Services
Special Education Program
4 Yankee Place
Ellenville, NY 12428-1510   845-647-6464
                                    FAX 845-647-3456
                                    http://www.centerforspectrumservices. org
                                    e-mail: questions@centerforspectrumservices.org
Mimi Werner, Coordinator

Provides educational programs, diagnostic evaluations and clinical services to children ages 2 to 12 with autism and Asperger Syndrome.

4175 EAC Nassau Learning Center
382 Main St
Port Washington, NY 11050-3136   516-883-3006
                                    FAX 516-883-0412
                                    http://www.eacinc.org
Jerry Stone, Executive Director

The purpose of EAC Learning Center is to help junior and senior high schools students who cannot function in a regular school environment obtain the necessary education which will make it possible for them to graduate from high school. EAC's first program, the Long Island Learning Centers have been serving learning disabled and emotionally disturbed students since 1971.

4176 Eden II Programs
150 Granite Ave
Staten Island, NY 10303-2718   718-816-1422
                                    FAX 718-816-1428
                                    http://www.eden2.org
                                    e-mail: jgerenser@eden2.org
Joanne Gerenser, Ph.D., CCC-S, Executive Director
Fred Bunker, Chief Operating Officer
Eileen Hopkins, Ph.D., Deputy Executive Director
The mission of the Eden II/Genesis Programs is to provide people with autism specialized community-based programs and other opportunities, with the goal of enabling them to achieve the highest possible quality of living across life

4177 Hallen School
97 Centre Ave
New Rochelle, NY 10801-7212   914-636-6600
                                    FAX 914-636-2844
                                    http://www.hallenschool.com
Angela Radogna, Executive Director

Hallen School is a private, special education school that serves children who exhibit learning disabilities, speech and language impairments, emotional difficulties, autistic features, and mid-health impairments.

4178 International Center for the Disabled
340 E 24th St
New York, NY 10010-4019   212-585-6000
                                    FAX 212-585-6262
                                    TTY: 212-585-6060
                                    http://www.icdnyc.org
                                    e-mail: ssegal@icdrehab.org

Serving children, adolescents, adults, and seniors with disabilities and other rehabilitative and developmental needs.

4179 Julia Dyckman Andrus Memorial
Andrus Children's Center
1156 N Broadway
Yonkers, NY 10701-1108   914-965-3700
                                   FAX 914-965-3883
        http://www.andruschildren.org
Residential treatment for youngsters who have moderate to severe emotional problems.

4180 Just Kids: Early Childhood Learning Center
35 Longwood Road
P.O. Box 12
Middle Island, NY 11953-0012   631-924-0008
                                   FAX 631-924-4602
        http://www.kidsschool.com
        e-mail: jkiep@optonline.net
Robin Stevens, Program Director

Offers developmentally appropriate curriculum to young children, ages birth to five years of age, who are disabled and non-disabled. Offers infant/toddler programs, pre-school education programs, mental health services, speech and language therapy and physical and occupational therapy services.

4181 Karafin School
PO Box 277
Mount Kisco, NY 10549-0277   914-666-9211
                                   FAX 914-666-9868
        http://www.karafinschool.com
        e-mail: karafin@optonline.net
Bart A Donow PhD, Direector

Private school serving students with disabilities in grades 9-12.

4182 Kildonan School
425 Morse Hill Rd
Amenia, NY 12501-5209   845-373-8111
                                   FAX 845-373-9793
        http://www.kildonan.org
        e-mail: admissions@kildonan.org
Benjamin Powers, Headmaster

Offers a fully accredited College Preparatory curriculum. The school is co-educational, enrolling boarding students in Grades 6-Postgraduate and day students in Grade 2-Postgraduate. Provides daily one-on-one Orton-Gillingham tutoring to build skills in reading, writing, and spelling. Daily independent reading and writing work reinforces skills and improves study habits. Interscholastic sports, horseback riding, clubs and community service enhance self-confidence.

4183 Maplebrook School
5142 Route 22
Amenia, NY 12501-5357   845-373-8191
                                   FAX 845-373-7029
        http://www.maplebrookschool.org
        e-mail: admin@maplebrookschool.org
Paul Scherer, President

A traditional boarding school enrolling students with learning differences and ADD. Offers strong academics and character development.

4184 Maplebrook School Learning Center
Maplebrook School
5142 Route 22
Amenia, NY 12501-5357   845-373-9511
                                   FAX 845-373-7029
        http://www.maplebrookschool.org
        e-mail: admin@maplebrookschool.org
Paul Scherer, President

CAPS offers a vocational program with employment skills and training, as well as a collegiate program with courses taken at the local community college and other support services.

4185 Mary McDowell Friends School
20 Bergen St
Brooklyn, NY 11201-6302   718-625-3939
                                   FAX 718-625-1456
        http://www.marymcdowell.org
        e-mail: debbiez@marymcdowell.org
Debbie Zlotowitz, Executive Director

An independent friends school for children with learning disabilities ages 5-12.

4186 New Interdisciplinary School
430 Sills Rd
Yaphank, NY 11980   631-924-5583
                                   FAX 631-924-5687
        http://www.niskids.org
        e-mail: information@niskids.org
Helen Wilder, Director

Offers educational and therapeutic services to children with disabilities from birth to five years of age.

4187 New York Institute for Special Education
999 Pelham Pkwy N
Bronx, NY 10469-4905   718-519-7000
                                   FAX 718-231-9314
        http://www.nyise.org
Bernadette Kappen, Executive Director
Thomas Burgett, Ph.D., Assistant Executive Director

Educational facility that provides quality programs for children who are blind or visually impaired, emotionally/learning disabled or developmentally delayed. Students ages 3 to 21 attend NYISE. The school offers residential and day programs, physical, occupational and speech-language therapy, career guidance and couseling.

4188 Parent Network of WNY
1000 Main St
Buffalo, NY 14202-1102   716-332-4170
                                       866-277-4762
        http://www.parentnetworkwny.org
Susan Barlow, Executive Director

A non-profit agency with the mission of parents helping parents and professionals enable individuals with disabilities to reach their own potential. Parent Network provides parents/caregivers of children with special needs, the tools necessary to allow them to take an active role in their child's education. this is accomplished through: information and referral services, workshops and conferences on various special education topics, library and resource materials, website & bimonthly newsletter.

4189 Program for Learning Disabled College Students:
Adelphi University
Chapman Hall Lower Level
Garden City, NY 11530   516-877-4710
                                       800-233-5744
                                   FAX 516-877-4711
                                   TDD:516-877-4777
        http://www.adelphi.edu
        e-mail: ldprogram@adelphi.edu
Susan Spencer-Farinacci, Assistant Dean & Director

4190 Responsibility Increases Self-Esteem (RISE) Program
Maplebrook School
5142 Route 22
Amenia, NY 12501-5357   845-373-9511
                                    FAX 845-373-7029
                    http://www.maplebrookschool.org
                    e-mail: admin@maplebrookschool.org
Paul Scherer, President

The RISE program provides the structure and support to awaken the learner in each student, promote responsibility and develop character, foster independence and growth and enhances social development.

4191 Robert Louis Stevenson School
24 W 74th St
New York, NY 10023-2497   212-787-6400
                                    FAX 212-873-1872
                    http://www.stevenson-school.org
                    e-mail: dherron@stevenson-school.org
Robert J Feiguine Psy D, Head of School
Dayana Jimenez, Clinical Director

Serves students who are functioning below their potential, whether because of adjustment difficulties, problems with peers mild depression or anxiety. Some have been diagnosed as learning disabled or Attention Deficit Disordered, but the program is for bright under-achievers. A college preparatory school.

4192 St. Thomas Aquinas College Pathways
125 Route 340
Sparkill, NY 10976   845-398-4230
                                    FAX 845-398-4229
                             http://www.stac.edu
                    e-mail: pathways@stac.edu
Richard F. Heath, Director
James M. Calisi, Assistant Director

Comprehensive support program for selected college students with learning disabilities and/or ADHD.

4193 Stephen Gaynor School
148 W 90th St
New York, NY 10024-1202   212-787-7070
                                    FAX 212-787-3312
                    http://www.stephengaynor.org
Scott Gaynor, Head of School

The school offers a unique educational experience for children ages 5-14 with learning differences.

4194 The Gow School
2491 Emery Road
P.O. Box 85
South Wales, NY 14139-0085   716-652-3450
                                    FAX 716-652-3457
                             http://www.gow.org
                    e-mail: admissions@gow.org
Bradley Rogers, Principal

A boarding school for boys, grades 7-12, with dyslexia and other language based learning disabilities.

4195 The Norman Howard School
275 Pinnacle Rd
Rochester, NY 14623-4103   585-334-8010
                                    FAX 585-334-8073
                    http://www.normanhoward.org
                    e-mail: info@normanhoward.org
Linda Lawerence, Executive Director

Norman Howard School is an independent day school for students with disabilities in 5-12th grade.

4196 Vocational Independence Program (VIP)
NYIT/VIP
300 Carleton Ave
Central Islip, NY 11722   631-348-3354
                                    FAX 631-348-3437
                        http://www.nyit.edu/vip
                    e-mail: sincorva@nyit.edu
Dr Ernst VanBergeijk, Assoc. Dean, Executive Director
Sheree Incorvaia, Recruitment/Admissions Director

A 3-year certificate program that focuses on vocational, social, and independent living skills, with academics, that support these areas. Also offers those that qualify, the ability to take credit courses towards a degree.

4197 Windward School
13 Windward Avenue
White Plains, NY 10605   914-949-6968
                                    FAX 914-949-8220
                        http://www.windwardny.org
Dr. John J. Russell, Head Master

Independent school for language-based, learning disabled students in grades 1-9.

North Carolina

4198 Exceptional Children's Assistance Center
907 Barra Row
Ste 102-103
Davidson, NC 28036-8103   704-892-1321
                                     800-962-6817
                                    FAX 704-892-5028
                    http://www.ecac-parentcenter.org
                    e-mail: ecac@ecacmail.org
Connie Hawkins, Executive Director

Parent Training and Information Program views parents as full partners in the educational process and a significant source of support and assistance to each other. Funded by the Division of Personnel Preparation, Office of Special Education Programs, these programs provide training and information to parents to enable such individuals to participate more effectively with professionals in meeting the educational needs of disabled children.

4199 Hill Center
3200 Pickett Rd
Durham, NC 27705-6010   919-489-7464
                                    FAX 919-489-7466
                        http://www.hillcenter.org
                    e-mail: smaskel@hillcenter.org
Sharon Maskel, Executive Director

Offers a unique half-day program to students in grades K-12 with diagnosed learning disabilities and attention deficit disorders. Also offers a comprehensive teacher training program.

4200 Huntington Learning Centers, Inc.
7101 Creedmoor Rd
Suite 105
Raleigh, NC 27613-1682   919-676-5477
                                     800-226-5327
                                    FAX 919-235-0093
           http://www.raleigh.huntingtonlearning.com
Mike Gallagher, President

Huntington Learning Center helps target your child's unique needs through diagnostic testing so they could better achieve their grades.

4201 Manus Academy
6203 Carmel Rd
Charlotte, NC 28226-8204   704-542-6471
                                         FAX 704-541-2858
                    http://www.manusacademy.com
Roseanne Manus, President

School for students with learning disabilties.

4202 Manus Academy
6203 Carmel Rd
Charlotte, NC 28226-8204   704-542-6471
                                         FAX 704-541-2858
                    http://manusacademy.com
Jeremy Ervin, Owner
Jeremy Ervin, Principal
Dana Mims, Business Administrator
Manus Academy works with students from kindergarten through college who experience learning disabilities, attention deficit disorder and other neurological and developmental difficulties. Their services include a middle and high school accredited by the Southern Association for College and Schools, after-school tutoring services for K-12 students who attend other schools, testing, consultation and parent and teacher training

4203 Piedmont School
815 Old Mill Rd
High Point, NC 27265-9679   336-883-0992
                                         FAX 336-883-4752
                http://www.thepiedmontschool.com
                e-mail: info@thepiedmontschool.com
John Yowell, President

Provides a unique, essential service to children with learning disabilites and/or an attention deficit disorder.

North Dakota

4204 Anne Carlsen Center for Children
701 3rd St NW
P.O. Box 8000
Jamestown, ND 58402   701-252-3850
                                         800-568-5175
                                         FAX 701-952-5154
                    http://www.annecenter.org
Marcia Gums, President

Offers education, therapy, medical care and social and psychological services for children and young adults with special needs.

Ohio

4205 Bellefaire Jewish Children's Bureau
22001 Fairmount Blvd
Shaker Heights, OH 44118-4819   216-932-2800
                                         800-879-2522
                                         FAX 216-932-6704
                    http://www.bellefairejcb.org
Adam Jacobs, President

Residential treatment center for adolescents, offering foster care, an adoption center, Monarch School for Children with Autism.

4206 Cincinnati Center for Developmental Disorders
Cincinnati Children's Hospital Medical Center
3333 Burnet Ave
Cincinnati, OH 45229-3039   513-636-4200
                                         800-344-2462
                                         TTY: 513-636-4900
                http://www.cincinnatichildrens.org

David Schonfeld, Executive Director

Established in 1957, the center provides diagnosis, evaluation, treatment, training and education for infants, children and adolescents with a variety of developmental disorders.

4207 Cincinnati Occupational Therapy Institute for Services and Study, Inc.
4440 Carver Woods Dr
Cincinnati, OH 45242-5545   513-791-5688
                                         FAX 513-791-0023
                    http://www.cintiotinstitute.com
Deborah Whitcomb, Executive Director

Cincinnati Occupational Therapy Institute provides evaluation and treatment directly to children and adults with occupational therapy needs. COTI is owned and operated by therapists. The therapists are uniquely skilled at helping clients of all ages achieve or regain independence by offering creative adaptations and alternatives for carrying out daily activities, as well as remediating dysfunction through appropriate therapeutic modalities.

4208 North Coast Education Services
31300 Salon Road
Suite 1
Solon, OH 44139-2718   440-914-0200
                                         FAX 440-542-1504
                    http://www.northcoasted.com
                    e-mail: info@northcoasted.com
Carole Richards, Director

Provides on-site education services to individual learners or groups. Uppermost in the delivery of these services is the development of self-esteem, expanding learner potential and utilizing problem-solving to identify strengths and weaknesses. Specializing in working with at-risk learners which include learning disabled students.

4209 Ohio Center for Autism and Low Incidence
470 Glenmont Avenue
Columbus, OH 43214   614-410-0321
                                         866-886-2254
                                         FAX 614-262-1070
                                         TTY: 614-410-1076
                                         http://www.ocali.org
                                         e-mail: ocali@ocali.org
Shawn A Henry, Executive Director

Serves parents and educators of students with autism and low incidence disabilities including Autism spectrum disorders, Deaf-blindness, Deafness and hearing impairments, Multiple disabilities, Orthopedic impairments, Other health impairments, Traumatic brain injuries, and Visual impairments.

4210 Ohio Coalition for the Education of Children with Disabilities
165 W Center St
Ste 302
Marion, OH 43302-3741   740-382-5452
                                         800-374-2806
                                         FAX 740-383-6421
                                         http://www.ocecd.org
                                         e-mail: ocecd@ocecd.org
Margaret Burley, Director

Non-profit parent training and information center serving Ohio families. Services are free.

4211 **RICHARDS READ Systematic Language**
North Coast Tutoring Services
31300 Solon Road
Suite 1
Solon, OH 44139   440-914-0200
800-335-7984
FAX 440-542-1504
http://www.northcoasted.com
e-mail: studentservices@northcoasted.com
Carole Richards, Executive Director

North Coast Tutoring Services strives to provide on-site education services to individual learners or groups. Uppermost in the delivery of these services is the development of self-esteem, expanding learner potential and utilizing problem-solving to identify strengths and weaknesses. We specialize in working with at-risk learners which include learning disabled students. Our systematic language program is extremely successful with language learning difficulties from age 5 to adult.

4212 **Springer School and Center**
2121 Madison Rd
Cincinnati, OH 45208-3288   513-871-6080
FAX 513-871-6428
http://www.springerschoolandcenter.org
e-mail: info@springer.hccanet.org
Shelly Weisbacher, Administrator

Springer School and Center is the only organization in the Greater Cincinnati area whose program is devoted entirely to the education of children with learning disabilities.

4213 **The Children's Home Of Cincinnati**
5050 Madison Road
Cincinnati, OH 45227-2784   513-272-2800
http://www.thechildrenshomecinti.org
Ellen Katz Johnson, President & CEO

Helps chldren with social, behavioral and learning challenges by helping them build the skills and confidence that they need in life to succeed in school, home, and the community.

Oregon

4214 **Thomas A Edison High School**
9020 SW Beaverton-Hillsdale Hwy
Portland, OR 97225-2436   503-297-2336
FAX 503-297-2527
http://www.taedisonhs.org
e-mail: thomasedison@taedisonhs.org
Patrick Maguire, Principal

A private high school in Oregon specifically designed to meet the needs of students with complex learning disabilities and attention deficit disorder issues. Thomas Edison High School empowers students with learning differences to experience academic success and personal growth, while preparing them for the future.

Pennsylvania

4215 **Center for Alternative Learning**
6 East Eagle Road
Havertown, PA 19083   610-446-6126
http://www.learningdifferences.com
e-mail: rcooper-ldr@comcast.net
Dr Richard Cooper, Ph.D., President

The Center for Alternative Learning was founded in 1987 to provide low cost and free educational services to individuals with learning differences, problems and disabilities.

4216 **Center for Psychological Services**
125 Coulter Ave
Ardmore, PA 19003-2410   610-642-4873
FAX 610-642-4886
http://www.centerpsych.com
e-mail: center12@verizon.net
Moss Jackson PhD, Director

Individual, family and group therapy psychoeducational evaluation and school consultation.

4217 **Devereux Mapleton**
Devereux Foundation
PO Box 275
Malvern, PA 19355-0275   610-296-6973
800-935-6789
FAX 610-296-5866
http://www.devereux.org
David Woodward, Executive Director

Residential and in-patient program for children, adolescents and young adults with emotional disorders and learning disabilities.

4218 **Dr Gertrude A Barber Center**
Barber National Institute
100 Barber Place
136 East Avenue
Erie, PA 16507-1899   814-453-7661
FAX 814-455-1132
http://www.barberinstitute.org
e-mail: BNIerie@barberinstitute.org
John Barber, President

Offers a complete range of educational services and support to children and adults with disabilities.

4219 **High Road School Of Baltimore County**
7707 German Hill Road
Baltimore, MD 21222   410-282-8500
FAX 410-282-1047
http://www.kids1inc.com
e-mail: kids1@kids1inc.com
Ellyn Lerner PhD, President

Offers programs serving the educational, social and emotional needs of children with specific learning disabilities, communication disorders and/or behavioral difficulties.

4220 **Hill Top Preparatory School**
737 South Ithan Avenue
Rosemont, PA 19010-1197   610-527-3230
FAX 610-527-7683
http://www.hilltopprep.org
e-mail: headmaster@hilltopprep.org
Tom Needham, Principal

Preparatory School for bright students in grades five through twelve with learning disabilities.

4221 **Hillside School**
2697 Brookside Rd
Macungie, PA 18062-9045   610-967-3701
FAX 610-965-7683
http://www.hillsideschool.org
e-mail: office@hillsideschool.org
Sue Straeter EdD, Head of School
Donna Henry, Asst Head of School

A day school for children with learning differences. One hundred and twenty-eight children in grades K-6 attend the school. Scholarships are available.

4222 KidsPeace Orchard Hills Campus

5300 KidsPeace Drive
Orefield, PA 18069-2098   610-799-8000
                                 800-8KID-123
                                 FAX 610-799-8900
                                 http://www.kidspeace.org
Richard Zelko, President

Offers various programs including community residential
care, specialized group homes, child and family guidance
center and student assistance programs.

4223 Melmark

2600 Wayland Rd
Berwyn, PA 19312-2313   610-325-4969
                               888-MEL-MARK
                               http://www.melmark.org
                               e-mail: admissions@melmark.org
Joanne Gillis-Donovan, President

Provides residential, educational, therapeutic and recreational services for children and adults with mild to severe
developmental disabilities.

4224 Parent Education Network

2107 Industrial Hwy
York, PA 17402-2223   717-600-0100
                              800-522-5827
                              FAX 717-600-8101
                              TDD:800-522-5827
                              TTY: 800-522-5827
                              http://www.parentednet.org
                              e-mail: lspaar@parentednet.org
Kay Lipsitz, Director
Lyn Spaar, Assistant Director

Parent training and information center of Pennsylvania.
Serves parents of all special needs children, birth to adulthood, to attain appropriate educational and support services
by providing specific knowledge of state and federal laws
and regulations; develops and disseminates material explaining the special education process and its relationship to
other systems.

4225 Pathway School

162 Egypt Rd
Norristown, PA 19403-3090   610-277-0660
                                    FAX 610-539-1973
                                    http://www.pathwayschool.org
Bill O'Flanagan, President
Diana Phifer, Director Of Admissions

Provides day and residential programming for individuals
ages 5-21, who have learning disabilities, neurological impairments and neuropsychiatric disorder. Special education,
counseling, speech and language therapy, reading therapy,
and other specialized services are provided in a small, warm
and supportive atmosphere.

4226 Stratford Friends School

2 Bishop Hollow Road
Newtown Square, PA 19073   610-355-9580
                                   FAX 610-355-9585
                                   http://www.stratfordfriends.org
                                   e-mail: tmadigan@stratfordfriends.org
Tim Madigan, Ph.D., Head Of School

A Quaker elementary school for children with language-based learning differences who have had difficulty
learning in a traditional classroom.

4227 The Children's Institute

1405 Shady Ave
Pittsburgh, PA 15217-1350   412-420-2400
                                    http://www.amazingkids.org

Jamie Calabrese MD, Director

Provides pediatric and adult rehabilitation services and programs.

4228 Vanguard School

1777 North Valley Road
P.O. Box 730
Paoli, PA 19301-0730   610-296-6700
                               FAX 610-640-0132
                               http://www.vanguardschool-pa.org
                               e-mail: info@vanguardschool-pa.org
Ernie Beattstrom, Principal

State licensed and approved private, non-profit, non-sectarian day school serving children from three to twenty-one
years of age who have been diagnosed with neurological disorders, emotional disturbance or autism/PDD.

4229 Woods Schools

Woods Services
Route 413 & 213
P.O. Box 36
Langhorne, PA 19047-0036   215-750-4000
                                   FAX 215-750-4591
                                   http://www.woods.org
Robert G Griffith, President

Provides a full range of residential, special education, rehabilitation, recreation and vocational training to children and
adults with Autism Spectru Disorder, Developmental Disabilities, Neurological Disorders, Traumatic Brain Injuries
and Emotional Disturbances.

Rhode Island

4230 Harmony Hill School

63 Harmony Hill Rd
Chepachet, RI 02814-1429   401-949-0690
                                   FAX 401-949-2060
                                   TDD:401-949-4130
                                   http://www.harmonyhillschool.org
                                   e-mail: djackson@hhs.org
Eric James, President

A private residential and day treatment center for
behaviorally disordered and learning disabled boys, age
eight through eighteen, who cannot be treated within their
local educational system or community based mental health
programs. Individual, group and family psychotherapy and
24-hour crisis intervention are available. Other programs include: Extended Day, Sex Offender, Diagnostic Day, Transition Programming, Summer Day, Career Education
Center, and a Formalized Life Skills Program.

4231 Rhode Island Parent Information Network

1210 Pontiac Avenue
Cranston, RI 02920   401-270-0101
                             800-464-3399
                             FAX 401-270-7049
                             TDD:800-464-3399
                             http://www.ripin.org
                             e-mail: info@ripin.org
Matthew B Cox, Executive Director

Rhode Island Parent Information Network is a statewide,
nonprofit organization that provides eleven programs and
services to families with children in RI, including families of
children with special needs due to disabilities.

South Carolina

4232 Parents Reaching Out to Parents of South Carolina
652 Bush River Rd
Ste 203
Columbia, SC 29210-7537   803-772-5688
                                        800-759-4776
                                        FAX 803-772-5341
                                http://www.proparents.org
                        e-mail: proparents@proparents.org
Mary Eaddy, Executive Director

Private nonprofit parent oriented organization providing information, individual assistance and workshops to parents of children with disabilities ages birth-21. Services focus on enabling parents to have a better understanding of special education to participate more effectively with professionals in meeting the educational needs of disabled children. Funded by a grant from the US Department of Education and tax deductible contributions.

4233 Sandhills School
1500 Halbrook Drive
Columbia, SC 29209   803-695-1400
                                        FAX 803-695-1214
                                http://sandhillschool.org
Anne Vickers, Head of School
Erika Senneseth, Assistant Head of School

A private, nonprofit school for children with learning disabilities. Serves students from grades 1-8 and also offers diagnostic evaluations, summer school and educational therapy for all ages. Boarding with local families is also available.

4234 Trident Academy
1455 Wakendaw Rd
Mt Pleasant, SC 29464-9767   843-884-7046
                                        FAX 843-881-8320
                                http://www.tridentacademy.com
                        e-mail: cnewton@tridentacademy.com
Joe Ferber, Principal

Trident Academy is for students with specific learning disabilities; offering an intensive, effective, multi-sensory program to remediate learning differences, tailored to each student's unique needs.

Tennessee

4235 Bodine School
2432 Yester Oaks Dr
Germantown, TN 38139-6400   901-754-1800
                                        FAX 901-751-8595
                                http://www.bodineschool.org
                        e-mail: info@bodineschool.org
Dr. Rene Friemoth Lee, Executive Director
Molly Cameron, Program Director

The Bodine School has provided students with language based learning disabilities a nurturing environment and a challenging academic curriculum for the last 30 years. The Bodine School program is designed specifically for the dyslexic student and is based on current research findings on reading and reading disorders.

4236 Camelot Of Kingston
The Camelot Schools
183 Fiddlers Ln
Kingston, TN 37763-4020   865-376-1190
                                        800-896-4754
                                        FAX 865-376-0369
                                http://www.thecamelotschools.com

Paul Hickling, Executive Director
Tammy Kropp, Principal

Accepts children ages 4-17 who have been referred by area school systems. The campus includes a horsebarn and pasture, in ground swimming pool, playground areaas and pet therapy dogs.

4237 Devereux Genesis Learning Centers
Genesis Learning Centers
430 Allied Dr
Nashville, TN 37211-3304   615-832-4222
                                        FAX 615-832-4577
                                http://www.genesislearn.org
                        e-mail: admin@genesislearn.org
Terance Adams, President

Day school and treatment programs for adolescents and young adults who have emotional disorders and learning disabilities.

4238 Genesis Learning Centers
430 Allied Dr
Nashville, TN 37211-3304   615-832-4222
                                        FAX 615-832-4577
                                http://www.genesislearn.org
                        e-mail: admin@genesislearn.org
Terance Adams, President

Genesis Learning Centers offer special educational services to children and youth with distinctive needs, including emotional and behavioral disorders, learning disabilities, mental retardation, developmental delays, and short-term severe illness, physical challenges, or misconduct.

Texas

4239 Achievers' Center for Education
University United Methodist Church
5084 De Zavala Rd
San Antonio, TX 78249-2025   210-690-7359
                                        FAX 210-690-7307
                        http://www.achieverscenterforeducation.org
                        e-mail: info@uchurch.tv
Roger Tetro, Chief Operating Officer
Stacey Arington, Program Assistant

Educational program for children and young adults in 6th through 8th grade who are behind academically due to dyslexia or other learning disabilities.

4240 Bridges Academy
901 Arizona Ave
El Paso, TX 79902-4506   915-532-6647
                                        FAX 915-532-8767
                                http://www.bridgesacademy.org
Irma Keys, Director

Private School for students with learning disabilities.

4241 Bright Students Who Learn Differently
Winston School
5707 Royal Ln
Dallas, TX 75229-5536   214-691-6950
                                        FAX 214-691-1509
                                http://www.winston-school.org
                        e-mail: info@winston-school.org
Polly Peterson, Head of School
Rebbie Evans, Division Head
Sara Collins, Director Admissons/Financial Aid

The environmment and curriculum of The Winston School are designed for bright students who learn differently. Through Winston's Testing and Evaluation Center, students are assessed and teachers are provided with the learning profiles, training, and resources needed to respond to the needs of each student.

4242   Crisman School

2455 N Eastman Rd
Longview, TX 75605-4057   903-758-9741
                                        FAX 903-758-9767
                    http://www.crismanschool.org
Laura Lea Blanks, Director

A private school designed to meet the needs of students with learning differences and/or Attention Deficit Disorder.

4243   Gateway School

2570 NW Green Oaks Blvd
Arlington, TX 76012-5621   817-226-6222
                                        FAX 817-226-6225
                    http://www.gatewayschool.com
Harriet Walber, Executive Director

Geteway School is dedicated to providing an appropriate education in a nurturing environment to individuals with learning disorders and/or attention deficit.

4244   Overton Speech & Language Center, Inc.

4763 Barwick Drive
Suite 103
Fort Worth, TX 76132-1531   817-294-8408
                                        FAX 817-294-8411
                    http://www.overtonspeech.net
                    e-mail: info@overtonspeech.net
Valerie Johnston, Director

Provides speech and language therapy.

4245   Parish School

11001 Hammerly Blvd
Houston, TX 77043-1913   713-467-4696
                                        FAX 713-467-8341
                    http://www.parishschool.org
Nancy Bewley, Principal

Offers a multi-age, language-based, developmental curriculum for children 18 months through fifth grade. Children served have communication and learning differences, but average to above average learning potential. The Parish School utilizes a classroom based therapy program implemented by certified teachers and speech/language pathologists.

4246   Partners Resource Network

1090 Longfellow Dr
Ste B
Beaumont, TX 77706-4819   409-898-4684
                                            800-866-4726
                                        FAX 409-898-4869
                    http://www.partnerstx.org
                    e-mail: partnersresource@sbcglobal.net
Janice Meyer, Executive Director

Statewide network of federally funded parent training and information centers. Provides servies to parents of infants, toddlers, children & youth ages brith to 26 with all types of diabilities.

4247   Scottish Rite Learning Center of Austin, Inc.

12871 N. U.S. Highway 183
Suite 105
Austin, TX 78750   512-472-1231
                                FAX 512-326-1877
            http://www.scottishritelearningcenter.org

Linda Gladden, Director
Doris Haney, Executive Director

Focuses on the evalation and treatment of dyslexia in children. The center also provides workshops, seminars and resources for educators and parents.

4248   Shelton School and Evaluation Center

Admissions Office
15720 Hillcrest Rd
Dallas, TX 75248-4161   972-774-1772
                                        FAX 972-991-3977
                    http://www.shelton.org
                    e-mail: wdeppe@shelton.org
Suzanne Stell, Executive Director
Linda Kneese, Head of School
Diann Slaton, Director of Admissions
A coeducational day school serving 865 students in grades Pre-K-12. The school focuses on the development of learning disabled students of average to above average intelligence, enabling them to succeed in conventional classroom settings. Services include on-site Evaluation Center for diagnostic testing, a Speech, Language and Hearing Clinic, an Early Childhood Program, Out Reach Program, open summer school and more.

4249   Starpoint School

Texas Christian University
Bailey Bldg & Palko Hall
3000 Bellaire Drive North
Fort Worth, TX 76129-0001   817-257-7660
                                        FAX 817-257-7480
                    http://www.sofe.tcu.edu
                    e-mail: education@tcu.edu
Marilyn Tolbert, Director

Provides individualized academic programs for children with learning disabilities.

Utah

4250   Mountain Plains Regional Resource Center

1780 North Research Parkway
Suite 112
Logan, UT 84341-1940   435-797-9009
                                        FAX 435-797-9018
                                        TDD:435-797-9018
                    http://www.rrfcnetwork.org
                    e-mail: Carol.Massanari@usu.edu
Carol Massanari, Director

The center is a United States Department of Education, Office of Special Education Programs funded project that helps build the capacity of State Education Agencies and Lead Agencies in improving programs and services for infants, toddlers, children and youth with disabilities.

4251   Reid School

2965 East 3435 South
Salt Lake City, UT 84109-3087   801-466-4214
                                            FAX 801-466-4214
                    http://www.reidschool.com
                    e-mail: ereid@xmission.com
Ethna Reid, Executive Director

Reid School is a private, innovative center for students who need more attention with reading, writing, speaking, and language arts education.

4252   SEPS Center for Learning

2120 S 1300 E
Ste 202
Salt Lake City, UT 84106-2828   801-467-2122
                                            FAX 801-467-2148
                    http://www.sepslc.com
                    e-mail: ava.eva.seps@sepslc.com

Avajane Pickering, Director

Designs educational programs that help adults and children succeed in school and life. Specializing in one-on-one tutoring in all areas for all age levels, assessment, day school and preschool programs, computer assisted cognitive and academic therapy, reading programs, summer recreation and academic programs, consultation for schools and businesses.

4253   Utah Parent Center
2290 E. 4500 South
Suite 110
Salt Lake City, UT 84117-4428   801-272-1051
                                        800-468-1160
                                    FAX 801-272-8907
                http://www.utahparentcenter.org
                e-mail: ftofninfo@utahparentcenter.org
Helen Post, Executive Director

Utah Parent Center offers free training, information, referral and assistance to parents and professionals through the provision of information, referrals, individual assistance, workshops, presentations and displays.

Vermont

4254   Stern Center for Language and Learning
135 Allen Brook Ln
Williston, VT 05495-9209   802-878-2332
                                 FAX 802-878-0230
                    http://www.sterncenter.org
                    e-mail: learning@sterncenter.org
Blanche Podhajski, President

Founded in 1983, the center is a nonprofit organization providing comprehensive services for children and adults with learning disabilities. The Center is also an educational resource serving all of Northern New England and Northern New York State. Programs include educational testing, individual instruction, psychotherapy, school consultation, professional training for educators and a parent/professional resource library.

Virginia

4255   Accotink Alternative Learning Center
Accotink Academy
6225-E. Rolling Road
Springfield, VA 22152-1508   703-644-9072
                                    FAX 703-644-9074
                http://www.accotinkacademy.com
                e-mail: preschool@accotinkacademy.com
Mark McConnell, Executive Director

Educational programs for students in grades 7-12 who have learning disabilities.

4256   BRAAC - Roanoke
Blue Ridge Autism and Achievement Center
312 Whitwell Dr
Roanoke, VA 24019-2039   540-366-7399
                               FAX 540-366-5523
                http://www.achievementcenter.org
                e-mail: braac.roanoke@gmail.com
Angela Leonard, Executive Director

A private day school offering many academic and educational programs for children with Autism and learning disabilities and their families.

4257   Behavioral Directions
626 Grant St
Ste I
Herndon, VA 20170-4700   703-855-4032
                               FAX 571-333-0292
                http://www.BehavioralDirections.com
        e-mail: behavioraldirections@smartneighborhood.net
Jane Barbin PhD BCBA, Psychologist

A resource for applied behavior analysis and behavior disorders

4258   Chesapeake Bay Academy
821 Baker Rd
Virginia Beach, VA 23462-1004   757-497-6200
                                       FAX 757-497-6304
                    http://www.cba-va.org

Mary Anne Dukas, Director

Chesapeake Bay Academy is the only accredited independent school in Southeastern Virginia specifically dedicated to providing a strong academic program and individualized instruction for bright students with LD and ADHD. With a student/teacher ratio of 5:1 a student:computer ratio of 2:1, qualified professionals tailor their techniques to individual needs, allowing students who have difficulty learning in traditional settings to finally succeed.

4259   Crawford First Education
Alternative Behavioral Services
825 Crawford Pkwy
Portsmouth, VA 23704-2301   757-391-6675
                                    877-227-7000
                               FAX 757-391-6651
                http://www.absfirst.com
                e-mail: info@absfirst.com

Jeff Gray, Director

Alternative education programs that are effective, comprehensive and fiscally responsible. Dedicated and committed to addressing and improving the problems of special needs students.

4260   Grafton School
Grafton, Inc.
120 Belleview Avenue
Winchester, VA 22601-1700   888-955-5205
                                   FAX 540-542-1722
                    http://www.grafton.org
                    e-mail: admissions@grafton.org
Mark Wilee, Principal

Grafton provides individualized educational and residential services and in-community supports for children, youth and adults with severe emotional disturbance, learning disabilities, mental retardation, autistic disorder, behavioral disorders, and other complex challenges, including physical disabilities.

4261   Learning Resource Center
909 First Colonial Rd
Virginia Beach, VA 23454-3111   757-428-3367
                                       FAX 757-428-1630
                http://www.learningresourcecenter.net
        e-mail: Nancy.Harris-Kroll@LearningResourceCenter.net

Nancy Harris-Kroll, Director

One-on-one remedial and tutorial sessions after school during the school year and all day and evening during the summer with specialists who have masters degrees. Advocacy services for parents of students with special needs. Psychoeducational testing is available. Special study skills and SAT courses given. Gifted, average, and learning disabled students attend.

4262 Leary School Programs
Lincolnia Educational Foundation
6349 Lincolnia Rd
Alexandria, VA 22312-1500   703-941-8150
                                    FAX 703-941-4237
                              http://www.learyschool.org
                              e-mail: mail@learyschool.org
Ed Schultze, President/Executive Director
Sharon Masin, Business Manager

A private, day, co-educational, special education facility
that serves 130 students with emotional, learning and behavioral problems. Along with individualized academic instruction, Leary School of Virginia offers a range of supportive
and therapeutic services, including physical education, recreation therapy, group counseling, individual
psychotherapy and art therapy.

4263 Little Keswick School
P.O.Box 24
Keswick, VA 22947-0024   434-295-0457
                                 FAX 434-977-1892
                         http://www.littlekeswickschool.net
                         e-mail: lksinfo@littlekeswickschool.net
Marc Columbus, Headmaster
Terry Columbus, M.Ed., Director Of Admissions

Little Keswick School is a therapeutic boarding school for
33 learning disabled and/or emotionally disturbed boys between the ages of 10 to 15 at acceptance and served through
17. IQ range accepted is below average to superior. LKS provides a structured routine in a small, nurturing environment
with services that include psychotherapy, occupational therapy, speech therapy and art therapy. Five week summer
session.

4264 New Community School
4211 Hermitage Rd
Richmond, VA 23227-3718   804-266-2494
                                  FAX 804-264-3281
                              http://www.tncs.org
                              e-mail: info@tncs.org

Julia Ann Greenwood, Principal

The New Community School is an independent day school
specializing in college preparatory instruction and intensive
remediation for dyslexic students in grades 6-12.

4265 New Vistas School
520 Eldon St
Lynchburg, VA 24501-3604   434-846-0301
                                   FAX 434-528-1004
                            http://www.newvistasschool.org
                            e-mail: cmorgan@newvistasschool.org
Charlotte Morgan, Head Of School
Lisa Thomas, Assistant Head of School
Sally Horner, Development Director
The New Vistas School provides individualized programs
for students in grades K-12 with Attention Deficit Disorder
and learning disabilities.

4266 Oakwood School
7210 Braddock Rd
Annandale, VA 22003-6068   703-941-5788
                                   FAX 703-941-4186
                            http://www.oakwoodschool.com
Robert Mc Intyre, Director

Oakwood School is a private, non-profit, co-educational day
school for elementary and middle school students with mild
to moderate learning disabilities. Students are of average to
above average potential and exhibit a discrepancy between
their potential and their current level of achievement.

4267 Parent Resource Center
Hopewell High School
11530 Beatties Ford Rd
Huntersville, NC 28078   980-343-5988
                                 FAX 980-343-5990
                         http://pages.cms.k12.nc.us/hopewell
Dr Louise Jones, Principal

4268 Riverside School
2110 McRae Rd
Richmond, VA 23235-2962   804-320-3465
                                  FAX 804-320-6146
                            http://www.riversideschool.org
                            e-mail: info@riversideschool.org
Patricia De Orio, Director

Private school for children grages 1-8 with specific language
based learning disabilities and Dyslexia.

Washington

4269 Children's Institute for Learning Differences
4030 86th Ave SE
Mercer Island, WA 98040-4198   206-232-8680
                                       FAX 206-232-9377
                              http://www.childrensinstitute.com
                              e-mail: info@childrensinstitute.com
Trina Westerlund, Executive Director

CHILD provides two therapeutic year-round day schools,
serving students who learn differently and who process information and life experiences in a unique way. On-site occupational and speech therapy, individual, group and family
counseling.

4270 Glen Eden Institute
19351 8th Avenue
Suite C
Poulsbo, WA 98370-8710   360-697-0125
                                 FAX 360-697-4712
                         http://www.glenedeninstitute.com
                         e-mail: director@glenedeninstitute.com
Ron Seifert, Director

Offers a unique educational alternative to meet the needs of
those complex students in grades k-12 who are unable to
function effectively in a school system due to medical, psychological or psychiatric causes.

4271 Hamlin Robinson School
1700 East Union Street
Seattle, WA 98125-1524   206-763-1167
                          http://www.hamlinrobinson.org
                          e-mail: ifno@hamlinrobinson.org
Jeanne Turner, Director

A nonprofit, state approved elementary day school for children with specific language disability (dyslexia), providing
a positive learning environment, meeting individual needs
to nurture the whole child. Small classes use the Slingerland
multi-sensory classroom approach in reading, writing, spelling and all instructional areas. It helps students discover the
joy of learning, build positive self-esteem, and explore their
full creative potential while preparing them for the
classroom.

4272 RiteCare Of Washington
Scottish Rite Masons
1207 North 152nd Street
Shoreline, WA 98133   206-324-6293
                              FAX 203-365-0270
                         http://www.srccld.org
Steve Anderson, Executive Director

Provides diagnostic and therapeutic services to children whose primary disorder is a severe delay in language or speech development.

4273   STOMP Specialized Training for Military Parents
6316 South 12th Street
Tacoma, WA 98465   253-565-2266
                                  FAX 253-566-8052
                                  TDD:283-588-1741
                        http://www.stompproject.org/
                        e-mail: stomp@wapave.org
Heather Hebdon, Director

STOMP (Specialized Training of Military Parents) is a federally funded center established to assist military families who have children with special education or health needs.

4274   St. Christopher Academy
Jevne Academy
4141 41st Ave SW
Seattle, WA 98116-4216   206-246-9751
                                  FAX 253-639-3466
                  http://www.stchristopheracademy.com
               e-mail: jevne@stchristopheracademy.com
Darlene Jevne, Director

St. Christopher Academy is a private school for learning disabled, ADD and/or academically at-risk students.

West Virginia

4275   Parent Training and Information
1701 Hamill Ave
Clarksburg, WV 26301-1666   304-624-1436
                                     800-281-1436
                                  FAX 304-624-1438
                                  TDD:304-624-1436
                        http://www.wvpti.org
                        e-mail: wvpti@aol.com
Pat Haberbosch, Executive Director

Provides information to parents and to professionals who work with children with disabilities.

Wisconsin

4276   Chileda Institute
1825 Victory Street
La Crosse, WI 54601-4724   608-782-6480
                                  FAX 608-782-6481
                        http://www.chileda.org
                        e-mail: info@chileda.org
Ruth Wiseman, President and CEO

Serves children and young adults ages 6-21 with learning disabilities. The Institute offers on-campus day school and residential programs, on/off campus summer school, after school and weekend respite programs and individualized consulting and training programs for educators and families.

Wyoming

4277   Parent Information Center of Wyoming
500 W Lott St
Ste A
Buffalo, WY 82834-1935   307-684-7441
                                     800-660-9742
                                  FAX 307-684-5314
                                  TDD:307-684-2277
                        http://www.wpic.org
                        e-mail: tdawson@wpic.org
Terri Dawson, Executive Director

Parent Training and Information Program views parents as full partners in the educational process and a significant source of support and assistance to each other. Funded by the Division of Personnel Preparation, Office of Special Education Programs, these programs provide training and information to parents to enable such individuals to participate more effectively with professionals in meeting the educational needs of disabled children.

Centers

4278   American College Testing Program
ACT Universal Testing
PO Box 168
Iowa City, IA 52243-168   319-337-1000
                                       FAX 319-339-3020
                                       http://www.act.org
                                 e-mail: sandy.schlote@act.org
Jon Whitmore, CEO
Janet E. Godwin, Chief of Staff
Thomas J. Goedken, Chief Financial Officer
Helps individuals and organizations make informed decisions about education and work. We provide information for life's transitions.

4279   Diagnostic and Educational Resources
115 Rowell Court
Suite 2
Falls Church, VA 22046-3126   703-534-5180
                                       FAX 703-534-5181
                                  http://www.DER-online.com
                              e-mail: aspector@DER-online.com
Annette Spector, M.S. Ed., Executive Director
Elisabeth Wester, Course Coordinator

Focuses on what the child can do and builds self-esteem. Provides a full range of psychoeducational testing, parent advocacy, case management, and tutoring services. Diagnostic testing determines individual needs, which are addressed in one-on-one tutoring sessions in the child's home or school. Staff trained in LD/ADHD methodologies remediate learning disabilities and offer practical suggestions for home programs and for working with school systems.

4280   Educational Diagnostic Center at Curry College
Curry College
1071 Blue Hill Ave
Milton, MA 02186-2302   617-333-0500
                                       FAX 617-333-2114
                                     http://www.curry.edu
                                 e-mail: curryadm@curry.edu
Jane Fidlery, Dean Of Admission
Keith Robichaud, Director Of Admission

A comprehensive evaluation and testing center specializing in the learning needs of adolescents and adults. The Diagnostic Center welcomes adolescents and adults in need of learning strategies, long term educational plans, and better understanding of their learning profiles.

4281   Educational Testing Service
Rosedale Road
Princeton, NJ 08541-0001   609-921-9000
                                       FAX 609-734-5410
                                       TDD:800-877-2540
                                       http://www.ets.org
                                   e-mail: etsinfo@ets.org
Kurt M Landgraf, President

Our mission is to help advance quality and equity in education by providing fair and valid assessments, research and related services.

4282   GED Testing Service
American Council on Education
1 Dupont Cir NW
Washington, DC 20036-1193   202-939-9300
                                       FAX 202-293-2223
                                     http://www.gedtest.org
                              e-mail: comments@ace.nche.edu
Molly Corbett Broad, President

The American Council on Education, founded in 1918, is the nation's coordinating higher education association. ACE is dedicated to the belief that equal educational opportunity and a strong higher education system are essential cornerstones of a democratic society.

4283   Georgetown University Center for Child and Human Development
P.O.Box 571485
Washington, DC 20057-1485   202-687-5000
                                       FAX 202-687-8899
                                       TTY: 202-687-5503
                               http://www.gucchd.georgetown.edu
                                 e-mail: gucdc@georgetown.edu
Phyllis R Magrab, Executive Director

To improve the quality of life for all children and youth, especially those with, or at risk for, special needs and their families.

4284   Huntington Learning Centers, Inc.
496 Kinderkamack Rd
Oradell, NJ 07649   201-261-8400
                                             800-226-7323
                               http://www.huntingtonlearning.com
Eileen Huntington, Founder

Helps students ages 5 to 17 achieve remarkable improvements in their grades, test scores and self esteem. Builds a personalized learning program for your child based on his or her individual strenths and needs, which is identified using their in-depth diagnostic evaluation. Helps child master a skill before moving on to more difficult tasks and mor advanced learning. Helps develop the skills to learn and solve problems independently.

4285   Munroe-Meyer Institute for Genetics and Rehabilitation
University of Nebraska Medical Center
42nd And Emile
Omaha, NE 68198-5440   402-559-4000
                                     http://www.unmc.edu/mmi
J. Michael Leibowitz, Ph.D., Director, Munroe-Meyer Inst.

Diagnostic evaluation therapy, speech, physical, occupational, behavioral therapies, pediatrics, dentistry, nursing, psychology, social work, genetics, Media Resource Center, education, nutrition. Adult services for developmentally disabled, genetic evaluation and counseling, adaptive equipment, motion analysis laboratory, recreational therapy.

4286   National Center for Fair & Open Testing FairTest
15 Court Square
Suite 820
Boston, MA 02108-2514   857-350-8207
                                       FAX 857-350-8209
                                       http://www.fairtest.org
                                    e-mail: info@fairtest.org
Monty Neill, Executive Director

Dedicated to ensuring that America's students and workers are assessed using fair, accurate, relevant and open tests.

4287   Plano Child Development Center
5401 S Wentworth Ave
Ste 14A
Chicago, IL 60609-6300   773-924-5297
                                       FAX 773-373-3548
                                     http://www.planovision.org
                                  e-mail: info@planovision.org
Stephanie Johnson-Brown, Executive Director
Ms. Addie Davis, Office Manager

A multi-disciplinary, not-for-profit optometric service organization that specializes in the identification, evaluation and treatment of individuals with learning related vision skills problems.

4288 Providence Speech and Hearing Center
1301 Providence Ave
Orange, CA 92868-3892   714-639-4990
                                          FAX 714-744-3841
                                          TTY: 714-532-4047
                                          http://www.pshc.org

Raul Lopez, Founder
Mary Hooper, Executive Director

Comprehensive services for testing and treatment of all
speech, language and hearing problems. Individual and
group therapy beginning with parent/infant programs.

4289 Reading Assessment System
Harcourt Achieve
6277 Sea Harbor Dr
Orlando, FL 32887   252-480-3200
                                          800-531-5015
                                          FAX 800-699-9459
                                          http://www.steckvaughn.com
                                          e-mail: info@steckvaughn.com
Steck-Vaughn Staff, Author
Tim McEwen, President/CEO
Jeff Johnson, Dir Marketing Communications
Lehmann Team Coordinator, Team Coordinator
The Reading Assessment System provides an ongoing
meaure of specific student's skills and offers detailed directions for individual instruction and remediation. Up to eight
reports are available. This popular program generates individual scores, class scores, school scores, and district
reports.

4290 Reading Group
3011A Village Office Place
Champaign, IL 61822-7674   217-351-9144
                                          FAX 217-351-9149
                                          http://www.readinggroup.org
                                          e-mail: info@readinggroup.org
Marlyn Rinehart, President
Betsy Wong, VP
Jennifer Bell, Executive Director
A non-profit learning center known for its work with students who have challenging learning difficulties/differ-
ences. Individualized one-on-one instruction is offered by
educational specialists in reading, writing, early childhood
development, giftedness, and English as a second language.

4291 Rehabilitation Resource
University Of Wisconsin - Stout
221 10th Avenue East
Room 101A
Menomonie, WI 54751   715-232-2470
                                          800-447-8688
                                          FAX 715-232-5008
                                          http://www3.uwstout.edu.com
                                          e-mail: luij@uwstout.edu
John W. Lui, Ph.D., Executive Director

Develops, publishes, and distributes a variety of rehabilitation related materials. Also makes referrals to other sources
on rehabilitation.

4292 Riley Child Development Center
Indiana University School of Medicine
702 Barnhill Dr
Room 5837
Indianapolis, IN 46202-5225   317-944-8167
                                          FAX 317-944-9760
                                          http://www.child-dev.com
                                          e-mail: info@child-dev.com
Dr. John Rau, M.D., Director

Provides an interdisciplinary evaluation for children with
behanvior, learning and other developmental disabilities.

4293 Rose F Kennedy Center
Albert Einstein College of Medicine
1410 Pelham Pkwy S
Bronx, NY 10461-1116   718-430-8600
                                          FAX 718-892-2296
                                          http://www.einsten.yu.edu.com
Herbert J Cohen, Director
Mark Mehler MD, Executive Director

Provides comprehensive diagnostic services and intervention services for children and adults with learning disabilities. The primary mission is to improve the quality of life of
persons with developmental disabilites and their families.

4294 Scholastic Testing Service
480 Meyer Rd
Bensenville, IL 60106-1617   630-766-7150
                                          800-642-6787
                                          FAX 630-766-8054
                                          http://www.ststesting.com
                                          e-mail: sts@ststesting.com
John Kauffman, Marketing VP

Publisher of assessment materials from birth to adulthood,
ability and achievement tests for kindergarten through grade
twelve. Publishes the Torrance Tests of Creative Thinking,
Thinking Creatively in Action and Movement, the STS High
School Placement Test and Educational Development
Series.

4295 Services For Students with Disabilities
PSAT/NMSQT Students With Disabilities
P.O.Box 6226
Princeton, NJ 08541-6226   609-771-7137
                                          FAX 609-771-7944
                                          TTY: 609-882-4118
                                          http://www.collegeboard.com/ssd
                                          e-mail: ssd@info.collegeboard.org
Provides services and reasonable accommodations that are
appropriate according to the type of disability and the pur-
pose of the exam.

4296 The Center for Learning Differences
45 North Station Plaza
Great Neck, NY 11201   516-487-4466
                http://www.centerforlearningdifferences.org
Susan Denberg Yellin J.D., Chairman/Executive Director
Stuart Rothman, PhD
Herman Davidovicz, PhD
A not-for-profit organization dedicated to providing information to families, physicians and other professionals in the
New York metropolitan area about issues they face in dealing with children and parents of children who struggle in
school with the hope that others can benefit from their experiences and the information they have learned. And by sharing your experinces with them, they hope to make them
available to other families who are dealing with similar
issues.

Behavior & Self Esteem

4297 BASC Monitor for ADHD
Pearson Assessments
PO Box 1416
Minneapolis, MN 55440-1416   800-627-7271
                                          FAX 800-232-1223
                http://www.pearsonassessments.com
           e-mail: clinicalcustomersupport@pearson.com
Randy W Kamphaus, Author
Cecil R Reynolds, Co-Author
Doug Kubach, Group President & CEO
The BASC Monitor for ADHD is a powerful new tool to help
evaluate the effectiveness of ADHD treatments using
teacher and parent rating scales, and database software for
tracking behavior changes.

4298 Behavior Assessment System for Children
Pearson Assessments
PO Box 1416
Minneapolis, MN 55440-1416

800-627-7271
FAX 800-232-1223
http://www.pearsonassessments.com
e-mail: clinicalcustomersupport@pearson.com
Randy W Kamphaus, Author
Cecil R Reynolds, Co-Author
Doug Kubach, Group President & CEO
A powerful assessment to evaluate child and adolescent behavior. Includes a self-report form for describing the behaviors and emotions of children and adolescents. Administration time: 10 - 20 minutes (TRS & PRS) 30 - 45 minutes for SRP.

4299 Behavior Rating Profile
Pro-Ed
8700 Shoal Creek Blvd
Austin, TX 78757-6816

512-451-3246
800-897-3202
FAX 512-451-8542
http://www.proedinc.com
e-mail: info@proedinc.com
Donald D Hammill, Owner
Linda Brown, Author

A global measure of behavior providing student, parent, teacher and peer scales. It helps to identify behaviors that may cause a student's learning problems. *$211.00*

4300 Child Behavior Checklist
University of Vermont
1 S Prospect St
St. Joseph's Wing
Burlington, VT 05401-3456

802-656-5130
FAX 802-656-5131
http://www.aseba.org
e-mail: mail@aseba.org
Dr TM Achenbach, Director/Professor
Ramani Sunderaju, Operations Manager

Psychological assessments

4301 Culture-Free Self-Esteem Inventories
Pro-Ed
8700 Shoal Creek Blvd
Austin, TX 78757-1648

512-451-3246
800-897-3202
FAX 512-451-8542
http://www.proedinc.com
e-mail: info@proedinc.com
Donald D Hammill, Owner
James Battle, Author

A series of self-report scales used to determine the level of self-esteem in children and adults. *$190.00*

4302 Devereux Early Childhood Assessment Program Observation Journal
Kaplan Early Learning Company
1310 Lewisville Clemmons Rd
Lewisville, NC 27023-9635

336-766-7374
800-334-2014
FAX 336-766-1586
http://www.kaplanco.com
e-mail: info@kaplanco.com
Hal Kaplan, President & CEO

Provides both sample and reproducible copies of suggested forms for early childhood programs to support appropriate observation and planning for individual children and the classroom. *$199.95*

4303 Disruptive Behavior Rating Scale Kit
Slosson Educational Publications, Inc.
538 Buffalo Rd
East Aurora, NY 14052

716-652-0930
888-756-7766
FAX 800-655-3840
http://www.slosson.com
e-mail: slosson@slosson.com
Bradley T Erford, Author
Steven Slosson, President
John H Slosson, Vice President
Identifies common behavior problems such as attention deficit disorder, attention deficit hyperactivity disorder, oppositional disorders and anti-social conduct problems. *$186.25*

4304 Draw a Person: Screening Procedure for Emotional Disturbance
Pro-Ed
8700 Shoal Creek Blvd
Austin, TX 78757-6816

512-451-3246
800-897-3202
FAX 512-451-8542
http://www.proedinc.com
e-mail: info@proedinc.com
Donald D Hammill, Owner
Jack A. Naglieri, Author
Timothy J. McNeish, Co-Author
A screening test that helps identify children and adolescents who have emotional problems and require further evaluation. *$145.00*

4305 Fundamentals of Autism
Slosson Educational Publications
538 Buffalo Rd
East Aurora, NY 14052

888-756-7766
FAX 800-655-3840
http://www.slosson.com
e-mail: slosson@slosson.com
Steven Slosson, President
Sue Larson, Author
Dr. Georgina Moynihan, Tech Support
The handbook and two accompanying checklists provide a quick, user-friendly approach to help in identifying and developing educationally related program objectives for the child diagnosed as Autistic. *$91.25*

4306 Multidimensional Self Concept Scale
Pro-Ed
8700 Shoal Creek Blvd
Austin, TX 78757-6816

512-451-3246
800-897-3202
FAX 512-451-8542
http://www.proedinc.com
e-mail: info@proedinc.com
Donald D Hammill, Owner
Bruce Bracken, Author

A thoroughly researched, developed and standardized clinical instrument. It assesses global self-concept and six context-dependent self-concept domains that are functionally important in the social-emotional adjustment of youth and adolescents. *$114.00*

4307 Revised Behavior Problem Checklist
Psychological Assessment Resources
16204 N Florida Ave
Lutz, FL 33549-8119

813-449-4066
800-899-8378
FAX 800-727-9329
http://www.parinc.com
e-mail: chairman@parinc.com
Bob III, President/CEO
Kay Cunningham, Director
Cathy Smith, Vice President

Psychological test products and software designed by mental health professionals. *$195.00*

4308   SSRS: Social Skills Rating System
Pearson Assessments
PO Box 1416
Minneapolis, MN 55440-1416
                                          800-627-7271
                                    FAX 800-232-1223
                http://www.pearsonassessments.com
            e-mail: clinicalcustomersupport@pearson.com
Kevin Brueggman, President
Frank M Gresham, Author
Stephen N Elliot, Co-Author
A nationally standardized series of questionnaires that obtain information on the social behaviors of children and adolescents from teachers, parents and the students themselves. Administration time is 10-15 minutes per questionnaire.

4309   Self-Esteem Index
Pro-Ed
8700 Shoal Creek Blvd
Austin, TX 78757-6816
                                          512-451-3246
                                          800-897-3202
                                    FAX 512-451-8542
                        http://www.proedinc.com
                    e-mail: info@proedinc.com
Donald D Hammill, Owner
Linda Brown, Author
Jacquelyn Alexander, Co-Author
A new, multidimensional, norm-referenced measure of the way that individuals perceive and value themselves. *$132.00*

4310   Social-Emotional Dimension Scale
Pro-Ed
8700 Shoal Creek Blvd
Austin, TX 78757-6816
                                          512-451-3246
                                          800-897-3202
                                    FAX 512-451-8542
                        http://www.proedinc.com
                    e-mail: info@proedinc.com
Donald D Hammill, Owner
Jerry Hutton, Author
Timothy Roberts, Co-Author
A quick, well-standardized rating scale that can be used by teachers, counselors and psychologists to screen students who are at risk for conduct disorders or emotional disturbances. *$154.00*

4311   Wings for Kids
476 Meeting Street
Suite E
Charleston, SC 29403
                                          843-442-2835
                                    FAX 866-562-8615
                        http://www.wingsforkids.org
                    e-mail: info@wingsforkids.org
Ginny Deerin, Founder
Paula Schwed, Communications Director
Bridget Laird, CEO
Wings for Kids is the only U.S. organization focused soley on social and emotional learning after school. Hot WINGS are social skill development activities that anyone can use to model, shape and reinforce the capabilities that equip a child to succeed. Through small lessons, you give kids the tools they need to navigate challenging situations and everyday problems. Activties include Positive Reinforcement, Cope with Anger and Stress, Express Emotions Constructively.

LD Screening

4312   ADD-H Comprehensive Teacher's Rating Scale: 2nd Edition
Slosson Educational Publications
538 Buffalo Rd
East Aurora, NY 14052   716-652-0930
                                          800-828-4800
                                    FAX 800-655-3840
                        http://www.slosson.com
                    e-mail: slosson@slosson.com
Rina Ullmann, Robert Sprague, Author
Steven Slosson, President
John H Slosson, Vice President
Dr. Georgina Moynihan, Tech Support
This brief checklist assesses one of the most prevalent childhood behavior problems: attention-deficit disorder, with or without hyperactivity. Because this disorder manifests itself primarily in the classroom, it is best evaluated by teacher ratings. Also available in a Spanish translation; please indicate when ordering. *$62.00*

4313   Attention-Deficit/Hyperactivity Disorder Test
Slosson Educational Publications
538 Buffalo Rd
East Aurora, NY 14052   716-652-0930
                                          800-828-4800
                                    FAX 800-655-3840
                        http://www.slosson.com
                    e-mail: slosson@slosson.com
James E Gilliam, Author
Steven Slosson, President
John H Slosson, Vice President
Dr. Georgina Moynihan, Tech Support
An effective instrument for identifying and evaluating ADHD. Contains 36 items that describe characteristic behaviors of persons with ADHD. These items comprise three subtests representing the core symptoms necessary for the diagnosis of ADHD: hyperactivity, impulsivity, and inattention. *$95.00*

4314   BRIGANCE Screens: Early Preschool
Curriculum Associates
PO Box 2001
North Billerica, MA 01862-901   978-667-8000
                                          800-225-0248
                                    FAX 800-366-1158
                http://www.curriculumassociates.com
                    e-mail: info@CAinc.com
Frank Ferguson, Chairman
Albert Brigance, Author
Robert Waldron, President and CEO
An affordable, easy-to-administer, all-purpose solution. Accurately screen key developmental and early academic skills in just 10-15 minutes per child. Widely used in Early Head Start programs, it meets IDEA requirements and provides consistent results that support early childhood educator's observations and judgement. *$110.00*

4315   BRIGANCE Screens: Infants and Toddler
Curriculum Associates
PO Box 2001
North Billerica, MA 01862-901   978-667-8000
                                          800-225-0248
                                    FAX 800-366-1158
                http://www.curriculumassociates.com
                    e-mail: info@CAinc.com
Frank Ferguson, Chairman
Albert Brigance, Author
Robert Waldron, President and CEO
An affordable, easy-to-administer, all-purpose solution. The Infant and Toddler Screen accurately assesses key developmental skills, and observes caregivers involvement and interactions. *$110.00*

4316 BRIGANCE Screens: K and 1
Curriculum Associates
PO Box 2001
North Billerica, MA 01862-901   978-667-8000
                                        800-225-0248
                                    FAX 800-366-1158
        http://www.curriculumassociates.com
                    e-mail: info@CAinc.com
Frank Ferguson, Chairman
Albert Brigance, Author
Robert Waldron, President and CEO
The K and 1 Screen is an affordable, easy-to-administer, all-purpose solution. Accurately screen key developmental and early academic skills in just 10-15 mintues per child. School districts nationwide rely on BRIGANCE for screening children before entering kindergarten, grade 1, and grade 2. It meets IDEA requirements and provides consistant results that support early childhood educators observations and judgement. *$110.00*

4317 Basic School Skills Inventory: Screen and Diagnostic
Pro-Ed
8700 Shoal Creek Blvd
Austin, TX 78757-6816   512-451-3246
                                        800-897-3202
                                    FAX 800-397-7633
            http://www.proedinc.com
                e-mail: info@proedinc.com
Lindy Jordaan, Marketing Coordinator
Donald D Hammill, Owner

Can be used to locate children who are high risk for school failure, who need more in-depth assessment and who should be referred for additional study. *$109.00*

4318 DABERON Screening for School Readiness
Pro-Ed
8700 Shoal Creek Blvd
Austin, TX 78757-6816   512-451-3246
                                        800-897-3202
                                    FAX 512-451-8542
            http://www.proedinc.com
                e-mail: info@proedinc.com
Donald D Hammill, Owner
Virginia Danzer, Author
Theresa Lyons, Co-Author
Provides a standardized assessment of school readiness in children with learning or behavior problems. *$176.00*
            Yearly

4319 Developmental Assessment for Students with Severe Disabilities
Pro-Ed
8700 Shoal Creek Blvd
Austin, TX 78757-6816   512-451-3246
                                        800-897-3202
                                    FAX 512-451-8542
            http://www.proedinc.com
                e-mail: info@proedinc.com
Mary Kay Dykes & Jane Erin, Author
Donald D Hammill, Owner

Offers diagnostic and programming personnel concise information about individuals who are functioning between birth and 8 years of age developmentally. *$217.00*

4320 Educational Developmental Series
Scholastic Testing Service
480 Meyer Rd
Bensenville, IL 60106-1617   855-532-0787
                                        800-642-6787
                                    FAX 630-766-8054
        http://http://www.ststesting.com/
                e-mail: sts@mail.ststesting.com
John Kauffman, Marketing VP
Scott Rich, J.D., Assessment Specialist

A standardized battery of ability and achievement tests. Administration time is approximately 2.5 - 5 hours, depending on grade level and subtests. The EDSERIES has the most comprehensive coverage of all the STS tests. It permits teachers, counselors and administrators to evaluate a student from the broadest possible perspective. A school may use the EDSERIES on a lease/score basis or it may purchase testing materials.

4321 Fundamentals of Autism
Slosson Educational Publications
538 Buffalo Rd
East Aurora, NY 14052   716-652-0930
                                        800-828-4800
                                    FAX 800-655-3840
            http://www.slosson.com
                e-mail: slosson@slosson.com
Sue Larson, Author
Steven Slosson, President
John H Slosson, Vice President
Dr. Georgina Moynihan, Tech Support
Provides a quick, user-friendly, effective, and accurate approach to help in identifying and developing educationally related program objectives for children diagnosed as autistic.

4322 Goodenough-Harris Drawing Test
Pearson
19500 Bulverde Rd
San Antonio, TX 78259-3701   210-339-5000
                                        800-627-7271
                                    FAX 800-232-1223
            http://www.psychcorp.com
        e-mail: clinicalcustomersupport@pearson.com
Aurelio Prifitera, President
Florence Goodenough, Author

This test focuses on mental maturity without requiring verbal skills. The fifteen-minute examination provides standard scores for children ages 3-15. *$178.00*

4323 Kaufman Assessment Battery for Children
Pearson
5601 Green Valley Dr
Bloomington, MN 55437-1099   952-681-3000
                                        800-627-7271
                                    FAX 800-632-9011
        http://www.pearsonassessments.com
        e-mail: clinicalcustomersupport@pearson.com
Alan Kaufman, Author
Nadeen Kaufman, Co-Author
Carol Watson, Publisher/Pres Clinical Asses
An individually administered measure of intelligence and achievement, using simultaneous and sequential mental processes.

4324 Kaufman Brief Intelligence Test
Pearson
5601 Green Valley Dr
Bloomington, MN 55437-1099   952-681-3000
                                        800-627-7271
                                    FAX 800-632-9011
        http://www.pearsonassessments.com
        e-mail: clinicalcustomersupport@pearson.com
Alan Kaufman, Author
Nadeen Kaufman, Co-Author
Doug Kubach, Group President & CEO
KBIT is a brief, individually administered test of verbal and non-verbal intelligence. Screens two cognitive functions quickly and easily.

4325 Marshall University: HELP Program
Higher Education for Learning Problems
520 18th St
Huntington, WV 25703-1530   304-696-6252
                                    FAX 304-696-3231
            http://www.marshall.edu/help

Kristina R. Pollard, M.Ed, Director

The HELP program is committed to providing assistance through individual tutuoring, mentoring and support, as well as fair and legal access to educational opportunities for students diagnosed with learning disabilities and related disorders such as ADD/ADHD.

4326   Peabody Individual Achievement Test
Pearson
5601 Green Valley Dr
Bloomington, MN 55437-1099   952-681-3000
                                FAX 800-632-9011
          http://www.pearsonassessments.com
      e-mail: clinicalcustomersupport@pearson.com
Frederick Markwardt Jr, Author
Matt Keller, Marketing Manager
Doug Kubach, Group President & CEO
Efficient individual measure of academic achievement. Reading, mathematics and spelling are assessed in a simple nonthreatning format that requires only a revised pointing response for most items.

4327   Peabody Test-Picture Vocabulary Test
Pearson
5601 Green Valley Dr
Bloomington, MN 55437-1099   952-681-3000
                                FAX 800-632-9011
          http://www.pearsonassessments.com
      e-mail: clinicalcustomersupport@pearson.com
Lloyd Dunn, Author
Leota Dunn, Co-Author
Doug Kubach, Group President & CEO
A measure of hearing vocabulary for Standard American English; administration time: 10-15 minutes.

4328   Restless Minds, Restless Kids
Slosson Educational Publications
538 Buffalo Rd
East Aurora, NY 14052   716-652-0930
                                    800-828-4800
                                FAX 800-655-3840
              http://www.slosson.com
          e-mail: slosson@slosson.com
Rick D'Alli, Author
Steven Slosson, President
John H Slosson, Vice President
Dr. Georgina Moynihan, Tech Support
Two leading specialists in the field of childhood behavioral disorders discuss the state-of-the-art approach to diagnosing and testing ADHD. They are joined by four mothers of ADHD children who share their experiences of the effects of this disorder on the family. *$67.00*

4329   School Readiness Test
Scholastic Testing Service
480 Meyer Rd
Bensenville, IL 60106-1617   855-532-0787
                                    800-642-6787
                                FAX 630-766-8054
              http://www.ststesting.com
          e-mail: sts@mail.ststesting.com
John Kauffman, Marketing VP
Scott Rich, J.D., Assessment Specialist

An effective tool for determining the readiness of each student for first grade. It allows a teacher to learn as much as possible about every entering student's abilities, and about any factors that might interfere with his or her learning.

4330   Slosson Intelligence Test
Pro-Ed
538 Buffalo Rd
East Aurora, NY 14052   716-652-0930
                                    800-828-4800
                                FAX 800-655-3840
              http://www.slosson.com
          e-mail: slosson@slosson.com

Steven Slosson, President
John H Slosson, Vice President
Richard.L Slosson, Author
A widely used individual screening test for those who need to evaluate the mental ability of individuals who are learning disabled, mentally retarded, blind, orthopedically disabled, normal, or gifted from ages 4 to adulthood. Revised by Charles Nicholson and Terry Hibpshman. *$147.00*

4331   TOVA
Universal Attention Disorders
3321 Cerritos Ave
Los Alamitos, CA 90720-2105   562-594-7700
                                    800-729-2886
                                FAX 562-594-7770
              http://www.tovatest.com
          e-mail: support@tovatest.com
Tammy Dupuy, Medical Director
Karen Carlson, Marketing Director

The TOVA (Tests of Variables of Attention) is a computerized, objective measure of attention and impulsivity, used in the assessment and treatment of ADD/ADHD. It is standardized from 4 to 80 years of age. TOVA's report contains a full analysis and interpetation of data. Variables measured include omissions, commisions, response time and response time variability.

4332   Test of Memory and Learning (TOMAL)
Pro-Ed
8700 Shoal Creek Blvd
Austin, TX 78757-6816   512-451-3246
                                    800-897-3202
                                FAX 512-451-8542
              http://www.proedinc.com
          e-mail: info@proedinc.com
Donald D Hammill, Owner
Cecil Reynolds, Author
Judith K Voress, Co-Author
TOMAL provides ten subtests that evaluate general and specific memory functions. *$376.00*

4333   Test of Nonverbal Intelligence (TONI-3)
Pro-Ed
8700 Shoal Creek Blvd
Austin, TX 78757-6816   512-451-3246
                                    800-897-3202
                                FAX 512-451-8542
              http://www.proedinc.com
          e-mail: info@proedinc.com
Donald D Hammill, President
Linda Brown, Author
Susan Johnson, Co-Author
A language-free measure of reasoning and intelligence presents a variety of abstract problem solving tasks. *$285.00*

4334   Vision, Perception and Cognition: Manual for Evaluation & Treatment
Therapro
225 Arlington St
Framingham, MA 01702-8773   508-872-9494
                                    800-257-5376
                                FAX 508-875-2062
              http://www.theraproducts.com
          e-mail: info@theraproducts.com
Karen Conrad, Owner
Barbara Zoltan, Author

Details methods for testing perceptual, visual and cognitive deficits, as well as procedure for evaluating test results in relation to cognitive loss. Clearly explains each deficit, provides step by step testing techniques and gives complete treatment guidelines. Also includes information on the use of computers in cognitive training. *$40.00*
232 pages

Math

4335 **3 Steps to Math Success**
Curriculum Associates
PO Box 2001
North Billerica, MA 01862-901   978-667-8000
800-225-0248
FAX 800-366-1158
http://www.curriculumassociates.com
e-mail: info@CAinc.com
Curriculum Associates, Author
Frank Ferguson, Chairman
Patricia Payette, Vice President, Financeÿ
Dave Caron, Chief Financial Officer
We developed an integrated approach to math that ensures
academic success long after the final bell has rung. To-
gether, these series create an easy-to-use system of targeted
instruction designed to remedy math weakness and reinforce
math strengths.

4336 **AfterMath Series**
Curriculum Associates
PO Box 2001
North Billerica, MA 01862-901   978-667-8000
800-225-0248
FAX 800-366-1158
http://www.curriculumassociates.com
e-mail: info@CAinc.com
Frank Ferguson, Chairman
Patricia Payette, Vice President, Financeÿ
Dave Caron, Chief Financial Officer
Galileo once said that mathematics is the alphabet in which
the universe was created. This series helps students master
that alphabet. As they puzzle their way through brainteasers
and learn math magic, students build critical-thinking skills
that are vital to comprehending and succeeding in today's
world.

4337 **ENRIGHT Computation Series**
Curriculum Associates
PO Box 2001
North Billerica, MA 01862-901   978-667-8000
800-225-0248
FAX 800-366-1158
http://www.curriculumassociates.com
e-mail: info@CAinc.com
Frank Ferguson, Chairman
Patricia Payette, Vice President, Financeÿ
Dave Caron, Chief Financial Officer
Close the gap between expected and actual computation per-
formance. The ENRIGHT Computation Series provides the
practice necessary to master addition, subtraction, multipli-
cation, and division of whole numbers, fractions, and
decimals.

4338 **Figure It Out: Thinking Like a Math Problem Solver**
Curriculum Associates
PO Box 2001
North Billerica, MA 01862-901   978-667-8000
800-225-0248
FAX 800-366-1158
http://www.curriculumassociates.com
e-mail: info@CAinc.com
Frank Ferguson, Chairman
Patricia Payette, Vice President, Financeÿ
Dave Caron, Chief Financial Officer
Critical thinking is the key to unlocking the mystery of these
nonroutine problems. Your students will eagerly accept the
challenge! Students learn to apply eight strategies in each
book including: draw a picture; use a pattern; work back-
wards; make a table; and guess and check.

4339 **Getting Ready for Algebra**
Curriculum Associates
PO Box 2001
North Billerica, MA 01862-901   978-667-8000
800-225-0248
FAX 800-366-1158
http://www.curriculumassociates.com
e-mail: info@CAinc.com
Frank Ferguson, Chairman
Patricia Payette, Vice President, Financeÿ
Dave Caron, Chief Financial Officer
NCTM encourages algebra instruction in the early grades to
develop critical-thinking, communication, reasoning, and
problem-solving skills. Getting Ready for Algebra exercises
these skills in lessons that focus on key algebra concepts:
adding and subtracting positive integers; patterns; set theory
notation; open sentences; inequality and more.

4340 **Learning Disability Evaluation Scale: Renormed**
Hawthorne Educational Services
800 Gray Oak Dr
Columbia, MO 65201-3730   573-874-1710
800-542-1673
FAX 800-442-9509
http://www.hes-inc.com
e-mail: info@hes-inc.com
Stephen McCarney, Author
Edina Laird, Director External Relations
Michele Jackson, Owner

The Learning Disability Evaluation Scale (LDES) is an initial screening and assessment instrument in the areas of listening, thinking, speaking, reading, writing, spelling, and
mathematical calculations based on the federal definition
(IDEA). The Learning Disability Intervention Manual
(LDIM) is a companion to the LDES and contains goals, objectives, and intervention/instructional strategies for the
learning problems identified by the LDES. *$152.00*
217 pages

4341 **QUIC Tests**
Scholastic Testing Service
480 Meyer Rd
Bensenville, IL 60106-1617   855-532-0787
800-642-6787
FAX 630-766-8054
http://www.ststesting.com
e-mail: sts@mail.ststesting.com
John Kauffman, Marketing VP
Scott Rich, J.D., Assessment Specialist

The Quic Tests are used to determine the functional level of
student comptetency in mathematics and/ or communicative
arts for use in grades 2-12. Administration time is 30 minutes
or less.

4342 **Skills Assessments**
Harcourt
6277 Sea Harbor Dr
Orlando, FL 32887   407-345-2000
800-531-5015
FAX 800-699-9459
http://http://www.harcourt.com/bu_info/harcourt
e-mail: international@harcourt.com
This handy, all-in-one resource helps identify students
strengths and weaknesses in order to determine appropriate
instructional levels in each of five subjects areas: reading;
language arts; math; science; and social studies. Assessments are identified by subtopics in each subject.

4343 **Test of Mathematical Abilities**
Pro-Ed
8700 Shoal Creek Blvd
Austin, TX 78757-6816   512-451-3246
800-897-3202
FAX 512-451-8542
http://www.proedinc.com
e-mail: info@proedinc.com

Donald D Hammill, Owner
Virginia Brown, Author
Mary Cronin, Co-Author
Has been developed to provide standardized information about story problems and computation, attitude, vocabulary and general cultural application. *$95.00*

Professional Guides

4344 Assessment Update
Jossey-Bass
111 River St
Hoboken, NJ 07030-5774   201-748-6000
                                 FAX 201-748-6008
                                 http://www.wiley.com
                                 e-mail: info@wiley.com

William J Pesce, CEO
Trudy Banta, Editor

Assessment Update is dedicated to covering the latest developments in the rapidly evolving area of higher education assessment. Assessment Update offers all academic leaders up-to-date information and practical advice on conducting assessments in a range of areas, including student learning and outcomes, factulty instruction, academic programs and curricula, student services, and overall institutional functioning.

4345 Assessment of Students with Handicaps in Vocational Education
Association for Career and Technical Education
1410 King St
Alexandria, VA 22314-2749
                                 800-826-9972
                                 FAX 703-683-7424
                                 http://www.acteonline.org
                                 e-mail: acte@acteonline.org

L Albright, Author
Jan Bray, Executive Director
Peter Magnuson, Senior Dir Strategic Marketing
Stephen Dewitt, Senior Dir Public Policy
Includes teachers, supervisors, administrators and others interested in the development and improvement of career & technical and practical-arts education.

4346 BRIGANCE Word Analysis: Strategies and Practice
Curriculum Associates
PO Box 2001
North Billerica, MA 01862-901   978-667-8000
                                 800-225-0248
                                 FAX 800-366-1158
                                 http://www.curriculumassociates.com
                                 e-mail: info@CAinc.com

Albert Brigance, Author
Frank Ferguson, Chairman
Patricia Payette, Vice President, Financeÿ
Dave Caron, Chief Financial Officer
Our comprehensive, two-volume resource combines activities, strategies, and reference materials for teaching phonetic and structural word analysis. Two durable binders feature reproducible activity pages. Choose from more than 1,600 activities for corrective instruction or to reinforce your classroom reading program.

4347 Career Planner's Portfolio: A School-to-Work Assessment Tool
Curriculum Associates
PO Box 2001
North Billerica, MA 01862-901   978-667-8000
                                 800-225-0248
                                 FAX 800-366-1158
                                 http://www.curriculumassociates.com
                                 e-mail: info@CAinc.com

Robert G Forest, Author
Frank Ferguson, Chairman
Patricia Payette, Vice President, Financeÿ
Dave Caron, Chief Financial Officer
Students career plans develop and evolve over several school years. Our portfolio will help keep track of their progress.

4348 Computer Scoring Systems for PRO-ED Tests
Pro-Ed
8700 Shoal Creek Blvd
Austin, TX 78757-6816   512-451-3246
                                 800-897-3202
                                 FAX 512-451-8542
                                 http://www.proedinc.com
                                 e-mail: info@proedinc.com

Donald D Hammill, Owner

Computer scoring systems have been developed to generate reports for many PRO-ED tests and to help examiners interpret test performance.

4349 Goals and Objectives Writer Software
Curriculum Associates
PO Box 2001
North Billerica, MA 01862-901   978-667-8000
                                 800-225-0248
                                 FAX 800-366-1158
                                 http://www.curriculumassociates.com
                                 e-mail: info@CAinc.com

Frank Ferguson, Chairman
Patricia Payette, Vice President, Financeÿ
Dave Caron, Chief Financial Officer
Using the Goals and Objectives program, you'll quickly and easily create, edit, and print IEPs. The CD allows you to install the program on your hard drive in order to save students data for future updates. You can easily export IEPs into any word processing program. CD-Rom for Windows and Macintosh.

4350 Occupational Aptitude Survey and Interest Schedule
Pro-Ed
8700 Shoal Creek Blvd
Austin, TX 78757-6816   512-451-3246
                                 800-897-3202
                                 FAX 512-451-8542
                                 http://www.proedinc.com
                                 e-mail: info@proedinc.com

Donald D Hammill, Owner
Randall M Parker, Author

Consists of two related tests: the OASIS-2 Aptitude Survey and the OASIS-2 Interest Schedule. The tests were normed on the same national sample of 1,505 students from 13 states. The Aptitude Survey measures six broad aptitude factors that are directly related to skills and abilities required in over 20,000 jobs and the Interest Schedule measures 12 interest factors directly related to the occupations listed in Occupational Exploration.

4351 Portfolio Assessment Teacher's Guide
Harcourt
6277 Sea Harbor Dr
Orlando, FL 32887   407-345-2000
                                 800-531-5015
                                 FAX 800-699-9459
                                 http://http://www.harcourt.com/bu_info/harcourt
                                 e-mail: international@harcourt.com

Roger Farr, Author
Tim McEwen, President
Patrick Tierrey, CEO
Jeff Johnson, Marketing Communication Director
Start your portfolio systems with tips from the expert. Roger Farr outlines the basic steps for evaluating a portfolio, offers ideas for organizing portfolios and making the most of portfolio conferences, and provides reproducible evaluation forms for primary through intermediate grades and above. *$23.60*

4352 Teaching Test Taking Skills
Brookline Books
PO Box 1209
Brookline, MA 02446   617-734-6772
                                        800-666-2665
                                    FAX 617-734-3952
                        http://www.brooklinebooks.com
                            e-mail: brbooks@yahoo.com
Margo Mastropieri,Thomas Scruggs, Author
Mike Beattie, Manager

Test-wise individuals often score higher than others of equal
ability who may not use test-taking skills effectively. This
work teaches general concepts about the test format or other
conditions of testing, not specific items on the test. *$21.95*

ISBN 0-914797-76-X

4353 Tests, Measurement and Evaluation
American Institutes for Research
1000 Thomas Jefferson St
Washington, DC 20007-3835   202-342-5000
                                    FAX 202-403-5454
                                      TTY: 877-344-3499
                                    http://www.air.org
                            e-mail: inquiry@air.org
David Myers, President/CEO
Jane Hannaway, Vice President and Director
Gary Phillips, Vice President
Our goal is to provide governments and the private sector
with responsive services of the highest quality by applying
and advancing the knowledge, theories, methods, and standards of the behavioral and social services to solve significant societal problems and improve the quality of life of all
people.

Reading

4354 3 Steps to Reading Success: CARS, STARS, CARS II
Curriculum Associates
PO Box 2001
North Billerica, MA 01862-901   978-667-8000
                                        800-225-0248
                                    FAX 800-366-1158
                        http://www.curriculumassociates.com
                            e-mail: info@CAinc.com
Frank Ferguson, Chairman
Patricia Payette, Vice President, Financeÿ
Dave Caron, Chief Financial Officer
Equipping your students with the skills and strategies they
need to achieve lifelong success can be a challenge. That's
why we developed an integrated approach to learning that
ensures academic success long after the final bell has rung.

4355 BRIGANCE Readiness: Strategies and Practice
Curriculum Associates
PO Box 2001
North Billerica, MA 01862-901   978-667-8000
                                        800-225-0248
                                    FAX 800-366-1158
                        http://www.curriculumassociates.com
                            e-mail: info@CAinc.com
Frank Ferguson, Chairman
Albert Brigance, Author
Dave Caron, Chief Financial Officer
Attend to the needs and differences of the children in your
program using Readiness: Strategies and Practice. Skills are
introduced, taught, and reinforced using both age-appropri-
ate and individual appropriate activties. *$174.00*

4356 Capitalization and Punctuation
Curriculum Associates
PO Box 2001
North Billerica, MA 01862-901   978-667-8000
                                        800-225-0248
                                    FAX 800-366-1158
                        http://www.curriculumassociates.com
                            e-mail: info@CAinc.com
Frank Ferguson, Chairman
Patricia Payette, Vice President, Financeÿ
Dave Caron, Chief Financial Officer
Capitalization and Punctuation features structured, easy to
understand lessons that are organized sequentially. Students
read the rules, study sample exercises, apply the skills in
practice lessons, and review the skills in maintenance
lessons.

4357 Dyslexia/ADHD Institute
148 Eastern Blvd
4th Floor
Glastonbury, CT 06033   860-633-2604
                                        877-342-7323
                                    http://www.diaread.com
                            e-mail: info@diaread.com
Les Fredette, Co-Operations
Susan Fredette, Co-Operations

Testing, diagnosis, and 1-on-1 tutoring for all ages and levels of need

4358 Extensions in Reading
Curriculum Associates
PO Box 2001
North Billerica, MA 01862-901   978-667-8000
                                        800-225-0248
                                    FAX 800-366-1158
                        http://www.curriculumassociates.com
                            e-mail: info@CAinc.com
Frank Ferguson, Chairman
Patricia Payette, Vice President, Financeÿ
Dave Caron, Chief Financial Officer
A unique new program teaching reading strategies and more.
Extensions offers rich experiences with nonfiction and fic-
tion. Each lesson extends to include: researching and writ-
ing; use of graphic organizers; vocabulary development; and
comprehension questions with test-prep format.

4359 Gray Diagnostic Reading Tests
Pro-Ed
8700 Shoal Creek Blvd
Austin, TX 78757-6816   512-451-3246
                                        800-897-3202
                                    FAX 512-451-8542
                                    http://www.proedinc.com
                            e-mail: info@proedinc.com
Donald D Hammill, Owner
Brian Bryant, Author
Diane Bryant, Co-Author
Uses two alternate, equivalent forms to assess students who
have difficulty reading continuous print and who require an
evaluation of specific abilities and weaknesses. Item #
10965. *$259.00*

4360 Gray Oral Reading Tests
Pro-Ed
8700 Shoal Creek Blvd
Austin, TX 78757-6816   512-451-3246
                                        800-897-3202
                                    FAX 512-451-8542
                                    http://www.proedinc.com
                            e-mail: info@proedinc.com
Donald D Hammill, Owner
J Lee Wiederholt, Author
Brian Bryant, Co-Author
The latest revision provides an objective measure of growth
in oral reading and an aid in the diagnosis of oral reading dif-
ficulties. *$233.00*

4361 Reading Assessment System
Steck-Vaughn Company
Specialized Curriculum Group
181 Ballardvale Street
Willmington, MA 01887
800-289-4490
FAX 800-289-3994
http://www.steckvaughn.com
The Reading Assessment System provides an ongoing measure of specific student's skills and offers detailed directions for individual instruction and remediation. Up to eight reports are available. This popular program generates individual scores, class scores, school scores, and district reports.

4362 Scholastic Abilities Test for Adults
Pro-Ed
8700 Shoal Creek Blvd
Austin, TX 78757-6816
512-451-3246
800-897-3202
FAX 512-451-8542
http://www.proedinc.com
e-mail: info@proedinc.com
Donald D Hammill, Owner
Brian Bryant, Author
James Patton, Co-Author
Measures scholastic competence, aptitude and academic achievement for persons with learning difficulties. *$186.00*

4363 Skills Assessments
Steck-Vaughn Company
PO Box 690789
Orlando, FL 32819-789
407-345-3800
800-531-5015
FAX 800-269-5232
http://www.steck-vaughn.com
e-mail: info@steck-vaughn.com
Connie Alden, Vice President
Michael Ruecker, Vice President

This handy, all-in-one resource helps identify students strengths and weaknesses in order to determine appropriate instructional levels in each of five subjects areas: reading; language arts; math; science; and social studies. Assessments are identified by subtopics in each subject. Each book is $13.99 each. *$69.95*

4364 Standardized Reading Inventory
Pro-Ed
8700 Shoal Creek Blvd
Austin, TX 78757-6816
512-451-3246
800-897-3202
FAX 512-451-8542
http://www.proedinc.com
e-mail: info@proedinc.com
Donald D Hammill, Owner
Phyllis Newcomer, Author

An instrument for evaluating students' reading ability. *$277.00*

4365 Test of Early Reading Ability
Pro-Ed
8700 Shoal Creek Blvd
Austin, TX 78757-6816
512-451-3246
800-897-3202
FAX 512-451-8542
http://www.proedinc.com
e-mail: info@proedinc.com
Donald D Hammill, Owner
D Kim Reid, Author
Wayne Hresko, Co-Author
Unique test in that it measures the actual reading ability of young children. Items measure knowledge of contextual meaning, alphabet and conventions. *$274.00*

4366 Test of Reading Comprehension
Pro-Ed
8700 Shoal Creek Blvd
Austin, TX 78757-6816
512-451-3246
800-897-3202
FAX 512-451-8542
http://www.proedinc.com
e-mail: info@proedinc.com
Donald D Hammill, Owner/Author
Virginia Brown, Co-Author
J Lee Wiederholt, Co-Author
A multidimensional test of silent reading comprehension for students. The test reflects current psycholinguistic theories that consider reading comprehension to be a constructive process involving both language and cognition. *$ 196.00*

Speech & Language Arts

4367 A Calendar of Home Activities
Curriculum Associates
PO Box 2001
North Billerica, MA 01862-901
978-667-8000
800-225-0248
FAX 800-366-1158
http://www.curriculumassociates.com
e-mail: info@CAinc.com
Frank Ferguson, Chairman
Donald Johnson, Author
Elaine Johnson, Co-Author
An activity-a-day: 365 activities for parents and children to share at home in just 10-15 minutes each day. Parents support their children's educational experiences in a meaningful and enjoyable way, such as cooking, playing ball, and sculpting clay.

4368 Adolescent Language Screening Test
Pro-Ed
8700 Shoal Creek Blvd
Austin, TX 78757-6816
512-451-3246
800-897-3202
FAX 512-451-8542
http://www.proedinc.com
e-mail: info@proedinc.com
Donald D Hammill, Owner
Denise Morgan, Author
Arthur Guilford, Co-Author
Provides speech/language pathologists and other interested professionals with a rapid thorough method for screening adolescents' speech and language. *$145.00*

4369 Advanced Skills For School Success Series: Module 4
Curriculum Associates
PO Box 2001
North Billerica, MA 01862-901
978-667-8000
800-225-0248
FAX 800-366-1158
http://www.curriculumassociates.com
e-mail: info@CAinc.com
Anita Archer, Mary Gleason, Author
Frank Ferguson, Chairman
Fred Ferguson, VP Corporate Development/CIO
Dave Caron, Chief Financial Officer
Develops oral and written language abilities. Students learn valuable strategies for note-taking, brainstorming, and effectively participating in class dicussions. *$19.90*

4370 Aphasia Diagnostic Profiles
Pro-Ed
8700 Shoal Creek Blvd
Austin, TX 78757-6816
512-451-3246
800-897-3202
FAX 512-451-8542
http://www.proedinc.com
e-mail: info@proedinc.com

Donald D Hammill, Owner
Nancy Helm-Estrabrooks, Author

This is a quick, efficient, and systematic assessment of language and communication impairment associated with aphasia that should be administered individually. The test can be administered in 40-45 minutes. *$175.00*

4371   BRIGANCE Assessment of Basic Skills
Curriculum Associates
PO Box 2001
North Billerica, MA 01862-901   978-667-8000
800-225-0248
FAX 800-366-1158
http://www.curriculumassociates.com
e-mail: info@CAinc.com

Frank Ferguson, Chairman
Albert Brigance, Author
Dave Caron, Chief Financial Officer
Critiqued and field tested by Spanish linguists and educators nationwide, the Assessment of Basic Skills meets nondiscriminatory testing requirements for Limited English Proficient students.

4372   BRIGANCE Comprehensive Inventory of Basic Skills
Curriculum Associates
PO Box 2001
North Billerica, MA 01862-901   978-667-8000
800-225-0248
FAX 800-366-1158
http://www.curriculumassociates.com
e-mail: info@CAinc.com

Frank Ferguson, Chairman
Albert Brigance, Author
Dave Caron, Chief Financial Officer
Designed for use in elementary and middle schools, the CIBS-R is a valuable resource for programs emphasizing individualized instruction. The Inventory is especially helpful in programs serving students with special needs, and continues to be indispensable in IEP development and program planning.

4373   BRIGANCE Employability Skills Inventory
Curriculum Associates
PO Box 2001
North Billerica, MA 01862-901   978-667-8000
800-225-0248
FAX 800-366-1158
http://www.curriculumassociates.com
e-mail: info@CAinc.com

Frank Ferguson, Chairman
Albert Brigance, Author
Dave Caron, Chief Financial Officer
Extensive criterion-referenced tool assesses basic skills and employability skills in the context of job-seeking or employment situations: reading grade placement; rating scales; career awareness and self-understanding; reading skills; speaking and listening; job-seeking skills and knowledge; pre-employment writing; math and concepts.

4374   BRIGANCE Life Skills Inventory
Curriculum Associates
PO Box 2001
North Billerica, MA 01862-901   978-667-8000
800-225-0248
FAX 800-366-1158
http://www.curriculumassociates.com
e-mail: info@CAinc.com

Frank Ferguson, Chairman
Albert Brigance, Author
Dave Caron, Chief Financial Officer
Assesses listening, speaking, reading, writing, comprehending, and computing skills in nine life-skill sections: speaking and listening; money and finance; functional writing; food; words on common signs and warning labels; clothing; health; telephone; travel and transportation.

4375   Bedside Evaluation and Screening Test
Pro-Ed
8700 Shoal Creek Blvd
Austin, TX 78757-6816   512-451-3246
800-897-3202
FAX 512-451-8542
http://www.proedinc.com
e-mail: info@proedinc.com

Donald D Hammill, Owner
Joyce West, Author
Elaine Sands, Co-Author
Access and quantify language disorders in adults resulting from aphasia. *$171.00*

4376   Boone Voice Program for Adults
Pro-Ed
8700 Shoal Creek Blvd
Austin, TX 78757-6816   512-451-3246
800-897-3202
FAX 512-451-8542
http://www.proedinc.com
e-mail: info@proedinc.com

Donald D Hammill, Owner
Daniel Boone, Author
Kay Wiley, Co-Author
Provides for diagnosis and remediation of adult voice disorders. This program is based on the same philosophy and therapy as The Program for Children but is presented at an adult interest level. *$153.00*

4377   Boone Voice Program for Children
Pro-Ed
8700 Shoal Creek Blvd
Austin, TX 78757-6816   512-451-3246
800-897-3202
FAX 512-451-8542
http://www.proedinc.com
e-mail: info@proedinc.com

Donald D Hammill, Owner
Daniel Boone, Author

Provides a cognitive approach to voice therapy and is designed to give useful step-by-step guidelines and materials for diagnosis and remediation of voice disorders in children. *$208.00*

4378   Connecting Reading and Writing with Vocabulary
Curriculum Associates
PO Box 2001
North Billerica, MA 01862-901   978-667-8000
800-225-0248
FAX 800-366-1158
http://www.curriculumassociates.com
e-mail: info@CAinc.com

Frank Ferguson, Chairman
Deborah P Adcock, Author
Dave Caron, Chief Financial Officer
This vocabulary enrichment series builds successful writers and speakers by implementing strategic word techniques. Students will add 120 writing words and other word forms to their word banks. Each lesson introduces ten vocabulary words in a variety of contexts: a letter, poem, story, journal entry, classified ad, etc.

4379   Diamonds in the Rough
Slosson Educational Publications
538 Buffalo Rd
East Aurora, NY 14052   716-652-0930
888-756-7766
FAX 800-655-3840
http://www.slosson.com
e-mail: slosson@slosson.com

Steven Slosson, President
Peggy Strass Dras, Author
Dr. Georgina Moynihan, Tech Support
College reference/rehabilitation guide for people with attention deficit disorder and learning disabilities. *$36.00*

4380 Easy Talker: A Fluency Workbook for School Age Children
Pro-Ed
8700 Shoal Creek Blvd
Austin, TX 78757-6816

512-451-3246
800-897-3202
FAX 512-451-8542
http://www.proedinc.com
e-mail: info@proedinc.com

Donald D Hammill, Owner
Barry Guitar, Author
Julie Reville, Co-Author
A diagnostic, criterion-referenced instrument to be used with children, to determine which stutterers would benefit from early intervention. Item #4855. *$45.00*

4381 Fluharty Preschool Speech & Language Screening Test-2
Speech Bin
PO Box 922668
Norcross, GA 30010-2668

800-850-8602
FAX 800-845-1535
http://www.speechbin.com
e-mail: info@speechbin.com

Shane Peters, Product Coordinator
Jan Binney, Owner
Andy Roussey, New Product Development Contact
Carefully normed on 705 children, the Fluharty yields standard scores, percentiles, and age equivalents. The form features space for speech-language pathologists to note phonological processes, voice quality, and fluency; a Teacher Questionnaire is also provided. Item number P882. *$153.00*

4382 Help for the Learning Disabled Child
Slosson Educational Publications
538 Buffalo Rd
East Aurora, NY 14052

716-652-0930
888-756-7766
FAX 800-655-3840
http://www.slosson.com
e-mail: slosson@slosson.com

Steven Slosson, President
John H Slosson, Vice President
Dr. Georgina Moynihan, Tech Support
Symptoms and solutions for learning disabled children. Features issues from a medical, psychological and educational basis and illustrates learning disabilities from emotional and mental impairment. *$48.75*

4383 Learning Disability Evaluation Scale
Hawthorne Educational Services
800 Gray Oak Dr
Columbia, MO 65201-3730

573-874-1710
800-542-1673
FAX 800-442-9509
http://www.hes-inc.com
e-mail: info@hes-inc.com

Stephen B McCarney Ed-D, Author
Tamara J Arthaud PhD, Co-Author

The Learning Disability Evaluation Scale - Renormed Second Edition (LDES-R2) was developed to enable instructional personnel to document those performance behaviors most characteristic of learning disabilities in children and youth. The LDES-R2 avoids the nature of a testing situation by relying on the performance observations of the classroom teacher or other instructional personnel. *$189.00*

4384 Oral Speech Mechanism Screening Examination
Pro-Ed
8700 Shoal Creek Blvd
Austin, TX 78757-6816

512-451-3246
800-897-3202
FAX 512-451-8542
http://www.proedinc.com
e-mail: info@proedinc.com

Donald D Hammill, Owner
Kenneth St Louis, Author
Dennis Ruscello, Co-Author
Provides an efficient, quick, and reliable method to examine the oral speech mechanism of all types of speech, language, and related disorders where oral structure and function are of concern. *$105.00*

4385 Peabody Picture Vocabulary Test
5601 Green Valley Dr
Bloomington, MN 55437-1099

800-627-7271
FAX 800-232-1223
http://www.pearsonassessments.com
e-mail: clinicalcustomersupport@pearson.com

Lloyd M Dunn, Author
Leota M Dunn, Co-Author
Doug Kubach, Group President & CEO
A wide-range measure of receptive vocabulary for standard English, and a screening test of verbal ability.

4386 Peabody Picture Vocabulary Test: Fourth Edition
Pearson Assessments
PO Box 1416
Minneapolis, MN 55440-1416

800-627-7271
FAX 800-232-1223
http://www.pearsonassessments.com
e-mail: clinicalcustomersupport@pearson.com

Karen Dahlen, Associate Director
Matt Keller, Marketing Manager
Lisa Dunttam, Development Assistant
A wide range measure of receptive vocabulary for standard English and screen of verbal ability. *$379.99*

4387 Preschool Motor Speech Evaluation & Intervention
Speech Bin
PO Box 922668
Norcross, GA 30010-2668

800-850-8602
FAX 800-845-1535
http://www.speechbin.com
e-mail: info@speechbin.com

Shane Peters, Product Coordinator
Jan Binney, Owner
Andy Roussey, New Product Development Contact
This comprehensive criterion-based assessment tool differentiates motor-based speech disorders from those of phonology and determines if speech difficulties of children 18 months to six years old are characteristic of: oral nonverbal apraxia; dysarthria; developmental verbal dyspraxia; hypersensitivity; differences in tone and hyposensitivity. Item number J322. *$59.00*

4388 Receptive One-Word Picture Vocabulary Test
Speech Bin
PO Box 922668
Norcross, GA 30010-2668

800-850-8602
FAX 800-845-1535
http://www.speechbin.com
e-mail: info@speechbin.com

Rick Brownell, Author
Shane Peters, Product Coordinator
Jan Binney, Owner
Andy Roussey, New Product Development Contact
This administered, untimed measure assesses the vocabulary comprehension of 0-2 through 11-18 years. New full-color test pictures are easy to recognize; many new test items have been added. It is ideal for children unable or reluctant to speak because only a gestural response is required. *$140.00*

4389   Receptive-Expressive Emergent Language Tests
Pro-Ed
8700 Shoal Creek Blvd
Austin, TX 78757-6816

512-451-3246
800-897-3202
FAX 512-451-8542
http://www.proedinc.com
e-mail: info@proedinc.com

Donald D Hammill, Owner
Kenneth Bzoch, Author
Richard League, Co-Author
Designed to use with at-risk infants and toddlers to provide a multidimensional analysis of emergency language skills. *$104.00*

4390   Say and Sign Language Program
Slosson Educational Publications
538 Buffalo Rd
East Aurora, NY 14052

716-652-0930
888-756-7766
FAX 800-655-3840
http://www.slosson.com
e-mail: slosson@slosson.com

Roger Hoffmann, Author
John H Slosson, Vice President
Dr. Georgina Moynihan, Tech Support
Addresses articulation skills, speech production, basic sign language skills, and finger spelling. *$71.50*

4391   Sequenced Inventory of Communication Development (SICD)
Speech Bin
PO Box 922668
Norcross, GA 30010-2668

800-850-8602
FAX 800-845-1535
http://www.speechbin.com
e-mail: info@speechbin.com

Shane Peters, Product Coordinator
Jan Binney, Owner
Andy Roussey, New Product Development Contact
SICD uses appealing toys to assess communication skills of children at all levels of ability, including those with impaired hearing or vision. SICD looks at child and environment, measuring receptive and expressive language. Item number W710. *$395.00*

4392   Skills Assessments
PO Box 690789
Orlando, FL 32819-789

407-345-3800
800-531-5015
FAX 800-269-5232
http://www.steck-vaughn.com
e-mail: info@steck-vaughn.com

Connie Alden, Vice President
Michael Ruecker, Vice President

This handy, all-in-one resource helps identify students strengths and weaknesses in order to determine appropriate instructional levels in each of five subjects areas: reading; language arts; math; science; and social studies. Assessments are identified by subtopics in each subject.

4393   Slosson Intelligence Test
Slosson Educational Publications, Inc.
538 Buffalo Rd
East Aurora, NY 14052

716-652-0930
888-756-7766
FAX 800-655-3840
http://www.slosson.com
e-mail: slosson@slosson.com

Steven Slosson, President
John H Slosson, Vice President
Dr. Georgina Moynihan, Tech Support

A quick and reliable individual screening test of Crystallized Verbal Intelligence. Tests include SIT-R3: Slosson Intelligence Test, Rev. - Third Edition; SORT-R3: Slosson Oral Reading Test, Rev. - Third Edition; S-VMPT: Slosson Visual Motor Performance Test; EASYOT: Educational Assessment of School Youth for Occupational Therapists. *$147.00*

4394   Slosson Intelligence Test Primary
Slosson Educational Publications
538 Buffalo Rd
East Aurora, NY 14052

716-652-0930
888-756-7766
FAX 716-655-3840
http://www.slosson.com
e-mail: slosson@slosson.com

Steven Slosson, President
Bradley Erford, Author
Gary Vitali, Co-Author
Designed to facilitate the screening identification of children at risk of educational failure. Provides a quick estimate of mental ability to identify children who may be appropriate candidates for deeper testing services. *$ 168.00*

4395   Stuttering Severity Instrument for Children and Adults
Pro-Ed
8700 Shoal Creek Blvd
Austin, TX 78757-6816

512-451-3246
800-897-3202
FAX 512-451-8542
http://www.proedinc.com
e-mail: info@proedinc.com

Donald D Hammill, Owner
Glyndon Riley, Author

With these easily administered tools you can determine whether to schedule a child for therapy using the Stuttering Prediction Instrument or to evaluate the effects of treatment using the Stuttering Severity Instrument. *$114.00*

4396   Test for Auditory Comprehension of Language: TACL-3
Speech Bin
PO Box 922668
Norcross, GA 30010-2668

800-850-8602
FAX 800-845-1535
http://www.speechbin.com
e-mail: info@speechbin.com

Shane Peters, Product Coordinator
Jan Binney, Owner
Andy Roussey, New Product Development Contact
The newly revised TACL-3 evaluates the 0-3 to 9-11-year old's understanding of spoken language in three subtests: Vocabulary, Grammatical Morphemes and Elaborated Phrases and Sentences. Each test item is a word or sentence read aloud by the examiner; the child responds by pointing to one of three pictures. Item number P792. *$261.00*

4397   Test of Adolescent & Adult Language: TOAL-3
Pro-Ed
8700 Shoal Creek Blvd
Austin, TX 78757-6816

512-451-3246
800-897-3202
FAX 512-451-8542
http://www.proedinc.com
e-mail: info@proedinc.com

Donald D Hammill, Owner/Author
Virginia Brown, Co-Author
Stephen Larson, Co-Author
This test is a measure of receptive and expressive language skills. In this revision easier items were added to the subtests, making them more appropriate for testing disabled students. *$202.00*

4398   Test of Auditory Reasoning & Processing Skills: TARPS

Speech Bin
PO Box 922668
Norcross, GA 30010-2668

800-850-8602
FAX 800-845-1535
http://www.speechbin.com
e-mail: info@speechbin.com

Morrison Gardner, Author
Shane Peters, Product Coordinator
Jan Binney, Owner
Andy Roussey, New Product Development Contact
TARPS assesses how 5-14 year old children understand, interpret, draw conclusions, and make inferences from auditorily presented stimuli. It tests their ability to think, understand, reason, and make sense of what they hear. Item number H787. *$64.00*

4399   Test of Auditory-Perceptual Skills: Upper TAPS-UL

Speech Bin
PO Box 922668
Norcross, GA 30010-2668

800-850-8602
FAX 800-845-1535
http://www.speechbin.com
e-mail: info@speechbin.com

Wayne Hresko, Shelley Herron, Pamela Peak, Author
Shane Peters, Product Coordinator
Jan Binney, Owner
Andy Roussey, New Product Development Contact
This highly respected, well-normed test evaluates a 13-18 year old's ability to perceive auditory stimuli and helps you diagnose auditory disorders in just 15-20 minutes. TAPS: UL measures the auditory perceptual skills of processing, word and sequential memory, interpretation of oral directions, and discrimination. Item number H769. *$95.00*

4400   Test of Early Language Development

Pro-Ed, Inc.
8700 Shoal Creek Blvd
Austin, TX 78757-6897

512-451-3246
800-897-3202
FAX 800-397-7633
http://www.proedinc.com
e-mail: info@proedinc.com

Wayne P Hresko, Author

4401   Test of Early Language Development: TELD-3

Pro-Ed, Inc.
8700 Shoal Creek Blvd
Austin, TX 78757-6897

512-451-3246
800-897-3202
FAX 800-397-7633
http://www.proedinc.com
e-mail: info@proedinc.com

Donald D Hammill, President/Author
Wayne Hresko, Co-Author
Kim Reid, Co-Author
An individually administered test of spoken language abilities. This test fills the need for a well-constructed, standardized instrument, based on a current theory, that can be used to assess spoken language skills at early ages. Now including scores for receptive language and expressive language subtests. Administration Time: 20 minutes. *$295.00*

4402   Test of Early Written Language

Pro-Ed
8700 Shoal Creek Blvd
Austin, TX 78757-6816

512-451-3246
800-897-3202
FAX 512-451-8542
http://www.proedinc.com
e-mail: info@proedinc.com

Donald D Hammill, Owner
Shelley Herron, Author
Wayne Hresko, Co-Author

Measures the merging written language skills of young children and is especially useful in identifying mildy disabled students. *$197.00*

4403   Test of Written Language: TOWL-3

Pro-Ed
8700 Shoal Creek Blvd
Austin, TX 78757-6816

512-451-3246
800-897-3202
FAX 512-451-8542
http://www.proedinc.com
e-mail: info@proedinc.com

Donald D Hammill, Owner/Author
Stephen Larson, Co-Author

Offers a measure of written language skills to identify students who need help improving their writing skills. Administration Time: 65 minutes. *$217.00*

4404   Test of Written Spelling

Pro-Ed
8700 Shoal Creek Blvd
Austin, TX 78757-6816

512-451-3246
800-897-3202
FAX 512-451-8542
http://www.proedinc.com
e-mail: info@proedinc.com

Donald D Hammill, Owner/Author
Stephen Larsen, Co-Author
Louisa Cook Moats, Co-Author
Assesses students' ability to spell words whose spellings are readily predictable in sound-letter patterns, words whose spellings are less predictable and both types of words considered together. *$88.00*

4405   Testing & Remediating Auditory Processing (TRAP)

Speech Bin
PO Box 922668
Norcross, GA 30010-2668

800-850-8602
FAX 800-845-1535
http://www.speechbin.com
e-mail: info@speechbin.com

Lynn Baron Berk, Author
Shane Peters, Product Coordinator
Jan Binney, Owner
Andy Roussey, New Product Development Contact
TRAP gives you an easy-to-implement program to assess and treat school-age auditory processing problems. It gives you two major components: Screening Test of Auditoring Processing Skills that identifies children at risk due to auditory processing deficits; and Remediating Auditory Processing Skills that presents interactional stories, sequence pictures, and illustrated activities. Item number 1233. *$38.00*

4406   Voice Assessment Protocol for Children and Adults

Pro-Ed
8700 Shoal Creek Blvd
Austin, TX 78757-6816

512-451-3246
800-897-3202
FAX 512-451-8542
http://www.proedinc.com
e-mail: info@proedinc.com

Donald D Hammill, Owner
Rebekah Pindzola, Author

Easily guides the speech pathologist through a systematic evaluation of vocal pitch, loudness, quality, breath features and rate/rhythm. *$78.00*

Visual & Motor Skills

4407 **BRIGANCE Inventory of Early Development-II**
Curriculum Associates
PO Box 2001
North Billerica, MA 01862-901   978-667-8000
                                        800-225-0248
                                     FAX 800-366-1158
            http://www.curriculumassociates.com
                   e-mail: info@CAinc.com
Albert H Brigance, Author
Frank Ferguson, Chairman
Dave Caron, Chief Financial Officer
The Inventory of Early Development simplifies and combines the assessment, diagnostic, recordkeeping, and instructional planning process, and it encourages communication between teachers and parents.

4408 **Benton Visual Retention Test**
Pearson Assessments
PO Box 1416
Minneapolis, MN 55440-1416
                                        800-627-7271
                                     FAX 800-232-1223
            http://www.pearsonassessments.com
       e-mail: clinicalcustomersupport@pearson.com
Abigail Benton Sivan, Author
Matt Keller, Marketing Manager
Doug Kubach, Group President & CEO
Assess visual perception, memory, visoconstructive abilities. Test administration 15-20 minutes. *$199.00*

4409 **Boston Diagnostic Aphasia Exam**
Speech Bin
PO Box 922668
Norcross, GA 30010-2668
                                        800-850-8602
                                     FAX 800-845-1535
                http://www.speechbin.com
              e-mail: info@speechbin.com
Harold Goodglass, Edith Kaplan, Barbara Barresi, Author
Jan Binney, Owner
Shane Peters, Product Coordinator
Andy Roussey, New Product Development Contact
BDAE-3 now gives you an instructive 90-minute video plus two separate forms of the test. Item number L235. *$150.00*

4410 **Developmental Test of Visual Perception (D TVP-2)**
Pro-Ed
8700 Shoal Creek Blvd
Austin, TX 78757-6816   512-451-3246
                                800-897-3202
                             FAX 512-451-8542
               http://www.proedinc.com
              e-mail: info@proedinc.com
Donald D Hammill, Owner/Author
Nils Pearson, Co-Author
Judith Voress, Co-Author
A test that measures both visual perception and visual-motor integration skills, has eight subtests, is based on updated theories of visual perceptual development, and can be administered to individuals in 45 minutes. *$207.00*

4411 **Differential Test of Conduct and Emotional Problems**
Slosson Educational Publications
538 Buffalo Rd
East Aurora, NY 14052   716-652-0930
                                888-756-7766
                             FAX 800-655-3840
                http://www.slosson.com
              e-mail: slosson@slosson.com
Steven Slosson, President
Edward Kelly, Author
Dr. Georgina Moynihan, Tech Support

Designed to address one of the most critical challenges in education and juvenile care. Administration of test is 15-20 minutes. *$120.75*

4412 **Educational Assessment of School Youth for Occupational Therapists**
Slosson Educational Publications
538 Buffalo Rd
East Aurora, NY 14052   716-652-0930
                                888-756-7766
                             FAX 800-655-3840
                http://www.slosson.com
              e-mail: slosson@slosson.com
Sharon Kenmotsu, Author
Katy Tressler, Co-Author
Dr. Georgina Moynihan, Tech Support
The E.A.S.Y. is a school-based occupational therapy assessment tool developed by occuaptional therapists. *$280.00*

4413 **Khan-Lewis Phonological Analysis: KLPA-2**
Pro-Ed
8700 Shoal Creek Blvd
Austin, TX 78757-6816   512-451-3246
                                800-897-3202
                             FAX 512-451-8542
               http://www.proedinc.com
              e-mail: info@proedinc.com
Donald D Hammill, President
Linda Klan, Author
Nancy Lewis, Co-Author
An in-depth measure of phonological processes for assessment and remediation planning. Administration Time: 10-30 minutes. *$144.00*

4414 **Peabody Developmental Motor Scales-2**
Speech Bin
PO Box 922668
Norcross, GA 30010-2668
                                        800-850-8602
                                     FAX 800-845-1535
                http://www.speechbin.com
              e-mail: info@speechbin.com
Shane Peters, Product Coordinator
Jan Binney, Owner
Andy Roussey, New Product Development Contact
PDMS-2 gives you in-depth standardized assessment of motor skills in children birth to six years. Subtests include: fine motor object manipulation; grasping; gross motor; locomotion; reflexes; visual-motor integration and stationary. Item number P624. *$43.00*

4415 **Perceptual Motor Development Series**
Therapro
225 Arlington St
Framingham, MA 01702-8773   508-872-9494
                                    800-257-5376
                                 FAX 508-875-2062
               http://www.theraproducts.com
              e-mail: info@theraproducts.com
Karen Conrad, Owner
Jack Capon, Author

Use these classroom tested movement education activities to assess motor strengths and weaknesses in preschool and early elementary grades or special education classes. The sequence of easily given tests and tasks requires minimal instruction time and your kids will find the activities to be interesting, challenging, and fun! Each book has 25-54 pages and costs $9.99 each. *$49.95*

4416 Phonic Reading Lessons
Academic Therapy Publications
20 Commercial Blvd
Novato, CA 94949-6120

415-883-3314
800-422-7249
FAX 888-287-9975
http://www.academictherapy.com
e-mail: sales@academictherapy.com

Jim Arena, President
Joanne Urban, Manager
Samuel Kirk, Author
A step-by-step program for teaching reading to children who failed to learn by conventional methods. Consistent sound-symbol relationships are presented and reinforced using a grapho-vocal method. A two book set (Book 1: Skills; Book 2: Practice). *$140.00*

ISBN 1-571284-68-6

4417 Preschool Motor Speech Evaluation & Intervention
Speech Bin
PO Box 922668
Norcross, GA 30010-2668

800-850-8602
FAX 800-845-1535
http://www.speechbin.com
e-mail: info@speechbin.com

Shane Peters, Product Coordinator
Jan Binney, Owner
Andy Roussey, New Product Development Contact
This comprehensive criterion-based assessment tool differentiates motor-based speech disorders from those of phonology and determines if speech difficulties of children 18 months to six years old are characteristic of: oral nonverbal apraxia; dysarthria; developmental verbal dyspraxia; hypersensitivity; differences in tone and hyposensitivity. Item number J322. *$59.00*

4418 Slosson Full Range Intelligence Test Kit
Slosson Educational Publications
538 Buffalo Rd
East Aurora, NY 14052

716-652-0930
888-756-7766
FAX 716-655-3840
http://www.slosson.com
e-mail: slosson@slosson.com

Steven Slosson, President
H Robert Vance, Author
Bob Algozzine, Co-Author
Intended to supplement the use of more extensive cognitive assessment instruments. Administration of test 25-45 minutes. *$175.00*

4419 Slosson Visual Motor Performance Test
Slosson Educational Publications
538 Buffalo Rd
East Aurora, NY 14052

716-652-0930
888-756-7766
FAX 716-655-3840
http://www.slosson.com
e-mail: slosson@slosson.com

Steven Slosson, President
Richard.L Slosson, Author
Dr. Georgina Moynihan, Tech Support
A test of visual motor integration in which individuals are asked to copy geometric figures increasing in complexity without the use of a ruler, compass or other aids. *$86.75*

4420 Test of Gross Motor Development
Pro-Ed
8700 Shoal Creek Blvd
Austin, TX 78757-6816

512-451-3246
800-897-3202
FAX 512-451-8542
http://www.proedinc.com
e-mail: info@proedinc.com

Donald D Hammill, Owner
Dale Urlich, Author

Assists you in identifying children who are significantly behind their peers in gross motor skill development and who should be eligible for special education services in phyiscal education. *$109.00*

4421 Test of Information Processing Skills
Academic Therapy Publications
20 Commercial Blvd
Novato, CA 94949-6120

415-883-3314
800-422-7249
FAX 888-287-9975
http://www.academictherapy.com
e-mail: sales@academictherapy.com

Jim Arena, President
Joanne Urban, Manager
Raymond Webster, Author
The TIPS (formerly The Learning Efficiency Test) provides a quick and accurate measure of a child or adult's information processing abilities, sequential and nonsequential, in both visual and auditory modalities. Additional subtests include Delayed Recall and Semantic Fluency. *$140.00*

ISBN 1-571284-68-6

4422 Visual Skills Appraisal
Academic Therapy Publications
20 Commercial Blvd
Novato, CA 94949-6120

415-883-3314
800-422-7249
FAX 888-287-9975
http://www.academictherapy.com
e-mail: sales@academictherapy.com

Jim Arena, President
Regina Richards, Author
Gary Oppenheim, Co-Author
This test identifies visual problems in children ages 5-9. Can be administered by an experienced examiner. Set includes manual, stimulus cards and test forms, design completion forms, and red/green glasses. *$100.00*

ISBN 0-878794-53-0

National Programs

4423 ACT Universal Testing
ACT
500 ACT Drive
P.O. Box 168
Iowa City, IA 52243-0168

319-337-1332
FAX 319-339-3021
TDD:319-337-1701
http://www.act.org
e-mail: sandy.schlote@act.org

Richard Ferguson, President

To help individuals and organizations make informed decisions about education and work. We provide information for life's transitions.

4424 American College Testing Program
ACT Universal Testing
500 ACT Drive
P.O. Box 168
Iowa City, IA 52243-0168

319-337-1000
FAX 319-339-3021
TDD:319-337-1701
http://www.act.org
e-mail: sandy.schlote@act.org

Richard L Ferguson, President

ACT provides a broad array of assessment, information, research and program management solutions pertaining to education and workforce development.

4425 Center For Accessible Technology
Alliance For Technology Access
2547 8th Street
12-A
Berkeley, CA 94710-2572

510-841-3224
FAX 510-841-7956
http://www.cforat.org
e-mail: info@cforat.orgg

Sharon Hall, Executive Director
Libbie Butler, Program Coordinator

A national organization dedicated to providing access to technology for people with disabilities through its coalition of 39 community-based resource centers in 28 states and in the Virgin Islands. Each center provides information, awareness, and training for professionals and provides guided problem solving and technical assistance for individuals with disabilities and family members.

4426 Division on Career Development
Council for Exceptional Children
1110 N. Glebe Road
Suite 300
Arlington, VA 22201-5704

888-232-7733
FAX 703-264-9494
TTY: 866-915-5000
http://www.cec.sped.org
e-mail: service@ces.sped.org

Liz Martinez, Director

Focuses on the career development of individuals with disabilities and/or who are gifted and their transition from school to adult life. Members include professionals and others interested in career development and transition for individuals with any exception at any age. Members receive a journal twice yearly and newsletter three times per year.

4427 Independent Living Research Utilization Program
2323 S. Shepherd
Suite 1000
Houston, TX 77019-7031

713-520-0232
FAX 713-520-5785
TTY: 713-520-0232
http://www.bcm.edu
e-mail: ilru@ilru.org

Lex Frieden, Director
Laurie Redd, Executive Director

A national resource center for information, training, research and technical assistance in independent living; produces and disseminates materials, develops and conducts training and publishes a monthly newsletter; provides a listing of Statewide Independent Living Councils (SILCS) in each state.

4428 Job Accommodation Network (JAN)
West Virginia University
PO Box 6080
Morgantown, WV 26506-6080

800-526-7234
FAX 304-293-5407
TDD:877-781-9403
http://www.jan.wvu.edu
e-mail: jan@jan.wvu.edu

Anne Hirsh, Co-Director

Source of free, expert, and confidential guidance on workplace accomodations and disability employment issues. Working toward practical solutions that benefit both employer and employee, helps people with disabilities enhance their employability and shows employers how to capitalize on the value and talent that people with disabilities add to the workplace.

4429 National Federation of the Blind
200 E. Wells St. At Jernigan Place
Baltimore, MD 21230-4914

410-659-9314
FAX 410-685-5653
http://www.nfb.org
e-mail: nfb@nfb.org

Marc Maurer, President
Patricia Maurer, Community Relations Director

Provides education, information, literature and publications to the public about blindness. The National Federation of the Blind also provides programs and jobs to blind individuals, which helps them build self-confidence and self-respect.

4430 U.S. Department of Education: Office of Vocational & Adult Education
400 Maryland Avenue, SW
Lyndon Baines Johnson, Dept Ed. Bldg.
Washington, DC 20202-0001

202-401-1576
800-872-5327
http://www.ed.gov
e-mail: ovae@ed.gov

John Sherrod, Executive Director

These agencies can provide job training, counseling, financial assistance, and employment placement to individuals who meet eligibility criteria.

Publications

4431 ADD on the Job
Taylor Publishing
7211 Circle S Road
Austin, TX 78745

512-444-0571
800-225-3687
FAX 512-440-2160
http://www.taylorpublishing.com
e-mail: Yearbooks@balfour.com

Lynn Weiss PhD, Author

Practical, sensitive advice for the ADD employee, his boss, and his co-workers. The book suggests advantages that the ADD worker has, how to find the right job, and how to keep it. Employers and co-workers will learn what to expect from fellow workers with ADD and the most effective ways to work with them.

232 pages Paperback
ISBN 0-878339-17-5

4432 Ability Magazine
Ability Awareness
PO Box 10878
Costa Mesa, CA 10878   949-854-8700
FAX 949-548-5966
http://www.abilitymagazine.com
e-mail: editorial@abilitymagazine.com
Chet Cooper, President

Brings disabilities into mainstream America. By interviewing high profile personalities such as President Clinton, Elizabeth Taylor, Mary Tyler Moore, Richard Pryor, Jane Seymour and many more, Ability Magazine is able to bring articles to the public's attention that may in the past have gone unnoticed.

80+ pages Bimonthly

4433 Current Developments in Employment and Training
National Governors Association
Ste 267
444 N Capitol St NW
Washington, DC 20001-1512   202-624-5300
FAX 202-624-5313
http://www.nga.org
e-mail: mjensen@nga.org
Martin Jensen, Editor
Dan Crippen, Executive Director
Barry Anderson, Deputy Director
Highlights issues and areas of interest related to employment and training.
Bimonthly

4434 Fundamentals of Job Placement
RPM Press
PO Box 31483
Tucson, AZ 85751-1483   520-886-1990
888-810-1990
FAX 520-886-1990
http://www.rpmpress.com
e-mail: pmccray@theriver.com
James Costello, Author
Paul McCray, President

Provides step-by-step guidance for educators, special counselors and vocational rehabilitation personnel on how to develop job placement opportunities for special needs students and adults.

4435 Fundamentals of Vocational Assessment
RPM Press
PO Box 31483
Tucson, AZ 85751-1483   520-886-1990
888-810-1990
FAX 520-866-1900
http://www.rpmpress.com
e-mail: pmccray@theriver.com
Paul McCray, President

Provides step-by-step guidance for educators, counselors and vocational rehabilitation personnel on how to conduct professional vocational assessments of special needs students.

4436 Handbook for Developing Community Based Employment
RPM Press
PO Box 31483
Tucson, AZ 85751-1483   520-886-1990
888-810-1990
FAX 520-866-1990
http://www.rpmpress.com
e-mail: pmccray@theriver.com
Paul McCray, President

Provides step-by-step guidance for educators and vocational rehabilitation personnel on how to develop community-based employment training programs for severely challenged workers.

4437 JOBS V
PESCO International
21 Paulding St
Pleasantville, NY 10570-3108   914-769-4266
800-431-2016
FAX 914-769-2970
http://www.pesco.org
e-mail: pesco@pesco.org
Joseph Kass, President

A software program matching people with jobs, training, employment and local employers. Provides job outlooks for the next five years.

4438 Job Access
Ability Awareness
PO Box 10878
Costa Mesa, CA 92627-4512   949-548-1986
FAX 949-548-5966
TDD:949-548-5966
http://www.jobaccess.org
e-mail: custserv@jobtarget.com
Chet Cooper, President

Job Access, a program of ability awareness, is an internet driven system dedicated to employ qualified people with disabilities. Employers can list job postings and review our resume bank. People with disabilities seeking employment can also search for jobs.

4439 Job Accommodation Handbook
RPM Press
PO Box 31483
Tucson, AZ 85751-1483   520-886-1990
888-810-1990
FAX 520-866-1990
http://www.rpmpress.com
e-mail: pmccray@theriver.com
Paul McCray, President

Provides how-to-do-it for counselors, job placement specialists, educators and others on how to modify jobs for special needs workers.

4440 Life Centered Career Education: Assessment Batteries
Council for Exceptional Children
2900 Crystal Drive
Suite 1000
Arlington, VA 22202-3557   703-620-3660
866-509-0218
FAX 703-264-9494
TTY: 703-264-5000
http://www.cec.sped.org
e-mail: service@ces.sped.org
Donn E Brolin, Author

The LCCE Batteries are curriculum-based assessment instruments designed to measure the career education knowledge and skills of regular and special education students. There are two alternative forms of a Knowledge Battery and two forms of the Performance Batteries. These assessment tools can be combined with instruction to determine the instructional goals most appropriate for a particular student.

827 pages

4441 National Governors Association Newsletter
Ste 267
444 N Capitol St NW
Washington, DC 20001-1512   202-624-5300
FAX 202-624-5313
http://www.nga.org
e-mail: mjensen@nga.org
Raymond Scheppach, Editor
Dan Crippen, Executive Director
Barry Anderson, Deputy Director
Highlights issues and areas of interest related to employment and training.
Bimonthly

4442 PWI Profile
Goodwill Industries of America
15810 Indianola Dr
Derwood, MD 20855-2674   301-530-6500
800-GOODWILL
http://www.goodwill.org
e-mail: contactus@goodwill.org
David Hadani, Director
Rev. Edgar J Helms, Founder

Newsletter that deals with employment of persons with disabilities.

4443 School to Adult Life Transition Bibliography
Special Education Resource Center
25 Industrial Park Rd
Middletown, CT 06457-1516   860-632-1485
FAX 860-632-8870
http://www.ctserc.org
e-mail: jlebrrun@ctserc.org
Jen Lebrun, Director
Marianne Kirner, Executive Director

A bibliography of references and resources.

4444 Self-Supervision: A Career Tool for Audiologists, Clinical Series 10
American Speech-Language-Hearing Association
10801 Rockville Pike
N Bethesda, MD 20852-3226   301-897-5700
800-638-2255
FAX 301-897-7358
TDD:301-897-5700
http://www.asha.org
e-mail: jjanota@asha.org
Arlene Pietrarton, Executive Director
Shelly S. Chabon, PhD, President
Carolyn W. Higdon, EdD, CCC-SLP, VP for Finance
Describes concepts of supervision, defines and presents strategies for self-supervision, discusses supervisory accountability and covers issues of self-supervision within supervisor format.

4445 Succeeding in the Workplace
Ste 707
2700 Virginia Ave NW
Washington, DC 20037-1909   202-333-1713
FAX 202-333-1735
http://http://www.ldanatl.org
e-mail: lathamlaw@gmail.com
Peter S Latham JD, Director
Patricia Horan Latham JD, Director

Comprehensive review: understanding disabilities, how to find and get the right job, how to succeed on the job, strategies, job accommodations, legal rights and personal experiences.

4446 Tales from the Workplace
Ste 707
2700 Virginia Ave NW
Washington, DC 20037-1909   202-333-1713
FAX 202-333-1735
e-mail: lathamlaw@gmail.com

Peter S Latham JD, Director
Patricia Horan Latham JD, Director

Easy to read. Explores through stories: What is the right job match? Should I disclose my disability? What are the signs of job trouble?

4447 Transition and Students with Learning Disabilities
Pro-Ed
8700 Shoal Creek Blvd
Austin, TX 78757-6816   512-451-3246
800-897-3202
FAX 512-451-8542
http://www.proedinc.com
e-mail: info@proedinc.com
Patton Blalock, Author
Donald D Hammill, Owner

Provides important information about academic, social and vocational planning for students with learning disabilities.

4448 Vocational Training and Employment of Autistic Adolescents
Charles C Thomas
2600 S 1st St
Springfield, IL 62704-4730   217-789-8980
800-258-8980
FAX 217-789-9130
http://www.ccthomas.com
e-mail: books@ccthomas.com
Michael P Thomas, President

Publisher of Education and Special Education books.

4449 Workforce Investment Quarterly
National Governor's Association (NGA)
Ste 267
444 N Capitol St NW
Washington, DC 20001-1512   202-624-5300
FAX 202-624-5313
http://www.nga.org
e-mail: info@nga.org
Dan Crippen, Executive Director
Barry Anderson, Deputy Director

Highlights issues and area interests related to employment and training. Contact NGA for more information.

Alabama

4450 Achievement Center
Easter Seals Of East Central Alabama
510 W Thomason Cir
Opelika, AL 36801-5499   334-745-3501
FAX 334-749-5808
http://www.achievement-center.org
e-mail: info@achievement-center.org
Thomas B. Whatley, Chairman

Provides vocational development and employment programs to developmentally and physically disabled individuals. The programs help individuals build self-esteem, self-confidence and helps to maximize their independent living skills.

4451 Easter Seals Alabama
5960 E Shirley Ln
Montgomery, AL 36117-1963   334-395-4489
800-388-7325
FAX 334-395-4492
http://www.alabama.easter-seals.org
e-mail: info@al.easterseals.comÿ
S.Lynne Stokley, CEO

Job training and employment services, senior community service employment program.

4452 Easter Seals Camp ASCCA
PO Box 21
Jacksons Gap, AL 36861-21   256-825-9226
                                     800-843-2267
                                FAX 256-825-8332
        http://www.alabama.easter-seals.org
               e-mail: matt@campascca.org
Matt Rickman, Director

Camp respite for adults and children, camperships, canoeing, day camping for adults, day camping for children, therapeutic horseback riding.

4453 Easter Seals Capilouto Center for the Deaf
5960 E Shirley Ln
Montgomery, AL 36117-1963   334-395-4489
                                     800-388-7325
                                FAX 334-395-4492
        http://www.alabama.easter-seals.org
             e-mail: info@al.easterseals.comÿ
S.Lynne Stokley, CEO

Job training and employment services, occupational skills training, job placement/competitive-supported employment, vocational evaluation/situation assessment, work adjustment.

4454 Easter Seals Disability Services
2448 Gordon Smith Dr
Mobile, AL 36617-2319   251-471-1581
                                    800-411-0068
                               FAX 251-476-4303
                               TTY: 334-872-8421
        http://www.alabama.easterseals.org
             e-mail: info@al.easterseals.comÿ
S.Lynne Stokley, CEO

Easter Seals has been helping individuals with disabilities and special needs, and their families, live better lives for more than 80 years. Whether helping someone improve physical mobility, return to work or simply gain greater independence for everyday living, Easter Seals offers a variety of services to help people with disabilities address life's challenges and achieve personal goals.

4455 Easter Seals Opportunity Center
United Way
217 West 13th St
Anniston, AL 36202-8407   256-820-9960
                               FAX 256-820-9592
        http://www.alabama.easter-seals.org
          e-mail: mikenancyoppcen@aol.com
Barry Cavan, President

Job training and employment services, occupational skills training, job placement/competitive-supported employment, vocational evaluation/situation assessment, work adjustment.

4456 Easter Seals Rehabilitation Center: Northwest Alabama

1450 Avalon Ave
Muscle Shoals, AL 35661-3110   256-381-1110
                               FAX 256-314-5101
        http://www.alabama.easter-seals.org
             e-mail: info@al.easterseals.comÿ
Shiella Phillips, Director

Job training and employment services, occupational skills training, job placement/competitive-supported employment, vocational evaluation/situation assessment, work services.

4457 Easter Seals: West Alabama
1110 Sixth Avenue East
Tuscaloosa, AL 35401-7446   205-759-1211
                                     800-726-1216
                                FAX 205-349-1162
        http://www.alabama.easter-seals.org
             e-mail: info@al.easterseals.comÿ
Jennifer Goode Davis, Director of Community Relations
Sherri Presley-Dumas, Program Coordinator
Alan Knox, Director of Vocational Services
Job training and employment services, occupational skills training, job placement/competitive-supported employment, vocational evaluation/situation assessment, work adjustment.

4458 Good Will Easter Seals
2448 Gordon Smith Dr
Mobile, AL 36617-2319   251-471-1581
                                    800-411-0068
                               FAX 251-476-4303
                               TTY: 800-411-0068
        http://www.alabama.easter-seals.org
Frank Harkins, President

Job training and employment services, occupational skills training, job placement/competitive-supported employment, vocational evaluation/situation assessment, work adjustment.

4459 State Vocational Rehabilitation Agency
Alabama Dept Of Rehabilitation Services
602 South Lawrence Street
Montgomery, AL 36104   334-293-7500
                                    800-441-7607
                               FAX 334-293-7383
                               TDD:334-613-2249
          http://www.rehab.state.al.us
          e-mail: sshivers@rehab.state.al.us
Steve Shivers, Director

State vocational rehabilitation agencies provide direct services to persons with disabilities, including persons with learning disabilities. The services may include evaluation and diagnosis; counseling, guidance, and referral services; vocational and other training services; transportation to rehabilitation services; and assistive devices.

4460 Workforce Development Division
Alabama Dept of Economic & Community Affairs
P.O.Box 5690
Montgomery, AL 36103-5690   334-242-5100
                               FAX 334-242-5099
          http://www.adeca.state.al.us
          e-mail: stevew@adeca.state.al.us
Tim Alford, Executive Director

Customer focused to help Americans access the tools they need to manage their careers through information and high quality services and to help US companies find skilled workers. Alabama's Career Center System is a network of one-stop centers designed to offer these services. These centers are co-located or electronically linked to provide streamlined services.

Alaska

4461 Alaska Department Of Labor & Workforce Development
Division Of Vocational Rehabilitation
801 W. 10th Street
Suite A
Juneau, AK 99801-1894   907-465-2814
                                    800-478-2815
                               FAX 907-465-2856
          http://www.labor.state.ak.us
Cheryl Walsh, Director

Services and programs for people with disabilities.

Arizona

4462   Arizona Vocational Rehabilitation
Arizona Department of Economic Security
3221 N. 16th Street
Suite 200
Phoenix, AZ 85016-7159   602-266-6752
                                 FAX 602-241-7158
                                 TTY: 602-241-1048
                                 http://www.azdes.gov
Michael Scione, Program Manager
Jon Ellerston, Assistant Program Manager

Programs provide a variety of specialized services for individuals with physical or mental disabilities that create barriers to employment or independent living. RSA offers three major service programs and several specialized programs/services.

4463   Rehabilitation Services Administration
Arizona Dept Of Economic Security
3221 N. 16th Street
Suite 200
Phoenix, AZ 85016-7159   602-266-6752
                                 FAX 602-241-7158
                                 TTY: 602-241-1048
                                 http://www.azdes.gov
                                 e-mail: azrsa@azdes.gov
Katharine Levandowsky, Director

The mission of the Rehabilitation Services Administration (RSA) is to work with individuals with disabilities to achieve increased independence and/or gainful employment through the provision of comprehensive rehabilitative and employment support services in a partnership with all stakeholders.

Arkansas

4464   Arkansas Department of Career Education
Luther Hardin Building
Three Capitol Mall
Little Rock, AR 72201-1005   501-682-1500
                                 FAX 501-682-1509
                                 http://www.arkansas.gov
Bill Walker, Jr., Director

Formerly the Dept. of Workforce Education, the Arkansas Dept. of Career Education (ACE) provides many resources to serve the educational needs of Arkansas individuals living with disabilities.

4465   Arkansas Department of Health & Human Services: Division of Developmental Disabilities
Donaghey Plaza North
P.O. Box 1437, Slot N505
Little Rock, AR 72203-1437   501-683-0870
                                 http://www.arkansas.gov
James Green PhD, Director

The mission of the Division of Developmental Disabilities Services is to provide a variety of supports to improve the quality of life for individuals with mental retardation, autism, epilepsy, cerebral palsy or other conditions that cause a person to function as if they had a mental impairment.

4466   Arkansas Employment Security Department: Office of Employment & Training Services
425 W. Capital Avenue
Suite 1620
Little Rock, AR 72201   501-324-8900
                                 http://www.arkansas.gov
Artee Williams, Director

Employment related services that contribute to the economic stability of Arkansa and its citizens. These services are provided to employers, the workforce and the general public.

4467   Arkansas Rehabilitation Services
26 Corporate Hill Dr
Little Rock, AR 72205-4538   501-686-2800
                                 FAX 501-686-9418
                                 TDD:501-686-9686
                                 http://www.arsinfo.org
                                 e-mail: ssholt@ars.state.ar.us
Robert Sanders, Director

For persons who are clients of Arkansas Rehabilitation Services, individual psychological/educational evaluations and college preparatory training are provided if approved by vocational rehabilitation counselor.

4468   Department of Human Services: Division of Developmental Disabilities Services
P.O.Box 1437
N501
Little Rock, AR 72203-1437   501-682-8665
                                 FAX 501-682-8380
                                 TDD:501-682-1332
                                 http://www.state.ar.us
Dr. Charlie Green, Director

Offers a wide range of services and supports to Arkansans with developmental disabilities and their families.

4469   Easter Seals Adult Services Center
Easter Seals Arkansas
11801 Fairview Rd
Little Rock, AR 72212-2406   501-221-1063
                                 877-221-8400
                                 FAX 501-227-7180
                                 TTY: 501-221-8424
                                 http://www.ar.easter-seals.org
                                 e-mail: info@easterseals.com
Lauren Zilk, President

Easter Seals Arkansas helps adults with disabilities gain greater independence through vocational and independent living programs.

4470   Office For The Deaf And Hearing Impaired
Arkansas Rehabilitation Services
26 Corporate Hill Drive
Little Rock, AR 72205   501-324-9521
                                 FAX 501-324-9579
                                 TDD:501-324-9520
                                 http://www.arsinfo.org
                                 e-mail: david.mcdonald@arkansas.gov
John Wyvill, Director

Providing opportunities for individuals with hearing impairment to work and have productive and independent lives.

4471   State Vocational Rehabilitation Agency of Arkansas
ARS, Vocational & Technical Education Division
P.O.Box 3781
Little Rock, AR 72203-3781   501-296-1600
                                 800-330-0632
                                 FAX 501-296-1655
                                 TDD:501-296-1669
                                 http://www.arsinfo.org
Bill Walker, Jr., Director

Provides direct services to persons with disabilities, including persons with learning disabilities. The services may include evaluation and diagnosis, counseling, guidance, and referral services, vocational and other training services, transportation to rehabilitation services, and assistive devices. Offering opportunities for individuals with disabilities to lead productive and independent lives.

4472   Workforce Investment Board
Arkansas State Employment Board
5401 S. University
Little Rock, AR 72209   501-682-8030
                                      http://www.arkansas.gov
Cindy Verner, Division Chief

Operates workforce centers that offer locally developed and operated services linking employers and jobseekers through a statewide delivery system. Conveinient centers are designed to eliminate the need to visit different locations. The centers integrate multiple workforce development programs into a single system, making the resources much more accessible and user friendly to jobseekers as well as expanding services to employers.

California

4473   Adult Education
California Department of Education
Ste 400
1430 N St
Sacramento, CA 95814-5901   916-319-0800
                                     FAX 916-319-0100
                                     http://www.cde.ca.gov
                                     e-mail: scheduler@cde.ca.gov
Jack O'Connell, Director

Elementary basic skills and tutor/literacy training are offered on or off site using language masters, audiocassettes, videos and computers with internet access. Workplace literacy training will also be provided, with groups of students physically coming into the Center or hooking up to the Center from their workplace by borrowing materials or going online. In the latter case, instructors will meet with students at the work site on a regular schedule for evaluation and consultation.

4474   California Department of Education
1430 N St
Sacramento, CA 95814-5901   916-319-0800
                                     800-331-6316
                                     TTY: 916-445-4556
                                     http://www.cde.ca.gov
                                     e-mail: gedoffic@cde.ca.gov
Nancy Edmunds, Program Coordinator

Provides access to a general high school education by providing many local classes and testing services.

4475   California Department of Rehabilitation
California Health & Human Services Agency
721 Capitol Mall
P.O. Box 944222
Sacramento, CA 94244-2220   916-324-1313
                                     FAX 916-558-5807
                                     http://www.dor.ca.gov
                                     e-mail: externalaffairs@dor.ca.gov
Catherine Campisi PhD, Executive Director

California Department of Rehabilitation works in partnership with consumers and other stakeholders to provide services and advocacy resulting in employment, independent living and equality for individuals with disabilities.

4476   California Employment Development Department
800 Capitol Mall
Sacramento, CA 95814-4807   916-654-8210
                                     FAX 916-657-5294
                                     TTY: 800-815-9387
                                     http://www.edd.ca.gov
                                     e-mail: phenning@edd.ca.gov
Patrick Henning, Director

The California Employment Development Department (EDD) offers a wide variety of services to millions of Californians under the Job Service, Unemployment Insurance, Disability Insurance, Workforce Investment, and Labor Market Information programs.

4477   Easter Seals Central California
9010 Soquel Dr
Aptos, CA 95003-4002   831-684-2166
                                     FAX 831-684-1018
                                     TTY: 831-684-1054
                                     http://www.centralcal.easter-seals.org
                                     e-mail: donna@es-cc.org
Bruce Hinman, President

Recreational services for adults, residential camping programs.

4478   Easter Seals Southern California
1801 E. Edinger Avenue
Suite 190
Santa Ana, CA 92705   714-834-1111
                                     FAX 714-934-1128
                                     http://www.southerncal.easterseals.com
Mark Whitley, President

Easter Seals provides job training and volunteer opportunities to those individuals with disabilities.

4479   Easter Seals Superior California
3205 Hurley Way
Sacramento, CA 95864-3853   916-485-6711
                                     888-887-3257
                                     FAX 916-485-2653
                                     http://www.superiorca.easterseals.com
                                     e-mail: info@easterseals-superiorca.org
Kathie Wright, President

Job training and employment services, occupational skills training, job placement/competitive-support employment, vocational evaluation/situational assessment and work adjustment.

4480   Easter Seals: Pacoima
Eastern Seals Southern California
12510 Van Nuys Blvd
Ste 103
Pacoima, CA 91331   818-996-9902
                                     800-996-6302
                                     FAX 818-975-8299
                                     http://www.essc.org
                                     e-mail: paula.pompa-craven@essc.org
Mark Whitley, President/CEO
Lupe Trevizo, Regional VP Day Programs

Job training and employment services, occupational skills training, job placement/competitive-support employment, vocational evaluation/situational assessment and work adjustment.

4481   Easter Seals: Redondo Beach
Ste 201
700 N Pacific Coast Hwy
Redondo Beach, CA 90277-2147   310-376-3445
                                     800-404-3445
                                     FAX 310-376-5567
                                     http://http://www.easterseals.com
                                     e-mail: dee.prescott@cssc.org
Dee Prescott, Regional VP
Mark Whitley, President

Job training and employment services, occupational skills training, job placement/competitive-support employment, vocational evaluation/situational assessment and work adjustment.

4482 **WorkFirst**
Easter Seals Of Southern California
Ste C
11110 Artesia Blvd
Cerritos, CA 90703-2546
562-860-7270
877-855-2279
FAX 562-860-1680
http://www.workfirst.us
e-mail: dee.prescott@essc.org
Sandra Meredith, Executive Director

WorkFirst helps individuals with disabilities to find work and keep working in a job that is more suited to their talents. The program also helps those individuals who are looking to open a business of their own.

Colorado

4483 **Colorado Department of Human Services: Division for Developmental Disabilities**
1575 Sherman Street
Denver, CO 80203-3111
303-866-5700
FAX 303-866-4047
TDD:303-866-7471
http://www.cdhs.state.co.us
Karen L. Beye, Executive Director

A state office that provides leadership for the direction, funding and operation of community based services to people with developmental disabilities within Colorado.

4484 **Easter Seals Colorado**
2644 Alvarado Road
Empire, CO 80436
303-569-2333
FAX 303-569-3857
http://www.co.easterseals.com
e-mail: info@eastersealscolorado.org
Lynn Robinson, President
Kelly Housman, Program Director

Job training and employment services, occupational skills training, job placement/competitive-support employment, vocational evaluation/situational assessment and work adjustment.

4485 **Human Services: Division of Vocational**
1575 Sherman St
4th Fl
Denver, CO 80203-1702
303-866-4150
866-870-4595
FAX 303-866-4905
TDD:303-866-4150
http://www.dvrcolorado.com
e-mail: drew.little@state.co.us
Nancy Smith, Director

Assists individuals whose disabilities result in barriers to employment to succeed at work and live independently. Building partnerships to improve opportunities for safety, self-sufficiency and dignity for the people of Colorado.

Connecticut

4486 **Department of Social Services: Vocational Rehabilitation Program**
25 Sigourney Street
Hartford, CT 06106-5033
860-424-5241
800-842-1508
TDD:800-842-4524
http://www.ct.gov
e-mail: pgr.dss@ct.gov
John Galiette, Director
Brenda Moore, Executive Director

Provides services to people with most significant physical or mental disabilities to assist them in their effort to enter or maintain employment. The agency also oversees a statewide network of community based, consumer controlled, independent living centers that promote independence for people with disabilities.

4487 **Easter Seals Connecticut**
85 Jones Street
P.O. Box 198
Hebron, CT 06248-0100
860-228-9496
800-874-7687
FAX 860-228-2091
http://www.ct.easterseals.com
John Quinn, President

Easter Seals Connecticut creates solutions that change the lives of children and adults with disabilities or special needs, their families and communities.

4488 **Easter Seals Employment Industries**
Easter Seals Rehabilitation Center
122 Avenue of Industry
Waterbury, CT 06705-3901
203-236-0188
FAX 203-236-0183
http://www.eswct.com
e-mail: eswct@eswct.com
Ron Bourque, President

Job training, employment services, vocational evaluation/situational assessment and work services.

4489 **Easter Seals Fulfillment Enterprises Easter Seals Connecticut**
24 Stott Ave
Norwich, CT 06360-1508
860-859-4148
FAX 860-455-1372
http://www.ct.easterseals.com
Job training, employment services, vocational evaluation/situational assessment and work services.

4490 **Easter Seals Job Training And Placement Services**
Easter Seals Waterbury, Connecticut
22 Tompkins Street
Waterbury, CT 06708
203-754-5141
FAX 203-757-1198
TTY: 203-754-5141
http://www.waterburyct.easterseals.com
Francis De Blasio, Executive Director

Offers a number of vocational rehabilitation services, application & interviewing support, individualized employment planning & supported employment, and on the job training.

Delaware

4491 **Division of Vocational Rehabilitation**
Delaware Department of Labor
4425 N Market St
PO Box 9969
Wilmington, DE 19809-0969
302-761-8085
FAX 302-761-6601
TTY: 302-761-8275
http://www.delawareworks.com
e-mail: cynthia.fairwell@state.de.us
Andrea Guest, Director

Mission is to provide information opportunities and resources to individuals with disabilities, leading to success in employment and independent living. Facebook: http://www.facebook.com/DE.DVR.1

4492 Easter Seals Delaware And Maryland's Eastern Shore
61 Corporate Circle
New Castle, DE 19720-2405
302-324-4444
800-677-3800
FAX 302-324-4441
TDD:302-324-4442
http://www.de.easterseals.com
William Adami, President

Offers early intervention services and outpatient rehab therapies for children and adults. Also offers day programs for adults with developmental disabilties.

4493 Easter Seals Dover Enterprise
Easter Seals Delaware & Maryland's Eastern Shore
100 Enterprise Place
Suite 1
Dover, DE 19904-8207
302-678-3353
800-677-3800
FAX 302-678-3650
http://www.de.easterseals.com
e-mail: gcassedy@esdel.org
Gary Cassedy, Vice President, Programs

Easter Seals offers a variety of programs and activities for children and adults with disabililties.

District of Columbia

4494 Department of Employment Services
District of Columbia
64 New York Ave NE
Suite 3000
Washington, DC 20002-3320
202-724-7000
FAX 202-724-5683
TDD:202-673-6994
TTY: 202-673-6994
http://www.does.dc.gov
Gregory Irish, Director

Helps consider career decisions and offer vocational and placement assistance at several area training locations.

4495 District of Columbia Department of Education: Vocational & Adult Education
400 Maryland Ave SW
Washington, DC 20202
202-842-0973
800-872-5327
FAX 202-205-8748
TTY: 800-437-0833
http://www.ed.gov
e-mail: ovae@ed.gov
Arne Duncan, Secretary of Education
Tony Miller, Deputy Secretary
Kiran Ahuja, Executive Director
To help all people achieve the knowledge and skills to be lifelong learners, to be successful in their chosen careers, and to be effective citizens.

4496 The DC Center For Independent Living, Inc.
1400 Florida Ave NE
Washington, DC 20002-5032
202-388-0033
FAX 202-398-3018
TDD:202-388-0277
TTY: 202-388-0277
http://www.dccil.org
e-mail: info@dccil.org
Richard Simms, Executive Director
Kandra Hall, Coordinator

Promotes independent life styles for persons with significant disabilities. Programs offered include advocacy/legal/information and referral services, and independent living skills training.

Florida

4497 Children's Therapy Services Center
Easter Seals Of Southwest Florida
350 Braden Ave
Sarasota, FL 34243-2001
941-355-7637
800-807-7899
FAX 941-358-3069
http://www.swfl.easterseals.com
Bill Lloyd, President

Job training, employment services, vocational evaluation/situational assessment and work services.

4498 College Living Experience
6555 Nova Drive
Suite 300
Davie, FL 33317-7404
954-370-5142
800-486-5058
FAX 954-370-1895
http://www.experiencecle.com
e-mail: secretary@cleinc.net
Ayme Sanchez, Admissions Coordinator
Beth Phillips, Program Director

A post-secondary program for students with Autism spectrum disorders, Dyslexia, Traumatic Brain Injury, ADD/ADHD, auditory/visual processing disorders and non-verbal learning disorders. The program offers students additional support with academic, social and living skills which helps them in adulthood.

4499 Division of Vocational Rehabilitation
Florida Department of Education
2002 Old Saint Augustine Road
Building A
Tallahassee, FL 32301-4862
850-245-3399
800-451-4327
FAX 850-245-3316
TDD:800-451-4327
http://www.rehabworks.org
Bill Palmer, Director

Statewide employment resource for businesses and people with disabilities. Our mission is to enable individuals with disabilities to obtain and keep employment.

4500 Easter Seals Florida, Inc.
6050 Babcock St SE
Suite 18
Palm Bay, FL 32909-3996
321-723-4474
FAX 321-676-3843
http://www.fl.easterseals.org
e-mail: scaporina@fl.easterseals.com
Gail Edwards, President

Offers vocational training to adults with disabilities and special needs, giving them the opportunity to receive job and life skills training so they gain greater independence.

4501 Easter Seals South Florida
1475 NW 14th Ave
Miami, FL 33125-1616
305-325-0470
FAX 305-325-0578
TTY: 305-326-7351
http://www.southflorida.easterseals.com
e-mail: lwelch@sfl.easterseals.com
Luanne K Welch, Executive President/CEO
Malerie Sloshay, VP Operations

Job training, employment services, vocational evaluation/situational assessment and work services, adult day services, outpatient medical rehabilitation.

4502 Florida Workforce Investment Act
Department of Labor & Employment Security
1580 Waldo Palmer Lane
Suite 1
Tallahassee, FL 32308   850-921-1119
                               FAX 850-921-1101
          http://www.workforceflorida.com
Kathleen McLeskey, Director

Provides job-training services for economically disadvantaged adults and youth, dislocated workers and others who face significant employment barriers.

4503 TILES Project: Transition/Independent Living/Employment/Support
Family Network on Disabilities, Inc.
2196 Main Street
Suite K
Dunedin, FL 34698-1610   727-523-1130
                                 800-825-5736
                            FAX 727-523-8687
                           http://www.fndfl.org
                          e-mail: fnd@fndfl.org
Richard Labelle, Executive Director
Betsy Taylor, Director

Provides training information to enable individuals with disabilities and the parents, family members, guardians, advocates, or other authorized representatives to participate more effectively with professionals in meeting the vocational, independent living and rehabilitation needs of people with disabilities in Florida.

Georgia

4504 Easter Seals East Georgia
1500 Wrightsboro Rd
P.O. Box 2441
Augusta, GA 30903-4079   706-667-9695
                                 866-667-9695
                            FAX 706-667-8831
          http://www.ga-ea.easterseals.com
             e-mail: shthomas@esega.org
Sheila Thomas, President/CEO

Job training for disabled individuals, employment services, vocational evaluation/situational assessment and work services.

4505 Easter Seals Middle Georgia
604 Kellam Rd
P.O. Box 847
Dublin, GA 31040   478-275-8850
                            FAX 478-275-8852
        http://www.middlegeorgia.easterseals.com
Wayne Peebles, President

Job training, employment services, vocational evaluation/situational assessment and work services.

4506 Easter Seals Southern Georgia
Easter Seals Southern Georgia
1906 Palmyra Rd
Albany, GA 31701-1575   229-439-7061
                                 800-365-4583
                            FAX 229-435-6278
       http://www.southerngeorgia.easterseals.com
          e-mail: benglish@swga-easterseals.org
Beth English, Executive Director

Helps individuals with disabilities and special needs by providing many services such as job training, employment services, vocational evaluation/situational assessment and work services.

4507 Vocational Rehabilitation Services
Georgia Department of Labor
10 Park Place South, SE
Suite 602
Atlanta, GA 30303-1732   404-657-2239
                            FAX 404-657-4731
                            TTY: 404-657-2239
                       http://www.vocrehabga.org
               e-mail: rehab@dol.state.ga.us
Peggy Rosser, Director

Operates 5 integrated and interdependent programs that share a primary goal — to help people with disabilities to become fully productive members of society by achieving independence and meaningful employment.

Hawaii

4508 Vocational Rehabilitation and Services For The Blind Division (VRSBD)
State Of Hawaii, Department Of Human Services
1901 Bachelot Street
Honolulu, HI 96817-0339   808-586-5268
                          http://www.hawaii.gov
Lilian Poller, Director

State vocational rehabilitation agencies provide direct services to persons with disabilities, including persons with learning disabilities. The services may include evaluation and diagnosis, counseling, guidance, and referral services, vocational and other training services, transportation to rehabilitation services, and assistive devices.

Idaho

4509 Goodwill Staffing Services
Easter Seals Goodwill Northern Rocky Mountain
1465 S Vinnell Way
Boise, ID 83709-1659   208-373-1299
                                 866-848-0331
           http://www.esgw-nrm.easterseals.com
Marcie Bailey, Director

Temporary staffing company which provides effective solutions to businesses in Idaho by customizing staffing solutions to fit individual needs, fill orders promptly, and monitors job performance to ensure customer satisfaction.

4510 Idaho Department of Commerce & Labor
State Of Idaho Department of Labor
317 W Main St
Boise, ID 83735-0001   208-332-3570
                            FAX 208-334-6430
                            TDD:800-377-1363
                       http://www.labor.idaho.gov
                        e-mail: labor.idaho.gov
Roger Madsen, Director

Provides vocational training services for economically disadvantaged adults and youth, dislocated workers and others who face significant employment barriers.

4511 Idaho Division of Vocational Rehabilitation Administration
Idaho State Board of Education
650 W. State Street
Room 150
Boise, ID 83702-0001   208-334-3390
                            FAX 208-334-5305
                       http://www.vr.idaho.gov
          e-mail: department.info@vr.idaho.gov
Michael Graham, Director

State vocational rehabilitation agencies provide direct services to persons with disabilities, including persons with learning disabilities. The services may include evaluation and diagnosis, counseling, guidance, and referral services, vocational and other training services, transportation to rehabilitation services, and assistive devices.

4512 State Of Idaho Department Of Labor
317 W Main St
Boise, ID 83735-0001   208-332-3570
FAX 208-334-6430
TDD:800-377-1363
http://www.labor.idaho.gov
e-mail: labor.idaho.gov
Roger Madsen, Director

An equal opportunity employer/program with auxiliary aids and services available upon request to individuals with disabilities.

4513 Workforce Development Services
Easter Seals-Goodwill Northern Rocky Mountains
1613 North Park Centre Place
Nampa, ID 83651-1705   208-466-2671
FAX 208-466-2537
http://www.esgw-nrm.easter-seals.org
e-mail: landisr@esgw.org
Kim Osadchuk, Director

Job training, employment services, vocational evaluation/situational assessment and work services.

Illinois

4514 State Vocational Rehabilitation Agency
100 S Grand Ave
Springfield, IL 62762-0001   217-782-2094
800-843-6154
FAX 217-558-4270
TDD:217-557-2507
TTY: 888-440-8982
http://www.dhs.state.il.us
e-mail: dhs.ors@illinois.gov
Rob Kilbury, Director

Assists people with physical, visual, and hearing disabilities in achieving their education, employment, and independent living goals, including preparing for and finding quality employment.

4515 Therapeutic School and Center For Autism Research
Easter Seals Metropolitan Chicago
1939 West 13th Street
Chicago, IL 60608   312-432-1751
FAX 312-432-9140
http://www.chicago.easterseals.com
e-mail: ndavenport@eastersealschicago.org
F. Timothy Muri, President & CEO
Barbara Zawacki, CEO
Nicole Davenport, School Administrator
Campus offers educational programs that help meet the special needs of students with autism, emotional behavior disorders and severe learning disabilities. Schools are also located in Rockford, Tinley Park and Waukegan.

4516 Timber Pointe Outdoor Center
Easter Seals Of Illinois
20 Timber Pointe Lane
Hudson, IL 61748   309-365-8021
FAX 309-365-8934
http://www.easterseals-ci.org
e-mail: info@easterseals-ci.org
Debbie England, President

Timber Pointe provides specialized camping and respite programs for individuals with disabilities or special needs and their families. For ages 7 and up. Children enjoy activities such as swimming, boating, fishing, sports, music and arts and crafts.

4517 UCP Easter Seals Heartland
13975 Manchester Road
Manchester, MO 63011   636-227-6030
FAX 636-779-2270
http://www.ucpesh.easterseals.com
Lynn Stonecipher, Director

Job training, employment services, vocational evaluation/situational assessment and work services.

Indiana

4518 Easter Seals Arc of Northeast Indiana
4919 Colwater Road
Fort Wayne, IN 46825-5380   260-456-4534
800-234-7811
FAX 260-745-5200
http://www.neindiana.easterseals.com
Steven Hinkle, President
Sue Dubay, Executive Assistant

The Easter Seals Arc of Northeast Indiana covers 16 counties and offers many services and programs to children and adults with special needs or disabilities.

4519 Easter Seals Crossroads
4740 Kingsway Dr
Indianapolis, IN 46205-1521   317-466-1000
FAX 317-466-2000
TTY: 317-479-3232
http://www.crossroads.easterseals.com
James Vento, President

Works with children and adults with disabilities or special needs to promote growth, dignity and independence.

4520 INdiana Camp R.O.C.K.S.
Easter Seals Crossroads
4740 Kingsway Drive
Indianapolis, IN 46205   317-466-1000
FAX 317-466-2000
TDD:317-479-3232
http://www.crossroads.easterseals.org
Anne Shupe, Director

Camp for chidlren and young adults ages 10-17 who have autism.

4521 Vocational Rehabilitation Services
1452 Vaxter Ave
Clarksville, IN 47129-7721   812-288-8261
877-228-1967
FAX 812-282-7048
TDD:812-288-8261
http://www.in.gov
Delbert Hayden, Director

Purpose is to assist the community by providing services which allow individuals to maximize their potential and to participate in work, family and the community. To do this we will provide rehabilitation, education and training.

Iowa

4522   Division of Community Colleges and Workforce Preparation
Iowa Department of Education
400 E 14th St
Des Moines, IA 50319-146
515-281-5294
FAX 515-242-5988
http://http://educateiowa.gov
e-mail: kathy.petosa@iowa.gov
Dr. Jason Glass, Director
Kathy Petosa, Administrative Assistant

The Iowa Department of Education (the Department) works with the Iowa State Board of Education (State Board) to provide oversight, supervision, and support for the state education system that includes public elementary and secondary schools, nonpublic schools that receive state accreditation, area education agencies (AEAs), community colleges, and teacher preparation programs.

4523   Easter Seals Center
2920 30th St
Des Moines, IA 50310-5299
515-274-1529
866-533-9344
FAX 515-274-6434
TDD:515-274-8348
TTY: 515-274-8348
http://www.ia.easterseals.com
e-mail: info@eastersealsia.org
Renee Bell, President

Job training, employment services, vocational evaluation/situational assessment and work services.

4524   Easter Seals Iowa
401 NE 66th Ave
Des Moines, IA 50313-1200
515-289-1933
866-533-9344
FAX 515-289-1281
TDD:515-274-8348
TTY: 515-289-4069
http://www.ia.easterseals.com
e-mail: info@eastersealsia.org
Sherri Nielsen, President

Offers many programs and services for children and adults with disabilities or special needs.

4525   State Vocational Rehabilitation Agency
Iowa Division of Vocational Rehabilitation Service
510 E 12th St
Des Moines, IA 50319-9025
515-281-4211
800-532-1486
FAX 515-281-7645
TDD:515-281-4211
TTY: 800-532-1486
http://www.ivrs.iowa.gov
Stephen Wooderson, Director

We work for and with individuals with disabilities to achieve their employment, independence and economic goals. Economic independence and more and better jobs are what we are about for Iowans with disabilities.

Kansas

4526   Office of Vocational Rehabilitation
Department of Vocational Rehabilitation
915 SW Harrison St
Topeka, KS 66612-1505
888-369-4777
TTY: 785-296-1491
http://www.srskansas.org
e-mail: cmxa@srskansas.org
Clarissa Ashdown, Director

Partnering to connect Kansans with support and services to improve lives. Vocational and transitional training.

Kentucky

4527   Easter Seals: West Kentucky
2229 Mildred St
Paducah, KY 42001-3067
270-442-9687
866-673-3565
FAX 270-442-4933
http://www.eswky.easterseals.com
George Kennedy, President

Provides programs and services for children and adults with disabilities and/or special needs. Provides job training, employment services, vocational evaluation/situational assessment and work services.

4528   Office of Vocational Rehabilitation
275 E Main St
Mail Drop 2EK
Frankfort, KY 40621
502-564-4440
800-372-7172
FAX 502-564-6745
TTY: 888-420-9874
http://www.kydor.state.ky.us
e-mail: wfd.vocrehab@mail.state.ky.us
Beth Smith, Executive Director
Pam Jarboe, Program Services Director

Provides direct services to persons with disabilities, including persons with learning disabilities. The services may include evaluation and diagnosis; counseling, guidance, and referral services, vocational and other training services, transportation to rehabilitation services, and assistive devices.

Maine

4529   State Vocational Rehabilitation Agency
Maine Bureau of Rehabilitation Services
150 State House Station
Augusta, ME 04333-0150
207-623-6799
800-698-4440
FAX 207-287-5292
http://www.maine.gov/rehab
Carolyn Lockwood, Executive Director
Betsy Hopkins, Director

Works to bring about full access to employment, independence and community integration for people with disabilities. Our three service provision units are Vocational Rehabilitation, Division for the Blind and Visually Impaired and Division of Deafness.

Maryland

4530   Maryland Technology Assistance Program
Maryland Department of Disabilities
217 E. Redwood Street
Suite 1300
Baltimore, MD 21202
410-767-3660
800-637-4113
http://www.mdtap.org
Beth Lash, Director

Offers information and referrals, reduced rate loan program for assistive technology, five regional display centers, presentations and training on request.

4531 State Vocational Rehabilitation Agency
Maryland State Dept Of Education/Div Rehab Svcs.
2301 Argonne Dr
Baltimore, MD 21218-1696

410-554-9442
888-554-0334
TTY: 410-554-9411
http://www.dors.state.md.us

Robert Burns, Director

Operates more than 20 statewide offices and also operates the Workforce and Technology Center, a comprehensive rehabilitation facility in Baltimore. Rehabilitation representatives also work in many Maryland One-Stop Career Centers.

Massachusettes

4532 Easter Seals: Massachusetts
89 South St
Boston, MA 02111-2629

617-226-2640
800-244-2756
FAX 617-737-9875
TTY: 617-226-2640
http://www.ma.easterseals.com

Alex Cassie, President

Job training, employment services, vocational evaluation/situational assessment and work services. Camp programs, assistive technology and augmentative communication.

4533 State Vocational Rehabilitation Agency
Massachusetts Rehabilitation Commission
59 Temple Place
Suite 905
Boston, MA 02111-1619

617-357-8137
800-245-6543
FAX 617-482-5576
TDD:800-223-3212
TTY: 800-245-6543
http://www.mass.gov

Elmer Bartels, Director

Provides public vocational rehabilitation, independent living and disability determination services for residents with disabilities in Massachusetts.

Michigan

4534 Easter Seal Michigan
2399 E. Walton Blvd.
Auburn Hills, MI 48326

248-475-6400
800-757-3257
TTY: 800-649-3777
http://http://mi.easterseals.com

Brent L. Wirth, President and CEO
Juliana Harper, Sr. Vice President
Rich Hollis, Sr. Vice President
Job training, employment services, vocational evaluation/situational assessment and work services.

4535 State Vocational Rehabilitation Agency
Dept Of Labor & Economic Grwth-Rehabilitation Svcs
201 N. Washington Square, 4th Floor
P.O. Box 30010
Lansing, MI 48909-7510

517-373-4026
800-605-6722
FAX 517-335-7277
TDD:888-605-6722
TTY: 888-605-6722
http://www.michigan.gov

Jaye Balthazar, Director

State vocational rehabilitation agencies provide direct services to persons with disabilities, including persons with learning disabilities. The services may include evaluation and diagnosis; counseling, guidance, and referral services; vocational and other training services; transportation to rehabilitation services; and assistive devices.

Minnesota

4536 Goodwill - Easter Seals Minnesota
553 Fairview Ave N
Saint Paul, MN 55104-1708

651-379-5800
FAX 651-379-5803
http://www.goodwilleasterseals.org
The Goodwill stores help individuals achieve their goals for employment, education, training and independence.

4537 Minnesota Vocational Rehabilitation Agency: Rehabilitation Services Branch
Department of Employment & Economic Development
390 Robert St N
Saint Paul, MN 55101-1805

651-296-3711
800-328-9095
FAX 651-297-5159
TTY: 651-282-5909
http://www.deed.state.mn.us
e-mail: VRS.CustomerService@state.mn.us
Paul Bridges, Director

Provides basic vocational rehabilitation services to consumers including vocational counseling, planning, guidance and placement, as well as certain special services based on individual circumstances.

4538 State Vocational Rehabilitation Agency: Minnesota Department of Economics Security
Rehabilitation Service Branch
332 Minnesota Street
Suite E200
Saint Paul, MN 55101-1351

651-296-7345
800-328-9095
FAX 651-296-3900
TTY: 651-296-3900
http://www.deed.state.mn.us
e-mail: paul.moes@state.mn.us

Paul Bridges, Director

State vocational rehabilitation agencies provide direct services to persons with disabilities, including persons with learning disabilities. The services may include evaluation and diagnosis, counseling, guidance, and referral services, vocational and other training services, transportation to rehabilitation services, and assistive devices.

Mississippi

4539 Office Of Vocational Rehabilitation
Mississippi Dept Of Rehabilitation Services
P.O.Box 1698
Jackson, MS 39215-1698

601-853-5100
800-443-1000
FAX 601-853-5158
TDD:601-351-1586
http://www.mdrs.state.ms.us

Gary Neely, President
H.S. McMillan, Executive Director

Helps individuals with physical or mental disabilities to find employment, retain employment and so they feel better about themselves and can live more independently.

Missouri

4540 Rehabilitation Services for the Blind
615 E 13th St
Ste 409
Kansas City, MO 64106-2829   816-889-2677
                                     800-592-6004
                                 FAX 816-889-2504
http://www.dss.mo.gov/fsd/rsb/index.htm
e-mail: Rachel.M.Labrado@dss.mo.gov
Rachel Labrado, District Supervisor

Provides services to people with varing degrees of visual impairment, ranging from those who cannot read regular print to those who are totally blind. Services may include: job training, job placement, vocational rehabilitation, assistive technology, independent living skills, personal and home management, meal preparation, communications assistance, independent travel instruction, counseling and guidance, leisure activities and client assistant program.

4541 State Vocational Rehabilitation Agency Department of Elementary & Secondary Education
3024 Dupont Cir
Jefferson City, MO 65109-6188   573-751-3251
                                        877-222-8963
                                    FAX 573-751-1441
                                    TDD:573-751-0881
http://www.dese.mo.gov

Jeanne Loyd, Director

State vocational rehabilitation agencies provide direct services to persons with disabilities, including persons with learning disabilities. The services may include evaluation and diagnosis, counseling, guidance, and referral services, vocational and other training services, transportation to rehabilitation services, and assistive devices.

Montana

4542 Easter Seals-Goodwill Career Designs Mountain
Regional Service Center
4400 Central Avenue
Great Falls, MT 59405-1641   406-761-3680
                                     800-771-2153
                                 FAX 406-761-5110
http://www.esg.easterseals.com
e-mail: sharonod@esgw.org
Michelle Belknap, President

Job skill training programs for adults with developmental disabilities.

4543 Easter Seals-Goodwill Store
951 S 29th St W
Billings, MT 59102-7434   406-656-4020
                              FAX 406-656-3750
http://www.esgw-nrm.easterseals.com
e-mail: gwbillings@mcn.net
Shalene Sparling, Director

Provides vocational training sites for individuals with emotional, developmental and physical disabilities. Employees develop and improve work skills while gaining work experience.

4544 Easter Seals-Goodwill Working Partners: Great Falls
4400 Central Avenue
Great Falls, MT 59405-1641   406-761-3680
                                     800-771-2153
                                 FAX 406-761-5110
                                 TDD:800-253-4093
http://www.esgrw-nrm.easter-seals.org
e-mail: joelc@csgw.org

Michelle Belknap, President
Russell Plath, Board Chair
Scott Wilson, 1st Vice Chair and Treasurer
Job training, employment services, vocational evaluation/situational assessment and work services.

4545 State Vocational Rehabilitation Agency
Department of Public Health & Human Services
111 North Sanders
P.O. Box 4210
Helena, MT 59604-4210   406-444-2590
                                877-296-1197
                            FAX 406-444-3632
http://www.dphhs.mt.gov
Robert Wynia, Executive Director
Joe Mathews, Director

State vocational rehabilitation agencies provide direct services to persons with disabilities, including persons with learning disabilities. The services may include evaluation and diagnosis, counseling, guidance, and referral services, vocational and other training services, transportation to rehabilitation services, and assistive devices.

Nebraska

4546 Camp Kaleo
Easter Seals Nebraska
2727 West 2nd Street
Suite 471
Hastings, NE 68901-4684   402-462-3031
                                  800-471-6425
                             TTY: 402-462-4721
http://www.ne.easterseals.com
Karen Ginder, President

Job training, employment services, vocational evaluation/situational assessment and work services.

4547 State Vocational Rehabilitation Agency: Nebraska
Nebraska Dept Of Educ. Vocational Rehabilitation
PO Box 94987
Lincoln, NE 68509-4987   402-471-3644
                                 877-637-3422
                             FAX 402-471-0788
                             TTY: 402-471-3659
http://www.vocrehab.state.ne.us
e-mail: vr_stateoffice@vocrehab.state.ne.us
Cherly Ferree, Director

We help people with disabilities make career plans, learn job skills, get and keep a job. Our goal is to prepare people for jobs where they can make a living wage and have access to medical insurance.

Nevada

4548 Bureau of Services to the Blind & Visually Impaired
Nevada Dept Of Employment,Training&Rehabilitation
2800 E. St. Louis Avenue
Las Vegas, NV 89713-5146   775-684-3849
                                   800-326-6868
                               FAX 775-684-4186
                               TTY: 775-684-8400
http://www.detr.state.nv.us
Gayle Sherman, Director

Services to the Blind and Visually Impaired (BSBVI) provides a variety of services to eligible individuals, whose vision is not correctable by ordinary eye care. Adaptive training, independence skills, low vision exams and aids, mobility training and vocational rehabilitation are offered.

4549 Nevada Governor's Council on Rehabilitation & Employment of People with Disabilities
2800 E. St. Louis Avenue
Carson City, NV 89713
775-684-3849
FAX 775-684-3850
TTY: 775-687-5353
http://www.detr.state.nv.us

Donna Sanders, Director

To help insure vocational rehabilitation programs are consumer oriented, driven and result in employment outcomes for Nevadans with disabilities. Funding for innovation and expansion grants.

4550 Rehabilitation Division Department of Employment, Training & Rehabilitation
Bureau of Services to Blind and Visually Impaired
500 East Third Street
Carson City, NV 89713
775-684-4040
FAX 775-684-4184
TDD:775-684-8400
http://www.detr.state.nv.us

Deborah Braun, Director

Providing options and choices for Nevadans with disabilities to work and live independently. Our mission will be accomplished through planning, implementing and coordinating assessment, employment, independent living and training.

New Hampshire

4551 Camp Sno Mo
Easter Seals New Hampshire
Hidden Valley Reservation
Gilmanton Iron Works, NH 03103-2684   603-364-5818
http://www.nh.easterseals.com
e-mail: cmcmahon@eastersealsnh.org

Larry Gammon, President
Robert Kelly, Camp Director

The camp gives children and young adults ages 11-21 with disabilties or special needs the chance to explore new adventures which develop confidence, gain courage and build new friendships. Some of the activities include swimming, canoeing, hiking, archery, woodcarving, and arts & crafts.

4552 Easter Seals: Keene
12 Kingsbury St
Keene, NH 03431-3825
603-355-1067
800-307-2737
FAX 603-358-3947
http://www.nheasterseals.com

Larry Gammon, President

Job training, employment services, vocational evaluation/situational assessment and work services.

4553 Easter Seals: Manchester
Joliceour School
1 Mammoth Road
Manchester, NH 03103-4800
603-623-8863
800-870-8728
FAX 603-625-1148
http://www.nheasterseals.com

Larry Gammon, President

Job training, employment services, vocational evaluation/situational assessment and work services.

4554 New Hampshire Department Of Health & Human Services
40 Terrill Park Drive
Concord, NH 03301-7325
603-271-6200
800-322-9191
TDD:800-735-2964
http://www.dhhs.nh.gov

Nick Toumpas, Director

Programs for individuals with disabilities or special needs.

4555 State Vocational Rehabilitation Agency
Department of Education
21 South Fruit Street
Suite 20
Concord, NH 03301-2428
603-271-3471
800-299-1647
FAX 603-271-7095
TDD:603-271-3471
TTY: 603-271-3471
http://www.ed.state.nh.us

Paul K Leather, Executive Director

Assisting eligible New Hampshire citizens with disabilities secure suitable employment, financial and personal independence by providing rehabilitation services.

New Jersey

4556 Assistive Technology Advocacy Center-ATAC
New Jersey Protection and Advocacy
210 South Broad Street
3rd Floor
Trenton, NJ 08608-2407
609-292-9742
800-922-7233
FAX 609-777-0187
TTY: 609-633-7106
http://www.njpanda.org
e-mail: advocate@drnj.com

Ellen Catanese, Director

Assists individuals in overcoming barriers in the system and making assistive technology more accessible to individuals with disabilities throughout the state.

4557 Division of Family Development: New Jersey Department of Human Services
Quakerbridge Plaza, Building 6
P.O. Box 716
Trenton, NJ 08625-0716
609-588-2000
FAX 609-588-3051
http://www.state.nj.us

Jeanette Page-Hawkins, Director

Offers programs to individuals with disabilities.

4558 Eden Family of Services
Eden Services
One Eden Way
Princeton, NJ 08540-5711
609-987-0099
FAX 609-987-0243
http://www.edenservices.org
e-mail: info@edenservices.org

Tom Mc Cool, President
David Holmes EdD, Executive Director

Provides year round educational services, early intervention, parent training, respite care, outreach services, community based residential services and employment opportunities for individuals with autism.

4559 New Jersey Council on Developmental Disabilities
P.O. Box 700
Trenton, NJ 08625-0700
609-292-3745
800-792-8858
FAX 609-292-7114
TDD:609-777-3238
http://www.njddc.org
e-mail: njddc@njddc.org

Elaine Buschbaum, Chair
Dr Allison Lozano, Executive Director
Douglas McGruher, Deputy Director
Promotes systems change, coordinates advocacy and research for 1.2 million residents with developmental and other disabilities.

4560 New Jersey State Department of Education
P.O.Box 500
Trenton, NJ 08625-0500 609-292-4469
http://www.state.nj.us
Lucille E Davy, Commissioner

Assists the disabled student with changes from the school environment to the working world.

4561 Programs for Children with Special Health Care Needs
NJ Department of Health & Senior Services
P.O. Box 360
Trenton, NJ 08625-0360 609-292-7837
800-367-6543
FAX 609-292-9288
http://www.nj.gov
Gloria Rodriguez, President

Assists families caring for children with long-term medical and developmental disabilities. Programs include early intervention and case management units

New Mexico

4562 New Mexico Department of Labor: Job Training Division
Office of Workforce Training and Development
401 Broadway NE
Albuquerque, NM 87103-3960 505-841-4000
http://www.dws.state.nm.us
e-mail: reese.fullerton@state.nm.us
Reese Fullerton, Executive Director
Veronica Moya, Office Assistant

Helps citizens of New Mexico from all walks of life find appropriate vocational trainings, and job placement.

4563 State of New Mexico Division of Vocational Rehabilitation
491 Old Santa Fe Trail
Santa Fe, NM 87501-2753 505-827-6328
877-696-1470
TTY: 505-476-0412
http://www.dvrgetsjobs.com
e-mail: rsmith@state.nm.us
Jim Parker, Director

Commited to improving the quality of life of those with disabilities by addressing program accessibility and economic self-sufficiency.

New York

4564 Commission for the Blind & Visually Handicapped
NYS Office Of Children & Family Services
40 North Pearl
15th Floor
Albany, NY 12210-2329 518-473-1675
TDD:518-473-1698
http://www.ocfs.state.ny.us
Professionals and paraprofessionals are available to help those with low vision or blindness with vocational rehabilitation services.

4565 Office of Curriculum & Instructional Support
New York State Education Department
89 Washington Ave
Albany, NY 12234-1000 518-474-8892
FAX 518-474-0319
http://www.emsc.nysed.gov
e-mail: jstevens@mail.nysed.gov
Jean Stevens, Director

Works with those seeking General Educational Development diplomas and technical training.

4566 Office of Vocational and Educational Services for Individuals with Disabilities
New York State Department of Education
1 Commerce Plaza
Room 1624e Plz
Albany, NY 12234-0001 518-436-0008
800-222-5627
TTY: 519-486-3773
http://www.emsc.nysed.gov
e-mail: speced@mail.nysed.gov
Harvey Rosenthal, Executive Director
Nancy Lauria, Director

Promotes educational equality and excellence for students with disabilities while ensuring that they receive the rights and protection to which they are entitled, assure appropriate continuity between the child and adult services systems, and provide the highest quality vocational rehabilitation and independent living services to all eligible people.

North Dakota

4567 North Dakota Department of Career and Technical Education
State Capital, 15th Floor
600 E Boulevard Ave, Dept. 270
Bismarck, ND 58505-0610 701-328-3180
FAX 701-328-1255
http://www.nd.gov/cte
e-mail: cte@nd.gov
Mark Nelson, Executive Director

The mission of the Board for Vocational and Technical Education is to work with others to provide all North Dakota citizens with the technical skills, knowledge, and attitudes necessary for successful performance in a globally competitive workplace.

4568 North Dakota Workforce Development Council
North Dakota Department of Commerce
P.O.Box 2057
Bismarck, ND 58502-2057 701-328-5345
FAX 701-328-5320
TTY: 800-366-6888
http://www.workforce.nd.gov
e-mail: jhirsch@state.nd.us
James Hirsch, Director

The role of the North Dakota Workforce Development Council is to advise the Governor and the Public concerning the nature and extent of workforce development in the context of North Dakota's economic development needs, and how to meet these needs effectively while maximizing the efficient use of available resources and avoiding unnecessary duplication of effort.

4569 Vocational Rehabilitation
North Dakota Department of Human Services
1237 West Divide Avenue
Suite 1B
Bismarck, ND 58501-1208 701-328-8950
800-755-2745
FAX 701-328-8969
TDD:701-328-8968
TTY: 701-328-8802
http://www.nd.gov/dhs/dvr
Nancy Mc Kenzie, Director

Assists individuals with disabilities to achieve competitive employment and increased independence through rehabilitation services.

4570 Workforce Investment Act
Governor's Employment & Training Forum
1000 E Divide Ave
POÆBox 5507
Bismarck, ND 58506-5507
701-328-2836
FAX 701-328-1612
TDD:800-366-6888
http://www.jobnd.com
e-mail: mdaley@nd.gov

Maren Daley, Executive Director

Job service North Dakota

Ohio

4571 Office of Workforce Development
Ohio Department of Job and Family Services
4020 E Fifth Ave
PO Box 1618
Columbus, OH 43216-1618
888-296-7541
FAX 614-728-8366
http://jfs.ohio.gov/owd

John Weber, Deputy Director

Operates several US department of labor-funded programs that focus on improving Ohio's workforce through career and job search realted services, assistance to employers, training and education.

4572 State Vocational Rehabilitation Agency
Ohio Dept Of Rehabilitation Services Commission
400 E Campus View Blvd
Columbus, OH 43235-4604
614-438-1255
800-282-4536
FAX 614-438-1257
TDD:614-438-1726
TTY: 614-438-1200
http://www.rsc.state.oh.us
e-mail: rsc_rir@vscnet.a1.state.oh.us

John M Connelly, Executive Director

State vocational rehabilitation agencies provide direct services to persons with disabilities, including persons with learning disabilities. The services may include evaluation and diagnosis, counseling, guidance, and referral services, vocational and other training services, transportation to rehabilitation services, and assistive devices.

Oklahoma

4573 State Vocational Rehabilitation Agency: Oklahoma Department of Rehabilitation Services
3535 NW 58th Street
Suite 500
Oklahoma City, OK 73112-4824
405-951-3400
800-845-8476
FAX 405-951-3529
TTY: 405-951-3400
http://www.okrehab.org
e-mail: info@okdrs.gov

Linda S Parker, Executive Director

State vocational rehabilitation agencies provide direct services to persons with disabilities, including persons with learning disabilities. The services may include evaluation and diagnosis counseling, guidance, and referral services, vocational and other training services, transportation to rehabilitation services and assistive devices.

4574 Workforce Investment Act
Oklahoma Employment Security Commission
Will Rogers Memorial Office Bldg.
2401 N. Lincoln Blvd., P.O. Box 52003
Oklahoma City, OK 73152-2003
405-557-7100
FAX 405-557-7256
TDD:800-722-0353
http://www.ok.gov

John Brock, Executive Director

Partnership of local goverments offering resource conservation and development and workforce development.

Oregon

4575 Oregon Employment Department
875 Union St NE
Salem, OR 97311
503-947-1470
877-345-3484
TTY: 503-947-1472
http://www.employment.oregon.gov

Laurie Warner, Director
Tom Fuller, Communciations Manager
Craig Spivey, Backup Manager
Supports economic stability for Oregonians and communities during times of unemployment through the payment of unemployment benefits. Serves businesses by recruiting and referring the best qualified applicants to jobs, and provides resources to diverse job seekers in support of their employment needs.

4576 Recruitment and Retention Special Education Jobs Clearinghouse
Teaching Research Institute
Western Oregon University
345 Monmouth Ave
Monmouth, OR 97361
503-838-8391
FAX 503-838-8150
TTY: 503-838-9623
http://www.tr.wou.edu
e-mail: samplesb@wou.edu

John Killoran, Director

A free on-line jobs clearinghouse with access to position openings in Oregon in the area of Special Education and related services. A Job Seeker Listing and resumes also sent via e-mail to districts and agencies looking for qualified individuals.

Pennsylvania

4577 State Vocational Rehabilitation Agency: Pennsylvania
Department of Labor & Industry
1521 N 6th St
Harrisburg, PA 17102-1104
717-787-5244
800-442-6351
FAX 717-783-5221
TTY: 717-787-5244
http://www.dli.state.pa.us
e-mail: wgannon@dli.state.pa.us

William Gannon, Executive Director

Provides individualized services to assist people with disabilities to pursue, obtain, and maintain satisfactory employment. Counselors are available for training, planning and placement services.

Rhode Island

4578 Rhode Island Vocational and Rehabilitation Agency
Rhode Island Department of Human Services
40 Fountain St
Providence, RI 02903-1898

401-421-7005
FAX 401-421-9259
TDD:401-421-7016
http://www.ors.ri.gov
e-mail: rcarroll@ors.ri.gov

Raymond A Carroll, Director

Assists people with disabilities to become employed and to live independently in the community. In order to achieve this goal, we work in partnership with the State Rehabilitation Council, our customers, staff and community.

4579 State Vocational Rehabilitation Agency: Rhode Island
Rhode Island Department of Human Services
40 Fountain St
Providence, RI 02903-1830

401-421-7005
FAX 401-421-9259
TDD:401-421-7016
http://www.ors.ri.gov
e-mail: rcarroll@ors.ri.gov

Raymond A Carroll, Director

Assists people with disabilities to become employed and to live independently in the community. In order to achieve this goal, we work in partnership with the State Rehabilitation Council, our customers, staff and community.

South Carolina

4580 Americans with Disabilities Act Assistance Line
Employment Security Commission
1550 Gadsden Street
Columbia, SC 29202-1406

803-737-9935
800-436-8190
FAX 803-737-0140
http://www.sces.org
e-mail: rratterree@sces.org

Regina Ratterree, Director

Provides information, technical assistance and training on the Americans with Disabilities Act.

4581 South Carolina Vocational Rehabilitation Department
PO Box 15
West Columbia, SC 29171-0015

803-896-6500
FAX 803-896-6529
TTY: 803-896-6500
http://www.scvrd.net
e-mail: info@scrvd.state.sc.us

Barbara G Hollis, Commissioner

Enabling eligible South Carolinians with disabilities to prepare for, achieve and maintain competitive employment.

South Dakota

4582 South Dakota Department of Labor
700 Governors Dr
Pierre, SD 57501-2291

605-773-3101
800-952-3216
FAX 605-773-6184
TDD:605-773-5017
TTY: 605-773-3101
http://www.state.sd.us
e-mail: miker@dol.pr.state.sd.us

Mike Ryan, Director

Job training programs provide an important framework for developing public-private sector partnerships. We help prepare South Dakotans of all ages for entry or re-entry into the labor force.

4583 South Dakota Department of Social Services
700 Governors Dr
Pierre, SD 57501-2291

605-773-3165
FAX 605-773-4855
http://www.dss.sd.gov

Deborah K Bowman, Director

4584 South Dakota Rehabilitation Center forthe Blind
Department of Human Services
Ste 101
2900 W 11th St
Sioux Falls, SD 57104-2594

605-334-4491
800-658-5441
FAX 605-367-5263
TTY: 605-367-5260
http://www.state.sd.us
e-mail: dawn.backer@state.sd.us

Gaye Mattke, Director

Helping people lead a full, productive life — regardless of how much one does or does not see. Upon completion of training, individuals usually return to their community and use these new skills in their home, school or job.

4585 State Vocational Rehabilitation Agency
Division of Rehabilitation Services
East Highway 34
Hillsview Plaza
Pierre, SD 57501-5070

605-773-3195
800-265-9684
FAX 605-773-5483
TDD:605-773-3195
http://www.dhs.sd.gov/drs
e-mail: steve.stewart@state.sd.us

Grady Kickul, Executive Director

Assists individuals with disabilities to obtain employment, economic self-sufficiency, personal independence and full inclusion into society.

Tennessee

4586 State Vocational Rehabilitation Agency
Tennessee Department of Human Services
15th Floor
400 Deaderick St
Nashville, TN 37248

615-313-4891
866-311-4288
FAX 615-741-6508
TTY: 615-313-4891
http://www.state.tn.us
e-mail: car.w.brown@state.tn.us

Terry Smith, Director

State vocational rehabilitation agencies provide direct services to persons with disabilities, including persons with learning disabilities. The services may include evaluation and diagnosis counseling, guidance, and referral services, vocational and other training services, transportation to rehabilitation services and assistive devices.

4587 Tennessee Department of Education
Tennessee Department of Education
710 James Robertson Parkway
Andrew Johnson Tower, 6th Floor
Nashville, TN 37243-0382

615-741-2731
800-531-1515
http://www.state.tn.us
e-mail: education.comments@tn.gov

Phil White, Director

Mission is to take Tennessee to the top in education. Guides administration of the state's K-12 public schools.

4588 Tennessee Department of Labor & Workforce Development: Office of Adult Education
11th Fl
500 James Robertson Pkwy
Nashville, TN 37243-1204
615-741-0466
800-531-1515
FAX 615-532-4899
TDD:800-848-0299
http://www.state.tn.us
e-mail: phil.white@state.tn.us

Phil White, Director
Bill Haslam, Governor

4589 Tennessee Services for the Blind
Tennessee Department Of Human Services
400 Deaderick Street
2nd Floor
Nashville, TN 37243-1403
615-313-4700
800-628-7818
FAX 615-313-6617
TDD:615-313-6601
TTY: 615-313-6601
http://www.state.tn.us
e-mail: Human-Services.Webmaster@state.tn.us

Terry Smith, Director

Offering training and services to help blind or low-vision citizens of Tennessee become more independent at home, in the community and at work.

Texas

4590 Department of Assistive & Rehabilitative Services
Texas Department of Health & Human Services
4800 N Lamar Blvd
Austin, TX 78756-3106
512-377-0500
800-628-5115
TTY: 866-581-9328
http://www.dars.state.tx.us

Glenn Neal, Director

Transitional and vocational programs aid independence in the home, community and at work for Texans who are blind, deaf, or have other impairments that would benefit from assistive technology.

4591 State Vocational Rehabilitation Agency
Texas State Rehabilitation Commission
4800 N Lamar Blvd
Austin, TX 78756-3106
512-424-4000
800-628-5115
FAX 512-424-4337
TTY: 800-628-5115
http://www.dars.state.tx.us
e-mail: dars@rehab.state.tx.us

Terry Murphy, Commissioner

State vocational rehabilitation agencies provide direct services to persons with disabilities, including persons with learning disabilities. The services may include evaluation and diagnosis, counseling, guidance, and referral services, vocational and other training services, transportation to rehabilitation services and assistive devices.

4592 Texas Department of Assistive and Rehabilitative Services
4800 N Lamar Blvd
Austin, TX 78756-3106
512-377-0500
800-628-5115
FAX 512-424-4730
TTY: 866-581-9328
http://www.dars.state.tx.us
e-mail: dars@rehab.state.tx.us

Terry Murphy, Commissioner

A place where people with disabilities and families with children who have developmental delays enjoys independent and productive lives. The mission is to wo

4593 Texas Workforce Commission
101 E 15th St
Austin, TX 78778-0001
512-463-2294
FAX 512-475-2321
TDD:800-735-2989
http://www.twc.state.tx.us
e-mail: larry.temple@twc.state.tx.us

Larry Temple, Executive Director

Provides oversight, coordination, guidance, planning, technical assistance and implementation of employment and training activities with a focus on meeting the needs of employers throughout the state of Texas.

Utah

4594 Adult Education Services
Utah State Office of Education
250 East 500 South
Salt Lake City, UT 84114-4200
801-538-7500
FAX 801-538-7882
http://www.schools.utah.gov
e-mail: marty.kelly@schools.utah.gov

Marty Kelly, Director

Provides oversight of state and federally funded adult education programs. Offers adult basic education, adult high school completion, English as a second language, and general education development programs.

4595 Utah State Office of Rehabilitation
250 E 500 S
Salt Lake City, UT 84111-3272
801-538-7530
800-473-7530
FAX 801-538-7522
TDD:801-538-7530
TTY: 801-538-7530
http://www.usor.utah.gov
e-mail: rthelin@utah.gov

Russell Thelin, Director

Assisting and empowering eligible individuals. Disabled, learning disabled, blind, low vision and deaf people can prepare for and obtain employment and increase their independence through job training and assistive technology.

Vermont

4596 Adult Education & Literacy
State Department of Education
120 State St
Montpelier, VT 05602-2703
802-828-3101
FAX 802-828-3146
http://wwww.education.vermont.gov
e-mail: edinfo@education.state.vt.us

Kay Charron, Director

Provides adults with educational opportunities to acquire the essential skills and knowledge to achieve career, post-secondary and life goals.

4597 State of Vermont Department of Education: Adult Education and Literacy
120 State Street
Montpelier, VT 05602
802-828-3101
FAX 802-828-3146
http://www.vermont.gov

Kay Charron, Director

Adult Education and Literacy Programs provide adults with educational opportunities to acquire the essential skills and knowledge to achieve career, post-secondary and life goals. The Department of Education supports and administers a number of programs that focus on essential literacy and academic skills as well as workplace and introductory occupational skills.

4598 Vermont Dept of Employment & Training

5 Green Mountain Drive
P.O. Box 488
Montpelier, VT 05601-0488
802-828-4000
FAX 802-828-4022
TDD:802-825-4203
http://www.labor.vermont.gov
Mike Calcagni, Director

The Disability Program Navigator Initiative provides professionals who help individuals with disabilities to find jobs, gain access to jobs, or help in re-entering the job market.

4599 Vermont Division of Vocational Rehabilitation

VocRehab Of Vermont
103 South Main Street
Weeks 1A Building
Waterbury, VT 05671-2303
866-879-6757
TTY: 802-241-1455
http://www.vocrehab.vermont.gov
e-mail: jana.sherman@ahs.state.vt.us
Diane Dalmasse, Director of VocRehab Division

VocRehab's mission is to assist Vermonters with disabilities, find and maintain meaningful employment in their communities. VocRehab Vermont works in close partnership with the Vermont Association of Business, Industry and Rehabilitation. Contact local VocRehab office for information about services.

4600 Vermont Family Network

600 Blair Park Road
Suite 240
Williston, VT 05495-7549
802-876-5315
800-800-4005
FAX 802-876-6291
http://www.vermontfamilynetwork.org
e-mail: info@vtfn.org
June Heston, President/CEO

Provides educational programs for children and young adults with special educational needs.

4601 VocRehab Reach-Up Program

VocRehab Of Vermont
103 South Main Street
Weeks 1A Building
Waterbury, VT 05671-2303
802-241-1455
866-879-6757
FAX 802-241-2830
http://www.vocrehabvermont.org
e-mail: jana.sherman@ahs.state.vt.us
Pamela Dalley, Director

The program helps individuals with disabilities find meaningful work at a level that is appropriate for them.

Virginia

4602 Adult Education and Literacy

Virginia Department of Education
101 N 14th St, James Monroe Bldg.
P.O. Box 2120
Richmond, VA 23218
804-225-2053
FAX 804-225-3352
http://www.doe.virginia.gov
e-mail: gedinfo@doe.virginia.gov
Randall Stamper, Director

Distributes funds and provides leadership and services related to adult education programs in Virginia. The goal is to raise the performance levels of adult education programs, increase the number of GED credentials issued by Virginia, and provide alternatives for youth who are at risk of dropping out of school.

4603 Virginia Department of Rehabilitative Services

8004 Franklin Farms Dr
Richmond, VA 23229-5019
804-662-7000
800-464-9950
FAX 804-662-9532
TTY: 804-662-9040
http://www.vadrs.org
e-mail: James.Rothrock@drs.virginia.gov
James Rothrock, Commissioner

In partnership with people with disabilities and their families, the Virginia Department of Rehabilitative Services collaborates with the public and private sectors to provide and advocate for the highest quality services that empower individuals with disabilities to maximize their employment, independence and engagement in the community.

Washington

4604 State Of Washington, Division Of Vocational Rehabilitation

P.O. Box 45340
Olympia, WA 98504-5340
360-725-3636
800-637-5627
FAX 360-438-8007
http://www1.dshs.wa.gov
e-mail: ruttllm@dshs.wa.gov
Lynnea Ruttledge, Director

Provides employment-related services to individuals with disabilities who want to work but need assistance. These individuals might experience difficulty getting or keeping a job due to a physical, sensory and/or mental disability. A DVR counselor works with each individual to develop a customized plan of services designed to help the individual achieve his or her job goal.

4605 State Vocational Rehabilitation Agency: Washington Division of Vocational Rehabilitation

Department of Social Services & Health
P.O.Box 45340
Olympia, WA 98504-5340
360-725-3636
800-637-5627
FAX 360-438-8007
TDD:360-438-8000
TTY: 360-438-8000
http://www.dshs.wa.gov
e-mail: obrien@dshs.wa.gov
Michael O'Brien, Director

State vocational rehabilitation agencies provide direct services to persons with disabilities, including persons with learning disabilities. The services may include evaluation and diagnosis, counseling, guidance, and referral services, vocational and other training services, transportation to rehabilitation services, and assistive devices.

West Virginia

4606 West Virginia Division of Rehabilitation Services

West Virginia Department of Education & the Arts
State Capitol
PO Box 50890
Charleston, WV 25305-0890
304-766-4601
800-642-8207
FAX 304-766-4905
TDD:304-766-4809
http://www.wvdrs.org
e-mail: susan.n.weinberger@wv.gov

Deborah Lovely, Director
Susan Weinberger, Supervisor, Ed. & Employment

A state agency responsible for the operation of the state and federal vocational rehabilitation program in West Virginia. Specializes in helping people with disabilities who want to find a job or maintain current employment.

Wisconsin

4607 Wisconsin Division of Vocational Rehabilitation
PO Box 7852
Madison, WI 53707-7852   608-261-0050
                                800-442-3477
                          FAX 608-266-1133
                          TDD:888-877-5939
                http://dwd.wisconsin.gov/dvr
                e-mail: dwddvr@dwd.wisconsin.gov
Charlene Dwyer, Administrator

Federal and state program designed to obtain, maintain and improve employment for people with disabilities by working with vocational rehabilitation consumers, employers and other partners.

Wyoming

4608 Wyoming Department of Workforce Services: State Vocational Rehabilitation Agency
1510 E Pershing Blvd
Cheyenne, WY 82002-0001   307-777-3704
                          FAX 307-777-5857
                          TTY: 307-777-7389
                http://www.wyomingworkforce.org
                e-mail: jmcint@state.wy.us
Norma Whitney, Vocational Rehabilitation

Assists Wyoming citizens with disabilities to prepare for, enter into, and return to suitable employment. Individuals with a disability that prevents them from working may apply for these services as long as a physical or mental impairment which constitutes or results in a substantial impediment to employment exists, and they have the ability to benefit in terms of an employment outcome from vocational services.

Georgia

Hawaii

Idaho

Illinois

Indiana

Iowa

Massachusetts

Michigan

Minnesota

Mississippi

Missouri

North Carolina

North Dakota

Ohio

Oklahoma

Rose State College, 3576
Southeastern Oklahoma State University, 3577
Southwestern Oklahoma State University, 3578
St. Gregory's University, 3579
State Vocational Rehabilitation Agency: Oklahoma Department of Rehabilitation Services, 4573
Tulsa Community College, 3580
Tulsa University, 3581
University of Oklahoma, 3582
Workforce Investment Act, 4570, 4574

Oregon

Andeo International Homestays, 1404
Central Oregon Community College, 3584
Clackamas Community College, 3585
Corban College, 3586
Department of Community Colleges and Workforce Development, 1764
Disability Rights Oregon, 1765
Easter Seals Medford, 588
Easter Seals Oregon, 293, 589
George Fox University, 3587
International Dyslexia Association of Oregon, 294
International Partnership for Service- Learning and Leadership, 1415
Lane Community College, 3588
Learning Disabilities Association of Oregon, 295
Linfield College, 3589
Linn-Benton Community College Office of Disability Services, 3590
Mobility International (MIUSA), 1418
Mount Bachelor Academy, 3591
Mt. Hood Community College Disability Services Department, 3592
Office of Vocational Rehabilitation Services, 1766
Oregon Bureau of Labor and Industry: Fair Employment Practice Agency, 1767
Oregon Council on Developmental Disabilities, 1768
Oregon Department of Education: School-to-Work, 1769
Oregon Department of Human Resource Adult & Family Services Division, 2216
Oregon Department of Human Services: Children, Adults & Families Division, 1770
Oregon Employment Department, 1771, 2217, 4575, 4575
Oregon GED Administrator: Office of Community College Services, 2218
Oregon Institute of Technology, 3593
Oregon State Library, 2219
Oregon State University, 3594
Oregon's Deaf and Hard of Hearing Services, 296
Portland Community College, 3595
Recruitment and Retention Special Education Jobs Clearinghouse, 4576
Reed College, 3596
Southwestern Oregon Community College, 3597
Thomas A Edison High School, 4214
Treasure Valley Community College, 3598
Umpqua Community College, 3599
University of Oregon, 3600
University of Oregon Center for Excellence in Developmental Disabilities, 297
Warner Pacific College, 3601
Western Oregon University, 3602
Willamette University, 3603

Pennsylvania

AAC Institute, 298
Albright College, 3604
Arcadia University, College of Global Studies, 1405
Bloomsburg University, 3605
Bryn Mawr College, 3606
Bureau of Adult Basic & Literacy Education, 1772
Cabrini College, 3607
Calm Down and Play, 840
Camp Lee Mar, 590
Carnegie Mellon University, 3608
Center for Alternative Learning, 4215

Center for Psychological Services, 4216
Client Assistance Program (CAP): Pennsylvania Division, 1773
College Misericordia, 3609
Community College of Allegheny County: College Center, North Campus, 3610
Community College of Allegheny County: Boy ce Campus, 3611
Community College of Philadelphia, 3612
Delaware County Community College, 3613
Delaware County Literacy Council, 2220
Delaware Valley College of Science and Agriculture, 3614
Delaware Valley Friends School, 3615
Devereux Mapleton, 4217
Dickinson College, 3616
Disability Rights Network of Pennsylvania, 1774
Dr Gertrude A Barber Center, 4218
Drexel University, 3617
East Stroudsburg University of Pennsylvania, 3618
Easter Seals Society of Western Pennsylvania: Fayette, 299
Forms for Helping the ADHD Child, 844
Gannon University, 3619
Gettysburg College, 3620
Gwynedd: Mercy College, 3621
Harcum Junior College, 3622
Harrisburg Area Community College, 3623
Hill Top Preparatory School, 3624, 4220
Hillside School, 3236, 4221
Huntingdon County PRIDE, 300
Indiana University of Pennsylvania, 3625
Institute for the Study of Adult Literacy, 1893
Institutes for the Achievement of Human Potential, 52
International Dyslexia Association of Pennsylvania, 301
Keystone Junior College, 3626
KidsPeace Orchard Hills Campus, 4222
King's College, 3627
Kutztown University of Pennsylvania, 3628
LDA Annual International Conference, 1009
Learning Disabilities Association of America, 340
Learning Disabilities Association of America, 58
Learning Disabilities Association of Pennsylvania, 302, 2221
Lebanon Valley College, 3629
Lehigh Carbon Community College, 3630
Literacy Council of Lancaster/Lebanon, 2222
Lock Haven University of Pennsylvania, 3631
Lycoming College, 3632
Manor Junior College, 3633
Mansfield University of Pennsylvania, 3634
Marywood University, 3635
Melmark, 4223
Mercyhurst College, 3636
Messiah College, 3637
Millersville University of Pennsylvania, 3638
Moravian College, 3639
National Center on Adult Literacy (NCAL), 1903
No Barriers to Study, 1420
Northampton Community College, 3640
Office of Civil Rights: Pennsylvania, 1775
Pace School, 3641
Parent Education Network, 4224
Pathway School, 3642, 4225
Pennsylvania Center for Disability Law and Policy, 303
Pennsylvania Department of Corrections, 1776
Pennsylvania Developmental Disabilities Council, 1777
Pennsylvania Human Rights Commission, 1778
Pennsylvania Institute of Technology, 3643
Pennsylvania Literacy Resource Center, 2223
Pennsylvania State University, 3644
Pennsylvania State University: Mont Alto, 3645
Pennsylvania State University: Schuylkill Campus, 3646
Pennsylvania State University: Shenango Valley Campus, 3647
Pennsylvania State University: Worthington Scranton Campus, 3648
Pennsylvania Training and Technical Assistance Network Workshops, 1021

Pennsylvania's Initiative on Assistive Technology, 1779
Point Park College, 3649
Reading Area Community College, 3650
Recording for the Blind & Dyslexic, 279, 304
Region III: US Department of Health and Human Services Civil Rights Office, 1780
Seton Hill University, 3651
Shippensburg University of Pennsylvania, 3652
Solebury School, 3653
Solutions Kit for ADHD, 854
State Vocational Rehabilitation Agency: Pennsylvania, 4577
Stop, Relax and Think, 857
Stop, Relax and Think Ball, 858
Stop, Relax and Think Card Game, 859
Stop, Relax and Think Scriptbook, 860
Stop, Relax and Think Workbook, 861
Stratford Friends School, 3654, 4226
Summer Matters, 3655
Temple University, 3656
Thaddeus Stevens College of Technology, 3657
The Children's Institute, 4162, 4227
Thiel College, 3658
University of Pennsylvania, 3659
University of Pittsburgh: Bradford, 3660
University of Pittsburgh: Greensburg, 3661
University of Scranton, 3662
University of the Arts, 3663
Ursinus College, 3664
Valley Forge Educational Services, 3665
Vanguard School, 3666, 4050, 4228, 4228
Washington and Jefferson College, 3667
Westmoreland County Community College, 3668
Widener University, 3669
Woods Schools, 4229
York County Literacy Council, 2224

Rhode Island

Brown University, Disability Support Services, 3670
Bryant College, 3671
Community College of Rhode Island: Knight Campus, 3672
Disability Services for Students, 3673
Harmony Hill School, 4230
International Dyslexia Association of Rhode Island, 305
Johnson & Wales University, 3674
Literacy Volunteers of America: Rhode Island, 2225
Literacy Volunteers of Kent County, 2226
Literacy Volunteers of Providence County, 2227
Literacy Volunteers of South County, 2228
Literacy Volunteers of Washington County, 2229
Literary Resources Rhode Island, 2230
Protection & Advocacy Agency, 1483, 1520, 1575, 1575, 1621, 1637, 1652, 1665, 1729, 1753, 1760, 1784
Providence College, 3675
Rhode Island College, 3676
Rhode Island Commission for Human Rights, 1785
Rhode Island Department of Elementary and Secondary Education, 1786
Rhode Island Department of Labor & Training, 1787
Rhode Island Developmental Disabilities Council, 1788
Rhode Island Human Resource Investment Council, 2231
Rhode Island Parent Information Network, 4231
Rhode Island Vocational and Rehabilitation Agency, 2232, 4578
Rhode Island Workforce Literacy Collaborative, 2233
Roger Williams University, 3677
State Vocational Rehabilitation Agency: Rhode Island, 4579

South Carolina

Aiken Technical College, 3678

Utah

Vermont

Virginia

Wyoming

Boldface indicates Publisher

All About Vision, 2803
All Children Learn Differently, 2728
All Kinds of Minds: Young Student's Book About Learning Disabilities & Disorders, 2329
Allan Hancock College, 3044
Allendale Association, 4067
Alliance For Technology Access, 4425
Alliance for Technology Access, 1034, 2410, 2431, 2447
Allyn & Bacon, 2945
The Almansor Center, 3994
Almansor Transition & Adult Services, 3963
Aloha Special Technology Access Center, 179
Alphabet Circus, 1114
Alpine Tram Ride, 1099
Alternate Assessments for Students with Disabilities, 2413
Alternative Behavioral Services, 4259
Alternative Learners Project, 3609
Alverno College, 3908
Alvin Community College, 3726
Ameri-Corp Speech and Hearing, 2834
America's Health Insurance Plans, 2
American Arbitration Association, 2376
American Association for Adult and Continuing Education, 1879
American Association of Collegiate Registrars and Admissions Officers, 3
American Bar Association Center on Children and the Law: Information Line, 4
American Camp Association, 5
American Camping Association, 437
American College Testing, 6
American College Testing Program, 4278, 4424
American Council on Education, 4282
American Counseling Association, 7
American Dance Therapy Association (ADTA), 8
American Educational Research Association, 2856
American Federation of Teachers, 2720
American Foundation for the Blind, 1069
American Government Today, 868
American Guidance Service, 2638
American Institute for Foreign Study, 1402
American Institutes for Research, 4353
American International College, 3222
American Journal of Occupational Therapy, 2846
American Journal of Speech-Language Pathology: A Journal of Clinical Practice, 2876
American Library Association, 2802
American Literacy Council, 1880
American Occupational Therapy Association, 9, 2846, 2870
The American Printing House for the Blind, Inc., 107
American Printing House for the Blind, 2639
American Psychiatric Publishing, Inc (APPI), 349, 371, 373, 411, 412, 417
American Psychological Association, 10, 2640, 406, 414, 1325, 2804, 2840, 2844, 2889, 2890
American Psychologist, 2840
American Public Human Services Association (APHSA), 11
American Red Cross American Red Cross National Headquarters, 12
American Rehabilitation Counseling Association (ARCA), 13
American School Board Journal, 2847
American School Counselor Association, 2378, 2566
American School for the Deaf, 3999
American Sign Language Concise Dictionary, 2414
American Sign Language Dictionary: A Comprehensive Abridgement, 2415
American Sign Language Dictionary: Software, 1115
American Sign Language Phrase Book Videotape Series, 2729
American Sign Language Video Dictionary & Inflection Guide, 1116
American Speech-Language-Hearing Association, 14
American Speech-Language-Hearing Association, 984, 2875, 2876, 2878, 4444

American University, 3125
American-Scandinavian Foundation, 1403
Americans with Disabilities Act (ADA) Resource Center, 1430
Americans with Disabilities Act Assistance Line, 4580
An Alphabet of Animal Signs, 2348
An Introduction to How Does Your Engine Run?, 836
An Open Book, 1332
An Open Book Unbound, 1333
Analogies 1, 2 & 3, 596
Anchorage Literacy Project, 1913
Andeo International Homestays, 1404
Anderson Center for Autism, 4171
Andreas: Outcomes of Inclusion, 2730
Andrew College, 3145
Andrews University, 3250
Andrus Children's Center, 4172, 4179
Andy and His Yellow Frisbee, 837
Angelina College, 3727
Animals of the Rainforest Classroom Library, 749
Ann Martin Children's Center, 3964
Ann Wood Literacy Center, 2161
Annals Publishing Company, 2848
Annals of Dyslexia, 2907
Annals of Otology, Rhinology and Laryngology, 2848
Anne Arundel County Literacy Council, 2087
Anne Carlsen Center for Children, 3499, 4204
Annual Postsecondary Disability Training Institute, 986
Another Door to Learning, 2416
Answers4Families: Center on Children, Families, Law, 2135
Answers4Families: Center on Children, Families and the Law, 1674
Antelope Valley College, 3045
Ants in His Pants: Absurdities and Realities of Special Education, 750, 2417
Aphasia Diagnostic Profiles, 4370
Appalachian State University, 3452
AppleSeeds, 751
AppleWorks Education, 1063
Aquarius Health Care Media, 2699
Aquarius Health Media Care, 2726, 2735, 2748, 2764, 2778
Aquinas College, 3251
Aquinas Literacy Center, 2015
Arcadia University, College of Global Studies, 1405
Archuleta County Education Center, 1960
Arizona Center Comprehensive Education and Lifeskills, 3957
Arizona Center for Disability Law, 122, 1463
Arizona Center for Law in the Public Interest, 1464
Arizona Department of Corrections, 1468
Arizona Department of Economic Security, 1465, 4462
Arizona Department of Education, 1466, 125, 1469, 1471, 2560
Arizona Dept Of Economic Security, 4463
Arizona Governor's Committee on Employment of the Handicapped, 1467
Arizona Vocational Rehabilitation, 4462
Arkansas Adult Learning Resource Center, 1919
Arkansas City Literacy Council, 2051
Arkansas City Public Library, 2051
Arkansas Council for Exceptional Children, 983
Arkansas Department of Career Education, 4464
Arkansas Department of Corrections, 1473
Arkansas Department of Education, 1474
Arkansas Department of Health & Human Services: Division of Developmental Disabilities, 4465
Arkansas Department of Special Education, 1475
Arkansas Department of Workforce Education, 1476, 1484
Arkansas Department of Workforce Services, 1477
Arkansas Disability Coalition, 3962
Arkansas Employment Security Department: Office of Employment & Training Services, 4466

Arkansas Governor's Developmental Disabilities Council, 1478
Arkansas Literacy Council, 1920
Arkansas Rehabilitation Services, 4467, 4470
Arkansas State Employment Board, 4472
Army & Air Force Exchange Service, 1406
Around the Clock: Parenting the Delayed ADHD Child, 2731
Art Academy of Cincinnati, 3509
Art for All the Children: Approaches to Art Therapy for Children with Disabilities, 2nd Ed., 2908
Art of Communication, 2732
Art-Centered Education & Therapy for Children with Disabilities, 2909
Artificial Language Laboratory, 1070
Ashe County 4-H, 572
Ashland Adult Education, 2063
Ashland Community & Technical College, 2063
Asnuntuck CC B-131, 1972
Aspen Education Group, 3046, 480
Assertive Option: Your Rights and Responsibilities, 2540
Assessing ADHD in the Schools, 365
Assessing Children for the Presence of a Disability, 2561
Assessing Learning Problems Workshop, 987
Assessing the ERIC Resource Collection, 2562
Assessment Update, 4344
Assessment of Students with Handicaps in Vocational Education, 4345
Assistive Technology, 1579, 1659, 1683, 1745, 1756
Assistive Technology Advocacy Center-ATAC, 4556
Assistive Technology Center, 1823
Assistive Technology Center (ATAC), 1704
Assistive Technology Office, 1603
Assistive Technology Partners, 1502
Assistive Technology Partnership, 1675
Assistive Technology Program, 1732, 1763, 1790, 1824
Assistive Technology Project, 1479, 1660, 1667
Assistive Technology Resource Centers of Hawaii (ATRC), 180
Assistive Technology System, 1838
Assistive Technology Training Program, 988
Assistive Technology of Alaska (ATLA), 1456
Associated Services for the Blind, 2641
Associated Talmud Torahs of Chicago, 4068
Association Book Exhibit, 989
Association Book Exhibit: Brain Research, 989
Association On Higher Education and Disability (AHEAD), 15
Association for Career and Technical Education, 4345
Association for Childhood Education International (ACEI), 216
Association for Educational Communications and Technology, 1071
Association for International Practical Training, 1407
Association for Supervision/Curriculum Development, 2705, 2708, 2712, 2770, 2845, 2855
Association of Educational Therapists, 16, 1881, 2841
Association of Higher Education Facilities Officers Newsletter, 2608
Association of State Mental Health Program Direct, 2384
Association on Higher Education and Disability, 1882
Association on Higher Education and Disability, 2642
Association on Higher Education and Disability, 2860, 3004, 3006, 3007, 3009, 3011, 3012
At-Risk Youth Resources, 2643
Atlanta Speech School, 4051, 3156, 4061
Atlantis Academy, 4038
AtoZap!, 597, 1117
Attack Math, 669
Attention Deficit Disorder, 2733

Boldface indicates Publisher

Boldface indicates Publisher

Boldface indicates Publisher

K

KC & Clyde in Fly Ball, 1108
KDES Health Curriculum Guide, 2947
KET Basic Skills Series, 2795
KET Foundation Series, 2796
KET, The Kentucky Network Enterprise Division, 2714, 2715, 2795, 2796, 2797, 2798
KET/GED Series, 2797
KET/GED Series Transitional Spanish Edition, 2798
KIND News, 2600
KIND News Jr: Kids in Nature's Defense, 2601
KIND News Primary: Kids in Nature's Defense, 2602
KIND News Sr: Kids in Nature's Defense, 2603
KY-SPIN, Inc., 4093
Kaleidoscope After School Program, 455
Kaleidoscope, Exploring the Experience of Disability Through Literature and Fine Arts, 2879
Kamp A-Kom-plish, 498
Kamp Kiwanis, 559
Kansas Adult Education Association, 1595, 2055
Kansas Board of Regents, 1600
Kansas Board of Regents Adult Education, 1602
Kansas Correctional Education, 2056
Kansas Department of Corrections, 2057
Kansas Department of Labor, 1596
Kansas Department of Social & Rehabilitation Services, 2058
Kansas Department of Social and Rehabilitation Services, 1597
Kansas Human Rights Commission, 1598
Kansas Literacy Resource Center, 2059
Kansas State Department of Adult Education, 2060
Kansas State Department of Education, 1599
Kansas State GED Administration, 1600
Kansas State Literacy Resource Center: Kansas State Department of Education, 2061
Kaplan Early Learning Company, 735, 736, 742, 743, 744, 745, 746, 4302
Karafin School, 4181
Kaskaskia College, 3165
Katie's Farm, 1137
Kaufman Assessment Battery for Children, 4323
Kaufman Brief Intelligence Test, 4324
Kaufman Speech Praxis Test, 615
Kayne Eras Center, 3076, 3975
Kean University, 3310
Keene State College, 3286
Keeping Ahead in School: A Students Book About Learning Disabilities & Learning Disorders, 2545
Kennedy Krieger Institute, 4102
Kent County Literacy Council, 2112
Kent State University, 2198
Kentucky Adult Education, 1604
Kentucky Client Assistance Program, 1605
Kentucky Department of Corrections, 1606
Kentucky Department of Education, 1607
Kentucky Laubach Literacy Action, 2064
Kentucky Literacy Volunteers of America, 2065
Kentucky Protection and Advocacy, 1608
Kentucky Special Ed TechTraining Center, 1326
Kentucky Special Parent Involvement Network, Inc., 4093
Ketchikan Campus: University of Alaska Southeast, 3033
Key Concepts in Personal Development, 2481, 2698
Key Learning Center, 3469
Keyboarding Skills, 887
Keystone Junior College, 3626
Khan-Lewis Phonological Analysis: KLPA-2, 4413
Kid Pix, 1138
KidDesk, 1319
KidDesk: Family Edition, 1320
KidTECH, 1281
Kids Behind the Label: An Inside at ADHD for Classroom Teachers, 2337
Kids Media Magic 2.0, 775, 1139, 1381
KidsPeace Orchard Hills Campus, 4222

Kildonan School, 3385, 4182
Kind News, 2601, 2602
Kindercomp Gold, 1280
King's College, 3627
Kingsbury Center, 4033
Kirkwood Community College, 2042
Klingberg Family Centers, 4010
Knoxville Business College, 3711
Kolburne School, 524
The Kolburne School Summer Program, 524
The Kolburne School, Inc., 3247
Kurtz Center, 4042
Kurzweil 3000, 1340
Kurzweil Educational Systems, 1340
Kutztown University of Pennsylvania, 3628

L

LAP-D Kindergarten Screen Kit, 742
LD Advocate, 2630
LD Child and the ADHD Child, 393
LD News, 2631
LD OnLine/Learing Disabilities Resource, 1027
LD OnLine/Learning Disabilities Resource, 1026
LD Online, 421
LD Online Math & Dyscalculia, 55
LD Pride Online, 2825
LDA Alabama Newsletter, 2621, 2864
LDA Annual International Conference, 1009
LDA Illinois Newsletter, 2622
LDA Learning Center, 4138
LDA Life and Learning Services, 274
LDA Minnesota, 4138
LDA Minnesota Learning Disability Association, 2119
LDA Rhode Island Newsletter, 2865
LDAT Annual State Conference, 1010
LDR Workshop: What Are Learning Disabilities, Problems and Differences?, 1011
LEARN: Regional Educational Service Center, 1966
LIFT: St. Louis, 2127
LILAC, 616
LINC, 1084
LRP Publications, 2383, 2852
LVA Richland County, 2133
The Lab School of Washington, 3129, 4035
Ladders to Literacy: A Kindergarten Activity Book, 2482
Ladders to Literacy: A Preschool Activity Book, 2483
Lafayette Advocacy Center, 210
Lake County Literacy Coalition, 1945
Lake Michigan Academy, 3255, 4135
Lakeshore Technical College, 3917
Lamar Community College, 3109
Lamar State College - Port Arthur, 3747
Landmark College, 3806
Landmark Elementary and Middle School Program, 3237
Landmark High School Program, 3238
Landmark Method for Teaching Arithmetic, 2981
Landmark School, 56, 515, 1012, 2484, 2526, 2972, 2980, 2981, 3237, 3238, 3239, 4118, 4119
Landmark School Outreach Program, 56, 1012, 3239, 4118
Landmark School Summer Boarding Program, 515
Landmark School and Summer Programs, 4119
Landmark School's Language-Based Teaching Guides, 2484
Landmark Summer Program: Exploration and Recreation, 516
Landmark Summer Program: Marine Science, 517
Landmark Summer Program: Musical Theater, 518
Lane Community College, 3588
Laney College, 3066
Language Activity Resource Kit: LARK, 617
Language Arts, 2880
Language Carnival I, 1140
Language Carnival II, 1141
Language Experience Recorder Plus, 1391
Language Learning Everywhere We Go, 2973

Language Master, 1142
Language and Literacy Learning in Schools, 2485
Language-Related Learning Disabilities, 2486
Laramie County Community College: Disability Support Services, 3947
Laredo Community College, 3748
Large Print Keyboard, 1048
Large Print Lower Case Key Label Stickers, 1049
Latest Technology for Young Children, 2760
Latter-Day Saints Business College, 3790
Laureate Learning Systems, 1321, 1101, 1152, 1172, 1173, 1174, 1175, 1188, 1190, 1191, 1192, 1194, 1195, 1202, 1272, 1275, 1354
Lawrence Hall Youth Services, 1565
Lawrence Productions, 1137
Lawrence University, 3918
League School of Greater Boston, 4120
Leap Program & Disability Services Office, 3710
Learn About Life Science: Animals, 818, 1363
Learn About Life Science: Plants, 819, 1364
Learn About Physical Science: Simple Machines, 820
Learn to Match, 1143
Learn to Read, 1992
Learning & Student Development Services, 3440
Learning About Numbers, 1241
Learning Accomplishment Profile Diagnostic Normed Screens for Age 3-5, 743
Learning Accomplishment Profile (LAP-R) KI T, 744
Learning Accomplishment Profile Diagnostic Normed Assessment (LAP-D), 745
Learning Ally, 57
Learning Ally: Colorado-Rocky Mountain Unit, 151
The Learning Camp, 458
Learning Center, 4011
The Learning Center (TLC), 3306, 4156
The Learning Center School, 4130
Learning Center for Adults and Families, 2250
The Learning Clinic, 4022
Learning Company, 1322
Learning Development Department, 3660
Learning Diagnostic Clinic, 3274
Learning Diagnostic Program, 3401
Learning Differences Program, 3636
Learning Disabilities & ADHD: A Family Guide to Living and Learning Together, 2487
Learning Disabilities A to Z, 2488
Learning Disabilities Association, 1813
Learning Disabilities Association Alabama, 2621
Learning Disabilities Association Illinois, 2622
Learning Disabilities Association of Hawaii, 214, 234, 340, 1609, 4063
Learning Disabilities Association of Alabama, 119
Learning Disabilities Association of Alabama, 2864
Learning Disabilities Association of America, 58, 2664
Learning Disabilities Association of America, 340, 1009, 2342, 2371, 2393, 2452, 2458, 2460, 2462, 2466, 2468, 2479, 2567, 2756, 2867
Learning Disabilities Association of Arkansas (LDAA), 130
Learning Disabilities Association of California, 142
Learning Disabilities Association of Central New York, 275
Learning Disabilities Association of Color ado, 152
Learning Disabilities Association of Conneecticut, 160
Learning Disabilities Association of Cuyahoga County, 290
Learning Disabilities Association of Florida, 171, 1993
Learning Disabilities Association of Georgia, 177
Learning Disabilities Association of Georgia, 394
Learning Disabilities Association of Hawaii (LDAH), 183
Learning Disabilities Association of Illinois, 191
Learning Disabilities Association of Indiana, 197

Boldface indicates Publisher

501

Boldface indicates Publisher

M

Boldface indicates Publisher

Boldface indicates Publisher

Boldface indicates Publisher

X

Y

Z

ADD/ADHD

Child Welfare

Clearinghouses

Cognitive Disorders

College

Communication Disorders

Community Integration

Comprehension

Conceptual Skills

Conferences

Consumer Resources

Consumer Skills

Contemporary Education

Cooperative Learning Centers

Baudhuin Preschool, 4039
Behavioral Directions, 4257
Bellefaire Jewish Children's Bureau, 4205
Berkshire Meadows, 3224, 4109
Bodine School, 4235
Bridges Academy, 4240
Camelot Care Center: Illinois, 4070
Center for Children with Disabilities, 4147
Center on Disability Studies, 4062
Chelsea School, 3207, 4099
Children's Institute for Learning Differences, 4269
Churchill Center & School for Learning Disabilities, 4140
Cincinnati Center for Developmental Disorders, 4206
Commonwealth Learning Center, 4112
Cotting School, 3230, 4113
Crisman School, 4242
DBTAC: Northeast ADA Center, 1718
Designs for Learning Differences Sycamore School, 4167
Developmental Disabilities Resource Center, 3997
EAC Nassau Learning Center, 4175
Educational Options, 4115
Evergreen Center, 3234, 4116
F.L. Chamberlain School, 4117
Focus Alternative Learning Center, 4005
Founder's Cottage, 4007
Frost Center, 4101
Frostig Center, 3071, 3971
Gateway School, 4243
Gillis Center, 4141
Hampshire Country School, 3284, 4148
Havern School, 3108, 3998
Heritage School, 4139
Hillside School, 3236, 4221
Huntington Learning Centers, Inc., 4200, 4284
Institute for the Redesign of Learning, 3074, 3974
Jacob's Ladder Helping Children Succeed One Step at a Time, 4057
Karafin School, 4181
KidsPeace Orchard Hills Campus, 4222
League School of Greater Boston, 4120
Leary School Programs, 4262
Living with a Learning Disability, 2496
Mary McDowell Friends School, 4185
Matheny Medical and Educational Center, 4157
Meredith-Dunn School, 4094
Mill Springs Academy, 3152, 4058
Morning Star School, 3137, 4044
Natchaug Hospital School Program, 4014
New Community School, 3825, 4264
New Vistas School, 4265
New York Institute for Special Education, 4187
Newgrange School, 4158
Newport Audiology Center, 3979
Office of Disability Employment Policy: US Department of Labor, 1444
Overton Speech & Language Center, Inc., 4244
Parish School, 4245
Paul Robeson School, 4034
Pine Hill School, 3982
Professional Assistance Center for Education (PACE), 4082
Readiness Program, 3410
Reading Success Plus, Inc., 4059
Reid School, 4251
Renaissance Learning Center, 4047
Ridge School of Montgomery County, 4105
Riley Child Development Center, 4292
Riverbrook Residence, 4126
Riverside School, 3836, 4268
Riverview School, 3244, 4127
Robert Louis Stevenson School, 4191
Saint Francis Home for Children: Highland, 4018
Schermerhorn Program, 3422
Sequel TSI, 3952
Special Education Day School Program, 3988
Starpoint School, 4249
Stratford Friends School, 3654, 4226
Summit School, Inc., 4085
Susan Maynard Counseling, 4049
The Almansor Center, 3994
The Center School, 4161

The Early Achievement Center, 4087
The Forbush School at Glyndon, 4106
The Foundation School, 4021
The Howard School, 4060
The Midland School, 4165
The Norman Howard School, 4195
The Perkins Day Treatment Program, 4132
Thomas A Edison High School, 4214
Trident Academy, 3693, 4234
VISTA Vocational & Life Skills Center, 4023
Van Cleve Program, 3447
Vision Care Clinic, 3996
Wilderness School, 4028
Willow Hill School, 3249, 4133
Windward School, 4197

Creative Expression

Affect and Creativity, 2883
Author's Toolkit, 935, 1386
Basic Skills Products, 1119, 1219
Create with Garfield, 1103
Create with Garfield: Deluxe Edition, 1104
Easybook Deluxe Writing Workshop: Immigration, 874, 944
Easybook Deluxe Writing Workshop: Rainforest & Astronomy, 875, 945
Once Upon a Time Volume I: Passport to Discovery, 1393
Painting the Joy of the Soul, 2342

Critical Thinking

Read and Solve Math Problems #3, 1262

Curriculum Guides

Print Module, 1324
Springer School and Center, 4212
Teaching Students with Learning and Behavior Problems, 2899

Daily Living

A Calendar of Home Activities, 4367
ABC's of Learning Disabilities, 2720
Aids and Appliances for Independent Living, 640
Aphasia Diagnostic Profiles, 4370
BRIGANCE Life Skills Inventory, 4374
Calendar Fun with Lollipop Dragon, 1184
Disabled Faculty and Staff in a Disabling Society: Multiple Identities in Higher Education, 3004
District of Columbia Department of Education: Vocational & Adult Education, 4495
District of Columbia Public Schools, 1983
Get Ready to Read!, 2629
Imagination Express Destination: Neighborhood, 1373
Imagination Express Destination: Pyramids, 1375
LD Advocate, 2630
LD News, 2631
Literacy Volunteers of the National Capital Area, 1984
Math Spending and Saving, 1200
Math for Everyday Living, 1247
Money Skills, 1201
Our World, 2632
Special Needs Program, 655
Succeeding in the Workplace, 4445
Travel the World with Timmy Deluxe, 666
U.S. Department Of Education, 1985
Upward Foundation, 3038
World Class Learning Materials, 1270
Zap! Around Town, 732, 1271

Databases

Dialog Information Services, 1080
www.apa.org/psycinfo, 2804
www.ntis.gov, 2829

Developmental Disabilities

Adirondack Leadership Expeditions, 546
Alabama Council for Developmental Disabilities, 1451
Birth Defect Research for Children (BDRC), 22
Body and Physical Difference: Discourses of Disability, 2912
California Association of Private Special, 132
California Association of Special Education & Services, 1942
Camp ASCCA, 441
Camp Akeela, 593
Camp Bari Tov, 547
Camp Buckskin, 531
Camp Kavod, 472
Camp Lee Mar, 590
Camp Northwood, 552
Camp Sky Ranch, 566
Center for Disabilities and Development, 199
Charis Hills, 591
Client Assistance Program (CAP): New Mexico Protection and Advocacy System, 1711
Colorado Developmental Disabilities, 1505
Defects: Engendering the Modern Body, 2921
Developmental Disabilities Council, 1619
Developmental Variation and Learning Disorders, 2922
EBL Coaching Summer Programs, 556
FAT City, 2749
Frames of Reference for the Assessment of Learning Disabilities, 2931
Gainesville Hall County Alliance for Literacy, 1995
Illinois Council on Developmental Disabilities, 1567
Institutes for the Achievement of Human Potential, 52
International Dyslexia Association Southwest Branch, 267
LDA Life and Learning Services, 274
LDA Minnesota Learning Disability Association, 2119
LDAT Annual State Conference, 1010
Landmark School Summer Boarding Program, 515
Learning Disabilities A to Z, 2488
Learning Disabilities Association, 1813
Learning Disabilities Association of Kentucky, 1609
Learning Disabilities Association of Maine (LDA), 214
Learning Disabilities Association of Alabama, 119
Learning Disabilities Association of Arkansas (LDAA), 130
Learning Disabilities Association of California, 142
Learning Disabilities Association of Colorado, 152
Learning Disabilities Association of Cuyahoga County, 290
Learning Disabilities Association of Florida, 171, 1993
Learning Disabilities Association of Iowa, 202, 1592, 2047
Learning Disabilities Association of Kansas, 206
Learning Disabilities Association of Missouri, 242
Learning Disabilities Association of New Mexico: Albuquerque, 268
Learning Disabilities Association of New York City, 276
Learning Disabilities Association of New Mexico: Las Cruces, 269
Learning Disabilities Association of Oklahoma, 292
Learning Disabilities Association of Oregon, 295
Learning Disabilities Association of Pennsylvania, 302, 2221
Learning Disabilities Association of Texas, 319
Learning Disabilities Association of Washington, 329
Learning Disabilities Association of Western New York, 277
Learning Disabilities Worldwide (LDW), 228
Learning Disabilities: Theories, Diagnosis and Teaching Strategies, 2491

Lily Videos : A Longitudinel View of Lily with Down Syndrome, 2768
Living Independently Forever, Inc., 4123
Maryland Developmental Disabilities Council, 1626
Massachusetts Association of Approved Private Schools (MAAPS), 229
Minot State University, 3505
Montana Council on Developmental Disabilities (MCDD), 1669
National Alliance on Mental Illness (NAMI), 341
National Association for Child Development, 66
National Council on Disability, 1437
National Dissemination Center for Children with Disabilities, 83, 344
National Organization on Disability (NOD), 90
New Hampshire Developmental Disabilities Council, 1698
New Hampshire Disabilities Rights Center (DRC), 256
New Jersey Council on Developmental Disabilities, 4559
New York Easter Seals Society, 278
North Carolina Council on Developmental Disabilities, 1734
North Dakota State Council on Developmental Disabilities, 1744
Northwestern State University, 3203
Ohio Developmental Disabilities Council, 1751
On Our Own Transition Series, 2800
Oregon Council on Developmental Disabilities, 1768
Oregon's Deaf and Hard of Hearing Services, 296
Pennsylvania Developmental Disabilities Council, 1777
Pennsylvania State University, 3644
Rhode Island College, 3676
Rhode Island Developmental Disabilities Council, 1788
SOAR Adventure Programs, 568
SUWS Wilderness Program, 480
Shield Summer Play Program, 564
South Carolina Developmental Disabilities Council, 1792
South Dakota Center for Disabilities, 309
Southwestern Indiana Easter Seal, 198
St. Louis Learning Disabilities Association, 244
Strong Center for Developmental Disabilities, 281
Survival Guide for Teenagers with LD Learning Differences, 2552
Teaching Developmentally Disabled Children, 2533
Teaching Gifted Kids in the Regular Classroom, 2963
Teaching Kids with Mental Health and Learning Disorders in the Regular Classroom, 863
Tennessee Council on Developmental Disabilities, 1810
University of Colorado: Denver, 3112
University of Idaho, 3158
University of New Mexico/School of Medicine, 3338
University of Tennessee, 3721
Vermont Developmental Disabilities Council, 1834
Victory Junction Gang Camp, 571
Washington State Developmental Disabilities Council, 1855
Wisconsin Board for People with Developmental Disabilities, 1867
YMCA Camp Glacier Hollow, 595
Yellin Center for Mind, Brain, and Education, 283
www.healthanswers.com, 2814
www.intelihealth.com, 2820
www.ldonline.org, 2824
www.optimums.com, 2832
3D Learner Program, 470

Directories

Directory for Exceptional Children, 2924
Directory of Organizations, 2564
Grey House Publishing, 2657
Guide to Private Special Education, 2453
ISS Directory of International Schools, 3008

Member Directory, 3010
National Toll-free Numbers, 2577

Discrimination

Civil Rights Division: US Department of Justice, 1431
Disability Rights California (California's Protection and Advocacy System), 1494
EEOC St. Louis District Office, 1661
Equal Employment Opportunity Commission, 1435
Eye-Hand Coordination Boosters, 901
Following Directions: Left and Right, 1194
Legal Center for People with Disabilities and Older People, 1507
Link N' Learn Activity Cards, 910
Nebraska Advocacy Services, 1677
New Hampshire Commission for Human Rights, 1697
New Jersey Department of Law and Public Safety, 1705
Office for Civil Rights: US Department of Health and Human Services, 1442
Office for Civil Rights: US Department of Education, 1443
Office of Civil Rights: California, 1498
Office of Civil Rights: District of Columbia, 1534
Office of Civil Rights: Georgia, 1544
Office of Civil Rights: Illinois, 1574
Office of Civil Rights: Massachusetts, 1635
Office of Civil Rights: Missouri, 1664
Office of Civil Rights: New York, 1725
Office of Civil Rights: Ohio, 1748
Office of Civil Rights: Pennsylvania, 1775
Office of Civil Rights: Texas, 1814
Office of Federal Contract Compliance Programs: US Department of Labor, 1445
Office of Federal Contract Compliance: Boston District Office, 1636
Region I: Office for Civil Rights, 1638
Region I: US Small Business Administration, 1639
Region II: US Department of Health and Human Services, 1730
Region III: US Department of Health and Human Services Civil Rights Office, 1780
Region IV: Office of Civil Rights, 1545
Region IX: US Department of Health and Human Services, 1500
Region V: Civil Rights Office, 1576
Region V: US Department of Labor: Office of Federal Contract Compliance, 1577
Region V: US Small Business Administration, 1578
Region VIII: US Department of Health and Human Services, 1509
Region VIII: US Department of Labor-Office of Federal Contract Compliance, 1510
Region X: Office of Federal Contract Compliance, 1848
Region X: US Department of Health and Human Services, Office of Civil Rights, 1850
Shape and Color Rodeo, 1282
US Department of Justice: Disabilities Rights Section, 2402
US Department of Justice: Disability Rights Section, 2403
Utah Antidiscrimination and Labor Division, 1828

Dispute Resolution Dyslexia

Dispute Resolution Journal, 2376

Dyscalculia

Dyscalculia International Consortium (DIC), 41
LD Online Math & Dyscalculia, 55

Dyslexia

About Dyslexia: Unraveling the Myth, 2408
Annals of Dyslexia, 2907
Atlantis Academy, 4038
Common Sense About Dyslexia, 2428

Connect Outloud, 1036
Cove School, 3162, 4074
Dyslexia/ADHD Institute, 4357
Dyslexia: A Different Kind of Learning, 2748
Easter Seals Central Alabama, 115
Easter Seals West Alabama, 116
Easter Seals of the Birmingham Area, 117
Eton Academy, 3254, 4134
IDA Conference, 1005
International Dyslexia Association - Illinois/Missouri, 189
International Dyslexia Association of Maryland, 220
International Dyslexia Association of Alabama, 118
International Dyslexia Association of Arizona, 124
International Dyslexia Association of New Jersey, 263
International Dyslexia Association of Pennsylvania, 301
International Dyslexia Association: Illinois Branch Newsletter, 2596, 2617
JAWS for Windows, 1047
Learning Ally: Colorado-Rocky Mountain Unit, 151
Legacy of the Blue Heron: Living with Learning Disabilities, 2493, 2766
McGlannan School, 4043
One To One Reading & Educational Tutoring, 3980
Open Book, 1051
Overcoming Dyslexia in Children, Adolescents and Adults, 2894
Reading and Learning Disabilities: A Resource Guide, 2992
Recording for the Blind & Dyslexic, 279, 304
Recording for the Blind & Dyslexic: Florida, 173
Recording for the Blind & Dyslexic: Phoenix Studio, 126
Recording for the Blind & Dyslexic: Sun Cities Studio, 127
Santa Cruz Learning Center, 3987
Teaching the Dyslexic Child, 2536
Washington State Branch of IDA, 331
www.ldteens.org, 2826

ESL

Center for Applied Linguistics, 27
KET/GED Series Transitional Spanish Edition, 2798
People at Work, 652
St. James ESL Program, 2306
TESOL Newsletter, 2627
The Eight Ball Club: Ocean of Fire, 2345
Write On! Plus: Spanish/ English Literacy Series, 974

Economic Skills

Arkansas Employment Security Department: Office of Employment & Training Services, 4466
Department of Community Colleges and Workforce Development, 1764
Department of Workforce Services, 1826
Illinois Department of Commerce and Community Affairs, 1568
Nebraska Department of Labor, 1678
Nebraska Equal Opportunity Commission, 1679
Texas Workforce Commission, 4593
Texas Workforce Commission: Workforce Development Division, 1822
Workforce Development Division, 4460
www.jobhunt.org/slocareers/resources.html, 2822

Education

ASCD Express, 2845
Academic Resource Center, 4098
Alternate Assessments for Students with Disabilities, 2413
American Camp Association, 5
American Counseling Association, 7

Elementary Education

Equality

Ethics

Evaluations

Eye/Hand Coordination

Family Involvement

Family Resources

Financial Resources

Fluency

Gameboards

Bozons' Quest, 1183
Curious George Preschool Learning Games, 734
Garfield Trivia Game, 1107
PCI Educational Publishing, 891

Gifted Education

CEC Today, 2851
Center on Disabilities Conference, 996
Council for Exceptional Children, 2611
State Resource Sheet, 2591
Teaching Gifted Kids in the Regular Classroom CD-ROM, 2962

Graphing

Data Explorer, 678, 1231
Graphers, 689

Health Care

America's Health Insurance Plans, 2
KDES Health Curriculum Guide, 2947
National Organization for Rare Disorders (NORD), 89
Programs for Children with Special Health Care Needs, 1727, 4561
Seven Hills Academy at Groton, 4128
www.HealthCentral.com, 2801
www.healthcentral.com, 2816

Hearing Impaired

American Sign Language Phrase Book Videotape Series, 2729
Beginning Signing Primer, 2350
Essential ASL: The Fun, Fast, and Simple Way to Learn American Sign Language, 2445
First Start in Sign Language, 2971
HearFones, 611
It's Your Turn Now, 2480
My Signing Book of Numbers, 2363
The Learning Center School, 4130
Volta Voices, 2598

Higher Education

ACCESS Program, 3043
ACT Universal Testing, 4423
Academic Resource Program, 3342
Adelphi University, 3343
Adirondack Community College, 3344
Aiken Technical College, 3678
Alaska Pacific University, 3030
Albert Einstein College of Medicine, 3345
Albright College, 3604
Alexandria Technical and Community College, 3259
Allan Hancock College, 3044
Alverno College, 3908
Alvin Community College, 3726
American College Testing, 6
American College Testing Program, 4278, 4424
American International College, 3222
American Printing House for the Blind, 2639
American Speech-Language-Hearing Association, 14
American University, 3125
Andrews University, 3250
Angelina College, 3727
Annual Postsecondary Disability Training Institute, 986
Antelope Valley College, 3045
Appalachian State University, 3452
Aquinas College, 3251
Arizona Center Comprehensive Education and Lifeskills, 3957
Art Academy of Cincinnati, 3509
Aspen Education Group, 3046
Auburn University, 3015
Auburn University at Montgomery, 3016

Augsburg College, 3260
Austin Peay State University, 3707
Averett College, 3811
Bacone College, 3566
Baker University, 3192
Bakersfield College, 3047
Baldwin-Wallace College, 3510
Ball State University, 3172
Bank Street College: Graduate School of Education, 3346
Banyan School, 3293
Barstow Community College, 3048
Bellevue Community College, 3850
Beloit College, 3909
Bennett College, 3453
Berkshire Center, 3223
Bethany College West Virginia, 3896
Binghamton University, 3347
Birmingham-Southern College, 3017
Bismarck State College, 3500
Black Hills State College, 3701
Blackhawk Technical College, 3910
Bloomsburg University, 3605
Bluffton College, 3511
Boston College, 3225
Bowling Green State University, 3512
Bramson Ort Technical Institute, 3348
Brescia University, 3196
Brevard College, 3454
Bridge School, 3049
Bridgewater State College, 3227
Bright Students Who Learn Differently, 4241
Bristol Community College, 3228
Brookhaven College, 3728
Brown Mackie College: Akron, 3513
Brown University, Disability Support Services, 3670
Bryan College: Dayton, 3708
Bryant College, 3671
Bryn Mawr College, 3606
Burlington College, 3800
Butte College, 3050
CUNY Queensborough Community College, 3349
Cabrillo College, 3051
Cabrini College, 3607
Caldwell College, 3294
Caldwell Community College and Technical Institute, 3455
California State University: East Bay, 3052
California State University: Fullerton, 3053
California State University: Long Beach-Stephen Benson Program, 3054
Camden County College, 3295
Campus Opportunities for Students with Learning Differences, 3000
Canisius College, 3350
Cardinal Stritch University, 3911
Career College Association (CCA), 25, 1883
Carnegie Mellon University, 3608
Carroll School, 3229
Carson-Newman College, 3709
Carthage College, 3912
Cascade College, 3583
Case Western Reserve University, 3514
Catawba College, 3456
Catawba Valley Community College, 3457
Cathedral High School, 3173
Catholic University of America, 3126
Cazenovia College, 3351
Cedar Valley College, 3729
Centenary College, 3296
Center for Adaptive Learning, 3966
Center for Child and Human Development, 167
Center for Disability Services, 3851
Central Carolina Community College, 3458
Central Ohio Technical College, 3515
Central Oregon Community College, 3584
Central Piedmont Community College, 3459
Central State University, 3516
Central Texas College, 3730
Centralia College, 3852
Chaffey Community College District, 3055
Champlain College, 3801
Chartwell School: Seaside, 3057

Chattahoochee Valley State Community College, 3018
Children's Care Hospital and School, 3702
Children's Institute for Learning, 3853
Chippewa Valley Technical College, 3913
Churchill Academy, 3019
Churchill Center and School for Learning Disabilities, 3272
Cincinnati State Technical and Community College, 3517
Cisco College, 3731
Citadel-Military College of South Carolina, 3680
Clackamas Community College, 3585
Clark College, 3854
Clark State Community College, 3518
Clearinghouse on Reading, English and Communications, 4089
Clemson University, 3681
Cleveland Institute of Art, 3519
Cleveland State University, 3520
Clinton High School, 3181
Coaching Program, 3252
Coastal Carolina University, 3682
Colgate University, 3355
College Board Services for Students with Disabilities, 30
College Internship Program, 4111
College Living Experience, 4498
College Misericordia, 3609
College Students with Learning Disabilities Workshop, 998
College of Alameda, 3058
College of Dupage, 3161
College of Eastern Utah, 3789
College of Marin, 3059
College of Mount Saint Joseph, 3521
College of New Jersey, 3298
College of New Rochelle: New Resources Division, 3356
College of Saint Elizabeth, 3299
College of Saint Rose, 3357
College of Saint Scholastica, 3261
College of Santa Fe, 3327
College of St. Joseph, 3802
College of Staten Island of the City University of New York, 3358
College of William and Mary, 3812
College of Wooster, 3522
College of the Canyons, 3060
College of the Mainland, 3732
College of the Redwoods, 3061
College of the Sequoias, 3062
College of the Siskiyous, 3063
Colleges for Students with Learning Disabilities or ADD, 3003
Collin County Community College, 3733
Columbia Basin College, Resource Center Program, 3855
Columbia College, 3064, 3359
Columbia-Greene Community College, 3360
Columbus State Community College Disability Services, 3523
Community College of Allegheny County: College Center, North Campus, 3610
Community College of Allegheny County: Boyce Campus, 3611
Community College of Philadelphia, 3612
Community College of Vermont, 3803
Comprehensive Services for the Disabled, 1077
Concordia College: New York, 3361
Connecticut College, 3115
Corban College, 3586
Cornell University, 3362
Corning Community College, 3363
Cornish College of the Arts, 3856
Cuesta College, 3065
Cumberland County College, 3303
Curry College, 3231
Cuyahoga Community College: Eastern Campus, 3524
Cuyahoga Community College: Western Campus, 3525
Dakota College at Bottineau, 3501
Dallas Academy, 3734

History

Hotlines

Human Services

Colorado Department of Human Services: Division for Developmental Disabilities, 4483
Connecticut Department of Social Services, 1515
Delaware Department of Education, 1527
Delaware Department of Labor, 1528
Department of Human Services: Division of Developmental Disabilities Services, 4468
Department of Human Services: Division of Rehabilitation Services, 1807
Disability Law Center, 1625, 1827
Disability Law Center of Alaska, 1459
Easter Seals Alaska, 121
Employment Security Division, 1460
Employment Service Division: Alabama, 1454
Governor's Council on Developmental Disabilities, 1472, 1543, 1587
Granite State Independent Living, 1695
Hawaii State Council on Developmental Disabilities, 1551
Human Services: Division of Vocational, 4485
Idaho Division of Vocational Rehabilitation, 1556
Idaho Human Rights Commission, 1558
Illinois Department of Human Rights, 1570
Increasing Capabilities Access Network, 1481
Indiana ATTAIN Project, 1580
Institute for Human Development: Northern Arizona University, 123
Institute on Disability, 1696
Kansas Department of Labor, 1596
Kansas Human Rights Commission, 1598
Maine Human Rights Commission, 1620
Michigan Protection and Advocacy Service, 1644
Minnesota Department of Children, Families & Learning, 1648
Minnesota Department of Human Rights, 1649
Minnesota Governor's Council on Developmental Disabilities, 1650
NYS Developmental Disabilities Planning Council, 1721
Nevada Governor's Council on Developmental Disabilities, 1690
New Hampshire Department Of Health & Human Services, 4554
New Mexico Human Rights Commission Education Bureau, 1713
North Carolina Division of Vocational Rehabilitation, 1735
North Dakota Department of Human Services, 1741
North Dakota Department of Human Services: Welfare & Public Assistance, 2188
Office of Human Rights: District of Columbia, 1535
Oregon Department of Human Resource Adult & Family Services Division, 2216
Oregon Department of Human Services: Children, Adults & Families Division, 1770
Pennsylvania Human Rights Commission, 1778
Pennsylvania's Initiative on Assistive Technology, 1779
Rhode Island Commission for Human Rights, 1785
Rhode Island Human Resource Investment Council, 2231
ServiceLink, 1702
South Carolina Human Affairs Commission, 1795
South Dakota Advocacy Services, 1801
South Dakota Department of Labor, 4582
South Dakota Department of Social Services, 4583
South Dakota Division of Human Rights, 1804
Texas Workforce Commission: Civil Rights Division, 1821
University of Oregon Center for Excellence in Developmental Disabilities, 297
University of Washington: Center on Human Development and Disability, 3889
Utah Developmental Disabilities Council, 1829
Vermont Family Network, 4600
Virginia Board for People with Disabilities, 1843
VocRehab Reach-Up Program, 4601
Washington Human Rights Commission, 1852

Inclusion

Andreas: Outcomes of Inclusion, 2730

Backyards & Butterflies: Ways to Include Children with Disabilities, 2421
Devereux California, 3968
Devereux Mapleton, 4217
Devereux Massachusetts, 4114
General Guidelines for Providers of Psychological Services, 2890
Inclusion Series, 2758
Inclusion: An Essential Guide for the Paraprofessional, 2943
Making School Inclusion Work: A Guide to Everyday Practices, 2948
Social-Emotional Dimension Scale, 4310
Southern Adventist University, 3717
Take Part Art, 2960

Infancy

New Jersey Programs for Infants and Toddlers with Disabilities: Early Intervention System, 1707
Programs for Infants and Toddlers with Disabilities, 1728

Information Resources

A Human Development View of Learning Disabilities: From Theory to Practice, 2902
Ablenet, 1032
Army & Air Force Exchange Services, 1406
Bethany House Publishers, 2644
Charles C Thomas, Publisher, Ltd., 2648
How to Organize Your Child and Save Your Sanity, 2466
Including Students with Severe and Multiple Disabilities in Typical Classrooms, 2941
Learning Company, 1322
National Bible Association, 2673
National Resources, 2576
Northwest Media, 2674
Reader's Digest Partners for Sight Foundation, 2679
Sunburst, 1330
Tales from the Workplace, 4446
Thomas Nelson Publishers, 2687
Thorndike Press, 2688
Underachieving Gifted, 2592
www.disabilityresources.org, 2808
www.hood.edu/seri/serihome.htm, 2818
www.specialneeds.com, 2838
www.wrightlaw.com, 2839

Integration

Division on Career Development, 4426
Division on Career Development & Transition (DCDT), 40
Inclusion: 450 Strategies for Success, 2942
Michigan Department of Community Health, 1643
Regular Lives, 2776
South Dakota Council on Developmental Disabilities, 1802

International Associations

American-Scandinavian Foundation, 1403
Andeo International Homestays, 1404
Association for Childhood Education International (ACEI), 216
Council on International Educational Exchange, 1409
International Dyslexia Association of Massachusetts, 227
International Dyslexia Association of Austin, 316
International Dyslexia Association of Central Ohio, 287
International Dyslexia Association of Dallas, 317
International Dyslexia Association of Houston, 318
International Dyslexia Association of New Hampshire, 255
International Dyslexia Association of Northern Ohio, 140, 288
International Dyslexia Association of Utah, 321
International Dyslexia Association of Virginia, 325

International Dyslexia Association of Washington, 328
International Dyslexia Association of Western New York, 273
International Dyslexia Association: Ohio Valley Branch, 289
International Dyslexia Association: Tennessee Branch, 311
International Reading Association, 54
International Reading Association Newspaper: Reading Today, 391, 2619
Lisle, 1417
People to People International, 1421
SUNY Buffalo Office of International Education, 1422
Sister Cities International, 1423
World Experience, 1425
www.familyvillage.wisc.edu, 2811

Intervention

Academic Skills Problems Workbook, 2903
Accessing Programs for Infants, Toddlers and Preschoolers, 2559
Behavior Change in the Classroom: Self-Management Interventions, 2998
Brief Intervention for School Problems: Outcome-Informed Strategies, 2913
Child Who is Ignored: Module 6, 2742
Division for Early Childhood of CEC, 39
Easy Talker: A Fluency Workbook for School Age Children, 4380
Focus on Exceptional Children, 2930
Guidelines and Recommended Practices for Individualized Family Service Plan, 2454
HELP Activity Guide, 2932
Intervention in School and Clinic, 2946
Just Kids: Early Childhood Learning Center, 4180
Practitioner's Guide to Dynamic Assessment, 2896
The Baby Fold, 4086
When Slow Is Fast Enough: Educating the Delayed Preschool Child, 29850d@MINOR HEADING = Job/Vocational Resources
A Student's Guide to Jobs, 2556
Adult Education & Literacy, 4596
Alabama Department of Industrial Relations, 1452
Alaska State Commission for Human Rights, 1455
Arizona Governor's Committee on Employment of the Handicapped, 1467
Arkansas Department of Workforce Services, 1477
BRIGANCE Employability Skills Inventory, 4373
California Department of Fair Employment and Housing, 1485
California Employment Development Department, 1488
Career Planner's Portfolio: A School-to-Work Assessment Tool, 4347
Colorado Department of Labor and Employment, 1504
DC Department of Employment Services, 1531
Department of Employment Services, 4494
Department of Employment, Training and Rehabilitation, 1686
Department of Personnel & Human Services, 1846
Different Way of Learning, 2791
District of Columbia Fair Employment Practice Agencies, 1533
Division of Family Development: New Jersey Department of Human Services, 4557
Easter Seal Michigan, 4534
Employment Initiatives Model: Job Coach Training Manual and Tape, 2792
Fair Employment Practice Agency, 1470
Florida Department of Labor and Employment Security, 1538
Florida Fair Employment Practice Agency, 1539
Florida Vocational Rehabilitation Agency: Division of Vocational Rehabilitation, 1991
Florida Workforce Investment Act, 4502
Goodwill - Easter Seals Minnesota, 4536
How Not to Contact Employers, 2794
Idaho Department of Commerce & Labor, 4510
Idaho Fair Employment Practice Agency, 1557
Illinois Department of Employment Security, 1569

Keyboards

Kits

Language Skills

Leadership

Legal Issues

Libraries

Listening Skills

Literacy

Literature

Logic

Mainstreaming

Matching

Mathematics

Maturity

Memorization Skills

Motivation

Motor Development

Multicultural Education

Multisensory Education

Music

Neurological Disorders

Newsletters

Occupational Therapy

Pathology

Perception Skills

Pets

KIND News Sr: Kids in Nature's Defense, 2603
National Association for Humane and
Environmental Education, 2605

Phonics

Chess with Butterflies, 754
Clues to Meaning, 756
Common Ground: Whole Language & Phonics
Working Together, 2427
First Phonics, 608, 1130
Fishing with Balloons, 767
High Noon Books, 770, 2661
I Can See the ABC's, 772
Lexia Phonics Based Reading, 1146
Lexia Primary Reading, 1343
More Primary Phonics, 782
Phonemic Awareness: The Sounds of Reading,
786, 2774
Phonic Ear Auditory Trainers, 1052
Phonology and Reading Disability, 2987
Phonology: Software, 1156
Primary Phonics, 789
Python Path Phonics Word Families, 622, 1157
Reading Who? Reading You!, 796, 1353
Sentence Master: Level 1, 2, 3, 4, 1354
Simon Sounds It Out, 1355

Physical Education

Adapted Physical Education for Students with
Autism, 2905
ECLC of New Jersey, 4152
Journal of Physical Education, Recreation and
Dance, 2620
Prentice School, 3087, 3983

Play Therapy

Children's Cabinet, 250
Flagship Carpets, 903
Link N' Learn Color Rings, 911
New Language of Toys, 2503

Program Planning

Adventure Learning Center at Eagle Village, 525
Calumet Camp, 539
Camp Frog Hollow, 1102
Camp Happiness, 576
Camp Joy, 504
Camp Kehilla, 551
Camp Lapham, 505
Camp Little Giant: Touch of Nature Environmental
Center, 482
Camp Moore, 543
Camp Shriver, 459
Camp Sunshine-Camp Elan, 553
Camp Winnebago, 535
Eagle Hill Summer Program, 461
Easter Seals Camp Hemlocks, 462
Groves Academy, 3262, 4137
Guide to ACA Accredited Camps, 437
Kamp A-Kom-plish, 498
Landmark Summer Program: Exploration and
Recreation, 516
Landmark Summer Program: Marine Science, 517
Landmark Summer Program: Musical Theater, 518
Lesley University, 3240
Marburn Academy, 3536
Marburn Academy Summer Programs, 584
Marvelwood, 3118
Patriots' Trail Girl Scout Council Summer Camp,
521
Pilgrim Hills Camp, 585
Project LEARN of Summit County, 2199
Recreation Unlimited Farm and Fun, 586
School Vacation Camps: Youth with
Developmental Disabilities, 563
Summer Day Programs, 465
The Kolburne School Summer Program, 524

The Kolburne School, Inc., 3247
Timber Trails Camps, 466
Wilderness Experience, 572

Public Awareness & Interest

Crotched Mountain, 253
New Hampshire Governor's Commission on
Disability, 1700
Parent to Parent of New Hampshire, 257
Public Agencies Fact Sheet, 2583
Vermont Governor's Office, 1835
Wisconsin Governor's Committee for People with
Disabilities, 1870
www.disabilityinfo.gov, 2807

Publishers

Academic Communication Associates, 2633
Academic Success Press, 2634
Academic Therapy Publications, 2635
Alexander Graham Bell Association for the Deaf
and Hard of Hearing, 2637
At-Risk Youth Resources, 2643
Blackwell Publishing, 2645
Brookes Publishing Company, 2646
Brookline Books/Lumen Editions, 2647
Concept Phonics, 757, 2650
Corwin Press, 2651
Decoding Automaticity Materials for Reading
Fluency, 760
Educators Publishing Service, 2652
Federation for Children with Special Needs, 47,
2653
Free Spirit Publishing, 2654
Gordon Systems & GSI Publications, 2656
Guilford Publications, 2658
Hazelden Publishing, 2659
Heinemann-Boynton/Cook, 2660
Love Publishing Company, 2668
Magination Press, 2669
Marsh Media, 1199, 2670
Nimble Numeracy: Fluency in Counting and Basic
Arithmetic, 708
Performance Resource Press, 2676
Peytral Publications, 2677
Research Press Publisher, 2680
Riggs Institute, 2681
Scholastic, 1328, 2682
Schwab Learning, 2683
Sounds and Spelling Patterns for English, 803
Stories from Somerville, 808
Teaching Comprehension: Strategies for Stories,
811
Teddy Bear Press, 2685
Therapro, 2686
Wadsworth Publishing Company, 2690
Woodbine House, 2691

Puzzles

ADA Quiz Book, 2374
Equation Tile Teaser, 680
Equation Tile Teasers, 1234
KIND News, 2600
KIND News Jr: Kids in Nature's Defense, 2601
KIND News Primary: Kids in Nature's Defense,
2602
Mind Over Matter, 1109
Puzzle Tanks, 715
Toddler Tote, 929
Wordly Wise ABC 1-9, 817

Recognition Skills

Creating Patterns from Shapes, 677
Curious George Pre-K ABCs, 601, 1125
Mind Matters, 284

Rehabilitation

AbleData, 1031

American Rehabilitation Counseling Association
(ARCA), 13
Answers4Families: Center on Children, Families,
Law, 2135
Answers4Families: Center on Children, Families
and the Law, 1674
Arizona Department of Economic Security, 1465
Arkansas Department of Corrections, 1473
Arkansas Rehabilitation Services, 4467
California Department of Rehabilitation, 1486,
4475
Client Assistance Program (CAP): Nebraska
Division of Persons with Disabilities, 2136
Client Assistance Program (CAP): Nebraska
Division of Persons with Disabilities, 1676
Cognitive Rehabilitation, 1122
Connecticut Bureau of Rehabilitation Services,
1514
Council on Rehabilitation Education, 34
Department of Assistive & Rehabilitative Services,
4590
Department of Correctional Services, 1719
Department of Social Services: Vocational
Rehabilitation Program, 4486
District of Columbia Department of Corrections,
1532
Division of Rehabilitation Services, 218
Fundamentals of Job Placement, 4434
Fundamentals of Vocational Assessment, 4435
Help for Brain Injured Children, 3973
Illinois Department of Rehabilitation Services,
1571
Iowa Vocational Rehabilitation Agency, 2045
Job Accommodation Network (JAN), 4428
Journal of Rehabilitation, 2861
Kansas Correctional Education, 2056
Kansas Department of Corrections, 2057
Kansas Department of Social & Rehabilitation
Services, 2058
Life After High School for Students with Moderate
and Severe Disabilities, 2799
Massachusetts Correctional Education: Inmate
Training & Education, 2106
Massachusetts Rehabilitation Commission, 1634
Minnesota Vocational Rehabilitation Agency:
Rehabilitation Services Branch, 4537
Minnesota Vocational Rehabilitation Services,
2124
Munroe-Meyer Institute for Genetics and
Rehabilitation, 4285
National Business and Disability Council, 75
National Council on Rehabilitation Education, 81
National Rehabilitation Association, 91
National Rehabilitation Information Center, 92
North Texas Rehabilitation Center, 320
Office For The Deaf And Hearing Impaired, 4470
Office of Vocational Rehabilitation Services, 1766
Rehabilitation International, 99
Rehabilitation Services Administration, 4463
Rhode Island Vocational and Rehabilitation
Agency, 2232, 4578
Section 504 of the Rehabilitation Act, 2391
Student Directed Learning: Teaching Self
Determination Skills, 2779
Texas Department of Assistive and Rehabilitative
Services, 1818
The Children's Institute, 4162, 4227
Virginia Department of Rehabilitative Services,
4603
Wiregrass Rehabilitation Center, 3953

Remediation

A Practical Parent's Handbook on Teaching
Children with Learning Disabilities, 2406
Art-Centered Education & Therapy for Children
with Disabilities, 2909
Auditory Skills, 1118
Boone Voice Program for Adults, 4376
Boone Voice Program for Children, 4377
Challenging Our Minds, 1120
Complete Learning Disabilities Resource Library,
2430
Cyber Launch Pad Camp, 460

Virginia Office for Protection & Advocacy Agency, 1844
West Virginia Assistive Technology System, 1862
Window-Eyes, 1062

Tourette Syndrome

Children with Tourette Syndrome, 2425

Training

125 Brain Games for Babies, 2404
ABC's, Numbers & Shapes, 934
Access Aware: Extending Your Reach to People with Disabilities, 2410
Access for All: Integrating Deaf, Hard of Hearing, and Hearing Preschoolers, 2984
Activities Unlimited, 833
Activities of Daily Living: A Manual of Group Activities and Written Exercises, 639
Activity Schedules for Children with Autism: Teaching Independent Behavior, 834
Advocates for Children of New York, 270, 4170
Alert Program with Songs for Self-Regulation, 835
Alliance for Technology Access, 1034
American Dance Therapy Association (ADTA), 8
An Introduction to How Does Your Engine Run?, 836
Andy and His Yellow Frisbee, 837
Arizona Vocational Rehabilitation, 4462
Arkansas Disability Coalition, 3962
Art for All the Children: Approaches to Art Therapy for Children with Disabilities, 2nd Ed., 2908
Assistive Technology Resource Centers of Hawaii (ATRC), 180
Autism Support Center: Northshore Arc, 1629
Baker Victory Services, 4173
Behavioral Institute for Children and Adolescents, 990
Best Practice Occupational Therapy: In Community Service with Children and Families, 2884
Beyond Drill and Practice: Expanding the Computer Mainstream, 1311
Breakthroughs Manual: How to Reach Students with Autism, 838
Busy Kids Movement, 839
CAST, 1074, 4110
Callirobics: Advanced Exercises, 936
Callirobics: Exercises for Adults, 937
Callirobics: Handwriting Exercises to Music, 938
Callirobics: Prewriting Skills with Music, 939
Career Assessment and Placement Center Whittier Union High School District, 1491
Center For Accessible Technology, 4425
Center for Alternative Learning, 4215
Center for Community, 1457, 3955
Child Who Appears Anxious: Module 4, 2739
Child Who Dabbles: Module 3, 2740
Child Who Wanders: Module 2, 2741
Children with Cerebral Palsy: A Parent's Guide, 2423
Classroom Success for the LD and ADHD Chil, 2426
Classroom Visual Activities, 642
Computer & Web Resources for People with Disabilities: A Guide to..., 2431
Correctional Education and Vocational Training, 1685
Courageous Pacers Classroom Chart, 841
Courageous Pacers Program, 842
Creative Community Services, 4055
Current Developments in Employment and Training, 4433
Curriculum Based Activities in Occupational Therapy: An Inclusion Resource, 2886
DBTAC: Great Lakes ADA Center, 1564
DBTAC: Pacific ADA Center, 1493
Delaware Assistive Technology Initiative(DATI), 1526
Developing Fine and Gross Motor Skills, 2437
Disability Rights Education & Defense Fund (DREDF), 36

Disc-O-Bocce, 897
Distance Education and Training Council (DETC), 37, 1886
Dysgraphia: Why Johnny Can't Write, 941
Dyslexia Training Program, 761
EPICS Parent Project, 4168
Eagle Hill School, 3116, 3233, 4004
Early Communication Skills for Childrenwith Down Syndrome, 602
Early Listening Skills, 603
Early Movement Skills, 737
Early Sensory Skills, 739
Early Visual Skills, 740
Eden Family of Services, 1002, 4558
Eden II Programs, 4176
Educating Children Summer Training Institute (ECSTI), 1003
Employment Development Department: Employment Services Woodland, 1496
Employment Development Department: Employment Services W Sacramento, 1497
Employment and Training Administration: US Department of Labor, 1434
Exceptional Children's Assistance Center, 4198
Exceptional Student Education: Assistive Technology, 4041
Face to Face: Resolving Conflict Without Giving in or Giving Up, 843
Families Together, 4091
Family Place in Cyberspace, 2447
Family Resource Center on Disabilities, 4078
Federation for Children with Special Needs Newsletter, 2615
FileMaker Inc., 1317
Fine Motor Activities Guide and Easel Activities Guide, 644
Fine Motor Skills in Children with Downs Syndrome: A Guide for Parents and Professionals, 2448
Fine Motor Skills in the Classroom: Screening & Remediation Strategies, 2449
Finger Frolics: Fingerplays, 645
First Words II Sterling Edition, 1191
From Scribbling to Writing, 948
Fun with Handwriting, 949
Fun with Language: Book 1, 609
Funsical Fitness With Silly-ous CD: Motor Development Activities, 845
Games we Should Play in School, 846
Gengras Center, 4008
Geometrical Design Coloring Book, 906
Get in Shape to Write, 907
Getting Ready to Write: Preschool-K, 950
Getting Started With Facilitated Communication, 2751
Getting it Write, 951
Goodwill Industries of Kansas, 205
Great Plains Disability and Business Technical Assistance Center (DBTAC), 1662
Gross Motor Skills Children with Down Syndrome: A Guide For Parents and Professionals, 2451
HELP for Preschoolers at Home, 741
Handbook for Developing Community Based Employment, 4436
Handling the Young Child with Cerebral Palsy at Home, 2457
Handwriting: Manuscript ABC Book, 953
Home/School Activities Manuscript Practice, 954
Horizons School, 3021, 4056
Horizons, Inc., 463
How Does Your Engine Run? A Leaders Guide to the Alert Program for Self Regulation, 2936
IN*SOURCE, 4090
Idaho Parents Unlimited, Inc., 4065
Inclusion: Strategies for Working with Young Children, 773, 2475
Independent Living Research Utilization Program, 49
Institute for Human Centered Design, 51, 1892
International Professional Development Training Catalog, 2759
JOBS V, 4437
KET Basic Skills Series, 2795
KY-SPIN, Inc., 4093

Kingsbury Center, 4033
Learning Disabilities Association of Hawaii, 4063
Learning Disabilities Association of Hawaii (LDAH), 183
Learning Disabilities Quarterly, 2866
Learning Strategies Curriculum, 888
Learning in Motion, 848
Let's-Do-It-Write: Writing Readiness Workbook, 956
Life Development Institute (LDI), 3959
Linden Hill School, 3241, 4122
Link Newsletter, 2623
MORE: Integrating the Mouth with Sensory & Postural Functions, 649
MPACT - Missouri Parents Act, 4142
Magicatch Set, 912
Maine Parent Federation, 215
Making Sense of Sensory Integration, 2769
Manus Academy, 4201
Manus Academy, 4202
Maryland Association of University Centers on Disabilities, 222
Maryland Technology Assistance Program, 1627, 4530
Memory Workbook, 650
Minnesota Literacy Training Network, 2123
Mississippi Project START, 1656
Myofascial Release and Its Application to Neuro-Developmental Treatment, 2950
National Center for Family Literacy (NCFL), 76
National Federation of the Blind, 85, 4429
National Governors Association Newsletter, 4441
National Institute of Art and Disabilities, 86
Nebraska Parents Training and Information Center, 4145
New Language of Toys: Teaching Communication Skills to Children with Special Needs, 849
Normal Growth and Development: Performance Prediction, 2771
Occupational Outlook Quarterly, 2871
Office of Adult Education and Literacy, 1840
Office of Curriculum & Instructional Support, 1726, 4565
Office of Workforce Development, 4571
Oh Say What They See: Language Stimulation, 2772
Ohio Coalition for the Education of Children with Disabilities, 4210
One-Handed in a Two-Handed World, 651
Opposites Game, 915
Out of Sync Child: Recognizing and Coping with Sensory Integration Dysfunction, 2508
Out of the Mouths of Babes: Discovering the Developmental Significance of the Mouth, 2509
PEAK Parent Center, 153, 2675
Parent Education Network, 4224
Parent Educational Advocacy Training Center (PEATC), 96
Parent Information Center, 1701, 4149
Parent Information Center of Delaware, 166, 4031
Parent Information Center of Wyoming, 4277
Parent Information Network, 125
Parent Network of WNY, 4188
Parent Resource Center, 4267
Parent Training and Information, 4275
Parents As Partners In Education Of Alabama, 3951
Parents Let's Unite for Kids, 4144
Partners Resource Network, 4246
Pennsylvania Training and Technical Assistance Network Workshops, 1021
Perceptual Motor Development Series, 4415
Plastic Cones, 918
Project PROMPT, 4097
Raising Special Kids, 3960
Reaching Out, Joining In: Teaching Social Skills to Young Children with Autism, 850
Reading Center of Bruno, 3986
Region VII: US Department of Health and Human Services, 1666
Rehabilitation Division Department of Employment, Training & Rehabilitation, 4550
Rehabilitation Resource, 4291

Transportation

Treatment

Visual Assistive Devices

Visual Discrimination

Lutheran Braille Workers, 144
Recording for the Blind & Dyslexic Learning, 236
Recording for the Blind & Dyslexic of
  Metropolitan Washington, 168
Recording for the Blind & Dyslexic:
  Berkshire/Williamstown, 230
Recording for the Blind & Dyslexic: Chicago Loop
  Studio, 193
Recording for the Blind & Dyslexic: Kentucky,
  208
Recording for the Blind & Dyslexic: Lois C Klein
  Studio, 194
Recording for the Blind & Dyslexic: Santa Barbara,
  148
Recording for the Blind and Dyslexic: Inland
  Empire-Orange County Unit, 1955
Recording for the Blind and Dyslexic: Inland
  Empire-Orange County Unit, 149
Same or Different, 1159
Sliding Block, 1300
South Dakota Rehabilitation Center forthe Blind,
  4584
Visual Perception and Attention Workbook, 2373

Vocabulary

Analogies 1, 2 & 3, 596
Bailey's Book House, 1334
Basic Signing Vocabulary Cards, 598
Bubbleland Word Discovery, 599
Carolina Picture Vocabulary Test (CPVT): For
  Deaf and Hearing Impaired Children, 600
Christmas Bear, 2351
Connecting Reading and Writing with Vocabulary,
  4378
Emergent Reader, 764
Explode the Code, 766
Following Directions: One and Two-Level
  Commands, 1195
Funny Bunny and Sunny Bunny, 2355
Halloween Bear, 2356
High Frequency Vocabulary, 1132
I Can Read Charts, 2358
Language Learning Everywhere We Go, 2973
Language Master, 1142
Learning Disabilities Resources, 2665
My Own Bookshelf, 1154
Nordic Software, 1296
Old MacDonald's Farm Deluxe, 1281
Once Upon a Time Volume II: Worlds of
  Enchantment, 1394
Once Upon a Time Volume III: Journey Through
  Time, 1395
Once Upon a Time Volume IV: Exploring Nature,
  1396
Peabody Picture Vocabulary Test, 4385
Peabody Picture Vocabulary Test: Fourth Edition,
  4386
Peabody Test-Picture Vocabulary Test, 4327
Reading Comprehension in Varied Subject Matter,
  794
Scare Bear, 2365
Secondary Print Pack, 1207
See Me Add, 801
Signs of the Times, 2976
Snowbear, 2368
Space Academy GX-1, 825
Speaking Language Master Special Edition, 1164
Stanley Sticker Stories, 1169
Story of the USA, 882
Summer@Carroll, 522
Talking Walls, 826, 1367
Talking Walls: The Stories Continue, 827, 1368
Tenth Planet Roots, Prefixes & Suffixes, 1357
Tenth Planet: Roots, Suffixes, Prefixes, 812
Test of Mathematical Abilities, 4343
Thinkin' Science ZAP, 664

Valentine Bear, 2372
Virtual Labs: Electricity, 832
Word Wise I and II: Better Comprehension
  Through Vocabulary, 1182
Wordly Wise 3000 ABC 1-9, 816

Voice Output Devices

Kurzweil 3000, 1340
Oral Speech Mechanism Screening Examination,
  4384
Reading Pen, 795, 1054

Volunteer

Aloha Special Technology Access Center, 179
Boy Scouts of America, 23
Delaware County Literacy Council, 2220
International Cultural Youth Exchange (ICYE),
  1414
International Partnership for Service-Learning and
  Leadership, 1415
Kentucky Literacy Volunteers of America, 2065
LDA Rhode Island Newsletter, 2865
Learning Disabilities Association of Michigan
  (LDA), 234
Literacy Chicago, 2027
Literacy Volunteers of America: Rhode Island,
  2225
Literacy Volunteers of Massachusetts, 2103
New York Literacy Volunteers of America, 2177
People Care Center, 2159
Teaching People with Developmental Disabilities,
  2711

Workshop Training

ACA Charlotte, 981
AVKO Educational Research Foundation, 1
Active Parenting Publishers, 985, 2636
Assessing Learning Problems Workshop, 987
Boston University, 3226
Computer Access Center, 1078
Dr. Peet's TalkWriter, 1380
Dyslexia Association Long Island Island, 271
Easybook Deluxe Writing Workshop: Colonial
  Times, 873, 943
Educational Options for Students with Learning
  Disabilities and LD/HD, 1004
Elim Christian Services, 4076
Handbook for Implementing Workshops for
  Siblings of Special Needs Children, 2455
How Difficult Can This Be?, 2754, 2935
Inclusion of Learning Disabled Students in Regular
  Classrooms Workshop, 1006
Interest Driven Learning Master Class Workshop,
  1007
International Dyslexia Association - Georgia, 176
International Dyslexia Association New York, 272
International Dyslexia Association Of Hawaii, 182
International Dyslexia Association of Michigan,
  233
International Dyslexia Association of Florida, 170
International Dyslexia Association of Indiana, 196
International Dyslexia Association of Iowa, 200
International Dyslexia Association of Los Angeles,
  139
International Dyslexia Association of Nebraska,
  248
International Dyslexia Association of Oregon, 294
International Dyslexia Association of Rhode
  Island, 305
International Dyslexia Association of San Diego,
  141
International Dyslexia Association of South
  Carolina, 307

International Dyslexia Association of Wisconsin,
  334
International Dyslexia Association: Philadelphia
  Branch Newsletter, 2618
LDA Learning Center, 4138
LDR Workshop: What Are Learning Disabilities,
  Problems and Differences?, 1011
Landmark School Outreach Program, 56, 1012,
  3239, 4118
Learning Disabilities Association of Nebraska, 249
Learning Disabilities Association of South Dakota,
  308
Learning Disabilities and the World of Work
  Workshop, 1013
Learning Problems and Adult Basic Education
  Workshop, 1014
Lindamood-Bell Learning Processes Professional
  Development, 1015
Lion's Workshop, 1198
Michigan Citizens Alliance to Uphold Special
  Education (CAUSE), 235
National Head Start Association, 1017
National Head Start Association Parent
  Conference, 1018
Parents Helping Parents, 97
Parents Reaching Out to Parents of South Carolina,
  4232
Rocky Mountain International Dyslexia
  Association, 155
Social Skills Workshop, 1022
State University of New York: Albany, 3430
Stockdale Learning Center, 3990
Switch to Turn Kids On, 1068
Teaching Math Workshop, 1025
The Fowler Center for Outdoor Learning, 529
Upper Midwest Branch of the International
  Dyslexia Association, 239
Washington PAVE: Specialized Training of
  Military Parents (STOMP), 111
Workshops, 3954

Writing

Advanced Skills For School Success Series:
  Module 4, 4369
Easybook Deluxe, 942, 1388
Easybook Deluxe Writing Workshop: Whales &
  Oceans, 946
Goals and Objectives Writer Software, 4349
Handwriting Without Tears, 952
Imagination Express Destination: Time Trip USA,
  1377
Making Handwriting Flow, 957
Making the Writing Process Work: Strategies for
  Composition & Self-Regulation, 2974
Making the Writing Process Work: Strategies for
  Composition & Self-Regulation, 2497
Media Weaver 3.5, 958, 1382
PAF Handwriting Programs for Print, Cursive
  (Right or Left-Handed), 960
Reading and Writing Workbook, 2549
Sunbuddy Writer, 963, 1383
Write On! Plus: Beginning Writing Skills, 966
Write On! Plus: Essential Writing, 968
Write On! Plus: Growing as a Writer, 969
Write On! Plus: Middle School Writing Skills, 972
Write On! Plus: Steps to Better Writing, 975
Write On! Plus: Writing with Picture Books, 976
Writer's Resources Library 2.0, 977
Writing Trek Grades 4-6, 978, 1399
Writing Trek Grades 8-10, 980, 1401

General Reference

America's College Museums
American Environmental Leaders: From Colonial Times to the Present
An African Biographical Dictionary
An Encyclopedia of Human Rights in the United States
Encyclopedia of African-American Writing
Encyclopedia of Gun Control & Gun Rights
Encyclopedia of Invasions & Conquests
Encyclopedia of Prisoners of War & Internment
Encyclopedia of Religion & Law in America
Encyclopedia of Rural America
Encyclopedia of the United States Cabinet, 1789-2010
Encyclopedia of War Journalism
Encyclopedia of Warrior Peoples & Fighting Groups
From Suffrage to the Senate: America's Political Women
Nations of the World
Political Corruption in America
Speakers of the House of Representatives, 1789-2009
The Environmental Debate: A Documentary History
The Evolution Wars: A Guide to the Debates
The Religious Right: A Reference Handbook
The Value of a Dollar: 1860-2009
The Value of a Dollar: Colonial Era
US Land & Natural Resource Policy
Weather America
Working Americans 1770-1869 Vol. IX: Revol. War to the Civil War
Working Americans 1880-1999 Vol. I: The Working Class
Working Americans 1880-1999 Vol. II: The Middle Class
Working Americans 1880-1999 Vol. III: The Upper Class
Working Americans 1880-1999 Vol. IV: Their Children
Working Americans 1880-2003 Vol. V: At War
Working Americans 1880-2005 Vol. VI: Women at Work
Working Americans 1880-2006 Vol. VII: Social Movements
Working Americans 1880-2007 Vol. VIII: Immigrants
Working Americans 1880-2009 Vol. X: Sports & Recreation
Working Americans 1880-2010 Vol. XI: Inventors & Entrepreneurs
Working Americans 1880-2011 Vol. XII: Our History through Music
World Cultural Leaders of the 20th & 21st Centuries

Business Information

Directory of Business Information Resources
Directory of Mail Order Catalogs
Directory of Venture Capital & Private Equity Firms
Environmental Resource Handbook
Food & Beverage Market Place
Grey House Homeland Security Directory
Grey House Performing Arts Directory
Hudson's Washington News Media Contacts Directory
New York State Directory
Sports Market Place Directory
The Rauch Guides – Industry Market Research Reports
Sweets Directory by McGraw Hill Construction

Statistics & Demographics

America's Top-Rated Cities
America's Top-Rated Small Towns & Cities
America's Top-Rated Smaller Cities
Comparative Guide to American Hospitals
Comparative Guide to American Suburbs
Profiles of... Series – State Handbooks

Health Information

Comparative Guide to American Hospitals
Complete Directory for Pediatric Disorders
Complete Directory for People with Chronic Illness
Complete Directory for People with Disabilities
Complete Mental Health Directory
Directory of Health Care Group Purchasing Organizations
Directory of Hospital Personnel
HMO/PPO Directory
Medical Device Register
Older Americans Information Directory

Education Information

Charter School Movement
Comparative Guide to American Elementary & Secondary Schools
Complete Learning Disabilities Directory
Educators Resource Directory
Special Education

Financial Ratings Series

TheStreet.com Ratings Guide to Bond & Money Market Mutual Funds
TheStreet.com Ratings Guide to Common Stocks
TheStreet.com Ratings Guide to Exchange-Traded Funds
TheStreet.com Ratings Guide to Stock Mutual Funds
TheStreet.com Ratings Ultimate Guided Tour of Stock Investing
Weiss Ratings Consumer Box Set
Weiss Ratings Guide to Banks & Thrifts
Weiss Ratings Guide to Credit Unions
Weiss Ratings Guide to Health Insurers
Weiss Ratings Guide to Life & Annuity Insurers
Weiss Ratings Guide to Property & Casualty Insurers

Bowker's Books In Print®Titles

Books In Print®
Books In Print® Supplement
American Book Publishing Record® Annual
American Book Publishing Record® Monthly
Books Out Loud™
Bowker's Complete Video Directory™
Children's Books In Print®
Complete Directory of Large Print Books & Serials™
El-Hi Textbooks & Serials In Print®
Forthcoming Books®
Law Books & Serials In Print™
Medical & Health Care Books In Print™
Publishers, Distributors & Wholesalers of the US™
Subject Guide to Books In Print®
Subject Guide to Children's Books In Print®

Canadian General Reference

Associations Canada
Canadian Almanac & Directory
Canadian Environmental Resource Guide
Canadian Parliamentary Guide
Financial Services Canada
Governments Canada
Libraries Canada
The History of Canada

Grey House Publishing
4919 Route 22, PO Box 56, Amenia NY 12501-0056 | (800) 562-2139 | www.greyhouse.com | books@greyhouse.com